A textbook that puts students at the center with a guided approach to Western Civilization

Newly designed and organized to ensure student success, **Making Europe: The Story of the West** guides Western Civilization students with an accessible writing style and extensive pedagogical features. Engaging students with a narrative that highlights individuals and the West's place in the world, the text then reinforces their understanding with focus questions, key-term reviews, and a comprehensive chapter review with bulleted summaries and *Test Yourself* questions.

The authors explore Western Civilization through five themes: politics, religion, social history, biography and personality, and individual and collective identity. Visually stunning images and maps further engage students while bringing the themes to life.

Explore **Making Europe: The Story of the West**. Your preview begins on the next page. ▶

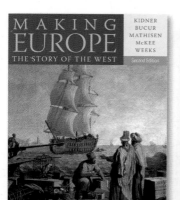

Complete Edition
978-1-111-84131-7

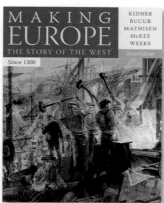

Since 1300
978-1-111-84132-4

"Making Europe has all the advantages we relished in older texts, with the added benefit of being accessible to a twenty-first century student audience. You won't find yourself frustrated either with lack of inclusiveness or failure to recognize the complexities of the past. Give it a try and see if you don't agree."

—Mark Rummage, Chair, History and Political Science Department, Holmes Community College

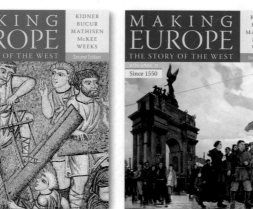

Volume 1: To 1790
978-1-111-84133-1

Volume 2: Since 1550
978-1-111-84134-8

"I actually enjoyed reading this textbook. The textbook keeps the information flowing nicely for easy understanding. It also has multiple resources for a student to use when studying, which as a busy college student is greatly appreciated."

—Morgan Colonna, Student, Longwood University

80% of instructors surveyed feel **Making Europe** will help students take a more active role in reading and learning than their current text.

82% of students said they were likely or very likely to recommend their instructor use **Making Europe**.

"This book makes history interesting and will help students do better on their exams."

—Haley Reinholz, Student, University of North Dakota

Improved understanding through unique pedagogy

Students begin each chapter with features designed to prepare them for the upcoming material.

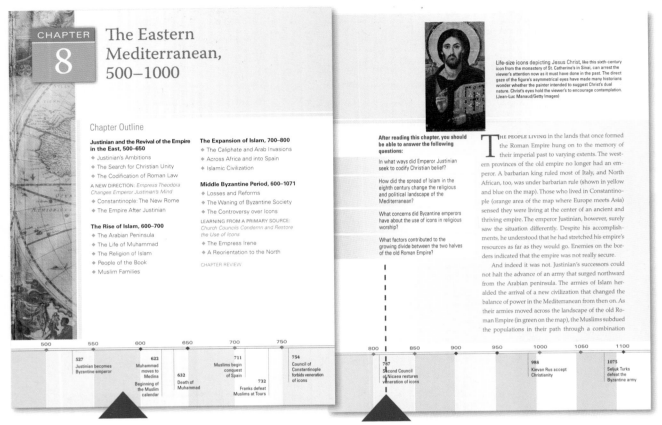

Chapter-opening timelines give students a broad overview of the chronology covered in the chapter.

Every chapter opener includes **new** focus questions that turn student attention to the central issues that will be explored in the chapter.

As students read the chapter, they are reminded of key ideas and terms.

The Rise of Islam, 600–700

- **What did Muhammad view as necessary to a worthy life?**
- **In which ways did Muslims view the world similarly to the way Christians and Jews viewed it, and in which ways did they view it differently?**

Each section begins with a series of questions that give students a preview of the coming material.

 Checking In

By yourself or with a partner, explain the significance of each of the following selected key terms:

Mecca	Five Pillars of Islam
Muhammad	mosques
Quran	Ramadan
Medina	Hajj

End-of-section *Checking In* exercises foster more active reading and thorough comprehension of the material.

Important names, terms, organizations, concepts, and events are explained or defined on the same page where they are introduced.

Mass Christian liturgical ceremony in which the officiating priest symbolically reenacts Jesus' Last Supper with his disciples.

laity (adj. **lay**) Collective term used to refer to everyone except the clergy.

nun Woman who has entered a monastic order for women to lead a life of prayer and contemplation.

ecclesiastical Pertaining to a church.

Body of Civil Law Justinian's three-volume codification issued between 533 and 563, containing the laws and jurist opinions of the Roman Empire and the canons issued by church councils.

patria potestas (in Latin, "paternal authority") Legal authority of a head of household, usually a father, over the members of his household, including his family, servants, and slaves.

The second edition is designed to meet instructors' needs by better preparing students for class

"I think the Chapter Review is the best part. Not many textbooks have this feature. It is a very good tool to help understand the material better and to help me study. This actually guided me through studying and I hope to see these specific features in future textbooks. I would recommend this textbook to any history professor."

—Itzel Guzman, Student, Borough of Manhattan Community College

CHAPTER
Review

Summary

◆ In the ninth century, the people of the eastern empire still thought of themselves as Roman, but so much had changed that a Latin-speaking resident of the city of Rome would not have understood the Greek-speaking inhabitants of Constantinople, "the New Rome."

◆ Disagreements over the nature of Christ continued. The Christians of sixth-century Constantinople had very strong and conflicting opinions about Jesus' humanity and divinity, which Emperor Justinian and empress Theodora at first tried to ignore. Eventually, the emperor suppressed those who disagreed with church doctrine, as threatening to Christian unity.

◆ Muhammad's new religion of Islam had from its start a firmer political and cultural foundation in the Arabian peninsula than Christianity had enjoyed in the Roman Empire.

◆ By the ninth century, Muslim territory encompassed more territory than had the Roman Empire.

◆ The Greek alphabet and the rites of the eastern church traveled with missionaries to the land of the Slavs and the Kievan Rus in the tenth century.

◆ Increasingly, sacred languages, practices, and leaders divided the people of the old Roman Empire. Religion was now a matter of loyalty as much as it was of belief.

A new, enhanced end-of-chapter section features a bulleted summary and a boxed chronology of events, followed by a *Test Yourself* multiple-choice self-quiz. This quiz is accompanied by critical-thinking questions that instructors can use to gauge student understanding of each major chapter division. Answers to the multiple-choice quizzes can be found in the back of the book.

Chronology

527	Justinian becomes emperor
532	Justinian's forces kills tens of thousands in the Nika Riot in Constantinople
533–563	Body of Civil Law is issued
534	Vandal kingdom of North Africa falls to Byzantine forces
542	Bubonic plague devastates Constantinople
552	Ostrogothic kingdom in Italy falls to Byzantine forces
ca. 570	Birth of Muhammad
610	Heraclius becomes emperor
613	Persians capture Jerusalem, destroy Church of the Holy Sepulcher
622	Muhammad flees to Medina in the Hejira; beginning of the Muslim calendar
628	Heraclius defeats the Persians
630	Heraclius returns relic of the True Cross to Jerusalem; Muhammad returns to Mecca
632	Muhammad dies in Medina
656	Election of Ali as caliph
661	Death of the caliph Ali and beginning of Umayyad dynasty, based in Damascus
711–714	Muslims conquer Spain
730	Leo III forbids use of icons in liturgical services
732	Franks halt Muslim advance at Tours
750	Umayyad dynasty is overthrown; Abbasid dynasty begins, based in Baghdad
787	Second Council of Nicaea reinstates veneration of icons
802	Removal of the empress Irene from power
803	Death of the empress Irene
988	Kievan Rus officially accept Christianity
1071	Turks defeat Byzantine army at Manzikert

Test Yourself

To gauge your mastery of the material in this chapter, answer the questions below. More than one answer may be correct.

Justinian and the Revival of the Empire in the East, 500–650

1. Which kingdom did Justinian **not** attempt to bring back into the empire?
   a. Visigothic
   b. Frankish
   c. Vandal
   d. Ostrogothic
   e. Persian

2. The empress Theodora endeavored to protect the followers of which sect declared heretical by church councils?
   a. Nestorians
   b. Monophysites
   c. Monotheletes
   d. Arians
   e. Chalcedonians

 CourseMate Visit the CourseMate website at **www.cengagebrain.com** for additional study tools and review materials for this chapter.

3. Which of the following sources of law did Justinian's commission **not** include in the Body of Civil Law?
   a. Germanic customs
   b. Church council rulings
   c. Jurists' opinions
   d. The legislation of previous emperors
   e. Recent legislation

4. What disaster reduced Constantinople's population nearly by half in 542?
   a. An earthquake centered in the Aegean Sea.
   b. An invasion of Alans from north of the Black Sea.
   c. The conquest of Constantinople by the Persian army.
   d. An outbreak of bubonic plague.
   e. The eruption of a volcano in Asia Minor.

5. Which emperor recovered much of the provinces in the east lost to the Persians?
   a. Hereclius
   b. Constantine
   c. Tiberius
   d. Leo III
   e. Constantine VI

Now that you have reviewed and tested yourself on this part of the chapter, take time to pull together all the important information by answering the following questions:

◆ In what ways did Justinian attempt to restore the Roman Empire to its former size and glory?

◆ Which of Justinian's accomplishments endured over the centuries? Which did not?

The Rise of Islam, 600–700

6. Which of the following descriptions best suit the people of the Arabian peninsula before Muhammad's lifetime?
   a. Farmers whose economy depended on agricultural production.
   b. Nomads who raised livestock.
   c. Merchants who traveled between Africa and Central Asia.
   d. Warriors who pillaged neighboring lands.
   e. City dwellers whose livelihoods depended on municipal employment.

7. Which of the following is **not** one of the Five Pillars of Islam?
   a. Jihad
   b. Charity
   c. Pilgrimage
   d. Fasting
   e. Admission of one god

8. Which of the following statements about Muslims, Christians, and Jews is most accurate:
   a. They have completely independent religious traditions.
   b. They are all polytheists.
   c. They have always rejected the use of images in religious worship.
   d. They all revere Abraham and the prophets of the Christian and Hebrew bibles.
   e. They all derive from religious cults from Persia.

9. Muhammad assumed leadership in which town when he was compelled to leave Mecca?
   a. Jerusalem
   b. Medina
   c. Riyaad
   d. Alexandria
   e. Antioch

10. Muhammad, the founder of Islam, died in which year?
   a. 622
   b. 711
   c. 630
   d. 542
   e. 632

"I don't feel that anyone should fail a test on this material if they use all the resources that are given to them with this book."

—Kaitlyn Mundie, Student, Longwood University

92%
of students rated the Chapter Review as helpful or very helpful.

Engaging students with a narrative that highlights individuals and the West's place in the world, *Making Europe* uses the

Vibrant, easy-to-understand maps—revised for the second edition—appear throughout each chapter. Many of the text's maps include questions that reinforce chapter material and help students develop geography and critical-thinking skills.

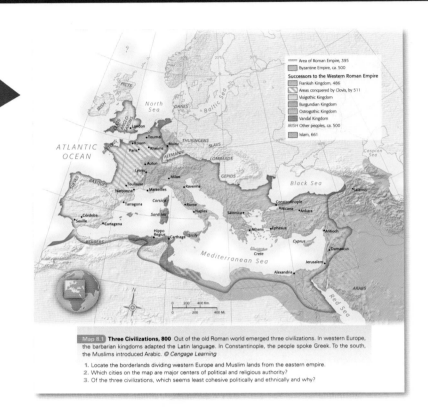

Map 8.1 **Three Civilizations, 800** Out of the old Roman world emerged three civilizations. In western Europe, the barbarian kingdoms adapted the Latin language. In Constantinople, the people spoke Greek. To the south, the Muslims introduced Arabic. © *Cengage Learning*

1. Locate the borderlands dividing western Europe and Muslim lands from the eastern empire.
2. Which cities on the map are major centers of political and religious authority?
3. Of the three civilizations, which seems least cohesive politically and ethnically and why?

A NEW DIRECTION

Empress Theodora Changes Emperor Justinian's Mind

In January 532, rioting throughout the city of Constantinople shook the imperial court to the core. Crowds attacked and burnt down the great church of Hagia Sophia, rebuilt by Constantine II in the 350s. Emperor Justinian I and the empress Theodora had barricaded themselves, with their supporters, in the royal palace, fearful of what would happen next. In the preceding days, Justinian's soldiers had tried to stop the violence that had broken out between the Greens and the Blues—the rival fans of chariot-racing teams who also held competing political and religious views. The emperor and empress preferred the Blues, but no one really knows what this uprising, which came to be called the *Nika Riot*, was about. The only person to write about the riot was the historian Procopius, who simply condemned the passions of all who confused their enthusiasm for sports and entertainment with politics and religion.

Nevertheless, the crowd was now contemplating an overthrow of the political order. The rioters forced two nephews of a previous emperor to join in their plans, which were to attack the imperial palace and kill the imperial couple. The danger to Justinian and Theodora increased by the hour. When the emperor and his advisers were told that the army could not guarantee his safety, Justinian decided to evacuate the city and try to regroup on the opposite side of the Bosporus.

But at this moment, according to Procopius, the empress Theodora made a courageous decision that Justinian was unable to make on his own: she urged her husband and his advisers to remain and fight. With great dignity, the empress reasoned:

If now it is your wish to save yourself, O Emperor, there is no difficulty. For we have much money, and there is the sea, here the boats. However, consider whether it will not come about after you have been saved that you would gladly exchange that safety for death. For as for myself, I approve a certain ancient saying that royal purple is fitting for a burial shroud.

With Theodora's support, Justinian resolved to stay in his palace. Summoning his general Belisarius, he ordered that the rioters be put down. Belisarius succeeded, but only by killing tens of thousands of the people of Constantinople. When the slaughter ended and peace returned to the capital, Justinian undertook the rebuilding of Hagia Sophia, this time on an unprecedented scale. The emperor and the empress entered the newly restored church five years after the Nika Riot. Thanks in part to Theodora's cool head and brave heart, the people of Constantinople once again accustomed themselves to the rule of this imperial couple.

It may seem surprising that Theodora should have been the one to give her husband courage because nothing in her background suggested she would succeed in any endeavor other than the popular theater. Her father reputedly worked in a circus, an atmosphere associated with prostitution and rough customers. Before she married Justinian, many people in Constantinople knew of her from her circus performances and as the lover of powerful men. Justinian, too, came from a humble family, but his military service under his uncle, an emperor who had first risen through the ranks of the Byzantine army, gave him the experience in commanding others that the office of emperor required. The young actress and courtesan Theodora, in contrast, must have possessed an exceptional intelligence and aptitude for politics that marriage to the ambitious soldier and future emperor released. Her influence over her husband aroused the envy of less powerful members of the imperial court, who spread rumors about her past to undermine her reputation. Whether the stories in circulation about her lewd behavior were true or false, never had a woman from as humble a background as Theodora's attained the rank of empress.

A New Direction essays focus on individuals who made choices that had important consequences and highlight the chapter's central themes.

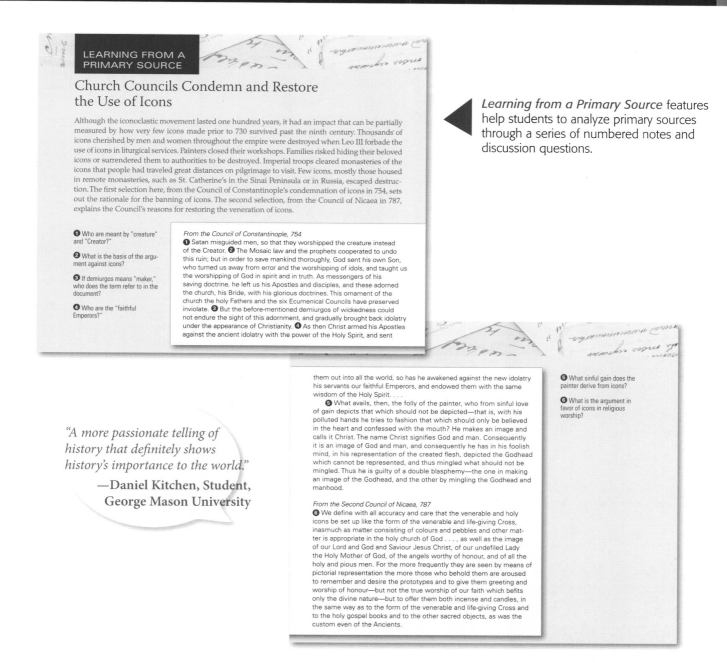

LEARNING FROM A PRIMARY SOURCE

Church Councils Condemn and Restore the Use of Icons

Although the iconoclastic movement lasted one hundred years, it had an impact that can be partially measured by how very few icons made prior to 730 survived past the ninth century. Thousands of icons cherished by men and women throughout the empire were destroyed when Leo III forbade the use of icons in liturgical services. Painters closed their workshops. Families risked hiding their beloved icons or surrendered them to authorities to be destroyed. Imperial troops cleared monasteries of the icons that people had traveled great distances on pilgrimage to visit. Few icons, mostly those housed in remote monasteries, such as St. Catherine's in the Sinai Peninsula or in Russia, escaped destruction. The first selection here, from the Council of Constantinople's condemnation of icons in 754, sets out the rationale for the banning of icons. The second selection, from the Council of Nicaea in 787, explains the Council's reasons for restoring the veneration of icons.

❶ Who are meant by "creature" and "Creator?"

❷ What is the basis of the argument against icons?

❸ If demiurgos means "maker," who does the term refer to in the document?

❹ Who are the "faithful Emperors?"

From the Council of Constantinople, 754
❶ Satan misguided men, so that they worshipped the creature instead of the Creator. ❷ The Mosaic law and the prophets cooperated to undo this ruin; but in order to save mankind thoroughly, God sent his own Son, who turned us away from error and the worshipping of idols, and taught us the worshipping of God in spirit and in truth. As messengers of his saving doctrine, he left us his Apostles and disciples, and these adorned the church, his Bride, with his glorious doctrines. This ornament of the church the holy Fathers and the six Ecumenical Councils have preserved inviolate. ❸ But the before-mentioned demiurgos of wickedness could not endure the sight of this adornment, and gradually brought back idolatry under the appearance of Christianity. ❹ As then Christ armed his Apostles against the ancient idolatry with the power of the Holy Spirit, and sent

them out into all the world, so has he awakened against the new idolatry his servants our faithful Emperors, and endowed them with the same wisdom of the Holy Spirit. . . .
❺ What avails, then, the folly of the painter, who from sinful love of gain depicts that which should not be depicted—that is, with his polluted hands he tries to fashion that which should only be believed in the heart and confessed with the mouth? He makes an image and calls it Christ. The name Christ signifies God and man. Consequently it is an image of God and man, and consequently he has in his foolish mind, in his representation of the created flesh, depicted the Godhead which cannot be represented, and thus mingled what should not be mingled. Thus he is guilty of a double blasphemy—the one in making an image of the Godhead, and the other by mingling the Godhead and manhood.

From the Second Council of Nicaea, 787
❻ We define with all accuracy and care that the venerable and holy icons be set up like the form of the venerable and life-giving Cross, inasmuch as matter consisting of colours and pebbles and other matter is appropriate in the holy church of God . . . , as well as the image of our Lord and God and Saviour Jesus Christ, of our undefiled Lady the Holy Mother of God, of the angels worthy of honour, and of all the holy and pious men. For the more frequently they are seen by means of pictorial representation the more those who behold them are aroused to remember and desire the prototypes and to give them greeting and worship of honour—but not the true worship of our faith which befits only the divine nature—but to offer them both incense and candles, in the same way as to the form of the venerable and life-giving Cross and to the holy gospel books and to the other sacred objects, as was the custom even of the Ancients.

❺ What sinful gain does the painter derive from icons?

❻ What is the argument in favor of icons in religious worship?

Learning from a Primary Source features help students to analyze primary sources through a series of numbered notes and discussion questions.

"A more passionate telling of history that definitely shows history's importance to the world."
—Daniel Kitchen, Student, George Mason University

"I really liked the way the whole chapter was set up. I didn't get tired or lose my place as much as in other books I've had to read. I feel like all the breaks and visuals kept me interested, and the timelines, Checking In features, maps, and definitions were great to have."
—Amanda Reoch, Student, John Tyler Community College

Aplia

Available August 2013

Aplia prompts history students to contextualize and analyze information. The exercises, written by trained historians who have taught undergraduates, ensure that students think critically and draw conclusions rather than merely memorize historical facts.

- Auto-assigned and graded activities hold students accountable for the material before class, increasing their effort and preparation.

- Primary source-based activities encourage critical thinking.

- Interactive maps provide practice interpreting this key historical medium.

- Grades are automatically recorded and instructors can monitor class performance and individual student performance on a topic-by-topic basis.

- Map and writing tutorials guide students through the process of interpreting information and effectively communicating their ideas within the framework of the history discipline.

Learn more at www.cengage.com/aplia.

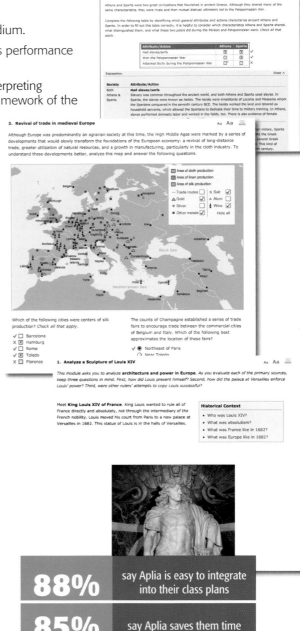

What instructors are saying about Aplia:

*"Thanks again for this great product. It **saved me as the instructor a lot of time in prep work** since it was already done for me, not to mention saving time in **grading as well**. I do **expect the quality of materials I select to be worth the dollars the students pay and this one definitely is**."*

—Abbylin Sellers, History and Political Science, Southeastern University, FL

*"Aplia gave students the primary source materials in a **comfortable digital format for students** to use in applying the general material they learned in the textbook."*

—Melissa Gayan, History, Georgia Southern University, GA

What students are saying about Aplia:

*"The Aplia homework assignments gave me a **better understanding** of the concepts in the textbook. The homework also prepared me for many tests that were taken during this school term. After I completed the questions, I started to see **better results on test scores**."*

—Rudy Hoff, Student, Normandale Community College, MN

*"It **raised my test scores 34 points when I took my second test in the class and it helped tremendously**. One hour a week or 30 minutes in 2 days can do wonders to your grade."*

—Steven O'Sullivan, Student, Georgia Southern University, GA

88% say Aplia is easy to integrate into their class plans

85% say Aplia saves them time

Create an affordable and customized online reader in minutes!

CourseReader: Western Civilization

CourseReader lets you choose from thousands of primary and secondary sources—including permissions-cleared readings, audio, and video selections.

CourseReader is Cengage Learning's easy, affordable way to build your own online customizable reader. Select exactly and only the material you want your students to work with. Each selection can be listened to (using the "Listen" button) to accommodate varied learning styles. Instructors can even add their own notes to readings to direct students' attention or ask them questions about a particular passage. Each primary source is accompanied by an introduction, and questions to help students understand the reading.

With **CourseReader**, you can:

- Easily search and preview source material for your course

- Publish your notes to students, assign due dates, assemble and re-order selections, archive readers from previous terms and adapt them for future classes

- Provide students with pedagogical support, including descriptive introductions that add context to many of the primary source documents, and critical-thinking and multiple-choice questions that reinforce key points

- Utilize Editor's Choice selections as time-saving starting points.

 Learn more and view a demo! www.cengage.com/coursereader

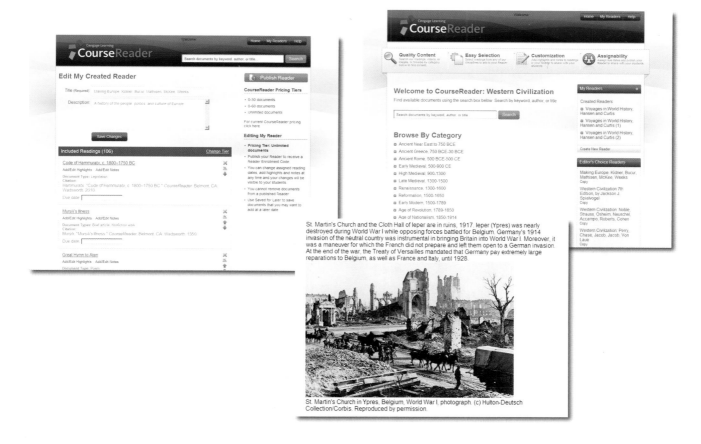

St. Martin's Church and the Cloth Hall of Ieper are in ruins, 1917. Ieper (Ypres) was nearly destroyed during World War I while opposing forces battled for Belgium. Germany's 1914 invasion of the neutral country was instrumental in bringing Britain into World War I. Moreover, it was a maneuver for which the French did not prepare and left them open to a German invasion. At the end of the war, the Treaty of Versailles mandated that Germany pay extremely large reparations to Belgium, as well as France and Italy, until 1928.

St. Martin's Church in Ypres, Belgium, World War I, photograph. (c) Hulton-Deutsch Collection/Corbis. Reproduced by permission.

History CourseMate

Complement your text and course content with study and practice materials. Cengage Learning's **History CourseMate** brings course concepts to life with interactive learning, study, and exam preparation tools that support the printed textbook. Watch student comprehension soar as your class works with the printed textbook and the textbook-specific website. **CourseMate** goes beyond the book to deliver what you need!

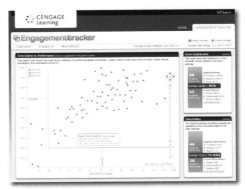

CourseMate has unique features!

- Use Engagement Tracker to monitor student engagement in the course and watch student comprehension soar as your class works with the printed textbook and the textbook-specific website.

- An interactive eBook allows students to take notes, highlight, search, and interact with embedded media (such as quizzes, flashcards, primary sources, and videos).

 Learn more at www.cengage.com/coursemate.

Save students time and money—direct them to Cengagebrain.com, a single destination for more than 10,000 new textbooks, eTextbooks, eChapters, study tools, and audio supplements. Students have the freedom to purchase a-la-carte exactly what they need, when they need it.

Making Europe

Making Europe

THE STORY OF THE WEST

Second Edition

Frank L. Kidner
San Francisco State University

Maria Bucur
Indiana University

Ralph Mathisen
University of Illinois at Urbana-Champaign

Sally McKee
University of California, Davis

Theodore R. Weeks
Southern Illinois University, Carbondale

WADSWORTH
CENGAGE Learning

Australia • Brazil • Japan • Korea • Mexico • Singapore • Spain • United Kingdom • United States

Making Europe: The Story of the West, 2e
Kidner/Bucur/Mathisen/McKee/Weeks

Editor-in-Chief: Lyn Uhl

Senior Publisher: Suzanne Jeans

Acquiring Sponsoring Editor: Brooke Barbier

Development Editor: Kate Scheinman

Associate Development Editor,
    Market Strategies: Laura Ross

Assistant Editor: Jamie Bushell

Editorial Assistant: Katie Coaster

Managing Media Editor: Lisa Ciccolo

Media Editor: Kate MacLean

Marketing Manager: Melissa Larmon

Marketing Coordinator: Lorreen R. Towle

Marketing and Communication Director:
    Talia Wise

Senior Content Project Manager: Carol Newman

Senior Art Director: Cate Rickard Barr

Manufacturing Buyer: Sandee Milewski

Senior Rights Acquisition Specialist:
    Jennifer Meyer Dare

Production Service/Compositor:
    Cenveo Publisher Services

Text Designer: Dutton & Sherman Design

Cover Designer: Dutton & Sherman Design

Cover Image: Zocchi, Giuseppe (171 1–1767), Italian. Oriental merchants at the port of Livorno, Italy, 1762. Detail rom a panel/Opificio delle Pietre Dure, Florence, Italy/Alfredo Dagli Orti/Art Resource, NY

For product information and technology assistance, contact us at **Cengage Learning Customer & Sales Support, 1-800-354-9706.**

For permission to use material from this text or product, submit all requests online at **www.cengage.com/permissions.** Further permissions questions can be emailed to **permissionrequest@cengage.com.**

Library of Congress Control Number: 2012945045

Student Edition:

ISBN-13: 978-1-111-84131-7

ISBN-10: 1-111-84131-4

Wadsworth
20 Channel Center Street
Boston, MA 02210
USA

Cengage Learning is a leading provider of customized learning solutions with office locations around the globe, including Singapore, the United Kingdom, Australia, Mexico, Brazil and Japan. Locate your local office at **international.cengage.com/region.**

Cengage Learning products are represented in Canada by Nelson Education, Ltd.

For your course and learning solutions, visit **www.cengage.com.**

Purchase any of our products at your local college store or at our preferred online store **www.cengagebrain.com.**

Instructors: Please visit **login.cengage.com** and log in to access instructor-specific resources.

Printed in the United States of America
2 3 4 5 16 15 14 13

Brief Contents

Contents

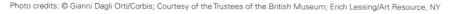

Photo credits: © Gianni Dagli Orti/Corbis; Courtesy of the Trustees of the British Museum; Erich Lessing/Art Resource, NY

Photo credits: Vanni/Art Resource, NY; Erich Lessing/Art Resource, NY; © The Trustees of the British Museum/Art Resource, NY; Scala/Art Resource, NY

Photo credits: Jean-Luc Manaud/Getty Images; Erich Lessing/Art Resource, NY; © Austrian Archives/Corbis; Culture and Sport Glasgow Museums, acc. #E. 1939.65.sn

Photo credits: Alinari/Art Resource, NY; Museo degli Argenti, Palazzo Pitti, Florence/The Bridgeman Art Library; bpk, Berlin/Skulpturesammlung und Museum fur Byzantinische Kunst, Staatliche Museen, Berlin/Art Resource, Inc.; © Derek Bayes-Art/Lebrecht Music & Arts/Corbis

Photo credits: Reunion des Musees nationaux/Art Resource, NY; © Science & Society Picture Library; Bibliotheque de L'Arsenal, Paris/Archives Charmet/The Bridgeman Art Library

Photo credits: NRM/SSPL/The Image Works; Pitt Rivers Museum, University of Oxford (1965.10.1); Private Collection/Photo © Bonhams, London/The Bridgeman Art Library; Ullstein Bilderdienst/The Image Works

Photo credits: © David Sutherland/Corbis; Visual Connection Archive; Thomas Kienzie/AP Images

Maps

Features

Preface

For years, we five professors from across the country have taught Western Civilization courses without the textbook we really wanted to have—a textbook with a coherent strategy for helping students to study and learn. In 1999 we commenced to develop such a text. This book is the result.

The five of us bring to this book a variety of backgrounds, interests, and historical approaches, as well as a combined total of nearly one hundred years of teaching history. Two of us completed graduate degrees in literature before turning to history. We have all studied, worked, or lived on three continents; we are all American citizens, but not all of us were born in the United States. Although we come from different parts of the country and have different historical specializations, all of us teach in large state university systems. We have a strong commitment to the kinds of students who enroll in our schools and in community colleges—young people and nontraditional students from richly diverse cultural and ethnic backgrounds who are enthusiastic and prepared to work but have little knowledge of history and few formal skills in historical analysis. We were gratified to be developing a new kind of textbook that met their needs.

We conceived of a textbook that would be lively and absolutely up-to-date but did not presume a great deal of prior knowledge of western civilization. We also wanted to include new types of learning aids that were fully integrated into the text itself. Our greatest hope is that students who use this book will come to understand how the West has developed and, at the same time, to see the importance of the past for the present. In other words, we want to help them value the past as well as understand it and thus to think historically.

Approaches and Themes

This textbook introduces the cultural unit we call "the West" from its beginnings in the ancient Near East to the present. It is focused around five themes: politics, religion, social history, biography and personality, and individual and collective identity.

Politics: Our book's first theme centers on western politics, states, and the state system from the emergence of civilization in Mesopotamia and Egypt down to our own century. Politics provides the underlying chronological backbone of the text. Our experience has taught us that a politically centered chronology is the most effective way to help inexperienced students get a sense of what came before and what came after and why. Political chronology helps them perceive trends and recognize the forces for historical continuity and change.

If there are sensible reasons for organizing the text around a political chronology, there are pitfalls as well. The chief one is the disaffection many students may have felt in the past with a history that seems little more than a list of persons, reigns, and wars ("Kings and Things") needing to be memorized. To avoid this pitfall we have adopted an approach that centers on dynamic exchanges between states and political elites on the one hand, and citizens or subjects on the other. In this textbook students will read and think about the ways taxation, the need for armies, and judicial protection affect ordinary people and vice versa—how the marginal and unrepresented affect the politically powerful. Our approach focuses both on what states and their political elites want from the people who live in them and on what benefits they provide to those people. In turn, we also consider what ordinary people do or do not want from the state, and what kinds of people benefit and do not benefit from the state's policies. When relevant, we also treat the state's lack of impact.

Religion: Our second theme takes up the history of western religion. We have aimed for an expansive treatment of religious activity that includes its institutions and beliefs but is not confined to them. Our textbook ranges widely over issues of polytheism, monotheism, civic religion, philosophically inspired religion, normative religion, orthodoxy and heresy, popular practices, ultimate spiritual values, and systematically articulated agnosticism or atheism. Since from beginning to end we emphasize religious issues, this book is set apart from most Western Civilization texts that treat religious matters fairly consistently up through the sixteenth century but then drop them.

Our distinctive post–1600 emphasis on religion arises from our sense that religious beliefs, values, and affiliations have continued to play a central role in European life up to and including the twenty-first century. Although in part compartmentalized or privatized in the last several centuries as states pursued various secularizing agendas, religious sensibilities still have had a considerable impact on economic behavior, social values, and political action, while simultaneously adjusting to or resisting changes in other aspects of life. In addition, of course, they regularly influenced European activity in colonies and empires.

In our treatment of religion we do not focus simply on the dominant religion of any time or place. Judaism, for example, is discussed throughout the text, while Islam, introduced in Chapter 8, is discussed again in connection with such issues as the Moriscos of Spain, the Habsburg re-conquest of Hungary, tension in Russian Central Asia and the Balkans before World War I, Soviet campaigns against religion, the arrival of Muslim immigrants in post–World War II Europe, and the dissolution of Yugoslavia. In addition, an emphasis on religious pluralism in European life leads to discussions of the variety of subcultures found in the West, many of which believe that their religious and ethnic identity is integral to their other values and practices. Indeed, our belief that religion continues to play an important role in modern European history rests in large part on the abundant evidence showing it to be a core component of life for subcultures within the larger western context. Catholic and Protestant Irish, Protestant northern Germans and Catholic southern Germans, Orthodox Russians, and Bosnian Muslims stand as examples of communities whose values and actions have been significantly shaped by ongoing religious allegiances and whose interactions with those practicing other religions have had lasting repercussions. Our intention is to present the religious past of the West in all its complex, multifold voices to students who are more and more self-consciously aware of racial, cultural, and ethnic diversity in their own world.

We also believe that attention to religion reflects the current public debate over values, using students' experience of this contested territory to stimulate their interest. Their awareness of current values-based programs can serve as a springboard for a study of the past. Does one choose aggression, persuasion, or passive resistance and nonaggression?

Social History: The theme of social history is integrated into the text as consideration is given to the way politics and religion affect people and societies. Discussions of daily lives and family structures are illuminated through occasional spotlights on the experience of a single, typical individual. We also pay close attention to issues of gender norms and roles in the past, drawing on the work of a generation of historians concerned with the history of ordinary men, women, and children. We see many possibilities for engaging the interest of students in this approach. We hope our book will stimulate productive class discussions of what it meant to live as a woman or a (male) citizen in the Athenian city-state, as a peasant or a landlord in the relatively stateless world of the early Western Middle Ages, as a man or woman during the French Revolution, and as a soldier or nurse in the trenches of World War I.

Biography and Personality: To give focus and immediacy to the themes we emphasize, we have chosen to highlight the biographies of important or representative figures in the past and, when possible, to give students a sense of their personalities. We want key figures to live for students through their choices and actions and pronouncements. Each chapter contains a feature, "A New Direction," that focuses on biography and personality. The person discussed in this box is integrated into the chapter narratives. Portraits of cities occasionally stand in for biographies by providing a picture of the places and spaces that have been important in a particular era or have continuing significance across centuries.

Identity: An emphasis on individual and collective identity is another distinctive feature of our book. By addressing matters of identity for each era, we believe that we can help students see themselves in—or as against—the experiences of those who preceded them. To this end, the relationship between the individual and the group is examined as well as changing categories of identity, such as religion, class, gender, ethnicity, nationality, citizenship, occupation or profession, generation, and race. In a real sense, this emphasis flows from the preceding four themes. It means that the political narrative is personalized, that history is not only an account of states, institutions, and policies, but also of people.

The West and the World

In addition to emphasizing the themes outlined above, we have adopted a view about the West that shapes this volume. It derives from our rejection of the tendency to treat the West as a monolithic entity or to imply that the West is "really" western Europe after 500 and, after 1500, specifically northwestern Europe. We define the West more broadly. Throughout the book, students remain informed about developments in eastern Europe, western Asia, and Africa. We show that, far from being homogeneous, the West represents a diversity of cultures. By taking this approach we hope to be able to engage students in a way that will lead them to understanding the causes, effects, and significance of the cultural diversity that exists in the modern world.

We also address the issue of cultural diversity by looking at the impact of the non-western world on the

West from antiquity to the present. We discuss both western knowledge and western fantasies about non-western peoples, the actual contact or lack of contact with non-western societies, and the growing global impact of Europe and Europeans during the last five hundred years. The emphasis is always on the West—on how the West did or did not make contact with other societies and, in the case of contacts, on their consequences for everyone involved—but the effect is to place the West in its larger global context as one of humanity's many cultural units.

Pedagogy and Features

One of the most common questions our students ask is: "What's important?" This textbook aims to help them answer that question for themselves. We have found that students can profit from a text that takes less for granted, provides a consistent and clear structure for each chapter, and incorporates primary documents. For both teachers and students, "Western Civ" is often the most difficult history course in the curriculum. With this textbook, we hope to change its reputation. For the second edition, we have developed a strong pedagogy, based on feedback from more than 500 instructors and students. This pedagogy is realized through a series of innovative features that will assist students in understanding the book's content and help them master it. The book itself becomes a complete study tool for students to ensure they are able to read and understand the material. In class tests with instructors who used chapters with the new pedagogy, students reported better understanding and interest in the material. We also kept instructors in mind, because we believe that carefully constructed chapters that convey basic information are the best support for teaching. Instructors may then build on the text or modify it to meet specific needs.

Chapter Openers: Every chapter begins with a list of focus questions previewing the content covered within that chapter. These questions direct students' attention to the central concerns and issues about to be examined. A timeline extending over the period is also featured, as well as a map with integrated questions to strengthen geography and critical-thinking skills.

Section Opening Questions: Before students begin reading the chapter sections, they will see focus questions related to the material they will read. These questions invite students to remain focused while going through the material.

Checking In: The Checking In feature appears at the end of every chapter section and provides students with a list of the key terms from that section. Students should review these terms before proceeding on to the next section to ensure thorough comprehension.

A New Direction: As noted earlier in this Preface, each chapter contains an account of an individual making a crucial choice that mattered, that had important consequences, and that can be used to highlight the chapter's central concerns. Our intention in this feature is to foreground human agency and to spark the interest of students. Thus, Chapter 12, which introduces students to the Renaissance in Italy and Northern Europe, features Michelangelo Buonarotti as a new kind of artist who changed the way the public viewed art and creativity. Chapter 22, which discusses the "triumph" of the nation-state in the late nineteenth century, contains an account of Theodor Herzl's endorsement of Zionism as a way to discuss the impact of nationalist ideology and to carry out the book's emphasis on religious diversity in the West.

Learning from a Primary Source: Each chapter also features a document from an individual who lived during the era of the chapter, sometimes from the same individual featured in "A New Direction." An explanatory headnote sets the context for the document. Students are then helped to analyze it historically through a series of numbered marginal notes, which are also designed to aid instructors seeking to integrate primary sources into their classrooms.

In addition, we have built into each chapter a strong framework of pedagogical aids to help students navigate the text. All the maps have been revised, and many are partnered with critical thinking questions. Photo captions have also been enriched with questions for students to ponder. Subheadings have been introduced throughout the chapters to clearly focus on the topics under discussion.

A distinctive feature of our text is the glossary—a system whereby boldfaced names, terms, organizations, concepts, and events are explained or defined on the same page where they are introduced. These definitions support students whose vocabulary and knowledge of history are weak, enhance the background a better-prepared student may have, and serve as a convenient review and study aid.

Chapter Review: A new, enhanced end-of-chapter section provides students with a number of ways to review the chapter. This thorough review features a bulleted summary and a boxed chronology of events, followed by a Test Yourself multiple-choice self-quiz. The questions for this quiz are broken down by section, allowing students to easily refer back to the sections or concepts that they need to review. This quiz is accompanied by critical thinking questions that instructors can use to gauge student understanding of each major chapter division. Answers to the multiple-choice quizzes can be found in the back of the book.

New to This Edition

The second edition of *Making Europe: The Story of the West* has been updated in a myriad of ways. The most significant of these revisions are:

- Chapter 1 includes an expanded discussion of cave painting, Sumerian iconography, Mesopotamian rule, the Great Pyramids, religious reforms of the pharaoh Akhenaton, Minoan culture, and Mycenaean architecture.

- Chapter 2 features more on naval warfare, the economic function of coinage, the first Jewish temple in Jerusalem, Assyrian military tactics, Babylonian iconography, Persian architecture, and the policies of Darius I of Persia.

- Chapter 3 contains new coverage of Greek technology and iconography, hoplite warfare, women's sports, and Greek coinage propaganda.

- Chapter 4 looks at urban architecture and interior decorating, Macedonian marriage practices, social and cultural integration in Hellenistic Egypt, Greek colonization, the survival of Greek architecture and multiethnicity in Hellenistic religion.

- Chapter 5 updates material on the use of archaeological evidence to understand the past, Etruscan views of the afterlife and of the Roman assimilation of Etruscan culture, Roman family life, use of propaganda by senators, the ultimate fate of Roman public buildings, the means by which Roman laws were preserved, and the deification of deceased rulers.

- Chapter 6 includes new coverage of the role of the emperor as commander in chief of the Roman army, the use of propaganda by Roman emperors, Roman urbanism, the role played by Pontius Pilate in the trial of Jesus, and the victory of the Persian king Shapur over the Roman emperor Valerian.

- Chapter 7's "A New Direction" focuses on Genevieve of Paris, thus increasing to an even greater extent the volume's commitment to gender balance in its coverage. Other Chapter 7 updates include a more direct connection made between Christianity and sun worship, an expanded discussion of the importance of church building and the role of churches in urban landscapes, discussion on the significance of senatorial withdrawal to the countryside, especially as evidenced by the construction of fortified villas, and the Roman adoption of barbarian customs.

- Chapter 8 contains new material that emphasizes the religious roots of medieval, Byzantine, and Muslim civilizations.

- Chapter 9 updates the coverage of feudalism, manors, and unfree status in light of the reservations scholars now have about their uniform applicability across western Europe.

- Chapter 10 includes updated material on the participants, goals, and outcomes of the crusading movement.

- Chapter 11's updates make it easier for students to understand the connections among climate, disease, warfare, and social unrest in the tumultuous fourteenth century.

- Chapter 12's "A New Direction" discusses the sculptor and painter Michelangelo, in the period when he was painting the Sistine Chapel.

- Chapter 13 adds material to its discussion of Antwerp, the expansion of Russia, Ivan IV, and European world expansion.

- Chapter 14 features revised coverage of church reform, including Martin Luther, the Jesuits, and Pope Paul III.

- Chapter 15, now called "A Century of Crisis, 1550–1650," expands the discussion on population growth and revolution, the Inquisition and witch trials, and the revolt in the Netherlands.

- Chapter 16 updates material on absolutism in France, the growth of Prussia, Peter the Great and Catherine the Great, partitioning of Poland, and the Seven Years' War.

- Chapter 17's "A New Direction" features Galileo Galilei. Additional changes cover the scientific revolution and the Enlightenment, including Rousseau and the concept of leisure.

- Chapter 18 features more on the expanding populations of Europe and resulting consumer revolution, as well as a closer look at the worldwide slave trade.

- Chapter 19 includes more on the French Revolution including both Louis XVI and Marie Antoinette, as well as Napoleonic Europe.

- Chapter 20 closely looks at coverage of ideological differences between conservatives, nationalists, and liberals during this period. A thoroughly revised introduction helps students orient themselves in the post-Napoleonic Era.

- Chapter 21 looks more closely at the effects of industrialization in the nineteenth century, including the expansion of railroads.

- Chapter 22 concentrates more specifically on nationalism throughout the European continent. A new image of Sacre Coeur cathedral in Paris emphasizes attempts by Catholic conservatives to reclaim industrial workers for the church in the post-commune period.

- Chapter 23 features new images from the fin-de-siècle period to help readers better make a connection among technology, leisure, commerce, and art.

- Chapter 24 contains new sections on missionary David Livingstone and on Germany's colonies. The new maps aid students in better making the connection between imperialism and world geography.

- Chapter 25's "A New Direction," focuses on the young assassin of Archduke Francis Ferdinand, Gavrilo Princip. New maps on World War I enable students to better understand the war both on the western and eastern fronts.

- Chapter 26 provides more connections between the photographs and the themes covered in the respective sections, such as asking students to identify important aspects of Kamal Ataturk's nationalism by examining his photograph.

- Chapter 27 provides two new maps, replacing the map of Nazi Germany's advances in WWII and the map representing the death camps and other aspects of the Holocaust. The description of *Guernica* also asks students to do a closer analysis of the symbology of peace and violence in that painting.
- Chapter 28 offers two replacement maps for East European Stalinism and De-Colonization, as well as added commentary for most images and questions to link those illustrations to the narrative.
- Chapter 29 has added commentary and questions for most images to better link them to the narrative.
- Chapter 30 includes an extended profile of Angela Merkel. This chapter also includes a discussion of the Arab Spring and of the most recent developments in the Iraq War and in Afghanistan. Developments in the European Union have been updated, together with a discussion of how the Eurozone has dealt with the financial woes of the last four years, including a discussion of the bailouts in Ireland, Greece, and Spain. The chapter has also updated important developments in the post Yugoslav wars' violence and peace building processes. An update on Russian politics since 2008 has also been added. There is now a new section on the "Global Economic Recession."

Flexible Format

Western Civilization courses differ widely in chronological structure from one campus to another. To accommodate the differing divisions of historical time into intervals for various academic year divisions, *Making Europe: The Story of the West* is published in three print versions, two of which embrace the complete work, and two electronic versions:

- One-volume hardcover edition: *Making Europe: The Story of the West*
- Two-volume paperback: *Making Europe: The Story of the West, Volume I: To 1790* (Chapters 1–17); *Volume II: Since 1550* (Chapters 15–30)
- *Making Europe: The Story of the West, Since 1300* (Chapters 12–30), for courses on Europe since the Renaissance
- An eBook of the complete one-volume edition
- A two-volume eBook of volumes one and two

Supplements

Instructor Resources

PowerLecture DVD with ExamView® and JoinIn®

ISBN-10: 1285062000 | ISBN-13: 9781285062006

This dual platform, all-in-one multimedia resource includes the Instructor's Resource Manual; Test Bank, prepared by Kathleen Addison of California State University - Northridge(includes key term identification, multiple-choice, essay, and true/false questions; Microsoft® PowerPoint® slides of both lecture outlines and images and maps from the text that can be used as offered, or customized by importing personal lecture slides or other material; and JoinIn® PowerPoint® slides with clicker content. Also included is ExamView, an easy-to-use assessment and tutorial system that allows instructors to create, deliver, and customize tests in minutes. Instructors can build tests with as many as 250 questions using up to 12 question types, and using ExamView's complete word-processing capabilities, they can enter an unlimited number of new questions or edit existing ones.

eInstructor's Resource Manual Prepared by Bethany Kilcrease of Aquinas College. This manual has many features, including learning objectives, chapter outlines, lecture suggestions, activities for using primary sources, activities for the text features, map activities, an audiovisual bibliography, and internet resources. Available on the instructor's companion website.

CourseMate

ISBN-10: 1285079604 | ISBN-13: 9781285079608 PAC
ISBN-10: 1285079493 | ISBN-13: 9781285079493 IAC
ISBN-10: 1285079426 | ISBN-13: 9781285079424 SSO

CourseMate Cengage Learning's History CourseMate brings course concepts to life with interactive learning, study, and exam preparation tools that support the printed textbook. History CourseMate includes an integrated eBook, interactive teaching and learning tools including quizzes, flashcards, videos, and more, and EngagementTracker, a first-of-its-kind tool that monitors student engagement in the course. Learn more at www.cengagebrain.com.

Aplia™

ISBN-10: 1285078993 | ISBN-13: 9781285078991
1-term PAC
ISBN-10: 1285079140 | ISBN-13: 9781285079141
1-term IAC
ISBN-10: 1285078977 | ISBN-13: 9781285078977
2-term PAC
ISBN-10: 1285079116 | ISBN-13: 9781285079110
2-term IAC

Aplia™ is an online interactive learning solution that improves comprehension and outcomes by increasing student effort and engagement. Founded by a professor to enhance his own courses, Aplia provides automatically graded assignments with detailed, immediate explanations on every question. The interactive assignments have been developed to address the major concepts covered in *Making Europe: The Story of the West*, 2e and are designed to promote critical thinking and engage students more fully in their learning Question types include questions built around animated maps, primary sources such as newspaper extracts, or imagined scenarios, like engaging in a conversation with Benjamin Franklin or finding a diary and being asked to fill in some blank words; more in-depth primary source question sets that address a major topic with a number of related primary sources and questions promote deeper analysis of historical evidence. Images, video clips, and audio clips are incorporated in many of the questions. Students get immediate feedback on their work (not only what they got right or wrong, but why), and they can choose to see another set of related questions if they want to practice further. A searchable ebook is available inside the course as well, so that students can easily reference it as they are working. Map-reading and writing tutorials are available as well to get students off to a good start.

Aplia's simple-to-use course management interface allows instructors to post announcements, upload course materials, host student discussions, e-mail students, and manage the gradebook; personalized support from a knowledgeable and friendly support team also offers assistance in customizing assignments to the instructor's course schedule. To learn more and view a demo for this book, visit www.aplia.com.

CourseReader: Western Civilization

ISBN-10: 1133045545 | ISBN-13: 9781133045540
CourseReader 0-30 PAC

ISBN-10: 1133045553 | ISBN-13: 9781133045557
CourseReader 0-30 IAC

ISBN-10: 1133045539 | ISBN-13: 9781133045533
CourseReader 0-30 SSO

ISBN-10: 1133045561 | ISBN-13: 9781133045564
CourseReader 0-60 PAC

ISBN-10: 1133211569 | ISBN-13: 9781133211563
CourseReader 0-60 IAC

ISBN-10: 1133211550 | ISBN-13: 9781133211556
CourseReader 0-60 SSO

ISBN-10: 1133211585 | ISBN-13: 9781133211587
CourseReader Unlimited PAC

ISBN-10: 1133211593 | ISBN-13: 9781133211594
CourseReader Unlimited IAC

ISBN-10: 1133211577 | ISBN-13: 9781133211570
CourseReader Unlimited SSO

CourseReader is an online collection of primary and secondary sources that lets you create a customized electronic reader in minutes. With an easy-to-use interface and assessment tool, you can choose exactly what your students will be assigned—simply search or browse Cengage Learning's extensive document database to preview and select your customized collection of readings. In addition to print sources of all types (letters, diary entries, speeches, newspaper accounts, etc., there collection includes a growing number of images and video and audio clips.

Each primary source document includes a descriptive headnote that puts the reading into context and is further supported by both critical thinking and multiple-choice questions designed to reinforce key points. For more information visit www.cengage.com/coursereader.

Cengagebrain.com Save your students time and money. Direct them to www.cengagebrain.com for choice in formats and savings and a better chance to succeed in your class. Cengagebrain.com, Cengage Learning's online store, is a single destination for more than 10,000 new textbooks, eTextbooks, eChapters, study tools, and audio supplements. Students have the freedom to purchase a-la-carte exactly what they need when they need it. Students can save 50% on the electronic textbook, and can pay as little as $1.99 for an individual eChapter.

Student Resources

Companion Website

ISBN-10: 113350681X | ISBN-13: 9781133506812

A website for students that features a wide assortment of resources to help students master the subject matter. The website, prepared by Ryan Swanson of George Mason University, includes a glossary, flashcards, learning objectives, maps, sample quizzes, and primary source links. Additionally, the list of Suggested Readings for each chapter from the first edition has now been placed on the student companion website so students can easily access this important information.

eBook

ISBN-10: 1285079264 | ISBN-13: 9781285079264

This interactive multimedia ebook links out to rich media assets such as video and MP3 chapter summaries. Through this ebook, students can also access chapter outlines, focus questions, chronology and matching exercises, primary source documents with critical thinking questions, and interactive (zoomable) maps. Available at www.cengagebrain.com.

Doing History: Research and Writing in the Digital Age, 2e

ISBN-10: 1133587887 | ISBN-13: 9781133587880

Prepared by Michael J. Galgano, J. Chris Arndt, and Raymond M. Hyser of James Madison University. Whether you're starting down the path as a history major, or simply looking for a straightforward and systematic guide to writing a successful paper, you'll find this text to be an indispensible handbook to historical research. This text's "soup to nuts" approach to researching and writing about history addresses every step of the process, from locating your sources and gathering information, to writing clearly and making proper use of various citation styles to avoid plagiarism. You'll also learn how to make the most of every tool available to you—especially the technology that helps you conduct the process efficiently and effectively. The second edition includes a special appendix linked to CourseReader (see below), where you can examine and interpret primary sources online.

The History Handbook, 2e

ISBN-10: 049590676X | ISBN-13: 9780495906766

eAudio History Handbook, 1e

ISBN-10: 084006344X | ISBN-13: 9780840063441

Printed Access Card for eAudio History Handbook, 1e

ISBN-10: 1111471266 | ISBN-13: 9781111471262

Prepared by Carol Berkin of Baruch College, City University of New York and Betty Anderson of Boston University. This book teaches students both basic and history-specific study skills such as how to take notes, get the most out of lectures and readings, read primary sources, research historical topics, and correctly cite sources. Substantially less expensive than comparable skill-building texts, *The History Handbook* also offers tips for Internet research and evaluating online sources. Additionally, students can purchase and download the eAudio version of *The History Handbook* or any of its eighteen individual units at www. cengagebrain.com to listen to on-the-go.

Writing for College History, 1e

ISBN-10: 061830603X | ISBN -13: 9780618306039

Prepared by Robert M. Frakes, Clarion University. This brief handbook for survey courses in American history, Western Civilization/European history, and world civilization guides students through the various types of writing assignments they encounter in a history class. Providing examples of student writing and candid assessments of student work, this text focuses on the rules and conventions of writing for the college history course.

The Modern Researcher, 6e

ISBN-10: 0495318701 | ISBN-13: 9780495318705

Prepared by Jacques Barzun and Henry F. Graff of Columbia University. This classic introduction to the techniques of research and the art of expression is used widely in history courses, but is also appropriate for writing and research methods courses in other departments. Barzun and Graff thoroughly cover every aspect of research, from the selection of a topic through the gathering, analysis, writing, revision, and publication of findings presenting the process not as a set of rules but through actual cases that put the subtleties of research in a useful context. Part One covers the principles and methods of research; Part Two covers writing, speaking, and getting one's work published.

Reader Program Cengage Learning publishes a number of readers, some containing exclusively primary sources, others devoted to essays and secondary sources, and still others provide a combination of primary and secondary sources. All of these readers are designed to guide students through the process of historical inquiry. Visit www.cengage.com/history for a complete list of readers.

Rand McNally *Historical Atlas of Western Civilization*, 2e

ISBN-10: 0618841946 | ISBN-13: 9780618841943

This valuable resource features over 45 maps, including maps that highlight classical Greece and Rome; maps documenting European civilization during the Renaissance; maps that follow events in Germany, Russia, and Italy as they lead up to World Wars I and II; maps that show the dissolution of Communism in 1989; maps documenting language and religion in the western world; and maps describing the unification and industrialization of Europe.

Document Exercise Workbook

Volume 1: ISBN-10: 0534560830 | ISBN-13: 9780534560836
Volume 2: ISBN-10: 0534560849 | ISBN-13: 9780534560843

Prepared by Donna Van Raaphorst, Cuyahoga Community College. A collection of exercises based around primary sources. Available in two volumes.

Custom Options

Nobody knows your students like you, so why not give them a text that is tailor-fit to their needs? Cengage Learning offers custom solutions for your course—whether it is making a small modification to *Making Europe: The Story of the West* to match your syllabus or combining multiple sources to create something truly unique. You can pick and choose chapters, include your own material, and add additional map exercises along with the *Rand McNally Atlas* to create a text that fits the way you teach. Ensure that your students get the most out of their textbook dollar by giving them exactly what they need. Contact your Cengage Learning representative to explore custom solutions for your course.

Acknowledgments

It is a pleasure to thank the many instructors who read and critiqued our text through its development:

Ken Albala, University of the Pacific
Steve Andrews, Central New Mexico Community College
Tom Backer, Covington Latin School
Brian Boeck, DePaul University
David Byrne, Santa Monica College
Dave Gould, Durham Academy
Jeffery Hankins, Louisiana Tech University
Andrew Keitt, University of Alabama at Birmingham
Randy Kidd, Bradley University
Frederic Krome, University of Cincinnati Clermont College
Fred Loveland, Broome Community College
Natasha Margulis, University of Pittsburgh at Greensburg
Patricia McGloine, Princess Anne High School
Jennifer McNabb, Western Illinois University
Andrew Nicholls, Buffalo State College
Janet Nolan, Loyola University Chicago
Patricia O'Neill, Central Oregon Community College
Kevin Robbins, Indiana University–Purdue University Indianapolis
Linda Scherr, Mercer County Community College
Robert Shaffern, University of Scranton
Lawrence Treadwell, Fort Lauderdale High School
David Weiland, Collin County Community College
John Weinzierl, Lyon College
Jessica Young, Oak Park and River Forest High School

The following instructors helped to shape the unique pedagogy offered in the second edition by participating in interviews, focus groups, reviews, or class tests:

Dr. Thomas Aiello, Gordon College
Dr. Charles Argo, Ball State University
Mary Axelson, Colorado Mountain College
Jean Berger, University of Wisconsin – Fox Valley
Kay Blalock, Saint Louis Community College – Meramec
Dr. Hans Peter Broedel, Assoc. Prof., History Dept., University of North Dakota
Bob Brown, Finger Lakes Community College
Rocco Campagna, Finger Lakes Community College
Stephanie E. Christelow, Idaho State University
Susan Cogan, Utah State University
David Coles, Longwood University
Elizabeth Collins, Triton College
Amy Colon, Sullivan County Community College
P. Scott Corbett, Ventura College
Gary Cox, Gordon College
Rob Coyle, Lone Star College

Brian R. Croteau, Adjunct Professor, Thomas Nelson Community College
Lawrence Cummings, North Central Michigan College
Dolores Davison, Foothill College
Sal Diaz, Santa Rosa Junior College
Rodney E. Dillon, Jr., Palm Beach State College
Ronald Dufour, Rhode Island College
Gordon Dutter, Monroe Community College – Rochester
Martin Ederer, Buffalo State College
Carrie Euler, Central Michigan University – Mount Pleasant
Linda Foutch, Walters State Community College
Barbara Fox, Suffolk Community College – Grant
Sharon Franklin-Rahkone, Indiana University of Pennsylvania
Thomas Freeman, Henderson State University
Annika Frieberg, Colorado State University – Fort Collins
Lori Fulton, Olivet Nazarene University
Paul George, Miami Dade Community College Miami – Wolfson
Marcos Gilmore, Greenville College
Michael Harkins, Harper College
Sharon Harmon, Pensacola Junior College – Pensacola
Charles Herrera, Paradise Valley Community College
Justin Horton, Thomas Nelson Community College
Carol Humphrey, Oklahoma Baptist University
Steven Isaac, Longwood University
Kay Jenkins, Holmes Community College – Ridgeland
Ryan Jones, Assistant Professor, Idaho State University
Barbara Klemm, Broward College – South
Edward Krzemienski, Ball State University
Chris Laney, Berkshire Community College
Dr. Charles Levine, Mesa Community College
Peter Linder, New Mexico Highlands University
John Maple, Oklahoma Christian University
Derek Maxfield, Genesee Community College
Maureen McCormick, Florida State College at Jacksonville
Darrel McGhee, Walters State Community College
Elizabeth Paige Meszaros, UNC Greensboro
Belinda Miles, Itawamba Community College Fulton
Alyce Miller, John Tyler Community College
Lynn W. Mollenauer, University of North Carolina – Wilmington
Mark Moser, University of North Carolina – Greensboro
Andrew Muldoon, Metrostate College of Denver
Lisa Ossian, Des Moines Area Community College – Ankeny
Kenneth Pearl, Queensboro Community College
Keith Pepperell, Columbus State Community College

Darren Pierson, Blinn College – Bryan

Greta Quinn, Lenoir Community College

Travis Ritt, Palomar College

Brian Rogers, Lake Sumter Community College

Ana Fodor, Danville Community College

Mark Rummage, Chair, History and Political Science Department, Holmes Community College

Nancy Rupprecht, Middle Tennessee State University

Professor Anne Ruszkiewicz, SUNY Sullivan

Tom Rust, Montana State University – Billings

Brian Rutishauser, Fresno City College

Stephen Ruzicka, University of North Carolina – Greensboro

Lisa Sarasohn, Oregon State University

Greg Sausville, Hudson Community College

Fred Schneid, High Point University

Barbara Shepard, Longwood University

Wayne E. Sirmon, Instructor, University of Mobile

Colleen Slater, Borough of Manhattan Community College

Greg Smith, Central Michigan University – Mount Pleasant

Sean Smith, Palm Beach State College

Richard Soderlund, Illinois State University

Ilicia Sprey, Saint Joseph's College

Dale Streeter, Eastern New Mexico University

William Strickland, Hazard Community College

Ryan Swanson, George Mason University

Mark Timbrook, Minot State University

Tristan Traviolia, Pierce College

Larry W. Usilton, University of North Carolina – Wilmington

David Valone, Quinnipiac University

Denis Vovchenko, Northeastern State University

Janet M.C. Walmsley, George Mason University

Clayton Whisnant, Wofford College

Steve Williams, New Mexico Highlands University

Laura Wood, Tarrant County College – Southeast

Bradley D. Woodworth, University of New Haven

Matthew Zembo, Hudson Valley Community College

And a big thank you to the hundreds of students who contributed to the development of the second edition by participating in focus groups and class tests.

Frank Kidner wishes to thank his colleagues Bob Cherney, Trevor Getz, Pi-Ching Hsu, Julyana Peard, and Jarbel Rodriguez for their help at various points in *Making Europe's* development.

Maria Bucur wishes to thank her husband, Daniel Deckard, for continued support and inspiration in matters intellectual and musical, and her children Dylan and Elvin, for putting up with the many hours mommy had to be away from them and reinvigorating her in the hours she was lucky to be with them.

Ralph Mathisen wishes to thank Frank Kidner for getting this project going and keeping it on track, as well as thousands of students who always have kept him on his toes. He would also like to thank his two children, Katherine and David, for putting up with piles of civ texts, notes, and drafts spread all over for many years.

Sally McKee wishes to thank her fellow authors for their mutual support, epicurean disposition, and good cheer over the years.

Ted Weeks would like to thank his history department colleagues at SIUC for intelligence, a sense of humor, and solidarity in the face of adversity. The same appreciation goes to my students whether in their first or tenth semester—you make it all worthwhile!

We also want to offer our warmest thanks to Kate Scheinman, our editor and guiding light during the preparation of this second edition of our book. Thank you Kate for all your hard work!

F. L. K.

M. B.

R. M.

S. M.

T. R. W.

About the Authors

Frank L. Kidner is Professor of History Emeritus at San Francisco State University, where he taught from 1968 until his retirement in 2006. He has also taught in the Western Civilization program at Stanford University and at Amherst College. His courses include Western Civilization, undergraduate and graduate courses in Early Modern Europe, and the history of the Christian Church as well as a graduate course in historical methodology. He has authored articles on topics in Late Antiquity and co-edited *Travel, Communication and Geography in Late Antiquity.*

Maria Bucur is Associate Dean in the College of Arts and Sciences and John V. Hill Professor in East European History at Indiana University, where she has taught an undergraduate course on "The Idea of Europe" and other topics in nineteenth- and twentieth-century eastern Europe. Her research focus is on social and cultural developments in eastern Europe, with a special interest in Romania (geographically) and gender (thematically). Her publications include *Eugenics and Modernization in Interwar Romania* and *Heroes and Victims: Remembering War in Twentieth-Century Romania.* When not writing and reading history or administrative memos, Maria is following her dream of being in a band (violin and bass) with her husband and children. You can find them jamming at a campground near you.

Ralph Mathisen is Professor of History, Classics, and Medieval Studies at the University of Illinois at Urbana-Champaign. He is a specialist in the ancient world with a particular interest in the society, culture, and religion of Late Antiquity. His teaching experience includes Western Civilization and topics in the Ancient Near East, Greece, Rome, Byzantium, coinage, and Roman law. He has written more than seventy scholarly articles and written or edited ten books, the most recent of which is *People, Personal Expression, and Social Relations in Late Antiquity.* He is also the editor of the *Journal of Late Antiquity* and Oxford Studies in Late Antiquity. He enjoys traveling, running, and ballroom dancing.

Sally McKee is Professor of History at the University of California at Davis, where she teaches courses on Western Civilization and medieval history. Her research focus has been Venice and its colonies and Mediterranean slavery, but her new project centers on nineteenth-century France and Italy. She is the author of numerous articles, one of which has won a prize and been anthologized, and she has also published a three-volume edition of Venetian-Cretan wills and a monograph, *Uncommon Dominion: Venetian Crete and the Myth of Ethnic Purity.* When she is not teaching, she travels the world in search of archives, modern art museums, and great street food.

Theodore R. Weeks is Professor of History at Southern Illinois University at Carbondale, where he teaches Western Civilization and World and European history. His research centers on nationality, inter-ethnic relations, and antisemitism in eastern Europe. He is the author of *Nation and State in Late Imperial Russia* and *From Assimilation to Antisemitism: The "Jewish Question" in Poland, 1850–1914,* and his articles have appeared in several languages, including Estonian and Hebrew.

Making Europe

The Origins of Western Civilization in the Ancient Near East, 3000–1200 B.C.E.

8000	3000	2500
8000 B.C.E. Neolithic Age begins	**3000 B.C.E.** Beginning of Bronze Age civilization in Sumeria and Egypt	**2700 B.C.E.** Old Kingdom in Egypt begins

The Sumerians believed that they needed to assist the gods when it came to doing the gods' work. For example, in order to help a god look after oneself, a Sumerian would place a statue representing her or himself in the god's temple. This would ensure that the god always looked out for the person. Statues could be made from inexpensive materials such as clay, or more expensive materials such as alabaster, as seen here. Men with shaved heads were priests, whereas those with beards were administrators and soldiers. The person was portrayed in an attitude of prayer. The wide-eyed look is typical of those who were in the presence of a god. Is the reverential attitude of this statue at all similar to the attitude of people in prayer in the modern day? (© Gianni Dagli Orti/Corbis)

After reading this chapter, you should be able to answer the following questions:

What were the social, economic, and cultural consequences of the adoption of agriculture?

How did geography influence the development of civilization in Mesopotamia and Egypt?

What part did religion play in the lives of the ancient Sumerians?

How did the ancient Egyptians view the concept of life after death?

In what ways were the Minoan and Mycenaean civilizations different from the civilizations of Mesopotamia and Egypt?

WESTERN CIVILIZATION as defined by modern historians arose around 3000 B.C.E. in the ancient Near East, in Mesopotamia (modern Iraq) and Egypt. The origins of human culture and society, however, go back over a million years to central and southern Africa, where early humans used stone tools and were primarily concerned with acquiring sufficient food—by hunting wild animals, gathering naturally growing foodstuffs, or scavenging—to meet their basic needs. It was not until 8000 B.C.E. that people in some parts of the world gained greater control over their food supply by herding animals and planting their own crops. The adoption of agriculture brought great changes in human society and culture. Populations increased. People could remain in the same place, build cities, and specialize in specific occupations. Metal technology advanced with the introduction of bronze weapons. The invention of writing brought the origin of written history. Taken together, these cultural advances created the first phase of civilization, known as the Bronze Age, around 3000 B.C.E.

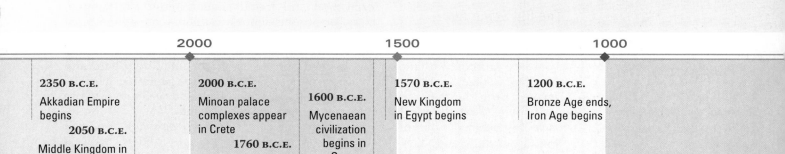

2000	1500	1000

2350 B.C.E.
Akkadian Empire begins

2050 B.C.E.
Middle Kingdom in Egypt begins

2000 B.C.E.
Minoan palace complexes appear in Crete

1760 B.C.E.
Old Babylonian Empire begins

1600 B.C.E.
Mycenaean civilization begins in Greece

1570 B.C.E.
New Kingdom in Egypt begins

1200 B.C.E.
Bronze Age ends, Iron Age begins

Geography played a major role in the rise of the first Near Eastern civilizations, which developed in fertile river valleys that offered rich soil and a dependable water supply. The most representative Bronze Age civilizations were based on the extensive exploitation of agriculture. In Mesopotamia, the Sumerians created a civilization in the Tigris and Euphrates River valleys. Because Mesopotamia had no natural barriers, Semitic and Indo-European peoples invaded, established the first empires, and absorbed the culture of the people they had conquered. In the Nile River valley, on the other hand, the civilization of Egypt grew largely in isolation, for it was protected by surrounding deserts. Outside the large river valleys, in Syria, Crete, and Greece, Bronze Age civilizations took advantage of their location on lines of communication and compensated for their lack of rich soil by creating economies based more heavily on trade. The end of the Bronze Age, around 1200 B.C.E., was marked by disruptions caused by Indo-European invaders known as the Sea Peoples.

Before History, 2,000,000–3000 B.C.E.

◆ **How did methods of acquiring food change during the course of the Stone Age?**

◆ **What social and economic factors influenced the rise of civilization?**

For the earliest humans, life was a constant struggle just to eat. People obtained food by hunting animals and gathering wild plant products, but food often ran short. Around 8000 B.C.E., people in a few places in the world learned how to grow plants for food. Thereafter food supplies were more dependable. The result was increasing populations and more organized societies. Humans gained a greater self-consciousness about how they related to the world around them, recognizing forces that seemed to control their fate and searching for ways to interact with these forces or even control them.

The Old Stone Age

The first, and by far the longest, period of human existence is known as the Old Stone Age, a name derived from the material used for making the most durable tools. People of the Old Stone Age left no written records, so their lives are known only from the study of the physical remains they left behind.

Getting to Know the Old Stone Age The remains left by the people of the Old Stone Age, known as **material culture**, consist primarily of stone tools and the bones of slaughtered animals. The material culture of past human societies is recovered and analyzed by the field of study known as **archaeology**. Using archaeological evidence, historians see that during the Old Stone Age human society gradually became increasingly complex as a result of biological evolution, technological development, and climate variation. Stone Age life also can be reconstructed by using **anthropology** to make comparisons with modern populations with similar lifestyles.

Early Human Populations The earliest human population, called Homo habilis ("skillful human"), evolved in central and southern Africa some two million years ago. These people were smaller than modern humans and used crude stone choppers to butcher animal carcasses. They banded together for protection and found shelter under overhanging cliffs. Beginning about a million years ago, a more advanced population, known as Homo erectus ("upright human"), about the same size as modern people, learned how to use fire. Flint, a very hard and easily worked stone, became the preferred material for making tools, which included weapons used to hunt big game, such as elephants.

Homo sapiens ("thinking human") appeared in Africa about 400,000 B.C.E. By 150,000 B.C.E. a European subspecies of humans known as the

material culture Physical remains left by past human societies.

archaeology Scientific study of the remains of past human societies.

anthropology Scientific study of modern human cultures and societies.

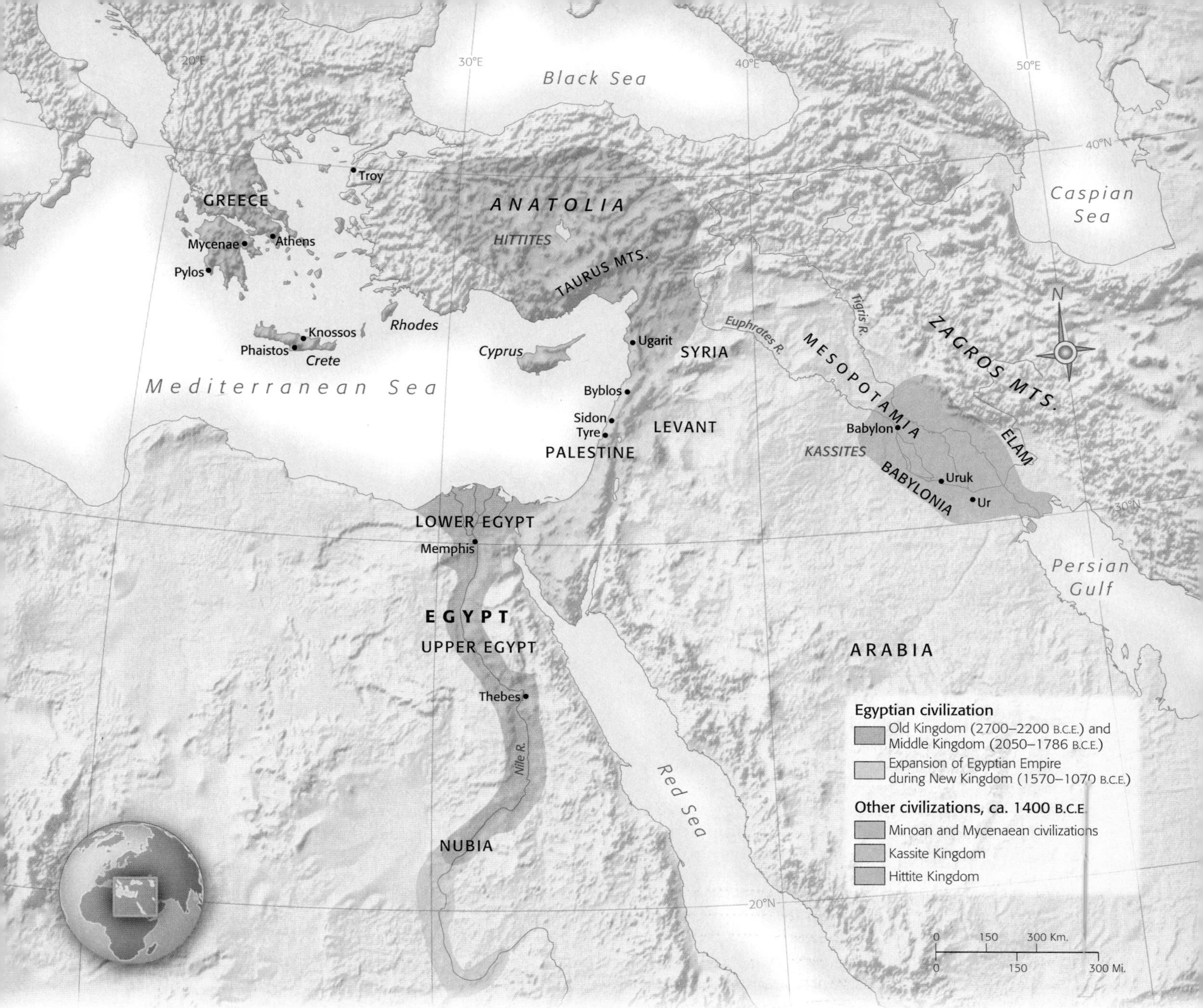

Black Sea
Caspian Sea
Mediterranean Sea
Persian Gulf
Red Sea
GREECE
Troy
Mycenae
Athens
Pylos
Knossos
Phaistos
Crete
Rhodes
Cyprus
ANATOLIA
HITTITES
TAURUS MTS.
Ugarit
SYRIA
Byblos
Sidon
Tyre
LEVANT
PALESTINE
Euphrates R.
Tigris R.
MESOPOTAMIA
ZAGROS MTS.
ELAM
Babylon
KASSITES
BABYLONIA
Uruk
Ur
LOWER EGYPT
Memphis
EGYPT
UPPER EGYPT
Thebes
Nile R.
NUBIA
ARABIA
Egyptian civilization
Old Kingdom (2700–2200 B.C.E.) and Middle Kingdom (2050–1786 B.C.E.)
Expansion of Egyptian Empire during New Kingdom (1570–1070 B.C.E.)
Other civilizations, ca. 1400 B.C.E
Minoan and Mycenaean civilizations
Kassite Kingdom
Hittite Kingdom
0 150 300 Km.
0 150 300 Mi.
20°E
30°E
40°E
50°E
40°N
30°N
20°N
N

Map 1.1 The Near Eastern World, ca. 1500 B.C.E. By 1500 B.C.E., the most important ancient western civilizations were located in the Near East in the areas of Mesopotamia and Egypt. Other centers of civilization arose rather later in the Levant on the east coast of the Mediterranean, on the island of Crete, and in Greece. *© Cengage Learning*

1. Locate on the map the Mediterranean Sea, Mesopotamia, Egypt, the Tigris, Euphrates, and Nile Rivers, Palestine, Anatolia, and Crete.
2. What geographical factors did Mesopotamia and Egypt share that contributed to the development of civilizations in these areas?
3. How are the civilizations of the Minoans, Mycenaeans, and Hittites geographically different from those of Mesopotamia and Egypt?

Neanderthals was making more advanced implements, such as axes, scrapers, and projectile points, from stone flakes chipped from larger pieces of flint. For shelter, the Neanderthals often made use of caves (hence the derogatory term *cave men*), which offered security from wild animals, protection from the weather, and storage space.

Initially, all human societies acquired food by hunting wild animals and gathering naturally growing plant products. Most food consisted of wild fruits, nuts, berries, roots, seeds, and grains. Early peoples supplemented this diet by hunting, fishing, or scavenging animal carcasses. Observing that some areas were better for hunting and gathering, humans traveled long distances, following migrating animals and seeking wild crops. But a change in animal migration routes or a drought could lead to starvation.

Males would have hunted and engaged in activities that took them far from their residences. Women would have gathered plant foods and overseen child care. In addition, the manufacture of stone tools, necessary during hunting expeditions, would have been primarily a male activity. Women, on the other hand, would have concentrated on tasks that could be performed in camp or at home, such as scraping and curing hides and preparing food or preserving it by drying it or storing it in pits.

About 100,000 years ago, another human subspecies known as Homo sapiens sapiens ("wise-thinking human")—essentially like modern humans—appeared in Africa and began to spread throughout the world. For unknown reasons, the other humans, including the Neanderthals, then gradually disappeared. About 40,000 years ago, new technologies helped people exploit the natural food-producing environment more effectively. For example, tree resin was used to bind tiny stone blades to wood or bone shafts to make sickles for harvesting wild grains.

The Origins of Religion At the same time, humans gave increasing attention to religion. Archaeological remains provide evidence for a belief in supernatural powers that governed the universe and controlled important aspects of life, such as food production, fertility, and death. Humans came to believe that they could influence these powers by means of religious rituals. For example, paintings found deep in caves in Spain and southern France show animals pierced by spears, suggesting that the painters hoped to bring about the same result in the real world. A cave painting

A cave painting from southern France called *The Sorcerer*, dating to about 13,000 B.C.E., depicts a man with a bearded face, an owl's eyes, a reindeer's antlers, a horse's tail, and a lion's claws. Interpretations of the painting vary. It could be part of some kind of hunting ritual, it might depict a horned god, or it might represent a shaman, a spiritual leader believed to be able to communicate with the supernatural world of animals and gods. What purpose do you think that this image could have served? (Visual Connection Archive)

from Spain showing nine women in knee-length skirts dancing around a small naked man probably represents a fertility ritual intended to promote the production of human offspring. The many large-breasted broad-hipped female figurines found on Stone Age sites also demonstrate the power attributed to female fertility in Stone Age societies, which may have been **matriarchal**—that is, governed by women. Elaborate burial rituals arose. The dead were buried sprinkled with red ocher (a mixture of clay and iron oxide) and accompanied by clothing, shells, beads, and tools, suggesting a belief in an afterlife.

The Neolithic Revolution

Soon after the end of the last ice age, about 10,000 B.C.E., great changes occurred in human lifestyles. These happened not only because of the warming climate but also because of continuing human social and technological evolution. These changes brought the end of the Stone Age, a period known as the "Neolithic (New Stone) Age."

Neanderthals Human subspecies that originated as early as 350,000 B.C.E. and became extinct soon after 40,000 B.C.E., discovered in Germany's Neanderthal ("Neander Valley") in 1856.

matriarchal society (from Greek for "rule by mothers") Society in which women have the primary authority.

The Neolithic Age The **Neolithic Age**, which began in the **Near East** about 8000 B.C.E., marked the final stage in stone tool technology. Finely crafted stone tools filled every kind of need. Obsidian, a volcanic glass, provided razor-sharp edges for sickles. Bowls and other items were made from ground as opposed to chipped stone. Long-distance trade brought ocher from Africa, flint from England, and obsidian from the islands of the Aegean Sea to markets in the Near East and elsewhere. Technologically, however, stone tools had reached their limits in durability and functionality. People now began to experiment with the use of metals, such as copper, for making weapons and jewelry.

The Rise of Pastoralism More significantly, the Neolithic Age brought two revolutions in food supply methods. One was the **domestication** of animals that could be used as a source of both food and raw materials. Sheep, goats, pigs, and cattle—which were not aggressive toward humans, had a natural herd instinct, matured quickly, and had an easily satisfied diet—were best suited for domestication. This helps to explain why animal domestication arose in Asia and the Near East, where these particular animals were found, rather than in Africa, where the native animals, such as buffalo, gazelles, and large carnivores, were less suited for domestication. Domesticated animals kept in flocks and herds gave people a dependable food supply in the form of milk products and clothing made from the animals' wool and hides. Only in times of need, or for ceremonial purposes, or when an animal died, were the livestock—which were also a form of wealth—actually eaten. Other animals, such as the dog and cat, also were domesticated.

People who kept domestic animals are called pastoralists because they are constantly searching for new pastures. Their diet was supplemented by hunting and gathering, but they still were subject to climatic changes. Prolonged periods of drought, for example, could have disastrous consequences. Nevertheless, **pastoralism** offered greater security than a purely hunting-and-gathering economy, and it quickly spread over nearly all of Europe, Asia, and Africa.

The Rise of Agriculture An even more revolutionary development of the New Stone Age was the domestication of certain kinds of plants, which led to **agriculture**, or farming. As early as 10,000 B.C.E., hunter-gatherers were experimenting with cultivating wild grains, such as rice in China and rye in Syria. Recent studies of ancient climate variations suggest that droughts also may have encouraged people to take greater control over their food supply. Around 8000 B.C.E., several Near Eastern populations began to cultivate grains including wheat, barley, and emmer. These grains evolved into greater usefulness both through natural selection (in which plants naturally mutate into more useful varieties) and selective breeding (in which humans select seeds for their desirable qualities). Other crops such as peas, beans, and figs supplemented the grain-based diet, and domestic animals provided meat and milk products.

Agriculture also arose in Africa, India, China, and Central and South America. This happened sometimes independently and sometimes by **cultural assimilation**, in which people who did not practice agriculture learned it from those who did. Gradually, the knowledge of agriculture spread throughout the world and brought increased economic productivity. In western Europe, social organizations based on agricultural economies mobilized great amounts of manpower. Beginning around 4000 B.C.E., massive standing stones called megaliths were erected, as at Stonehenge in England. Such feats required hundreds or thousands of participants. Beyond the physical achievement of their erection, the stones also demonstrate an elementary knowledge of astronomy. They were aligned with the heavens and permitted people to predict the seasons based on the alignment of certain stars, such as Sirius, in relation to the stones.

The Consequences of Settled Lifestyles Agriculture brought two main changes to human existence: it required people to remain in the same place year after year, and it created a dependable food supply that yielded a surplus, which created wealth. The food surplus also meant that larger populations could be supported. People settled together in villages—permanent settlements with several hundred residents and houses made from local materials such as reeds, mud brick, or timber. Agricultural productivity was limited only by the amount of land placed under cultivation and the availability of water. A larger population then meant that more land could be brought into cultivation and that even more food could be produced.

A settled lifestyle also opened up the opportunity for individuals to pursue specialized occupations, such as pottery making, carpentry, and home building.

Neolithic Age (from Greek for "new stone") Period between 8000 and 4000 B.C.E., during which people gained greater control over their food supply.

Near East In antiquity, Egypt, the Levant, Mesopotamia, Anatolia, and Iran; in the modern day also known as the Middle East.

domestication Practice of adapting wild animals to live with humans or wild plants for cultivation.

pastoralism Mobile lifestyle based on keeping flocks and herds.

agriculture Sedentary style of life based on the cultivation of crops.

cultural assimilation Acquisition by one group of people of the cultural traits of another people.

Some farmers and craftworkers were more successful than others, which led to social differentiation—that is, the division of society into rich and poor. By 7000 B.C.E., villages such as Jericho, near the Jordan River in Palestine, were home to several thousand persons and were protected by thick walls.

Life in permanent settlements also brought problems. Too much emphasis on grain could result in an unbalanced diet and greater susceptibility to disease. Larger populations living close together and surrounded by their own waste increased the possibility of the spread of communicable diseases such as tuberculosis, smallpox, malaria, and plague. Farmers also sometimes destroyed their own environment. As land was deforested for agriculture or overgrazed by domestic animals, the soil could be eroded by being washed or blown away. In addition, the watering and fertilization of cropland could result in a buildup of salt that reduced soil fertility. And to make matters even worse, villages with food surpluses could be targets for raids by pastoralists who were short of food. Hunter-gatherers or pastoralists could always move when living conditions deteriorated in one location, but once farmers had committed themselves to an agricultural economy, they were compelled to make do with the agricultural economy as best as they could.

Religious practices also continued to evolve during the Neolithic period. Maleness was seen as the source of the rain that brought fertility to the land and was represented by phallic imagery. Great Mother cults, evidenced by female statuettes, suggest that femaleness was associated with the earth as the provider of the bounty of herds and crops. Clay-covered skulls found at Jericho suggest a form of ancestor worship in which deceased loved ones remained with the living.

Fertile Crescent Arc of fertile land running through Egypt, the Levant, and Mesopotamia, in which early agriculture was practiced.

Levant Lands between the eastern coast of the Mediterranean and Mesopotamia, including Palestine, Lebanon, and Syria.

Mesopotamia (Greek for "between the rivers") Lands surrounding the Tigris and Euphrates Rivers and the site of a Bronze Age civilization; modern Iraq.

history (from Greek for "narrative") Accounts of the human past that use written records.

The Emergence of Near Eastern Civilization

The most extensive exploitation of agriculture occurred in river valleys, where there was both good soil and a dependable water supply regardless of the amount of rainfall. In the Near East, this occurred in Egypt and Mesopotamia.

The Fertile Crescent Near Eastern agriculture was most heavily developed in the area known as the **Fertile Crescent**, a region extending up the Nile River valley in Egypt, north through the **Levant** (Palestine, Lebanon, and Syria), and then southeast into the Tigris and Euphrates River valleys of **Mesopotamia**. The richest soil was located in the deltas at the mouths of the rivers, but the deltas were swampy and subject to flooding. Before they could be farmed, they needed to be drained, and irrigated and flood control systems had to be constructed. These activities required administrative organization and the ability to mobilize large pools of labor.

The Criteria of Civilization In Mesopotamia, perhaps as a consequence of a period of drought, massive land reclamation projects were undertaken after 4000 B.C.E. to cultivate the rich delta soils of the Tigris and Euphrates Rivers. The land was so productive of crops that many more people could be fed, and a great population explosion resulted. Villages grew into cities of tens of thousands of persons.

These large cities needed some form of centralized administration. Archaeological evidence indicates that the organization initially was provided by religion, for the largest building in each city was a massive temple honoring one of the many Mesopotamian gods. In Uruk, for example, a sixty-foot-long temple known as the White House was built before 3000 B.C.E. There were no other large public buildings. This suggests that the priests who were in charge of the temples also were responsible for governing the city and organizing people to work in the fields and on irrigation projects, building and maintaining systems of ditches and dams.

The great concentration of wealth and resources in the river valleys brought with it further technological advances, such as wheeled vehicles, multicolored pottery and the pottery wheel, and the weaving of wool garments. Advances in metal technology just before 3000 B.C.E. resulted in the creation of bronze, a durable alloy (or mixture) of about 90 percent copper and 10 percent tin that provided a sharp cutting edge for weapons.

By 3000 B.C.E., the economies and administrations of Mesopotamia and Egypt had become so complex that some form of record keeping was needed. As a result, writing was invented. Once a society became literate, it passed from the period known as prehistory into the historic period, leaving written records that can be used along with archaeology to learn more about the life of its people. In fact, the word **history** comes from a Greek word meaning "narrative": not until people were able to write, could they provide a detailed permanent account of their past.

Collectively, these developments resulted in the appearance, around 3000 B.C.E., of a new form of

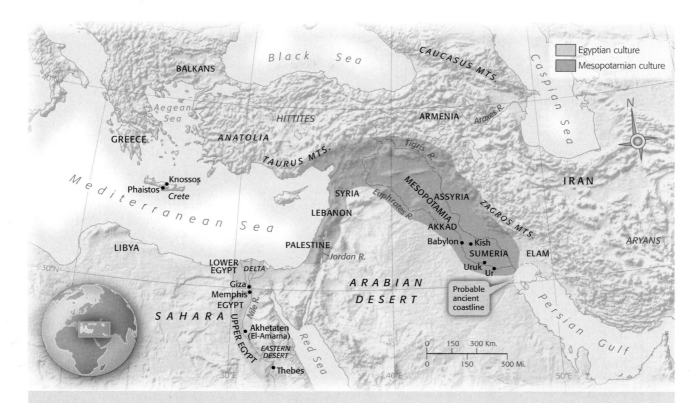

Map 1.2 **The Fertile Crescent** During the Bronze Age, civilizations based on the extensive exploitation of agriculture arose in a "Fertile Crescent" extending north from the Nile valley in Egypt and then eastward through the Tigris and Euphrates valleys in Mesopotamia. © *Cengage Learning*

1. What kinds of geography characterized the areas in the Fertile Crescent?
2. What kinds of geographical conditions existed outside of the Fertile Crescent that might have inhibited the large-scale use of agriculture?
3. What peoples lived outside the large river valleys during the Bronze Age?

culture called **civilization**. The first civilizations had several defining characteristics. They had economies based on agriculture. They had cities that functioned as administrative centers and usually had large populations. They had different social classes, such as free persons and slaves. They had specialization of labor, that is, different people served, for example, as rulers, priests, craftworkers, merchants, soldiers, and farmers. And they had metal technology and a system of writing. As of 3000 B.C.E., civilization in these terms existed in Mesopotamia, Egypt, India, and China.

The Bronze Age This first phase of civilization is called the **Bronze Age** because of the importance of metal technology. In the Near East, the most characteristic Bronze Age civilizations, those of Mesopotamia and Egypt, were located in river valleys, were based on the extensive exploitation of agriculture, and supported large populations. Bronze was a valuable commodity; the copper and tin needed for its manufacture did not exist in river valleys and had to be imported—tin from as far away as Britain. Bronze, therefore, was used mainly for luxury items, such as jewelry or weapons, but not for everyday domestic items, which were made from pottery, animal products, wood, and stone. In particular, bronze was not used for farming tools. Thus, civilizations based on large-scale

civilization A form of human culture that includes agriculture, urbanization, social classes, metal technology, and writing.

Bronze Age In the Near East, the period from 3000 to 1200 B.C.E., when bronze was used for weapon making and when the most characteristic civilizations were located in river valleys, based on extensive agriculture, and had large populations.

agriculture, such as those of Mesopotamia and Egypt, were feasible only in soils that could be worked by wooden scratch-plows pulled by people or draft animals such as oxen. Other Bronze Age civilizations, however, such as those that arose in the Levant and the eastern Mediterranean, took advantage of their location on communication routes to pursue economies based on trade.

 Checking In

By yourself or with a partner, explain the significance of each of the following selected key terms:

- material culture
- Neolithic Age
- domestication
- cultural assimilation
- Fertile Crescent
- history
- civilization
- Bronze Age

Mesopotamian Civilization, 3000–1200 B.C.E.

- ◆ **How did geography influence Mesopotamian civilization?**
- ◆ **How did Mesopotamians seek to gain control of their world?**

Mesopotamian civilization was greatly influenced by geography. The Tigris and Euphrates River valleys were subject to unexpected floods and open to invasion. This led to uncertainties in their lives that gave the Mesopotamians a pessimistic outlook on the world. Every Mesopotamian city had one chief god. At first, priests ruled each city in the name of its god, but later military leaders also arose. Because the Mesopotamians did not trust the gods to impose order on the world, they sought to do so themselves, often by issuing elaborate law codes. Over time, the Mesopotamians came into contact with neighboring Semitic and Indo-European peoples, who invaded Mesopotamia and adopted Mesopotamian culture.

cuneiform (from Latin for "wedge-shaped") Mesopotamian writing system that put wedge-shaped indentations on clay tablets.

myths Stories, often about gods, explaining things that people did not understand.

legends Accounts of people and events in the distant past that have been passed on orally.

Anatolia Modern-day Turkey, also known as Asia Minor.

polytheism Belief in the existence of many gods.

anthropomorphic (from Greek for "human-shaped") Looking and behaving like people.

The Rise of Sumeria

Mesopotamian civilization began around 3000 B.C.E. in Sumeria, the rich agricultural delta where the Tigris and Euphrates Rivers empty into the Persian Gulf. Sumerian civilization was built on cities. Twenty principal cities, such as Uruk, Kish, and Ur, had populations of over 50,000 each and occupied all of the good farmland close to the rivers.

Sumerian Writing What is known about Sumerian civilization comes from both archaeological remains and written records. The Sumerian writing material was clay, and the writing instrument was a stylus, or pointed stick, that made wedge-shaped indentations in the clay. The writing system, called **cuneiform**, began as a multitude of pictograms, signs that looked like what they represent, such as a star. By 3000 B.C.E., about a hundred of the signs had come to stand for syllabic sounds—that is, a consonant plus a vowel (*ba, be, bi, bo,* and so on)—and could be used to spell any word. Significant numbers of texts, however, do not appear until about four hundred years later. Sumerian accounts of their earlier history, such as their lists of kings, are therefore often based on **myths** and **legends**—stories passed down orally about gods and heroes—that often seem fantastic but usually are based on a core of truth.

The Role of Geography in Mesopotamia Sumerian ideas about their place in the world stemmed largely from their geography. Mountains rose to the north of Mesopotamia, and to the south and west lay the Syrian-Arabian Desert, a semiarid area that supported substantial pastoralist populations. Sumeria proper received less than ten inches of rainfall a year, but the upper reaches of the rivers in the mountains of **Anatolia** (modern Turkey) often received heavy rainfalls that surged downriver. These inundations were useful for agriculture, but they also sometimes flooded the cities without any warning and Mesopotamians lived in constant fear of floods. They also feared raids by mountain peoples from the north and desert dwellers from the south. Life in Sumeria thus was full of uncertainties. This gave the Sumerians a pessimistic outlook on life and a great concern for organizing their world to make it as safe as possible.

The Sumerians and Their Gods The Sumerians were **polytheists** who believed that the world was controlled by gods who had created people to do the gods' work. The gods were conceived of as being **anthropomorphic**—that is, looking like people. Making the world secure meant being able to influence the gods. Because life was uncertain, the gods also were considered to be unpredictable and not to be trusted to look out for the people's best interests. The Sumerians, therefore, tried to assert some control over the gods. People placed small statues of themselves in temples to ensure that the gods would be watching over them. They attempted to learn what the gods intended by looking for signs in dreams, animal entrails, and even wisps of smoke—a practice known as **divination**.

The most important gods were assigned numbers proportional to their relative status. An, the father of all the gods, was the god of the universe. He dwelt somewhere among the stars and was rarely concerned with what happened on earth. An was assigned the number 60, the basis of the Sumerian number system. Enlil (50), a sky god who controlled lightning and thunder, was the god most directly concerned with life on earth. Enki (40), the water god, was thought to have brought civilization to humanity. Other important gods included the moon god, Nanna (30); the sun god, Shamash (20); and Ishtar (15), the goddess of fertility. Ranking the gods by numbers gave the Sumerians an additional feeling of having control over them.

Sumerian pessimism was reflected in their perceptions of the afterlife. They believed that the underworld, or "Land of No Return," was ruled by Ereshkigal, the sister of Ishtar, and her partner, the war god Nergal. The dead were buried with offerings that were believed to be stolen by demons when the spirits of the dead traveled to the underworld. The dead then ate clay and dust and spent eternity weeping over their fate. The dream of every Sumerian was to become immortal and escape being sent to the underworld. The most famous Sumerian legend tells how the hero Gilgamesh, the king of Uruk, became upset by the death of his friend Enkidu and attempted to escape his own death. He traveled the world searching for the tree of life, which bore a magic fruit that kept one eternally young. Gilgamesh eventually found the fruit, only to have it stolen by a serpent. Not even a great hero could escape his fate.

Another legend involving Gilgamesh exemplifies Sumerian relations with their unpredictable gods. During his travels, Gilgamesh met Ut-Napishtim, who told Gilgamesh that long ago the sky god Enlil had decided to destroy humanity. The water god Enki advised Ut-Napishtim to build an ark and to fill it with every species of animal. They all survived the flood, and Ut-Napishtim became the only man ever to become immortal. According to Sumerian lists of their kings, this great flood occurred around 2600 B.C.E. and separated a period when legendary kings ruled for thousands of years from a period of kings with normal life spans. It is quite likely that the legend recollects an actual flood, such as one that left an eleven-foot layer of silt found at Ur. Legends like these, used in conjunction with

archaeology, offer the opportunity to reconstruct the history of periods for which no written records survive.

Sumerian Government and Society

The Sumerian cities were **city-states**, independent nations, and were rarely united politically. In fact, disunity was a defining characteristic of Mesopotamian politics. Nevertheless, the cities all shared the same culture—the same religious practices, the same kinds of government, and the same traditions. Each city had one primary god. At Ur, for example, the main god was Nanna, the moon god. The god's temple, called a **ziggurat**, was a massive step-pyramid, 150 feet on a side and over 100 feet high, built of fired brick laid over a mud-brick core. Looking like a staircase rising to heaven, it was the most visible building in the city. There also were numerous smaller temples of other gods.

Sumerian Society The Sumerians believed that the true ruler of each city was its god but that the god delegated the work of ruling on earth to priests. The earliest rulers were priest-kings who, along with being religious leaders, also were responsible for organizing the agricultural and irrigation work of the city. By around 2600 B.C.E., conflicts had arisen between cities over access to river water, bringing further uncertainties to Sumerian life. For defense, cities constructed massive walls several miles long, and a class of professional soldiers arose. Because of a need for effective military leaders, some cities replaced the priest-kings with generals as rulers. But all rulers continued to act as representatives of the city's god.

Sumerian society had a **hierarchical structure**—that is, people were ranked according to their social, economic, and legal status. This hierarchy is apparent in art, for example, where more important people, such as the king, appear larger than less important people. Ranking below the king were the nobles, who served as administrators and generals and owned large tracts of land, and the priests, who oversaw the temples and the property of the gods. Next in status were civil servants and soldiers. Ranking below them, in a sort of middle class, were artisans and specialized laborers, including potters, artists, metal and leather workers, weavers, bricklayers, stonemasons, teachers, scribes, fishers, sailors, and merchants.

divination Religious practice in which people looked for signs to determine future events and the will of the gods.

city-state City that is also an independent nation.

ziggurat Step-shaped pyramid serving as the main temple in Mesopotamian cities.

hierarchical structure Social structure organized according to rank, status, and privilege.

The so-called Standard of Ur was found in a royal grave in the city of Ur dating to about 2500 B.C.E. It consists of a two-sided trapezoidal wooden box with scenes made of a mosaic of red limestone, lapis lazuli, and shells on two sides. Each side depicts three registers of scenes from Sumerian life. This side shows the nation at peace. In the top register the king, at the left, presides over a banquet with his nobles. They drink a toast accompanied by a lyre player on the far right. In the lower two registers, Sumerian workers, including farmers, fishermen, and merchants, bring taxes and offerings. The other side of the standard shows Sumeria at war, with troops marching on foot and riding into battle on carts and with bodies of slain enemies lying at the bottom. How does this item portray the different segments of Sumerian society? (Courtesy of the Trustees of the British Museum)

The majority of the population, which ranked below the artisans, was occupied in farming. A few small farmers owned their own land, but most worked plots belonging to nobles or priests and paid rents of about one-seventh of their produce. Lowest in status were the slaves, who included war captives, persons born as slaves, and those who had been sold into slavery for debt. Slaves usually performed household tasks. Even slaves were full-fledged members of the community, for they, too, were believed to be doing the work of the gods, and it was understood that after performing enough work, they deserved to be set free.

The Sumerian Economy Economic activity was largely controlled by the government. There was no coined money. Economic transactions took place by **barter**, the exchange of goods and services. The government collected taxes in produce and in labor. Landowners paid a percentage of their crops, which were stored in government warehouses and redistributed to pay the salaries of government employees such as soldiers, shepherds, fishermen, craftworkers, and even snake charmers. The annual salary of a typical government worker was thirty bushels of barley and one ounce of silver. Labor taxes were paid with work on public works projects ranging from temple building to digging and cleaning irrigation ditches. Government bureaucrats kept detailed records of every tax payment, distribution of rations, and bit of labor.

The lack of any local resources besides water, mud, and plant materials created a need for raw materials, which could be acquired only through trade—often under government supervision. Sumerian exports included woolen textiles, grain, and worked-metal items. Imports were primarily raw materials, such as copper, tin, timber from the mountains to the north, and gemstones and spices from as far away as India, Arabia, and Africa. Imports were used to manufacture products such as jewelry and weapons. In the course of their manufacturing activities, the Sumerians invented the dyeing and bleaching of fabrics, the art of engraving, and accounting.

barter Form of exchange using goods and services rather than coined money.

Sumerian Gender Roles Sumerian society also was **patriarchal**, a form of hierarchical social organization in which customs and laws generally favor men. For example, in cases of adultery, a guilty man was forgiven, but a woman was sentenced to death. Married women were expected to provide children, and infertile women could be divorced. A husband could even sell his wife and children into slavery to pay off debts. Women whose fathers could not support them or find husbands for them could be devoted to a god as sacred prostitutes, known as "sisters" of the god. But women did have some rights. A wife kept control over her **dowry**—the money provided by her father when she married to support her and her children—and had equal authority with her husband over their children. Family property was usually managed by the husband or a grown son, but if they were lacking the wife was in charge. Women also could engage in business in their own name. Children, however, had no legal rights and could be disowned by their parents and expelled from the city at any time.

Daily Life in Sumeria In the countryside, Sumerians lived in houses made of bundles of reeds that had beaten-earth floors and were plastered on the outside with **adobe**, a mixture of clay and straw. Farm animals lived with the family. City houses, made of sun-dried mud brick, were small—just a few hundred square feet—and packed together on narrow streets that sometimes were only four feet wide in order to make maximum use of the protected space within the city walls. Thick walls and a lack of windows helped keep the houses cool, and their flat roofs were used for cooking and for sleeping in hot weather. Furniture was minimal. Food and water were stored in large clay pots. A rudimentary sewage system conducted waste to the river but did little to keep down the stench.

The Sumerian diet consisted primarily of grain products, lentils, onions, lettuce, fish, and beer. Clothing was made from woven wool. The usual garment was a rectangular piece of cloth that women draped around themselves from the left shoulder and men wrapped around their waist. Sumerians wore sandals and protected their heads from the hot sun with caps. Women adorned themselves with bracelets, necklaces, anklets, and rings for their fingers and ears.

Semitic and Indo-European Peoples

The Sumerians occupied only a tiny geographical area of the Near East and were surrounded by non-Sumerian peoples with whom they regularly came into contact. Over the course of centuries, many of the economic, technological, and religious practices that arose in Mesopotamia spread outward and were adopted by other peoples. The first people to assimilate Mesopotamian civilization were the **Semitic peoples**—pastoralists who lived in the semiarid regions of Syria and northern Arabia to the south and east of Mesopotamia and whose similar Semitic languages gave them a sense of shared identity.

Sargon and the Akkadians The Semitic peoples had a long history of contact with the Sumerians, whom they knew had the ability to grow and store large food surpluses. Soon after 3000 B.C.E., the **Akkadians**, one of the Semitic peoples, moved into the river valleys themselves, just upstream from the Sumerians. They created an agricultural civilization of their own that assimilated the culture of the Sumerians. Subsequently, in what became a regular pattern of invasion and assimilation, other peoples likewise moved into the river valleys and adopted the civilized style of life.

Around 2350 B.C.E., the Akkadian leader Sargon embarked on a career of conquest. By his own account, the infant Sargon had been set adrift in a basket in the Euphrates River by his mother, perhaps because he was of illegitimate birth. He was rescued by a gardener, entered the service of the king of Kish, and even claimed to be the lover of the goddess Ishtar. Sargon seized power and defeated Uruk, Ur, and the other Sumerian cities. Claiming to have conquered territory all the way to the Mediterranean Sea, he called himself King of Sumer and Akkad and established the Akkadian Empire, the first Near Eastern empire.

Sargon had to administer an **empire** made up of cities that did not get along with one another. In some ways he tried to be conciliatory. For example, even though he favored Ishtar, he respected Enlil, the most important Sumerian god, by calling himself the Great King of Enlil. In other ways, however, Sargon was excessively domineering. He humiliated defeated rulers, tore down the walls of Sumerian cities, and installed Akkadian governors. He even made his daughter Enheduanna priestess of Nanna at Ur, where she wrote several surviving poems in Sumerian, including one called "Praise of Ishtar." After his death, Sargon's empire crumbled. His successors confronted revolts

patriarchal society (from Greek for "rule by fathers") Society in which men have the primary authority.

dowry Financial contribution provided to a bride by her family.

adobe Mixture of clay and straw dried in the sun, used to make plaster or bricks.

Semitic peoples Pastoral peoples living in semiarid regions of Syria and northern Arabia who spoke versions of the same language.

Akkadians Semitic people who established the first Near Eastern empire, the Akkadian Empire, in 2350 B.C.E. under their king, Sargon.

empire Political unit incorporating different peoples and nations under a single government.

Elam Ancient kingdom located in western Iran.

Amorites Western Semitic peoples, including the Assyrians and Babylonians, who moved into Mesopotamia around 2000 B.C.E.

Assyrians Semitic people who settled in the upper Tigris River valley around 2000 B.C.E.

Babylonians Semitic people who settled in central Mesopotamia around 2000 B.C.E and established the Old Babylonian Empire in 1760 B.C.E.

Hammurabi (r. 1790–1750 B.C.E.) Mesopotamian ruler who created the Old Babylonian Empire and issued a famous law code around 1760 B.C.E.

talent Mesopotamian unit of weight, about 56 pounds, comprised of 60 minas, with each mina being composed of 60 shekels.

astrology (from Greek for "knowledge of the stars") Branch of learning based on the belief that the future was ordained by the gods and could be read in the motions of the stars and planets.

Indo-European peoples Pastoral peoples of central Asia who settled in areas from India to Europe and spoke versions of the same language.

steppe Treeless grass-covered plain covered by short grass.

Aryans Indo-European peoples who settled in Iran around 2000 B.C.E.

Hittites Indo-European people who settled in Anatolia around 2000 B.C.E.

Balkans Southeastern Europe, including modern Greece, Bulgaria, and Romania.

Kassites Indo-European people who invaded Mesopotamia around 1500 B.C.E.

by the conquered peoples and raiders from the northern mountains and the kingdom of **Elam** in eastern Iran. Mesopotamia soon returned to its customary disunited condition. The empire's most lasting legacy was the establishment of the Akkadian language, written in Sumerian cuneiform characters, as an international language that was used throughout the Near East for centuries.

Hammurabi and the Babylonians Once Sumeria was free of the Akkadians, the city of Ur attempted to establish its authority over Sumeria. But Mesopotamia soon faced further invasions. Around 2000 B.C.E., Semitic peoples known collectively as the **Amorites** moved into Mesopotamia from the west. They included the **Assyrians**, who settled in the upper reaches of the Tigris River valley, and the **Babylonians**, who occupied central Mesopotamia. Like earlier pastoralists who had settled in Mesopotamia, the Babylonians assimilated Sumerian culture. They used cuneiform to write their language, and they adopted many Sumerian gods, but they did retain their own supreme god, Marduk, a storm god whom they equated with Enlil. They also gave their name to Babylonia and established a capital city at Babylon.

In 1790 B.C.E., **Hammurabi** (r. 1790–1750 B.C.E.) became king of the Babylonians. Using a shrewd mixture of diplomacy and military might, he brought all of Mesopotamia under his control and created the Old Babylonian Empire, the second Near Eastern empire. He introduced measures

intended to unify the many different peoples of his empire. For example, in the marketplaces he required the use of standard weights based on the **talent**, which weighed about fifty-six pounds. There were sixty minas in a talent and sixty shekels in a mina. Around 1760 B.C.E., Hammurabi issued a standard legal code that placed everyone under the same laws.

The Babylonians also advanced the study of mathematics and astronomy. Using the cumbersome 60-based number system, Babylonian mathematicians dealt with concepts such as square roots and algebraic unknowns (which they called a false value). Lacking a symbol for zero, Babylonians substituted a blank space. These innovations had practical applications, such as calculating compound interest or the amount of building material needed for a ziggurat. Babylonian astronomers divided the year into 360 days (6 times 60), the day into 6 parts, and the hour into 60 minutes. By keeping detailed records of the movements of the sun, moon, and planets, they were able to predict the phases of the moon. They also believed that the positions of astronomical bodies had a predictable effect on what happened on earth, giving rise to **astrology**.

The Indo-European Peoples In spite of Hammurabi's best efforts to create unity, his empire disintegrated soon after his death around 1750 B.C.E. A new group of invaders then appeared, the **Indo-European peoples**. Like the Semitic peoples, the Indo-Europeans consisted of different groups of pastoralist peoples speaking versions of the same language. Their homeland lay in the grassy **steppes** of Central Asia north of the Black and Caspian Seas. Every so often, groups of Indo-Europeans left to seek new homes because of overpopulation or food shortages. The earliest known Indo-European migration occurred around 2000 B.C.E. One group, the **Aryans**, settled in modern-day Iran. Another, the **Hittites**, moved into Anatolia, and yet others migrated into the **Balkans**.

The first Indo-Europeans to invade Mesopotamia were the Hittites, who raided Babylonia in 1595 B.C.E. Shortly thereafter, around 1500 B.C.E., one group of Aryans invaded India, destroying the Bronze Age civilization there. At the same time, another Aryan group, the **Kassites**, occupied Mesopotamia, making use of new military technology, the horse and chariot. They assimilated Mesopotamian culture—including religion, dress, and language—so thoroughly that nearly the only element of their native Indo-European culture they preserved was their names. The Kassites continued to rule much of Mesopotamia until about 1200 B.C.E.

The Code of Hammurabi

The most important document to survive from ancient Mesopotamia is the law code of Hammurabi.

It placed everyone in the Old Babylonian Empire under a single legal system. The code was a compilation of existing laws and customs relating to civil and criminal procedures. It recognized three classes of people: nobles, free persons, and slaves. Many laws dealt with property and business, setting prices for manufactured items and wages for laborers such as sailors, barbers, physicians, veterinarians, home builders, artisans, and farm workers. Other laws dealt with agriculture: For example, someone whose dam broke and caused flooding was to be sold as a slave to pay for the damages.

Gender Relations in the Code of Hammurabi Of the 282 laws in the code, 49 dealt with marriage. First marriages usually were arranged by a girl's family. Men were permitted to have two wives, but women were allowed only one husband. The code acknowledged that marriages did not always work out. If a wife was childless, her husband could pay her a mina (about a pound) of gold for a divorce or take a second wife, who would rank beneath the first wife. If a wife became incapacitated by disease, a husband could marry a second wife but had to support the first wife as long as she lived. A man who divorced a wife who had borne him children had to support her until the children were raised; she then received part of his property so she "could marry the man of her heart." A woman who "ruined her house, neglected her husband, and was judicially convicted" could be divorced but would be forced to remain with her ex-husband as a servant even if he remarried. A woman whose husband left her received a divorce, but a woman who left her husband was thrown into the river (and presumably drowned).

Crime and Punishment in the Code of Hammurabi In the case of criminal law, many crimes—such as making false accusations, stealing temple property, receiving stolen property, kidnapping, stealing or harboring escaped slaves, breaking and entering, robbery, rape, and shoddy construction—were punished by death. Some death sentences were quite gruesome. Sons and mothers guilty of incest and looters who burned houses were burned alive. Male and female lovers who killed their spouses were **impaled**. Other punishments involved physical mutilation. Cutting off the hands was the penalty for physicians who bungled operations, for farm workers who stole grain, and for sons who struck their fathers. Men who slandered women were branded on the forehead. Punishments also could vary according to a person's social status. A free person who struck a noble received sixty blows from an ox-whip, but if he struck someone of equal rank, he merely paid a fine. A slave who struck a free person lost an ear. A noble who put out the eye

A six-foot tall black basalt obelisk created around 1760 B.C.E. and preserved in the Louvre Museum in Paris bears the Code of Hammurabi. Hammurabi, like all Mesopotamian monarchs, ruled not in his own right but as a representative of the gods. As a consequence, Hammurabi, standing at the left, is shown here receiving the code from the sun god Shamash. In the text, Hammurabi said, "The gods called me, Hammurabi, who feared God, to bring about the rule of righteousness and to destroy the wicked and the evil-doers, so that the strong would not harm the weak." Copies of the law code were posted throughout the empire. Why do you think Hammurabi stresses his relationship to the gods? (Erich Lessing/Art Resource, NY)

of another noble was subject to the law of retaliation and had his own eye put out. But if a noble put out the eye of a free person, he paid a fine of one mina of gold.

In other regards, the Code of Hammurabi attempted to provide fair treatment for everyone. Judges who made bad decisions were removed from

impalement Form of execution in which a victim was skewered on a sharpened stake.

office, and victims of crimes were reimbursed by the community. Even slaves had legal rights. Male slaves were allowed to marry free women. The children of such unions were free, but when the slave died, the marital property was divided between the wife and the slave's owner. If a free man had children by a slave woman, they and the woman were freed at his death. If a man sold his children, his wife, or himself into slavery to pay off a debt, they were set free after three years of labor. The code not only reflected contemporary Mesopotamian standards of justice but also provided a model for future lawmaking.

Checking In

By yourself or with a partner, explain the significance of each of the following selected key terms:

myths	Semitic peoples
polytheism	empire
city-state	Hammurabi
ziggurat	Indo-European peoples

Egyptian Civilization, 3000–1200 B.C.E.

- ◆ **How did geography influence Egyptians' views of themselves, the world, and the afterlife?**

- ◆ **How and why did the role and status of the pharaoh change during the course of Egyptian history?**

Generally speaking, civilization developed in Egypt in much the same way as it did in Mesopotamia. But in more detailed ways, the two civilizations were very different. Unlike the Mesopotamians, the Egyptians were geographically isolated, and for more than a thousand years they experienced no foreign invasions. Their country was usually unified. The Egyptians trusted their gods to look after them, had an optimistic outlook on life, and believed that they would enjoy a delightful afterlife. Each of the three periods of Egyptian history—the Old, Middle, and New Kingdoms—had particular identifying characteristics. During the Old Kingdom, the pharaohs had absolute authority. Only the pharaohs were believed to have afterlives, and they constructed gigantic pyramids as their tombs. During the Middle Kingdom, the pharaohs had less authority, and Egyptians believed that all had access to the afterlife. The New Kingdom saw the rise of the Egyptian army and the Egyptian Empire.

Nubia Region of Africa located in the upper Nile valley just south of Egypt.

The Gift of the Nile

As in Mesopotamia, civilization in Egypt arose around 3000 B.C.E. in a fertile river valley, with extensive exploitation of agriculture and the use of bronze for weapons and jewelry. Unlike the Tigris and Euphrates Rivers, however, the flooding of the Nile River was predictable. Every summer, heavy rains in central Africa fed water into the Nile, causing it to overflow its banks in mid-August. By November, the river had returned to its banks, leaving behind a layer of fertile soil. Irrigation ditches were dug, and the land was planted. Agricultural life was organized according to three seasons: Inundation of the Nile, Emergence (planting), and Deficiency (low water and harvest). To forecast the seasons and the Nile floods, the Egyptians created a calendar based on the moon. It had twelve months of 30 days each. Five feast days added at the end made a 365-day year that serves as the basis of our own calendar.

The Land of Egypt Egypt was the richest agricultural land in the Mediterranean world, and Egyptian life was focused on the Nile. The Egyptians' own word for their land was Kemet, the "black land," a reference to the rich, dark soil of the Nile River valley. Because people were never far from the river, they traveled by boat and at first had no need for wheeled carts or horses to pull them. The Nile valley was a thin strip of agricultural land six hundred miles long but only four to twenty miles wide, surrounded on the east and west by the inhospitable and sparsely populated Sahara Desert. The Egyptians divided the Nile valley into two sections, Lower Egypt (the Nile Delta) and Upper Egypt (the rest of the river valley south to **Nubia**). These designations are used because water flows from higher to lower ground.

Geography also isolated Egypt from the rest of the world. If the approaches to Egypt in the north and south were protected, as they were until the eighteenth century B.C.E., the country was safe from invasion. The predictable renewal of the soil and the lack of concern about invasion or floods gave the Egyptians an optimistic outlook on life. They were convinced they had the best life of anyone on earth. They thought themselves superior to the black peoples of Africa to the south and to the Semitic and other peoples of the Levant and Mesopotamia to the north. Geographical isolation also meant that influence from outside was restricted. Change came slowly.

The Unification of Egypt Before 3000 B.C.E., Upper and Lower Egypt were separate kingdoms, but around 3000 B.C.E. the two kingdoms were united by a ruler named Narmer. Political unity then became the normal condition of Egypt. To unify Egypt further, Narmer founded a new capital city at Memphis, where Upper and Lower Egypt met. This unity further contributed to the Egyptians' sense of optimism. Narmer was the first of a multitude of rulers known as **pharaohs**. Subsequently, pharaohs belonging to the same family were organized into **dynasties**.

During the first two dynasties of pharaohs (3000–2700 B.C.E.), all the fundamental aspects of Egyptian culture, religion, and government evolved. Egyptian writing, known as **hieroglyphics**, had more than seven hundred symbols that represented different words, thoughts, or meanings. Only highly educated scribes could write. The usual writing materials were stone, for large monuments, or papyrus (the source of our word "paper"), for record keeping. Hollow papyrus reeds were split down the middle, flattened, and glued together in a two-layer crosshatched pattern to form sheets about fifteen inches square. Writing was done with a pen and ink.

Egypt was divided into forty-two smaller territories called **nomes**, each administered from a city center. As in Mesopotamia, cities served as centers for administration and for the storage and distribution of food supplies. Each Egyptian city—again, as in Mesopotamia—had its own main god. Egyptian cities were not large population centers, however, and they were not walled. Most of the people lived securely in the countryside, close to their fields.

Early Egyptian Religion The Egyptians had a multitude of gods, many of whom were depicted as animals, such as Anubis, the jackal god. Several important gods were connected to the sun. In the time of Narmer, Ra, the god of the noonday sun, became the most important god of Egypt. In addition, rather than just being representatives of the gods, as in Mesopotamia, Egyptian pharaohs were considered to be gods in their own right. Pharaohs also took on the personality of other gods, such as Ra. The Egyptians were confident that their pharaohs, and their other gods, would take care of them. The goddess **Ma'at**, for example, provided order, stability, and justice. Even the pharaoh was expected to rule according to Ma'at.

Egyptian Government and Society

The pharaoh stood at the peak of Egyptian government and society. The pharaoh was assisted in governing by an increasingly large bureaucracy. His main assistant was the vizier, a chief executive officer in charge of administrative details. Upper and Lower Egypt each had governors, and nomarchs managed the nomes. The government oversaw tax collection and the administration of justice. As in Mesopotamia, taxes were paid in produce, a percentage of the crops, or in labor, including work on irrigation projects and the upkeep of temples and palaces.

Crime and Punishment in Egypt All free persons were equal under the law. Criminal law was based on getting a confession from the accused party, often by torture, which included whipping and mutilation. Accused persons who refused to confess could be set free. Many crimes carried physical punishment. The penalty for extortion, for example, was one hundred blows and five open wounds; the penalty for interfering with traffic on the Nile was cutting off the nose and exile. The death sentence—in forms including impalement, burning, drowning, or decapitation—was exacted for crimes such as treason, sacrilege, murder, and tax evasion.

Egyptian Society In contrast to Mesopotamia, however, Egypt had no professional soldiers at this time, for there was no fear of invasion. If the pharaoh needed a military force to raid a neighboring region, a band of farmers and artisans would be armed and then disbanded when the campaign was over.

Like Mesopotamian society, Egyptian society was hierarchical. The pharaoh had the highest rank. Next came the pharaoh's family, which consisted of a chief wife, who often was also the pharaoh's sister (by this means, pharaohs behaved like gods and kept power in the family); additional wives and **concubines**; and the pharaoh's children. The pharaoh's successor usually was a son, although female pharaohs were not prohibited. Pharaohs advertised their divine status with large stone sculptures of themselves, such as the Great Sphinx, which showed the pharaoh as a man-headed lion.

Ranking after the royal family were nobles and priests. Nobles held high state offices and owned large amounts of land. Priests administered the lands belonging to the temple. Next in status were specialized workers such as scribes, acrobats, singers, dancers, musicians, artists, stonemasons, perfume makers, and professional mourners at funerals. Most of these positions were open to both men and women. Lower in status was the majority of the population, which labored in farming or on public works projects

pharaoh (in Egyptian, "great house") Ruler of ancient Egypt.

dynasty Group of rulers belonging to the same family.

hieroglyphics (from Greek for "sacred writing") Earliest form of Egyptian writing.

nomes Smaller geographical and administrative regions of ancient Egypt, governed by nomarchs.

Ma'at Egyptian goddess who represented order, justice, and stability.

concubine Female sexual partner ranking below a wife.

The three largest Egyptian pyramids were constructed at Giza beginning about 2600 B.C.E. The "Great Pyramid" of the pharaoh Khufu, on the far right, is 781 feet at the base, 481 feet tall, and contains 2.3 million stone blocks weighing from two to fifteen tons each. The pyramids of Khafre and Menkaure are in the center and at the left, respectively. The uncompleted smaller pyramids in the foreground were intended for other members of the royal family, who thus were able to share the pharaoh's afterlife. In the twelfth century C.E. the Sultan of Egypt attempted to destroy Menkaure's pyramid, but gave up after eight months of fruitless effort. How do you think the pharaohs were able to mobilize the resources needed to build the pyramids?

such as digging and cleaning irrigation ditches. Lowest in status were slaves, who were either Egyptians who had been sold for debt or captives acquired by occasional raids into Nubia to the south or Asia to the north. Some slaves were set free and even became governmental officials. Most, however, were employed in domestic and farm work.

Daily Life in Egypt Egyptians treasured their family life. Many scenes in Egyptian art depict affection between husbands and wives or of parents for their children. Egyptians usually married in their teens. An Egyptian proverb advised men, "Take a wife while you are young." Even though marriages were usually arranged by families, young people still composed love poems. One young woman wrote, "He torments my heart with his voice, he makes sickness take hold of me." Marriage contracts specified the rights of the husband and wife to their own possessions, the amount of the allowance that the husband

would provide to his wife, and how the property would be divided in case of a divorce. The marriage ceremony consisted of the bride moving her possessions to her husband's house. Either party could initiate a divorce, and divorced wives were entitled to continued support from their ex-husbands. Male and female children inherited the family property equally. In general, women had parity with men when it came to having careers, owning property, and pursuing cases in court.

Egyptian homes were made of adobe brick, and doors and windows were covered with mats to keep out insects. A room on the upper storey with an open wall could be used for sleeping on hot nights. Furniture consisted of stools, mats for sleeping, and large and small jars for storing food and personal items. The diet was primarily bread, along with fruit, fish, and beer made from barley. Household sewage flowed directly into the Nile. Clothing was made from linen. At work, men wore loincloths and women wore short skirts. For special occasions, women wore dresses held up by straps and men wore kilts. Both men and women wore jewelry made from copper, gold, and semiprecious stones, including anklets, rings, bracelets, earrings, and beaded necklaces. The use of cosmetics, such as black and green eye shadow and red cheek and lip gloss, was also common.

The Old Kingdom: The Age of the Pyramids

Historians identify three periods during which Egypt was united: the Old, Middle, and New Kingdoms. These periods were separated by "intermediate periods" when Egyptian unity broke down. Each period had its own distinctive traits. Even though Egyptian civilization began around 3000 B.C.E., it was not until the Old Kingdom (2700–2200 B.C.E.), from which written records survive in significant numbers, that the history of ancient Egypt begins to be clearly known.

The Nature of the Pyramids The Old Kingdom was characterized by all-powerful pharaohs who built tombs in the shape of gigantic stone pyramids. The largest pyramids were built during the Fourth Dynasty, beginning around 2600 B.C.E. The pharaoh's burial chamber was hidden deep inside the pyramid—safe, it was hoped, from grave robbers. It preserved all the wealth, jewelry, and domestic objects that the pharaoh would need in the afterlife. It even contained clay figures of servants to take care of the pharaoh's future needs. The tomb chamber also had "pyramid texts," magical spells written on the walls to ensure that the pharaoh's transition to the afterlife would go smoothly. At the beginning of the Old Kingdom, only the pharaohs were thought to have an afterlife. As a result, nobles hoping to share the pharaoh's afterlife placed their tombs next to a pyramid.

Building a pyramid required a vast supply of material and workers that only a pharaoh, who had the authority of a god, could mobilize. Stone quarried from the cliffs next to the Nile was ferried during the flood season to the royal burial ground just west of Memphis. Tens of thousands of Egyptian workers were fed and housed at the pharaoh's expense while they dragged the massive stone blocks up earthen ramps to the top of the new pyramid. A large pyramid took fifteen years or more to complete.

The Rise of the Nobles Pharaohs did all they could to ensure that work proceeded as quickly as possible, and here lay the seeds of future problems. Pharaohs gave private estates, tax exemptions, and special privileges to nomarchs who fulfilled their labor and supply quotas, and the sons of nomarchs were allowed to succeed them, thus strengthening the noble class. These policies helped individual pharaohs in the short term but made fewer resources available to their successors. Pyramids became smaller and smaller, reflecting a decline in the pharaohs' resources. At the same time, nobles gained a greater sense of self-importance and began to build tombs for themselves with pyramid texts in their own nomes, a sign that they believed they now had their own individual afterlives. Powerful nobles began to challenge the pharaoh's authority and to compete with one another for power. The last pharaoh of the Sixth Dynasty (2350–2200 B.C.E.) was Nitocris, the first woman to rule Egypt. After her death, revolts among nobles broke out, and Egypt lost its customary unity and stability.

The Middle Kingdom: The Age of Osiris

The loss of unity during the First Intermediate Period (2200–2050 B.C.E.) caused a breakdown in irrigation, and famines occurred. Not until 2050 B.C.E., was the nomarch of Thebes able to reunify Egypt, beginning the Middle Kingdom (2050–1786 B.C.E.). As a symbol of the change of rule, the bull god Amon, the chief god of Thebes, became the most important god of Egypt. Ra, Egypt's previous main god, often was linked with Amon, creating a composite second chief god, Amon-Ra. Pharaohs of the Middle Kingdom, however, were weaker than those of the Old Kingdom. They still were seen as living gods and buried in small pyramids, but their authority was threatened by ambitious nobles and priests who controlled more and more of Egypt's land and produce.

The Egyptian Afterlife For most of the population, the biggest change during the Middle Kingdom was that the afterlife now was available to everyone. The result was a great increase in reverence for Osiris, the god of the underworld. Egyptians believed that Osiris, who had brought civilization to Egypt, had been killed and chopped up by his envious brother Set. Isis, the wife of Osiris, put the pieces back together and breathed life back into him. Osiris then became the judge who decided whether the dead deserved a good afterlife. Osiris's son Horus, the falcon god, defeated Set and became the defender of the dead when they were judged.

The Egyptians believed that if Osiris could live happily after death, so could they. They anticipated continued enjoyment of all the best spiritual and material things they had enjoyed during life—providing their bodies were preserved by **mummification**. All the internal organs except the heart were removed and mummified separately. The brain was scrambled, pulled and sucked out through the nose, and discarded. The remaining skin, bones, and

mummification Drying process by which bodies are preserved after death.

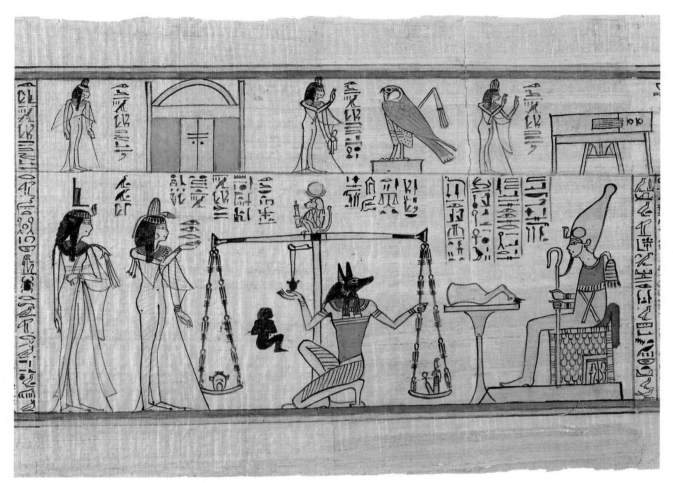

The "Papyrus of Nany" shows on the left Nany, a woman who died in her seventies and who had served as a ritual singer of the god Amon-Ra, holding her mouth and eyes in her hand. She is being judged by Osiris, dressed like the pharaoh with the tall white crown of Upper Egypt, sitting on the right. In the center, the jackal god Anubis weighs Nany's heart against Ma'at to see whether she had led a just life. Anubis keeps his hand on the weighing pan to ensure that her heart does not fail the test, for in the Egyptian view, the gods ensured that everyone would receive an afterlife. Why do you think the Egyptians were so confident that everyone would have a happy afterlife? (Image copyright © The Metropolitan Museum of Art. Image source: Art Resource, NY)

muscle then were soaked in natron, a salt solution that removed moisture. The dried corpse was wrapped with linen bandages and buried underground in an elaborately decorated coffin, accompanied by grave goods such as food, jewelry, and domestic items. Those who could not afford this expensive process made do with a simpler burial in the desert sand, which often resulted in natural mummification.

Egyptians believed that before receiving a good afterlife they would be questioned by Osiris to determine whether they had lived according to Ma'at. Those judged unworthy were devoured by the Eater of the Dead, a demon that was part crocodile, part hippopotamus, and part lion. To ensure that they passed the test, Egyptians wrapped mummies with a collection of answers to Osiris's questions known as the **Book of the Dead**. It contained advice such as, "Say 'No' when asked if you ever stole anything." Thus, even in death, Egyptian optimism prevailed; Egyptians believed that everyone would pass the test and receive a good afterlife.

The Hyksos Invasion About 1730 B.C.E., the Middle Kingdom came to an end when Egypt was invaded by a Semitic people known as the **Hyksos**. Using the latest military technology, including the

Book of the Dead Catalogue of magical spells that was buried with mummies to ensure that Egyptians received a good afterlife.

Hyksos (from Semitic for "rulers of foreign lands") Semitic people who conquered Egypt in 1730 B.C.E.

horse and chariot and the compound bow—a bow made from laminated layers of wood and animal horn for extra strength—the Hyksos easily overcame the undefended cities and untrained armies of the Egyptians. Egypt again entered a period of disunity, the Second Intermediate Period (1730–1570 B.C.E.). The Hyksos became pharaohs in northern Egypt but allowed the rest of Egypt to be governed by Egyptian subordinate rulers called **vassals**, who were left alone as long as they acknowledged Hyksos authority.

The Hyksos enthusiastically assimilated Egyptian culture and even preserved documents from the Old Kingdom that otherwise would have been lost. The Egyptians, however, could not tolerate being ruled by foreigners. They mastered the use of the chariot and compound bow and created professional armies. In 1570 B.C.E., led by the ruler of Thebes, they counterattacked. The Hyksos were expelled and pursued up the coast of Palestine, where they were completely destroyed. The Egyptians then obliterated nearly every trace of the Hyksos and were determined never again to let foreigners invade Egypt.

The New Kingdom: The Warrior Pharaohs

The reunification of Egypt after the expulsion of the Hyksos marked the beginning of the New Kingdom (1570–1070 B.C.E.), an era characterized by strong pharaohs, a standing army, and the creation of an **Egyptian Empire**. Pharaohs became military leaders. Their armies included both native Egyptians, who often were rewarded with land, and hired foreign soldiers called **mercenaries**, many from Nubia. Support from the army gave pharaohs the means to reassert their dominance over unruly nobles and priests. In Egyptian art, the pharaoh now was customarily shown shooting a bow from a war chariot, a forceful reminder to everyone of the source of his power. At the same time, the pharaoh's chief wife was promoted to the status of "God's Wife." By these measures, the royal family was able to regain much of the authority that it had lost during the Middle Kingdom.

Protecting Egypt The pharaohs' first task was to ensure the security of Egypt. They did this by defending the borders and by establishing a military presence outside of Egypt. Pharaoh Thutmose I (r. 1527–1515 B.C.E.) campaigned into Nubia in the south and all the way to the Euphrates River in the north, thus impressing Egypt's neighbors with his military might. His daughter Hatshepsut (r. 1498–1483 B.C.E.) was crowned pharaoh, and to enhance her stature, she claimed she was the daughter of the bull god Amon. She wore male royal clothing and a false royal beard. As commander in chief of the army, she led an attack into Nubia. Hatshepsut also constructed border fortifications and a huge terraced temple in honor of Amon, considered to be one of the most beautiful buildings of the ancient world. The building activities of other pharaohs, too, were focused on temples, which often advertised their military achievements. Pharaohs no longer built pyramids but were buried in underground stone tombs.

The Egyptian Empire Hatshepsut's son, Thutmose III (r. 1483–1450 B.C.E.), subdued the peoples of Palestine and Syria and created an Egyptian Empire that served as a buffer between Egypt and potential enemies, thus increasing Egypt's security. Rather than making conquered lands part of Egypt, Thutmose followed the Hyksos' model of making defeated rulers into vassals. Egyptian vassals were permitted to remain in power as long as they remained loyal, paid tribute, and sent hostages to Egypt to guarantee their good behavior. Every year or so, the pharaoh assembled the Egyptian army, marched north, and reminded the vassals—who were always ready to revolt—of his overwhelming power. These demonstrations reinforced the pharaoh's position as military commander and renewed the army's loyalty to him.

The Religious Revolution of Akhenaton The empire remained stable for about a hundred years, until Amenhotep IV (r. 1350–1334 B.C.E.) ascended the throne. Even though Egypt had the most conservative culture of all the ancient Near Eastern peoples, Amenhotep departed from Egyptian tradition. He declared that **Aton**, a minor sun god, was the only god who could be worshiped (see A New Direction: Akhenaton Decides to Make Aton the Main God of Egypt). He even changed his own name to Akhenaton to honor the god. The move so distressed the Egyptians that the army was compelled to remain in Egypt to maintain order, which gave the Hittites an opportunity to occupy parts of the Egyptian Empire. Akhenaton then disappeared from history, perhaps a victim of the unrest that his reforms had caused.

The Successors of Akhenaton Akhenaton was followed by several short-lived boy pharaohs. One of them, Tut-ankh-aton, soon

---

vassals Subordinate rulers who declare loyalty to a higher-ranking ruler.

Egyptian Empire Egyptian conquests in Palestine and Syria that served to protect Egypt from invasion, created by Thutmose III (r. 1483–1450 B.C.E.).

mercenaries Hired soldiers who often are foreigners.

Hatshepsut (r. 1498–1483 B.C.E.) Female pharaoh who fortified Egypt.

Aton Sun god whom the pharaoh Akhenaton (r. 1350–1334 B.C.E.) attempted to make the supreme god of Egypt.

Akhenaton Decides to Make Aton the Main God of Egypt

In the fourteenth century B.C.E., the Egyptian Empire was at its height, and its ruler, the pharaoh Amenhotep IV, was considered to be a living god. The Egyptians worshiped many gods, such as the sun god Ra, the bull god Amon, and Osiris, the god of the dead. All these gods played important roles in the everyday life of an Egyptian society that had been remarkably stable for sixteen centuries. But then Amenhotep, a man of strong beliefs who had complete authority over Egyptian government and religion, decided to make a revolutionary change in Egyptian religious practices. For reasons that remain unclear, Amenhotep became completely committed to the worship of an obscure sun god named Aton, whom he attempted to make the primary god of Egypt.

To demonstrate his devotion to Aton, Amenhotep changed his own name to Akhenaton ("Glory of Aton") and established a new capital city in honor of Aton, calling it Akhetaton ("The Horizon of Aton"), on the site of today's El-Amarna. Akhenaton forbade the worship of all other gods, but at the same time he decreed that only the royal family would be allowed to worship Aton. Artworks were created that showed only Akhenaton and his family, no one else, receiving the beneficial rays of Aton. To ensure that no other gods would be worshiped, Akhenaton closed and defaced their temples.

Akhenaton's religious reforms deeply affected the Egyptian people. The priests who oversaw the worship of all the other gods lost their livelihood, and ordinary Egyptians could no longer worship Osiris, the god who, they believed, gave them their afterlife. Civil unrest arose, and the Egyptian army had to be called out to maintain order. Over time, the army became so occupied with controlling internal strife that it could no longer defend the Egyptian Empire and ultimately turned against Akhenaton. His name and the name of Aton were erased from the monuments; the temples of Aton were destroyed, Akhetaton was abandoned, and Akhenaton disappeared from history. It may be that the army decided to get rid of this unpopular pharaoh.

It remains a mystery why Akhenaton introduced measures that had such disastrous consequences. One school of thought sees his reforms as a calculated effort to undercut the power of the priests and increase the power of the pharaoh. If so, Akhenaton seriously miscalculated, and the plan went badly wrong. So perhaps a more likely suggestion is that Akhenaton was a true religious reformer. He was determined to make his god the primary god in Egypt regardless of what kinds of misery and disasters doing so brought upon the Egyptian people and nation.

Akhenaton's favoring of Aton in spite of the consequences can be viewed as a clash between Akhenaton's personal beliefs about the nature of God and his responsibilities as a ruler. And the reaction of the Egyptian people can be seen as an example of how attempts to change deeply felt religious beliefs and rituals can inspire resistance to political authority. Both of these themes recur often in western history.

changed his name to **Tut-ankh-amon** (r. 1334–1325 B.C.E.), a sign that the god Amon had returned to favor. When Tut-ankh-amon died, he was buried so secretly that his was the only pharaoh's tomb not to be robbed in antiquity. After its discovery in 1922 C.E., the boy king was nicknamed King Tut.

The next pharaohs were army generals, suggesting that the army had taken over. The pharaohs of the Nineteenth and Twentieth Dynasties (1293–1070 B.C.E.), most of whom were named Ramses, struggled to restore and maintain the Egyptian Empire. **Ramses II** (r. 1279–1212 B.C.E.), the greatest of the warrior pharaohs, fought the Hittites for twenty years. In 1259 B.C.E., the two empires made peace by establishing fixed boundaries and agreeing to defend each other against outside aggressors. To seal the bargain, each ruler married a daughter of the other. Ramses spent the remainder of his reign engaged in massive building projects. He not only constructed many temples in his own name but also put his name on monuments of his predecessors. By the time of his death in 1212 B.C.E., Ramses II was over ninety years old, and great changes were soon to occur. The Bronze Age was

Tut-ankh-amon (r. 1334–1325 B.C.E.) Also known as King Tut; the only Egyptian pharaoh whose tomb was not robbed in antiquity.

Ramses II (r. 1279–1212 B.C.E.) Egyptian pharaoh who made peace with the Hittites and constructed many temples.

drawing to a close and, with it, the days of Egypt's greatest glory.

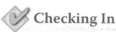

Checking In

By yourself or with a partner, explain the significance of each of the following selected key terms:

pharaoh	Egyptian Empire
dynasty	Hatshepsut
Ma'at	Aton
Hyksos	Ramses II

Lost Civilizations of the Bronze Age, 2500–1200 B.C.E.

◆ **What factors encouraged the development of trading economies during the Bronze Age?**

◆ **What factors helped bring about the decline of Bronze Age civilization?**

The Bronze Age was the great age of river valley civilizations based on the extensive exploitation of agriculture. At the same, however, other peoples living outside large river valleys in the Levant, on the island of Crete, and in Greece created civilizations of their own. These peoples focused on trade as a means of expanding their economies. Around 1200 B.C.E., Bronze Age civilization came to an end as the result of disruptions caused by the arrival of Indo-European invaders known as the Sea Peoples.

Ebla and Canaan

The assumption by historians that Egypt and Mesopotamia were the only important civilizations of the Near Eastern Bronze Age was stunningly disproven in 1968 when Italian archaeologists discovered **Ebla**, a Syrian city mentioned in Akkadian and Egyptian records but whose location previously had been unknown.

Ebla and the Role of Trade Excavations at Ebla revealed eighteen thousand cuneiform tablets showing that as early as 2500 B.C.E. Ebla was a thriving commercial center. The city walls enclosed about 125 acres and housed some thirty thousand persons. Ebla was a cultural crossroad, as demonstrated by the many languages used in the tablets, including Assyrian, Akkadian, Sumerian, Hittite, and the previously unknown language of the Eblaites. Some tablets listed the meanings of Eblaite words in Sumerian and other known languages, making Ebla's Semitic language easy for scholars to decipher. The tablets tell us much about the people who lived there.

Controlling territory from southern Anatolia to the Euphrates River, Ebla was able to oversee trade south to Egypt, east to Mesopotamia, north to Anatolia, and west into the Mediterranean. Like all ancient peoples, the Eblaites had an agricultural economy, but their farmland did not produce a large surplus. To expand their economy, they traded manufactured products, such as linen and wool textiles and fine inlaid wooden furniture, and raw materials, such as timber, copper, and silver.

In the course of their commercial activities, the Eblaites assimilated religious practices from neighboring cultures. They worshipped the western Semitic god **Ba'al** and the Mesopotamian Shamash and Ishtar. The tablets also contained names like U-ru-sa-li-ma (Jerusalem), Ab-ra-mu (Abraham), and Da-u-dum (David), which would reappear centuries later in Jewish scripture. In about 2250 B.C.E., Ebla was sacked and burned by the Akkadians. The fires baked the clay tablets in the palace archives, thus preserving them.

The Cities of Canaan The Levant continued to be a center of commercial activities after 2000 B.C.E. The Assyrians on the upper Tigris River sent caravans of woven textiles to Anatolia, where the Hittites attempted to gain control of the lucrative metal trade. Trading cities such as Byblos, Sidon, Tyre, and Ugarit arose around 1500 B.C.E. on the coast of **Canaan**. Sometimes they were independent and sometimes they were under the domination of **imperialist** states such as Egypt or the Hittite kingdom. The Canaanite cities experimented with writing systems using symbols that represented not ideas, words, or syllables but consonants. These vastly simplified systems were the forerunners of the **alphabet** and made writing more accessible to the general population, especially to merchants, and less the monopoly of priests and scribes.

The Minoans of Crete

Another Bronze Age civilization based on trade, the **Minoan civilization**, arose on Crete, a Mediterranean

---

Ebla Syrian city that established a civilization with a trading economy around 2500 B.C.E.

Ba'al (from Semitic for "master") Name given to several western Semitic gods.

Canaan Area of the Levant bordering the Mediterranean coast (modern Lebanon and Palestine).

imperialist Having to do with building empires.

alphabet (in Greek, "alpha beta") System of writing in which symbols represent individual consonants or vowels.

Minoan civilization Bronze Age civilization that developed on the island of Crete soon after 3000 B.C.E.

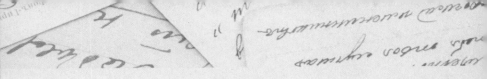

Akhenaton, "Great Hymn to Aton"

The pharaoh Akhenaton's "Great Hymn to Aton," found engraved on the tomb of the pharaoh Ay at El-Amarna, expresses Akhenaton's personal devotion to the god Aton in formal and ceremonial language. The hymn begins with praises of Akhenaton and his wife, Nefertiti, and Akhenaton also is referred to by his coronation name, Nefer-kheperu-Ra Wa-en-Ra ("Sole-One-of-Ra"). The text has similarities to the scriptures of other world religions.

❶ Why does Akhenaton think Aton is important?

❷ Who is this son?

❸ What is the significance of the transition from darkness to light?

❹ Who benefits from the blessings of Aton?

Praise of the King of Upper and Lower Egypt, who lives on truth, the Lord of the Two Lands: Nefer-kheperu-Ra Wa-en-Ra, the Son of Ra, who lives on truth, the Lord of Diadems, Akhenaton, long in his lifetime; and praise of the Chief Wife of the King, his beloved, the Lady of the Two Lands: Neferneferu-Aton Nefertiti, living, healthy, and youthful forever and ever.

Akhenaton says:
❶ Thou appearest beautifully on the horizon of heaven,
Thou living Aton, the beginning of life!
Thou art gracious, great, glistening, and high over every land;
Thy rays encompass the lands to the limit of all that thou hast made.
As thou art Ra, thou reachest to the end of the lands;
❷ Thou subduest them for thy beloved son.
❸ When thou settest in the western horizon,
The land is in darkness, in the manner of death.
Darkness is a shroud, and the earth is in stillness.
At daybreak, when thou arisest on the horizon,
When thou shinest as the Aton by day,
Thou drivest away the darkness and givest thy rays.
❹ The Two Lands are in festivity every day,
Their arms are raised in praise at thy appearance.
All beasts are content with their pasturage;
Trees and plants are flourishing.

island south of Greece. It is named after King Minos, a legendary Cretan king. Soon after 3000 B.C.E., an advanced culture centered on coastal towns appeared.

Minoan Palace Complexes By 2000 B.C.E., several small urban centers known as "palace complexes" had been built near the coast of Crete, including Knossos in the north and Phaistos in the south. They seem to have been independent of each other, and their lack of walls indicates that they were at peace with one another and not threatened by foreign attack. Most people lived in the palace suburbs or in the countryside, in houses that had doors, windows, and even indoor plumbing.

Minoan palaces complexes had rooms of roughly equal size organized around a central plaza. As the complex expanded, additional rooms were added on the periphery. The palace complexes were administrative centers overseeing the manufacture, storage, and distribution of goods rather than population centers. As an administrative aid, the Minoans created their own writing system, known as Linear A. It was unlike the writing of Mesopotamia or Egypt. Characters were scratched on clay with a pointed wooden stylus. Linear A has not yet been deciphered, but the purpose of Minoan documents is clear. Most are lists of words followed by a number and clearly represent inventories and accounts.

The birds that fly from their nests,
Their wings are stretched out in praise to thy ka [soul].
❺ Creator of seed in women,
Thou who makest fluid into man,
Thou who maintainest the son in the womb of his mother …
O sole god, like whom there is no other!
Thou didst create the world according to thy desire:
The countries of Syria and Nubia, the land of Egypt,
Thou settest every man in his place,
Thou suppliest their necessities:
Everyone has his food, and his time of life is reckoned.
❻ Their tongues are separate in speech,
And their natures as well;
Their skins are distinguished,
As thou distinguishest the foreign peoples.
Thou makest a Nile in the underworld,
Thou bringest forth water as thou desirest
To maintain the people of Egypt.
All distant foreign countries, thou makest their life also,
For thou hast set a Nile in heaven,
That it may descend for them and make waves upon the mountains,
To water their fields in their towns.
How effective they are, thy plans, O lord of eternity!
❼ The Nile in heaven, it is for the foreign peoples,
While the true Nile comes from the underworld for Egypt.
❽ Thou are in my heart,
And there is no other that knows thee
Save thy son Nefer-kheperu-Ra Wa-en-Ra,
For thou hast made him well-versed in thy plans and in thy strength.

Source: Pritchard, James, *Ancient Near Eastern Texts Relating to the Old Testament*, 3rd edition with supplement. © 1950, 1955, 1969, renewed 1978 by Princeton University Press. Reprinted by permission of Princeton University Press.

❺ How does Akhenaton portray Aton's relation to the other gods? What similarities are there between Akhenaton's hymn and the scriptures of other world religions?

❻ How did the Egyptians feel about foreign peoples?

❼ Why does Akhenaton speak of two Niles?

❽ How does Akhenaton emphasize his special relationship with Aton?

Minoan Trade Crete did not have fertile river valleys that could be used for large-scale grain production. For economic expansion, the island location encouraged trade by sea, and Minoan ships traveled the Mediterranean. Most were merchant vessels propelled by sails, but some were oar-driven warships whose purpose was to protect the Minoan trading fleet. The Minoans imported metal from the Aegean islands and Italy and amber that had reached the Mediterranean from the Baltic Sea. Their exports included olive oil, made from olive trees grown on sunny hillsides, and manufactured goods such as fine pottery, stoneware, carved gemstones, and intricate metal jewelry, which they shipped to Greece, Anatolia, the Levant, and Egypt. Egyptian wall paintings record a people called the Keftiu who came from "the islands in the great green sea," generally thought to be a reference to Minoan traders. The Minoans also established trading colonies on islands, such as Thera, in the Aegean Sea, and even on the coast of Anatolia. From about 2000 to 1400 B.C.E., the Minoans had a virtual monopoly on Mediterranean trade.

Minoan Religion In other ways, too, Minoan civilization was different from its Near Eastern counterparts. The Minoans had no high-profile gods worshiped in elaborate temples. Minoan religion was personal rather than public, practiced in caves and small shrines in the countryside. Worshipers demonstrated

Scala/Art Resource, NY

The Minoan activity known now as "bull leaping" may reflect either sport or religious ritual and is one of many examples of the importance of bulls in ancient societies. This comic-strip-like portrayal from the Minoan palace at Knossos shows a long-horned bull charging a young man or woman who grasps the horns, flips over the bull, and lands with arms outstretched—much like a modern gymnast—behind the bull. The importance of bulls in Minoan culture also may be reflected in the Greek legend of the Minotaur, or bull-headed man. What do you think might have been the purpose of this activity?

their devotion by depositing **cult objects**, such as small golden double-axes, in the shrines. Many deities represented the forces of nature. One was a goddess known later to the Greeks as the Lady of the Wild Things. Small statuettes depict her wearing an open-breasted, flounced dress and holding two snakes in her upraised hands. Artistic portrayals, in which men and women are represented equally, suggest that Minoan worshipers dressed like the deity they were worshiping and worked themselves into a religious ecstasy in which they believed they could see the god or goddess.

Minoan Views of the World Also unlike other Near Eastern civilizations, the Minoans did not have self-conscious kings who erected monuments commemorating their great deeds. In fact, there are few representations of rulers in Minoan artwork. The so-called throne room at Knossos is a modest chamber with an unpretentious

cult object Any object associated with the performing of religious rituals.

stone chair that may have been used by a low-key administrator.

Minoan art focused on nature. Typical pottery decorations include geometric designs (such as lines and circles), leaves and other vegetation, and animals such as octopuses and bulls. Some of the rare Minoan artworks portraying people depict what seem to be sporting events, such as boxing.

The Dark Side of Minoan Civilization The impression of peaceful, unassuming nature worshipers that emerges from the archaeological evidence is very different, however, from the picture of the Minoans provided by the ancient Greeks. According to Greek historians writing nearly a thousand years later, Minos, king of Knossos, created a sea-based power that dominated the Mediterranean Sea. It was said that Minos's wife Pasiphaë mated with a sacred bull and produced the Minotaur, a bull-headed man. Minos compelled the Greeks to provide seven maidens and seven youths annually to feed the Minotaur. Like most ancient legends, this one had a basis in truth. It correctly recalled Minoan skill at seafaring and interest in bulls, and the Minotaur's cannibalism might be somehow related to a recent archaeological discovery of infants who were butchered and eaten at Knossos.

The Fall of the Minoans Around 1400 B.C.E., the major Minoan cities were destroyed, and the Minoan civilization collapsed. It once was thought that a cataclysmic volcanic explosion on the island of Thera created huge tidal waves that overwhelmed Crete. More recent studies indicate, however, not only that the eruption—which did destroy the Minoan colony on Thera—had relatively little impact on Crete but also that it occurred two hundred years earlier.

It now is thought that the fall of the Minoan civilization was caused by an aggressor people. As of 1400 B.C.E., the Minoan Linear A script was replaced in Crete by Linear B script, which used the Minoan symbols to write a different language. Linear B tablets also were found on the Greek mainland, and in 1953 Linear B was deciphered and discovered to be an early form of Greek. The presence of Linear B on Crete suggests, therefore, that mainland Greeks destroyed the Minoan civilization and even occupied some of the Cretan cities.

The Mycenaeans of Greece

The Linear B tablets proved that Greek civilization began much earlier than once believed. The Greeks who occupied Crete were the descendants of Indo-Europeans who had settled in the Balkans beginning around 2000 B.C.E. and are called **Mycenaeans**, after the Bronze Age fortress of Mycenae in central Greece.

The Origins of Mycenaean Civilization The Mycenaeans had much in common with the Minoans. Greece, like Crete, lacked big river valleys, but its hills and sunny, dry climate were ideal for cultivating olives and grapes. The early Mycenaeans came into contact with Minoan traders and assimilated much of Minoan culture, often adapting it to their own needs. They mimicked Minoan pottery manufacture and copied Minoan art. The Mycenaeans built their own palaces to serve as centers for the accumulation and distribution of resources. As their economy expanded, a means of keeping records was needed and the Mycenaeans developed their own Linear B writing system, adapting Minoan Linear A to the Greek language. By 1600 B.C.E., the Mycenaeans had created the first civilization on the European mainland.

Mycenaean Society Mycenaean cities, such as Mycenae in central Greece, Pylos in the west, and Athens

Massive Mycenaean fortifications like the Lion Gate of Mycenae, ca. 1250 B.C.E., indicate a need for defense against attack. Inside the walls can be seen the circular foundations of the "grave circle" where early Mycenaean kings were buried; unlike most ancient graves, these were not robbed in antiquity, and were not rediscovered until the late nineteenth century. The later Greeks believed that these walls had been built by the Cyclops, the one-eyed giants of Greek myths. How successful do you think walls like these would be at defending the city from possible enemies? (Benaki Museum Photographic Archives. Photo: Dimitrios Harissiadis)

in the east, were built on defendable hills, not right on the coast, and were surrounded by massive walls built from huge roughly hewn blocks. These fortified sites suggest that the Mycenaeans were more security-minded than the Minoans and felt vulnerable to attack. Later Greek legends suggest that the cities were independent and that there was no unified Mycenaean nation. City government consisted of an obsessively bureaucratic administration headed by a king. The possessions of each citizen were minutely catalogued each year, presumably for the purposes of tax assessment.

Mycenaeans Indo-European people who settled in Greece and established the first Greek civilization around 1600 B.C.E.

Every bit of palace income or disbursement was likewise recorded. Manufacturing, ranging from weaving to the crafting of gold ornaments, was controlled from the palace.

Mycenaean art is full of unpeaceful activities, such as hunting and warfare. Lions, boars, and bulls were the favorite prey of Mycenaean hunters. Men's graves contained bronze swords, daggers, armor, and headgear made of boars' tusks. Women as well as men are depicted driving chariots. These images suggest that violence was an everyday aspect of Mycenaean culture.

Mycenaean Trade From the Minoans, the Mycenaeans learned that trade was an effective means of economic expansion. They took to the sea and began to trade in the same markets as the Minoans. Competition arose, and the Mycenaeans made good use of their warlike ways: by 1400 B.C.E., they had invaded Crete and defeated the Minoans. For the next two hundred years, the Mycenaeans controlled trade in the Mediterranean. They established trading colonies in Crete, Syria, Anatolia, and Cyprus. Their trading income made them wealthy, and Mycenaean kings were buried in massive stone-lined underground tombs capped by beehive-shaped ceilings more than forty feet high and containing gold ornaments such as elaborate death masks.

The Sea Peoples and the End of the Bronze Age

By 1200 B.C.E., the Bronze Age was ending in Mesopotamia and Egypt. For a long time, there had been no major technological, economic, cultural, or intellectual advances in the river valleys; most innovations had been occurring in places like Syria, Crete, and Greece. Archaeological evidence from around 1200 B.C.E. shows massive population movements that began with an invasion of several groups of Indo-Europeans from the Central Asian steppes. Collectively, the Egyptians called the invaders the **Sea Peoples**. The disruption they caused was remembered in both contemporary documents and later legends.

The Invasion of the Sea Peoples Evidence for the first appearance of the Sea Peoples can be found in the Greek legend of a Mycenaean attack on **Troy**, a rich and powerful trading city in northwestern Anatolia. Centuries later, the Greek poet **Homer** wrote in a poem called the *Iliad* that King Agamemnon of Mycenae led a Greek coalition of a thousand ships (each carrying about fifty men) against Troy. The city was captured, sacked, and burned after a ten-year siege. For centuries it was thought that Homer's account was just a legend and that Troy could not have existed at that place and time. In the late nineteenth century, however, archaeologists discovered Troy, which was just as Homer had described. In addition, the legendary date of the Trojan War, 1184 B.C.E., is consistent with the movements of the Sea Peoples just after 1200 B.C.E. So, too, are the Egyptian accounts of groups of Sea Peoples called the Danuna and Akawasha, names strikingly similar to the Danaans and Achaeans, as Homer's Greeks were called. It is possible, therefore, that groups of Mycenaeans were caught up in the southward movement of the Sea Peoples and that Troy was one of the first places to be attacked.

The Sea Peoples threatened the entire eastern Mediterranean. Surviving correspondence among local kings shows concern about impending attacks. Ammurapi, king of Ugarit, reported the sighting of enemy ships to the king of Cyprus, who replied, "If this is true, then make yourself very strong. Be on the lookout for the enemy." Ammurapi's answer depicts a dire situation: "Enemy ships have come and set my ships ablaze, and have done wicked things to the country." In the end, the Hittite kingdom was destroyed and Ugarit was sacked and burned.

The Defeat of the Sea Peoples Around 1180 B.C.E., the Sea Peoples smashed into the rich Nile Delta, where they were met by pharaoh **Ramses III** (r. 1182–1151 B.C.E.). The Egyptian account of the battle is the longest surviving hieroglyphic inscription. It began, "The foreign countries made a conspiracy in their islands. No land could stand before their arms. They were coming toward Egypt and thinking, 'Our plans will succeed!'" Ramses was ready. He said, "I had the river mouths prepared like a strong wall with fully equipped warships. On land, the charioteers consisted of picked men, prepared to crush the foreign countries." The battle ended in an overwhelming Egyptian victory. Ramses boasted, "Those who reached my frontier, their heart and their soul are finished forever. They were enclosed and prostrated on the beach, killed and made into heaps." Those Sea Peoples who escaped scattered about the Mediterranean, creating further destruction. Egypt, after this great victory, sank into obscurity.

Sea Peoples Large group of Indo-European peoples who attacked eastern Mediterranean lands shortly after 1200 B.C.E.

Troy City of northwestern Anatolia destroyed by the Mycenaeans shortly after 1200 B.C.E.

Homer Blind Greek poet of about 800 B.C.E. whose *Iliad* and *Odyssey* told of the Trojan War and its aftermath.

Ramses III (r. 1182–1151 B.C.E.) Egyptian pharaoh who defeated the Sea Peoples around 1180 B.C.E.

The End of the Bronze Age In Greece, disorder continued. The Mycenaean trading economy declined as a consequence of the devastation in the eastern Mediterranean. About 1150 B.C.E., Indo-Europeans known as the **Dorians** took advantage of Mycenaean weakness and made their way from northern to southern Greece. Documents from the city of Pylos tell of the approaching peril. One reports, "The enemy grabbed all the priests and murdered them by drowning. The northern strangers continued their attack, terrorizing and plundering." In spite of Mycenaean efforts, Pylos was sacked and burned. By 1100 B.C.E., all the Mycenaean centers except the stronghold of Athens had fallen to the invaders. The Dorians enslaved many of the local people they conquered. Some Mycenaeans fled to **Ionia**, on the western coast of Anatolia, and founded new cities. Additional disruption occurred at roughly the same time in Mesopotamia, where shortly after 1200 B.C.E., the Kassite kingdom was destroyed by the Elamites of Iran. Throughout the Near East, the Bronze Age ended in chaos.

Dorians Indo-Europeans who began to settle in southern Greece about 1150 B.C.E.

Ionia Western coastal region of Anatolia, the site of Greek colonies founded by the Mycenaeans.

Checking In

By yourself or with a partner, explain the significance of each of the following selected key terms:

Ebla	Mycenaeans
Ba'al	Sea Peoples
alphabet	Troy
Minoan civilization	Ramses III

Review

Summary

- Of the million-plus years of the human past described in this chapter, only 1800 years, from 3000 to 1200 B.C.E., cover periods of human civilization. Almost all of the entire human past took place in the period before civilization, when people lived a wandering existence focused on finding food and shelter.

- Beginning around 8000 B.C.E., humans gained greater control over their food supply through the domestication of animals and plants. Expanded agriculture brought increased food supplies, larger populations, and, ultimately, the creation of cities.

- Around 3000 B.C.E., the first phase of civilization—a form of culture defined by the presence of agriculture, cities, writing, metal technology, social differentiation, and specialization of labor—arose in the river valleys of Egypt, Mesopotamia, India, and China.

- The first period of civilization is known as the Bronze Age. In the Bronze Age, the most representative civilizations were located in fertile river valleys.

They produced vast food surpluses through the extensive exploitation of agriculture and supported large populations.

- The use of writing marked the beginning of history, for people now could create permanent narrative accounts of their past.

- Over time, pastoral peoples such as the Semitic and Indo-European peoples interacted with the river valley peoples and assimilated their culture. Civilization spread out of the river valleys.

- Western civilization began with the civilizations of Mesopotamia and Egypt. Although these two civilizations were similar in their general outlines, they had very different specific traits. The Mesopotamians were geographically exposed, politically disunited, and generally pessimistic. The Egyptians were geographically protected, usually united into a single kingdom, and extraordinarily optimistic. The Mesopotamians had little faith that their gods would take care of them; the Egyptians had complete confidence in their gods.

◆ The Mesopotamians and Egyptians both made fundamental contributions to western civilization in the areas of government and law, economic development, technology, religious belief, and literary and artistic expression.

◆ Both the strength and the weakness of river valley civilizations was that they were based very heavily on agriculture, which provided a dependable food supply but also had few opportunities for economic expansion through trade.

◆ At the same time, experiments in economic activity that focused more heavily on trade were occurring elsewhere in the Levant, Crete, and Greece.

◆ By 1200 B.C.E., the initial phase of civilization, based on the extensive exploitation of agriculture in river valleys, was over. Destructive attacks by the Sea Peoples brought the Bronze Age to an end.

Chronology

2,000,000 B.C.E.	Homo habilis uses crude stone choppers to butcher animals
1,000,000 B.C.E.	Homo erectus learns the use of fire
40,000 B.C.E.	Homo sapiens create cave paintings
8000 B.C.E.	Neolithic Age begins
4000 B.C.E.	Sumerians drain Tigris and Euphrates River valleys for agriculture
3000 B.C.E.	Beginning of Bronze Age civilization Narmer unifies Egypt
2700 B.C.E.	Old Kingdom in Egypt begins
2600 B.C.E.	Building of the largest Egyptian pyramids
2500 B.C.E.	Ebla becomes a commercial center
2350 B.C.E.	Sargon creates Akkadian Empire
2050 B.C.E.	Middle Kingdom in Egypt begins
2000 B.C.E.	Amorites settle in Mesopotamia Indo-Europeans settle in Iran, Anatolia, and the Balkans Minoan palace complexes appear in Crete
1790 B.C.E.	Hammurabi becomes king of Babylon
1730 B.C.E.	Hyksos invade Egypt
1600 B.C.E.	Beginning of Mycenaean civilization in Greece
1570 B.C.E.	New Kingdom in Egypt begins
1500 B.C.E.	Kassites settle in Mesopotamia
1498 B.C.E.	Hatshepsut becomes pharaoh of Egypt
1483 B.C.E.	Thutmose III becomes pharaoh of Egypt
1400 B.C.E.	Mycenaeans destroy Minoan civilization
1350 B.C.E.	Akhenaton institutes religious reforms in Egypt
1200 B.C.E.	Invasion of the Sea Peoples End of the Bronze Age
1180 B.C.E.	Ramses III defeats the Sea Peoples

Note: B.C.E. means "Before the Common Era."

© Cengage Learning

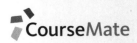

Test Yourself

To gauge your mastery of the material in this chapter, answer the questions below. More than one answer may be correct.

Before History, 2,000,000–3000 B.C.E.

1. What are the surviving remains of a culture known as?
   a. Technology
   b. Material culture
   c. Cultural assimilation
   d. Myths and legends
   e. Pastoralism

2. The "Neolithic Revolution" resulted in the acquisition of what new kinds of food production methods?
   a. Hunting
   b. Agriculture
   c. Pastoralism
   d. Gathering
   e. Flint tools

3. The adoption of agriculture provided people with what opportunities?
   a. To settle in one place
   b. To migrate with flocks and herds
   c. To have a dependable food supply
   d. To acquire wealth
   e. To harvest wild berries

4. To qualify as a "civilization," a society must possess which of these characteristics?
   a. Metal technology
   b. Stone tools
   c. Writing
   d. Agriculture
   e. Cities

Now that you have reviewed and tested yourself on this part of the chapter, take time to pull together all the important information by answering the following questions:

◆ How did methods of acquiring food change during the course of the Stone Age?

◆ What were the social, economic, and cultural consequences of the adoption of agriculture?

Mesopotamian Civilization, 3000–1200 B.C.E.

5. Irregular flooding of the Tigris and Euphrates Rivers caused Mesopotamians to develop which of these concepts?
   a. A pessimistic view of the world
   b. Large step pyramids called ziggurats
   c. Unpredictable gods
   d. An unpleasant afterlife
   e. Cuneiform writing

6. What were the lives of the ancient Sumerians fixated on?
   a. Warfare
   b. Entertainments
   c. Religion
   d. Pursuing public service
   e. Trade

7. Mesopotamians tried to gain control over their world by doing what?
   a. Placing trust in the gods
   b. Issuing laws
   c. Assigning numbers to the gods
   d. Putting statues of themselves in temples
   e. Conquering the desert peoples

8. Which of these peoples invaded Mesopotamia during the Bronze Age?

    a. Babylonians
    b. Aryans
    c. Mycenaeans

    d. Kassites
    e. Akkadians

Now that you have reviewed and tested yourself on this part of the chapter, take time to pull together all the important information by answering the following questions:

◆ How did geography influence the development of civilization in Mesopotamia?

◆ What part did religion play in the lives of the ancient Sumerians?

Egyptian Civilization, 3000–1200 B.C.E.

9. The regular flooding of the Nile River valley caused the Egyptians to develop which of these concepts?

    a. A warlike attitude
    b. Optimism
    c. Trust in their gods

    d. Belief in a single god
    e. Wheeled vehicles

10. In the mind of the Egyptians, what could they expect after they died?

    a. To be tortured by demons
    b. To enjoy a wonderful afterlife
    c. To be gathered into "the well of infinity"

    d. To be reborn in animal form
    e. To have their bodies cremated

11. During the Old Kingdom, what was the primary role of the Egyptian pharaohs?

    a. Army generals
    b. Administrators of the nomes
    c. Living gods

    d. Servants of the priests
    e. Figurehead rulers

12. The pharaoh Akhenaton tried to make which god the main god of Egypt?

    a. Ra
    b. Isis
    c. Osiris

    d. Amon
    e. Aton

Now that you have reviewed and tested yourself on this part of the chapter, take time to pull together all the important information by answering the following questions:

◆ How did geography influence the development of civilization in Egypt?

◆ How did the ancient Egyptians view the concept of life after death?

Lost Civilizations of the Bronze Age, 2500–1200 B.C.E.

13. During the Bronze Age, where did peoples who concentrated on trade live?

    a. Outside large river valleys
    b. In mountains where there were gold and silver mines
    c. In deserts where they did not fear being attacked

    d. In small self-sufficient villages
    e. In the Nile River valley

14. Which cultures developed economies focusing on trade during the Bronze Age?
    a. The Sumerians
    b. The Minoans
    c. Ebla
    d. The Kassites
    e. The Mycenaeans

15. What marked the end of the Bronze Age?
    a. The invention of writing
    b. The exploitation of agriculture in river valleys
    c. The invasion of Egypt by the Hyksos
    d. The attacks by the Sea Peoples
    e. The expansion of the Minoan civilization

Now that you have reviewed and tested yourself on this part of the chapter, take time to pull together all the important information by answering the following questions:

◆ What factors encouraged the development of trading economies during the Bronze Age?

◆ In what ways were the Minoan and Mycenaean civilizations different from the civilizations of Mesopotamia and Egypt?

CHAPTER 2

Iron Age Civilizations, 1200–500 B.C.E.

1200	1150	1100	1050	1000	950	900	850

1200 B.C.E.
Bronze Age ends, Iron Age begins

1100 B.C.E.
Dorians settle southern Greece

970 B.C.E.
Solomon becomes Hebrew king

900 B.C.E.
Rise of the Assyrian Empire

This finely made gold chariot was part of a hoard of 170 gold and silver objects dating to the Persian Empire of the fifth or fourth century B.C.E. found by the Oxus (present-day Amu) River in modern Tajikistan, in the far reaches of the empire. One of the items, reproduced here, shows a chariot carrying a driver and a high-ranking official, probably a Persian satrap. Both are dressed in clothing of the Medes. On the front of the chariot is an image of the Egyptian god Bes. The multicultural nature of the chariot reflects the multi-cultural nature of the Persian Empire, which incorporated a vast number of peoples representing different places and cultures. It has been suggested that the chariot was intended as an offering at a temple. Can you think of any other purposes that this chariot might have served? (Courtesy of the Trustees of the British Museum)

After reading this chapter, you should be able to answer the following questions:

How was the Iron Age different from the Bronze Age?

How did trade, commerce, and acquisition of wealth affect the development of empires during the Iron Age?

What was the nature of the relationship between the Hebrews and their god?

What kinds of factors made the Assyrian Empire such an unsuccessful empire?

How were the Persians able to create such a large and successful empire?

B
Y 1200 B.C.E., the river valley civilizations of the Bronze Age had expanded to their limits. Future technological, economic, and political developments would occur outside the river valleys, facilitated by the growing use of a new metal—iron, which was much less expensive to manufacture than bronze. If bronze was the metal of society's elite, iron was the common person's metal, and it gave its name to the Iron Age. Iron could be used for tools such as plows, which permitted agriculture to spread to areas with tougher soils outside the river valleys. Another important characteristic of the Iron Age was the vastly increased use of trade as a means of economic and political expansion by peoples of the eastern Mediterranean coast.

The Iron Age also saw the creation of empires much larger than those of the Bronze Age, first in Assyria and then in Persia. Unlike the empires of the Bronze Age, these empires were no longer obsessed with the extensive exploitation of agriculture in the heart of fertile river valleys: the Assyrian homeland was far upstream

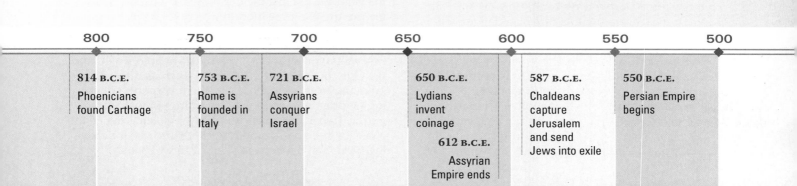

800	750	700	650	600	550	500

814 B.C.E.
Phoenicians found Carthage

753 B.C.E.
Rome is founded in Italy

721 B.C.E.
Assyrians conquer Israel

650 B.C.E.
Lydians invent coinage

612 B.C.E.
Assyrian Empire ends

587 B.C.E.
Chaldeans capture Jerusalem and send Jews into exile

550 B.C.E.
Persian Empire begins

on the Tigris River, and Persia was nowhere near a river valley. The Iron Age empires were more concerned with economic expansion, the encouragement of trade, and the accumulation of wealth. They also were characterized by powerful rulers overseeing vast administrative systems.

At the same time, the Hebrews, a people descended from the Semitic groups that inhabited the fringes of Mesopotamia, created in Palestine a religious culture incorporating not only belief in a single God but also concepts of morality and ethics. This culture would have great influence on the subsequent evolution of western civilization. The story of the Hebrews' struggle to preserve their cultural and religious identity continues to resonate in the modern day.

Merchants and Traders of the Eastern Mediterranean, 1200–650 B.C.E.

◆ **Why did the importance of trade increase during the Iron Age?**

◆ **What was the role of iron in the Iron Age?**

The new patterns of Iron Age civilization first appeared about 1200 B.C.E. in the lands bordering the eastern coast of the Mediterranean Sea. Here, peoples who previously had existed in the shadows of the civilizations and empires of Mesopotamia and Egypt were able to achieve a greater degree of political, economic, and religious self-expression. They made tools and weapons of iron, engaged in widespread trade, and, outside of the major river valleys, built small, fortified cities that were lively centers of commerce. Over time, the Iron Age way of life diffused out of western Asia and westward into Europe.

From Bronze to Iron

Even though the Iron Age began in the Near East around 1200 B.C.E., the use of iron actually had begun in the Bronze Age, when it was a luxury item. In the nineteenth century B.C.E., for example, Assyrian merchants valued iron at forty times its weight in silver. King Tut was buried with a rare iron dagger, still unrusted when the tomb was opened in 1922.

Iron Production For a long time, however, iron did not enter into widespread use. It was much more difficult to mine and smelt than bronze. Unlike the copper and tin used in making bronze, iron in its metallic form was extremely rare,

cast iron Raw molten iron that is poured into molds and allowed to cool.

found mainly in meteorites. Most iron occurred in combination with other elements, such as sulfur and oxygen, in ores that had to be smelted to release the iron. The relatively low melting point of bronze, 950 degrees Celsius (1,742 degrees Fahrenheit), made it an easy alloy to work in ordinary pottery kilns. The smelting of iron ore, however, required a much higher temperature, 1,538 degrees Celsius (2,800 degrees Fahrenheit).

The early production of iron often is associated with the Hittites, but they produced only limited quantities of iron implements before their empire collapsed around 1200 B.C.E. Not until then—at the same time as and perhaps even because of the disruptive movements of peoples that ended the Bronze Age—did the knowledge of ironworking technology spread throughout western Asia (Iran, Mesopotamia, Anatolia, and the Levant). By 1100 B.C.E., ironworking technology had diffused into southwestern Europe, reaching all the way to Britain by about 700 B.C.E. The Egyptians, however, clung to the old ways. Iron did not become widely used in Egypt until the seventh century B.C.E.

Once iron making became widespread and economical, the transition from bronze to iron occurred quickly. Iron could be used for manufacturing commonplace items, such as tools and household utensils, that would have been prohibitively expensive if made from bronze. Metal implements now became available to everyone, not just the rich. Only in weapons manufacture did the transition to iron take longer because early **cast iron** was soft and brittle and did not keep a sharp edge. Initially, therefore, bronze remained the best metal for weapons, which had to hold up in battle. Only over time did processes such as carburizing (alloying iron with about 1 percent carbon), quenching (sudden immersion of heated iron in water), tempering (reheating quenched iron and allowing it to cool slowly), and hammering come into use for creating hard, non-brittle, and sharp iron weapons.

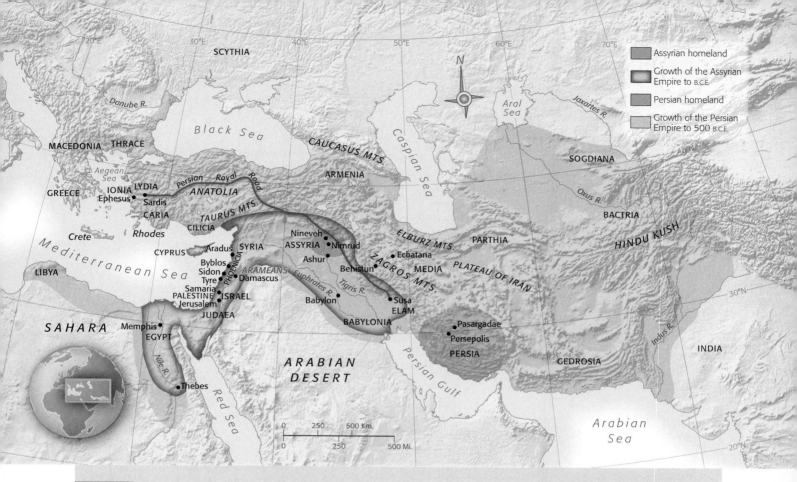

Map 2.1 **The Assyrian and Persian Empires, 900–500 B.C.E.** The Assyrian and Persian Empires were the greatest Iron Age empires. The Assyrian Empire was the first to incorporate both Egypt and Mesopotamia under the same rule, and the even vaster Persian Empire contained parts of India and Europe. © *Cengage Learning*

1. Geographically, how is the Assyrian Empire related to the "Fertile Crescent?" Why do you think this might have been the case?
2. How is the geographical extent of the Persian Empire different from the geographical coverage of earlier empires?
3. Which major river valleys were incorporated into the Persian Empire?
4. To what extent did the Assyrians and Persians expand their empires beyond their original homelands? What kinds of administrative problems might have been caused by doing this?

The Iron Age The use of iron brought great economic changes. Iron plows could work tough soils, such as those in the Danube and Rhine valleys in Europe, that wooden scratch plows could not. Large-scale agriculture thus expanded out of the Near Eastern river valleys. But Iron Age societies could never be as completely dependent on agriculture as the river valley civilizations of the Bronze Age, for their soils were not nearly as rich. Thus, in the Iron Age, people had to find other ways of expanding their economies. They did so by focusing much more heavily on manufacturing and trade, which became another of the distinguishing characteristics of the Iron Age.

During the Iron Age, peoples living outside river valleys gained a greater opportunity to expand their political and economic influence. The centers of civilization, culture, and economic development moved out of the river valleys and, in general, toward the

west, first to the Levant, then to Anatolia and the Balkans, and then to western Europe. The Iron Age was a period of smaller, fortified cities, located either in uplands for protection or near seacoasts for access to water transportation, with economies based largely on commerce. Artisans no longer concentrated on luxury goods, as in the Bronze Age, but on mass-produced pottery and textiles. Merchants grew wealthy transporting goods from one trading center to another. Typical Iron Age culture arose first on the eastern coast of the Mediterranean, represented by the Phoenicians, Arameans, and Philistines. It then spread to the Lydians in western Anatolia.

The Phoenicians

Many of the seacoast cities of Phoenicia (modern Lebanon) recovered after the attacks of the Sea Peoples.

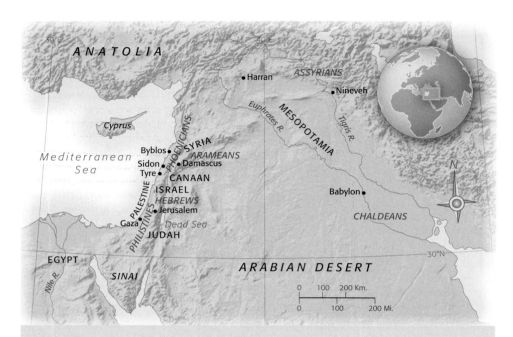

Map 2.2 **Peoples of the Early Iron Age** Four peoples living on or near the eastern coast of the Mediterranean Sea, the Phoenicians, Arameans, Philistines, and Hebrews, provide examples of early Iron Age life. © *Cengage Learning*

1. How were the areas occupied by the peoples of the early Iron Age different from the areas occupied by the civilizations of Mesopotamia and Egypt? In what ways did this limit these peoples' economic opportunities?
2. What kinds of economic opportunities became available to the peoples of the early Iron Age as a result of their geography?
3. What were some of the cities that were important for the peoples of the early Iron Age? How were these cities different from the cities of the Bronze Age?

The hilly and forested coastal land was unsuitable for extensive agriculture, so the **Phoenicians**, another of the Semitic peoples, turned to trade as a means of economic expansion. The great trading city of Ugarit was never rebuilt, but other cities, such as Tyre, Sidon, and Byblos, became centers of a reinvigorated seaborne commerce. Each Phoenician city was an independent city-state, governed by a king who was advised by a council of nobles.

Phoenician Trade Borrowing nautical technology from the Sea Peoples, the Phoenicians built ships with keels for improved strength and maneuverability. They traveled the Mediterranean and beyond, navigating by the sun and the stars. Because rowers were expensive and took up valuable deck space, Phoenician merchant ships were driven by sails. Ancient sailing ships were unable to sail against the wind effectively, so trading ships could be delayed for weeks in port waiting for a favorable wind. Like all ancient sailors, the Phoenicians hugged the coast rather than striking out for the open sea, and they headed for shore at the first sign of bad weather. Each Phoenician city also maintained a navy to protect its trade. Warships had to be maneuverable and ready to go at a moment's notice, regardless of the wind, so they were propelled by oarsmen. With two banks of oars, rows of shields, a bronze ram, and an armed body of marines, a Phoenician galley (an oar-driven ship) would have been a fearsome sight to any pirate.

Phoenician merchants became legendary. The Bible describes the Phoenicians of Tyre as those "whose merchants are princes, whose traders are honored in the world." The Phoenicians imported luxury goods such as ivory, gemstones, and peacocks from Africa and India; papyrus from Egypt; spices such as myrrh and frankincense from Arabia; and metals such as gold, silver, tin, and copper from Cyprus, Spain, Britain, and Africa. These raw materials were either re-exported or used in local manufacturing. The city of Byblos exported so much papyrus that the Greek word for

Phoenicians Semitic people engaged in sea trade who inhabited modern-day Lebanon.

A Phoenician warship on a stone relief of about 800 B.C.E. has two banks of oars, a fortified upper deck protected by a row of shields, and a ram for piercing the side of enemy ships. Ships such as these were necessary for the protection of Phoenician trading ships and would have been a terrifying sight even to the boldest of pirates. Warships were driven by oars rather than sails because they had to be able to travel even when there was no wind and to go in any direction, regardless of where the wind was coming from. How do you think that these cities might have been able to afford these expensive navies? (© The Trustees of the British Museum/Art Resource, NY)

"book," *biblion*, and hence the word *Bible*, come from the city name. Fine furniture was made from the extensive cedar and hardwood forests. Phoenician glassblowing, including the creation of transparent glass, began a tradition that lasted for centuries. Other local products such as timber, salted fish, and wine also were exported. But the Phoenicians were best known for "Tyrian purple," a dye used for coloring royal garments that was made from a local shellfish.

The Alphabet As an aid in keeping business records, the Phoenicians perfected the alphabet. The Phoenician alphabet had twenty-two consonants beginning with the letters *aleph* (originally a consonant), *beth*, and *gimel*. This alphabet was later borrowed by the Greeks, from whom it made its way to the Romans and then to us. And as another means of assisting in their commercial enterprises, the Phoenicians established colonies along their trade routes. Carthage, founded on the coast of modern Tunisia in 814 B.C.E. by Princess Elissa of Tyre, later became a major power in its own right. Cadiz, on the Atlantic coast of Spain just beyond the Strait of Gibraltar, was a port for ships that traded all the way to the British Isles.

Phoenician Religion The Phoenicians worshiped a triad of three primary gods, who were reflected in the architecture of Phoenician temples, which had three chambers. The creator god was El, a word that meant simply "god." El, who was called the "father of the gods" and "the creator of the creators," was often worshiped at an altar in a "high place." The son of El was Ba'al, a storm god who was viewed as the most important god on earth. Ba'al eventually eclipsed El,

much as the god Enlil had overshadowed his father An in Sumeria. Ba'al had many forms: in Tyre he became Melqart and under that name was exported to Carthage. The third primary deity was Astarte, a goddess representing fertility, sexuality, and war. Astarte was known under different names to many different peoples: she was called Ishtar in Mesopotamia, Ashtoret in the Bible, and Aphrodite in Greece. A surviving **cult statue** of Astarte has holes punctured in her breasts that could be stopped up with wax. When the wax was subtly melted during a ceremony, milk (stored in the statue's hollow head) flowed from her breasts. Early Phoenician worship also included human sacrifice, a practice that continued in Carthage even after it had been abandoned in the Phoenician homeland.

Like the Egyptians, the Phoenicians believed in an afterlife and attempted to preserve their dead in elaborate tombs and coffins, even though Phoenician mummies soon decomposed in the damp seacoast climate. A Phoenician king inscribed on his coffin these words: "I, Tabnit, priest of Astarte, King of Sidon, am lying here. Whoever might find this coffin, do not disturb me, for such a thing would be an abomination to Astarte." Tabnit's tomb, unlike the thousands of others that were plundered in

Carthage Phoenician trading colony founded on the coast of modern Tunisia in 814 B.C.E. by the city of Tyre.

Strait of Gibraltar Strait between Spain and North Africa that connects the Mediterranean Sea with the Atlantic Ocean.

triad Group of three.

Astarte Goddess of fertility, sexuality, and war worshiped by many Near Eastern peoples.

cult statue Statue serving as a stand-in for a deity in a temple.

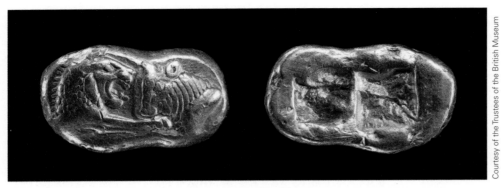

A crude gold coin, known as a shekel, issued by the Lydian king Croesus about 550 B.C.E. bears the facing heads of a lion and a bull on one side and two punch marks on the other. Because these coins all had the same weight and because gold was a commodity that was valued by all societies, the coins were readily accepted in markets everywhere in exchange for any sort of merchandise. The symbols identified who had issued the coin and guaranteed its weight and purity. Croesus was so wealthy that he still serves as the basis for the saying to be "rich as Croesus." Why do you think gold was so highly valued in antiquity and continues to be in the modern day?

antiquity, lay undisturbed until its discovery in the 1800s.

Other Eastern Mediterranean Traders

Other eastern Mediterranean peoples also represented Iron Age culture in various ways. These included the Arameans and Philistines on the eastern Mediterranean coast, and the kingdom of Lydia in western Anatolia.

The Arameans The **Arameans**, a Semitic people from northern Arabia, established city-kingdoms, such as Damascus, to the east of the Phoenicians just before 1200 B.C.E. and gained a virtual monopoly on trade by land. Aramean caravans carried goods ranging from agricultural products to textiles south to Egypt and Arabia, north to Turkey and Central Asia, and east all the way to India. Because Arameans traveled everywhere, their language, Aramaic, replaced Akkadian as a common language that allowed people from different countries to communicate.

The Philistines To the south of the Phoenicians, on the seacoast of modern-day Palestine, lived the **Philistines**, an Indo-European people descended from the warlike Sea People known to the Egyptians as the Peleset, who had settled there just after 1200 B.C.E. The Philistines established their own city-states, such as Ashkelon and Gaza, each ruled by its own lord. They left no written records and so are known only from writings of their enemies and from a few archaeological remains, such as a furnace used for making iron swords. They appear in the Bible as warriors known for their iron weapons who threatened the peoples around them. In spite of their military reputation, however, the Philistines were primarily farmers, for they had productive agricultural land. Lacking good seaports, they never became sailors, but they did become wealthy by controlling the land and sea traffic passing north and south between Egypt and Phoenicia. They worshiped the Canaanite deity Dagon, a crop, fertility, and war god, and Dagon's wife Astarte.

The Kingdom of Lydia Iron Age civilization soon spread to the western seacoast of Anatolia, where the kingdom of **Lydia** arose after the destruction of the Hittite kingdom around 1200 B.C.E. Their coastal cities on the Aegean Sea gave the Lydians access to the trading markets of the Mediterranean. The Lydians also controlled gold-bearing streams, giving rise to the legend of King Midas, who was said to turn everything he touched into gold. The Lydians thus grew rich through gold mining and trade. They also made one of the most important economic advances of all time by inventing coinage. Previously, gold and silver had been recognized by traders as having great value but had been traded by weight. Around 650 B.C.E., the Lydians began using lumps of gold and silver that all had the same weight, and thus the same value, as a means of exchange in business transactions. These lumps were the first coins. They were so useful that other trading peoples soon adopted them, and the use of coinage rapidly spread throughout the Mediterranean and Near Eastern worlds.

Arameans Semitic people living in Syria who engaged in trade by land.

Philistines Indo-European people who gave their name to Palestine, where they settled just after 1200 B.C.E. Lydia Trading kingdom in northwestern Anatolia that invented coinage.

Lydia Trading kingdom in northwestern Anatolia that invented coinage.

The Hebrews and Monotheism, 1800–900 B.C.E.

◆ **What made the Hebrew people distinct from other peoples?**

◆ **How did the Hebrews relate to their God?**

The Hebrews originated as Semitic pastoralists living on the fringes of the civilized world and went on to form a powerful Iron Age kingdom. But their primary importance was religious rather than political, for they created a religious culture that would have great influence on later western civilization. The Hebrews' intensely personal relationship with a single God made their religion different from every other religion of pre-Christian antiquity. In addition, written teachings gave the Hebrews a sense of identity, and the Hebrew Bible became one of the most influential documents of western history.

Hebrew Origins

The Hebrews, later known to history as the Jews, played a major role in the history of the early Iron Age. They were the first **People of the Book**; that is, people who, like the Christians and Muslims after them, based their beliefs on teachings that were preserved in written form, known as **scripture**. Because they were written down, these teachings were resistant to change over the centuries.

Sources of Hebrew History Hebrew scripture, known to Jews as the **Tanakh** and to Christians as the Hebrew Bible or the Old Testament, describes not only the relations of the Hebrews with their God but also the history of the Hebrew people. It begins with five books called the **Torah**, and also contains nineteen books of Prophets and eleven books known as the Writings. For the ancient Hebrews, scripture provided an accurate portrayal of their ancient history. Today, a comparison of Hebrew scripture with other evidence, such as archaeology or contemporary Near Eastern records, shows that the Bible is about as accurate as any other historical sources surviving from the early Iron Age. In many instances, archaeological evidence strikingly confirms the outlines of what is reported in scripture, but in other cases, such as the dates of the creation of the world and the Hebrew Exodus, startling inconsistencies have produced debates among theologians and historians. The following discussion is based primarily on the Hebrews' view of their history as preserved in the Tanakh.

The Hebrew Covenant In Hebrew scripture, the human past began with God's creation of the world and the first two humans, Adam and Eve, over 6,000 years ago. The Hebrews believed that their special relationship with their God began about 1800 B.C.E., when God, at that time known as **El Shaddai** (God Almighty), made a **covenant**—a binding agreement—with Abraham, the **patriarch**, or head, of a group of Semitic pastoralists. In the book of Genesis, God said to Abraham, "I will establish My covenant as an everlasting covenant between Me and you and your descendants after you for the generations to come, to be your God and the God of your descendants after you. The whole land of Canaan, where you are now an alien, I will give as an everlasting possession to you and your descendants after you." God also said, "You are to undergo circumcision, and it will be the sign of the covenant between Me and you." By keeping this covenant, the Hebrews became the "chosen people" of God.

Previously, like other peoples of that time, the Hebrews had believed in many gods, but God's covenant with Abraham set them on the path to **monotheism**, the belief that there is only one god. The Hebrew God was incorporeal, having no shape or form that could be represented in physical form, and was everywhere. God also had humanlike emotions and could be loving, jealous, angry, and demanding. The Hebrew relationship with their God was very personal. God was a real presence and spoke directly to the Hebrews through **prophets**, of whom Abraham was the first. Prophets could be anyone, regardless of social

People of the Book People who base their beliefs on teachings that are preserved in written form.

scripture Sacred or religious writings of a religion.

Tanakh Jewish scriptures, consisting of the Torah, the Prophets, and the Writings.

Torah First five books of Jewish scripture.

El Shaddai Original name of the Hebrew god, meaning "God Almighty."

covenant Agreement by which God agreed to make the Hebrews His chosen people and the Hebrews agreed to follow God's law.

patriarch (from Greek for "father") In early Hebrew history, the male leader of an extended family group; later, the spiritual leader of the Jews, and in the later Roman Empire, the bishops of the most important Christian cities.

monotheism (from Greek for "one god") Belief in the existence of only one god.

prophets Persons through whom God communicated to the Hebrews.

status or gender. Prophets were able to converse and even negotiate with God, and they exercised leadership over the Hebrew people as a consequence of their direct contact with God.

The Age of the Patriarchs The period of Hebrew history that began with Abraham is known as the Age of the Patriarchs, when the Hebrews were one of many **clans** of wandering Semitic pastoralists who lived on the semiarid fringes of the Mesopotamian river valley civilizations. An elderly male patriarch led each clan. The people kept sheep and cattle, lived in tents, and traveled about in search of pasturelands. Sometimes they stayed long enough in one place to plant a crop of grain, but they never settled for long. In this male-dominated society, women had an inferior status. Property belonged to the clan and was controlled by the men. Men had both wives and concubines. Men could divorce their wives for several reasons, such as infertility, and could take second wives to provide children.

Even though they rejected urban life, the ancestors of the Hebrews assimilated much of Mesopotamian culture, such as its legal concepts, the Sumerian word *edin* (a flat plain), stories of a great flood, descriptions of ziggurats, and tales of heroes who were cast adrift as infants. These elements reappeared in Hebrew scripture in the judicial concept of "an eye for an eye," and in stories of the garden of Eden, Noah's flood, the tower of Babel, and the infant Moses being cast adrift in the Nile.

The Hebrew Sojourn in Egypt The Hebrew people expanded. According to scripture, the twelve sons of Abraham's grandson the patriarch Jacob, also known as Israel, gave rise to twelve **tribes**, or extended clans. The tribes were later known as the children of **Israel**. During a period of famine, Jacob's son Joseph moved his family to northern Egypt, possibly between 1700 and 1600 B.C.E., during the Hyksos period, when Egypt's northern frontiers were open to outsiders. There, the Hebrews became agricultural laborers and slaves working on building projects. Their stay in Egypt thus turned the Hebrews from wandering pastoralists into settled farmers and artisans.

Aside from scripture, however, there is little record of the Hebrews' stay in Egypt. Near Eastern documents of the thirteenth century B.C.E. and later make generic, often derogatory, references to the Ha-bi-ru, a word meaning "the dusty people." They appear as slaves, laborers, bandits, and mercenaries. Egyptian records, for example, speak of "the Ha-bi-ru who drag stone for the great building of Ramses II." Eventually, the word Ha-bi-ru came to be applied to the Hebrews alone. It has also been suggested, but with little justification, that Hebrew monotheism influenced Akhenaton's belief that Aton was the one primary god.

The Exodus and the Age of Judges

One of the greatest events in Hebrew history was the **Exodus**, in which the prophet **Moses** led several thousand Hebrew slaves out of captivity in Egypt.

Moses and the Exodus According to scripture, the infant Moses was placed in a basket and set adrift in the Nile River by his mother because the pharaoh had ordered all male Hebrew children to be killed. Moses was rescued downstream by an Egyptian princess and raised in the Egyptian royal household. This scriptural account is consistent with the Egyptian origin of Moses's name, which is similar to that of the pharaoh Thutmose. The biblical book of Exodus goes on to report that after killing an Egyptian overseer, Moses took refuge in the Sinai Desert, where God addressed him from a burning bush and revealed His true name: "I appeared to Abraham, to Isaac, and to Jacob by the name of El Shaddai, but my name YHWH was not known to them." In Hebrew scripture, the name of God was never completely spelled out but was represented by the Hebrew letters for YHWH (in English, Yahweh, the Christian Jehovah), which means something like "the one who is." God then ordered Moses to free the Hebrews from bondage in Egypt. After several confrontations with the pharaoh, Moses successfully guided the refugee Hebrews across the Red Sea and into the Sinai Desert, where Moses received the **Ten Commandments** of Hebrew law from God.

After forty years in the wilderness, the Bible continues, the Hebrews entered Canaan. Led by Joshua, the Hebrews successfully occupied some territory, often in the uplands, but they were constantly threatened by neighboring peoples. There were atrocities on both sides, and the Hebrews sometimes massacred Canaanite populations to protect Hebrew religious practices from foreign influence.

The dating of the Exodus and the settlement in Canaan is one of the great controversies of biblical studies. The Bible states that the Hebrews departed "from the city of Ramses," thus placing the Exodus during the reign of one of the eleven pharaohs named Ramses, whose rule began around 1300 B.C.E. The biblical references to massive building projects

---

clan Extended family group of people descended from a common ancestor.

tribes Descendants of the twelve sons of the Hebrew patriarch Jacob, who also was known as Israel.

Israel Another name for the patriarch Jacob; it became the name for the Hebrew people in general and also for the northern Hebrew kingdom.

Exodus (from Greek for "departure") Departure of the Hebrews from Egypt, led by Moses.

Moses Hebrew prophet who led the Hebrews out of Egypt and received the Ten Commandments from God.

Ten Commandments Laws that the Hebrews received from God in the Sinai Desert after the Exodus.

Deborah Leads the Hebrew People Against the Canaanites

The biblical book of Judges reports that not long after the Hebrews settled in Canaan they faced an attack by the Canaanite king Jabin and his general Sisera. The male Hebrew leaders were reluctant to act, so it was a woman, Deborah, who led the Hebrew resistance. Deborah must have been a woman of great character, for at this time political leadership was almost always exercised by men. Deborah overcame convention and served as one of the Hebrew judges, leaders who arose to help the Hebrews overcome spiritual or military troubles. Deborah may have been able to take charge of the Hebrew resistance because she also was called a prophetess, meaning that she was thought to be in direct communication with God.

When Deborah's story begins, she is holding court under a palm tree where Hebrews come to have their disputes settled. The Hebrew people call out to God for help against the Canaanites, and when the Hebrew men do nothing, it is Deborah who acts. Summoning the Hebrew general Barak, she reminds him that God had commanded him to assemble ten thousand men to fight the Canaanites. Barak timidly responds, "If you will go with me, I will go; but if you will not go with me, I will not go." It was unusual for women to accompany armies into battle, but Deborah replies, "I will go with you, but you will not gain any honor, for God will surrender Sisera into the hands of a woman." The Hebrews were especially afraid because Sisera's army included 900 iron chariots. Iron had only recently begun to be used for weapons and was thought to bestow a great military advantage. Deborah again encourages Barak to take action, saying, "Get up, for this is the day that God has delivered Sisera into your hands."

Then Barak led his ten thousand men to face the Canaanites, and Deborah went with him. Sisera called out his chariots, but a fierce storm turned the ground into mud and Sisera's chariots were unable to maneuver. The Hebrews attacked and put the Canaanites to flight. Sisera fled and took refuge in the tent of Jael, a distant female relative of Moses. She cunningly welcomed him, tucking him into bed with a bottle of milk. But when he was fast asleep, she hammered a tent peg into his head and killed him. Barak arrived in pursuit to discover that Deborah's prophecy had been fulfilled—Sisera had been surrendered into the hands of a woman.

Deborah then sang a victory song, which may well be the oldest original composition to survive in Hebrew scripture. Her story provides a brief insight into a world dominated by men where one woman serving as God's spokesperson took a leadership role in the Hebrew resistance and another woman slew an enemy general. One has to wonder whether there were other occasions when women also provided leadership—occasions that were not preserved in the historical sources, almost all of which were written by and about men.

Source: Scripture taken from the NEW AMERICAN STANDARD BIBLE®, Copyright © 1960, 1962, 1963, 1968, 1971, 1972, 1973, 1975, 1977, 1995 by The Lockman Foundation.

---

at this time fit the known activities of Ramses II (r. 1279–1212 B.C.E.). In addition, the earliest non-biblical evidence for the Palestinian Hebrews is a monument erected in 1208 B.C.E. by the pharaoh Merneptah, who bragged after a campaign in Canaan that "Israel lies desolate." This shows that a Hebrew nation existed in Palestine by that time. A similar date is provided by Palestinian archaeological finds showing destruction in the thirteenth century B.C.E. that is attributed to the campaigns of Joshua. This evidence would put the Exodus around 1270 B.C.E. and the settlement in Canaan forty years later, around 1230 B.C.E. The book of Kings, however, states that the Hebrew king Solomon's temple, constructed around the year 966 B.C.E., was built in the 480th year after the Exodus, thereby dating the Exodus to around 1446 B.C.E. The controversy over the date of the Exodus is still unresolved, but at present, the later date, 1270 B.C.E., generally is thought to be more consistent with the evidence. The Hebrew invasion of Canaan thus provides one more example of the movement of peoples that occurred toward the end of the Bronze Age.

The Hebrew Judges After the settlement in Canaan, the Hebrew tribes were united religiously by a shared shrine at Shiloh, where a sacred container known as the **Ark of the Covenant** preserved the Ten Commandments. But the Hebrews lacked any political unity, which made them easy prey to enemies such as the Canaanites to the north and the Philistines on the coastal plain to the west. The most important Hebrew leaders now were called **judges**. Believing themselves to be acting under Yahweh's authority, judges led short-lived coalitions of tribes against foreign threats, especially the Philistines. The unsettled

Ark of the Covenant Sacred container that held the stone tablets inscribed with the Ten Commandments.

judges Leaders of the Hebrews after the settlement in Canaan.

The Song of Deborah

The account in the biblical book of Judges of the Hebrew victory over the Canaanite general Sisera is followed by "Deborah's victory song," in which the Hebrew judge Deborah expresses her thanks to Yahweh for bringing victory to the Hebrews. It is generally considered to be one of the oldest texts in Jewish scripture, having been composed in the late twelfth century B.C.E., and is one of the rare instances in which a primary source was inserted directly into the text of the Bible. The song recapitulates much of the story told in the previous chapter of Judges. Even though the song begins with the names of both Deborah and her general Barak, the text clearly shows that it is Deborah who is speaking, and it provides a rare portrayal of a woman's point of view.

❶ Why might Deborah have been called a "mother" here and not a judge or prophetess as she is called elsewhere?

❷ How many of the Hebrew tribes actually resisted the Canaanite army?

1 Then sang Deborah and Barak the son of Abinoam on that day: 2 "That the leaders took the lead in Israel, that the people offered themselves willingly, bless Yahweh! 3 Hear, O kings; give ear, O princes; to Yahweh I will sing, I will make melody to Yahweh, the God of Israel ... 6 In the days of Shamgar, son of Anath, in the days of Jael, caravans ceased and travelers kept to the byways. ❶ 7 The peasantry ceased in Israel, they ceased until you arose, Deborah, arose as a mother in Israel ... 12 Awake, awake, Deborah! Awake, awake, utter a song! Arise, Barak, lead away your captives, O son of Abinoam. ❷ 13 ... The people of Yahweh marched down for Him against the mighty. 14 From Ephraim they set out thither into the valley, following you, Benjamin, with your kinsmen; and from Zebulun those who bear the marshals staff; 15 the princes of Issachar came with Deborah, and Issachar faithful to Barak; into the valley they rushed forth at his heels. Among the clans of Reuben there were great searchings of heart. 16 Why did you tarry among the sheepfolds, to hear the

times gave persons who ordinarily were lacking in privilege the opportunity to assume significant leadership roles, as when Deborah served as a judge around 1150 B.C.E. and led an army to victory against the Canaanites (see A New Direction: Deborah Leads the Hebrew People Against the Canaanites). Another Hebrew judge, Samson, was a warrior of very great strength. According to Hebrew scripture, he killed many Philistines in single combat and did great damage to Philistine crops, but he then was captured, blinded, and enslaved. The Philistines continued to dominate the Hebrews, even capturing the Ark of the Covenant and forbidding the Hebrews to make use of iron technology.

The Evolution of Hebrew Identity

The Exodus was understood as a sign that Yahweh was performing His part in the covenant with the Hebrews. Those who had escaped from Egypt came to be called the children of Israel. During the forty years of wandering in the wilderness, Moses finalized the Hebrews' covenant with God when he received the Ten Commandments. God renewed his promise to make the Hebrews His chosen people and to lead them into Canaan, the promised land of good fortune, and the Hebrews, in turn, agreed to obey God's laws as set forth in the Ten Commandments and to recognize Yahweh as their only god, to the exclusion of all others. Over the centuries, many other regulations written in the Torah and elsewhere specified the Hebrews' religious duties toward God and their moral conduct toward other people.

Hebrew Laws Under the guidance of the prophets, Hebrew laws and traditions emphasized ethical behavior, personal morality, and social justice involving both governments and individuals. The prophets taught that all people were equal before God, and the rich and powerful were reminded to protect the poor and weak. Rulers were expected to rule justly and to obey God's law. If they did not do so, then the prophets were justified in rebuking them. As individuals, the Hebrews learned to value righteousness, justice, kindness, and compassion.

Hebrew laws were in many ways much more comprehensive than the laws of other Near Eastern peoples, for they dealt not only with religious, civil, piping for the flocks? Among the clans of Reuben there were great searchings of heart. **17** Gilead stayed beyond the Jordan; and Dan, why did he abide with the ships? Asher sat still at the coast of the sea, settling down by his landings ... **19** The kings came, they fought; then the kings of Canaan fought, at Taanach, by the waters of Megiddo [a great Canaanite city]; they got no spoils of silver. **20** From heaven fought the stars, from their courses they fought against Sisera. **21** The torrent Kishon [a flash flood] swept them away ... **22** Then loud beat the horses hoofs with the galloping, galloping of his steeds. **23** Curse Meroz [a village that let the Canaanite fugitives escape], says the angel of Yahweh, curse bitterly its inhabitants, because they came not to the help of Yahweh ... ❸ **24** Most blessed of women be Jael, the wife of Heber, of tent-dwelling women most blessed. **25** Sisera asked for water and she gave him milk, she brought him curds in a lordly bowl. **26** She put her hand to the tent peg and her right hand to the workmen's mallet; she struck Sisera a blow, she crushed his head, she shattered and pierced his temple. **27** He sank, he fell, he lay still at her feet; at her feet he sank, he fell; where he sank, there he fell dead. **28** Out of the window she peered, the mother of Sisera gazed through the lattice: 'Why is his chariot so long in coming? Why tarry the hoof beats of his chariots?' **29** Her wisest ladies make answer, 'Nay.' She gives answer to herself, **30** 'Are they not finding and dividing the spoil? A maiden or two for every man; spoil of dyed stuffs for Sisera, spoil of dyed stuffs embroidered, two pieces of dyed work embroidered for my neck as spoil?' ❹ **31** So perish all thine enemies, O Yahweh! But thy friends be like the sun as he rises in his might.'"

---

❸ Why does Deborah include this poignant portrait of the Canaanite women?

❹ How does this account compare to the account given in "A New Direction?"

and criminal law but also with intimate aspects of personal behavior, such as personal hygiene and food preparation. Laws often were expressed as prohibitions that began with the words "Thou shalt not" and were addressed not to society in general, as were the laws of most other nations, but to individuals. Four of the Ten Commandments had to do with honoring Yahweh, including not worshiping any other gods and respecting the **Sabbath**, the day of worship. The remaining six commandments regulated human society and prohibited behaviors such as adultery, theft, murder, false testimony, and covetousness. These briefly stated regulations did not specify punishments for guilty parties, but other sections of Hebrew law did. In many cases, violations of the law, such as not respecting the sanctity of the Sabbath, were punishable by death. But most Hebrew adherence to the law was self-imposed. It was the individual responsibility of every Hebrew to live an upright life.

In some ways, Hebrew law, religion, and society were similar to those of other Near Eastern peoples. For personal injuries, Hebrew law specified the same "eye for an eye" law of retaliation found in the Babylonian Code of Hammurabi. As in many other Near Eastern societies, women were disadvantaged and could not own or sell property or initiate lawsuits or divorces. Initially, women participated in some religious rituals, but, over time, they lost this right. Just as Mesopotamian gods were believed to be the true rulers of Mesopotamian cities and kingdoms, Yahweh was believed to be the true ruler of the Hebrews, and individual Hebrew leaders acted on His authority. In other Near Eastern societies, only a small royal or priestly segment of the population was thought to be in communication with the god, whereas any Hebrew could potentially serve as Yahweh's spokesperson. In addition, other Near Eastern societies acknowledged the existence of some form of afterlife, but, on this point, Hebrew scripture was divided. The book of Isaiah, for example, stated, "The dead shall live, their bodies shall rise," but the book of Psalms said, "The dead cannot praise the Lord."

Sabbath Jewish holy day, modern Saturday.

The Chosen People Their belief that a single God had made them God's chosen people, along with their following of Yahweh's laws and their pursuit of a life based on moral and ethical behavior, united the Hebrews, gave them a unique identity, and kept them separate from other peoples. But meeting all of Yahweh's expectations was not always easy. The Bible reports numerous occasions on which Hebrews were caught engaging in the worship of other gods, making Yahweh angry and causing Him to punish them. Nevertheless, the Hebrews persevered and never abandoned their devotion to their God no matter what tribulations they faced. The Hebrew God continues to be worshiped in the present day, whereas the worship of nearly all the other Near Eastern gods ended thousands of years ago. The Hebrew code for living a moral and ethical life likewise provided a model that was later assimilated by Christianity and Islam.

The Hebrew Kingdom

Eventually, scripture relates, the Hebrews realized that their disunity was a weakness, and they asked the prophet Samuel, the last Hebrew judge, to give them a king. Samuel attempted to dissuade them, but the people insisted, saying, "No! We will have a king over us, so we may be like all the nations." Samuel therefore anointed two kings in succession, consecrating them with holy oil, first **Saul** (r. 1050–1010 B.C.E.) and then **David** (r. 1010–970 B.C.E.). Under their leadership, the Hebrews defeated and expelled the Philistines from Canaan. In the process, David captured the heavily fortified Canaanite city of Jerusalem and made it the Hebrew capital. He also expanded the borders of the kingdom all the way to the Mediterranean coast. The creation of this expanded Hebrew kingdom was seen as the fulfillment of Yahweh's promise to Abraham to provide a land for His chosen people.

anoint To consecrate by applying holy oil.

Saul (r. 1050–1010 B.C.E.) First king of the Hebrews.

David (r. 1010–970 B.C.E.) Hebrew king who made Jerusalem the Hebrew capital city.

Solomon (r. 970–930 B.C.E.) Hebrew king who built the Hebrew Temple in Jerusalem.

Judah One of the twelve Hebrew tribes; also the name for the southern Hebrew kingdom.

King Solomon David was succeeded as king by his son **Solomon** (r. 970–930 B.C.E.), who centralized Hebrew worship by constructing in Jerusalem a temple to contain the Ark of the Covenant. The Temple was designed by architects from Tyre and built, over seven years, at great cost, with 70,000 haulers, 80,000 quarryers, and 3,300 foremen taking part in its construction. It became the focus of Hebrew religious rituals, and once a year a high priest entered the Holy of Holies, the sanctuary of the Temple, to pray and sacrifice on behalf of the people.

Like other Near Eastern rulers, Hebrew kings had great authority. Solomon ruled wisely and was famous for his fair settlements of lawsuits and quarrels. But Hebrew kings also sometimes abused their power. David, for example, connived to take the woman Bathsheba from Uriah the Hittite, a foreign mercenary serving in Israel's army. He sent Uriah into the front line of battle, where he was soon killed. But David did not go unpunished. The prophet Nathan rebuked him, saying, "Because you have utterly scorned the Lord, the child that is born to you shall die." Other prophets, also acting under Yahweh's authority, advised and censured other Hebrew kings to ensure that they ruled according to the law.

By the time of Solomon, the Hebrews had changed from a loosely organized group of pastoral peoples bound together by a shared religion into an urbanized and politically centralized kingdom that was a full participant in the political and economic life of the early Iron Age. The Hebrew kingdom now extended from the Euphrates River to the Sinai Peninsula. The Hebrews controlled the trade routes between the Mediterranean and Red Seas, and they taxed caravans traveling from the east. Trade brought a profitable return on goods such as gold, silver, ivory, and exotic animals, and tribute and gifts came from foreign rulers. Solomon's international relations extended to Phoenicia in the northwest and to Arabia in the south. Using Phoenician expertise, Solomon constructed a fleet of trading ships and engaged in joint trading expeditions with the Phoenicians. Camel caravans from Sheba, an Arabian kingdom on the Red Sea, provided gold, as well as the frankincense and myrrh needed for Hebrew religious rituals. During a famous visit, the queen of Sheba brought camels, spices, gold, and gems. These mercantile and diplomatic initiatives brought great wealth into the Hebrew kingdom. The Bible declares, "King Solomon exceeded all the kings of the earth for riches." Solomon's army had more than ten thousand cavalry and a thousand chariots, and his international reputation was so great that he married a daughter of the Egyptian pharaoh.

The Split of the Hebrew Kingdom After Solomon's death, popular unrest over high taxes caused the kingdom to split in two. In the south, the tribes of Judah and Benjamin became the kingdom of **Judah**, with its capital at Jerusalem, and its inhabitants became known as "Judaeans," or Jews. The remaining ten tribes were incorporated into the northern kingdom of Israel, with its capital at Samaria, and became known as Samaritans. Having lost its unity, the Hebrew kingdom also lost its economic and political importance, and the

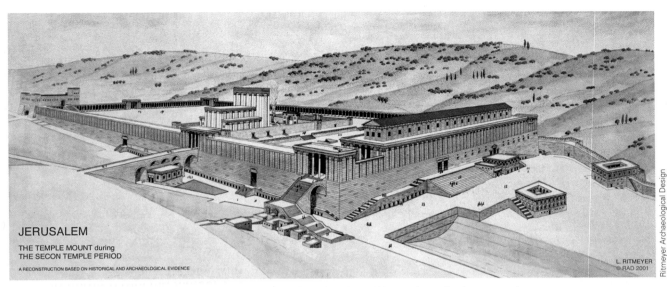

JERUSALEM

THE TEMPLE MOUNT during
THE SECON TEMPLE PERIOD

A RECONSTRUCTION BASED ON HISTORICAL AND ARCHAEOLOGICAL EVIDENCE

L. RITMEYER
© RAD 2001

Ritmeyer Archaeological Design

This reconstruction of the temple built in Jerusalem by King Solomon about 966 B.C.E. shows its three-part plan, with two side sections and a larger central section. The style is similar to the three-chambered temples of the Phoenicians and may be attributed to Solomon's use of Phoenician architects and artisans. The Temple provided a centralized site for the performance of Hebrew religious rituals and gave the Hebrew kings great religious authority. The only surviving section of the Temple, known as the "Wailing Wall," is the foundation from a later rebuilding of the Temple dating to 19 B.C.E. How do you think building the Temple helped Solomon to solidify his control over the Hebrew kingdom?

Hebrews once again suffered attacks by their more powerful neighbors. They also came under foreign religious influence. The Bible tells of prophets rebuking Hebrews who worshiped foreign gods. Prophets were uncompromising. Their fearlessness in criticizing even the policies of kings provided models for later Christian holy men and women who challenged kings and emperors.

The northern kingdom of Israel continued to evolve along typical Iron Age lines, with much trade and exchange of ideas with foreign peoples. The Bible shows the northern Hebrews adopting elements of Phoenician culture, such as the worship of the god Ba'al, who was portrayed as the primary competitor of Yahweh. King Ahab reportedly lived in an ivory palace and married a Phoenician princess named Jezebel. After Ahab built a temple to Ba'al for Jezebel, the two were said to have been punished by Yahweh for their sins: Ahab bled to death in battle, and Jezebel was thrown from a building and eaten by dogs. The southern kingdom of Judah, however, remained more conservative and less affected by foreign influences. The kings of Judah supported the monotheistic movement and consolidated the position of the Temple in Jerusalem as the religious center of Jewish worship. At the same time, Hebrew oral traditions of their past history and their relations with Yahweh began to be committed to writing, using the alphabet borrowed from the Phoenicians.

 Checking In

By yourself or with a partner, explain the significance of each of the following selected key terms:

covenant	Ten Commandments
monotheism	judges
Israel	Solomon
Exodus	Judah

The Assyrians and Their Successors, 900–550 B.C.E.

◆ **What effect did the growth of the Assyrian Empire have on the Assyrian economy?**

◆ **What methods did the Assyrians use for gaining and retaining their empire?**

The age of small nations that characterized the beginning of the Iron Age came to an end with the creation of the first Iron Age empire by the Assyrians. The Assyrian Empire was the first Near Eastern empire to incorporate both the Nile and the Mesopotamian river valleys. The Assyrians reflected Iron Age patterns by showing great concern for economic expansion and the accumulation of wealth. They also created a model of an empire based on military might, and their economic exploitation of the peoples they conquered led to their fall.

The Rise of the Assyrian Empire

The Assyrians were a Semitic people who had settled along the upper reaches of the Tigris River around 2000 B.C.E. They assimilated Mesopotamian culture and in language, culture, and religion were very similar to the Babylonians.

The Origins of the Assyrians From the beginning, the Assyrians were confronted by economic challenges. Because the soil in Assyria was not as rich as that farther downstream, the Assyrians could not exploit agriculture to the same extent as the people of lower Mesopotamia. Instead they took advantage of their access to profitable trade routes on all sides and turned to commerce as a means of expanding their economy. As early as 1900 B.C.E., the Assyrians maintained a trading colony in Anatolia.

For a thousand years, the Assyrians engaged in a struggle for survival. Not only did the Assyrian kingdom have no natural defenses, it also was situated squarely on the routes used by armies going back and forth across Mesopotamia. This left the Assyrians exposed to attack from Arameans to the west, wild mountain peoples from the north, and ambitious empire builders downriver in Mesopotamia. In response, the Assyrians created the most effective military machine the world had yet seen.

The Assyrian Army The Assyrian army consisted of the Assyrian people under arms. Indeed, the Assyrians originated the concept of a standing army—that is, an army always on call. Native Assyrian farmers made up the backbone of the army. The Assyrians assimilated the most up-to-date military tactics from the steppe **nomads** to the north. Cavalry mounted on horseback replaced old-fashioned chariots. Cavalrymen had no saddles or stirrups but sat on a blanket and held a set of reins. A long lance was useless—a warrior would slide off the back of his horse if he stabbed anyone—but swords and short spears could be used to hack or jab downward at a foe. Mounted archers were particularly effective as mobile shock forces. Specialist troops included engineers skilled in siege warfare, which involved battering rams, tunnels to undermine walls, scaling ladders, and movable towers. The Assyrians also created the first army based on iron weapon-making technology. In fact, nearly 150 tons of unworked iron bars found in the palace of one Assyrian king probably were meant to be used for making weapons.

The Assyrian kingdom became focused on institutionalized warfare. Even Assyrian religion was militaristic. The Assyrian people were named after Assur, their god of war, and Ishtar was imported from Babylon as the goddess not only of fertility but also of war. For the Assyrians, conquest became a mission from the gods.

The Expansion of the Assyrian Empire Around 900 B.C.E. the Assyrians began to expand. King Shalmaneser III (r. 858–824 B.C.E.) repeatedly defeated the Arameans and Babylonians. A monument recording his victory over the Arameans of Damascus bragged: "They marched against me to offer battle. The king of Damascus sent 1,200 chariots, 1,200 horsemen, and 20,000 men. … Ahab of Israel sent 10,000 men. With the noble might granted by the lord Assur, I fought with them. I slew 14,000 of their soldiers. I desolated and destroyed the city, I burnt it." Shalmaneser later forced Jehu, king of Israel, to pay tribute. Later, the Assyrian queen Sammuramat, who ruled around 800 B.C.E. and was known in later Greek legend as Semiramis, was said to have fought many successful wars. She was so famous as a builder that many Near Eastern monuments, including huge levees that kept the Euphrates River from flooding, were later attributed to her.

The greatest Assyrian king was **Tiglath-Pilezer III** (r. 745–727 B.C.E.). Said to have begun life as a gardener, he later became a soldier and was made king by the army because of his great military ability. Tiglath-Pilezer made the territorial acquisitions that created the final phase of the Assyrian Empire. He conquered the Arameans and Phoenicians, thereby giving the Assyrians access to the timber of Lebanon and the ports of the Mediterranean Sea. He also seized Babylonia, where a Semitic people known as the **Chaldeans** had recently settled, and claimed to have **annexed** the **Medes**, an Indo-European people of western Iran.

Subsequent kings continued to expand the empire. In 721 B.C.E., Samaria, capital of the northern Hebrew kingdom of Israel, fell to Sargon II (r. 721–705 B.C.E.). Soon afterward, the Philistines were annexed, giving the Assyrians control of the entire eastern Mediterranean coast. Under **Sennacherib** (r. 704–681 B.C.E.), the Assyrians invaded the southern Hebrew kingdom of Judah, as attested not only by Hebrew and Assyrian documents but also by archaeology. In preparation for his defense, the Jewish king Hezekiah built a tunnel, which still exists, 1,750 feet long that led to wells outside the walls and gave Jerusalem a dependable water supply. The Assyrians besieged Jerusalem in 701 B.C.E., and Sennacherib boasted: "Hezekiah the Jew did not submit. I besieged his cities, and conquered them with earthen ramps, battering rams, and tunnels. Himself I shut up in Jerusalem, like a bird in a cage." Nevertheless, the

nomad Pastoralists who travel on horseback rather than on foot.

Tiglath-Pilezer III (r. 745–727 B.C.E.) Assyrian king who annexed Phoenicia, the Arameans, and Babylonia.

Chaldeans Semitic people who settled in Babylonia in the eighth century B.C.E.

annex To incorporate a conquered territory into an empire or kingdom.

Medes Indo-European people occupying western Iran.

Sennacherib (r. 704–681 B.C.E.) Assyrian king who attacked Jerusalem in 701 B.C.E.

Assyrian rulers customarily erected monuments that displayed scenes of their conquests. Here, the Black Stele, an inscribed stone pillar of the Assyrian king Shalmaneser (r. 858–824 B.C.E.), shows King Jehu of Israel humbly paying tribute to the Assyrians about 840 B.C.E.; the legend reads: "I received the tribute of the Tyrians, Sidonians, and Jehu." The palace attendants standing behind Jehu announce to the king the amount that Jehu has paid. Shalmaneser had been unable to defeat Jehu completely, but realizing that he could not resist an all-out Assyrian attack, Jehu shrewdly chose to submit and become an Assyrian vassal. This is the earliest surviving depiction of an ancient Israelite. How does this scene exemplify Assyrian attitudes toward conquered peoples?

city held out. According to Hebrew scripture, Hezekiah, guided by the prophet Isaiah, sought the help of Yahweh, and 186,000 Assyrian besiegers died in a single night by divine intervention. By listening to a prophet, Hezekiah became a model of a good king. Eventually, he persuaded the Assyrians to leave by agreeing to pay tribute to Sennacherib.

In 671 B.C.E., the Assyrian king **Esarhaddon** (r. 681–668 B.C.E.) invaded Egypt, where a southern dynasty from Nubia had assumed power. Esarhaddon occupied Lower Egypt and declared himself king not only of Upper and Lower Egypt but of Ethiopia as well. For the first time in history, both major river valleys of the Near East were controlled by the same power.

Assyrian Economy and Government

In the Assyrian Empire, warfare was a way of life. The Assyrians went to war for three reasons: defense, territorial expansion, and economic growth.

The Organization of the Assyrian Empire Peoples who had attacked the Assyrians in the past, such as the Arameans or Babylonians, were defeated. Conquered territories also created a defensive buffer zone, as they had for the Egyptians. The Assyrians consolidated their military gains by placing army garrisons in the hills and on trade routes and by granting land to Assyrian settlers. Important conquests were annexed, made into **provinces**, and directly governed by Assyrian administrators. More distant or marginal conquests were made into vassals and permitted to

govern themselves as long as they followed Assyrian orders.

The empire was a moneymaking enterprise. Foreign trade benefited the state, and luxury goods were funneled into the royal court. Warfare created income in several ways. Tribute was assessed on defeated peoples, and additional contributions also were extorted from them. Raiding parties plundered beyond the empire's frontiers. Wherever they went, the Assyrians siphoned off as much wealth as possible. In general, they had no concern for the economic well-being of subject peoples and did not incorporate them into Assyrian society or give them a share in the benefits of empire. Trading peoples such as the Phoenicians and Arameans, who helped meet the insatiable Assyrian demand for luxury goods, did have a privileged legal status, but their resources were drained for the benefit of the Assyrians. These shortsighted policies resulted in constant unrest, resistance, and revolt in the conquered territories,

Assyria as a Terrorist State The Assyrians used terror tactics to maintain control of their subject populations. Opposition was punished by enslavement, expulsion, and harsh treatment. For example, Assyrian records report that when some Phoenicians resisted paying their taxes, Assyrian soldiers "made the people jump around" with the

Esarhaddon (r. 681–668 B.C.E.) Assyrian king who conquered Egypt in 671 B.C.E.

provinces Foreign territories annexed and administered by another nation.

This relief from the Assyrian palace at Nimrud shows King Tiglath Pilezer III (r. 745–727 B.C.E.) and the Assyrian army besieging a city with scaling ladders and a battering ram, all under the protection of showers of arrows. The Assyrians showed no quarter when a city resisted. At the top here prisoners are impaled, and at the bottom the wounded have their throats slit. The Assyrians' ability to capture heavily fortified cities was a primary factor in their army's, and their empire's, success. Who do you think the Assyrian kings intended to be the audiences for monuments like these?

points of their spears. When a Syrian leader revolted, he was captured and skinned alive.

To demoralize newly conquered peoples, the Assyrians often **deported** large numbers of them, especially the well-to-do, to other conquered territories far across the empire. There, as newcomers, they would be unlikely to cause trouble. After the conquest of Israel in 721, for example, thousands of Hebrews were deported to Iran, and conquered peoples from other areas were settled in Israel. These Hebrew exiles were later known as the **ten lost tribes of Israel**. King Sargon II proclaimed, "In the first year of my reign I besieged and conquered Samaria. I deported 27,290 inhabitants. I settled prisoners there, people from all lands." These relocations also promoted economic expansion, as the Assyrians moved persons with skilled trades, such as artisans and merchants, into economically underdeveloped regions, thus creating new sources of income for the empire. Most of the deported peoples became integrated into the populations among whom they were settled and lost their previous cultural identity. Yet even these extreme measures could not extinguish unrest, and Assyrian kings were constantly suppressing revolts.

The Assyrian Kings To administer their growing empire, the Assyrians created the first unified system of **imperial** government. Past empires, such as those of the Akkadians, Babylonians, and Egyptians, had dealt with conquered peoples individually. In contrast, the Assyrians created a centralized administrative system that applied equally to all conquered territories. At the top of the Assyrian administrative and social structure was the king, who, like all Mesopotamian kings, was seen as the representative of the primary god, in this case Assur. Assyrian art, however, often depicts the king as even more prominent than the god. The king was the supreme political, military, judicial, and religious leader. In short, he was the state, and, in a very personal way, it was the king who unified the otherwise diverse empire. As ruler of an empire perpetually at war, he was primarily a military leader.

Each year the army visited conquered and neighboring peoples, extorting financial contributions along the way. Grandiose monuments catalogued the peoples the king had defeated and the plunder he had accumulated. In fact, one of the reasons so much is known about the Assyrians is that Assyrian rulers recorded so many of their achievements. After several campaigns, for example, King Shalmaneser III gloated, "I carried away their possessions, burned their cities with fire, demanded from them hostages, tribute, and contributions, and laid on them the heavy yoke of my rule." As warrior kings, Assyrian rulers often are depicted in artwork participating in a pastime considered appropriate for a military monarch: hunting the most dangerous quarry of all, lions, which still lived wild in the Near East. The king hunted with bow and arrow, either on foot or on horseback. Units of the Assyrian army accompanied him and served as beaters, driving the lions into the center of a circle, where the king awaited. One king claimed that on a single hunt he killed 10 elephants, plus 120 lions on foot and 800 from his chariot.

The king was at the heart of the centralized administrative web. All imperial officials were servants of the king and responsible directly to him, as were the nobles and the priests. The king kept close watch on government officials through a system of royal messengers

deportation Removal of people from their home country.

ten lost tribes of Israel Ten Hebrew tribes of the kingdom of Israel that were deported by Sennacherib in 721 B.C.E.

imperial Relating to an empire.

Table 2.1   Assyrian Rulers

Shalmaneser III (r. 858–824 B.C.E.)
Sammuramat (r. 800 B.C.E.)
Tiglath-Pilezer III (r. 745–727 B.C.E.)
Sargon II (r. 721–705 B.C.E.)
Sennacherib (r. 704–681 B.C.E.)
Esarhaddon (r. 681–668 B.C.E.)
Assurbanipal (r. 671–627)

© Cengage Learning

who reported personally to him. A class of scribes, using standard Mesopotamian cuneiform writing, kept yearly chronicles of events such as military campaigns and eclipses, thus permitting modern historians to establish Assyrian chronology with a great degree of accuracy. State control even extended to traders and craftsmen, who were organized into government-run associations. And multitudes of slaves, many of whom were war captives, performed a wide range of duties. Slaves were protected from harsh treatment by their owners and had the right to own property, to make binding contracts, and to testify in court.

Assyrian kings built magnificent palaces that served as the administrative and social centers of the empire. Sennacherib established Nineveh as the primary Assyrian capital, where he built what he called "the palace without a rival," 600 by 630 feet in size. Later kings added additional palaces there, along with temples to Ishtar, Nergal, Nanna, and other deities. The palaces housed the king's family, which included multiple wives and many children. It was expected that a king would be succeeded by a son, and male children plotted to be named as the next king. Also living in the palaces were rulers and nobles of conquered and vassal peoples, who were kept in honorable captivity to ensure the good behavior of their people.

The Assyrians, who considered books and learning to be another form of plunder, originated the concept of libraries. Assurbanipal (r. 671–627 B.C.E.), for example, assembled at Nineveh an extensive collection of texts dealing with history, mythology, religion, law, mathematics, astronomy, grammar, and, in particular, magic. Some twenty thousand clay tablets from Assurbanipal's library have been discovered during excavations of the ruins of Nineveh, and it is thanks to him that many of the literary works of ancient Mesopotamia have survived to the present day.

The Fall of the Assyrian Empire and Its Successors

Eventually the Assyrian method of governing resulted in the fall of their empire. Several subject peoples revolted and then established new kingdoms of their own.

Threats to the Assyrian Empire Because the king and his court enjoyed most of the profits of empire, free peasant farmers, who made up the bulk of the army, and rural nobles often went unrewarded, causing internal unrest; on one occasion, the entire royal family was assassinated. In addition, Assyrian rule was so oppressive that only Assyrians could be trusted to serve in the army. As the empire expanded, the army was spread more and more thinly. Moreover, because they always were on campaign, Assyrian farmers who served as soldiers were unable to work the land back home, and the Assyrian agricultural economy fell into decline. Tiglath-Pilezer attempted to confront the recruitment problem by allowing some subject peoples to serve in the army instead of paying taxes. Troops were also recruited from vassals, such as the Medes. These measures provided a larger but inferior army, which became less homogeneous, less dependable, and less Assyrian.

The Fall of the Assyrian Empire Even though the empire appeared to be enjoying its greatest success during the reign of Assurbanipal, there were signs of trouble. The Medes and Chaldeans continued to resist Assyrian rule, and a new threat appeared from the north in the form of the **Scythians**, Indo-European steppe nomads from Central Asia. The best that the Assyrians could do was to enlist the Scythians as mercenaries. In the 650s B.C.E., the Assyrians were expelled from Egypt and soon thereafter faced revolts in Babylon and Phoenicia. The final swift decline began in the 620s B.C.E., when the Chaldeans and Medes revolted and formed an alliance against the Assyrians. The Assyrians initially were able to hold them off by using Scythian mercenaries, but the conclusive blow came in 612 B.C.E. The Scythians changed sides, and a joint army of Medes and Chaldeans defeated the Assyrian army and captured, sacked, and destroyed Nineveh. The Assyrian Empire had been held together by the Assyrian army. With the destruction of the army, the empire was no more. In the future, the Assyrians would provide an example of how not to run an empire.

The Successors of the Assyrians The Assyrian Empire was succeeded by four smaller, regional powers: Egypt, the Medes, Lydia, and the New Babylonians. Egypt experienced a momentary revival of influence. The Egyptians finally entered the commercial spirit of the Iron Age by establishing a trading colony in the Nile Delta, where they received silver in exchange for wheat, papyrus, and linen textiles. They also began to construct a canal linking the Mediterranean and Red Seas, and they sent an expedition all the way around Africa. The Medes created a

Assurbanipal (r. 671–627 B.C.E.) Assyrian king who created a magnificent library at Nineveh.

Scythians Indo-European nomads from Central Asia.

long, thin kingdom that extended north of Mesopotamia from Iran to central Anatolia. In the west, the kingdom of the Medes bordered on the rich and powerful trading kingdom of Lydia.

The New Babylonian Empire The strongest of the Assyrian successor states was the New Babylonian Empire, established in Mesopotamia by the Chaldeans. It extended from the Persian Gulf to the Mediterranean and incorporated what was left of the Assyrian people. The most effective Chaldean king was Nebuchadrezzar (Nebuchadnezzar in the Bible) (r. 605–562 B.C.E.). He strengthened the walls of Babylon, making the city virtually impregnable, and built an elaborately decorated gate dedicated to the goddess Ishtar. For his queen he built the famous hanging gardens of Babylon, one of the Seven Wonders of the Ancient World. No designs for the gardens survive, but they probably incorporated some kind of terraced arrangement, perhaps associated with the ziggurat of Marduk, who continued as the national Babylonian god.

The New Babylonian Empire was a center of scientific learning. Chaldean priests were famous for their knowledge of astronomy, the study of the positions and motions of stars, moon, and planets, and astrology, the belief that these heavenly bodies contained messages from the gods. The Chaldeans devised the zodiac, an astronomical map that divided the heavens up into twelve constellations. By compiling and studying lists of eclipses, they also were able to calculate future eclipses. Chaldean astronomical learning had much influence on later Greek and Roman science.

Nebuchadrezzar proposed to conquer the southern Hebrew kingdom of Judah, something the Assyrians had never done. The prophet Jeremiah already had predicted that, because of the Jews' failure to follow the law, Jerusalem would be destroyed and the Jews would be scattered and persecuted. Jeremiah also foretold: "'The days are coming,' declares the Lord, 'when I will raise up a king who will reign wisely and do what is just and right in the land.'" Such prophecies by Jeremiah and other prophets gave rise to a belief in a messiah,

At Babylon, the Ishtar Gate, built about 575 B.C.E. under the New Babylonian king Nebuchadnezzar (r. 605–562 B.C.E.), provided a massive ceremonial entrance for the city and was one of the original Seven Wonders of the Ancient World. Although the gate was artistically crafted, covered with blue-glazed tiles depicting dragons and aurochs (a now-extinct form of large wild cattle), the entrance also was well protected on three sides, making it virtually impossible for enemies to approach the gate. Why do you think cities such as Babylon needed such powerful fortifications?

Bildarchiv Preussischer Kulturbesitz/Art Resource, NY

or "anointed one," a descendant of King David who would be sent by Yahweh to restore the Jews' political independence and bring peace to the world. In 587 B.C.E., Nebuchadrezzar attacked Judah. According to Jewish tradition, the heroine Judith charmed the Babylonian general Holofernes, got him drunk, and then cut off his head. In spite of Jewish resistance, however, Nebuchadrezzar captured Jerusalem, destroying its walls and Solomon's Temple.

Following the Assyrian model, Nebuchadrezzar deported large numbers of influential Jews to Mesopotamia in what later became known as the Babylonian Captivity. Some of the exiles prospered. They were permitted religious freedom, and worship at the Temple was replaced by the study of scripture in synagogues, as Jewish places of worship came to be known. The exile caused the Jews to renew their commitment to maintaining a separate

New Babylonian Empire Empire established by the Chaldeans that succeeded the Assyrian Empire in Mesopotamia.

Nebuchadrezzar (r. 605–562 B.C.E.) Chaldean king of the New Babylonian Empire who captured Jerusalem in 587 B.C.E.

zodiac Astronomical map used in astrology that divides the heavens into twelve constellations.

messiah (from Hebrew for "the anointed one") The person the Jews believed would be sent by Yahweh to restore their independence and bring peace.

Babylonian Captivity Deportation of thousands of Jews to Babylon after the capture of Jerusalem by the New Babylonians in 587 B.C.E.

synagogue (from Greek for "assembly") Jewish place of worship, prayer, and study.

identity in the midst of foreign influences. Jewish law forbade marrying non-Jews and working on the Sabbath. For most of the rest of their history, up to the year 1948, Jews would be under the domination of foreign rulers. But Jewish history has been one of resilience, of being able to survive terrible oppression because of their conviction that they were the chosen people of God.

✓ Checking In

By yourself or with a partner, explain the significance of each of the following selected key terms:

Chaldeans	Assurbanipal
Medes	New Babylonian Empire
Sennacherib	messiah
deportation	Babylonian Captivity

The Persian Empire, 550–500 B.C.E.

- ◆ **How did King Darius try to unify the Persian Empire?**
- ◆ **How were Persian policies toward subject peoples different from those of the Assyrians?**

A little more than fifty years after the end of the Assyrian Empire, an even greater Iron Age empire arose, that of the Persians. The Persian homeland was in southern Iran, marking the first time a major Near Eastern empire had not originated in a large river valley. The Persian Empire was similar to the Assyrian Empire in that the Persians also were interested in economic expansion and the accumulation of wealth. It was very different, however, insofar as the Persians were much more successful in convincing their subject peoples that they had a share in the benefits of the empire.

Cyrus and the Creation of the Persian Empire

Like the Medes, the Persians were descended from Indo-European Aryan peoples who had settled in Iran beginning around 2000 B.C.E. The Persians occupied the southern part of Iran, and the Medes the western part. The Persian kingdom was established around 700 B.C.E., but for the next century and a half the Persian kings were vassals of the Medes.

Origin of the Persian Empire The founder of the Persian Empire was the Persian king Cyrus. As in the case of Sargon of Akkad, Moses, and other ancient leaders, popular legends arose regarding Cyrus's childhood. It was said that Astyages, the king of the

Medes, had a dream that a giant vine grew from the womb of his daughter Mandane, who was married to the king of Persia, and covered the entire world. Astyages's priests, called **Magi**, interpreted this as meaning that Mandane's son would overthrow him. Astyages therefore ordered the nobleman Harpagus to kill the baby. But the shepherd that Harpagus ordered to carry out this deed substituted his wife's stillborn infant, and they raised baby Cyrus themselves. Eventually, Cyrus's royal character was revealed, and when Astyages discovered what had happened, he slaughtered Harpagus's own son, invited Harpagus to dinner, and served him the head of his son on a platter. Harpagus took revenge by encouraging Cyrus to revolt. In 550 B.C.E., Cyrus (r. 550–531 B.C.E.) defeated the Medes and became king of the Medes and Persians, marking the beginning of the Persian Empire.

Cyrus Expands the Empire Like the Assyrians, the Persians had a great interest in economic development and expanded commercial activity. An outlet to the Mediterranean was essential. Thus, in 547 B.C.E., Cyrus attacked the seacoast kingdom of Lydia. In the climactic battle, the Lydian horses caught the scent of the camels in the Persian baggage train and fled, resulting in a total Persian victory. The Persians thereby gained control not only of Lydia but also of the Greek cities of Ionia, on the western seacoast of Anatolia.

Cyrus then turned to Mesopotamia, where Nebuchadrezzar's successors were facing local unrest because of conflicts with the influential Chaldean priests. In particular, the Chaldean king had attempted to favor the moon god Sin over the Babylonian national god Marduk, thereby arousing great popular opposition led by the powerful priests of Marduk. When Cyrus invaded Babylonia in 539 B.C.E., the people welcomed him as their savior, and Cyrus captured Babylon without striking a blow. Instead of imposing himself as a conqueror, Cyrus showed respect for local traditions by claiming the support of Marduk and taking the ancient Mesopotamian title of King of Sumer and Akkad. As a result of this spirit of conciliation, the cities of Syria and Palestine also acknowledged Cyrus's authority. Under Cyrus, the Persians gained a reputation for lenient and accommodating treatment of their subject peoples. Recognizing that they could not hope to rule such a large empire without local cooperation, the Persians often made native leaders officials in the Persian administration.

Cyrus and the Jews In 535 B.C.E., Cyrus demonstrated

Persians Indo-European people who settled in southern Iran.

Magi Priests of the Medes, they gave their name to the modern word *magic*.

Cyrus (r. 550–531 B.C.E.) Persian king who established the Persian Empire.

The remains of the Persian capital city of Persepolis, begun by King Darius I (r. 522–486 B.C.E.) and expanded by subsequent Persian kings, illustrate the mountainous geography of Iran. Persian cities were not population centers and consisted of little more than the king's palace, the treasury, and military quarters. Persian kings had several such palaces, and traveled among them during the course of the year. Much of the superstructure of these palaces does not survive because the Persians used wood for all but the largest columns. What does the landscape in which Persepolis was built suggest to you about how the Iron Age was different from the Bronze Age?

Robert Harding World Imagery

additional consideration for his subjects by allowing the deported Jews of Babylon to return home to Judah. Cyrus was praised in the Hebrew Bible, which reported: "Thus says Cyrus, king of Persia: The Lord has given me all the kingdoms of the earth. Whoever is among you of his people, let him go up to Jerusalem and rebuild the house of the Lord." The Temple was completed in 515 B.C.E., beginning the Second Temple period of Jewish history. Some Jews chose to remain in Babylon, and Jewish communities also arose in other places, such as Egypt. Thus began the Jewish **Diaspora**, the dispersion of Jews throughout the world. Because the Jews of the Diaspora were considered just as much a part of the Jewish world as the Jews of Palestine, the Jewish people came to define themselves not by place of residence but by belief and cultural identity.

Some Jews prospered under Persian rule. For example, Jewish scripture relates that Esther, a Babylonian Jew, was raised in the household of a Persian king and eventually married him. After the king had been tricked into authorizing a plan to destroy the Jews, she persuaded him to change his mind. In 445 B.C.E., Nehemiah, another Babylonian Jew, was made governor of Judah by the Persians and was permitted to rebuild the walls of Jerusalem. At the same time, the Torah assumed its final official form under the prophet and scribe Ezra. As a consequence of this written scripture, many Jewish concepts and practices were transmitted to the two subsequent great "religions of the book," Christianity and Islam.

The Death of Cyrus Cyrus expanded the Persian Empire to the frontiers of India. In 530 B.C.E., he attacked the Scythians, who had been raiding Persian territory and disrupting Persian trade routes to the east. After Cyrus captured the son of the Scythian queen Tomyris, she sent a message to him saying, "If you return my son to me, you may leave my land unharmed, but if you refuse, I swear by the sun, the lord of the Scythians, that I will give you your fill of blood." Cyrus refused this request and was killed in the ensuing battle. Tomyris then was said to have filled an animal skin with blood and dipped Cyrus's head into it, saying, "Thus I make good my promise," and the Scythians continued to threaten the Persian northern frontier. Cyrus was succeeded by his son **Cambyses** (r. 530–522 B.C.E.), who continued to expand the empire by invading Egypt in 525 B.C.E. The Persians were victorious, and Cambyses was installed as pharaoh, once again demonstrating Persian respect for native customs. In 522 B.C.E., Cambyses was on his way home when he died under curious circumstances, reportedly falling on his sword while getting off his horse.

Darius and the Consolidation of the Empire

The successor of Cambyses was **Darius** (r. 521–486 B.C.E.), a distant relative of the royal family. Darius's primary achievement was the establishment of an administrative system that tied the empire together and ensured its long-term survival, even under undistinguished rulers.

Diaspora (from Greek for "dispersion") Spread of the Jews throughout the Near Eastern and Mediterranean worlds.

Cambyses (r. 530–522 B.C.E.) Persian king, the successor of Cyrus, who conquered Egypt in 525 B.C.E.

Darius (r. 521–486 B.C.E.) Persian king who established the administrative procedures of the Persian Empire.

The Persian Kingship At the head of the Persian administration was the king. Like other Mesopotamian monarchs, Persian kings saw themselves not as gods but as the earthly representatives of their primary god, **Ahura Mazda**, the god of light. Nevertheless, their subjects treated them as if they were gods. Everyone living in the Persian Empire was considered a slave of the king, and the Persian king was known as "the Great King, the King of Kings." He wore elaborate gold and purple robes, sat on a golden throne, and was attended by a court of worshipers. Those introduced into his presence prostrated themselves face down on the floor. To publicize their great deeds, Persian rulers had huge **reliefs** carved on the sides of cliffs—one, for instance, depicts how Darius became king by suppressing a revolt by the Medes. As absolute monarchs, Persian kings could act on their whims, and sometimes did so cruelly: those who had particularly angered the king were impaled.

Darius's Organization of the Persian Empire The king's court was centered on palaces located in several capital cities, such as Susa and Persepolis. In fact, Persian cities often consisted of little more than the palace, for most of the population lived in the countryside. The palaces were staffed by **eunuchs** because only castrated men were allowed into the personal chambers of the royal women. Reliefs lining the walls of Darius's palace at Persepolis display the Persian court in operation: rows of humble rulers bring offerings, and Darius's bodyguard still keeps watch.

Darius's plan for administering the empire's subject peoples was based on respect for their traditions and a willingness to give them a share in the responsibilities and the benefits of empire. The Persians expected three things from their subject peoples: loyalty, taxes, and troops. Taxes were moderate, and, to keep costs down, troops were called up only as they were needed. The only standing professional army was the king's personal bodyguards, ten thousand elite Persian soldiers known as the Immortals. The remainder of the army was recruited from the subject peoples, who provided contingents based on local specialties: Medes provided cavalry, Mesopotamians infantry, Phoenicians warships, and so on. That most of the Persian army was composed of subject peoples demonstrates how much the Persians trusted their loyalty. This system put immense military forces, about a quarter of a million soldiers, at the Persians' disposal. The army's most effective branch was its archers, both mounted and on foot, for the infantrymen were lightly armored, often protected only by wicker shields. The Persians usually defeated their enemies not by fighting skill but by sheer numbers. A built-in weakness of the Persian recruitment system was the length of time necessary—up to two years—to mobilize the army, thus leaving the Persians vulnerable to sudden attacks.

Like the Assyrians, the Persians organized their subject peoples into annexed territories and vassals. Vassals remained under native rulers as long as they stayed loyal. The annexed territories—most of the empire—were divided up into twenty very large units called **satrapies**. Egypt, Lydia, and Babylonia, for example, were separate satrapies. A satrap appointed by the king governed each satrapy. Sometimes the satraps were local people, but usually they came from an elite group of Persian noble families known as The Seven. Satraps were very powerful, almost like petty kings, and it took a strong-willed king to control them. When a king died, the next king was chosen from the royal family by The Seven. Sometimes they chose a weak king so that they would have more freedom of action.

The Persian Empire was much more loosely organized than the Assyrian Empire. Local officials, thousands of miles from the court, had much **autonomy**. Darius did what he could to keep officials under his authority and sent out spies, known as "the eyes and ears of the king," who reported back to him regarding what was going on in the satrapies. There was no direct oversight, however, of a satrap's day-to-day activities, and a prudent king always had to be prepared to deal with satraps who abused their authority.

The Persian Economy Darius and later kings introduced policies intended to unify their huge empire, to facilitate trade, and to increase economic productivity. Standardized law codes reduced confusion about which laws applied to whom. A simplified cuneiform system reduced the number of signs from several hundred to forty-two alphabetic symbols, thus making record keeping much easier. Aramaic was used as a universal language of commerce and diplomacy. Good communications were crucial, and Darius introduced the first large-scale road system in antiquity. The Royal Road, which extended 1,600 miles from Susa in Persia to Sardis in Lydia, was used by merchants and imperial couriers who could carry a message its full length in a week by changing horses at regular stops. A nautical trade route from India to Egypt was opened, and the canal connecting the Mediterranean and Red Seas was completed, permitting merchant ships to sail from Spain to India.

Economic exchange and productivity were facilitated by Darius's introduction of a standardized coinage system, and the gold daric and silver siglos were accepted throughout the Near Eastern

Ahura Mazda God of light who was the chief Persian deity.

relief Image carved in relief (raised form) on a stone surface.

eunuch Male who has been castrated.

satrapy Large administrative unit of the Persian Empire, governed by a satrap.

autonomy (from Greek for "self-rule") A degree of independence or self-government of a territory or people within a larger political unit.

The Persian kings advertised their deeds on huge rock carvings on the sides of cliffs. This carving at Behistun in Iran depicts the initial proclamation of the Persian king Darius, and shows him reviewing nine captives—he is trampling on one of them—who had opposed his rule. The Immortals, armed with bows and spears, stand behind him, and the god Ahura Mazda looks down from above. The accompanying inscription reads, "I overthrew nine kings and I made them captive," and regarding one of them Darius said, "Then did I crucify him in Ecbatana; and the men who were his foremost followers, those at Ecbatana within the fortress, I flayed and hung out their hides, stuffed with straw." What do you think Darius hoped to accomplish with this particular rock carving?

world. Persian kings amassed incredible wealth, with huge gold and silver reserves stored in palace treasuries, and were often more concerned with hoarding their money than with using it for necessary expenditures.

Persian Society and Religion

Persian society was organized around the family. Members of the seven noble families led a privileged existence. According to a Greek historian, young Persian nobles were taught only "horse-riding, archery, and speaking the truth." An elderly male headed each Persian clan, and fathers had absolute authority over their children. It was important to have legitimate heirs, and men could therefore have several wives. The most prosperous Persians were landowners, for Persian soldiers were granted land by the king in exchange for their military service. The Persians were not known as artisans; for this kind of work, they generally made use of the skills of their subject peoples. Among skilled workers, scribes were particularly favored for their importance in keeping royal records relating to matters such as tax payments and military recruitment. Most of the remaining Persian people were herders and small farmers. Much menial labor was performed by a large population of slaves, many of whom were seized in the regular wars in which the Persian kings engaged. Slaves served on the vast imperial properties, in the mines, on building projects, and in the imperial palaces.

Persian Religion Persian religion was dualistic; that is, it viewed the universe in terms of a perpetual conflict between good and evil. It had two kinds of deities: daevas, skygods who were bad, and ahuras, abstract moral qualities that were good. The chief deity was Ahura Mazda, a god of light who represented truth and justice and who was worshiped at fire altars, for fire represented purity. Ahriman, a daeva, represented darkness and evil. Around 750 B.C.E., the Persian prophet Zarathustra, called **Zoroaster** in Greek and known now chiefly by that name, formalized the teachings of Persian religion. In the Gathas, poems believed to have been written by Zoroaster himself, Zoroaster declared, "There is one God, the Wise Lord, he called Ahura Mazda." Zoroaster taught that the universe was a battle between the forces of good and evil. Spiritual things represented good and material things, evil. At the end of time the good would triumph.

The essential teaching of Zoroaster was to "be like God." People did so by making it their personal responsibility to follow the path of good rather than the path of evil and thus to assist in the triumph of good. Good was equated with order, law, justice, and truth, and evil with disorder and lies. It was believed that, at the end of time, everyone would be judged

Zoroaster Persian prophet (in Persian, Zarathustra) who established the Persian religion known as Zoroastrianism.

in the fire by Ahura Mazda and that, after death, the soul came to the "Bridge of the Separator," where all one's actions, words, and thoughts would be evaluated in terms of good and evil. The good would be allowed to cross the bridge into the heavenly world, but the evil would fall down below. These concepts of the end of the world and salvation through a savior god are consistent with and influenced similar beliefs in other world religions, such as Christianity.

Zoroaster's teachings, which later bore the name Zoroastrianism, were preserved by Magi in scriptures known as the **Zend Avesta**. Zoroastrianism became the Persian state religion, with the Persian king at its head. For example, a huge rock carving proclaimed: "King Darius says: Ahura Mazda granted me the empire. I always acted by the grace of Ahura Mazda. Ahura Mazda brought me help because I was not wicked, nor was I a liar, nor was I a tyrant. I have ruled according to righteousness. Whoever helped my house, him I favored; he who was hostile, him I destroyed. You who shall be king hereafter, protect yourself vigorously from lies; punish the liars well." Persian kings saw their rule as reflecting the eternal conflict between good and evil and viewed the expansion of the empire as part of their religious responsibility to further the ultimate victory of Ahura Mazda. Their expressed desire to rule justly is one of the reasons the Persian Empire was administered more effectively than earlier empires. Zoroastrianism still survives in small pockets of the Middle East and in India, where it is known as Parsiism.

Persia, the West, and the Future

Like his predecessors, Darius expanded the Persian Empire. He conquered the Indus River valley in India, marking the first time that three of the major river valleys of the ancient world had been brought under one rule. Confronted by problems on the northern frontier, where the Scythians continued to raid Persian territory, Darius also mounted a massive invasion of Central Asia in 513 B.C.E. Like other invaders of the area, however, Darius soon learned that Central Asia was bigger than he had thought. The Scythians refused to be drawn into battle and lured the Persian army farther and farther into the steppes. Running low on supplies, Darius finally had no choice but to return home. In an exercise of good generalship, he got his army out intact, but just barely. Darius's invasion was, however, in some ways a success. Even though his army had not defeated the Scythians, the latter were sufficiently demoralized that they no longer posed a serious menace. In addition, the Persians gained **Thrace** (modern-day Bulgaria), a new satrapy south of the Danube River.

The Persian occupation of Thrace marked the first time that a Near Eastern empire had occupied territory in Europe, and it brought the Persians into direct contact with the first European civilization, that of the mainland Greeks. The confrontation between these two civilizations became one of the most important focal points of the future history of western civilization.

> **Zend Avesta** Scriptures of the Zoroastrians.
>
> **Thrace** Persian satrapy in modern Bulgaria.

 Checking In

By yourself or with a partner, explain the significance of each of the following selected key terms:

Persians	Darius
Magi	Ahura Mazda
Cyrus	satrapy
Diaspora	Zoroaster

Review

Summary

- The Iron Age built on the Bronze Age to mark the next progressive step in the evolution of western civilization. The Bronze Age civilizations of Egypt and Mesopotamia had exhausted the possibilities for the expansion of a river valley economy based almost exclusively on agriculture using wooden farm implements.

- The Iron Age gave increased importance to trade as a means of economic expansion and an economic advantage to peoples who had ready access to raw materials and were located on transportation routes.

- The widespread availability of cheap iron implements made it possible to work the tougher soils outside of the Near Eastern river valleys. Most of the world now could be effectively farmed.

- During the Iron Age, the centers of new political, economic, and cultural developments moved out of the river valleys. The first examples of Iron

Age economies are found on the east coast of the Mediterranean, where peoples like the Phoenicians, Arameans, Philistines, and Hebrews all benefited in their own ways from the opportunities to expand their economies through mercantile activities.

◆ Empires arose based on the Iron Age economic model.

◆ The Assyrian Empire focused on short-term economic gains by exploiting the economic resources of the peoples it conquered and by making no effort to give its subject peoples a share in the empire. The Assyrians thus aroused distrust and resentment that often flared up into open resistance and resulted in the destruction of the Assyrian Empire at the end of the seventh century B.C.E.

◆ The most successful Near Eastern empire was that of the Persians. The Persian Empire succeeded because of its ability to recruit a large and loyal army, its good treatment of its subject peoples, its effective system of administration, and its Zoroastrian religion, which advocated ethics and morality. On the other hand, the empire also had two weaknesses: an administrative structure that put great power in the hands of the satraps and required an effective king to keep them under control, and a cumbersome army recruitment system that took up to two years to assemble the empire's full military strength.

◆ The aspect of the Iron Age having the greatest future impact was the evolution of the religious beliefs and practices of the Hebrews. The Hebrews' belief that they were the chosen people of a single God, coupled with their moral and ethical teachings, made their religion different from all of the other Near Eastern religions. The Hebrews' creation of written scripture was especially important in preserving their beliefs and identity in the course of many centuries during which they had lost their political independence. Their struggle to preserve their religious identity and cultural heritage would result in the creation of a great world religion that in the future also would have an enormous influence on the birth and development of Christianity and Islam. The Hebrews thus laid the religious foundations for the subsequent religious history of western civilization.

◆ In many ways, we still are in the Iron Age. Our cities still focus on economic expansion through manufacturing and trade. Wide-ranging commercial and political powers still search for unifying factors that can bring people together and give them common ground. Last, religions still are based on written scriptures, moral and ethical teachings, and the belief in a single God.

Chronology

1270 B.C.E.	Hebrew Exodus from Egypt
1230 B.C.E.	Hebrews settle in Canaan
1200 B.C.E.	Beginning of Iron Age in the Near East
1150 B.C.E.	Deborah serves as Hebrew judge
1050 B.C.E.	Saul becomes first Hebrew king
1010 B.C.E.	David becomes Hebrew king
970 B.C.E.	Solomon becomes Hebrew king
814 B.C.E.	Carthage founded by the Phoenicians
800 B.C.E.	Semiramis becomes queen of Assyria
750 B.C.E.	Zoroaster formalizes teachings of Persian religion
721 B.C.E.	Assyrians conquer Israel
701 B.C.E.	Assyrians besiege Jerusalem
700 B.C.E.	Persian kingdom is founded
671 B.C.E.	Assyrians conquer Egypt
650 B.C.E.	Lydians invent coinage
612 B.C.E.	Chaldeans and Medes capture Nineveh
587 B.C.E.	Chaldeans capture Jerusalem; Babylonian Captivity begins
550 B.C.E.	Persian Empire begins
547 B.C.E.	Persians conquer Lydia
539 B.C.E.	Persians conquer Babylon
535 B.C.E.	Babylonian Jews return to Judah
525 B.C.E.	Persians conquer Egypt
513 B.C.E.	Darius attacks the Scythians

Test Yourself

To gauge your mastery of the material in this chapter, answer the questions below. More than one answer may be correct.

Merchants and Traders of the Eastern Mediterranean, 1200–650 B.C.E.

1. The characteristics of the Iron Age include the following:
   - a. Small fortified cities
   - b. Exploitation of agriculture in river valleys
   - c. Centers of civilization move toward the west
   - d. Expanded use of trade
   - e. Very large cities

2. Which eastern Mediterranean peoples participated in commerce in the early Iron Age?
   - a. Persians
   - b. Hittites
   - c. Phoenicians
   - d. Arameans
   - e. Akkadians

3. Who perfected the use of the alphabet?
   - a. Persians
   - b. Hittites
   - c. Phoenicians *phonics*
   - d. Arameans
   - e. Akkadians

Now that you have reviewed and tested yourself on this part of the chapter, take time to pull together all the important information by answering the following questions:

◆ How was the Iron Age different from the Bronze Age?

◆ How was iron used during the Iron Age?

The Hebrews and Monotheism, 1800–900 B.C.E.

4. The Hebrews were the first ancient people to practice which of the following?
   - a. Polytheism
   - b. Human sacrifice
   - c. Monarchy
   - d. Monotheism
   - e. Henotheism

5. What is the agreement the Hebrews made with their god known as?
   - a. Bible
   - b. Covenant
   - c. Tanakh
   - d. Clan
   - e. Torah

6. Which Hebrew judge led the Hebrews to victory over the Canaanites?
   - a. Eve
   - b. Jezebel
   - c. Deborah *woman!*
   - d. Sisera
   - e. Ahab

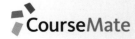

7. Which kings ruled the Hebrew kingdom at its height?
   a. Joseph
   b. Moses
   c. David
   d. Solomon
   e. Jezebel

Now that you have reviewed and tested yourself on this part of the chapter, take time to pull together all the important information by answering the following questions:

◆ What was the nature of the relationship between the Hebrews and their god?

◆ What made the Hebrew people distinct from other peoples?

The Assyrians and Their Successors, 800–550 B.C.E.

8. At various times during their history, the Assyrians recruited their army from which of the following?
   a. Assyrian peasants
   b. Scythian mercenaries
   c. Phoenician slaves
   d. Babylonian priests
   e. Egyptian nobles

9. What was the Assyrian army known for?
   a. Mounted cavalry   1st to use it
   b. Siege warfare
   c. Extensive use of chariots
   d. Extensive use of iron technology
   e. The use of untrained peasants

10. Which of the following peoples and places were conquered by the Assyrians?
   a. The Arameans
   b. The Chaldeans
   c. Egypt
   d. The Persians
   e. The Lydians

11. The Assyrian Empire was succeeded by which smaller regional powers?
   a. Egypt
   b. Lydia
   c. Persia
   d. The Medes
   e. The New Babylonian Empire

Now that you have reviewed and tested yourself on this part of the chapter, take time to pull together all the important information by answering the following questions:

◆ What factors made the Assyrian Empire such an unsuccessful empire?

◆ What happened to the lands controlled by the Assyrians after the fall of the Assyrian Empire?

The Persian Empire, 550–500 B.C.E.

12. Who founded the Persian Empire?
   a. Cyrus
   b. Cambyses
   c. Croesus
   d. Darius I
   e. Tomyris

13. King Darius organized and consolidated the Persian Empire by using which of the following?
   a. Coinage
   b. Satrapies
   c. Respect for conquered peoples
   d. "The Eyes and Ears of the King"
   e. The alphabet

14. Who were the primary gods of the Zoroastrian religion?
    a. Ahriman
    b. Ahura Mazda
    c. Ba'al
    d. Zoroaster
    e. Astarte

15. The Persian Empire was the first ancient empire to include what river valleys?
    a. Tiber
    b. Nile
    c. Tigris and Euphrates
    d. Indus
    e. Ganges

Now that you have reviewed and tested yourself on this part of the chapter, take time to pull together all the important information by answering the following questions:

◆ How did trade, commerce, and the acquisition of wealth affect the development of empires during the Iron Age?

◆ How were the Persians able to create such a large and successful empire?

CHAPTER 3

The Rise of Greek Civilization, 1100–387 B.C.E.

Chapter Outline

1200	1100	1000	900	800

1100 B.C.E.

Dorians settle southern Greece

First wave of Greek colonization begins

Greek Dark Ages begin

776 B.C.E.

First recorded Olympic games

Archaic Age begins

The Greeks were expert sculptors in both marble and bronze. But whereas many marble statues survive, few bronze ones do, because they were melted down for their metal in subsequent periods. This heroic statue, over two meters tall and dated to around 475 B.C.E., was recovered in 1926 from a Roman shipwreck in the Aegean Sea off Cape Artemisium. The statue is an early example of the classical style of Greek art that would establish the standard of excellence for ancient sculpture. There is an ongoing debate regarding whether it represents the god Zeus, who would be hurling a lightning bold, or Poseidon, who would be throwing a trident. Which possibility do you think makes the most sense? (Erich Lessing/Art Resource, NY)

After reading this chapter, you should be able to answer the following questions:

What was the role of competition in the evolution of Greek society and politics?

In what ways did the Greeks borrow from the cultures of other peoples?

How was the Spartan social system designed to preserve the Spartan way of life?

How did the Athenian democracy function?

What were the consequences of the Peloponnesian War for the Greeks?

AT THE END OF THE BRONZE AGE, the Greeks lost the complex civilization of the Mycenaeans and entered a period called the Greek Dark Ages. During this dimly known period, Greek city-states began to take shape and the Greeks grew intensely competitive. It took hundreds of years for Greek civilization to revive. During the subsequent Archaic Age, the pressure of overpopulation brought great changes, including a renewal of trade, the founding of foreign colonies, and the rise of recurrent warfare. The governance of most Greek cities progressed through a series of stages, from rule by a king to rule by aristocrats to rule by the wealthy. Subsequently, the city of Athens achieved democracy—rule by the people.

Greek culture also recovered during the Archaic Age as a consequence of contacts with the civilizations of the Near East. In spite of their political differences, the Greeks were culturally united and created a spectacular civilization in which all Greeks took pride. During the following Classical Age, Greek artistic, architectural, and literary achievements were at their height. Greek architecture, sculpture, and pottery were circulated throughout

700	600	500	400	300

B.C.E.
Rome is nded in Italy

750 B.C.E.
Second wave of Greek colonization begins

508 B.C.E.
Cleisthenes creates the Athenian democracy

500 B.C.E.
Classical Age begins

480 B.C.E.
Greeks fight Persians at Thermopylae and Salamis

431 B.C.E.
Peloponnesian War begins

387 B.C.E.
King's Peace ends warfare between Sparta and Athens

399 B.C.E.
Death of Socrates

the Mediterranean by Greek traders and colonists, as was Greek philosophy, poetry, drama, and history. The Greek culture of the Archaic and Classical Ages left a legacy that significantly shaped western civilization.

During the sixth century B.C.E., the two largest Greek cities, Sparta and Athens, also became politically the strongest. In many ways they were opposites. Sparta was politically conservative; Athens was liberal. Sparta retained its kings, whereas Athens introduced democracy. Sparta's economy depended on agriculture; that of Athens, on trade. Sparta's military power was based on its army; that of Athens, on its navy. When Greece was invaded by the mighty Persian Empire in the early fifth century B.C.E., Sparta and Athens joined with other city-states to defeat the invaders. But Greek rivalry soon reasserted itself. Sparta and Athens resumed their competition for power and influence. At the end of the fifth century, a lengthy war between them led to the defeat of Athens and a collective weakening of the Greeks that soon brought about their political downfall.

The Development of Greek Identity, 1100–776 B.C.E.

◆ **How did Greek political organization evolve during the Dark Ages?**

◆ **What role did competition play in the creation of Greek identity?**

During the Dark Ages, the Greeks lost the civilization that had been created by the Mycenaeans. Long-distance commerce disappeared, and the Greek economy became purely agricultural. No historical records survive from this period, and thus only the most general changes can be identified, including the evolution from monarchy to aristocracy as the main form of government, the development of the city-state, and the expansion of competition as a characteristic of the Greek way of life.

The Greek Dark Ages

Unlike the Near East, Greece did not recover quickly from the disruptions that ended the Bronze Age. After the Dorian settlement and the final collapse of the Mycenaean Bronze Age civilization around 1100 B.C.E., Greece entered the Iron Age with a period of cultural reversion known as the **Greek Dark Ages** because so much of the period is hidden from history.

Greek Dark Ages Period from 1100 to 776 B.C.E. in which the Greeks lost the culture developed during the Mycenaean Bronze Age civilization.

The complex administrative and economic systems of the Mycenaeans vanished, taking with them urbanization, large-scale political organization, massive stone architecture, a trading economy, writing, and the manufacture of fine pottery, sculpture, and metalwork. As a result, little is known of post-Mycenaean Greece.

Evidence for the Dark Ages There was no written literature in the Dark Ages, but folk memories were preserved in myths and legends passed orally from generation to generation. Collections of myths described how the gods had created and continued to control the world, and cycles of legends described the deeds of Greek heroes. These tales were put into verse and memorized by wandering bards who were welcomed wherever they went, for they provided a rare kind of entertainment. The Greeks considered these stories to be their ancient history, and because the myths and legends were so well known, they provided material for later Greek art and literature that any Greek would at once understand.

Two epic poems composed around 800 B.C.E. by the blind poet Homer and then passed on orally deal with the most famous Greek legend, the story of the massive Greek attack on the city of Troy in northwestern Anatolia. The *Iliad* tells of the events leading up to the capture of Troy, including the arrival of a thousand Greek ships (each carrying about fifty men) and the quarrel between king Agamemnon of Mycenae and the Greek hero Achilles, son of a goddess and a mortal man. And the *Odyssey* describes the ten-year struggle of the Greek hero Odysseus to return home from Troy and the stratagems used by his wife Penelope

Map 3.1 **The Greater Greek World During the Peloponnesian War, 431–404 B.C.E.** The Peloponnesian War was the ancient equivalent of a world war, as it involved not only Sparta and Athens but also other cities and powers ranging from Syracuse (Sicily) in the west to the Persian Empire in the east. © *Cengage Learning*

1. What differences in geography do you notice comparing Athens and its allies to Sparta and its allies?
2. Why do you think so many of the allies of Athens were concentrated in the area in and around the Aegean Sea?
3. Why do you think so many different regions, in and out of Greece, would have become involved in a war between Athens and Sparta?

to fend off a crowd of suitors. Homer's poems became two masterpieces of Greek poetry and mark the beginning of European literature. Although Homer's stories are based on fact, they also contain a vast amount of exaggeration that makes it difficult to separate fact from fiction. For example, the poems contain some recollections of the Bronze Age, as when king Agamemnon is described as "glorious in his armor of gleaming bronze." But they also reflect the later life of the Iron Age, as when Agamemnon proposes to give Achilles "twenty iron cauldrons." Aside from these general impressions, the later written remains are of

little help in compiling a narrative of the Dark Ages. Nor does archaeology help much in this regard, for only very meager material remains survive.

The Settlement of the Dorians Several general developments, however, can be identified for this era. One was the settlement of the Dorian Greeks, who destroyed the Mycenaean culture. Although it is difficult to find archaeological evidence for the Dorian occupation, the distribution patterns of Greek dialects (different versions of the Greek language) show that by the end of the Dark Ages the most fertile agricultural

Map 3.2 **Ancient Greece, ca. 1050 B.C.E.** During the Dark Ages, the Greeks inhabited both the Greek mainland and Ionia, the western coast of Anatolia. City life developed in Ionia and in the southern part of Greece to a much greater extent than in Macedonia and in the north. © *Cengage Learning*

1. Why do you think Greek cities were concentrated in southern Greece as opposed to the north?
2. Why do you think so many Greek cities were located close to the sea?
3. What effect do you think so many Greek cities concentrated in such a small area might have on the Greeks' ability to become united?

acropolis (Greek for "high point of the city") Fortified high point that provided a refuge for people living in a Greek city.

subsistence economy Economy in which necessary products are produced locally and there is no surplus food supply.

lands of southern Greece were inhabited by people speaking Dorian Greek. The Mycenaean versions of Greek virtually disappeared from the Greek mainland, being preserved only by Greeks who held out on the Acropolis, a fortified rocky bluff, at Athens and who settled in Ionia on the coast

of Anatolia, where, around 1100 B.C.E., some Mycenaeans fled to avoid the Dorians. This migration was the first wave of Greek colonization.

Dark Age Communities During the Dark Ages, people lived in isolated rural villages where agriculture was virtually the sole basis of economic life. They were supported by a **subsistence economy** in which all resources, ranging from grain (wheat, barley, oats) and animals (sheep, goats, pigs, cattle) to home-smelted iron, were locally produced. Social organization was based on the family. It was the family's responsibility, for example, to retaliate against another family for wrongs done to a family member, and such retaliations could lead to long-term cycles of blood feuds. The smallest family unit was the household, and several households made up an extended family. Extended families were organized into larger units, the clan and the tribe. People's status in society was determined largely by the family, clan, and tribe to which they belonged.

Villages were independent political units administered by petty kings whose original function was to serve as war leaders. Most Greek governments, therefore, began as **monarchies**, ruled by kings. Gradually, economic and political power gravitated into the hands of those who acquired the most and best land. These people came to identify themselves as aristocrats, a word meaning "the best people." Eventually, the only way to become an aristocrat was to be born one. The eldest aristocrats were members of a council that advised the king. During the more peaceful times after the initial Dorian settlement, the need for kings who served as war leaders declined, and nearly all of the kings were replaced by a new kind of **constitutional**, or legal, government called an **aristocracy**. In an aristocracy, the aristocrats continued to be members of the chief legislative body, the council, and shared the most important offices, as generals, city priests, and annual presiding officials known as **archons**.

Other free members of Dark Ages communities included a few craftworkers and traders as well as a larger number of commoners who owned small plots of land, rented land from an aristocrat, or worked as shepherds or farmworkers. Commoners could not hold office or serve on the council, but they did attend a citizen assembly. The assembly, however, had little authority except to approve decisions already reached by the council. Finally, at the bottom of the social ladder were slaves, owned mostly by aristocrats. Slaves were not always well treated and were often ready to revolt.

The Rise of the Polis Another development during the Dark Ages was the rise of the **polis**, or city-state. City-states were created when several villages coalesced for the purpose of physical security and economic and political consolidation. A polis often was centered on a fortified acropolis, which provided a place of refuge and overlooked an **agora**, or marketplace. The city of Athens had formed by about 1000 B.C.E. Not long afterward, five villages joined to form Sparta, and eight villages combined to create Corinth. By about 800 B.C.E., more than a hundred other cities had formed in a similar manner, and all of Greece south of Macedonia was divided into city-states. The polis became the focus of Greek political life.

Greek cities introduced new concepts in government. Unlike Near Eastern kingdoms and cities, which were ruled by kings or gods, Greek cities, to a greater or lesser degree, were ruled collectively by their citizens. Someone was a citizen if one of his or her parents was one. Slaves and resident foreigners, therefore, were not citizens. A city could make a foreigner a citizen, but this did not happen very often. Citizens were equal under the law, and all adult male citizens had some degree of participation in the government, even if only to vote in the assembly. This degree of popular rule was unheard of in the Near East, and it gave citizens a special sense of identity with their cities. Civic loyalty could be just as important as family loyalty. Even though some cities were very small, just a few thousand people and covering less than a hundred square miles, each Greek thought that his or her polis was the best one in Greece.

Competition and Conflict

During the Dark Ages competition and conflict became characteristic aspects of the Greek way of life. Individuals competed for status, power, wealth, and influence. Social classes clashed with each other as the privileged tried to protect their interests against the unprivileged, and cities competed for resources.

The Nature of Greek Competitiveness The Greeks saw all of human activity as a competition. Even the gods were worshiped through athletic competitions, which also were held at funerals to honor the dead. Nor was it enough simply to win. The Greeks believed that the joy of victory was magnified if a defeated rival was humiliated. In Greek unconditional warfare, it was customary for the victors to extend no mercy to the losers, and it was acceptable, even if it did not often happen, for the men to be killed and the women and children to be sold into slavery. The Greeks had no good losers and no moral victories. At the Olympic games, for example, there was no prize for second place. Competitors prayed for "either the wreath of victory or death."

The Importance of Aretē Greek competitiveness grew out of a desire to demonstrate **aretē**, or personal excellence. In the epics of Homer, aristocrats were

monarchy (Greek for "rule by one person") Constitutional form of government based on rule by a king.

constitution Written or unwritten legal basis for the government of a city.

aristocracy (Greek for "rule by the best people") Constitutional form of government based on rule by aristocrats who own the best land and are related by blood.

archons (Greek for "leaders") Chief officials in Greek aristocracies and oligarchies.

polis (Greek for "city") Greek city-state and source of the English word politics, which means "life in a city."

agora (Greek for "marketplace") Central market and gathering place of a Greek city.

aretē (Greek for "excellence") Greek sense of personal excellence.

expected to embrace a warrior code that valued honor above all else. Aretē had to be displayed in some outward form. External appearances were what mattered, not intentions. Most of all, bravery in war was glorified, whereas cowardice, such as throwing away one's shield and running away from a battle, carried the greatest disgrace. Aretē also was demonstrated by excelling in a competitive endeavor, such as politics, speechmaking, warfare, or athletic competition, as well as by openly caring for one's parents, showing hospitality to strangers, and honoring the gods. Successful pursuit of excellence brought fame and public recognition. Failure to demonstrate aretē led to dishonor, loss of reputation, and shame.

For male aristocrats, military glory was what counted most. When the Greek hero Achilles was given the choice between a short, glorious life and a long, colorless one, his choice was obvious. These attitudes could create conflicts between the desire for glory in warfare and devotion to family at home. Homer sympathetically portrayed this tension in his account of the Trojan hero Hector's farewell to his wife Andromache and son Astyanax:

> Andromache spoke to him, "My dear husband, your warlike spirit will be your death. You have no compassion for your infant child, for me, your sad wife, who before long will be your widow. For soon the Greeks will attack you and cut you down." Great Hector answered her: "Wife, all this concerns me, too. However, I'd be disgraced, dreadfully shamed if I should slink away from war like a coward." With that, Hector reached toward his son, who shrank back, terrified by the horsehair plume on his father's helmet. Laughing, glorious Hector pulled the glittering helmet off. Then he kissed his dear son, holding him in his arms.*

No matter how dear his family was to him, Hector had to demonstrate his bravery publicly, even if that meant putting himself into a situation in which he would almost surely be killed.

The Greek competitive spirit was both a blessing and a curse. It encouraged the Greeks to great achievements in literature, art, and architecture, but it also produced constant conflict and warfare that weakened the Greeks so much that they eventually succumbed to invaders.

Gender Roles

Another way that Greek men demonstrated their superiority was by controlling Greek women. Most Greek women were disadvantaged in several ways.

The Role of Women In nearly every Greek city, women were an underclass in both public and private life, a subordinate position that began at birth. Male children were preferred, and it was not uncommon for families to abandon unwanted infants, females in particular. Abandoned infants could be taken by anyone, and many were raised as slaves. Male children of citizens gained full citizenship rights after they reached adulthood. Citizen women were protected by the city's laws and passed citizenship on to their children, but they could never exercise any public citizenship rights. They could not attend assembly meetings, could not hold office, and did not serve in the military. Their public activities were limited to participation in religious ceremonies restricted to women. Women could not inherit property, which passed to sons or, if there were none, to the eldest male member of the family. Married women often were prohibited from controlling any more money than could be used to buy a bushel of grain.

A woman's primary duties were to keep house and bear and raise children. Women were married as young as fourteen years of age, often to a man forty or fifty years old. Well-to-do women did not appear in public unless accompanied by a male, even if only a boy. Because respectable women spent most of their time with other women, very close friendships, including sexual ones, were common between them. Less privileged women, on the other hand, and in particular slaves, appeared regularly in public and often were badly treated. Many poor women engaged in prostitution. Two things in particular worried Greek women. Childbearing was filled with risk, for medical care was minimal, and it was not uncommon for women to die in childbirth. And Greek women also feared violence at the hands of their husbands. There was no defense against battering, which was prevalent because of the competitive nature of Greek public life. If a man was not doing well outside the home, he might take out his frustrations on his wife.

The Role of Men Greek men were equally segregated and were rarely in the company of women who were not mothers, wives, or prostitutes. Male citizens spent most of their time with each other out of the house, exercising nude in the gymnasium, participating in politics, and serving together in the military. Male homosocialization was fostered by a system in which a man around thirty years of age mentored a fourteen- or fifteen-year-old youth, instructing him in what it meant to be a citizen. This bond usually involved sexual activity, although actual penetration was forbidden, as this disqualified a man from citizenship. A favorite male activity was the symposium, or drinking party. Female company was provided by high-class prostitutes, known as companions, who were often well educated and trained in such activities as music, dance, and sex play—things that men did not expect from their wives.

---

*Ian Johnston, trans., Homer, The Iliad, A New Translation. http://records.viu.ca/~johnstoi/copyright.htm

In ancient Greek society, a woman's place was in the home, where she oversaw the domestic economy. One of a woman's responsibilities was to oversee making clothing for the family. This scene of the everyday life of women, from an Athenian vase painting of about 540 B.C.E., depicts women weaving cloth on a loom. In this vertical "warp weighted loom," commonly used in ancient Greece, the warp threads were attached at the top and kept taut in bundles by weights at the bottom. The long pointed shuttle was used to guide the horizontal weft threads through alternating warp threads. In general, in what ways were the activities of women and men different in ancient Greece?

Image copyright © The Metropolitan Museum of Art/Art Resource, NY

Greek Religion and Culture

Although they were politically and socially disunited, the Greeks were culturally united. Collectively, they thought of themselves as **Hellenes**—that is, those who came from Hellas, or Greece. Anyone who spoke Greek was a Hellene. The Greeks believed they were culturally superior to all other peoples. Those who did not speak Greek were called **barbarians** because, to the Greeks, their speech sounded like bar-bar-bar.

Greek Gods and Goddesses Greeks shared the same gods and religious practices. In Greek mythology, the most important twelve deities were called the **Olympian gods** because they were believed to meet on Mount Olympus, in northern Greece. The chief Olympian god was Zeus, the god of lightning and thunder, and the others were his siblings and children. The siblings were his wife Hera, the goddess of marriage and childbirth; Poseidon, who ruled the sea and caused earthquakes; Aphrodite, the goddess of love and sex; and Demeter, the goddess of the harvest. Zeus's Olympian children included Ares, the god of war; Athena, the goddess of wisdom; Artemis, the goddess of hunting; her brother Apollo, god of

the sun, prophecy, medicine, and music; Hephaestus, the craftsman; Hermes, the messenger of the gods; and Dionysus, the god of wine. Other important gods were Zeus's sister Hestia, in charge of hearth and home, and Zeus's brother Hades, who ruled the underworld. Each Greek city identified one god who was believed to take special care of that city: Athena, for example, was the patron goddess of Athens, and Artemis, of Sparta.

Greek gods were anthropomorphic, and the Greeks believed that their gods had the same kinds of quarrels, friendships, and personal relationships as humans. In Greek mythology, mortals often interacted with gods in a way that most Near Eastern mortals never did. Zeus, for example, fathered many sons by mortal women and, like Greek men, was fond of boys. There also were half-gods,

Hellenes (from Greek Hellas, for "Greece") Collective name of the ancient Greeks for themselves.

barbarians (Greek for "a person who speaks bar-bar-bar") Greek term for anyone who did not speak Greek and therefore was not Greek.

Olympian gods Important Greek gods and goddesses who were said to meet on Mount Olympus in northern Greece.

Erich Lessing/Art Resource, NY

This Athenian black-figure ointment container of about 570 B.C.E. shows what happened in Greek mythology after Zeus, the king of the gods, received a prophecy that Metis, the goddess of wisdom, would bear a son stronger than he—he swallowed her when she became pregnant. When Zeus began to have terrible headaches, the god Hephaestus chopped open his head with an ax to see what was wrong. This scene shows the resultant birth of Athena, the goddess of wisdom and war, who sprang fully armed from the head of Zeus, shown here wielding his ever-present thunderbolt. Zeus is flanked by two birth goddesses with their arms raised. On the far left stands Hephaestus holding his ax and to the right stands Poseidon with his trident. This scene also demonstrates how, in Greek art, gods and goddesses could be recognized by their attributes, that is, the items that they wore or carried. Why do you think it was so important that people be able to recognize the figures in ancient Greek art by their attributes?

such as Hercules and Perseus, whose parents were a human and a god. Humans who accomplished great deeds, such as the winners of athletic contests or victorious generals, were thought to share in the divinity of the gods. In most regards, however, the gods had a less pervasive presence in Greece than in the Near East. The Greeks did not have a large class of publicly supported priests and did not believe that gods actually ruled their cities. For the Greeks, the gods put order into the world but then left people to carry on their own business. The gods were fundamentally just and would punish evildoers, especially those who did not pay respect to the gods, and therefore the Greeks performed rituals designed to maintain the goodwill of the gods.

oracle Message about future events believed to come from the gods; also used for the priest or priestess who delivered the message.

Greek Religious Practices

In each city, public religious rituals were carried out at temples by local officials who also served as state priests. The priests offered sacrifices, usually a slaughtered animal, intended to ensure that the god would look favorably on the city. Bones wrapped in fat were burned as offerings to the god, and the meat was cooked and served to the people. Temples usually were not frequented for personal religious purposes, although they could provide asylum for those whose personal safety was at risk. In general, the worship of a city's patron deity aroused little emotional enthusiasm but was considered necessary to keep the god well disposed toward the city.

In order to receive personal attention from the gods, individual Greeks left offerings in temples for favors received, such as being cured of a disease; for help in the future, as on an upcoming sea voyage; or as amends for a terrible crime, such as killing a relative or disrespecting the gods. At shrines in the countryside, people could receive **oracles**, messages from the gods about the outcomes of future events.

Oracles could be received in many forms, such as through the interpretation of dreams or the sounds in a brook. The shrines of gods who provided oracles were some of the few places in Greece where there were permanent staffs of priests and priestesses.

The Growth of Shared Identity By the eighth century B.C.E., Greek cities were in more frequent contact. The fame of the oracle of Apollo at Delphi, in northern Greece, spread, and even foreigners came to seek advice on matters ranging from settling quarrels to undertaking wars. A priestess inhaled volcanic fumes and then recited a cryptic answer that could often be interpreted in several ways. Consulting the oracle provided a means whereby local disputes, such as crimes involving bloodguilt that followed from the killing of a relative, could be resolved once the oracle's advice had been given.

In 776 B.C.E., the first firmly attested date in Greek history, the Greeks began to record the meetings of a pan-Hellenic (Greece-wide) festival in honor of the god Zeus held at Olympia in southern Greece. Zeus was honored with athletic contests known as the Olympic games, which subsequently were held every four years. The names of the victors were preserved with great care, and the four-year periods, known as Olympiads, became a standard means of dating. The great statue of Zeus at Olympia, designed by Phidias, the most distinguished sculptor of Greek antiquity, became one of the Seven Wonders of the Ancient World. In theory, warfare was supposed to cease during the games so that athletes and spectators could attend with relative personal security. Customs such as these gave the Greeks an even stronger sense of being Greek.

 Checking In

By yourself or with a partner, explain the significance of each of the following selected key terms:

Greek Dark Ages	Hellenes
aristocracy	barbarians
polis	Olympian gods
aretē	oracle

The Archaic Age, 776–500 B.C.E.

◆ **How did foreign contacts influence the revival of Greek culture?**

◆ **How did the growth of Greek trade affect political evolution?**

By the eighth century B.C.E., the people of Greece were emerging from the isolation and cultural regression of the Dark Ages. Population growth brought a need for larger food supplies, which was met by trade, by establishing colonies, and by warfare to seize another city's land. These activities brought increased contacts among the peoples of the Mediterranean world, resulting in cultural interchanges that stimulated a revival of Greek culture. At the same time, a handful of Greek cities gained exceptional economic and political importance. By the end of the Archaic Age, Sparta and Athens had become the most powerful cities in Greece, and Greece had become a major economic and political force in the Mediterranean world.

The Revival of Trade and Culture

The year 776 B.C.E., when the winners of the Olympic games were first recorded, also marks the beginning of a new period of Greek history, the **Archaic Age**, which brought a revival of culture, the economy, and political significance to Greece. During the Dark Ages, populations had gradually increased to the point where Greece's rocky and hilly soil could not produce enough agricultural staples. Methods for dealing with larger populations had to be found.

Greek Trade One solution to overpopulation was to import additional foodstuffs. As a consequence, Greek commerce and production of trade goods expanded. In exchange for grain imported from Egypt and the lands around the Black Sea, the Greeks traded olive oil, fine pottery, and silver. This explosion of commerce brought the Greeks into direct conflict with the existing Mediterranean trading power, the Phoenicians. The warlike Greeks constructed fleets of maneuverable iron-beaked fifty-oared galleys. The unwieldy Phoenician two-decked warships were no match for these, and the Greeks soon wrested control of important Mediterranean trade routes from the Phoenicians.

Greek Colonization A second solution to the overpopulation problem was to seek new farmland elsewhere. In a second wave of colonization, lasting roughly from 750 to 550 B.C.E., Greek cities established colonies on the shores of the Black Sea, the Adriatic Sea, and the Mediterranean Sea in North Africa, France, and Spain. Because colonists wanted access to the sea for trade, they occupied only coastal sites. Corinth, for example, founded the great city of Syracuse in Sicily. The most extensive immigration

pan-Hellenic Relating to or including all the Greeks.

Olympiad Four-year period that separated each holding of the Olympic games.

Phidias Greek sculptor of the fifth century B.C.E. who designed the statue of Zeus at Olympia and the statue of Athena at Athens.

Archaic Age (based on Greek *archaios*, "ancient") Period of Greek history from 776 to 500 B.C.E., during which Greek culture and civilization were revived.

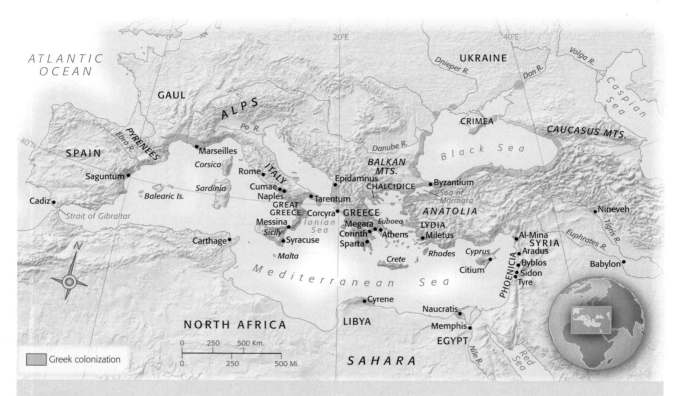

Greek Colonization, ca. 750–550 B.C.E. During the second wave of Greek colonization, Greek colonies were established along the shores of the Black, Adriatic, and western Mediterranean Seas and carried Greek culture far beyond the Greek mainland. © *Cengage Learning*

1. Why do you think Greek colonies were founded only on seacoasts?
2. How might you explain areas of seacoast where the Greeks founded no colonies?

was into southern Italy and western Sicily, which became known as "Great Greece."

Colonies had the same culture, social structure, and government as the cities that founded them. Although they maintained sentimental ties to their mother city, they were completely independent. Because the colonists were mostly male, they found wives, and slaves, among the local populations whose land they also had taken. A consequence of this intermingling was the spread of Greek culture, which became a common culture throughout the Mediterranean world and diffused into central Europe through the colony of Marseilles in southern France and into southern Russia via the colonies on the Black Sea.

The Revival of Greek Culture The revival of Greek trade also brought Near Eastern culture into Greece. From the Phoenicians the Greeks borrowed the alphabet, for they now had a need to keep records. From the Lydians, they picked up coinage, and the silver coins of Corinth and Athens became standard currency throughout the Mediterranean world. The Greeks also assimilated artistic styles. The simple geometric patterns of the Dark Ages gave way to the "Orientalizing" style. Greek sculpture assumed a very Egyptian look, and Greek pottery depicted many eastern designs, such as sphinxes, lions, and bulls. Almost always, however, the Greeks modified what they borrowed to suit their own preferences. For example, they were the first people to put designs on both sides of coins. They changed some letters of the Phoenician alphabet from consonants into vowels. And Greek potters and sculptors soon used designs from their own myths and legends.

Greek pottery was a particularly important trade good. Some pots, such as large urns used as grave monuments, were made for ceremonial purposes, but most were utilitarian. Four-foot-tall jars called amphorae stored wine, olives, and other edibles. Many kinds of bowls, plates, and cups served as tableware. Greek potters soon were the acknowledged Mediterranean masters of pottery making. All Greek cities produced pottery for local use, and the pottery of important trading cities was valued throughout the ancient world. During the sixth century B.C.E., Corinth was famous for pottery featuring black figures on a lighter background, but by 500 B.C.E., Athenian pottery with red figures on a black background had become the preferred style.

During the Archaic Age the Greeks also began to build stone temples as focal points of civic pride as well as to honor their primary gods. Temples usually were constructed in simple rectangular form, with a tile roof supported by external rows of stone columns. The **column style** evolved from the simple Doric style, with vertical grooves running up the column; to the Ionic style, with spiral rolls on the capital (the top section of the column); to the Corinthian style, with elaborate floral capitals. Temples often housed a statue of the god and an altar. They also were places where offerings made to the god by individuals or cities were put on display.

The Evolution of Greek Literature and Thought

The Archaic Age also brought the creation of Greek literary culture. Rather than using writing primarily to keep business records, the Greeks also used it to create literature.

The Origins of Greek Literature As early as 750 B.C.E., the *Iliad* and the *Odyssey* were committed to writing. Fifty years later, the poet **Hesiod** composed written poems such as the *Theogony*, a catalogue of the gods, and the *Works and Days*, practical advice about farming. Soon afterward, Greeks began to express personal feelings in **lyric poetry**, which displayed a growing sense of individualism and provides the first examples of the modern concept of heterosexual and homosexual love. The poet Anacreon, for example, wrote, "Boy with a maiden's looks, I love you but you heed me not." And **Sappho** of Lesbos said of a young man she fancied: "The youth who sits next to you seems to me to be the equal of the gods. My tongue grows numb; a subtle fire runs through my body. I sweat, I tremble, I turn pale, I faint." The poems of **Pindar**, the greatest lyric poet, glorified Olympic victors and traditional Greek aretē.

Poems of other authors praised warfare as a means of demonstrating excellence. The Spartan poet Tyrtaeus wrote, "It is a noble thing for a brave man to die falling in the front ranks struggling for his own land." Poems also extolled the city, as when **Solon** of Athens wrote, "Our polis is destined never to perish." But there also was a contrary trend toward realism. The poet Archilochus violated conventional aristocratic standards when he admitted to his own cowardice by writing, "Some Thracian now enjoys the shield I left in the bushes. I didn't want to lose it, but I got away alive."

The Development of Greek Philosophy Greek scientific thought, also known as **philosophy**, also arose. Influenced by Babylonian astronomy and mathematics, Ionian Greeks speculated on cosmology, the nature of the universe. Rather than attributing everything to the activities of gods, as in mythology, they looked for rational explanations that usually did not directly involve any gods. **Thales**, for example, proposed in the early sixth century B.C.E. that the world had originated from water, but in the fifth century B.C.E. **Democritus** taught that all matter was made up of "atoms," tiny particles that could not be divided, providing the origin of our atomic theory. **Pythagoras**, an Ionian who migrated to southern Italy in the sixth century B.C.E., believed the universe could be understood in terms of mathematical harmony and devised a formula for calculating the lengths of the sides of a right triangle, known as the Pythagorean theorem. Heraclitus rejected the concept of underlying harmony and saw the world as perpetually in conflict. His famous phrase, "Everything flows," illustrates his view that nothing is constant. Heraclitus did, however, believe in an overall rational governing force, the **Logos**, behind the universe. The search to understand the Logos would challenge philosophers well into the Christian period. The approach of early Greek philosophers was to propose a theory and then make rational arguments in its favor. They did not, however, perform experiments that would have actually proved or disproved their theories.

column style Doric, Ionian, and Corinthian artistic styles used in designing columns for temples and other public buildings.

Hesiod Greek poet, about 700 B.C.E., who wrote the *Theogony* and *Works and Days*.

lyric poems Poems expressing personal feelings, called "lyric" because they were meant to be accompanied by the lyre.

Sappho Female Greek lyric poet from the island of Lesbos who wrote about 600 B.C.E.

Pindar Greek lyric poet who wrote in the first half of the fifth century B.C.E.

Solon Politician and poet of Athens in the early sixth century B.C.E. who created the oligarchy at Athens in 592 B.C.E.

philosophy (Greek for "love of wisdom") Greek system of scientific thought that looked for rational explanations of the workings of the universe and human society.

Thales Greek philosopher of the early sixth century B.C.E. who taught that the universe had originated from water.

Democritus Greek philosopher of the fifth century B.C.E. who taught that matter was composed of tiny atoms that could not be divided.

Pythagoras Greek philosopher of the sixth century B.C.E. who devised a formula for calculating the length of the sides of a right triangle, known as the Pythagorean theorem.

Logos (Greek for "speech," "word," or "reason") The rational force that Greek philosophers such as Heraclitus believed governed the universe.

Scala/Art Resource, NY

A Corinthian vase dating to about 650 B.C.E. shows a phalanx of Greek hoplites advancing in formation to the tune of a flute player, whose music helps them to keep in step. It was important for a phalanx to stay in formation because each hoplite's shield protected not only his own left side but also the right side of the man next to him. Another phalanx attacks from the right. As long as the hoplites maintained their discipline, there would be a great shoving match and the phalanxes would tend to rotate counterclockwise because the left side of the last hoplite on the left end of each line was unprotected. But eventually, a gap would appear in one of the lines, enemy soldiers would force their way into the gap, and the phalanx would disintegrate when the men lost their discipline, dropped their heavy shields, and fled for their lives. At what point during a battle between Greek phalanxes do you think there would have been the greatest loss of life?

The Rise of Militarism

A third means by which a city could deal with overpopulation was to seize additional land in Greece. During the Archaic Age warfare between the city-states increased. Sparta, for example, conquered the fertile plains of the southern half of the **Peloponnesus**. Conflict also developed over the control of trade routes. After Corinth seized control of the shortest passage across the narrow isthmus connecting northern and southern Greece, it became the wealthiest Greek trading city.

Changes in Greek Military Recruitment The growth of trade and warfare had important consequences for Greek society and government. The expansion of trade led to the rise of a new moneyed class whose wealth came from trade rather than land. No matter how wealthy or influential these newly rich people became, however, they could never become aristocrats, for aristocratic status was based on birth. Wealthy merchants could not hold

Peloponnesus Southern section of Greece.

office or serve on the council as these duties were limited to aristocrats. Merchants grew discontented about having no voice in decisions that affected their ability to do business. The increase in warfare brought them opportunities to gain greater rights. In the past, fighting had been limited to aristocrats because only they could afford the necessary arms and armor. This situation changed when merchants grew rich. Trading cities that feared they would lose the next battle began to permit all those who could afford arms and armor to perform military service. As a result, many rich merchants and well-to-do but nonaristocratic farmers became full-fledged citizen soldiers. There was no way that a city with a small aristocratic army could hope to compete with a city fielding an army of all who could afford to serve. As a result, by 650 B.C.E., all the Greek cities had adopted the larger armies.

The Rise of Hoplite Armies The wealthiest citizens, who could afford a horse, served in the cavalry, but most of the army consisted of heavily armed infantrymen called **hoplites**. A hoplite carried weapons and protective gear made from bronze or iron, including a helmet, cuirass (chest protector), shield, sword, spear, and greaves (shin guards). The primary weapon was not the sword but a long thrusting spear. These larger armies fought in a packed mass called a **phalanx** that was four or more rows deep. Hoplites in the front few ranks pointed their eight-foot spears forward. Those in the rear ranks held their spears upward to keep them out of the way. In battle it was crucially important for hoplites to stay in formation. If a phalanx's discipline broke down, it would disintegrate, and its hoplites would discard their heavy shields and attempt to escape. That was when the slaughter started, as pursuing hoplites and cavalrymen cut down fleeing enemies from behind. The Greeks gained a well-deserved reputation as excellent soldiers, giving rise to another way for dealing with overpopulation. Many adventurous Greeks went overseas to serve as mercenaries. As early as 650 B.C.E., Greek mercenaries, called "men of bronze," were serving in Egypt.

New Forms of Government

The rise of hoplite armies led to the decline of aristocratic governments. Once well-to-do merchants had gained a place in the army and had, on the basis of ability, gained military leadership positions, they demanded greater political rights. When aristocrats resisted, merchants joined with other disadvantaged social and economic groups, including poor farmers and resident foreigners. In most Greek cities, discontent reached the point that the aristocrats had to make concessions.

The Rise of Oligarchies One complaint of the nonaristocrats was that they did not know the laws, which were known only to aristocratic "law rememberers," whom the nonaristocrats did not always trust to remember the law correctly. Thus, in an effort to head off discontent, aristocrats in many cities appointed aristocratic **lawgivers** to write down the laws. Many of the written laws, however, were designed to protect aristocratic interests, especially their control of land, and to keep them in power. The law codes thus did little to lessen the discontent of nonaristocrats.

In some cities, aristocrats made common cause with the most wealthy nonaristocrats and changed their constitutions to create a new form of government called **oligarchy**, in which the ability to participate in government was determined by wealth. All the old aristocrats plus the richest nonaristocrats became oligarchs, who could serve as archons or on a council that had the right to introduce laws. Citizens who did not qualify as oligarchs still belonged to the assembly, which could only vote yes or no on measures introduced by the council. Oligarchies were more stable than aristocracies because oligarchies could incorporate new members, thus providing some insurance against rebellion. Oligarchy became the standard form of Greek government, and once a city acquired an oligarchy, it usually kept it.

The Age of Tyrants In some cities, the aristocrats resisted making any changes. In these cases, discontented groups, such as rich merchants, ruined farmers, and the urban poor, eventually overthrew the aristocracy and replaced it with an illegal ruler with absolute power called a **tyrant**. Not all tyrants were bad, as the modern sense of the word would suggest. Some governed responsibly, some not, but all were illegal rulers who could remain in power only as long as they kept their supporters happy. They did this by distributing free seed grain to small farmers, sponsoring grandiose building projects that kept the urban poor employed, and giving tax breaks to merchants to encourage economic expansion. These shows of favoritism gave previously disadvantaged groups a feeling of empowerment.

The period 650–500 B.C.E. is known as the Age of Tyrants because so many Greek cities replaced aristocracies

hoplite (based on Greek *hoplon*, "large shield") Heavily armed.

phalanx Closely packed and well-organized body of Greek infantrymen.

lawgivers Aristocrats who were appointed to write down the laws of a city.

oligarchy (Greek for "rule by the few") Constitutional form of government based on rule by the wealthy.

tyrant Illegal, unconstitutional Greek ruler who opposed the aristocrats.

with tyrannies. Big commercial cities, which had the most newly rich people, were the ones most likely to have tyrants. At Corinth, for example, Cypselus, the son of an aristocratic woman and a commoner, became commander of the army and seized power. He exiled the aristocrats and established a hereditary tyranny. His son **Periander** gained a reputation as the most wicked of tyrants. He murdered his wife and sent three hundred boys from a rival city to Lydia to be made into eunuchs. But he also initiated many popular programs. He built a stone ramp across the Isthmus of Corinth and charged tolls for dragging ships between the Aegean Sea and the Gulf of Corinth, thus eliminating the dangerous coastal voyage around southern Greece. Corinth became so rich that Periander was able to eliminate taxes. He also increased the city's status by creating a powerful navy and establishing the Isthmian Games, which were held every four years (in between the Olympics). In spite of his evil reputation, Periander later was known as one of the "seven wise men of Greece" for his motto, "Forethought in all things."

Tyranny, because it was illegal, was fundamentally unstable. No matter how effective or popular a tyrant was, he always faced the threat of assassination. Eventually, all the Greek cities replaced tyrannies with much more stable oligarchies.

✔ Checking In

By yourself or with a partner, explain the significance of each of the following selected key terms:

Archaic Age	hoplite
Sappho	lawgivers
philosophy	oligarchy
Pythagoras	tyrant

Sparta and Athens

♦ **What were the reasons for and consequences of Sparta's adoption of a militaristic life?**

♦ **How did the Athenian democracy function?**

During the Archaic Age, two cities in particular, Sparta and Athens, increased in strength, and by 500 B.C.E. they had become the two most powerful cities in Greece. They were similar in that they controlled large amounts of territory, but in many other ways they were opposites. They also were different from most other Greek cities.

Periander Tyrant of Corinth in the seventh century B.C.E. who made Corinth into a major commercial center. Greek infantryman.

Lycurgus Spartan lawgiver of about 700 B.C.E. who established the Spartan way of life known as the Good Rule.

The Spartan Way ↑Greece

Sparta was one of the many Dorian city-states that arose in the Peloponnesus. Unlike other important Greek cities, however, it was located inland, far from the sea. Sparta therefore always retained a purely agricultural economy, remaining poor at the time when coastal cities were becoming wealthy through commerce. The Spartans were so unsophisticated economically that they never issued coins; their money consisted of cumbersome iron rods. Sparta's military was its army, for Sparta did not need (and could not afford) an expensive navy. The only way the Spartans could expand their economic resources was by seizing the land of their neighbors, and by about 700 B.C.E. they had conquered the southern half of the Peloponnesus.

Spartan Government Like many agricultural communities, the Spartans had a very conservative outlook on the world. They always were wary of foreigners and new ideas. They were the only Greek polis not to get rid of its kings, although they did move in the direction of aristocracy by devising a dual monarchy in which two kings were chosen from the two leading aristocratic families. The kings were advised, and supervised, by a Council of Elders comprised of twenty-eight men over sixty years old. An assembly of all male Spartan citizens over thirty approved measures submitted by the Council of Elders. The power of the kings was limited by five annually elected ephors, who presided over meetings of the council and assembly.

The Good Rule of Sparta According to Spartan tradition, about 700 B.C.E., the Spartan lawgiver **Lycurgus** established the Spartan system of life known as the Good Rule. It was intended to unify the Spartan people, to make all male citizens equal, and to focus everyone's loyalty on the polis. Lycurgus established a militaristic society designed to do only one thing: raise good soldiers. Whereas the soldiers of other Greek cities were amateurs, a citizen militia, the Spartans were professional career soldiers. The Spartans had so much confidence in their army that they refused to build a wall around the city, trusting to their army for defense.

A child's participation in the Good Rule began at birth, when infants were inspected by a group of elders. If they seemed unhealthy, they were exposed on a mountainside and left to die. Children's military training began early. Boys went off to live in the military barracks when they were seven years old. They learned what it meant to be Spartan: to fight under all sorts of conditions, to live off the land by stealing food, and not to complain about bad weather or bad food. When they reached the age of twenty, young men would be elected into a military dining club of about fifteen men and become one of the Equals, the full citizens of Sparta. A single negative vote prevented a man from becoming a citizen: he would still live in Sparta, but it would be as if he did not exist. All the Equals were given a land grant that made them economically independent and thus able to concentrate on their military training. Because of the need to produce offspring to supply the army, men were encouraged to marry by the age of thirty. Marriage ceremonies were militaristic. The bride dressed up as an enemy soldier, and the groom had to fight his way into her house and carry her off as a prisoner. Men then lived in the barracks until they were sixty years old, when they finally could return home.

Spartan Women Spartan women also were part of this militaristic system. Girls remained at home, but they learned to be just as tough as the men. According to the Greek historian Plutarch, Lycurgus "ordered the young women to exercise themselves with wrestling, running, and throwing the javelin, so that they would conceive their offspring in strong and healthy bodies. To toughen them, he ordered that they should go naked in the processions. It taught them simplicity and a care for good health." Instead of wearing the enveloping clothing typical of other Greek women, Spartan women wore a single tunic slit down the side, which led other Greeks to call them "thigh flaunters." And whereas other Greek women often were married by the age of fourteen, Spartan women usually did not marry until eighteen, when they were considered more suitable for childbearing.

Spartan women also had a reputation for fearlessness. Once, when a Spartan woman was being sold as a slave, her buyer asked her what she knew how to do. "To be free," she replied. When he ordered her to do menial tasks not fitting for a free woman, she committed suicide. Spartan women even undertook military duties, something unheard of in other Greek cities. Another time, when the Spartan army was away at war, a Greek general attacked the city and was defeated by the Spartan women. Spartan mothers perpetuated the Spartan dislike of defeat. When a mother handed her son his shield before he went off to war, she told him, "Come back with this or on top of it." Being brought back dead was deemed better than abandoning one's shield to escape alive.

Spartan women were less restricted than other Greek women. Although they could not hold office, they appeared in public and had a voice in politics. Once when an Athenian woman asked a Spartan woman why "the women of Sparta were the only women in the world who could rule men," she arrogantly replied, "Because we are the only women who are the mothers of men." While the men were away on campaign, Spartan women oversaw the household economies. They were responsible for providing each Equal's contribution to his army dining club.

This bronze statuette of about 500 B.C.E., now in the British Museum in London, shows a Spartan girl running in the women's race at Olympia known as the Heraea, in honor of Hera, the wife of Zeus. The women raced on the same course as the men did for the Olympic games, although the length was shortened by one-sixth. They did not compete completely naked like the men, but did race with the right breast bared. Most of the competitors were Spartans, who were very athletic. Spartan girls received training in dance and gymnastics and took part in public performances in the nude just like the boys. The entire Spartan population had to be well trained in order to defend the Spartan way of life. How do you think Greeks like the Athenians would have felt about the Spartan way of life?

And they were the only women in Greece who were permitted to inherit property. In fact, it was said that nearly half of the land in Sparta eventually belonged to women.

Sparta and the Helots The Spartans needed to maintain this military lifestyle because Sparta's agricultural land was worked by **helots**, agricultural slaves whose ancestors had been enslaved when Sparta conquered their territory. The Spartans were greatly outnumbered: only about 5 percent of the total population, never more than 8,000 soldiers, was Spartan; about 15 percent

Plutarch Greek writer of biographies and history of the second century C.E.

helots Agricultural slaves of Sparta.

were free noncitizens; and the remaining 80 percent were helots. Plutarch commented that in Sparta, "those who were free were the most free anywhere, and those who were slaves were the most enslaved." The primary goal of the Spartans was to preserve their system and to keep the helots in their place. The helots were always ready to revolt. So that they would learn this point, Spartan men in their late teens were sent to spy on the helots and authorized to kill any who appeared disloyal. This duty impressed on young Spartans how greatly outnumbered they were and helped to justify the sacrifices they had to make in the service of the city.

To protect themselves further against the helots, the Spartans also organized a mutual-defense alliance of Greek cities in the Peloponnesus, called the **Peloponnesian League**. Any member who was attacked could call on the help of any other member. The Spartans thus had a core of local allies to help them whenever the helots revolted. The constant fear of a helot uprising meant that the Spartans were very reluctant to send their army very far away from home.

The Evolution of the Athenian Government

The territory of Athens, known as Attica, extended over a thousand square miles and had a population of around six hundred thousand. It was second in size only to Sparta but in other regards the two cities were very different. The Athenians, descendants of the Mycenaeans, spoke the Ionian version of Greek, whereas the Spartans spoke the Dorian dialect. Unlike Sparta, Athens was located on the coast and developed an economy focused on trade. Whereas Sparta was poor, Athens was rich. Athens' military might lay not in its army but in its navy, which was funded by its mercantile profits. And whereas Sparta was exceptionally conservative, Athens had the most liberal political ideology of all the Greek cities and was open to ideas about new kinds of government.

The Evolution of Athenian Government Politically, Athens initially followed the standard Greek pattern. By 800 B.C.E., the monarchy had been replaced by an aristocracy. Each year, nine archons were chosen from among the aristocrats to run the government. Ex-archons became members of a council that initiated legislation, served as a supreme court, and chose the archons, always other aristocrats. The remaining male citizens were members of the assembly, but all the assembly could do was to vote yes or no on measures introduced by the council. During the 600s B.C.E.,

increasing involvement in trade, based largely on the production of olive oil, brought great wealth to Athens, and a new moneyed class arose whose wealth was based on commerce. By 650 B.C.E., nonaristocrats who could afford their own weapons were eligible to serve in the army, but this service did not gain them any additional political rights.

By the late seventh century B.C.E., several Athenian groups had cause to be discontented. Rich merchants could never become aristocrats and therefore could not be part of the government. Newcomers, in particular merchants and craftworkers who had immigrated from other Greek cities, could not become citizens. Small farmers could be sold into slavery if they fell into debt to aristocrats who were eager to gain possession of their land. The urban poor often had no jobs. Dissatisfaction with aristocratic rule became so great that in 621 B.C.E. the aristocrats appointed a lawgiver named **Draco** to write down the laws. From a positive perspective, the law code attempted to end blood feuds by taking away from families the right to punish murder and creating instead a state-run court to try homicide. But Draco's code also was legendary for its harshness. It preserved the right of aristocrats to enslave debtors, and the punishment for even minor crimes was death. Draco's code thus created even greater dissatisfaction among nonaristocrats.

The Reforms of Solon In response to the heightened unrest, in 594 B.C.E., the aristocrats appointed the aristocrat Solon to deal with social and economic complaints. Solon introduced a program known as the Lifting of Burdens, which abolished all of Draco's laws except for the murder court, forbade debt slavery and freed those who had been enslaved for debt, allowed foreign artisans who settled in Athens with their families to become citizens, and even established uniform weights and measures to stimulate the economy.

Solon's reforms not only helped end the economic unrest but also made Athens into a major commercial center. Their success led to Solon's reappointment in 592 B.C.E., as Reformer of the Constitution, to deal with political discontent. Solon then did what many other Greek cities were doing at the same time—changed the form of government from an aristocracy to an oligarchy. Solon divided the Athenian male citizen body into four groups based on wealth and made the ability to participate in the government dependent on one's contribution to the city's economic productivity. Archons were chosen from the most wealthy two groups. The right to initiate new legislation was given to a Council of 400, drawn from the top three groups. As before, all citizens were members of the assembly, and their only right continued to be to vote yes or no on measures already passed by the council. To compensate the poor for their lack of privileges, only the top three classes were taxed.

Peloponnesian League Allies of Sparta in the Peloponnesus.

Draco Athenian lawgiver whose legal code issued in 621 B.C.E. was known for its harshness.

The Athenian Tyranny In most Greek cities, the establishment of an oligarchy brought political stability, but not in Athens. Its large territory created regional differences. Three groups competed for influence: wealthy, aristocratic, and conservative inhabitants of the coastal plain; poor farmers living in the hills; and liberal artisans, merchants, and sailors living on the coast. Each group had its own agenda. Those living on the plain wanted an aristocratic constitution, those in the hills wanted jobs, and those on the coast wanted increased foreign trade. In 546 B.C.E., the war hero **Peisistratus** seized power as tyrant. His policy for staying in power was to keep the support of the coastal and hill dwellers at any cost. He provided seed grain and jobs for the poor and loans to merchants. To ensure that there were no unemployed troublemakers, he sponsored massive building projects. His measures were largely successful. Under his rule, Athens overtook Corinth in the vase market. Moreover, he instilled pride in the city by creating an annual festival in honor of the god Dionysus at which plays were performed, with the Athenians voting afterward on which plays were the best.

The Athenian Democracy

Peisistratus was succeeded as tyrant by his two sons. One was assassinated, and the other was expelled in 508 B.C.E. The aristocrat **Cleisthenes** then gained the support of the people and was given the authority to reform the constitution in order to end factional fighting and create stability.

The Reforms of Cleisthenes To break down regional loyalties, Cleisthenes first divided the Athenian citizen body into three groups: the city (craftworkers and merchants), the coast (sailors and fisherman), and the plain (farmers). He then created ten new tribes, each of which had members from all three groups, so none would have obvious familial or regional affiliations.

Cleisthenes's new form of government was called **democracy**, or "rule by the people." All male citizens over thirty years old had an equal chance to participate in the government. The old Council of 400 was replaced by a Council of 500, to which each tribe contributed 50 members. Members of the council were chosen randomly by lot to serve for one year, and each day a member of one of the tribes was chosen by lot to serve as the chief official of the Athenian state. The archons likewise were chosen by lot. The assembly, which all male citizens over age twenty could attend, became the primary legislative body of Athens, and any member could propose legislation.

The Operation of the Democracy This kind of democracy, in which all citizens are equally responsible for participating in governing, is known as radical democracy. It was different from American representative democracy, in which people elect representatives to participate in government on their behalf. Athenian democracy also was different from modern democracies in another way. It was much less democratic in that only a small percentage of the Athenian population actually had full citizenship rights. About 40 percent of the population were slaves, and another 20 percent were noncitizen foreigners. Citizens thus made up 40 percent of the population, and half of these, the females, had no voting rights. Of the remaining 20 percent, the male citizens, about half would have been under the age of twenty and so did not have voting rights. Thus, only about 10 percent of the Athenian population, about sixty thousand persons at most, could actually participate in government. This level of participation was still much greater than in any non-democratic Greek city, and far greater than in any Near Eastern state. In Greek oligarchies, for example, only about 1 percent of the population had full participation rights.

The Athenian democracy was cumbersome to operate. Meetings of the assembly could have six thousand or more members present, all with equal rights to speak and to introduce legislation. Discussion of a topic would begin with a herald asking, "Who wishes to speak?" Men over fifty were allowed to speak first, and no one under thirty could speak at all. In addition, any man convicted of not supporting his parents, throwing away his shield in battle, or being a prostitute was barred from speaking. Those advocating unpopular opinions ran the risk of simply being shouted down. Voting was by a show of hands and thus was called "arm stretching."

Making the Democracy Work The majority of the assembly was made up of **thetes**, landless poor who often would vote for any measure that would improve their economic circumstances. Good speakers with glib tongues, called demagogues, could sway the assembly by introducing moneymaking measures. To restrict frivolous legislation, those whose bills did not pass were fined. And to keep bickering from getting out of hand, the Athenians introduced the practice of **ostracism**. Each year there was a vote for the "most unpopular man in

Peisistratus (d. 527 B.C.E.) Athenian tyrant of the sixth century B.C.E. who created the festival of Dionysus.

Cleisthenes Athenian leader who established Athenian democracy in 508 B.C.E.

democracy (Greek for "rule by the people") Constitutional form of government based on rule by the people.

thetes Athenian citizens who did not own any land.

ostracism Ten-year exile imposed on one man each year by vote of the Athenians.

Athens." If anyone received more than one-tenth of the vote of the entire citizen body, or about six thousand votes, he was compelled to leave Athens for ten years—a good way for ambitious politicians to get rid of their enemies.

Choosing officials by lot may have been democratic, but it was not a good method for filling jobs that required special talents. The Athenians therefore chose one important official by vote: each of the ten tribes elected a general known as a **strategos**. This arrangement made sense, for a city would at least want experienced generals. But because strategos was the most powerful elective office, ambitious politicians with no military abilities campaigned to be chosen, and Athens often was burdened with bad generals.

It soon became clear that only the well-to-do had the liberty to participate in government on a regular basis. To increase participation by Athenians who had to work for a living, citizens were paid for their services, a practice that made the Athenian democracy very expensive to operate. Poor Athenians such as the thetes looked on the government as a source of income, and Athens was continually looking for ways to raise money to pay for its democracy. The expensive nature of Athenian democracy helps to explain why it was so rarely adopted by other Greek city-states. Only an economic powerhouse like Athens could afford it.

 Checking In

By yourself or with a partner, explain the significance of each of the following selected key terms:

Lycurgus	democracy
Peloponnesian League	thetes
Peisistratus	ostracism
Cleisthenes	strategos

The Classical Age, 500–387 B.C.E.

♦ **What were the reasons for the Persian successes and failures in their conflicts with the Greeks?**

♦ **What were the causes of Athens' rapid rise and fall?**

strategos (Greek for "general") Only elective office in the Athenian democracy.

Marathon Battle in 490 B.C.E. in which the Athenians defeated the Persians.

The fifth century B.C.E. is known as the Classical Age, the period when Greece was at its height both politically and culturally. By 500 B.C.E., the Greeks had established a unified culture and had become a great economic force in the Mediterranean world. Politically, however, they were divided. Hitherto, the Greeks had not faced any foreign threats, but soon after 500 B.C.E. they were drawn into a conflict with the greatest power the world had yet known, the Persian Empire. The Greeks later looked back on their victory over the Persians as their defining moment. Subsequently, however, they again fell to fighting among themselves, conflicts that culminated in the ruinous Peloponnesian War between Sparta and Athens. Yet this period of warfare also saw major achievements in sculpture, architecture, literature, and thought that had a permanent influence on western civilization.

The Persian Wars

Because the Greeks considered all foreigners to be barbarians, no Greek could tolerate being ruled by a non-Greek. As the Persian Empire expanded westward, it incorporated more and more Greeks, who chafed under Persian rule, resulting in a series of conflicts between the Greeks and the Persians.

The Origin of the Persian Wars The first conflict between Greeks and Persia began in 498 B.C.E., when the Ionian Greek cities, led by the city of Miletus, revolted against the Persian king Darius. The Ionians, realizing they could not hold out for long, appealed for help to the European Greeks. The Athenians sent twenty ships and helped to burn the Persian provincial capital but then lost interest and went home. It took Darius a few years to raise an army to retaliate, but once he had done so, he burned Miletus and deported its inhabitants to the frontiers of India.

To prevent future Greek interference in the Persian Empire, Darius decided to attack the mainland Greeks. Before his invasion, Darius sent ambassadors to the Greek cities demanding earth and water, the Persian sign of surrender. Several Greek cities saw an alliance with the Persians as a way to gain an advantage over Greek rivals and allied themselves with the Persians. Athens refused to surrender, and when the Persian ambassadors arrived at Sparta, the Spartans threw them into a well and told them to get the earth and water themselves. The ambassadors died in the fall.

The First Persian Invasion of Greece The first Persian attack on Greece came in 490 B.C.E. Two hundred ships carrying 25,000 soldiers sailed across the Aegean Sea and landed on the plain at Marathon, about twenty-six miles from Athens. The Athenians sent a messenger to Sparta asking for help, but the Spartans replied that they were performing a religious ceremony and could not leave for several days. The Athenian army of 10,000 heavily armed hoplites thus advanced almost alone to meet the 25,000 Persians. In the ensuing Battle of **Marathon**,

The trireme was the preferred Greek warship of the fifth century B.C.E., and Athens' fleet of 200 triremes made the city the greatest naval power of ancient Greece. The effective use of a trireme's three banks of oars, manned by 180 rowers, required extensive training and coordination. A trireme had a top speed of about 15 miles per hour and was maneuvered so that its iron ram could punch a hole in the side of an enemy ship. In the 1980s, a trireme named the Olympias, shown here, was reconstructed using Oregon oak and Virginia pine. Its bronze ram weighed 200 kg. With a crew of 170 male and female rowers, it reached a top speed of about 11 miles per hour. Why do you think Athens was able to build such a large navy?

the lightly armed and inexperienced Persian infantrymen proved no match for the Greek hoplites. The Athenians posted most of their troops on the Persian flanks and allowed the Persians to push back the center of their line. The Athenian wings then closed behind the Persians, who fled for their ships and escaped as best as they could. The final toll was 6,400 Persian dead to 192 Athenians. A runner was sent to Athens with the news, the first running of the marathon. He fell dying in the marketplace, gasping, "Nenikekamen" ("We have won!"). The Spartans arrived the next day and could only congratulate the Athenians and lament that they had not been there to share in the glory.

The Battle of Marathon showed that the Persians could be beaten. But it was by no means the end of Persian attempts to defeat the Greeks. The Greeks realized that the Persians would be back. When a huge silver mine was discovered near Athens, the strategos Themistocles convinced the Athenians to invest the money in a new fleet of 200 triremes, warships driven by three banks of oars. The thetes backed this measure because each ship required 180 rowers, who were recruited from thetes too poor to serve in the army and were handsomely paid. In the future, any proposals that would use the navy would be supported by the thetes.

The Second Persian Invasion of Greece Darius died in 486 B.C.E. His son Xerxes soon prepared a massive attack on Greece by land and sea. In 481 B.C.E., the Greek cities met at Corinth to plan their defense but immediately fell to quarreling

over who would be in charge. Meanwhile, hoping to split up the Greeks, the Persians sent ambassadors to all the Greek cities except Sparta and Athens, demanding earth and water and promising them good treatment. About one-third of the Greek cities went over to the Persians. Another third decided to wait and see who was going to win. Only Sparta and Athens, and their trustworthy allies, resolved to resist the Persians. The situation looked bleak for the Greeks. Even the Delphic oracle foresaw failure, telling the Spartans that "they must lose their city or one of their kings" and recommending to the Athenians that they "flee to the world's end." When the Athenians asked for another oracle, they were told to "trust to their wooden walls," which many interpreted as meaning the wooden wall around the city.

In 480 B.C.E. a Persian force numbering about 250,000 soldiers and 1,200 warships advanced out of Anatolia toward Greece by land and sea. The primary Persian advantage lay in numbers; Xerxes hoped simply to overwhelm the Greeks. The Greeks realized that to neutralize the Persian numerical superiority they would have to fight in confined quarters. Therefore, as a first line of defense they chose a narrow mountain pass in northern Greece at Thermopylae. A force of 7,000

Themistocles Athenian leader who organized the resistance against the Persians in the 480s B.C.E.

Thermopylae (Greek for "hot gates") Battle at a narrow pass in northern Greece where 300 Spartans were annihilated by the Persians in 480 B.C.E.

Greek silver coins served both economic and propaganda purposes. During the fifth century B.C.E., the economic power of Athens made its large silver coin, called a tetradrachm (or four-drachm piece; 1 drachm weighed about 4 grams), into one of the most recognized and accepted coins of the Mediterranean world. The tetradrachm's images proclaimed its Athenian origin, for it had the head of Athena, the patron goddess of Athens, on one side, and an owl, Athena's bird, on the other, with an olive branch, a symbol of Athens' primary manufactured product, to the upper left. The crescent moon on the owl's shoulder, which was added in 490 B.C.E., is thought to be a reference to the phase of the moon at the time of the Battle of Marathon. How much purchasing power do you think such a coin might have had? (Ashmolean Museum, University of Oxford/The Bridgeman Art Library)

Greeks led by 300 Spartans under King Leonidas was sent to delay the Persian advance. As the Spartans prepared to meet the Persian attack, a local farmer attempted to frighten a Spartan soldier by saying that the sky would go black when the Persian archers shot their arrows. The Spartan bravely replied, "Well, then we'll get to fight in the shade." The initial Persian attacks on the pass failed. Finally, Xerxes sent in his elite force, the Immortals, but they, too, were defeated by the well-trained Spartans. As Xerxes began to despair, a Greek traitor showed the Persians a narrow mountain path around behind the Spartans. Betrayed, the Spartans, who by that time had sent away their allies, were surrounded. But even then the Persians could not defeat them. Eventually, Xerxes ordered his archers to send volleys of arrows down on the Spartans until they all were dead. King Leonidas was killed, and the oracle's prophecy thus was fulfilled. The Greeks later put up an epitaph to the 300 Spartans, reading: "Stranger, go tell the Spartans that we lie here, obeying their orders."

The Persians then marched south, capturing and burning Athens without a fight, for the Athenians had withdrawn to the island of **Salamis**, just off the coast. A great naval battle ensued when the Persian navy attempted to occupy Salamis, which was defended by a Greek fleet comprised mainly of the Athenian navy. The well-drilled Greeks won a spectacular victory. It now became clear what the oracle had meant by "wooden walls"—not the walls around Athens but the wooden hulls of the ships. Having lost the better part of his navy, and fearing for his safety, Xerxes returned to Persia by land, leaving his army in Greece. The following year, in 479 B.C.E., the Persian army was defeated at Plataea. The Spartans performed heroically, standing stoically under Persian arrow fire until it was their turn to charge. On the same day, it was said, the Athenians destroyed what was left of the Persian fleet in Ionia, and the Ionian cities again revolted from the Persians.

The Rise and Fall of Athens

The Persians' defeat marked their last attempt to conquer the Greek mainland. Later in their history, the Greeks looked back at the defeat of the Persians as their finest hour. Sparta and Athens now were the most powerful cities in Greece. Many Greeks wanted to continue the war against Persia. Athens was the natural leader, for it had a large navy, and the Spartans were reluctant to have their army away from home.

The Delian League In 478 B.C.E., Athens organized an anti-Persian league of Greek cities called the **Delian League** because it was headquartered on the

Salamis Naval battle in 480 B.C.E. at an island off the coast of Athens where the Greeks defeated the Persians.

Plataea Battle in 479 B.C.E. in which the Greeks defeated the Persians.

Delian League Anti-Persian alliance of Greek cities organized by Athens in 478 B.C.E.

Aegean island of Delos. Its goal was to set free the Ionian Greeks. League members contributed either ships or money. Under the leadership of Athens, the Greeks repeatedly defeated the Persians. As Athens grew in prestige, the Athenians tried to turn what had begun as a voluntary alliance into an empire, treating members of the league as if they were Athenian subjects. League membership became mandatory. Cities that attempted to resign were forced to accept Athenian-style democracies and to continue their payments, which now could be called **tribute**, as they were diverted directly into the Athenian treasury. In 448 B.C.E., the Persians made peace with Athens, giving up their claim to the Ionian cities. Once the war was over, many cities of the Delian League stopped making their contributions. But Athens forced them to continue paying, and the transition from Delian League to Athenian Empire was complete.

The Rise of Pericles The strategos Pericles was the most effective Athenian leader of this period, in good part because he focused his attentions on domestic matters rather than on costly foreign wars. His mother was the niece of Cleisthenes, and his father had been ostracized but had returned to Athens to become a distinguished general. As a young man he had studied with philosophers, from whom he learned to remain calm in the face of adversity. In the 460s B.C.E., Pericles began a political career based on an anti-aristocratic, pro-people platform. He was an effective speaker able to manipulate the otherwise unruly electorate. He gave the people everything they wanted, including full employment and free entertainment. In 451 B.C.E., he sought to protect the privileges of poor citizens with a law limiting Athenian citizenship to those whose mother and father were both Athenian citizens. This maximized the amount of benefits available to each thete.

Pericles was greatly influenced by his mistress Aspasia, a courtesan from Miletus who, unlike most Athenian women, appeared regularly in public and spoke her mind. She was greatly envied for her political influence. It was said that Pericles was so fond of her that he kissed her every morning when he left the house and every evening when he returned—a display of affection very unusual among the Greeks.

The Peloponnesian War When Athens began to interfere in the affairs of Spartan allies on the Greek mainland, these cities appealed for help to the Spartans, who were duty bound to support them. The result was the **Peloponnesian War**, which lasted from 431 until 404 B.C.E. On one side were Sparta and its allies, including not only most of the Peloponnesian cities but also much of northern Greece and the powerful Sicilian city of Syracuse. Sparta could raise an

The homes of well-to-do Greeks often contained portrait busts of famous people, especially people from a city's own past. This Roman marble copy of a Greek original depicts Pericles, the leader of Athens from about 461–429 B.C.E. The inscription at the bottom of the bust reads simply "Pericles." As the only Athenian politician who was able to control the Athenian voters, Pericles did his best to keep the Athenians out of disastrous wars and to focus their attentions on beautifying the city. What purpose do you think these portrait busts served for the Greek people? (Alinari/Art Resource, NY)

army of 50,000 hoplites, but only about 100 ships. Athens was supported by its empire of some 300 cities, which could muster about 30,000 hoplites and more than 400 ships. A third interested party was Persia, which was ready to use its huge financial resources to gain any benefit it could from the conflict.

In the first phase of the war, the Athenians ravaged the Spartan coast with their navy, and the Spartans marched their army into Attica each year, destroying the crops. The Athenians

tribute A form of taxation paid as a fixed annual amount by a subject territory or people to a central government.

Pericles (d. 429 B.C.E.) Athenian leader during the Golden Age of Athens in the fifth century B.C.E. who sponsored many building projects.

Peloponnesian War War between Athens and Sparta lasting from 431 to 404 B.C.E.

The Athenian Acropolis was the most famous complex of temples in the ancient world. Most of the monuments were either begun or built during the time of Pericles, between about 447 and 430 B.C.E. On the left end of the Acropolis in this aerial view, the grand entrance, known as the Propylaeum, leads up to the sacred area on top. On the right side of the Propylaeum is the tiny temple of Athena Nike, goddess of victory. At the center of the Acropolis can be seen the Parthenon, the great temple of "Athena the Virgin," 101 feet wide and 228 feet long. To the left of the Parthenon stands the Erechtheum, with its distinctive caryatids, female statues that serve as columns. These building projects were extremely expensive. Where do you think the Athenians got the money to pay for them?

withdrew behind their walls and refused to fight, supplying themselves by sea. A result of so much crowding was a terrible plague in Athens, graphically described by the historian **Thucydides:** "Many who were in perfect health were suddenly seized with illness. The disease brought on vomiting of bile and the body broke out in ulcers. The internal fever was intense, and sufferers were tormented by unceasing thirst. Either they died on the seventh or ninth day, or the disease then produced violent diarrhea. Severe exhaustion then usually carried them off." One of the victims was Pericles himself.

At first, neither Athens nor Sparta gained an advantage. Eventually, however, the Spartans devised a strategy to win the war. They realized that to defeat Athens they needed

a navy, but navies were expensive and Sparta was poor. So the Spartans made an alliance with Persia, agreeing that in exchange for Persian money they would permit Persia to reoccupy Ionia if the Spartans won the war. Yet even with Persian money the Spartans were unable to defeat the Athenians at sea.

The Decline of Greece Finally, in 405 B.C.E., the Spartans surprised the Athenian fleet, which was pulled up on shore in Anatolia, destroying it and executing three thousand Athenians. Athens was financially drained and could not continue to fight, and the following year the Spartans occupied Athens. Given the hard-fought nature of the war, the Spartans were remarkably lenient and did not kill the men and enslave the women and children. Instead, they compelled the Athenians to abandon their empire and their fleet, to dismantle their city walls, and to obey Spartan foreign policy. The Spartans

Thucydides Greek historian of the late fifth century B.C.E. known for his account of the Peloponnesian War.

also forced the Athenians to abandon their democracy and accept an oligarchic government. They then went home. The following year, the Athenians restored their democracy, but the Spartans, believing that Athens had been suitably weakened, made no response.

Sparta now was the strongest city in Greece, but the Persian reoccupation of Ionia put it in an awkward position. The Ionians appealed to Sparta, and to maintain their reputation, the Spartans felt obliged to abandon their agreement with Persia and send an army to Ionia. The Persians then threw their support to Athens. Using Persian money, the Athenians rebuilt their walls and their fleet, and the war with Sparta was renewed. Both sides were exhausted, but neither would allow the other to dictate terms of peace. The two sides finally asked the king of Persia to arbitrate. The **King's Peace** of 387 B.C.E. declared that the fighting would stop, that all the Greek cities were free, and that the Persian king would receive the cities of Ionia. Thus, after over forty years of warfare, the Greeks had succeeded only in weakening themselves. The only people to gain from the conflict were the Persians. The previous hundred years of conflict had demonstrated the fundamental inability of the Greeks to get along with each other.

The Golden Age of Greek Culture

At the same time that the Greeks were fighting self-destructive wars, they also were engaged in a great outpouring of artistic and literary production known as the **Classical Age**.

The Golden Age of Athens Many cultural endeavors took place in Athens, which enjoyed its own Golden Age. The Athenians undertook monumental building projects, paid for by tribute from their empire. These projects were popular with the Athenian people because they gave work to the urban poor. In 449 B.C.E., Pericles passed a law allocating 9,000 talents (about 500,000 pounds) of silver for temple construction work and began a large-scale rebuilding of the temple of Athena on the Acropolis known as the **Parthenon**, now recognized as the most beautiful temple of the ancient world. Except for its terra-cotta roof, the Parthenon was made entirely of marble. It contained a gold-plated statue of Athena designed by the sculptor Phidias, whose pupils created the many marble sculptures that decorated the temple. In the 430s B.C.E., a monumental gateway to the Acropolis known as the Propylaea was built, and during the 420s B.C.E., two more temples were added on the Acropolis—one, the Erechtheum, in honor of Poseidon and Erechtheus (a legendary early king of Athens), and the other dedicated to Nike, the goddess

of victory. Taken together, these monuments made the Acropolis the most renowned ancient temple complex.

Greek Drama The Golden Age of Athens also was the Golden Age of Greek drama. Every year, at the festival of Dionysus, the city financed dramatic productions. There were two kinds of drama, tragedy and comedy. Both dealt with important matters, but tragedies did so seriously and had sad endings, whereas comedies did so lightheartedly and had happy endings. The underlying theme of tragedies was that whoever failed to obey the will of the gods suffered greatly. The plots of tragedies were drawn from well-known myths and legends, meaning that the audience already knew the ending. But the characters in the play did not, and dramatic tension resulted from the manner in which the characters were inexorably drawn to discover their awful fates.

Aeschylus, for example, dramatized the betrayal and murder of the Greek high king Agamemnon by his wife and her lover. **Sophocles** told how Oedipus unknowingly married his mother and, when the truth was discovered, blinded himself. And **Euripides** described how Medea took revenge on her husband, Jason, by killing their own children. Comedies, on the other hand, were risqué and full of sexual innuendo. Because they allegedly were not meant to be taken seriously, they could deal with issues from current events. A comedy of **Aristophanes** called the *Lysistrata*, for example, responded to a pervasive desire to end the war with Sparta without sounding unpatriotic. No public figure was safe from ridicule. In another play of Aristophanes, the philosopher Socrates was depicted as living in "cloud cuckoo-land." Because Greek tragedies dealt with timeless themes of human emotion, faith, and morality, they continue to be meaningful today, whereas the many references to fifth-century events means that Greek comedies now seem less relevant.

The Invention of History
The Classical Age also was the great age of historical writing. The Greeks were the first people to believe that one can learn from studying the past and thus not only avoid making the

King's Peace Peace treaty arbitrated by the Persian king that ended the war between Sparta and Athens in 387 B.C.E.

Classical Age The height of Greek artistic and literary endeavor, lasting from 500 until 323 B.C.E., which included the Golden Age of Athens.

Parthenon Athenian temple on the Acropolis built in honor of Athena.

Aeschylus, Sophocles, and **Euripides** Athenian writers of tragedy during the fifth century B.C.E.

Aristophanes Athenian writer of comedies in the late fifth century B.C.E., author of the play *Lysistrata*.

Aristophanes Suggests How to End the War

When dissent was expressed in Athens, it had to be done in a roundabout manner if its author hoped to avoid criminal charges. Comic plays permitted politically dangerous ideas to be raised in an ostensibly nonserious way. In Aristophanes's play *Lysistrata*, presented about 410 B.C.E., the women of Greece come up with a plan for how to end the Peloponnesian War, which had been devastating Greece for nearly twenty years. The Athenians would have found this concept humorous because in all Greek cities except Sparta women were expected to remain at home and not participate in politics. The selection begins when Lysistrata, who had summoned women from various Greek cities to a meeting, meets her friend Cleonice in the street in Athens. She is worried because the women she is expecting have not arrived.

❶ What does this tell us about the role of Athenian women?

❷ What does Greece need to be saved from during this period?

❸ What does this exchange tell us about views of Spartan women?

❶ Cleonice: Oh! They will come, my dear; but it's not easy, you know, for women to leave the house. One is busy pottering about her husband; another is getting the servant up; a third is putting her child to sleep or feeding the brat.

Lysistrata: But I tell you, the business that calls them here is far more urgent.

Cleonice: And why do you summon us, dear Lysistrata?

Lysistrata: It means just this, Greece saved by the women! Our country's fortunes depend on us. ❷ If the Boeotian and Peloponnesian women join us, Greece is saved.

Cleonice: But look! Here are some arrivals.

Myrrhine: Are we late, Lysistrata? Tell us, pray. What, not a word?

Cleonice: No, let's wait until the women of Boeotia arrive and those from the Peloponnesus.

Lysistrata: Yes, that is best…. Ah! Here comes Lampito. [*Lampito, a husky Spartan woman, enters with two women from Boeotia and one from Corinth.*] ❸ Good day, Lampito, dear friend from Sparta. How handsome you look! What a rosy complexion! And how strong you seem. Why, you surely could strangle a bull!

same mistakes over again but also anticipate how to behave in similar circumstances in the future. The three most influential early Greek historians all worked in Athens. During the 440s B.C.E., **Herodotus**, who has been called the father of history, composed a massive study intended to explain how the Greeks and Persians had become involved in the greatest war the world had yet known. Even though Herodotus portrayed the war as a conflict between civilization and barbarism, he was sympathetic to Near Eastern culture. He was the first historian to use the historical method, the system by which historians gather evidence, form hypotheses, test the validity of their evidence, and come to conclusions based on the most reliable evidence. Much of Herodotus's evidence was drawn from myth and legend, and, like the writers of tragedy, he adopted a moral approach to human behavior in which the gods rewarded the

Herodotus Author, during the 440s B.C.E., of a history of the Persian Wars, known as the father of history.

Lampito: Yes, indeed, I really think I could. It's because I do gymnastics and practice the bottom-kicking dance. But who has called together this council of women, pray?

Lysistrata: I have.

Lampito: Well then, tell us what you want of us.

Lysistrata: First answer me one question. Don't you feel sad because the fathers of your children are far away with the army?

Cleonice: Mine has been the last five months in Thrace.

Myrrhine: It's seven since mine left.

❹ Lampito: If mine ever does return, he's no sooner home than he takes down his shield again and flies back to the wars.

Lysistrata: And not so much as the shadow of a lover! Now tell me, if I have discovered a means of ending the war, will you all second me?

Cleonice: Yes, verily, by all the goddesses.

Lampito: Why, to secure peace I would climb to the top of Mount Taygetus [a mountain outside Sparta].

❺ Lysistrata: Then I will out with it at last, my mighty secret! Oh! Sister women, if we would compel our husbands to make peace, we must refrain …

Cleonice: Refrain from what?

Lysistrata: We must refrain from the male altogether…. Nay, why do you turn your backs on me? So, you bite your lips, and shake your heads, eh? Why these pale, sad looks? Why these tears? Come, will you do it—yes or no?

Cleonice: I will not do it, let the war go on. Anything, anything but that! To rob us of the sweetest thing in all the world, Lysistrata, darling!

Lysistrata: You, my dear, you from hardy Sparta, if you join me, all may yet be well. Help me, I beg you.

❻ Lampito: 'Tis a hard thing, by the two goddesses [Demeter and Persephone], it is! For a woman to sleep alone without ever a strong male in her bed. But there, peace must come first.

Lysistrata: Oh, my darling best friend, you are the only one deserving the name of woman!

Cleonice: Very well, if you must have it so, we agree.

Source: From "Lysistrata," in The Eleven Comedies, vol. 1 (London: Athenian Society, 1912), pp. 254ff.

❹ What was the role of the shield in Greek society?

❺ How does Lysistrata suggest the women can coerce the men into ending the fighting?

❻ How does Aristophanes intend the relations among these women to serve as a model for the men?

good and punished the wicked. For Herodotus, there were fundamental rights and wrongs, with no middle ground.

Thucydides, an Athenian general who had lost a battle and been sent into exile, wrote a history of the Peloponnesian War up to the year 411 B.C.E. In his view, the gods were not involved in the making of history. People were, and they were responsible for their own actions. For Thucydides, the most fundamental human motivation was a struggle for power. He observed, "The strong do what they can and the weak suffer what they must." Thucydides relied on written documents and first-person evidence for his conclusions and argued that there were two sides to every quarrel, without any absolute right or wrong. He believed it was possible to detect underlying patterns in events. He wrote for "those who wish to have a clear view of events that likely will occur again" and hoped that a critical study of the factors leading up to the Peloponnesian War could help to prevent ruinous wars in the future.

Socrates Chooses Death

In 399 B.C.E., the Athenian philosopher Socrates was put on trial on false charges and sentenced to death. He was given the chance to go into exile, but to show his commitment to his beliefs, he chose to abide by the sentence and died by drinking poison. At this time, Athens was in turmoil. Five years earlier the Athenians had lost a hard-fought war with Sparta, and they were looking for people to blame for the political instability that followed.

In his early life, Socrates seemed much like an average Athenian. He was the son of a sculptor and a midwife and fought heroically in the lengthy war against Sparta. After the war, however, rather than taking part in public life by attending meetings of the assembly or holding public office, he chose to become a philosopher—in Greek, a "lover of wisdom." Socrates was interested in concepts of right and wrong, justice, virtue, and love. He believed that vice came from ignorance and that people had a natural tendency to be good if they could only be taught what good was. Feeling that he could serve Athens best by teaching the Athenians to look into their souls, he spent his time in the marketplace, questioning people about their beliefs and guiding them by his questions to a greater understanding of goodness. What is the nature of the gods, he asked; what is the role of government? Is striving for wealth, office, and status more important than seeking wisdom, morality, goodness, and the health of one's soul?

By challenging some of the Greeks' most fundamental beliefs, Socrates made enemies. Raising such questions was dangerous at a time when Athens was having political difficulties, and in a democracy where any citizen could bring a legal charge against anyone else. Socrates was well aware that he was taking risks. But when asked whether his choice to challenge conventional values concerned him, he replied, "You are wrong, sir, if you think that a man who is any good at all should take into account the risk of life or death; he should look to this only in his actions, whether what he does is right or wrong, whether he is acting like a good or a bad man."

Eventually Socrates was accused of neglecting the gods and corrupting the youth by teaching that the gods did not exist. He was put on trial before a jury of five hundred Athenian citizens. Instead of respectfully defending himself against the charges, he used the occasion to present his teachings, thereby insulting the jury, which convicted him and sentenced him to death. Socrates declined to make an appeal, which might well have been granted, and asserted not only that Athens could kill his physical body but never his soul, but also that by killing him, his judges were harming their own souls.

The Athenians had a tradition that those sentenced to death could escape the penalty by going into exile, and many of those who voted to convict Socrates may have done so simply to get him out of town. However, when his friends urged Socrates to flee, he refused, claiming that he must respect the law: if he were to flee, it would seem that he was arguing that the laws should be disobeyed, which is the last thing he wanted to do. Rather than being executed by the state, Socrates was given the opportunity to commit suicide. On the designated day, surrounded by his friends, Socrates told them that his soul soon would be in the realm of the blessed and that only his body would be left behind for burial. He then drank a cup of hemlock, a common poison used for suicide in those days, and a fatal numbness crept up from his legs to his vital organs.

To maintain his self-respect, as a Greek and as a philosopher, Socrates chose death. As a Greek, he was expected to display his virtue publicly, and once he had taken his stand, he was committed to following through. As a philosopher, he had to remain true to his beliefs, even at the cost of his life.

Source: From the Greek philosopher Plato (c. 424–347).

Xenophon, another Athenian general, continued the history of Greece from 411 to 362 B.C.E. Unlike Herodotus and Thucydides, however, Xenophon wrote his history mostly as narrative—first this happened, then this, then this—without any attempt to make events fit a particular model. His *March of the 10,000*—an account of how a band of trapped Greek mercenaries fought their way out of the Persian Empire in 401 B.C.E.—is one of the great adventure stories of all time. Most subsequent historians followed Xenophon's narrative style.

Xenophon Historian of the period after 411 B.C.E., author of the "March of the 10,000."

Socrates and Plato The Greeks also continued their study of philosophy. Philosophers turned from explaining the nature of the universe to examining the nature of human interactions. Educators known as **sophists**, who sometimes passed as philosophers, taught how to make effective arguments using debate and rhetoric, a useful skill to have in Athenian politics. Sophists often taught how to argue both sides of a question, for to them there was no absolute truth: everything was relative to the side of the argument one decided to support. Some Greeks thus viewed the sophists as immoral. The relativism of the sophists was opposed by the Athenian philosopher **Socrates** (see A New Direction: Socrates Chooses Death), who taught during the latter part of the Peloponnesian War. He believed that truth could be discovered by question and answer, an approach still known as the Socratic method. Because he questioned some fundamental Athenian values, Socrates was sentenced to death in 399 B.C.E.

 Checking In

By yourself or with a partner, explain the significance of each of the following selected key terms:

Thermopylae	Classical Age
Delian League	Herodotus
Pericles	sophists
Peloponnesian War	Socrates

Socrates left no writings of his own, and his teachings have come down to us in the books of his pupil **Plato**. Plato established his own school of philosophy in Athens, known as the Academy. His written works investigate abstract questions such as, "What is justice?" Plato assumed the existence of a divinely established perfection that humans should strive to copy. The world we live in, he taught, is a very imperfect copy of the perfect forms and ideas that exist in the perfect static universe. Plato was particularly disillusioned with the democracy that had condemned Socrates to death. Plato's most influential book, *The Republic*, presented a model for a perfect human society that was lacking the strife and contention so characteristic of the Greeks. Everyone living in Plato's republic was under the control of the state and had his or her fixed place. Some people were soldiers, and others were workers. The rulers, of course, were the philosophers, who could be either women or men.

> **sophists** Greek teachers who taught the art of making effective arguments using debate and rhetoric.
>
> **Socrates** (d. 399 B.C.E.) Athenian philosopher of the late fifth century B.C.E. who used a question-and-answer method of teaching, now known as the Socratic method.
>
> **Plato** Athenian philosopher of the early fourth century B.C.E. who wrote *The Republic* and established a school called the Academy.

Review

Summary

◆ Between 1100 and 387 B.C.E., the Greeks evolved from a rudimentary agricultural society to the most important cultural and political presence in the Mediterranean world. Their development was fueled by a great sense of competition among individuals, social classes, and cities, as every Greek strove to gain some advantage over every other Greek. Competition extended to every aspect of Greek life, including politics, warfare, religion, athletics, literature, and art.

◆ Greek life revolved around the polis, or city-state. Most Greek cities followed a sequence of political evolution from monarchy, rule by a king; to aristocracy, rule by the aristocrats; to oligarchy, rule by the wealthy. An intermediate stage, tyranny, often intervened between aristocracy and oligarchy.

◆ The two most important Greek cities during this period, Sparta and Athens, were political exceptions, and very different from each other. Sparta scarcely got past monarchy, whereas Athens went one step beyond oligarchy to democracy, rule by the entire male citizen body. Sparta's need to control a large enslaved population resulted in its creation of a militaristic society, whereas Athens became the wealthiest trading city of the Greek world. At first, the great differences between the two cities meant that they had nothing to compete over, and together they led the Greeks in their resistance against the Persians between 490 and 479 B.C.E.

◆ The Greek victory over Persia was followed by a contest between Sparta and Athens over which would be the leader of the Greeks.

◆ To fund their expensive democracy, the Athenians created an empire of hundreds of other Greek cities, which paid tribute to Athens. This income funded the marvelous Athenian architecture and literature still admired today.

◆ Athenian interference in other Greek cities eventually resulted in the ruinous Peloponnesian War, in which Sparta and Athens engaged in mutual destruction. At the end of the conflict, all Greek cities were weakened.

◆ The most lasting legacies of the Archaic and Classical Greeks were intellectual rather than political. The Greeks invented drama, history, and philosophy. In particular, the Greeks were the first people of antiquity to believe that they could understand the universe through speculative thought or through observation, without the need to attribute everything to the activities of the gods.

Chronology

1100 B.C.E.	Dorians settle in southern Greece; Greek Dark Ages begin; First wave of Greek colonization begins	490 B.C.E.	Athenians defeat Persians at Battle of Marathon
776 B.C.E.	First recorded Olympic games; Archaic Age begins	480 B.C.E.	Persians defeat Spartans at Battle of Thermopylae; Greeks defeat Persians at Battle of Salamis
ca. 750 B.C.E.	Homer's *Iliad* and *Odyssey* are committed to writing	479 B.C.E.	Greeks defeat Persians at Battle of Plataea
750–550 B.C.E.	Second wave of Greek colonization occurs	440s B.C.E.	Herodotus writes *The Histories*
ca. 700 B.C.E.	Lycurgus establishes Spartan Good Rule	431–404 B.C.E.	Peloponnesian War
650–500 B.C.E.	Age of the tyrants	430–427 B.C.E.	Plague devastates Athens
621 B.C.E.	Draco composes Athenian law code	410 B.C.E.	Aristophanes writes the play *Lysistrata*
592 B.C.E.	Solon creates the Athenian oligarchy	404 B.C.E.	Sparta occupies Athens
546 B.C.E.	Peisistratus becomes tyrant of Athens	401 B.C.E.	Xenophon's March of the 10,000
508 B.C.E.	Cleisthenes creates the Athenian democracy	399 B.C.E.	Socrates dies
500 B.C.E.	Classical Age begins	387 B.C.E.	King's Peace ends warfare between the Spartans and Athenians

© Cengage Learning

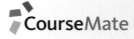 Visit the CourseMate website at **www.cengagebrain.com** for additional study tools and review materials for this chapter.

Test Yourself

To gauge your mastery of the material in this chapter, answer the questions below. More than one answer may be correct.

The Development of Greek Identity, 1100–776 B.C.E.

1. General developments that occurred during the Greek Dark Ages included

    a. The settlement of the Dorian Greeks.
    b. The development of a trading economy.
    c. The development of the polis.
    d. The evolution of competition.
    e. Conflicts with the Persians.

2. A Greek woman's primary duties were

    a. To keep house.
    b. To serve in the army.
    c. To raise children.
    d. To exercise in the gymnasium.
    e. To serve in the Assembly.

3. During the Greek Dark Ages, how did Greek political organization evolve?

    a. From aristocracy to democracy
    b. From aristocracy to oligarchy
    c. From aristocracy to tyranny
    d. From monarchy to aristocracy
    e. From monarchy to tyranny

4. Which Greek gods' shrines and festivals attracted attention from throughout Greece?

    a. Apollo
    b. Zeus
    c. Hades
    d. Hestia
    e. Osiris

Now that you have reviewed and tested yourself on this part of the chapter, take time to pull together all the important information by answering the following questions:

◆ How did Greek political organization evolve during the Dark Ages?

◆ What was the role of competition in the evolution of Greek society and politics?

The Archaic Age, 776–500 B.C.E.

5. Which of these cultural attributes did the Greeks assimilate from non-Greeks?

    a. The Olympic games
    b. Coinage
    c. The alphabet
    d. Eastern artistic styles
    e. A competitive nature

6. What was a packed mass of Greek heavily armed infantrymen called?

    a. Hoplite
    b. Oligarchy
    c. Hellene
    d. Phalanx
    e. Minotaur

7. During the Archaic Age, how did Greek political organization evolve?

    a. From aristocracy to democracy
    b. From aristocracy to oligarchy
    c. From aristocracy to tyranny
    d. From monarchy to aristocracy
    e. From monarchy to tyranny

8. During the Archaic Age, what was the illegal ruler discontented groups of Greeks sponsored known as?

   a. King
   b. Aristocrat
   c. Tyrant
   d. Hoplite
   e. Oligarch

Now that you have reviewed and tested yourself on this part of the chapter, take time to pull together all the important information by answering the following questions:

◆ In what ways did the Greeks borrow from the cultures of other peoples?

◆ How did the growth of Greek trade affect political evolution?

Sparta and Athens

9. The Spartan militaristic way of life included which of these attributes?

   a. Athletic training for girls
   b. Inspection of infants at birth
   c. The development of a trading economy
   d. The creation of a powerful navy
   e. Life in military barracks for boys and men

10. What was the Spartan way of life designed to do?

    a. Prevent revolts by the helots
    b. Create the best poets
    c. Develop an advanced commercial economy
    d. Encourage individualism and imagination
    e. Encourage the building of defensive walls

11. What did the law code of the Athenian lawgiver Draco provide?

    a. Eliminated the death penalty
    b. Established a court to try murder cases
    c. Created the Athenian democracy
    d. Allowed debtors to be enslaved
    e. Was known for its leniency

12. Which Athenians had full citizen rights, including the right to speak in the Assembly?

    a. All men and women over the age of eighteen
    b. All those whose parents were Athenian citizens
    c. All male citizens over thirty years of age
    d. All males living in Athens except for slaves
    e. Any foreigner who settled in Athens for fifteen years

Now that you have reviewed and tested yourself on this part of the chapter, take time to pull together all the important information by answering the following questions:

◆ How was the Spartan social system designed to preserve the Spartan way of life?

◆ How did the Athenian democracy function?

The Classical Age, 500–387 B.C.E.

13. When the Persians invaded Greece in 480 B.C.E., who opposed them?

    a. All the Greek cities except for Sparta and Athens
    b. The Greek cities of Ionia
    c. Sparta and its allies
    d. Athens and its allies
    e. The Greeks and the Macedonians

14. What were the "wooden walls" the Oracle at Delphi had said would protect Athens later understood to mean?

    a. The wooden walls of Athens
    b. The walls of the temple of Athena on the Acropolis
    c. The Athenian navy
    d. The wood of the trees of the Athenian olive groves
    e. The wooden shields of Athenian hoplites

15. What were the contributions provided by the members of the Delian League used for by the Athenians?

    a. Pay for Athenian building projects

    b. Rebuild the cities of Ionia

    c. Pay for the Athenian democracy

    d. Hire mercenaries to fight in Athens' army

    e. Pay tribute to Persia

Now that you have reviewed and tested yourself on this part of the chapter, take time to pull together all the important information by answering the following questions:

◆ What were the reasons for the Persian successes and failures in their conflicts with the Greeks?

◆ What were the consequences of the Peloponnesian War for the Greeks?

CHAPTER 4

From Polis to Cosmopolis: The Hellenistic World, 387–30 B.C.E.

380	360	340	320	300	280	260	240	220	200

338 B.C.E.
Macedonians defeat the Greeks

336 B.C.E.
Alexander becomes king of Macedonia

330 B.C.E.
Third wave of Greek colonization begins

331 B.C.E.
Battle of Guagamela

300 B.C.E.
Ptolemy I founds Alexandria Museum

Euclid publishes theorems of geometry

Zeno begins teaching Stoicism

280 B.C.E.
Final partition of Alexander's empire

In ancient Egypt, gods and goddesses were depicted with specific attributes: Isis, for example, usually was portrayed crowned with a solar disk and horns, and holding a rattle. During the Hellenistic period, old cultural barriers began to break down, and through the process of syncretism, the attributes associated with deities became less fixed. Thus, this bronze statuette, thought to represent Isis, portrays her wearing the measuring bushel of the god Sarapis, and holding in her right hand the cornucopia (representing plenty) and in her left the rudder associated with Fortuna, the goddess of good fortune. Syncretism became so widespread that in some cases, as here, it is not even clear which deity is being represented. How does the depiction of the human form in this statuette compare with that of earlier Egyptian and Greek art? (Vanni/Art Resource, NY)

After reading this chapter, you should be able to answer the following questions:

Why was Alexander the Great able to conquer the Persian Empire?

How and why did the empire of Alexander disintegrate after his death?

In what ways did the Greeks demonstrate an interest in the non-Greek world during the Hellenistic Age?

In what ways was the Hellenistic Age an age of science and technology?

How did the people of the Hellenistic Age use religion to take control of their lives?

D URING THE ARCHAIC AND CLASSICAL AGES, the history of Greece had been focused on the Greek mainland and on great cities such as Athens and Sparta. Believing that their culture was superior to that of all other peoples, the Greeks considered non-Greeks to be barbarians. But wars among themselves during the fifth century B.C.E. weakened the southern Greeks to the point that the Macedonian Greeks to the north, under King Philip II, were able to defeat them. *338 BCE year south*

Led by Philip's son, Alexander the Great, the Greeks conquered the Persians and created a great empire that extended from Greece to western India. After the death of Alexander, however, his empire broke apart. Families of his generals gained control of large parts of it, and smaller powers took over the rest. Wherever the Greeks went, they brought their culture with them, especially by founding colonies. At the same time, they also absorbed much of eastern culture. The result was a hybrid Hellenistic culture that extended from the Strait of Gibraltar all the way to the Indus River valley.

The Hellenistic Age was a period of exploration, scholarship, and scientific investigation. Merchants and

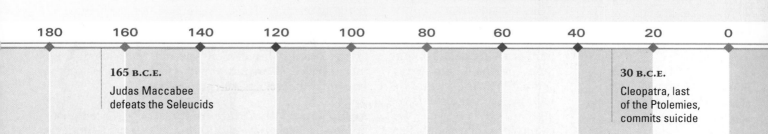

180	160	140	120	100	80	60	40	20	0

165 B.C.E.

Judas Maccabee defeats the Seleucids

30 B.C.E.

Cleopatra, last of the Ptolemies, commits suicide

explorers wrote accounts of their travels to distant places, including India, Africa, and Britain. Hellenistic science, based on observation and experimentation, resulted in discoveries in astronomy and mathematics. Practical applications of scientific findings included the development of water clocks, steam engines, and even primitive computers.

But the opening up of a wider world also created an identity crisis for many Greeks, for whom the old Greek polis no longer provided the same sense of belonging. People now were part of the much larger world of the cosmopolis, or world-city, and had to learn how to relate to the new world around them. Many looked for meaning in religion. Some found comfort in mystery religions that promised an afterlife; others used philosophical beliefs to give them a model for their lives.

Alexander the Great, 387–323 B.C.E.

- ◆ **Why was Alexander able to conquer such a large empire?**
- ◆ **What methods did Alexander use to make his empire secure?**

After the King's Peace of 387 B.C.E., the Greek cities continued to be nonunified, and consequently the northern Greek kingdom of Macedonia imposed its authority over Greece. Led by the Macedonian kings Philip II and Alexander III, the Macedonians then attacked the Persian Empire. Young Alexander, later called the Great, went on to create the greatest empire the world had yet seen.

The Rise of Macedonia

For over six hundred years, from 1100 B.C.E. until 490 B.C.E., the Greeks had been able to develop their culture with little to fear from foreign invaders. One of the reasons they could do so was that the **Macedonians**, who inhabited Macedonia in far northeastern Greece, had served as a buffer zone between the southern Greeks and any hostile peoples farther north.

Macedonia and the Greeks The Macedonians pursued a life of hunting, drinking, and blood feuds. Even though they were of Greek ancestry, because of their difficult-to-understand northern Greek dialect and their rude manners, many southern Greeks were reluctant to accept them as being Greek. In 496 B.C.E., for example, when the Macedonian king Alexander I

Macedonians Northern Greeks who lived in the kingdom of Macedonia.

Philip II (r. 359–338 B.C.E.) King of Macedonia who defeated the Greeks in 338 B.C.E.; father of Alexander the Great.

attempted to participate in the Olympic games, his Greekness was challenged. Only after proving that he was a direct descendant of the Greek hero Hercules was he permitted to compete, and he tied for first in the footrace.

Some Macedonian aristocrats, and especially Macedonian royalty, were much attracted to southern Greek culture and served as patrons for Greek poets and teachers. Socrates was invited to Macedonia, but declined. The poet Euripides accepted an invitation and wrote a play about a Macedonian king before being attacked and torn to pieces by savage Macedonian hunting dogs.

The Macedonians were open to almost constant attack, and, like the Assyrians, in order to survive they eventually developed a powerful army. Because of their constant need for military leaders, the Macedonians, unlike the Greeks to the south, always kept their kings, who were chosen by a warrior assembly comprised of the Macedonian army. Rich silver mines gave the kings a dependable source of income. The Macedonian aristocrats, known as the king's companions, held their land from the king. They made up the Macedonian cavalry, which initially was the only effective part of the Macedonian military.

When the Persians invaded Greece in 480 B.C.E., the Macedonians were unable to resist and became Persian vassals, but they secretly supported the Greeks. They supplied the Athenians with ship timber and ambushed the retreating Persians after the Battle of Plataea. The Macedonians took advantage of the Persian defeat to expand their kingdom. Conquered territory known as spear land was distributed by the king to Macedonian peasants in exchange for their service in an untrained infantry that became known as the king's foot companions.

Philip II and the Macedonian Army Macedonia became a major power during the 350s B.C.E. under the leadership of king **Philip II** (r. 359–338 B.C.E.).

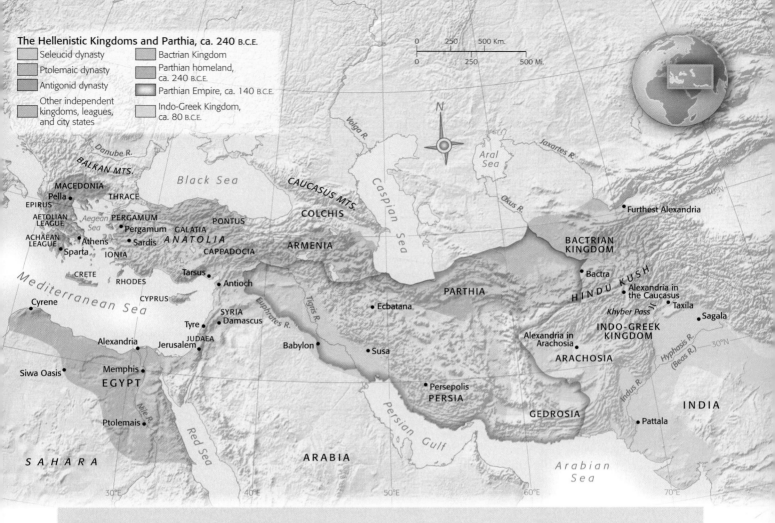

The Hellenistic Kingdoms and Parthia, ca. 240 B.C.E.

- Seleucid dynasty
- Ptolemaic dynasty
- Antigonid dynasty
- Other independent kingdoms, leagues, and city states
- Bactrian Kingdom
- Parthian homeland, ca. 240 B.C.E.
- Parthian Empire, ca. 140 B.C.E.
- Indo-Greek Kingdom, ca. 80 B.C.E.

Map 4.1 **The Hellenistic Kingdoms in 280 B.C.E.** After Alexander's death in 323 B.C.E., his empire broke up into three large kingdoms, ruled by the Antigonid family in Macedonia, the Ptolemies in Egypt, and the Seleucids in Asia. Smaller powers included the kingdom of Pergamum and the island city of Rhodes. © *Cengage Learning*

1. What new areas of the world were opened up to Greek culture during the Hellenistic Age?
2. Which of these Hellenistic kingdoms might have been the most difficult to keep together? Why?
3. How was the geography of areas settled by the Greeks during the Archaic and Classical Ages different from the areas settled in the Hellenistic Age?

Philip molded the infantry into an effective fighting force by rigorously drilling it and arming it with sixteen-foot-long spears. The spears of the men in the front ranks were pointed forward, whereas those of the men in the rear were pointed upward to keep them out of the way and to deflect incoming arrow fire. The tightly packed Macedonian phalanx looked like a porcupine. It could go only in one direction— forward—and it cut through anything in its path. With its heavy cavalry protecting its flanks, the Macedonian army became the most formidable fighting force in the ancient world.

The Unification of Greece

During the fourth century B.C.E., the Greeks continued quarreling. Greek intellectuals suggested that the discord could be ended if the Greeks united politically in the same way that they were united culturally. Doing so would allow them to demonstrate their superiority over the Persians, for the one thing that all Greeks could agree on was dislike for the Persians.

Concepts of Greek Unification The philosopher **Aristotle**, for example, suggested that non-Greeks, like the Persians, were only fit to be slaves. Greeks also believed that an attack on the Persian Empire could help solve a recurrence of overpopulation by providing land for settlement. But Greek thinkers were unsure about how this unity could be created. The Athenian orator Isocrates thought that Philip of Macedon, whom he described as "a Greek, but a leader of barbarians," was the kind of person who could unite the Greeks.

Aristotle (384–322 B.C.E.) Greek philosopher who established scientific classification methods and the school known as the Lyceum.

Ultimately, Philip was drawn into factional conflicts in Greece. In 338 B.C.E., at **Chaeronea** in central Greece, he defeated a Greek coalition led by Athens. The decisive Macedonian cavalry charge was led by his impetuous eighteen-year-old son, Alexander. For the first time, Greece had been conquered. Declining the impossible task of actually ruling Greece directly, Philip formed the **League of Corinth**, a coalition of Greek cities, with himself at its head, whose ostensible purpose was to attack the Persian Empire. Philip hoped to seize Anatolia from the Persians and place Greece's excess population there. But two years later, before he could pursue his plans, Philip was assassinated by a disgruntled Macedonian.

Alexander Becomes King Young Alexander (r. 338–323 B.C.E.) was proclaimed king, and many wondered whether he, only twenty years old, would be able to manage the kingdom, let alone put his father's plans into effect. Several Greek cities revolted. Alexander responded by attacking the ancient city of Thebes. The historian Plutarch not only describes what happened but also provides insight into Alexander's personality: "The city was stormed and sacked. Only one house, that of the poet Pindar, was left standing. Alexander hoped that a severe example might terrify the rest of Greece into obedience. Thirty thousand Thebans were sold as slaves and upward of six thousand were put to the sword." When he felt it was necessary, Alexander could be brutal, and his show of force brought the Greek cities back into line. But Alexander also could be merciful, as Plutarch demonstrates in the story of Timoclea, a respectable Theban matron who was raped and robbed by a Thracian mercenary. When she was asked if she had any other valuables, she said they were hidden in a well, and "when the greedy Thracian stooped to look in the well, she pushed him in, and then flung great stones on him, until she had killed him." Alexander was so taken by her bravery that he let her and her children go free.

Alexander's Wars

Alexander proved any remaining doubters wrong. Believing himself the son of Zeus, he planned to conquer not just Anatolia but the whole world, all the way to the great eastern ocean that geographers believed lay on the far side of India.

Alexander Defeats the Persians In 334 B.C.E., Alexander led his army into Anatolia. He had only 35,000 men, whereas against him the Persians could raise 250,000. But Alexander took the Persians by surprise, before they had time to assemble their entire army. Anatolia was defended only by an army of Greek mercenaries, who put up a very stiff resistance. At the Battle of the **Granicus River**, as in every battle, Alexander was in the thick of the fighting. According to Plutarch, one of the opposing mercenaries "gave Alexander such a blow with his battle-axe on the helmet that he cut off its crest and the edge of the weapon touched the hair of his head." Only after a desperate fight were the mercenaries defeated.

By 333 B.C.E., the Persian king **Darius III** (r. 338–331 B.C.E.) had been able to mobilize only the western half of his empire. Alexander met the Persian army at **Issus** in northern Syria. The sight of the advancing Macedonian phalanx sent Darius fleeing, and his army fled with him. Taken captive were Darius's mother, wife, and daughters, who were fearful of what would befall them at Alexander's hands. Alexander gained much credit for receiving them kindly. Before pursuing Darius, Alexander thought it prudent to occupy Egypt and the eastern Mediterranean coast so as not to leave any enemies in his rear. Most cities surrendered peacefully and were well treated, but the island city of Tyre held out, emboldened by Alexander's lack of a navy. Alexander used eight valuable months building an earth and stone jetty out to the city, which he then stormed and sacked. In Egypt, Alexander was welcomed as the pharaoh and as the son of Ra and the son of Zeus. At this point, Darius offered to turn over to Alexander all of the Persian Empire west of the Euphrates, but Alexander declined, for he had much more ambitious goals.

Alexander advanced into Mesopotamia in 331 B.C.E. By then, Darius had been able to assemble the full Persian army. The armies met on a flat plain at **Gaugamela**. The Macedonians were greatly outnumbered, and the battle began badly for them. Their cavalry was driven off by the Persian cavalry, leaving the flanks and rear of the phalanx open to attack. But at this point, thinking the battle was won, the Persian cavalry rode off to loot the Macedonian camp. Alexander then led a cavalry charge directly at Darius, who once again fled from the battlefield. His army followed, and the Persians had lost their last chance for organized resistance.

Alexander now laid claim to the throne of the Persian Empire. Like foreign conquerors of the past, he assumed all the titles of Near Eastern monarchs, becoming the Great King of Persia and the King of Sumer and Akkad. When he occupied the Persian capital of Persepolis, he discovered 180,000 talents (over 10,000 tons) of silver hoarded in the Persian treasury, which he used to pay his own mounting expenses. Indeed, Alexander issued so many silver coins that the price of silver plummeted throughout the Mediterranean world. When Persepolis burned

Chaeronea Battle in which Philip II of Macedon defeated the Greeks in 338 B.C.E.

League of Corinth Organization of Greek cities led by the king of Macedonia for the purpose of attacking Persia.

Granicus River Battle in northern Anatolia in which Alexander the Great defeated the Persians' Greek mercenaries in 334 B.C.E.

Darius III (r. 338–331 B.C.E.) Last ruler of the Persian Empire.

Issus Battle in northwestern Syria in which Alexander the Great defeated Darius III in 333 B.C.E.

Gaugamela Battle in Mesopotamia in which Alexander the Great defeated the full Persian army in 331 B.C.E.

Scala/Art Resource, NY

The walls of the homes of well-to-do Greeks, not to mention Romans, would be covered with mosaics and frescoes depicting scenes from Greek mythology and history. This mosaic of the first century C.E. from the buried Roman city of Pompeii depicts the Battle of Issus in 333 B.C.E. between Alexander the Great and the Persian king Darius III. Here, Darius, standing in his chariot and looking worried, looks back at Alexander pursuing him from the left. Darius's charioteer resolutely whips the horses into flight. Meanwhile, in between Darius and Alexander, Darius's brother Oxyathres heroically holds off Alexander to allow Darius to escape. Alexander's breastplate depicts the legendary snake-haired Medusa, whose look turned people into stone. This was the crucial moment of the battle, for when Darius fled, his army then followed and Alexander won a great victory. What does this painting tell you about how Darius was portrayed in ancient art?

soon afterward, some claimed it was in retribution for the Persians' burning of Athens in 480 B.C.E., but others said it was an accident.

Alexander Expands His Empire It took Alexander four more years to conquer the rest of the Persian Empire. **Bactria**, modern Afghanistan, proved especially difficult, but Alexander eventually won the allegiance of the natives by his bravery and magnanimity as well as by his marriage to a local princess named Roxanne. In 327 B.C.E., not content with having conquered the Persian Empire, Alexander invaded India. The Indians resisted desperately, village by village. Alexander himself was wounded many times. In one hard-fought battle, the Macedonians defeated Porus, an Indian king whose army included war elephants. Alexander always emerged victorious, but the Macedonian army had been away from home for eight years, many soldiers had died, and the survivors were tired of fighting. With every hill they crossed, they expected to see the eastern ocean, but all they found were more hostile Indians.

The exhausted army finally refused to take one step farther east. Alexander sulked in his tent for three days

and then agreed to return home, but not the way they had come, for that would look too much like a retreat. The Macedonians, therefore, advanced down the Indus River valley, fighting every step of the way. In one encounter, Alexander was so badly wounded that he nearly died. After reaching the Indian Ocean, the army had to make a difficult trek along the desert coast of the Persian Gulf to get back to Persia. Many never made it back at all. Alexander finally returned to Persia in 324 B.C.E.

Alexander's Empire

In only ten years, Alexander had been able to create the largest empire the world had yet known. He next attempted to consolidate his territorial gains.

Alexander Consolidates His Rule To provide some Greek presence in the conquered territories, and land for thousands of army veterans who were disabled, ill, or whose services were no longer needed, Alexander founded more than seventy colonies throughout

Bactria Modern Afghanistan, a center of Greek civilization in the east.

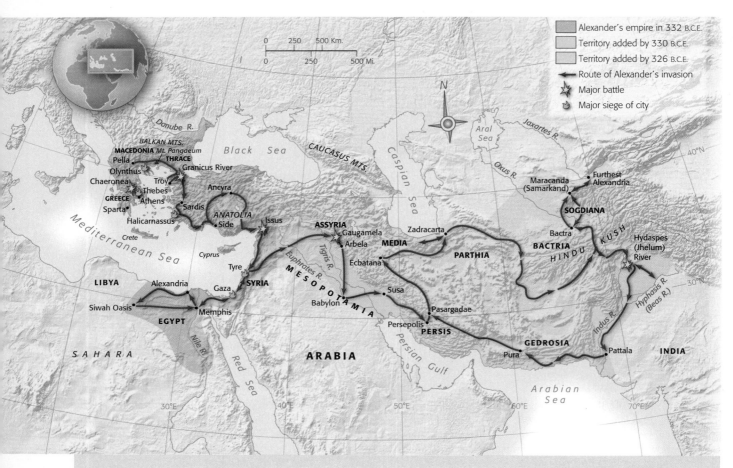

1. How was the geographical coverage of Alexander's empire the same as the coverage of the Persian Empire? How was it different?

2. What geographical factors might have made it difficult for Alexander to hold his empire together?

the empire. All of them were named **Alexandria** except for one that he named after his horse, Bucephalus. Alexander's colonies extended from Alexandria in Egypt to the one called Last Alexandria in Afghanistan. They began what can be called the third wave of Greek colonization, which lasted from about 332 to 250 B.C.E. Unlike the first two waves, which resulted in many seacoast colonies, these colonies were inland. After the fighting was over, Greek settlers continued to emigrate to Asia. The colonies brought Greeks and Greek culture to the far corners of the Asian world.

In spite of the colonies, there were far too few Macedonians to be able to administer the empire directly. Alexander realized that he would need the cooperation of the conquered peoples and therefore adopted the Persian model of showing respect for native

Alexandria Name given to Greek colonies established by Alexander the Great, the most famous of which was in Egypt.

customs. He copied the Persian method of administration by dividing his empire up into satrapies, and he integrated native peoples into his government. Furthermore, Alexander developed a vision for unifying the Greek and Persian peoples. He already had recruited 30,000 Bactrians into his army and trained them in Macedonian fighting styles. He also adopted Persian dress and customs and attempted to introduce the Persians to the Macedonians by having 5,000 Macedonians marry 5,000 Persian women. He himself took a second wife, Statira, the daughter of Darius.

Many conservative Macedonians objected to Alexander's adoption of so many Persian customs, and when Alexander suggested he would like his subjects to prostrate themselves before him, in the Persian manner, the Macedonians simply refused. But they could not resist the effects of their exposure to eastern culture. Most chose to remain in the east, and those who did return home brought eastern culture and customs with them.

In one way or another, therefore, the Greeks were assimilating the ancient culture of the Near Eastern world.

In 323 B.C.E., Alexander established his capital at Babylon, on the borderland between the eastern and western halves of his empire. Ambassadors came from far and wide to congratulate him on his victories and to establish good relations. There were representatives not only from the powerful trading city of Carthage in North Africa but also from Rome, a city in central Italy that was just beginning to expand. Meanwhile, Alexander's plans to conquer the world continued. He intended first to attack the Arabs of Arabia and then to expand west into the Mediterranean, all the way to the Strait of Gibraltar.

The Death of Alexander Alexander's Babylonian astrologers, however, had received bad omens and were concerned for his safety. They even seated a commoner on Alexander's throne to absorb the bad luck they saw coming for him. In spite of this precaution, after a typical Macedonian drinking party, Alexander

A first-century C.E. wall fresco from Pompeii depicts the marriage of Alexander the Great to Statira, the daughter of the Persian king Darius III, in 324 B.C.E. Alexander is portrayed as Ares, the god of war, and Statira as Aphrodite, the goddess of beauty and sex, reflecting not only the idea that powerful monarchs shared some of the divinity and the qualities of the gods but also the mythological tale that Ares and Aphrodite were lovers. Statira thus became Alexander's second wife, in addition to Roxanne. Why do you think Alexander decided to also marry Statira?

Vanni/Art Resource, NY

became very ill and died a few days later. Suggested causes of his death have ranged from the cumulative effects of past war wounds to malaria to poison. Almost immediately, Alexander passed into legend, remembered as Alexander the Great. Many believed that he became a god. Exotic tales of his adventures, known as the **Alexander Romance**, were widely circulated and are still popular more than a thousand years later.

Checking In

By yourself or with a partner, explain the significance of each of the following selected key terms:

Macedonians	Issus
Philip II	Gaugamela
League of Corinth	Bactria
Darius III	Alexandria

The Hellenistic World, 323–30 B.C.E.

- **What happened to Alexander's empire after his death?**
- **How did Greek views of the non-Greek world change during the Hellenistic period?**

After the death of Alexander, his empire was divided among the families of three of his generals, the Antigonids, the Ptolemies, and the Seleucids. The expansion of the Greek world into Africa and Asia brought Greeks into contact with many non-Greek cultures, and there was a growing popular interest in foreign places. Greek explorers and merchants wrote accounts of the peoples they encountered. The resulting awareness and appreciation of other cultures gave rise to an amalgamation of cultures known as Hellenistic civilization.

The Hellenistic Kingdoms

Alexander did not name an heir. As he was dying, he was asked who should inherit his kingdom. Some thought that he answered, "The strongest man." Alexander's only legitimate son, Alexander IV, was not born to Roxanne until after his death. The infant was hardly able to rule, and Alexander's generals began to carve out pieces of the empire for themselves.

The Division of Alexander's Empire By 280 B.C.E., after years of civil war, the empire had been divided into three main kingdoms ruled by the families of three of Alexander's generals. The period between the death of Alexander and the

Alexander Romance Legends about Alexander the Great circulated after his death.

Plutarch and Arrian Describe Alexander's Mass Marriages

One of Alexander's goals was to integrate the Macedonian and Persian populations. Given past incompatibilities between Greeks and Persians, this would not have been an easy task. He decided that intermarriage would be a good way for the two peoples to get to know each other. He himself married two eastern women, and in 324 B.C.E. he supported the marriages of 5,000 Greek men to 5,000 Persian women. The following accounts are from two Greek historians who wrote in the second century C.E., during the Roman Empire. Plutarch, in his Life of Alexander, describes the events associated with Alexander's marriage to Roxanne in 327 B.C.E. Arrian of Nicomedia, in Campaigns of Alexander, reports Alexander's marriage to the daughter of the Persian king Darius III in early 324 B.C.E., after he had returned from India.

❶ Was this a sensible strategy?

❷ How did Alexander display his respect for native customs?

Plutarch

❶ Now, also, he more and more accommodated himself in his way of living to that of the natives, wisely considering that it would be wiser to depend on the good-will which might arise from intermixture and association as a means of maintaining tranquility, than on force and compulsion. As for his marriage with Roxanne, whose youthfulness and beauty had charmed him at a drinking entertainment, where he first happened to see her taking part in a dance, it was, indeed a love affair, yet it seemed at the same time to be conducive to the object he had in hand. ❷ For it gratified the conquered people to see him choose a wife from among themselves, and it made them feel the most lively affection for him, to find that in the only passion that he was overcome he yet restrained himself until he could obtain her in a lawful and honorable way.

end of the last of these kingdoms, from 323 until 30 B.C.E., is known as the **Hellenistic Age**.

Hellenistic Age (based on Greek for "Greek-like") Period from 323 until 30 B.C.E. that resulted in a mixing of Greek and eastern culture.

Antigonids Family that ruled Macedonia after the death of Alexander the Great.

Ptolemies Family that ruled Egypt after the death of Alexander the Great.

Cleopatra (r. 69–30 B.C.E.) Queen and pharaoh of Egypt, last of the Ptolemies; committed suicide in 30 B.C.E.

The Antigonids of Macedonia The Macedonian homeland fell to the **Antigonids**, the descendants of Alexander's general Antigonus. But Macedonia was no longer a world power. The constant departure of soldiers had left the land depopulated, and the wars also had drained the economy. The best that the Antigonid kings could hope for was to remain the strongest power in Greece, and they did this by establishing strategic fortresses that kept the Greeks under control.

Another Antigonid concern was the growing power of Rome, just across the Adriatic Sea.

The Ptolemies of Egypt Alexander's general Ptolemy seized control of Egypt, the wealthiest and most geographically secure satrapy of Alexander's empire. His family, the **Ptolemies**, was confronted by the need to rule over two populations, one Greek and one Egyptian. To their Greek subjects, the Ptolemaic kings were Macedonian kings and successors to Alexander. But to the Egyptians, they were a new dynasty of pharaohs. Like pharaohs of the past, Ptolemaic kings married their sisters and were worshiped as if they were gods. Ptolemy II, for example, took an Egyptian name meaning "Loved by Amon, Chosen by Ra." He married his sister Arsinoë and was known after his death as Ptolemy the Sister-Lover.

Ptolemaic queens with names like Berenice, Arsinoë, and **Cleopatra** often were virtual rulers of the kingdom. According to one source, Arsinoë accompanied her troops and rallied them when a battle was

Arrian of Nicomedia

❸ Then Alexander also celebrated weddings in Persia, both his own and those of his Companions. He himself married Statira, the eldest of Darius' daughters. He had already married previously Roxanne, the daughter of Oxyartes of Bactria. He gave Drypetis to Hephaestion, she too a daughter of Darius—his intention was that the children of Hephaestion should be cousins to his own children.... To Ptolemy the bodyguard and to Eumenes the royal secretary he gave the daughters of Artabazus, Artacama to one and Artonis to the other. To Nearchus he gave the daughter of Barsine and Mentor, and to Seleucus he gave Apame, the daughter of Spitamenes of Bactria.

❹ Similarly he gave to the other Companions the noblest daughters of the Persians and Medes, some 80 in all. The marriages were celebrated according to Persian custom. Chairs were placed for the bridegrooms, and the brides came in and sat down, each by the side of her groom. They took them by the hand and kissed them. **❺** The king began the ceremony, for all the weddings took place together. More than any action of Alexander this seemed to show a popular and comradely spirit. After receiving their brides, the bridegrooms led them away, and to all Alexander gave a dowry. And as for all the Macedonians who had already married Asian women, Alexander ordered a list of their names to be drawn up; they numbered over 10,000, and Alexander offered them gifts for the wedding.

Source: Reprinted by permission of the publishers and the Trustees of the Loeb Classical Library from *Arrian: Volume II*, Loeb Classical Library® Volume 269, translated by P. A. Brunt on the basis of E. Iliff Robson's edition, Cambridge, Mass.: Harvard University Press, Copyright © 1929, 1976 by the President and Fellows of Harvard College. The Loeb Classical Library® is a registered trademark of the President and Fellows of Harvard College.

❸ Why are these particular women being married to Alexander's most important generals?

❹ Why did Alexander follow Persian rather than Greek custom?

❺ Do you think performing these marriages was an effective way of uniting the Macedonian and Persian peoples?

going badly: "She exhorted them to defend themselves and their children and wives bravely, promising to give them each two minas [about two pounds] of gold if they won the battle. And so it came about that the enemy was routed, and many captives were taken."

The Ptolemaic administration of Egypt was very centralized. The top officials were Greeks, but lower-level bureaucrats, such as scribes, often were Egyptians. The economy was closely supervised by an extensive bureaucracy to ensure maximum income for the government. The kings sponsored irrigation, drainage, and land reclamation projects. To attract Greek settlers, the Ptolemies offered them land grants on the condition that they also provide military service. These Greek farmers were scattered throughout Egypt and, as a result, there was growing integration between the Greek and Egyptian populations.

The Seleucid Kingdom The Asian parts of Alexander's empire fell into the hands of the **Seleucids**, the family of Alexander's general Seleucus. The Seleucid kingdom was the least unified and the most difficult to hold together, for it extended from Anatolia all the way to India. It contained a huge non-Greek population, and Seleucid kings found it hard to attract additional Greek settlers. More than any of Alexander's successors, the Seleucids knew they had to conciliate their subjects. Thus, after Alexander died, Seleucus was one of the few Macedonians who did not divorce his Persian wife. Understanding that he could not hope to hold India, Seleucus traded his Indian territories to an Indian king in exchange for five hundred war elephants. Other Seleucid territories were controlled by making alliances with powerful local leaders. For example, in Mesopotamia, the Seleucids allied themselves with priests who were afraid of a renewed Persian takeover. Elsewhere, native rulers were allowed local rule as long as they provided tribute and military aid. The Seleucid army was composed

Seleucids Family that ruled Asia after the death of Alexander the Great.

Visual Connection Archive

A relief from Tanis in Egypt shows king Ptolemy II (r. 283–246 B.C.E.), portrayed as an Egyptian pharaoh, and his wife and sister Arsinoë II, depicted as the goddess Isis, thus illustrating the efforts of the Macedonian rulers of Egypt to demonstrate their respect for Egyptian customs. Following Egyptian tradition, Ptolemy also took the name "Loved by Amon, Chosen by Ra." For their Greek subjects, they would have been kings and queens in the Greek tradition. How would the typical ancient Greek have felt about Greek kings and queens being portrayed as Egyptians?

not of Greeks, as in Macedonia and Egypt, but mostly of contingents recruited from the subject peoples, as the Persians had done.

In spite of Seleucid efforts, parts of their kingdom slipped away. Beginning about 250 B.C.E., for example, an Indo-European people known as the **Parthians** occupied Iran. They split the Seleucid kingdom in half, leaving the Bactrian Greek colonies in complete isolation.

Parthians Indo-European people that invaded Iran beginning in 250 B.C.E.

inflation Process by which the cost of goods and services increases and the value of money declines.

market economy Economy in which goods and services are exchanged between buyers and sellers.

Hellenistic Life During the Hellenistic period, concepts of rule changed. Greek city-states, including Greek colonies, continued to be administered by oligarchies and democracies as in the past, but nearly all were incorporated into, or under the influence of, a Hellenistic kingdom ruled by an absolute monarch. As a consequence of their great authority, Hellenistic kings and queens, like Alexander before them, were believed to have godlike qualities, a concept previously foreign to the Greeks but consistent with Near Eastern thought. Kings and queens often were granted divine honors not only after their deaths but even while they were living. One Seleucid king, for example, took the title God Made Manifest.

Hellenistic economic life also functioned on a grand scale. The great infusion of Persian gold and silver into the Mediterranean world brought with it not only **inflation**, caused by the pouring of millions of silver coins into the economy, but also increased prosperity, caused by the greater availability of money to more people. Many Greeks, not just rulers, became wealthy. Goods were manufactured and foodstuffs grown not just for local consumption but also for export, creating a **market economy**. Huge estates in Anatolia and Sicily, worked by hundreds or thousands of slaves, produced grain for cities throughout the Hellenistic world.

Eventually, all the Hellenistic kingdoms fell to Rome. The last was Ptolemaic Egypt. In 30 B.C.E., the Macedonian queen and pharaoh Cleopatra admitted defeat and committed suicide, ending not only the Hellenistic Age but also a line of pharaohs that stretched back three thousand years.

Hellenistic Cities

Hellenistic civilization, like the civilization of the Archaic and Classical Ages, was built around cities that served as commercial centers. But Hellenistic cities outside Greece proper were different in that almost all were ruled by kings and no longer were centers of independent political life. They also were the places where Greeks settled, preserved their learning and culture, and retained their identity. Hellenistic monarchs also were great supporters of scholarly studies, and some major Hellenistic cities became famous centers of learning.

Hellenistic Colonies The Seleucids, for example, realized that their Greek population was far too small to disperse throughout the countryside, so they continued Alexander's policy of establishing colonies that could be centers of Seleucid rule. Greek colonies could be found across the length and breadth of the vast Seleucid territories. The most important Seleucid city was the great city of Antioch in Syria, named after the Seleucid king Antiochus I. It became the core of the Seleucid kingdom, with a reputation as a center for literature and the arts. By the first century B.C.E., it had a population of five hundred thousand.

The Hellenistic colonies left a curious legacy in the easternmost part of the Seleucid kingdom. After 250 B.C.E., the Greek cities of Bactria were cut off from the rest of the Greek world by the Parthians and forgotten by the western Greeks. Against all the odds, however, they maintained their Greek way of life as best as they could. They enlisted native help and incorporated native customs much more extensively than any other Greeks. For example, their coins carried lettering in both the Greek and Indian languages. And when the Bactrian king Menander invaded India, not only was he supported by the local Buddhists but, according to legend, he even became a Buddhist himself. He was later considered one of the four great Buddhist rulers of India. The last Greek rulers in India finally succumbed to invaders from central Asia about 50 B.C.E. The Greek kings of Bactria and India are known primarily through their coins and the archaeological remains of their cities.

In Egypt, the greater number of Greek settlers allowed the Ptolemies to continue the ancient Egyptian custom of having farmers live in villages rather than in cities. The exception was the capital city of the Ptolemaic kingdom, Alexandria, founded by Alexander in 332 B.C.E. on the Mediterranean coast at the mouth of the Nile and the only Macedonian colony in Egypt. The harbor entrance to the city was marked by a gigantic 384-foot-tall lighthouse that became one of the Seven Wonders of the Ancient World. Its mirror used sunlight or light from a fire to cast a beam of light that could be seen for more than thirty-five miles.

Within a hundred years, Alexandria was the largest city in the world, with well over half a million inhabitants, including many Jews of the Diaspora. It became the cultural capital of the Greek world. There the Ptolemies founded the **Museum**, a university named after the Muses, the goddesses of learning, where a community of scholars pursued literary and scientific studies. Associated with the Museum was the great library of Alexandria, where books were deposited from throughout a Greek world that now extended from Spain to India.

Small Hellenistic Powers Smaller powers also established important Hellenistic cities. The small kingdom of **Pergamum** in western Anatolia broke away from the Seleucids and was centered on a city of the same name. The kings of Pergamum saw themselves as the inheritors of the cultural traditions of Athens and built a massive acropolis modeled on the Athenian one. The huge marble Altar of Pergamum depicted in sculpture the origin of the gods and later appeared in the Christian book of Revelation, where it was described as "Satan's Throne." Pergamum also became a center of learning, with a library second only to the one in Alexandria and a famous school of medicine. One of the goods exported from Pergamum was *pergamene*, modern **parchment**, a writing material developed from stretched sheepskins at a time when there was a shortage of papyrus from Egypt.

South of Pergamum, the city of **Rhodes** controlled an island of the same name located off the southwestern coast of Anatolia. As the primary stopping point for commercial traffic traveling along the Anatolian coast, Rhodes became rich on harbor tolls. Its coins, which depicted a rose (*Rhodos* means "rose" in Greek), circulated throughout the Mediterranean world. In the early third century B.C.E., to commemorate a military victory, the city constructed a 110-foot-tall statue of the sun god known as the Colossus of Rhodes, another of the Seven Wonders of the Ancient World. To ensure the safety of the cargoes that passed through the city and to suppress pirates, Rhodes maintained a powerful navy. Like other Hellenistic cities, Rhodes became a center of learning, providing instruction in philosophy, rhetoric, literature, and science.

Voyages of Exploration

Greek expansion during the Hellenistic period brought the Greeks into direct contact with a multitude of foreign cultures, stimulating a great interest in geographical exploration. A popular genre of travel literature known as the **periplus** described the strange places and peoples that travelers encountered in the course of their journeys. These works often were of a practical nature. Many were commissioned by rulers interested in the nature of the territories to which they had laid claim or were authored by merchants seeking the best places to trade and the safest routes for getting there. In contrast to earlier geographical accounts, which had been based on myth and legend, these were based on firsthand observations. Much of the impetus for these works came from the campaigns of Alexander the Great, especially his travels in India.

The Voyages of Nearchus In 325 B.C.E., Alexander's admiral, **Nearchus**, was ordered to survey the coast between India and Persia. He did so in great detail, and after his return, around 310 B.C.E., he wrote a book about India. He told of trees so large that one of them could shade ten thousand people, and he discussed the habits of elephants, which Mediterranean peoples found fascinating: "If there is an intelligent animal, it is the elephant. I myself saw an elephant clanging the cymbals while other elephants danced; two cymbals were fastened to the player's forelegs and one on his trunk.

Museum (from Greek for "home of the Muses") University established in Alexandria by the Ptolemies.

Pergamum Small Hellenistic city-kingdom in western Anatolia.

parchment (based on Greek *pergamene*, "from Pergamum") Writing material made from cured and stretched animal skins.

Rhodes (from Greek *rhodos*, "rose") Island city-state located off the southwestern coast of Anatolia.

periplus (Greek for "sailing around") Hellenistic genre of travel literature.

Nearchus Admiral of Alexander the Great who in the fourth century B.C.E. wrote a book about India.

As he rhythmically beat the cymbal on either leg in turn the dancers danced in a circle." During the voyage in the Indian Ocean, Nearchus traveled so far south, he reported, that at noon the sun cast no shadow at all and at night some of the familiar stars could not be seen. According to another writer, Nearchus once encountered a pod of spouting whales, and when the rowers of the warships became distressed at the sight of these huge beasts, "Nearchus signaled them to turn the ships' bows toward the whales as if to give battle and to raise their battle cry and make a great deal of noise. When they neared the monsters, they shouted with all the power of their throats, and the bugles blared, and the rowers made the greatest splashing with their oars. So the whales were frightened and dove into the depths."

The Periplus of the Red Sea A report of a voyage along the coast of the Red Sea (which extended all the way to India in this version) was written in the first century B.C.E. by an anonymous merchant who catalogued market towns and the kinds of goods that could be traded. He reported that, after leaving Egypt, a traveler encountered along the east coast of Africa the fish-eaters, the Berbers (a variation on the word *barbarians*), the flesh-eaters, and the calf-eaters. The merchant traveled no farther, however, than the Horn of Africa (modern Somalia), writing, "Beyond these places the unexplored ocean curves around toward the west, and running to the south of Africa it mingles with the western sea." A voyage down the coast of Arabia, on the other side of the Red Sea, was rather more dangerous. According to the merchant, "The country inland is peopled by rascally men who plunder those who approach the coast and enslave those who survive shipwrecks." Beyond this, in modern Yemen, lay the "frankincense country." Producing frankincense, one of the most sought-after spices of antiquity, was a dangerous business. The merchant noted, "The frankincense is gathered by the king's slaves. These places are very unhealthy, and almost always fatal to those working there." From there, the merchant sailed past Arabia toward India, reaching the Indus River. In India, the merchant obtained turquoise, lapis lazuli, silk, and indigo in exchange for frankincense, gold, and silver. Finally, the merchant made the first known western mention of China, here called Thinae, saying, "Silk, silk yarn, and silk cloth are exported by way of the river Ganges. But this land is not easy of access; few men come from there, and seldom."

Voyages into the Atlantic Ocean Other merchants traveled west, out of the Mediterranean and into the Atlantic. One voyage story told of a fifth-century B.C.E.

Modern Ai-Khanum in Afghanistan, shown here with the mountains of the Hindu Kush looming in the background, is the site of a Hellenistic city that was located on the very fringes of the world known to the Greeks. It included temples, colonnaded walks, a theater, gymnasium, and the other amenities of a Greek polis intended to make Greek colonists feel at home. The ancient name of the city is unknown, although it may have been one of the many "Alexandrias" founded by Alexander the Great. It later was one of the centers of the Greek kingdom of Bactria. The city was destroyed around 140 B.C.E. by Indo-European invaders from central Asia, and not rediscovered until 1961. It was excavated by French archaeologists between 1964 and 1978; the site was later looted under the Taliban. How do you think the Greek settlers in such a place would have coped with being so far away from their homeland in the midst of peoples so different from themselves?

expedition by the Carthaginian sailor **Hanno** down the west coast of Africa, as far as the equator or beyond. Sailing up one river, Hanno encountered crocodiles and what he called hippopotamuses, a word meaning "water horses." At a later landing point, he wrote, "We could see nothing but forest by day, but at night many fires were seen and we heard the sound of flutes and the beating of drums and tambourines, which made a great noise. We were struck with terror and our fortune-tellers advised us leave the island." Farther along, he reported encountering an "island full of savages. They had hairy bodies and the interpreters called them gorillas." If this account is true, Hanno must have gone as far as the Congo River. According to one account, Hanno eventually turned back because of a lack of supplies, but another version has him sailing around Africa and eventually arriving in Arabia.

Finally, a Greek sailor from Marseilles named **Pytheas** described a voyage he made up the Atlantic coast of Europe around 300 B.C.E. looking for a sea route to sources of tin and amber. He traveled to Britain, which he called Albion, and then continued even farther north to a place called Thule, six days' sail north of Britain, which has been identified as the Shetland Islands or even Iceland, places previously unknown to the Greeks. Pytheas noted that on June 21, the sun never set, suggesting that he even reached the Arctic Circle. He described sailing conditions in which there was no distinction between the earth, air, and sea, perhaps a reference to a very thick fog. He also was the first Greek to report on the tides and to connect them with the motion of the moon.

Checking In

By yourself or with a partner, explain the significance of each of the following selected key terms:

Hellenistic Age	Parthians
Antigonids	Museum
Ptolemies	Pergamum
Seleucids	periplus

Hellenistic Culture and Science

◆ **In what ways did Hellenistic scientists use methods different from those of earlier philosophers?**

◆ **What was the nature of Hellenistic scientific discoveries?**

The incorporation of the Persian and even the Indian worlds into the Greek experience brought a new form of Greek culture called Hellenistic culture, through which the Greeks lost the Greek-centered view of the world of the Classical Age and learned to value other peoples and cultures. The old distinction between the

Hellenes and barbarians became less clear as populations and cultures from Greece to the Indus River valley became mixed. As during the Archaic Age, eastern influences in art, government, and thought flowed into Greece. Greek culture became a hybrid, an amalgamation of western and eastern culture that gave western and eastern people new common ground.

Art and Literature

Whereas classical Greek culture was marked by general agreement among the Greeks about what constituted excellence, Hellenistic culture was characterized by variety and **syncretism**, a melding of elements of different cultures. The cultural assimilation that came with the Hellenistic Age was affirmed by the Roman historian **Livy**, who commented, "The Macedonians, who have colonies in Egypt and Babylon and elsewhere in the world, have become Syrians, Parthians, and Egyptians."

Hellenistic Art In the world of art, the simplicity and clean lines of classical art were replaced by ornate Hellenistic extravagance. In architecture, for example, by the mid-fourth century B.C.E. the floral Corinthian column capital replaced the simple Doric and Ionic capitals as the preferred style for columns. In the eastern Greek colonies, eastern and western artistic traditions merged. Religious syncretism occurred in Egypt, where, to provide common ground between Greeks and Egyptians, the Ptolemies created a composite god, **Serapis**, who had attributes of the Greek Zeus and the Egyptian Osiris.

Hellenistic Literature Hellenistic literature, on the other hand, could not rival the literature of the Archaic and Classical Ages. Form became more important than content, quantity more important than quality, and writers were more concerned with appealing to a larger audience. Comedies no longer dealt with current events but were concerned with everyday domestic life and were full of slapstick. Tales of the absurd multiplied, such as an account of a country where it was so cold that words spoken in the winter immediately froze and were not heard until they thawed out in the spring. Stories that combined love and adventure resulted in an early form of the novel. The primary literary contribution

Hanno Fifth-century B.C.E. Carthaginian explorer who wrote of a voyage down the west coast of Africa.

Pytheas Greek sailor from Marseilles who wrote about his voyage to Britain around 300 B.C.E.

syncretism (from Greek for "bringing together") The mixing of elements of different cultures or religions.

Livy (59 B.C.E.–7 C.E.) Roman historian who wrote the history of Rome.

Serapis Composite Egyptian god with aspects of the Greek god Zeus and the Egyptian god Osiris.

A head of the Egyptian god Serapis, who developed during the Hellenistic Age as a combination of the Egyptian Osiris and Greek Zeus, demonstrates the attempts of the Ptolemies to create a meeting ground between Greek and Egyptian culture. The hairstyle and beard are reflective of Zeus, but the kindly facial expression reminds one of Osiris. It was found in the harbor of Alexandria during recent underwater excavations. In what ways does this composite god demonstrate how Greek feelings about the cultures of other peoples changed during the Hellenistic period?

Sandro Vannini/Corbis

created in Hellenistic times became the models for all later ones. In general, Hellenistic literature is best known for its attention to practical applications. Geographical treatises, scientific thought, school handbooks, and philosophical systems all would have great influence on western civilization. At the same time, a form of Greek known as **koinē** Greek became the standard language of both commerce and intellectual discourse throughout the Mediterranean and Near Eastern worlds. These regions became culturally united in a way they had never been before and never would be again.

Aristotle and the Rise of Practical Philosophy

During the Hellenistic period, Greek scientific thought turned from theory based on speculation and convincing argument to theory based on observation and experimentation.

The Teaching of Aristotle The first practical scientific thinker was Aristotle, a native of northern Greece whose father had been the personal physician and friend of King Philip II of Macedonia. After studying medicine with his father, the young Aristotle pursued his studies at Plato's Academy in Athens. He taught for a while at the Academy and then moved to Ionia, where he turned his attention to biology and began his practice of collecting observations. He then returned to Macedonia, where he is said to have tutored Alexander the Great. Eventually, in 335 B.C.E., Aristotle returned to Athens and founded his own school, called the **Lyceum**.

As Plato's most influential pupil, Aristotle reacted against the view that scientific problems could be solved simply by contemplation. Aristotle's method of understanding the universe and human behavior was to collect evidence, analyze it, and then come to conclusions based on observation. Rather than focusing purely on theory, as did the Academy, the Lyceum undertook broad scientific study of the real world of nature. Whereas Plato's Academy looked for a unified system that would explain everything in the world, Aristotle's interests were much more eclectic. He and his pupils believed in categorizing and subdividing all the fields of study and looking at each one individually. His work on animals and plants, for example, resulted in the categorization of different kinds of species. Aristotle published books on biology and zoology, astronomy, chemistry, poetry, rhetoric, mathematics, logic (a field he virtually invented), ethics, politics, sociology, and economics. His book *The Politics* formulated his own idea of an ideal society that was not theoretical, like Plato's, but fixed firmly in the real world and based on a collection of the constitutions of many different governments, including even those of barbarians like the Carthaginians. Aristotle believed that people could govern themselves, but only if they were virtuous.

of the Hellenistic Age, however, was the genre of biography. This was an age of great personalities, and accounts of the lives of great men and women were very popular.

In academic circles, creative literature gave way to scholarship. Many authors became more interested in collecting and cataloguing the learning of the past than in dealing with grand, timeless issues of meaning and morality. Hellenistic scholars collected and edited the literature of Greek antiquity, such as the *Iliad* and *Odyssey*, creating editions that, by and large, are still in use. Likewise, the grammars and dictionaries

koinē (Greek for "common") Common version of Greek in the Hellenistic Age.

Lyceum School of philosophy established in Athens by Aristotle.

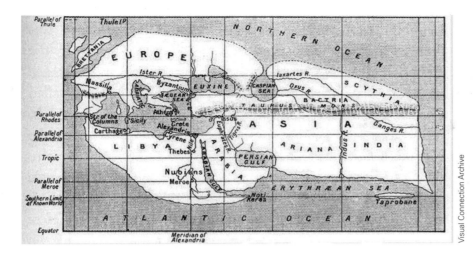

A reconstruction of Eratosthenes's map of the world from the third century B.C.E. In Eratosthenes's model, the world had three more or less equally sized continents—Europe, Asia, and Libya (Africa)—and was surrounded by a single large ocean. In this view, Asia and the east, through India at least, took up nearly half of the known world. But how well do you think this part of the world was known to the Greeks? And, in general, to what degree does Eratosthenes's map correspond to modern maps of these areas?

Visual Connection Archive

Aristotle and the Scientific Method Plato had denied the importance of change by arguing that the transitory things of this world are just imperfect reflections of the world of perfect unchanging forms. In contrast, Aristotle thought that the world was defined by the manner in which things do change. Every change, he believed, occurs for a reason, by means of some material cause and for some purpose. There was little room for gods in Aristotle's universe. He acknowledged that some kind of divinity had originally set the universe in motion, but it then became self-perpetuating. He created a method for understanding the world based on observation, logic, and common sense that could also be replicated—that is, proved by someone else—thus making Aristotle's model very different from the methods of earlier philosophers. Aristotle laid down many of the rules for what later would be known as the scientific method, in which evidence is collected, studied, classified, and analyzed, with conclusions based on the evidence, not on who could make the best argument. His approach was adopted by other Hellenistic scientists, whose experiments, observations, and conclusions in fields such as mathematics, medicine, physics, and astronomy were not superseded until the seventeenth century or later.

Hellenistic Science

The Hellenistic period was the most important period of antiquity for scientific investigation based on practical applications. Many Hellenistic discoveries anticipated scientific applications of the modern day.

The Rise of Hellenistic Science Alexander the Great himself was a believer in scientific investigation, and his armies included a staff of scientists who observed and recorded discoveries in fields ranging from geography to botany. The works of his botanist **Theophrastus**, for example, served as the foundation for modern botany. Alexandria was especially famous as a center of science and mathematics, and the most influential of the Alexandrian scientists was the mathematician **Euclid**, who wrote a textbook on plane geometry around 300 B.C.E. that is said to be, after the Bible, the most influential book ever published. Euclid's textbook presented five **axioms** that were obviously true, such as that only one line parallel to another line can be drawn through a given point, and then combined them to prove more complex propositions, called **theorems**, which then could be used to prove other theorems. Modern geometry textbooks do little more than reproduce Euclid's theorems.

Hellenistic Astronomy Alexandria also was home to many famous astronomers. One topic of investigation was the place of the earth in the universe. Aristotle and other Greek scientists had assumed that the sun, moon, and planets revolved around the earth. Contrary to this view, **Aristarchus**, around 250 B.C.E., proposed a heliocentric universe, with the sun at the center and the earth rotating on its own axis. Shortly thereafter, Eratosthenes devised a method for computing prime numbers—numbers that cannot be divided by any other number—and estimated the circumference of the earth by comparing the difference in length between shadows cast at noon at two different places in Egypt. His figure of 24,887 miles was almost exactly correct (the actual circumference is

Theophrastus Third-century B.C.E. Greek philosopher and naturalist.

Euclid Hellenistic mathematician who around 300 B.C.E. wrote a textbook on geometry.

axioms and theorems In geometry, axioms, statements that are assumed to be true without needing to be proved, are used to prove theorems, hypotheses that must be proved by using axioms and previously proved theorems.

Aristarchus Alexandrian astronomer who in about 250 B.C.E. proposed a heliocentric (from Greek for "sun-centered") universe.

24,902 miles). Eratosthenes also made a map of the world and predicted that there were other continents in the Southern Hemisphere and that one could reach India by sailing west from Spain.

The most notable Hellenistic astronomer was **Hipparchus**, who around 140 B.C.E. established the field of observational astronomy by creating the first western star catalogue. He measured the exact positions of some five hundred stars with an astrolabe, a device using a long thin tube to pinpoint a star's location. To create his catalogue, Hipparchus had to devise a standard reference system, using lines of latitude and longitude that could be used to define positions both on the earth and in the sky. Hipparchus rejected Aristarchus's heliocentric model because it could not be proven observationally and returned to the traditional geocentric system, with the earth in the center of the universe. To explain the occasional looping motion of the planets against the stars, Hipparchus proposed a system whereby the planets moved not in perfect circles but in a complex pattern of circles within circles.

Medical Science Hellenistic scientists also made advances in medical science, which had begun at the very end of the Classical Age with the work of **Hippocrates**. Known as the father of medicine, Hippocrates was the first Greek physician to reject the idea that illness was caused by the gods. He believed that sickness was caused by diet and environment and that an important point in an illness was the crisis, after which the patient would either recover or die. Because he believed that the body was largely capable of healing itself, through rest, he was reluctant to administer medicines. Hippocrates also taught the importance of observing symptoms so that similar illnesses could receive similar treatments. He established a school of medicine that included many later Greek doctors, and the medical ethics he developed are preserved in the modern Hippocratic Oath. During the Hellenistic period, medical science was expanded by an Alexandrian school of medicine that studied human anatomy and physiology by dissecting the bodies of condemned criminals. By this means, Alexandrian physicians discovered the function of nerves and the flow of blood through vessels.

Hipparchus Alexandrian astronomer who believed in a geocentric (from Greek for "earth-centered") universe and in about 140 B.C.E. created the first western star catalogue.

Hippocrates Greek physician of the early fourth century B.C.E. who established Greek medicine and whose ethical model provides the oath taken by modern physicians.

Ctesibius of Alexandria Alexandrian Greek inventor of the water clock, after 250 B.C.E.

Hero of Alexandria Inventor of an ancient steam engine.

Archimedes Greek scientist from Syracuse who about 225 B.C.E. invented mathematical physics and developed the concept of specific gravity.

Hellenistic Technology

During antiquity, technology generally evolved slowly, and antiquity is not generally thought of as a great age of invention. The Hellenistic Age, however, stimulated by the intellectual interaction of eastern and western thought, was a period of great technological advancement. Machines were invented both for practical purposes and as curiosities; some prefigured modern technological developments.

Hellenistic Inventors The first great Hellenistic inventor, **Ctesibius of Alexandria**, was the son of a barber. His first invention was a counterweighted mirror that could be adjusted to the height of a customer's head. His realization that air was a substance that could be manipulated led to the invention of a number of devices based on the use of water pressure and compressed air. He created a water clock in which a system of valves turned the supply of water on and off, a high-pressure pump used to shoot streams of water at fires, and an organ that used water pressure to create airflow through sets of pipes—the first keyboard instrument.

Hero of Alexandria, nicknamed "the machine man," likewise devised machines based on air and water pressure. He invented the first steam engine, which transformed steam into circular motion by means of jets placed on the sides of a hollow sphere. The same principle is used in the modern jet engine. Instead of being put to practical use, Hero's engine was used only as a toy, to make puppets dance. Other curiosities invented by Hero included automatic door openers for temples. More practical were his hydraulic devices to force the oil out of olives. He also invented an odometer, a system of gears connected to a wheel that could be used to measure distances. During the Roman Empire, Hero's odometer was used to place the mile markers on the famous Roman road system.

Archimedes of Syracuse The most famous Hellenistic inventor was **Archimedes**, a native of Syracuse in Sicily, who had been a pupil of Aristarchus at Alexandria. Around 225 B.C.E., Archimedes invented the field of mathematical physics. According to one story, Archimedes was once sitting in a bath when he observed that his body had displaced its own volume of water. On this basis, he was able to calculate specific gravity of any object, the ratio of the object's weight to the weight of the same volume of water. He also invented the Archimedes screw, a device for boosting water out of rivers and canals for irrigation.

Hellenistic inventions also could be used for warfare, as happened in 212 B.C.E., when Syracuse was attacked by the Romans. According to Plutarch, Archimedes used his engineering knowledge to attack the Roman navy: "huge poles thrust out from the walls over the ships sunk some by the great weights that they dropped down upon them; others they lifted up into the air by an iron hook and whirled about until the sailors were all thrown out, when at length they were dashed against the rocks below." Archimedes also was said to have built a gigantic lens that set Roman ships afire by focusing sunlight on them. When the Romans finally took the city, Archimedes was in the midst of diagramming a problem in the sand. Plutarch reports, "A soldier commanded him to follow him, which he declined to do before he had completed working out his problem. The soldier, enraged, drew his sword and ran him through."

The Anticythera Device Other machines were equally complex. The ability to predict the motions of the sun, moon, and planets had practical significance for astrologers, for it permitted them to cast **horoscopes** for any date in the past, present, or future. Elaborate geared mechanical devices were constructed

that allowed the user to portray the position of the heavenly bodies at any time. One such device, the first known mechanical computing machine, was discovered by a Greek sponge diver in 1900 off the coast of Crete near the island of Anticythera, hence the name "the Anticythera device." Built around 80 B.C.E., it is the most complicated machine to be preserved from antiquity. The surviving section alone (part of it is missing) contains thirty-two gears. The device is based on the theories of Hipparchus and can predict the position of the sun, moon, and planets in the zodiac, along with the phases of the moon, with an accuracy of one part in 86,000.

✓ Checking In

By yourself or with a partner, explain the significance of each of the following selected key terms:

syncretism	Hipparchus
Serapis	Hippocrates
koinē	Hero of Alexandria
Euclid	Archimedes

The octagonal Tower of the Four Winds in Athens, about forty feet tall and built of marble, was designed by the Hellenistic scientist Andronicus of Cyrrhus (a Seleucid colony in Syria) around 150 B.C.E. to be used on the outside as a sundial and weathervane (now vanished from the top) and on the inside as a water clock. The name comes from the depictions of the eight winds carved on the eight sides: Boreas, for example, represented the north wind, and Zephyros the west wind. The tower survived because it was first converted into a church and then largely buried under earth and debris. In what ways was the science of the Hellenistic period different from the science of the Greek Archaic and Classical periods?

Ronald Sheridan/Ancient Art & Architecture Collection

Identity in a Cosmopolitan Society

◆ **How did religion give people a sense of identity?**

◆ **How and why did the Jews resist Hellenistic culture?**

For many Greeks, the Hellenistic period created a crisis of identity. The city-states that had been major participants in world politics had been superseded by Hellenistic kingdoms and no longer provided the same focal points for loyalty and personal identity. The importance of Greece itself had declined to the point that even being a Greek no longer created the same sense of self-satisfaction as before. Both Greeks and non-Greeks felt adrift in the new Hellenistic multicultural world. To hold on to their old identity or find a new sense of identity, many people turned to philosophy and religion.

An Age of Anxiety

During the Hellenistic period, there was no opportunity for a Greek polis to play an important role in world politics. This was a time of kings and kingdoms in which cities were shuffled around from one kingdom to another. As cities lost their political independence, Greeks lost part

horoscope (from Greek for "looking at the hours") Diagram of the positions of heavenly bodies used to forecast future events in a person's life.

of their personal identity. Being a subject of a king simply could not replace the sense of belonging that came from being a citizen of an independent polis.

The Cosmopolis The feeling now arose that one was a citizen of the **cosmopolis**, or world-city. People encountered the wider world every day—in the street, in literature, and in the schoolroom. In the marketplace, they heard not only Greek but also Persian, Aramaic, and Egyptian. Because they were constantly exposed to foreign cultures, the Greeks could no longer be supremely confident that their culture was the best in the world, and they felt that their sense of cultural identity was threatened. In fact, foreign cultures had many attractions for the Greeks, and they no longer felt that all foreign things were barbarian. Greek culture now was Hellenistic culture, which meant the assimilation of the cultures of many foreign peoples.

Astrology and Magic These changes made the Greeks uncomfortable. They were used to being in control, to being able to understand and feel integrated in their world. Now they felt lost. Life seemed unpredictably governed by **Tyche**, a goddess who represented blind chance, who could bring either good fortune or complete ruin. To try to regain a sense of control, many Greeks turned to personal religion. Some sought supernatural guidance, adopting some of the very same Near Eastern ideas that had made them uncomfortable in the first place. Babylonian astrology, which taught that the future had been ordained by the gods and could be read in the motions of the stars and planets, gained a great following. The famous Babylonian astrologer Berossus even moved to Greece around 290 B.C.E. and opened up a school. The use of magical spells also gave average people a sense of empowerment. An Egyptian charm was used to command a god to do one's bidding: "Hear me, because I am going to say the great name, Aoth, before whom every god prostrates himself and every demon shudders. Your divine name is Aeeioyo Iayoe Eaooyeeoia. I have spoken the glorious name, the name for all needs." In this case, it was believed a god could be controlled by speaking the god's secret name.

Magical charms also were used for self-medication, for then, as now, people were very concerned about their health. An ancient pregnancy test suggested, "You should make the woman urinate on the Great-Nile plant. When morning comes, if you find the plant scorched, she will not conceive. If you find it green, she will conceive." Incubation—that is, sleeping in the sanctuary of a healing god such as Asclepius—was thought to be a means of curing maladies ranging from psoriasis to lameness to cancer. Temple walls were hung with plaques attesting to various cures. One, regarding a wounded soldier, read, "As he was sleeping in the Temple the god extracted the spearhead. When day came he departed, cured." People also believed that they could receive help from the gods in dreams received while they slept in temples. According to one report, "Arata, a woman of Sparta, was dropsical. While she remained at home, her mother slept in the temple and saw a dream. It seemed that the god cut off her daughter's head and hung her body upside-down. Out came a huge quantity of fluid matter. Then he fitted the head back on the neck. Afterward she went home and found her daughter in good health."

The Hellenistic Mystery Cults

Another way people tried to gain greater control over their lives was by attempting to find happiness after death. Many believed this could be done by participating in **mystery cults**, which promised a blissful afterlife gained by participating in secret rituals.

The Nature of Mystery Cults Mystery cults taught that people could obtain **salvation** from the cares of this world by following the model of a god who had endured terrible suffering or death on earth and then had been restored or reborn. If the god could triumph over the troubles of this world, people believed that they could too. But participants in mystery cults could not obtain salvation by their own efforts. They needed help, in the form of going through the proper rituals, to understand the mystery of how the god they were worshiping had obtained salvation. Unlike modern religions of redemption, moreover, mystery religions were not intended to help someone obtain forgiveness and avoid punishment for past sins, but simply to ensure that a participant received an afterlife. There was no concept of guilt, repentance, or regret for past sins. Indeed, most mystery cults had no concept of sin at all.

A participant in a mystery cult was thought to obtain salvation by participating in an initiation ceremony that allowed one to share the identity of the god and thus the god's immortality. Different cults created this mystical union in different ways, although there were several general similarities. Initiates were sworn to secrecy, but enough information slipped out to give a general picture of the rites. The ceremony often began with a purification ritual that made the initiate fit to come into contact with the deity. The initiate then sat through, or participated in, an elaborate performance that explained the cycle of life and death.

cosmopolis (Greek for "world-city") Universal city that people in the Hellenistic Age believed they belonged to; the origin of the modern word cosmopolitan.

Tyche Greek goddess representing blind chance.

mystery cult (based on Greek mysterion, "secret") Form of worship modeled on the experiences of a god and promising a happy afterlife through secret initiation rituals.

salvation Process by which people believed they were saved from the suffering and troubles of this world and gained eternal life; also known as redemption.

The Eleusinian Mysteries To be initiated into most mystery cults, all one had to do was attend the ceremony, although some cults had more demanding initiations than others. The **Eleusinian mysteries** at Athens honored the grain goddess Demeter. In Greek mythology, Demeter's daughter Persephone had been carried off to the underworld by the god Hades but was allowed to return to earth six months of the year. The initiation began with a ritual purification in which initiates carried a piglet into the sea. Then the piglet was sacrificed, and the initiates were baptized by being sprinkled with its blood. They then took part in a torchlight procession to holy places in the Athenian countryside that appeared in the myth of Demeter and Persephone, thus sharing in the goddesses' experiences. The climax of the ceremony occurred in the Hall of Initiation, where a religious drama depicting the return of Persephone from the underworld was presented. Sacred objects, such as ancient wooden statues of the goddesses and wheat stalks, also were displayed. The poet Pindar wrote about these mysteries, "Blessed are those who have seen these things for they understand the end of mortal life and the beginning of a new life given by god."

The Cult of Isis Initiation into the Eleusinian mysteries took place only in Athens, but initiation into most other cults could occur anywhere. During the Hellenistic period, the ancient Egyptian cult of Isis, whose brother Osiris had been brought back from the dead after being torn to pieces, was revived. This cult was similar to the Eleusinian mysteries, but it also made greater demands. Initiates were expected to purify themselves by living in the temple with the priests and attending worship services, even if only for a day. Participants then viewed sacred books and were baptized in water representing the life-giving Nile River. For the next ten days, initiates abstained from eating meat, drinking wine, and having sex. These requirements were a form of death, in which participants assumed the role of Osiris. The actual initiation began at sunset on the tenth day, when the candidate was taken into the innermost sanctuary of the temple of Isis. There then was a performance of a ritual death and resurrection, with the initiate, as Osiris, being reborn with the rising of the sun. At this point the initiates returned to the temple to be viewed as living gods. In one account, Isis herself addressed the initiate, "When you descend to the underworld, there you will see me shining and you will worship me as the one who has favored you."

The Cult of Cybele The most demanding cult of all was that of the Asian Great Mother goddess, **Cybele**. She had caused her lover Attis, a vegetation god, to go mad and castrate and kill himself with a sharp stone so that no other woman could have him. Like vegetation, Attis was reborn every year in the spring. Initiation into the cult of Cybele occurred during a spring festival that began with the cutting of a pine tree to represent Attis. Participants were expected to fast for one day by not eating fruits and vegetables, although eating meat was permitted. The rites came to a head on "the day of blood," in which participants worked themselves into a frenzy dancing to the sounds of horns, drums, and cymbals. They slashed their bodies with knives, sprinkling blood on the sacred tree as a means of calling Attis back to life. The Greek satirist Lucian described what happened next: "Frenzy comes on many who have come simply to watch and they subsequently perform this act on themselves. The initiate throws off his clothes, rushes to the center with a great shout, takes up a sword, and immediately castrates himself. Then he runs through the city holding the parts he has cut off. He takes female clothing and women's adornment from whatever house he throws the parts into." Having taken this irrevocable step, the initiate—if he survived—then became one of the wandering priests of Cybele.

The mystery cults required no faith. Salvation was gained by one's personal, albeit brief, devotion to the mystery deities. There was no need to engage in any continuing ritual. Nor were the cults exclusive. People could be initiated into as many mystery cults as they wished. These were the first religions offering personal salvation that were open to all, and they were extremely popular.

The Intellectual Approach to Identity

Greeks with intellectual inclinations sought to find their place in the universe through philosophical beliefs. The old philosophical schools of Plato and Aristotle usually had speculated about the nature of the universe and humanity in a broad sense, rarely on the level of the individual. For many, the teachings of these schools seemed out of date, and in the Hellenistic period, before and after 300 B.C.E., new philosophical teachings aimed to fulfill the needs of individuals.

The Cynics In the mid-fourth century B.C.E., the philosopher **Diogenes**, for example, taught that people could find their proper place in the world, and also become invulnerable to the unpredictability of Tyche, by discarding all human social conventions and "living according to nature." His followers gained the name Cynics, from the Greek word for "dog," because they lived like dogs, performing all of their natural functions—eating, sleeping, defecating, and having sex—in the street. Cynics were self-sufficient and indifferent to suffering. Their lack of respect for social conventions also meant they were outspoken

Eleusinian mysteries Mystery cult at Athens that honored the grain goddess Demeter.

Cybele Asian mother goddess, the lover of Attis, whose worship included ritual castration.

Diogenes Mid-fourth century B.C.E. Greek Cynic philosopher.

A fresco from the buried Italian city of Herculaneum, destroyed by the eruption of Mt. Vesuvius in 79 C.E., depicts a ceremony at a temple of Isis. In the center, at the top of the steps, a priest holds a covered urn. The priestess to his right shakes a rattle, and to his left a black priest holds a staff. The multiethnic worshipers gather below, where another black priest watches over a priestess sacrific- ing ducks, joined by one musician playing a flute and others shaking rattles. This and other polythe- istic (or "pagan") religious ceremonies were held in full public view, consistent with the policies of ancient governments that generally forbade secret meetings of any kind of organization. Why do you think there might have been black participants at religious rites honoring the goddess Isis?

social critics and took no account of rank or status. In a famous story, one day Alexander the Great vis- ited Diogenes, who lay naked sunning himself. When Alexander asked Diogenes what he could do for him, Diogenes replied, "You could move to the side a bit and stop blocking the sun."

The Epicureans The philosopher Epicurus, from the Aegean island of Samos, took a materialistic ap- proach to life. Beginning just before 300 B.C.E., in the philosophy known as **Epicureanism**, he taught that the universe was comprised of atoms randomly fall- ing through space. There was no guiding principle and no underlying struc- ture. There were no gods, no chance, no good or bad fortune, just falling atoms.

Sometimes these atoms would swerve, clump to- gether, and create the material world. The swerve also gave people free will by introducing an element of variation into the falling atoms. A person's only goal should be to pursue a form of pleasure that Epi- curus defined as preventing one's atoms from being disturbed, and this meant avoiding pain. Thus, any pleasure that later caused pain, such as drunkenness or overeating, was to be avoided. To avoid pain, one also needed peace of mind and the ability not to be affected by circumstances. Epicurus thus advocated withdrawal from public life in favor of a calm life of seclusion spent with like-minded friends. But the focus on pleasure led to misunderstanding of Epi- curus's teachings; today, the term *Epicurean* refers to someone who overdoes pleasure seeking, exactly the opposite of what Epicurus meant. Epicurus's school was unusual in that he admitted women.

Epicureanism Philosophy founded by Epicurus (341–270 B.C.E.) that advocated the avoidance of pain.

The Stoics Just after 300 B.C.E., Zeno, a native of Cyprus, presented a different view in the philosophy known as **Stoicism**. He also taught that the universe was materialistic, but for him it was highly structured and had an unalterable pattern established by a divine governing force called the Logos. The universe was like a finely organized machine, full of wheels and gears, that repeated the same cycle about every twenty-six thousand years. Just as every part of the machine played its part in the smooth functioning of the mechanism, it was everyone's duty to perform his or her individual role in the pattern established by the Logos. Zeno, therefore, also taught that one should live by nature, but his point was that all must accept the role that they had been assigned in nature. The Stoic prayer was, "Lead me, O Zeus, wherever you will, and I will follow willingly, and if I do not, you will drag me." The only choice a person had was either to accept what already had been determined or to fight against it and inevitably be destroyed as a consequence. The importance given to performing one's duty made Stoicism attractive to individuals who were committed to political service.

Hellenistic Judaism

At the same time that mystery cults and new philosophies were emerging, a very significant religion of antiquity was once again facing challenges from outside. Under Persian rule, the Jews of Judaea, as the Jewish homeland now was called, had been permitted, and even encouraged, to pursue their worship with little or no interference from the government.

Jews in the Hellenistic World When Judaea was absorbed into the empire of Alexander, the Jews continued to enjoy the same religious freedom. Following the disintegration of Alexander's empire, Judaea lay in the disputed border area between the Ptolemaic and Seleucid kingdoms and thus was often drawn into border wars. Eventually the Seleucids prevailed, and the Seleucid kings initially maintained the Jews' freedom to worship as they saw fit.

The situation changed with the Seleucid king **Antiochus IV Epiphanes**, who, desiring to unify his still vast and very disparate kingdom, sought to implant Greek culture in Judaea much more actively than had his predecessors. Many Jews, mostly from among the well-to-do, already had become **Hellenized** by learning Greek, studying Greek literature, and adopting Greek religious and philosophical practices and beliefs. Because Greeks, who exercised in the nude, believed that circumcision was a gross deformity, some Jews even underwent surgical processes to undo circumcision. The enthusiasm of these Hellenized Jews may have led Antiochus to believe that the rest of the Jews also were ready to adopt Greek culture.

The Revolt of the Maccabees Many conservative Jews, however, opposed Hellenization. The book of Maccabees in the Jewish Septuagint reported, "In those days certain renegades came out from Israel and misled many, saying, 'Let us go and make a covenant with the **Gentiles** around us.' So they built a gymnasium in Jerusalem, according to Gentile custom, and removed the marks of circumcision, and abandoned the holy covenant." The greatest opposition to Antiochus's policies arose among less privileged Jews, led by the **Hasidim**, who feared that any adoption of Greek culture not only violated Jewish beliefs but also would lead to their destruction. Nevertheless, Antiochus pursued his policy of Hellenization by actively attempting to undermine Jewish practices. He issued laws forbidding circumcision, study of the Torah, and the observance of the Sabbath. The book of Maccabees continued, "They put to death the women who had their children circumcised, and they hung the infants from their mothers' necks." Antiochus Hellenized the Jewish Temple in Jerusalem by instituting ritual prostitution and placing in the Temple a statue and altar to Zeus on which pigs, which the Jews believed to be unclean, were sacrificed. The Jews referred to this affront to the Jewish religion as the "abomination of desolation." Antiochus even demanded that he himself be worshiped as a god.

In 167 B.C.E., rebellion broke out, led by the elderly Jewish priest Mattathias and his son Judas, nicknamed Maccabee ("The Hammer"). The rebels, joined by the Hasidim and other discontented Jews, became known as the **Maccabees**. Their goal was political independence, which they now believed was necessary for true religious freedom. Against all odds, Judas defeated Antiochus in 165 B.C.E. and liberated Jerusalem (see A New Direction: The Maccabees Decide to Revolt). In the following year, the Temple was cleansed and reopened to the regular Jewish sacrifices, an event that is still commemorated each year in the Jewish festival of **Hanukkah**. The Seleucids, however, did not concede defeat easily. Fighting continued, and Judas and several of his brothers were killed. Ultimately, the revolt of the Maccabees resulted in the creation of an independent

Stoicism Greek philosophy founded by Zeno just after 300 B.C.E. that advocated doing one's duty in the universe.

Antiochus IV Epiphanes (r. 175–164 B.C.E.; his name means "God Made Manifest") Seleucid king who attempted to Hellenize the Jews.

Hellenization Process of implanting Greek culture.

Gentiles (Latin for "peoples") Non-Jews.

Hasidim (Hebrew for "pious ones") Jews who resisted the adoption of Greek culture.

Maccabees Jewish rebels against the Seleucids in the 160s B.C.E.

Hanukkah (Hebrew for "dedication") Jewish festival commemorating the defeat of the Seleucids by the Maccabees and the reopening of the Temple in Jerusalem.

The Maccabees Decide to Revolt

In the 160s B.C.E., the faith of the elderly Jewish priest Mattathias was put to the test. He could remain true to his religious convictions, or he could follow the orders of a Greek king and sacrifice to non-Jewish gods. Mattathias was in this position because ever since the fall of Jerusalem in 587 B.C.E., the Jews of Judaea had been under foreign domination. Their rulers—first the Chaldeans, then the Persians, then Alexander the Great—usually had allowed them religious freedom, and the Jews were confident that they would be able to continue to practice their religion without outside interference.

In 167 B.C.E., however, the Seleucid ruler of Judaea, King Antiochus IV, attempted to impose Greek culture on the Jews. As described in the book of the Maccabees in the Hebrew Bible, when the king's men attempted to force Mattathias to sacrifice a pig, an animal considered unclean by the Jews, Mattathias and his sons were horrified: they "tore their clothes, put on sackcloth, and mourned greatly." A royal official addressed old Mattathias: "You are a leader, honored and great in this town. Now be the first to come and do what the king commands, as all the Gentiles and the people of Judah and those that are left in Jerusalem have done. Then you and your sons will be numbered among the Friends of the king." Mattathias, however, knew where his duty lay and fearlessly replied, "I and my sons and my brothers will continue to live by the covenant of our ancestors. We will not obey the king's words by turning aside from our religion." He then killed both the official, who was about to make a sacrifice on a Jewish altar, and the king's officer. Crying, "Let every one who is zealous for the law and supports the covenant come out with me!" Mattathias fled into the hills with his five sons and was soon joined by many other Jews.

Mattathias's decision to resist the king's orders must have looked like certain suicide to most observers. The Jews were outnumbered and were facing an army that included professional mercenary soldiers. But the Jews were fighting for their religious freedom and were willing to die, whereas mercenary soldiers generally were used in battles in which both sides strove to limit their losses.

At first, the Greek army had an unfair advantage, for many Jews refused to fight on the Sabbath, the holy Jewish day of rest. On one occasion, thousands of Jewish men, women, and children were slaughtered when they refused to fight. Mattathias and his army, therefore, had another crucial choice to make: Would they abide by their law and be slaughtered, or put the law aside to be able to defend themselves? They said to each other, "If we do as our kindred did and refuse to fight with the Gentiles on the Sabbath, they will quickly destroy us." Thus they decided, "Let us fight against anyone who comes to attack us on the Sabbath day; let us not all die as our kindred died in their hiding places."

Mattathias soon died, and his son Judas took his place as the leader of the Jewish revolt. He, too, chose to continue the fight against all odds. When Antiochus's huge army approached, the Jewish rebels began to lose heart, saying "How can we, few as we are, fight against so great and so strong a multitude?" But Judas gave them courage by replying, "It is not on the size of the army that victory in battle depends, but strength comes from Heaven. They come against us in great insolence and lawlessness to destroy us and our wives and our children, and to despoil us; but we fight for our lives and our laws. God himself will crush them before us; as for you, do not be afraid of them." Judas then led the attack, and the enemy was routed. By refusing to adopt Greek culture and by choosing to fight for their beliefs, even if it meant doing so on the Sabbath, the Jews were not only able to preserve their way of life but even to overcome what, at the outset, appeared to be insurmountable odds.

Source: Excerpts from 1 Maccabees 2.

Jewish kingdom, ruled by members of Judas's family, that would last for another hundred years.

The Jewish Kingdom Jewish independence did not mean an end to unrest and disagreements among the Jews themselves. There were conflicts over how Jewish law was to be interpreted and over the assimilation of non-Jewish culture. A group called the **Sadducees**, who represented the wealthy and were in charge of overseeing the temple in Jerusalem, embraced many Hellenistic beliefs and formed a secular-oriented group that cooperated with foreign rulers. They took a narrow interpretation of Jewish law, relying on written scripture only. Sadducees usually controlled the supreme legal and legislative body of the Jews, the **Sanhedrin**, which met in the Temple in Jerusalem and had seventy-one members, including the High Priest.

On the other hand, the **Pharisees**, the successors of the Hasidim, who tended to come from well-to-do but not rich backgrounds, opposed Hellenization and supported a rigorous enforcement of Jewish religious law. They studied and interpreted scripture in

Sadducees Class of wealthy Jews who were in charge of the Temple in Jerusalem.

Sanhedrin Supreme legal and legislative body of the Jews.

Pharisees Class of Jews who supported a rigorous interpretation of Jewish law.

synagogues and created a more religiously oriented party. During the reign of Queen Salome Alexandra (r. 76–67 B.C.E.), the Pharisees gained control of the Sanhedrin and were able to impose many elements of religious law. Their oral interpretations of the laws of Moses increased the number of prohibitions and regulations necessary for living a life acceptable to Yahweh. For example, biblical law identified 39 kinds of work prohibited on the Sabbath, a number eventually raised to 1,521 by oral interpretations. Even some Pharisees, however, were influenced by foreign religious beliefs to the extent that they adopted a belief in an afterlife that included the resurrection of the body.

The Jewish Diaspora At the same time, the Jewish Diaspora expanded as Jews settled throughout the Mediterranean world. There continued to be a large Jewish population in Mesopotamia, and a large colony of Jews comprised of exiles, merchants, and mercenaries arose in Alexandria in Egypt, eventually outnumbering the Jews in Palestine. These foreign Jews were remarkably successful at preserving the fundamental aspects of their culture, such as adhering to dietary regulations, building synagogues, and keeping the Sabbath, in the midst of foreign cultures.

But in other respects, especially language, foreign Jews were compelled to accommodate themselves to local conditions. The Jews of Alexandria eventually spoke Greek rather than Hebrew, and to make scripture available to these Greek-speaking Jews, a translation was needed. According to tradition, seventy Jewish translators went to work on their own translations into koinē Greek, each of which turned out to be exactly the same. This Greek version of the Old Testament was known as the **Septuagint**.

> **Septuagint** (based on Latin for "seventy") Greek translation of Jewish scripture said to have been made by seventy translators.

Checking In

By yourself or with a partner, explain the significance of each of the following selected key terms:

cosmopolis	Hellenization
mystery cult	Maccabees
Epicureanism	Pharisees
Stoicism	Septuagint

Review

Summary

- At the beginning of the Hellenistic period the conflicts between the Greeks and the Persians came to an end. Led by Alexander the Great, Macedonian Greek armies repeatedly defeated the Persians, resulting in the creation of an empire that extended from the Adriatic Sea to the Indus River.

- Before his death in 323 B.C.E., Alexander attempted to unify his empire by planting colonies of Greeks throughout the empire and by respecting the customs of conquered peoples.

- After Alexander's death, his empire disintegrated into three large pieces, ruled by the families of three of his powerful generals: the Antigonids, Ptolemies, and Seleucids.

- The Macedonian rulers of Egypt and western Asia were remarkably successful in creating a composite society that continued to respect the customs of their very culturally and ethnically diverse populations.

- Cities such as Alexandria and Antioch served not only as royal capitals but also as centers of learning. Smaller powers, based in the cities of Pergamum and Rhodes, also became centers of learning and economic wealth.

- The conquests of Alexander had unforeseen cultural consequences for the Greeks, who were forced to reckon with the non-Greek world. Greeks no longer could hold the view that they were the best people in the world and that all non-Greeks were barbarians. Geographers brought accounts of the cultures of peoples living as far away as India, central Africa, and Britain. Foreign influences affected every aspect of Greek art and thought, creating a composite Hellenistic culture that extended from India across the Mediterranean. Never at any time in history has the western world, broadly defined, been so culturally united.

◆ The study of science and technology emerged during the Hellenistic period. Most large cities were centers of some branch of learning. In Athens, the philosopher Aristotle introduced scientific classification. At the Museum of Alexandria, mathematicians created standard concepts of geometry, astronomers and geographers mapped both the heavens and the earth, physicians studied human anatomy, and inventors experimented with the uses of water and steam pressure.

◆ The Hellenistic world also brought a sense of personal crisis to many Greeks, who felt lost now that the polis was no longer the focus of their lives. Many Greeks even lost the feeling of being Greek. Foreign languages and culture were everywhere. In an effort to discover a sense of identity and find their place in the world, many people turned to mystery religions, which promised an afterlife and to philosophies that provided guidelines for life. And in Judaea, the Jews strengthened their hold on their own identity by establishing their political independence for the first time in more than 400 years.

Chronology

387 B.C.E.	King's Peace ends warfare between the Spartans and Athenians
359 B.C.E.	Philip II becomes king of Macedonia
338 B.C.E.	Philip II defeats the Greeks at Chaeronea
336 B.C.E.	Alexander III becomes king of Macedonia
335 B.C.E.	Aristotle founds the Lyceum
334 B.C.E.	Alexander invades the Persian Empire
332 B.C.E.	Third wave of Greek colonization begins
331 B.C.E.	Alexander defeats Persians at Battle of Gaugamela
327 B.C.E.	Alexander invades India
323 B.C.E.	Alexander dies
c. 300 B.C.E.	Ptolemy I founds Alexandria Museum; Euclid publishes geometry theorems; Epicurus teaches Epicureanism; Zeno teaches Stoicism; Pytheas of Marseilles explores Atlantic coast of Europe
280 B.C.E.	Final partition of Alexander's empire
250 B.C.E.	Parthians invade Seleucid kingdom; Aristarchus proposes heliocentric universe; Ctesibius uses air and water pressure in inventions
225 B.C.E.	Archimedes develops theories of physics
220 B.C.E.	Eratosthenes creates a map of the world
175 B.C.E.	Antiochus IV becomes Seleucid king
165 B.C.E.	Judas Maccabee defeats Seleucids
140 B.C.E.	Hipparchus creates first western star catalogue and defends geocentric universe
80 B.C.E.	Anticythera device is first known mechanical computing machine
50 B.C.E.	Greek rulers in India are defeated by Central Asian invaders
30 B.C.E.	Cleopatra commits suicide after defeat by Romans

© Cengage Learning

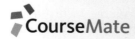 Visit the CourseMate website at **www.cengagebrain.com** for additional study tools and review materials for this chapter.

Test Yourself

To gauge your mastery of the material in this chapter, answer the questions below. More than one answer may be correct.

Alexander the Great, 387–323 B.C.E.

1. What kinds of factors characterized ancient Macedonia?

    a. The pursuit of literature and poetry
    b. Lives of hunting, drinking, and blood feuds
    c. A retention of monarchy
    d. The need to build a powerful army
    e. The expansion of a trading economy

2. Alexander the Great defeated the Persians at what battles?

    a. Gaugamela
    b. Babylon
    c. Issus
    d. Granicus
    e. Marathon

3. Alexander's empire included which of these river valleys?

    a. Tiber
    b. Nile
    c. Tigris and Euphrates
    d. Indus
    e. Ganges

4. What methods did Alexander use to try to unify his empire?

    a. Marriages between Greeks and Persians
    b. Founding colonies
    c. Using military force to control the population
    d. Adopting Persian methods of administration
    e. Imposing Greek culture on the entire population

Now that you have reviewed and tested yourself on this part of the chapter, take time to pull together all the important information by answering the following questions:

◆ Why was Alexander the Great able to conquer the huge Persian Empire?

◆ What methods did Alexander use to try to make his empire secure?

The Hellenistic World, 323–30 B.C.E.

5. Which of these families took control of parts of Alexander's empire?

    a. The Achaemenids
    b. The Antigonids
    c. The Ptolemies
    d. The Seleucids
    e. The Sargonids

6. What was the university established in Alexandria by the Ptolemies called?

    a. Agora
    b. Acropolis
    c. Periplus
    d. Museum
    e. Temple

7. Who told accounts of sea voyages about encounters with strange peoples and places?

    a. Nearchus
    b. Hanno
    c. Aristotle
    d. Pytheas
    e. Hero

Now that you have reviewed and tested yourself on this part of the chapter, take time to pull together all the important information by answering the following questions:

◆ How and why did the empire of Alexander disintegrate after his death?

◆ How did Greek views of the non-Greek world change during the Hellenistic period?

Hellenistic Culture and Science

8. What term represents mixing together aspects of different cultures?
   a. Stoicism
   b. Syncretism
   c. Civilization
   d. Navigation
   e. Philosophy

9. On what did the philosopher Aristotle base his method for understanding the world?
   a. Unproven speculation
   b. Logic
   c. Observation
   d. Common sense
   e. Mathematical proofs

10. What was the Hellenistic scientist Aristarchus known for?
    a. Creating the first western star catalogue
    b. Inventing medical science
    c. Suggesting that the earth revolved around the sun
    d. Writing a textbook on plane geometry
    e. Inventing machines using water pressure

11. The inventor Hero of Alexandria created machines that
    a. Anticipated the jet engine.
    b. Pumped water from the Nile River to irrigate crops.
    c. Measured distances along roads.
    d. Calculated the positions of astronomical bodies.
    e. Caused ships to be set afire at a distance.

Now that you have reviewed and tested yourself on this part of the chapter, take time to pull together all the important information by answering the following questions:

◆ In what ways was the Hellenistic Age an age of science and technology?

◆ In what ways did Hellenistic scientists use methods different from those of earlier philosophers?

Identity in a Cosmopolitan Society

12. In the Hellenistic Age, people sought supernatural guidance and assistance by using which of the following?
    a. Daily prayers to pagan saints
    b. Magical spells
    c. Human sacrifice
    d. Astrology
    e. Philosophical rituals

13. Initiation into a mystery cult involved participation in
    a. A purification ritual
    b. A performance that explained life and death
    c. Regular attendance at temple rituals
    d. Dedicating oneself to a savior god
    e. Human sacrifice

14. Which philosophical systems helped people find their place in the universe?
    a. Astrology
    b. The Eleusinian mysteries
    c. Cynicism
    d. Stoicism
    e. Epicureanism

15. Which groups of Hellenistic Jews had rather different views about how to relate to the world?
    a. Pharisees
    b. Galileans
    c. Hasidim
    d. Cosmopolites
    e. Sadducees

Now that you have reviewed and tested yourself on this part of the chapter, take time to pull together all the important information by answering the following questions:

◆ How did the people of the Hellenistic Age use religion to take control of their lives?

◆ How and why did the Jews resist Hellenistic culture?

CHAPTER 5

The Rise of Rome, 753–27 B.C.E.

800	750	700	650	600	550	500	450	400

753 B.C.E.
Rome is founded by Romulus and Remus

509 B.C.E.
Roman Republic is established

390 B.C.E.
Rome is sacked by Gauls

This fresco from the buried city of Pompeii depicts the baker Terentius Neo and his wife. Terentius is wearing a toga that signifies his status as a Roman citizen and holding a scroll with a red seal that probably indicates an official appointment probably connected with the city council. His unnamed wife holds a folded wax-coated writing tablet and a pointed stylus that stress her own educated status and probably suggest her role in the family business. Her curly hairstyle was in vogue during the reign of the emperor Neo. Neo's direct gaze and his wife's rather pensive look reflect the realistic nature of Roman portrait art. How does the appearance of these two individuals compare with that of the Roman senators depicted below? How might you account for the differences? (Erich Lessing/Art Resource, NY)

After reading this chapter, you should be able to answer the following questions:

In what ways did the Romans adopt the cultures of foreign peoples during the Roman Republic?

How were the plebeians able to gain greater rights during the Conflict of the Orders?

What were the reasons the Romans got involved in so many wars during the Roman Republic?

How did powerful Roman senators try to gain power in the years after 145 B.C.E.?

What were the reasons for the fall of the Roman Republic?

WHEN ROME WAS FOUNDED around 750 B.C.E., it was just one of thousands of small agricultural villages around the Mediterranean. Nothing marked it for future greatness. Rome's location at a crossroads between northern and southern Italy brought the Romans into contact with other peoples, including the Etruscans, Greeks, and Celts, all of whom would influence the future development of Roman culture. Over time, the Romans learned not only to survive but to prosper by assimilating the culture and customs of the peoples around them.

The early Romans were hardy farmers who valued their traditions. They had a strong work ethic based on duty to their gods, to their families, and to Rome. Their religious and family values made them close-knit, willing to resolve disputes without resorting to violence, and able to settle internal conflicts peaceably. The Romans' perseverance and ability to work together were major factors in their future success.

After first being ruled by kings, the Romans in 509 B.C.E. created a form of government called the Republic,

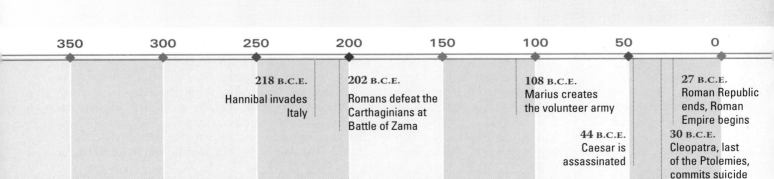

350	300	250	200	150	100	50	0

218 B.C.E.
Hannibal invades Italy

202 B.C.E.
Romans defeat the Carthaginians at Battle of Zama

108 B.C.E.
Marius creates the volunteer army

44 B.C.E.
Caesar is assassinated

27 B.C.E.
Roman Republic ends, Roman Empire begins

30 B.C.E.
Cleopatra, last of the Ptolemies, commits suicide

in which the members of a governing body called the Senate shared power among themselves. Early in its history, the Republic was engaged in a struggle for existence against hostile neighbors. Beginning in the fourth century B.C.E., for reasons ranging from a fear of strong neighbors to a desire by senators for military glory, the Romans became involved in a series of wars first in Italy and then in the western and eastern Mediterranean. By 146 B.C.E. they had emerged victorious in all their wars and had become the strongest Mediterranean power. Nevertheless, the Romans resisted becoming an empire and taking full responsibility for governing their conquered territories.

The acquisition of great power had enormous consequences for Roman life. Some of the foreign customs and concepts that the Romans assimilated, especially from the Greeks, conflicted with traditional Roman values. During the first century B.C.E., the government of the Roman Republic collapsed as a result of its unwillingness or inability to deal with problems such as poorly administered foreign territories, armies that could no longer be controlled, and senators who put personal ambitions ahead of the best interests of Rome.

The Development of Roman Identity, 753–509 B.C.E.

◆ **What values were important to the Romans?**

◆ **In what ways did Rome assimilate foreign peoples and customs?**

At the time of its founding, Rome was a small agricultural village. Romans had a strong sense of duty that subordinated individuals to the greater good of family, nation, and religion. They adopted what they believed were the best elements of foreign cultures and even accepted foreign peoples into their midst while at the same time preserving their own unique identity. The Romans' social and religious values gave them a strong sense of being able to work together and to overcome adversity.

Latins Peoples living in Latium in central Italy, distinguished from the neighboring Italian peoples by their dialect; they gave their name to the Latin language.

Romulus and **Remus** Twin brothers, the legendary founders of Rome in 753 B.C.E.

A City on Seven Hills

The early Romans had no written history. The beliefs of later Romans about how Rome was founded were based on oral legends that had been passed down for centuries. Eventually—by around 200 B.C.E.—Greek and Roman historians created a standardized account of early Roman history that was drawn from many sources.

Legends of Rome One story started with Aeneas, a Trojan who had escaped from the burning city of Troy around 1184 B.C.E. and fled to Italy. There he established a city not far from the future site of Rome that was populated by his Trojan followers and local people known as **Latins**.

One of Aeneas's distant descendants was a woman named Sylvia, who gave birth to twin sons, **Romulus** and **Remus**, claiming that the god Mars was their father. Their uncle, who had stolen the throne, ordered the twins to be put to death, fearing that they would replace him. But the executioner did not have the heart to kill the boys, so he set them adrift in a basket in the Tiber River. Downstream, a shepherd found them being suckled by a wolf and raised them as shepherds. Subsequently, the legend continues, the two boys discovered their true identity and decided to establish their own city on a site with seven hills on the south bank of the lower Tiber River. In the course of an argument, Remus was killed by Romulus, and the new city was named Rome, after him. The date was April 21, 753 B.C.E. Romulus became the first king of Rome and began the period known as Rome of the Kings.

According to legend, Romulus's city was first populated by Latin men who needed wives. They therefore kidnapped women from the Sabines, a nearby Italian people who spoke a slightly different dialect. Romulus established a monarchy and became the first of seven kings of Rome. Later Romans

Map 5.1 **Roman Expansion to 44 B.C.E.** Between 227 and 44 B.C.E., Rome gained control of provinces extending from Spain in the west to Syria in the east. Even though historians call this period the Roman Republic, the Romans were in fact creating an empire. © Cengage Learning

1. What does the map tell you about the rate over time at which Rome acquired new territory?
2. What was the geographical distribution of most of the territory controlled by the Romans? Why do you think this might have been the case?
3. What kinds of problems could arise when Rome gained control of so much foreign territory but refused to take complete responsibility for governing it?

believed that these kings had established many of Rome's most ancient traditions and customs, such as that the kings had two powers: the **imperium**, which gave them the authority to lead armies, and the **auspicium**, the right to consult the gods.

These foundation legends played an important role in defining Roman identity. They exemplified the Roman willingness to integrate newcomers into their society. They also connected Rome to Greek antiquity and to Greek gods. They reveal that the Romans wanted to be part of the broader, civilized Mediterranean world and to show the Greeks that they, too, had a distinguished history and were not barbarians.

Rome and the Etruscans
Even though the legends were based on a core of truth, they also added many elaborations. Archaeological excavations offer more concrete information about the early history of Rome

imperium Power of Roman kings and consuls to govern Rome and command armies.

auspicium Power of Roman kings and consuls to determine the will of the gods.

Terra cotta urns in the shape of the huts in which people lived were used for burying the ashes of the cremated dead in early Rome, thus allowing people to remain after death in the same kinds of quarters they inhabited when they were alive. These urns can be used in conjunction with archaeological evidence, the surviving postholes that held the support posts of early Roman huts on the Palatine Hill, to reconstruct the homes of the early Romans. What kinds of indications do these urns provide about what the future history of the Romans might be?

Scala/Art Resource, NY

and demonstrate that the first settlement of the hills of Rome did in fact take place around 750 B.C.E. The presence of two populations is attested by the use of two different burial techniques: cremation, in which bodies were burned, and inhumation, in which bodies were buried without being burned. At first, Rome was just a small farming village of straw huts perched on some of the hills. The southern part of Italy was inhabited by Greeks in the coastal areas and Italian peoples in the uplands. Just north of Rome lived the **Etruscans**, a people who may have emigrated from the coastal region of Anatolia about 800 B.C.E. In several ways the Etruscans were like the Greeks. They were not unified, and they lived in twelve independent cities ruled by warrior aristocracies. They had a highly developed economy based on trade and manufacturing, and they were especially expert at metalworking. Much Etruscan trade was with the Greeks; in fact, some of the best-preserved Greek pottery comes from graves in Etruria. The Etruscans used an alphabet adapted from Greek to write a language that is still undeciphered.

Etruscans Inhabitants of northwestern Italy whose culture greatly influenced early Rome.

Forum The center of public life in Rome, with markets, temples, law courts, and the Senate house.

Republic (in Latin, "the public thing") System of government introduced by the Romans after the expulsion of kings in 509 B.C.E., based on collegiate rule and rule by law.

Around 600 B.C.E., the Etruscans began expanding south and occupied Rome. The site attracted them because it was strategically positioned at the best crossing of the lower Tiber River, providing a means of good communications between northern and southern Italy. The Etruscans brought urbanization and civilization to Rome. They drained the swampy land between the hills and constructed the first paved roads, the first stone buildings, and the **Forum**, or central meeting place. They introduced new occupations, such as trading and pottery manufacturing, and made Rome a commercial center. Their religious practices and version of the Greek alphabet also were adapted by the Romans. Under Etruscan influence, Rome developed from a village into a city.

The Etruscans also provided the last three kings of Rome. Patriotic legends told how the wicked son of the autocratic Etruscan king Tarquin the Proud raped the virtuous Roman matron Lucretia, who then committed suicide for having disgraced her family. An uprising of enraged native Roman aristocrats expelled Tarquin in 509 B.C.E., and the Romans resolved never again to have a king. To do so, in the same year they created the Roman **Republic**.

What It Meant to Be Roman

During the era of the kings, the defining elements of Roman character and identity took shape.

Roman Values The Romans were fundamentally conservative and resistant to change. Reverence for the past guided their behavior, which was based on the concept of *mos maiorum*, "the ways of the ancestors." When faced with a problem, they first would ask, "What would our ancestors have done?" But the Romans were not blindly conservative. They also were very sensible and willing to adapt to changing conditions if circumstances required it. The Romans valued moral qualities such as responsibility, discipline, industry, frugality, temperance, fortitude, and modesty. Except on a very few occasions, such as after a great military victory, they refrained from self-promotion. The greatest Roman virtue was *pietas*, the sense of duty toward gods, family, friends, and country. Romans did their duty because of *religio* (from which our word *religion* is derived), a sense of subordination to external forces that included the gods, state officials, and family members. Everyone in Rome was subordinate to some greater authority and thus knew how he or she related to everyone else. Even when Romans pursued their personal ambitions, they always expressed themselves in terms of these traditional Roman values.

Early Roman Society Early Roman society was composed mostly of free citizens belonging to three tribes (from the Roman word for "thirds") believed to be the descendants of original populations of Latins, Italians,

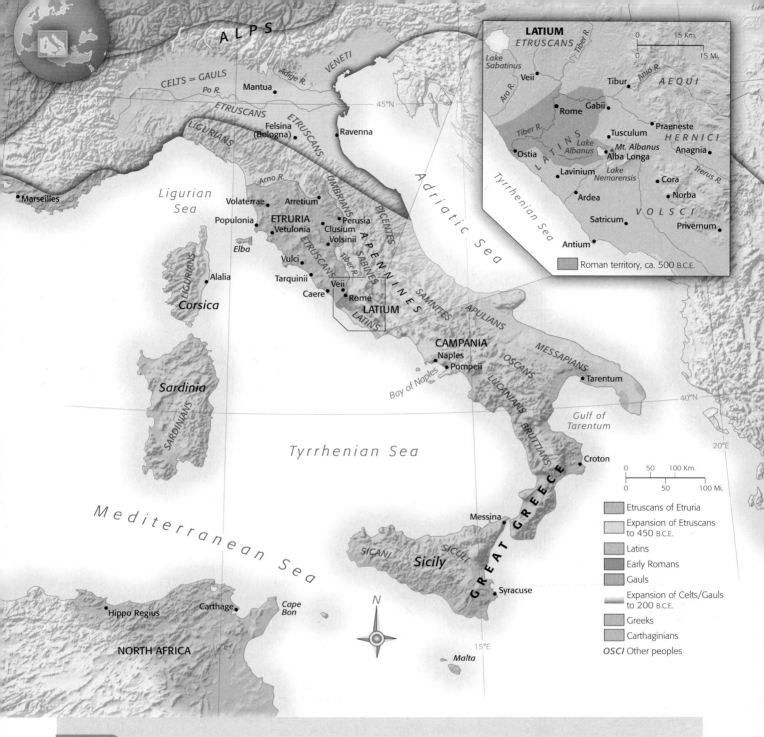

LATIUM

Roman territory, ca. 500 B.C.E.

Etruscans of Etruria

Expansion of Etruscans to 450 B.C.E.

Latins

Early Romans

Gauls

Expansion of Celts/Gauls to 200 B.C.E.

Greeks

Carthaginians

OSCI Other peoples

Map 5.2 **Early Italy, ca. 760–500 B.C.E.** When Rome was founded about 750 B.C.E., it was just a small agricultural village perched on hills adjoining the Tiber River. The rest of Italy was inhabited by other peoples who greatly influenced the development of Roman culture. © *Cengage Learning*

1. Who were the other peoples who inhabited early Italy along with the Romans?
2. Into what area of Italy did both the Etruscans and Celts attempt to expand?
3. In what areas of the map would you expect that the Greeks and Carthaginians might come into conflict? Why?
4. What areas of Italy did the Samnites and other Italian peoples occupy?

and Etruscans. Citizens enjoyed both private rights, which allowed them to marry, inherit property, and carry on business under Roman law, and public rights, which permitted male citizens to vote and run for public office. At this time, the population of foreigners and slaves was small because Rome was not yet very prosperous. Unlike in other ancient societies, slaves of Roman citizens who were set free gained full Roman citizenship rights, providing another example of how the Romans were willing to integrate newcomers into their society.

Even as a city, Rome remained a primarily agrarian society. As some farmers grew more successful than others, two social orders evolved: the **patricians** and the **plebeians** (or plebs). The patricians were the equivalent of the Greek aristocrats; the only way to become a patrician was by being born one. The patricians owned the best land, and the heads of the patrician families were members of the **Senate**, a hereditary body of about one hundred that originally advised the king. The senators were the most powerful persons in Rome. They saw themselves as preservers of Roman tradition and as models of Roman virtue, which they believed was best exemplified through military service. The plebeians, on the other hand, were mostly farmers, working either their own small plots or land that belonged to the patricians. As a result of the expansion in commerce and manufacturing under the Etruscans, some plebeians became very wealthy, but even so they could not enter the hereditary patrician class. At the other extreme, plebeians who defaulted on loans could be sold into slavery.

The Patron-Client Relationship Roman social relations revolved around the idea of bilateral (two-way) duty that was viewed in terms of contractual commitments. If someone did a Roman a favor, the Roman was obligated to that person until the favor had been repaid. This practice lay behind one of Rome's most important social institutions, the **patron-client relationship**, in which persons owed services to each other and were bound together in an almost religious union. At this time, the patrons were usually patricians, who would have many plebeians as their clients. A patrician patron provided physical protection, civil and criminal legal services, and economic support, including foodstuffs, seed grain, and even land to rent when times were tough. In return,

the plebeian client accompanied the patrician in time of war (the patricians did most of the actual fighting), helped to raise a ransom if he should be captured, and contributed to a dowry when a patrician's daughter was married. This system of reciprocal responsibility knit Roman society together in a way that Greek society was not. As a result, Romans were much less likely to resort to violence against each other when disputes arose. The system also was designed to preserve the position and privileges of the patricians.

Early Roman Religion

Religious beliefs and practices were deeply embedded in early Roman society, culture, and politics. Much of the Romans' sense of subordination to a greater power derived from their religion.

The Nature of Early Roman Gods The Romans believed that their most ancient religious institutions had been established by Numa, the second king of Rome. But the Romans also adopted other religious practices from the Etruscans and the Greeks. Roman religion was polytheistic, with many gods who took many forms. Some gods looked after the welfare of the state as a whole, and others were concerned with Roman private life. The earliest Roman gods were *numina*, vague and shapeless forces of nature that controlled the environment. The numen Janus, for example, who could be visualized with two faces pointing in opposite directions, was in charge of comings and goings and beginnings and endings. Each family had its own household gods, known as *Lares*, who looked after the well-being of the family, and *Penates*, who ensured that the storeroom was never empty. The *Manes* were spirits of beloved ancestors. The *Lemures*, on the other hand, were restless spirits of the dead who had to be placated every May with an offering of black beans. It was said that Romulus had begun this festival to pacify the spirit of Remus.

The Romans' social values were mirrored in their religious convictions. They believed that deities, too, had duties to perform, and they attempted to force the gods to do their duties by making ritualized contracts with them. Thus, each year a red dog was sacrificed at a crossroads to ensure that the numen Robigus did his duty and kept the red leaf blight from infecting the crops. Religious rituals were marked by compulsive attention to detail. The slightest deviation from a ritual, such as a sneeze or whisper, would neutralize its effectiveness. The greatest personal sacrifice that an individual Roman could make was the ritual called devotion. When a Roman battle was going badly, a Roman commander sometimes devoted himself to the gods and then committed suicide by charging into the enemy ranks. His men then regained confidence in the belief that the gods would fulfill their part of the bargain by granting victory.

---

patricians The most privileged of the early Roman citizens, equivalent to aristocrats.

plebeians (or plebs) The less privileged of the early Roman citizens; later, the generic term for Roman citizens.

Senate Primary governing body of the Roman Republic; its members were senators.

patron-client relationship The rendering of mutual services between a senior party (a patron) and a junior party (the client).

numina (sing. *numen*) Formless forces of nature that controlled the natural environment.

The Etruscans initially had a very positive view of the afterlife, but later in their history their attitude changed. This scene from an Etruscan tomb of about 300 B.C.E. depicts the execution of Trojan captives during the Trojan War to placate the ghosts of the dead. The underworld demon Charu (Greek Charon), who will hit the deceased with his hammer, and his winged female companion Vanth wait to escort the dead man to the underworld. Their fear of being tortured in the underworld led the Etruscans to try to satisfy the demons with ceremonies, such as fights to the death, that could include forms of human sacrifice. In what form were these fights to the death later adopted by the Romans?

The Evolution of Roman Religious Practices As a consequence of their contacts with the Etruscans and Greeks, the Romans also began to worship anthropomorphic gods and goddesses in permanent stone temples. Thus, Jupiter, along with being the formless numen of lightning and thunder, also could be visualized as a bearded man throwing a lightning bolt. In the course of creating Rome as a city, the Etruscans built several temples in the area of the Forum. The most important was a three-chambered temple on top of the **Capitoline Hill**, the highest hill in Rome, where it could be seen from far out in the countryside. This was the temple of the gods who looked after the welfare of the Roman state: **Jupiter the Best and Greatest**; his wife, Juno; and Minerva, a war goddess—the Roman equivalents of the Greek Zeus, Hera, and Athena. The temple served as an important symbol of Roman power and authority. Sacrifices of oxen and other animals were made in exchange for the gods' support of the well-being of the Roman people.

State priests saw to it that the government functioned according to religious law and that the *pax deorum* ("peace of the gods") was maintained between the gods and the Roman people. The most important Roman priest was the ***pontifex maximus***, who was in charge of other state priests and priestesses, including the vestal virgins, who kept the sacred hearth fire of the goddess Vesta burning in the Forum. The *pontifex maximus* also kept official lists of government officials and of important events. He also controlled the calendar; every so often, he added an extra month after February to keep the months synchronized with the seasons because the year as established by King Numa was 10 days short of a 365-day solar year.

Many Roman religious rituals were borrowed from the Etruscans, who used divination to discover the will of the gods. Etruscan priests observed flights of birds and examined sheep livers, looking for good or bad omens. Roman state priests used the same rituals to discover whether the

Capitoline Hill The tallest hill in Rome, site of the Capitoline temple of Jupiter, Juno, and Minerva.

Jupiter the Best and Greatest Most important Roman state god.

pontifex maximus (Latin for "the greatest bridge builder") An ancient title for the chief priest of Rome.

decisions of the Roman government had the support of the gods. If the priests found bad omens, government business could not proceed. Etruscan religious practices also found their way into Roman private life. Etruscan funeral ceremonies, which included wrestling matches, combats to the death, and human sacrifices intended to placate the demons of the underworld, evolved into Roman **gladiatorial** matches.

Roman Family Life

Roman society was very family oriented. In early Rome, a person's Roman citizenship depended on being a member of a Roman family. And within each family, the "father of the family" had absolute authority.

Roman Families   In early Rome, every Roman citizen belonged to a gens, or clan, and bore a clan name ending in *-ius* or *-ia*, such as Julius for men or Julia for women. Shortly after birth, Roman infants also received a first name. The first names of boys came from a standard list of twenty-two names, such as Marcus or Gaius. Certain first names ran in the family, so someone named Marcus Tullius probably had a father and grandfather also named Marcus Tullius. Female children, on the other hand, were simply identified by sequence numbers. Thus the second daughter of a Marcus Julius would be Julia Secunda. Romans also had a third name identifying their family, a subset of a clan. Family names often referred to a physical characteristic of a distant ancestor, such as Caesar ("hairy"). Thus, a Roman citizen had three names, for example, Gaius Julius Caesar. Senators were extremely proud of their heritage. The foyers of their houses contained wax portraits of ancestors that were paraded during funerals. Roman fathers expected to have a son to carry on the family name and inherit the family property. If a man had no natural sons, a son could be brought into the family by adoption.

The Paterfamilias   The concept of subordination to a greater authority carried over into Roman family life. The chief authority within each nuclear family (a father and all of his dependents) was the *paterfamilias*, who had life-and-death power over the household. A newborn baby was placed at the feet of its father; if he refused to pick it up, the infant was exposed and left to die. The father had the legal authority to execute any of those in his power as long as the cause (such as a violation of family or national honor) warranted doing so. In one legendary case, a Roman general executed his son, who had just won a battle, for disobeying orders; he was praised for putting loyalty to Rome before loyalty to his family. It was possible for a young man to become a *paterfamilias* in his own right if his father pretended to sell him as a slave three times and then set him free. Many men, however, simply waited for their fathers to die before becoming free of paternal authority.

Roman Marriage   Girls were permitted to marry young, and some were wed as young as age twelve, often to much older men. Men generally waited until a later age, around thirty. For a Roman marriage to be legally valid, the two parties both had to be Roman citizens. Marriages between Romans and foreigners or Romans and slaves did not convey any legal rights to offspring, whereas children of married Roman citizens also were citizens. Marriage was a private matter between two consenting persons who agreed to treat a relationship as a marriage. No legal or religious ceremonies were required, although a wedding feast often was held as a means of publicizing the union, and the parents of girls usually provided a dowry.

In a type of marriage common at the beginning of the Republic, called purchase, a father fictitiously sold his daughter to her husband, who then assumed legal authority over her. In another type of marriage, called usage, the wife remained under her father's authority as long as she spent three nights away from her husband's house each year. This kind of marriage gradually evolved into marriage "without authority," in which a woman came under her own authority when her father died. Even then, however, she needed a cooperative male guardian to carry out any business, such as buying property or making a will, on her behalf.

Either party in a marriage could obtain a divorce simply by declaring "I divorce you" three times before a witness. It was only in the matter of the disposition of property that fault was considered. For example, if a divorce occurred by mutual consent or if a husband declared a divorce without cause, the husband was required to return the entire dowry—a consideration that inhibited men from seeking divorce. But if the wife was guilty of adultery, the husband could keep one-sixth of the dowry. Any children went to the father, and a divorced mother had no right even to see them again.

Roman Children   Children in early Rome were educated mainly in the home by mothers and fathers, who shared the responsibility equally. Boys were instructed in law and history and engaged in physical training that would prepare them for military life. Girls learned household economy and were taught to perform the most virtuous feminine activity of all: spinning wool to make the family's clothing. Mothers instilled Roman virtues, such as reverence for the gods and respect for authority. Fathers took their sons along on their daily round of business activities and public life. In senatorial families, mothers and fathers both were responsible for forwarding the careers of their sons and for securing good marriages for their daughters.

gladiator (Latin for "sword bearer," from Latin gladius, "sword") A person, usually a slave, who fought in an arena against animals or other gladiators for the entertainment of the audience.

paterfamilias (Latin for "father of the family") Head of a Roman family, with life-and-death power over family members.

Scala/Art Resource, NY

In ancient Rome, past traditions supplied examples for living life in the present. Roman senators were extremely proud of their ancestors, who provided models of how good Romans should behave. Roman senators thus felt that they had to live up to the examples of their ancestors, and if possible even to surpass them. In this statue of the first century C.E., a senator carries busts of his ancestors that would have been displayed in the foyer of his house and paraded during funerals of family members. How does this Roman method of remembering family ancestors compare to modern methods of doing so?

Roman Women Roman women were expected to be modest, obedient, and loyal. The primary duty of a married woman was to bear children. Poor women in particular were expected to have as many children as possible—often ten or more—to ensure that at least some of them, given the high infant mortality rate, survived to maturity. Many women died in childbirth. A Roman gravestone, for example, tells of a woman named Veturia, who was married at eleven, bore six children (only one lived to adulthood), and died at twenty-seven. Women's duties also included supervising any household slaves and overseeing domestic activities such as cooking, clothing production, and child care.

Plebeian women who were not fully occupied at home could help support themselves and their families by working in a senatorial household; in the clothing industry; in service positions, such as hairdressers, masseuses, midwives, maids, and wet nurses; or as entertainers, such as dancers and prostitutes. In several regards, Roman women had greater liberties and responsibilities than their Greek counterparts. Roman women regularly appeared outside the home, with or without their husbands, engaging in such activities as visiting the public baths and attending religious ceremonies and dinner parties.

The most honored Roman women were the six vestal virgins, who also were the only women completely free of male legal authority. They were permitted to manage their own property and make wills in their own names. Girls became vestals before the age of ten and served for thirty years. After they retired, they were permitted to marry, but many continued to serve the goddess and to keep their legal independence. Because the welfare of the state was tied to the vestals' purity, those convicted of unchastity were sentenced to being buried alive.

Checking In

By yourself or with a partner, explain the significance of each of the following selected key terms:

Romulus and Remus	plebeians
imperium	Senate
Etruscans	patron-client relationship
Republic	*paterfamilias*

The Evolution of the Roman Republic, 509–146 B.C.E.

- ◆ **How was the collective will of the Roman people expressed in Roman government?**
- ◆ **Why were the Romans initially reluctant to create an empire?**

After the expulsion of the kings, the Romans created the Roman Republic, a system of government based on the sharing of power among several magistrates (officials). The Roman people were governed by the rule of law, which represented the collective will of the people. During the early Republic, a nonviolent conflict arose between the patricians, who monopolized economic and political influence, and the plebeians, who wished to gain greater self-expression. By the early third century B.C.E., the Senate, the primary governing body of Rome, included both patricians and influential plebeians. The Senate guided Rome through many wars, first in Italy and then throughout the Mediterranean world. At first, the only goal of these wars was to weaken potential enemies, and the Romans were reluctant to assume responsibility for

Table 5.1   **Officials of the Roman Republic (by 146 B.C.E.)**

Title	Number	Duties	Term
Annually Elected Officials (in rank order)			
Consul	2	Leads Roman army, presides over assemblies	1 year
Praetor	6	Oversees law courts, governs some provinces	1 year
Aedile	4	Oversees buildings and markets in Rome	1 year
Quaestor	6	Oversees financial matters	1 year
Tribune	10	Presides over Council of the Plebs	1 year
Nonannual Officials			
Dictator	1	Outranks consuls during emergencies	6 months maximum
Censor	2	Assesses property, appoints senators	18 months
Proconsul	varies	Governs provinces	1–3 years
Legate	varies	Governor's assistant	Will of the governor

© Cengage Learning

administering foreign territory. But during the second century B.C.E., the Romans became more willing to take direct control over foreign territories, known as provinces. By 146 B.C.E. Rome had become the strongest power in the Mediterranean world.

Roman Republican Government

The Roman monarchy was superseded by the Republic, a government based on the concept of **collegiality**, in which offices and responsibilities were shared by the members of the Senate, which now became the most important governing body in Rome.

collegiality Shared responsibility for the same office.

consul Highest-ranking annual Roman official, whose primary duty was to lead the army.

legion Largest unit of the Roman army, roughly 5,000 men.

triumph Victory ceremony given to a Roman general who had won a great victory.

census Assessment of property carried out by the censors for taxation purposes.

Roman Magistrates The king was replaced by two **consuls**, who were elected by the people every year. Like the king, the consuls had the powers of imperium and auspicium. They had the right to introduce laws, but their primary duty was to lead the Roman **legions** in war. The greatest honor that a senator could receive was to be granted a ceremony called a **triumph** after a military victory during his term as consul. The consul, with his face painted red like the god Jupiter, led a procession of cheering soldiers and pitiful captives through the streets of Rome and up to the temple of Jupiter on the Capitoline Hill. Only in grave emergencies did the Romans return to a very restricted form of one-man rule. In such cases the consuls would appoint a dictator, the highest ranking of all magistrates. But there were severe limitations on the dictator's authority: he could serve only until the crisis was over and never for more than six months.

Over time, lower-ranking officials, elected by the people, also were introduced. These included, in descending rank, two praetors, who were the chief legal officials; four aediles, who managed the markets, streets, and public buildings; and six quaestors, who oversaw state finances. In addition, every five years, two censors, who ranked even higher than the consuls, were elected. They served for eighteen months, and their duties included assessing property for taxation purposes (the **census**) and appointing new members to the Senate. Because all Roman magistrates except the dictators served in groups of two or more, it was crucially important for the smooth operation of the government that they get along with each other. Table 5.1 provides a listing of the most important officials in the Roman Republic.

Roman Assemblies The Republican government operated according to a constitution that was a combination of customary practices and unwritten law. Supreme authority lay with the people, whose will was expressed by the votes of assemblies to which all male citizens belonged. The assemblies elected all officials except the dictators and voted on declarations of war, trials involving the death penalty, and laws regulating everyday Roman life. But the assemblies did not have the right to introduce laws. They could vote only on measures presented to them by the consuls, who were expected to have consulted with the Senate before they introduced any laws. The Senate thus was the primary governing body of Rome.

The Power of the Patricians At the beginning of the Republic, the patricians controlled the government because all three hundred or so members of the Senate were patricians and could instruct their plebeian clients how to vote in the assemblies. The patricians controlled the elections in the same way, and given that new senators were appointed by the censors, there was no chance that a plebeian would be chosen. In addition, only the patricians knew the laws, which were passed down by word of mouth from one generation to the next. At the beginning of the Republic, therefore, the patricians held virtually all the political, legal, social, and economic authority.

A People Ruled by Law

Beginning around 500 B.C.E., a period of domestic unrest known as the Conflict of the Orders disturbed the Republic as plebeians attempted to gain social, economic, legal, and political power.

The Conflict of the Orders During the Conflict of the Orders, the patricians were determined to maintain their privileged status and resisted plebeian calls for change. Two factors permitted the plebeians to pursue their goals. First, Rome could not be defended adequately from foreign enemies without plebeian military assistance. Therefore, soon after 500 B.C.E., the Senate sponsored reforms allowing wealthy plebeians who could afford their own weapons to fight in the army. Through their military service, these plebeians gained personal authority and found common ground with the patricians.

The plebeians also found strength in numbers by creating their own assembly, the Council of the Plebs, which only plebeians could attend. It issued rulings that were binding on the plebeians. Each year the plebeians elected ten tribunes of the plebs, who had the responsibility of defending the plebeians against patrician oppression. The plebeians swore to kill any patrician who ever harmed a tribune. The tribunes appropriated the right to say "Veto" ("I forbid") if the patricians did anything against plebeian interests. On such occasions, the plebeians went on strike until the tribune had been satisfied. In extreme cases, the plebeians threatened to secede and to establish their own nation.

The Twelve Tables The plebeians' earliest demand was to know the laws. Therefore, in 451 B.C.E., to avoid a secession of the plebeians, the Senate appointed a board of ten men, the decemvirs, to write down the existing laws. The result was the **Twelve Tables**, issued in 450 B.C.E., which became the basis for all later Roman law. One of Rome's most important contributions to western civilization is the concept of **rule of law**, the idea that governments and officials are subordinate to the law. Roman law represented not the will of the gods or the whims of godlike rulers, as in the Near East, but the collective will of the people. Once the law was written down, the plebeians became more confident that it would be fairly enforced, and what was already a stable society became even more stable.

The Twelve Tables reveal much about how Roman society functioned. They dealt with trial procedures, inheritances, property ownership and transfer, lawsuits, and religious law. They reflect both the harsh nature of early Roman life and the Roman virtues of responsibility, discipline, fortitude, and frugality. Romans were expected to maintain proper decorum in times of stress, and it was decreed that "women shall not weep on account of a funeral." There was no place for nonproductive persons: another regulation stated, "A dreadfully deformed child shall be quickly killed." Serious crimes such as treason, arson, and perjury were punished by death. Some laws did appear to benefit less privileged persons. For example, a patron who "devised any deceit against his client" could be legally killed. But overall, the laws were designed to maintain the favored position of the patricians. One law specified that plebeian debtors could be loaded down with chains and sold as slaves, and another prohibited marriages between patricians and plebeians, blocking the one means by which members of a plebeian family could enter the aristocracy.

The Plebeians Gain Rights The plebeians became so angered by such laws that they seceded. The patricians responded with laws that recognized the existence of the Council of the Plebs and guaranteed the personal safety of the tribunes of the plebs. At the same time, a new assembly, the Council of the People, was created, modeled on the Council of the Plebs but also including patricians.

Continued agitation by the most wealthy and influential plebeians soon brought the repeal of the ban on intermarriage. Plebeians married into patrician families, and the children of a plebeian woman who married a patrician were patricians. Plebeians also were permitted to hold military offices that gained them entry into the Senate. The patricians eventually acknowledged that to avoid future unrest they would have to give at least some plebeians a share in government, and they did so by

> **Twelve Tables** First written collection of Roman law, created by the decemvirs in 451–450 B.C.E.
>
> **rule of law** The idea that the law has higher authority than governments and officials.

Polybius Describes the Roman Constitution

During the 130s B.C.E., the Greek historian Polybius, a Roman hostage who became a good friend of Scipio Aemilianus and other leading Roman senators, described the constitution of the Roman Republic as an evenly balanced combination of monarchy, aristocracy, and democracy. He equated the consuls with monarchy, the Senate with aristocracy, and the Roman people with democracy. By explaining Roman government in terms of various forms of Greek government, Polybius demonstrated both that Greeks were trying to understand Rome in terms of their own experiences and that Romans wanted their own traditions to be understood in terms of the more ancient Greek past.

❶ How did these three forms of government function?

❷ How is Polybius putting Roman government into a Greek context?

❸ What is the relationship between the consuls and the Senate?

❹ How would the Senate expect its "friendly advice" to be received?

❺ How does Polybius's description of the role of the Senate compare with the description given in the chapter text?

❻ In what ways do the people not have as much power as Polybius suggests?

Three kinds of government shared in the control of the Roman state with such fairness that it was impossible even for a native to pronounce with certainty whether the system was aristocratic, democratic, or monarchical. **❶** For if one fixed one's eyes on the consuls, the constitution seemed completely monarchical; if on that of the Senate, it seemed again to be aristocratic; and when one looked at the power of the masses, it seemed clearly to be a democracy. The parts of the state falling under the control of each element are as follows. **❷**

The consuls, before leading out their legions, exercise authority in Rome over all public affairs. Besides this, they consult the Senate on matters of urgency, they carry out in detail the provisions of its decrees. **❸** It is their duty to summon assemblies, to introduce legislation, and to preside over the enforcement of the popular decrees. As for warfare, their power is almost uncontrolled, for they are empowered to make whatever demands they choose. They also have the right of inflicting punishment on anyone under their command, and they are authorized to spend any sum from the public funds. So that if one looks at this part of the administration alone, one may reasonably pronounce the constitution to be a pure monarchy.

To pass to the Senate. It has the control of the treasury, all revenue and expenditure being regulated by it. In addition, crimes committed in Italy, such as treason, conspiracy, poisoning, and assassination, are under the jurisdiction of the Senate. It also occupies itself with the sending of all embassies to countries outside of Italy for the purpose either of settling differences, or of offering friendly advice, **❹** or indeed of imposing demands, or receiving submission, or of declaring war; and in like manner with respect to embassies arriving in Rome it decides answer should be given to them. All these matters are in the hands of the Senate, so that without the consuls the constitution appears to be entirely aristocratic. **❺**

After this we might ask what part in the constitution is left for the people, considering that the Senate controls all the particular matters I mentioned, and that the consuls have uncontrolled authority as regards armaments and military operations. But nevertheless there is a very important part left for the people. The people alone have the right to confer honors and inflict punishment. They are the only court that may try capital charges. The people bestow office on the deserving, the noblest reward of virtue in a state. The people have the power of approving or rejecting laws, and they deliberate on the question of war and peace. Further, in the case of alliances, terms of peace, and treaties, it is the people who ratify all these or the reverse. Thus, here again one might plausibly say that the people's share in the government is the greatest, and that the constitution is a democratic one. **❻**

source: From the Greek historian Polybius (200–118 B.C.).

allying themselves with the most wealthy and influential plebeians. A law of 367 B.C.E. declared that from then on, one consul had to be a plebeian. Subsequently, all other government offices also were opened up to plebeians.

The Roman Oligarchy The Conflict of the Orders finally came to an end in 287 B.C.E., when the Hortensian Law gave the Council of the Plebs the right to pass laws binding on all the Roman people. These laws were introduced by the tribunes of the plebs, who, like the consuls, were expected to consult with the Senate before proposing any legislation. The result of the Conflict of the Orders was an evolution, just as had occurred in Greece, from an aristocracy, in which Rome was effectively governed by the patricians alone, to an oligarchy, in which both patricians and important plebeians served in the Senate and held high office.

The key to the success of Roman republican government lay in the willingness of the senators to share rule among themselves. But sharing rule was not always easy, for senators constantly competed with each other for status. Every five years, the censors drew up a list of senators in rank order, and every senator's ambition was to be the **princeps**, the "first man" on the list. Senators whose ancestors had been consuls became an inside group, called the nobles, who jealously monopolized access to this office. Only the most able non-nobles could be elected consuls, and someone who did so was called a **new man**. Though rare, the election of a new man demonstrated that an ambitious Roman man did have a chance to rise to the very top of Roman politics and society.

Going to War

The early years of the Republic were a struggle for survival as the Romans defended themselves against neighboring peoples who sought to control Rome's fertile agriculture lands and strategic location on the Tiber River.

The Celts and Early Rome The Romans fought off Etruscan attempts to recapture the city and competed with neighboring Latins and Italians for control of the rich agricultural plain of Latium. The combined army of patricians and plebeians was able to defend Rome until 390 B.C.E., when a raiding party of Gauls from northern Italy attacked. The Gauls, more generally known as the **Celts**, were an Indo-European people who inhabited the British Isles, **Gaul** (modern France), and the rest of Europe except for Greece and Italy. There were many independent Celtic groups, each governed either by a king or by a council of warrior aristocrats. The Celtic economy was based primarily on farming, the Celts also had a highly developed trading network, and Celtic metalwork was particularly prized.

It was for their fighting style, however, that the Celts were best known. Celtic warriors wore an ornate metal ring called a torque, often of gold or silver, forged around their necks. Believing that their torques' magical powers would protect them from harm, the most enthusiastic warriors fought in the nude. Before a battle, Celtic warriors smeared wet lime into their hair to make it stand straight back when it dried and give them a more terrifying appearance. Celtic battles began with warriors leaping about and shouting insults at their enemy as they worked themselves up into the famous Celtic fury. Then came their terrifying charge, with naked six-foot-tall warriors wildly swinging their yard-long swords. At first, no Mediterranean people could resist them.

The Romans were completely dumbfounded by the wild and undisciplined charge of the howling Gauls. The Romans' tightly packed phalanx, a military formation they had adopted from the Greeks of southern Italy, collapsed, and the Romans fled. The Gauls then sacked and burned the city of Rome, departing only after they had exacted a large ransom. The Romans were determined that such a disaster would never happen again. It took them about fifty years to recover from the Gallic sack, after which they initiated a long series of military actions that ultimately resulted in Rome's becoming the most powerful nation in the Mediterranean world.

Rome's Reasons for Going to War Rome's development as a world power has interested historians because the Romans got involved in so many wars and yet at first seemed uninterested in building an empire. The Romans could decide to go to war for several reasons. One was fear. Following the sack by the Gauls, the Romans were frightened by strong neighbors and sometimes made preemptive strikes against peoples they believed were becoming too powerful. In addition, to gain social and political status, Roman consuls often felt that they needed military glory and almost always voted for war if the opportunity arose. The Romans also took their treaty responsibilities seriously, and a Roman ally that was attacked could usually count on Rome to come to its assistance. Occasionally, the Romans went to war to gain land for distribution to poor plebeians. Finally, of course, there were genuine threats, for the Romans had to resist when they were attacked by a foreign power.

Rome's Reluctance to Create an Empire Even though the Romans defeated a great many peoples in Italy and throughout the Mediterranean world, they

princeps (Latin for "first") The first man on the list of senators drawn up by the censors.

new man A consul who did not have an ancestor who had been a consul.

Celts The people of inland Europe, also known as Gauls.

Gaul Modern France, homeland of the Gauls.

Erich Lessing/ Art Resource, NY

A Roman copy of a Hellenistic statue shows a Gaul wearing a torque killing himself and his wife so they would not be taken captive by the Romans and enslaved. Many Greek and Roman statues of Celts show them dead or dying, reflecting the fear that the Celts created. Like many Gallic warriors, this one is portrayed in the nude, protected by the magical power of the torque that he wears around his neck. Do you think this is a favorable depiction of the Gauls? Why or why not?

low, and there was no regular tax collection system—and the Roman economy was so undeveloped that the Republic did not issue coinage for more than two centuries after it began. Because there was no money to support a standing army, Rome's army was a citizen **militia**. Soldiers were recruited from among farmers and artisans only when a consul was assigned a war. They had to be able to supply their own weapons and largely to pay their own way as part of their civic duty. Thus, poor people were unable to serve in the army. When the war was over, the soldiers returned to civilian life, and the Senate did not have any responsibility for them. A citizen militia was not the kind of army that empire building required, and the Senate had no desire to expand Rome's government to administer an empire.

The Expansion of Rome

By about 350 B.C.E. the Romans had finally recovered from the Gallic sack. Soon thereafter, they became drawn into wars against other people, first in Italy and then in the Mediterranean. The end result was that Rome was left as the only power in the Mediterranean world.

Wars in Italy Shortly after 350 B.C.E., the Samnites, an Italian mountain people, began expanding west toward the Bay of Naples. Fearful of a threat to their security, the Romans fought three wars between 343 and 290 B.C.E. against the Samnites and their allies. After losing several battles, the Romans finally defeated a combined force of Samnites, Etruscans, and Gauls in 295 B.C.E., and the Samnites soon capitulated. Soon afterward, the Greeks of the southern Italian city of Tarentum, fearing Rome's growing power, summoned the able Greek general, King **Pyrrhus of Epirus**, to help them. Pyrrhus invaded Italy in 280 B.C.E. and won three hard-fought battles, but his losses were very heavy. His comment after one battle, "Another victory like this and I will be totally ruined," gave rise to the term Pyrrhic victory, meaning a victory so costly that one might as well have lost. The losses of the Romans were even greater, but they simply refused to give up, and in 275 B.C.E., Pyrrhus withdrew and returned to Greece. The Greeks of southern Italy then made peace on Roman terms. In these campaigns, the Romans prevailed primarily because of their persistence and their willingness to take greater losses than their opponents. They lost

at first were reluctant to take over, administer, or exploit the territory of the peoples they defeated. This policy was different from that of the Near Eastern and Greek peoples of the past for several reasons. First, the Roman justifications for going to war, explained above, did not support empire building. In addition, the Romans had no tradition of conquest for economic or political gain. They did not believe that gaining territory contributed to the greater glory of Rome.

The Romans also recognized that building and keeping an empire would require a large professional army, something the Senate neither wanted nor could afford. The Roman government had very little tax revenue—taxes were very

militia Military force of nonprofessional citizen soldiers.

Pyrrhus of Epirus (318–272 B.C.E.) Greek king who fought the Romans between 280 and 275 B.C.E.

more battles than they won, often because the consuls who led their armies were in office for only one year and were not experienced generals.

The Consolidation of Roman Authority Even though the Romans had defeated all the peoples of Italy by 268 B.C.E., they showed little interest in imposing direct control over them. Primarily, they wanted to keep their neighbors from posing a threat, and they did so in several ways. To be able to concentrate their forces quickly, they created a network of all-weather military roads. The first, the Appian Way, was begun in 312 B.C.E. and went from Rome to southern Italy.

The Romans also occupied enough land to establish military colonies at strategic points such as mountain passes or river fords. These colonies also allowed the Romans to give land there to poor plebeians and thus make them eligible for military service. The keystone of Roman foreign policy was to impose treaties on defeated enemies in which Rome was the patron and the enemy was the client. The former enemy remained independent but became a Roman ally. Whenever Rome went to war, its allies were expected to provide military units to assist the Roman legions, which were manned only by Roman citizens. This **Italian alliance** gave Rome access to a manpower reserve of half a million men.

The First Punic War Rome soon became engaged in even bigger wars outside Italy. The first were with the powerful North African trading city of Carthage. The Carthaginians worshiped the goddess Tanit, who commanded that the first-born sons of Carthaginian families be sacrificed to her. Excavations of Carthaginian infant cemeteries testify that many devout Carthaginians observed this practice. During the third century B.C.E., Carthage attempted to gain control of the island of Sicily. The prospect of such a powerful neighbor only a few miles offshore from Italy worried the Romans. When Sicilian Greeks asked for Roman protection, a consul who was eager to win personal glory convinced the people to vote for war. Rome thus became committed to its first overseas conflict, the First **Punic War** (264–241 B.C.E.).

To get to Sicily, the Romans, who had little seafaring tradition, were compelled to create a navy. They won their first battle by simply running their ships alongside the Carthaginian ships, boarding them with soldiers, and effectively changing a sea battle into a land battle. The Carthaginians were not fooled again, but this unexpectedly easy victory only strengthened the Roman commitment to fight on until they had won. After a long war, the Carthaginians made peace in 241 B.C.E., agreeing to evacuate Sicily and to pay an **indemnity** of 3,200 talents of silver, for the Romans expected the defeated party to pay the cost of the war.

The Romans then had to decide what to do about the territory Carthage had abandoned. Fearful of having the rich island of Sicily become another source of trouble, in 227 B.C.E. the Romans made it their first province, a foreign territory over which Rome assumed direct control. Two years later, Sardinia and Corsica, which in the past had been Carthaginian bases, became Rome's second province. Having no method for governing foreign territories, the Romans created two new praetors to serve as provincial governors. Otherwise, they did little with the new provinces, content simply to keep them from Carthaginian control.

The Second Punic War Meanwhile, the fortunes of the Carthaginians revived under the leadership of **Hannibal**, one of the ablest generals of all time. After losing the First Punic War, the Carthaginians rebuilt their army using silver and Celtic mercenaries from Spain. In 218 B.C.E., after the Romans had attempted to interfere in Carthaginian-controlled Spain, Hannibal led an army of Celtic infantry, **Numidian** cavalry, and thirty-seven war elephants out of Spain, through the Alps, and into Italy. This began the Second Punic War (218–201 B.C.E.), the most difficult war the Romans ever fought. Hannibal's goal was to break up Rome's Italian alliance. He quickly won three spectacular victories. At Cannae, in 216 B.C.E., a Roman army of more than 50,000 men was surrounded and virtually annihilated by Hannibal's smaller 30,000-man army. Subsequently, for fear of losing another battle, the Romans simply refused to fight Hannibal in Italy, and he marched about unopposed for another thirteen years.

Hannibal finally met his match in the Roman general **Scipio**. Scipio's father and uncle had been killed fighting Hannibal, but Scipio was determined never to surrender. As a young man, he was placed in command of the Roman armies in Spain, where he gained a reputation for fair treatment of prisoners. By 206 B.C.E., Scipio had defeated three veteran Carthaginian armies and forced the Carthaginians to evacuate Spain. Chosen consul for the year 205 B.C.E., Scipio began training an army to invade Africa, which he did the next year. He convinced many Numidians to change sides, thus gaining some excellent cavalry. Scipio defeated the Carthaginians, who then recalled Hannibal from Italy.

Italian alliance Defeated cities and peoples of Italy who were required to follow Roman foreign policy and supply Rome with soldiers.

Punic Wars (from the Latin *Poenus*, "Phoenician") Series of three wars (264–241, 218–201, and 149–146 B.C.E.) that Rome fought against Carthage in North Africa.

indemnity Monetary penalty imposed by the Romans on a defeated enemy.

Hannibal (ca. 247–183 B.C.E.) Carthaginian general who invaded Italy in 218 B.C.E., beginning the Second Punic War.

Numidia Region of western North Africa famous for horsemanship.

Scipio Africanus (ca. 236–183 B.C.E.) Roman general who defeated Hannibal at the Battle of Zama in 202 B.C.E.

The final confrontation came in 202 B.C.E. at the Battle of Zama, where the Roman cavalry was able to slip behind the Carthaginian army and attack from the rear. Hannibal was defeated, and Scipio received the nickname "Africanus" ("the conqueror of Africa") in recognition of his victory. The next year, Carthage surrendered. The Romans did not take over any territory in Africa, but they did compel Carthage to give up Spain (which was made into two new Roman provinces), destroy its navy, and pay an indemnity of 20,000 talents. Scipio generously permitted Hannibal to live, but Carthage never again was a strong military power.

The Romans looked back to the Second Punic War as their defining moment. They had never considered surrendering. All of Rome pulled together: Roman women donated their jewelry to the war effort, and contractors provided war supplies on credit. The war also demonstrated the strength of Rome's Italian alliance, for nearly all Rome's allies had stayed loyal. Rome now was the only power in the western Mediterranean.

Wars in the East   The war also left Rome completely exhausted. Tens of thousands of soldiers had been killed, Italian property losses were staggering, and the Roman government was deep in debt. Nevertheless, Rome immediately was drawn into conflicts with two of the three great Hellenistic kingdoms to the east: Antigonid Macedonia, Seleucid Syria, and Ptolemaic Egypt.

In 200 B.C.E., the Romans declared war on Macedonia because the Macedonians had made an alliance with Hannibal. Three years later, they soundly defeated the Macedonians and compelled them to pay a war indemnity, give up their navy, and evacuate their territory in Greece. Shortly thereafter, the Romans also defeated the Seleucids of Syria, who had frightened the Romans by invading Greece. The Seleucids were compelled to pay a large indemnity, give up their war elephants, and abandon their territories in Anatolia. In both cases, the Romans had the opportunity to take over foreign territory but chose not to do so. Their goal was simply to keep potential enemies weak. Then, in 171 B.C.E., it was rumored that the Macedonians planned to hire Celts to invade Italy. War again was declared, and the Macedonians were defeated in 168 B.C.E. This time the Romans took stronger measures to weaken Macedonia, dividing it into four independent countries. The Romans then went home, confident that the Macedonian threat finally had been eliminated.

But the wars still were not over. Carthage had rebuilt itself as an economic, although not as a military, power, creating jealousy in Rome. The hawkish senator **Cato the Elder**, an ambitious new man, ended each of his speeches in the Senate by declaring, "And I also think that Carthage must be destroyed." He got his wish in 149 B.C.E., when the Romans again attacked Carthage. The war dragged on until 146 B.C.E., when **Scipio Aemilianus**, the grandson by adoption of Scipio Africanus, captured the city in desperate house-to-house fighting. Many Carthaginians committed suicide by leaping into the burning temple of Tanit. In the same year, the Romans were victorious in yet another Macedonian war.

The Beginnings of Empire   At this point, the Roman attitude to foreign territories changed. Recognizing that allowing defeated enemies to remain independent caused problems later, the Romans changed their response in two ways. First, they taught a lesson to any people contemplating resistance by destroying two of the most famous cities of the Mediterranean world, Carthage in North Africa and Corinth in Greece. In addition, they annexed North Africa and Macedonia as new provinces and shortly after added the province of Asia in western Anatolia, and the southern part of Gaul. The building of what would become the Roman Empire now was well under way.

✔ Checking In

By yourself or with a partner, explain the significance of each of the following selected key terms:

collegiality	princeps
consul	Italian alliance
triumph	Punic Wars
Twelve Tables	Cato the Elder

The Effects of Roman Expansion, 146–88 B.C.E.

◆ **How did Roman expansion create problems for the Romans?**

◆ **What were the consequences of changes in Roman military recruiting policies?**

The growth of Roman power had many consequences for Roman life. To cope with the acquisition of far-flung provinces, the Romans had to restructure their society and economy. They also were confronted by an influx of foreign cultural ideas, especially from Greece. Some Romans welcomed new cultural concepts; others saw them as a challenge to old Roman values. Administering the provinces effectively was difficult because the Senate was reluctant to make changes in the Roman system of government. Recruiting soldiers for the Roman army also became difficult.

Cato the Elder (ca. 234–149 B.C.E.) Conservative Roman senator who represented old Roman values and opposed the assimilation of Greek culture.

Scipio Aemilianus (185–129 B.C.E.) Roman senator who defeated Carthage and favored the assimilation of Greek culture.

The denarius, first issued in 212 B.C.E., became the standard Roman silver coin. It was used by senators as a form of advertising to glorify their families. This denarius, issued in 43 B.C.E. by the Brutus who had just assassinated Julius Caesar, commemorates the Brutus who was one of the first two Roman consuls in 509 B.C.E. The consul is accompanied by two lictors bearing the rods and axes symbolizing the consul's authority. Why do you think the assassin Brutus would have issued a coin that referred to the very beginning of the Roman Republic? (Snark/Art Resource, NY)

Efforts to deal with some of these problems met stiff resistance and flared into the first violence ever experienced in Roman politics.

The Transformation of Rome

By 120 B.C.E., Rome controlled territory extending from Spain to Anatolia. Roman expansion had far-reaching social, cultural, and economic effects.

The Equestrian Class and Roman Wealth The influx of wealth from overseas brought the most noticeable changes. So many riches were seized from Macedonia in 168 B.C.E. that taxes on Roman citizens were eliminated. The Romans realized that provincial resources, such as the silver mines of Spain, could be made into a permanent source of income. Because of the financial opportunities created by Roman expansion, a new social class arose, the **equestrians**, who ranked just below the senators. They made fortunes in trade, manufacturing, moneylending, tax collecting, and selling supplies to the army. Senators, who preferred to invest in land, became even more wealthy than before through their service as provincial governors.

Expansion also created the need for money to pay for it. A Roman silver coin, the **denarius**, was finally introduced in 212 B.C.E. when tremendous amounts of coinage were needed to meet the expenses of the Second Punic War. The denarius soon became the standard currency of the Mediterranean world.

The old Roman virtues of frugality and modesty gave way to taking pleasure in luxury and display. On one occasion, women protested against a law that no woman should own more than a half-ounce of gold, or wear multicolored clothing, or ride in a carriage in Rome. They blockaded the Forum and confronted the senators, engaging in an unprecedented form of political activism. The conservative consul Cato the Elder complained, "Our freedom is conquered by female fury, we even now let them meddle in the Forum," but the offensive law was repealed nonetheless.

Popular Expenditures New construction adorned the city of Rome. New temples were built, and old ones, such as the temple of Jupiter on the Capitoline Hill, were rebuilt on a grander scale. The first **basilica**, a large rectangular public building used for hearing legal cases, was built in the Forum. New aqueducts brought fresh water into Rome. For their building projects, the Romans used stone blocks, bricks, and concrete made from *pozzolana*, a fine, wear-resistant volcanic sand. They also made extensive use of the arch, the vault, and the dome, pioneering building types that would continue to be characteristic of western architecture in the Middle Ages, the Renaissance, and modern day.

The Roman people came to expect expensive entertainments, which were held in honor of funerals, religious festivals, and military victories. One popular festival was the Saturnalia, a period of merriment held December 17–23 in honor of the god Saturn. People exchanged gifts, and slaves traded places with their masters. Chariot racing, borrowed from the Greeks and the Etruscans, attracted ever-larger crowds. Beginning in 211 B.C.E., an annual festival in honor of Apollo included two days of chariot racing. Races were held on racecourses known as **circuses**, and in the 170s B.C.E. the Circus Maximus, or "Greatest Circus," was rebuilt. Gladiatorial contests, which had been borrowed from the Etruscans, became increasingly popular. At first, gladiators fought only at the funerals of important persons. In 174 B.C.E., for example, the senator Flamininus, who had defeated Macedonia, celebrated his father's funeral by matching seventy-four gladiators against each other. Eventually, however, gladiatorial combats were put on purely for entertainment.

equestrians (from Latin "eques," a person wealthy enough to own a horse) Roman social class ranking just below the senators.

denarius Silver coin introduced by the Romans in 212 B.C.E.; it became the standard coin of the Mediterranean world.

basilica A large rectangular public building with a large middle aisle and two side aisles.

circus Long oval racecourse for chariot races and other forms of entertainment.

The Roman Forum was the center of Roman public life and contained temples and other public buildings. This view of the forum as it appears in modern day shows several monuments initially built during the Republic. The remains of the house of the Vestal Virgins appear on the left. Adjoining it, three surviving columns of the ancient temple of Castor and Pollux stand in front of the site of the basilica Julia, dedicated by Julius Caesar in 46 B.C.E., where the praetors heard legal cases. On the slopes of the Capitoline Hill in the background is the *tabularium*, the official archives. And on the far right stands the Senate house. Why do you think some ancient Roman buildings, such as the Senate house and tabularium, survived to the modern day virtually intact, whereas most others have disappeared?

Scala/Art Resource, NY

The Assimilation of Greek Culture

Roman expansion also exposed the Romans to foreign cultural influences, especially from Greece. Many Romans enthusiastically embraced Greek thought, literature, language, and culture.

Roman Education The Romans patterned their educational system on the Greek model. Well-to-do Romans often hired or purchased a Greek schoolmaster for their children. Rich and poor boys and girls also attended private schools for a small fee. Grammar schools, for children aged twelve through sixteen, taught grammar and literature. Rhetoric schools, for children aged sixteen and up, taught public speaking, an important skill for a young man who wanted a career in public life. Corporeal punishment, such as hitting with a wooden switch, was regularly administered in the belief that it made students more attentive. Educated Roman youngsters grew up to be bilingual, often learning to read Greek before they learned Latin. Many went on to pursue their studies in Greece.

Polybius (ca. 203–120 B.C.E.) Greek who was held as a hostage in Rome and wrote a history of Rome's rise to world power.

The Assimilation of Greek Literature Greek literature provided a model for Roman literature, which first developed in the second century B.C.E. Roman playwrights such as Plautus and the ex-slave Terence wrote Latin comedies based on Greek originals. The first histories of Rome, written in the years after 200 B.C.E., were written in Greek, not only by Romans but also by Greeks such as **Polybius**, a Greek hostage who was an eyewitness to the fall of Carthage. And the Stoic philosophy, which taught that doing one's duty was the highest virtue, found many followers in Rome. These undertakings were supported by influential Roman senators, such as Scipio Aemilianus.

Roman Opposition to Foreign Influence Not all Romans thought that the acceptance of Greek culture was a good thing. Some conservative senators, such as Cato the Elder, feared that old Roman values would be destroyed by what he perceived as Greek luxury, extravagance, and immorality. He advised his son, "Take this as a prophecy: when those Greeks give us their writings, they will corrupt everything." As censor, Cato expelled from the Senate any senator who did not meet his moral standards. When Greek Epicurean philosophers, who Romans thought advocated a life of self-indulgence, visited Rome, Cato saw to it that they were deported. And in a personal protest against Greek literature, Cato wrote his own history

During the Roman Republic, decrees of the Senate and laws passed by the popular assemblies were first haphazardly stored in the Temple of Saturn, and then, after 78 B.C.E., in the tabularium, the new state archives. But there was no standardized compilation of laws, and all of these records have long since been lost. But some Roman laws were inscribed on stone or bronze tablets and posted where people could see them, either in Rome itself or in cities under Roman control. Some of these laws, engraved on more substantial material, still survive, such as this bronze copy of the Decree of the Senate on the Baccanalians, which was issued in 186 B.C.E. and forbade the organized worship of the wine-god Bacchus. How likely do you think it is that original copies of laws issued in the modern day will still survive 2,000 years from now?

of Rome in Latin. Later Roman authors followed his example, and by the end of the second century B.C.E., Latin had become an established literary language in its own right. The Romans even developed their own literary genre, satire, which used parody, obscenity, and abuse to project a critical but humorous view of society, morality, and personal behavior.

Romans' concerns about their values also surfaced with regard to foreign religious practices, which Rome also assimilated. At the end of the third century B.C.E., for example, the worship of the eastern mother goddess Cybele was introduced into Rome. The uninhibited practices associated with these religions caused anxiety in some conservative senators. In 186 B.C.E., a Roman consul received a report that worshipers of the wine god Bacchus were holding secret orgies. The Senate not only saw such behavior as a threat to conventional morality but also feared that the covert gatherings might lead to conspiracies against the government. According to the Roman historian Livy, many Romans were sentenced to death, with women being turned over to their families "so they could inflict the punishment in private." In spite of Roman resistance, Greek culture continued to infiltrate Rome.

Problems in the Provinces

The most significant consequence of Rome's wars was the acquisition of an increasing number of foreign provinces. By 146 B.C.E., these provinces had made Rome into an empire in everything but name.

Provincial Government It soon became clear that Rome was unable to cope with the administration of its foreign territories. Even though the Romans had the best intentions of fulfilling their responsibilities in the provinces, they lacked the institutions for doing so, and the conservative Senate saw no reason to alter Rome's form of government to accommodate the provinces. As a result, direct Roman administration was minimal. When a new province was created, a senatorial commission created a Law of the Province that established general administrative guidelines, but otherwise local customs were respected and native laws remained in effect. Roman governors held the office of either praetor or **proconsul** (a senator who in the past had held the office of consul). Governors served for two or three years and had very small staffs, consisting only of a quaestor to handle the finances and a few legates, deputies to whom their authority could be delegated.

The governors' primary responsibilities were to provide military defense, oversee the administration of justice, and collect taxes. Every effort was made to minimize expenses. Roman taxes were not excessive, but the Romans did expect the provinces to pay for themselves. To keep costs down, armies were sent to provinces only when needed. Because the governor did not have the staff to govern the province directly, local government was left in the hands of city governments. If a province did not already have cities, as in the case of much of Europe, the Romans created them. In Spain, for example, Romans redefined the territory of a Celtic people as belonging to a city created to serve as an administrative center. This process eventually would foster the urbanization of western Europe. Governors made a regular circuit of provincial cities to resolve legal disputes that could not be settled locally.

Ineffectiveness of Roman Government The rudimentary Roman provincial administration led to several problems. Provincial people had no rights in Rome, and the governor was the highest court of appeal. Corrupt governors therefore could enrich themselves by selling legal decisions to the highest bidder or by confiscating property, and there was nothing the provincials could do about it. Nor was there any established procedure by which provincials could become Roman citizens. But the provincials' greatest complaint involved tax collection.

> **proconsul** A senator who in the past had held the office of consul and later served as a provincial governor with the power of imperium.

In some provinces tribute, a fixed annual sum, was collected and in others the **tithe**, a tenth of the crops. Because the Roman governor did not have staff to collect the taxes, the right to do so was auctioned off. Tax collection companies paid the Roman government a lump sum for tax-collection rights and then went out into the countryside and extorted as much as they could. In provinces with the tithe, tax collectors known as publicans had a reputation for seizing large quantities of crops and calling it a tenth. Even if a governor protested against this practice, as many did, he did not have the workforce to prevent it.

At best, the Roman attitude toward the provinces could be called benign neglect. The Romans did not intend to exploit the provinces, and they did not make much money from them. Any corruption that arose benefited individual governors or profiteers, not the Roman government. The government simply did not have any centralized procedures for policing the provinces. One of the primary failures of the Republic was that it was unable to integrate the provinces, and their inhabitants, into the mainstream of Roman government and society.

The Gracchi and the Military Recruitment Crisis

Fighting wars and acquiring provinces created a need for armies, which led to another serious problem. Ever since the Samnite Wars, Roman armies had been fighting farther and farther from home for longer and longer periods. Because military recruiting policies required soldiers to be property owners, thousands of property-owning farmers were fighting far from home instead of farming, and Rome's agricultural economy suffered as a consequence. Moreover, many farmer-soldiers did not come back, and those who did often chose not to return to a life of drudgery on the farm and sold their land to senators, who always were looking to expand their landholdings. As a result, many landless plebeians settled in Rome, and senators acquired huge farms known as **latifundia**.

These developments created a military recruitment crisis because there were fewer and fewer landowners eligible to serve in the army. The Senate could have addressed the crisis either by abandoning the property requirement for military service or by distributing state-owned public land to landless plebeians and thus making them eligible for military service. In typical fashion, however, the conservative Senate did nothing.

tithe Form of taxation, one-tenth of everyone's crops, imposed on some Roman provinces; other provinces paid tribute, a fixed annual amount.

latifundia (in Latin, "widespread estates") Large estates belonging to Roman senators.

Gracchi Tiberius (163–133 B.C.E.) and Gaius (154–122 B.C.E.) Gracchus, Roman reformers from about 133–122 B.C.E.

The Reforms of the Gracchi Two brothers, Tiberius and Gaius Gracchus, attempted to deal with this and other problems. The **Gracchi**, as they were known, were related to the noblest Roman senatorial families. Their mother, Cornelia, was the daughter of Scipio Africanus, and after the death of her husband, she raised the two boys herself. She became the model Roman mother. According to one story, when a friend was showing off her jewelry and asked to see Cornelia's jewelry, Cornelia called in her two sons and said, "These are my jewels." It came as a great surprise to many when these two distinguished senators became reformers.

As a tribune of the plebs in 133 B.C.E., Tiberius Gracchus introduced legislation to distribute public land to poor plebeians to make them prosperous enough for military service. His proposal met great resistance from senators who had been renting public land and saw it as their personal property. Suspecting that the Senate would not approve his legislation, Tiberius decided not to seek the Senate's advice. Instead, he took his law directly to the Council of the Plebs, where it was passed and put into effect. His ignoring of traditional procedures threatened the authority of conservative senators, who organized an armed mob. In the ensuing riot, Tiberius and several hundreds of his supporters were killed.

Several years later, in 123 B.C.E., Tiberius's younger brother Gaius also was elected tribune and proposed additional reforms, including a law to confiscate land from senators and give it to poor plebeians. A year later, conservative senators organized another mob, and Gaius committed suicide rather than be captured alive. Over a thousand of his supporters reportedly were killed.

The deaths of the Gracchi and their supporters marked not only the first appearance of serious violence in republican politics but also the breakdown of the carefully cultivated cooperation among senators that had made the Republic work. Increasingly, senators looked out for their own self-interest as they competed to gain political influence and high office. Instead of working with the Senate, many ambitious senators now took their legislation directly to the assemblies, appealing to the urban poor by offering jobs, entertainment, subsidized food, free land, and reduced army service.

Marius and the Volunteer Army

The new land distribution policy did not meet the need for army recruits. The old recruitment system was sufficient as long as there were no large demands on it, but it broke down completely beginning around 113 B.C.E.

The Military Crisis The first crisis came when two large groups of northern European Celts, the

Cimbri and Teutones, arrived in southern Gaul looking for land and defeated one Roman army after another. At the same time, Rome went to war against the Numidian chieftain Jugurtha, whose army had massacred some Italian merchants, but Roman armies had little success against Jugurtha's hit-and-run tactics. In addition, there was a massive slave revolt in Sicily in 104 B.C.E. It was simply impossible to recruit enough soldiers to handle these emergencies.

The Creation of the Volunteer Army The recruitment problem was solved by **Marius**, a member of a previously undistinguished equestrian family. After gaining a military reputation in Spain, Marius pursued a political career. As a newcomer, he had a difficult time and lost several elections, but he persevered. He also married Julia, a member of the distinguished Julius Caesar family. In 108 B.C.E., Marius was elected consul and thus became a new man. He was appointed to take command in Africa, and to raise an army, he enlisted men who had no property at all. Other generals soon did the same, thereby creating a **volunteer army** of professional soldiers whose livelihood was based on their military service. Soldiers no longer fought to protect their homes, but for pay and any other kinds of personal profit.

When the Senate refused to pay for these new armies or to reward the soldiers with land grants after the war was over, these responsibilities were left to the generals. The armies, therefore, began to feel more loyalty toward their generals than toward the state. Using this new army, Marius soon was able to defeat Jugurtha, the Cimbri and Teutones, and the Sicilian slaves. By 101 B.C.E., the military threats to Rome had been averted, and the military recruitment crisis was over. But Rome was now left with an even more serious problem—armies whose loyalty to the state was dependent on the goodwill of the senatorial generals who commanded them.

Revolt of the Italian Allies Military recruitment policies also created another problem for the Republic. Over time, Rome's Italian allies had provided an ever-greater percentage of Rome's armies, increasing from half in the third century B.C.E. to two-thirds by the early first century B.C.E. The allies believed they were bearing more of the burden for Rome's wars but sharing less in the benefits. These concerns grew into Italian demands to be granted Roman citizenship. The Senate repeatedly refused, resulting in a massive revolt of the Italian allies in 90 B.C.E. The Romans could not hope to win such a war and once again showed that they could change if they had to. Citizenship was quickly granted to the Italians, and the fighting soon stopped. Nearly all of the free people living in Italy thus became Roman citizens. This unification of Italy, even though it was long in coming, provides another example of the long Roman tradition of being able to make outsiders into insiders.

 Checking In

By yourself or with a partner, explain the significance of each of the following selected key terms:

equestrians	latifundia
denarius	Gracchi
proconsul	Cimbri and Teutones
tithe	volunteer army

The End of the Republic, 90–27 B.C.E.

◆ **In what ways did senators put their own interests ahead of those of the Republic?**

◆ **What caused the fall of the Roman Republic?**

By 90 B.C.E., the Republic faced grave problems that the Senate had been unwilling and unable to deal with. The most serious problem was ambitious and powerful senators who controlled large armies. Although these senators tried to maintain their duty to Rome, too often their conflicts erupted into civil war. In the end, contests among ambitious senators led to the collapse of Roman republican government and Rome was left under the control of a single powerful general.

Sulla Seizes Rome

Following the Italian revolt, the Roman Republic confronted three overwhelming problems: ineffective administration of the provinces, lack of control over the volunteer army, and ambitious senators who put their personal interests ahead of the best interests of Rome.

The War with Mithridates Dissatisfaction with provincial administration was especially widespread in prosperous provinces such as Sicily and Asia in Anatolia, where there was more opportunity for corruption. In 88 B.C.E., resentment of tax collection methods boiled over into open revolt in the province of Asia. This provided an opening for Mithridates, the ambitious king of Pontus on the southeastern coast of the Black Sea, to invade the Roman province. Eighty thousand Romans reportedly were murdered on a single day, and a Roman general was executed by having molten gold poured down his throat while being told, "And now let the Roman thirst for gold be satisfied."

Cimbri and **Teutones** Celtic peoples who attacked Roman territory beginning in 113 B.C.E.; finally defeated by Marius in 101 B.C.E.

Marius (157–86 B.C.E.) Roman general who created the volunteer army about 108 B.C.E.

volunteer army Professional Roman army comprised of men without any property.

Back in Rome, the Senate assigned the war against Mithridates to the consul **Sulla**, a shrewd member of a penniless patrician family who was hoping to restore his family's fortunes. Marius, however, who had hoped to get the command for himself, convinced the Council of the Plebs to transfer the command to him. Rather than accepting this disappointment, Sulla appealed to his army for support. His soldiers seized Rome, and Sulla forced the Senate to reconfirm his command. Sulla then sailed off to the east, where he eventually defeated Mithridates.

The Rule of Sulla Five years later, in 83 B.C.E., Sulla returned and again seized Rome. To retain absolute power, he had himself appointed dictator, but without the customary six-month limitation. In order to raise the money to pay off his army, he issued the **proscriptions**, a list of fifteen hundred enemies condemned to execution and the loss of their property. Before his death in 78 B.C.E., Sulla attempted to strengthen the authority of the Senate to prevent anyone else from doing what he had done, but it was his example of using an army to take control of the government that was his most important legacy.

Other ambitious senators also discovered uses for an army. Away from Rome, military victories allowed a general to gain clients in the provinces, to acquire wealth, and to win glory, and by doing so to fulfill Roman ideals of virtue. In Rome, soldiers could be used to manipulate votes in the Senate and assemblies. The only way to get authorization to recruit an army was to be assigned a war somewhere in the provinces. Ambitious senators therefore became even more eager for military commands.

Late Republican Politics

After Sulla's death, three ambitious senators struggled for power: **Crassus**, the richest man in Rome; **Pompey**, a young supporter of Sulla; and **Julius Caesar**, a member of an old patrician family.

The Revolt of Spartacus
The next crisis for the Republic was another consequence of Roman expansion.

Hundreds of thousands of war captives had been sold in Italy as slaves. Those with useful skills could look forward to a comfortable urban life and eventual freedom, but unskilled slaves were considered no more than "speaking tools," and large numbers were put to work, and often badly treated, in the fields of senatorial *latifundia*. Cato the Elder recommended that agricultural slaves be bought cheaply, often as war captives, fed little, worked to death, and then replaced with additional cheap slaves.

Occasionally, slaves revolted and were brutally punished. This was the case in the slave revolt begun by **Spartacus** in 73 B.C.E. (see A New Direction: Spartacus Decides to Revolt). Crassus was assigned the war against the slaves, raised his own volunteer army, and suppressed the revolt with great severity. This victory made Crassus one of the most powerful senators in Rome, but it also made the Senate reluctant to grant him another military command that would enable him to become even more powerful.

The Career of Pompey Pompey had gained a military reputation as a supporter of Sulla; for his enthusiastic execution of Sulla's enemies he was nicknamed "the Teenage Butcher." In 67 B.C.E., he was assigned the task of wiping out the pirates who infested the Mediterranean. He swept from Gibraltar to Anatolia, clearing out the pirates as he went. In the following year, he undertook and won another war against Mithridates. He then abolished the Seleucid kingdom and made Syria into a Roman province. He also annexed part of the Jewish kingdom, leaving the rest in the hands of a Jewish **client king**, who owed his position to Rome. When he returned home, Pompey discovered that the Senate was so jealous of his successes that it refused to approve his organization of Syria and Judaea and to grant land to his army veterans.

Cicero and Catiline An ambitious senator who made his reputation not in the army but with his legal and oratorical talents was **Cicero**, who came from a previously undistinguished equestrian family. After a string of successful court cases, he was elected consul as a new man for the year 63 B.C.E. The senatorial conservatives had supported Cicero because they preferred him to his opponent Catiline, who was appealing to the poor by proposing to cancel all their debts. The disappointed Catiline then formed a conspiracy to overthrow the government. The conspirators raised an army, and Cicero himself narrowly escaped being assassinated. In a series of famous speeches, Cicero warned the Senate about Catiline's plans, and Catiline fled. Cicero had Catiline's supporters in Rome arrested and illegally executed without a trial, and Catiline himself then was defeated and killed. This incident demonstrates that Roman politics had reached the point where any ambitious senator was willing to act illegally.

Sulla (ca.138–78 B.C.E.) Roman senator who used his army to overthrow the government in 88 B.C.E.

proscriptions List of enemies published by Sulla.

Crassus (ca.115–53 B.C.E.) Very rich senator, member of the First Triumvirate.

Pompey (106–48 B.C.E.) Excellent general, member of the First Triumvirate.

Julius Caesar (100–44 B.C.E.) Member of the First Triumvirate who conquered Gaul and seized control of Rome after a civil war.

Spartacus (d. 71 B.C.E.) Thracian slave who led a revolt of slaves against Rome in 73 B.C.E.

client king Foreign ruler appointed by and dependent on the Romans.

Cicero (106–43 B.C.E.) Roman senator known as an excellent speaker who was consul in 63 B.C.E. and suppressed the conspiracy of Catiline.

Spartacus Decides to Revolt

By the early first century B.C.E., the Romans had enslaved hundreds of thousands of non-Italian foreigners. Many of these slaves were very badly treated. One was Spartacus, a native of Thrace, a mountainous region north of Greece. According to the Greek historian Plutarch, "He was a Thracian belonging to one of the nomad peoples, and a man not only brave and of high spirit, but also rich in understanding. He was unexpectedly gentle, and more of a Greek than the people of his country usually are." It was said that when Spartacus was first sold as a slave in Rome, a snake coiled itself on his face and his wife, a prophetess and worshiper of the god Bacchus, saw the snake as a sign of future greatness but also of a bad end.

Spartacus was forced to become a gladiator at Capua, a city on the Bay of Naples. Gladiators performed at public spectacles, either individually or in groups, fighting in an arena until their opponents were either wounded or killed. Spartacus and his fellow gladiators realized that they would probably die in the arena, but they had no choice. Revolt would have seemed out of the question, for no slave revolt had ever succeeded, and slaves who tried to rebel were savagely punished.

Even though Spartacus knew the odds against him, he decided to fight for his freedom and, in 73 B.C.E., he led his fellow slaves in revolt. Breaking out of their cells, they grabbed knives in the kitchen, overpowered their guards, and seized weapons in Capua. Many of the rebels had formerly been soldiers, and under Spartacus's leadership, they defeated several units of Roman soldiers sent against them and even captured a Roman army camp. Their numbers were constantly increased by additional slaves who escaped from neighboring estates, and Spartacus soon had more than seventy thousand soldiers. They could be as brutal as the Romans they were fighting against, looting the countryside and dividing the spoils equally among themselves. When a friend was killed in combat, Spartacus sacrificed three hundred Roman prisoners to his dead friend's ghost. In the conflict between the rebels and the Romans, no mercy was expected, or given, on either side.

In spite of his successes, Spartacus realized that the rebels could not resist the Romans indefinitely. He therefore made another important decision: to lead his people out of Italy. He first planned to go north across the Alps, where the rebels could scatter and attempt to return to their homes, but the rebels preferred to continue their looting in Italy. Spartacus then planned to hire pirates to ferry the slaves across to Sicily, where he thought the large slave population also would be ready to revolt, but the pirates ran off with the payment, leaving Spartacus trapped in Italy.

In 71 B.C.E., the Roman general Crassus led eight legions (more than forty thousand soldiers) against Spartacus. When one of his armies was defeated by the rebels, Crassus showed that he was as tough as Spartacus by imposing the punishment called decimation: one of every ten of his disgraced soldiers was executed. By doing so, he demonstrated that he would not tolerate failure. Crassus finally cornered Spartacus in southern Italy, and Spartacus had no choice but to fight the large, well-trained Roman army. In the ensuing battle, Spartacus and many of his followers were surrounded and slaughtered. Rebels who tried to escape were killed or captured, and six thousand captives were crucified along the road leading south from Rome.

The great slave revolt was over, but if the example of Spartacus taught Italian slaves the futility of revolt, it also taught the Romans something too. To prevent future slave revolts, they improved the conditions in which slaves were forced to live.

Source: From the Greek biographer Plutarch, on Spartacus (c. 46–120).

The Rise of Julius Caesar The third powerful general of this period was Julius Caesar, a member of a patrician family supposedly descended from the goddess Venus. Caesar was the nephew of Sulla's enemy Marius and had barely escaped after his name appeared on Sulla's proscription list. His political career therefore started slowly, but he still had great ambitions. Once, in his early thirties, he burst into tears when reading about Alexander the Great. When asked what was wrong, he replied that at his age Alexander had conquered the world, whereas he, Caesar, had not yet done anything memorable. Caesar was popular with the people, and in 60 B.C.E. he was elected consul for the next year. Like any ambitious senator, he wanted to be assigned a province where he would be able to recruit a large army and gain military glory. The Senate, however, insultingly assigned him "the cattle trails of Italy" as his province.

The Triumvirates

By 60s B.C.E., ambitious generals were taking greater and greater control of Rome. Lacking armies, the only way that the Senate could resist this trend was by refusing to grant additional powers and army commands to its generals. This brought senatorial generals into direct conflict with the Senate.

The First Triumvirate Crassus, Pompey, and Caesar all had been disrespected by the Senate.

In 60 B.C.E., therefore, they formed an unofficial alliance known as the First **Triumvirate**, whereby they agreed to use their influence on one another's behalf. As consul, Caesar saw to it that Pompey's legislation was passed and that land was given to his soldiers. Caesar himself was reassigned two provinces in Gaul, giving him an opening for military adventures to the north. And Crassus, who desired to refurbish his own military standing, eventually was granted a military command against the Parthians in the east. The triumvirs thus controlled affairs in Rome by cooperating and avoiding competition with one another. Conservative senators were troubled by this arrangement but could do nothing about it.

Caesar's Gallic Wars In 58 B.C.E., Caesar took his army to Gaul, where he remained for nine years. One of the best generals of antiquity, Caesar played off one Celtic people against another and ultimately defeated them all. His reports of his campaigns, the *Gallic* Wars, are one of the best historical works of antiquity. By 50 B.C.E., Caesar had annexed all of Gaul up to the Rhine River, gained great wealth, and created a battle-hardened army. Meanwhile, Crassus waged a disastrous war against the Parthians. His army became bogged down in the Mesopotamian desert. At the Battle of Carrhae in 53 B.C.E., Crassus was killed and thirty thousand of his troops were killed or enslaved. Crassus's head ended up being used as a stage prop in a production of a Greek play in the Parthian capital.

Civil War Between Caesar and Pompey In Rome, Cicero and other senators turned Pompey against Caesar by playing on his vanity. In 50 B.C.E., with Pompey's support, the Senate ordered Caesar to disband his army and return to Rome as a private citizen. Caesar realized that if he did so, he probably would be killed by his enemies. He therefore decided to bring his army back to Rome with him. In 49 B.C.E. he led his army across the shallow Rubicon River, the boundary between Gaul and Italy, an act that automatically put him in rebellion against the Roman state. Pompey and his supporters fled to Greece to prepare their own army. Caesar soon followed, and at the Battle of Pharsalus in 48 B.C.E. Pompey was defeated. Pompey fled to Egypt, the last independent Hellenistic kingdom, where King Ptolemy XIII, thinking to do Caesar a favor, beheaded him. But when Caesar arrived, he was not pleased that an Egyptian king had murdered a distinguished Roman senator. He therefore deposed Ptolemy in favor of Ptolemy's sister (and wife) Cleopatra.

The Assassination of Caesar After his return to Rome, Caesar, like Sulla before him, had to decide what his official position would be. He attempted to make his one-man rule look legal by regularly serving as consul and by holding the position of dictator for life. But his unconstitutional policies and monopolization of high offices aroused hostility and jealousy in several senators, who conspired against him. At a meeting of the Senate on the Ides of March (March 15), 44 B.C.E., Caesar was stabbed to death.

The Second Triumvirate Caesar's assassins presumed that after he was gone, the old Republic would be restored, but they were mistaken. Two of Caesar's generals, **Lepidus** and Marcus Antonius (known to us as **Mark Antony**), made an alliance against the assassins with **Octavian**, Caesar's eighteen-year-old grandnephew, whom Caesar had adopted in his will. The three divided up Caesar's armies and in 43 B.C.E. formed the Second Triumvirate. To honor Caesar's memory, they had him **deified**, or declared to be a god, by the Senate. Initially, Roman politicians thought little of young Octavian, but he soon showed that he possessed a political shrewdness well beyond his years. The triumvirs seized control of the government, and Cicero, who had delivered a series of speeches against Antony, was murdered. In 42 B.C.E., the assassins were defeated at the Battle of Philippi in Macedonia. Another struggle then began among the triumvirs to see who would gain sole control of the state.

Civil War Between Antony and Octavian Lepidus soon was forced to retire, and Antony and Octavian divided up the Roman world, Octavian receiving Italy and the west, and Antony obtaining Syria and the east. Antony spent most of his time in Egypt, where Queen Cleopatra helped him to build up his forces. In 31 B.C.E., Octavian and Antony attacked each other, and their armies met at the Battle of Actium on the western coast of Greece. Antony and Cleopatra were defeated and fled back to Egypt. The following year, 30 B.C.E., Octavian and his massive army arrived in Egypt. Antony and Cleopatra, not wishing to be disgraced by being displayed in Octavian's triumphal procession, committed suicide, and Octavian annexed Egypt as a new province. Once again, a powerful senatorial general had been able to use his army to eliminate all his rivals and to take control of the entire Roman world. The civil wars had demonstrated that the Republic could no longer work. By 27 B.C.E., it was at its end.

Society and Culture at the End of the Republic

By the end of the Republic, Rome had experienced many social and cultural changes, as reflected, in

---

triumvirate A group of three men; the First Triumvirate (Caesar, Crassus, and Pompey) was formed in 60 B.C.E., and the Second Triumvirate (Antony, Lepidus, and Octavian) in 43 B.C.E.

Lepidus (d. 13 B.C.E.) One of Caesar's generals and a member of the Second Triumvirate.

Mark Antony (ca. 80–30 B.C.E.) One of Caesar's generals and a member of the Second Triumvirate; defeated by Octavian, committed suicide in 30 B.C.E.

Octavian (63 B.C.E.–14 C.E.) Adopted son of Caesar and a member of the Second Triumvirate who gained control of the Roman world in 30 B.C.E.

deification An act whereby the Senate declared that a deceased Roman was a god.

The life and death of Cleopatra, the last queen and pharaoh of Egypt, fascinated the people of the Roman world, and she often appeared in artwork. This fourth-century C.E. fresco from the Via Latina Christian catacombs in Rome shows Cleopatra, whose halo suggests a form of divinity, committing suicide as she holds a poisonous asp to her breast. Thus, even Christians were fascinated by the career of a non-Christian such as Cleopatra. Why do you think the life and death of Cleopatra had and continues to have such a great fascination for people?

particular, in the changing role of Roman and the flowering of Latin literature.

Roman Women at the End of the Republic Roman women now enjoyed a freedom that would have been unthinkable in the past, and high-ranking women were even more visible in public life. In one famous case, the Second Triumvirate attempted to tax the wealthiest women of Rome, whereupon the women assembled in the Forum. There, Hortensia, the daughter of the orator Hortensius, delivered a speech in which she argued, "If we have no share in government or army commands or public office, why should we pay taxes?" The triumvirs responded by reducing the tax on women and raising that on wealthy men.

Origins of the Golden Age of Latin Literature This period also marked the beginning of the **Golden Age of Latin Literature**, which lasted from 70 B.C.E. until 14 C.E. Some Latin writers made their reputations solely on the basis of their literary accomplishments. These included the poets **Catullus**, known for his love poetry, and **Lucretius**, who gained fame with a lengthy poem called *On the Nature of Things*, which described the Epicurean view of the universe. But many late Roman writers also were active in public life because the senatorial ideal included the expectation that a senator would engage in literary activities. Politicians such as Caesar and Cicero also were well-known authors. Cicero, in fact, was later considered by many to be Rome's greatest writer, publishing not only speeches and letters but also works on oratory and philosophy. Roman politicians and generals thus also saw themselves as the representatives of Roman culture and values.

> **Golden Age of Latin Literature** Period of Latin literature beginning around 75 B.C.E. and lasting until 14 C.E.
>
> **Catullus** (ca. 84–54 B.C.E.) Writer of Latin love poetry.
>
> **Lucretius** (ca. 94–49 B.C.E.) Epicurean philosopher who wrote the poem *On the Nature of Things*.

 Checking In

By yourself or with a partner, explain the significance of each of the following selected key terms:

proscriptions	Octavian
Julius Caesar	deification
Spartacus	Golden Age of Latin
Cicero	Literature
triumvirate	

CHAPTER
Review

Summary

◆ After its founding as a small farming village on the banks of the Tiber River in the eighth century B.C.E., Rome slowly grew to become the ruler of the entire Mediterranean world.

◆ Early in their history, the Romans learned to assimilate the cultures of other peoples, such as the Etruscans to the north and the Greeks to the south.

◆ Their shared values and sense of social responsibility gave the Romans a sense of community that permitted them to solve internal disputes peacefully, without resorting to violence.

◆ The Romans' concept of rule by law is one of their most important contributions to western civilization.

◆ Under constant threat of attack, the early Romans also developed an army that was used not only for defense but also to attack peoples who were seen as threats. Eventually, the Romans defeated all the peoples in Italy and the Mediterranean world. Although they initially were reluctant to take over direct administration of the peoples they had defeated, by 30 B.C.E. they had annexed nearly all the lands surrounding the Mediterranean Sea.

◆ Numerous foreign wars and the acquisition of overseas provinces had profound effects on Roman society and institutions. The Romans were exposed to many new cultural influences, especially from Greece and the east.

Chronology

1184 B.C.E.	Aeneas escapes from Troy and later settles in Italy	186 B.C.E.	Romans investigate Bacchus worshipers
753 B.C.E.	Traditional date of the foundation of Rome by Romulus and Remus	133–122 B.C.E.	Reforms of Tiberius and Gaius Gracchus
		108 B.C.E.	Marius creates the volunteer army
ca. 600 B.C.E.	Etruscans bring civilization to Rome	90 B.C.E.	Italian allies revolt against Rome
509 B.C.E.	Etruscan kings are expelled from Rome; Roman Republic is established	88 B.C.E.	Sulla uses his army to seize Rome
		73–71 B.C.E.	Spartacus leads a slave revolt
500–287 B.C.E.	Conflict of the Orders	63 B.C.E.	Cicero suppresses Catiline's conspiracy to overthrow Roman government
451–450 B.C.E.	Twelve Tables of Roman law are issued		
390 B.C.E.	Rome is sacked by Gauls	60 B.C.E.	Crassus, Pompey, and Caesar form First Triumvirate
343–290 B.C.E.	Romans fight Samnite Wars		
264–146 B.C.E.	Romans fight Punic Wars against the Carthaginians	44 B.C.E.	Caesar is assassinated on Ides of March
		43 B.C.E.	Lepidus, Mark Antony, and Octavian form Second Triumvirate
227 B.C.E.	Sicily becomes first Roman province		
216 B.C.E.	Hannibal defeats Romans at Battle of Cannae	31 B.C.E.	Octavian wins Battle of Actium against Antony and Cleopatra, who commit suicide the next year
212 B.C.E.	Denarius is introduced	27 B.C.E.	Roman Republic ends; Roman Empire begins
202 B.C.E.	Scipio defeats Hannibal at Battle of Zama		

- Roman expansion created problems of military recruitment and provincial administration that the conservative Senate was unable to deal with.

- The old Roman virtues of duty and modesty were superseded by military ambition, as powerful senators put their personal interests ahead of the best interests of the state as a whole. Nevertheless, even in pursuit of personal glory, Roman senators always attempted to adhere to standards of Roman virtue and strove to show that they were good Romans. Generals such as Sulla and Julius Caesar saw themselves as Roman senators, not as kings or autocrats.

- Contests between powerful senators with their large armies brought strife and civil war to the Republic. Sulla, Caesar, and Octavian all used their armies to gain sole control of the Roman government, and all confronted the question of what their role in the government would be.

- By 27 B.C.E. the Roman Republic was at an end. Governing the Roman world had become the responsibility of Octavian, the adopted son of Julius Caesar and the final victor in the civil wars.

Test Yourself

To gauge your mastery of the material in this chapter, answer the questions below. More than one answer may be correct.

The Development of Roman Identity, 753–509 B.C.E.

1. Which people brought civilization to the city of Rome?
   a. The Carthaginians
   b. The Celts
   c. The Etruscans
   d. The Greeks
   e. The Samnites

2. The Romans believed that the three Roman tribes had originated from which peoples?
   a. The Greeks
   b. The Celts
   c. The Etruscans
   d. The Latins
   e. The Italians

3. What was the social institution that bound the Roman people together known as?
   a. Numen
   b. Pietas
   c. Religio
   d. The patron-client relationship
   e. Collegia

4. What types of early Roman marriage existed?
   a. Usage
   b. Bride theft
   c. Love matches
   d. Purchase
   e. Arrangement

Now that you have reviewed and tested yourself on this part of the chapter, take time to pull together all the important information by answering the following questions:

- In what ways did the Romans adopt the cultures of foreign peoples during the Roman Republic?

- What values were important to the Romans?

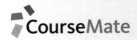

The Evolution of the Roman Republic, 509–146 B.C.E.

5. What were the duties of the Censor?

   a. Appointing members of the Senate
   b. Assessing property values for taxation
   c. Leading Roman armies
   d. Presiding at meetings of the Senate
   e. Issuing coinage

6. Which of these things characterized the Conflict of the Orders?

   a. Constant resistance from the patricians
   b. Plebeian threats to secede
   c. The organization of the plebeians
   d. Violent conflicts
   e. The freeing of slaves

7. Which of these were reasons the Romans went to war during the Republic?

   a. Fear of strong neighbors
   b. A desire to create an empire
   c. To gain glory for Roman consuls
   d. To support their allies
   e. For economic exploitation

8. What was Hannibal's strategy during the Second Punic War?

   a. Capture Rome and end the war quickly
   b. Launch a naval blockade of Roman ports
   c. Break up Rome's Italian alliance
   d. Fight a long-term guerilla war
   e. Encourage a slave revolt

Now that you have reviewed and tested yourself on this part of the chapter, take time to pull together all the important information by answering the following questions:

◆ How were the plebeians able to gain greater rights during the Conflict of the Orders?

◆ What were the reasons the Romans got involved in so many wars during the Roman Republic?

The Effects of Roman Expansion, 146–88 B.C.E.

9. The financial opportunities created by Roman expansion led to the growth of what Roman social class?

   a. Plebeians
   b. Equestrians
   c. Senators
   d. Patricians
   e. Slaves

10. Which of these types of literature did the Romans adopt from the Greeks?

    a. History
    b. Drama
    c. Satire
    d. Philosophy
    e. Oral tradition

11. What were the primary responsibilities of governors of Roman provinces?

    a. Collect taxes
    b. Refer complaints of the provincials to Rome
    c. Provide defense
    d. Oversee the administration of justice
    e. Grant Roman citizenship

12. What was the plan of Tiberius Gracchus for ending the military recruitment crisis?

    a. Abolish the requirement that army recruits had to own property
    b. Hire foreign mercenaries
    c. Give the Italian allies citizenship so they could serve in the Roman legions
    d. Distribute public land to landless plebeians to make them eligible for army service
    e. Free slaves to serve in the army

Now that you have reviewed and tested yourself on this part of the chapter, take time to pull together all the important information by answering the following questions:

◆ How did Roman expansion create problems for the Romans?

◆ What were the consequences of general Marius's changes in Roman military recruiting policies?

The End of the Republic, 90–27 B.C.E.

13. Who was the senatorial army general who first used his army to seize control of Rome?

   a. Marius
   b. Pompey
   c. Sulla
   d. Scipio
   e. Hannibal

14. Who were the members of the First Triumvirate?

   a. Crassus
   b. Spartacus
   c. Pompey
   d. Caesar
   e. Cicero

15. Who was the final winner of the Republican civil wars?

   a. Sulla
   b. Caesar
   c. Octavian
   d. Mark Antony
   e. Cicero

Now that you have reviewed and tested yourself on this part of the chapter, take time to pull together all the important information by answering the following questions:

◆ What were the reasons for the fall of the Roman Republic?

◆ How did powerful Roman senators try to gain power in the years after 145 B.C.E.?

CHAPTER 6

The Roman Empire, 27 B.C.E.–284 C.E.

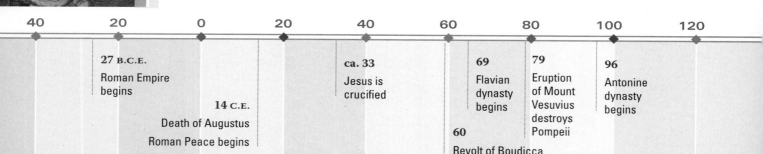

40	20	0	20	40	60	80	100	120

27 B.C.E. Roman Empire begins

14 C.E. Death of Augustus Roman Peace begins

ca. 33 Jesus is crucified

69 Flavian dynasty begins

60 Revolt of Boudicca

79 Eruption of Mount Vesuvius destroys Pompeii

96 Antonine dynasty begins

Roman emperors needed to justify not only the vast resources expended on the Roman army but also the need for an emperor at all. One way they did this was by magnifying their role in defending Rome against hordes of supposedly hostile barbarians. Imperial art thus is full of portrayals of defeated barbarians, as in this scene of chained, dejected barbarians being paraded in a triumphal procession in Rome, probably after Trajan's final defeat of the Dacians in 107 C.E. Small matter that defeated barbarians then were often allowed to settle on Roman lands and become Roman citizens. Do you think that the commanders of large modern armies also look for "barbarian" enemies to use these armies against and thus appear to be doing their jobs? (© The Trustees of the British Museum/Art Resource, NY)

After reading this chapter, you should be able to answer the following questions:

How did Augustus attempt to solve the problems that had caused the fall of the Roman Republic?

What was the significance of the Roman army during the Principate?

Why are the first two centuries of the Roman Empire known as the "Roman Peace?"

What was the place of Christianity in the Roman world during the Principate?

What factors caused the imperial crisis of the third century C.E.?

HISTORIANS PLACE the beginning of the Roman Empire in 27 B.C.E., when Octavian, the winner of the civil wars of the Roman Republic, received the title of *augustus*, which he then used as his name. As the first Roman emperor, Augustus created the Principate, the first phase of the Roman Empire. He ensured that he and his successors were able to maintain control of the army. He created a system of frontier defenses. He gained the support of the Senate by claiming that he had restored the Republic and was sharing power with the senators. He gained the support of the people in the provinces by allowing them the opportunity to become Roman citizens. The empire incorporated many diverse peoples. Some peoples willingly opted to come under Roman authority. Others, such as Boudicca and the Britons, resisted for a while, but ultimately a multitude of peoples were gathered peacefully under Roman rule.

The Roman emperors created the most successful empire that the western world had yet known. What made it work was the belief of its inhabitants that the best interests of the empire were their own best interests.

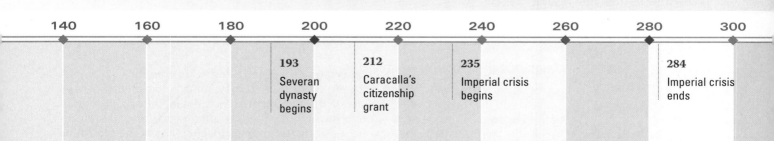

140	160	180	200	220	240	260	280	300

193
Severan dynasty begins

212
Caracalla's citizenship grant

235
Imperial crisis begins

284
Imperial crisis ends

The first two centuries of the Roman Empire are known as the Roman Peace. The empire was well governed, well defended, and economically prosperous. People throughout the empire lived in peace and harmony and felt they shared in the benefits and opportunities the empire had to offer. It was possible for provincials to rise in society and even to become emperor. A common Mediterranean culture gave people a sense of shared identity, especially in cities.

The most important development during the Roman Empire was the rise of Christianity, a religion that grew out of Judaism and spread from Palestine throughout the Roman world. Ease of travel during the Roman Peace facilitated the spread of new religious ideas, and Christianity filled spiritual and social needs that other religions failed to address. It developed a large following, especially in urban areas and among underprivileged people. But some of its beliefs and practices brought it into conflict with the Roman government, leading to occasional persecutions.

By the third century, however, new problems, including economic decline and an unruly military, confronted the empire, problems that the methods introduced by Augustus could no longer effectively solve. The result was a period of imperial crisis that nearly destroyed the empire.

Augustus and the Creation of the Roman Empire, 27 B.C.E.–14 C.E.

- ◆ **How did Augustus attempt to unify the Roman Empire?**
- ◆ **How did Roman government function during the Principate?**

The year 27 B.C.E. marks the beginning of the Roman Empire and the beginning of the reign of Augustus, the first Roman emperor. Augustus was a singularly talented administrator who was largely responsible for establishing the Principate, as the first phase of the Roman Empire is known. He shrewdly gained the support of both the army and the Senate. He created an image of the emperor as the embodiment of Roman virtue and of Rome itself. The measures he introduced not only gave him the powers that made him an emperor but also brought unity to the previously disorganized Roman world. It was largely as a result of his efforts that the Roman Empire became the most successful empire that the world has ever known.

Suetonius (ca. 70–ca.135 C.E.) Secretary of the emperor Hadrian who wrote biographies called *The Twelve Caesars.*

Augustus the Emperor

Once Octavian had defeated all his rivals, his first concern was to decide what his own position was

to be. He had two choices: he could either retire, or he could find a way to stay in power that was more effective than the methods used by Sulla and Caesar. The solution that Octivian chose resulted in the creation of what we call the Roman Empire.

Staying Alive In 30 B.C.E., after the suicides of Antony and Cleopatra, Octavian, the adopted son of Julius Caesar, was left in undisputed control of the Roman world. He commanded eighty legions, and all of his significant opponents were defeated or dead. He faced some difficult choices, such as whether he should retire or try to hold on to power. According to the Roman biographer **Suetonius**, Octavian "thought that he himself would not be safe if he retired and that it would be dangerous to trust the government to more than one person." He would have realized that to protect himself and to keep the peace he would have to retain control of the army, and to do that, he had to stay in power. Octavian was a shrewd politician, with a good sense of what would work and what would not. Sulla and Caesar had tried to stay in power by using the office of dictator, but their approach was considered by the other senators to be unconstitutional and autocratic and had created great opposition. Octavian could not repeat their mistakes.

Octavian and the Senate To remain in power peacefully, Octavian knew that he needed the support of the people and the Senate. After sixty years of civil war, the people wanted peace, and, therefore, being a better administrator than a general, Octavian

Map 6.1 **The Roman Empire in 117 C.E.** The Roman Empire surrounded the Mediterranean Sea, which the Romans referred to as "Our Sea." At its maximum extent, the empire stretched from Scotland to the Straits of Gibraltar to the cataracts of the Nile River to the Persian Gulf. © *Cengage Learning*

1. Do you think the Roman Empire was land-oriented or sea-oriented? Why?
2. What areas were controlled only for short periods by the Romans? Why do you think this was?
3. Based on geography, from what directions do you think might come the greatest possibilities of attacks on the Roman Empire? Why?
4. How much territory did the Romans add to the empire after the death of Augustus in 14 C.E.? Is this consistent with popular ideas about the Roman Empire as a period of conquest?
5. What significant battles were fought during the first three centuries of the Roman Empire? Why do you think there were so few?

committed himself to creating a peaceful world. Gaining the support of the Senate was even more crucial. The senators were the only experienced military and civil administrators; they controlled most of the economic resources of the Roman world; and as the most influential patrons, they also were able to mobilize the Roman people. The Senate also represented all the ancient traditions of Rome, including the power to oversee legislation and the election of officials. Octavian could not rule without them. So, to gain support from the Senate, Octavian portrayed himself as the representative of Roman tradition and virtue, as a supporter of the rights of the Senate, and as the restorer of the Roman Republic.

The Creation of the Roman Empire Octavian soon was confident that the Senate would support any legislation that he desired, thus ensuring that anything he did was legal. In 27 B.C.E., he offered to give up all his powers, but the Senate not only declined this proposal but also granted Octavian additional honors, including the title of *augustus* ("the revered one"), which was not a power or an office but a mark of great admiration and respect. Octavian was so proud of this new title that he used it as his name, and it later became a title used by subsequent Roman emperors. Augustus, however, claimed neither to have established the Roman Empire nor to have become Roman emperor, but to have restored the Republic. But in spite of this pretense, it is clear that the Roman Republic was dead and that one individual, the emperor, now controlled the army and was in charge of the government.

The Roman Empire thus is said to have begun in 27 B.C.E. In this form it is called the **Principate**, from the emperor's title of princeps, the highest-ranking member of the Senate. There always had been a princeps, so the emperor could claim he was still just another senator. The Principate was based on the understanding that the emperor and the Senate governed as partners. To hold on to the real power without upsetting the Senate, Augustus initially proposed to serve as one of the two consuls every year. Being consul allowed him to command the army, with the power of imperium, and to introduce laws. But by monopolizing the highest office, Augustus aroused the same kind of jealousy that Sulla and Caesar had experienced.

The Emperor's Powers In 23 B.C.E., Augustus adopted a new solution. He stopped being consul and had the Senate grant him the power of a proconsul with a "greater" imperium that allowed him to outrank any other general. Augustus also received the power of a tribune, enabling him to introduce legislation and to veto the actions of other officials. The knowledge that he had veto power meant that he never had to use it, for any senator planning to introduce any legislation made sure to clear it with Augustus in advance. Augustus also took over the censor's right to appoint new senators, which allowed him to pack the Senate with his own supporters. He also became pontifex maximus, the head of the Roman state religion, the only actual office that he held. This made him the intermediary between Rome and the gods. His general policy of holding powers rather than offices allowed him to keep a low profile and to avoid seeming arrogant or autocratic.

Augustus created a model of empire that was used by his successors. The powers of a proconsul and

A marble statue from Prima Porta in Italy and now in the Vatican Museum in Rome shows Augustus in military uniform as a victorious army general. In his left hand he holds the ivory scepter that symbolized the power of a consul, and he extends his right arm as if he were addressing the soldiers. The scene on the breastplate depicts the return to the Romans of the standards the Parthians had captured from Crassus in 53 B.C.E. In spite of his own lack of military expertise, Augustus, as commander-in-chief of the army, took credit for the victories of his generals. At his feet is a tiny figure of Cupid, the son of Augustus's supposed distant ancestress Venus. By subtly showing that he was descended from gods, Augustus was able to lay claim to divine authority for his rule. Why do you think Augustus was so concerned to have himself shown as a victorious army general?

a tribune became the two primary sources of the authority of the Roman emperors during the Principate, permitting them to control the army and the laws while at the same time keeping a low profile. Everything the emperor did was done according to the Republic's constitution. The Senate still met; consuls still were appointed; and being a senator or consul continued to be a great honor. But the Senate, senators, and consuls no longer had any real power. Augustus's restoration of the Republic was a fiction, but a fiction that everyone was happy to go along with.

The Unification of the Roman World

Once Augustus had solved the problem of what his own position was to be, he then was able to tackle

augustus (Latin for "the revered one) Title given to Octavian in 27 B.C.E. that he used as his name; also used as the title of all subsequent Roman emperors.

Principate (based on Latin *princeps*, "first man") Roman Empire from 27 B.C.E. to 284 C.E., as established by Augustus.

several long-standing problems the Republic had never confronted or dealt with: how to control the army, and how to integrate the provinces into the mainstream of the Roman world. His solutions to these problems provided a model for the Roman Empire that lasted for nearly three centuries.

Augustus and the Army Augustus used his authority to bring stability and unity to the Roman world and to create internal cohesiveness where none had existed before. He turned what in the past had been problems, such as the army and the provinces, into opportunities for unity. The most important institution in the Roman Empire was the army, for the empire could not succeed if the army was not fully integrated into the life of the empire. The army was responsible for defending the empire from foreign attacks and for maintaining internal order (there was no civil police force). It was by far the biggest drain on the imperial treasury. There also was a constant threat of its becoming involved in politics.

The emperor's top priority always was to maintain the army's loyalty, and Augustus created a standing, professional army that was loyal directly to him. To minimize expenses, he reduced the army to twenty-eight legions—about 140,000 men—a number considered barely sufficient for defense plus a single offensive campaign. To keep the army out of politics, Augustus stationed it on the frontier, as far away from Rome as possible. The only troops in Italy were the **Praetorian Guard**, an elite 10,000-man unit camped on the outskirts of Rome.

Augustus's Frontier Policy The army was responsible for overseeing thousands of miles of frontier. During the Republic, there had been no coherent plan for expansion or defense. Augustus changed that. He terminated the practice of helter-skelter expansion that had characterized the Republic. He expanded the empire to fixed boundaries that were easy to defend and then stopped. In the south was the Sahara desert. To the east lay the Parthian Empire, which extended from the Euphrates River to India. Augustus realized there was nothing to be gained by attacking the Parthians, so he negotiated a favorable treaty and established peaceful relations.

The most dangerous frontier was in the north, where Celtic and Germanic peoples posed threats of raids, if not organized invasions. To safeguard the northern border, Augustus expanded the Roman frontier to the Danube River. A related attempt to expand to the Elbe River in Germany, however, ended in disaster in 9 C.E. when the Germanic leader Arminius ambushed and destroyed three Roman legions led by the Roman general Varus in the Teutoburg Forest. The Romans withdrew to the Rhine River, and the Danube and the Rhine became the permanent northern frontier. Elsewhere, border areas not considered important enough to annex were left in the hands

of client kings, such as Herod (r. 41 B.C.E.–4 C.E.) in Judaea, who were permitted to remain in office as long as they did not antagonize Rome.

After this period of strategic expansion, Augustus focused on guarding the frontiers, regulating commerce and interaction with the outside world, and consolidating the territories that Rome controlled. This policy was followed by nearly all of his successors. The Roman army became a **garrison army**, spread out along the frontiers but doing little actual fighting. This single line of defense worked well as long as no enemy was able to break through and make its way into the undefended inner regions of the empire.

The Spread of Romanization The army also held the empire together and unified it in other ways. Roman army camps brought **Romanization**, the extension of Roman culture, to the very edges of the empire. Augustus allowed provincials to serve in the army, and the first thing these soldiers had to learn was Latin. Romanization also was promoted by the elaborate Roman road system, which had been designed for military transport but was used primarily for personal and commercial traffic. In addition, during Augustus's reign, eighty colonies were established for hundreds of thousands of army veterans who received land in Spain, North Africa, and Greece, creating additional centers of Roman culture in the provinces.

The army was a constant presence in the Roman world, but often a benign one. It was rarely used against provincial populations; in fact, there were only two rebellions against the Romans after a province had been completely conquered—both by the Jews—a remarkable record for an empire supposedly based on military might. The army was more likely to be engaged in constructing defenses or building roads than in fighting.

Provincial Administration The empire now consisted of some twenty-five provinces and a population of between forty and sixty million persons. Augustus tried to unify the many different peoples of the empire in several ways. He standardized the provincial administration. Governors and army generals were chosen from the members of the Senate on the basis of their ability. Augustus established a permanent civil service in both Rome and the provinces. Many officials were equestrians, including the **praetorian prefect**, the commander of the Praetorian Guard in

Praetorian Guard Ten thousand–man elite Roman army unit stationed at Rome.

garrison army Professional army stationed permanently in the same place that does little fighting.

Romanization Extension of Roman culture throughout the empire.

praetorian prefect Commander of the Praetorian Guard.

Rome, and procurators who supervised tax collection. To remove tax inequities, Augustus replaced the tithe with fixed tribute in all the provinces. He also implemented a regular census that required all inhabitants of a province to register their property, thus providing a basis for fair tax assessment. City councils, whose members were known as **decurions**, continued to be in charge of local government in the provinces.

The Role of Coinage An effective integrating tool developed by Augustus and his successors was the Roman coinage system, which served both economic and propaganda purposes. A system of interchangeable copper, silver, and gold coins facilitated economic exchange inside the Roman Empire and well beyond the imperial frontiers. The coinage was based on the denarius, a silver coin that the emperors used primarily to pay the army. The salary of a soldier in the legions was 225 denarii per year. Copper denominations included the large sestertius (four per denarius) and the as (sixteen per denarius). A gold aureus, worth 25 denarii, was issued for special occasions, such as when a new emperor was named. Coins also conveyed a multitude of messages to a mass audience. Their words and images announced military victories and building projects, reminded people of the emperor's virtues, and reassured them of the army's loyalty. Table 6.1 summarizes the Roman coinage system.

The Imperial Cult Augustus also wanted to integrate the inhabitants of the provinces fully into the Roman world, to give them a sense of shared identity, and to allow them to feel that Rome's interests were their own. To provide provincials with a unified voice, he established provincial councils, where city representatives met annually to convey their concerns to the emperor. Augustus also established the **imperial cult**, the worship of the divine nature of living emperors and of deceased emperors who had been deified by the Senate. Even though Augustus and later emperors did not claim to be gods, the imperial cult implied that there was something godlike about the emperor's spirit.

People participated in the imperial cult in temples honoring Rome and Augustus located in provincial capitals throughout the empire. Taking part in the imperial cult was more of a political than a religious act. By dropping a pinch of incense into a fire on the altar, people symbolically renewed their loyalty to Rome and to the emperor. Standard rituals

decurions Members of the city councils in the provinces.

imperial cult Worship of the divinity of living and deified emperors in which provincials renewed their loyalty to Rome and the emperor; carried out in temples of Rome and Augustus.

Table 6.1 The Roman Coinage System

Metal	Denomination	Value
Gold	aureus (aurei)	25 denarii = 100 sesterces = 400 asses
Silver	denarius (denarii)	4 sesterces = 16 asses
Copper	sestertius (sesterces)	4 asses
Copper	as (asses)	

© Cengage Learning

like these gave the people of the empire a shared sense of belonging.

The Spread of Roman Citizenship The benefit that gave the people of the provinces the greatest sense of identification with Rome was Roman citizenship, a privilege that few provincials had been able to obtain under the Republic. Augustus opened citizenship to two classes of people who served the empire: decurions and soldiers. Decurions could become citizens by requesting citizenship from the emperor, who granted it to encourage influential provincials to identify their interests with Rome. Once they became citizens, decurions could work their way up to being equestrians or even senators. Augustus also allowed provincials to become citizens by serving in the Roman army—not in the legions, which were open only to citizens, but in the auxiliary forces. The auxiliary forces were specialized troops (such as the Numidian cavalry) and skirmishers (lightly armed troops sent into battle first). After twenty-five years of military service, provincials received citizenship. They and their descendants then likewise had opportunities to advance in Roman society.

The Age of Augustus

The reign of Augustus established the values, the literary models, and the forms of public entertainments that would characterize the Roman Empire.

The Preservation of Roman Values Augustus was a master of public relations. In law, literature, art, and architecture, he created an image of himself as the restorer of peace, stability, virtue, and morality. He believed that conservative Roman virtues had gained the support of the gods and created the greatness of Rome. It was his responsibility, he felt, to provide a model for these virtues. In his memoirs, Augustus expressed his pride in a golden shield that the Senate had hung up in his honor, "testifying to his virtue, mercy, justice, and piety." Using his authority as censor, he encouraged other Romans to live up to his

After his death, Augustus, like Caesar before him, was deified, that is, made into a god. In the upper register of the Gemma Augustea, a cameo carved from blue and white Arabian onyx and now in Vienna, Augustus, seated next to the goddess Roma, is depicted as the god Jupiter. Jupiter's eagle stands under the throne, and the goddess Oikumene, representing the whole world, crowns him from behind with the "civic crown" bestowed on those who saved the lives of Romans. Neptune, signifying rule of the sea, and Italia, representing Italy, are behind him; in front of his head is Capricorn, Augustus's astrological sign; and the goddess Roma sits in front of him. At the far left Tiberius, Augustus's successor, descends from a chariot after celebrating a military triumph. In the lower register, the Roman soldiers who had won the victory raise a trophy over defeated barbarian captives, demonstrating where the real power of the emperors lay. In what way did pieces of artwork such as this provide propaganda value for the Roman emperors?

Kunsthistorisches Museum, Vienna/ Erich Lessing/Art Resource, NY

ideals of virtue and morality and promoted an ancient version of family values.

Augustus was particularly concerned about sexual morality and passed legislation against adultery, fornication, and homosexuality. He tried to reduce prostitution by taxing it. He promoted marriage not only because it encouraged appropriate sexual behavior but also because it produced offspring who could join the Roman army. Widows and widowers were required to remarry within three years. Mothers and fathers of large families received tax exemptions. Augustus's implementation of his moral agenda was undercut, however, by the behavior of his own family, as he had to send his own daughter Julia into exile for adultery.

The Golden Age of Latin Literature To promote his image of Rome further, Augustus became a patron of the arts. His sponsorship brought the height of the Golden Age of Latin literature. The works of writers whom he subsidized conveyed the glory of Rome, with Augustus as the divinely supported leader. In 17 B.C.E., Augustus celebrated the ancient secular games, which were held only every 110 years and marked the beginning of a new age each time they were held. In honor of the occasion, the poet Horace wrote a hymn that identified Augustus as the leader who had permitted "virtue, long dishonored, to return." Horace also wrote satires that described conventional morality and everyday life in Rome and showed that, with Augustus, everything had returned to normal.

The poet Vergil composed an epic poem, the *Aeneid*, that recounted the story of the founding of Rome and was memorized by every Roman schoolchild. Vergil stressed Aeneas's sense of duty, and readers recognized that their emperor had the same qualities. The historian Livy authored a massive history of Rome that commenced with the city's foundation and showed how the reign of Augustus was a continuation of the Roman Republic. There also was a flowering of poetry by poets such as Ovid, whose *Metamorphoses* provided a summary of Greek and Latin mythology that placed Rome in the context of the ancient Greek classical tradition.

Popular Expenditures Augustus also demonstrated his commitment to tradition by building and remodeling many Roman buildings, especially temples. In his memoirs, he stated, "I rebuilt in the city eighty-two temples of the gods, omitting none that needed to be repaired." One of these temples, honoring Mars, was located in the new Forum of Augustus, which adjoined a forum built by Julius Caesar. Augustus also built an Altar of Peace that showed Augustus, his family, and the Senate performing a religious sacrifice and portrayed Augustus as the person who had brought peace to the Roman world. Augustus did additional remodeling work on the Senate house, the Capitoline temple of Jupiter, and Julius Caesar's basilica in the Forum. He also built a great circular mausoleum to hold his own remains and those of his family and successors. Augustus's efforts to adorn and beautify Rome

> **Aeneid** Epic poem, written in the late first century B.C.E. by the poet Vergil, describing the origins of Rome and Roman virtue.

The literature of the Golden Age of Roman literature provided a common cultural meeting ground for educated persons throughout the Roman world. A second-century North African mosaic shows the poet Vergil writing the *Aeneid*, the greatest of all Roman literary works, on a papyrus scroll. Behind him stand Clio, the muse of history, on the left holding a scroll, and Melpomene, the muse of tragedy, on the right holding an actor's mask. The muses were the nine goddesses of literature and the arts who were thought to provide inspiration for authors and artists. Why do you think Vergil is shown here with the muses of history and tragedy?

C.M. Dixon/Ancient Art & Architecture Collection

were so extensive that he claimed he had changed Rome from a city of brick into a city of marble.

Finally, Augustus also showed his devotion to the Roman people by presenting many kinds of entertainments. He reported that he paid for eight shows of gladiators in which 10,000 men fought and twenty-six wild beast hunts in which 3,500 animals were killed. Later emperors followed his example by sponsoring building projects and extravagant entertainments in Rome.

Beginning with Augustus, therefore, the emperor became the patron of the Roman world, whose inhabitants became his clients. The emperor provided honors and offices for the senators and equestrians, salaries and employment for the soldiers, citizenship for the provincials, and public works and entertainment for the people of Rome.

Roman Peace Period from 14 B.C.E. until 192 C.E., when the Roman Empire was at its height.

 Checking In

By yourself or with a partner, explain the significance of each of the following selected key terms:

augustus	praetorian prefect
Principate	decurions
Praetorian Guard	imperial cult
Romanization	*Aeneid*

The Roman Peace, 14–192 C.E.

◆ **Describe how the Roman Empire functioned during the Roman Peace.**

◆ **Describe the life of an average citizen during the Roman Peace.**

The first two centuries of the Principate are known as the Roman Peace, the period when the Roman Empire was at its height. The Roman world was well administered by generally able emperors. With a few exceptions, the army was kept under control, and there was little threat of foreign invasion. Nearly all the empire's inhabitants had chances for social advancement. Urban life flourished, and economic opportunities abounded. A unified culture and society extended from Britain in the northwest to Arabia in the southeast.

The Successors of Augustus

The empire created by Augustus brought a long period of peace and prosperity known as the **Roman Peace**. The empire reached its absolute height during the Antonine dynasty (96–192 C.E.), named after the emperor Antoninus (138–161 C.E.), whose reign was so uneventful that it is curiously undocumented. Antoninus was so popular with the Senate that it granted him the title pius ("dutiful"), which, like the title augustus, was used by many subsequent emperors.

The Imperial Succession One of Augustus's most difficult tasks had been to find someone to succeed him. Because Augustus claimed that he had reestablished the Republic, there was no constitutional position of emperor and thus no constitutional process for **imperial succession**, the choosing of a new emperor. Augustus had to satisfy both the Senate and the army. To please the Senate, he had to do everything legally. Therefore, before he died, he had the Senate grant to his intended successor, his stepson Tiberius, the same powers that he had. To please the army, he had to designate a family member, preferably a son, for in Rome, loyalty, including military loyalty, was inherited. Augustus did not have any blood sons, so to show the army whom he wanted to succeed him, he adopted Tiberius.

This method for choosing a successor by satisfying both the Senate and the army also worked for Augustus's successors, but only when an emperor had the foresight to put his successor in place before he died. If he failed to do so, a crisis could arise if the Senate and different armies around the empire disagreed over who the next emperor should be.

Augustus died in 14 C.E. at the age of seventy-eight. He was immediately deified by the Senate, and Tiberius (r. 14–17 C.E.) smoothly succeeded him as emperor. It now had been more than seventy years since the Republic had actually worked. Few remembered it as anything but ancient history, and everyone expected that Rome henceforth would be ruled by emperors. The succeeding Roman emperors are organized into families known as dynasties (shown in Table 6.2); Augustus was the first emperor of the Julio-Claudian dynasty (27 B.C.E.–68 C.E.).

Several important political developments occurred during the Principate, including the increasing influence of the army, the declining importance of the Senate, and the growing power of the emperor. The emperors were well aware that their power was based on the army, and newly appointed emperors felt compelled to give the soldiers a gold offering known as a **donative** to ensure their loyalty. When an emperor died without naming a successor, the power of the army became even clearer. Even though the Senate had the legal authority to grant the powers that made an emperor, it rarely acted quickly. Thus, it was almost always the army that took the lead in finding a new emperor.

Problems with Imperial Succession In 37 C.E., Tiberius died without having named his successor. The Praetorian Guard in Rome immediately hailed Tiberius's nephew Caligula (r. 37–41 C.E.) as the next

Table 6.2 **Dynasties of Emperors**
Julio-Claudian Dynasty (27 B.C.E.–68 C.E.)
Augustus (27 B.C.E.–14 C.E.)
Tiberius (14–37 C.E.)
Caligula (37–41 C.E.)
Claudius (41–54 C.E.)
Nero (54–68 C.E.)
Flavian Dynasty (69–96 C.E.)
Vespasian (69–79 C.E.)
Titus (79–81 C.E.)
Domitian (81–96 C.E.)
Antonine Dynasty (96–192 C.E.)
Nerva (96–98 C.E.)
Trajan (98–117 C.E.)
Hadrian (117–138 C.E.)
Antoninus (138–161 C.E.)
Marcus Aurelius (161–180 C.E.)
Commodus (180–192 C.E.)
Severan Dynasty (193–235 C.E.)
Septimius Severus (193–211 C.E.)
Caracalla (211–217 C.E.)
Elagabalus (218–222 C.E.)
Severus Alexander (222–235 C.E.)

© Cengage Learning

emperor, and the Senate had no choice but to agree. In 41 C.E., the army acted even more directly by assassinating Caligula and naming his uncle Claudius (r. 41–54 C.E.) as emperor. Once more, the Senate had to concur.

A more serious crisis occurred in 68 C.E., when Nero (r. 54–68 C.E.), the last Julio-Claudian emperor, died without naming a successor. There were no family members left to succeed him, and when armies around the empire sponsored their own candidates, civil war broke out. The winner was Vespasian (r. 69–79 C.E.), a general who was in the process of putting down a revolt by the Jews in Palestine when his soldiers declared him emperor. After he defeated his last rival, the Senate granted him the powers of an emperor and he founded the Flavian dynasty (69–96 C.E.). A series of effective emperors then

imperial succession Means by which power was transferred from one emperor to the next.

donative Gift of gold coins distributed to soldiers by new emperors.

Nero (r. 54–68 C.E.) Roman emperor who blamed the Christians for a great fire in Rome in 64 C.E.

Boudicca Chooses to Revolt Against Rome

During the early years of the Roman conquest of Britain, Boudicca, the queen of the Celtic people known as the Iceni, decided to lead a revolt against the mighty Roman Empire. Boudicca's husband, Prasutagus, had been a client king whom the Romans had allowed to continue to rule as long as he acknowledged Roman authority. Prasutagus had hoped to leave his kingdom to his two daughters when he died, but he was afraid the Romans would simply annex it. In his will he therefore left half his kingdom to the emperor Nero, hoping that Nero would then allow his daughters to rule the rest. But Prasutagus's plan failed. According to the Roman historian Tacitus, after Prasutagus's death in 60 C.E., "the kingdom was ransacked by soldiers as if it was conquered territory. The king's wife Boudicca was beaten, and his daughters were raped. The leaders of the Iceni were stripped of their property, and those close to the king were enslaved." The Romans had decided to demoralize the Iceni in every way that they could, using rape to humiliate their leaders, and to occupy the entire kingdom.

Boudicca, whose name may be derived from Boudiga, the Celtic goddess of victory, took over the leadership of the Iceni. She faced a difficult dilemma: she could permit the Romans to loot and occupy the kingdom, or she could rebel. If she led a revolt, she knew the odds were against her, for almost all past resistance against Roman occupation had failed. But she also would have known of the victory of Arminius, who had successfully resisted the Romans in Germany forty years earlier.

Unwilling to suffer further disgrace at the hands of the Romans, Boudicca chose to revolt. She convinced other Celtic peoples to do the same, and at first the rebels had great success. The Roman city of Colchester was captured and the inhabitants slaughtered. One Roman legion was ambushed and destroyed, and another was so terrified that it hid in camp and refused to march against the rebels. Paulinus, the Roman commander in Britain, evacuated London, which the Celts then sacked and burned in a fire so hot that a ten-inch layer of melted red clay still can be found fifteen feet below London's streets. The only other Roman city in Britain, St. Albans, also was destroyed. In the end, the Celts were said to have killed 70,000 Romans and Roman sympathizers, and it appeared that their uprising would succeed.

Paulinus then gathered what was left of the Roman army. In the decisive battle, 10,000 Romans faced nearly 100,000 Celtic warriors accompanied by family members and encumbered by wagons filled with loot. According to Tacitus, Boudicca, riding in her chariot with her daughters in front of her, addressed her army thus:

> Just as I have summoned each of the peoples, it also is customary for the Britons to be led by women in war. I come to avenge not my kingdom and riches but my lost liberty, my wounded body, and my ravished daughters. The lusts of the Romans have grown to the point that they respect the bodies of no one; they leave untouched neither old age nor undefiled virginity. Now, the gods of avenging justice are at hand. One legion that dared to fight us already has been destroyed; the others have fled or are hiding in their camps. We must conquer in the line of battle or fall. That is the fate of this woman; let men live on as slaves if they wish.

The wild Celtic charge then was met by the disciplined Romans, who were drawn up on a hillside with forests protecting their flanks and rear. The Britons were thrown back, became entangled in their own wagons, and then were slaughtered. It was said that 80,000 Celts were killed, but only 400 Romans.

Boudicca, like Cleopatra before her, committed suicide to avoid the disgrace of being paraded in triumph in Rome. After this last attempt at independence, the British Celts accommodated themselves to Roman rule. In modern times, Boudicca, also known as Boadicea, became the symbol of British resistance to any foreign invader.

Source: From the Roman historian Tacitus, on Boudicca (c. 56–117).

Trajan (r. 98–117 C.E.) Roman emperor whose conquests of Dacia and Mesopotamia violated the policy of Augustus against foreign conquests.

Hadrian (r. 117–138 C.E.) Roman emperor who concentrated on defending the empire and built Hadrian's Wall.

successfully kept the army out of politics until 192 C.E.

The End of Roman Expansion Only two emperors violated Augustus's policy that the empire should cease expanding, and both were motivated by a desire to increase the empire's economic resources. Claudius undertook the conquest of Britain in the belief that it contained pearls and silver mines. After the revolt of Boudicca in 60 C.E. was suppressed (see A New Direction: Boudicca Chooses to Revolt Against Rome), southern Britain was successfully incorporated into the empire. But the Romans found little silver and few pearls.

More significantly, **Trajan** (r. 98–117 C.E.) conquered Dacia, on the north side of the Danube River, for its gold mines and captured Mesopotamia from the Parthians. His successor, **Hadrian** (r. 117–138 C.E.), realized that Mesopotamia could not be defended and returned it to the Parthians in exchange for trading privileges. He kept Dacia, however, for its gold. Otherwise, the empire remained on a defensive footing, and the army was a garrison army. Hadrian, for example, strengthened the empire's defense with a program that included putting the army to work building a ninety-mile wall, known as Hadrian's Wall, across northern Britain to control traffic across the frontier. The emperors also used the army on public works projects such as building roads, bridges, and aqueducts. Many soldiers went their entire careers without fighting in a single war.

The Emperor's Authority More and more authority fell into the hands of the emperor, for he was the person who had the power to get things done. The emperor assumed control of foreign affairs and took charge when emergencies arose, such as foreign attacks, food shortages, or natural disasters. The imperial bureaucracy expanded as emperors took on responsibility for dealing with additional administrative details. The Senate simply implemented the emperor's will; if the emperor requested a law, the Senate passed it. During the second century C.E., the emperors assumed the right to issue laws in their own name, bypassing the Senate altogether. Before making decisions, emperors consulted not with the Senate but with their amici ("friends") and with a private council made up of high officials and legal specialists. Thus, even more authority fell into the hands of the emperor. One of the few independent rights the Senate had came after an emperor's death. If the Senate liked an emperor, it would deify him, but if the Senate despised an emperor, it passed a decree of "damnation of memory," which permitted his name and images, on coins and statues, to be mutilated—an act that ordinarily was an act of treason.

Most emperors followed Augustus's lead by ruling responsibly according to law. Some, however, were less suited to rule. Emperors who had a suspicious nature listened to informers known as **delators**, who accused people of treason and received one-fourth of the property of any condemned person they had informed on. Some emperors acted irrationally or autocratically. Caligula, for example, reportedly made his horse consul and believed that he was the god Jupiter. Domitian (r. 81–96 C.E.) liked being addressed as "lord and god." And Commodus (r. 180–192 C.E.) portrayed himself on coinage as the Greek hero Hercules and fought as a gladiator. Emperors who exhibited such extreme behavior ran the risk of being assassinated, as in fact happened to the three just mentioned.

Society and Culture

During the Roman Peace, a unified society and culture extended from Britain in the northwest to Arabia in the southeast. The extension of Roman culture to the provinces was balanced by continued Roman assimilation of provincial culture.

Greco-Roman Culture

The culture of the Roman Empire usually is called **Greco-Roman culture** but might be better called Mediterranean culture, for the culture of the Roman world was an amalgamation of the cultures of all the peoples incorporated under the Roman umbrella, including not only Romans and Greeks but also Egyptians, Syrians, Jews, Germans, and many others.

The Rise of the Provinces The two things that bound Roman society together were Roman citizenship and urban life. Those who enjoyed both were fully integrated into a homogeneous Roman system. But even noncitizen country dwellers and foreigners felt the impact of Roman culture. During the Roman Peace, legal and political privileges were extended to larger numbers of people, and many provincials attained Roman citizenship, intensifying the sense of collective identity. This process culminated in 212 C.E. when the emperor **Caracalla** (r. 211–217) granted citizenship to everyone (except slaves and certain ex-slaves) who did not yet have it. Foreigners who settled within the empire also became citizens. Everyone in the empire was under the same legal system—even slaves had legal rights.

Political power also filtered out from Rome into the provinces. By the beginning of the second century C.E., emperors such as the Spaniards Trajan and Hadrian were coming from the provinces. The Senate included North Africans, Greeks, and Syrians along with Italians and other western Europeans. People living outside Rome saw themselves as Romans first and Greeks, Gauls, or Egyptians second. In a speech entitled "To Rome," the Greek orator Aristides expressed to the emperor Hadrian the sense of satisfaction provincials felt: "No one fit for office or a position of trust is an alien. There exists a universal democracy under one man, the best prince and administrator. You have made the word Roman apply not to a city but to a universal people." Aristides was speaking, of course, primarily for the privileged male population of the empire, which was able to enjoy the benefits of Roman citizenship to its fullest extent. Only males, for example, were able to hold office or be members of the Senate.

The Rights of Disadvantaged Persons Other previously disadvantaged segments of the population

delators (from Latin for "betrayers") Informers who accused people of treason and received part of their property at their conviction.

Greco-Roman culture Composite culture shared by people living in the Roman Empire.

Caracalla (r. 211–217 C.E.) Roman emperor who raised the pay of the soldiers and gave Roman citizenship to almost everyone in the empire.

gained new rights. It became easier for both sons and daughters to get out from under the authority of their fathers and establish their legal independence. Women gained greater authority to choose their own husbands. A **jurist** stated, "Engagements, like marriages, come about by the consent of the parties and, therefore, the consent of a daughter of a family is needed for an engagement just as it is for a marriage." Some women could even act in court without a guardian.

The lot of many slaves also improved. They were much more valuable than they had been in the days of the Republic, for the wars of conquest and the cheap slaves they brought as spoils were long gone. Slaves' legal rights included the opportunity to accumulate money to buy their freedom. The regulations for slaves on one imperial estate stated that baths and hospitals were to be provided and that slave women were to be set free after bearing a specified number of slave children. But not all slaves were treated well. The enslaved gold miners of Dacia, for example, spent their lives chained underground and were left lying where they died.

Education in the Empire The empire also offered career opportunities. The emperors sponsored an extensive education system, for the expanding imperial bureaucracy had an insatiable need for educated civil servants. There were municipal and imperial salaries for teachers of grammar and public speaking. The school curriculum was purely literary, based on studying texts such as Vergil's *Aeneid*, with little inclusion of mathematics and science. Law became the most popular field of advanced study; even if orators had fewer chances to rise in politics than in the Republic, they still could argue cases in court.

The Silver Age of Latin Literature The period from 14 C.E. until about 200 C.E. is called the **Silver Age of Latin Literature**. Around 100 C.E., **Tacitus**, the greatest Roman historian, examined the times from Caesar through Domitian in the *Annals* and the *Histories*. Shortly thereafter, Suetonius, secretary of the emperor Hadrian, wrote a collection of biographies of emperors called *The Twelve Caesars*. Much silver-age literature, moreover, was practical in nature. The rhetorician Quintilian's manual on oratorical training became a standard school text. Pliny the Elder, a Roman admiral who died while investigating the eruption of Mount Vesuvius in 79 C.E., authored a massive *Natural History* that dealt with geography, ethnography, zoology, botany, and geology.

In the second century, the astronomer and geographer **Ptolemy of Alexandria** refined Hipparchus's concept of an earth-centered universe to create the complex Ptolemaic model, which was so convincing that it remained the standard model of the universe for the next seventeen hundred years. Ptolemy also created a world map and compiled a star catalogue containing 1,048 stars organized into 48 constellations whose names still are in use. And around 180 C.E. the physician **Galen of Pergamum**, who had gained extensive knowledge of human anatomy by serving as the imperial physician to gladiators, wrote the most important medical works of antiquity, including books called *On the Natural Faculties* and *On the Use of the Parts of the Human Body*.

Urban Life

Urbanism provided another unifying factor, for life during the Principate was centered on cities. The countryside, of course, remained important because farming was the backbone of the Roman economy. But cities were the focus of cultural, social, religious, and economic development.

The City of Rome Of all the cities in the empire, Rome was easily the most important and provided a model for urban life elsewhere. Rome now was home to one million inhabitants who had come from places both within and outside the empire. In the streets, one would encounter Greeks, Celts, Egyptians, and Syrians as well as red-haired and blue-eyed Germans, black Africans, and dark-skinned Arabs and Indians. Commercial goods flowed into Rome from throughout the world, as did foreign languages, cultures, and religious practices. About the year 100 C.E., the Roman satirist Juvenal wrote, "The Syrian river Orontes now flows into the Tiber, bringing its language and customs." Rome had become a melting pot of peoples and cultures.

Rome was the showcase of the Roman world as emperors continued to adorn the city. Vespasian's Forum of Peace portrayed Vespasian, like Augustus, as one who had brought peace after a period of civil war. Vespasian and his sons sponsored the construction of the Flavian **Amphitheater**, commonly known as the Colosseum, one of the most enduring Roman monuments. Trajan built baths, a forum, and a market used for the distribution of subsidized food. Hadrian constructed the circular Pantheon, a temple of "all the gods," and a new mausoleum for himself and his successors. Caracalla built a huge public bath complex that is still used for opera performances. Many emperors

jurist Legal expert who commented on the law and advised emperors.

Silver Age of Latin Literature Period of Latin literature lasting from the death of Augustus until the end of the second century C.E.

Tacitus (ca. 56–117 C.E.) Roman historian who about 100 C.E. wrote histories from Julius Caesar through the emperor Domitian.

Ptolemy of Alexandria (ca. 90–168 C.E.) Astronomer and geographer who favored an earth-centered universe and created a star catalogue and world map.

Galen of Pergamum (ca.129–200 C.E.) The most influential medical writer of antiquity.

amphitheater Large circular structure with seats around a circular arena, used for entertainments.

contributed to the upkeep of roads, bridges, aqueducts that brought in fresh water from up to forty miles away, and a sewer system that flushed Rome's waste into the Tiber River. The most destitute residents of Rome could expect the emperor to provide basic foodstuffs, such as bread and olive oil, and perhaps even some occasional cheese and wine. On special occasions, such as an imperial birthday, the emperors even distributed money.

Provincial Cities Outside Rome, city life also formed the basis for the enjoyment and extension of Roman culture. Many western European cities, such as Lyons in Gaul, had been created out of nothing to meet the needs of the Roman administration. They now served as focal points for the dissemination of Roman civilization. So did colonies of Roman citizens that had been established early in the empire, such as Merida in Spain, and the restored cities of Carthage in North Africa and Corinth in Greece. Even on the frontiers, army garrison posts gave rise to cities such as Bonn, Mainz, Strasbourg, Vienna, Budapest, and Belgrade. By the second century, Alexandria in Egypt, Antioch in Syria, and Carthage in North Africa had populations of over a quarter of a million.

Members of city councils, the decurions, patterned themselves on the Senate of Rome and manifested their civic pride by competing with one another to endow their cities with the same amenities as Rome, including theaters, amphitheaters, temples, town halls, and libraries. Aqueducts delivered fresh water, which was made available at street-corner fountains. Public latrines were equipped with constantly flushing toilets. And elaborate public baths provided enormous hot and cold pools along with exercise and massage rooms, libraries, and lecture halls. The emperors often aided cities with imperial assistance for public works projects, and army troops sometimes provided the labor.

Daily Life in the Roman World The noise, smell, and dust in a Roman city were overpowering. In spite of sewer systems, the trash and filth that accumulated in the streets, much of it left behind by draft animals, bred insects, rodents, and disease. The rich did their best to shut the city out by building homes with blank external walls and elaborate central gardens. But the living quarters of an average laborer would have been a single room, without running water or indoor plumbing, on the fifth or sixth floor of a downtown apartment building. Such an individual would be fortunate to earn one denarius a day when working, an amount that provided little more than the most basic necessities—two sets of clothing, some pottery kitchen utensils, and a few pieces of furniture.

The average person's diet consisted primarily of olive oil, wine diluted with water, and grain, which was made into bread or porridge. Bread was eaten with honey, cheese, or sausage. Vegetables included

cabbage, asparagus, onions, and radishes. Fish and pork, if one could afford them, were the most common meats and had to be eaten quickly, before they spoiled. Honey was a common sweetener. The Romans particularly enjoyed strongly flavored sauces. The main meal was eaten at noon; morning and evening meals were often little more than snacks.

City governments in large cities also provided entertainments, including theatrical productions, mime performances, and athletic contests such as footraces. Violent forms of entertainment were very popular. Chariot races, which often featured disastrous wrecks, were held in circuses. Blood sports took place in an amphitheater on a sand-covered arena where wild beasts and gladiators (both male and female) fought against each other in different combinations. Public entertainment in arenas also was provided by the execution of condemned criminals who were not Roman citizens: they might be hunted down by starved wild animals, gored to death by bulls, or forced to fight each other. The provision of food and entertainment served a useful purpose: by keeping the urban population preoccupied and content, emperors and city governments ensured that there would be no bored and starving mobs rioting in the streets. In all of the cities in the empire, one encountered the same kinds of institutions and services, all of which gave people a sense of unity and shared identity.

The Last Days of Pompeii Today's most extensive knowledge about life in Roman cities comes from **Pompeii**. At the beginning of the Roman Empire, Pompeii was a thriving city of about twenty thousand people, located on the Bay of Naples at the base of Mount Vesuvius, a volcano that had produced earthquakes but no recent eruptions. All this changed on August 24, 79 C.E., when the volcano erupted. A cloud of superheated gas, ash, mud, and rock known as pyroclastic flow surged down the mountainside, slamming into Pompeii at a temperature of about 650 degrees Fahrenheit. Ash filled the air and made it impossible to see. Some people fled to the seacoast and were rescued by Roman naval vessels. Others took refuge underground, where they were asphyxiated by the poisonous gases. Still others died in collapsing buildings or in the streets. The entire city was buried under thick layers of rock, mud, and ash. Over ten thousand inhabitants were killed. The city was not rediscovered until the seventeenth century, and excavations of the site are still ongoing.

The city preserves the tiniest details of everyday life. Like most Roman cities, Pompeii had a forum, a theater, an aqueduct, public baths, a senate house, a temple of the imperial cult, and even its own small amphitheater for putting on gladiatorial contests. The poor lived in large

Pompeii City on the Bay of Naples destroyed by an eruption of Mount Vesuvius in 79 C.E.

O. Louis Mazzatenta National Geographic Image Collection

In this view of the site of Pompeii, Mt. Vesuvius overlooks the ruins of the city. Pompeii had all of the amenities that one expected to find in a typical Roman city, such as a forum, public baths, a small amphitheater where local gladiators fought, and a theater, shown here in the foreground, for the performance of Greek and Roman plays. When the city was buried under six feet of volcanic ash in 79 C.E., it became a time capsule that provides an intimate look into the everyday life of a typical Roman city. The city streets, seen stretching back here, were lined with businesses and the houses of rich and poor alike. Archaeological excavations of the city began in the seventeenth century and continue in the modern day. How do you think that the inhabitants of Pompeii would have felt about living next to a smoking volcano?

bread. Street musicians entertained passersby. A **mosaic** at the front entrance to one house depicts a dog and the warning, "Beware the Dog." Graffiti carved into the walls preserve the actual words of inhabitants, such as "Marcus loves Spendusa," or "Money doesn't smell." Like no other Roman remains, Pompeii brings the Romans back to life.

Economic Activity

The Roman economy was primarily rural and agricultural, but during the Roman Peace a great expansion of manufacturing and commerce brought, at least in the cities, a great rise in prosperity. Even peoples living beyond the frontiers of the empire were affected by Rome's economic reach.

Roman Agriculture Although cities have the greatest visibility in the literary and archaeological source material, they could not exist without the produce of the countryside. The Roman economy remained primarily rural, and most of the population lived in rural areas. Ninety percent of the government's tax income came from the tax on agricultural land. Some farmland was owned by small farmers, but most was consolidated into the large *latifundia* of senators. Initially, *latifundia* had been farmed primarily by a combination of slave and day labor, but by the second century C.E., there was an increasing use of tenant farmers known as **coloni**, who paid a portion of their crop to the landowner and kept the rest for themselves. Many senators were absentee landlords and left the administration of their estates to privileged slaves. The largest landowner of all was the emperor, whose estates grew ever larger as a result of purchases, bequests, and confiscations. These, too, often were overseen by high-ranking imperial slaves.

Roman Commerce Manufacturing and trade expanded dramatically during the Roman Peace, as an empire-wide free market was facilitated by two centuries of peace and lack of government restrictions. The second century C.E. was the great age of the Roman middle class. Ease of travel by water, by both sea and river, made it possible to ship bulk products great distances. In addition, the Roman road system, which extended to the most distant frontiers, made land commerce much less costly than it had been. Road tolls and port dues were low, banditry had been suppressed, and piracy was virtually eliminated. A unified and trustworthy currency system facilitated monetary transactions. Long-distance commerce also was supported by imperial subsidies that kept frontier armies well supplied with foodstuffs and material goods. Much of the trade was in the hands of easterners, primarily Greeks, Syrians, and Jews, resulting in a gradual shift of the economic center of the empire from the western Mediterranean to the east.

apartment buildings, the rich in villas built around a central garden. The streets were laid out on a grid plan, at right angles to each other. Steppingstones allowed inhabitants to avoid the animal droppings and other refuse that littered the streets; sewers under the streets carried away the waste when it rained. Street corner lunch counters served soup, vegetables, and beverages. Vendors sold round loaves of

mosaic Work of art made from small colored pieces of stone or glass cemented together.

coloni (Latin for "tenants") Tenant farmers who worked sections of large estates in exchange for a percentage of their crops.

The trade in luxury items such as gold, spices, and gems was complemented by large-scale commerce in smaller-value items ranging from agricultural products such as wine to manufactured items such as pottery, glassware, and clothing. Different regions were known for different kinds of products. Italy and Gaul were recognized for their ceramics; Sidon in Phoenicia and northern Gaul were famous for glass; Spain and Britain were centers of mining. Amber was imported from the Baltic Sea area and exotic animals from sub-Saharan Africa. The most important grain-growing areas were Egypt, North Africa (which was heavily irrigated), and Sicily. Every year, a huge grain fleet departed from Alexandria and struck out across the Mediterranean for Rome to help to meet Italy's voracious need for grain. In addition, olive oil was produced in North Africa, Italy, and Spain; wine in Italy and southern Gaul; and a popular fish sauce in Spain.

Rome and the Barbarians Rome's economic reach extended beyond the frontiers, to the peoples the Romans knew collectively as barbarians. For the Romans, as for the Greeks, barbarians were people whose culture was different from their own. None of the northern barbarian peoples had any written history prior to their contact with Rome. Greek and Roman accounts are full of stereotypes about them—they dressed in skins, liked to fight, and smelled—and offer little information on the actual details of their lives and customs independent of Mediterranean influence. The most numerous barbarians were on the northern frontier, for in the south was the sparsely populated Sahara desert and to the east were the Parthians, who were just as civilized as the Romans. The northern barbarians, mostly Celtic and Germanic peoples, were settled farmers and had been living in contact with the Romans for centuries, so they were not uncivilized savages.

Roman and barbarian traders and travelers exchanged not only trade goods but also elements of culture, and barbarians could not help picking up Roman culture, including the Latin language. A third-century historian remarked, "The barbarians were adapting themselves to the Roman world. They did not find it difficult to change their lives, and they were becoming different without realizing it." Rome's influence extended even to modern Poland, where an ironworking industry fluctuated according to economic and political conditions within the empire. **Hoards** of Roman coins found hundreds of miles beyond the frontiers also demonstrate Rome's economic reach.

Roman trade routes extended to the Far East, India, and even China. Roman gold, silver, fabrics, glassware, and wine were exchanged for eastern silks, spices, gems, and perfumes. The emperor Trajan dredged out a canal between the Nile River and the Red Sea, and every year a fleet of more than a hundred trading ships set out from Egypt to the east. The journey from Italy to India took about sixteen weeks. An Indian poet of the second century wrote, "Drink the cool and fragrant wine brought by the Greeks in their vessels." In 166 C.E., traders claiming to be the representatives of the emperor **Marcus Aurelius** (r. 161–180) visited the Chinese court. One consequence of all this foreign commerce was a huge trade deficit of some 550 million sesterces per year—enough to pay the annual salaries of the entire Roman army three times over. So many silver denarii flowed out of the empire that the denarius became the standard coinage used in India.

Checking In

By yourself or with a partner, explain the significance of each of the following selected key terms:

Roman Peace	Caracalla
imperial succession	Tacitus
donative	coloni
delators	Marcus Aurelius

Religion in the Roman Empire and the Rise of Christianity

◆ **Describe the religious practices and beliefs of the early Roman Empire.**

◆ **How did early Christians relate to the Roman world?**

The Principate was a period of great religious development and change, caused, in part, by the expanded contact among peoples of different religious beliefs under a unified government. Eastern religious practices, including mystery cults, philosophical beliefs, and Judaism, spread throughout the Mediterranean world. But the most important religious development of the Principate was the appearance of Christianity, a religion that grew out of Judaism and would shape the development of western civilization.

State and Private Religion

Nearly all the people living in the Roman world were polytheists, worshiping many gods. Polytheistic religions included both state religion and private religion.

hoard Coins that were hidden, usually in the ground, either as a means of saving or in times of trouble.

Marcus Aurelius (r. 161–180 C.E.) Roman emperor who fought German invasions and practiced Stoicism.

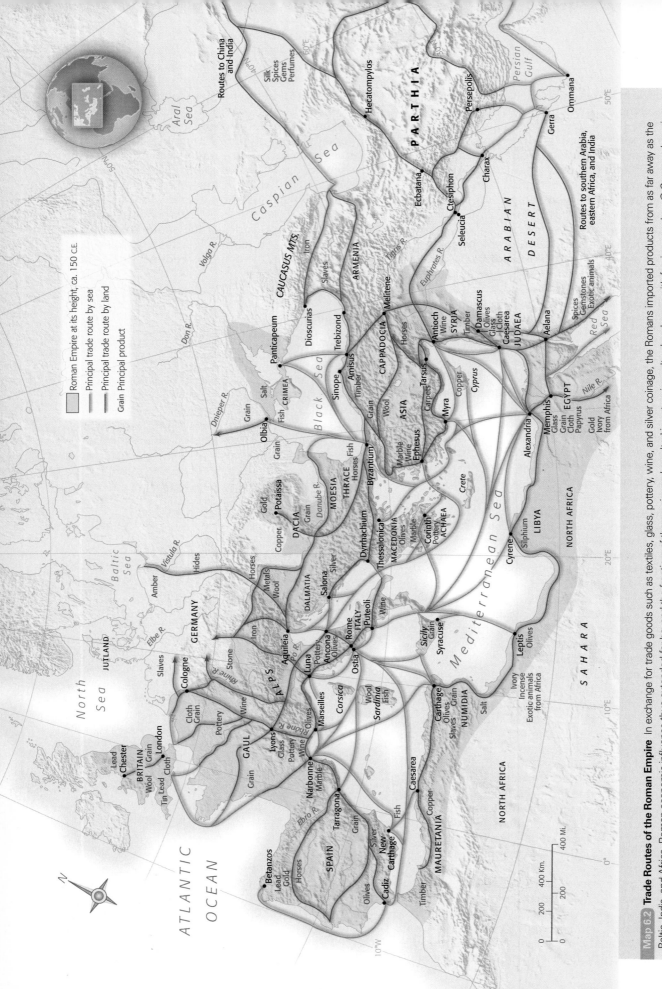

Map 6.2 Trade Routes of the Roman Empire In exchange for trade goods such as textiles, glass, pottery, wine, and silver coinage, the Romans imported products from as far away as the Baltic, India, and Africa. Roman economic influence thus extended far beyond the frontiers of the empire and resulted in extensive cultural exchange with foreign peoples. © Cengage Learning

1. What kinds of trade goods did the Romans receive from beyond the southern and eastern frontiers? What kinds of people would have made use of these products?

2. What were the primary grain producing areas of the empire?

3. Do you think the Roman armies stationed on the northern frontier would have been able to supply their needs locally? Why or why not?

4. What were the silver producing areas of the empire? Do you think these would have been sufficient to meet the empire's need for coinage? Why or why not?

5. How much of the Roman trade network was on inland routes? What kind of transportation system would have been needed to carry out this trade?

Roman State Religion State religion was exercised in public and revolved around the imperial cult. Emperors served as *pontifex maximus* and made regular sacrifices on behalf of the Roman people to Jupiter, Juno, and Minerva, the gods who looked after the welfare of Rome. For the general population, participation in the imperial cult was a political act, a way of declaring loyalty to Rome and the emperor, and did not entail a great deal of spiritual devotion.

Roman Private Religion In private religion, people sought personal religious satisfaction within a small circle of family and friends. Romans were exposed to many different kinds of private religious practices. Many participated in mystery cults, such as the cult of Isis, that promised an afterlife to their initiates. Magic, which allowed people to feel that they were empowered by the gods, was widely practiced. Astrology was used to cast horoscopes that predicted the future outcome of people's lives. It was illegal, however, to cast the horoscope of an emperor for fear that a bad forecast could lead to unrest or revolt. The study of philosophy continued to bring spiritual satisfaction. Stoicism, with its focus on duty and responsibility, had great attraction for the Roman ruling class. One stoic was the emperor Marcus Aurelius, whose *Meditations* preserve his personal thoughts on what it meant to be emperor. Some philosophers went to extremes to put their beliefs into practice. For example, a Cynic philosopher named Proteus burned himself alive to show that death was nothing to be feared.

Roman Holy Men People also believed in "divine men" who were able to use the power of the gods to perform miracles, including curing disease, raising the dead, and controlling the weather. The most famous miracle worker was Apollonius, a native of Anatolia who lived in the first century C.E. Apollonius attracted disciples and healed the sick. He was believed to have overpowered a vampire and to have expelled a demon that was bringing the plague. It even was said that he could be in two places at the same time. Some supposedly divine men, however, were opportunists who took advantage of people's gullibility. The satirist Lucian made fun of "swindlers who deal in magic; they will guide your love life, defeat your enemies, find you treasure, or get you an inheritance." Lucian also suggested, "These scoundrels are completely unprincipled. They understand that human life is ruled by fear and hope, and that anyone who can control these two things will become rich."

By the third century, as a result of religious syncretism, the many different polytheistic gods often were seen as being representations of a single universal deity. Many believed that the sun, which was worshiped as Jupiter, Apollo, or the Unconquered Sun, represented a single, primary god. The emperor Aurelian (r. 270–275 C.E.) even attempted to make the Unconquered Sun into the main god of the Roman Empire, and December 25, when the sun began to rise higher in the sky, was declared to be his birthday.

The Jews in the Roman World

Of all the peoples living in the Roman world, the Jews were the most resistant to assimilation and were, in fact, the only provincials to engage in organized resistance to Rome. They continued to await the arrival of a Messiah who would restore their political independence.

Rome and the Jews In general, the Roman government was tolerant of the Jewish insistence on worshiping only a single god and exempted the Jews from making sacrifices to the imperial cult. But some emperors offended Jewish religious sensibilities. Caligula ordered a statue of himself to be set up in Jerusalem, and the Jews were at the point of revolt until a sensible Roman official refused to implement the order.

The Jewish Revolts In 66 C.E., Jewish dissatisfaction with Roman rule broke into open rebellion. Four years later, Titus, the son of the emperor Vespasian, captured and sacked Jerusalem, destroying the Jewish Temple. Many Jews fled Palestine and settled elsewhere in the empire, adding to the continuing Jewish Diaspora. Following Jewish uprisings in Egypt and Palestine in 117 C.E., the emperor Hadrian introduced anti-Jewish measures that included prohibitions on circumcision, reading of the law, and observance of the Sabbath. In 132 C.E., Hadrian announced his intention to build a temple of Jupiter on the site of the Jewish Temple in Jerusalem. The Jews revolted again under Simon bar Kochba ("son of the star"), whom many Jews believed to be the Messiah, and it took the Romans three years to suppress the rebellion. A Roman colony then was built on the site of Jerusalem, and thousands more Jews were expelled from Judaea, resulting in a further expansion of the Diaspora. By the second century C.E., there was scarcely a city in the empire that did not have a Jewish community.

Maintaining Jewish Identity In spite of Roman efforts to destroy Jewish unity, Jews living in the Roman Empire maintained their unique identity. After the Bar Kochba revolt, a new Sanhedrin assembled outside Jerusalem and continued to receive Jewish contributions that previously had gone to the temple. The Jewish leader, now called a patriarch, served as an intermediary between the Jewish people and the Roman government. With the Temple gone, synagogues became the centers of Jewish religious life in cities with a Jewish population. There, Jews met under the guidance of a **rabbi** to pray, hear preaching based on scripture, and read and study scripture and commentaries on scripture. Learned Jewish rabbis met in Palestine to discuss and write down interpretations of God's will.

About the year 200 C.E., oral interpretations of Jewish law were collected into a volume known as the **Mishnah**, which became part of a larger collection of Jewish teachings called the **Talmud**, a comprehensive guide to Jewish life that included oral tradition, interpretations of the Law of Moses, statements on faith and morality, biblical commentaries, and historical narratives. Jews preserved their way of life by living according to **Halakha**, a set of guidelines that determined how Jews related to God and to fellow human beings. Halakha established a common bond among all Jews everywhere.

The Talmud shows that Jews were ambivalent about Rome. According to one passage, "Rabbi Judah said, 'How excellent are the deeds of this nation. They have instituted market places, they have instituted bridges, they have instituted baths.' Rabbi Simeon ben Yohai answered, 'All that they have instituted they have instituted only for their own needs. They have instituted market places to place harlots in them, baths for their own pleasure, bridges to collect toll.'" Whether they admired the Romans or not, Jews were living in a Roman world. And some Jews did benefit, for the Jewish interest in commerce depicted in this passage reflects the unparalleled opportunities to pursue business activities that were open to Jews in cities throughout the Roman world and beyond that had Jewish communities.

rabbi Respected Jewish teacher who decides questions of ritual and law.

Mishnah Written collection of interpretations of Jewish law, compiled about 200 C.E.

Talmud Collection of Jewish teachings that serve as the comprehensive guide to Jewish life.

Halakha Guidelines that specify how Jews relate to God and people.

Jesus of Nazareth (d. 33 C.E.) Founder of Christianity, whom Christians believe was the Son of God and the Jewish Messiah.

New Testament Books of scripture that the Christians added to the Hebrew Bible.

Apostles Original twelve disciples of Jesus Christ.

crucifixion Form of execution in which the victim is hung from a wooden crossbar and left to die a lingering death; Jesus was crucified.

Christ (from Greek "Christos," or "anointed") The Greek translation of the Hebrew word for the Messiah, and the name given to Jesus of Nazareth.

The Teachings of Jesus of Nazareth

The most significant religious development of the early Principate was the appearance of Christianity, a religion that over the next four centuries would come to pervade every aspect of life in the Roman world and beyond.

The Life of Jesus Christianity grew out of Judaism and was based on the teachings of **Jesus of Nazareth**. Knowledge of the life of Jesus comes mainly from Matthew, Mark, Luke, and John, the first four books of the **New Testament** of the Bible, known collectively as the Gospels. The next book, the Acts of the **Apostles**, discusses the activities of Jesus' disciples after his **crucifixion**. The remainder of the New Testament consists of letters (or epistles) written by followers of Jesus. From a historical perspective, the evidence of the New Testament is considered to be very reliable.

Jesus of Nazareth was born at the end of the reign of the Jewish king Herod, a time when many Jews were expecting the arrival of the Messiah, a word translated into Greek as Christos, or **Christ**. According to Christian scripture, Jesus' mother, Mary, had been told by the angel Gabriel that even though she was a virgin, she would conceive by the Holy Spirit and give birth to the Son of God. Mary thus already was pregnant when she married Joseph, a distant descendant of King David and a carpenter in the town of Nazareth. Christian tradition placed the birth of Jesus on December 25 in a stable in the town of Bethlehem. Jesus' humble origins also were indicated by his early life as a carpenter.

When he was about thirty years old, Jesus was baptized in the Jordan River by his cousin John the Baptist, a Jewish holy man whom some Jews had already identified as the Messiah. The book of Luke said of Jesus, "The Holy Spirit descended on him as a dove, and a voice came from heaven, 'You are my beloved Son; with you I am well pleased.'" Jesus then began to take his message to the people. He gathered twelve disciples from varying backgrounds who accepted him as their rabbi. Several, such as Peter, were fishermen. Matthew was a tax collector and thus disliked by many people. Simon belonged to the Zealots, a group that advocated the violent overthrow of the Romans.

The Ministry of Jesus For the following three years, Jesus traveled about Palestine, teaching in synagogues like any Jewish rabbi and also preaching in the streets. He carried his message not just to the rich and educated but also to the poor and oppressed. He taught that the kingdom of God was open to all equally, including people who were customarily looked down on, such as prostitutes and tax collectors.

Roman emperors often erected triumphal arches meant to commemorate their achievements. An arch built by the emperor Titus shows scenes of the Roman sack of the Jewish Temple in Jerusalem in 70 C.E. Here, Roman soldiers carry off Jewish sacred items including the seven-branched Menorah that was used at Hanukkah to celebrate the liberation from the Seleucids by the Maccabees. Why do you think Roman emperors often erected monuments to commemorate military victories such as this?

He also taught that the kingdom of God was coming quickly and that people needed to prepare themselves for it. People of high social status would not have any special privileges, as indicated by Jesus' lesson that it was easier for a camel to go through the eye of a needle than for a rich man to enter the kingdom of Heaven. Jesus recommended that the rich should give their wealth to the poor. As a demonstration of the power of God, he performed miracles such as changing water into wine, expelling demons, curing the sick, and raising the dead.

Jesus taught that the old Jewish covenants of Abraham and Moses with Yahweh now were replaced with a new covenant based on faith in the grace of God. Many of the most important points of Jesus' teachings appear in his Sermon on the Mount, delivered on a hillside to his disciples and a large crowd. Jesus made clear his message of peace and

love, saying, "You have heard that it was said, 'You shall love your neighbor and hate your enemy.' But I say to you, love your enemies, bless those who curse you, do good to those who hate you, and pray for those who spitefully use you and persecute you." Unlike other Jewish popular leaders, however, and consistent with his message of peace, Jesus did not preach rebellion. When asked whether it was proper for Jews to pay taxes to the Romans, Jesus responded, "Give to Caesar the things that are Caesar's and to God the things that are God's," thus clearly expressing his teaching that the world of God was separate from the world of politics.

The Trial of Jesus Those who believed Jesus' message saw him not only as the Messiah but also as the

grace The gift of God by which people receive salvation.

After the legalization of Christianity in the fourth century C.E., well-known scenes from the life of Christ were portrayed in churches throughout the Roman world. In this mosaic from the sixth-century C.E. church of Sant'Apollinare Nuovo in Ravenna, Italy, Jesus is shown on trial before Pontius Pilate. On Pilate's right, Jews present Jesus to Pilate and ask for his execution. Behind Pilate stand a soldier wearing a military cloak and two bailiffs responsible for keeping order. Pilate himself, likewise wearing a military cloak signifying his right to command soldiers, disclaims responsibility for his order that Jesus be crucified by washing his hands. In later history, who do you think received the most blame for the death of Jesus, the Romans or the Jews? Why do you think this was the case?

Son of God, but many Jews, especially Jewish leaders, saw him as a dangerous revolutionary. In the third year of his ministry, around the year 33 C.E., Jesus entered Jerusalem a few days before Passover, a Jewish spring holy day that commemorates the Exodus. Many Jews hailed him as the Messiah, causing the Sanhedrin, which oversaw Jewish religious and civil administration, to feel threatened by his increasing influence and to plot against him. Jesus foresaw his own death, and called his disciples together for a meal. He distributed to them bread and wine, which he told them to interpret as his body and blood, saying, "This is my blood of the new covenant, which is shed for many for the remission of sins." The Sanhedrin bribed one of Jesus' disciples, Judas, to identify him, and on that night Jesus was arrested and questioned by the Sanhedrin.

Witnesses testified that Jesus had blasphemed against God, a capital crime under Jewish law. But only the Roman governor had the authority to impose the death penalty, so on Friday, Jesus was brought before Pontius Pilate, the Roman **prefect**, or governor, of Judaea, who sentenced Jesus to death. Because Jesus was not a Roman citizen, he was

prefect Equestrian military and tax collection official, or a governor of a small province.

subjected to the humiliating punishment of crucifixion. He died that evening and was buried in the tomb of one of his followers. Two days later, on Sunday, the Gospels report that Jesus rose from the dead. In the book of Matthew, Jesus appeared to his disciples and commanded them, "Go and make disciples of all nations," thus making it clear that his message was to be delivered not just to Jews but to all the people in the world. Forty days after his resurrection, his followers believed, Jesus rose to heaven.

Early Christian Communities

During the first three centuries of the Roman Empire, Christianity gradually spread out of Palestine into the rest of the Roman world. At this time, characteristic Christian practices also developed as Christians came to a collective understanding of just who they were.

The Spread of Christianity After Jesus' death, his followers, who were known as Christians, or the followers of Jesus the Christ, continued to **proselytize**—that is, to seek converts—for his teachings. The spread of Christianity was helped by three factors. First and foremost, Christianity met spiritual and social needs that other religions failed to address. Second, it attracted gifted adherents who were able to communicate its message and convince polytheists to convert. And third, it arose at a time when travel was easy and religious ideas could spread among multitudes of people.

The Ministry of Paul Initially, efforts at conversion were directed mainly at Jews, but this changed under the leadership of Paul of Tarsus, also known as Saul. A Jewish Pharisee and also a Roman citizen, Paul originally had persecuted the Christians and had stood by when Stephen, the first Christian **martyr**, was stoned to death by Jews in Jerusalem. While on his way to Damascus to arrest Christians, Paul had a vision in which Christ said to him, "Saul, Saul, why do you persecute me?" causing Paul to convert to Christianity and become one of its greatest promoters. Paul convinced the Christians of Jerusalem that Gentiles (non-Jews) who converted to Christianity should not be required to follow the Jewish laws, which would have required circumcision and adherence to a multitude of dietary and other restrictions. The primary requirement of converts was that they have faith in Christ, an emphasis that allowed Christians to deliver their message to all the peoples of the empire and beyond.

Paul tirelessly spread Christ's teachings throughout the Roman world, preaching that in the Christian world, there was "no Gentile and Jew, no circumcised and uncircumcised, no barbarian and Scythian, no slave and free freeman, but Christ in all things." During the 40s and 50s C.E., Paul visited Anatolia, Greece, and the Levant. He pursued his mission not just with visits, but also with letters—addressed to peoples such as the Galatians, the Hebrews, and even the Romans—in which he clarified the nature of Christian belief and the Christian life. Several of his letters later were incorporated into the New Testament. In the late 50s C.E., Paul was accused of plotting revolt and was arrested. He exercised his right as a Roman citizen to appeal his case to the emperor and was transported to Rome, where he continued to preach. According to Christian tradition, he eventually was tried, found guilty, and beheaded, an execution that befitted a Roman citizen.

Christian Identity Early Christians felt that Christianity offered them a much greater feeling of personal identity and spiritual fulfillment than the polytheistic religions. Like the mystery religions, Christianity promised an afterlife, but it also offered much more. Christians believed that Christ died to gain forgiveness for their sins. But they also believed it was their Christian duty to try not to sin, for Christianity offered a moral code according to which they were expected to live. The Christian message that all were equal in the sight of God regardless of wealth or social rank gave Christianity a degree of inclusivity that made it popular among less privileged people such as slaves, women, and the poor.

Christianity also provided a sense of community, for along with offering the opportunity for private spirituality, Christianity had a communal side. Christians met together to worship, very often in someone's house. Unlike Jewish synagogue meetings, which favored men, men and women participated together in early Christian worship services. Christian communities supported the poor, elderly, and sick. Early Christians also lived in the expectation that Christ soon would return. They believed that this Second Coming, also known as the **Apocalypse** and Judgment Day, would bring the kingdom of God and the destruction of the earthly world.

Christian Rituals The early Christian church recognized two sacraments, rituals that symbolized the bestowing of God's grace. One was baptism, which Christians believed washed away their past sins. Some Christians felt that people should wait

proselytize To recruit new members actively for an organization or belief.

martyr (Greek for "witness") One who suffers for his or her faith.

Apocalypse The revealing of Jesus as the Messiah, a reference to the Second Coming of Christ, also known as Judgment Day.

to be baptized until they were old enough to profess their faith publicly. Others, however, thought that infants should be immediately baptized because even they were tainted with the **original sin** of Adam and Eve, who had disobeyed God's command not to eat the fruit of the tree of knowledge in Eden.

The other sacrament was the Eucharist, also known as Communion, a distribution of bread and wine based on Christ's Last Supper with his disciples. By taking Communion with each other, Christians shared their sense of community in God's grace. The worst punishment that could be inflicted on a Christian was **excommunication**, denial of the right to take Communion with other Christians. Christians who repented of sins committed after baptism were expected to confess them publicly before the other members of the Christian community. The penance that Christians performed to atone for their sins also was performed publicly. In this way, a sinner was reintegrated into the Christian community.

Christian Communities Christianity prospered earliest in urban environments for several reasons. The communal nature of early Christianity required a sufficiently large population, not found in the countryside. Cities also had diverse and often rootless populations looking for spiritual fulfillment. In cities, the Christian refusal to participate in traditional Roman religious practices did not attract as much attention as it would have in the countryside. In addition, the Jewish communities from which Christians often came were located in cities. The fact that early Christians often competed with Jews for converts may be one reason the writers of the Gospels placed the blame for Christ's death not on the Romans but on the Jews, a consequence of which has been centuries of **antisemitism**.

Many Roman cities, especially in the east, gained Christian communities during the first few centuries of the Principate. Christian congregations in each city were under the overall authority of a male **bishop**. Christians believed that their bishops received their authority by **apostolic succession**— that is, by being the direct successors to the Apostles of Christ. Lower-ranking

Christian clergy included priests, who oversaw spiritual matters, administered sacraments, and mediated between God and the congregation, and **deacons**, who initially could be either male or female and whose duties included managing church property, caring for the poor, and overseeing the instruction of new converts. The first Christian communities had little contact with each other. They often used different scriptures, had different rituals, and based their practices as much on oral tradition as on written texts.

The Christians in the Roman World

At first, the Romans took little notice of the Christians and had difficulty distinguishing Christians from Jews. But it soon became clear that there were differences, and Christianity went through a difficult period of negotiating for acceptance from the rest of the Roman world.

Misconceptions About Christianity Christians, for example, met not on the Jewish Sabbath (Saturday) but on "the day of the Sun" (Sunday). Like the Jews, the Christians refused to worship other gods— a potential problem, for the imperial government saw participation in the cult of Rome and Augustus as the test for loyalty to the state. Jews were exempt from participation, but Christians were not. Normally, only high-ranking dignitaries were expected to sacrifice during cult rites, so Christians rarely had to worry about being tested. But if Christians were accused of atheism (not believing in the gods) or disloyalty, they could be ordered to sacrifice. If they refused, they could be found guilty of treason and executed.

Because Christianity was different from other religions, misconceptions arose among the general public. Unlike polytheists, Christians worshiped in private, out of the public view, leading to suspicions that they were a secret society engaged in subversive activities. It also was thought that Christians were cannibals because they ate the flesh and drank the blood of their god (a misunderstanding of the sacrament of Communion) and that they practiced incest because they called each other "brother" and "sister."

Christianity and the Roman Government When the Roman government noticed the Christians at all, it sometimes was tolerant. In 111 C.E., for example, Pliny the Younger, a Roman governor in Anatolia, consulted the emperor Trajan about how to deal with Christians. Trajan replied, "These people must not be hunted out; if they are brought before you and the charge against them is proved, they must be punished, but anyone who denies that he is a Christian, and makes this clear by offering prayers to our gods, is to be pardoned." Even in Trajan's lenient policy,

original sin Sin committed by Adam and Eve when they disobeyed God's command not to eat from the tree of knowledge.

excommunication The denial of Communion to a Christian; later, the exclusion from other Christian sacraments as well.

antisemitism Racial, religious, or ethnic hostility directed against Jews.

bishop Leader of the Christian community in a city.

apostolic succession Belief that Christian bishops receive their authority by being direct successors to Jesus' Apostles.

deacons Christian clerics responsible for overseeing church finances and carrying out good works of the church.

Vibia Perpetua Records the Events Leading to Her Martyrdom

Vibia Perpetua was a young Christian woman of Carthage in North Africa. In 202 C.E. she was arrested, convicted of being a Christian, and sentenced to fight wild animals in the arena. Her first-person account of the events leading up to her martyrdom on March 7, 203 C.E.—including her trial before the Roman procurator and several visions she had during the course of her imprisonment—is preserved in *The Passion of Sts. Perpetua and Felicitas,* from which the following selection is taken. The following day Perpetua was sent into the arena to die. When a mad cow failed to kill her, she guided the executioner's sword to her throat with her own hand. Her account then provided a model for later Christians for how to live their lives.

❶ What kinds of pressures are put on Perpetua to sacrifice?

❷ What role did dreams play in the ancient world?

❸ Does Perpetua show any fear? Why or why not?

❹ Why does Perpetua see herself as a male gladiator?

❺ What does the "Gate of Life" signify?

Another day we were suddenly snatched away to be tried; and we came to the forum and a very great multitude gathered together. We went up to the tribunal. The others being asked if they were Christians, confessed. So they came to me. And my father appeared there also, with my son, and tried to draw me from the step, saying, "Perform the sacrifice; have mercy on the child." ❶ And Hilarian the procurator said: "Spare your father's gray hairs; spare the infancy of the boy. Make sacrifice for the emperors' prosperity." And I answered, "I am a Christian." Then Hilarian passed sentence on us all and condemned us to the beasts; and cheerfully we went down to the dungeon. ❷ The day before we fought, I saw in a vision that Pomponius the deacon had come to the door of the prison and knocked hard on it. And I opened to him, and he said to me: "Perpetua, we await you; come." And he took my hand, and we went through rugged and winding places. At last he led me into the arena. And he said to me: "Be not afraid." And he went away. And I saw many people watching closely. ❸ And because I knew that I was condemned to the beasts I marveled that beasts were not sent out against me. And there came out against me a repulsive Egyptian, to fight with me. Also there came to me comely young men as my helpers. ❹ And I was stripped naked, and I became a man. And my helpers rubbed me with oil as their custom is for a contest. And there came forth a man of very great stature, wearing a purple robe and holding a green branch on which were golden apples. And he besought silence and said: "If this woman shall conquer the Egyptian, she shall receive this branch." And he went away. And we came close to each other. The Egyptian tried to trip up my feet, but with my heels I smote his face. And I rose up into the air and began so to smite him. And I caught his head, and he fell on his face; and I trod on his head. And I went up to the master of gladiators and received the branch. And he kissed me and said to me: "Daughter, peace be with you." ❺ And I began to go with glory to the gate called the Gate of Life. And I awoke; and I understood that I should fight, not with beasts but against the devil; but I knew that mine was the victory. Thus far I have written this, till the day before the games; but as for the deed of the games themselves let him write who will.

Source: Excerpt from "Vibia Perpetua Records the Events Leading to Her Martyrdom," W. H. Shewring, trans., *The Passion of Perpetua and Felicity* (London: Sheed & Ward, 1931). Reproduced by kind permission of Continuum International Publishing Group.

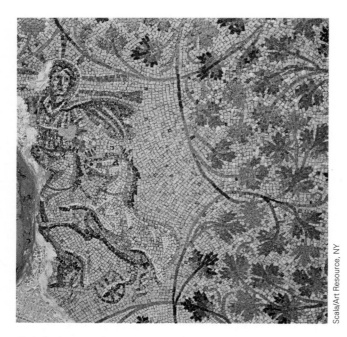

Scala/Art Resource, NY

Christianity sometimes was thought to be a form of sun worship, as seen in this depiction of Christ as the sun god in a third-century mosaic from a Christian mausoleum beneath St. Peter's basilica in Rome. Here Christ is shown driving the sun god's four-horse chariot across the sky. His head is surrounded with rays of the sun that inspired the later Christian halo. How might non-Christian perceptions of Christianity have been affected if Christ was viewed as a form of the sun god?

Christians who refused to sacrifice to the state gods still were liable to execution.

persecution The seeking out and punishing of Christians by the imperial government.

Decius (r. 249–251 C.E.) Roman emperor who sought to reunify the empire by ordering all citizens to sacrifice at the altar of the imperial cult.

apostasy A Christian's denial of his or her faith.

saint (from Latin, "holy") Christian martyr believed to be able to intercede with God.

relics Pieces of the bodies or clothing of saints, thought to possess miraculous powers.

apologists Christian intellectuals who attempted to defend Christianity against attacks by polytheists.

On other occasions, Christians were harshly treated. The historian Tacitus reports that in 64 C.E., a great fire incinerated a section of Rome where the emperor Nero had wanted to build a new palace. When suspicions arose that Nero himself had ordered the fire to be set, he blamed the Christians, and many were executed in what came to be known as their first **persecution**. Christians also were persecuted in other parts of the empire at other times. In 250 C.E., for example, the emperor **Decius** proposed to use religion to reunify the empire. He ordered all citizens to revalidate their loyalty by sacrificing at the altar of the imperial cult. Many

Christians were martyred when they refused to sacrifice, although others did sacrifice and later were accused by other Christians of **apostasy**, or abandoning their faith.

Convicted Christians often were sentenced to die in the arena because they were noncitizens and therefore not entitled to a more honorable form of execution, such as decapitation. Those who were executed became martyrs and were revered for having died for their faith. Many martyrs also became **saints**, who lived model Christian lives and were believed to have the power to intercede with God. Two early martyrs and saints were the Apostles Peter and Paul, executed in Rome during the reign of Nero. Items associated with martyrs, such as their bones and clothing, were called **relics** and were thought to possess miraculous powers. The official court records of Christians' trials sometimes were preserved and later served as the basis for biographies known as "lives of the saints," which provided models for Christian behavior. One well-known biography, that of Vibia Perpetua, included her own autobiographical account of the events leading up to her martyrdom at Carthage in 203 C.E.

Christianity Goes Mainstream As of the late second century C.E., there were growing enclaves of Christians in cities throughout the Roman world. Christianity had shown remarkable staying power, not only enduring, but even being strengthened by periods of persecution. Christian intellectuals known as **apologists**, some of them converted polytheists, made an intellectual case for Christianity to the larger polytheist population. They argued that Christian teachings were compatible with the teachings of polytheistic philosophers such as Plato and that Christians were responsible subjects of the emperor.

In addition, Christianity was gradually becoming part of the mainstream of Roman religion. For example, many people thought the Christians were sun worshipers because they met on the day of the Sun and their god had the same birthday as the sun. Even some Christians had a special reverence for the sun. But there still was no feeling among the general public that Christianity would ever be anything more than just one more eastern mystery religion.

 Checking In

By yourself or with a partner, explain the significance of each of the following selected key terms:

Halakha	bishop
Christ	persecution
martyr	saint
excommunication	apologists

The Roman Empire in Crisis, 193–284 C.E.

◆ **In what ways did the Principate no longer work in the third century C.E.?**

◆ **How did the army contribute to the empire's instability?**

By the third century C.E., the Principate was not functioning nearly as well as it had in the past. New political and economic problems arose that Augustus's approach could not solve. The supposed partnership of the emperors with the Senate fell apart as the emperors exercised more and more direct authority. At the same time, the army became more difficult to control, and the coinage lost much of its value. The inability of emperors to deal with these problems resulted in a period of civil wars and invasions that nearly destroyed the empire.

The Severan Dynasty

Beginning in the late second century C.E., the Roman Peace began to break down. During the reign of Marcus Aurelius, soldiers brought back a devastating plague from a Parthian war, and for the first time there were serious problems on the northern frontier. Marcus spent most of his reign campaigning against Germanic peoples who were seeking to move south of the Danube, and by the time of his death, in 180 C.E., the Germans had been pushed back. But difficulties again surfaced after the assassination of Marcus's son Commodus in 192 C.E. Different armies named their commanders emperors. Civil war broke out, and the winner, **Septimius Severus** (193–211 C.E.), established the Severan dynasty (193–235 C.E.).

Severus was a native of Libya, and his wife, Julia, was a Syrian. They had little in common with the senators of Rome, who had supported one of his rivals and ridiculed his African accent. Realizing that he was completely dependent on the army, Severus began to abandon the pretense that he ruled in partnership with the Senate. The army also had changed. Few Italians enlisted anymore. Most soldiers came from the provinces, especially from the backwoods of the Rhine and Danube Rivers. To meet the need for troops, barbarian units from beyond the frontiers sometimes were hired. These soldiers had little in common with their cultured senatorial commanders and were much more difficult to control. They were less interested in defending the idea of Rome than in seeking personal gain.

The last emperor of the Severan dynasty was Severus Alexander (r. 222–235 C.E.), only thirteen years old when he came to power. He was much too young to rule on his own, and the government was in the hands of his aunt and mother, both named Julia, who received the title of *augusta*. This was the closest that Rome ever came to being ruled by women. Alexander's mother attended meetings of the Senate and attempted to restore its authority to counteract the growing influence of the army.

The Ruin of the Roman Economy

In the third century the Roman economy, which hitherto had been a great source of Roman strength, became one of its greatest weaknesses as a result of mismanagement of both the coinage and urban finances.

The Debasement of the Currency Septimius Severus was said to have advised his two sons, "Treat the soldiers well, and despise everybody else." He followed his own advice by granting the soldiers additional privileges. He allowed them to marry while still in service—making them happier but also less mobile because they became reluctant to serve far from home. He also raised military salaries from 300 to 500 denarii a year. His son Caracalla (r. 211–217 C.E.) followed suit and increased military pay to 750 denarii per year. The treasury did not have nearly enough income to meet these increases.

To deal with the financial crisis, the emperors debased the money—that is, they mixed copper in with the silver. Soon the coins were only 50 percent silver, and their value fell accordingly. In addition, more than twice as many coins as usual were being poured into circulation every year. As the value of the coins decreased and the money supply increased, the cost of goods and services went up, resulting in runaway inflation. To make matters even worse, people hoarded the old all-silver coins and used the new debased ones to pay their taxes. Thus, every year when the incoming coins were melted down, there was less and less silver with which to mint new coins. In repeated cycles of debasement and inflation, the silver coinage lost almost all its value. By 260 C.E., the amount of silver in the coinage had fallen to 5 percent, and the salaries of the soldiers, rather than being increased, became virtually worthless.

Problems in Urban Life Financial catastrophe also hit the cities, many of which had been misspending and overspending as a consequence of poor management. Some cities had begun massive building projects, such as new

Septimius Severus (r. 193–211 C.E.) Roman emperor who preferred the army to the Senate.

augusta (feminine form of "augustus") Title given to Roman imperial women.

Dr. Stephen Coyne/Ancient Art & Architecture Collection

Rather than putting up triumphal arches like the Roman emperors, New Persian kings advertised their achievements on huge rock carvings on the sides of cliffs. In this relief, from Naqsh-e Rostam in Iran, the captured Roman emperor Valerian begs for mercy from King Shapur I, who had captured Valerian in 260 C.E. In his own words, Shapur reported, "And beyond Carrhae and Edessa we had a great battle with Valerian Caesar. We made prisoner ourselves with our own hands Valerian Caesar and the others, chiefs of that army, the praetorian prefect, senators; we made all prisoners and deported them to Persis." Valerian spent the rest of his life as a slave of the New Persians. How would his capture of Valerian have been of propaganda value to Shapur?

aqueducts and amphitheaters, that they could not pay for. The emperors often made up the difference, resulting in another drain on the treasury. In some cases, emperors appointed caretakers to oversee a city's finances, thus increasing the size of the imperial bureaucracy. There also were problems with tax collection, which traditionally had been in the hands of the decurions. Shortfalls, which occurred more and more often, had to be made up by the decurions from their own resources. In addition, philanthropy by decurions that in the past had been optional, such as sponsoring entertainments, by the third century C.E. had become mandatory. As a consequence, being a decurion sometimes no longer was the great honor it once had been, and the emperors were in danger of losing local support.

imperial crisis Period of civil war and foreign invasions between 235 and 284 C.E.

The Imperial Crisis

In 235, the unruly army murdered Severus Alexander, marking the beginning of one of the most disastrous periods in Roman history, the **imperial crisis**, during which the Roman Empire nearly collapsed completely.

Civil Wars For several reasons, armies throughout the empire went out of control and began naming their commanders as emperors. First, the uncultured soldiers just could not be effectively commanded by cultured senators. In addition, because their salaries had become virtually worthless, their only meaningful pay became the gold donatives received when a new emperor was named, a situation that naturally encouraged them to make new emperors. Armies abandoned their frontier posts and marched on Rome to try to defeat the current emperor and force the Senate to recognize their candidate. No emperor was able to get the army back under control or to establish a new dynasty.

Foreign Invasions The borders could not have been left unguarded at a worse time, for several powerful enemies were menacing the frontiers.

Germanic peoples north of the Rhine had co-alesced into larger, more formidable coalitions, the **Franks** ("swordsmen") on the lower Rhine and the **Alamanni** ("all men") on the upper Rhine. The **Goths**, a Germanic people living north of the Black Sea, threatened Roman provinces on the Danube. And in the east, the Parthians were overthrown in 227 C.E. by the Persians, who created the **New Persian Empire** and proposed to reestablish the Persian Empire of the fifth century B.C.E. The Persians laid claim to Egypt, Palestine, and Anatolia, resulting in an immediate state of war with the Roman Empire. All these foreign enemies were eager to take advantage of Roman weakness.

Disaster followed on disaster. The Franks, Alamanni, and Goths broke through the frontier defenses and ravaged the heart of the empire. In 251 C.E., the emperor Decius was killed by the Goths, an event that the Christians interpreted as the judgment of God against this persecuting emperor. The New Persians invaded the eastern provinces and captured and enslaved a Roman emperor. The provinces of Gaul, Spain, and Britain broke away and established their own empire.

The Soldier Emperors Then, just as it seemed that the empire was about to collapse, emperors known as the **soldier emperors**, who had risen through the ranks in the army and then been made emperor by their troops, began to get the army back under control and put the empire back together. Aurelian (r. 270–275 C.E.), who gained the nickname "the Restorer of the World," drove the Goths and other invaders back across the Danube. In the east, he defeated Queen Zenobia of the desert city of Palmyra, who had declared her independence and seized several Roman provinces. Palmyra was destroyed, and the proud queen was taken captive. The Gallic empire capitulated without a fight. The empire now was on the road to recovery.

Franks, Alamanni, and Goths Barbarian peoples who threatened Rome's northern frontier in the third century C.E.

New Persian Empire Eastern empire extending from Mesopotamia to Iran that succeeded the Parthian Empire in 227 C.E.

soldier emperors Emperors during the latter part of the imperial crisis who had risen through the ranks in the army and been made emperor by their troops.

 Checking In

By yourself or with a partner, explain the significance of each of the following selected key terms:

Septimius Severus	Alamanni
augusta	Goths
imperial crisis	New Persian Empire
Franks	soldier emperors

CHAPTER
Review

Summary

- Augustus established the Roman Empire in 27 B.C.E. in a form known as the Principate, based on the concept that the emperor had restored the Republic and was sharing power with the Senate.

- The Roman Empire was the most successful empire the world had yet seen. It brought peace and prosperity, and people throughout the provinces were able to share in the opportunities the empire offered.

- Even though the empire was based on the military might of the Roman army, the army was hardly ever visible.

- The empire offered many opportunities. Citizenship became available to all. Provincial men could become senators or even emperors. Previously disadvantaged groups, such as women, foreigners, and slaves, gained greater rights under the law than persons in any other ancient society.

◆ Trade and urban life flourished. A common culture extended to the most distant frontiers.

◆ In this context of empire-wide peace and security, a new religion, Christianity, arose as a movement within Judaism. It was based on the teachings of Jesus of Nazareth. Christianity quickly developed as a separate religion. It met the spiritual needs of large numbers of people, and it attracted converts who were effectively able to spread its message. There soon were Christian communities in most of the large urban centers of the Roman world.

◆ Christians also came into conflict with the Roman government when they refused to sacrifice to the imperial cult. Many were martyred, and it was not clear whether Christianity would be able to survive in the face of Roman persecution.

◆ During the third century C.E., the empire established by Augustus began to fall apart. Emperors became more dependent on the army, and the Senate was shut out of power. The empire and its cities fell into financial difficulties. The government lost control of the armies, which revolted and made their own commanders emperors.

◆ Civil wars broke out, which gave foreign enemies the chance to raid and invade the empire. Parts of the empire were lost to invaders or to secession. By the middle of the third century C.E., it appeared that the empire might not survive.

◆ Soldier emperors, who had spent their lives in the army, then began to regain control of the armies and restore the empire.

Chronology

31 B.C.E.	Octavian defeats Antony and Cleopatra at Battle of Actium		69–96	Flavian dynasty rules Roman Empire
30 B.C.E.	Cleopatra and Antony commit suicide		79	Eruption of Mount Vesuvius destroys Pompeii
27 B.C.E.	Roman Empire begins when the Senate gives Octavian the title of Augustus		96–192	Antonine dynasty rules Roman Empire
27 B.C.E.–68 C.E.	Julio-Claudian dynasty rules Roman Empire		193–235	Severan dynasty rules Roman Empire
9	Germans defeat Romans at Teutoberg Forest		203	Perpetua is martyred for being a Christian
14	Death of Augustus		212	Caracalla grants Roman citizenship to everyone but slaves
14–192	Peace and prosperity prevail during the Roman Peace		227	New Persian Empire begins
ca. 33	Jesus of Nazareth is crucified		235	Imperial crisis begins
60	Boudicca leads British revolt against the Roman Empire		250	Decius institutes loyalty oath
64	Great fire burns part of Rome		270	Aurelian begins to restore the Roman Empire
			284	Imperial crisis ends

© Cengage Learning

Note: C.E. means "common era."

Test Yourself

To gauge your mastery of the material in this chapter, answer the questions below. More than one answer may be correct.

Augustus and the Creation of the Roman Empire, 27 B.C.E.–14 C.E.

1. In order to gain the support of the Senate, Augustus claimed that he
   a. Had restored the Roman Republic.
   b. Was a living god.
   c. Was working in partnership with the Senate.
   d. Was just another senator.
   e. Planned to retire.

2. What powers did Augustus and later emperors use to rule the Roman Empire?
   a. The power of a proconsul
   b. Dictatorial powers
   c. The "power of persuasion"
   d. The power of a tribune
   e. Command of a large police force

3. What means did Augustus use to encourage the people in the provinces to identify with Rome?
   a. Grants of Roman citizenship
   b. The opportunity to serve in the army
   c. Land grants to provincial leaders
   d. The Cult of Rome and Augustus
   e. The forced adoption of Roman culture

4. In order to show his commitment to Roman tradition, Augustus
   a. Campaigned against sexual immorality.
   b. Took the ancient title of "King of the Romans."
   c. Remodeled many ancient Roman buildings.
   d. Sponsored literature that portrayed him as a leader appointed by the gods.
   e. Reestablished the office of Dictator

Now that you have reviewed and tested yourself on this part of the chapter, take time to pull together all the important information by answering the following questions:

◆ How did Augustus attempt to solve the problems that had caused the fall of the Roman Republic?

◆ How did Roman government function during the Principate?

The Roman Peace, 14–192 C.E.

5. Newly appointed emperors were expected to distribute an offering of gold coins to the soldiers for what purpose?
   a. "Free will offering"
   b. Campaign contribution
   c. Service bonus
   d. Donative
   e. Tithe

6. Which emperors violated Augustus's policy of no more expansion?
   a. Vespasian
   b. Claudius
   c. Trajan
   d. Hadrian
   e. Commodus

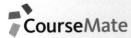 Visit the CourseMate website at **www.cengagebrain.com** for additional study tools and review materials for this chapter.

7. Typical Roman cities around the empire contained which of these amenities?

    a. Military garrisons
    b. Theaters
    c. Amphitheaters
    d. Aqueducts
    e. Step pyramids

8. What was the land that senators consolidated into large estates called?

    a. Tenant farms
    b. Truck farms
    c. Plantations
    d. *Latifundia*
    e. Public land

Now that you have reviewed and tested yourself on this part of the chapter, take time to pull together all the important information by answering the following questions:

◆ Why are the first two centuries of the Roman Empire known as the "Roman Peace?"

◆ Describe the life of an average Roman during the Roman Peace.

Religion in the Roman Empire and the Rise of Christianity

9. The sun god was worshiped in which of these forms?

    a. The Unconquered Sun
    b. Hercules
    c. Apollo
    d. Jupiter
    e. Isis

10. What were the guidelines for the Jewish way of life known as?

    a. Halakha
    b. The New Testament
    c. Bar Kochba
    d. The Exodus
    e. "The Law of Joshua"

11. Jesus of Nazareth taught that

    a. The kingdom of god was open to all.
    b. The old Jewish covenant had been replaced by a new covenant based on faith.
    c. Rebellion against Rome was necessary.
    d. People with high social status did not have special privileges.
    e. All slaves should be set free.

12. Misconceptions about the Christians included stories that they

    a. Practiced incest.
    b. Engaged in subversive activities.
    c. Had originally come from China.
    d. Were cannibals.
    e. Worshiped the son of Jupiter.

Now that you have reviewed and tested yourself on this part of the chapter, take time to pull together all the important information by answering the following questions:

◆ Describe the religious practices and beliefs of the early Roman Empire.

◆ What was the place of Christianity in the Roman world during the Principate?

The Roman Empire in Crisis, 193–284 C.E.

13. The Severan emperors ruined the Roman silver coinage by

    a. Making the coins so small that they lost their value.
    b. Mixing the silver with large amounts of copper.
    c. Issuing so much good silver coinage that the value of the coins fell.
    d. Withdrawing all the silver coins from circulation.
    e. Exporting huge quantities of silver to Britain.

14. During the imperial crisis, who attacked the Roman Empire?

    a. New Persians   d. Alamanni

    b. Goths   e. Assyrians

    c. Franks

15. Whom did the emperor Aurelian (270–275 C.E.) defeat before becoming, known as the "Restorer of the World?"

    a. Queen Zenobia   d. The Gallic empire

    b. The New Persians   e. The Carthaginians

    c. Dacia

Now that you have reviewed and tested yourself on this part of the chapter, take time to pull together all the important information by answering the following questions:

◆ In what ways did the Principate no longer work in the third century C.E.?

◆ How did the army contribute to the empire's instability?

CHAPTER 7

Late Antiquity, 284–527

Chapter Outline

280	300	320	340	360	380	400
284 Diocletian becomes emperor	**306** Constantine becomes emperor	**325** Nicene Creed is issued		**378** Battle of Adrianople	**392** Christianity becomes the empire's legal religion	**395** Roman Empire splits into east and west

This gigantic porpyry sarcophagus traditionally is thought to have held the remains of the empress Helena, the mother of Constantine the Great, who died around 328 C.E. But the scenes of Roman cavalrymen riding down and killing barbarians hardly seems suited for the tomb of an empress. It therefore has been suggested that the sarcophagus might initially have been designed for Constantine himself, or perhaps for another male member of the imperial family. Why would the scenes on the sarcophagus have been suitable for a Roman emperor? (Scala/Art Resource, NY)

After reading this chapter, you should be able to answer the following questions:

How were Diocletian and Constantine able to restore the Roman Empire?

How did the legalization and growing acceptance of Christianity affect life in the Roman Empire?

What were the reasons for the fall of the Western Roman Empire?

What kinds of social, political, and cultural changes occurred during Late Antiquity?

D URING FIFTY YEARS of nearly constant civil war in the third century, the empire had seemed on the verge of extinction. Beginning in 284, it was largely the reforms of two able emperors, Diocletian and Constantine, that allowed the empire, which now can be called the Late Roman Empire, to survive. Yet some of these emperors' reforms had an unforeseen consequence: instead of unifying the empire, they led to greater fragmentation.

The middle of the third century marks the beginning of the period known as Late Antiquity, which lasted until the mid-seventh century and fills the gap between the Greek and Roman classical world and the Middle Ages. Whereas the Principate was a time of social, political, and cultural stability and uniformity, Late Antiquity was marked by change and diversity. Political authority became decentralized, and the empire gradually split into eastern and western halves. Christianity became a favored religion with the full support of the imperial government. The emperor sometimes saw himself as the leader of the church, but powerful bishops contested

Roman Peace

420	440	460	480	500	520	540

410
Visigoths sack Rome

476
Fall of the Western Roman Empire

481
Clovis becomes king of the Franks

527
Justinian becomes Byzantine emperor

this claim. Christian bishops took over many responsibilities that in the past had been held by civil officials. But the Christian church, which was intended to unify the empire, was itself racked by debates over authority and belief. The character of urban life changed as resources that once had been expended on municipal public works were reallocated to church building and as aristocrats reduced their support for the central government and withdrew to the countryside, where they were able to consolidate their influence.

During the fifth century, the western empire was infiltrated by non-Roman barbarian peoples from the north and east who sought security and a better life. Through a process of military conquest and largely peaceful settlement, the barbarians ultimately established independent kingdoms that later would develop into several modern-day European nations. The eastern part of the empire, however, continued as before and even prospered, in the form known today as the Byzantine Empire. In general, the Mediterranean world, once unified by Rome, now was breaking up.

△ = change

The Restoration of the Roman Empire, 284–337

- ◆ What did Diocletian and Constantine do to try to restore order in the Roman Empire?
- ◆ How did the administration of the empire change during the late Roman period?

In 284, the Roman Empire still was in crisis. The army had spent fifty years in repeated revolts: there was no effective method for choosing emperors, the borders were under attack by barbarian peoples, and many people felt disadvantaged or alienated. In addition, the economy was in a shambles, imperial control over the army was shaky, the expanding bureaucracy was increasingly difficult to afford, and the imperial cult no longer fulfilled its unifying purpose. Beginning in the 270s, a series of soldier emperors brought some stability. Order was fully restored under Diocletian and Constantine, who introduced many reforms. They brought the army back under control, devised ways to revive the failing economy, and assumed a much greater level of personal responsibility for the survival of the empire.

Diocletian (r. 284–305) Emperor who began the creation of the Late Roman Empire.

Late Roman Empire Second phase of the Roman Empire, from 284 to 476, and the first phase of Late Antiquity.

dominus (Latin for "lord and master") Title of Roman emperors during the Late Roman Empire.

Diocletian and the Return to Order

In 284, **Diocletian**, a tough Balkan soldier, was named emperor by the Roman army. Like the first Roman emperor, Augustus, Diocletian was a better administrator than general, but a competent administrator was just what the empire needed.

The Personality of Diocletian Diocletian's origins were obscure: some said he was the son of a clerk, others that he was a freed slave. Like many Romans who wanted to improve their positions, he joined the army, where he rose through the ranks and did well. According to one Roman historian, "He was crafty, but also very wise and insightful. He was disposed to cruelty, but was nonetheless a very able ruler." Diocletian believed that it was the emperor's duty to oversee every aspect of life within the empire to ensure its future. First, he needed to end the military revolts, after which he could implement other long-term reforms. Diocletian's reign marks the beginning of the period known as the **Late Roman Empire**.

Getting the Army Under Control To reduce the threat of rebellion, Diocletian raised the status of the emperor from *princeps* ("first man") to ***dominus*** ("lord and master"), thus transforming the emperor from a high-ranking senator into a virtual living god. As emperor, Diocletian exchanged the general's cloak for a floor-length purple robe encrusted with gemstones and wore a pearl diadem as a crown. Everything associated with the emperor's person—the laws, the government, the coinage, his every word— became "sacred." Those who met with Diocletian were expected to fall facedown before him. These changes made it more difficult for potential rivals to pass themselves off as emperors.

As another means of reducing the possibility of a revolt, Diocletian limited the power of possible rivals

1. What effect do you think these many provinces and separate capitals might have on emperors' attempts to keep the empire unified?
2. From what regions do you think the greatest threats from barbarians might come?
3. Which half of the empire had the greater concentration of cities? What significance do you think this might have had?
4. Which half of the empire was responsible for defending the larger part of the dangerous northern frontier? What consequences might result from this?

and took away all remaining power from the Senate. Political authority now belonged to the emperor and army alone, and the Senate was reduced to the status of a city council for Rome. To lessen senators' influence even further, Diocletian also limited the opportunities for senators to hold high-ranking government posts, especially military ones. He divided up possible sources of power. He split the army by pulling the most able troops back from the border and creating a mobile field army stationed in the interior, leaving the remaining troops as a border army guarding the frontier. He separated civil careers from military careers so provincial governors did not command troops and generals did not govern provinces. By subdividing the provinces, he increased their number from fifty to one hundred, thereby decreasing the power of each governor.

These subdivisions of authority helped end the cycle of revolts but also greatly increased costs. Soon there were approximately 40,000 officials on the imperial payroll, and the army had a paper strength of about 450,000.

Diocletian and the Economy Once Diocletian had solidified his authority over the army and the government, he turned his attention to the economy. Tax income had been reduced because farms in border areas had been abandoned owing to the constant warfare. In addition, the debased silver coinage was virtually worthless; soldiers complained that their entire annual salary was used up on one small purchase. Taxes paid in these coins were hardly worth collecting. There was not enough gold and silver in the treasury to issue good gold and silver coins, so in an attempt to make the money worth something again, Diocletian issued a large copper coin coated with silver. No one, however, was fooled. He then tried to restore value to the money by issuing a law that set maximum prices for goods and services, but the law was blatantly disregarded.

Diocletian finally recognized that the value of the money could not be restored, so he required that the land tax be paid in produce rather than in the worthless coinage. A farmer, for example, paid roughly 20 percent of a harvest as taxes. Sheep owners paid in wool; the owners of iron mines paid in iron. Foodstuffs and other raw materials were gathered into imperial storehouses, processed in imperial factories, and used to pay soldiers with food rations, clothing, and weapons. A soldier's only significant monetary compensation was the donative, which now was issued in pure gold and silver at five-year intervals. This system was cumbersome, requiring an even larger bureaucracy, but it worked. In a further attempt to keep the empire going, Diocletian identified "compulsory services" that had to be performed. Those who performed these occupations—such as soldiers, bakers, decurions, and tenant farmers—were prohibited from changing jobs, and their children were required to hold the same jobs. Enforcement of this requirement, however, proved virtually impossible.

Great Persecution Last official persecution of Christians, begun by Diocletian in 303 and ended by Constantine's Edict of Milan in 313.

Tetrarchy (in Greek, "rule by four") Four-emperor system established by Diocletian.

Helena (ca. 250–330) Mother of the emperor Constantine who believed she had discovered the cross on which Christ was crucified.

The Great Persecution Like earlier emperors, Diocletian believed that participation in the imperial cult could be used to unify the empire. But this belief brought him into conflict with Christianity, which rejected participation in the imperial cult. Diocletian saw this as a direct threat to the well-being of the empire, all the more so because Christianity now attracted not just less privileged persons but also soldiers and even the occasional senator. As a result, in 303, Diocletian began the **Great Persecution**. Christians were ordered to sacrifice in the imperial cult or die. Some Christians actually were executed, especially in the east, and were added to the growing catalogue of Christian martyrs. But in most parts of the empire, the orders were ignored. Christianity by now had become too popular and widespread to be eliminated.

The Tetrarchy and the Rise of Constantine

Diocletian introduced a system of multiple emperors that was designed to solve the problem of the imperial succession. But his plan failed, and the empire fell into the hands of Constantine.

The Tetrarchy Believing that the empire was too large and complex to be governed by a single emperor, Diocletian divided it into four parts and appointed three of his army colleagues as co-emperors. This created the **Tetrarchy**, shown in Table 7.1. Two emperors, Diocletian and Maximian, had the rank of augustus (senior emperor) in the eastern and western halves of the empire, respectively, whereas the other two, Galerius and Constantius, were their junior emperors and had the title of caesar. To create family ties among themselves and cement their alliance, the emperors married one another's daughters. Constantius, for example, was compelled to dismiss his concubine **Helena** to marry Maximian's daughter Fausta. Each emperor's court, consisting of his household, chief officials, and bodyguard, accompanied him wherever he went. The multiple emperors dealt effectively with matters of internal and external security. Maximian, for example,

Table 7.1 The Tetrarchy

	Augustus	Caesar
East	Diocletian (r. 284–305)	Galerius (r. 293–311)
	(Anatolia, Syria, Egypt)	(the Balkans)
	(retired in 305)	(promoted to augustus in 305)
West	Maximian (r. 286–305)	Constantius (r. 293–306)
	(Italy, Africa, Spain)	(Gaul, Britain)
	(retired in 305)	(promoted to augustus in 305)
	Son: Maxentius	Son: Constantine

© Cengage Learning

A statue in porphyry (a purple stone found only at a single quarry in Egypt), originally in Constantinople but now in Venice, shows the four emperors of the Tetrarchy demonstrating their solidarity with each other. The emperors all are depicted in the same way, with few or no individual characteristics. Each emperor has one arm around his imperial colleague and his other hand on his sword, making clear the source of his authority. The message was that even though there are four emperors, there was only one empire. Do you think that this was an effective way of showing unity among the four emperors? (Scala/Art Resource, NY)

crushed rebellious peasants in the west, and Galerius defeated the New Persians and brought peace to the eastern frontier. But it always was clear that Diocletian was in control. His personal authority forced his three colleagues to rule peacefully together.

The Imperial Succession This system of multiple emperors also gave Diocletian a way to deal with the imperial succession, which had been the greatest cause of instability during the Principate. The successor of each senior emperor would be his junior emperor, who then would become the new senior emperor and name a new junior emperor. In 305, claiming that he had ruled long enough, Diocletian retired and made his co-augustus Maximian do the

same. This ensured that the succession system took effect. A second Tetrarchy was formed: Galerius and Constantius assumed the rank of augustus, and they appointed two new caesars. A potential difficulty with the new Tetrarchy, however, was that it ignored Maxentius and Constantine, the sons of Maximian and Constantius. There was muttering in the army, which had always preferred emperors to be succeeded by their sons. A year later, while visiting York in Britain, Constantius became very ill. Before dying, he recommended his son to his soldiers, who then loyally proclaimed Constantine emperor.

The Collapse of the Tetrarchy The Tetrarchy then collapsed. Its fatal flaw was that it could not overcome the army's preference for sons to succeed their fathers. In Rome, Maxentius also was declared emperor, making a total of six emperors. Civil war again erupted as each emperor attempted to expand his authority. In 312, Constantine attacked Maxentius and defeated and killed him at the battle of the **Milvian Bridge** just outside Rome. Early in the next year, Constantine demonstrated his support for Christianity by issuing the **Edict of Milan**, which decreed religious freedom for Christians and returned confiscated Christian property. This brought the persecutions to an end. By 324, Constantine's rivals were dead. Once again a single emperor controlled the empire.

Constantine and Late Roman Government

Constantine faced the same problems as Diocletian, but he tried some different solutions that were more successful than Diocletian's.

The Policies of Constantine Constantine reversed Diocletian's policy toward senators by welcoming them into imperial offices in the hope that they then would support the imperial government. Regarding the economy, Constantine decided that a trustworthy hard currency was needed to meet the needs of the army and bureaucracy. Rather than trying to revive the discredited silver coinage, he put the empire on the gold standard by introducing a new gold coin, the **solidus**. Taxpayers who preferred the convenience of cash to payments in produce could pay in gold. Other taxes, such as the merchants' income tax, were assessed in gold. These policies resulted in a recycling of the gold coinage: it was constantly paid out in

Constantine (r. 306–337) Roman emperor who completed the restoration of the Roman Empire and made Christianity a favored religion.

Milvian Bridge Battle in which Constantine attributed his victory over Maxentius, outside Rome in 312, to the support of the Christian God.

Edict of Milan Law issued by Constantine in 313 making Christianity a legal religion.

solidus (Latin for "solid") Gold coin introduced by Constantine, weighing 1/72 pound.

URBS CONSTANTINOPOLITANA NOVA ROMA.

Bodleian Library, University of Oxford, MS. Canon. Misc. 378, fol. 84r

The city of Constantinople as depicted in the *Notitia dignitatum*, a list of Roman offices compiled about 400 C.E., showing the city's protected location on a heavily fortified peninsula. A large round church dome emphasizes the Christian orientation of the city. The legend reads, "The City of Constantinople, New Rome." What effect do you think the creation of a second capital city had on the unity of the Roman Empire?

expenses and received back in taxes. The solidus was so successful that it remained the standard means of exchange in the Mediterranean world for nearly seven hundred years.

The Foundation of Constantinople Constantine recognized that the empire's greatest source of economic and population resources lay in the east. Therefore, in 330 he established a second imperial capital on the site of the old Greek city of Byzantium on the Bosporus. This strategic strait linked the Mediterranean and Black Seas and controlled traffic between Asia and Europe. Constantine named the new city **Constantinople**, after himself. In many ways, Constantinople (modern Istanbul) was a carbon copy of Rome. It soon had its own imperial administration and officials as well as its own chariot racecourse, the **Hippodrome**. New senators were created to populate a new Senate. Constantine also made Constantinople into a purely Christian city, in contrast to Rome, by building churches such as the Church of **Hagia Sophia** and a cross-shaped Church of the Holy Apostles, where he planned

Constantinople Second capital of the Roman Empire, established by Constantine in the east in 330.

Hippodrome (from Greek for "running horse") Chariot racecourse in Constantinople and a site for gatherings of the people.

Hagia Sophia (Greek for "holy wisdom") Church built in Constantinople by Constantine.

masters of soldiers Highest-ranking generals in the late Roman army.

to be buried. But Constantine did not neglect Rome. Along with his triumphal arch, he built churches, such as the Church of Saint John Lateran, which became the official church of the bishop of Rome. He also completed the construction of a large basilica that he used as an audience hall, the last monument to be built in the old Roman Forum.

Constantine and the Imperial Succession Constantine established a method for choosing emperors on the basis of dynastic succession that proved to be remarkably stable. Whenever possible, fathers were succeeded by sons. If an emperor had no sons and the position became vacant, the army had the authority to acclaim a new emperor. The reigning emperor or emperors also had the authority to create new emperors. The Senates of Rome and Constantinople had no role in choosing emperors except to deliver congratulations. Male emperors still bore the title augustus, and imperial women could be granted the title augusta. Women were not constitutionally excluded from ruling although for more than four hundred and fifty years no woman ruled in her own name.

Late Roman Government Late Roman government was cumbersome, but it worked. The government had civil and military branches. The highest-ranking generals were eight **masters of soldiers**, and the chief civil officials were the four praetorian prefects. Ranking below them were many layers of other officials. The Late Roman Empire, including the emperors themselves, continued to be ruled by law. Indeed, emperors preferred to deal with problems by issuing laws, many thousands of which survive. Every word that came from the emperor, even brief replies to questions, had the force of law. All of this legislation makes the late empire look like it regulated all aspects of Roman life, such as who could marry whom or who could pursue what kind of career. In reality, however, emperors were unable to enforce all these laws, and the laws often were disobeyed. They worked well enough to keep the empire going, but not so well that it became a complete dictatorship.

When Constantine died in 337, his new succession policy went into effect, and the empire was divided among his three sons. The empire appeared as sound and stable as it had been in the time of Augustus.

Checking In

By yourself or with a partner, explain the significance of each of the following selected key terms:

Diocletian	Helena
Late Roman Empire	Constantine
Great Persecution	solidus
Tetrarchy	Constantinople

The Christian Empire, 312–415

[handwritten: was it for better or worse?]
[handwritten: was christianity popularized?]

◆ How did the Roman Empire change after Christianity was legalized?

◆ In what ways did people express their devotion to Christianity?

Raised to worship the sun, Constantine became Roman emperor when Christianity was a persecuted religion. Soon afterward, he began to support Christianity. Several stories circulated about why Constantine had made this decision. Some believed he had received signs directly from God, as seen in this fresco in the papal palace in Rome, painted about 1500 by Raphael Sanzio, which is based on a popular story that Constantine had seen a vision of the Christian cross in the sky. The cross Constantine saw may well have been a rare solar phenomenon involving parhelia, or sun dogs. If so, it would have helped Constantine to make a connection between sun worship and Christianity. In what ways at this time was sun worship seen as having similarities to Christianity?

The most momentous change that occurred during Late Antiquity was the growing influence of the Christian church. Constantine himself is best known for beginning the process of making Christianity into the predominant religion of the Mediterranean world. His example and initiatives had a profound effect on the life, culture, and religion of the Roman world. In only eighty years, Christianity went from a persecuted religion to the only legal religion (aside from Judaism) in the Roman Empire. Conversions to Christianity, which in the past would have occurred in an atmosphere of fearful secrecy, now were celebrated with joyous publicity. Christianity soon pervaded late Roman culture, society, and politics.

Constantine and the Church

Constantine's most lasting legacy was to begin the process by which Christianity became the primary religion of the Roman world. Making the transition to a Christian empire, however, was full of problems.

Constantine Favors the Christians Like his predecessors, Constantine believed that religion could be used to unify the empire, but he felt that Christianity was a better choice than the imperial cult. If Christian support could be acquired, the organizational structure and public services of the Christian church could be mobilized on behalf of the empire. Constantine, therefore, favored the Christians in various ways, such as exempting Christian priests from burdensome service on city councils; making Sunday, the Christian day of worship, an official day of rest; and forbidding Jews from keeping Christian slaves. At the same time, social services, such as the care of the sick and poor, something the emperors had never had the resources or resolve to undertake, were delegated to the church. In addition, Constantine's support for Christianity allowed him to confiscate polytheist temple treasures and use the gold to mint his new gold coins and also to finance the magnificent churches he constructed in Rome, Constantinople, and elsewhere.

[handwritten sidebar: Shows favoritism to Christains]

Constantine Deals with Christian Conflicts Constantine soon discovered that he had been mistaken in assuming the Christians were unified. The Christian community in each Roman city was in many ways an independent enclave under the authority of its bishop. Christians in different parts of the empire spoke different languages. There were no higher-ranking church authorities to enforce unity. Christians did not even agree on which books belonged in the Bible. The church was racked by disputes over **theology**, church practices, and authority. To deal with these issues, Constantine assumed the responsibility for encouraging, or even compelling, churchmen to settle their disputes. Just as the emperor had appropriated authority from the Senate during the Principate, Constantine appropriated authority from the church, and as a result he accumulated even greater power.

The Arian Controversy The most troubling Christian conflict involved questions about the nature of the Christian God. It was believed that God consisted of three persons, the Father, the Son, and the Holy Spirit, known collectively as the **Trinity**.

theology Study of religious teachings and beliefs.

Trinity The three persons—Father, Son, and Holy Spirit—making up the Christian God.

Conflict over how the three related to each other burst forth in the 320s when an Alexandrian priest named Arius taught that Christ the Son was subordinate to and of a different nature from God the Father. This teaching became known as **Arianism**. Many others, however, believed that the Father and Son were equal in status and of the same nature.

The Council of Nicaea In 325, Constantine dealt with this problem by assembling an **ecumenical** church council at Nicaea, a city in northwestern Anatolia. It was attended by 318 bishops from throughout the empire. The bishops were ordered to come up with a definition of Christian belief that everyone could agree with. The Council of Nicaea condemned Arianism as a **heresy**, that is, an illegal belief. The bishops issued the **Nicene Creed**, which stated what all Christians were expected to believe and became the official statement of faith of the Roman Empire. The council also put the church on the Roman administrative model. Each city in each province was placed under the spiritual authority of a bishop and each province under the oversight of a higher-ranking bishop, called an archbishop. The bishops of three cities—Alexandria, Antioch, and Rome—were given the even higher rank of patriarch, as were the bishops of Jerusalem and Constantinople soon afterward. The bishop of Rome, the original capital city of the empire, claimed the greatest status of all based on apostolic succession from the apostle Peter, the first bishop of Rome. But many bishops, including those who had their own apostolic succession, refused to acknowledge this claim.

Constantine's last official act left a troublesome legacy, for his deathbed baptism in 337 was carried out by an Arian bishop who, in spite of his refusal to repudiate his belief, had isen in the emperor's favor. Shortly after Constantine's death, Arian bishops gained much influence, and it appeared that Arianism might yet triumph. The Goth Ulfilas learned the Arian form of Christianity while living in the empire and returned home to convert many of his people. They and other barbarian peoples then adopted Arianism.

The Impact of Christianity

During the fourth century C.E., Christianity triumphed over competing religions surprisingly quickly. Soon, the only significant surviving non-Christian religion was Judaism.

The Expansion of Christianity The expansion of Christianity in the fourth century induced great personal and spiritual soul searching. Many people rethought their religious beliefs and the role that religion played in their lives. Christianity continued to offer the same attractions it had in the past: a moral code, communal worship services, a sense of community, economic support, an emphasis on personal spirituality, and hope of an afterlife. To this list now was added government preference, which resulted in increasing social and even official pressure for non-Christians to convert.

Christians also could seek converts more openly than in the past. Conversion efforts were focused within the empire, where large numbers of people, especially in the countryside, clung to the religious practices of their ancestors. In addition, the senators of Rome, who believed that Rome's past successes were the result of faithfulness to the ancient Roman deities, continued to support traditional Roman religious practices. Convincing people such as these to change their religious identity was difficult work. There was little official interest, therefore, in converting foreigners. Conversions of foreign peoples, such as the work of Ulfilas the Goth, usually were carried out privately. Another private missionary was **Patrick**, a native of Britain who undertook to convert the Irish to Christianity around 430. Not until the sixth century, when most of the rural population of the empire finally had been brought into the Christian fold, was formal missionary activity initiated outside the Roman world.

Alternatives to Christianity There continued to be alternatives to Christianity. Paradoxically, the rise of Christianity led to a momentary revival of polytheism. When Constantine's nephew Julian, who had been raised as a Christian, succeeded to the throne in 361, it turned out that he had been a secret sympathizer with polytheism. He abandoned Christianity and openly worshiped the traditional gods, thus gaining the nickname "Julian the Apostate." Julian attempted to weaken Christian influence. He prohibited Christian professors from teaching classical literature, arguing that it was hypocritical to teach about gods in whom one did not believe. He also used the Christian church as a model for an organized polytheist church. But Julian's efforts failed, for Christianity had gained too strong a hold on the devotion of the people. In 363, during an invasion of the New Persian Empire, Julian was killed—some said by a Christian soldier in his own army. He was the last non-Christian ruler of the whole empire. All serious

Arianism Form of Christian belief introduced by the priest Arius, who taught that Christ the Son was subordinate to God the Father; condemned at the Council of Nicaea in 325.

ecumenical Relating to church councils made up of bishops from throughout the Christian world.

heresy A prohibited form of Christian belief as defined by church councils and the imperial government.

Nicene Creed Standard statement of Christian belief, issued at the Council of Nicaea in 325 and still recited in many Christian churches.

Patrick (ca. 385–450) British missionary who brought Christianity to Ireland.

Christianity was not the only late Roman religion that offered believers salvation gained through baptism. In this scene, the Persian sun god Mithras slaughters the bull in whose blood initiates were baptized. Christianity and Mithraism also had other points of contact; indeed, December 25, the date of Mithras's birth, also was adopted by Christians as the date of Jesus' birth, another example of a connection between Christianity and sun worship. And because Mithras was believed to have slain the bull in a cave, his worshipers met in an actual or artificial subterranean place of worship called a Mithraeum. The cult of Mithras, which excluded women, was especially popular in the Roman army. In the competition for religious supremacy, why do you think Christianity ultimately triumphed over Mithraism? (Werner Forman/Corbis)

hope of imperial support for the old Roman religion died along with him.

Other non-Christian forms of belief and worship continued to attract followers. **Neoplatonism**, which had evolved from the teachings of Plato, was the most influential philosophical teaching of Late Antiquity. It viewed the universe as a hierarchy, with earthly matter at the lowest level of existence and a single, impersonal, divine principle called "The One" at the highest and most distant level. An adherent's duty was to try to leave earthly existence behind and attain a higher level of consciousness. Neoplatonism's stress on morality and self-discipline made it attractive to Christians. On the other hand, the cult of the Persian sun god **Mithras** was particularly popular with soldiers. The cult shared many aspects with Christianity, such as a moral code, group worship, communal meals, and baptism (in the blood of a slaughtered bull). Mithras's birthday, December 25, was even adopted by the Christians as the birthday of their own god, giving additional support to the idea that Christians were sun worshipers. Mithraism's appeal was limited, however, by its exclusion of women. In the case of Neoplatonism and Mithraism, the attractiveness of a non-Christian belief was influenced by how much it resembled Christianity, indicating the degree to which Christianity had become the standard by which other religions were measured.

The only non-Christians who successfully retained their ancestral beliefs were the Jews. There still was a sizable Jewish population in Palestine, overseen by the Jewish patriarch. In addition, the Diaspora had placed Jewish communities in many cities in the empire and beyond, including over a million Jews living under New Persian rule in Babylon. Two versions of the Talmud were created by the Jews, who valued scholarship more than any other activity: a Palestinian one, which was completed in the late fourth century; and a Babylonian one, which was in circulation by around 500 and continues to be the authoritative basis for Jewish life. Even though the Christian population generally acknowledged the Jews' right to practice their religion, sporadic attempts were made to convert them to Christianity. Roman emperors attempted to pressure Jews to convert by issuing legislation that prohibited them from holding government posts, from making wills, from receiving inheritances, and from testifying in court. In 425, the Jewish

Neoplatonism Late Roman philosophical belief descending from Plato that taught the existence of a single overall god and stressed morality and self-discipline.

Mithras Persian sun god popular with the Roman army.

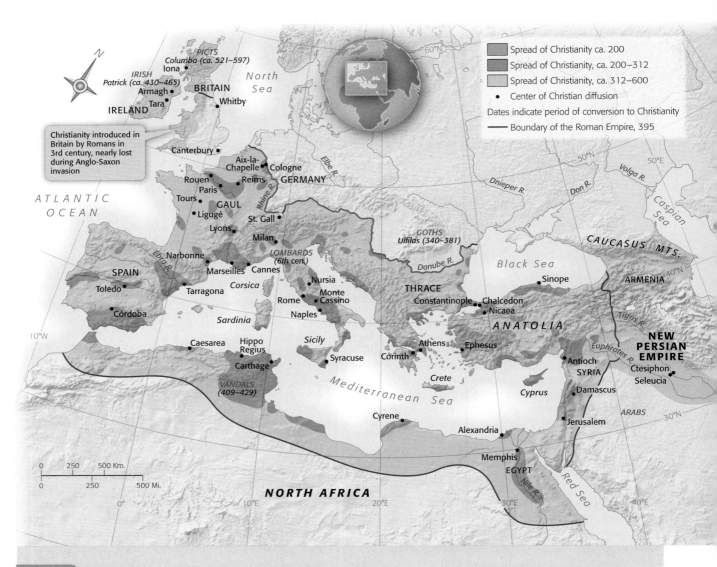

Map 7.2 **The Spread of Christianity to 600 C.E.** During the first six centuries C.E., Christianity spread throughout the Roman world, with the greatest acceptance of Christianity coming after Constantine began making it into a favored religion after 312 C.E. © *Cengage Learning*

1. In what kinds of areas did Christianity first flourish?
2. What geographical factors would have aided the spread of Christianity?
3. When did the various barbarian peoples become Christian?
4. What kind of religion would Roman Christians have encountered in the New Persian Empire?

patriarchate was abolished. Few Jews, however, abandoned their faith, and there continued to be a Jewish presence in virtually all the cities of the Roman world.

The Christian Life

The adoption of Christianity affected almost every aspect of life in the Roman world as people adapted their beliefs and customs to the new religion.

pagans (from Latin *paganus*, "country dweller") Derogatory term used by Christians to describe participants in traditional religious practices.

Christian Worship The imperial acceptance of Christianity brought an end to the old distinction between personal and state religion. Regardless of whether one was worshiping privately at home or publicly in church, the same scriptures were used and the same God was being worshiped. Christian worship included personal, private, communal, and ceremonial elements. Christians also rethought their role in the Roman world. Now that Christianity was becoming a favored religion, Christians began to treat non-Christians in a more disparaging manner. They described the believers in the traditional gods as **pagans**, a word meaning "country dwellers."

As the Roman Empire evolved into a Christian empire, emperors showed their support for the new religion just as they had supported the polytheistic religions of the past. Beginning with Constantine, Roman emperors sponsored the construction of many Christian churches. Constantine himself built churches in Constantinople, such as the church of the Holy Apostles, and Rome, including the churches of St. Agnes and St. John. The round church of St. Costanza (Constantina) in Rome, shown here, was built by Constantine as a tomb for his daughters Constantina and Helena but later was converted into a church. How do you think urban landscapes would have been affected when emperors and other powerful persons transferred their financial support to the construction of churches?

Scala/Art Resource, NY

Eventually nearly everyone in the Roman world, except for the Jews, converted to Christianity. Certain kinds of behavior were expected of them. Attendance at Sunday church services was considered an outward demonstration of a Christian's internal devotion. The presence of a church in a city, town, or village demonstrated the existence of an active Christian community. The simplest kind of church could be a converted house. Churches in cities, on the other hand, could be very large. Some were built in the shape of a cross, but most were constructed in the basilica style that in the past had been used for large public audience halls. **Chapels** often were attached to the sides of larger churches and dedicated to particular saints. Churches could be elaborately decorated, with fine mosaics or frescoes on the walls and marble columns. The holiest section, or **chancel**, was on the east end. The chancel housed the altar and was accessible only to the clergy and choir. A screen divided the chancel from the remainder of the church, or **nave**, where the congregation of men and women stood to worship. The main entrance was on the west end, where a baptismal font, or baptistery, for the performance of baptisms often was located. Many churches also had an underground crypt, usually below the chancel, for burials and the preservation of relics.

Christian church services in Late Antiquity included prayers; readings from scripture; the singing and chanting of hymns and biblical psalms by both choir and congregation; and sermons by bishops and priests, who often were trained speakers. The church calendar included saints' days that marked the date of the death of Christian martyrs and other holy men

and women. Social life increasingly revolved around the church, with people visiting with one another before and after the service. In these ways, Christianity differed greatly from paganism, which had no concept of regular attendance at religious services.

Christian Lifestyles Christians also were expected to live a virtuous private life. In addition to the three Christian virtues of faith, hope, and charity (Christian love), Christians adopted the Greek and Roman cardinal virtues of temperance, prudence, courage, and justice. Private worship involved prayer and fasting. Christians also were expected to perform good works. Christians were taught to distribute their wealth to the poor and to make offerings to the church. Christians also believed that the only acceptable sexual relations were those sanctified by the marriage bond and undertaken for the procreation of children. Senior Christian clerics, such as bishops and priests, were expected to give up sexual relations even if they were married.

Christians continued to live in constant expectation of the Second Coming of Christ. Apocalyptic literature, such as the biblical book of Revelation, attempted to predict when the end would come. Some Christians combined the creation of the world in seven days with the scriptural passage that "every

chapel Small building or room used for Christian worship, often in association with a larger church.

chancel Part of a church containing the altar.

nave Main part of a church, especially the long, narrow central section.

day is like a thousand years" to predict that the Apocalypse would occur around 400 or 500 C.E. Others thought that sinister signs would predict the approach of the Apocalypse. For example, Bishop Cyprian of Carthage wrote, "Wars continue to prevail, death and famine accumulate, the human race is wasted by the desolation of pestilence. The Day of Judgment is now drawing near, the censure of an indignant God."

Christian Conversion To prepare themselves for the Last Judgment, many Christians experienced a second conversion, after which they devoted their lives completely to religion. One of these was **Augustine**, a North African who was raised as an unbaptized Christian and also received a classical education based on the traditional Greek and Latin authors. Augustine became a successful teacher and public speaker but felt there was something lacking in his life. In the midst of a spiritual crisis, he heard a child chanting "Tolle, lege" ("Take up and read"). He therefore picked a random spot in the Bible and read, in Paul's letter to the Romans, "Arm yourself with the lord Jesus Christ; spend no more thought on nature's appetites." Taking this passage as a sign, he committed himself to religion and was baptized on Easter Day, 387, by Bishop **Ambrose of Milan**. Augustine's later account of his conversion, known as the *Confessions*, is the most important autobiography to survive from antiquity. Augustine later was named bishop of Hippo in North Africa and wrote a great many letters, sermons, theological tracts, and interpretations of scripture. One of his most important teachings was that, because humanity was polluted by the original sin of Adam and Eve, people could not receive eternal life through their own efforts but only by receiving God's gift of grace. Many of Augustine's teachings on the church's authority, the Christian view of history, and Christian doctrine became the standard views of the Christian church and continue to influence Christian thought.

Christian Asceticism and Monasticism

Some Christians believed that to reach a higher level of spirituality and become closer to God, they had to separate themselves from the everyday world. These Christians practiced **ascetism**, or physical self-denial. Christian ascetics rejected earthly pleasures, such as comfortable living quarters, fine food and clothing, and sexual relations. The greater self-deprivation one suffered, the greater the degree of holiness and spiritual authority one was thought to have gained.

Monasticism As early as the third century, some Egyptian ascetics gave up all contact with the ordinary world and lived as hermits in isolated huts and desert caves, becoming the first **monks**. Other monks soon began living communally in monasteries. Male monasteries were directed by **abbots** and female monasteries by abbesses. Ascetic and monastic practices soon were adopted in the west by persons such as **Martin of Tours**, who in the fourth century abandoned a military career and became a hermit. Some monastic communities attempted to re-create the isolation of the desert, whereas others concentrated on performing charitable services. Monasticism created an alternate world, separated from urban life. Monks also attempted to distance themselves from the authority of bishops, who resided in cities, and in this way contributed to a decentralization of church authority.

Holy Men and Women Famous Christian ascetics, known as holy men and women, gained great moral and spiritual authority. Because they distanced themselves from earthly concerns and were thought to be in close touch with God, they were seen as impartial arbitrators, advisers, and judges. As a result, women, who were excluded from holding church offices, and unprivileged men could have great authority outside the normal channels of church or government jurisdiction. For example, the holy man Simeon, the son of a shepherd, sat exposed to the weather atop a column in northern Syria for thirty years and was consulted by rich and poor alike on account of his reputation for holiness. And Matrona of Constantinople, to escape her abusive husband, disguised herself as a man and entered a male monastery. She later became abbess of a female monastery and had such great spiritual power that she instructed the emperor on church teaching.

The Power of the Church

As time went on, Christianity acquired more and more influence and authority, not only in the religious sphere, but also in the secular world.

The Consolidation of Christian Authority The impact of Christian beliefs and practices was felt everywhere. Christians even asserted that the Roman Empire itself had arisen by the will of God. As the Roman Empire became a Christian empire, Christian ideologies made their way into public life. The church used

Augustine Bishop of Hippo in North Africa from 396 to 430; one of the most important Christian writers and thinkers, author of the *City of God*.

Ambrose of Milan Bishop of Milan from 374 to 397; one of the leading teachers of the Christian church; established Christian authority over Theodosius the Great.

ascetism A life of physical deprivation.

monks (from Greek for "solitary") Christians who withdrew from society to live together in monasteries.

abbot Head of a male monastery; abbesses were the heads of female monasteries.

Martin of Tours (ca. 316–397) Soldier who converted to Christianity, became a monk, and later served as bishop of Tours.

church councils assembled under imperial authority to establish official positions on matters of authority, belief, and proper behavior. The canons, or rulings, issued by church councils created an increasing body of church law known as **canon law**. After much debate, an official list of books to be included in the Christian Bible was agreed on. Some books that were excluded, such as the Gospels of Peter and Thomas and the Revelation of Peter, continued to be used, however, by heretical Christian sects. Around 400, the Old and New Testaments were translated from the original Hebrew and Greek into Latin by the priest **Jerome** of Bethlehem in a definitive form known as the **Vulgate**, which gradually replaced earlier versions of the Latin Bible used by different churches.

Christianity and the Roman Government What went on in the Roman world came to be viewed not from a Roman imperial perspective but from a Christian perspective. Powerful Christian clerics such as Ambrose of Milan exercised great influence even over Roman emperors. Ambrose represented a new kind of bishop. Rather than humbly rising through the ranks of the church, he was the son of a Praetorian prefect. Like his father, he embarked on a career of government service and was appointed as a governor in Italy. But his career took an unexpected turn when the people of Milan, an imperial capital in northern Italy, elected him bishop even though he had no previous experience in the church. He quickly adopted an ecclesiastical lifestyle, but he also brought to the office his experience in the world of Roman politics.

Ambrose soon became engaged in a power struggle with the emperor **Theodosius I**. Theodosius was a strong supporter of Nicene Christianity and an open opponent of Arianism. In 381, he convened the second ecumenical church council at Constantinople. Arianism again was condemned and faded among the Roman population even as it prospered among barbarians. But Theodosius angered Ambrose by ordering Christians who had destroyed a Jewish synagogue to restore it. Subsequently, Ambrose blamed Theodosius when Roman soldiers in Greece massacred seven thousand rioting citizens. Ambrose excommunicated the emperor. Theodosius was not readmitted to Christian Communion until he had publicly and humbly begged forgiveness from God. The sight of this powerful and determined emperor's humiliation by an equally powerful and determined bishop demonstrated the high status of Christian clerics and the degree to which the church was able to act independently of imperial control.

Theodosius then issued pro-Christian legislation that culminated in 392 with a law definitively prohibiting all pagan practices. As a result, Christianity became the only fully legal religion and Theodosius was called "The Great" by the Christian community. Zealous Christians now persecuted non-Christians. In 415, **Hypatia**, the first female head of the school of Neoplatonic philosophy at Alexandria, was assaulted and torn limb from limb by a band of fanatical Christians. Pagan statues were either smashed or "converted" by having crosses carved on their foreheads. Many pagan temples were demolished, sometimes against violent opposition. Others, such as the Parthenon in Athens and the Pantheon in Rome, were converted into Christian churches and survived until the modern day.

Checking In

By yourself or with a partner, explain the significance of each of the following selected key terms:

heresy	ascetism
Nicene Creed	Jerome
Mithras	Theodosius I the Great
Augustine	Hypatia

Late Romans and Their World

◆ **How did late Romans find security and new opportunities?**

◆ **How did Christianity affect culture and society during the late Roman period?**

Unlike the people of the Principate, who thought of themselves as citizens of Rome, the people in Late Antiquity tended to identify themselves as Gauls, Italians, Egyptians, and so on. The empire no longer unified people as effectively as it once had. Nor did the empire protect people as well as before. The government issued laws attempting to strengthen the empire and to protect everyone's interests, but the laws were full of loopholes and exceptions and were regularly disregarded. Powerful persons often operated outside the law. The loss of imperial legal protection made it important for everyone, privileged or not, to look for a more powerful protector. Increasing numbers of the poor became dependents of the rich and powerful. But the changing times also brought new opportunities. Ambitious individuals from all segments of society could better themselves if they had enough initiative,

canon law Law of the church, as issued by church councils or, later in history, by the bishop of Rome.

Jerome (ca. 347–420) Priest of Bethlehem and translator of the Vulgate Bible; one of the leading teachers of the Christian church.

Vulgate Standard Latin translation of the Bible, made by Jerome around 400.

Theodosius I (r. 379–395) Emperor who made Christianity the only legal religion of the empire.

Hypatia Head of the Neoplatonic philosophy school of Alexandria who was murdered by fanatical Christians in 415.

good luck, and the right friends. The Christian church in particular provided new prospects for personal expression and social advancement to men and women, rich and poor alike.

The Pursuit of Personal Security

By the fourth century, everyone living in the Roman Empire was looking for physical, spiritual, and economic security that the Roman government was less able to provide. Powerful persons such as senators could be threatened by government demands or by rivals willing to take the law into their own hands. The less privileged were threatened by influential individuals who would take advantage of them in any number of ways. Declining trade reduced economic prosperity. Everyone was threatened by barbarian attacks.

The Senators The most influential people in the empire were still the senators, but there now were many more of them, both male and female, and many ways to become one. The easiest ways to become a senator were to be the child of a senator or for a woman to marry a senator. In addition, holding a high imperial office or being a Christian bishop automatically made a man a senator. Anyone with enough money could purchase senatorial rank from the emperor. Eventually an empire-wide aristocracy of thousands of senators arose that stood in stark contrast to the elite six-hundred-member senate of the early Principate. Senators still possessed great economic influence: the wealthiest had incomes of over two thousand pounds of gold a year. But because the Senates of Rome and Constantinople had no real power, senators were less committed to making the empire work. They continued to hold high government offices, which emperors granted to secure their support, but senators often saw these offices as a way to pursue their own self-interests rather than the good of the empire as a whole.

Instead of living in Rome or Constantinople, most senators now resided in the provinces. They kept their distance from the emperor. Especially in the west, senators expanded their landholdings, consolidated their local authority, and pursued a life of leisure in the security of their self-sufficient country **villas**. They did their best to avoid paying taxes and often defied the law. Some recruited bands of armed retainers who were little better than hired thugs. Most senators preferred being big men at home to being under the thumb of the emperor. As a result, the central government had less authority in the provinces, and the empire became less unified.

villa A largely self-sufficient country estate of a wealthy aristocrat.

Middle Ages The broad historical period between the ancient and modern periods.

The Decurions Lower on the social scale were the decurions, whose primary responsibility continued to be tax collection. Because many senators refused to pay their taxes, decurions had to squeeze what they could out of the rest of the population, and for this they were hated. In addition, the imperial government forced more responsibilities for local administration onto them, such as carrying out expensive road repairs. Municipal offices, once an honor, now became a burden. Many decurions attempted to escape their duties. Some claimed to be senators or became Christian clerics, groups exempted from serving as decurions. Others simply ran away. As a result, city services suffered, and many cities fell into decline.

The Economy More and more wealth, in particular landed property, was concentrated in the hands of the wealthy. The gap between the rich and the poor became even greater. Less privileged people faced increasing economic hardship. The gold standard was convenient for the wealthy but did nothing to benefit the poor, for whom a single solidus represented four months' wages. The value of the copper coinage, the only form of small change, continued to decline. By the late fourth century, it took 450,000 tiny copper coins to purchase one solidus. People whose businesses used small change found it difficult to make a living. For merchants, opportunities shrank. The trend toward local self-sufficiency brought a decline in long-distance commerce. When troops were pulled back from the borders, government subsidies for trade to frontier areas were lost. And the construction of imperial factories for supplying the army meant an end to military contracts.

Tenant Farmers Small peasant farmers who owned their own land often fell into debt, transferred their property to land-hungry aristocrats, and became *coloni* (tenant farmers) on land they once had owned. Coloni were legally tied to the land unless they could repay what their patrons had invested in them, and in this regard they anticipated the serfs of the **Middle Ages**. But restraints on their freedom were usually outweighed by the security they gained from having a regular livelihood and being under the protection of a powerful aristocrat. They had few other options, except to become migrant laborers traveling from job to job.

Slaves Some slaves, on the other hand, experienced an improvement in their living conditions. Now that tenant farming was the preferred method for cultivating large estates, some landlords promoted slaves to coloni so they would not have to feed, clothe, and shelter them. Among the most valued and privileged slaves were castrated males known as eunuchs. Because castration was illegal in the empire, most eunuchs had to be imported, usually from Persia and the east. Eunuchs were used by the wealthy, mainly in the eastern empire, in positions of trust. They could rise to have great authority. In the imperial palace

During the Late Roman Empire, local life became centered on self-sufficient villas, as seen on this fifth-century mosaic depicting a villa in North Africa that belonged to a land-owner named Julius. The villa itself is fortified, with turreted towers at the corners and blank walls facing out, indicating its role as a place of refuge in troubled times. Surrounding it are scenes from everyday life, such as gathering ducks and harvesting fruit from trees at the upper left. On the right, a fowler accompanied by dogs carries nets for snaring birds. And at the bottom, Julius himself, seated, and his wife, standing, oversee their domain. By withdrawing to their villas, senators could pursue local authority outside the direct oversight of the emperor and imperial officials. What effect do you think the existence of these country villas might have had on the efforts of emperors to preserve the unity of the empire? (Gilles Mermet/akg-images)

the "Keeper of the Sacred Bedchamber" had to be a eunuch. He had the ear of the emperor and empress and often had great influence. It remained quite common for slaves to be set free, especially on the death of their owners.

New Opportunities

The changes and flux that occurred during Late Antiquity brought new opportunities for individuals who in the past had been restricted in the ways that they could find personal fulfillment.

Opportunities in the Church The rise of the Christian church brought new social and economic opportunities for men and women. Less privileged persons could find work in churches as doorkeepers, readers, and grave diggers. Some even became deacons, who oversaw church finances, or priests, who provided spiritual guidance. But the greatest honor was the office of bishop. As the most important institution in the Roman world, the church became increasingly wealthy as a result of offerings and bequests made by emperors, aristocrats, and the general public. The person who controlled that wealth—the bishop—thus had great economic and political authority as well as spiritual authority. Bishops served for life, and **episcopal** office became increasingly attractive to talented and ambitious individuals, such as Ambrose and Augustine, as an alternative to state office. Indeed, a prominent pagan senator reportedly said, "Elect me bishop of Rome and I'll become a Christian too." Bishops were elected by the people, and intense, sometimes violent, politicking could go on before an election as the supporters of different candidates lobbied for support.

Episcopal office allowed bishops not only to display their Christian piety but also to demonstrate their public spirit and to enhance the local authority they cherished. Bishops supervised the care of the poor, elderly, and sick for which the church now was responsible. They intervened on behalf of those accused or even convicted of crimes. They ransomed captives. They were permitted to judge some kinds of civil and criminal cases. They also could influence public opinion by speaking out during church services, in contrast to the days of the Principate, when public assemblies had been carefully regulated by the government. These activities gained bishops status and supporters.

Opportunities for Women Women, whose activities continued to center on the family, also found new opportunities in Christianity. It often was the women in the family, for example, who converted male pagan senators to Christianity. Moreover, women who devoted themselves to the Christian life were able to escape traditional subordination to males. Spending their money on charitable works gave single women and widows greater control over their property than they would have had if they were married. Imperial women provided role models for female piety. One was Helena, the mother of

episcopal Relating to a bishop.

Constantine, who rose from humble beginnings as a stable girl to become the concubine of Constantine's father, Constantius. After Constantine adopted Christianity, Helena also took up the Christian life. She decorated churches, gained freedom for prisoners, and supported the poor. While on a **pilgrimage** to the **Holy Land**, she believed that she had discovered the True Cross on which Jesus had been crucified. The Cross then became one of the most sacred relics of the Christian church. Part of it was placed in the **Church of the Holy Sepulcher** in Jerusalem, which Helena had built on the site of Christ's tomb; the rest was taken to Constantinople.

Other rich and influential women also demonstrated Christian piety. Some built churches; others cared for the poor. For example, the Roman aristocrat **Melania** the Elder, daughter of a consul, made a pilgrimage to the Holy Land after the deaths of her husband and two of her three children. To minister more freely to the poor, she dressed in slave clothing. When she was arrested by a provincial governor, she boldly declared: "I am the daughter of the consul Marcellus, but now I am the servant of Christ. I can dress any way I choose. You can't threaten me without getting into real trouble." The governor apologized and ordered that she be allowed to carry out her charitable works. Melania then established monasteries for men and women. Around 400, she returned to Rome and converted her granddaughter, Melania the Younger, to the ascetic life. The younger Melania convinced her husband to live chastely with her. They used their wealth for charitable works in Italy, Sicily, and North Africa, where they established men's and women's monasteries. Eventually they moved to the Holy Land, where Melania built a monastery for herself, virgins, and ex-prostitutes. She also converted her uncle, a devoted pagan, to Christianity.

Literary Culture

Late Antiquity was an age of great literary creativity, and a great deal of both secular and religious literature survives from the period.

Secular Literature Some literary production was due to the efforts of senators who took pride in participating in and supporting intellectual endeavors. The senators of Rome, for example, sponsored the work of the last great historian of antiquity, Ammianus Marcellinus, whose history went up to the year 378 and painted a glowing picture of the pagan emperor Julian. With their own hands, senators made **manuscript** copies of the literature of the past.

Christian Literature The greatest expansion of literary creativity took place in the Christian church, where many of the brightest minds were attracted. Christian writers such as Augustine, Ambrose, and Jerome wrote sermons, letters, theological treatises, commentaries on scripture, and even Christian versions of Roman history that had an immense effect on Christian belief and practice. Christian intellectuals debated the role pagan literature should have in the Christian world. Some argued that the Greek and Latin classics should be abandoned, but the influence of classical tradition was irresistible. Augustine and Ambrose recognized that the Greek and Roman literary education, with its emphasis on grammar, public speaking, and argumentation, could be pressed into the service of the church. For example, many Christian concepts, such as the idea of a single transcendent god, were found embedded in the teachings of Neoplatonism. Of course, Christian thinkers sometimes disagreed with their pagan predecessors. For example, in his *City of God*, Augustine promoted a progressive, linear concept of history, which moved from a beginning (the Creation) to an end (the Second Coming of Christ), as opposed to the classical view that history was cyclical and constantly repeated itself.

Thanks to Augustine and other like-minded Christians, the church ultimately became the primary means by which Greek and Latin classical literature was preserved in the Middle Ages and transmitted to the modern day. Christian monks and clerics copied and recopied manuscripts that previously had been copied by and for Roman senators. In general, the preservation of both Christian and pagan writings was promoted by the use of the **codex**, the modern day book format, as opposed to the scroll. For writing material, codices used virtually indestructible parchment, made from preserved sheep and calfskins, rather than from papyrus, which tended to become fragile and disintegrate.

The Changing Landscape

The changing times of Late Antiquity also were reflected in the material culture of both cities and the countryside.

The Transformation of City Life Roman senators and local elites concentrated more on expanding and embellishing their country estates than on maintaining cities. They decorated their estates with works of art, including sculptures, frescoes, and mosaics modeled on those of the Greek and Roman past. City populations shrank as rich and poor sought security in the countryside. At the same time, the withdrawal of much of the Roman army from frontier areas caused

pilgrimage Journey made to a holy place for religious devotion.

Holy Land Areas around Jerusalem and Bethlehem mentioned in the Bible.

Church of the Holy Sepulcher Church built by Helena in Jerusalem on the site of Christ's tomb.

Melania The Elder (d. 410) and the Younger (d. 439), grandmother and granddaughter; famous for leading lives of Christian asceticism and doing good works.

manuscript (from Latin for "written by hand") Handwritten document or book.

codex (pl. codices) Modern book format, as opposed to the scroll.

Genevieve Chooses to Become a Christian Activist

During Late Antiquity, authority in the Christian church came to be limited more and more to men, with women being restricted to supporting roles as wives or in convents. On some occasions, however, the political and social disruption of the times gave assertive women an opportunity to assume roles that generally were adopted by men. Their decisions to do so, however, sometimes had dire consequences.

In the mid-fifth century, Genevieve, a young woman of Paris, adopted the religious life in a very visible way, as reported in a "saint's life" written not long after she died. When her mother opposed her choice, Genevieve replied, "I shall haunt the threshold of the church," and her uncooperative mother was stricken blind for two years. According to her biographer, Genevieve performed miracles, including curing the sick, casting out demons, and raising the dead. She also could create wine and oil from nothing, light candles, and cause doors to open.

Other miracles were rather sinister in nature and were viewed by some as sorcery. Genevieve could summon and subdue sea monsters, control the weather, and cause people who provoked her, such as her mother, to become ill or disabled. She even could predict the future and read minds.

Because of her reputation for holiness, Genevieve was asked to intercede on behalf of people who had nowhere else to go for help. On one occasion, for example, she threatened a man who refused to forgive a misbehaving servant:

She said, "If you despise my supplications, the Lord Jesus Christ will not do so." When the man returned home he became feverish, his mouth gaping and drooling like that of an aurochs [an extinct form of huge wild cattle]. He rolled at Genevieve's feet and begged her to give him pardon. After she had blessed him, all fever and illness left him, and he then pardoned his servant.

These kinds of activities were more typical of male holy men, and they aroused popular resentment against Genevieve. On one occasion, she was nearly lynched: "The citizens of Paris rampaged against her. They conspired to punish Genevieve by pelting her with stones or drowning her in a vast pool." Only at the last minute did they change their minds.

Genevieve also gained popular approval by freeing captives and relieving a famine. Then, in 451, during the invasion of Gaul by Attila and the Huns, the men of Paris panicked and were on the verge of abandoning the city. Genevieve, however, persuaded the women to undertake fasts, prayers, and all-night vigils. She also warned the men that they should not remove their goods from Paris because other cities they considered safer would be devastated by the Huns, whereas Paris would remain untouched. Genevieve's initiative bore fruit. The Huns did turn aside, and Paris was saved.

As a result of her activities, Genevieve was subsequently recognized as a Christian saint. Her example was followed by other assertive women who decided to violate the norms of society. But the activities of many other women saints are poorly known, for unless they had biographers, as Genevieve did, their activities would be lost in the mists of time.

Source: From the anonymous biographer of St. Genevieve of Paris (c. 422–512).

---

the cities that had arisen there to decline. The result was a contraction of urban life. In Gaul, the areas of cities protected by defensive walls were as little as a tenth of what they had been in the second century.

But cities did not vanish. They still functioned as administrative centers and as the seats of bishops, who by the fifth century had assumed many responsibilities for local administration, including the upkeep of city services and the administration of justice. There also was a great deal of new building activity, but it had a different orientation. Resources that previously had been devoted to constructing public meeting halls, bath complexes, theaters, amphitheaters, and aqueducts now were used for building churches, which became a city's primary architectural monuments.

Personal charitable contributions also were directed toward the church. Whereas in the past a rich benefactor might have funded a town hall, now he or she underwrote the construction of a basilica. Earlier public monuments that fell into disrepair were quarried for materials to be used in church building. Thus the old urban centers decayed at the same time that Christian centers, often located outside the old city limits, prospered. Some cities even were reoriented around the churches, and the old city center was just abandoned.

 Checking In

By yourself or with a partner, explain the significance of each of the following selected key terms:

villa	Church of the Holy Sepulcher
Middle Ages	Melania the Elder
pilgrimage	manuscript
Holy Land	codex

The Fall of the Western Roman Empire, 364–476

◆ **How did Romans and barbarians interact during Late Antiquity?**

◆ **What were some of the causes of the fall of the Western Roman Empire?**

In many ways, in 364 the empire looked as peaceful and prosperous as it had been in the first century C.E. But appearances were misleading. Forces were in motion that soon would produce the most significant political development of Late Antiquity: the fall of the Western Roman Empire. By 395, the empire had effectively split into eastern and western halves. The eastern empire proved more durable than the western one. During the fifth century, bands of foreign barbarians carved the western empire into independent kingdoms, and by 476, it was no more.

Rome's Last Golden Age

In the third quarter of the fourth century C.E. the Roman Empire appeared to be as strong as ever. But there were continuing problems with military recruitment, and the western and eastern sections of the empire tended to pursue their own self-centered interests.

Valentinian I In 364, soon after the death of the last member of Constantine's family, the army selected Valentinian, one of its officers, as emperor. **Valentinian I** (364–375 C.E.) immediately made his younger brother, **Valens** (364–378 C.E.), co-emperor and gave him responsibility for the eastern provinces while he took the west. Valentinian's reign later was looked on as the third Golden Age of the Roman Empire (the first two were the reigns of Augustus and Trajan). The borders were securely defended. The empire still extended from Scotland in the northwest to the Euphrates River in the east. Rural life flourished on large western villas and on smaller farms in the east. Now that Constantine's gold standard had been established, the imperial treasury had enough income to meet expenditures. Disputes among Christians were subdued, and debates between pagans and Christians were politely conducted. It looked like the empire would last forever.

Problems on the Horizon But there were ominous signs. Military recruitment continued to be a problem. Landowners, who were responsible for providing recruits as part of their tax assessment, either sent men unsuited for army life or chose to pay an exemption fee. Men eligible for military service sometimes cut off fingers or thumbs in an attempt to avoid it. In addition, in distributing resources, the government sometimes favored the eastern part of the empire at the expense of the west. This made sense because the east was more defensible, more economically prosperous, more populous, and even more cultured, but the west suffered as a consequence. But it meant that the west was increasingly unable to meet its expenses. In addition, the separate administrations at Rome and Constantinople meant that sometimes one half of the empire adopted policies that were detrimental to the interests of the other half. There, thus, was an accelerating tendency for the two halves of the empire to go their own ways.

The Barbarians and Rome

The most worrisome problem faced by late Roman emperors was the barbarians, who became harder and harder for the Romans to control.

The Barbarian Peoples The Romans had dealt with barbarian peoples successfully for centuries, but barbarians now became a much greater threat, in part because other, more distant barbarians, now also threatened Rome. (See Table 7.2.) The empire was surrounded by barbarians. In Ireland and Scotland, there were Celtic peoples who had never been incorporated into the Roman Empire. North and east of the Rhine River were west Germans such as the **Franks**, Angles, Saxons, and Alamanni. In eastern Europe lived east Germans such as the **Visigoths**, **Ostrogoths**, **Vandals**, and Burgundians. Farther east, on the Central Asian steppes, were nomads such as the **Huns**, a Mongolian people who had been forced westward out of Mongolia centuries earlier (see Learning from a Primary Source).

Valentinian I (r. 364–375) Emperor responsible for the last Golden Age of the Roman Empire.

Valens (r. 364–378) Co-emperor of the eastern empire during reign of Valentinian I; killed by the Visigoths at the Battle of Adrianople.

Franks West Germanic people living near the lower Rhine River who established the Merovingian dynasty in the fifth century.

Visigoths East Germanic people who crossed the Danube into Roman territory in 376 and in 418 established a kingdom in Aquitaine.

Ostrogoths East Germanic people from north of the Black Sea who invaded Italy in 489 and established their own kingdom.

Vandals East Germanic people who invaded the Roman Empire in 406; their destructiveness gave rise to the term vandalism.

Huns East Asian barbarian people originally from Mongolia who invaded the Western Roman Empire in 451.

Table 7.2 Barbarian Peoples

West Germans	East Germans	Steppe Nomads
Alamanni	Visigoths (west Goths)	Huns
Franks	Ostrogoths (east Goths)	
Angles	Burgundians	
Saxons	Vandals	

© Cengage Learning

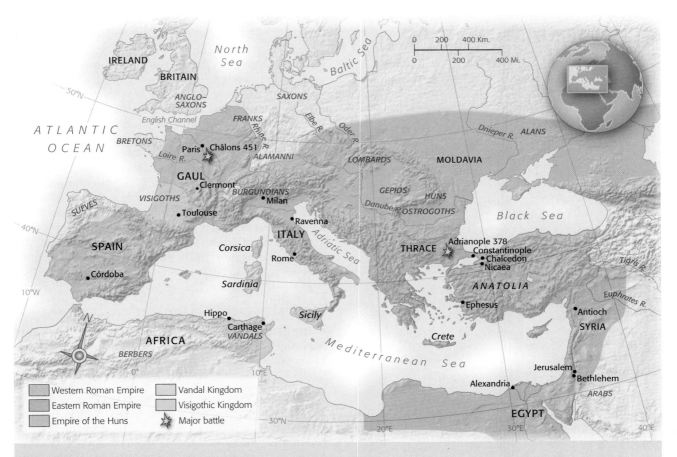

Map 7.3 **The Barbarians and Rome** By the middle of the fifth century C.E., the occupation of the Western Roman Empire by various barbarian peoples was well under way. The Anglo-Saxons, Franks, Visigoths, Burgundians, Sueves, and Vandals already had established independent kingdoms on Roman territory. At the same time, the entire Roman world was threatened by the Huns. © *Cengage Learning*

1. Which parts of the Roman Empire were first occupied by barbarian peoples?
2. What barbarian peoples became associated with the Huns?
3. What factors do you think made the Huns such a formidable threat?
4. How do the locations of barbarian peoples on this map compare to their locations on the map at the beginning of this chapter? How might you account for the changes?

As the Huns continued to move west, they created a barbarian empire and came ever closer to Roman territory.

Roman-Barbarian Cultural Exchanges

Cultural interchange between barbarians and Romans continued. Several Germanic peoples already had picked up the Arian form of Christianity from the Romans. And Romans adopted aspects of barbarian culture. Barbarian long hair and dress, such as trousers, fur coats, and boots, became all the rage in Rome. The Roman army even adopted the barbarian custom of raising a newly acclaimed ruler on a shield.

The primary point of contact between Rome and its barbarian neighbors was the Roman army. When barbarians were not fighting against the Roman army,

they were serving in it. Faced with profound recruitment difficulties, late Roman emperors employed barbarian mercenaries. Bands of Franks and Alamanni, for example, would be hired for a campaign and then return home, bringing back Roman coinage, commodities, and culture, along with tales of the riches, prosperity, and opportunity that lay within the empire. Some barbarian chieftains even rose to the rank of master of soldiers in the regular Roman army. The large-scale recruitment of barbarians resulted in the loss of the Roman military superiority that had been taken for granted during the Principate. By the middle of the fourth century, Roman and barbarian armies were using the same personnel and the same tactics.

The Arrival of the Visigoths In 375, a group of defeated Germans were so insolent that Valentinian

This panel of a two-sided ivory plaque, known as a diptych, from the early fifth century depicts Stilicho, a half-Vandal, in the uniform of a Roman general, with his military cloak pinned at the right shoulder with an elaborate fibula. Stilicho was but one of many barbarians who became a Roman general. In addition, the Roman adoption of barbarian customs is seen in the use of the long thrusting spear, as opposed to the old Roman throwing javelin, and the oblong barbarian shield. Stilicho married Serena, the daughter of the emperor Honorius, but his hope that his son Eucherius would become emperor did not come to pass, for Stilicho eventually was executed by Honorius. What effect do you think the infiltration of barbarians and barbarian customs into the Roman world might have had on the survival of the Roman Empire?

Alinari/Art Resource, NY

Adrianople Location of a battle in 378 in which the Romans were disastrously defeated by the Visigoths.

fleeing from the Huns had appeared on the banks of the Danube River. The Visigoths offered military service in exchange for the right to settle on deserted lands located safely inside the Roman frontier. Valens agreed, believing that doing so would allow him to find more army recruits and also to get more land into cultivation and on the tax rolls. But once inside the empire, the Visigoths began raiding and looting. In 378, Valens attacked the Visigoths at the Battle of **Adrianople**, northwest of Constantinople. His army was virtually annihilated and he was killed. His successor, Theodosius I, was unable to defeat, much less expel, the Visigoths. The best he could do was to recognize them as Roman allies. This face-saving measure left the Visigoths free to roam about under their own leaders, one of whom was the able general Alaric. The barbarian invasions of the Roman Empire had begun.

The Disintegration of the Western Empire

During the fifth century, barbarian peoples gradually occupied all of the Western Roman Empire. By the year 500, the western empire was no more.

The Split of the Empire When Theodosius died in 395, he was succeeded by his two young sons. The empire was divided between them, and the split of the empire into eastern and western halves now became permanent. Constitutionally, there still was only one empire, and the emperors continued to issue laws and coins in each other's names. But in reality, the eastern and western empires had their own emperors and administrations and looked out for their own interests. During the fifth century, the eastern government watched as the west collapsed.

Invasions of the Western Empire At the beginning of the fifth century, the barbarian invasions shifted to the western empire. Although the barbarian peoples had no unity and no common agenda, the attacks of several different peoples at the same time overwhelmed the west. First, a band of Visigoths led by Alaric invaded Italy. Then, on the last day of 406, after Roman troops had been withdrawn from the north to defend Italy, a horde of barbarians, including the Vandals and Burgundians, walked across the frozen Rhine River. They traveled south, looting and burning as they went. The Vandals made their way into the fertile, undefended provinces of Spain. In 410, Alaric and the Visigoths captured and sacked Rome. The pillaging lasted only three days, and the churches were left untouched, but the point had been made. "Unconquered Rome," as it had been called, was no longer unconquered. The psychological damage was even greater than the material destruction. The emperor Honorius, who had retreated to the safety of Ravenna in the swamps of

became enraged, suffered a stroke, and died. A year later, Valens was faced with a momentous decision. A large group of Visigoths

Ammianus Describes the Huns

The Romans' fear of the barbarians often led them to portray barbarians as uncouth savages who represented the opposite of everything a civilized Roman or Greek stood for. For Romans of the late fourth century, the Huns, who had only recently appeared on the Roman frontiers, were the most savage barbarians of all, hardly better than animals. In the following selection from his *Histories*, the late Roman historian Ammianus Marcellinus, a former army officer who personally observed all kinds of barbarians, describes the Huns as they appeared to the Romans in the 390s. His account is full of stereotypes and would have made the Romans feel justified in the repugnance that they felt toward the Huns.

❶ Why are the Huns compared to beasts?

❷ What role did horses play in the life of the Huns?

❸ How does Ammianus portray the Hun government?

❹ Does Ammianus's description of Hun fighting tactics compare to Roman tactics?

❺ How does Ammianus portray the life of the Huns as being different from Roman life? Why does he do so?

❻ Why might you decide not to believe all of what Ammianus says about the Huns?

The people of the Huns exceed every degree of savagery. Because the cheeks of the children are deeply furrowed with steel from their very birth, in order that the growth of hair may be checked by the wrinkled scars, they grow old without beards and without any beauty, like eunuchs. ❶ They all have compact, strong limbs and thick necks, and are so monstrously ugly and misshapen that one might take them for two-legged beasts. They are so hardy that they have no need of fire nor of savory food, but eat the roots of wild plants and the half-raw flesh of any kind of animal whatever, which they put between their thighs and the backs of their horses, and thus warm it a little.

They are never protected by any buildings, but they avoid these like tombs. Roaming at large amid the mountains and woods, they learn from the cradle to endure cold, hunger, and thirst. They dress in the skins of field mice sewn together. When they have once put on a faded tunic, it is not taken off until by long wear it has been taken from them bit by bit. ❷ They are almost glued to their horses, and sometimes they sit on them woman-fashion and thus perform ordinary tasks. From their horses every one of that nation buys and sells, eats and drinks, and bowed over the narrow neck of the animal relaxes into sleep. ❸ And when deliberation is called for, they all consult as a common body on horseback. They are subject to no royal restraint, but they are content with the disorderly government of their important men.

❹ You would not hesitate to call them the most terrible of all warriors, because they fight from a distance with missiles having sharp bone, instead of the usual metal points. Then they gallop over the intervening spaces and fight hand-to-hand with swords, regardless of their own lives; and they throw nooses over their opponents and so entangle them that they fetter their limbs.

❺ No one in their country ever plows a field or touches a plow-handle. They are all without fixed abode, without hearth, or law, or settled mode of life, and keep roaming from place to place, accompanied by the wagons in which their wives weave their hideous garments, cohabit with their husbands, bear children, and rear them to the age of puberty. None of their offspring, when asked, can tell you where he comes from, because he was conceived in one place, born far from there, and brought up still farther away.

❻ In truces they are faithless and unreliable. Like unreasoning beasts, they are utterly ignorant of the difference between right and wrong; they are deceitful and ambiguous in speech, never bound by any reverence for religion or for superstition.

northeastern Italy, eventually got the Visigoths out of Italy by allowing them to settle in Aquitaine in southwestern France. They soon established an independent kingdom on Roman soil, the first of several barbarian peoples to do so.

The disintegration of the western empire continued during the reign of the emperor Valentinian III (r. 425–455). The Vandals left Spain and occupied North Africa, depriving Italy of its best grain supply. In 451, the Huns, led by their ferocious king **Attila**, invaded Gaul. The Roman master of soldiers Aëtius, sometimes called "the last of the Romans," patched together a shaky alliance of Romans, Visigoths, and Franks. At the **Battle of Châlons**, the previously undefeated Huns were put to flight, but they returned the next year to invade Italy. An embassy led by **Leo the Great**, the powerful bishop of Rome, paid off the Huns to withdraw.

Attila (r. 435–453) King of the Huns who terrorized the Eastern Roman Empire and was defeated at the Battle of Châlons.

Battle of Châlons Battle in 451 in north-central France in which the Romans under the master of soldiers Aëtius defeated the Huns.

Leo the Great Bishop of Rome from 441 to 460 who persuaded Attila the Hun to withdraw from Italy.

puppet emperors Western Roman emperors between 455 and 476 who were manipulated by barbarian generals; a puppet ruler also is any ruler manipulated by another person.

Romulus (r. 475–476) Last emperor of the western empire; deposed in 476; nicknamed "Augustulus" ("little Augustus").

Odovacar (r. 476–493) Barbarian chieftain who deposed Romulus, the last western emperor, in 476 and became king of Italy.

Arthur A sixth-century ruler in Britain; stories of his exploits and companions were popular in the Middle Ages and into modern times.

The End of the Western Empire Avoiding conquest by the Huns was the west's last victory. After Valentinian III's death in 455, the western throne was occupied by nine emperors known as the **puppet emperors** because they often were manipulated by their barbarian masters of soldiers. What remained of the western empire was occupied by barbarians. In 476, the boy emperor **Romulus**, nicknamed "Augustulus" ("little Augustus"), was deposed by the barbarian general **Odovacar**, who called himself King of Italy and notified the eastern emperor Zeno that the west no longer needed its own emperor. Romulus was the last emperor to rule in Rome, and the year 476 generally is said to mark the fall of the western empire, even though some areas still resisted. Britain, for example, continued to fight the Angle and Saxon invaders. Led by warlords such as **Arthur**, the Britons held out until about the year 500, when they became the last of the western Romans to fall to the barbarians.

Interpretations of the Fall of the West

The question of why Rome fell has been debated ever since it happened. In antiquity, religious explanations were common. Pagans argued that Rome fell because the Romans had abandoned their old gods. Some Christians suggested that the fall of Rome was God's punishment of Christians for their immoral lives. Augustine proposed in his *City of God* that what happened on earth was God's will and had to be accepted by Christians; what was really important was what took place in God's "heavenly city."

In the late eighteenth century, the British historian Edward Gibbon wrote *The Decline and Fall of the Roman Empire,* which described the fall of the western empire as the "triumph of Christianity and barbarians." He suggested that Christianity had weakened the will of the Romans to resist, opening the way for invasions by more warlike barbarians. This explanation now is seen as overly simplistic. After all, most barbarians were Christians themselves. And as for the invasions, the emperors had dealt effectively with barbarian threats for centuries. Aside from the Battle of Adrianople, the barbarians did not win many significant military victories. The west was occupied more by means of infiltration, peaceful settlement, and persistence than by military conquest. The real question, it seems, is what made it possible for barbarians to succeed in the fifth century when in the past they had been unable to occupy virtually any Roman territory.

More recently, historians have proposed many interrelated causes. Some suggestions, ranging from drastic climatic change to ethnic mixing to lead poisoning, can easily be dismissed. More plausible suggestions include the withdrawal of senatorial support for the emperors, increased administrative decentralization, too many barbarians in the army, economic collapse, excessive taxation, corruption, military recruitment shortages, excessive bureaucracy, poor leadership, lack of organized resistance, and just plain bad luck. In addition, any explanation for the political decline of the west also must explain why the east did not fall. In this regard, it is clear that the east had more secure geographical frontiers, a stronger economy, a larger population, and a more dependable Roman military recruitment base. In view of the east's advantages, it may be that once the empire split in two, the downfall of the west was inevitable.

 ## Checking In

By yourself or with a partner, explain the significance of each of the following selected key terms:

Valentinian I	Attila
Franks	Leo the Great
Vandals	puppet emperors
Adrianople	Odovacar

The Post-Roman World, 400–527

◆ How did Roman and barbarian populations and customs become integrated?

◆ How did eastern emperors survive the challenges of the fifth century?

By the beginning of the sixth century, the Mediterranean world was vastly different from what it had been in the time of Augustus. The unity so carefully constructed by the Romans had disappeared. The western part of the Roman Empire had been partitioned among several barbarian peoples. The most powerful were the Visigoths, who occupied Aquitaine and Spain, and the Vandals, who held the rich provinces of North Africa. Elsewhere, the Angles and Saxons settled in Britain, the Franks on the lower Rhine, the Alamanni on the upper Rhine, the Burgundians in central Gaul, and the Ostrogoths in Italy. During the sixth and seventh centuries, the western European world evolved into what we now call the Middle Ages. But the eastern half of the Roman Empire, the Byzantine Empire, continued and even flourished, adapting to changing times as it had in the past.

Romans and Barbarians in the Post-Roman West

After the fall of the Western Roman Empire, Romans and their new barbarian neighbors needed to find ways to get along with each other. They were remarkably successful in doing so.

Roman-Barbarian Interactions By the end of the fifth century, the government of the Western Roman Empire was gone, but the west remained populated by Romans who had to respond to the barbarian presence. Some fled, some were killed, and others faced captivity or enslavement. Most simply became free citizens of the kingdoms in which they resided and made whatever private peace they could with their new rulers. In most respects, life went on as before, but now with barbarians not only as rulers but also as neighbors, social acquaintances, and marriage partners. For many Romans, barbarian kings provided new sources of rewards, patronage, and career opportunities. Some powerful senators may even have preferred a local barbarian ruler who respected their property rights to a distant, yet intrusive, Roman emperor.

The barbarian peoples adopted Roman ways as they created their own nations on Roman soil. Barbarian kings realized the necessity of maintaining the goodwill of their Roman subjects, for there were many more Romans than barbarians. If they lost the support of the Roman population, in particular of the Roman senators, they risked provoking uprisings in which they might be overwhelmed. Thus, except in Britain, all the barbarian rulers used the Roman Empire as a model, adopting Roman administrative practices. Barbarian kings also accepted the Roman concept of the rule of law: they issued laws in their own names but also recognized the validity of Roman law. Romans continued to serve as city administrators, military governors, and royal advisers. None of the kingdoms, however, had a bureaucracy that was nearly as complex as that of the Roman Empire, especially at the local level. As a result, even more of the responsibility for local government fell into the hands of Christian bishops, who undertook most of the duties that in the past had been performed by government officials and city councils. Many European cities were transformed into centers of Christian administration and worship.

A potential incompatibility between Romans and some barbarians involved religion. Barbarians such as the Visigoths, Burgundians, and Vandals were Arian Christians, whereas the Romans followed the Nicene Creed. In practice, however, Arian and Nicene Christians were generally tolerant of one another and even attended each other's services. Eventually all Arian barbarians converted to Nicene Christianity. In addition, unlike Roman emperors, barbarian kings usually stayed out of theological disputes, leaving those to churchmen, although they sometimes interfered in the election of bishops.

Another possible source of conflict concerned property. Incoming barbarians were primarily seeking land on which to settle, and barbarian kings provided land for them in several ways. Sometimes, in a process called hospitality, barbarians received one-third of the land of a large Roman landowner. The Roman then was confirmed in the ownership of the rest. Barbarian kings also granted to their supporters property that had been abandoned by Romans who had fled or land that had fallen behind on its taxes. Barbarian governments also controlled the Roman tax collection structure and could use tax money collected from Romans to purchase land. Only rarely, as in North Africa or Britain, did barbarians forcibly evict Roman landowners. As a result, the barbarian settlement was much more peaceful than it might have been.

The Nature of the Post-Roman World With the exception of Britain, Roman culture continued as before in the barbarian kingdoms. Latin remained the predominant language, eventually evolving into modern **Romance languages** such as Italian, French, Spanish, Portuguese, and Romanian. Classical literature was appreciated and preserved by the educated elite, both Roman and barbarian. It was once thought that the creation of the barbarian kingdoms resulted in a period of cultural barrenness known as the Dark Ages, but this attitude arose largely

Romance languages Modern European languages that derive from Latin.

from a failure to appreciate the importance of the new Christian literature of the early Middle Ages. It is more accurate to speak of the transformation of the Roman world, not its decline and fall, terminology that refers only to politics. Western Europe undeniably went into a period of reorganization during the barbarian settlement.

In many ways, however, it was the Roman Empire itself, not its aftermath, that was the anomaly. Rome had brought to western Europe an artificially high degree of administrative and economic complexity that was designed to suit the needs of the empire. When the Western Roman Empire collapsed, it took its administrative and economic superstructure with it. Western Europe returned to a condition that was more suited to western European needs. European culture during the early Middle Ages was not necessarily worse than classical culture, but it was different. As time went on, any sense of ethnic or cultural identity separating Romans and barbarians became meaningless. The peoples of western Europe created a hybrid culture that both preserved and reinterpreted classical culture.

The Barbarian Kingdoms

The western empire was replaced by several barbarian kingdoms, the most significant of which were those of the Visigoths, the Franks, and the Ostrogoths.

The Visigoths The kingdom of the Visigoths included Aquitaine and Spain. As the first barbarians to settle on Roman soil, the Visgoths readily adapted themselves to Roman practices. They issued a law code that contained selections from existing Roman law; thus Roman law became Visigothic law. Visigothic kings also issued new laws in their own names, which likewise applied to all of the people in their kingdom. Visigoths and Romans created a culture so integrated that it is virtually impossible to distinguish Visigoths from Romans in archaeological remains.

The Franks The Franks originated as several independent groups located on both sides of the lower Rhine. In the late fifth century they were united by King **Clovis**, a member of the **Merovingian** family, which gave its name to the first dynasty of Frankish kings. Clovis was ruthless in his quest to unify the Franks, murdering several relatives who ruled

The barbarians who settled in the Roman Empire in the fifth century initially were either pagans or Arian Christians, creating problems of assimilation with the Roman population. Around 496 C.E., Clovis, the king of the Franks, chose to be baptized as a Christian, as shown in this re-creation by an unnamed French artist known as the Master of St. Gilles. By adopting the same religion as most of the Roman population, Clovis then was portrayed as a "new Constantine" and gained a political advantage over his barbarian rivals. What role do you think Christianity might have had in the eventual integration of Romans and barbarians in the early medieval world?

Clovis (r. 481–511) King of the Franks who converted to Christianity in 496 and defeated the Visigoths in 507.

Merovingian Family name of the Frankish kings, named after a fifth-century king Merovech.

Salic law Frankish law code introduced by Clovis in the early sixth century, named after the Salians, one of several Frankish peoples.

Theoderic the Great (r. 493–526) Ruler of the Ostrogothic kingdom in Italy.

their own Frankish subgroups. But Clovis also was politically savvy and knew how to use diplomacy when diplomacy suited his purpose. Advised by his wife, Clotilde, around 496, Clovis shrewdly adopted the Nicene Christian faith. As a consequence of becoming a Nicene Christian, Clovis gained support from the Roman population. In 507, he defeated the Visigoths at the Battle of Vouillé, and the Franks occupied most of Gaul. Like Germanic kings, Clovis issued a law code, the **Salic law**. It incorporated a Germanic practice whereby the perpetrators of crimes like murder, theft, or vandalism made fixed payments to their victims. Not long afterward, Clovis's sons annexed the Burgundian kingdom, and the Franks thus became the most important power in Gaul, eventually giving their name to modern France.

The Ostrogoths In 489, **Theoderic the Great**, king of the Ostrogoths, invaded Italy from the Balkans.

Four years later, Odovacar was defeated and the Ostrogoths created a kingdom that looked much like the Roman Empire. Theoderic made the Roman imperial city of Ravenna his capital and worked closely with the wealthy and powerful Italian senators. He issued legislation virtually indistinguishable from that of the empire. Many of the highest-ranking officials in the kingdom were Romans. The Senate of Rome even regained some of its old powers, such as the right to issue coins. The bishop of Rome, freed from imperial supervision, expanded his authority and began to monopolize the title of **pope**, which in the past had been applied to any distinguished bishop.

Bad Barbarians A few barbarian peoples, however, were less conciliatory. The Vandals of North Africa simply confiscated large tracts of Roman land and savagely persecuted Nicene Christians. And in Britain, the Roman population was forced to move out, to Wales or to Brittany in western France, by the Angles (whose name survives in modern England) and Saxons who, for the time being, retained their own Germanic culture.

The Byzantine Empire

In the fifth century, the eastern half of the Roman Empire, which can now be called the **Byzantine Empire** (after Byzantium, the original name of Constantinople), survived and even prospered.

The Emperor Theodosius II The Byzantine Empire experienced many of the same problems as the west, but it was better equipped to deal with them. The emperor **Theodosius II** (402–450 C.E.), the grandson of Theodosius the Great, ruled for nearly half a century. Theodosius was more of a scholar than a soldier. He expanded the university at Constantinople to contain thirty-one professors teaching law and philosophy along with grammar and public speaking. Greek became the preferred language, with Latin used mainly by administrators and lawyers. In 437, Theodosius issued the Theodosian Code, a comprehensive compilation of the legislation of Roman emperors going back to the time of Constantine. A treasure trove of information on administration, society, and the economy, it provides insights into what the emperors thought were the most important issues of their day.

The Huns The east, like the west, was threatened by barbarian attacks. In 400, the people of Constantinople responded to the barbarian menace by massacring several thousand Visigothic mercenaries. Theodosius then strengthened Constantinople's defenses by building massive walls on the city's landward side, doubling the size of the city. The greatest pressure came from the Huns, whose king, Attila, was kept from attacking by bribes of thousands of pounds of gold. After Theodosius's death in 450, the Byzantines stopped the tribute payments. The Huns then turned to the west, where, as already discussed, they were defeated in 451. In 453, Attila died, mysteriously, on his wedding night. The power of the Huns was broken forever when their subjects revolted and defeated them the next year. For the time being, the barbarian threat to the Byzantine Empire was reduced.

The New Persians During the fifth century, Byzantine relations with the New Persian Empire improved. The New Persians also were menaced by the Huns, and therefore the two empires made peace so each could concentrate on the more serious threat. The New Persians, who were Zoroastrians, also ceased persecuting their Christians subjects. By the early fifth century, Christians had become a tolerated minority in the New Persian Empire. Some Jews and dissident Christians even fled Byzantine religious oppression and took refuge with the New Persians.

Byzantine Politics Economic prosperity returned to the Byzantine world at the end of the fifth century. The introduction of a copper coinage that was interchangeable with the gold coinage restored confidence in the small-change currency that facilitated exchange at the local level. Revitalized trade brought increased tax revenues. Political problems, however, surfaced in the early sixth century with the growth of mob politics. Chariot-racing fan clubs known as the Blues and the Greens (from the colors that the racing teams wore) became thinly veiled political activist groups. They met in the Hippodrome and often used violence to support their views on matters ranging from theology to imperial appointments. During one riot, an emperor presented himself bareheaded and offered to resign. The fickle mob, impressed by his bravery, declined the offer.

Byzantine Religion In contrast to the west, where Christians were generally content with the Nicene faith, eastern Christians continued to dispute the nature of Christ, and the emperors often were compelled to intervene. The **Nestorians**, named after Nestorius, bishop of Constantinople, argued that while on earth Christ was just a man and that he was not divine until after the crucifixion. This viewpoint angered Nicene Christians, who believed that the divine and human natures of Christ were intermixed in a single substance and who viewed Mary as the Theotokos, or "mother of God."

pope (from Latin for "father") Title originally used for any distinguished bishop; by the sixth century, referred mainly to the bishop of Rome.

Byzantine Empire The continuation of the Roman Empire in the east after 476.

Theodosius II (r. 402–450) Byzantine emperor who issued the Theodosian Code in 437.

Nestorians Christians who believed that the divine and human natures of Christ were completely separate; the belief was condemned at the Council of Ephesus in 431; named after Nestorius, bishop of Constantinople.

In 431, at the third ecumenical council, summoned by Theodosius II at Ephesus on the Anatolian coast, Nestorianism was condemned. Many Nestorians then chose to go into exile in the New Persian Empire; some eventually even made their way to China.

Discussions about the nature of Christ then were revived by the **Monophysites**, who believed that Christ's human nature was was completely absorbed by his divine nature. In 451, a fourth ecumenical council, held at Chalcedon, just east of Constantinople, confirmed the belief that the divine and human natures of Christ were intermixed in a single substance and declared Monophysite teachings to be heresy. But the Monophysites refused to surrender their beliefs and continued to have a wide following in Egypt (where they survive as the modern Copts), in Syria (where a few thousand survive as the Jacobites), and in the New Persian Empire. The Council of Chalcedon also granted the bishop of Constantinople a status equal to that of the bishop of Rome. Bishop Leo the Great of Rome and his successors refused to accept the bishop of Constantinople as an equal, creating dissension between the eastern and western Christian churches.

Monophysites (from Greek for "single nature") Christians who believed that Christ had a single, divine nature; the belief was condemned at the Council of Chalcedon in 451.

The Emperor Justinian By 527, when the emperor Justinian came to the throne, the Byzantine Empire seemed secure. Economic prosperity had been restored, the barbarian threat had been contained, and religious dissent had been suppressed if not completely eliminated. It seemed that the empire in the east had avoided the misfortunes that caused the fall of the west, and its inhabitants could look to the future with optimism.

Checking In

By yourself or with a partner, explain the significance of each of the following selected key terms:

Arthur	Byzantine Empire
Clovis	Theodosius II
Theoderic the Great	Monophysites
pope	

CHAPTER
Review

Summary

- During Late Antiquity, momentous changes occurred in the Mediterranean world. The Roman Empire recovered from the civil wars of the third century and was revived by able emperors such as Diocletian and Constantine.

- During the Late Roman Empire, emperors took personal responsibility for ensuring the continued survival of the empire by issuing thousands of laws intended to deal with problems they identified.

- The emperors' efforts to restore the empire were hindered by difficulties in military recruitment, declining support from senators, and a growing split of the empire into eastern and western halves. A growing inability of the imperial government to provide security led many people to look for it elsewhere, such as under the protection of a powerful person.

- The most significant development of Late Antiquity was the expansion of Christianity beginning in 312, when the emperor Constantine began to favor the Christians openly. In a remarkably short period, Christianity evolved from a religion that was persecuted by the government to a universal state-sponsored religion that transformed the politics, society, and culture of the Roman world.

- Christianity changed how individual people thought about themselves and their world. Many people lived Christian lives that emphasized self-denial, personal spirituality, and community service. For many, the church now provided a place to find forms of spiritual and economic security the empire no longer was able to provide.

- In the middle of the fourth century, it looked like the Roman Empire was as sound as it had ever been, but this changed in 378, when the Roman army was defeated by the Visigoths at Adrianople, marking the beginning of the barbarian invasions.

- During the fifth century, barbarian peoples settled in the western half of the empire and established independent kingdoms, some of which eventually evolved into modern nations such as France and England.

- The synthesis of Roman and barbarian culture preserved classical culture, and western Europe evolved into an era known as the Middle Ages. In the eastern Mediterranean, what remained of the Roman Empire continued in the form now known as the Byzantine Empire.

◆ By the beginning of the sixth century, the political and cultural unity created by the Romans had disappeared and was replaced by diversity and fragmentation. New governments and religious institutions were introduced that continue, in various forms, to the modern day.

Chronology

284	Diocletian becomes emperor	392	Theodosius I makes Christianity the legal religion of the empire
303	Great Persecution begins	395	Roman Empire splits into eastern and western halves
306	Constantine becomes emperor		
312	Constantine defeats Maxentius at Battle of Milvian Bridge	406	Barbarians cross Rhine River
		410	Alaric and the Visigoths sack Rome
313	Edict of Milan grants religious freedom to Christians	437	Theodosius II issues Theodosian Code
325	Nicene Creed states official Christian beliefs	451	Romans defeat Huns at Battle of Châlons; Council of Chalcedon condemns the Monophysites
337	Constantine is baptized a Christian		
364	Valentinian I becomes emperor	476	Western Roman Empire falls
		481	Clovis becomes king of Franks
378	Visigoths defeat Romans at Battle of Adrianople	489	Ostrogoths invade Italy
387	Augustine baptized as a Christian	527	Justinian becomes Byzantine emperor

© Cengage Learning

Test Yourself

To gauge your mastery of the material in this chapter, answer the questions below. More than one answer may be correct.

The Restoration of the Roman Empire, 284–337

1. What measures did Diocletian use to reduce the chances of revolts?
   a. Raising the status of the emperor
   b. Removing power from the Senate
   c. Issuing legislation that made revolts illegal
   d. Dividing up sources of power
   e. Making mass arrests of dissidents

2. The Tetrarchy was designed to
   a. Deal with an empire too large and complex to be ruled by a single emperor.
   b. Divide the empire up into four separate and independent nations.
   c. Create a chain of command leading to Diocletian at the top.
   d. Deal with the problem of imperial succession.
   e. Provide for equal distribution of tax income.

3. Why did the Tetrarchy collapse?
   a. It failed to take into account the army's preference for emperors' sons.
   b. It was too cumbersome to function effectively.
   c. People had a hard time accepting the concept of four emperors.
   d. Diocletian chose colleagues who did not have military and administrative experience.
   e. Barbarian invasions could not be defeated.

4. Constantine built on the reforms of Diocletian by

   a. Creating a second capital of the empire in the east.
   b. Allowing the Senate to issue legislation.
   c. Putting the empire on the gold standard.
   d. Replacing the Tetrarchy with a system of dynastic succession.
   e. Using Christianity in the service of the empire.

Now that you have reviewed and tested yourself on this part of the chapter, take time to pull together all the important information by answering the following questions:

◆ What did Diocletian and Constantine do to try to restore order in the Roman Empire?
◆ How did the administration of the empire change during the late Roman period?

The Christian Empire, 312–415

5. How did Constantine show his support for Christianity?

   a. Issued the Edict of Milan
   b. Appointed bishops to government offices
   c. Convened church councils to settle Christian disputes
   d. Made Sunday a day of rest
   e. Required government officials to become Christian

6. Christians insulted non-Christians by referring to them as

   a. Bishops.
   b. Nicenes.
   c. Arians.
   d. Pagans.
   e. Barbarians.

7. Christians referred to the time when the world would end as the

   a. Apocalypse.
   b. Last Judgment.
   c. Second Coming of Christ.
   d. Golden Age.
   e. Consulate.

8. Who was the female philosopher murdered by Christian monks?

   a. Helena
   b. Hypatia
   c. Melania
   d. Monica
   e. Genevieve

Now that you have reviewed and tested yourself on this part of the chapter, take time to pull together all the important information by answering the following questions:

◆ In what ways did people express their devotion to Christianity?
◆ How did the Roman Empire change after Christianity was legalized?

Late Romans and Their World

9. One could become a senator by

   a. Holding a high-ranking office.
   b. Purchasing senatorial rank from the emperor.
   c. Being the child of a senator.
   d. Serving twenty-five years in the Roman army.
   e. Becoming wealthy.

10. Late Roman women could show their devotion to Christianity by

    a. Building churches.
    b. Serving as Christian bishops.
    c. Taking part in persecutions of pagans.
    d. Spending money on charitable works.
    e. Destroying pagan buildings.

11. Christians helped to preserve the pagan literary culture of antiquity by

    a. Copying manuscripts.
    b. Using Greek and Roman education in the service of the church.
    c. Burning only those pagan books that were considered to be heretical.
    d. Creating secret repositories where pagan classics could be stored.
    e. Reading pagan classics during church services.

Now that you have reviewed and tested yourself on this part of the chapter, take time to pull together all the important information by answering the following questions:

◆ Wht kinds of social, political, and cultural changes occurred during Late Antiquity?
◆ How did late Romans find security and new opportunities?

The Fall of the Western Roman Empire, 364–476

12. What problems confronted the western empire in the reign of Valentinian I?

   a. A government preference for the eastern part of the empire.
   b. Finding suitable recruits for the army.
   c. Excess agricultural production that could not be distributed quickly enough.
   d. Conflicts of interest between the eastern and western governments.
   e. A barbarian reluctance to settle on deserted land within the empire.

13. Which Roman emperor was killed at the Battle of Adrianople in 378?

   a. Diocletian
   b. Constantine
   c. Valentinian I
   d. Valens
   e. Theodosius

14. Which barbarian peoples followed the Arian version of Christianity?

   a. Franks
   b. Vandals
   c. Huns
   d. Burgundians
   e. Visigoths

15. What were Christians called who believed that Christ was just a man while he was on earth?

   a. Arians
   b. Nicenes
   c. Nestorians
   d. Monophysites
   e. Pagans

Now that you have reviewed and tested yourself on this part of the chapter, take time to pull together all the important information by answering the following questions:

◆ How did Romans and barbarians interact during Late Antiquity?
◆ What do you think were the causes of the fall of the Western Roman Empire?

The Post-Roman World, 400–527

16. What practices did barbarian kingdoms adopt from the Romans?

   a. Issuing laws
   b. Administrative practices
   c. Pagan religious rituals
   d. Using Roman officials
   e. Brewing beer

17. What was the dominant language in western Europe after the fall of the Romen Empire?

   a. Celtic
   b. German
   c. Latin
   d. Greek
   e. Gothic

18. Which barbarian peoples were least conciliatory toward the Roman population?

   a. Angles
   b. Visigoths
   c. Saxons
   d. Vandals
   e. Franks

19. The emperor Theodosius II is known for

   a. Defeating the Huns
   b. Issuing a law code
   c. Solving quarreling among Christians
   d. Introducing a new coinage system
   e. Reconquering the western Empire

Now that you have reviewed and tested yourself on this part of the chapter, take time to pull together all the important information by answering the following questions:

◆ In what ways did barbarian kingdoms preserve Roman culture and traditions?
◆ In what ways was the Byzantine Empire a continuation of the Roman Empire?

CHAPTER 8

The Eastern Mediterranean, 500–1000

Chapter Outline

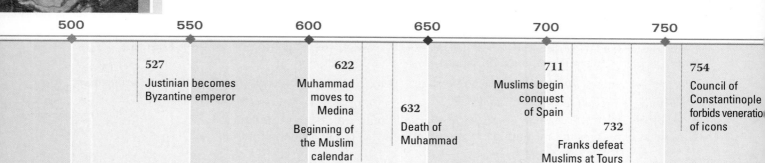

500	550	600	650	700	750

527
Justinian becomes Byzantine emperor

622
Muhammad moves to Medina

Beginning of the Muslim calendar

632
Death of Muhammad

711
Muslims begin conquest of Spain

732
Franks defeat Muslims at Tours

754
Council of Constantinople forbids veneration of icons

Life-size icons depicting Jesus Christ, like this sixth-century icon from the monastery of St. Catherine's in Sinai, can arrest the viewer's attention now as it must have done in the past. The direct gaze of the figure's asymmetrical eyes have made many historians wonder whether the painter intended to suggest Christ's dual nature. Christ's eyes hold the viewer's to encourage contemplation. (Jean-Luc Manaud/Getty Images)

After reading this chapter, you should be able to answer the following questions:

In what ways did Emperor Justinian seek to codify Christian belief?

How did the spread of Islam in the eighth century change the religious and political landscape of the Mediterranean?

What concerns did Byzantine emperors have about the use of icons in religious worship?

What factors contributed to the growing divide between the two halves of the old Roman Empire?

THE PEOPLE LIVING in the lands that once formed the Roman Empire hung on to the memory of their imperial past to varying extents. The western provinces of the old empire no longer had an emperor. A barbarian king ruled most of Italy, and North African, too, was under barbarian rule (shown in yellow and blue on the map). Those who lived in Constantinople (orange area of the map where Europe meets Asia) sensed they were living at the center of an ancient and thriving empire. The emperor Justinian, however, surely saw the situation differently. Despite his accomplishments, he understood that he had stretched his empire's resources as far as they would go. Enemies on the borders indicated that the empire was not really secure.

And indeed it was not. Justinian's successors could not halt the advance of an army that surged northward from the Arabian peninsula. The armies of Islam heralded the arrival of a new civilization that changed the balance of power in the Mediterranean from then on. As their armies moved across the landscape of the old Roman Empire (in green on the map), the Muslims subdued the populations in their path through a combination

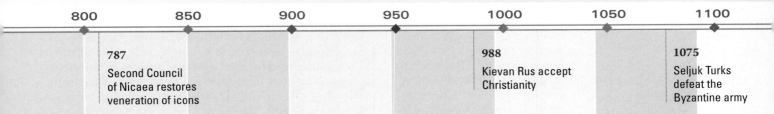

800	850	900	950	1000	1050	1100

787
Second Council of Nicaea restores veneration of icons

988
Kievan Rus accept Christianity

1075
Seljuk Turks defeat the Byzantine army

of brute force and persuasion. Islam spread westward across Africa into Spain and northward up to the gates of Constantinople. The Christian world saw a formidable adversary in Islam.

Even without the threat from the Muslims, the Byzantine emperors—as the rulers in the east are now called—faced problems that threatened to provoke political unrest and even civil war. Theological controversies were so serious that they destabilized the government. In the eighth century, an emperor's ban against the use of images, or icons, in Christian worship deeply divided the empire's subjects. By the eleventh century, the old Roman Empire had irreversibly dissolved into political blocs, divided between Christian and Muslim. Islam, relying on one language, stood in strong contrast to Christianity, whose sacred texts and commentaries existed in both Greek and Latin. By 1000, few Christians could read both. The political and religious unity that had been so important to Justinian and his predecessors was gone, as was the idea of the Mediterranean world as Roman.

Justinian and the Revival of the Empire in the East, 500–650

- ◆ **What were the causes and consequences of Justinian's attempt to reunify the old empire?**
- ◆ **What were the lasting achievements of Justinian's reign?**

Of all the emperors to rule the Byzantine Empire, Justinian left the longest-lasting legacy. When he ascended the throne in 527 at age forty-five, he shared it with his uncle, Justin I, an old peasant from the Balkan region in the western provinces who had risen through the ranks of the army and been acclaimed emperor for lack of any legitimate heirs or stronger candidates. The co-emperors ruled together for only one year before Justin died. From then on, Justinian's most trusted adviser was his wife, Theodora, and together they set out to restore lost territory to imperial rule and to unify the people under their rule in one church. Recovered territory, glorious new monuments adorning the largest city in the empire, and the codification of ancient imperial law all represented a level of achievement not experienced within living memory. That Justinian managed to stay in power for nearly half a century and die of old age should by itself be considered an accomplishment, given the fate of many Roman emperors before him.

Justinian's Ambitions

From an imperial perspective, the old Roman Empire was gone. Barbarians had established kingdoms in Italy, Spain, Gaul, Britain, and the provinces of North Africa. The western provinces had not had an emperor for nearly half a century, and many eastern provinces had fallen into the control of the Persians. When **Justinian I**, a common soldier from the Balkans, succeeded to the imperial throne, he would have seen restoring the empire as his mission.

Reconquest Reconquering territory was accomplished in arduous stages. After his first target, the Crimea, succumbed easily, Justinian turned his attention to the Vandal kingdom of North Africa, which fell to the forces of his brilliant general **Belisarius** in 534. The conquest of Italy, now in the hands of the Ostrogoths, proved much more difficult. Belisarius arrived in 535; it took seventeen years to end Ostrogothic rule. Though Italy once again came under Byzantine rule in 552, the triumph was costly. Not only were Italy's cities and countryside devastated, but the Byzantine army and treasury were also much weakened.

Justinian's insistence on recapturing Italy put an enormous strain on the empire's resources. He sometimes had to cancel the salaries of his own troops for lack of funds—and then put down their rebellions. With his attention focused on the western provinces, he was compelled to pay off the Persians in the east to discourage them from invading. By building costly fortifications along the border, he managed to keep the **Slavs** on the far side of the northern frontier.

Justinian I (r. 527–565) Byzantine emperor noted for his reconquest of lost territory, building program, and comprehensive law code.

Belisarius (505–565) Sixth-century general who led the Byzantine army to successes in Persia, North Africa, and the Italian peninsula.

Slavs A loose confederation of peoples originating in eastern Europe who pressed into the empire at various times, becoming a serious threat in the seventh century.

Map 8.1 **Justinian's Empire** Out of the old Roman world emerged three civilizations. In western Europe, the barbarian kingdoms adapted the Latin language. In Constantinople, the new center of the old empire, the people spoke Greek. To the south, the Muslims introduced Arabic to North Africa, Syria, and Palestine. © *Cengage Learning*

1. Why would possession of the city of Antioch matter to Justinian?
2. Locate where the emerging frontiers separating the three civilizations lay.
3. Looking at the civilizations on either side of Justinian's empire, what challenges did his armies confront in those parts of the world?

But his treasury's resources were stretched to their limits. As the old Romans knew, maintaining an empire never came cheaply.

Ceremony Maintaining the emperor's dignity was also difficult, especially since this emperor did not come from an aristocratic family. Unprecedented grandeur and increased rigidity in court ceremonies, designed to instill obedience to the emperor, may have been Justinian's way of asserting his legitimacy to rule. In every aspect of his person—from his appearance to his role in church policy—Justinian projected his belief that he ruled with God's sanction. Even his daily life was orchestrated to impress on those around him the measure of his authority. While visitors waited in the large audience hall in Constantinople to see

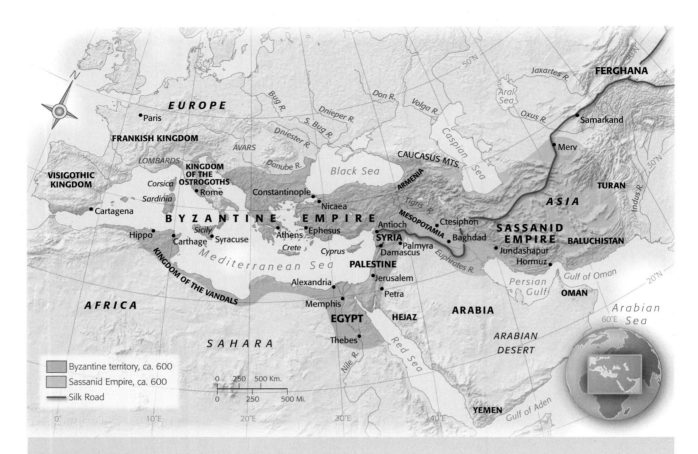

Map 8.2 **From the Roman Empire to the Byzantine Empire** Justinian's armies restored much of the old empire's territories and luster. By the year 600, the greatest power in the Mediterranean region was the eastern half of the old Roman Empire, now called the Byzantine Empire. Its main rival was not the Frankish kingdom to the northwest, but the Sassanid Empire to the east. © *Cengage Learning*

1. Looking at the detail in this map, which region of the Byzantine Empire was economically vital to its interests? Why?
2. Which frontiers would the Byzantine emperors be concerned to protect? Why?
3. Why did the Italian peninsula matter to Justinian and his successors?

him, he and the empress **Theodora**, dressed in sumptuous robes of royal purple bordered in gold, entered an area behind a curtain. On the other side of the curtain, the hushed, expectant crowd would have examined the imposing mosaics that covered the walls and floor. Once the royal couple took their places on their thrones, attendants placed jeweled crowns on their heads. Then, when all was ready, royal attendants drew back the curtain to reveal Justinian and Theodora in all their awesome splendor. Instantly, the supplicants prostrated themselves.

For all the majesty the imperial couple projected, it annoyed some visitors, especially the aristocrats, that they had to bend down and touch their foreheads to the floor and then kiss the knees of first the emperor and then the empress. Being forced to grovel was bad enough. Acting like a cowering slave before two people from humble origins made it that much worse. Never before, some believed, had two people of such base origins demanded such extravagant displays of submission to imperial authority.

Their insistence on excessive homage notwithstanding, Justinian and Theodora had reason to be proud of themselves. It had been a long time since the empire's fortunes had looked as good as they did in the first half of the sixth century, thanks to Justinian's energy and Theodora's mostly beneficial influence on her husband.

The Search for Christian Unity

Long before Justinian came to the throne, church leaders had taken notice of imperial court ceremony. Recognizing the power of presentation, they designed churches to resemble the emperor's audience hall, placing the altar at one end of a long rectangular room, screened from public view by a curtain. By staging the

Theodora (497–548) Emperor Justinian I's wife and empress, who had much influence on her husband's political and religious policies.

most important elements of the Communion ceremony behind the curtain, out of sight of the congregants, they heightened the mystery of the **Mass**. Once the priest had consecrated the bread and wine and given Communion to the clergy around the altar, he passed through the curtain to dispense Communion to the **laity** waiting on the other side. Imperial ceremony had provided a model to the clergy seeking to enhance the central mystery of the Christian religion. And Justinian fully supported whatever strengthened the church.

Authority The respect commanded by the emperor—no matter how low his social origins—bore a close resemblance to the authority owed a bishop or priest. Justinian, as a successor of Constantine the Great, claimed the right to convene and preside over church councils—something no barbarian king in the west had the right to do. Although he could not celebrate the Mass or administer the sacraments, the emperor was the only layman to witness the Eucharist ceremony behind the curtain that separated the people from the altar area, and he was allowed to preach in church. For this reason, the Byzantine emperors saw themselves as on a par with the patriarch of Constantinople and thus equal to all other patriarchs and archbishops, including (most controversially from a western point of view) the pope, who saw himself as the spiritual head of all Christendom. Justinian, then, wielded religious authority that enhanced his imperial authority, although no one at the time would have perceived a distinction between the two.

Belief Theology was one area in which this royal husband and wife diverged in their outlooks. Although the Council of Chalcedon in 451 had formally condemned the Monophysites, many people in the eastern empire continued to believe that Christ had only one nature—a divine, not a human nature. The empress Theodora was one of them. Justinian, a staunch supporter of the Nicene Creed, disliked all viewpoints that disagreed with the church, but he believed that persecuting Monophysites would diminish the chances of reconciling them with the church. His tolerant approach early in his reign was also influenced by his Monophysite-leaning wife. Theodora protected Monophysite monks, **nuns**, and clergy who faced persecution from local **ecclesiastical** authorities. It was the empress who made it possible for Monophysites to form churches in Armenia, Egypt, and Syria.

Nonetheless, Justinian had to enforce the church's condemnation of Monophysites. When his attempts to bring prominent Monophysites into line with church teachings failed, he sent them into exile. He showed a strong inclination to stamp out those who did not adhere to church teachings or to the church itself. On his orders, Jews and followers of pre-Christian religions suffered persecution. Although earlier Christian thinkers had produced valuable theological works that employed Platonic philosophy, Justinian forbade the study of any pre-Christian philosophy and closed Plato's Academy in Athens. In an intellectual environment that discouraged critical examination of non-Christian texts, Christian thinkers placed those ancient works on their library shelves and forgot about them.

The Codification of Roman Law

Early in his reign, Justinian commissioned legal scholars to gather into one work the legislation of previous Roman emperors and the canon law of all the church councils as well as the legal opinions of Roman jurists. The project, which sought to extend the great Theodosian Code of the early fifth century, lasted decades, from the issuance of the first volume in 533 to the publication of the most recent laws in 565. This **Body of Civil Law** provided a systematic approach to law that had as its underlying principle: "Justice is the constant and perpetual wish to render to every one his due." The Civil Law remained the law of the Byzantine Empire until the fifteenth century and became the foundation of every modern-day legal system in continental Europe.

One basic distinction laid down by Justinian's law was that between a free person and a slave. A free person was someone endowed with the right to conduct affairs in civil society. A slave was the opposite: not quite a "thing," but not a person either, endowed with freedom by nature but deprived of civil rights by human society. Roman law proceeded on the convoluted logical grounds that a slave could not own property because he was property. A free man could not be property because he could own property. In this way, when Justinian's commissioners began to work out which ancient laws fit into their framework of legal principles, they provided the institution of slavery—already long in existence—with a rationale that governments would also rely on for more than a thousand years.

Family Law Family life also profoundly felt the impact of Roman law. At the heart of this legal system was the **patria potestas**, the legal head of household. In Justinian's day, the head of the household was the guardian of everyone in his household, all of whom were legally subordinated

Mass Christian liturgical ceremony in which the officiating priest symbolically reenacts Jesus' Last Supper with his disciples.

laity (adj. **lay**) Collective term used to refer to everyone except the clergy.

nun Woman who has entered a monastic order for women to lead a life of prayer and contemplation.

ecclesiastical Pertaining to a church.

Body of Civil Law Justinian's three-volume codification issued between 533 and 563, containing the laws and jurist opinions of the Roman Empire and the canons issued by church councils.

patria potestas (in Latin, "paternal authority") Legal authority of a head of household, usually a father, over the members of his household, including his family, servants, and slaves.

Empress Theodora Changes Emperor Justinian's Mind

In January 532, rioting throughout the city of Constantinople shook the imperial court to the core. Crowds attacked and burnt down the great church of Hagia Sophia, rebuilt by Constantine II in the 350s. Emperor Justinian I and the empress Theodora had barricaded themselves, with their supporters, in the royal palace, fearful of what would happen next. In the preceding days, Justinian's soldiers had tried to stop the violence that had broken out between the Greens and the Blues—the rival fans of chariot-racing teams who also held competing political and religious views. The emperor and empress preferred the Blues, but no one really knows what this uprising, which came to be called the *Nika Riot*, was about. The only person to write about the riot was the historian Procopius, who simply condemned the passions of all who confused their enthusiasm for sports and entertainment with politics and religion.

Nevertheless, the crowd was now contemplating an overthrow of the political order. The rioters forced two nephews of a previous emperor to join in their plans, which were to attack the imperial palace and kill the imperial couple. The danger to Justinian and Theodora increased by the hour. When the emperor and his advisers were told that the army could not guarantee his safety, Justinian decided to evacuate the city and try to regroup on the opposite side of the Bosporus.

But at this moment, according to Procopius, the empress Theodora made a courageous decision that Justinian was unable to make on his own: she urged her husband and his advisers to remain and fight. With great dignity, the empress reasoned:

> If now it is your wish to save yourself, O Emperor, there is no difficulty. For we have much money, and there is the sea, here the boats. However, consider whether it will not come about after you have been saved that you would gladly exchange that safety for death. For as for myself, I approve a certain ancient saying that royal purple is fitting for a burial shroud.

With Theodora's support, Justinian resolved to stay in his palace. Summoning his general Belisarius, he ordered that the rioters be put down. Belisarius succeeded, but only by killing tens of thousands of the people of Constantinople. When the slaughter ended and peace returned to the capital, Justinian undertook the rebuilding of Hagia Sophia, this time on an unprecedented scale. The emperor and the empress entered the newly restored church five years after the Nika Riot. Thanks in part to Theodora's cool head and brave heart, the people of Constantinople once again accustomed themselves to the rule of this imperial couple.

It may seem surprising that Theodora should have been the one to give her husband courage because nothing in her background suggested she would succeed in any endeavor other than the popular theater. Her father reputedly worked in a circus, an atmosphere associated with prostitution and rough customers. Before she married Justinian, many people in Constantinople knew of her from her circus performances and as the lover of powerful men. Justinian, too, came from a humble family, but his military service under his uncle, an emperor who had first risen through the ranks of the Byzantine army, gave him the experience in commanding others that the office of emperor required. The young actress and courtesan Theodora, in contrast, must have possessed an exceptional intelligence and aptitude for politics that marriage to the ambitious soldier and future emperor released. Her influence over her husband aroused the envy of less powerful members of the imperial court, who spread rumors about her past to undermine her reputation. Whether the stories in circulation about her lewd behavior were true or false, never had a woman from as humble a background as Theodora's attained the rank of empress.

Source: From Procopius's biography of the empress Theodora (c. 500–565).

to his will, including not only his family but also his servants and slaves. A husband governed his wife, his children, his servants, and his slaves in the same way a ruler governed his people. In contrast to women in western Europe, however, Byzantine women enjoyed property rights and retained ownership over their dowries after marriage, although their husbands had the authority to manage their investments.

Commerce By regulating the relationship between people and property, Roman law also had a deep and lasting effect on commerce. By the sixth century, the head of a family who wanted to transfer property in a way that ensured that enforcement of the agreed-upon terms (such as price or length of possession) would resort to a **contract**. Contracts, most of which were verbal but just as binding as written ones, invoked the power of the law in case one party did not abide by the terms. Traders made the greatest use of them, but contracts were also used in the transmission of property within and between families. In his lifetime, a father would hand over property to children by means of a contract but

contract Framework of rules and legal remedies for an agreement.

resort to the laws relating to succession and inheritance to direct the distribution of his property after death. Marriage amounted to little more than a contract to sanction the legal union of members of two families so that the couple's children would have a legal right to inherit both families' property. Because it provides instruments to manage relationships between people and between people and property, Roman law remains the foundation of legal systems throughout western Europe and the United States.

Constantinople: The New Rome

Standing under the immense dome of Hagia Sophia in Constantinople, a subject of Justinian might be forgiven for thinking that this was the center of the world. Under severe financial constraints when he rebuilt the basilica following its destruction in the Nika Riot of 532 (see A New Direction: Empress Theodora Changes Emperor Justinian's Mind), Justinian hired two amateur builders whose daring must have horrified professional architects of the time. Indeed, that immense dome, 180 feet above the stone pavement, would collapse in 558, only to be rebuilt even more steeply within a few years.

To the ordinary person, the effect of standing under the dome in the immense central nave must have been spectacular. The awed observer would have noticed subtle gradations of colors in the marble walls and, on the flat surfaces at the top of arches on either side of the nave, mosaic images depicting sacred figures against a shimmering background of gold leaf. Light entered through arched windows set around the base of the dome and the exterior walls. Hagia Sophia made worshipers feel God's majesty.

Crowds standing outside Hagia Sophia in the hot sun felt no less a sense of overwhelming majesty. The immense bulk of the building dominated the space around it, with the imperial palace complex on one side, near the Hippodrome, itself capable of seating thousands of spectators at the chariot races. To the east was the Sea of Marmora. A merchant sailing into port would have seen Hagia Sophia first, for it towered over the city. With its exceptional harbor, the Byzantine capital drew merchants not only from the Mediterranean but also from as far away as India and Scandinavia. Spices, glass, ceramics, silks, furs, and timber—almost anything a person might want— were for sale in the city's **bazaars**. For the people of Constantinople, if Hagia Sophia was the center of the world, then their city was the epicenter of commerce.

The commercial world was a very masculine place. Men of all ages, origins, and social status crowded the narrow streets lined with low, flat-roofed buildings and bazaars. Respectable Byzantine women stayed out of sight in the women's quarters of their households and wore veils when they ventured into public. Servant men and women did the household shopping. Only disreputable women, such as actresses,

Erich Lessing/Art Resource, NY

Hagia Sophia's immense dome was meant to instill in the visitor a sense of awe. When the Ottoman Turks converted the church into a mosque in the fifteenth century, they replaced many of the mosaics of Christian imagery with Quranic quotations. Is the enormous space you see in the photo meant to be a public space where all were welcome? Or was it meant to be an awe-inspiring sacred space exclusively for the emperor and clergy?

prostitutes, slaves, and tavern keepers, circulated freely and unveiled in the streets of cities and towns.

Constantinople reflected the achievements of Justinian's reign in the jostle of the market crowds, the white marble of its monuments, and the throngs of galleys moored in its harbor. But its very density made it vulnerable to natural disasters. In 542, the same year in which an earthquake flattened parts of the city, a horrifying epidemic of **bubonic plague** devastated the population. It killed indiscriminately, ceased, and then flared up again somewhere else. By some accounts, nearly half the population living around the Mediterranean died during the following thirty years. Once bustling cities seemed empty of residents. In the Syrian city of Antioch, a man by the name of Evagrius left an account that reveals an elementary idea of contagion:

> Some perished by merely living with the infected, others by only touching them, others by having entered their chamber,

bazaar Market in a Muslim city that can be either enclosed or in the open.

bubonic plague Disease caused by the bacillus *Yersina pestis* that attacks the lymph glands and is nearly always fatal if not treated with antibiotics.

Justinian's Hagia Sophia (Holy Wisdom) stands out in the skyline of modern Istanbul just as it did in the sixth century. When an architectural wonder such as this church dominates an urban landscape like this church did in Constantinople, how might the people of the city view it?

others by frequenting public places. Some, having fled from the infected cities, escaped themselves, but imparted the disease to the healthy.... Some, too, who were desirous of death, on account of the utter loss of their children and friends, and with this view placed themselves as much as possible in contact with the diseased, were nevertheless not infected; as if the pestilence struggled against their purpose.

The high mortality rate led to hardship throughout the empire. Landowners took possession of lands left vacant by the epidemic and ruthlessly pushed peasants off their small plots of land and into poverty. Heavy taxation forced many others to give up farming. The landless peasants moved to urban centers in the hope of finding work or at least charity. Once there, they found soaring prices and rents, but also higher wages, because labor had become scarce. In 544, the emperor attempted to halt the rise in the cost of living by issuing an edict prohibiting wage and price increases: "In the future no businessman, workman, or artisan in any occupation, trade, or agricultural pursuit shall dare to charge a higher price or wage than that of the custom prevalent from antiquity." Such stern measures in hard times barely kept a bad economic situation from becoming much worse.

Justinian, who lived until his seventies, brought back into the empire the territory it had lost; he constructed some of the most beautiful churches and public monuments his subjects had ever seen; and he and his wife had averted their overthrow by mobs. Plagues and earthquakes, however, disrupted his ability to lay down a solid basis for the empire's continued geographical expansion and military defense.

The Empire After Justinian

The pressures on the empire only increased after Justinian's death in 565. Even if his successors had been his equal in energy, administrative ability, and shrewdness, ruling the empire was not an enviable task. The **Lombards**, a people from northern Europe, began their gradual conquest of the Italian peninsula after Justinian's death. By the end of the eighth century, they had taken most of northern Italy. Large bands of people living beyond the borders of the empire pressed harder and harder on the frontiers. Epidemics of plague continued to weaken the empire's economy and reduce its population. Tensions among Christians with divergent views of Christ's nature increased and became entrenched along regional lines. The long decline of the Byzantine Empire had begun.

New Pressures By the time of **Heraclius**, in the seventh century, the empire was in sore need of a strong military leader. What began as a migration of Slavs into the empire looked more and more like an invasion when they resisted efforts to hold back their advances. The **Avars**, a people related to the Huns, also tried to force their way over the frontier. They pushed into the Balkans and, by 617, had reached the outskirts of Constantinople. At the same time, the Persians on the eastern flank chipped off pieces of Mesopotamia, Syria, and Armenia. In 613, the capture of Jerusalem by the Persians stung the Christian empire, particularly when Persian soldiers looted and destroyed the Church of the Holy Sepulcher, founded by Helena, Constantine the Great's mother, in the fourth century. The Persians took away with them what the faithful believed to be a piece of the True Cross on which Jesus had been crucified. The problem for Heraclius, then, was to stop further erosion of the empire's territory and to reclaim land already lost, especially Jerusalem.

With an almost empty treasury, Heraclius devised ways to generate the revenue he needed to maintain an army in the field. These methods did not make him popular, but they helped him achieve his goals. He confiscated church furnishings made of

Lombards A northern German people who crossed the Alps and in 572, and established a kingdom based in northern Italy.

Heraclius (r. 610–641) Emperor who recovered the Byzantine Empire's eastern provinces and defeated the Persian Empire.

Avars A people originally from western Asia who settled in eastern Europe in the sixth century.

Vanni/Art Resource, NY

precious metals to melt them into much-needed coinage. He reformed the tax system, making it harsher but more efficient. Extensive as these and other measures were, they were barely enough. It took Heraclius more than fifteen years to recapture all the lands lost to the Persians. The situation looked grim when the Avars to the north allied with the Persians to the east and attacked Constantinople. After bribing the Avars to cease their attack, Heraclius turned his attention to the Persians. He pushed them so far back into their own territory that their utter defeat in 628 took place close to their own capital of Ctesiphon.

Humiliated, the Persians returned the relic of the True Cross, which Heraclius himself carried back to Jerusalem. In 630, the emperor entered the holy city, reportedly dressed as a humble pilgrim, walking barefoot into the old, ruined Church of the Holy Sepulcher. There he prostrated himself on the floor before placing the relic, now sealed in a protective container, back in its original place.

Neither the relic, nor the church, nor Jerusalem remained in Christian hands for long. No sooner had Heraclius achieved his goal of regaining the territory lost to the Persians than he had to face a surprising and even more formidable threat from the south: a new religion called *Islam*.

Checking In

By yourself or with a partner, explain the significance of each of the following selected key terms:

Justinian I	Body of Civil Law
Theodora	patria potestas
Mass	bubonic plague
laity	Lombards

The Rise of Islam, 600–700

◆ **What did Muhammad view as necessary to a worthy life?**

◆ **In which ways did Muslims view the world similarly to the way Christians and Jews viewed it, and in which ways did they view it differently?**

In the late sixth century, few people in the Byzantine Empire remembered the ties they had once had with the people in the western half of the old Roman Empire. Not even a shared faith kept alive the bond that had once existed. The demise of the western empire reoriented the Byzantines toward Syria and Palestine, where Christianity began and where the empire's frontiers needed protection. In the markets of Jerusalem, merchants from Byzantium encountered traders from the Arabian peninsula, Egypt, and even as far away as India. The mix of people of many faiths and from many cultures created an atmosphere of religious and cultural exchange whose influence could be felt across the entire region. In this spiritually fertile environment, a new religion took root and flourished.

The Arabian Peninsula

Located between Africa to the west and the Persian Empire to the east, the Arabian peninsula had long been accustomed to seasonal **caravans** of traders and pilgrims. It was, and is, a harsh, forbidding desert land. The western coastline of the Red Sea contains the peninsula's only fertile soil, and in the seventh century even that land was sparsely cultivated. The area's chief value was that it lay on the route from the Syrian and Persian market centers in the north and east to the markets across the Red Sea in Egypt and Libya. Few cities enlivened the barren landscape.

Instead of relying on agriculture, the Arabian peoples were nomads who depended for their food largely on date palms and goats. Left pretty much to themselves, the people of the coastal plain, including communities of Jews, lived and worked in places where caravans stopped to sell their wares. Unlike the cities of Asia Minor, which were teeming with visitors, merchants, traders, and pilgrims, Arabian towns saw only traders on their way to the ferries that crossed the Red Sea or pilgrims coming to worship at local shrines dedicated to gods believed to reside in sacred rocks and trees. The region seemed so uninviting that even would-be conquerors, like the Romans, did not spend much time there. Indeed, Arabian towns benefited from the disruptive warfare to the north between the Byzantine and Persian armies, which compelled traders to find safer southern routes to the distant markets of Africa.

Before Muhammad At the center of the town of **Mecca**, located about fifty miles inland from the Red Sea, stands a fifty-foot-high cube-shaped building called the **Kaaba**. It has only one door, seven feet above the ground on its northeastern side, which leads into a room containing only hanging lamps and inscriptions on the wall. Embedded in the outside wall of the building's eastern corner is a black rock—perhaps made of lava, or even meteoric— that today is held together by a band of silver. No building is holier to Muslims than this cube, surrounded by a broad plaza and a covered walkway. It stands at the heart of Islamic ritual and at the heart of Islam itself. Tradition has it that it was built by Abraham, whom Muslims call "the first submitter," the first human to submit to the will of God. Having long served as a shrine for

caravan Group of merchants traveling with their wares to distant markets.

Mecca City of Muhammad's birth, located in the western part of the Arabian peninsula, toward which Muslims pray.

Kaaba Shrine in the form of a large cube—its name derived from the Arabic word for *cube*—located in Mecca (today, in Saudi Arabia).

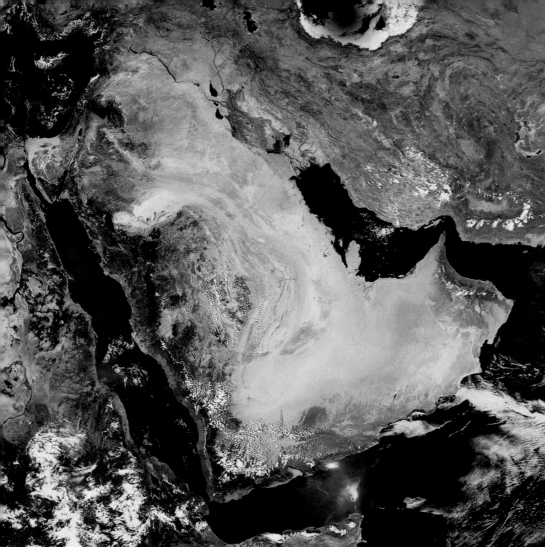

Nearly all of the fertile land in the Arabian peninsula lies on its western coast along the Red Sea. A trade route connected Jerusalem to Medina and Mecca. Looking at the satellite image, which areas most likely to be in contact? Which regions would likely be in touch by sea and which by land?

NASA/Getty Images

the local gods, the Kaaba almost certainly predates the city of Mecca itself, which grew up around the shrine. By the end of the sixth century, one large tribe or clan, the Quraysh, dominated the town's economy. Among the wealthiest merchants in Mecca, the Quraysh also served as political leaders. Given their role as guardians of Mecca's pilgrimage and caravan trade, the Quraysh elders would not have approved of anyone who threatened to undermine their economic dominance, even if the threat came from one of their own.

The Life of Muhammad

About five years after the death of Justinian in Constantinople, the life of a man who would found one of the great monotheistic religions of the world began in this town of Mecca, far from the centers of cosmopolitan living in the Byzantine Empire. Around the year 570, **Muhammad**, whom Muslims call the Last Prophet, was born into a humble family belonging to the Quraysh tribe. Orphaned at an early age, Muhammad had the good fortune to marry a merchant's widow, Khadidja, for whom he was working. By taking over the management of Khadidja's trading business, he improved his social standing. Occasionally, he traveled to Palestine and Syria, where he encountered Christians and Jews, whose sacred writings impressed him greatly.

Conversion After he turned forty, Muhammad's conception of the world and of humanity's duties toward God began to take clearer shape. He often withdrew to a remote place on the outskirts of Mecca to meditate. One day, he believed he had a vision of the archangel Gabriel standing astride the horizon in the distance. The angel three times commanded, "Muhammad, recite!" When he opened his mouth, Muhammad began to utter the sayings Muslims believe to be the words of God. Eventually Muhammad's recitations, called **sura**, were written down by his followers and compiled to form the **Quran**. They expressed a belief in one God—Allah—and described the path to achieving salvation.

At first, the messages Muhammad received went no farther than his own household. His wife, Khadidja, became Islam's first convert. But others, too,

Muhammad (570–632) Founder of Islam; Muslims believe he was the last prophet in a line of biblical prophets stretching back to Abraham.

sura Quranic verses representing the word of God.

Quran Sacred book of Islam (formerly written in Roman letters as "Koran").

began to find Muhammad's exhortations to live lives of prayer and charitable purpose appealing. Muhammad was offering the Meccans Allah as a substitute for the tribal gods and, ultimately, for tribal loyalty. As the number of converts grew and Muhammad began to speak out against the traditional gods of Mecca, the town's powerful families, who benefited financially from the pilgrimages to the Kaaba, viewed Muhammad with increasing hostility.

Exile As tensions between Muslims and the authorities in Mecca grew, it seemed likely that Muhammad and his followers would be banished. Just then, the people of **Medina**, a smaller town a few hundred miles to the north, invited Muhammad and his followers to come and lead them. The prominent families of Medina, who frequently engaged in disputes that threatened the peace of the town, felt the need for an objective outsider to come among them as a mediator. The Medinans were looking for a political leader, not a religious one. Instead, they got both in one man. The year Muhammad left Mecca to go to Medina, 622, marks the beginning of the Muslim calendar, and his journey there is called the **Hejira**.

Muhammad brought political and religious unity to Medina, primarily by forcing out the Jews, most of whom would not convert to his new religion. Up to that point, the early Muslims had prayed facing in the direction of Jerusalem because they, like the Jews, revered the holy city. But not long after he and his followers moved to Medina, Muhammad substituted the town from which they had been exiled, Mecca, as the focal point of worship, thereby reducing Jerusalem to the rank of the second holiest city of Islam. But Muhammad was determined to become a political and economic force whom the leaders of Mecca could not afford to ignore. To undermine the Meccan economy, he conducted raids on caravans heading there. Eventually, in 630, the leaders of Mecca had to negotiate with Muhammad. At the head of his community of followers, Muhammad returned to Mecca and took up the role as head of the Quraysh clan and the ruler of the city. Now the political leader of both Medina and Mecca, Muhammad set out to convert the tribes of Arabia to his new way of life.

By the time he died in Medina in 632, Muhammad had very nearly realized his ambition. The peoples of the Arabian peninsula had accepted him as their spiritual and political leader, and in his last years he had established the rituals and practices of Muslim life. Nine days before his death, Muhammad passed on his last recitation to the supporters whose responsibility was to write them down.

The Religion of Islam

It is important to understand that Muhammad's role in Islam is not analogous to Jesus' role in Christianity.

Built prior to Muhammad's lifetime, the Kaaba is constructed of bricks and mortar, draped with a cloth embroidered with Quranic quotations, and serves as the focus of pilgrims to Mecca. What kinds of services would Meccans have provided for the many pilgrims arriving to worship at the Kaaba?

Instead, Jesus is to Christianity what the Quran is to Islam: both are believed to be physical manifestations of God's Word. Christians understand the New Testament Gospels as divinely inspired historical witnesses of sacred events, but Muslims view the Quran itself as a sacred event. In other words, it represents the very words of God, which came through the mouth of a mortal man, Muhammad, for whom Muslims claim no supernatural powers.

Five Pillars The words *Islam* and *Muslim* share a common linguistic root, which means "surrender" or "submission to God's will." In establishing his new religion, Muhammad envisioned a new way of life that would enact that obedience to God's will. A worthy life proceeds from the **Five Pillars of Islam**, actions that shape every individual Muslim's life and the life of the Muslim community as a whole.

Medina Town to which Muhammad and his followers emigrated from Mecca and where he served as a civic leader.

Hejira Muhammad's flight, or "pilgrimage," to Medina in the year 622, the first year in the Muslim calendar.

Five Pillars of Islam The basic duties of every Muslim: acknowledgment of one God, prayer five times a day, fasting at set times of the year, charity, and a pilgrimage to Mecca at least once in a lifetime.

The first pillar is the admission that "there is no God but God and Muhammad was his prophet," the first line heard in the calls to prayer that ring out at set times during the day in **mosques** everywhere. This profession of faith is so important to Muslims that the only action necessary to convert to Islam is to repeat the admission three times in the presence of qualified witnesses.

Once God is acknowledged, every Muslim has a duty to pray five times throughout the day, the second pillar of Islam. Muslims pray for the same reasons that Christians and Jews pray: to express their devotion to God. Facing in the direction of Mecca (no matter where they are in the world), Muslims kneel and press their heads to the floor several times before sitting upright on the back of their heels with their outstretched palms opened on either side of the body. The third pillar of Muslim life is fasting. Muhammad intended fasting to be a reminder of how temporary life is and how inconsequential material possessions are. During **Ramadan**, the ninth and holiest month in the Islamic calendar, Muslims fast during the daytime, not eating until after sunset. Muhammad designated charity as the fourth pillar in the belief that Muslims were responsible for one another and for the Islamic community as a whole. More than a set of beliefs and a set of practices, Islam involved political allegiance from the very beginning. In this respect it is unlike Christianity, which did not become the exclusive religion of the Roman Empire until nearly three centuries after the death of its founder.

Finally, Muhammad expected every believer to make at least one pilgrimage to Mecca—the **Hajj**. But, by not making the pilgrimage strictly mandatory, he took into account the limited means of the poor and sick to fulfill this obligation. Over the course of a set week in the Muslim calendar, pilgrims who do go to Mecca perform a series of rituals established by Muhammad in the last year of his life. Muhammad meant for the five pillars of Islam to give shape to the lives of all Muslims by uniting them in common purpose and action.

People of the Book

According to the Quran, Muslims, Jews, and Christians are all people of the book—namely, the Hebrew Bible. All three religions consider themselves descendants of the biblical patriarch Abraham, whose god became the God of Jews, Christians, and then Muslims. Muhammad acknowledged the figures in the Hebrew Bible and Jesus as prophets, but he did not believe, as Christians do, that through Jesus' death and resurrection God offered salvation to humanity. In Muhammad's view, humans still had not heeded God's injunctions to live righteous and moral lives. Since Muslims revere as prophets the same biblical figures that Jews and Christians do and believe in the same God, Muslims consider the Hebrew and Christian Bibles (the Old and New Testaments) to be sacred texts, but in their view, the compilation of God's messages in the Quran is the final and most authoritative divine statement.

Christians and Jews From the start, religious authority and political authority in Islam were the same. When Muhammad became the political leader of Arabia, the religious and the political aspects of his authority, and that of his successors, blended into one. In contrast, in the western church, political authority over Christians came to be mediated through kings and emperors. Jesus never held political power, and his religious authority until his death was limited to a small group of followers. Because the church developed independently of the authority of kings in the west, it remained distinct from political institutions even where it assumed political responsibility in cities with weak governments. Consequently, a Christian living somewhere in western Europe looked to the king for protection and justice, whereas a Muslim in Damascus looked to religious leaders. Regardless of these differences, both Muslims and Christians thought of themselves in the first place as sons or daughters of the city or province in which they were born. Within the Muslim and Christian worlds, local culture and language distinguished people from one another more than religion united them. But when Muslims and Christians met, they would have regarded each other first in terms of their Muslim and Christian identities.

At first, Muslim relations with Jews and Christians were friendly. The Quran suggests that Muhammad tried to accommodate the beliefs and rituals of Judaism early in his residency in Medina. But the period of tolerance did not last because the Jews refused to recognize Muhammad's religious leadership. Before the Muslims returned to Mecca, the Jews of Medina faced the choice of converting or emigrating, and most chose to emigrate. Although the first Muslims did not encounter many Christians before their conquests took them north to Palestine and Syria, they maintained a stance toward them similar to the one they held toward Jews.

This half-respectful, half-critical attitude toward Judaism and Christianity meant that Muslims much preferred Jews and Christians to adherents of polytheistic religions yet considered Judaism and Christianity to be inferior to Islam. In practice, although Jews and Christians living under Islamic rule paid more taxes than Muslims, they were allowed to worship as they pleased as long as they did not proselytize.

mosque Building where Muslims worship together.

Ramadan Ninth and holiest month of the Muslim lunar calendar when Muslims fast during the day.

Hajj Pilgrimage to Mecca expected of all Muslims at least once in a lifetime.

Scala/Art Resource, NY

Muslims include Jerusalem among the holy cities of Islam. They believe that Muhammad ascended to heaven from the rock covered by the dome of this mosque. Look closely at the tiled upper sections of the mosque exterior. How would you describe the decoration on the mosque?

Labeled **dhimmi**, they were thus able to survive, and at times prosper, within Muslim society. Some even became wealthy and politically influential. Quranic prohibitions against Muslims lending money at interest to fellow Muslims presented opportunities to Jewish and Christian moneylenders to offer credit to Muslim merchants. And members of both groups entered the employment of city governments as administrators and financial managers. On the whole, more Jews and Christians prospered under Muslim rule than Jews or Muslims did in Christian lands.

Muslim Families

Muslim families lived according to certain rules that placed them within the Judeo-Christian tradition. Like Jews, Muslims both prohibited the eating of pork and required their sons to be circumcised. Unlike Jews, however, they banned alcohol. Sharing a fear of idolatry with Christians and Jews, Muslims prohibited images of living creatures partly on the grounds that such depictions competed with God the Creator. And like the Byzantine Christian women, Muslim women wore veils in the presence of men who were not their kin and were confined to sections of their homes where male guests were not permitted.

But Muslims set themselves apart from the traditions of those older religions by allowing **polygamy**, the practice of multiple spouses. Muhammad set a limit of four wives for every Muslim man, but he himself did not take more than one wife until after the death of his first wife, Khadidja. Islam accords a place of honor to Khadidja, a capable woman who had been married to a prosperous merchant before marrying Muhammad. After her death, Muhammad took other wives in part as a way to cement alliances with the heads of other powerful families in areas of the Arabian peninsula. To mark a tribe's acceptance of Muhammad's religious and political leadership, the tribal head would offer him a female relative in marriage. Muhammad's last wife, Aisha, played a significant role in the power struggles among Muhammad's successors, even leading an army into battle.

dhimmi Arabic word for people of the book—that is, Jews and Christians.

polygamy Practice of taking multiple spouses.

Women Before Muhammad revolutionized Arabian society with his new code of living, women occupied a low rung on the social ladder. They could not own property outright, and their legal rights amounted to little more than those of children. In this respect, they were not much worse off than women in Christian lands, who likewise had limited property rights and lived perpetually under the guardianship of a father, husband, or other male relative. As in Judaism, divorce was an option in Arabian society for both men and women, although men more easily initiated an end to their marriages than women did. The practice of having multiple wives existed prior to Islam, but only wealthier men with the financial resources to support a large household could avail themselves of the right.

In Muhammad's lifetime and thereafter, the Muslim family became an even more private realm than before. The word **harem** has come to mean in the west a group of women, including wives, concubines, and slaves, segregated in quarters closed to the outside world. In Arabic, however, *harem* means "protected" or "forbidden" and refers to any space deemed a sanctuary or refuge and closed to certain groups thought to be potential threats or polluters of holy ground. Thus, the region around Mecca and Medina is "harem" to non-Muslims in the same way that women's quarters in private homes are "harem" to men who are not closely related to the women living there. What appears to non-Muslims as constraints on women's behavior and mobility Muslims themselves perceive as protection of women.

Undoubtedly, such protection felt like a burden to many women. After Muhammad's lifetime, Muslim laws pertaining to women grew increasingly harsh. Stoning became the punishment for a woman's adultery. Women now prayed in a segregated area of the mosque screened from the sight of men. Divorce became an option that only men could initiate. Women had to veil themselves whenever they moved outside the harem of their homes—in theory, to diminish the sexual temptation they posed to men. The seclusion and veiling of women had existed in certain circles prior to Muhammad's lifetime, and the Quran indicates that Muhammad's wives followed these practices. But sequestration and veiling became widespread in Islamic territory only in the period following Muhammad's death. In the view of many Muslims, men and women, the veil stood for a woman's sobriety, modesty, and virtue. It constituted her protection and her badge of honor.

harem (in Arabic, "sacrosanct") A protected and inviolate area, often women's quarters in a Muslim home, but also the area around Mecca and Medina, forbidden to non-Muslims.

caliph Spiritual and political leader of the Muslim community.

Despite the restrictions placed on them, Muslim women played an active role in the management of their family's property. Occasionally, women even appeared in court to defend their own rights, although their testimony counted less than men. Because men considered the proper place of women to be in the home, many women succeeded in wielding considerable moral authority within that sphere, particularly if they had sons whose choices in life they could influence.

Checking In

By yourself or with a partner, explain the significance of each of the following selected key terms:

Mecca	Five Pillars of Islam
Muhammad	mosques
Quran	Ramadan
Medina	Hajj

The Expansion of Islam, 700–800

◆ **Identify some of the causes and consequences of Muslim expansion.**

◆ **What aspects of Islamic culture did Muslim conquests spread from Baghdad to Spain?**

In the same year that Muhammad and his followers returned to Mecca, the Byzantine emperor Heraclius returned the relic of the True Cross to the ruined Church of the Holy Sepulcher in Jerusalem. With the Persians crushed and their empire extinguished, Heraclius may have believed Byzantine Christian rule secure. But when the city of Damascus, seat of a Christian bishop, fell to the armies of Muslim Arabs in 635, Byzantine imperial and religious unity was threatened anew. A century later, far to the west, even Frankish kings grew alarmed as adherents of this new religion pushed into their territory. Within just one hundred years, the religion of Islam and armies of Muslim Arabs had captured Egypt, raced across North Africa, and seized Spain. The Mediterranean had ceased to be Roman.

The Caliphate and Arab Invasions

Muhammad died in 632 before indicating clearly who would succeed him as leader of the Muslim community. From a field of four candidates, Muslim leaders chose Abu Bakr, one of Muhammad's fathers-in-law and a highly respected member of the Quraysh, to become the first **caliph**, or successor.

The caliph, a position patterned after Muhammad's role among his followers, served as both the political and the spiritual leader of the community. For two years until he died in 634, Abu Bakr carried on the campaign to bring all Arabian peoples under Muslim authority. Another of Muhammad's fathers-in-law, Umar, next served as caliph for ten years. During this time Muslim forces conquered Byzantine Syria, Palestine, and Egypt. Old Persian lands, in disarray following defeat by Heraclius, fell to them too.

Schism After internal dissent led to the murder of the third caliph, Uthman, in 655, tensions among the Muslim leaders intensified. Some believed Ali, Muhammad's cousin and son-in-law, stood next in line to be elected as Uthman's successor. Because only he among the Muslim leadership belonged to Muhammad's family, Ali claimed to be the rightful leader of the Muslim community. In his and his supporters' view, the first three caliphs had been illegitimately chosen. Others, however, wished to reserve the office for senior members of the Quraysh tribe. Ali's election as caliph in 656 did not end the disagreement. A civil war ensued between the supporters of Ali (the Shi'ites) and the Quraysh-led majority sect of Islam (the Sunni) that led to the defeat and murder of Ali and the beginning of the **Umayyad dynasty** of caliphs in 661.

The **schism** between the Shi'ites and the Sunnis came at a time when the leaders of Islam increasingly resorted to military conquest to extend their authority. Making no distinction between their political and religious authority, the religious leaders were rulers of territory as well as people. Like most rulers, they sought to expand the territory they controlled. More territory meant more wealth for the leaders of Islam. The Umayyad caliphs' decision to relocate the capital of Islam from Mecca to Damascus in 661 after the death of Ali was as much a military decision as an economic one. Damascus, the capital city of Syria then and now, was situated on the path of a number of intersecting trade routes running east to west and north to south. Once the Muslim leaders conquered Syria, they benefited not only from improved lines of communication, as Muslim armies moved westward along the North African coast, but also from increased commercial revenue.

Expansion Within thirty years after Muhammad's death, Arab armies had conquered the lands stretching from Iran in the east to the Black Sea in the north as well as around the Mediterranean from Antioch to Alexandria. Not since the time of Alexander the Great had an army moved so far so fast. The dissatisfaction of populations subject to Byzantine rule made the Muslim conquest relatively easy and quick. High taxes and harsh treatment had undermined Byzantine authority in Syria, Palestine, and Egypt. Once those provinces were conquered, Muslim rule imposed taxes that were lighter than those the conquered people had paid to the emperor. Moreover, the Muslim authorities proved to be more tolerant of their subjects' religious diversity than the Byzantine emperor or patriarch of Constantinople had been. Although some Christians fled following Muslim conquests, many chose to remain. Under Muslim rule, Monophysite Christians no longer had to worry about persecution. The rebuilt Church of the Holy Sepulcher remained Christian.

When the Muslims brought new territory under their rule, they continued local political bodies but placed them under the supervision of a small number of Muslim military administrators. As a result, the newly created provinces of the Islamic empire enjoyed a degree of autonomy that lessened the humiliation of being conquered. At the height of its power, during the relatively short period of political and religious unity from the death of Muhammad to the early eighth century, the Muslim world embraced distinct cultural units whose people all turned in prayer toward Mecca.

Across Africa and into Spain

Having conquered the eastern provinces of the Byzantine Empire, the Muslims set out to capture Constantinople itself. Twice, from 674 to 678 and from 717 to 718, Muslim armies under Umayyad caliphs laid siege to the city. Both times they failed. The fall of Christian Constantinople to a Muslim army was still seven hundred years in the future. For now, Muslim leaders focused on extending Islam westward.

Westward Quickly Muslim armies moved west across the North African coast, which had been under Byzantine rule since Justinian's army brought down the Vandal kingdom in the mid-sixth century. The Muslims' advance succeeded in part because of the leaders' ability to recruit new soldiers along the way, and the **Berber** people in North Africa were willing converts. In 711, Muslim forces under **Tariq ibn Ziyad**, a general of Berber origins, crossed the narrow straits from Africa to Spain, seizing the mountain that eventually bore his name, **Gibraltar** (Gibr al-Tariq,

Umayyad dynasty First line of hereditary caliphs whose capital was in Damascus.

schism (in Greek, "split") Division in a religion or church on theological principles.

Berbers An indigenous people of North Africa in modern Algeria and Tunis.

Tariq ibn Ziyad (d. 720) Muslim general who led the invasion and conquest of the Iberian Peninsula.

Gibraltar (from Jabal Tariq, "mountain of Tariq") Mountain at the southern tip of Spain.

The Spread of Islam After Muhammad died in 632, Muslim forces brought the Arabian peninsula, Syria, Palestine, all of northern Africa, and the Iberian Peninsula under Muslim rule within one hundred years. *© Cengage Learning*

1. How much of this vast territory had once formed part of the Roman Empire?
2. What were the advantages of moving the political capital of Islam from Mecca to Damascus?
3. Given the amount of territory the Muslim rulers had conquered, how easy would it have been to maintain centralized rule?

Arabic for "Mountain of Tariq"). Basing his army there, Tariq advanced to conquer Spain, under the rule of Visigothic kings since the beginning of the sixth century. His first conquest was Toledo, the capital of the Visigoths' kingdom. By 714, he had conquered all of Spain. To the Christians in neighboring Gaul, the Muslims appeared unstoppable, but in 732 the Franks stopped them at **Tours**.

When news of the conquest of Spain reached Damascus, the Umayyad caliph placed the territory under the command of the governor of North Africa and ordered that land be distributed to supporters. The first allotments went to Muslim military leaders, but Berbers from North Africa and Arabs from the Arabian peninsula, including members of the Quraysh tribe, also migrated to Spain to claim land for themselves. A fifth of all revenue from Spain belonged to the caliph in Damascus, and his portion passed through the hands of the governor of North Africa, an arrangement that did much to increase the governor's wealth. In time, the provinces of Spain and North Africa became separate administrative districts, and governors of Spain were allowed to keep most of the revenue that once had gone to North Africa and Damascus.

Resistance to the Muslims in Spain was minimal in the first centuries of their rule. As long as Christians paid a poll tax and did not proselytize or in any other way undermine the Muslim faith, they could keep their property and practice their faith. Muslim authorities offered the same condition to the Jews, who had suffered from periodic persecutions under the Visigoths and may have aided the Muslims during their conquests.

From the mid-eighth century on, the empire created by the caliphs proved very difficult to rule from

Tours Battle in 732 in which the Franks defeated Muslims advancing north from Spain.

one center. The same techniques of conquest that allowed for a degree of local autonomy also weakened a centralized Islamic empire, with the caliph ruling from a capital. Problems in long-distance communications and regular tax collection plagued the caliphs just as they had the Roman emperors. When the Umayyads were overthrown in 750 and the new **Abbasid dynasty** moved its capital to Baghdad, Muslim leaders in Spain took advantage of the political chaos in Syria to establish a **caliphate** of their own in the **Iberian** city of Cordoba. For the first time since its inception, Islam had no political center or single caliph. The Abbasid caliphs in Baghdad looked to expand eastward. The caliphs of Spain aspired to crossing the **Pyrenees** into the Frankish kingdoms. These breakaway caliphates encouraged the development of local cultural traditions. Islamic religious unity had ended shortly after Muhammad's death. Now the political unity of Islam was at an end.

Islamic Civilization

From Persia in the east, through Mesopotamia and Arabia, north to Palestine and Syria, west through Egypt, arcing across North Africa and penetrating Spain to the Pyrenees, Muslims ruled a vast portion of the old Roman Empire—more, in fact, than Justinian had in his control when the Byzantine Empire was at its greatest extent. As the Muslims came into contact with older civilizations, they absorbed aspects of these cultures that enriched Islamic thought, art, and society. Muslim philosophers translated many philosophical and medical works of ancient Greek writers, which had survived in Syrian monasteries. Astronomers provided maritime traders with the elements of celestial navigation. Mathematicians studied Euclid's geometry and developed trigonometry and calculus. The Arabic origin of the word *algebra* demonstrates how much western mathematics owes to Muslim scientists. The very concept of zero, unknown in the Roman system of numerals, was developed by these thinkers. Later, in the fourteenth century, when Arabic numerals were adopted in the west, all kinds of new mathematical calculations became possible.

Literature Through intellectual pursuits and law, Islamic society achieved a cultural unity that was visually apparent in its distinctive style. Rejecting representations of human figures, Islamic art favored a highly ornamental form of decoration that used brilliant colors, images of lush foliage, and elaborate curved lines to display calligraphic Quranic quotations on manuscript pages, ceramics, metalwork, and the walls of buildings. The architecture and decoration of mosques and public and private structures in Islamic Spain at one end of the Mediterranean displayed features similar to those found in Syria at the other end.

The greatest masterpieces of Muslim literature—lyrical and passionate love poems, biting political satire, and profound religious inquiry—were written during the Abbasid dynasty, after 750, when a high standard of composition in the Arabic language was attained. The poetry of **Abu Nuwas**, considered the best in that period, reflected the urban culture that flourished in Baghdad. The popularity of this poet's drinking songs makes it clear that, prohibitions against drinking alcohol notwithstanding, life in Muslim cities had much in common with cities in the west.

Commerce Following its start in the town of Mecca, Muslim civilization continued to be urban and commercial. In fact, commercial prosperity underlay much of the wealth and power of Muslim society. The Abbasid caliphs promoted trade and intellectual pursuits in all regions regardless of religion. Muslim prosperity drew merchants from western Europe, particularly from the Italian port cities, to the ports and markets of Egypt, Palestine, and Syria. The traders from far away brought ideas and skills as well as products. By 793, for instance, Central Asian traders had brought from China to Baghdad the technique of papermaking, whose inexpensive manufacture made manuscripts and notebooks available more cheaply to literate people.

Though centralized control was lax, the one feature all Muslim provinces shared was a new language of religion, learning, and administration. When the peoples around the southern rim of the Mediterranean accepted the Muslim religion of their new rulers, they had to learn Arabic, the language of the Quran. Because Muslim leaders had decreed that the word of God as revealed in the Quran must remain untranslated, Arabic was the only language of worship and study. Those who did not convert had incentives to learn Arabic, too, because the Muslims used it in their political administration. Thus, the Muslim advances of the seventh and eighth centuries brought about an Arabization of conquered lands that was linguistic as well as religious. Arabic, once spoken only in the Arabian peninsula, became the dominant language wherever Islam made itself

Abbasid dynasty Second line of hereditary caliphs, who came to power in 750 and moved the political center of Islam to Baghdad.

caliphate Muslim state ruled by a caliph.

Iberia Peninsula in southwest Europe today comprising Spain and Portugal.

Pyrenees Mountain chain separating France from the Iberian Peninsula.

Abu Nuwas (ca. 747–813) Poet of Persian descent who lived in Abbasid Baghdad, considered one of the greatest poets in the Arabic language.

Islamic architecture and art retained its distinctive features throughout the Muslim world. By the ninth century, the style and details of this mosque in Cordoba, Spain, would have reminded a Muslim from Syria of the mosques he knew at home. What does the decoration of this mosque have in common with the mosque shown on page 227?

the law. In the eighth and ninth centuries, however, with political unity increasingly fragmented, the Arabic language took on local characteristics, each region developing a dialect of its own.

 Checking In

By yourself or with a partner, explain the significance of each of the following selected key terms:

Caliph	Tours
Umayyad dynasty	Abbasid dynasty
Berber	caliphate
Gibraltar	Iberian

Middle Byzantine Period, 600–1071

- **In what ways did the Byzantine Empire decline?**
- **How did debate at the highest levels of political and church authority over the use of icons in worship touch ordinary people?**

The Muslim conquest of the southern and eastern regions of the Byzantine Empire brought far-reaching and permanent changes. With the loss of Syria, Palestine, and Egypt, three of the most important cities of Christianity—Jerusalem, Antioch, and

Alexandria—no longer had Christian rulers. In losing them, the Byzantine Empire also lost important revenue. Despite territorial decline, the Byzantine Empire had energetic emperors in the seventh and eighth centuries. Sending missionaries north to convert the people living along the Volga River, they spread Byzantine culture. Some emperors attempted to shore up their defenses along the frontiers and to strengthen the imperial army. But societies need more than missionaries and military might to prosper. As Muslim raids from the south and Slavic harassment from the north continued, sheer survival became the emperors' most pressing priority. These external pressures, in addition to more outbreaks of plague, had economic, military, and cultural repercussions that made life precarious and strained the empire itself, in what is known as its middle period.

Losses and Reforms

A mere four years after the death of the founder of Islam, in 632, the caliph Umar led Muslim forces to confront the emperor Heraclius's army at the river of Yarmuck in Syria. Muslim chroniclers of the time estimated that tens of thousands of Arabian combatants faced hundreds of thousands Byzantine, Armenian, Mesopotamian, and Syrian soldiers in a showdown for possession of the Byzantine province. Despite the daunting odds against them, the Muslim forces smashed their opponents, and Heraclius had no choice but to retreat to the safety of Constantinople. Syria became, and would remain, in religious, political, and cultural terms, a Muslim land.

Military Reform The Byzantine emperors relied on three methods to hold off the threats to the empire's borders. First, to maintain the Byzantine army in the face of diminishing revenues, lost when Egypt, Syria, and eastern Anatolia fell to Muslim forces, Heraclius's grandson, **Constans II**, divided the empire into administrative units called **themes** and placed each *theme* under a military governor who commanded a battalion garrisoned there. As each battalion had to provision itself from the revenue of the *theme* in which it was stationed, the burden of maintaining an army of three hundred thousand was distributed across the empire. The system also partially relieved the imperial government in Constantinople from having to administer such far-flung provinces.

Second, Constans's successors extended his efforts to strengthen Byzantine defenses by building a navy and reorganizing the cavalry. Muslim Arabs were now raiding the Anatolian coast, coming uncomfortably close to Constantinople by way of the **Dardanelles Strait**. In response, the imperial navy made effective use of **Greek fire**, which

had been invented by a Christian refugee from Syria. Believed to be made of petroleum-based substances that water could not extinguish, Greek fire launched from Byzantine ships forced the Muslim Arabs to withdraw. Though Greek fire was dangerous to launch and used sparingly, its lethal reputation constrained Byzantium's enemies for the time being. Beginning in the seventh century, heavy cavalry, known as **cataphracts** and recruited mainly from the more affluent levels of the peasantry, played an important part in the Byzantine land forces. Together, the Byzantine fleet and cavalry gained for the empire a reputation as a formidable military state. The Byzantine Empire also became known for its third method of protecting itself: military intelligence and subterfuge. Military leaders created dissension among Byzantium's enemies through spying and by bribing one foe to attack another.

The administrative reforms and strengthening of the military in the empire gave the impression to Muslim and western Christian observers of a large superpower with unlimited resources. In reality, by the end of the eighth century, the Byzantine Empire had been reduced in size and population. If there was more religious unity, it was only because the loss of Syria, Palestine, and Egypt, which had removed the major dissenters from the orthodoxy of the eastern church. What remained of the old Roman Empire was scarcely recognizable to its inhabitants or to its enemies.

The Waning of Byzantine Society

Though its territory was shrinking, the Byzantine Empire from the seventh to the eleventh centuries had a stronger economy than did western Europe, and its subjects had a higher standard of living. The city of Constantinople, the center of urban life, retained its awe-inspiring powers. Long-distance trade in luxury goods and agricultural products between Christian and Muslim lands continued in the eastern Mediterranean, whereas commercial traffic toward western Europe had begun to decline even before the advent of Muslim merchants. In contrast to the great number of cities in the Muslim

Constans II (630–668) Emperor responsible for extensive administrative and military reforms of the Byzantine Empire.

themes Administrative units of the Byzantine Empire corresponding to the dispersal of military battalions throughout the empire.

Dardanelles Strait The water passage connecting the northern Aegean Sea to the Sea of Marmora and Constantinople.

Greek fire Petroleum-based substance that ignited on contact with water; used by the Byzantine army in warfare.

cataphracts Units of heavy cavalry that dominated Byzantine military tactics on land by the seventh century.

world, however, the Byzantine Empire had very few urban centers apart from the capital city. Rarely did Byzantine traders venture with their merchandise very far from Constantinople. Instead, traders came to them.

Plague When the Middle Byzantine period is compared to the fifth and sixth centuries, a decline in almost all aspects of society can be seen. Most catastrophically, periodic outbreaks of the plague reduced the population everywhere. By the ninth century, Constantinople's population had dropped from nearly 500,000 to around 100,000. Nearly every other city in the empire similarly shrank in size and population. Some disappeared altogether. Athens no longer resembled at all the classical city-state that had produced the philosophers Socrates and Plato and graceful temples like the Parthenon. Only the city of Thessalonica prospered a little in hard times. Most people resided in small villages in the countryside, where livelihoods and diets were restricted. Villagers ate bread from local grain as well as beans, honey, and olives. For meat and dairy products, they relied on sheep and goats. Imported spices, dried fruits, and other products were rarely available outside of Constantinople, so the difference in the quality of life between Constantinopolitans and provincial peasants was stark.

Decline of Literacy The high level of cultural and intellectual expression attained during the Roman Peace was no longer possible. Higher education had mostly disappeared by the seventh century, after Justinian I closed Plato's Academy in Athens, but few people had access to education at any level. The primary and secondary schools that remained offered practical vocational training. But from then on, education, which had always been private, declined. By the seventh century, it would have been very unusual to meet a man of great learning anywhere outside of a small social circle in Constantinople. Even church intellectuals did not exhibit the mastery of texts and theological thinking that earlier Christian thinkers had.

As fewer people could read and write, the quality of literature declined. Byzantine writers produced no works of enduring fame or merit. Even the copying of ancient manuscripts to preserve classical works fell behind, and many writings of the ancient Athenians thus disappeared. Knowledge of Latin became scarce. Byzantine lawyers read Justinian I's great Body of Civil Law not in the language in which it was written—Latin—but in a simplified Greek version. The Christians of the east read the Bible in Greek, the language in which most of the books

of the New Testament had been written. But very few could read at all, and those who could were most often clergy. To a merchant from Baghdad—a city famous for its writers, physicians, astronomers, and artists—Byzantine culture would have seemed unsophisticated and, if he was a snob, lacking in taste.

Increasingly over the sixth, seventh, and eighth centuries, the Mediterranean populations of the old Roman Empire made distinctions between themselves and others. How people defined themselves depended on whom they were defining themselves in relation to. A fisherman living in the eighth century in the port city of Antioch, situated on the coastline where Asia Minor meets Syria, might have thought of himself as a Christian when he was dealing with the tax collectors of his Muslim rulers. But as a Monophysite, he knew he would not be welcomed in lands ruled by Christians. He spoke to his Muslim and Jewish neighbors in Aramaic or Arabic, but he did not know Greek well enough to talk to visiting Christian and Jewish traders from the empire or farther west. All the new political and religious divisions apparent in the world made life very complicated and confusing. It was difficult to know where people's allegiances lay.

In either the Christian or Muslim worlds, the wonder was that any one facet of a person's identity, like religion, could count for so much, given that gender, birthplace, language, and social rank sometimes made more of a difference in daily life than did prayers and devotions. Nevertheless, religion became the standard that Christians and Muslims carried into battle against each other over the succeeding centuries.

The Controversy over Icons

The extraordinary variety of sights, colors, and sounds common today make it difficult to imagine the spectacular impact a church interior could have had on an ordinary person in the Byzantine Empire. A woman coming to pray for her sick child, for example, would have paused at the entrance to let her eyes adjust to the darkness. There were few windows, and the only light came from candles, whose smoke stains had made the interior even darker over time. But then, illuminated by candlelight, she might have stopped to study the stern faces of the early **church fathers**, depicted on the walls in frescoes. If the church had wealthy patrons, she could have gazed up at scenes from the life of Christ, portrayed in richly decorated mosaics against a background of gold. Above her, embedded into the surface of the central dome, there might be a huge mosaic of a forbidding rather than a compassionate Christ, in keeping with the Byzantine emphasis of Christ as ruler rather than as dispenser of mercy. At eye level, she

church fathers Early Christian writers, such as Augustine, Ambrose, Jerome, and Leo the Great.

would have seen **icons**, paintings made on panels of wood showing Christ; his mother, the Virgin Mary; or the saints—all close enough to touch or to kiss in the fervency of prayer. The flickering candlelight would animate the gold and multicolored pigments in these portraits. It is little wonder that, for many, these icons made visible the presence of the holy figures they represented. In her devotions, the mother of the sick child may have prayed to the Virgin in the icon, taking comfort in the Virgin's closeness even as the church interior evoked in her a deep sense of awe and humility.

Idolatry? By the middle of the eighth century, however, people's attachment to icons had made some high-ranking members of Byzantine society uneasy. Most prominently, Emperor **Leo III** was preoccupied with the biblical commandment against the worship of "graven images": Were icons, as the focus of believers' prayers, almost the same as idols—objects embodying the "false gods" that the Hebrew prophets of old had warned against? Then, in the summer of 726, a volcano erupted in the middle of the Aegean Sea, spreading ash and smoke as far as northern Greece. God was evidently highly displeased with the people of the Christian empire, concluded Leo, and he removed an icon of Christ on the Chalke Gate, at the entrance to the imperial palace, that was greatly revered by the people of Constantinople. Riots ensued. The emperor had struck a nerve in the city populace, but he continued to urge the people to give up their icons and to pressure the clergy to remove icons from their churches.

Debate over the sinfulness—or righteousness—of religious images escalated into a full-scale church controversy. Those who persisted in their attachments to icons argued that the Old Testament prohibition of images had never been strictly observed, as angels were depicted in the Temple in Jerusalem. More positively, they argued that the birth of Christ, the God-Man, removed the old prohibitions. As the theologian John of Damascus explained, "In former times, God who is without body, could never be depicted. But now when God is seen in the flesh conversing with men, I make an image of the God whom I see." In other words, Christ's human nature deserved to be shown in the form God himself had chosen. Nevertheless, the church hierarchy fell into line with the emperor's wishes. In 730, Leo banned all icons depicting holy figures, except the Cross, reinforced by a subsequent ban in 754 by the Council of Constantinople. In reaction, the church in western Europe dissented, following Pope Gregory II's lead, and declared iconoclasts ("smashers of icons") and the doctrine of **iconoclasm** to be heretical. Thus, the division between the eastern and the Roman church deepened.

Erich Lessing/Art Resource, NY

Few icons survived the period of iconoclasm. Only icons in monasteries located far from the heart of the Byzantine Empire managed to escape destruction. This depiction of Jacob's ladder dates to the twelfth century. Can you infer who the human figures in the icon are meant to represent by their clothing or their placement within the composition?

Leo III's son and grandson took the policy further and persecuted those who venerated icons. Monks and nuns, whose spiritual authority among the poor and the rural population rested in part on their association with revered icons, went into hiding. But when Leo's grandson, Emperor Leo IV, died in 775, and his widow, **Irene**, became **regent**, ruling until her nine-year-old son, Constantine VI, would be old enough to be named emperor, imperial policy toward icons changed. An ambitious woman, empress Irene sought to consolidate her power by initiating the theological reform she

icon A representation of sacred figures on wood panels, mosaics, or wall paintings.

Leo III (r. 717–741) Byzantine emperor who took the first steps toward the prohibition of icons.

iconoclasm Policy initiated by Emperor Leo III in 731 forbidding the veneration of icons in religious worship.

Irene (ca. 752–803) Widow of Emperor Leo IV, who usurped power from her son, Constantine VI, to rule in her own right.

regent Person authorized to rule in the name of a monarch who has not yet come of age.

Church Councils Condemn and Restore the Use of Icons

Although the iconoclastic movement lasted one hundred years, it had an impact that can be partially measured by how very few icons made prior to 730 survived past the ninth century. Thousands of icons cherished by men and women throughout the empire were destroyed when Leo III forbade the use of icons in liturgical services. Painters closed their workshops. Families risked hiding their beloved icons or surrendered them to authorities to be destroyed. Imperial troops cleared monasteries of the icons that people had traveled great distances on pilgrimage to visit. Few icons, mostly those housed in remote monasteries, such as St. Catherine's in the Sinai Peninsula or in Russia, escaped destruction. The first selection here, from the Council of Constantinople's condemnation of icons in 754, sets out the rationale for the banning of icons. The second selection, from the Council of Nicaea in 787, explains the Council's reasons for restoring the veneration of icons.

❶ Who are meant by "creature" and "Creator?"

❷ What is the basis of the argument against icons?

❸ If demiurgos means "maker," who does the term refer to in the document?

❹ Who are the "faithful Emperors?"

From the Council of Constantinople, 754

❶ Satan misguided men, so that they worshipped the creature instead of the Creator. **❷** The Mosaic law and the prophets cooperated to undo this ruin; but in order to save mankind thoroughly, God sent his own Son, who turned us away from error and the worshipping of idols, and taught us the worshipping of God in spirit and in truth. As messengers of his saving doctrine, he left us his Apostles and disciples, and these adorned the church, his Bride, with his glorious doctrines. This ornament of the church the holy Fathers and the six Ecumenical Councils have preserved inviolate. **❸** But the before-mentioned demiurgos of wickedness could not endure the sight of this adornment, and gradually brought back idolatry under the appearance of Christianity. **❹** As then Christ armed his Apostles against the ancient idolatry with the power of the Holy Spirit, and sent them out into all the world, so has

knew would win her support from many clergymen and ordinary people. In 784, when the office of patriarch of Constantinople became vacant, Irene appointed a man who wished to end the policy of iconoclasm. Three years later, in 787, the Second Council of Nicaea debated the matter, and the leaders of the eastern church reversed themselves. At its concluding session, Irene and her son, Constantine VI—now twenty-one years old and ruling in his own right—signed a declaration officially restoring the use of icons in religious services and worship in the Byzantine Empire. The iconoclasm controversy was at an end. Symbolically, Irene replaced the Christ icon at the Chalke Gate, but very few other icons had survived. Irene's popularity rose, in large part because the people of the empire

viewed her as responsible for restoring their beloved icons.

The Empress Irene

When, in 769, Emperor Constantine V had chosen Irene to marry his son Leo, designated heir to the imperial throne, the young woman from a provincial family in Athens must have been terrified. Life in the great palace complex in Constantinople, a labyrinth of reception rooms, galleries, gardens, churches, stables, and military barracks, would mean an unending series of exhausting ceremonies. From now on her days would be filled with prescribed movements and rituals, with coronations, judicial sessions, receptions for dignitaries, he awakened against the new idolatry his servants our faithful Emperors, and endowed them with the same wisdom of the Holy Spirit. . . .

❺ What avails, then, the folly of the painter, who from sinful love of gain depicts that which should not be depicted—that is, with his polluted hands he tries to fashion that which should only be believed in the heart and confessed with the mouth? He makes an image and calls it Christ. The name Christ signifies God and man. Consequently it is an image of God and man, and consequently he has in his foolish mind, in his representation of the created flesh, depicted the Godhead which cannot be represented, and thus mingled what should not be mingled. Thus he is guilty of a double blasphemy—the one in making an image of the Godhead, and the other by mingling the Godhead and manhood.

From the Second Council of Nicaea, 787

❻ We define with all accuracy and care that the venerable and holy icons be set up like the form of the venerable and life-giving Cross, inasmuch as matter consisting of colours and pebbles and other matter is appropriate in the holy church of God . . . , as well as the image of our Lord and God and Saviour Jesus Christ, of our undefiled Lady the Holy Mother of God, of the angels worthy of honour, and of all the holy and pious men. For the more frequently they are seen by means of pictorial representation the more those who behold them are aroused to remember and desire the prototypes and to give them greeting and worship of honour— but not the true worship of our faith which befits only the divine nature— but to offer them both incense and candles, in the same way as to the form of the venerable and life-giving Cross and to the holy gospel books and to the other sacred objects, as was the custom even of the Ancients.

Source: The Seven Ecumenical Councils of the Undivided Church, trans. H. R. Percival, in Nicene and Post-Nicene Fathers, 2nd Series, ed. P. Schaff and H. Wace, (repr. Grand Rapids MI: Wm. B. Eerdmans, 1955), XIV, pp 543–44.

❺ What sinful gain does the painter derive from icons?

❻ What is the argument in favor of icons in religious worship?

commemorative Masses, holy **feast days**, and other occasions that created a mystical aura around the emperor's person. So elaborate had the public and private court rituals become that specially trained courtiers oversaw their performance and instructed the imperial family in their proper roles.

Eunuchs The court specialists who trained Irene were likely tall, long-limbed, blond, and beardless eunuchs, men who had been surgically neutered when they were boys. Since they were unable to procreate, the eunuchs were trusted with access to the women's quarters, acting as servants and advisers to the female members of the imperial family. Irene would spend much of her life largely in the company of these court servants, many of whom she appointed to key positions in her government.

The empress Irene, once regent, enjoyed the power she wielded while her son was underage. Unlike previous imperial mothers who promoted their sons' interests, she had no intention of letting her son assume his role as senior emperor. Although of age to assume full control of the state, Constantine lived under a form of house arrest in Porphyra, the imperial palace paneled with slabs of purple marble where he was born. In 788, his mother sent a commission of judges throughout the empire to find him a wife from among his subjects.

feast day Holiday marking a religious date, like the birth of Jesus or the birthday of a saint.

With a list of ideal standards in hand, the judges measured the physical and moral qualities of young aristocratic women presented to them for inspection. These **bride shows** produced about thirteen possible candidates, from which Irene chose Maria, a young woman from the province of Armenia, to be her son's wife. The marriage turned out badly, in part because Constantine saw his wife as his mother's ally. After having two daughters but no son to succeed him, Constantine divorced Maria and married Theodote, his mistress, actions that church leaders strongly condemned but were unable to prevent.

In 790, with the support of military regiments unhappy with Irene's rule, Constantine took control of the government, alienating key sectors of Byzantine society. By 792, Irene had managed to rally enough support for her return to the position of empress mother. Constantine had no choice but to allow his mother a place in his court. Within a few years, support for Constantine had once again eroded. Relations between mother and son became so tense in 797 that Constantine fled, was captured, and, on the order of his mother, blinded, a common punishment for conspirators and political rivals. He did not die, but Irene ruled the empire alone for five more years. However, important segments of the army were still opposed to being ruled by a woman, and Irene's own connivances contributed to the growing instability of the throne and the empire. A group of military commanders deposed her and installed one of their own as emperor. Exiled to an island in the Aegean Sea, Irene died eight months after her deposition in 802. The son she had had blinded outlived her by a few years.

Irene's reign was an experiment that was not repeated. For the rest of the Middle Ages, no other woman in the Byzantine Empire or in western Europe came as close as she had to exercising the full power of a monarch.

A Reorientation to the North

Even as Byzantine authority and control were declining, Byzantine culture was expanding in response to continued threats on its northern border. Over the tenth century, the Kievan **Rus**, a Scandinavian-Slavic people, pushed deep into the Byzantine Empire to raid, trade, and settle. On trading expeditions, they brought timber, furs, and slaves from the north and took back with them silver in the form of coin and vessels. When raiding, they carried their terror farther and farther into Byzantium. They continued their ancestors' tradition of taking captives to sell in the ports where they found customers. Their attempts to settle in the interior caused the displacement of people and chaos in the empire.

Whether the Rus traded or raided, all observers, Muslims and Christians alike, reported the harsh conditions in which they lived. Groups of ten or twenty, crammed into small wooden structures along the Volga River, engaged in sexual behavior that greatly shocked Christian and Muslim visitors. Women wore pendants from their neck that indicated the social rank of the husbands. From childhood, their breasts were bound to discourage their growth. Equally shocking was the Rus custom of cremating their dead in boats. A wealthy man could count on sailing into the afterlife with his horse, dog, and one of his slave women, who would be slain and laid beside him. When all was ready, the boat with all its contents was set on fire and shoved into the sea. The advent of Christianity, with its emphasis on bodily resurrection, slowly changed these customs.

Mission Work To confront the problem of the Rus pressing against their border, the Byzantine emperors devised a three-pronged strategy: diplomacy, military recruitment, and conversion. Diplomacy seemed the wisest course to all observers at the time and, in fact, did prevent the Rus from engulfing the empire. In the face of attacks and threats of siege, the emperors continued granting trading privileges, but these only stimulated the Rus to seek new advantages. Ultimately, the Rus extended their dominion over territory along the Volga and in Bulgaria. Military recruitment also failed. Although the Rus supplied a relatively reliable source of troops and once, in 989, even rescued the emperor from a plot, they also (much like the barbarian contingents of the Roman army in earlier centuries) were increasingly attracted to Byzantine salaries and Byzantine culture—and were an increasing menace.

Conversion to Christianity seemed the best way to deal with the peoples north of the border. When the Byzantines sent missionaries, Christianity took root in Kiev. The brothers **Cyril** and **Methodius** are credited with introducing Christian worship in Slavonic, the language of the people they missionized, and providing the Slavs with an alphabet derived from the Greek, called **Cyrillic**. In 988, after missionaries

bride shows Presentation of prospective brides to imperial representatives charged with finding a bride for an unmarried emperor or heir to the throne.

Rus Scandinavian-Slavic people who established themselves in Novgorod and Kiev by the late ninth century.

Cyril (ca. 827–869) and **Methodius** (ca. 825–885) Missionaries and brothers sent to the Kievan Rus to oversee their conversion; they created the Cyrillic alphabet.

Cyrillic alphabet System of letters, named for the ninth-century missionary Cyril, used to write Ukrainian, Russian, Bulgarian, and other Slavic languages.

brought Christianity to neighboring peoples, Kiev also became a Christian land when its rulers and people converted, and Byzantine culture now penetrated beyond the Volga River. Ancient customs were prohibited; like Christians elsewhere, the Rus buried their dead in the ground, in hopes of bodily resurrection. But as much as the Byzantine emperor and the patriarch of Constantinople would have liked to bring the Rus completely under the control of the eastern church, the new Kievan church instead developed its own liturgical customs and language, Old Church Slavonic.

Meanwhile, in the south, the Muslim threat strengthened. By the beginning of the ninth century, the Byzantine Empire encompassed little more than Anatolia and the mainland of what is today Greece. Then **Seljuk** Turks, newcomers from the steppes of Asia, threatened even Anatolia. When they soundly defeated the Byzantines at the Battle of **Manzikert** in 1071, the Byzantine Empire lost its core territory.

With only the Greek peninsula south of the Danube River under its control, plus the islands of Crete and Cyprus, the emperor decided to seek assistance from the west.

Seljuk Turkic people from the steppes of Central Asia who migrated westward into Byzantine territory and eventually converted to Islam.

Manzikert Battle in 1071, in which Seljuk Turkic forces defeated the Byzantine army and extended their control into Anatolia.

Checking In

By yourself or with a partner, explain the significance of each of the following selected key terms:

Constans II	Leo III
Greek fire	iconoclasm
church fathers	Irene
icons	Cyrillic alphabet

CHAPTER
Review

Summary

◆ In the ninth century, the people of the eastern empire still thought of themselves as Roman, but so much had changed that a Latin-speaking resident of the city of Rome would not have understood the Greek-speaking inhabitants of Constantinople, "the New Rome."

◆ Disagreements over the nature of Christ continued. The Christians of sixth-century Constantinople had very strong and conflicting opinions about Jesus' humanity and divinity, which Emperor Justinian and empress Theodora at first tried to ignore. Eventually, the emperor suppressed those who disagreed with church doctrine, as threatening to Christian unity.

◆ Muhammad's new religion of Islam had from its start a firmer political and cultural foundation in the Arabian peninsula than Christianity had enjoyed in the Roman Empire.

◆ By the ninth century, Muslim territory encompassed more territory than had the Roman Empire.

◆ The Greek alphabet and the rites of the eastern church traveled with missionaries to the land of the Slavs and the Kievan Rus in the tenth century.

◆ Increasingly, sacred languages, practices, and leaders divided the people of the old Roman Empire. Religion was now a matter of loyalty as much as it was of belief.

Chronology

527	Justinian becomes emperor		632	Muhammad dies in Medina
532	Justinian's forces kills tens of thousands in the Nika Riot in Constantinople		656	Election of Ali as caliph
533–563	Body of Civil Law is issued		661	Death of the caliph Ali and beginning of Umayyad dynasty, based in Damascus
534	Vandal kingdom of North Africa falls to Byzantine forces		711–714	Muslims conquer Spain
542	Bubonic plague devastates Constantinople		730	Leo III forbids use of icons in liturgical services
552	Ostrogothic kingdom in Italy falls to Byzantine forces		732	Franks halt Muslim advance at Tours
ca. 570	Birth of Muhammad		750	Umayyad dynasty is overthrown; Abbasid dynasty begins, based in Baghdad
610	Heraclius becomes emperor		787	Second Council of Nicaea reinstates veneration of icons
613	Persians capture Jerusalem, destroy Church of the Holy Sepulcher		802	Removal of the empress Irene from power
622	Muhammad flees to Medina in the Hejira; beginning of the Muslim calendar		803	Death of the empress Irene
628	Heraclius defeats the Persians		988	Kievan Rus officially accept Christianity
630	Heraclius returns relic of the True Cross to Jerusalem; Muhammad returns to Mecca		1071	Turks defeat Byzantine army at Manzikert

© Cengage Learning

Test Yourself

To gauge your mastery of the material in this chapter, answer the questions below. More than one answer may be correct.

Justinian and the Revival of the Empire in the East, 500–650

1. Which kingdom did Justinian **not** attempt to bring back into the empire?
   - a. Visigothic
   - b. Frankish
   - c. Vandal
   - d. Ostrogothic
   - e. Persian

2. The empress Theodora endeavored to protect the followers of which sect declared heretical by church councils?
   - a. Nestorians
   - b. Monophysites
   - c. Monotheletes
   - d. Arians
   - e. Chalcedonians

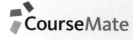
Visit the CourseMate website at **www.cengagebrain.com** for additional study tools and review materials for this chapter.

3. Which of the following sources of law did Justinian's commission **not** include in the Body of Civil Law?

   a. Germanic customs
   b. Church council rulings
   c. Jurists' opinions
   d. The legislation of previous emperors
   e. Recent legislation

4. What disaster reduced Constantinople's population nearly by half in 542?

   a. An earthquake centered in the Aegean Sea.
   b. An invasion of Alans from north of the Black Sea.
   c. The conquest of Constantinople by the Persian army.
   d. An outbreak of bubonic plague.
   e. The eruption of a volcano in Asia Minor.

5. Which emperor recovered much of the provinces in the east lost to the Persians?

   a. Hereclius
   b. Constantine
   c. Tiberius
   d. Leo III
   e. Constantine VI

Now that you have reviewed and tested yourself on this part of the chapter, take time to pull together all the important information by answering the following questions:

◆ In what ways did Justinian attempt to restore the Roman Empire to its former size and glory?

◆ Which of Justinian's accomplishments endured over the centuries? Which did not?

The Rise of Islam, 600–700

6. Which of the following descriptions best suit the people of the Arabian peninsula before Muhammad's lifetime?

   a. Farmers whose economy depended on agricultural production.
   b. Nomads who raised livestock.
   c. Merchants who traveled between Africa and Central Asia.
   d. Warriors who pillaged neighboring lands.
   e. City dwellers whose livelihoods depended on municipal employment.

7. Which of the following is **not** one of the Five Pillars of Islam?

   a. Jihad
   b. Charity
   c. Pilgrimage
   d. Fasting
   e. Admission of one god

8. Which of the following statements about Muslims, Christians, and Jews is most accurate:

   a. They have completely independent religious traditions.
   b. They are all polytheists.
   c. They have always rejected the use of images in religious worship.
   d. They all revere Abraham and the prophets of the Christian and Hebrew bibles.
   e. They all derive from religious cults from Persia.

9. Muhammad assumed leadership in which town when he was compelled to leave Mecca?

   a. Jerusalem
   b. Medina
   c. Riyaad
   d. Alexandria
   e. Antioch

10. Muhammad, the founder of Islam, died in which year?

    a. 622
    b. 711
    c. 630
    d. 542
    e. 632

Now that you have reviewed and tested yourself on this part of the chapter, take time to pull together all the important information by answering the following questions:

◆ How would you describe the way of life Muhammad required his followers to follow? What are its essential elements?

◆ What are some of the beliefs and practices shared by Muslims, Christians, and Jews?

The Expansion of Islam, 700–800

11. Which of the following Muslim leaders became the first caliph after Muhammad's death?
   - a. Umar
   - b. Uthman
   - c. Abu Bakr
   - d. Ali
   - e. Hussein

12. The Shi'ites supported which of the first four caliphs?
   - a. Umar
   - b. Uthman
   - c. Abu Bakr
   - d. Ali
   - e. Hussein

13. The caliphs of the Umayyad dynasty relocated the political capital of Islam to which city?
   - a. Baghdad
   - b. Damascus
   - c. Jerusalem
   - d. Constantinople
   - e. Cairo

14. Muslim armies entered Iberia in which year?
   - a. 642
   - b. 700
   - c. 711
   - d. 632
   - e. 750

15. The dynasty that replaced the Umayyad dynasty was:
   - a. Fatimid
   - b. Abbasid
   - c. Cordoban
   - d. Quranic
   - e. Abu Nuwas

Now that you have reviewed and tested yourself on this part of the chapter, take time to pull together all the important information by answering the following questions:

◆ What were the underlying causes of the split between the Sunnis and Shi'ites?

◆ Describe some of the key characteristics of Islamic culture?

Middle Byzantine Period, 600–1071

16. Iconoclasts are:
   - a. Rebels who seek to subvert the dominant culture.
   - b. Worshippers who venerate icons.
   - c. Clergy in charge of the care of a church's icons.
   - d. A person who objects to the use of images in religious worship.
   - e. The custodians responsible for the care and preservation of icons.

17. The empress Irene was notable for which of the following?
   - a. The only woman to reign in her own right in the Byzantine Empire.
   - b. A mother who had her son blinded in order to preserve her control of the imperial throne.
   - c. Instrumental in bringing an end to the ban on the use of icons in religious worship.
   - d. The object of hostility by the army and the nobility because she was a woman.
   - e. All of the above.

18. Which invaders settled, intermarried with locals, and gave rise to the Kievan Rus?
    a. Muslims
    b. Byzantine Greeks
    c. Franks
    d. Visigoths
    e. Vikings

19. The brothers Cyril and Methodius are credited with introducing what to the Kievan Rus?
    a. Christianity and the Greek alphabet
    b. Islam
    c. Arianism
    d. Pasta
    e. Viking culture

20. The Byzantine Empire faced a new threat at the beginning of the ninth century. Who were they?
    a. Mongols
    b. Persians
    c. Ottomans
    d. Iberians
    e. Seljuk Turks

Now that you have reviewed and tested yourself on this part of the chapter, take time to pull together all the important information by answering the following questions:

◆ Why might the people of the Byzantine Empire have objected to the ban on images in religious worship?

◆ What challenges did the empress Irene face when she assumed power in her own right?

Chapter Outline

400	450	500	550	600	650	700
	476 Fall of the western Roman Empire	**511** Clovis's lands are divided among his sons	**525** Benedict founds monastery at Monte Cassino	**ca. 563** Columba founds monasteries in Scotland and Britain		

Charlemagne spent nearly his entire reign on military campaign. Late in life, he settled in his capital at Aachen in northern Germany. This bronze statue of Charlemagne on horseback shows him wearing a crown and holding an orb. What do the crown and orb symbolize about his authority? (Erich Lessing/Art Resource, NY)

After reading this chapter, you should be able to answer the following questions:

What impact did the disappearance of centralized authority have on the economy in western Europe?

How did bishops and monasteries help to preserve social order and literacy after the end of the empire in the West?

Which factors played a role in perpetuating the warfare and violence among the ruling families of the Frankish kingdoms?

IN THE EIGHTH CENTURY, in the territory that was once the Roman Empire, three very different civilizations dominated. Strong centralized authority persisted in the Byzantine Empire and also characterized the rule of the caliph over Muslim territory. But rule in the western part of the Roman Empire was decentralized. Almost no one had the power to defend public order beyond a city wall or a village boundary. By 750, constant warfare among rival Frankish kings and nobles had undermined what little prestige the title of king of the Franks held.

To the peasants who made a meager living off the land, the men who called themselves kings acted more like warlords with troops they could barely control. There was little anyone could do to prevent crops from being burned or trampled by armies. Some peasants belonged to plots of land that belonged to a lord, for whom they were compelled to work. Hardened by custom over time, relationships between people of different social status grew rigid. No matter how low or high their rank, many people had obligations to someone more powerful. When the pope asserted the right

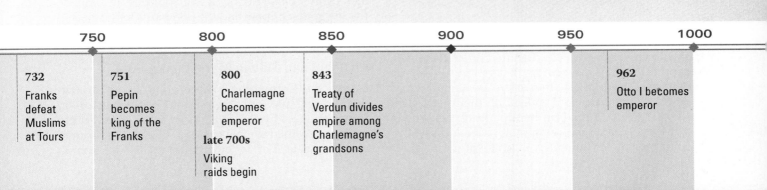

750   800   850   900   950   1000

732
Franks defeat Muslims at Tours

751
Pepin becomes king of the Franks

800
Charlemagne becomes emperor

late 700s
Viking raids begin

843
Treaty of Verdun divides empire among Charlemagne's grandsons

962
Otto I becomes emperor

to legitimize kings, even kings came to feel they had obligations to a higher order, but they also resisted these obligations.

What little sanctuary existed from disaster and arbitrary violence was provided by the church. At its least effective, the church promised the distressed and poor a better world to come. At its most effective, it filled the gap left by the disappearance of public authority. Missionary monks fanned out across the northern lands to persuade the people living there, first, that they needed salvation and, second, that no salvation was possible without the church. Kings saw church teachings as a way to bolster their subjects' loyalty and obedience to public authority. In southern Europe, bishops stepped into the role of municipal leaders and ferociously defended the people under their care against kings and lords.

Charlemagne, king of the Franks and subsequently emperor, brought greater security to the inhabitants of his lands by sending out inspectors to check on the management of his lands and by taking war to his neighbors rather than by waging war in his empire's heartland. He brought the forces of church and government together to create a period of relative peace and stability for the people living in his empire.

But then order and security disappeared again, as Charlemagne's grandsons and great-grandsons fought among themselves over land and power. Only in the eastern portion of Charlemagne's old empire was one king, Otto I, able to restore some semblance of order. The system he devised to rule his empire created problems of its own, however, as it came to rely on the clergy for its personnel. In the newly revived empire, the clergy served one master, the emperor, a situation a subsequent generation of popes would find hard to accept. There and elsewhere in western Europe, rulers and popes began their long competition for the loyalty of their subjects.

Regional Rule, Local Views, 500–750

◆ **What caused the fragmentation of political power in the west?**

◆ **How did the decline in long-distance trade affect the cities of western Europe?**

Although no one realized it at the time, Romulus Augustulus, deposed in 476, would be the last Roman emperor in the west. When that office remained vacant in the late fifth century, rulers in the western provinces, once labeled "barbarian" by their Roman masters, stepped forward to lead on their own. Partially as a result, the world became local. No longer did the peoples of the western interior look to the Mediterranean for direction or innovation, and no longer did the lands bordering the Mediterranean give direction. Europe underwent a long, difficult transformation as Rome slipped further back into memory and new, smaller political units emerged. Western Europe was turning inward.

These new political units were often violent and unstable. In Gaul, the Merovingians managed to build the longest-lived kingdom in the political vacuum created by the collapse of the western empire. In contrast, the Visigoths in Spain and the Lombards in Italy lasted for little more than a century.

Kingship and Rule in Merovingian Gaul

Unlike the Ostrogoths, whose adoption of Roman methods of rule, nonetheless, did not protect them from conquest by the Byzantines in 552, the Frankish kings seemed unable to adopt a consistent Roman model of rule. The order maintained by the Roman

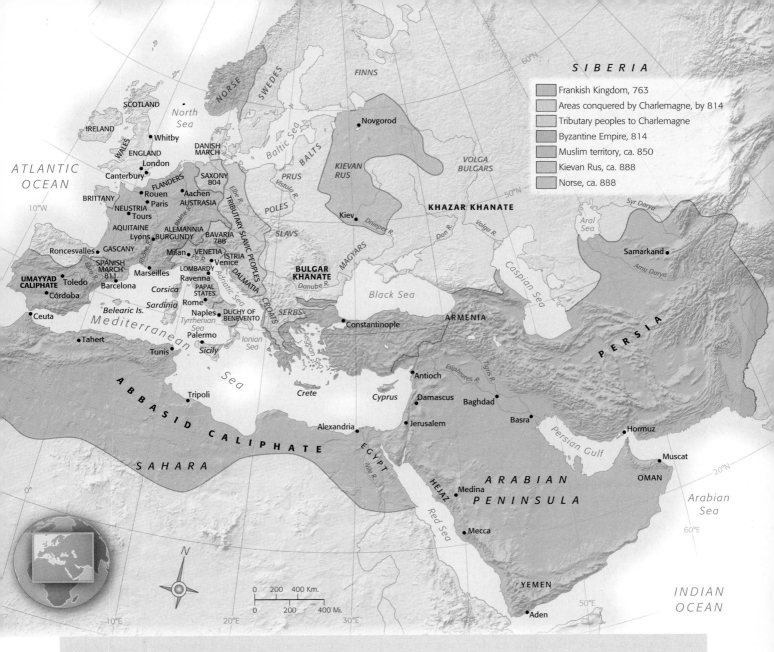

Map 9.1 **Europe and the Mediterranean, ca. 800** In the Treaty of Verdun, Charlemagne's grandsons, Louis the German, Lothar, and Charles the Bald, divided the Frankish kingdom among themselves. They continued the Frankish inheritance custom of dividing kingdoms equally among male heirs. © *Cengage Learning*

1. On the map, locate the area that Charlemagne's empire covered. What land mass does it correspond to today?
2. Once you have located the Byzantine Empire in orange and the Muslim territory in green, does the Frankish kingdom seem integrated into the old Mediterranean world or isolated from it?
3. If the Frankish kingdoms turned away from the Mediterranean as their main highway of commerce, which other bodies of water would they have access to?

frontier garrisons and the municipal services administered by provincial governors disappeared when the Romans withdrew from northern Europe. The Frankish kings and their warrior supporters were not interested in ruling or in overseeing the welfare of ordinary people. They sought only to increase their own land and wealth. The disorder that ensued actually suited them because becoming a powerful warlord depended on the absence of order. Thus it took centuries for order and security to return to western Europe. From the sixth to the seventh centuries, the Franks repeatedly expanded into new regions and then withdrew, but out of the ensuing chaos the society and culture of the Middle Ages was born.

Erich Lessing/Art Resource, NY

The sword hilts pictured here reveal the high quality of Merovingian crafts. The delicate gold leaf on the handle indicates that the king who wielded these weapons used them for display more than for battle. What do you think the red shapes on the pieces are? Can you deduce something about how the pieces were made?

A Father's Estate Today, a kingdom calls to mind a tract of territory over which one king or queen rules the people who live in it, as the monarch of Great Britain (a territory) reigns over the people living in Great Britain today. Such was not the case in Merovingian Gaul. A king viewed the territory in which his subjects lived as his personal estate, which he would bequeath to his heirs. This Merovingian attitude came into clearest focus at the death of a king. When Clovis, king of the Franks, died in 511, each of his sons inherited—and became king of an equal portion of the land their father had conquered. This division of a father's estate was custom, and custom had the force of law. In other words, the division of Clovis's kingdom was not so much a political division as a familial one.

Thinking of a kingdom as a family's estate makes it easier to understand why the temptation to restore the father's territory overcame brotherly affection in nearly every generation after Clovis. The Merovingian kings of the seventh century spent much of their time and wealth conducting wars against family members. Every time a king died, his sons fought each other, each seeking to acquire the power and wealth their father had possessed. The result was constant violence and murder. With alarming predictability, brothers slaughtered brothers, mothers attempted to kill daughters, and uncles massacred nephews.

Warrior Chieftains Thus, Merovingian kings were not so much rulers of territories who sought to govern as they were warrior chieftains who sought to seize and subdue land and the people who lived on it. A king was only as powerful as he was wealthy and forceful, so he was always at war, always on the move in search of gain. Wherever he was, there was the government, but governance involved little more than rewarding supporters with land. This kind of kingship and rule encouraged instability and continual warfare. Only slowly, over the course of the sixth, seventh, and eighth centuries, did kings evolve from warrior chieftains to rulers of subjects. But when kings designated towns or castles as their seats of government, royal authority increased. These places, where they kept treasuries and records and from which they issued decrees, provided some stability. In the meantime, the overwhelming majority of the population working on the land hoped to escape the notice of passing armies and thereby survive.

The Iberian and Italian Peninsulas

Following their defeat by the Franks in 507, the Visigoths retreated over the Pyrenees to the Iberian Peninsula, where they found the population easier to subdue. As a province of the Roman Empire, Spain had had close cultural and religious ties to the imperial city. The upper levels of society were descendants of Roman military and civilian administrators and people indigenous to the region. These Christians looked to the bishop of Rome as their spiritual leader. The Visigoth kings, who were Arian Christians, came to understand that as long as they appeared to be heretics in the eyes of their subjects, their legitimacy would be in question. So they converted to Roman Christianity. Thereafter, Visigoth kings cooperated closely with the bishops to bolster one another's authority. The arrival of the Muslims in 711 and the Muslim conquest of the peninsula in 718 brought Visigothic rule and society to an end.

Italy In the same period the Lombards from the north of Germany crossed the Alps into northern Italy and drove the Byzantines out. The Italian cities that had survived the collapse of the western empire owed their existence largely to their bishops, who assumed many of the responsibilities as well as the grandeur of imperial power. Now the Lombards used the municipal buildings and organizations they found in these cities to good effect, trying to rule as they imagined

The Visigoths converted to Arian Christianity centuries before they settled in Spain. Their conversion to Roman Christianity made them more acceptable as rulers to the people of the Iberian Peninsula. Why did the builders of this church make the windows small? Does the church remind you more of a fortress than a place of worship? What does that suggest about the role churches sometimes played in the sixth century?

Foto Marburg/Art Resource, NY

the Romans would have done. Once they had established their capital at the inland town of Pavia in 572, they gave themselves the titles, offices, and authority of the old Christian Roman Empire. Not surprisingly, the bishops did not welcome these new competitors for civic authority, some of whom were Arian Christians and therefore, in their opinion, heretics. The ill will between bishops and kings went both ways, as the Lombard kings rejected the church's claims to authority within the cities. Whereas the Visigoth kings saw cooperating with the bishops as a means for gaining power, the Lombard kings viewed bishops as impediments to their rule. The pope, in particular, became their target. As bishop of Rome, he ruled most of central Italy. Good relations between the Lombard kings and the church seemed impossible while the pope had the central portion of the peninsula in his control.

Protecting the Pope This threat to the pope, however, drew the attention of the Frankish kings in Gaul, who did not welcome the Lombards' attempts to take possession of the entire Italian peninsula. Just as it took Muslim invaders to bring down the Visigothic kingdom, it would take an invader from the north to put an end to the Lombard kingdom in Italy at the end of the eighth century.

The Decline of Trade

Merovingian warfare and political instability throughout the region contributed to a decline in trade between western Europe and the Mediterranean. What is more, as commercial contact between east and west dwindled, the Frankish kings had less

cause to maintain cultural and political contacts with Greek Byzantium. The arrival of Muslim raiders in Mediterranean waters in the early eighth century further dampened enthusiasm for travel and trade around the Mediterranean. Up to that point, the axis of long-distance trade routes ran on sea and land from northwestern Europe in a southeasterly direction toward Constantinople. Now the dangers of long-distance trade caused a shift in the principal trade routes to an axis running north-south within western Europe, from the Baltic Sea to the shore of the Mediterranean.

Economic Changes These economic and political changes in the old Roman world had three effects on western Europe: a decrease in the quantity of luxury goods that reached the royal and aristocratic courts of eighth-century Gaul, a change from gold to silver coins, and a heightened self-sufficiency in the population of western Europe as a whole. Merchants still brought wares from the east to markets near the residences of nobles and bishops, but in smaller quantities and less often. Spices, gold, silk cloth, and ceramics became extremely difficult to find in the markets of the west. Trade became increasingly local and regional as western Europe came to rely more and more on its own resources.

By the eighth century, people in Europe had little access to or use for gold coinage. What little there was entered Europe from Byzantine and Muslim lands as Europe's only gold mines had been depleted by the eighth century. Moreover, because trading occurred most frequently on a local level, ordinary people found it more convenient to use a silver coin, the solidus, for their purchases.

The delicate decoration and faded frescoes in this Lombard church in central Italy signal a church of some importance. What can you say about the faded figures in the frescoes? What feature marks them as special figures?

Gold coins were simply impractical for the small purchases people typically made. The switch to silver coins from gold reveals much about the kinds of commercial transactions taking place in early medieval Europe.

The use of silver coins does not mean that these transactions always involved coinage. Often coinage only supplemented exchanges of goods. For example, a peasant woman might want to purchase a pig from a neighbor. She had only three hens and some rough woolen cloth she wove herself to give for the pig, but those items did not come close to what a pig was worth. Pigs were valuable, and therefore expensive, not only for their meat but also for their low maintenance because they wandered freely and could feed themselves off the growth in pastures and forests. The peasant woman did have some silver coins, which she could use to make up the difference between the value of her goods and the value of the pig. Barter, or exchange in kind, predominated in very isolated areas where coins were rarest and persisted throughout the early Middle Ages, particularly among people of humble status.

Fewer Markets In general, people had less need of markets than they had had in the past. Markets had become places where peasants made purchases or bartered to supplement the foods they grew. There they encountered neighbors, and perhaps a few traders displaying locally or regionally produced goods. But there were no traders hawking wares from distant lands. And the peasants did not purchase much. Whether in times of plenty or of famine, people produced most of their own food and clothing.

The Decline of Cities

The decline in trade contributed to a decline in both the number and size of cities in western Europe. This decline began in the fifth century and lasted until the end of the tenth century. Under Roman rule, cities had been seats of provincial governments and military garrisons, with markets drawing merchants from far away. Residents of cities in the Roman world saw themselves as cosmopolitan and distinguished themselves from the humbler, less cultivated folk who toiled in the countryside. Living in a city meant, for those more sophisticated men and women, access to a wider range of goods in the market, better clothing, better housing, and the benefits of the services municipal governments provided such as courts of justice. Lyons, located in central Gaul where the Saône and Rhône Rivers converged, became an important market city connecting the Mediterranean with the north.

Little Safety in Numbers When warfare among the Merovingian kings made life insecure and trade with the eastern Mediterranean declined, city dwellers gradually dispersed to the relative safety of the countryside, where, even if their quality of life diminished, they at least could avoid marauding armies and grow their own food. In the countryside they also would be more likely to avoid epidemics like those that had devastated the Byzantine Empire in the sixth and seventh centuries. The cities of Britain started to shrink and then disappear as early as the late fifth century, once the Romans withdrew from the island. On the continent, the contraction of city size and population began in the sixth and continued into the seventh century. With no one needing services—few merchants and even fewer bureaucrats and royal officials—the service economy underlying the basis of most cities dried up. Public authority shifted away from cities to the countryside, where the lords resided. Bandits in the forest or simply a more powerful stranger encountered on a path could prey on the defenseless without much fear that any public authority would pursue them. Troops following ambitious leaders in search of loot and land posed as great a danger as did the bandits and ordinary thieves.

Cities in the Italian Peninsula The cities that survived the economic shifts in western Europe shared certain features. In northern Italy, those cities whose bishops had assumed municipal authority and those that served as capitals of the Lombard kingdom made the transition to the medieval period. Roman buildings and monuments were put to new uses or were torn down for the stone, which was then used for new structures. Italian cities maintained portions of the grid-like street plans the Romans imposed on the cities they founded. Even some of the old city sewer systems built by the Romans lasted into the seventh century. North of the Alps, however, fewer Roman cities survived the end of the empire because the Frankish rulers lacked the resources to maintain the city walls, streets, drainage systems, and roads provided by Roman imperial rule.

Even to call the places where a few hundred or thousands of people lived in this era cities seems an exaggeration. Certainly to a visitor from far to the east—rare enough in the Merovingian period—the muddy settlements would not have qualified as cities. Jewish merchants, practically the only traders who still occasionally came from the Byzantine world to the Frankish kingdoms, would have thought them primitive. To the people of Constantinople, the west had little appeal. Its rude living conditions, limited diet, and lack of personal hygiene were in strong contrast to the urban centers of Islam, with their learning and lively markets.

Urban life in the west ultimately began to revive, but at different times in different places. Britain, one of the first places where cities declined, experienced the earliest revival. In the seventh century, even as Frankish cities were beginning to contract, London and other urban settlements showed signs of increased activity, especially with an upsurge in trading via the North Sea. The cities of Italy that managed to survive the decline in trade had to wait until the tenth century for better times, when the port cities took up trading with Muslim countries on distant shores of the Mediterranean. Not until the warfare among Frankish kings died down could rulers in the old Roman province of Gaul turn their attention to protecting and regulating trade in cities.

The Western Church, 500–800

- How did the church provide continuity between the old Roman world and the new Frankish one?

- What role did monasteries play in the preservation of learning?

At first, in the aftermath of the empire's collapse in the west, no one seemed to be in charge. Public authority had dwindled to nothing. The Germanic tribes hacked away at one another's territories in bids to increase their own holdings, thereby aggravating the violence and insecurity that marked the lives of all who lived in the western lands once ruled by Rome. Only in the northern Italian peninsula and southern Gaul could people feel a sense of continuity and a little security between the old world and the new. There, leaders of the church stepped into the breach created by the disappearance of municipal institutions and administrators. In northern Europe, the Roman past quickly receded and, along with it, the church, which had barely been established there. It would take an invasion of missionaries to resuscitate Christianity in the extreme reaches of the old Roman Empire.

The Christianization of Northern Europe

Across the channel from the Frankish kingdom, the newly arrived Angles and Saxons pushed the Celts and descendants of the Roman population to the margins of the island or off it altogether. Those who remained vied to dominate Britain. By the late sixth century, the region was divided among numerous kings whose fortunes rose and fell. A Saxon kingdom took shape in Wessex in the southwest and another in Northumbria in the north. In the southeast, King **Aethelbert** of Kent established his capital in the town of **Canterbury**, and his kingdom lasted a century. Then the kingdoms of Wessex in the south and Mercia in the Midlands overtook the kingdom of Kent, and they in turn were overpowered in the mid-seventh century by the Northumbrian kings. Rivalry among Britain's kingdoms meant almost constant warfare on the island. In the midst of the fighting, groups of monks walked tirelessly across the land, seeking to speak of the Gospels.

These sixth-century monks had not yet withdrawn completely from the world. Though monasticism remained connected to the asceticism of the eastern Mediterranean, the monks of western Europe

Aethelbert (r. ca. 593–ca. 617) King of Kent, a region in southeastern Britain bordering on the English Channel.

Canterbury Capital of the kingdom of Kent and seat of the archbishop and head of the English church.

perceived a greater need for active proselytizing and seeking support for the establishment of new monastic communities. To them, there was still much to be done to extend and deepen the Christian religion among the rulers and the common people of the British Isles and the land of the Franks.

Mission to Britain In 597, **Pope Gregory I** dispatched a small group of missionaries to the British Isles, headed by a monk who had adopted the name **Augustine** in honor of the early fifth-century Christian thinker from North Africa. Although Christianity had long before reached the Anglo-Saxon territory in Britain, Augustine and his companions worked to improve the people's understanding of the religion and extend its influence. Augustine converted King Aethelbert to Christianity and became the archbishop of Canterbury. From then on, even after the kingdom of Kent declined, the archbishop of Canterbury remained the spiritual and administrative leader of the church in all of Britain.

Augustine's mission has received most of the credit for initiating the spread of Christianity in Britain, but his missionaries received powerful support from royal women. When King Aethelbert married **Bertha**, daughter of a Frankish king, to reinforce an alliance with the Merovingians, he allowed her to practice her religion and to promote it through the churchmen who accompanied her as a bride to her new home. Similarly, Edwin, king of Northumbria, agreed to accept Christianity when he married Aethelbert's daughter. The missionaries who had accompanied Bertha north then began to convert the followers of Edwin. Thus marital alliances between powerful families combined with missionary activity ensured the gradual spread of Christianity throughout England.

Missionaries in the British Isles encountered monks from Ireland, which Patrick had Christianized a century before.

Pope Gregory I (r. 590–604) Pope who dispatched missionaries to northern Europe and wrote theological works and saints' biographies.

Augustine (d. 604) Augustine of Canterbury, a monk who converted King Aethelbert to Christianity and became the first archbishop of Canterbury.

Bertha (539–ca. 612) Christian daughter of a Frankish king who married King Aethelbert and helped establish Christianity in Britain.

Synod of Whitby Meeting in 664 at which Roman usages and the date for Easter were adopted, thus bringing English Christianity into the Roman tradition.

Columba (521–597) Irish monk who founded monasteries off the coast of Scotland and in northern England.

Columbanus (543–615) Irish monk who founded monasteries in the Frankish kingdoms.

Luxeuil Monastery founded by Columbanus in 590 in modern northeastern France that became a famous center of learning.

Pope Gregory I sent missionaries to convert the peoples of northern Europe and the British Isles. He also wrote theological works that led to his inclusion among the Church Fathers. Is this depiction of the pope meant to be a true likeness? If you did not know that the figure was meant to be Pope Gregory, what can you deduce from the features of the carving?

Since then, the church in Ireland had developed in relative isolation, depending on abbots more than on bishops for pastoral and administrative services. The Irish calculated the date of Easter differently from the method followed in Rome, a distinction that caused considerable tension among Pope Gregory's missionaries and the Irish monks when they met in the courts of the British kings. In the end, representatives of the pope convinced Oswy, the king of Northumbria, to follow their calculation at the **Synod of Whitby** in 664, and Roman Christianity took the first step toward becoming the dominant form in England.

Irish Monks **Columba**, an Irish monk, crossed the Irish Sea around 563 to establish monastic communities, first on islands off the coast of Scotland and later in northern Britain, that became important centers of learning. In the 590s, another Irish monk, **Columbanus**, with a group of assistants from his homeland, traveled through the Frankish kingdom, founding monasteries wherever he went. One of them, **Luxeuil**, on the site of a Roman town in eastern France that had been destroyed by Attila in 451, became renowned as a center of learning. Columbanus's success depended in large part on the financial support and encouragement of the Merovingian rulers and aristocracy.

Another monk from the British Isles, **Boniface**, began the conversion of the northern Germanic peoples. Born with the name Winfrid, this missionary received in 719 the title of bishop from Pope Gregory II, who conferred on him the new name of Boniface to mark his exalted status. Boniface set out to make converts out of the Frisians, Hessians, and Thuringians in what is today northern Germany. His efforts complemented the efforts of the Franks to submit the non-Christian German peoples to their rule. Christianizing the people of the north made it easier to integrate them into the Christian Frankish kingdom.

The Bishops

Boniface's elevation to the office of bishop of the German lands reflects the kind of work bishops undertook in northern Europe, where there were not yet many practicing Christians. In these regions, bishops resembled missionaries more than they did ecclesiastical administrators. In southern Gaul, Spain, and Italian cities, on the other hand, bishops became the caretakers not only of the early medieval church but also of early medieval society. In addition to overseeing the spiritual care of the Christians living under their jurisdiction, they became the effective rulers of many Italian and southern French cities. The bishops of Milan and Lyons acquired reputations for their courts of justice. In northern Europe, bishops acted more as advisers to kings in the absence of other officials.

Regional Consultation The bishops of a region met occasionally to discuss and address problems in their areas. But their primary role centered on their status as spiritual head of an administrative unit called the **bishopric** or **diocese**, which had authority over local churches, in smaller administrative units called **parishes**, within it. Parish priests assigned to local churches to perform religious services answered to the bishop in whose diocese their churches were located. The bishopric was centered on a city, and at the heart of the bishop's city stood the **cathedral**, the principal church of a diocese, and at the heart of the cathedral were preserved the relics and tombs of local holy figures considered saints by ordinary people. The cathedral of Tours attracted pilgrims from all over Gaul who desired to pray to Saint Martin, a Roman soldier-turned-monk whose remains and relics lay under the altar. The proximity of sacred relics to the bishop's seat by the altar was meant to instill pious obedience in the hearts of the men and women living in the bishopric.

Wealth and Masses A bishop's authority nevertheless rested on more than an aura of holiness. His spiritual authority derived as well from worldly wealth and political power, in the form of revenue from land belonging to the bishopric. Throughout the Middle Ages, the church was the single largest landowner, if all the land belonging to bishoprics and monasteries is counted. Other sources of income also contributed to a bishop's authority. When bishops allied themselves to the ruling and noble families of western Europe, they received gifts of land from wealthy men and women who wished to have **commemorative Masses** performed for the benefit of their souls or those of their relatives after they died. Bishops also relied on **tithes**, a tax placed on all Christians for the maintenance of the church. Bolstered by revenue from land and the tithes, and endowed with the gifts of the royal and noble patrons, bishops became very wealthy.

The bishops' wealth, combined with the authority delegated to them by kings, made these churchmen very powerful in both ecclesiastic and **secular** spheres. They exerted influence over ordinary Christians by virtue of their role as spiritual pastors. Bishops oversaw the instruction of the laity in Christian **dogma**, the administration of relief to the poor and to the general populace in times of famine, and the supervision of the clergy in their duties. These ecclesiastical responsibilities alone afforded them considerable power.

Secular Cooperation Everywhere in Europe bishops developed mutually beneficial relationships with rulers. Kings found in bishops capable advisers and administrators, and bishops looked to kings and their royal families for support in the extension and deepening of the Christian faith in western Europe. With the help of royal women, bishops organized missionary work and the establishment of new monastic communities. They served as judges in the kings' courts and oversaw the maintenance not only of churches but also occasionally of city walls and other municipal structures.

Boniface (ca. 672–754) Missionary appointed by Pope Gregory II to oversee the conversion of the northern Germanic peoples.

bishopric/diocese Ecclesiastical administrative unit over which a bishop presides.

parish Smaller ecclesiastical administrative unit, in which a parish priest serves a local church.

cathedral Official church of the bishop's authority.

commemorative Masses Religious services during which the officiating priest prays for the souls of the dead.

tithe Tax of one-tenth of property levied by the church on all Christians to help sustain its activities.

secular Pertaining to the worldly as opposed to the spiritual or ecclesiastical realm; relating to the state as opposed to the church.

dogma Official teachings of the church.

Pope Gregory Sends Instructions to a Missionary

In the 720s, Boniface, an English-born bishop appointed by Pope Gregory II to proselytize among the Germanic tribes, wrote to Rome to ask for advice. In spite of some years in the north, Boniface still did not have a solid knowledge of the practices of the church and its rituals. The pope's letter is important evidence of eighth-century religious practice. Gregory demonstrates, too, an understanding of how to win the trust and confidence of people.

❶ Why does Gregory call the people of Germany uncivilized?

❷ What does it mean to be in "a state of continence"?

❸ What does this say about the degree of authority parents had over their children?

❹ How might Pope Gregory's understanding of contagious disease differ from our own?

❺ What can you infer from this letter about the standards of behavior imposed on the clergy?

❻ How would you describe the role of the priest and bishop in a community of people not yet well acquainted with the church and Christianity?

You ask first within what degrees of relationship marriage may take place. We reply: strictly speaking, in so far as the parties know themselves to be related they ought not to be joined together. **❶** But since moderation is better than strictness of discipline, especially toward so uncivilized a people, they may contract marriage after the fourth degree. **❷** As to your question, what a man is to do if his wife is unable on account of disease, to fulfill her wifely duty: it would be well if he could remain in a state of continence. But, since this is a matter of great difficulty, it is better for him who cannot refrain to take a wife. He may not, however, withdraw his support from the one who was prevented by disease, provided she be not involved in any grievous fault....

In the celebration of the Mass, the form is to be observed which our Lord Jesus Christ used with his disciples. He took the cup and gave it to them, saying: "This cup is the new testament in my blood; this do ye as oft as ye take it." Wherefore it is not fitting that two or three cups should be placed on the altar when the ceremony of the Mass is performed....

You ask further, if a father or mother shall have placed a young son or daughter in a cloister under the discipline of a rule, whether it is lawful for the child after reaching the years of discretion to leave the cloister and enter into marriage. This we absolutely forbid, since it is an impious thing that the restraints of desire should be relaxed for children offered to God by their parents.... **❸**

❹ You ask whether, in the case of a contagious disease or plague in a church or monastery, those who are not yet attacked may escape danger by flight. We declare this to be the height of folly; for no one can escape from the hand of God.

❺ Finally, your letter states that certain priests and bishops are so involved in vices of many sorts that their lives are a blot upon the priesthood and you ask whether it is lawful for you to eat with or to speak with them, supposing them not to be heretics. We answer, that you by apostolic authority are to admonish and persuade them and so bring them back to the purity of church discipline. If they obey, you will save their souls and win reward for yourself. **❻** You are not to avoid conversation or eating at the same table with them. It often happens that those who are slow in coming to a perception of the truth under strict discipline may be led into the paths of righteousness by the influence of their table companions and by gentle admonition. You ought also to follow this same rule in dealing with those chieftains who are helpful to you.

Source: Taken from Pope Gregory II's letter to Boniface.

To a modern eye, many Frankish bishops look very much like city mayors.

Because of the cooperation between rulers and bishops, Frankish kings felt they had the right to appoint churchmen to ecclesiastical positions within their kingdoms, although this notion went against long-established church law. In some respects, the kings' expectations were reasonable. After all, the duties of bishops extended far beyond the walls of their cathedrals, and, as practically the only literate people in society, the lower clergy such as priests and deacons performed critically important services in royal and municipal administration.

Some bishops were inclined to agree with the king's view of appointments, but many bishops, and especially the pope, did not approve of secular appointments to church positions at any level, which they felt diminished the church's authority. Such appointments raised a question of loyalty: should a bishop owe his first loyalty to the church or to the layman who appointed him to his office? By the eleventh century, more and more people believed the health of the church depended on keeping the clergy out of the king's business and on keeping the king out of the church's affairs.

The Bishop of Rome

No one in the Christian world at either end of the Mediterranean in the sixth through the eighth centuries denied the bishop of Rome his special place among the church's leaders. Bishops and archbishops in the east and west agreed that, through apostolic succession, he possessed the authority of Saint Peter, the Apostle to whom Christians believe Jesus conveyed his authority after his death. All Christians recognized the pope as an especially important bishop, but the Christians of the west viewed the authority of the pope as directly descended from Saint Peter himself.

A Prestigious Office To the Christians of the east, the pope did not rank quite as high. The pope, in their view, was no more than the first among equals and certainly not the supreme head of the church. The archbishops of Alexandria, Antioch, and Jerusalem each had a claim to apostolic authority by virtue of the Apostles who had worked and died in those cities. Constantinople's patriarch, in particular, claimed at least as much authority as the pope on the basis of his proximity to the emperor. Nevertheless, regardless of the details, all Christians everywhere turned to the pope as a figure of extraordinary spiritual and moral authority. Such was his prestige that clergy everywhere appealed to him to settle disputes over appointments and church property.

The pope's court and staff, collectively known as the **papacy**, thus acquired a reputation in western Europe and in the east as a highly authoritative court of appeals. The popes of the early Middle Ages and their officers came to believe that the office of pope was heir to the western half of the empire and viewed it as their right to take over many of the emperor's responsibilities and privileges. That sphere of jurisdiction included a sizable portion of central Italy, the **Papal States**, over which they ruled as secular rulers.

Far-Reaching Claims Some time after the year 750, a document came to light that gave the office of the pope the legitimacy it needed to rule territory. The **Donation of Constantine** purported to be a fourth-century agreement between the emperor Constantine the Great and the bishop of Rome, Silvester, in which Constantine, departing for his new capital in Constantinople, transferred to Silvester authority not only over the institution of the church but also directly over much of the territory of central Italy and indirectly over the secular rulers of the west. The document made it appear that Constantine was leaving Silvester in charge of the western half of the empire. In the fifteenth century, the Italian scholar Lorenzo Valla proved the document was a forgery, but even in the ninth century some doubted its authenticity.

The Donation of Constantine reveals, however, the ambitions of the popes in contrast to the limits of their practical power. Frankish kings, in emulation of the eastern emperors, could still convene church councils, a prerogative that the pope claimed in principle exclusively for himself. Also, there was little the pope could do at this point to prevent kings from appointing bishops or prevent lords from appointing priests on their lands. Although they viewed the pope as the head of the church, western secular rulers and even bishops and archbishops outside of Rome felt no obligation to recognize, much less put into practice, the pope's laws. It would not be until the end of the twelfth century that the papacy would begin to realize its claim to hold supreme authority in spiritual and secular affairs. But the desire to do so had long been apparent.

Monasticism and Learning

In 525, in the vicinity of Monte Cassino, south of Rome, **Benedict of Nursia**,

papacy Institution that carries out the duties of the bishop of Rome, the pope.

Papal States Large territory in central Italy ruled by the pope and from which the papacy derived a large proportion of its wealth.

Donation of Constantine A forged mid-eighth-century document purporting to be a transfer of land and power in the western empire from Emperor Constantine to Pope Silvester.

Benedict of Nursia (ca. 480–543) Founder of the Benedictine Order of monks who devised a mode of monastic living that proved successful and was widely adopted.

an educated man from a noble Roman family who had become a hermit, founded a small community of men who dedicated their lives to constant prayer. Benedict adapted and expanded on the **rules** of earlier monastic communities in Egypt and Syria to suit the conditions in which he and his fellow monks lived. The rules he put together—emphasizing poverty, chastity, and obedience and establishing a schedule of prayers, meals, and sleep—attracted others, who established further monasteries adhering to the Benedictine rule. Benedict made manual labor a daily obligation for the monks in his community. Each monastery had an abbot, whose authority was absolute.

A Way of Life and Prayer The Rule of Saint Benedict gave structure to a monk's day. Benedict understood how the seemingly insignificant decisions in a spiritual life, such as what to eat, how to pray, and when to sleep, could undermine a community's peace if those decisions were left to individual choice. All monks took vows of poverty, chastity, and obedience. The fewer decisions the monks had to make about how to live together, so Benedict's thinking went, the fewer disagreements they would have. The Rule called for a regular rotation of religious services, called the **Divine Office**, that ensured the monks would recite the entire Bible at least once over the course of a year.

In the early Middle Ages, monks engaged in manual labor, such as farming, to support themselves. But as noble families donated more and more land to the monks in exchange for prayers, they did less and less manual labor. By the year 1000, monasteries had become self-sufficient, wealthy corporations engaged in a variety of revenue-producing activities, such as agriculture, milling, mining, and animal husbandry. In the two centuries following Benedict, a monastery's reputation depended on its strict adherence to his Rule; in the ninth and tenth centuries, monasteries became known instead for their wealth as well as their holiness. As monasteries grew wealthy and the violence and chaos of western Europe subsided, the monks secluded themselves in their **cloisters** to spend more time in prayer and study, leaving their duty to perform manual labor to their servants and the peasants living on their lands.

Intellectual Work The monks' obligatory study of Holy Scripture had the effect of preserving some of Rome's literary heritage. With the decline of education in the post-Roman world, learning retreated with the monks behind monastery walls, where the only schools in the early Middle Ages persisted. The necessity of reading scripture in services prompted monasteries to maintain at least a minimal level of literacy among monks, who read and copied ancient works by Christian and non-Christian writers. In addition to the works of Ambrose, Augustine, Jerome, and other early church fathers, monastic libraries contained the works of the great Roman authors, such as Cicero and Virgil.

Some monastic **scribes** composed works of their own in addition to reading, copying, and commenting on works from the past. The pages of the manuscripts were made of either parchment or vellum—sheep and calf skins, respectively—that were treated to remove the hair and soften it. For a complete manuscript of the Bible, the skins of nearly two hundred sheep were required; only the very wealthy could afford such a luxury. In northern England, **Bede**, a monk in the isolated monastery of Wearmouth, relied on the ancient texts in his library to write a history of the English church. The monks of northern England and Ireland became known for their beautiful and intricate manuscript **illuminations**, decorations in gold leaf and brightly colored inks. Still, the monks' tendency to neglect the non-Christian works led to the permanent loss of many classical works.

Religious Women Since women, too, had their own monastic communities, it was common prior to the tenth century for only a wall to separate women's monasteries from those of men, allowing the priest monks to celebrate the Mass in the women's section, as women were not allowed to do so. At the monastery of Luxeuil, a few women even served as abbesses of both the men's and the women's communities. But medieval society was always deeply suspicious of communities with both male and female members, even though sharing resources and providing mutual protection made sense in those violent and chaotic times. By the tenth century, conjoined religious establishments had been separated, and the religious women suffered materially. Unlike men's monasteries, women's communities could not attract lucrative donations, to say, commemorative Masses. With some notable exceptions, poverty burdened many women's monasteries throughout the Middle Ages.

rule Set of regulations followed by a religious community that established the schedule of worship and manual labor.

Divine Office Daily cycle of prayers and services in a monastery.

cloister Enclosed courtyard of a monastery; also the entire monastery itself.

scribe Someone who serves as a secretary or copies manuscripts in a formal script.

Bede (ca. 673–735) Monk known as the Venerable Bede for his great learning; author of *The Ecclesiastical History of the English People*.

illuminations Colorful decorations in gold leaf and brightly colored inks on medieval manuscripts.

Monks spent part of their day walking in silent contemplation around the cloister with their prayer books. What purpose did the enclosed walkway, or portico, serve?

Women's monasteries served a social function as well as a religious one. Royal and noble families unable to provide dowries commensurate with their status often compelled their daughters to become nuns. The financial contribution required to place a woman in a monastery was more than most ordinary families could afford but less than the dowry expected of a noble bride. With no choice in the matter, noble daughters spent their lives in seclusion from the secular world. Widowed queens and noblewomen often chose to retreat from the world. The *History of the Franks*, by Gregory of Tours, indicated that entering a monastery meant the end of a Merovingian queen's political influence at court, but the start of a new life working for the poor and surrounded by kinswomen and attendants. One queen, Radegund, wife of King Chlotar I, left her husband to found a monastery in which she acquired a reputation for great sanctity and sacrifice.

Some women undoubtedly resented confinement in a secluded community. Others found that monastic life offered them opportunities for spiritual and intellectual growth not easily available in the lay world. Although women's monasteries did not possess libraries like those in men's monasteries, a nun nevertheless stood a better chance of learning to read and of having access to written texts than did a woman at the king's court. Women's monasteries outnumbered men's in the early centuries of medieval Europe, so the monastic life clearly had an appeal for women.

 Checking In

By yourself or with a partner, explain the significance of each of the following selected key terms:

Canterbury   papacy

Pope Gregory I   Donation of Constantine

Synod of Whitby   Benedict of Nursia

parishes   cloisters

Charlemagne and the Revival of Empire in the West, 700–900

- **How did the pope view his authority in relation to Charlemagne's?**
- **What factors helped revive the title of emperor in the west?**

By the late eighth century, most people in western Europe associated the office of emperor with the Byzantine emperors. For the eastern emperors, there had been no break in continuity from the golden days of Rome to the less glorious present of a much-reduced eastern empire. But the Frankish king and nobility also remembered that there had once been a system of two emperors, one in the east and one in the west, and so the possibility of a revival of the western title existed. The time was especially favorable because a woman occupied the imperial throne in Constantinople. For many in the west, that meant that the office of emperor was, in effect, vacant.

From Mayor to King

Over the seventh and early eighth centuries, the infighting among the Merovingians contributed to the decay of the office of king, as did pressure from powerful noble families. The nobles benefited from their position as the king's chief supporters, as the estates granted to them by the kings allowed them to create strongholds where they exercised authority equal to and eventually surpassing that of the kings. In fact, the kings became so insignificant politically that the most powerful nobles of the moment chose the king from the pool of Merovingian descendants.

As early as 600, the Frankish kingdom had consisted of three provinces—Neustria, Austrasia, and Burgundy. Each province had its own king, but a court official called the mayor of the palace, or **major domus**, effectively ruled in the place of the king. Instead of the kings fighting among themselves, the struggle for power shifted to the mayors, who fought for dominance over as much of one another's provinces as they could manage to acquire. The Merovingian kings had become little more than puppets for the ambitions of land-hungry mayors.

The Carolingian Family One family in particular rose to power from its base in Austrasia, the northeastern region of the Frankish kingdom. **Charles Martel**, the mayor of Austrasia, waged war against his fellow mayors in the adjacent regions and eventually brought the heartland of Europe under his rule. Once he had set up a puppet Merovingian king in Neustria, he turned his attention to east of the Rhine River. The populations there had had little previous contact with Frankish culture, nor had they yet converted to Christianity. When Charles incorporated them by force into his realm, he brought them into Christendom at the same time.

Charles Martel also battled for Christianity in the southwest, where he faced a Muslim foe. A little more than a century after

Charlemagne, seen here in this manuscript page with his wife, was the first ruler in the West to bear the title of emperor in over three hundred years. Which figure is Charlemagne and which is his wife? What might the difference in their size signify besides relative height? How would you describe their clothing? Rich? Modest? (Erich Lessing/Art Resource, NY)

conquering the Iberian Peninsula, Abd-ar-Rahman, the Muslim ruler based in the city of Cordoba, led an army over the Pyrenees and headed north, claiming the Frankish land he passed through by right of conquest. At Tours, in 732, Charles stopped the Muslim advance, and the invaders withdrew to the south. By the time he died in 741, Charles had more territory under his control than any Merovingian king had ever accumulated. Although he never assumed the title of king, Charles lent his name to the **Carolingian dynasty**, founded by his son, **Pepin**.

Acting Like a King Unlike his father, Pepin desired the title of king. The problem was how and under what pretext he could claim it because the title of king had always belonged to the Merovingian family. It would have been unprecedented in Frankish history for it to pass to another family. Before he could resolve this problem, however, Pepin first had to reconsolidate his father's territory, as after Charles died, all the rulers of the conquered regions pulled away from his son's rule. Continual warfare marked the first eight years of Pepin's reign.

major domus (in Latin, "mayor of the palace") Merovingian kings' military commander and chief governor of a province.

Charles Martel (686–741) Known as "the Hammer," the mayor of the palace in Austrasia who established the Carolingian dynasty.

Carolingian dynasty (750–987) named for Charles (Carolus) Martel that replaced Merovingians as kings of the Franks.

Pepin (c. 714–768) Son of Charles Martel, the first of his family to assume, in 750, the title of king of the Franks.

When he had achieved a relatively stable state of affairs in the kingdom, Pepin turned his attention to the title of king. Writing to Pope Zacharias in 750, he asked if it was right that a king should hold the title of king but not wield a king's power. The pope wrote back a convoluted answer that said, essentially, no, and he then ordered the Frankish bishops to consecrate Pepin as king. Pepin found the pope's validation useful, but he resisted the idea that the pope had the power to make (and, by implication, unmake) kings. Pepin locked away the last Merovingian king in a monastery and had himself consecrated king in a religious ceremony. The Carolingian dynasty had formally begun.

From King to Emperor

A change in dynasty did not lead to a change in inheritance customs. It would no more have occurred to the Carolingians than to the Merovingians to bequeath their kingdoms in one piece to one son, thereby disinheriting the other sons. When Pepin died, he left his territory to his two sons, Charles and Carloman, but before they began fighting each other for their father's territories they first had to subdue the rulers of these territories. Once accomplished, Carloman, very likely under pressure, turned his half of Pepin's kingdom over to his brother Charles. Charles's success at maintaining and even enlarging this kingdom would win for him immortality in history and legend as Charles the Great, otherwise known as **Charlemagne**.

Assuming the Title of King Pepin's assumption of the title of king opened the door to a revival of the title of emperor in the west. In the old days, the Roman emperor could claim to be the ruler of nearly every people, or ethnic group, known to exist at that time. A conglomerate of different lands and different peoples under one rule indeed became the definition of an empire. Charlemagne had the title of emperor in mind when he took an innovative step and had himself crowned king of a people other than his own. In 773, he invaded the Lombard kingdom in northern Italy, partly as a favor to Pope Hadrian I, some of whose lands the Lombard king had taken. Instead of forcing regular payments of tribute or making the Lombard king swear allegiance to him—the usual choices for a conqueror after conquest—Charlemagne removed the Lombard ruler and proclaimed himself king of the Lombards in 774. It made little sense to most people at the time, for Charlemagne was already king of the Franks. But it made sense to Charlemagne: as the king of a people other than his own, he was just a step away from calling himself an emperor of many.

Three factors were working together to create this possibility. First, Pepin's taking of the title of king from the Merovingian family, which had held it for two centuries, produced a different political understanding of kingship. After him, it was understood that the title of king could be transferred from one person or one family to another. Second, the diminished splendor and the much-reduced military might of the eastern empire opened Charlemagne's mind to the idea of restoring the old title of emperor in the west. So did the fact that the ruler in Constantinople was a woman, Irene, and thus not regarded as legitimate by rulers in the west or by many in the east. Finally, an ongoing relationship of mutual support between the Carolingian kings and the pope created the possibility that the king of the Franks might claim to be the defender of the church, as Constantine the Great had done in the fourth century.

Reviving the Title of Emperor Toward the end of 800, Charlemagne and his army crossed the Alps to give aid to a pope, as he and his father had already done several times before. In this instance, the noble Roman families had physically attacked and expelled the unpopular Pope Leo III from the city of Rome. To restore order, Charlemagne first had to subdue the Romans. He then brought the unlamented Leo back to Rome, restored him to his position, and confirmed his possession of huge tracts of land stolen from him by the Lombards.

The situation in Rome now settled, the pope crowned the king as emperor at a Christmas Mass (see A New Direction: The Pope Crowns Charlemagne Emperor). It was not only the first time the pope had formally conferred the title of emperor on a king but also the first time—in the west or the east—that a member of the clergy had placed a crown on the head of a king. In crowning Charlemagne, Pope Leo signaled that the authority of a pope, as God's representative, gave the king, or the emperor, his authority as a secular ruler. Thus, for Charlemagne, to be crowned emperor by the pope was something of a mixed blessing. He did not wish to be obligated to the pope for his imperial authority. On the contrary, Charlemagne felt the pope should be obliged to *him*. After all, the pope owed his position to Charlemagne's army. To make this point clear, thirteen years later, Charlemagne stage-managed a coronation ceremony of his own when he watched his son, Louis, crown himself co-emperor with no help from the pope.

To resist the idea that popes were the source of their authority, emperors thereafter came to view popes as mere messengers of God's will. They may have had the model of the Byzantine emperor's superior relationship to the patriarch of Constantinople in mind. But in neither the

Charlemagne (r. 768–814) Son of Pepin; king of the Franks who became emperor of the west in 800.

The Pope Crowns Charlemagne Emperor

Pope Leo III stood waiting, off to the side in front of the altar in the ancient Church of Saint Peter's in Rome. The priests assisting him at the Christmas Mass in the year 800 were helping Charles, king of the Franks and king of the Lombards, don once again the robes and symbols of his royal authority. Earlier in the Mass, the king had divested himself and prostrated himself before the altar as a humble gesture of an ordinary man—which he most definitely was not. The king was as proud a man as they come.

All his life, Charles exhausted everyone he came into contact with. Tall for his time (a little more than six feet) and burly, this new emperor in the west wore out officials, armies, horses, clergy, and family. From the time he became king in 768 until he died as emperor in January 814, Charles spent every year of his reign except the last four conducting war and conquering territory. His empire stretched from the Pyrenees Mountains in the southwest of Gaul to the river Elbe in eastern Europe. He conquered the Aquitainians, Lombards, Romans, Friulians, Saxons, Bretons, Beneventans, Bavarians, Slavs, Avars, Bohemians, Linonians, Abodrites, Alamannians, Gascons, Catalans, Pannonians, Dacians, Dalmatians, and others too many to name. Wherever he conquered, he forced his new subjects to convert to Christianity. The king seemed never to rest. The Byzantines, nervously pondering where lay the limits of Charles's ambitions, had a proverb: "Have a Frank as a friend, never as a neighbor."

Now, his prayers finished, the time had come for Charles to reassume his mantle and crown. Pope Leo took the crown from the altar and prepared to set it again on the king's head. He had done the same at Christmas Mass in years past, when Charles had come to Rome in the winter after safeguarding the pope's lands and position in central Italy. But this time, the pope deviated from past practice. Setting the crown on the king's head, Leo declared that Charles was now emperor of the Roman Empire, the first to bear that title in the west since the end of the fifth century.

When the news that the pope had crowned Charles emperor reached Constantinople, it made the Byzantines especially uneasy, for their ruler at the time was the empress Irene, and to some—in both the east and the west—rule by a woman meant that the throne in Constantinople might as well have been vacant. To call Charles emperor was at least presumptuous; at the worst, it could be threatening. There was little, however, the Byzantines could do about it, under pressure as they were from invaders on their southern borders.

The monk Einhard, Charles's biographer, claimed much later that Charles reluctantly accepted the title of emperor. Charlemagne "made it clear that if he would not have entered the cathedral that day at all, although it was the greatest of all the festivals of the Church, if he had known in advance what the Pope was planning to do." As unlikely as it was that Charles did not know in advance what the pope intended to do, Charles had good reason to dislike the pope's action, or at least to feel ambivalent about it. Symbolically, the pope's crowning of the emperor suggested that the emperor received his authority from the pope and, therefore, owed the pope the respect due a superior. Was the emperor actually beholden to the pope? Or was the pope merely the conduit of God's approval? The question took centuries to resolve.

Source: From Einhard, Charles's biographer (c. 775 –840).

---

emperor's nor the pope's mind did government stand to one side and the church to the other. Today, church and state constitute two distinct entities. For most of the early Middle Ages, people made no such distinction.

Imperial Rule in the West

Charlemagne's reign represents a change in the expectations people in the Middle Ages had of their rulers. In contrast to the Merovingian kings, who felt little need to justify their possession of the title, Carolingian kings and emperors justified their rule by ministering to Christian society. Conceiving themselves as lay ministers, Charlemagne and his successors considered it their duty to defend and extend the church, bring justice to their subjects, punish their enemies, and make their own lives a moral example to others.

King as Governor Ministerial kingship became the standard by which medieval rulers measured themselves and were measured by others. Charlemagne viewed the church as well as his subjects to be under his care. Identifying himself as a Christian king and the source of social order, Charlemagne gained the loyalty of his subjects to a

ministerial kingship Concept of kingship introduced by Charlemagne in which the king assumes responsibility for government and church affairs.

degree his Merovingian predecessors had been unable to achieve. Whether the emperor was always able to live up to his own expectations of his authority was a different matter, but by overseeing government and church affairs, Charlemagne imposed a greater degree of order and peace in his kingdom than any of the earlier Frankish kings had done.

Still, government in Charlemagne's day amounted to little more than maintaining peace and granting justice. No bureaucracy yet existed to prepare reports, no courts to hear pleas, and no services offered to towns and villages. In practice, government accomplished little more than organizing the leading members of society for annual military campaigns, rewarding them for their work, settling disputes among them, and ensuring social order on a local level throughout the kingdom.

To these ends, Charlemagne delegated his authority to royal officials, or **counts**, whose wealth derived from the large tracts of land the king had granted to them as reward for their administrative and military services. To ensure that the counts were doing their job properly, he sent out royal emissaries, called **missi dominici**, to make inspections of his kingdom. The problem with this system of government, even with the help of the missi, is that it took a strong, energetic king to prevent the counts from viewing the authority they exercised locally as their own. While Charlemagne was alive, there was no question of who was in charge of the kingdom. After his death, power began to slip out of the hands of the kings and into the hands of the local counts.

A New Capital Even before he was crowned emperor, Charlemagne wanted a cultural life around him that was reminiscent of the Roman Empire. Later in life, he no longer felt the need to be always leading his army to increase his conquests, and he spent more and more time in **Aachen**, a town in northern Europe once popular among the Romans for its hot springs. In his new capital, Charlemagne created a court life that became known for its learning and sophistication, and he encouraged intellectual and religious studies as they had once existed in earlier centuries. Viewing his office as a ministry, Charlemagne hoped to deepen understanding of Christianity within the ruling ecclesiastic and lay circles of his realm. To achieve these goals, he worked to improve the standard of literacy among the clergy and laypeople of high social status.

Even if government bureaucracy during Charlemagne's time was minimal, there was still a need for literate men who knew how to draw up documents. Although the number of **cartularies**, or records of royal law, did not significantly increase until the thirteenth century, people in the Carolingian period had a growing appreciation for writing down important information. The more often people turned to the king to settle their disputes, the greater the need for documents to preserve the outcome of those settlements.

Charlemagne and his advisers recognized that his authority could not be imposed, or order in society brought about, without literate men. In an age when education had retreated to the monasteries, knowing how to read and, more rarely, to write became a skill scarcely found among the laypeople of Charlemagne's empire. For this reason, Charlemagne relied heavily on clergymen to carry out the bureaucratic tasks of government. Yet the clergy in the service of the king found themselves in a potentially difficult position as the interests of the king increasingly diverged from the interests of the institutional church.

A Cultural Revival As a man who admired great learning, Charlemagne sponsored the establishment of schools throughout his kingdom, the most important of which was the one in his own court. To direct his palace school he chose the bishop **Alcuin of York**, reputed to be the greatest intellectual of the day. As head of the school, Alcuin promoted cultural reform that extended beyond the confines of Charlemagne's court. In addition to making the **liturgy** conform to the rites of the Roman Mass, he also revived the study of the **seven liberal arts** (grammar, logic, rhetoric, arithmetic, music, geometry, and astronomy), which had fallen out of use centuries before. Then he turned his attention to the Vulgate (the Latin Bible), eliminating the scribal errors and mistakes that had corrupted it over generations of copying and recopying since Saint Jerome completed his translation in the third century. Through this work and a program for copying manuscripts of religious and classical literature,

counts Major landowners and supporters of Frankish kings; a count's territory corresponded to a county.

missi dominici (in Latin, "emissaries of the lord") Inspectors appointed by Charlemagne to oversee how counts used his authority.

Aachen Charlemagne's capital; today in northwest Germany and known to the French as Aix-la-Chapelle.

cartularies A register of laws and varying kinds of documents used in monasteries and secular courts.

Alcuin of York (ca. 732–804) Important scholar and cleric appointed by Charlemagne to oversee the school established at his court in Aachen.

liturgy Collection of Christian rites, like the Mass, performed in church services.

seven liberal arts The classic course of study comprising the Trivium (grammar, rhetoric, and logic) and the Quadrivium (astronomy, geometry, music, and arithmetic).

Charlemagne and Alcuin helped ensure the transmission of late classical learning into medieval Europe's cultural heritage.

This program of preservation included a reform in script that increased legibility. Handwriting had deteriorated considerably in the last centuries of the Roman Empire and in Merovingian Gaul. At the height of the empire, Romans had used relatively clear capital letters with punctuation and breaks between words. By the beginning of the eighth century, not only had handwriting come to resemble today's cursive script, with each letter connected to the next, but word breaks and punctuation had disappeared. Some Merovingian handwriting was as difficult for monastic intellectuals of the early Carolingian empire to read as it is today. To improve handwriting, Carolingian scribes emphasized clarity in letter forms and divisions between words. They also modeled their letter forms on the inscriptions on the decayed Roman structures and buildings. Their imitation of Roman capital letters was so successful that the fifteenth-century humanist intellectuals of Italy believed that the old and dusty manuscripts they were discovering in monastic libraries around Europe dated back to Roman times.

The Partition of Charlemagne's Empire

Like the Merovingian kings before him, Charlemagne submitted to custom regarding the inheritance of property and planned for an equal division of his empire among his three sons after his death. But two sons died before him, leaving only his third son, Louis, to inherit the empire. To ensure a smooth succession after his death, Charlemagne arranged in 813 for Louis, known to his contemporaries as **Louis the Pious**, to come to his capital at Aachen. There in the cathedral Charlemagne had Louis place a crown on his own head, making himself co-emperor with his father until his father's death would leave him sole emperor.

This coronation without the pope would have set a lasting precedent had it not been for Louis's insecurity following his father's death in 814. Wishing to bolster his claim to the title, Louis reverted to his father's precedent. In 816, he had himself recrowned by Pope Stephen V in the cathedral at Rheims. From that point on, the central role of the pope in the coronation of all western emperors was established.

No doubt mindful of the premature deaths of his brothers, Louis began early in his reign to plan for the division of the empire after his own death. In 817, he allotted the bulk of the empire and the title of emperor to his oldest son, Lothar, who would hold a rank superior to that of his two younger brothers, Pepin and Louis. These last two were to receive smaller shares of their father's domain, a distinct innovation for its time. In 823, Louis had Lothar crowned co-emperor and king of Italy.

Thereafter, however, Lothar viewed his father and co-emperor as a rival, while the younger brothers resented both their emperor-brother and their emperor-father. When, after his first wife died, Louis had another son, **Charles the Bald**, by a second wife, the three older sons perceived this new brother as a threat to their inheritance. In 833, Louis's sons captured their father and placed him in a monastery. Louis gained his freedom and his authority in 835, but in spite of the death of Pepin, the potential for warfare only increased. Louis's death in 840 signaled a new, violent phase in the civil wars of the Carolingian dynasty.

In the generations after Louis's death, the empire was divided up among succeeding Carolingian kings. The political divisions of modern Europe can be seen in the first important division among Louis's heirs. In the **Treaty of Verdun** in 843, his sons agreed to the partition of the Frankish kingdom into three segments. Charles claimed the western portion, corresponding roughly to modern France; Lothar, the central portion that covered the **Low Countries** (today Belgium and the Netherlands), the French provinces of Burgundy and Provence, and Italy. Louis's eastern portion became the basis of what would later be called the Holy Roman Empire and still later, Germany.

The political divisions reflected linguistic ones as well. In the western kingdom, Latin mixed with local dialects gave rise to early dialects of French. German and Slavic languages emerged as the dominant languages in the eastern Frankish kingdom. The dialects in the northern Italian peninsula retained close relationships to Latin. Overall, however, the people of the Frankish kingdom did not have to travel far beyond their own regions before hearing dialects that they could barely understand. Only in the very small group of educated clergy and court secretaries, scattered across the kingdom, did the Latin language serve as a common language.

The Treaty of Verdun did not prevent further bloodshed. Each generation waged war against

---

Louis the Pious (r. 814–840) Charlemagne's only surviving son who had already assumed the title of emperor within his father's lifetime.

Charles the Bald (r. 840–877) The king of the western Franks, a position inherited from his father, Emperor Louis the Pious.

Treaty of Verdun Division of the Frankish empire in 843 among Emperor Louis's heirs into the three portions that laid the basis for the future political divisions of Europe.

Low Countries Modern Belgium and the Netherlands, so described because they are on a low plain along the North Sea.

kinsmen to gain greater territory and wealth. The title of emperor was stolen from one branch of the family, passed from heir to heir for a couple of generations, and stolen once again by another branch of Charlemagne's descendants. In this maneuvering, the pope looked out for his own interests. The constant and debilitating warfare at the imperial level was made worse by the infighting among aristocratic families over their own acquisition of land and wealth. In the second half of the ninth century, the last vestige of the central authority once wielded by Charlemagne disappeared. Once again, kings were little more than military leaders constantly on campaign and minimally concerned with government. By 870, in another division of Charlemagne's empire that also soon collapsed, the old "Middle Kingdom" of Lothar was divided between Charles and Louis. By 924, even the title of emperor had fallen into disuse.

Checking In

By yourself or with a partner, explain the significance of each of the following selected key terms:

major domus	liturgy
Charles Martel	seven liberal arts
Charlemagne	Treaty of Verdun
missi dominici	Low Countries

Order and Disorder in the Ninth and Tenth Centuries

◆ **How did patterns of loyalty and obligation provide some sense of order and security in early medieval society?**

◆ **What were the forces for disorder?**

Charlemagne had a notion of the orderly and highly cultured world of the Roman Empire in the west, but he could not restore it. Life on all levels of society had changed dramatically since the fifth century, when the last western emperor was deposed. In the face of almost perpetual warfare, relations between the powerful and the powerless had been fundamentally altered. Now, lords and kings—often no more than warlords—compelled peasants to supply them with goods and food in exchange for a small measure of security, and peasants had no choice but to agree. In addition, raiders from distant lands periodically brought death and destruction.

Lords and Vassals

In the early Middle Ages, kings devoted more time and energy to warfare than to governing. Only when Charlemagne set up his court at Aachen did the government find a permanent place in the kingdom—for a time. The highest lord in a realm, a king was only as powerful as he was wealthy, energetic, and ready to wage war. To wage war in a time when not much money was in circulation, kings developed ways to raise armies and ensure their loyalty through grants of land.

During the Carolingian period in the Frankish kingdoms north of the Alps, kings granted a portion of their land to some of their supporters, or **vassals**. This grant of property was called a **fief**, and in exchange, a vassal swore an **oath of fealty** that obligated him to provide military support to the king. At first, the concession of a fief to a vassal made it possible for kings to raise an army without having to pay for it out of their own pockets: the oath of fealty required vassals to bring their troops to the field of battle for their king for specified lengths of time, usually forty days a year, and to spend time at their own expense in the king's court, where they advised the king on matters pertaining to his kingdom. The king also kept in his court a troop of soldiers to whom he did not grant land. Instead, they ate in his household and received gifts or wages for their service. Royal armies consisted of warriors who depended on the king in different ways.

More than elsewhere in western Europe, the Frankish kings relied on this system of land grants in exchange for military service, but, even among the Franks, there were many variations of this system. In general, however, vassals retained a large portion of the fief and disbursed the rest to their own supporters, who thus became vassals of the king's vassals. Only exceptionally did women become vassals, usually when they had no brother to inherit their fathers' commitments. **Feudal armies**—made up, in part of vassals performing their obligatory military service to their king and, in part, of soldiers directly under the command of the king—were notoriously unreliable. The strength of a sworn oath rarely overcame the reluctance of most lords to leave their lands

vassal Typically, a man of combat who swore an oath of fealty to bring both fiscal and military aid to a lord, usually in exchange for property with which to support himself.

fief Unit of property, usually real estate, granted by a lord to a vassal in exchange for military service and counsel.

oath of fealty Formal pledge of fidelity made by a vassal to his lord to support him in his military efforts.

feudal armies In theory, a force comprising all who owed military service to the king or a lord, but in practice vassals rarely met this obligation.

to go fight their king's battles. Over time, the great nobles of the Frankish kingdoms greatly preferred to make cash payments instead of performing military service, and kings came to prefer cash payments too because they could then hire an army of professional soldiers, or mercenaries.

In the ninth century, when the power of the Carolingian kings dwindled as a consequence of the warfare among Charlemagne's descendants, the nobility exercised powers within their fiefdoms that kings had once sought to regulate. Nobles dispensed justice without concern that a king would step in to impose royal law on them. Nobles kept more of the taxes they collected from the peasants living on their lands. Their armies functioned like militias, policing the fiefdom, guarding the borders, and occasionally raiding their neighbors' lands. Just as in the Merovingian period, the world of those without land or power—in other words, the vast majority of the population—had once again become local, violent, and arbitrary.

Peasants and the Manor

The king, his vassals, and all the nobles in the Carolingian kingdom depended for their material welfare entirely on the labor of the peasantry. More than 25 million people lived in western Europe in the ninth century, 98 or 99 percent of them peasants. Nobles and clergy made up the rest. To many, the world seemed naturally organized into lords, priests, and peasants.

And Europe's territory was divided into forestland, fields, villages, and smaller hamlets. A lord's property might consist of various **manors**—each a collection of peasant dwellings, a residence for the lord, and surrounding fields under cultivation—spread across the territory he held from his lord or king. A manor resembled a village where a community of agricultural workers who tended fields belonging to the lord lived, but everything was designed to increase the wealth of the lord. The lord compelled some peasants to work certain fields whose harvest he retained entirely, known as the **desmesne**. Not only did he insist that

the peasants take their grain to his mill to be ground and their food to his communal oven to be cooked, he charged them for it. Peasants had to put aside a portion of everything they tended, collected, or made—from hens' eggs to woven baskets—for the lord's rents. The manor was a revenue-generating machine that functioned for the benefit of the lord and solely through the work of the peasants.

Not all the people who lived on a manor had the same relationship to their lord. Some peasants were **serfs**, tied so tightly to the manor's agricultural obligations that they were not considered to be free and were said to belong to the manor rather than to the lord. The lord exacted more labor than rent from them. They could not leave the manor, and when the manor passed into the possession of another lord, the serfs went with it. Among their neighbors might be free peasants, who owed their lord goods or cash more than services. Both serfs and free peasants suffered from the heavy burdens their lords placed on them, but only free peasants had the right to bequeath whatever property they had to their heirs. At the bottom of the manor's society were slaves, who had no rights at all and endured the grimmest existence. By the tenth century, however, slaves were extremely rare and mostly women in the Carolingian kingdom. Overseeing the work of all free and unfree laborers on the manor, the **bailiff** stood at the top of peasant society. He represented the lord on the manor, making sure that the peasants' customary obligations were fulfilled.

Peasants spent their entire lives struggling to produce enough to live on after they turned over what they owed to their lord. Both men and women worked in the fields, although men usually handled the plowing and women the harvesting. In addition, peasants wove their own cloth, made their clothes, tended livestock, constructed tools, and built shelters and furniture—that is, if they could find the wood and other materials. No wonder children were set to work around the home almost as soon as they could walk. On the manor, the lord's requirements meant a lifetime of work.

Saracens, Vikings, and Magyars

As if life in ninth- and tenth-century northern Europe was not violent and hard enough, thanks to Carolingian warfare, the people also had to endure the harsh, bloody impact of three migratory populations: from the southwest came the Muslims (called Saracens by the people of the west); from the north, the **Vikings**; and from the southeast, the **Magyars**.

After their defeat at Tours, the Muslims returned to Spain, and they never again posed a serious threat to the Frankish rulers. But their raids continued. Just before Tours, they had seized Luxeuil and killed most

manor Collection of peasant dwellings and a lord's residence surrounded by agricultural land that the peasants cultivated for the lord.

desmesne Portion of an estate whose produce was reserved for the lord's use.

serfs Peasants whose residence on a plot of land that they cultivated for a lord was compulsory and hereditary.

bailiff Peasant who served as the lord's overseer and manager on a manor.

Vikings Scandinavian warriors who raided the coasts of Europe and the British Isles.

Magyars Nomadic people from Central Asia who invaded the Frankish kingdom and the Byzantine Empire; known eventually as Hungarians.

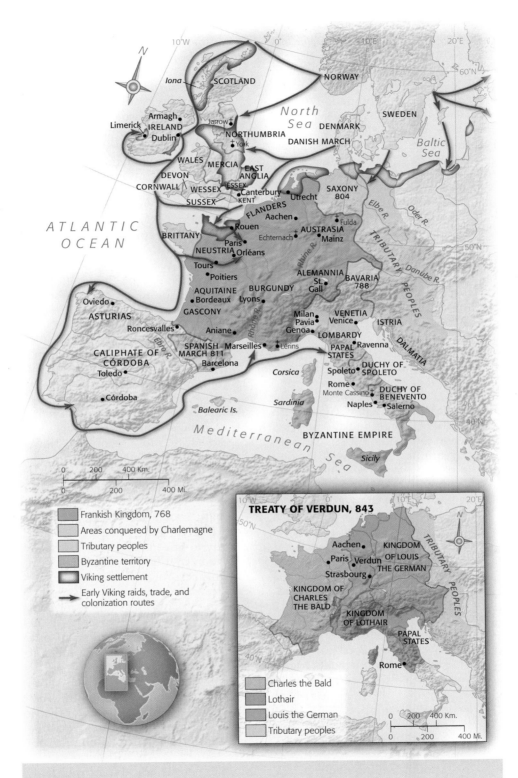

Map 9.2 legend:
- Frankish Kingdom, 768
- Areas conquered by Charlemagne
- Tributary peoples
- Byzantine territory
- Viking settlement
- → Early Viking raids, trade, and colonization routes

TREATY OF VERDUN, 843

Inset legend:
- Charles the Bald
- Lothair
- Louis the German
- Tributary peoples

Map 9.2 The Carolingian World Merchants in Europe never ceased to supply slaves to the Byzantines and Muslims. Captives were sold in the major slave markets of Constantinople, Cordoba, Rome, and Alexandria. © *Cengage Learning*

1. Which regions did the Vikings raid and which did they settle?
2. In which direction—north, south, or east—did most trade run? Who were the Carolingian's trading partners?
3. Which other civilization was the Carolingian empire's closest neighbor? Where did their territories meet?

of its monks. In the next century they sacked Monte Cassino and burned it to the ground. Their harassments around the Mediterranean discouraged maritime trade.

From the north came the Vikings of Scandinavia. Historians believe that overpopulation set the peoples of Scandinavia on the move in the late eighth century. At home, they were settled farmers. But after they planted their crops in the spring, they set off in their longboats, well designed for ruthless raiding and trading. These oar-propelled vessels, each with one main sail, were large enough to carry thirty warriors over rough seas but also shallow enough to carry them up rivers into Europe's interior. Wherever they went, they caused havoc, repeatedly sailing up the Seine River, for example, to attack, loot, and burn settlements all the way to Paris. When the season of raiding was over, the Vikings returned home to harvest their crops.

Viking pillaging was widespread along the coasts of northwestern Germany, the Low Countries, France, and Spain, and it occurred at a time when Carolingian warfare made organized defense impossible, though some local kings paid the raiders to leave them alone. (See Map 9.2 on page 265.) Viking raiders from what is now Sweden headed for Russia, where they followed the Volga River south deep into the interior. There they settled and married into the local population to become the Kievan Rus, who harassed the Byzantines. The Danes headed west, raiding northern France and the eastern coast of England, while Northmen, as they were called by the people they attacked, raided the western coast of England and the eastern coast of Ireland. Some traveled as far as Iceland and Greenland; a few explored the coastline of North America. At first, monasteries were their primary targets, and the Vikings seized their gold and silver liturgical objects, provisions, and even tools and implements. Many monasteries quickly moved deeper into the forested interior of Europe.

Well stocked with captured goods, Viking raiders became traders on their way home, selling their prizes when terrified Europeans were willing to deal with them. Some of the "prizes" were slaves, captured men and women who would be sold before their captors

returned home. Most slaves were brought back to Scandinavia, however, where they were pressed into heavy labor during the summer growing and harvesting season, when the Viking men were on their raiding journeys.

Eventually, and only gradually, the various groups of northerners ceased returning to their homelands in the winter and instead settled near the areas where they regularly raided. For this reason, historians sometimes refer to the Viking experience as a migration instead of an invasion. Each time the Danes pushed their way into northeastern England, some managed to settle, in spite of the efforts of **Alfred**, king of Wessex, to prevent them. In 878, his army halted their advance into his southwestern region of the island. The Norwegians, or **Norsemen**, who settled on the northern coast of modern-day France, became so much associated with the region that it came to be called Normandy. As Normans, they would continue ventures of conquest—of England and Sicily—in the eleventh century.

By the time the Vikings began to settle down, both literally and figuratively, at the end of the tenth century, poet-singers had made them famous. The **sagas** of their adventures describe their violence and heavy drinking as well as their rough treatment of women. Yet Viking male society allowed women considerably more property rights and granted them more responsibilities outside the domestic sphere than other societies at that time. An accurate reflection of Viking life is found in the epic poem, *Beowulf*, written between 700 and 1000. It narrates the battles of a Germanic hero from Scandinavia with the fearsome monster Grendel. Composed in the Anglo-Saxon language, the poem combines pre-Christian myths with Christian symbolism, reflecting the merging of pagan and Christian cultures that transformed Viking culture. Epics like *Beowulf* kept the Viking's reputation for brutality alive long after they had ceased raiding. As their thuggish behavior diminished, Vikings' customs and language blended into the regional cultures of the lands they had penetrated.

In southeastern Europe, another threat was emerging in the same period, this time from the Russian steppes. The Magyars, a nomadic people whose origins were much farther east in Asia, burst into the territory along the northern shore of the Danube River. Although the Bulgars, another steppe people on the move, had pushed them there, the Magyars aggressively preyed on the populations of the regions where they had been forced to migrate. Now known as Hungarians, the Magyars acquired a reputation for savagery similar to that of the Vikings. Some sold their services as mercenary soldiers to the Byzantine emperor

Alfred (r. 871–899) King of Wessex in southwestern and south-central England who stopped the invasion of the Danes.

Norsemen Raiders and traders from the region now known as Norway who settled on the northern coast of modern France.

sagas Poems relating ancient stories.

Beowulf Epic poem written between 700 and 1000 in Anglo-Saxon that tells the story of a hero from Scandinavia who defeats the monster Grendel.

The isolated setting of the monastery at Conques in southwestern France is typical of monasteries seeking refuge from invaders and warlords. What does such isolation imply about the means of sustaining themselves?

and even to the Bulgar king who had forced them westward. The remainder crossed the eastern Alps and raided the towns of northern Italy in 899. Defeated by **Otto I**, king of the eastern Franks, at Lechfeld in 955, they withdrew to lands along the Danube and settled in the region that would one day be Hungary and Ukraine.

The Empire Under Otto

When Otto I, king of the eastern Franks, defeated the Magyars in 955, it had been some thirty years since a king had called himself emperor. But, following Roman practice, Otto's troops hoisted their king on their shoulders and proclaimed him Emperor Otto the Great. Seven years later, in 962, Pope John XII crowned Otto emperor in Rome in more dignified circumstances. As emperor, Otto grabbed firm hold of spiritual authority. Like his father and Frankish kings dating back to Pepin in the eighth century, he regularly marched an army over the Alps to come to the aid of a harassed pope in Rome. This practice had become a tradition, and it made the church reliant on kings, in particular on those ruling directly to the north of Italy, now heralded again as Roman emperors. Like the eastern emperor, Otto convened church councils and synods, something only an archbishop or the pope was supposed to be able to do. He, not the pope, appointed bishops, abbots, and archbishops in his lands. Wherever he conquered territory and compelled the people there to convert to Christianity, Otto established a diocese, whose bishop acted like a colonial governor. Bringing Christianity—as well as his dominion—to the peoples of eastern Europe preoccupied him, although the Magyar disturbances on his frontier distracted him from conquering and converting the Slavs and Danes.

Otto's empire in the heartland of the eastern Franks consisted of provinces ruled by **dukes**, all of whom made oaths of fealty to the emperor. To minimize

Otto I (r. 936–973) King of the eastern Franks, crowned emperor in 962.

duke (from Latin dux, "leader") A title similar to but superior in rank to that of count.

University Museum of National Antiquities, Oslo

Seventy feet long and sixteen feet wide, a Viking long ship like the one shown here was capable of navigation over deep-sea water and up shallow river routes. How efficient would a vessel like this have been for carrying crew, provisions, and cargo?

dissension among them and to increase the number of obedient and compliant dukes, Otto installed bishops as dukes whenever a duke died. Thus he created a generation of dukes who owed their position to him and who, because as clergy they could not marry, would not produce successors, thus giving Otto even tighter control over the next generation of dukes. The benefits of using a bishop to administer territory increased when the bishop was a member of Otto's family, as in the case of his brother Bruno, who was both the archbishop of Cologne and the duke of Lotharingia. The methods Otto developed to increase his authority in the empire disturbed the leaders of the church in Rome, but as yet they were unable to resist.

Kinship and spiritual authority did not always guarantee good relations, however. Otto frequently had to contend with his other brother, Henry, duke of Bavaria, and his sons, who seized what opportunities they could to undermine Otto's rule. In the early years of his reign, rebellions by the dukes, often stirred up by Henry, kept Otto from extending his realm eastward. After he had subdued his rebellious dukes or replaced them with churchmen, Otto could turn to other pressing matters, like the Magyar invaders. But rebellious dukes remained a problem for Otto I, his son Otto II, and his grandson Otto III, all of whom worked hard to integrate the church into imperial administration. They saw no contradiction in the emperor's acting as the head of the church in the west.

 Checking In

By yourself or with a partner, explain the significance of each of the following selected key terms:

vassals	Norsemen
fief	sagas
feudal armies	*Beowulf*
desmesne	Otto I
serfs	

CHAPTER
Review

Summary

◆ The disappearance of imperial authority at the end of the fifth century ushered in an era of social disorder in the west.

◆ Kings—who were warlords more than rulers—and their supporters fought incessantly to defend or expand their territory.

◆ As a result of the chaos, interregional trade declined and cities contracted.

◆ By the tenth century, monasteries, the primary place where an education could be had, relocated deep into the interior, as far as possible from the paths of armies, and continued to grow rich.

◆ Charlemagne's revival of the title of emperor led to the revival of—or at least the pretension to—imperial culture.

◆ Following his reign, Charlemagne's empire was divided and warfare returned.

◆ In the tenth century, the western emperor, Otto I, appointed bishops—many of whom also happened to be his relatives—to the position of duke, the rulers of the provinces into which his empire was divided.

◆ The kings of the Franks and their vassals used their armies to fight among themselves and to confront incursions by Vikings, Magyars, and Muslims into their territories.

Chronology

507	Franks defeat the Visigoths, who then migrate to Spain	768	Charlemagne becomes king of the Franks
525	Saint Benedict founds monastery	774	Charlemagne proclaims himself king of the Lombards
552	Byzantine forces conquer Ostrogothic Italy	late 700s	Viking raids begin
ca. 563	Columba founds monasteries off Scotland and in northern Britain	800	Pope Leo III crowns Charlemagne emperor
572	Lombards establish their capital in Pavia, Italy	813	Charlemagne has son Louis crown himself co-emperor
ca. 590s	Columbanus begins missions to Germanic tribes	816	Pope Stephen V recrowns Louis emperor
597	Pope Gregory I sends Augustine to establish Christianity in British Isles	843	Treaty of Verdun divides Charlemagne's empire among his grandsons
718	Muslim armies end Visigothic rule of Spain	878	King Alfred of Wessex defeats Danes in Britain
732	Charles Martel defeats Muslim forces at Tours	899	Magyars cross Alps and enter Italy
751	Pepin consecrates himself as king of the Franks	c. 924	The title of emperor falls into disuse in the west
ca. 750s	Donation of Constantine supposedly puts pope in charge of western empire	936	Otto becomes king of the eastern Franks
		962	Pope John XII crowns Otto I emperor

© Cengage Learning

CourseMate Visit the CourseMate website at **www.cengagebrain.com** for additional study tools and review materials for this chapter.

Test Yourself

To gauge your mastery of the material in this chapter, answer the questions below. More than one answer may be correct.

Regional Rule, Local Views, 500–750

1. How did early medieval kings view their kingdoms?
   a. As land that they held in fealty to the Church
   b. As land that they ruled by agreement of Church leaders and nobles
   c. As their own personal estate to be divided among their sons after death
   d. As their family's property, which their heirs had to rule jointly
   e. As property that custom prevented from going to their heirs

2. Which peoples ruled in Iberia and in Italy in the sixth century?
   a. The Alans in Iberia and the Ostrogoths in Italy
   b. The Ostrogoths in Iberia and the Saxons in Italy
   c. The Lombards in Iberia and the Franks in Italy
   d. The Visigoths in Iberia and the Lombards in Italy
   e. The Huns in Iberia and the Ostrogoths in Italy

3. When trade across the length of the Mediterranean became too dangerous in the eighth century, what economic impact did it have on Europe?
   a. Western Europe turned inward and became more self-sufficient and had less use of coin.
   b. The Franks sought new regions to explore across the Atlantic Ocean.
   c. Rulers of western Europe sought treaties of cooperation and trade with Muslim rulers.
   d. The Byzantine Empire sent armies to invade western Europe.
   e. Newly discovered gold mines in Europe made up for the decline in trade.

4. The disappearance of gold coin and the increasing use of silver coin in western Europe reflected which economic change?
   a. A severe economic crisis that pushed the people into dire poverty
   b. An economic boom that raised the standard of living for everyone in Europe
   c. An economic boom that raised the standard of living only for the people in the Italian peninsula
   d. An increase in local manufacturing
   e. A contraction in the scale of exchange within regions

5. Where were the only cities of the old Roman Empire to survive the end of the empire in the west?
   a. In Britain
   b. In the Italian peninsula
   c. In Iberia
   d. In Hungary
   e. In Scandinavia

Now that you have reviewed and tested yourself on this part of the chapter, take time to pull together all the important information by answering the following questions:

◆ How would you distinguish between the ways Merovingian kings viewed their subjects and the land they conquered?

◆ Given the decline in trade and in the number of cities, how would you characterize life in western Europe in the seventh and eighth centuries?

The Western Church, 500–800

6. Who were the main agents who Christianized Britain in the sixth century?

    a. The formerly Arian Franks who took up missionary work
    b. The Visigoths who sent monks to Britain on a diplomatic mission
    c. Old Roman families who survived the end of Roman rule in Britain
    d. Pope Gregory I, who came to Britain to meet with the island's kings
    e. Monks sent by Pope Gregory and monks from Ireland who both carried out missionary work in the same period

7. In the absence of an emperor, which leaders stabilized the surviving cities in western Europe?

    a. Local noble families
    b. Bishops
    c. City councils
    d. Church councils
    e. Kings

8. Which of the following archbishops claimed as much apostolic authority as the bishop of Rome?

    a. Constantinople
    b. Antioch
    c. Jerusalem
    d. Alexandria
    e. Paris

9. According to the Rule of St. Benedict, what were the primary duties of monks?

    a. Healing the sick and feeding the poor
    b. Missionary work
    c. Prayer
    d. Manual labor
    e. Assisting in religious services

10. What advantages might life in a women's monastic community have for a family's daughter?

    a. A life of contemplation and prayer
    b. The opportunity to be educated
    c. Escaping an arranged marriage by her family
    d. For women from royal families, safety from dynastic intrigue
    e. All of the above

Now that you have reviewed and tested yourself on this part of the chapter, take time to pull together all the important information by answering the following questions:

◆ What roles did Church leaders envision the Church playing in the societies of western Europe?

◆ Describe the prominent part that monastic communities played in the Christianization and the preservation of literacy in western Europe.

Charlemagne and the Revival of Empire in the West, 700–900

11. The family of Charles Martel was based in which region of the Merovingian kingdom?

    a. Bavaria
    b. Neutria
    c. Burgundy
    d. Austrasia
    e. Swabia

12. Charlemagne used which administrative means to exert oversight over his kingdom?

    a. Military leaders who imposed order by force throughout the kingdom
    b. Bishops who exercised royal authority
    c. Royal emissaries who performed regular inspections
    d. Peasants trained to manage his great estates
    e. Priests who administered the laity in parish churches

13. Which of the following statements about Charlemagne describes his ambitions?

    a. He sought only to enhance his own prestige by assuming the title of emperor.
    b. He sought only military glory.
    c. He was a man of little energy who squandered many opportunities to expand his empire.
    d. He promoted educational reform that sought to improve literacy among the clergy and legibility in manuscripts.
    e. His goal was to conquer Constantinople in order to reunite the Roman Empire.

14. What is a cartulary?

    a. A record of royal law
    b. A deed to a church
    c. A card game popular in Charlemagne's court
    d. A written history of a monastery
    e. A document that allowed the king's servant to judge a case

15. The Treaty of Verdun in 843 had which effect?

    a. It settled the problem of succession to the title of emperor for all time.
    b. It divided Charlemagne's empire into three parts among his heirs.
    c. It settled a dispute between the pope and the emperor over rights to church land.
    d. It declared Charles the Bald to be Charlemagne's rightful heir to his entire empire.
    e. It declared Louis the German to be Charlemagne's rightful heir to two-thirds of his empire.

Now that you have reviewed and tested yourself on this part of the chapter, take time to pull together all the important information by answering the following questions:

◆ What long-lasting effects did the inheritance customs have on Frankish society?

◆ How did Charlemagne and his heirs justify the legitimacy of their rule?

Order and Disorder in the Ninth and Tenth Centuries

16. Which of the following elements best describe the makeup of a feudal army?

    a. Mercenaries from the Byzantine Empire
    b. Muslim mercenaries from Iberia
    c. Vassals holding land from the king and soldiers from the king's household
    d. Monks who specialized in warfare
    e. Serfs required to perform military service for their lord

17. What is the desmesne?

    a. The tax levied on peasants on a manor
    b. The official in charge of managing the lord's estate
    c. The fields owned by the peasants who lived on a manor
    d. The village where the peasants of a manor live
    e. The land held directly by the lord on which some peasants were compelled to work

18. Which region of Europe did the Vikings *not* eventually settle in?

    a. Iberia
    b. Northern France
    c. Along the Volga River
    d. Sicily
    e. Western Scotland

19. Emperor Otto I reduced his dependency on the dukes of his empire by relying on which of the following to govern?

   a. Greek intellectuals imported from the eastern emperor's court
   b. Bishops
   c. Commoners trained to be secretaries
   d. Vikings who had settled in the empire
   e. Magyars captured in warfare

Now that you have reviewed and tested yourself on this part of the chapter, take time to pull together all the important information by answering the following questions:

◆ Imagine a village on a manor. How would you describe the people who lived there and the work they carried out?

◆ What impact did the Vikings have on Europe other than that of violence?

CHAPTER 10

The High Middle Ages, 1000–1300

Chapter Outline

960	980	1000	1020	1040	1060	1080	1100	1120	1140
962 Otto I becomes emperor					**1066** William, duke of Normany, conquers England	**1076** Pope Gregory VII excommunicates Emperor Henry IV	**1095** Pope Urban II's sermon provokes the crusading movement		

The gold and precious gems that decorate this crown evoke the splendor of the emperor's court that Charlemagne and his descendants created in Aachen. Although it is thought to have been made in the late tenth or early eleventh century, the crown reflects various influences—Byzantine ones, in particular—that were contemporary with Charlemagne. What do the various elements of the crown symbolize? Is this an object that would have been in daily use? Or would it have been used mainly in ceremonies? (© Austrian Archives/Corbis)

After reading this chapter, you should be able to answer the following questions:

How would you describe the overall aim of the church reform movement?

What were the positive and negative consequences of the military expeditions known as the Crusades?

What are a few of the ways in which education changed during the eleventh and twelfth centuries?

BY THE START OF THE ELEVENTH CENTURY, the church's dependence on secular rulers for protection and its inability to prevent lay interference in ecclesiastical appointments had undermined its role as supreme authority in Christian society. To become the spiritual leader of society, the church needed to live up to its own standards, set standards of behavior for everyone under its authority, and regulate the expressions of devotion among the common people that so easily got out of hand. It would take a reform movement that engaged everyone from the pope to the laity to bring these changes about.

Secular rulers, on the other hand, recognized that to extend their authority they had to impose much needed order in society. The only way to restore social order was to dispense justice, prohibit private warfare, and collect taxes. To regularize the harvesting of crops and the collecting of revenue from the harvest, peasant families needed to live without fear of being plundered by land-hungry knights. How to contain the warlike impulse of the nobility was a problem that preoccupied kings and popes.

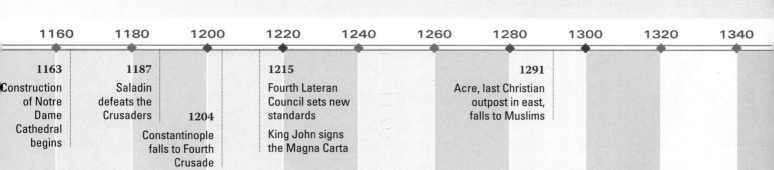

1160	1180	1200	1220	1240	1260	1280	1300	1320	1340

1163 Construction of Notre Dame Cathedral begins

1187 Saladin defeats the Crusaders

1204 Constantinople falls to Fourth Crusade

1215 Fourth Lateran Council sets new standards

King John signs the Magna Carta

1291 Acre, last Christian outpost in east, falls to Muslims

The pope saw a solution to the problem in holy war. Encouraging large numbers of nobles and knights to conquer Jerusalem discouraged them from fighting closer to home. But the establishment of Christian rule over the birthplace of Christianity came at a high cost. From the eleventh century on, even though merchants trading with Muslims in eastern Mediterranean ports brought to Europe a wider and more expensive range of goods to sell in markets, relations between Christians and Muslims were strained.

Those people who stayed close to home slowly began to feel the changes in the wider world. Peasant families had more to eat, found more in their local market to look at if not to buy, and had more obligations to the church than did people at the start of the twelfth century. As later generations of peasants saw more people on the road—merchants, wandering monastic scholars, royal messengers as well as troops—they heard about towns, which aroused their hopes for something better than what they could find on the land. Many laypeople chose a life of holiness as they understood it, not as the church had taught them. Others attacked Jews and Muslims out of a conviction that the world should be entirely Christian, no matter the cost. Still others sought new worlds through the life of the mind. Not in centuries had the people of western Europe had such a variety of opportunities to choose from.

Church Reform and Spiritual Renewal

- ◆ **What goals did reform-minded popes set for reforming the church?**
- ◆ **How did laypeople take a greater role in religious life?**

By the year 1000, the standards the church had set for itself had sunk on all fronts. Rich monasteries, ecclesiastical offices for sale, married priests, and secular rulers appointing bishops all indicated that the church was losing sight of its mission. Some clergy were determined to turn the church around. Their campaign for reform inspired many laypeople to dedicate themselves to God's work among the poor and infirm. Yet church leaders also worried that religious enthusiasm would create an atmosphere in which the church's essential role in salvation would be ignored. The task was to find a way for the laity to participate more fully in the life of the church without challenging its authority.

Reform from Within

Since the Merovingian period, monasteries had grown wealthy. Many derived large incomes from land they had received from noble and royal patrons, and they acquired reputations more for opulence than for austerity. Gold and silver liturgical instruments adorned monastic altars. Servants tended to the needs of the monks. Abbots resembled noblemen more than leaders of contemplative communities.

A Desire to Change The wealth of monasteries was bound to offend those still committed to the Benedictine ideal of poverty, charity, and obedience. In the tenth century, some church leaders had taken steps to restore discipline among the clergy living a monastic life and to advocate for similar reforms among the parish priests. They took their inspiration from Cluny, a monastery founded in 910 in central France that had set a standard for austerity.

There, monks adhered to a rigorous schedule of prayers that required them to rise several times during the night. So popular did this reform-minded monastery become that monks everywhere sought permission from Cluny's abbot to found monastic houses obedient to him. By the thirteenth century, the abbot of Cluny headed more than three hundred affiliated monasteries across Europe.

In the eleventh century, Cluny's highly educated monks helped direct church and papal policy. They prescribed a stricter adherence to celibacy, a minimal level of literacy, and a ban on the purchase of ecclesiastical office. Viewing human sexuality in mostly negative terms by associating all that is good with the spirit and all that is bad with the flesh, the church in western Europe reinforced its long-standing requirement that the clergy be chaste and unmarried. The requirement, dating back to 390, had been increasingly

Cluny Influential reform-minded monastery founded in 910, known for its austerity.

Map 10.1 **Merchants, Pilgrims, and Migrants on the Move, 1000–1300** By the end of the eleventh century, people at different ends of the Mediterranean came once more into contact with one another, mostly through trade, but sometimes through pilgrimage and holy war. © *Cengage Learning*

1. Which cities under Byzantine and Muslim rule drew traders and pilgrims from Europe to the east and why?

2. Locate where the crusading armies started and then find where the lands of the Roman church, the eastern church, and the Muslims were located. The longest part of the crusaders' journey passed through which lands?

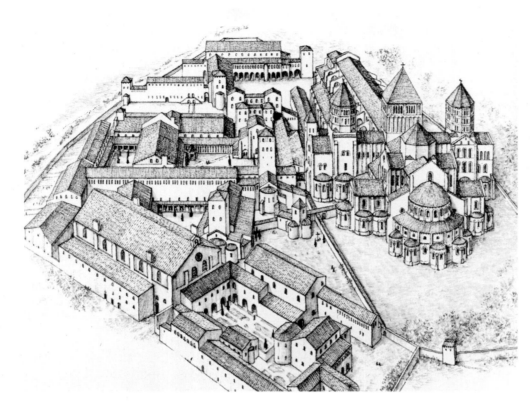

The church at Cluny was the largest structure in western Europe in the Middle Ages. What does that suggest to you about how the monks of Cluny viewed their monastery? (Based on a drawing from *Cluny des Églises et la Maison du Chef d'Ordre*, by R. J. Conant. Courtesy Medieval Academy of America)

ignored, as priests and deacons had taken wives and concubines and had children by them. In the late eleventh and twelfth centuries, a series of church councils invalidated such marriages and reduced the wives and children of priests and deacons to servile status.

Not for Sale At the same time, the reformers instituted a rule that required clergymen to be literate enough to be able to read the Bible and the prayers involved in the liturgy. They also put on notice those clergymen who had purchased their positions, a practice known as **simony**. It had been customary for lords to accept fees from priests in exchange for the rights to officiate in the churches located on the lords' lands, despite the fact that bishops claimed to control these rights. Some bishops and archbishops even accepted payment for the lower-ranking offices in their jurisdiction. Now, all such payments were condemned.

Like most successful reform movements, over time the products of reform became themselves in need of reform. By the end of the eleventh century, the Cluniac Order, too, had become rich. The abbey church at Cluny was the largest structure in Europe, and

simony Purchase of ecclesiastical office from a layperson or church official.

Saint Bernard of Clairveaux (1090–1153) Cistercian monk who was an influential preacher and adviser to French kings and the pope.

Leo IX (r. 1049–1054) Pope who initiated the church reform movement.

the monastery resembled more a bustling city than a sanctuary for silent prayer. Cluny's influence can be measured by the great number of papal, royal, and noble delegations—similar to the elaborate ceremonial visits secular rulers paid each other—sent to pay respects to the order's abbot. Important visitors required accommodations and banquets befitting their exalted status. The order's own high standards had collapsed under the weight of its success.

The Cistercians A new set of reformers then sought to revive the standards the Cluniac Order had attempted to set. In 1098, monks from a monastery associated with Cluny established the Cistercian Order, which acquired a reputation for austerity it never lost. One of the most famous preachers of the Middle Ages, **Saint Bernard of Clairveaux**, belonged to this community in central France. He not only helped establish other Cistercian communities but also became an influential adviser to the French kings of the early twelfth century.

The Church and Secular Authority

The German emperor Henry III's selection of German-born **Leo IX** as pope in 1049 made few people happy. Supporters of reform within the church viewed the emperor's role as interference. In Rome, the noble families had trouble accepting a non-Roman pope over whom they exercised little influence. Bishops who had purchased their office were particularly nervous about the arrival of a man known to be intolerant of simony. Ordinary priests with wives feared that this new bishop of Rome might compel them to give up their families. They were right to be worried.

The Reform Begins From the start, Leo set the tone for reform by dressing in the humble garb of a pilgrim. One of his first official acts was to depose the bishops and priests who had attained their positions through simony. He was equally aggressive in attacking clerical marriage. The response of the married clergy was clear and heartfelt: they accused the church hierarchy of driving them into poverty. Who, they cried, would tend to their material needs while they ministered to spiritual ones? Who would make and wash their clothing, clean their house, brew their ale, and in general maintain their household if not women? Affection undoubtedly entered into the clergy's concerns, but the ban's repercussions had a practical side as well.

Leo IX's successor, **Pope Gregory VII**, continued to raise standards for the clergy and also expanded papal authority, protecting the liberties of the church against interference from secular rulers. The greatest obstacle to the new pope's plans was Henry IV, the emperor who, like his father Henry III, considered it his right not only to appoint the pope but also to appoint clergy to church positions within his empire. Intending to end that custom, Gregory decreed in 1075 that only the pope had the authority to appoint clergy to offices. He also forbade secular rulers from conferring the symbols of a bishop's authority on newly appointed bishops, a ceremony known as investiture.

Enraged, Henry responded by removing Gregory from office and calling for the election of a new pope. To punish the emperor, Gregory excommunicated him in 1076. "I release all Christian men from the allegiance which they have sworn or may swear to him, and I forbid anyone to serve him as king," the pope declared. Relations between the emperor and the pope could hardly have been more tense.

Canossa In the winter of 1077, wearing the garb of a penitent pilgrim, Henry went to meet the pope at Canossa, a village in the mountains of central Italy where the pope was visiting the castle of a powerful family. For three days, it was said, Henry stood barefoot in the snow waiting for the pope to receive him. In the face of such a public act of contrition, the pope was compelled to forgive the seemingly penitent emperor. The **Investiture Controversy**, as the confrontation between Gregory VII and Henry IV is known, appeared to be over.

In fact, the battle for an end to lay interference in church affairs was just beginning. A compromise between Gregory's and Henry's successors was reached in the **Concordat of Worms** in 1122, which distinguished between the earthly and spiritual powers of a bishop. From then on, the emperor would confer the symbols of a bishop's temporal authority over lands and property, and church authorities would invest bishops with the symbols of their spiritual jurisdiction. Despite the clarity of the compromise, the liberties of the church remained an important issue as popes continued to challenge the right of not only the emperor but also kings, dukes, counts, and barons to interfere in church affairs.

Innocent III and the Fourth Lateran Council

The Gregorian reform lived much longer than its namesake. In the early thirteenth century, another pope, this one a young, highly skilled lawyer, turned reform into law. The reform legislation of **Innocent III** was intended to define what it meant to be Christian and to distinguish Christians from the non-Christians living among them. In 1215, with Innocent presiding, the **Fourth Lateran Council** issued seventy canons that set standards for clergy behavior, declared the pope to be the preeminent bishop in Christendom, condemned heresy, and required all Christians to confess their sins to a priest once a year. But it was the council's pronouncements on marriage and the presence of Jews in Christian society that had the greatest impact on ordinary Christians.

Marriage Reform Since Carolingian times, the church had had an unofficial role in the formal arrangements of marriage, usually no more than a priest's blessing of a couple wed by contract. As in the Roman world, marriage signaled an alliance between families and the passage of property between them. By the eighth century, the church had made the consent of the couple, not of their families, the defining feature of a legal marriage. Starting in the twelfth century, to prevent marriages between close kin, priests required the publishing of **banns**, a public announcement of a couple's intention to marry that invited anyone with information that would hinder the marriage to come forward. Clandestine marriages—unions contracted between a man and a woman in secret—were

---

Pope Gregory VII (r. 1073–1085) Pope who expanded papal authority, raised clerical standards, and protected the church from interference by secular rulers.

Investiture Controversy Conflict between Pope Gregory VII and Emperor Henry IV over the secular role in the investiture, or appointment, of bishops.

Concordat of Worms Agreement between the papacy and the emperor in 1122 that allowed the emperor to confer secular, but not spiritual, authority on bishops.

Innocent III (r. 1198–1216) One of the most influential popes of the Middle Ages, responsible for the Fourth Lateran Council and the crusade against heretics within Europe.

Fourth Lateran Council Church council of 1215, presided over by Pope Innocent III, whose decrees set standards for the clergy, declared the pope to hold supreme authority in the church, and required all Christians to take confession once a year.

banns Declaration by a priest of a couple's intention to marry.

strongly condemned by the church. After the Fourth Lateran Council, marriages had to be announced publicly in advance, contracted openly, and publicly acknowledged; they were also forbidden between closely related kin.

Jews and Muslims in a Christian World In seeking to reinforce Christian identity, the council decreed that Jews and Muslims must wear distinguishing clothing in public. In addition, on the grounds that only Christians should exercise authority over Christians, Jews were barred from holding public office. Finally, Jews who had converted to Christianity were forbidden to return to their former religion. At this time Jews in the Diaspora lived mainly in the German territories, southern France, and Sicily, working as merchants, moneylenders, cobblers, and tanners. The constraints placed on them only increased from this point forward.

Innocent died in 1216, less than a year after the council adjourned. The church had benefited from having such an able canon lawyer as pope for eighteen years. The reforms that Leo IX and Gregory VII had fought for took on substance in the legislation Innocent III shepherded through the council sessions. Not all of his measures would succeed in the long run, but he provided the papacy with the legal and theological instruments to impose order on the church and Christian society and to delineate the boundaries of Christian identity.

Lay Leaders and Friars

Starting in the late tenth century and throughout the eleventh, wandering monks carried the spirit of reform through the towns and villages of western Europe, preaching and engaging laypeople in the movement to define what it meant to be Christian and live accordingly. Inspired by the biblical text "If you wish to be perfect, then go and sell everything you have, and give to the poor" (Matthew 9:21), many laypeople formed communities dedicated to prayer and helping the sick and poor. Unlike monasteries, the new lay communities did not withdraw from but worked in the world and lived according to rules they devised for themselves.

The Waldensians The church welcomed these initiatives but worried that untrained preachers might misrepresent the teachings of the church. So laypeople had to receive permission to preach. Permission became an issue in the French city of Lyons, when, in the late twelfth century, the public preaching of a merchant, **Peter Waldo**, attracted attention. Waldo sought permission to preach from the archbishop of Lyons and from the pope but was denied. This refusal led him to question the church's authority and, later, the necessity of the sacraments for salvation. When he continued to preach, the church formally condemned him in 1184. This condemnation caused the Waldensians to question the value of some of the sacraments, at which point the church undertook their suppression with vigor. Members of the sect were declared heretics, imprisoned periodically, excommunicated, and, finally, in the early thirteenth century, expelled from the region.

The Cathars In the mid-twelfth century, another heretical sect, the **Cathars**, adopted a dualist conception of the world, seeing everything of the spirit as good and the material world as evil. Also known as Albigensians (for the southern French town, Albi, where many lived), Cathars rejected the special role of the priesthood in salvation. By the early 1200s, Catharism had spread over much of southern France and into Spain. In many towns, under the protection of noblemen who had joined the sect, Cathars set up their own churches, which attracted more people than did the Roman churches.

Although missionary efforts aimed to bring the Cathars back into obedience failed, the church did not always discourage new religious orders, provided they respected church authority and adhered to church teaching. In the early thirteenth century, the spirit of reform combined with a new religious enthusiasm among the laity to produce a new kind of religious order, the **mendicants**, who repudiated property ownership and embraced poverty. Unlike monks in isolated monasteries, **friars** lived according to a monastic rule in the world and carried out the church's mission, working or begging to provide for their very simple needs.

Francis Succeeds Where Others Failed The Order of the Minor Brothers, commonly known as the Franciscan Order, vowed obedience to the pope, renunciation of property, and chastity. Relief of the poor and preaching stood at the center of their mission. Their founder, **Francis of Assisi**, was born in 1182 in Assisi, a hill town in central Italy, to a family of prosperous cloth merchants. After serving in a war, he renounced his claim on his father's goods in 1207, gave away all his clothing and goods, and dedicated his life to the poor and infirm. The powerful example of his conversion convinced many of his friends to join him.

Within two years, in 1209, Pope Innocent III approved the rule Francis wrote. The Franciscan friars wandered over Italy, preaching repentance and aiding the sick; within ten years, they numbered in the thousands. Their wanderings took them not only across Europe but also to Muslim territories, where

---

Peter Waldo (ca. 1170s–1218) Devout merchant in Lyons, France, who defied church authorities and exhorted Christians to live more piously.

Cathars Heretical religious sect, also known as Albigensians, who rejected the role of the priesthood in salvation.

mendicants (from Latin, "beggars") Members of religious orders that repudiated the ownership of personal and communal property.

friars (from Latin, "brothers") Members of mendicant orders.

Francis of Assisi (1182–1226) Founder of the Franciscan friars, the first mendicant order.

Scala/Art Resource, NY

Dominicans vs. Cathars

Giotto's magnificent frescoes in the basilica in Assisi tell the story of how the Franciscan Order was founded. In this panel, Francis receives the blessing of Pope Innocent III. Compare the two groups of men in the image. What differences between them do you see and what do you think those differences reflect?

they sought converts. Women followed a more traditional path in the order. With support from Francis, a young woman from Assisi, **Clare**, founded an order of nuns in 1212 that became known later as the Order of the Poor Clares. Unlike the friars, however, they lived in strict seclusion.

Although Francis resisted pressure from members of his order to modify his principle that Franciscans could own no property, either individually and collectively, he reluctantly lessened the physical hardship the brothers were expected to endure in their life of poverty. After his death in 1226 from years of physical self-deprivation, the Franciscans became divided between those who wanted to follow Francis's original rule to the letter and those who believed the order needed to own some property to be able to function. The majority of the members and the papacy favored a modified rule that permitted the order to acquire missions and schools to teach their members how to preach and convert. By the start of the fourteenth century, the Franciscans had brothers working in missions as far away as Africa.

The Dominicans A Spanish contemporary of Francis, **Dominic Guzman**, founded another order of mendicant friars, the Order of Preachers, or the Dominicans. In contrast to the Franciscans, few of whom were priests, the Dominicans were an order of priests who specialized in preaching with the special aim of combating heresy, in particular the Cathars. Founded in 1216, the Dominican Order proved so effective against heretical groups that bishops relied on theologically trained Dominican friars to interrogate possible heretics and apostate Jews—Jews who had converted and later renounced Christianity. Dominicans placed great value on education in theology as a way to combat religious beliefs at odds with church doctrine.

The friars' work made a deep impression on religious life in Europe. By setting an example of apostolic poverty, they made people question their attachment to

Clare of Assisi (1194–1253) Follower of Francis of Assisi who established an affiliated order of nuns, the Poor Clares, in 1212.

Dominic Guzman (ca. 1170–1221) Founder of the Order of Preachers, or Dominican Order.

material things and made them more sympathetic to the poverty surrounding them. They placed a greater emphasis on learning. They also participated in the papacy's campaign to impose uniformity of belief on Christian society.

 Checking In

By yourself or with a partner, explain the significance of each of the following selected key terms:

simony	Fourth Lateran Council
Pope Gregory VII	mendicants
Investiture Controversy	Clare of Assisi
Innocent III	Dominic Guzman

The Crusades

- ◆ **What were the causes and outcomes of the Crusades?**
- ◆ **How did the Crusades change relations between Christians and Muslims?**

The belief that Jerusalem—the holiest spot in Christendom—needed rescue gave a focus to an enthusiasm few people suspected lay behind the spirit of reform. Beginning in the late eleventh century, the church—until then an advocate of peace—sent armies across the continent for the purposes of war and conquest. Thousands left homes and families to travel great distances and fight non-Christians for possession of land they thought of as theirs but that, in fact, had not been under Christian rule since the seventh century. Crusading armies attacked not only Muslims but also Jews, other non-Christians, Christians believed to be heretics, and the Christians of the Byzantine Empire. The march of Christian armies changed the nature of the Christian religion and created deep and lasting enmities that persist to this day.

A War to Renew the Church

Beginning in the eleventh century, the papacy had campaigned for reform on many fronts. In addition to raising the standards of clerical behavior and defending the liberties of the church, reformers also felt compelled to do something about the near-constant warfare among the nobles of western Europe that they perceived as harmful to the well-being of the church and its members. Noble families had long engaged in combat to seize land and build wealth. Now, as the custom of **primogeniture** began to take root in northern Europe, with the eldest son inheriting his father's entire estate, landless younger sons had even more incentive to make war and seize land. While some served as **knights**—in this period, little more than soldiers in the households of other nobles—others fought almost constantly. Few people felt secure.

Secular rulers did not have the means to control this violence because their armies were made up of the same men they sought to rein in. But the pope, who saw himself as the shepherd of an enormous flock, nobles and commoners alike, looked for ways to redirect the violence elsewhere. At local councils, bishops declared Truces of God, outlawing violence on certain days, and the Peace of God, prohibiting attacks on clergy, women, and the poor. These measures proved only partially effective, however.

Pope Urban's Call to Arms In 1095, **Pope Urban II** received a letter that allowed him to give the nobility a new focus for their hostilities. The Byzantine emperor, **Alexius I Comnenus**, asked for aid against the Seljuk Turks, who had seized land in Asia Minor, Syria, and Palestine from both Byzantine and Muslim rulers. Instead of appealing to the German emperor or the king of the French, Alexius applied to the pope, whose status in western Europe he understood to resemble his own in his empire.

Even before receiving Alexius's request, the pope had heard that the Church of the Holy Sepulcher had been destroyed in 1010 by a Muslim ruler of Jerusalem. Rumors about the mistreatment of Christians there were widespread in the west. In reality, the Muslims, who by then had ruled Jerusalem for centuries, and Seljuks, who replaced them, benefited economically from the great number of pilgrims who came to worship at Christian shrines and so were inclined to leave the Christians in peace. The pope was in possession of mistaken and outdated news.

Yet, on November 25, 1095, Pope Urban II preached a sermon to a large crowd in Clermont, in central France, where he had been presiding over a local council. Enemies of the faith, he reportedly declared, were intent on conquering the Holy Land. He urged "men of all ranks whatsoever, knights as well as foot-soldiers, rich and poor, to hasten to exterminate this vile race from our lands and to aid the Christian inhabitants in time." He promised a remission of sins for any of those who went to fight non-Christians, making war an act of penance. Christians fighting Muslims for control of the Iberian Peninsula would also have their sins remitted. This war, said the pope, unlike the noblemen's violence, was a **just war**.

Just War The church taught that war in itself was not sinful, especially when it was defensive. Since Saint Augustine in the fourth century, Christians had

---

primogeniture System of inheritance that directs the majority of or the entire estate from a father to his eldest son.

knights Armed supporters of nobles who lived and served in the households of their lords.

Urban II (r. 1088–1099) Pope who in 1095 inspired the crusading movement.

Alexius I Comnenus (r. 1081–1118) Byzantine emperor whose request for aid from the west served as the pretext for the Crusades.

just war The idea and theological explanation of when it is legitimate to wage war.

In this fourteenth-century manuscript illumination, Pope Urban II arrives at the council and gives the sermon that galvanized thousands to march to Jerusalem. But who is he shown preaching to and why? (Bridgeman-Giraudon/Art Resource, NY)

considered violence, when necessary, lawful if the proper authorities condoned it, if the cause was deemed just, and if the soldiers themselves meant good by it. In Alexius's letter, Urban saw an occasion for a just war that met all those criteria.

Crusading Armies and Crusader States

When monks spread word of Urban's sermon throughout Europe, the response was dramatic. Within a year, two armies—one an unorganized army of knights and peasants with little leadership, the other contingents of knights led by noblemen experienced in warfare—planned to depart. In the first wave, fifty thousand people or more incited by the sermons they had heard set out for Jerusalem, the city they believed to be in need of rescue. Jerusalem had for centuries been a city that Christians in western Europe dreamed of seeing but which only pilgrims willing to endure the dangers of a ruinously expensive journey ever reached. Now pious determination mixed with the allure of plunder and the thirst for adventure in the crowds that set out to rid Jerusalem of people who were not Christian. "Deus le volt!" ("God wills it!") became the rallying cry of the masses marching east.

Attacks on Jews Some saw enemies closer to home. In numerous cities, mobs massacred the only non-Christians in their midst, the Jews. One witness described how pilgrims in the northern French city of Rouen "armed themselves, rounded up some Jews in a church—whether by force or by ruse I don't know—and led them out to put them to the sword regardless of age or sex. Those who agreed to submit to the Christian way of life could, however, escape the impending slaughter." The massacres were the first widespread violence against Jews in western Europe.

Having accomplished what they believed God desired, many crusading Christians returned home, but thousands pushed on. When they reached Constantinople in 1097, Emperor Alexius did not recognize in these ragged, mostly unarmed, and mostly poor men and women a response to his request. His army quickly escorted them out of his territory. On a road in Asia Minor, the Seljuk Turks put a bloody end to what became known, somewhat inaccurately, as the Poor People's Crusade.

1st wave of crusaders

A Professional Army Meanwhile, more seasoned soldiers prepared for a military undertaking endorsed by the pope. The First Crusade, led by nobles from France, Germany, and southern Italy, lasted over two years, during which the Crusaders besieged walled towns, fought Muslim powers that stood in their way, and slaughtered indiscriminately—even Christians, whose faith they either ignored or were unaware of. Enduring hardship and starvation, more Crusaders died of disease than in combat. After capturing the port of Antioch from a Muslim ruler, they reached the walls of Jerusalem in June 1099. Since their journey began, however, not only had rival Muslim powers in Egypt expelled the Seljuks from Jerusalem but now Muslims, Jews, and Christians once again coexisted under Muslim rule in the city they all considered sacred. Nevertheless, on July 15, 1099, after a month-long siege, the Crusaders captured the city and massacred nearly the entire population.

Anna Comnena Describes the Crusaders

Around 1120, Anna, the daughter of the Byzantine emperor Alexius I Comnenus, wrote The Alexiad, an admiring history of her beloved father and the events of his reign. The last five of the fifteen chapters describe the First Crusade (1099–1102), and Anna's account of the crusading warriors who showed up unannounced at the gate of Constantinople provides insight into the way western Europeans were perceived in the old, highly ceremonial culture of the Byzantine court. In addition to calling them Franks, as most Byzantines did, Anna also calls them Kelts (Celts). In her world, northern Europe was populated by primitive "barbarian" peoples whom Roman geographers had labeled long ago. ❶ ❷

❶ What does Anna appreciate about the Crusaders and what does she dislike?

❷ How would you describe the Byzantine court based on what Anna says?

❸ What is it about the language Anna uses that tells you her impressions of the Crusaders are mostly negative?

❹ Why does Anna object to the way the Crusaders speak to her father?

❺ Does Emperor Alexius show diplomacy or a lack of sensitivity in dealing with the Crusaders?

❸ The Keltic counts are brazen-faced, violent men, moneygrubbers and where their personal desires are concerned quite immoderate. These are natural characteristics of the race. They also surpass all other nations in loquacity. So when they came to the palace they did so in an undisciplined fashion, every count bringing with him as many comrades as he wished; after him, without interruption, came another and then a third—an endless queue. Once there they did not limit the conversation by the water-clock, like the orators of ancient times, but each, whoever he was, enjoyed as much time as he wanted for the interview with the emperor. ❹ Men of such character, talkers so exuberant, had neither respect for his feelings nor thought for the passing of time nor any idea of the by-standers' wrath; instead of giving way to those coming behind them, they talked on and on with an incessant stream of petitions. Every student of human customs will be acquainted with Frankish verbosity and their pettifogging love of detail; but the audience on these occasions learnt the lesson more thoroughly—from actual experience. When evening came, after remaining without food all through the day, the emperor would rise from his throne and retire to his private apartments, but even then he was not free from the importunities of the Kelts. They came one after another, not only those who had failed to obtain a hearing during the day, but those who had already been heard returned as well, putting forward this or that excuse for more talk. ❺ In the midst of them, calmly enduring their endless chatter stood the emperor. One could see them there, all asking questions, and him, alone and unchanging, giving them prompt replies. But there was no limit to their foolish babbling, and if a court official did try to cut them short, he was himself interrupted by Alexius. He knew the traditional pugnacity of the Franks and feared that from some trivial pretext a blaze of trouble might spring up, resulting in serious harm to the prestige of Rome. It was really a most extraordinary sight. Like a statue wrought by hammer, made perhaps of bronze or cold-forged iron, the emperor would sit through the night, often from evening till midnight, often till third cock-crow, sometimes almost until the sun was shining clearly. The attendants were all worn out, but by frequently retiring had a rest and then came back again—in bad humour.

Source: Excerpt from The Alexaid of Anna Comnena translated by E.R.A. Sewter (Penguin Classics, 1969). Copyright © E.R.A. Sewter, 1969. Reproduced by permission of Penguin Books, Ltd.

The new kingdom of Jerusalem established by the Crusaders could not depend on western kings for consistent, timely support, so early in the twelfth century professional soldiers came to be garrisoned in immense stone fortifications. These soldiers were not ordinary knights. They belonged to religious orders of laymen who had taken vows similar to those taken by monks. Their original purpose had been the care of sick pilgrims, but now, in addition to their vows of poverty, chastity, and obedience, these monk-knights considered the defense of the Crusader kingdom to be their primary responsibility.

Military Orders One such order was the **Knights Hospitaller** of Jerusalem, which acquired a reputation as a superior military unit. Another, which took its name from the location of its headquarters near the ruins of what was reputedly Solomon's Temple, was the **Knights Templar**. Bernard of Clairveaux praised "the new knighthood" for its services to Christendom, but the Templars engaged in far more than relief of the poor and military defense. Their military skill made them the ideal guards of money moving between western Europe and Palestine, and they gained immense wealth from moneylending.

As creditors of kings, the Knights Templars had not only wealth but also political influence. In 1305, one of the Templars' debtors, King Philip IV of France, charged them with heresy and homosexual activity, confiscated their vast properties, imprisoned all the Knights Templar in his kingdom, and burned many of them as heretics at the stake. Their destruction produced a windfall of cash for the nearly empty royal treasury.

Crusader States For nearly a century, the Franks maintained Crusader states in the cities they conquered in Syria and Palestine. These were multicultural societies with legal and political institutions that blended western European and local traditions. But the Crusaders' presence, brutality, and ignorance of the religion and customs of the people in the land they had conquered galvanized opposition to them.

Crusades in the East and in Europe

Meanwhile, a Second Crusade had organized to support the gains of the First. The German emperor Conrad III gathered his troops and pressed the kings of Poland and Bohemia to join him. With **Louis VII** of France, accompanied by a host of other nobles, the Crusaders arrived in Syria in the spring of 1148, where they chose to attack Damascus, the one city in the region whose Muslim ruler was most inclined to join forces with the Christians. The resulting siege was a disaster. The arrival of a massive Muslim army from the south forced the Christian kings to retreat and find their way home. The failure of the Second Crusade had a devastating impact on the morale of Christians in western Europe. Bernard of Clairveaux attributed the failure to the sins of Christians, many of whom were willing to accept the blame.

It took a while for the Muslims of the region to unify behind a leader, but when they did, the **jihad**, as holy war is called in Islam, brought an end to Christian rule in the Near East. The Muslim leader, a Kurd based in Egypt, was **Saladin**, a legend in both the Muslim and Christian worlds. Saladin drew the crusading armies into a trap.

The Battle of Hattin On July 3, 1187, his army crushed the Frankish army, weakened by internal rivalries, on the ground between two hills, the Horns of Hattin, near the Sea of Galilee. Only one Crusade leader survived the battle. Saladin then took possession of the cities under Frankish rule one by one until he finally entered Jerusalem in October, a loss that deeply shocked the Christian west. Barely alive, Frankish refugees retreated to the ports of Tyre, Tripoli, and Antioch.

The Third Crusade To recapture Jerusalem, **Richard I**, king of England, and **Philip II Augustus** of France led the Third Crusade, but they succeeded in seizing only the port of **Acre** on the coast of Palestine in 1191. King Philip shortly returned to France. For nearly a year, Richard and Saladin fought indecisive skirmishes. But when reports of problems at home reached Richard and reports of disagreements among his allies reached Saladin, the two warriors looked for a way out of the war.

In the end, they agreed to a three-year truce in September of 1192 that ended shortly before Saladin died in 1193, but Jerusalem remained out of reach for the crusading armies. Meanwhile, a hospital set up by a group of German merchants to assist Richard and his forces in the siege of Acre was transformed, within a decade, into the **Teutonic Knights**, an order whose military mission was identical to that of the Hospitallers and the Templars but whose members came from German lands.

Knights Hospitaller (from the Hospital of St. John in Jerusalem) Monastic order of knights formed to defend Christian possessions in Syria and Palestine.

Knights Templar Military order founded in the 1120s in Jerusalem to defend the land the Crusader forces had captured.

Louis VII (r. 1137–1180) King of France, first husband of Eleanor of Aquitaine and leader of the failed Second Crusade.

jihad Religious duty imposed on Muslims to defend and extend Islam.

Saladin (r. 1169–1193) Muslim leader, of Kurdish ancestry, who defeated the Crusaders at Hattin and captured Jerusalem.

Richard I (r. 1189–1199) Son of Henry II of England and Eleanor of Aquitaine; king of England and leader of the Third Crusade; known as Richard the Lion-Hearted.

Philip II Augustus (r. 1179–1223) King of France and co-leader of the Third Crusade.

Acre Mediterranean port, today in Israel; last Christian territory in the Holy Land to fall to Muslims, in 1291.

Teutonic Knights Order of German knights founded in Jerusalem who shifted their area of operation in 1211 to eastern Europe to convert non-Christians.

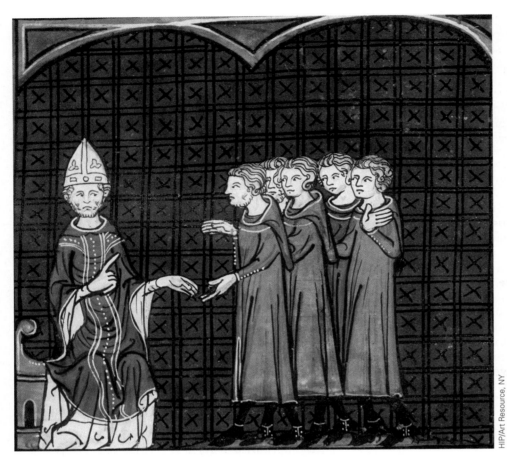

Innocent III, seen here, was the first to turn the weapon of crusade against inhabitants of western Europe when he called for a crusade against those the church deemed heretics. Look at the background of this image. Is it naturalistic? Does it mean to indicate a specific place?

HIP/Art Resource, NY

The Fourth Crusade In Rome, Pope Innocent III called for a Fourth Crusade to the Holy Land. But in 1204, instead of fulfilling the mission defined by the pope, the crusading army seized Constantinople, the capital of the Byzantine Empire. It was the first time in a thousand years that the mighty walls had been breached by invaders. Once inside, the army burned and pillaged the city. Churches, palaces, libraries, and public buildings were ransacked and stripped of their treasures. The crusading leaders then divided the old empire among themselves. The principal funder of the crusade, Venice, received the island of Crete and two ports on the southern coast of the Peloponnesus. There eastern clergy were compelled to recognize the pope as their spiritual leader and the Christian population was made to feel like conquered people. The crusading movement had now become an open hunt for plunder and territory.

Reconquista (from Spanish, "reconquest") War to bring all Muslim territory in Spain under Christian rule.

Albigensian Crusade War waged in the first half of the thirteenth century against the Cathar sect in southwestern France.

Crusading in Europe Closer to home, the crusade to seize Spain from the Muslims continued. Known as the **Reconquista**, the effort to bring all of the Iberian Peninsula under Christian rule succeeded in limiting Muslim rule to the province of Granada in the south by 1236. In 1208, Pope Innocent III also called for war against the Cathar heretics, thus using crusading as a tool to impose religious uniformity in western Europe. Responding to his call, knights from England and nobles from northern France undertook the **Albigensian Crusade**, attacking Cathar cities and massacring thousands. It took several armies and nearly twenty years to suppress the Cathars.

The Teutonic Knights now applied their crusading zeal to the conquest and conversion of the peoples of eastern Europe. In 1211, they arrived in Hungary to serve the king, Andrew II, whose kingdom suffered from incursions from a non-Christian people, the Cumans. The knights next subdued and converted the Prussians and in 1226 received permission to settle. Within fifty years they were masters of the region, controlling the lucrative grain trade to the Baltic Sea. In eastern Europe, the land-rich, commercially active Teutonic Knights remained a military, political, and economic force.

Meanwhile, all attempts to reestablish a Christian presence in the Holy Land stalled. In 1215, King Louis IX of France, later Saint Louis, led a crusade to Egypt as its target, but, like his great-grandfather, Louis VII, he went home in defeat. The few remaining Christian outposts in Syria and Palestine survived until 1291, when Acre, the last city in the region under Christian rule, fell to Muslim forces.

The Impact of the Crusades

Two centuries of fighting had resulted in a tremendous loss of life, on all sides. By openly endorsing the idea of slaughter as penance, the papacy created the conditions for legitimating violence toward Jews, Muslims, other non-Christians, and Christians who did not recognize the pope as the head of the universal church. The massacre of Jews at the start of the Poor People's Crusade was only the first episode in centuries of violence against them. Although Christians and Muslims had fought against each other in centuries past, now their confrontations were cast in starkly sectarian terms. For each side, it was a matter of "we the believers" against "the **infidels**"—the nonbelievers—despite the fact that for centuries Muslim and Christian merchants had done business on largely peaceful terms in eastern markets.

In the northern reaches of Europe, whole peoples joined the church when faced with the choice of conversion or death. In southwestern France, the Cathars were destroyed. Christians living in the conquered Byzantine Empire thought of the Crusades as the last of the barbarian invasions. Following the Crusader conquest, eastern clergy were no longer allowed to be ordained according to the Greek rite. With the Crusades, reform of the church had come to mean uniformity of belief and practice, and western Christianity became a militant religion.

Plunder and Profit Many profited from the Crusades. The merchants of western Europe, especially in Italian cities, benefited from contact with the markets of Palestine and Syria. Following close behind the crusading conquerors in the First Crusade were Italian merchants, who immediately established trading outposts in the Crusader states. Venetian traders predominated in the port of Tyre, while merchants from Amalfi, Pisa, and Genoa traded in Jerusalem, Acre, and other Christian strongholds. Having access to local markets where traders from as far away as India and even China brought their goods meant that the Italian merchants could now create a demand in European markets for luxury goods: spices, silk and linen fabrics, carpets, and brassware.

In the twelfth century northern Italian cities began to produce their own silk instead of importing it from the east, setting the conditions for the rise of the silk industry in the next century. The great distances between Italy and the Levant gave rise to banking techniques for the long-distance transfer of credit instead of coin, always vulnerable to theft and piracy. Thus the Crusades accelerated the pace of economic changes that had already begun prior to the fall of Jerusalem in 1099.

 **Checking In**

By yourself or with a partner, explain the significance of each of the following selected key terms:

primogeniture	Louis VII
Pope Urban II	Saladin
Alexius I Comnenus	Philip II Augustus
Knights Templar	Reconquista

The Growth of Royal Authority

◆ **By what means did kings manage to centralize and increase their authority?**

◆ **Describe the different government structures in France, England, and the Holy Roman Empire.**

In the eleventh century, kings had limited power over their kingdoms. The disorder created by the warring nobility made it difficult for any authority, except that of the church, to extend beyond a local level. Even the authority of the emperors had eroded since Otto I in the tenth century. But in the next two centuries, kings imposed their authority. They brought additional land into direct royal possession, replaced customary law with royal law, claimed the exclusive right to declare and wage war, and asserted their right to tax subjects. By the end of the thirteenth century, the imposition of royal authority had brought stability to the lives of ordinary people, and secular rulers had created within their kingdoms the mechanisms of strong and lasting monarchies.

From Weak Kings to Strong Monarchs

In France, royal authority rose in direct proportion to the increase in the royal domain. When France's longest-lasting line of kings, the Capetians, replaced the Carolingians in 987, kings were poorer and weaker than their nobles. Although in theory the kingdom of the Capetian kings consisted of most of the land of modern-day France, their income derived principally from the region around Paris, which formed the royal domain. The rest of their kingdom was parceled out to the great lords who were their vassals.

The Royal Domain Over the twelfth and thirteenth centuries, the French kings added much territory to the royal domain—mainly by confiscating their chief vassals' lands—and made significant progress in turning royal law into the law of the kingdom. In the thirteenth century, the French kings convened their judicial court, called **Parlement**, where they and their judges took the

infidel (from Latin, "unbeliever") From a Christian or Muslim perspective, anyone who is not a member of their religion.

Parlement In the fourteenth century, the French king's court of appeals located in Paris.

counsel of vassals, tried cases reserved for royal justice, and heard appeals from the towns and provinces.

The English Kings In England, the consolidation of royal authority occurred more swiftly than in France. Following invasions by Angles and Danes in the ninth and tenth centuries, at **Hastings** in 1066, **William**, the duke of Normandy, defeated the Danish king of England. After this **Norman Conquest**, William and his successors ruled England from Normandy until the early thirteenth century by delegating the tasks of government in England to royal representatives. Their main concern was to raise money.

Henry II After a long contest among William's heirs, **Henry II** restored order in part by adapting pre-Norman administrative structures to his needs. He instituted a system whereby royal representatives in the counties, known by their Anglo-Saxon name as **shires**, collected taxes and delivered them to the royal treasury, called the **Exchequer**. Henry and his sons, Richard I and **John I**, all tried to curtail the ability of their nobles to wage war against them by prohibiting the construction of castles without royal license. Henry's relations with the church were marred by his fight with Thomas Becket, archbishop of Canterbury. Though Henry hoped Becket's loyalty to him would survive his appointment to the highest church office in his kingdom, the archbishop defended the liberties of the church, and lost his life (see A New Direction: Thomas Becket Defends the Liberties of the Church).

In France and England, kings launched military campaigns more easily than they managed to raise regular funds from their subjects. Throughout the Middle Ages, direct taxation—that is, the levying of taxes on individuals rather than on goods and services—was associated with low social status and local authority. Kings expected financial support from their vassals, but the amounts set by long-standing custom were tiny in comparison to royal fiscal needs. Beyond the customary financial aid, nobles viewed the royal treasury as the personal concern of the king. The church was exempt from all taxation. Not surprisingly, then, royal pressure on the nobility and the church to contribute more often led to rebellion.

Restraint on the King When the demands of England's King John I exceeded the limits of what he was owed by custom, a group of nobles compelled him to sign the **Magna Carta** in 1215. Although this document restored the traditional rights of the barons and the clergy, especially protection from the king's excessive fiscal demands, its defense of "free men" created a powerful precedent for the rights of all subjects of the king, not just the nobility. Later generations used it to protect themselves from unlawful seizures and oppressive government.

The king's need for financial aid from his free, property-owning subjects played a role in the emergence of a representative assembly, the English **Parliament**. When the king needed money, he met with representatives from the nobility, clergy, and merchants to request the amount. When these representatives used the meetings to raise issues of concern to them with the king, the interaction became a negotiation, though the king usually maintained the upper hand. In France, by contrast, the king never instilled in the nobility the expectation of financial support.

The Politics of Dynastic Families

Because the dowries of royal and noble daughters consisted of large amounts of money and even land, marriages at that social level often had important political consequences. Deprived of a direct role in political life, royal and aristocratic women served as the vehicles that transferred property from one family to another. The custom of not allowing women in possession of large amounts of territory to inherit noble and royal titles led to some of the period's most disruptive conflicts within and between families.

A Powerful Heiress When **Eleanor**, the heiress of the duke of Aquitaine, married the heir to the French throne in 1137, the land she brought to the marriage more than doubled the size of the kingdom. Over fifteen years of marriage, Eleanor and Louis VII produced several daughters, but no sons. She acquired a reputation for bold, even scandalous behavior at her husband's court, which was only heightened when she accompanied him to Syria on the Second Crusade and stayed close to the fighting. Well-educated, Eleanor gathered around her poets and intellectuals.

For reasons having mostly to do with the lack of a male heir to the throne, Louis and Eleanor's marriage was **annulled** by the pope in 1152. She took all

Hastings Battle in 1066 in which William, duke of Normandy, defeated the Danish king of England.

William I (r. 1066–1087) King of England, who, as duke of Normandy, invaded England, defeated the Danish king, and assumed the crown; known as William the Conqueror.

Norman Conquest Invasion and conquest of England in 1066 by William, duke of Normandy, and his army of Norman nobles.

Henry II (r. 1154–1189) King of England who, through his marriage to Eleanor of Aquitaine, held in vassalage a large portion of the French kingdom.

shire Administrative unit in England equivalent to a county, represented to the king by the sheriff.

Exchequer English royal treasury, so-called for the checked cloth covering a table on which accounts are calculated.

John I (r. 1199–1216) King of England who lost most of his territory in France and was forced by nobles to sign the Magna Carta in 1215; known as John Lackland.

Magna Carta A document confining the English king to his traditional rights and obligations, signed by King John in 1215.

Parliament The representative assembly of England.

Eleanor of Aquitaine (1122–1204) Queen of France and later queen of England, who inherited the province of Aquitaine in southwestern France.

Thomas Becket Defends the Liberties of the Church

On the evening of December 29, 1170, Thomas Becket, archbishop of Canterbury, had unexpected visitors. Four armed knights approached the archbishop in his cathedral—and murdered him. They believed that they were acting according to the wishes of their king, Henry II of England. With this murder, a long-standing quarrel between Thomas and his king over the church's freedom from secular interference came to an end. It did not, however, put an end to the problem.

Thomas and Henry had not always been enemies. As Henry's chancellor, Thomas had administered Henry's government, assisting him in a variety of judicial, fiscal, and military reforms. Thomas was one of the so-called new men—literate commoners elevated to positions of power by virtue of their skills in the exercise of government. Originally from London and of Norman descent, Thomas was a tall man and fond of lavish display. He aroused the resentment of the English barons, who felt that new men were unworthy of powerful and lucrative positions in the king's service. But Thomas was also in the service of the church. Prior to entering Henry's service, Thomas had served Theobald, the archbishop of Canterbury, and in 1154—the same year that Henry made Thomas his chancellor—Theobald made Thomas cathedral archdeacon. Yet Thomas had served Henry faithfully, even supporting the king's attempts to curtail the authority of the church. Theobald, who was slowly dying, regretted his archdeacon's activities.

Upon the death of the old archbishop, Henry appointed Thomas archbishop of Canterbury, intending that Thomas would retain his position as chancellor as well. But as archbishop, Thomas experienced a political, personal, and ultimately spiritual transformation. As archbishop, he was head of the church in England, and in this position Thomas decided that his interests were no longer the same as the king's. The role of an archbishop, it was now clear to him, lay in the defense of the church's liberties against the attempts of the king to limit them. Thus Thomas gave up being a king's man, resigned the position of chancellor, and took up the role of church defender.

A confrontation was soon in coming. In a departure from canon law and tradition, Henry claimed the right to try clergymen suspected of crimes in his royal court rather than in ecclesiastical courts, where they usually received lighter penalties. Thomas immediately objected and set himself against the will of the king. The hostility between the two men forced Thomas into exile in France and at the pope's court in Rome for six years. The geographic distance did not lessen their enmity. Henry confiscated the archbishop's property and forced his relatives into exile. Thomas excommunicated Henry and all those who supported him in his cause. The bishops of England were split on the matter, but most came down on the side of the king.

Eventually, Henry, fearing isolation from his fellow Christian rulers, met with Thomas and agreed that Thomas would return to Canterbury. When he did so, Thomas was greeted by cheering crowds. But he would not overturn the excommunications he had issued against Henry and those who supported him, and Henry took that as an insult. It was at that point that Henry's knights sped to Canterbury and murdered Thomas.

Almost immediately, Thomas Becket's grave in the cathedral became a focal point for pilgrims. So strong was Thomas's reputation for holiness and defense of the church that Pope Alexander III canonized him three years after his murder in 1173.

---

her lands with her out of the marriage. Louis married twice more before he had a son, Philip II Augustus. Two months after the annulment, Eleanor married Henry Plantagenet, duke of Normandy, count of Anjou, soon to become Henry II, king of England, in 1154. The new king and queen of England now held more land in the French kingdom than did Eleanor's former husband, Louis VII, king of the French.

One King's Loss Is Another's Gain Politics shaped King Henry's relations with his wife and children. He saw four of his five sons and three daughters all married to wealthy, titled men and women. The daughters married a German duke, a Spanish king, and a Neapolitan king. After his eldest son died, Henry had the next son, his namesake, crowned king in 1170. Eleanor made her third son, Richard, the duke of Aquitaine. Another son, Geoffrey, became the duke of Brittany through his marriage to the heiress of the province. Only John, the youngest, had to be content with nothing for the time being, thereby earning the nickname John Lackland.

Henry's refusal to allow his sons a role in ruling the territories attached to their titles alienated both his sons and his queen. Henry the Young King led one unsuccessful revolt against his father and died during another. The surviving brothers continued to plot against their father. As punishment for her support of her rebellious sons, Henry had Eleanor imprisoned, where she remained for sixteen years until Henry died, in 1189. While her son Richard I was on crusade in the east, Eleanor ably administered the government of England. Richard's brother and successor, John I, could not prevent Philip, the French king, who was looking to increase the French royal domain, from capturing most of his land

> **annulment** Invalidation of a marriage as if it had never existed.

Richard I, king of England, probably would have appreciated laying next to his mother, Eleanor, his main support and ally in his wars against his father. Looking at these idealized effigies of two kings and a queen, describe their poses and what they hold. What do the differences tell you about ideal kings and queens?

Erich Lessing/Art Resource, NY

in France and thereby reducing his income by a third. By the mid-thirteenth century, the English kings held little more than Gascony in southwest France. (See Map 10.2 on page 291.)

Over the thirteenth century, dynastic marriages between the French and English royal families punctuated an almost continuous state of hostility between the two kingdoms. In 1299, King John's grandson, Edward I, took as his second wife Margaret, the sister of France's King Philip IV, and married his son, the future Edward II, to Isabelle, the French king's daughter. The two marriages represented attempts at peace in recurring wars over Gascony. Tensions between the two kingdoms intensified in 1328, when the last of Philip IV's sons died. A long struggle for the French crown between descendants of the French royal family was about to begin.

The Holy Roman Empire and Frederick II

In the western empire, the successors to Otto III reinforced imperial control over church appointments. Not only had bishops become provincial governors, but the emperor had acquired a free hand in choosing the pope. With Emperor Henry III's selection of Leo IX, the first pope to make church reform a priority, the empire became the first battleground in the church's struggle to gain independence from

secular interference. Despite seeming resolutions in the Investiture Controversy and the Concordat of Worms, the pope and the emperor continued to contest each other's authority over clergy in the empire.

In the early twelfth century, a new dynasty, the Hohenstaufen, restored prestige and authority to the office of emperor. The ongoing rivalry between the papacy and the emperor over whose authority was superior made the new emperors highly conscious of their title's symbolic power, and so the empire now acquired a new name, the **Holy Roman Empire**, a political entity that would last until 1806. In the twelfth century, the designation *holy* signaled the emperor's claim to defend the church and to involve himself in its affairs.

Holy Roman Empire   The first to designate the empire as "holy," **Frederick I** reinforced imperial power by claiming the same rights and laws wielded by the ancient Roman emperors, which became known collectively as **regalia**. Frederick's revival of Roman imperial authority was as short-lived as it was ambitious. He died, apparently of a heart attack, on his way to join the Third Crusade in 1190. His son who succeeded him, Henry VI, married Constance, heiress to the Norman kingdom of Sicily, who, because she was a woman, could wear the crown only as consort of her husband, not in her own right.

Frederick II   In 1198, Henry VI died. When his son, **Frederick II**, an infant, became the ward of Innocent III, the pope hoped to raise an obedient son of the church, but he was disappointed. Frederick's kingdom consisted not only of the Holy Roman Empire in the north but also, in the south, Sicily and southern

Holy Roman Empire Name first used for the old eastern Frankish empire from the twelfth century on.

Frederick I (r. 1155–1190) Emperor of the Holy Roman Empire known as Barbarossa ("Red Beard").

regalia Instruments and symbols of either ecclesiastical or secular authority.

Frederick II (r. 1197–1250) Emperor of the Holy Roman Empire and ruler of Sicily and southern Italy who engaged in a long war against the papacy.

Map 10.2 **The Growth of the Kingdom of France** The French king's revenue derived from the royal domain. At the start of the twelfth century, the royal domain consisted mainly of the region surrounding Paris. Over the succeeding two centuries, the royal domain grew larger as the king took land away from one vassal in particular. © *Cengage Learning*

1. Where are the boundaries of the French kingdom?
2. How much of the kingdom did the French king rule directly? Which parts were ruled by his chief nobles?
3. Locate regions the French king first set out to confiscate; who did he confiscate them from and why?

Italy. In between lay the Papal States. In 1215, the year before he died, Innocent gave his approval to Frederick's being crowned emperor in Aachen—Charlemagne's old capital.

Soon Frederick attempted to join the two portions of his empire by depriving Innocent's successors of their lands. He marched his armies through the Italian peninsula, causing the cities of Italy much suffering from urban warfare between factions loyal to him and to the pope. He also forced the Muslims from Sicily to leave the island and settle in a village in southern Italy, where he allowed them to practice their religion without hindrance but required them to pay heavy taxes and serve in his armies.

Because he began his reign at such a young age, by the time Frederick II died in 1250 at least two generations of people living in the empire and in Italy could not

remember a time when he had not been emperor. His great learning, military exploits, and reputation for both good and bad government led the people of his time to call him Stupor Mundi ("Wonder of the World")—an epithet he had no reason to reject.

The Instruments of Rule

As kings in France, England, and the Holy Roman Empire sought to centralize their authority, and popes sought to maintain theirs, written records became increasingly useful and in the thirteenth century proliferated. By 1300, many people in western Europe had reasons to consult a written document at least once in their lives. Managers of estates kept account books of inventories and sales of estate produce. Knights preserved charters to show they had rights to the land granted to them by their lords. Noblemen sent instructions to their vassals in letters. Merchants relied heavily on written documents to communicate with their partners and employees traveling on business and to keep accounts of the business they conducted.

Record Keeping By far, the record offices of secular rulers and popes produced the most documents. The chief secretary of a king's or pope's records acquired the title of **chancellor**. His responsibility was to draft letters in response to requests for the king's advice. At the start of the thirteenth century, the records of the French king traveled with him. By the end of the same century, the king's business had become so complex that it was necessary to store his correspondence and account books in a fixed, permanent place.

The Law of Merchants The commercial culture of Italian cities gave rise to needs that brought about changes in record keeping and legal documents for which customary law had few answers. Merchants looked to the law of the Roman Empire, specifically the Body of Civil Law, to supply legal formulas that would protect the interests of both parties to contracts. Two merchants forming a company or a short-term business venture called on a **notary**—a public official charged with drawing up legal documents—to write a contract with the proper legal formula. The revival of Roman business law and practice in the thirteenth century made merchants adept at the intricacies of loans, bills of sale, receipts, wills, and other documents involving the management of property.

Universities began to specialize in teaching law. At the University of Bologna, the most famous and prestigious of law faculties in the Middle Ages, law students absorbed principles of law and legal remedies through the study of Justinian's Body of Civil Law. Once graduated, as jurists, they applied their learning by writing opinions in court cases that judges referred to when making their decisions. Similarly, jurists reconciled Roman law with canon law. The law of the church governed the clergy, ecclesiastical property, and procedures against heretics, but it also covered matters of intimate concern to laypeople, such as penance, marriage, and wills. In many places in western Europe, inheritance and marital disputes were decided in ecclesiastical courts.

The influence of Roman law did not reach far north of the Alps. In southern France, Provence adapted Roman law to the needs of its merchants. Feudal law combined with royal law and statutory law prevailed in northern Europe. England developed a judicial system that had no comprehensive code book like the Body of Civil Law

but relied instead on the accumulation of decisions rendered in past cases. England's **common law** was made applicable everywhere in the kingdom as the law common to all. Itinerant justices made regular circuits of the shires to hear the civil and criminal cases under the king's jurisdiction. Out of this system of law evolved the English legal system and, much later, that of the United States.

 Checking In

By yourself or with a partner, explain the significance of each of the following selected key terms:

Norman Conquest	Magna Carta
Henry II	parliament
shires	Holy Roman Empire
exchequer	common law

The Growth of Towns and Trade

♦ **How and why did economies begin to grow in the eleventh century?**

♦ **How did trade encourage the growth of towns?**

The expansion of church and royal authority from the eleventh through the thirteenth centuries owed much of its success to generally improved conditions in the countryside and to the growing concentrations of population at key points along expanding trade routes. More surplus on the land meant more food, but also more rents to pay to landowners. Merchants brought merchandise from the eastern end of the Mediterranean to sell to kings, nobles, and church officials. Negotiating one's way through the world was becoming increasingly complex—new technology, new courts, documents, taxes, and financial obligations. New opportunities for trade led some to traffic in human beings.

Expansion in Agriculture

Throughout the Middle Ages, land was the measure of most aspects of life. A person's wealth was measured by the amount of land in his or her possession. The amount of land under cultivation determined how much food was available. Toward the end of the tenth century, an increase in the amount of crop-producing land was accompanied by an increase in population, with the potential for that number to rise even higher. The increase in agricultural production came about as a result of a combination of factors, the most prominent of which were changing methods of field management and improvements in agricultural technology.

Changes in the Land For much of the early Middle Ages, peasants, like the Romans before them, had divided their fields in two, left one-half fallow, or uncultivated,

chancellor Office of chief secretary in a king's household.

notary Public official who draws up private legal documents, such as deeds and wills.

common law Body of English law and case precedents applicable to all free persons.

for a year, and planted their crops in the other half. Fallow land replenished its nutrients, but the practice meant that half the land produced nothing every year. In southern Europe—with its drier climate—this system of two-field crop rotation continued, but in northern Europe, peasants improved on this system by dividing their land into three parts. One they left fallow, another they planted in the spring, and the third they planted with winter crops. This three-field crop rotation, dependent on more rainfall than southern Europe received, meant that two-thirds instead of half of a peasant's land was under production in one year.

Related to the changes in crop rotation were improvements in plows and animal harnessing. More land under cultivation spurred experimentation in the construction of plows. Peasants attached wheels to their plows, which made it easier for oxen to pull them through the heavier, wetter soil of northern Europe. A vertical blade, or coulter, made a narrow slice through the soil, followed by the plowshare, an iron-covered blade that cut horizontally. The moldboard tipped the cut soil over, creating the ridge of a row. Wheels made it possible for a plow to move more quickly down a row—provided it had a speedy animal pulling it.

New Technology Oxen are slow and unintelligent compared to horses. But because the strap that circles an ox's neck under a yoke would strangle a horse, peasants could not use horses to pull plows until they devised a different kind of harnessing. With a harness resting on its shoulders rather than its neck, a horse could be used to plow, and horses could walk more quickly and work longer hours than oxen. They also required less guidance because they understood verbal signals from the plower to turn or to stop.

Heavier, wheeled plows pulled by suitably harnessed horses meant that peasants could work more land in a day than ever before. Whether an increase in population across western Europe, but particularly in the north, stimulated innovations or whether such innovations contributed to a rise in the population, the cumulative effect of these changes in agriculture made itself apparent in the tenth century. Conditions in Europe were ripe for an economic and cultural upsurge.

Revival of Trade and Town

Even before the Crusades brought western Europe into increased contact with the people and markets of the eastern Mediterranean, trade and towns were on the rise. Travel was still dangerous, but merchants were willing to risk transporting goods long distances. By the late thirteenth century, a few merchants from Italy, like the Venetian Marco Polo, had even reached China. Greater surpluses in crops meant people had more to sell at market. More people and goods led to regularly held markets in the most populated location in a region. It would be impossible to say whether trade gave rise to towns or vice versa. What is clear is that each fostered the other in conditions of greater social stability.

Trade Fairs Travel on trade routes increased, and some towns sprang up to provide rest and refreshment to traders. The distance between towns often corresponded to the distance that traders could cover in a day. Merchants kept their eyes open for customers with money to spend. Kings, lords, bishops, and their household dependents were good customers, eager to buy the luxury items merchants had for sale. Thus, royal, noble, and ecclesiastical residences became sites of markets for local and long-distance traders. In Champagne, in northeastern France, six large annual markets attracted merchants from all over Europe during the twelfth century. Their different currencies prompted the first development of banking techniques. With the use of coins now the norm, money changers daily posted changing exchange rates so that merchants would know the worth of their coins in relation to the worth of other merchants' coins. The fairs of Champagne declined in the 1200s, when merchant galleys reached northern Europe through the Strait of Gibraltar. By 1300, trade had transformed life for the better throughout western Europe.

Maritime Trade Italian seaports benefited from their proximity to the markets of the eastern Mediterranean. They became urban far faster than most towns north of the Alps. Because of their location, merchants from Genoa, Venice, Pisa, and Amalfi functioned as middlemen carrying goods from the eastern Mediterranean to north of the Alps. In northern Europe, urbanization occurred at a slower pace. Towns grew fastest in the cities of **Flanders**, a region in modern-day Belgium, whose merchants took an active part in trade with the British Isles, the Baltic region, and, eventually, Italy. Starting in the thirteenth century, Flemish textiles, made with imported wool from England, were sold in markets all over Europe and the Mediterranean. By the beginning of the fourteenth century, commerce and manufacturing industries experienced explosive growth throughout western Europe. (See Map 10.3 on page 294.)

Guilds Merchants and craftworkers organized themselves into **guilds** according to the goods they specialized in. Guilds for goldsmiths, masons, leatherworkers, furriers, carpenters, glassworkers, drapers, and many other skilled workers as well as merchants wrote statutes that governed their professional behavior and built halls in which they could meet. Members relied on their guilds to represent them to municipal authorities. Some guilds were only for master craftsmen, who owned their own businesses. Others also admitted **journeymen**, those who had completed

Flanders Most urban region of northern Europe in the Middle Ages, today a province of Belgium.

guilds Associations of merchants or craftworkers for mutual protection and regulation of their field of business.

journeymen (from French, "day") Skilled, salaried workers who labored for master craftsmen.

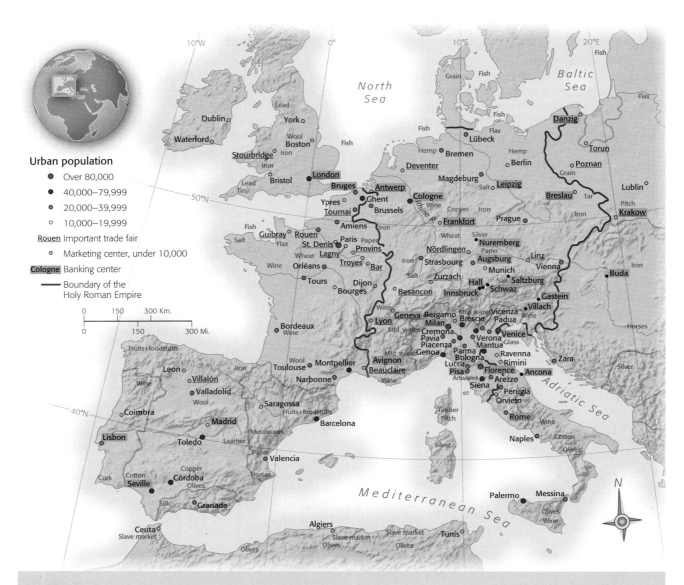

Map 10.3 **Population and Economic Centers** Improved agricultural techniques contributed to the rise in population across most of Europe. Cities grew in size and population between the tenth and twelfth centuries, but few had more than a few thousand inhabitants. © *Cengage Learning*

1. Compare this map with the one at the beginning of the chapter. Where are the largest cities located in this map?
2. Which regions are most active in trade in the chapter-opening map? Are they the same or different here?

apprenticeships and now worked in a master's business for a wage. Craftsmen and merchants generally had shops open to the public on the street level and their private residence above. In spite of the expertise they could acquire working in their husbands' businesses, women were generally excluded from guilds, except in the textile trade.

Urban life required new forms of government. A city government's highest priority was to protect the city's economy, and that almost always meant protecting the interests of its wealthy merchants and craftsmen. In most cities, the craft and merchant guilds

effectively became municipal governments: what was good for trade was considered good for the city, and vice versa. City governments assigned guilds large warehouses that also served as hostels to traveling merchants; others granted them entire neighborhoods in which to live and conduct their business. The working poor played no political role in their cities.

The Interests of Business

For long-distance trade and manufacturing to be profitable, some cooperation among competitors was necessary for all the businesses to be secure. Merchants and craftworkers in western Europe formed companies that directed capital into potentially profitable ventures. Often business was a family matter. Brothers and sons pooled their family's assets in ventures designed to turn a profit. The younger male members of a family spent years working in the family's branch offices throughout Europe and the Mediterranean. Galleys bearing cargo and business correspondence voyaged several times a year in convoy for mutual protection against pirates.

Insurance   To protect themselves from the hazards of sea travel and piracy—in addition to the risky nature of business ventures—merchants developed various kinds of contracts that allowed investors different degrees of involvement and profit. One kind of contract between two merchants promised greater profit to the partner who supplied most of the funds but stayed home than to the one who contributed fewer funds but traveled to purchase goods elsewhere. Early forms of insurance also offered merchants protection. Traders who understood how profitable long-distance trade could be also came to recognize how intricate the methods of turning a profit had become.

Credit   Not everyone who wished to conduct business had the means to do so. Borrowing money at interest enabled merchants with little or no capital to embark on commercial ventures. If they made back what they borrowed plus the interest and still had profit, their venture was a success. The church's view was different. On the basis of the Old Testament ban on charging interest, or **usury**, the church forbade interest-bearing loans between Christians. Credit was essential to the economic expansion of the thirteenth century, so merchants found ways around the prohibition.

Written agreements between lenders and borrowers recorded only the amount to be repaid, thereby hiding the interest charged. Long-distance trade merchants hid rates of interest—12 percent on ordinary loans was standard—in the exchange rates of loans made in one currency and repaid in another. What began as protection of poorer traders from richer ones inhibited bold economic initiatives. Over time, the church adjusted its definition of usury to the charging of *excessive* interest, to allow money to move into the hands of those who needed and were willing to pay for it.

Christians turned over the job of lending money mostly to Jews, whose religion allowed them to take interest from Christians but not from other Jews. For Jews practicing humble crafts like shoemaking and leatherworking, moneylending offered a chance for prosperity. Even though not all Jews became moneylenders and Christians, too, lent money at interest in certain places and periods, Jews came to be associated with the practice and to bear the brunt of the hostility people always feel toward their creditors. When cash-strapped King Philip Augustus of France in 1182 defaulted on his debts to Jewish moneylenders, he also

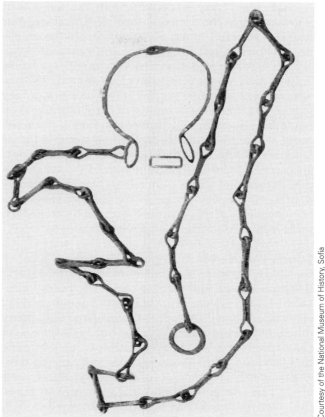

Courtesy of the National Museum of History, Sofia

A slave trader restrained his captive by slipping the chain through the loops in the neck collar (top), fastening it securely, and then attaching the chain to the captive's limbs. Why is the chain made up of short, rather than longer, links? What does its construction tell you about the way slaves were transported from one place to another?

confiscated their property and expelled them from his kingdom. He was not the only Christian king to deal with debt in this way.

The Trade in Slaves

Throughout the Middle Ages, goods from the Muslim world were in greater demand in western Europe than goods from the Christian world were in Muslim countries. Christian merchants supplied Muslim traders with three basic commodities: furs, timber, and slaves. Since the Carolingian period, Christians from western Europe had sold slaves to Muslims on the southern shore of the Mediterranean. As long as western merchants had minimal contacts with their Muslim counterparts, the trade persisted on a small scale. When long-distance trade intensified over the eleventh and twelfth centuries, Christian merchants once again found the sale of slaves to Muslims a good way to make a profit—only, this time, they now found a growing market for slaves at home as well.

usury Originally, the charging of interest on a loan, revised in the later Middle Ages to mean the charging of excessive interest.

The word *slave* is derived from the word *Slav,* a general term for someone from eastern Europe or Russia. At certain times, Slavs constituted the majority of captives sold into slavery, but never for long. Yet the association between slavery and Slavs stuck. Traders native to the forested regions around the Black Sea captured men and women in the same places they logged for timber and hunted for animal fur. They made the slaves haul the timber and furs to Black Sea ports, where they sold them. Raiders stripped the islands and coastlines of the Aegean Sea of its occupants and carried their captives to markets in Constantinople, Thebes, and Crete. Genoese and Venetian traders dominated the slave trade in the eastern Mediterranean, while the Catalans from Barcelona controlled the trade from North Africa at the western end.

Sources of Slaves In the twelfth century, most of the slaves Christian merchants sold came from North Africa, Sardinia, and Corsica. After the Fourth Crusade in 1204, Greeks, Turks, Tatars, Bulgars, Abkhazians, Georgians, Russians, Circassians, and many others fell victim to slavery. The old Viking trade in slaves along the Volga River continued well into the tenth century. Christian merchants met Muslim merchants in the slave markets of the old Byzantine ports around the Aegean Sea and in North African ports. Both were willing to pay high prices for slave women from north of the Black Sea, but Muslim merchants also bought large numbers of men to use as rowers on galleys and soldiers in their armies. The young women who constituted the majority of slaves sold to Christians in Italian and Spanish markets worked as domestic servants, unskilled laborers in crafts and trades, and sexual servants of their masters.

Religion and Slavery Muslims were forbidden to enslave other Muslims, and Christians of the Roman rite could not enslave other Christians of the Roman rite or, later, someone of western European descent. Nor were Christians allowed to sell Christians to Muslims. But Christian merchants defined *Christian* narrowly. For example, until the early fifteenth century, they considered Greek Christians to be heretics and so beyond the protection of the church. After the fall of the Byzantine Empire, the growing power of Turkish states in Asia Minor inspired Italian cities to bring Greeks within the circle of those protected by law from enslavement.

During the economic expansion of the thirteenth century, the number of slaves increased and the demand for them rose, especially in Italy and Spain. In 1300, the French conquerors of Italy sold the Muslims whom Frederick II had transported to southern Italy. Those cities with the most slaves were the same ones whose merchants dominated the trade: Barcelona, Genoa, Venice, and Palermo. The high cost of slaves made them luxury items, symbols of status. Great distances and the destitute origins of most slaves made redemption by relatives highly unlikely. At the close of the thirteenth century, the Mediterranean trade in slaves

had not yet reached its peak. Before the focus of the slave trade shifted to Africa, both Christian and Muslim slave traders had swept up whole populations of the eastern Mediterranean into servitude. It was just getting started.

 Checking In

By yourself or with a partner, explain the significance of each of the following selected key terms:

Flanders

guilds

journeymen

usury

The Building of Cathedrals and the Spread of Learning

◆ **What did cathedrals do and symbolize?**

◆ **How did knowledge and learning change and grow?**

In the twelfth century, signs of increased prosperity were apparent not only in the marketplaces and the wealth of royal courts but also in the towns of western Europe, where enormous cathedrals were begun and new universities attracted communities of scholars and students. As townsfolk watched enormous churches rise up to the sky, they were aware of the benefits wrought by increased trade, better diets, social stability, and increased money in circulation. Teachers and scholars took learning to new levels and changed the nature of intellectual debate.

The Great Cathedrals

A trader with goods to sell approaching a large town in western Europe would have seen its cathedral first. These enormous churches, the seat of the bishop, were always taller than any other structure, though in the twelfth century many were still under construction. Cathedrals were an integral part of the revival of cities. Their magnificence reflected the growing wealth of the church. Their construction gave work to hundreds of people and drew workers in from the countryside. They functioned as a city's spiritual heart, where the relics of the city's patron saint were kept. In turbulent times, they provided sanctuary for those seeking shelter from arbitrary violence. Most of all, the dizzyingly high vaulted ceilings and walls that seemed to contain more glass than brick evoked wonder both in regular worshipers and in those who saw them for the first time.

New Structures, New Styles In the early Christian period, churches tended to be built first and decorated later. Flat walls went up before mosaics and paintings were applied to them. In the tenth century, decorative stone sculpture on entries and columns required planning from the outset of construction.

Foto Marburg/Art Resource, NY

This photograph was taken in the early twentieth century when the town of Chartres still retained its medieval character. What does it tell about the role of cathedrals in the lives of town and city dwellers?

Two styles of cathedral architecture emerged. Incorporating elements taken from ancient Roman arches, the **Romanesque** style, popular in the eleventh century, had rounded arches over doors and window tops. The small windows and broad, unbroken wall space of cathedrals built in the Romanesque style made them resemble fortresses. Emerging in the mid-twelfth century, the **Gothic** style's central features were pointed arches on doorways and windows and ceilings pushed up to unprecedented heights. Because walls consisting more of brilliantly colored stained glass windows than of brick could not support heavy timber roofs, braces called flying buttresses propped up the exterior walls.

Notre Dame Such large buildings required innovative feats of engineering, and their costs put severe strains on episcopal and municipal treasuries. The long stretches of time when construction ceased for lack of funds help explain why cathedrals took a century or more to complete. In 1163, construction began on **Notre Dame de Paris**, one of the most impressive Gothic cathedrals in western Europe. Twenty years later, the area around the altar, the apse, was completed, followed nearly fifteen years later by the central aisle, or nave, which was covered by a timber roof 115 feet above the floor.

It took another half century to complete the enormous round stained-glass window on the western wall and the decorations on the cathedral's façade. Generations of Parisians passed their lives in the shadow of

a never-ending construction site. Only someone born after 1250 would have seen the cathedral that we still see today. Finished or not, once the great towers went up, their visibility from a great distance gave a focus to travelers approaching Paris. In later years, Notre Dame would be the site of coronations, royal weddings, and the most important public ceremonies in France.

From Cathedral Schools to Universities

In the late eleventh century, as part of the movement for church reform, cathedrals established schools where young men could prepare to become clergy. Aspiring scholars, too, found teachers in cities like Paris, Bologna, Pavia, and Salerno, whose bishops licensed men who had demonstrated their expertise in a subject such as **logic** or theology to give lectures and organize students' readings. These masters acquired reputations for their deep knowledge

Romanesque Style of architecture beginning in the eleventh century that evoked features of ancient Roman structures.

Gothic Style of architecture that emerged in the mid-twelfth century and diverged from the slightly earlier Romanesque style in its pointed arches and the use of much more stained glass made possible by flying buttresses.

Notre Dame de Paris Cathedral of Paris, begun in 1163 and completed in the late thirteenth century.

logic Systematic study of philosophical and theological propositions.

of a subject or ancient author. When cathedral schools first started, students worked with one master until they were ready to move on to a master of another subject, who might live in another, distant town. By the mid-twelfth century, it became common for masters and students to converge on cities, like Paris or Bologna, where the one group would always be sure of finding the other.

A Typical Education The career of John of Salisbury, a secretary of Thomas Becket and a famous intellect in his own right, offers a good example of the education of a wandering scholar of the twelfth century. Born in England in the 1130s, John arrived in Paris as a young man to study under the most illustrious minds teaching in Europe at that time. There he studied with a succession of eight different masters of theology for more than ten years before, in 1150, he took the position of secretary to the archbishop of Canterbury in England. His education under those eight masters consisted of the seven liberal arts. When he had completed all seven courses, John achieved the level of master of arts, the ancestor of the modern postgraduate degree today.

By 1200, the large number of students seeking higher education forced the replacement of the loosely related cathedral schools with the more organized structure of a university. Universities acquired specialties. The University of Paris, founded in the late twelfth century, became the preeminent place to study theology. Bologna's university attracted students from all over Europe who wished to study law. Following study at one of these universities, young men entered not only church positions but also government service, as expanding royal bureaucracies needed men trained in letters and law.

But before they finished school, students worked and enjoyed themselves as much as their modern-day counterparts do. Twelfth- and thirteenth-century students stayed up too late, caroused, neglected their studies, and caused havoc in the cities. A group of cleric scholars, the Goliards, wandered from city to city, singing songs that celebrated gambling, drinking, and revelry.

When we are in the tavern,
we do not think how we will go to dust,
but we hurry to gamble,
which always makes us sweat.
What happens in the tavern,
where money is host,
you may well ask,
and hear what I say.

Notre Dame became one of the most recognizable buildings in the world. Even in the Middle Ages, people associated the cathedral closely with the city of Paris. Can you locate in this exterior view the nave, flying buttresses, and stained-glass rose window of the cathedral?

David R. Frazier/Photo Researchers

Some gamble, some drink,
some behave loosely.
But of those who gamble,
some are stripped bare,
some win their clothes here,
some are dressed in sacks.
Here no-one fears death,
but they throw the dice in the name of Bacchus.*

New Learning, New Thinking

Meanwhile ancient texts, both classical and Christian, continued to be preserved and copied in monastery libraries. The epics of the Roman poets fascinated the monks, who sought in such works as Virgil's *Aeneid* foreshadowings of the birth of Christ. They had copies of a few of Plato's works, which the fourth-century writings of Saint Augustine helped them to understand, but they struggled to understand Aristotle. Only a few of his texts were preserved in the west, and the isolation of monasteries made it difficult for monastic scholars to communicate with one another about their studies. Moreover, the monastic scholar's goal was to know a text and its author thoroughly, not to question them. The reasoning underpinning the text tended to be accepted at face value.

Reasoning Beginning in the tenth century, however, a new generation of clerical scholars began to pay greater attention to how philosophy worked—in other words, to reasoning. Instead of relying on scriptural authority, scholars now aimed to support arguments with logic, the systematic principles of reasoning. Their aim to uncover the mysteries of the universe through applied logic came to be called **Scholasticism**.

Scholastics like Anselm of Bec and Berengar of Tours believed the mind possessed the tools needed to understand God, while other intellectuals believed that God's essence could not be contained within human understanding. Anselm devised a famous proof of God's existence in the formula that God is "that than which no greater can be conceived." It was a brave attempt to apply logic to faith but easily refuted, as other scholars pointed out that the ability to imagine something, however great, did not mean that it necessarily existed. Other thinkers came up with logical proofs of God, but none withstood close analysis. Fierce debates galvanized students and scholars on one side or the other.

Abelard and Heloise The career of one of the most brilliant scholars of the Middle Ages exemplifies the intensity of debate. **Peter Abelard**, who first described his field of study as theology, believed in the power of logic to answer all questions, and he put logic to use to debate and defeat his teachers with an arrogance that gained

him enemies. While previous scholars had followed the prayer of St. Augustine—"I believe in order to understand"—Abelard reversed the sequence, asserting he wanted to understand in order to believe. His approach put him at odds with many church leaders, who insisted that faith had to remain a mystery. In their view, having proof of God's existence deprives humanity of the free choice to believe in a supreme being. Abelard, however, had his mind set as much on the means of his intellectual reasoning as he did on the ends. Higher learning's purpose was no longer exclusively spiritual. Abelard loved learning for learning's sake.

Abelard also loved a young woman named Heloise, whose reputation for great learning was widespread among the intellectuals of Paris. In addition to an excellent command of Latin and a knowledge of Greek, she could even read a little Hebrew, a language that practically no Christian in western Europe knew. Her uncle, a clergyman attached to the Cathedral of Notre Dame, hired Abelard to tutor her, and as Abelard admits in his autobiography, their tutoring sessions became love-making sessions. Their marriage, after she gave birth to a son they named Astrolabe, put an end to Abelard's career in the church. When Heloise's uncle learned of their marriage, he sent his niece to a convent and a band of men to Abelard's rooms, where they castrated him. Abelard retreated to a monastery, where he tried to revive his school, but church leaders vehemently opposed him. Called to an inquiry, he supplied an intellectual basis for faith and church doctrine. But his works were condemned and burned.

Aristotle Debates over the utility of logic to answer questions of faith continued, however, especially after new translations into Latin, from Arabic, made Aristotle's *Meta physics* and other previously unknown works available. These addressed the relationship of the natural world to the soul, and they forced monastic scholars to reconsider all they thought they had understood about Aristotelian logic. To help them understand these works, they also had commentaries written by Muslim scholars, translations of which reached them around the turn of the thirteenth century. The earliest commentator was **Avicenna**, a physician and philosopher in early eleventh-century Persia. His writings on Aristotle's medical and scientific works reached the scholars of Spain and then France in translations around the time Aristotle's new works arrived.

Another Muslim philosopher, **Averroës**, wrote his

Scholasticism School of theology that applied logic to matters of faith.

Peter Abelard (1079–1142) Brilliant theologian and charismatic lecturer in Paris, notable for his attempts to reconcile faith and reason.

Avicenna (ca. 980–1037) Persian physician and philosopher who specialized in Aristotle's work relating to medicine.

Averroës (1126–1198) Important Muslim philosopher, born in Muslim Spain, whose interpretations of Aristotle's work were influential in Christian Europe.

influential interpretation of Aristotle's philosophy in Cordoba, Spain, where he was a judge and a jurist in the late twelfth century. In the same period in the same city, a Jewish philosopher and physician, **Moses Maimonides**, wrote interpretations of Aristotle's work in both Hebrew and Arabic. In his *Guide for the Perplexed*, he reconciled Aristotle's thinking with Judaism so clearly that Jewish communities across Europe and around the Mediterranean requested copies of the work. When the works of these three thinkers had been translated into Latin by Christian scholars working in Spain, they gave the scholars in northern Europe and in Italy much to ponder about the natural world and the role of God in it.

Aquinas In the thirteenth century, a Dominican friar, **Thomas Aquinas**, became well known for his effort to reconcile Christian doctrine with Aristotelian philosophy. Thomas excelled at composing **summae**, treatises containing the "highest," or most complete, summary of a given topic. The most important of these was his *Summa Theologiae*, which he meant to be a complete statement of Christian philosophy. Although Thomas's brilliance gave him enormous influence over theological debates of this time, some church leaders objected to his attempts to render God and human existence perfectly intelligible. In 1270, a few years before he died, Thomas stood accused of trying to do the impossible: reconcile reason with faith. The bishop of Paris condemned as heretical portions of his *Summa* but accepted Thomas's essential position that logic prepares the mind for faith rather than determines it.

> **Moses Maimonides** (1135–1204) Jewish philosopher and physician from Muslim Spain whose *Guide for the Perplexed* and other works influenced Christian scholars interested in Aristotelian philosophy.
>
> **Thomas Aquinas** (1225–1274) Dominican theologian whose works are a synthesis of Aristotelian philosophy and Scholasticism.
>
> **summae** Works that seek to be the most complete statements about a subject.

Checking In

By yourself or with a partner, explain the significance of each of the following selected key terms:

Romanesque	Peter Abelard
Gothic	Avicenna
logic	Averroës
Scholasticism	summae

CHAPTER
Review

Summary

- From the eleventh through the thirteenth centuries, church leaders carried out reforms aiming to set higher standards of behavior and belief for the clergy and the laity and to end lay interference in church affairs.

- In 1215, the energetic Pope Innocent III oversaw the Fourth Lateran Council, whose decrees turned reform measures into law.

- At the end of the eleventh century, enthusiasm for an expedition to rid Jerusalem of nonbelievers surged beyond the power of the church to control it.

- Kings also sought to expand their authority, but their power did not increase at the same pace or in a uniform fashion.

- Improved agricultural technology increased food supplies. Long-distance trade revived, and towns grew.

- Merchants, craftsmen, and those who supplied services to them had more money than previous generations to spend on goods from near and far, to invest in business ventures, and to educate themselves.

- The church and inhabitants of the young cities devoted some of this wealth to building cathedrals, monuments to the glory of God.

- At new universities, scholars debated new approaches to learning and faith. In the High Middle Ages, everyone from peasants and townsfolk to kings experienced an improvement in the conditions of their lives.

Chronology

910	Monastery of Cluny is founded	1184	Church condemns Peter Waldo
987	Capetian dynasty replaces Carolingians in France	1187	Saladin crushes crusading army at Hattin
1049	Leo IX elected pope	1191	Richard I of England and Philip II Augustus of France capture Acre
1076	Pope Gregory VII excommunicates Emperor Henry IV	1192	Richard I and Saladin conclude three-year truce
1095	Pope Urban II's sermon prompts crusading movement	1204	Constantinople falls to Fourth Crusade
1096	First wave of Crusaders sets off for Jerusalem	1208	Pope Innocent III calls for crusade against Albigensian sect
1098	Cistercian Order is formed	1209	Pope Innocent III approves Franciscan Order
1099	Jerusalem falls to First Crusade	1215	King John I signs Magna Carta; Fourth Lateran Council
1120	Order of the Templars is founded in Jerusalem	1216	Dominican Order is founded
1163	Construction on Notre Dame begins	1291	Acre, last Christian outpost in east, falls to Muslims
1182	Philip II expels Jews from France		

© Cengage Learning

Test Yourself

To gauge your mastery of the material in this chapter, answer the questions below. More than one answer may be correct.

Church Reform and Spiritual Renewal

1. Which monastery promoted the goals of reform?
   - a. Cluny
   - b. Luxeuil
   - c. Montecassino
   - d. Clermont
   - e. Paris

2. Pope Gregory VII and Emperor Henry IV disagreed strongly about which issue?
   - a. The emperor's right to conquer land inhabited by Christians
   - b. The pope's insistence on his authority over monasteries
   - c. The emperor's right to invest bishops with the symbols of their authority
   - d. The pope's right to hear appeals in ecclesiastical disputes
   - e. Henry IV's right to the title of emperor

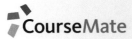
Visit the CourseMate website at **www.cengagebrain.com** for additional study tools and review materials for this chapter.

3. The Fourth Lateran Council had what effect on marriage?

   a. Clandestine marriages were invalid.
   b. Marriages now had to take place inside a church and be officiated by a priest.
   c. No marriage could be annulled.
   d. Marriages between second cousins were permitted.
   e. Priests could not be present at a betrothal ceremony.

4. Why did church leaders take issue with Peter Waldo?

   a. Peter Waldo preached that Jesus was fully human.
   b. Peter Waldo proposed a Monophysite understanding of God the Father and God the Son.
   c. Peter Waldo preached in public on his own initiative after being denied permission to do so.
   d. Peter Waldo believed the Patriarch of Constantinople to be the head of the church.
   e. Peter Waldo denied the existence of God.

5. How did Francis and the Franciscans succeed in gaining papal approval?

   a. He acknowledged that the pope was the leader of the Universal Church.
   b. His theology was more in line with church teachings than other groups that sought recognition as independent orders.
   c. He organized a monastic order without the approval of the pope, who had eventually to accept its existence.
   d. Francis acknowledged the authority of the pope and the church and sought to work within its strictures.
   e. Francis attracted so much popular support that the papacy had no choice but to give in.

Now that you have reviewed and tested yourself on this part of the chapter, take time to pull together all the important information by answering the following questions:

◆ What were the aims of the movement to reform the church, and in what ways did it succeed?

◆ Why did Francis and the Franciscan order succeed and the Waldensians and the Cathars fail to gain ecclesiastical approval?

The Crusades

6. Pope Urban II called on Christians to go expel non-Christians from the Holy Land in response to:

   a. A Muslim fleet's attack on southern France.
   b. A challenge sent to the pope from the leader of the Seljuk Turks.
   c. A demand by Christian kings.
   d. The Muslim conquest of Constantinople.
   e. An appeal from the Byzantine Emperor for military aid against the Seljuk Turks.

7. Which group in Europe suffered first from the fervor stirred up by Pope Urban's sermon?

   a. The merchants
   b. The Jews
   c. The parish priests
   d. Women
   e. Married clergy

8. The goal of the First Crusade leaders was to reach which city and why?

   a. Cairo, because it was the base of Muslim power.
   b. Baghdad, because it was the base of Muslim power.
   c. Damascus, because the Muslim ruler was an ally of the Christians.
   d. Antioch, because that was the city where the word, "Christian," was first used.
   e. Jerusalem, because the city holiest to Christians was in the hands of non-Christian rulers.

9. The Third Crusade ended when:

     a. Richard I and Saladin agreed to a truce.

     b. The leaders disagreed and they abandoned the mission.

     c. Richard I defeated Saladin and recaptured Jerusalem.

     d. Richard I and Philip II Augustus could not agree on a strategic goal.

     e. Saladin made an alliance with Philip II Augustus against Richard, who fled.

10. Which of the following was *not* a consequence of the Crusades?

     a. In the crusader states, the eastern clergy could not be ordained according to their own rites.

     b. The increase in long-distance trade led to improvements in banking techniques.

     c. The English who participated in the Crusades dominated trade in the Holy Land thereafter.

     d. Hostility between Christians and Muslims increased thereafter.

     e. Italian merchants brought back new goods from the markets of the Crusaders states to trade in Europe.

Now that you have reviewed and tested yourself on this part of the chapter, take time to pull together all the important information by answering the following questions:

◆ How did preaching the Crusades fit into the pope's plans for church reform?

◆ Why were the military orders a necessary and mostly successful development in the Crusades?

The Growth of Royal Authority

11. The battle of Hastings in 1066 between William, duke of Normandy, and the Danish king of England led to:

     a. The establishment of Norman rulers over Denmark.

     b. The conquest of the Danes over the western half of Britain.

     c. The establishment of Norman rulers over England.

     d. The expulsion of the Normans from England.

     e. The French king's claim to the throne of England.

12. Magna Carta created a precedent for the rights of all the king's subjects in England, but its principal aim was to:

     a. Restrain the rights of the church in England

     b. Restrain the king's fiscal demands on his subjects.

     c. Reject the role of the king in England's judicial system.

     d. Impose the authority of the Archbishop of Canterbury over the king.

     e. Impose the authority of the English king over the church in England.

13. As vassal of the French king, King Henry II of England held in fief to him:

     a. Nearly one-half of the French kingdom

     b. The territory surrounding the city of Paris

     c. Burgundy

     d. Flanders

     e. Champagne

14. What are regalia?

     a. The clothing worn by the clergy when celebrating the mass

     b. The crown and scepter borne by the Holy Roman Emperor in court

     c. A queen's attire in court

     d. The secular rights enjoyed by the bishops of the Holy Roman Empire

     e. The rights and laws wielded by the Holy Roman Emperor

15. What is a notary?

    a. The king's representative in the shires

    b. The chief secretary of the pope

    c. A judge who travels around the country hearing cases

    d. A public official who draws up legal documents

    e. The official who records the king's law as he pronounces it

Now that you have reviewed and tested yourself on this part of the chapter, take time to pull together all the important information by answering the following questions:

◆ In which ways did secular rulers seek to enhance their authority?

◆ Who stood to gain from inhibiting the grown of centralized royal authority?

The Growth of Towns and Trade

16. Which technological innovations accompanied the changes in agricultural production?

    a. The invention of the stirrup

    b. Improvements in plows and animal harnessing

    c. Innovations in the design of mills

    d. Metallurgical innovation

    e. The understanding of germination

17. At the fairs of Champagne in the twelfth century, which new techniques emerged?

    a. Currency exchange and banking

    b. A more precise system of barter

    c. The provision of services, like inns and taverns, for traveling merchants

    d. The beginnings of a postal system

    e. The association of games with the sale of agricultural produce

18. Which of the following statements about the practice of usury is accurate?

    a. Christians forbade Jews and Muslims from lending money at interest.

    b. Jews refused to lend money at interest.

    c. Lending money at interest was one of the only occupations allowed Muslims in Europe.

    d. The church promoted the lending of money at interest in order to promote profits.

    e. The church forbade Christians from lending money at interest to one another.

19. Christian slave traders in the Mediterranean depended on which regions for sources of slaves?

    a. Sub-Saharan Africa

    b. Ireland

    c. Eastern Europe and Central Asia

    d. Iberia

    e. Sicily

Now that you have reviewed and tested yourself on this part of the chapter, take time to pull together all the important information by answering the following questions:

◆ What changes occurred in people's daily lives when more land was put under agricultural production and more merchants traveled greater distances for goods?

◆ What role did religion play in the enslavement of people beyond the borders of Europe?

The Building of Cathedrals and the Spread of Learning

20. What were the two main styles of architectural decoration preferred by builders in the Middle Ages?

    a. Romanesque and Moorish

    b. Romanesque and Italian

    c. Romanesque and Gothic

    d. Romanesque and Byzantine

    e. Romanesque and Anglo-Saxon

21. What did the cathedral schools of Paris specialize in?

    a. Law
    b. Medicine
    c. Astronomy
    d. Mathematics
    e. Theology

22. The influential commentaries of Avicenna and Moses Maimonides deepened scholars' understanding of:

    a. The works of Aristotle
    b. The writings of St. Augustine
    c. The Hebrew Bible
    d. The works of Peter Abelard
    e. The Summa of Thomas Aquinas

23. Which of the following statements best describes Peter Abelard's method of intellectual reasoning?

    a. I believe in order to understand.
    b. I understand and therefore do not need to believe.
    c. I understand and I believe.
    d. I believe because I will never understand.
    e. I seek to understand in order to believe.

24. What are summae?

    a. Another word for God
    b. Treatises containing the most complete summary of a given topic
    c. The portions of the Christian Bible that contained the Epistles
    d. Collections of Parisian students' notes passed down from generation to generation
    e. The bookkeeping records of merchants

Now that you have reviewed and tested yourself on this part of the chapter, take time to pull together all the important information by answering the following questions:

◆ In what ways does learning in the Middle Ages differ from university learning today?

◆ What was the relationship between education and the church?

CHAPTER 11

Reversals and Disasters, 1300–1450

Chapter Outline

1200	1220	1240	1260	1280	1300	1320	1340
	1215 King John signs the Magna Carta					**1305** Avignon papacy begins	**1337** Hundred Years' War begins

Crossbows were as feared as semi-automatic assault weapons are today. Church leaders preached that crossbows were deadly to an unnecessary and immoral degree. The one represented here is a relatively simple device to use, but, like all crossbows, it had disadvantages in battle. Which kind of bow would be more quickly reloaded in battle, a crossbow or a conventional bow? What do you surmise would be the advantage of a weapon like this? (Culture and Sport Glasgow Museums, acc. #E. 1939.65.sn)

After reading this chapter, you should be able to answer the following questions:

What were the key social and economic consequences of famine and plague in the fourteenth century?

In what ways did warfare and violence contribute to social unrest?

How did the prestige of the church suffer as a result of the Avignon papacy and the Great Schism?

What external pressures changed the borders of Christian Europe?

Throughout the thirteenth century, the ties that bound people of western Europe to their rulers were often strained and weak. Widespread famine, climatic changes, and epidemics starting in the first half of the fourteenth century caused suffering to a degree that no one, not even kings, could lessen. Warfare only made things worse.

In spite of a century and a half of unprecedented hardship, by the mid-fifteenth century patriotic sentiment bound people to their rulers more than ever before. The change, however, had less to do with the order reestablished by rulers in their realms during the fifteenth century than it did with the government's and the church's manipulation of people's attachment to their town, region, country, and now their ruler.

The fourteenth century was a time of reversals and disasters. The growth of towns and trade slowed as colder, wetter weather in the north had a catastrophic effect on agriculture. Famine was ever-present, and then a terrifying illness, first seen in the port cities of the Mediterranean, spread across Europe. Men, women, and children, high and low, died in days, overnight,

1360	1380	1400	1420	1440	1460	1480

1347 Black Death first appears in Italy

1356 French defeated at Battle of Poitiers

1378 Great Schism begins

1417 Great Schism ends

1453 Fall of Constantinople Hundred Years' War ends

within hours. Meanwhile France and England were engaged in a long war, and in the east Turks and Mongols made advances against the surviving portions of the Byzantine Empire. Three kings of England waged war on the Welsh, Scots, and the Irish when they were not fighting their own rebellious barons. To finance the fighting that was taking place all over the continent, rulers stretched their sources of revenue to their limits. Heavy taxes burdened people already oppressed by the climate changes and failed crops.

New, extended wars and new threats from the east made life seem much more precarious than it had been in the thirteenth century. The common people bore the brunt of the consequences of their rulers' territorial ambitions. From far away, reports of infidels marching right up to the frontiers of Christendom alarmed both governments and their subjects. The ancient Byzantine Empire dwindled away under the pressure of first the Mongol advances. A new empire ruled by the descendants of the warrior chieftain Osman took its place. The reality of the expanding Ottoman Empire pushing against Europe's borders put secular rulers and the pope on alert. After economic expansion slowed and as the borders of Europe seemed threatened, few looked into the future with optimism. Survival was all.

Famine and Plague

- **What factors caused widespread death throughout Europe?**
- **What were the economic consequences of the plague?**

By 1300, the benefits of more land in cultivation, increased long-distance trade, and strengthened royal authority were felt throughout western Europe. Population expanded: some 4 million people lived in the British Isles and 10 million or so in the Italian peninsula. More towns and villages dotted the landscape. People had a little more to eat, better clothes to wear, and a wider range of goods to buy. As long as harvests were plentiful and families well nourished, peasants and townsfolk could look forward to living longer than previous generations.

The Spread of Hunger

Then, around the start of the fourteenth century, the weather and even the climate changed noticeably. Winters were colder and longer. Heavy rains poured down summer after summer on France, Germany, the Low Countries, and England, depriving crops of warmth and sunlight.

Little Ice Age Period of cooler weather in Europe beginning around the start of the fourteenth century.

Cities on the coastlines of northern Europe experienced severe flooding. In the North Atlantic, sheets of ice permanently covered Greenland, so named when its land had been green, not white. The inhabitants of England and the Low Countries turned to brewing beer instead of making wine once the colder weather put an end to grape cultivation there. The **Little Ice Age** had descended on northern Europe.

Soil Exhaustion To make matters worse, much of the previous century's increase in agricultural production occurred in regions with unsuitable soil. Signs of soil exhaustion appeared early in the fourteenth century. Because it now took more seed to yield the same amount of crops as before, peasants had to put aside a larger share of their grain for the next year's sowing. Meager harvests in the years when rains did not wash away the entire crop meant less food for the peasant family and less to sell at market. A ten-acre plot of land would have fed a peasant family a generation earlier, but no longer. The land was overworked.

Changes in Climate By 1315, rain, colder weather, and soil exhaustion had created the conditions for a severe famine across much of northern Europe. Failed crops and the difficulties of transporting food from where it could be found to where it was needed meant that most people experienced the pain of hunger, and thousands starved to death. The famine lasted three years, faded, and then recurred intermittently in succeeding decades whenever harvests

Map 11.1 **Europe Ravaged from Within** Along the trade routes and sea lanes that linked Europe to the Middle East and Asia traveled merchants, pilgrims, and armies. These travelers also brought deadly diseases that killed a third to half the population of Europe. © *Cengage Learning*

1. Is there a pattern to the spread of the epidemic, or does it seem random?
2. Comparing the dates and the regions affected, why might the plague not have arrived in Vienna until 1350 even though it appeared in southern England two years earlier?
3. What might account for the pockets that were spared?

were poor. Livestock, too, declined, and peasants resorted to eating whatever they could find: cats, dogs, rodents, and horses. By the middle of the fourteenth century, northern Europe's population increases had been reversed.

Fear of starvation set people in motion. From the northern English city of York to the trading posts of Poland, rain, flooding, and perpetual winter turned thousands of people into refugees. Villages became ghost towns, and cities became temporarily overcrowded, until their populations, too, succumbed to starvation. Bands of beggars roamed the countryside, and in cities most crimes involved theft of food. Like the Frankish kings of the early Middle Ages, secular rulers could offer little protection to their subjects. Disorder prevailed, and for most people the situation could not have gotten much worse.

The Specter of Death

And then it did. In the summer of 1347, a deadly plague, later called the **Black Death**, swept across Europe. The symptoms were unlike any seen before. Swollen, bruised lumps on the lower abdomen, in the armpits, or on the throat were the first indicators. Lymph glands swelled to the size of an egg or larger in the groin and armpits. If the glands burst, causing internal hemorrhaging, the suffering was unbearable and death was inevitable. If they did not, then the victim might survive, but most often they burst. Someone retiring to bed in the evening with a slight fever might never wake up. An airborne form of the bubonic and pneumonic plague affecting the lungs could bring death within hours. Other symptoms—bruises and spots appearing all over the body—led some physicians (and a few modern historians) to wonder if more than one disease was at work.

Bubonic Plague Most historians agree that the disease that made death a daily, if not hourly, possibility was the bacillus *Yersinia pestis*, or bubonic plague, so called for the inflamed swellings, or buboes, of the lymph glands. Beginning in Central Asia, spreading westward, the plague was carried—though its victims did not know it at the time—by fleas on rats. Rats hidden on vessels heading west carried the disease to the Aegean Islands and then to Sicily, where it was first seen in September 1347. Six months later, the disease had spread north to Florence, where it killed half the population between March and September 1348. Over the course of 1349, the plague spread across Spain and northern Europe, reaching eastern Europe in 1350. Between a third and a half of the people of Europe died.

The cities and towns of Italy were hardest hit, for they had the greatest concentrations of population. In Florence, the devastation was reported in *The Decameron* by the poet and storyteller **Giovanni Boccaccio**: "Many dropped dead in the open streets, both by day and by night, whilst a great many others, though dying in their own homes, drew their neighbours' attention to the fact more by the smell of their rotting corpses than

Werner Forman/Art Resource, NY

This fourteenth-century illumination from a collection of sermons by Thomas of Stitny, a Czech cleric, depicts people's fear about the bubonic plague. The disease could take hold so quickly that people died in their sleep hours after contracting it. Do you think this image was meant to reassure or alarm the reader of this collection?

by any other means. And what with these, and the others who were dying all over the city, bodies were here, there and everywhere." After the first wave, the plague recurred every ten years or so until the early fifteenth century, when the number of outbreaks increased even more.

No Remedies Physicians had few remedies for the suffering taking place around them. Weakened immune systems made people vulnerable to other diseases, such as smallpox and influenza, the symptoms of which complicated physicians' understandings of what they observed in their patients. Because the number of deaths in heavily populated areas was so high, physicians believed the disease spread by contact between persons. Because everyone, not just physicians, lacked an understanding of germs, poor hygiene and filth contributed to the spread of disease. The only option open to medical men and the women who worked more informally as healers was to fall back on methods familiar to them: astrology, bloodletting, and herbal medicine. Inadvertently, some

Black Death Epidemic of bubonic plague that killed one-third to one-half of the people of Europe between 1347 and 1351.

Giovanni Boccaccio (1313–1375) Influential Florentine author of *The Decameron* and other literary works.

"The Dance of Death" (detail), 1463, attributed to Bernt Notke. St. Nicolai's Church, Tallinn, now the Niguliste Museum

The "Dance of Death" became a common scene in manuscript illuminations, frescoes, and statuary. Given that the poor died in greatest numbers, why is the figure of Death depicted here shown to lead off to the afterlife a pope, an emperor, and a noble woman?

of these methods may have helped in certain situations, but in general, physicians proved to be as helpless as everyone else in the face of the plague's virulence. Mostly, they urged people to flee the congested areas where the plague was rampant. But the working poor and the destitute had nowhere to go, and so the plague claimed more victims among the humble than among the rich, who fled to their country estates. Parents abandoned their children, children abandoned their parents, and priests deserted their flocks.

Endurance and Adaptation

In the face of so much suffering, the people of Europe searched for spiritual comfort and a means of understanding the disasters. Rulers and clergy could do little for people. Locally, the comfort church services and rituals could provide depended on the survival and courage of local priests. Many laypeople sought a deeper involvement in religious life. Others, believing that God had abandoned humanity because of its sins, assumed a despairing, cynical attitude toward life. In the face of so much inexplicable death, it took fortitude to survive.

Collective Guilt Some felt the need to take responsibility for the catastrophe by joining penitential groups. Believing that the plague represented God's punishment for their sins, people living mainly in cities flocked to join **confraternities**, associations dedicated

to the performance of acts of charity and whose processions through city streets were now meant as public penance. A few groups went to extremes by ritually whipping themselves in public. When the **flagellants**, as they were called, drew blood with their scourges, they drew the admiration of some and aroused revulsion of others. Groups of flagellants had existed in the thirteenth century, but their popularity waned after the church condemned their activity in 1261. After the plague hit, flagellants went from town to town in processions, scourging themselves as they walked, until, in 1349, Pope Clement VI again condemned the activity.

Scapegoats Others felt the Jews to be convenient **scapegoats**. Across Europe, whole communities of Jews died at the hands of rioting Christians who believed that the Jews had poisoned the water supply or in some other mysterious way introduced the disease. Such persecutions caused some Jews to leave western Europe, migrating east toward Poland and Russia, where they remained in large numbers until the twentieth century, or southeast toward Muslim lands, where they received a slightly warmer welcome.

confraternities Associations dedicated to the public performance of acts of charity and penance during the plague.

flagellants Groups who ritually whipped themselves in public to atone for the sins of humanity during the plague.

scapegoats Any group that innocently bears the blame of others.

Economies Under Stress

At first the commercial boom of the thirteenth century continued into the next century. The economic outlook in long-distance trade looked much brighter than did the outlook in agricultural production. Refinements in merchants' arrangements, improvements in navigation, and the development of new commercial techniques in the decades prior to the arrival of the plague helped keep economies going during difficult times. Long-distance trade became so complex that merchants reorganized the ways in which their companies operated. Each company delegated its business among the merchants who remained at the company's base, the operators of the ships that conveyed the company's goods from market to market, and the agent-representatives residing in foreign cities who oversaw the buying and selling of those goods. Regular convoys of galleys bearing goods and mail between merchants and their home offices made the networks of trade run more smoothly and profitably.

Navigation The same commercial networks benefited from improvements in navigation. Oar-driven galleys were redesigned to hold more cargo and a new type of vessel was introduced to the Mediterranean trade. Round-hulled sailing vessels called **cogs**, which, with their small crews and great storage capacity, had been developed for the rough waters of the Atlantic Ocean and the Baltic Sea, were adapted for use in the smoother waters of the Mediterranean. Still, galleys, whose oars offset the disadvantages of low wind, remained the principal means of Mediterranean naval transport until the eighteenth century. In the fourteenth and fifteenth centuries, the governments of Venice, Genoa, and Florence annually sponsored enormous convoys of merchant galleys to Flanders, England, Crete, the Black Sea, and the ports of the Levant.

Maritime Trade The two major trading regions continued to be the Mediterranean and the Baltic Sea. In the Mediterranean, the merchants of Venice, Genoa, and Barcelona dominated maritime trade. Nobles, kings, manufacturers, and even popes took advantage of the credit services offered by Florentine merchants, whose interest rates for loans were far below those of merchants elsewhere. On the Baltic Sea, the city of Lübeck (in present-day northern Germany) was unrivaled in the import-export traffic that passed through its port. In 1358, it became the official headquarters of the **Hanseatic League**, an association of German merchants with branches throughout the Holy Roman Empire.

cog Sailing cargo ship with a rounded hull.

Hanseatic League (from German *hansa*, "trading association") Association of north German merchants formed to protect their trading interests.

Signs from the East Yet even before the plague arrived in Europe, trade with the eastern end of the Mediterranean had begun to decline, and economies were weakening. Migrations and disturbances far to the east in Central Asia and China made the long treks to the markets there increasingly difficult. Muslim conquest of the Black Sea region also hampered Christian trading in the east. Venetians, Genoese, and Catalans still traveled to the Black Sea to do business, but Muslim merchants offered them stiff competition. Then, with famine and plague, population decreases and the disruptions of warfare, the demand for luxury goods decreased. Many trading companies went bankrupt.

Overall, the economic consequences of the plague were mixed. Death emptied rural areas of workers, causing rents to fall. At the same time, although some cities experienced an increase in population—mostly refugees from the countryside—the scarcity of labor drove up wages. Skilled and unskilled workers earned more than ever before, but had less to buy than they would have had at the start of the century. By the middle of the fifteenth century, population levels had still not recovered, trade with the east was still difficult, and the people of Europe had learned to endure the new realities of a frightening world.

Checking In

By yourself or with a partner, explain the significance of each of the following selected key terms:

Little Ice Age	flagellants
Black Death	scapegoats
Giovanni Boccaccio	cogs
confraternities	Hanseatic League

One Hundred Years of Warfare

♦ **What caused the Hundred Years' War, and why did it last so long?**

♦ **How did the war create national sentiment in the English and the French?**

Famine and plague arrived in the midst of a war between France and England that continued, intermittently, for more than one hundred years. The war began for dynastic reasons, created at the time of the Norman Conquest, when William, the duke of Normandy, added king of England to his titles and lands across the English Channel to his realm. Henry II inherited his great-grandfather's lands in northern France and, through his marriage to Eleanor, assumed control of the Aquitaine, making him a greater landowner in France than the French king. By the end of the thirteenth century, the French king had deprived the English king of most of his lands in France and was intent on taking them all.

Buildup to War

Frustrated by their loss of land in France, the English kings of the thirteenth century looked northward to Scotland to compensate for their losses. Scottish barons resisted English sovereignty over Scotland in a series of rebellions between 1295 and 1304. Prominent among the rebel lords was **Robert Bruce**, who exploited the dissension among the barons to claim the throne of Scotland. He was crowned in 1306, an event that did not stop Edward I—and afterward his son, Edward II—from pressuring the Scottish king to become a vassal of the English king. With France's support, King Robert's army defeated the English army at Bannockburn in 1314. Fourteen years passed before, in the Treaty of Northampton, the English crown formally—but, in practice, only temporarily—recognized Robert as king and renounced all claims to overlordship in 1328.

Edward III By then, a new king, **Edward III**, sixteen years old, sat on the throne of England. His widowed mother, Queen Isabella, sister of the French king, and her lover Roger Mortimer insisted that her brother the French king, Charles IV, not make further incursions into **Guyenne**, the English territory in southwestern France, and cease undermining English authority there. But then Charles died with no male heir to succeed him. The French nobles could choose the late king's cousin or his nephew, son of his sister. In addition to a prejudice against the female line of succession, crowning the nephew posed a special problem because the nephew was Edward III, already king of England. Thus the majority of French noblemen supported his cousin, who was crowned king of France in 1328 as Philip VI, the first of the Valois dynasty.

To most observers of this dynastic dispute, war between the English and French kings, with Scotland in alliance with France and the Low Countries sympathetic to England, seemed increasingly likely from this point on.

An Occasional War

Within a decade, the conflict had begun. The nobles of Guyenne were divided between those who supported King Edward's overlordship and those who preferred the direct lordship of the king of France. Each side repeatedly tested the limits of authority, leading to occasional outbreaks of violence. By the late 1330s, Edward III believed the only way to compel the French king to accept England's sovereignty over Guyenne was to defeat him in war. In 1337, what

would eventually be known as the **Hundred Years' War** began.

Crécy In 1338, Edward arrived in Flanders with an army, hoping that his presence on France's northeastern frontier and his army in Guyenne in the southwest would squeeze the French king into compliance. But the first six years of war produced little result. Short of money and soldiers and now calling himself king of France, Edward avoided the French king's larger army until August 1346, when, at **Crécy**, he arranged his troops across a low rise and faced oncoming French forces. He had only 4,000 men-at-arms and 10,000 archers, but the archers had **longbows** that shot arrows faster and farther than the crossbows of the French archers. A shower of English arrows destroyed the contingent of French crossbowmen and the cavalry of French nobles. Their superior position and the success of the longbows allowed the English army to drive the much larger French army from the field, where France's greatest nobles lay dead.

Poitiers Ten years later, Edward III's son, Edward—called the Black Prince for the color of his armor—repeated his father's victory at **Poitiers** in 1356: the longbowmen again overwhelmed an attack of mounted French nobles, with the same lethal results. This time, the king of France, John II, was captured, taken to England, and held for ransom. The humiliation of the French aristocracy and monarchy seemed complete.

A Lull in the Fighting After the catastrophic French defeat at Poitiers, diplomacy produced a truce in 1360. Neither side was prepared to continue the fight. Edward III's death in 1377, one year after the death of his son, the Black Prince, meant that Edward III's grandson, Richard II, a boy too young to lead a war, became king. The war seemed to be over.

But it was not yet half over. In its first phase the

Robert Bruce (r. 1306–1329) King Robert I of Scotland, who successfully resisted English attempts to impose lordship over his kingdom.

Edward III (r. 1327–1377) King of England whose claim to the throne of France was largely responsible for the Hundred Years' War.

Guyenne Region in southwest France, originally a part of Aquitaine, under English rule from the twelfth to the mid-fifteenth century.

Hundred Years' War (1337–1453) The long conflict between the kings of England and France.

Crécy Battle in 1346 between English and French armies in which the English gained advantage with the longbow and France lost much of its nobility.

longbow Bow six feet high that had been used by the Welsh to resist the English and then adopted by the English army, where it proved decisive in Edward III's battles in France.

Poitiers Battle in 1356 that marked the second defeat of the French army by the English, during which the French king was captured and held in England for ransom.

At the battle of Crécy in 1346 in northeastern France, the six-foot-tall longbow, carried by the archers in the right-hand foreground of this fifteenth-century manuscript illumination, was decisive in the English army's devastating victory over French forces. How would you explain to a friend why the illuminator placed the longbow archers prominently in the foreground? Did the use of the longbow fit the chivalric ideal?

Bibliotheque nationale de France/The Art Archive at Art Resource, NY

war was not so much between the countries of England and France as it was between the kings of England and France. To persuade his subjects to finance his war through taxation, Edward III fostered a connection between the crown and the people by holding public pageants to celebrate his army's victories. In France, on the other hand, support for the war had never been strong. From the start, the people of northern France, where most of the fighting occurred, viewed the dispute as their ruler's problem. Sieges of ports and cities focused the hardship of warfare on civilians as much as on soldiers. When the French king was captured, the government of his eldest son, known as the **dauphin**, levied heavy taxes to raise the huge ransom. By 1360, the people of France had enough of the war—but the periods of peace were beginning to take their toll as well.

Violence Against Civilians

Military commanders in the fourteenth century faced considerable difficulties in controlling their armies on and off the field of battle. The source of their difficulties lay chiefly in methods of recruitment and in the

periods of demobilization. Feudal service, mass **conscription**, mercenary forces, or a combination of all three each had advantages that were often outweighed by the disadvantages of poor accountability, the political consequences of an armed peasantry, and the chaos created by out-of-work professional fighters.

A Selective Code of Honor The French army consisted largely of noblemen and their troops who fought out of loyalty to their king, to whom they owed feudal service. Military discipline did not emerge easily from the feudal army, bound together as it was by a loose sense of common purpose among quasi-autonomous troops under the French king. Although an informal code of **chivalry** meant noble combatants could expect mercy if they were captured by noblemen of the opposing army, they could also expect financial ruin from the enormous ransoms their families would have to pay to liberate them. Common soldiers taken captive could expect death. Evading capture at all cost—even if that meant leaving the field prematurely—led to chaos on the battlefield.

King Edward of England, in contrast, hired commanders through contracts binding their service. The commanders promised to recruit a certain number of troops, equipped with agreed-on types of weaponry, for predetermined lengths of military service. Long experience had taught the kings of England that relying on the feudal army meant going to war with

dauphin Title of the eldest son of the king of France, usually the heir to the throne.

conscription Military draft; involuntary recruitment of soldiers from among the people.

chivalry Code of military and courtly conduct among the nobility that valued mercy in battle, Christian duty, and defense of women.

In a fifteenth-century chronicle of the Hundred Years' War, an illumination shows soldiers opening barrels of wine and carrying off the furnishing of a house in Paris. Soldiers' violence against civilians caused nearly as much harm as their warfare. What effect might the English army's pillaging have had on the French population's support of their king's war?

Erich Lessing/Art Resource, NY

an insufficient number of troops and that recruiting commoners led to an armed population capable of rebellion. A system of paid contingents was expensive, but more reliable.

Chevauchées During the Hundred Years' War, deliberately inflicted violence became military policy. The Black Prince instituted a strategy of terror to undermine the morale and economic resources of the French. Companies of mounted fighters and foot soldiers stormed through northern France, burning crops and houses and randomly killing anyone they encountered. These campaigns of terror, known as *chevauchées*, were a brutal way to wage war that stood in contrast to the often gallant consideration knights and nobles on opposing sides showed one another.

Many parts of France had no peace, for people had more to fear from the cessation of fighting than they did from pitched battles. If the soldiers were not fighting, they were not paid. So between military campaigns, companies of unemployed soldiers moved from place to place, looting as they went or demanding to be paid off instead. Everyone knew neither the king nor the nobility could provide protection for their subjects or for the kingdom as a whole.

The Final Stage

In 1399, Edward III's grandson, the former boy-king Richard II, had alienated his nobles so severely that

they forced him to abdicate at the age of thirty-two. In his stead, his cousin, Henry of Bolingbroke, leader of the rebel nobles, became King Henry IV. Viewed as a usurper of the English throne by many, Henry successfully put down Scottish raids on the border, Welsh assertions of independence, and powerful English nobles who attempted to capture the throne. In 1413, Henry IV died with his claim to the English throne and his son's succession secured.

Henry V This son, **Henry V**, revived the claim to the French throne. Since Henry needed money and moral support to restart the war, he organized a campaign to win the hearts of all his subjects, noble and commoner alike. Priests delivered sermons justifying war. The bishop of Rochester even insisted to his congregation that since God was an Englishman, they had a duty to fight for England. Triumphal processions filled with colorful floats carried religious and royal symbols whenever the king left for war or returned from France. The crowds lining the streets to see the processions were moved to feel pride and loyalty. The people of England came to think of themselves as united in being English.

The End of the War After forming a secret alliance

chevauchées (in French, "horse charges") Mounted warriors whose purpose was to destroy crops and terrorize the people of the countryside.

Henry V (r. 1413–1422) King of England who revived the Hundred Years' War.

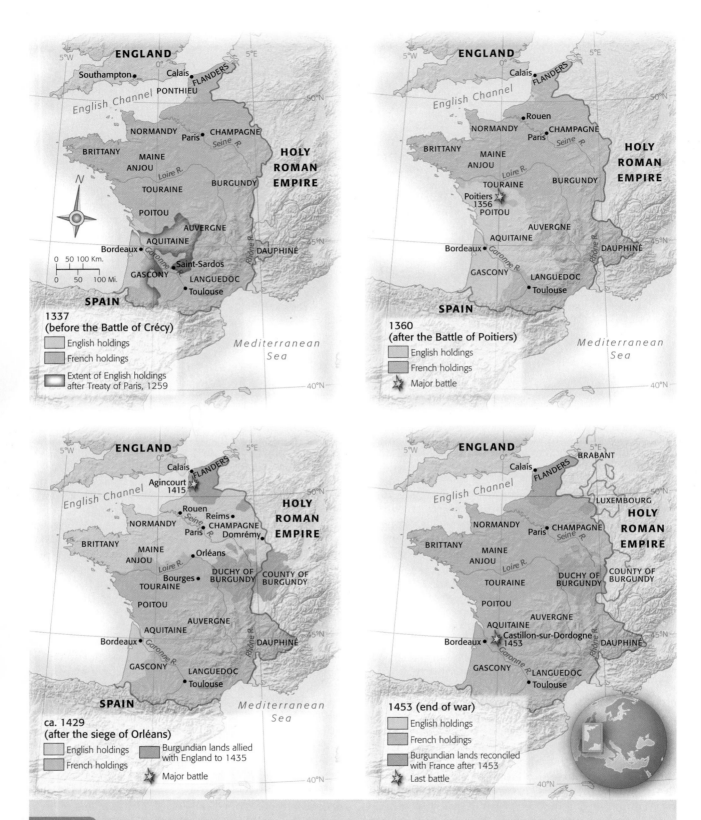

Map 11.2 **Hundred Years' War** As the sequence of four maps showing the stages of the Hundred Years' War indicates, a large proportion of the kingdom of France came under the rule of the English king after 1360. By the 1430s, France stood in danger of becoming entirely a possession of the English king. © *Cengage Learning*

1. Locate the territory in the French kingdom ruled by the English king in the 1330s. How much had it changed by 1360?
2. In which part of the French kingdom did the majority of the battles throughout the war take place? What might account for it?
3. What factors led to the changes in the maps between 1429 and 1453?

Joan of Arc Recants, Then Retracts Her Recanting

In 1428, Joan of Arc, a peasant girl around sixteen years of age from the province of Lorraine, claimed to hear the voices of Saints Michael, Catherine, and Margaret. They told her she must convince the leaders of the French forces fighting the English to put her at the head of the army. Joan sought out the captain of the French army garrisoned near her village to ask him to send her to the dauphin, the late French king's uncrowned son and commander of the army. When the captain refused, Joan returned home. A year later, she tried again and this time received permission to make the eleven-day journey to the castle where the dauphin was lodged. Dressed in men's clothing, Joan reached the dauphin's court.

Perhaps the most extraordinary aspect of her story is that Joan, who had never before traveled far from her village, much less fought in a battle, suc-ceeded in convincing the dauphin to let her lead the troops in an attack on the walls of Orléans in 1429. Against tremendous odds, the troops she led raised the siege. Joan led French troops into other battles and opened the way into captured territory so that the dauphin could be crowned King Charles VII at the Cathedral of Rheims, the traditional site of royal coronations in France.

A year later, Joan was captured by England's Burgundian allies. A court of English and Burgun-dian judges condemned her as a witch—someone who, they claimed, had dealings with the Devil—and a heretic. The judges sought to end the inspira-tion she could provide to the French, for the English were slowly losing ground to France in the war. Just nineteen years old, Joan stood her ground before the judges. She refused to exchange her men's clothes for women's and to deny that the voices she heard came from Heaven. She refused to tell the judges what she had said to the dauphin to convince him to let her lead the French armies. She refused to acknowledge that the church's authority took precedence over the instructions she received from the voices. The judges threatened her with torture and made it clear that if she did not cooper-ate, she would be burned at the stake.

After Joan was found guilty of witchcraft and heresy, and turned over to the secular authorities for execution, her courage faltered. Terrified of being burned at the stake, she signed a document in which she recanted, renouncing her voices and admitting that her claim to having heard them was heretical. The judges condemned her to life im-prisonment and required her to give up the men's clothing she had worn since she first led the French army. Dressed once again in women's clothing, Joan entered her prison cell.

A few days later, her jailers found her in men's clothing once more. She put on the clothes she wore in battle to symbolize her decision to retract her recanting and once more to obey the voices of the saints that she believed she had heard. The possession of courage, it must be remembered, does not mean the absence of fear. Joan bravely went to her death at the stake in terror of the agony she was about to endure. After the war against the English ended, the people of France cherished the memory of Joan's short life and career as a soldier for her king. She became a symbol of France and in 1920 was canonized.

Bridgeman-Giraudon/Art Resource, NY

Key to the story of Joan of Arc is the men's clothing she wore. It was considered improper for women to dress like men, and her attire implied she had the ability to act like a man. Though trial records indicate Joan wore male attire to her death, the illuminator depicts her at her execution in women's clothing. What reasons might the illuminator have had to paint Joan in women's clothing at the stake?

with the duke of Burgundy, for a while the regent ruling in place of the intermittently mad French king Charles VI, Henry V took his army across the English Channel. In September 1415 at **Agincourt**, the French army went down to defeat for the third time. Henry quickly annexed Normandy while the dauphin organized an army in the south of France. When the English army laid siege to Orléans, southwest of Paris, the town's resis-tance slowed their advance. **Joan of Arc** (see A New Di-rection: Joan of Arc Recants, Then Retracts Her Recant-ing) convinced the dauphin that the voices she heard told her she could raise the siege. Inspired by her courageous leadership, the French army won decisive victories that undermined

Agincourt Battle in 1415 in northern France in which the army of Henry V defeated the army of Charles VI of France.

Joan of Arc (1412–1431) Peas-ant girl who led French troops to victory over the English at Orléans in 1429; later captured by the English and burned at the stake as a witch.

the alliance between the English and the Burgundians. After the duke of Burgundy made his peace with Charles VII in 1435, the French army slowly recaptured nearly all the territory that the English had taken. When the French army captured Guyenne in 1453, all the English king had left in France was the port of Calais. The century-old conflict was over.

The peoples of England and of France paid a heavy price for their kings' war. Overtaxed, the English grew tired of King Henry's military adventure. The French endured sustained and serious losses in crops, income, and lives. Yet, despite the suffering, the peoples of England and of France now each regarded their kings as symbols of their country. The kings' rallying support for the war forged a new bond between rulers and their subjects, the strength of which was tested repeatedly. For victorious France, the war also united French territory, at least theoretically.

 Checking In

By yourself or with a partner, explain the significance of each of the following selected key terms:

Robert Bruce	chivalry
Edward III	*chevauchées*
Crécy	Henry V
dauphin	Joan of Arc

Resistance and Revolt

- **What elements did the revolts of the fourteenth century have in common?**
- **From which ranks of society did the rebels emerge?**

The people of Europe endured famine, plague, and war. When bonds between kings and their subjects strengthened, many asked their rulers for greater freedom and political participation, especially since they had to pay heavy taxes. But when their hopes for protection, relief, and political rights were disappointed, many vented their anger on those they held responsible for their problems. Across Europe, and throughout the fourteenth century, revolts broke out and were ultimately put down.

Flanders

The cities of Flanders, just beyond France's northeastern border, were among Europe's largest by the end of the thirteenth century. Ghent, with more than sixty thousand inhabitants, ranked second only to Paris in population. These cities owed their size and economic vitality to the textile industry. From England

came vessels carrying raw wool, which would be washed, carded, spun, woven, fulled, dyed, and finished as cloth before being sent out along trade routes heading south toward the Mediterranean and north toward the Baltic ports. The process of turning wool into cloth involved both rural and city workers. Although textiles made many Flemish cloth producers wealthy, the economy nevertheless depended on agricultural production, mainly grain, and on livestock on rural estates belonging to the merchant families in the cities. Whoever ruled Flanders stood to benefit richly from custom duties and taxes.

Heavy Taxation By 1320, the Flemish were caught between the French king, on one hand, who was interested primarily in revenue from taxation and customs duties, and the English king, on the other. Their own ruler, Louis, count of Flanders and a vassal of the French king, favored the French. Louis's subjects felt differently. Dependent on the wool trade with England, Flemish peasants and merchants resented the heavy tax burdens the count imposed on them as well as the pressure the French king put on their economy. A Flemish army had already defeated the French king's army at Courtrai in 1302. Just when their economy was improving, not only were the count's taxes crushing them, but his corrupt government was making him wealthy at their expense.

The Peasants Revolt In 1323, peasants in the countryside rioted against the count's oppressive taxation. Well-to-do textile merchants and less well-off workers in the city allied with them and forced the governors of their cities to flee. Ghent, Bruges, Ypres, and other cities of Flanders formed a federation of rebel governments, made up of rebels from the upper levels of Flemish peasant and urban society. The first action the new rulers took was to cancel tax collection. They organized themselves into an army that defeated the count's forces on more than one occasion.

The Flanders revolt that began in 1323 changed character over the five years it lasted. What began as a tax revolt of prosperous merchants and peasants against the count of Flanders eventually gained the support of poorer peasants and workers in the cities. Ordinary people spoke out against the privileges of the nobility. Popular preachers delivered sermons that advocated social equality. Once the revolt took on characteristics of a social revolution, the count and the Flemish nobles appealed to the French king for help.

Repression In the summer of 1328, the French king sent an army through Flanders, slaughtering tens of thousands of people as they went. The rebellion was brutally suppressed, but it lasted far longer than any other subsequent rebellion in the fourteenth century. One change initiated by the rebels was lasting. When they assumed control of a city at the start of the revolt, the merchants experienced political power for the first time. Although the end of the revolt ended their dominance of Flemish politics, merchants continued to hold seats on the governing councils of their cities.

France

Unlike Flanders, whose merchants and peasants fought for a greater say in the management of their economy and government, the dire conditions in France made peasants desperate and angry. After the French defeat at Poitiers, when the English massacred or captured almost all of the nobles, including the king himself, the peasants were forced to raise the king's ransom. The situation was worse in the areas where the English armies conducted their *chevauchées*. More than any other rebellion of the fourteenth century, the **Jacquerie**—so called for the name the nobles called peasants, "Jacques"—arose from the ranks of the much-oppressed peasants.

A Revolt Spreads to Paris The violence began in May 1358 as resistance to plundering soldiers in the countryside. It very quickly turned into an expression of rage toward the nobility. Soon peasants from all over northeastern France destroyed castles and slaughtered nobles and their families. Word of the rebels' violence spread far beyond the region affected. As rebels traveled along the Loire and the Seine Rivers, moving in the direction of Paris, noble families fled.

In the same period, the city of Paris was experiencing political turmoil of its own. There the need to raise the king's ransom forced the government to make political concessions to the merchants of Paris, who sought reforms in the way they were governed. Reluctant to cede any authority to the Parisians but much in need of their money, the government, led by the dauphin, granted some of the merchants' demands in February 1358, but the concessions were not enough. A mob murdered two of the king's closest advisers. Parisians joined forces with the peasants, but, in June 1358, the French army defeated the combined forces of peasants and Parisians occupying the city of Meaux.

The Jacquerie rebellion was quickly brutally suppressed and inflicted new suffering on an already much-burdened population. But chroniclers who wrote about the war for their noble patrons, such as Jean Froissart, attributed the brutality to the rebels, and that is what the French people remembered.

Florence

As in Flanders, the workers and well-to-do inhabitants of Italian cities grew increasingly dissatisfied with the way they were being governed, taxed, and excluded from political decisions. Many people questioned—in private, for the most part—the privileges that aristocratic families demanded as their due.

Periodic riots against city governments contributed to a growing sense of disorder, most notably in Florence.

The Signoria Florence was governed by a system of councils, chief of which was the Signoria. Made up of representatives from the city's twenty-one guilds, it acted like an executive council overseeing all the other councils charged with governing the large mercantile city. The rotation every two months of the guild members on councils made it look like a republican government, as so many of Florence's guild members proudly insisted that it was. In reality, a small group of wealthy merchants and their male relatives and clients were repeatedly elected to the city's public offices, and guilds representing the most prestigious occupations—lawyers, merchants from the textile trade, bankers, shopkeepers, and furriers—dominated Florentine political life. Middling businessmen, artisans, and poor skilled workers belonging to smaller and less prestigious guilds were not represented on the city council. Entirely excluded from power, workers and peasants sought power in republican Florence in the only way available to them—through force.

Wool Carders The **Ciompi Revolt** of 1378 began as a revolt of the wool carders, the *ciompi*, who combed wool into manageable strands prior to its being woven. The production and sale of woolen cloth made the city wealthy, but not all of those who worked in the industry benefited equally. The ciompi ranked lower in Florentine society than weavers and wholesale woolen merchants. Their radical inclinations had up until then caused the Signoria to forbid them to form a guild. Shut out of political life, they grew increasingly frustrated.

Revolt Their anger finally exploded into riots in the summer of 1378. Other workers, who felt shut out of Florence's political life, joined them. For a few weeks that summer, Florentines flooded the streets with riotous demonstrations or they hid in their houses. Crowds milling around in the **piazza** of the Palace of the Signoria called for the government to lower taxes, abolish the public debt, and allow the ciompi to form their own guild. The city council refused to compromise. Finally, on July 22, 1378, a crowd pushed into the large, fortress-like palace and took the council room and its occupants by force. The minor guilds gained the political power they had long desired, and the ciompi at last announced the formation of their own guild.

Jacquerie Peasant revolt of 1358 in northern France directed mainly at the nobility.

Ciompi Revolt (in Italian, "wool carders") Revolt in Florence in 1378 instigated by wool carders.

piazza Public square in an Italian city.

The minor guilds dominating the new government despised lower-class ciompi just as the major guilds had when they were in power. The wool carders soon felt themselves again pushed to the margins of political power. Within a month, conflict once more threatened to engulf the city. To avert another civil war, the lesser guilds on the city councils suppressed the wool carders' guild and thus ended their participation in Florence's government. But the minor guilds themselves, despised by the more prestigious guilds, did not last long in power.

Four years later, in 1382, the major guilds regained control of the city council, expelled the lesser guilds, and pushed the middling and lower ranks of Florentine society out of political power. An oligarchy of wealthy guild members monopolized civic authority in Florence once more.

England

In 1381, horsemen and men on foot, armed with bows and pikes, proceeded along the roads of Essex and Kent toward London, recruiting artisans and farmers as they went. They were men of property intent on making someone suffer for the heavy taxes imposed on them by the king's ministers. Earlier that year, the government had imposed the third **head tax** in four years on all property owners. Finally, they had had enough. Wars, famine, inflation, and disease placed the heaviest burden on the poor, but the social standing of the people on their way to London reflected the profound changes taking place in English society.

Seeds of Revolt Well-to-do peasants, merchants, artisans, and craftworkers profited from cheap real estate, abandoned property, and the shortage of food. By buying land cheaply or simply taking possession of abandoned farmland and by selling the food produce they grew at inflated prices where food was scarce, they earned more than they ever had before. Some of the marchers were technically still serfs, even if they were quite well off. Reeves, or managers of noble estates, came from the countryside north of London to join in with the rebels. In their towns and villages, they were respectable men of modest property, but they had no political representation at the king's court and wanted some say about taxes. The **Peasants' Revolt** of 1381 represented the first large-scale rebellion of commoners demanding greater participation in the political life of the kingdom in which they were tax-paying subjects.

Military Experience To the dismay of the government, the rebels behaved like a trained army, as indeed, in some ways, they were. Although the war with France had entered a period of relative inactivity, the government of England still feared an invasion from across the English Channel. **Militias** organized in the towns and villages of Essex and Kent had gathered in local pastures to practice archery; some men actually served as archers in the king's army. These trained men now became a rebel army, marching to London in an orderly manner to rid their young king of ministers they viewed as corrupt.

Along the way, the rebels stopped to burn down the homes of particularly unpopular noblemen. In London, they decapitated the archbishop of Canterbury and murdered the king's chancellor. Rushing to London's Newgate Prison, notorious for its barbaric conditions, the rebels forced open the gates to release all those imprisoned in it. By the time King Richard II, fourteen years old at the time, and a company of his nobles had organized to put down the revolt, the rebels had gone on to murder London merchants and set fire to portions of the city. With a small troop for protection, the young king on horseback confronted the leaders of the revolt, **Wat Tyler** and the renegade priest John Ball, inside the city walls. To show their loyalty to their king, the leaders and their rebel army followed Richard through the city gates and into a field. He knew they would follow him because they had made it clear their complaints were directed at the king's officials, not him. But Richard led them into a trap. His army was waiting for them. The rebels who were not slaughtered that day were later executed.

Another Revolt Suppressed Like the revolts in Flanders, France, and Florence, the English uprising ended without having significantly altered the society that the rebels sought to change. The hopes and radical ideas of the rebels did not disappear entirely, but the conditions for their fulfillment still lay far in the future.

---

head tax Fixed tax all residents of a locality are expected to pay.

Peasants' Revolt An uprising in the summer of 1381 of commoners from mainly southeast England seeking greater political liberty that was quickly suppressed by King Richard II's forces.

militia An armed group of people from one town or region whose self-appointed or assigned purpose was to protect their locality.

Wat Tyler (d. 1381) Leader of the English Peasants' Revolt.

 ### Checking In

By yourself or with a partner, explain the significance of each of the following selected key terms:

Jacquerie	Peasants' Revolt
Ciompi Revolt	militias
piazza	Wat Tyler
head tax	

On the right of this illumination, King Richard II persuades the army of the Peasants' Revolt of 1381 to follow him outside London's walls. To the left of the illumination, once outside the city walls, the king watches his guards murder Wat Tyler, the leader of the rebels. Why did the rebels fall into the trap?

British Library, London/HIP/Art Resource, NY

A Worldly Church

- What factors contributed to the papacy's loss of prestige?

- How did the mystics reflect the religious sentiment of ordinary people?

To many in western Europe in the fourteenth century, it seemed that raising funds, not saving souls, had become the papacy's first priority. The popes saw things differently. The papacy still claimed authority over ecclesiastic and secular rulers, but, lacking the resources to make its claims effective, it turned to adornments—to gold, silver, marble, and silk vestments—that would give the impression of authority. Secular rulers of western Europe were either indifferent to or irritated by the pope's claim that his power was superior to theirs. Ordinary people, alienated by the papacy's opulent appearance and apparent corruption, sought ways to privately and publicly express their own spirituality.

Papal Ambitions

Rome's population consisted of wealthy, modest, and poor families, all of whom depended on the city's biggest employer—the church—for jobs, patronage, and business. It now took a manager as much as a spiritual leader to oversee the bureaucracy of the papacy. The pope had the authority to appoint clergy to lucrative positions within the church, and the competition among clergy for positions with good incomes, called **benefices**, was fierce and corrupt. Bribes paid to papal officials opened doors for those who had the money. The noble families of Rome pressured the pope to favor their kinsmen. The pope had his own kinsmen to give positions to, as did the cardinals.

A New Pope When Pope Nicholas IV died in 1292, the cardinals of the church withdrew into a **conclave** to elect a new **pontiff**. A process that usually consumed a few days or occasionally a few weeks at most, the conclave this time lasted until 1294. The cardinals could not agree on anyone. After two years of stalemate, they settled on an elderly monk with no talent for administration. Six months later, Celestine V became the only pope in history to **abdicate**, an action that did not prevent his canonization in 1313. Fearful of another deadlock, the cardinals quickly elected **Boniface VIII**, an elderly canon lawyer who was also a good administrator. Boniface's sharp temper, however, alienated the cardinals. His popularity sank even lower when he had the

benefice Right to the income from a church office.

conclave Meeting of church leaders to elect a new pope.

pontiff One of the pope's titles, derived from *pontifex maximus*, the title of the chief priest of the state religion in pre-Christian Rome.

abdicate To resign from an office, usually one with a life term.

Boniface VIII (r. 1294–1303) Pope who reasserted the papacy's supreme authority over secular rulers.

former pope, Celestine, put in prison, where the old monk soon died.

Despite his lack of support, Boniface energetically tackled the major problems facing the church. Of them, the fact that the papacy's income did not meet its expenses was the most serious. Though head of the extensive lands in the Papal States, the pope had difficulty exacting taxes from the nobles who ruled in his name but preferred to keep the revenue for themselves. Papal troops—always a major expense—had to be maintained there to keep order. Tithes, gifts, a tax to pay for a new crusade, and fees for appointments earned the papacy much revenue, but its expenses continued to outstrip what the church took in.

Dispute with the French King In 1296, Philip IV of France and Edward I of England taxed the clergy in their kingdoms despite the canon law exempting the church from taxation by secular rulers. Boniface threatened to excommunicate any clergy who paid the taxes. In turn, Philip and Edward promised to banish them if they did not. Philip also stopped all shipments of gold and silver coin to the papacy from leaving his kingdom. Starved of his revenue, Boniface backed down.

Unam Sanctam Five years later, in 1301, Philip tried a bishop in the royal court, also against canon law, which exempted clergy from trial in secular courts. Boniface condemned this act and, a year later, issued a bold statement of his authority, *Unam sanctam*, in which he claimed ultimate temporal and spiritual authority over all humanity. Boniface declared that "it is absolutely necessary for salvation that every human creature be subject to the Roman Pontiff." The claim, in fact, had no force behind it. In 1303, determined to end Boniface's opposition to Philip's right to try a member of the clergy, the king sent a troop of noblemen to intimidate the pope, who was residing at his summer home at Anagni, south of Rome. The eighty-six-year-old man died a few weeks later, after the French nobles reportedly physically mistreated him. His successor, Benedict XI, lived barely a year after his election, and discord among the cardinals in Rome left the papal throne once again empty for nearly two years.

The Avignon Papacy

When, in 1305, after two years of stalemate, the French king pressured the cardinals to choose a French bishop, the new pope—Clement V—was in no hurry to reach the papal palace in Rome. The city of Rome had become a contentious place, torn apart by the rivalries among the cardinals' families and now especially unhappy to have a pope who was not Roman. Resigned to waiting until the political climate in Rome improved, Clement settled in Avignon, a town on the Rhone River outside the borders of the French kingdom. But as a Frenchman and now within easy reach of Philip's letters and ambassadors, Clement gave the impression of being the French king's puppet. He made so many Frenchmen cardinals that they soon constituted the majority, thus ensuring that the succeeding seven popes all came from France.

A French Papacy What was intended to be a short stay at Avignon lasted more than seventy years. During the **Avignon papacy**, Clement V and his successors established a court that resembled those of the wealthiest secular rulers. The Avignon popes bought sumptuous fabrics, spices, and foods for their banquets as well as gold and silver objects to adorn their rooms and chapels. A new palace that looked like an imposing fortress became their residence and workplace. Emissaries of secular rulers from all of Europe found in Avignon a papal court with all the attributes of a major center of diplomatic power.

Indulgences Residence in Avignon made it difficult for the pope to collect income from the Papal States, so they looked for new sources of revenue. Because the pope continued to receive appeals in ecclesiastical disputes, the papacy became an international court of appeal to which laypeople could also apply—for a fee. Aristocratic couples, for instance, seeking annulment of their marriages, sought the pope's authoritative ruling on their problems. The Avignon popes found additional income by issuing **indulgences** to sinners seeking forgiveness. An indulgence wiped away any punishment still owing in this life or in **Purgatory** for sins confessed and repented. The church's original acceptance of a contribution to facilitate the granting of an indulgence had grown into their outright sale. The temptation was too great to resist, although many laypeople and even church leaders deplored the crass exchange of money for salvation.

No matter how hard the Avignon popes tried to reassert the moral authority of their office, they always had to contend with the widespread conviction that the papacy had become a worldly institution more interested in its own financial health than in the spiritual health of ordinary Christians. Moreover, it remained mildly scandalous for the papacy to continue to remain in Avignon, far from its spiritual base in Rome. The honorable return of the papacy to Rome became a problem to which church leaders gave increasing attention.

Unam sanctam ("One Holy Church") Declaration issued by Pope Boniface VIII in 1302 that defined the supreme authority of the pope.

Avignon papacy From 1309 to 1377, the period of the papacy's residence in the city of Avignon in what is today southern France.

indulgence Cancellation of any punishment still due to sin after the sacrament of penance.

Purgatory Place in which the souls of the dead spend time to atone for sins still remaining at the time of their death.

Allegiance to Rome
Allegiance to Avignon
Area of Hussite Revolt, 1415–1436
Boundary of the Holy Roman Empire

1. Compare this map with the ones of the Hundred Years' War. Are there similarities?
2. Locate Avignon and then locate Rome. Name some of the advantages and disadvantages each side of the Schism derived from their locations.

The Great Schism

When Clement V settled in Avignon in 1305, bureaucrats and their families moved to Avignon or to other towns in search of employment. With so many of the church's higher clergy too far away to look after them, Rome's buildings and churches fell into decay. Ancient monuments, such as the Pantheon, were stripped of their marble for use in other buildings. An earthquake caused portions of the Coliseum to collapse, giving it the appearance it retains to this day. Marshland that had been filled in during the thirteenth century returned to its previous unhealthy condition. Without the papacy, Rome reverted to a small, run down town of crumbling walls and malarial marshes.

An Attempted Return to Rome Maintaining the papacy in Avignon had become so unpopular that Pope Gregory XI, another Frenchman, moved to Rome in 1377. When he died soon after, the corruption and luxury of his successor, Urban VI, provoked the cardinals into invalidating their election of him and electing another Frenchman, Clement VII, who returned the papacy to Avignon. But Urban VI refused

to recognize his removal, and he excommunicated the newly elected pope, who, in turn, excommunicated Urban. Two men, each claiming to be pope, appointed their own cardinals and established rival bureaucracies. The enemies in the Hundred Years' War took sides, even though there had been little fighting in over two decades: the French king supported the pope at Avignon, and the English king supported the pope at Rome. By 1378, the split in the church, known as the **Great Schism**, threatened to divide the Roman Church in two.

Too Many Popes The Great Schism brought shame on the church, but the two popes and secular rulers found it to their advantage to let the situation continue. Even though only the pope had the authority to convene councils, the cardinals of both popes at last jointly convened the Council of Pisa in 1409 to settle the matter. They deposed both popes and elected a new pope, Alexander V. When the two popes refused to leave office, the cardinals faced the challenge

Great Schism (1378–1417) Split within the western church at the end of the Avignon papacy over the three rivals to the office of the pope.

of three men claiming to be pope. Another five years passed before the church was prepared to end the confusion. At the Council of Constance in 1414, the Roman pope was forced to resign, the Avignon pope continued to resist, and church officials imprisoned the third pope elected at Pisa. With two of three popes disposed of, removing the third depended on political maneuvering and timing. In 1417, when the last Avignon pope gave in, the council elected Martin V as pope. The church was at last reunited.

Conciliar Movement During the Great Schism, when the prestige of the papacy was very low, some church theologians and lawyers argued for limits on the pope's authority. They studied the history of the church and concluded that ultimate church authority derived from councils, consisting of high church officials, including the pope. This position, known as **conciliarism**, surfaced in a period when the weakened papacy could do little to counter it. The conciliar movement initiated the Councils of Pisa and Constance, and at the Council of Basel (1431–1439) new canons set limits on the pope's finances and his courts and reserved the right to hear appeals against his decisions. The council also officially endorsed seven **sacraments**.

The new pope and his cardinals tried to restore the papal authority that the Great Schism had damaged. In 1420, Pope Martin moved the papacy back to Rome after instigating a program of urban improvement to make the city habitable. He also rejected the very process that had brought about his election. Thenceforth, he proclaimed, the pope would not answer to the authority of church councils.

The Laity and the Church

Laypeople, too, had their opinions about the state of the church. For many, religion was their only comfort in the face of starvation, disease, and random violence, but church leaders seemed too embroiled in the schism to minister to the people. Some men and women joined chaste communities dedicated to prayer. Like the mendicant orders of the thirteenth century, these laypeople chose to remain active in the world while carrying out acts of pious charity. In contrast

to the cloistered Poor Clares, however, some women stepped into the public sphere to make an example of their spirituality.

A Woman Saint One such woman, **Catherine of Siena**, made many church leaders uneasy. Born to artisan parents, Catherine discovered a vocation for religious life at young age. She renounced marriage and, when she was eighteen, joined a Dominican order that allowed her to live in her parents' home while wearing the special tunic worn by members of the order. She became known for long fasts that over the years wore down her body's reserves. So famous for holiness did Catherine become that she felt free to express her opinions about the political events of her day. Although she never received an education, Catherine dictated hundreds of letters to church leaders, rulers, and the pope. She gave counsel to the mighty and comfort to the weak through her works and the prayers she composed.

An Outspoken Woman Catherine's reputation for speaking out in public about the need for the Avignon papacy to return to Rome and her service as the pope's ambassador to Florence went against all notions of how a proper, devout woman should act. Religious women belonged, most people felt, in a nunnery or in their homes. Yet Catherine captured the affections of pious men and women throughout Italy and southern Europe, who tolerated her untraditional behavior because they believed her when she said that, in a vision, she had become a spouse of Christ. In 1378, when the papacy returned from Avignon to Rome, Catherine moved there and spent the last two years of her life helping the church reestablish itself. Only thirty-three years old but suffering from extreme physical self-deprivation, she died in Rome in 1380.

Women Mystics In contrast to the Scholastic theologians, whose intellectual efforts involved philosophical tools like logic, mystics such as Catherine spoke and wrote about the experience of religious passion and rapture. Her **mysticism** inspired a movement of clergy and laypeople who sought a direct experience of God that appealed to people's spiritual sensibilities instead of to their reason. In the Low Countries, laywomen, known as **Beguines**, took vows of chastity and lived in communities, although they could leave to marry if they chose. In 1415, a church council arranged for incorporation of the Beguines into the Franciscan lay order. Many mystics were highly educated men and women, one of whom, Meister Eckhart, a German Dominican, advocated that everyone, not just the clergy, should embark on his or her own spiritual searches. For that opinion, he came under suspicion for heresy.

When religious belief combined with anger toward the leaders of the church, the church's response

---

conciliarism Theory that councils are the highest authoritative body in the church.

sacraments Religious practices or ceremonies that symbolize a deeper religious reality; the seven sacraments are baptism, communion (Eucharist), confirmation, confession (penance), ordination, marriage, and unction in sickness.

Catherine of Siena (1347–1380) Holy woman known for her long fasts and mystic religious experiences; canonized in 1461.

mysticism Belief that God can be experienced directly through contemplation and prayer.

Beguines Laywomen, mainly in the Low Countries of northern Europe, who lived communally to devote themselves to a spiritual life.

was harsh. **John Wycliffe**, a theologian at Oxford University in England, wrote works that questioned clerical authority, excommunication, and monasticism. After his death, his followers, known as **Lollards**, endured persecution or went into hiding. A more serious challenge to church authority occurred in the Czech region of Bohemia, under the rule of the Holy Roman Emperor. **Jan Hus**, a theologian, expressed many of the same opinions as Wycliffe, but unlike the Lollards, the **Hussites**, as they were called, enjoyed the protection of the Bohemian nobility. After Hus was captured and burned at the stake in 1415, his followers led a revolt that drew support from all levels of the population. The Hussites developed a radical program of reform that dispensed with the distinction between clergy and laity. The popularity of the revolt among the Czechs and the strength of the rebels' army forced the emperor, as the church's defender, to negotiate a settlement in 1436. The success of the Hussite Revolt represents a turning point in the church's monopoly over lay religious expression.

Checking In

By yourself or with a partner, explain the significance of each of the following selected key terms:

benefices	sacraments
Unam sanctam	Catherine of Siena
indulgences	mysticism
Purgatory	Hussites

The Contraction of Europe's Borders

◆ **How did the old Roman Empire finally come to an end?**

◆ **Compare the multiethnic society of the Ottoman Empire to western Europe.**

Already aware of Muslim states in Spain and on the southern shore of the Mediterranean, the people of the later Middle Ages learned of a new threat to their eastern borders. Turkish tribes were slowly destroying the Byzantine Empire. One tribe in particular, the Ottomans, came uncomfortably close to the frontier between the old empire and western Europe. Farther east and northward in Russia lay the lands of people whom the Roman Church scarcely considered Christian. Although some in the west, especially merchants, felt that distant markets represented opportunities, others felt that Christendom was contracting, and with it the boundaries of what was safe and familiar.

Old Empires and Newcomers

In 1261, thirty-six-year-old Michael VIII Paleologus, the emperor of the much-reduced Byzantine Empire, centered on the city of Nicaea, recaptured Constantinople from the Frankish rulers who had held it since 1204. From there, he fought to retake all the territory lost earlier in the century. His first priority was northern Greece. Unable to expel the Frankish rulers of the Peloponnesus, he forced them to recognize him as their overlord. Yet, expecting invasion from Turkish powers to the east and Slavs from the north, the Byzantine emperor was surrounded by hostile forces.

An Attempt to Unify the Churches With such pressure on his borders, Michael sent delegates to the Council of Lyons in 1274 to gain the support of the pope with a promise to reunite the Latin and Greek churches, which had formally ended relations with each other in 1054 mostly over the Greek church's refusal to recognize the pope as the supreme head of both churches. When the council and the pope agreed that the eastern church could continue some of its rituals, Michael authorized the union. The idea of union between the churches had long been unpopular among ordinary Byzantines and especially among the Byzantine clergy. After his death in 1282, his son, Andronicus II, could afford to repudiate the union. A new threat emerging from the east that menaced his empire and the Muslims in Syria and Palestine made the issue of the reunification of the churches less of a priority to either side.

The Mongols In the thirteenth century, with the arrival of **Mongols** from the east, the Muslims were placed on the defensive for the first time. The great Mongol leader **Genghis Khan** led his armies all the way to Russia in the west and Beijing in the east. His successors drove their forces even farther. In 1240, they sacked Kiev. In the 1260s they ended Seljuk rule, already in decline, in Anatolia. The Abbasid dynasty in Baghdad fell in 1258, thus bringing to an end the centuries-old caliphate. Wherever the Mongols went, news of their terrifying

John Wycliffe (ca. 1330–1384) Theologian from Oxford who questioned the fundamental teachings of the church.

Lollards Followers of John Wycliffe, whose beliefs and social agenda drew the condemnation of the church.

Jan Hus (ca. 1369–1415) Czech theologian and reformer condemned as a heretic and burned at the stake.

Hussites Followers of Hus, whose execution in 1415 sparked a revolt and led to the establishment of a Hussite government in Czech Bohemia and the Hussite church.

Mongols An Asiatic people whose empire at its height in the thirteenth century stretched from the Pacific to the Mediterranean.

Genghis Khan (c. 1204–1227) Mongol ruler who conquered northern China and established the Mongol Empire.

mounted archers and savagery preceded them. Now, when merchants from Christian and Muslim territories reopened land routes to Asian markets, they had to pass through a new and unfamiliar empire whose borders seemed endless.

The Khans From eastern Siberia to western Russia, from Siberia in the north to Iran, modern-day Iraq, and Syria in the south and southwest, the Mongol Empire was so extensive that it could not be governed by a central power. So the Mongols established **khanates** that relied on local populations to do much of their ruling for them. Each of the khans reported to the great khan (the equivalent of the western title of emperor) based no longer in Mongolia but in China after the 1220s. The huge distances gave the khans a good deal of autonomy. Political, cultural, or social cohesion was nearly impossible, given the size of the empire. An empire like the Mongols' could be held together only by force and the cooperation of local elites. As with previous empires, however, the strains of ruling such far-flung provinces, together with the impact of the bubonic plague that devastated Asia before reaching western Europe in 1347, contributed to their decline in the mid-fourteenth century.

The Mamluks The fall of the Abbasid caliphate in Baghdad allowed for the emergence of other independent caliphates in Egypt and India. In thirteenth-century Egypt, the position of caliph became the prerogative of the descendants of **Mamluks**, or slave soldiers, many of them Turkish in origin, who had gained control over the caliphs. Under the Abbasids, Muslim armies relied on slave soldiers who over time acquired influence over their masters to such a degree that they became, in effect, the rulers. Eventually, in Egypt and in India they replaced the caliphs altogether and established dynasties that lasted until the sixteenth century.

The Rise of the Ottoman Turks

After the Mongols withdrew from Anatolia, the Turkish warrior leader **Osman**, whose ancestors had probably arrived in Anatolia early in the thirteenth century, emerged as the strongest power in the region. By the time Osman died in 1324, he had conquered

In 1478, the Senate of Venice sent Gentile Bellini, a member of the talented family of painters, to visit the Ottoman court in Constantinople, where the Venetian painted the aged Sultan Mehmed the Conqueror's portrait. Here, Mehmed wears the large turban typical of Ottoman rulers. Men of lower rank wore smaller turbans. How would you describe the setting that Bellini places his subject in? Is it classical, Islamic, Italian, or a little bit of each?

Erich Lessing/Art Resource, NY

most of northwestern Anatolia. His successors, the Ottomans—whose name derives from Osman—steadily added new territory. They conquered Thrace in northern Greece after 1357 and Adrianople in 1361. Bulgaria came under their rule in 1389. They whittled down the Byzantine Empire until it consisted of little more than its capital, Constantinople, and the surrounding region. Even before the capture of the capital in 1453, the Ottoman **sultans** ruled an empire that stretched from Anatolia to the Balkans. The **Ottoman Empire** would last more than six centuries, until the end of the First World War in 1918.

The Conqueror After being defeated by a Tartar army led by **Timur**, the Ottoman Empire ceased to exist for ten years. Timur's death in 1405 gave Mehmed I, a son of the last sultan, an opportunity to reassert Ottoman rule once he had united rivals under his leadership. Mehmed (r. 1413–1421) reestablished a bureaucracy and Islamic judicial system. He reinstated a system whereby he allotted a unit of land, called a **timar**, to a mounted soldier who was expected to equip himself with its revenue. The sultan restored

khanate Geographical unit ruled by a Mongol ruler, or khan.

Mamluks Slave soldiers in Muslim Egypt who first served the sultan ruler but later assumed power themselves.

Osman (1258–1324) Turkish founder of the Ottoman dynasty.

sultan Ruler of a Muslim country or empire called a sultanate.

Ottoman Empire Empire ruled by the sultan descendants of the house of Osman.

Timur (ca. 1370–1405) Tartar conqueror, also known as Tamerlane.

timar In the Ottoman Empire, a unit of property in exchange for which military service was required, similar to the western European fief.

The Rise of the Ottoman Empire and the End of the Byzantines The Ottoman Turks first ruled the region around Nicaea before expanding across Asia Minor, north into the Balkans and eastern Europe, and south into Muslim territories. Their expansion occurred mainly at the expense of Byzantine power, but the older Muslim dynasties ruling Egypt also succumbed to their might. © *Cengage Learning*

1. Which powers in Europe were most likely to perceive earliest the threat of an approaching Ottoman army?
2. Where were merchants from the Italian cities most likely to encounter Ottoman merchants?
3. What factors promoted communication between the people of Italy and Spain, on one hand, and the subjects of the Ottoman Empire, on the other?

the practice of seizing Christian boys from conquered territories, compelling them to convert to Islam, and raising them to serve in an elite unit of warriors known as the **janissaries**. Once the basic elements of state were in place, Mehmed set out to reconquer all the Balkan territory his predecessors had once ruled.

The Fall of an Empire By 1450, the Balkan lands were once again under Ottoman rule. **Mehmed II** was determined to breach the thick walls of Constantinople and take the city. Help from the west was unlikely and unwelcome, as the Fourth Crusade's conquest of Constantinople and the Byzantine emperor's favor shown to Venetian and Genoese merchants to

the disadvantage of Byzantine merchants had instilled a deep hostility toward the west in the subjects of the Byzantine emperor. The pope's insistence that the clergy of the eastern church recognize his supreme authority intensified the hostility. Though representatives of the western and eastern churches had tried to achieve reunion at the Council of Florence in 1439, so many Byzantine Christians resented

janissaries Ottoman infantry composed mainly of Christian boys either captured or given in tribute to the sultan to be raised as Muslim soldiers.

Mehmed II (r. 1451–1481) Sultan who conquered Constantinople and established the city as the capital of the Ottoman Empire.

Scala/Art Resource, NY

Although the Venetian painter Giacomo Palma the Younger painted this scene a century after the fall of Constantinople in 1453, it captures the monumental undertaking that the conquest required of the Ottoman Turks. The painting shows on the left Ottoman forces breaching the city walls built by Theodosius II in the fifth century. Are there indications that the painter has an opinion about the conquest of the city? Does he admire the Ottomans' magnificent military achievement or deplore the catastrophic fall of a great Christian city?

the agreement that the reunion had to be abandoned. But without friends in the west, the people of the Byzantine Empire had nowhere to turn.

Mehmed set about bringing down the capital of the Byzantine Empire and all the vestiges of the old Roman Empire. In addition to nearly 100,000 troops, he deployed a relatively new technology to achieve his goal: cannon. Mehmed's huge cannons, forged by Christian Hungarians in his employ, battered the city walls that had only twice before been breached. On May 29, 1453, Mehmed's janissary troops entered Constantinople through a hole the cannons had created in the walls. Its capital city conquered, the Byzantine Empire vanished.

A Multiethnic World

While the people of western Europe often cast their world in terms of religion—Muslim or Jew versus Christian—the people of the Ottoman Empire experienced their world differently. Men and women of Turkish descent held a privileged position in Ottoman society, but not one that was exclusively theirs. The new empire encompassed lands occupied by many different ethnic groups that followed the Christian, Jewish, or Muslim religion. No matter their ancestry, converts to Islam entered fully into the rights and privileges of Muslim life. Even some who remained

Christians and Jews achieved positions of wealth and power. But most of the non-Turkish population entered Ottoman society involuntarily and on an inferior social footing.

Slaves in the Ottoman Empire Slaves were central to the households of early Ottoman sultans and the ruling elite. Although most slaves performed menial labor, slaves also formed the backbone of the army, served as advisers and ministers in the bureaucracy, and bore the sultan's children. Slaves in the army and government had usually been brought as children from Christian and other non-Muslim lands to Ottoman territory. They were raised as Muslims and expected to display unswerving loyalty to the sultan. Endowed by Islamic law with limited power to act on their master's behalf, slaves could exercise some authority. At the level of the sultan, eunuch slaves served as officials in various departments of government.

Sultans and Slave Women Slaves factored heavily into sexual relations and reproduction in Ottoman society. It was common for slave concubines to bear their master's children, who inherited their free father's status. Once she gave birth to a boy, her position in her master's household was protected. The head of the household, whether the sultan or an Ottoman official, was not allowed to sell her once she had borne him a son, and at his death she would be freed. By the middle of the fifteenth century, the sultans had given up marrying and had children exclusively with slaves, whose offspring provided the sultan with a pool of potential heirs—and had also created conditions for their rivalry. Men of lower social rank continued to take legal wives.

After the fifteenth century, all Ottoman sultans had mothers who had been slaves in their father's household, which also means that sultans had mothers of different ethnic origins from their fathers because Muslims are forbidden to enslave other Muslims. The mother of a ruling sultan often wielded great political power through her influence over her son. Mothers raised their sons in their harem quarters until they reached the age of twelve, when the sons were appointed provincial governors. When the father died, his sons, by tradition, fought one another for the succession to the sultanate, and the slave mothers conspired with their sons for the office of sultan. Through their sons and through the networks of informants and clients that they established in the sultan's household, the concubines could achieve a significant level of political power and influence.

Jews Under Christian and Ottoman Rule

The condition of Jews under Ottoman rule contrasts markedly to their life in the Christian west. Ottoman Turks regarded all non-Muslims as second-class subjects of the empire, but, like most Muslim societies, appreciated that, as People of the Book, Muslims, Jews, and Christians all venerated the ancient Hebrew prophets. Jews fared at times as well and as poorly as Christians under the sultan's rule.

Jews in Christendom But in the west, Christian antipathy toward Jews had been increasing ever since the massacres preceding the First Crusade at the end of the eleventh century. The Lateran Council of 1215 compelled Jews to wear badges that identified them in public. Beginning in the twelfth century, accusations of **blood libel**—false charges that Jews sacrificed Christian children at Passover to obtain their blood—incited attacks on Jews. Occasionally all the men of a community were arrested and executed, as happened in Trent in 1475. The hostility many Christians directed toward Jews made them easy scapegoats when explanations for the devastation caused by the plague were sought. Jews throughout the Diaspora in Europe endured the hardship of expulsion from the lands where they had lived and worked for generations. In 1492, the rulers of the newly united Spanish kingdom expelled Jews and Muslims from their lands, initiating a migration of tens of thousands of **Sephardim**, or Spanish Jews, to the Low Countries; Italian cities; the northwestern frontiers in Poland, Lithuania, and Russia; and the Ottoman Empire.

In between periods of violence and open hostility, the Jews of Europe, especially the communities in the German cities of the Holy Roman Empire, Italy, and southern France, lived productive and even prosperous lives in the narrow range of occupations they were permitted to enter, such as moneylending and shoemaking. German and Polish Jews, the **Ashkenazim**, spoke and wrote in **Yiddish**, a language derived from German and Semitic languages and written in Hebrew characters. A rich literary culture began to flourish in the twelfth century in the cities along the Rhine River and eastern Europe. Unwelcome and often persecuted, Jewish communities responded by emphasizing among themselves their bonds of kinship, common faith, and vibrant culture.

At the same time that the religious and political climate in Christian Europe worsened for Jews, it improved in the newly established Ottoman territories. While Christendom was unable to incorporate Jews as Jews, the Ottomans were willing to let Jews prosper in relative security. Ottoman cities such as Constantinople (now called Istanbul) and Edirne had Jewish residents. Thessalonica had had prosperous Jewish communities well before 1453.

The inclusion of Jews in Ottoman society was not entirely voluntary. Soon after the conquest of Constantinople, which had been depopulated and in decline in the years leading up to its capture, Mehmed II forcibly relocated Jews from the Balkans and Anatolia to his new capital to help revive the economy.

Thereafter, he encouraged Jewish immigrants from the west. Jewish physicians, merchants, and bankers became much sought after in the new empire. Opportunities to live in peace, make a living, and even join the ranks of the wealthy (despite a tax rate higher than Muslims paid) were available to Jews under the Ottomans as they were not in the west.

Russia After 1000

Medieval Russia had been divided into principalities, each ruled by a prince. The descendants of Vikings and Slavs, Christianized in the tenth century, ruled the region surrounding the city of Kiev along the Dnieper River. With the city's commercial power and military strength, Kiev's princes dominated the other Russian princes until the arrival of the Mongols around 1237 drastically changed the political and economic landscape.

The Mongols Retreat When Genghis Khan died in 1227, he was on the verge of entering the steppes north of the Black Sea and south of the land of the Russians. His sons and grandsons received a portion of his empire, the western portion falling to his grandson Batu, who ruled the population of Mongols, Turks, and Russians known to the west as the Empire of the **Golden Horde**. In 1240 Batu's army laid waste to the city of Kiev, the populous capital of trade and government. Only the death of his uncle, the great khan, stopped Batu from pushing farther westward.

Once Batu had conquered all the Russian principalities, he and his people settled in the steppes and south of the Volga River. As the overlord of the Russian princes, he organized the collection of tribute and the conscription of soldiers for the army of the Golden Horde. Important caravan routes—known as the **Great Silk Road**—connecting China with the Byzantine Empire passed through their land. Silk, spices, precious jewels, and ceramics came west to be exchanged for Scandinavian slaves, fur, hides, salt, and Caspian caviar in demand in the east. The khans granted

blood libel Accusation that Jews sacrificed Christian children to use their blood in rituals for Passover, the commemoration of the ancient Hebrews' deliverance from slavery in Egypt.

Sephardim Jews expelled from Spain in 1492.

Ashkenazim Jews of Europe who settled mainly in the Holy Roman Empire, Poland, Lithuania, and other eastern regions.

Yiddish Language spoken by the Ashkenazim, derived from German and Semitic and written in Hebrew characters.

Golden Horde Collection of Tartar-Mongol tribes who conquered and ruled the land of the Rus from the mid-thirteenth to the late fifteenth century.

Great Silk Road Long trade route from China to the Mediterranean coast; so-called because it was the route by which silk goods arrived in the west.

Eleazar of Mainz Writes His Last Testament

Mainz, Germany, was one of the cities whose Jewish population was massacred by crusading zealots in 1096. More than 250 years later, around 1357, a member of the small, barely revived Jewish community, Eleazar ben Samuel HaLevi, wrote a kind of last testament for his children known as an ethical will. Unlike most wills, which dispose of the testator's worldly goods among his or her heirs, ethical wills bequeath to the heirs the testator's moral and spiritual legacy. Eleazar's will is the last lesson in life that he passed on to his children.

❶ Who does Eleazar mean by "Gentile?"

❷ What does Eleazar consider to be the marks of membership among Jews?

❸ What impression of himself does Eleazar hope to give in the manner of his burial?

These are the things which my sons and daughters shall do at my request…. **❶** Their business must be conducted honestly, in their dealings both with Jew and Gentile. They must be gentle in their manners and prompt to accede to every honorable request. They must not talk more than is necessary; by this will they be saved from slander, falsehood, and frivolity. They shall give an exact tithe of all their possessions: they shall never turn away a poor man empty-handed, but must give him what they can, be it much or little. If he beg a lodging over night, and they know him not, let them provide him with the wherewithal to pay an innkeeper. Thus shall they satisfy the needs of the poor in every possible way….

❷ If they can by any means contrive it, my sons and daughters should live in communities, and not isolated from other Jews, so that their sons and daughters may learn the ways of Judaism. Even if compelled to solicit from others the money to pay a teacher, they must not let the young of both sexes go without instruction in the Torah. Marry your children, O my sons and daughters, as soon as their age is ripe, to members of respectable families. Let no child of mine hunt after money by making a low match for that object; but if the family is undistinguished only on the mother's side, it does not matter, for all Israel counts descent from the father's side….

On holidays and festivals and Sabbaths seek to make happy the poor, the unfortunate, widows and orphans, who should always be guests at your tables; their joyous entertainment is a religious duty. Let me repeat my warning against gossip and scandal. And as you Speak no scandal, so listen to none; for if there were no receivers there would be no bearers of slanderous tales; therefore the reception and credit of slander is as serious an offense as the originating of it. The less you say, the less cause you give for animosity, while "in the multitude of words there wants transgression" [Proverbs 10:19].

❸ I beg of you, my sons and daughters, my wife, and all the congregation, that no funeral oration be spoken in my honor. Do not carry my body on a bier, but in a coach. Wash me clean, comb my hair, trim my nails, as I was wont to do in my lifetime, so that I may go clean to my eternal rest, as I went clean to synagogue every Sabbathday. If the ordinary officials dislike the duty, let adequate payment be made to some poor man who shall render this service carefully and not perfunctorily….

Put me in the ground at the right hand of my father, and if the space be a little narrow I am sure that he loves me well enough to make room for me by his side. If this be altogether impossible put me on his left, or near my grandmother, Yura. Should this also be impractical, let me be buried by the side of my daughter.

Source: Reprinted from Jacob R. Marcus, *The Jew in the Medieval World*, with permission of the Hebrew Union College Press, Cincinnati.

Genoese merchants the use of Caffa, a port on the Crimean peninsula in the Black Sea, as a base for their trade in slaves and other commodities. The Venetians had the use of Tana, another port on the Black Sea, where they engaged in similar commerce.

Trade To the north, in the lands of the Russian princes, the fur and timber of Russia forests attracted merchants from everywhere. The Baltic Sea served as a highway for the cogs sailing from Scandinavian and German ports, and rivers gave access to merchants from Christian Europe and Muslim lands. Whoever ruled this land—spectacularly rich in resources, with few towns and a relatively small and entirely rural population—had the potential of possessing great economic and political power.

The fall of Kiev and the princes who ruled it opened the way for other Russian leaders to emerge. Although Novgorod in the north survived the Mongol invasion, Moscow, once an isolated military post, began to emerge as a center of power in the late thirteenth century. **Alexander Nevsky**, prince of Novgorod and grand prince of Vladimir, made sure not to alienate the khan of the Golden Horde but fought back Swedish, Lithuanian, and German troops from the west. His son, Daniel, was the first prince of a dynasty centered on Moscow in the principality of Muscovy, which would benefit from the political vacuum created by the fall of Kiev.

> **Alexander Nevsky** (r. 1236–1263) Russian ruler who stopped the advance of German, Swedish, and Lithuanian troops from the west.

Checking In

By yourself or with a partner, explain the significance of each of the following selected key terms:

Genghis Khan	Sephardim
Mamluks	Ashkenazim
Ottoman Empire	Golden Horde
janissaries	Alexander Nevsky

CHAPTER
Review

Summary

- The fourteenth century in western Europe brought intense hardship, disasters, and epidemics.

- Weather changes in northern Europe brought wet summers, even colder winters, and extensive flooding; poor harvests led to severe shortages of food in many regions.

- An epidemic of the bubonic plague claimed the lives of a third to half of the population of Europe in the middle of the century.

- In the Hundred Years' War between the kings of England and France, the English armies trampled planted fields, set fire to villages, and besieged walled towns as a way to undermine support for the French king.

- After a long lull in the hostilities, when the English and the French resumed the fighting in 1415, the hold that kings had on their subjects' loyalty had strengthened.

- Loyalty to kings, however, was hard won. Over the second half of the fourteenth century, the populations of western Europe grew increasingly frustrated by the inability of their rulers to protect them from violence, high taxation, and their lack of political influence.

- In the 1350s, discontented men and women began the Jacquerie, a bloody rampage in the countryside of France.

- In 1381, an army from the counties surrounding London tried to impose social change on the English king, Richard II, but was quickly defeated.

- The church, governed for most of the fourteenth century in Avignon, had become a huge bureaucracy concerned primarily with its own unhealthy finances.

- The Ottomans had emerged from Anatolia by 1300 and slowly chipped away at the Byzantine Empire over the fourteenth century.

- When in 1453 the great city of Constantinople fell for the second time in its long history, it was to its new Muslim master, the Ottoman sultan Mehmed II.

Chronology

1261	Michael VIII Palaeologus recaptures Constantinople
1301	Pope Boniface VIII issues *Unam sanctam*
1305	Clement V becomes pope; Avignon papacy begins
1323	Flanders revolt begins
1346	English defeat French at Battle of Crécy
1347	Black Death first appears in western Europe
1356	English defeat French at Battle of Poitiers
1358	Jacquerie revolt takes place in France
1360	Truce ends first phase of Hundred Years' War
1361	Ottomans conquer Adrianople
1378	Gregory XI returns papacy to Rome
1378	Great Schism begins
1378	Ciompi Revolt takes place in Florence
1381	Peasants' Revolt takes place in England
1402	Timur invades Anatolia
1409	Council of Pisa attempts to solve problem of multiple popes
1415	Henry V defeats French at Battle of Agincourt
1415	Revolt in Bohemia following the execution of the religious reformer John Hus
1417	Council of Constance resolves Great Schism; Martin V becomes pope
1429	Joan of Arc defeats English at Orléans
1453	Constantinople falls to Ottomans; Hundred Years' War ends

© Cengage Learning

Test Yourself

To gauge your mastery of the material in this chapter, answer the questions below. More than one answer may be correct.

Famine and Plague

1. Which of the following statements does *not* describe disastrous changes in the first half of the fourteenth century?

   a. The people of Europe experienced a one-degree increase in average temperatures over the year.
   b. Winters were cold and summers were wetter.
   c. Cities on the northern coasts of Europe suffered severe flooding.
   d. The people of England changed from making wine to brewing beer.
   e. Ice covered Greenland.

2. What part of the body was primarily attacked by the bubonic plague?

   a. Liver
   b. Heart
   c. Lymph glands
   d. Central nervous system
   e. Spleen

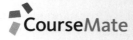
Visit the CourseMate website at **www.cengagebrain.com** for additional study tools and review materials for this chapter.

3. What did laypeople organize across Europe to promote repentance and carry out good works to help the sick and poor?

a. Guilds
b. Hospitals
c. Monastic orders
d. The College of Cardinals
e. Confraternities

4. What was the principal means of maritime transport in the Mediterranean during this time?

a. Cogs
b. Caravels
c. Caravans
d. Galleys
e. Skiffs

5. The primary purpose of the Hanseatic League was:

a. To provide shelter and food to the poor.
b. To protect and advance the interests of German merchants in the Holy Roman Empire.
c. To wage war against the infidel in the Holy Land.
d. To combat heresy in the French kingdom.
e. To govern Italian cities in the interests of its merchants.

Now that you have reviewed and tested yourself on this part of the chapter, take time to pull together all the important information by answering the following questions:

◆ Describe some of the ways in which people reacted to the impact of the plague. In what ways did people respond positively and negatively?

◆ What were some of the economic consequences of the plague? What opportunities emerged as a result of the devastating loss of life?

One Hundred Years of Warfare

6. Edward III of England claimed the throne of France on what basis?

a. He believed that the kings of England had had a claim to the French throne since Anglo-Saxon times.
b. His wife was the daughter of the French king.
c. His mother was the daughter of the French king.
d. His father had conquered a major portion of it.
e. He invented his claim to the French throne to pressure the French king.

7. At the battle of Crécy, the English prevailed over the French in spite of:

a. The French army's superior numbers.
b. The French army's use of the longbow.
c. The English army's use of the crossbow.
d. The French army's use of primitive cannon.
e. The well-trained cavalry of French noblemen.

8. What were the campaigns to inflict violence and destruction of property on the French people and countryside called?

a. Chevaliers
b. Chivalry
c. Chevauchées
d. Crécy
e. Cîteaux

9. Henry V was successful in rallying support among his subjects for the renewed war by:

a. Lowering taxes and holding free fairs.
b. Manipulating public sentiment and patriotism so that his war became his subjects' war.
c. Promising money to anyone who attended pageants and processions to promote the war.
d. Manipulating church leaders to insist that the people of England support the war in penance for their sins.
e. Manipulating his noblemen to reform the feudal army so that it worked.

10. The English and the Burgundians used which pretexts to convict Joan of Arc of witchcraft?

   a. She dressed like a man and claimed to hear the voices of saints.
   b. She attempted to escape from her prison through the use of magic.
   c. She knew how to wield weapons in a way that seemed magical.
   d. They claimed she denied the existence of God to her confessor.
   e. She declared she had the right to be ordained a priest.

Now that you have reviewed and tested yourself on this part of the chapter, take time to pull together all the important information by answering the following questions:

◆ How did Edward I's wars in Scotland prepare the English for war in France?

◆ How would the map of Europe look in the late fifteenth century if the English had won the war instead of losing it?

Resistance and Revolt

11. The revolt in Flanders began as a result of:

   a. The English and French kings' pressure on the Flemish each to control the Flemish economy.
   b. The French king's refusal to let the Flemish sell their textiles in his kingdom.
   c. The refusal of the English to buy wool from the Flemish.
   d. The competition with French textile producers.
   e. The Flemish wanting to expel the Count of Flanders and unite with France.

12. The Jacquerie was:

   a. The French king's high court in Paris.
   b. A jacket worn by French soldiers in the Hundred Years' War.
   c. The prison in Paris where rebels were kept.
   d. The negative word peasants used to describe noblemen.
   e. A rebellion aimed at the nobility that began in the countryside.

13. Why did the wool carders of Florence rebel against the rulers of Florence?

   a. Their wages had been cut to the point where they were destitute.
   b. The conditions of their work were unhealthy and wages were low.
   c. The guilds of more powerful textile professions shut them out of political life.
   d. As the most powerful guild in Florence, they sought total control over city government.
   e. The cost of their work tools had risen so high they were unable to practice their trade.

14. The army that led the Peasants' Revolt in England consisted of:

   a. Destitute peasants from the countryside.
   b. Impoverished noblemen from northern England.
   c. Butchers and other food service workers in London.
   d. Well-off peasants, merchants, artisans, and craftsworkers.
   e. Slaves employed in agricultural production.

15. For what purpose did King Richard II invite the rebel army to accompany him beyond the walls of London?

   a. To sign a treaty granting the rebels what they wanted.
   b. To bring them to the king's army waiting to slaughter them.
   c. To chase them out of the vicinity.
   d. To negotiate with them out of the sight and hearing of the Londoners.
   e. To warn them that an army waited for them in central London.

Now that you have reviewed and tested yourself on this part of the chapter, take time to pull together all the important information by answering the following questions:

◆ Which factors contributed more to the revolts and uprisings of the fourteenth century: the desperation and poverty of the rebels, or the desire for greater political input into how they were governed?

◆ What did it take to bring most of these revolts to a conclusion?

A Worldly Church

16. Pope Boniface VIII's papal bull, *Unam sanctam*, made what controversial assertion?
    - a. That he had no power over the bishops in France.
    - b. That he was the ultimate temporal and spiritual authority.
    - c. That he would abdicate in favor of a favorite of the French king's.
    - d. That secular rulers would have to come to Rome in order to be crowned.
    - e. That clergy had the right to marry.

17. How did the Avignon papacy compensate for the loss of revenues from the Papal States?
    - a. It sold churches in Rome to Roman noble families.
    - b. It received a pension from the French king.
    - c. It sold indulgences and charged a fee to hear appeals of judicial disputes.
    - d. It increased the tithes that Christians paid in western Europe.
    - e. It borrowed money from the Patriarch of Constantinople.

18. Which movement played a major part in bringing to an end the Great Schism?
    - a. Conciliarism
    - b. Chivalry
    - c. Chevauchées
    - d. Cistercian
    - e. Cluniac

19. What are Lollards?
    - a. Wool workers in monasteries
    - b. An order of monks in England who followed Wat Tyler
    - c. A group of religious dissenters who followed John Wycliffe
    - d. A group of religious dissenters who followed Jan Hus
    - e. A group of laywomen who took vows of poverty and chastity

20. Who were the Hussites?
    - a. German merchants banded together for mutual protection
    - b. A group of religious dissenters in Florence
    - c. A group of laywomen accused of sexual impropriety
    - d. A group of theologians at the University of Paris
    - e. A group of religious dissenters who followed Jan Hus

Now that you have reviewed and tested yourself on this part of the chapter, take time to pull together all the important information by answering the following questions:

◆ What factors contributed to laypeople's disillusionment with the papacy and the church?

◆ How would you compare and contrast the experiences of the Lollards and the Hussites?

The Contraction of Europe's Borders

21. Which people from the east threatened the lands on the borders of western Europe in the thirteenth century?

    a. Mingherelli

    b. Seljuk Turks

    c. Mongols

    d. Kievan Rus

    e. Varengi

22. In the early fourteenth century, Osman founded which dynasty?

    a. Abbasid

    b. Ayubbid

    c. Fatimid

    d. Ottoman

    e. Umayyad

23. Who was the sultan responsible for capturing Constantinople?

    a. Mehmed II

    b. Osman

    c. Suleiman

    d. Michael Palaeologus

    e. Timur

24. After the fifteenth century, it was the standard practice that sultans had children by:

    a. Christian noble women

    b. Jewish women

    c. Turkish women

    d. Slave women

    e. Peasant women

25. Sephardim Jews are those who came from:

    a. The Fertile Crescent

    b. Spain

    c. Poland

    d. Hungary

    e. Germany

Now that you have reviewed and tested yourself on this part of the chapter, take time to pull together all the important information by answering the following questions:

◆ What political changes occurred beyond Europe's borders that gave the people of western Europe cause for concern?

◆ What opportunities did Jews have under Christian and Ottoman rule? In which civilization did they have had a better chance of prospering?

CHAPTER 12

The Renaissance in Italy and Northern Europe, 1350–1550

Chapter Outline

1340	1360	1380	1400	1420	1440

1347
Black Death first appears in Italy

1417
Great Schism ends

1440s
Gutenberg invents printing process

Giovanni Bellini painted this altarpiece depicting the coronation of the Virgin Mary for a Franciscan church in Pesaro in the early 1470s. What purposes do the tile pavement and the white frame and columns above the Virgin serve? Would fifteenth-century viewers be able to identify the figures in the painting by what they are wearing? Who do you think they are? (Alinari/Art Resource, NY)

After reading this chapter, you should be able to answer the following questions:

How did perceptions of painters, sculptors, and architects change over the fourteenth and fifteenth centuries?

What is the purpose of applying linear perspective in painting?

What were the differences in the ways painters in Italian cities and those in Flanders achieved depth and dimension in their work?

How did the scholarly interests of humanists in Italy differ from humanists in northern Europe?

B Y THE EARLY SIXTEENTH CENTURY, a cultural flowering of art and literature had begun in Italy. Further generations would call this period the Renaissance. It was more, however, than an artistic movement. At the same time, new forms of expression affirming faith in God and the worth of human creativity had been developing for more than a century. Even before famine and plague afflicted Italy in the fourteenth century, its intellectuals and artisans had begun to explore new techniques, new ideas, and new ways to analyze old texts, and the hardships ahead did not hinder them. Over time, commerce and industry revitalized the Italian urban economies hurt by crop failures and population loss. A mutually beneficial relationship developed between wealthy families looking to display their high social status and talented scholars and artisans. The products of those relationships—extraordinary lifelike paintings and bronze statuary, philosophical treatises displaying great learning, and breathtaking monuments to God or man—caught the attention of the rest of the continent.

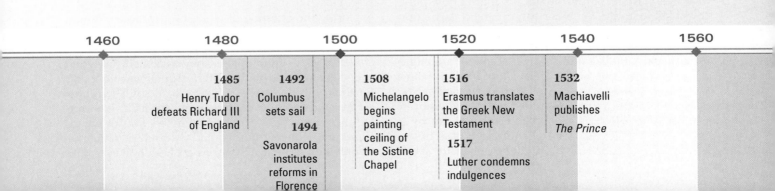

1460	1480	1500	1520	1540	1560

1485 Henry Tudor defeats Richard III of England

1492 Columbus sets sail

1494 Savonarola institutes reforms in Florence

1508 Michelangelo begins painting ceiling of the Sistine Chapel

1516 Erasmus translates the Greek New Testament

1517 Luther condemns indulgences

1532 Machiavelli publishes *The Prince*

No longer confined to the world of the clergy, scholars rejected the old methods of analysis in favor of a rigorous, questioning approach to the study of classical and Christian texts. In Italy, intellectuals discovered new joy in reading ancient Latin texts, taking pleasure foremost in the literary qualities of Cicero and Virgil instead of testing their compatibility with Christian doctrine. When Greek texts that no one in the west had previously read arrived in the baggage of refugees from the east, the scholars dedicated themselves with enthusiasm to the study of Greek. In northern Europe, the same love of inquiry drove scholars to re-examine with newly critical eyes authoritative Christian texts. The invention of the printing press made all these texts available to a far greater number of readers than ever before.

[handwritten note: why did society start to break away from focus on christain theology?]

[handwritten note: How did Renaissance women differ during this period?]

A New Climate of Cultural Expression

◆ **How did the humanists differ from monks and scholastic thinkers?**

◆ **What factors caused artisans to emerge as artists?**

Even before the Black Death completely subsided, an entirely new spirit began to be felt in Italy. Between the middle of the fourteenth and the middle of the fifteenth centuries, an explosion of cultural expression of astonishing and extravagant proportions permeated every aspect of life. No one, no matter how poor, could fail to notice. Whether passing the construction site of an enormous cathedral dome rising to an awe inspiring height, praying before an altar painting of an unusually lifelike and colorful scene, or watching a bejeweled husband and wife clothed in rich fabric trimmed with gold embroidery and surrounded by a large entourage pass by on a city street, even the most ordinary person was aware of living in an extraordinary time. People believed they, or at least their societies, had reached unprecedented wealth and ease. This impression was only partly an illusion.

The Spirit of Humanism

The new spirit began with a broadening of learning. Universities no longer held a monopoly on intellectual pursuits. Now laymen studied texts with private tutors in the hopes of employment in the governments of Italian cities. Women from well-to-do families, too, studied philosophy and theology, but solely out of a love of learning because careers outside of home and marriage were closed to them. Lay scholars became interested in exploring the question of what it meant to be human. They were called humanists because their intellectual interests centered on the study of humanity (*studium humanitatis*), or **humanism**. They esteemed the works of ancient Romans for their literary qualities rather than for their usefulness for Christian theology. Their interest in language and the technical aspects of literature led them to criticize Scholastic thinkers for not paying closer attention to grammar and vocabulary in their interpretation of biblical texts. In general, however, they

humanism Philosophical and literary study of what it means to be human.

Largest cities, ca. 1500
- ● Over 125,000
- ● 100,000 to 125,000
- ● 50,000 to 100,000
- ○ 25,000 to 50,000
- • Other city
- ── Boundary of the Holy Roman Empire

Map 12.1 **The Spread of New Cultural Expression, 1300–1500** In the fifteenth century, artists and thinkers across northern Italy produced extraordinary artistic and intellectual work that attracted attention throughout Europe. Byzantine refugee scholars brought previously unknown classical works with them to Italy.
© Cengage Learning

1. Look closely at the Italian peninsula. Where are most of the cities located?
2. Thinking back to past chapters and locate the most urban and industrialized centers in western Europe. Then locate the places where the cultural movements covered in this chapter took place. Is there a correspondence?
3. Looking at eastern Europe in the map, the major cities are all located on rivers. Where do those rivers lead, and what might that tell you about the cultural contacts of each of those cities?

Petrarch (1304–1374) Francesco Petrarca, one of the first humanist scholars, was responsible for the recovery of numerous works of classical Latin Roman writers.

vernacular In medieval and Renaissance Europe, the dialects spoken in everyday life, in contrast to the literary language of Latin.

bibliophile Lover and collector of books.

Emmanuel Chrysoloras (1355–1415) Important Greek scholar who introduced the scientific works of ancient Greek philosophers to the west.

autocrat Ruler who possesses absolute power.

patron Person, usually wealthy or powerful, who financially supports the intellectual or artistic work of a client.

client Artist or intellectual supported by a wealthy patron.

Lorenzo de' Medici (r. 1469–1492, "the Magnificent") Ruler of Florence and patron of artists, poets, and humanist scholars during the Italian Renaissance.

civic humanism Study and appreciation of classical republican forms of government.

renaissance Literally, "rebirth," signifying a revival.

Michelangelo Buonarotti (1475–1564) Painter, sculptor, poet, and architect, considered in his time to be the greatest artist Italy had ever produced.

Giotto di Bondone (1267–1334) Best-known and most influential painter of the Middle Ages.

artisan Skilled craftsmen, such as a cabinetmaker, painter, or shoemaker.

celebrated human potential and downplayed the theological emphasis on the sinful nature of humanity.

Petrarch One of the earliest humanists, Francesco Petrarca, born in 1304 in Tuscany and known as **Petrarch**, belonged to the generation of scholars that joined the clergy to acquire a higher education. His father wanted him to study canon law, but a love of literature directed the young scholar toward poetry both in Latin and in the everyday **vernacular** language. Petrarch's poems made him famous throughout Italy, southern France, and eventually all of Europe, but his love of manuscripts made a greater impact on literature. As ambassador to the Avignon popes, Petrarch traveled all over Europe, stopping in monasteries along his way. A **bibliophile** of the first order, Petrarch searched through their libraries for old manuscripts and discovered lost works by Cicero. Writing to the ancient Roman as if he were alive, Petrarch chastised Cicero for contributing to the downfall of the Roman Republic. He emulated the style and content of the ancients with such success that readers took a new interest in the language and texts associated with Rome.

Byzantine Refugees Ancient Greek texts benefited from the arrival of refugees from the Byzantine Empire in the 1390s. Fleeing the Ottomans, they emigrated to Italy and stimulated a great interest in the literature of the past. After a tour of Europe in 1394, the great Greek scholar **Emmanuel Chrysoloras** made Florence a new center of Greek learning,

thanks to his skills as a teacher and to the manuscripts he brought with him. Other Byzantine scholars found employment elsewhere in Italy, where they not only taught Greek but also introduced intellectuals to the previously unknown body of scientific works by Plato, Aristotle, and others.

Patronage Not all intellectuals worked as papal secretaries or scribes in city government. Some worked directly for **autocratic** rulers and wealthy merchants who enjoyed the prestige that came with being **patrons** of humanists. These men employed scholars in their households to instruct their children or to converse when visitors came to call. Humanist **clients** encouraged their patrons to collect manuscripts and, later, books that would form the basis of some of Europe's most important libraries. **Lorenzo de' Medici**, the ruler of Florence in the late fifteenth century, amassed an important collection of manuscripts and books under the guidance of the humanist scholars whose patron he was.

Although humanists tended to embrace the values of the patrons for whom they worked, they admired Cicero's involvement in Roman public affairs and valued political engagement in city life. The Florentine humanists took from Cicero an appreciation for republicanism, which rejected autocractic rule in favor of government by the people. **Civic humanism**, the study of ancient texts to develop ideological support for Florence's republican government, gave the humanists an opportunity to express their patriotism. Through the study of these texts, the humanists sought to bring what they perceived to be the best of the ancient world to life again in their own time—hence their conviction that they lived in a period of rebirth, or **renaissance**.

From Artisan to Artist

By the end of the fifteenth century, when the Renaissance in Italy was at its height, patrons like Lorenzo de' Medici would have viewed the painter, sculptor, and architect **Michelangelo** much as we do today, as an artist of outstanding genius. Two centuries earlier, the early-fourteenth-century Italian painter **Giotto** would have been viewed as an **artisan** of exceptional talent. The emergence of artists from the world of artisans had everything to do with the same cultural climate in which humanist scholars worked.

Giotto Giotto painted in a time when the function of a painting mattered as much as the beauty or creativity it displayed. The male and female patrons who hired Giotto would have specified what they wanted to see in the painting. Giotto's role in the process was simply to execute the patron's desire. Although Giotto received much praise for the beauty and spiritual qualities of his painting, he was only a craftsman in

Scala/Art Resource, NY

At the behest of Pope Julius II, Michelangelo worked on the Sistine Chapel for four years. Because he stood with his head back for long hours on scaffolding, his health and his eyesight suffered damage. How visible would the details of this ceiling fresco be to observers standing sixty-eight feet below?

the eyes of the people who employed him. Religious and secular patrons hired artisan painters, sculptors, and architects to create devotional objects whose beauty was meant to enhance, reinforce, and remind viewers of what they should believe or do. Painted frescoes like the ones Giotto painted celebrating the life of Saint Francis in the basilica at Assisi (see image on page 281) depicted stories that taught the laity the elements of Christian belief.

Sculptors created statues out of stone or bronze that portrayed holy or historical figures, celebrated warriors, or secular rulers. Craftsmen builders designed churches, government buildings, and private residences whose size or grandeur suggested the glory of God or its occupants. Even the finely crafted gold and silver objects on display in churches had practical uses in the Mass. All artistic creations had a purpose and a function.

Artisans Those who painted portraits or religious works, made statues, and designed buildings would have described themselves as artisans, not as painters, sculptors, or architects. They were also businessmen. If a painter was successful, he very likely owned and operated his own workshop and employed other painters who assisted him, even to the extent of painting the background of a scene that would eventually be associated with his name alone.

Gentile Bellini Gentile Bellini, a renowned Venetian painter and the son and brother of two other famous painters, was the master of his own workshop, where he and his assistants together painted scenes of Venice's ceremonial life. The contract he signed with his patrons specified precisely what images the painting would contain, the pigment colors that would be used, and the date when the project would be completed. Once all the conditions had been agreed upon, Bellini's assistants worked on drafting and painting the buildings in the background while the master focused his creative attention on the figures that required technical precision and artistic vision. Sculptors and architects made similar contractual arrangements with their patrons, who tended to view themselves as the real creative force behind artistic productions.

The workmanlike relationship between a painter and his patron changed slowly over the fifteenth century as the creative expression of the artisan became more highly valued. By the end of the century, not only did people think of painters, sculptors, and architects as artists, as we understand the term, but the artisans also began to regard their skills and talent more highly than previously. Michelangelo, a devoutly

Gentile Bellini (ca. 1429–1507) Important Venetian painter whose subject matter mainly concerned Venetian political and religious history.

Michelangelo—A New Kind of Artist

In 1512, after nearly four years of hard labor, Michelangelo Buonarotti hurried to finalize his almost-finished fresco paintings on the ceiling of the Sistine Chapel in Rome. For over a year, his employer, Pope Julius II, had badgered him repeatedly to complete the work. Each time the pope asked when he would be done, Michelangelo would answer impatiently, "When I can get it done, Your Holiness."

At last, the pope had had enough. He ordered the high scaffolding on which Michelangelo worked to be dismantled. Michelangelo rushed to apply the last touches to the ceiling before the scaffolds came down. Then the pope had the doors to the chapel opened to allow the public to view the painter's masterpiece. Everyone in Rome had been talking about it and its creator for months. Now when they bent their heads back to look up at the ceiling sixty-five feet above them, they were amazed to see a profusion of color and a multitude of human forms. Standing somewhere to the side of the awe-struck crowd, however, Michelangelo was not a happy man.

Not yet forty years old, Michelangelo had a clear estimation of his own talents and accomplishments. He had already gained a reputation as the finest sculptor for the beauty of his *Pietà*. The monumental statue of *David* in his native city Florence was already famous throughout Europe. With the Sistine Chapel's frescoes, he now demonstrated to many people's surprise that no painter then working in Italy had more skill or more genius than the man known until then mainly for his mastery over marble.

But Michelangelo resented being treated disrespectfully, as he believed the pope treated him. If it was the artist's judgment that there was still work to do on the frescoes, then he expected the pope to respect that assessment. Instead, Michelangelo had had to accede to the wishes of Pope Julius, a church man notorious for spending as much time leading an army as he did in prayer. Perpetually short of money, the pope had frequently delayed paying the sculptor, as if he were an ordinary craftsman rather than a great artist, as Michelangelo saw himself.

Michelangelo's relationship with Pope Julius had never been an easy one. They irritated each other from the start, when the pope invited the twenty-nine-year-old sculptor to come to Rome to make his tomb. Once Michelangelo showed what he was capable of creating in stone, Julius put him to work instead on the Sistine ceiling (reportedly on the advice of Michelangelo's rival painters, Raphael and Bramonte), who were convinced he would fail. Contrary to expectations, Michelangelo displayed a formidable talent for painting—but Pope Julius still treated him like a servant.

As temperamental as both the pope and the painter were, only Michelangelo made a lasting impression on how the public viewed his occupation. Thanks to the artist's friend Giorgio Vasari, who wrote a much-read biography of Michelangelo, people came to associate great artistry with extreme emotion, even though Pope Julius could match Michelangelo in tantrums and ill-temper. From then on, no longer viewed primarily as *artisans*—painters, sculptors, and architects became *artists* and were associated in the public mind with high-strung personalities, whose genius excused misbehavior or melodrama. When they saw what he had created in the Sistine Chapel, many people felt Michelangelo could behave however he liked. He was an artist, after all.

Source: Attributed to Michelangelo (1475–1564).

---

religious man, who painted the ceiling of the Sistine Chapel and designed Saint Peter's Church, both at the **Vatican**, evoked the highest praise of any artist in his time from his contemporaries, yet he revealed his ambivalence about the life of an artist in a poem:

> *My cherished art, my season in the sun, name, fame, acclaim—that cant I made a run for, left me in servitude, poor, old, alone.*
> *O death, relieve me soon. Or soon I'm done for.*

By the sixteenth century, the artisan had become an artist, and his work was now art. This change is reflected clearly in a collection of biographical sketches by a painter whose reputation rests more firmly on his writings than on his paintings. **Giorgio Vasari's** *The Lives of the Most Eminent Painters, Sculptors, and Architects,* published in 1550, preserves details about the life, work, and character of Renaissance Italy's most famous artists, from Giotto in the thirteenth century to Michelangelo in the sixteenth. In this work, the stereotype of artist as temperamental genius emerges clearly for the first time.

Perspectives and Techniques

One man's career best personifies the changes in cultural expression and production during the

Vatican Area on the north side of the Tiber in Rome where the pope was living by the end of the fifteenth century.

Giorgio Vasari (1511–1574) Italian architect and artist who wrote biographies of Renaissance artists.

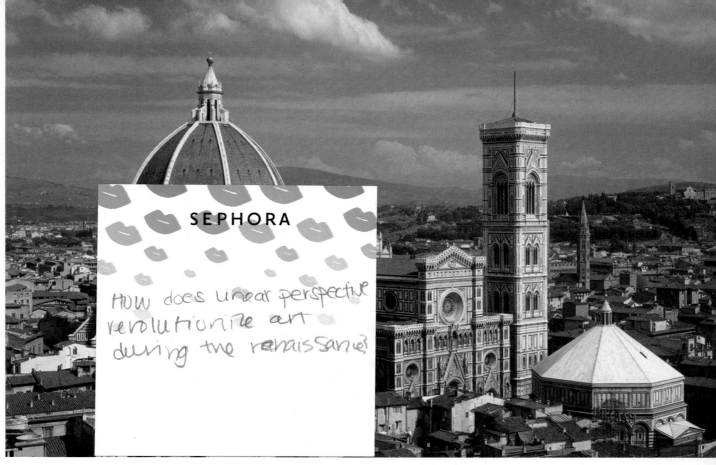

Brunelleschi's reputation rests on his engineering of the dome of Florence's cathedral, finished in 1436 and pictured here. Italians refer to cathedrals by their word for "dome," *duomo*. The Duomo stands out so clearly in Florence's skyline that it epitomizes the city today as much as it did in the fifteenth century. Looking at how close the surrounding buildings are to the cathedral walls, do you think the exterior of the cathedral was meant to impress from near or afar? (Scala/Art Resource, NY)

Italian Renaissance. **Filippo Brunelleschi**, like most of his colleagues, did not confine himself exclusively to one creative medium. He was an exceptionally talented painter, metalworker, engineer, and architect, all in one. Born and raised in Florence, Brunelleschi became, even in his own day, one of the most famous artists Italy ever produced. His two most significant contributions to the cultural movements of his time related to his experiments with **linear perspective** in painting and to his engineering innovations in architecture.

Like the humanists, Brunelleschi believed the ancient Romans had much to teach him. His studies in the art and architecture of Rome led him to develop the mathematical principles of linear perspective that the Romans had used in their wall paintings to convey a sense of depth. Linear perspective creates the illusion of three dimensions on a two-dimensional surface. To convey a sense of depth or distance, the painter drew lines on the flat surface of his canvas or wall that all converged on one point, called the **vanishing point**.

Brunelleschi's own paintings in which he demonstrated this technique have not survived, but his peers credit him with bringing the principles of linear perspective to the attention of working painters and sculptors. Among the very first to make use of perspective were **Masaccio** in Florence and Jacopo Bellini, the father of Gentile Bellini, the prominent Venetian painter.

Brunelleschi's fame, in his own time and today, however, stems mainly from his architectural and engineering accomplishments. Although the foundation of Florence's cathedral was laid at the very end of the thirteenth century, it still lacked a roof and a dome in the first decades of the fifteenth century. In 1420, Brunelleschi, chief architect of the ongoing construction, implemented his plan to build an enormous and immensely heavy octagonal

Filippo Brunelleschi (1377–1446) Outstanding architect, painter, and engineer who introduced linear perspective in painting and designed the dome of Florence's cathedral.

linear perspective Illusion of depth and three-dimensional space in an image achieved by drawing the lines of the composition toward a vanishing point.

vanishing point In a painting, the point at which all the lines converge to give the illusion of depth and three dimensions.

Masaccio (1401–1428) Italian artist notable for his early experimentation with linear perspective.

Did the rise of the acquisitive spirit cause an economic rise in Renaissance Italy?

Scala/Art Resource, NY

Before beginning his painting, the Adoration of the Magi, in 1482, Leonardo sketched on paper its composition, using linear perspective in the architectural elements. The painting was never finished, but Leonardo's sketches have taught art historians much about how painters in the fifteenth century worked. Can you find the vanishing point in this drawing?

dome on top of the completed cathedral walls. It was a daring project, involving updated Roman engineering equipment and ancient brick and stone methods of construction. In the end, Brunelleschi's plan worked, and the dome was consecrated in 1436. A friend of all the great artists at the time, Brunelleschi represents the extraordinary combination of talent, skill, and great learning found in many of the artists who emerged in the fifteenth century.

Leonardo Leonardo da Vinci rivaled Brunelleschi and Michelangelo in breadth of knowledge, skill, and talent. He worked as a painter of portraits and of the large frescoes in monasteries and civic buildings that only ecclesiastical institutions and governments could afford to commission. His skills as a military engineer made him just as well known. He was a scholar, too, who read widely in many fields. The humanist quest to celebrate all that was human inspired Leonardo to investigate the inner workings of the human body through dissections of cadavers, an illegal practice condemned by the church. Understanding how tendons connected muscle to bone enabled him to depict human forms with detailed accuracy. Everything that was human fascinated Leonardo. His wide range of expertise and his genius made him the prototype of the Renaissance man.

The Pleasure of Things

The explosion of cultural creativity in Renaissance Italy was not confined to the works of art in churches and government buildings. All wanted to adorn themselves and their surroundings with more possessions than had ever been available before, but, as always, only a minority could afford to. When the economy began to revive after the reversals and disasters of the fourteenth century, a new acquisitive spirit took hold in Italian cities as trade, manufacturing, and a rise in imported goods provided people with opportunities to spend money on objects that pleased them, enhanced their status, or both.

Domestic interiors in the late fourteenth century would have seemed as uncomfortable to someone at the start of the sixteenth century as they would to someone today. Medieval homes lacked good seating. Most families of modest means in the fourteenth century owned very few pieces of furniture. One or two beds sufficed for all members of the family; the servants slept on rushes piled on the floor.

Leonardo da Vinci (1452–1519) One of the world's greatest artists and engineers, most famous for his painting the *Mona Lisa*.

One table provided a surface to eat on, socialize around, or write on. Perhaps there was a stool or a wooden bench to sit on. Against a wall might be a rough-hewn wooden chest for storage. With so little furniture, families spent most of their days outside in the courtyard of a house, working in the fields, or sitting under a tree with their neighbors, whether they lived in the countryside or in a city. When they had to come indoors, family members piled on the bed for seating.

The home of a well-to-do family would not have contained a greater variety of furniture, although there were likely to be a few more seats, wooden chests, and tables. Nor was there much in the way of decoration. Only wealthy families could afford to have their walls hung with tapestries, whose main function was, in any case, to retain heat. Everyday utensils, like serving dishes and cookware, tended to be uniform and utilitarian in shape, color, and material.

As the fifteenth century progressed, people bought more and more things because, in large part, there were now more things to buy. Italian cities were becoming societies of consumers, intent on spending money in ways that would show off their status and taste. The wealthiest families directed their money toward building palaces that would reflect their social status. Domestic architecture emerged as a style distinct from ecclesiastic and governmental architecture.

relating to church

Domestic Spaces Builders designed palaces for their patrons that looked magnificent and imposing from the outside and luxurious and ceremonial on the inside. Spacious reception rooms, where the members of the family met with visitors, now contained more kinds of furniture than before. Larger and more ornately decorated wooden storage chests lined the wall. More chairs were available. A sideboard held the family's silver plate in a room now specifically designated for eating. Framed devotional paintings or frescoes depicting all the members of the family and their patron saints filled in the spots on the wall not covered by tapestries. People spent their money on luxury goods that would impress a visitor with the family's wealth, prestige, and cultivated taste.

Clothing In addition to decorating their homes, consumers spent a good deal of money on what they wore. Until the fifteenth century, people's social status could be judged by the quality of their clothes. Renaissance Italians now had a greater variety of apparel to choose from, and the clothes themselves became more ornate, more complex in design, and made of expensive material. This greater availability of luxurious clothing, however, caused social tension. When a greater variety of

fabrics came on the market at prices humble people could afford, even the wife of a shoemaker could look like a member of the upper classes. People could no longer be sure of a stranger's social rank from his or her clothing.

Many city governments in Italy passed **sumptuary laws**, which prohibited people of middle and low social status from wearing the kinds of fabrics and accessories associated with the rich. Ordinary women, for instance, could not use mink to trim the necklines of their dresses. In Venice, only patrician men could wear a red *giubba*, the gown worn by men of the city's highest rank. Of course, these laws proved very difficult to enforce. The consumer societies coming into being in the fifteenth century had the unintended effect of blurring some social distinctions that the ruling elites depended on to maintain order in society and themselves in power.

 Checking In

By yourself or with a partner, explain the significance of each of the following selected key terms:

humanism	artisan
Petrarch	Vatican
patrons	linear perspective
Lorenzo de' Medici	Leonardo da Vinci

The Northern European Renaissance

◆ **What distinguished Flemish from Italian painters?**

◆ **How did the invention of movable type and the printing press bring about a revolution?**

The Renaissance in northern Europe contrasted sharply with the busy, chaotic workshops of Italian artists and the offices in government palaces occupied by busy scribes. In Flanders, France, and England, quiet chambers in universities and libraries lined with tall bookcases—with the soft light of northern Europe streaming through glass windows—characterized the more tranquil environment of intellectuals and artists at work. What was produced in the northern Renaissance struck contemporary observers as no less stunning, however, for its less dramatic and less noisy emergence onto the cultural scene. If northern Europe benefited much from exposure to Italian scholars and

sumptuary laws Municipal legislation restricting modes and expense of attire according to social status, profession, and, in the case of Jews, religion.

artists, then the people of the north more than balanced the exchange of innovation by providing everyone with the printing press.

Northern European Art

The other center of artistic innovation in the fifteenth century lay in northern Europe, particularly in the cities of Flanders, where a style of painting and decoration very much different from Italian painting evolved. Although Flemish and Italian painters were interested in one another's work, they took from the other basic ideas and molded them to fit their own cultural environment. So subtle was the cultural exchange that it has been a matter of considerable debate as to whether the fifteenth-century fashion for portrait painting began in Italy or in Flanders. By the end of that century, however, two distinct styles of painting and sculpture had emerged.

Manuscripts Manuscripts from the late fourteenth century reveal the earliest signs of northern European artists' approach to representing the world around them. Wealthy women and men paid copyists to compile prayer books for use in daily worship and artists to illuminate the pages with designs and figures in brilliant colors and gold leaf. A so-called **Book of Hours** contained a calendar with feast days and saints' days marked, the Psalms, and readings from the Gospels. Typically, illuminating the calendar offered the artist an opportunity to use bright and costly blue, red, and gold pigments to illustrate a month. In the manuscript collections of the Psalms (**Psalters**) and the schedule of church services throughout the year, which were small enough to fit conveniently in the hand, artists rendered painstakingly detailed scenes of the banquets, hunts, and other recreations of the nobility and urban elites. *The Very Rich Hours of the Duke of Berry*, executed around 1416, offers an exquisite example of the artistry to be seen in northern Europe.

Jan van Eyck From the detailed miniature manuscript illuminations to oil paintings was a short step. Unlike Italian artists, who used paints made of pigments mixed with egg yolks—known as **tempera**—either on fresh wall plaster or on wooden boards joined to form a smooth surface, Flemish painters set their scenes in pigments mixed

National Gallery, London/The Bridgeman Art Library

Above, in his 1434 portrait of a newly married couple, the Flemish painter Jan Van Eyck used light and color to achieve depth of field. In contrast, the Italian Fra Angelico, a painter and Dominican friar, employed linear perspective—the use of lines converging on a vanishing point—for a similar effect in his fresco of the Annunciation from the 1440s on the right (page 349). Using your own words, how would you describe the differences between the two painting?

Book of Hours Book or manuscript containing a calendar, prayers, and biblical passages for private devotion.

Psalter Book or manuscript containing the Psalms.

tempera Egg-based medium that binds paint pigments, used in Renaissance Italy.

Jan van Eyck (ca. 1390–1441) Influential Flemish painter whose pioneering use of rich colors and light conveyed unprecedented depth of field.

with linseed oil and on linen canvas. The practice of painting in oil migrated from Flanders to Italy by the start of the sixteenth century, once Italian artists saw the superb work of **Jan van Eyck**, court painter to Philip, duke of Burgundy, and other Flemish artists.

Technique Apart from this difference in painting medium, two other differences in technique between the Italians and the Flemish are immediately noticeable. Whereas Italian painters relied on linear perspective to convey depth and dimension, the Flemish used gradations in color and the optical effect of painted light to achieve the same effect. And Italian painters presented their paintings in an architectural frame within the painting that separated the viewers from the painting's subject, while Flemish painters placed their subjects in a setting that seemed to include the viewer of the painting in the same space.

In contrast to the monumental, spare quality of Italian painting, the oil painting of Flanders looked cluttered and busy, with too many objects claiming the viewer's attention. Nothing in the world around them—from sacred figures to the buttons on the jacket worn by a portrait's subject—seemed insignificant to van Eyck and his fellow painters. They sought to realistically depict things and people as they looked to the human eye. It was the ordinariness of life that interested them. Not everyone appreciated the effort. Michelangelo, for one, thought Flemish painters were far too obsessed with the minutiae of life and not attentive enough to its spiritual essence.

Symbols The things that cluttered Flemish paintings possessed meanings not easily apparent. In his portrait commemorating the marriage of an Italian merchant residing in Bruges, the objects van Eyck placed around the wedding couple standing beside a bed include a little dog and one lighted candle in the chandelier, both objects seemingly irrelevant to the event the painting honored. To the people of the time, it has long been believed, the bed was a familiar symbol of the sexual union in marriage, the little dog recalled fidelity, and the candle signaled the presence of Christ at the marriage. Thus, the painting works on both literal and symbolic levels at the same time.

Flemish artists invited viewers to look not just at the objects in their paintings but through the objects to find their symbolic meaning.

Northern Humanists

Scholars from all over Europe undertook the arduous journey through the mountain passes into Italy to learn from the humanist scholars, especially those in Florence, whose works displayed a refreshing approach to classical literature. Frenchmen, Englishmen, and scholars from the Low Countries, in particular, came to Florence, Pisa, Venice, and other cities, where they found tutors in Greek and specialists in Latin literature to study with.

New Scholarship When they returned home, they took with them new methods for the analysis of texts, a deeper appreciation for Greek and Roman literature, and plans to apply their newly acquired learning in the service of the church. In contrast to the Italian humanists, who believed public service was as important as private study, the scholars from the north mostly came from and returned to either the cloister or the university. Because they were not in the public eye, the impact they had on their societies was less obvious and provoked less fanfare, but it was equally profound.

Like many of the Italian humanists, the humanists of northern Europe focused on the languages and literature of the past, but their interests reflected their close ties to the church and universities. By examining the language and history of texts written by early Christian writers more closely than had been done before, these fifteenth-century Christian humanists placed Christianity in history.

They traced the evolution of doctrine from the church's earliest days to their present. In France, Italian-trained humanists such as Jacques Lefèvre d'Étaples produced new editions of texts written by the early church fathers. Others, like John Colet at Oxford University in England, studied early Christian texts written in Greek and Latin. They were the first generation of scholars to question the accuracy of the translations from Greek into Latin of scripture and the writings of early church thinkers. These editing projects and textual analyses formed the basis of a new field, **patristics**. Likewise, German scholars studied early Hebrew texts to gauge their influence on the development of early Christian thought.

Erasmus The new fields and methods of study were controversial. From the perspective of the Christian humanists, the texts they studied and edited suggested that the church had wandered far from its original mission. More controversially, a few questioned the translation of certain words and verses in the New Testament, a text whose accuracy the church prohibited anyone from questioning. **Desiderius Erasmus**, a theologian born in Rotterdam in the Low Countries, believed not only that literate lay Christians ought to read scripture in the languages they spoke, but also, that scholars ought to reexamine the Vulgate Bible, which he found to contain errors in translation from the Greek New Testament. After a number of years of comparing manuscripts of the Greek New Testament he found in western Europe, Erasmus produced in 1516 a corrected Greek version with an updated Latin translation and extensive notes. Even this corrected version did not satisfy the standards set by humanist scholars, including Erasmus himself, and in 1522 he issued an improved edition of his Greek Testament that corrected his own errors.

Erasmus faced stiff criticism from church leaders, most of whom objected to his undertaking the translation

In 1523, Hans Holbein the Younger, one of the best known painters in northern Europe, painted this portrait of Erasmus. Although the scholar is shown seated in a room, he wears heavy robes and a hat. The interiors of houses in northern Europe were so difficult to heat that people dressed very warmly while indoors. What details in the painting suggest to you that Erasmus led a comfortable life?

Erich Lessing/Art Resource, NY

without the authorization of the church. They also felt ambivalent about making scripture available in vernacular languages to people liable to read whatever they wished into the translations. Even many of Erasmus's friends warned him that allowing laypeople to read and interpret the Bible for themselves would lead to disorder and rebellion. Although he and his fellow humanists believed that reading scripture for themselves in their own language would strengthen laypeople's faith, Erasmus came to see that it would not necessarily lead to continued obedience to church authority.

Jewish Scholarship Jewish scholars, too, participated in the humanist study of texts. Their works incorporating humanist principles into the study of Judaism and the Hebrew Bible drew the interest of some Christian scholars. The study of Hebrew texts posed a challenge to those who objected in principle to the idea that Judaism had any influence on Christianity. Anti-Jewish sentiment within the church

---

patristics Study of the writings of the early church fathers, such as Jerome, Ambrose, Augustine, and Pope Gregory I.

Desiderius Erasmus (1469–1536) Dutch humanist, theologian, and textual scholar whose writings influenced the movement for church reform.

kabbalah (From Hebrew, "tradition") Field of Jewish mysticism dating to the twelfth century but of greater interest in the sixteenth.

Erich Lessing/Art Resource, NY

Printer's shops, like this re-creation of Johannes Gutenberg's in Mainz, Germany, were crowded places. The printing press took up most of the room. Printers hung freshly printed pages on lines across the shop so that the ink would dry. In the background appear frames with many compartments in which letter types were stored. Although printer's shops resembled workshops more than libraries, how might these commercial places have fostered intellectual exchange? Was it necessary for printers to be men of learning?

and among traditional scholars made ecclesiastical authorities look with suspicion on scholars like Johannes Reuchlin, a German theologian at the university in Württemberg, who studied the **kabbalah**, a Jewish mystical text.

Neither northern humanists nor their Italian counterparts sought to challenge the authority of the church and the papacy. But to varying degrees, the humanist project in northern Europe and in Italy helped to create the conditions out of which powerful critiques of the church emerged in the sixteenth century.

Printing, a New Medium

Scholarship in both northern Europe and in Italy underwent a profound change when a new invention, the printing press, made it possible to reproduce many identical copies of a work quickly for distribution. A goldsmith from the German city of Mainz, **Johannes Gutenberg**, is believed to have invented in the 1440s

the process in which a printer pressed ink-coated movable type onto paper.

Printing Technology Although the Chinese had centuries before devised a printing process by carving the characters that made up their written language onto blocks of wood, Gutenberg's innovation was, first, to cast small pieces of metal type, each with a raised face in the shape of a letter. A typesetter arranged the metal type, letter by letter, in horizontal rows to spell out the text to be published. Setting the type was the most time-consuming part of the printing process. After the rows were locked within a frame, the printer brushed the set type with ink, laid paper on it, and then slid it under a heavy press. When all the pages of the text had been printed, the metal type was disassembled so that it could be set again for another text.

Johannes Gutenberg (d. 1468) Inventor of the printing press, and printing from movable type, in the west.

Erasmus Defends His Translation of the Greek New Testament

Erasmus, a theologian and editor and translator of the Greek New Testament, faced strong criticism for undertaking his translation from church leaders and other theologians, who feared what would happen if laypeople studied the text on their own. Erasmus had an enormous circle of friends throughout Europe. All his life, he wrote letters to them in which he discussed whichever work he was composing at the time, debated with them about political trends, and defended his belief in church reform. In the following letter, written in 1515, he responds to Martin Dorp, a Dutch theologian who in a previous letter had questioned the need for and legitimacy of the New Testament translation that Erasmus was about to begin. In his reply, Erasmus aggressively defends his translation at the same time as he insinuates that someone like Dorp, who could not read scripture in its original language of Greek, was in no position to lecture a theologian who could.

❶ What does Erasmus seem to have learned from his reading of the church fathers?

What you write about the New Testament really makes me wonder what's happened to you…. You don't want me to change a single thing unless an idea is expressed more significantly in the Greek, and you deny that in the edition we know as the Vulgate there is any error at all. You think it would be sacrilege to alter in any way a text authenticated by agreement over so many centuries and endorsed by so many councils. **❶** But if what you say is true, let me ask you, most learned Dorp, why Jerome often cites scripture in a form that varies from ours, and Augustine in another form, and Ambrose in still another? Why does Jerome censure and correct many specific passages which still remain uncorrected in the Vulgate?…. Are you going to dismiss all these authorities to follow a manuscript that may be full of scribal errors? Nobody says that the scriptures contain lies, though you seem to assume this is my attitude; nor does the matter relate in any

Paper The development of the printing process depended on the availability and low cost of paper in western Europe. Originally a product from China that Muslim merchants brought back along the caravan routes to the Mediterranean, paper attracted the attention of Christian merchants—and possibly the crusaders—who had dealings in the Muslim world. They recognized that paper, made from pulverized cotton cloth, cost far less to produce than parchment and vellum, the treated sheep or calfskins that served as writing surfaces in western Europe. Depending on its size, a complete Bible consisting entirely of parchment or vellum pages could require the skins of nearly two hundred sheep or calves, which explains why manuscripts were so expensive to produce. By the late thirteenth century, paper production in Italy had begun. Scribes continued to use parchment and vellum for their luxury manuscripts, but in everyday life people increasingly used paper for their account books, records, and private documents.

Books and Pamphlets The affordability of paper and the speed of printing on it brought about a revolution in ideas and beliefs in the sixteenth century, as unprecedented amounts of information were put into circulation. The first products of the printing press certainly included books, but short and inexpensive political pamphlets, religious tracts, and bureaucratic forms appeared for sale in Mainz's first print shops right away. The artistry and craftsmanship that went into large luxury books, like the beautiful three-volume Bibles Gutenberg printed around 1455, kept their price prohibitively high.

way to the various controversies between Jerome and Augustine. ❷ But the situation cries aloud; it would be plain, as they say, to a blind man: often, because of the ignorance or carelessness of a translator, the Greek has been imperfectly rendered, and often the original true reading has been corrupted by an ignorant copyist. We see this happen every day: texts are changed by thoughtless or sleepy scribes. Who does more to promote a lie, the man who corrects and removes a mistake, or the man who, out of reluctance to make a change, lets it stand? Besides, it's the nature of corrupt texts that one error leads to another. For a fact, more of these changes that I've made relate to the emphasis than to the basic sense, though frequently the emphasis is itself part of the sense, and not infrequently the whole passage has been drawn out of shape. When such a thing happens, I ask you, where does Augustine turn, where do Ambrose, Hilary, and Jerome look, if not to the Greek original?…

…I have translated the entire New Testament afresh from the Greek originals with a Greek text across the page for easy comparison. My annotations are separate; they show, partly on the evidence and partly on the authority of ancient theologians, that my emendations were not rashly undertaken, that they can be accepted with confidence, and that they cannot be lightly dismissed. I only hope I have succeeded in a venture which has cost me so much labor…. ❸ Finally, I don't doubt that you too will congratulate me on the book you now deplore, provided only that you acquire a little taste of that language without which you can't possibly form a reasonable judgment of the matter.

Source: From *The Praise of Folly and Other Writings* by Desiderius Erasmus, translated by Robert M. Adams. Copyright © 1989 by W. W. Norton & Company, Inc. Used by permission of W. W. Norton & Company, Inc.

❷ How did printing change the problems inherent in the process of manuscript copying?

❸ Why does Erasmus stress the need for Dorp to learn Greek before he can offer informed criticism?

Printing shops spread quickly, first across Germany and then throughout Europe. Within a few years of Gutenberg's Bibles, the printing press reached other German cities—Strasbourg in 1460, Cologne in 1464. Sixty towns in Germany had printing shops by 1500. But in that same year Venice could boast of 150 printing presses. One Venetian printer, **Aldus Manutius**, joined with humanist scholars to print texts in the Greek alphabet that refugee scholars from the Byzantine Empire had brought to Italy.

Less than a century following the invention of movable type and the printing press, an estimated 9 million books were in circulation. Moreover, a great many more people knew how to read, especially in Italy, where literacy had accompanied the expansion of commerce and lay education. As the print culture expanded, reliance on memory and recitation diminished. The very way people thought and learned and remembered was changing.

Aldus Manutius (1449–1515)
Important Venetian printer noted for publishing Byzantine texts in the Greek alphabet.

 Checking In

By yourself or with a partner, explain the significance of each of the following selected key terms:

Book of Hours	Desiderius Erasmus
Psalters	kabbalah
tempera	Johannes Gutenberg
Jan van Eyck	Aldus Manutius

Map 12.2 **The Growth of Printing in Europe** Bills of sale, sermons, bibles, and scholarly works were among the first printed texts that printers produced. Compare the dates of when printing reached Sweden, Denmark, Lisbon, Madrid, Constantinople, and Warsaw. © *Cengage Learning*

1. Did distance from Mainz play a part in the arrival of printing in a city?
2. Do you see a correlation between trade centers and major printing centers?

The Cities of Renaissance Italy

◆ **How were the cities of Italy governed?**

◆ **What was the relation of the Papal States to the politics of Renaissance Italy?**

The cities of the northern Italian peninsula took pride in their nearly complete autonomy, although in theory the German Holy Roman emperor still ruled them. For some, like the city of Milan, that autonomy had come at a bloody price. The end of the fourteenth century brought an end to that autonomy. Now military strongmen, wealthy merchants, and royal foreigners each saw a chance to grab as much Italian territory as they could manage. While an army brought some to power, fabulous wealth put others in charge of their cities. The republican liberty and human potential that humanist scholars and artists celebrated remained an ideal that the reality of politics in the cities of Italy nearly always defeated.

The Medici of Florence

Florentine merchants considered themselves the inheritors of the ideals of the Roman Republic, which they read about in history books now being written for their pleasure by a new generation of humanist intellectuals espousing the ideals of civic humanism. In reality, these city governments only inadvertently resembled the Roman Republic because, like the small elite that had ruled Rome more than fifteen hundred years before, they, too, constituted a small minority of wealthy men who monopolized the political life of their cities.

Within those small groups of mercantile families, competition to exert the most influence on the government was fierce. Wealthy patrons granted business and political favors to less wealthy clients, who then were expected to vote according to the interests of their patrons. A family's political power stemmed from such supporters, friends, and relatives who felt beholden to their benefactors and their families.

The Medici In Florence, the Medici family came to power through the steady and generous distribution of fiscal, political, and commercial favors to those less fortunate than they. Those favors bought the political loyalty of those who accepted the Medici's help. The first member to achieve nearly complete but unofficial dominance of the Florentine government was **Cosimo de' Medici,** who inherited his father's lucrative role as banker to the pope in addition to the responsibility of representing the family in Florence's public life.

Cosimo was elected to the Signoria and other city councils, like many of his peers, but his real power far exceeded the authority of any public office he held. Through his network of clients, Cosimo directed—out of sight from public view—Florentine fiscal and diplomatic affairs. He dressed modestly, ate sparingly, and often retreated to Florence's most exclusive monastery, San Marco, spending days in quiet reflection and prayer. Behind that humble exterior lay a hunger for power as sharp as his splendid palace was opulent. The city governing councils did nothing relating to taxation, foreign policy, or the economy without taking their direction from Cosimo de' Medici. His supreme authority was so taken for granted—even if an open secret and resented by many—that foreign powers knew to negotiate directly with him, not with the elected councils.

Lorenzo the Magnificent Despite opposition, Cosimo's grandson, Lorenzo, strengthened his family's hold on power. Called "the Magnificent" for the grandeur of his palaces and building projects, Lorenzo shared with his grandfather a similar passion for power. Displaying a subtle diplomatic skill, he prevented the pope and other Italian rulers from banding together against him, but within his own city he faced continual challenges to his power, including an attempted assassination in 1478. Although severely wounded, he lived to exact revenge on his would-be killers. Opponents of Medici rule had to wait until two years after Lorenzo's death in 1492 before they ousted the family from power and exiled them from the city.

Savonarola After the ouster of the Medici in 1494, **Girolamo Savonarola,** a friar from the monastery of San Marco, used his great popularity as a church reform–minded preacher to become the next ruler of Florence. Savonarola's establishment of a new government dedicated to eradicating the corruption associated with the Medici and the papal court alarmed both the Medici allies and the pope. He ruled Florence with the support of the majority of Florentines, while a small faction of families conspired with the papacy to bring about his downfall. On the grounds that his calls for church reform constituted heresy, Savonarola was tried and burned at the stake in 1498. After four more years of turmoil in the city, the Medici returned to power in 1512.

Maritime Republics

The Florentines were not the only people of Italy who

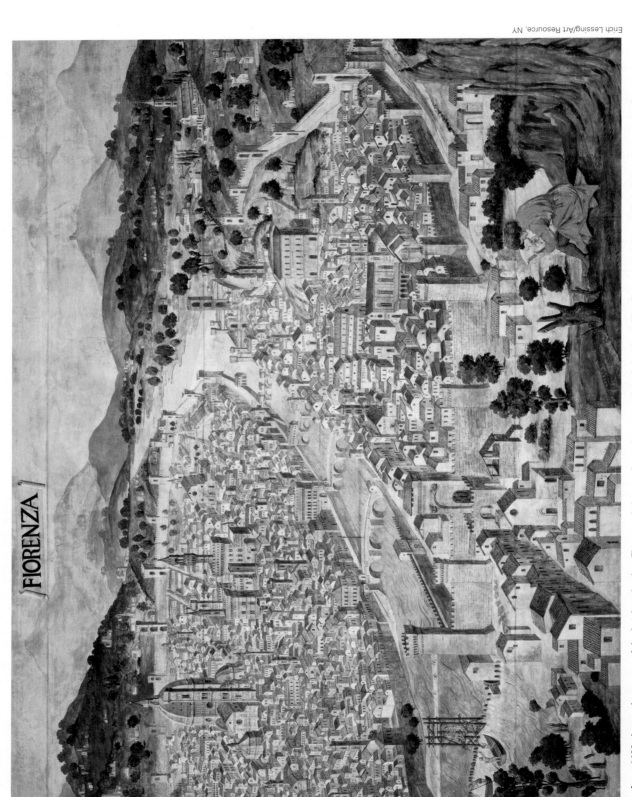

FIORENZA

This map from 1480 shows that many of the landmarks that Florence is known for today were already in place. The Duomo and the public buildings appear in the center of the map. The expansion of the city across the river Arno, to the right, required extending the city walls. What impressions do you think the mapmaker wanted to convey about Florence?

claimed their city embodied the classical virtues of civic humanism. Similar to the elites of Florence, small, hereditary groups of merchant families ruled the republics of Venice and Genoa by the end of the fourteenth century. The governments of both city-states consisted of councils, over each of which a **doge** presided as the official head of state. In Venice, the members of the ruling councils considered themselves to be nobles, but the term they used to describe themselves was reminiscent of ancient Rome—patricians. They represented only about 1 percent of the population of Venice, which fluctuated just above and below 100,000. A similarly tiny percentage of Genoa's population exercised complete political authority there. The families that rose to the top of Venetian and Genoese societies became wealthy through long-distance trade. Trading companies had extensive networks of branch offices around the Mediterranean and in the ports of northern Europe.

Venice and Genoa Economic competition between Genoa and Venice at times led to open hostilities and even warfare between the two republics. Four times—in 1258, 1298, 1350, and 1380—the fleets of the two cities met in sea battles in the vicinity of their trading operations in the east and in the Venetian lagoon. They fought over access to and commercial dominance of the Aegean Islands and the Black Sea.

During the last and decisive conflict known as the **War of Chioggia** in 1380, the Venetians relied on cutting-edge military technology by mounting cannon on their war galleys, which they aimed both at attacking ships and at on-shore military defenses. Venice's victory over Genoa had as much to do with its advanced weaponry as it did with Genoa's internal weaknesses. Factional fighting among Genoa's ruling elite led to frequent changes in Genoa's government and the shifting of the responsibility for the city's overseas trade to the **Maona**, a private mercantile company in Genoa that assumed the role of the state in the Aegean Islands under Genoese rule.

Genoa's instability gave the edge to Venetian merchants, who benefited from the stable and mature institutions of their government, which maintained a war fleet in the region that protected them. By the turn of the fifteenth century, Venice had emerged as the stronger power.

Venice Prevails Of the two cities, Venice had the more illustrious—certainly the more notorious—reputation. By the fifteenth century, Venetians lived as much by means of the sea as literally in the sea. A city made up of more than a hundred tiny islands connected by bridges, Venice had thoroughfares that were either footpaths or navigable canals, punctuated now and then by a campo, or field, with a public well in its center. In the seventeenth century, when the campi were paved, the Venetian government banned horses and compelled Venetians to move around the city either on foot or by gondola, a long, black vessel propelled by an upright oarsman. Even in the fifteenth century, Venice exerted a fascination on people from elsewhere. Its jewel-like appearance, lying off the mainland and surrounded by a shimmering sea, impressed visitors. So did its growing reputation for vice. Contemporaries expressed astonishment at the number of prostitutes and **courtesans** in public view in certain quarters of the city.

The Most Serene Republic Beginning with Petrarch in the 1360s, humanists received a warm welcome in Venice, provided they did nothing to disturb the oligarchic serenity of Venice's patricians. In the city itself, the lack of visible social unrest among the humble sections of its population and its ruling elite impressed visitors and Venetians themselves to such an extent that its government proudly called itself The Most Serene Republic in its official documents. The Aegean islands occupied by Venetian troops in the fourteenth century and the mainland Italian cities subordinated to Venetian authority in the fifteenth had a different experience of Venice's serenity. By the middle of the fifteenth century, as Ottoman Turks undermined Venetian authority in the eastern Mediterranean and Venice attempted to extend its territory on the mainland, the other Italian powers felt increasingly threatened.

Autocrats and Humanists

In the late fourteenth century, northern Italian city dwellers lived in fear of rioting workers, bloody **vendettas** between warring families, and the violent overthrow of civic institutions by ambitious men. Personal and collective liberty required from the city residents constant vigilance and active defense. Urban violence reached such alarming levels that city authorities resorted to the services of professional

doge (from Latin *dux*, "leader") Head of state in Venice and Genoa.

War of Chioggia Conflict between Venice and Genoa in 1380, in which Venice won a decisive victory.

Maona Private mercantile company in Genoa that assumed the role of the state in the Aegean Islands under Genoese rule.

courtesan A woman, very often highly educated and refined, who served as a mistress to wealthy men in exchange for support.

vendetta Campaign of revenge fought between two factions or families.

military men—**condottieri**—to keep the peace. These captains and their salaried armies acted at first like a police force and a militia, but they soon made themselves lords of the cities whose safety they had been hired to defend.

These military rulers of Italian cities owed their power to brute force, but disguised it behind the elegant and refined behavior typical of a Renaissance court. Among humanists, two types of the ideal ruler took shape. *The Courtier*, a widely read work published in 1528 by **Baldassare Castiglione**, a diplomat and intellectual from Milan, described the ideal ruler as a battle-tested as well as a highly educated commander with elegant manners. Castiglione's "Renaissance man" combined a chivalrous knight with a humanist scholar.

Machiavelli A Florentine presented another type of ideal ruler that reflected a grittier understanding of how the world worked. The son of a poor Florentine lawyer who belonged to a distinguished family, **Niccolò Machiavelli** gained considerable experience as a diplomat in Florence's government between the death of Savonarola in 1498 and the Medici's return to power in 1512. On the grounds that employment in Florence's government prior to their return made Machiavelli their enemy, the Medici family had him arrested and tortured. After a brief, painful period in prison, he went into exile.

The Prince To win his way back to Florence, Machiavelli dedicated to the new Medici ruler his work *The Prince*. Published in 1532 only after Machiavelli died, *The Prince* offers political advice on how heads of states, particularly those who seize power, should govern. Machiavelli advanced a strategy for domination requiring rulers to show no mercy to their enemies, to act decisively and ruthlessly, and to rule by expediency rather than morality. The ends, Machiavelli famously argued, justified the means. Like the humanists, he looked to ancient Roman writers for solutions to the problems he saw plaguing the cities of Italy. But he studied those texts with the autocratic behavior he had witnessed when on diplomatic business for Florence in Milan and the Papal States in mind and came to conclusions that sat uneasily with humanist ideals.

Milan Milan in the province of Lombardy enjoyed the rights and privileges of an autonomous city. A council made up of the leading Milanese families governed the city until 1311, when the **Visconti** family imposed its rule on the population. Under their rule, Milan grew into a powerful state founded on its rulers' military requirements. Its armaments and textile industries made the city wealthy. Milanese armor was in demand throughout Europe, and its silk cloth rivaled what Florentine weavers produced.

The Visconti family's ambition to govern did not stop, however, at the city walls. Throughout the 1380s and 1390s, Visconti forces conquered Siena and Pisa (both near Florence) as well as Verona and Vicenza (close to Venice), subdued the city of Bologna (a papal possession), and took control of the commercially important passes over the Alps. The alliance formed by Florence, Venice, and the pope to stop the Visconti was only partly successful. In 1447, when Filippo Maria Visconti died without a legitimate male heir, the people of Milan saw an opportunity to form a republic. Filippo Maria's son-in-law, **Francesco Sforza**, the condottiere hired to keep public order, had other plans. By 1450, attempts to form a republic had failed and Sforza had declared himself duke of Milan.

The new autocratic rulers of Milan enjoyed the prestige that came from patronizing the humanists and artists inspired by Renaissance ideals of republican liberty. In return, the republican-minded humanists, painters, and architects did not object to working in the military state that Milan had become. They easily found employment in the city's monasteries and ducal government. The most prominent artist of all, Leonardo da Vinci, spent nearly two decades in Milan in the employ of Ludovico Sforza, duke of Milan, who asked him to cast a bronze equestrian statue commemorating his father, Francesco, the first Sforza duke of Milan. His fresco of the Last Supper in the Convent of Santa Maria delle Grazie in Milan remains to this day one of the most recognizable paintings in the world.

The Papal States and the Church

Unlike Florence and Milan, where many people clung to republican ideals even when ruled by autocrats, the Papal States made no accommodation to those who would have preferred to live in a republic. In all of western Europe, only the pope could claim legitimacy dating back to Emperor Constantine in the

condottieri Mercenary captains employed by Italian city-states to maintain internal order.

Baldassare Castiglione (1478–1529) Diplomat and humanist who wrote *The Courtier* (1528), in which he describes the "Renaissance man."

Niccolò Machiavelli (1469–1527) Diplomat and political writer most famous for *The Prince*, a work instructing rulers on how to govern.

Visconti The family of ruling Milanese dukes from 1395 until 1447, when replaced by the Sforza family.

Francesco Sforza (r. 1447–1466) Mercenary captain hired to protect Milan; the first of a dynasty to rule Milan.

third century, even if that claim had been discredited in certain circles.

A Forged Document Over half a century before, in 1440, the humanist **Lorenzo Valla** performed a feat of scholarship that drew the admiration of scholars all across Europe, including Erasmus. Using humanist methods of textual analysis, he convincingly proved that the Donation of Constantine, on the basis of which the papacy laid claim to central Italy, was forged. Valla's work had little practical impact, as the papacy's power had been reinforced simply by the passage of centuries and the weight of tradition. The Papal States remained a theocratic and autocratic dominion until the nineteenth century.

The Papal States When the papacy left Rome and settled in Avignon, the nobles who governed the Papal States on behalf of the papacy took the opportunity to extricate themselves from its lordship. During the fourteenth century, several of the cities and towns under papal rule, such as Bologna, refused to recognize the lordship of the Avignon popes. The Visconti family of Milan, whose territory abutted the northwestern borders of the pope's lands, also saw an opportunity to add to their territory. Resistance to papal overlordship grew so strong that the papacy's income dropped significantly. Hiring an army in the 1350s to reimpose papal rule over the rebel lands sapped the pope's treasury even more.

The Borgias Initially, restoring order in the Papal States was the first order of business when the popes returned to Rome permanently at the end of the Great Schism in 1417. The popes of the fifteenth century appointed their own family members to secular and ecclesiastic offices in the cities of central Italy as a way of securing the loyalty of public authorities there. At the end of the century, Pope **Alexander VI** of the Borgia family put family loyalty ahead of the papacy's interests by creating a new, independent state carved out of the Papal States for his illegitimate son, Cesare Borgia, whom he had made a cardinal in 1493 when Cesare was not yet twenty. Five years later, Cesare exchanged his position as cardinal for that of military commander. The army he led conquered the three principal regions in the Papal States: Emilia, Romagna, and Umbria. When his father died in 1503, Cesare lost access to the funding he needed to pay his army. Without an army, and with a new pope intent on restoring dignity to the papacy and its lands, Cesare fell from power.

Pope Julius II The death of Alexander VI's successor within a year of his election put Pope **Julius II**

in charge of imposing papal rule over central Italy. Not content with hiring a mercenary army to enter battle for him, Julius led his own troops in 1508 to restore papal authority in the cities of Bologna and Perugia, contrary to church law, which forbade clergy to fight in wars. Alexander VI's death and Cesare Borgia's inability to defend his possession of the Papal States had given Venice an opportunity to expand its mainland holdings. Now, in an alliance with other powers in Italy, Julius forced the Venetians out of his lands in 1509. Julius, the patron of the arts responsible for Michelangelo's ceiling in the Sistine Chapel, conquered the land that had been lost to the papacy since the Avignon popes of the fourteenth century.

✓ Checking In

By yourself or with a partner, explain the significance of each of the following selected key terms:

Girolamo Savonarola	Condottieri
doge	Niccolò Machiavelli
War of Chioggia	Lorenzo Valla
courtesans	Julius II

Renaissance Ideals in Transition, 1400–1550

- ◆ **How did many of the cultural benefits of the Italian Renaissance reach France?**
- ◆ **What factors contributed to their slow passage to England?**

Pope Julius, the Sforza dukes, and the Medici demonstrated that the appreciation of humanist ideals could coexist with autocratic domination over their subjects. Similarly, the people of other countries and their rulers absorbed the cultural and intellectual innovations of Italy and Flanders at different rates and in their own ways. The French king admired the Italian Renaissance so much that, when he invaded the peninsula to conquer it, he made sure to acquire as many works of art—and artists—as he could

Lorenzo Valla (1407–1457) Humanist scholar whose influential treatise, written in 1440, showed the Donation of Constantine to be a forgery.

Alexander VI (r. 1492–1503) Pope who was a member of the Spanish Borgia family and notorious for the promotion of his illegitimate children and the corruption of his papal court.

Julius II (r. 1503–1513) Pope who was a great patron of artists, especially Michelangelo, and who restored the Papal States to papal control.

along the way. For most of the fifteenth century, civil war distracted the nobility of England from the pleasures of patronage. In Germany, painters took some notice of the Italian and Flemish artists, but farther east, the Russians clung to the stylized forms icon painters had absorbed from the Byzantines long ago.

The Court of Francis I

Chivalry—the medieval code of heroism, piety, and the idealization of noblewomen—was the consuming passion of one man, whose interests and predilections shaped the character of the Renaissance in France, King **Francis I**. As a fatherless teenager, heir to his cousin Louis XII, Francis took no interest in academic learning. Warfare and the ceremony associated with aristocratic knighthood absorbed all of the spoiled boy's attention. With no one able to guide him or restrain him apart from his mother, Francis trained himself to wage war rather than to rule.

When he succeeded to the throne in 1515, Francis I made his mother, Louise, regent so that she could rule in his absence and then left to conquer Italy. His first target was the duchy of Milan, under the rule of the Sforza family, whose forces he defeated. The French king was outmaneuvered by the adroit Pope Leo X, who took back possession of his territories in central Italy while recognizing Francis's overlordship. The Sforza duke of Milan achieved the same arrangement.

Francis, the Renaissance Prince Francis failed to conquer Italy, but Italy, in a sense, conquered him. During his time at the papal court, the French king was deeply impressed with the culture of the Italian Renaissance and, over time, patronized some of its leading artists. He drew to his court in France the finest painters, poets, musicians,

and scholars, who, perceiving their patron's chivalric passions, produced paintings, poetry, and songs that glorified the arts of war. Leonardo da Vinci and the sculptor Benvenuto Cellini were his guests.

The royal place at **Fontainebleau** melded traditional French architecture with the new Italian style, and the king's lavish court life there was modeled on the magnificence of the great Italian courts in Florence and Milan. Moreover, Francis took an interest in the Christian humanists and their reform-minded critiques of the church. As an adult, he acquired the intellectual interests that his martial training in youth had precluded. The combination of chivalric ceremonial displays and his promotion of the arts and learning created a lasting legacy for Francis as his kingdom's Renaissance king.

England Before Its Renaissance

After the last battles of the Hundred Years' War in the mid-fifteenth century, English men and women associated king with country more than they had ever done, partly as a result of patriotic pageants, popular **ballads**, and other propaganda meant to rally financial and moral support for the war against France.

Tales of King Arthur Throughout the war, the **Arthurian legends** idealized knighthood and offered a powerful model of chivalric kingship in the character of King Arthur. After the war, in the 1470s, **Thomas Malory** reworked many of the old tales about the legendary king and his knights for the first time in English in an epic account of the Knights of the Round Table, *Le Morte d'Arthur* (*The Death of Arthur*). The printer **William Caxton** published it in 1485, making it one of the earliest printed works of English literature. The stories about the adventures of King Arthur, Lancelot, Guinevere, and the knights offered a model of heroic kingship that the English looked for in their own king.

Dynastic Instability Henry V's son and heir, Henry VI (r. 1421–1461, 1470–1471), did not, however, inspire much confidence. Mentally unstable and unfit to rule for periods of time, he survived repeated attempts to remove him from power until kinsmen and rival claimants to the throne deposed him in 1461. The leader of his opponents and his cousin from the House of York ascended the throne as Edward IV (r. 1461–1470, 1471–1483). Henry fled to allies in Scotland but was captured and confined in the **Tower of London** in 1465. The new king Edward spent his entire reign fighting off supporters of the deposed Henry in the ongoing

---

Francis I (r. 1515–1547) King of France who centralized royal rule, created at his court a vibrant Renaissance culture, and unsuccessfully fought Charles V for control of Italy.

Fontainebleau Castle, or château, and chief residence of Francis I, king of France.

ballad Popular song that usually told a story.

Arthurian legends Stories associated with the deeds and lives of the mythical King Arthur and the Knights of the Round Table.

Thomas Malory (d. 1471) Author of *Le Morte d'Arthur*, an English-language collection of the Arthurian legends, published in 1485.

William Caxton (ca.1415–1492) England's first printer, who published Malory's *Le Morte d'Arthur*.

Tower of London Norman fortification situated on the banks of the Thames River where political prisoners were confined.

series of civil wars known collectively as the **Wars of the Roses** (1455–1485), after the red and white roses symbolizing Edward IV's York and Henry VI's Lancaster families. After his coronation, Edward ruled for ten years before his early death put his young son, Edward V (r. 1483), on the throne.

The young king's reign, too, soon ended. His uncle, Richard of York, imprisoned the young king and his younger brother in the Tower of London, where they both died under mysterious circumstances. Rumors that their uncle, now **Richard III**, had had his nephews murdered turned the nobles and the population against the king, thus presenting an opportunity for the supporters of Henry VI's House of Lancaster to reassert their claim to the throne. In 1485, Richard's chief Lancastrian opponent, Henry Tudor of Wales, defeated Richard at **Bosworth Field**. When Henry married Elizabeth of York in 1486, he united the Lancastrian and Yorkist factions. Crowned **Henry VII**, the founder of the **Tudor** dynasty set out to restore stability to England and replenish the nearly empty royal treasury. Only under later Tudors would England achieve its Renaissance.

The Holy Roman Empire and Eastern Europe

In the lands to the east of the French kingdom in the late fourteenth and fifteenth centuries, the flourishing trade among the Baltic Sea countries inspired the rulers in the region to consolidate their authority and claim their share of the profits. The Holy Roman emperors concentrated their efforts on their German lands. The princes of Moscow wrested control over their lands from their Mongol conquerors. The kings of Bohemia and Hungary insinuated themselves into the center of the Holy Roman Empire's political life, while new states were emerging along the northern shorelines of the Baltic Sea.

Prince Electors Unlike his predecessors, the Holy Roman emperor Charles IV (r. 1347–1378) faced the difficult truth that he could not sustain an empire that stretched from Germany in the north to Italy in the south. In a proclamation issued in 1356 and known as the **Golden Bull**, he laid out a system by which his successors would be chosen by seven permanent electors: the archbishops of three German cities and the rulers of four principalities. Three of the **prince electors** were German; the fourth was the king of Bohemia.

Although Charles's plan provided political stability to the civil war–prone empire, the permanent exclusion of certain princely families deepened resentments and competition among the German nobles that had already led to sporadic warfare. Charles's choice

of electors, however, had an unforeseen but timely impact on the empire's security. After deposing Charles's son and successor, the electors chose as emperor his grandson, Sigimund, king of Bohemia and Hungary in 1410, largely because his kingdom was viewed as the front line in the effort to hold back the Ottoman Turks, whose armies pushed the empire's eastern borders in the first half of the fifteenth century.

The Hanseatic League Although the system of prince electors offered some stability to the empire, merchants in German and Slavic territories competed fiercely over trade in Scandinavian and Baltic lands. In the final decades of the thirteenth century, guilds of German merchants with branch offices in England and Flanders joined with German merchants based in the Baltic and Scandinavian regions to form the Hanseatic League, a commercial association whose purpose was to provide its members with protection against piracy at sea and to regulate trade in German cities and in the Baltic states farther north. They specialized in the major commodities of the Baltic region, especially in fish, timber, and furs. Because public order was conducive to trade, league members served as city managers and police forces in the hundred-odd cities in which they were based during the fourteenth century. But the lack of centralization among the branches of the Hanseatic League led to their decline in the face of the growing power of the states around them, particularly to the east.

Poland and Lithuania On the eastern borders of the empire and the Hanseatic cities of Prussia lay Poland and, beyond it, Lithuania, whose duke, Jagiello, became king of Poland in 1386 when he married Poland's heiress to the throne, Jadwiga. Jagiello's conversion to the Roman church at his marriage ensured that the majority of Lithuanians adhered to the Roman Catholic Church rather than the Eastern Orthodox tradition. Although the two countries

Wars of the Roses Civil wars between the descendants of Edward III for the throne of England, 1455–1485.

Richard III (r. 1483–1485) King of England after his young nephew, Edward V, died in captivity; defeated and killed by Henry Tudor at the Battle of Bosworth Field.

Bosworth Field Battle in 1485 in which the Yorkist forces, led by the English king Richard III, were defeated by the Lancastrian faction commanded by Henry Tudor.

Henry VII (r. 1485–1509) First Tudor king of England, who ended the Wars of the Roses and consolidated royal power.

Tudor Dynastic family ruling England from 1485 to 1603.

Golden Bull Decree issued by Emperor Charles IV in 1356 that established the method for electing the Holy Roman emperor.

prince electors Noblemen and bishops with the hereditary right to elect the Holy Roman emperor.

were ruled by the same man, they did not merge into one kingdom. Within a generation, Poland had one grandson of Jagiello's as king and Lithuania had another as grand prince.

The power of conjoined Poland-Lithuania succeeded in defeating the military order of Teutonic Knights, the major competitor for conquering and ruling the unchristianized Baltic territory to the north. Based in Prussia, to the west of Poland and Lithuania, the order protected the Hanseatic cities and made incursions into Polish territory in an effort to claim land there. In 1410, Jagiello defeated the order in a battle that set back its efforts to occupy the northern parts of Lithuania. But it was only at the conclusion of a thirteen-year war in 1466 that the Teutonic Knights were finally and decisively defeated.

The Russian Principalities Even farther to the east, the grand prince of Moscow, **Basil I**, brought together Russian principalities under his rule by conquering his neighbors between 1392 and 1398. To discourage an invasion of his lands by the Mongol Empire of the Golden Horde—to whom he paid tribute to prevent just that possibility—he made an alliance with Lithuania in 1392. Within three years, a larger threat appeared on his eastern borders: Timur, the Tartar ruler, who attacked Basil's lands and inflicted even more damage on the Mongols. Basil's death in 1425 left his ten-year-old son, Basil II (r. 1425–1462), to defend his inheritance of his father's lands from his uncles. Political stability came to Basil's Russian lands only after decades of warfare against his uncles and cousins, the slow collapse of the Golden Horde, and, once Basil had died in 1462, the coming to power of his capable son, Ivan III. By the end of the fifteenth century, Basil's heirs had transformed Moscow into the strongest power in the east, beholden to no other.

Basil I (r. 1389–1425) Grand prince of Moscow who expelled the Mongols from Russia and maintained his independence from Lithuania.

Checking In

By yourself or with a partner, explain the significance of each of the following selected key terms:

Francis I	Tudor
Arthurian legends	Golden Bull
Thomas Malory	prince electors
Wars of the Roses	Basil I
Henry VII	

CHAPTER
Review

Summary

◆ Out of the long, bleak period of high mortality rates emerged a cultural movement that emphasized humanity's essential worth.

◆ Humanists, painters, sculptors, and architects celebrated mind and body in their work.

◆ In the birthplace of the long-gone Roman Republic, many scholars found a new inspiration that felt like a rebirth, a renaissance.

◆ The rediscovery of classical texts refreshed knowledge of a past world and stimulated a new type of critical textual analysis.

◆ Artisans strove to depict the human form in life-like dimensions, which included situating figures realistically within a painted scene. The skills required were more than those of a technician. It took an artist to render the soul in human form.

◆ In northern Europe scholars focused on the Bible and the writings of the church fathers.

◆ Humanists such as Erasmus came to believe that it was time to review the translations from Greek of the New Testament.

◆ The spread of printing presses across western Europe assisted the humanists in their goals. Communities of scholars now had identical texts to study.

◆ The Medici family of Florence, the republics of Venice and Genoa, and the Sforza family of Milan conducted campaigns of conquest and ruthlessly squashed republican sentiment.

◆ Francis I of France introduced many of the achievements of the Italian Renaissance and lured many of its artisans, like Leonardo, to follow him.

◆ The absorption of Renaissance ideals by the peoples of England, the Holy Roman Empire, and Russia occurred at a slower pace.

Chronology

1356	Emperor Charles IV issues Golden Bull	**1485**	William Caxton publishes Malory's *Le Morte D'Arthur;* Henry Tudor defeats Richard III of England
1362	Lithuanians capture Kiev	**1494**	Ludovico Sforza becomes duke of Milan; the Medici of Florence enter exile
1380	Venice and Genoa fight War of Chioggia		
1417	Great Schism ends		
1436	Brunelleschi's dome atop the cathedral of Florence is consecrated	**1496**	Savonarola assumes power in Florence
		1498	Savonarola is burned at the stake
1440	Lorenzo Valla refutes authenticity of Donation of Constantine	**1508**	Pope Julius II reconquers Papal States
1440s	Gutenberg invents printing press	**1508–1512**	Michelangelo paints ceiling of Sistine Chapel
1450	Francesco Sforza becomes duke of Milan	**1512**	Medici return to power
1455–1485	House of Lancaster and House of York fight Wars of the Roses	**1516**	Erasmus translates Greek New Testament into Latin; Leonardo settles in France
ca. 1455	Gutenberg Bible is published		
1470	Thomas Malory writes *Le Morte d'Arthur (The Death of Arthur)*	**1520**	Francis I becomes king of France
		1532	Publication of Machiavelli's *The Prince*
1478	Lorenzo de' Medici survives assassination attempt		

© Cengage Learning

CourseMate Visit the CourseMate website at **www.cengagebrain.com** for additional study tools and review materials for this chapter.

Test Yourself

To gauge your mastery of the material in this chapter, answer the questions below. More than one answer may be correct.

A New Climate of Cultural Expression

1. Petrarch is considered a humanist because:
   a. He was the first intellectual who questioned the existence of God.
   b. He wrote works that advanced a theory of human rights.
   c. He had a deep interest in the authors of Classical Rome such as Cicero.
   d. He denounced the cruel treatment of animals.
   e. He rejected intellectual work for mystical communion with God.

2. What contributions did refugees from Constantinople bring to Italian cities?
   a. The first copies of the Quran
   b. Copies of the Talmud
   c. Previously unknown letters of the Apostle Paul
   d. Icons that survived the period of Iconoclasm
   e. Ancient scientific texts of Plato, Aristotle, and others

3. Artists and architects in the Italian cities occupied a place in society much like:
   a. Master craftsmen and artisans
   b. Poorly paid unskilled workers
   c. University lecturers
   d. Highly esteemed and well-educated professionals
   e. Mercenaries

4. Filippo Brunelleschi was responsible for the architectural design of:
   a. St. Peter's in Rome
   b. Westminster Abbey in London
   c. The Coliseum in Rome
   d. The Palazzo de la Signoria in Florence
   e. Florence's duomo

5. When Italian painters used linear perspective in their work, they relied on what to convey depth and dimension?
   a. The vanishing point
   b. The frame of the painting
   c. An assumed stationary viewer
   d. Gradations of color
   e. Charcoal

Now that you have reviewed and tested yourself on this part of the chapter, take time to pull together all the important information by answering the following questions:

◆ How would you describe the differences the use of linear perspective would have made in a painting?

◆ Imagine and describe the rooms in which a well-to-do Florentine family lived in the fifteenth century. What furniture would they have?

The Northern European Renaissance

6. Italian artists relied on linear perspective to convey depth and dimension; what did Flemish painters use to achieve the same effect?

   a. Trick mirrors
   b. Gradations in color and light
   c. Tracery
   d. Tempura
   e. Brushwork

7. The humanists of northern Europe differed from those of the Italian peninsula in which ways?

   a. They were open to exploring whether God existed.
   b. They rejected as heretical classical texts in Greek and Latin.
   c. They did not differ.
   d. They did not believe in the worthiness of humanity.
   e. They maintained a closer relationship to the church and universities.

8. Erasmus issued a new translation of which work?

   a. The Hebrew Bible
   b. The Talmud
   c. Aristotle's *Politics*
   d. The Greek New Testament
   e. The Psalms

9. What is the kabbalah?

   a. A shrine in Mecca
   b. A collection of canon laws
   c. A Christian mystical text
   d. A Cathar mystical text
   e. A Jewish mystical text

10. The printing process that Gutenberg is believed to have invented depended on what prior condition for it to succeed?

    a. The ability to create small metal letters
    b. A reduction in the price of parchment and vellum
    c. The availability and low cost of paper
    d. A higher level of literacy throughout western Europe
    e. The importation of ancient Greek texts that suggested the idea

Now that you have reviewed and tested yourself on this part of the chapter, take time to pull together all the important information by answering the following questions:

◆ How would you describe the differences between the style of painting in northern Europe and the style of painting in Italian cities?

◆ Think about how handwritten manuscripts and printed books are produced. What consequences do you infer about the dissemination of knowledge from the way the two kinds of texts are made?

The Cities of Renaissance Italy

11. The Medici family dominated Florence through which means?

    a. Their monopoly of seats on the city councils
    b. Steady and generous donations to those less fortunate and a network of clients
    c. The maintenance of a private army ready to apply force
    d. Hereditary rule
    e. The support of the pope

12. The rivalry between Venice and Genoa culminated in which conflict?

   a. The War of the Roses
   b. The War of Calabria
   c. The Hundred Years' War
   d. The War of Chioggia
   e. The War of Otranto

13. In his work, *The Prince*, Niccolò Machiavelli offered what kind of advice?

   a. How rulers should govern, especially after seizing power
   b. How to prepare a royal son to rule
   c. How to dress and act in a ruler's court
   d. How to train the clergy to attend royal courts
   e. How to promote monarchy in a newly conquered territory

14. When Lorenzo Valla showed that the Donation of Constantine was a forgery, he undermined what claim by the pope?

   a. He was the head of the entire church.
   b. The bishopric of Rome dated back to the first century.
   c. The pope had the right to tax secular rulers.
   d. He was the temporal lord of central Italy.
   e. He had the right to the title of emperor in the west.

Now that you have reviewed and tested yourself on this part of the chapter, take time to pull together all the important information by answering the following questions:

◆ What factors contributed to making the cities of the northern Italian peninsula the most urban and economically powerful in western Europe?

◆ In what way did the rulers of northern Italian cities differ from monarchs? On what did their power depend?

Renaissance Ideals in Transition, 1400–1550

15. Where did King Francis I of France establish a court that rivaled the splendor of the Medici's in Florence?

   a. Faenza
   b. Fontainebleau
   c. Ferrara
   d. Firenze
   e. St. Foy

16. The War of the Roses was a conflict between which two branches of Edward III's descendants?

   a. York and Lancaster
   b. Clarence and Tudor
   c. Richmond and York
   d. Lancaster and Richmond
   e. Tudor and York

17. What was the Golden Bull?

   a. A statue that belonged to the papal treasury
   b. A papal letter claiming the pope's rights over central Italy
   c. The name of the vessel that carried Francis I back to France
   d. A decree that set out how the Papal States would be ruled
   e. A decree that established seven electors to elect the Holy Roman emperor

18. The dynasty ruling Poland-Lithuania defeated which rival in the competition to conquer the Baltic territories?

    a. The Knights Hospitallers
    b. The grand prince of Moscow
    c. The Vikings

    d. The Teutonic Knights
    e. Papal troops

19. What was the Golden Horde?

    a. A principality near Moscow
    b. Another name for the Mongol Empire that threatened the Russian principalities

    c. Another name for the Russian principalities
    d. Another name for the Baltic lands
    e. The nickname of a Russian dynasty

Now that you have reviewed and tested yourself on this part of the chapter, take time to pull together all the important information by answering the following questions:

◆ What factors played a part in the arrival of the Renaissance in England so much later than elsewhere in western Europe?

◆ What challenges did the powers in eastern Europe face?

CHAPTER 13

Europe's Age of Expansion, 1450–1550

1440	1450	1460	1470	1480	1490
1440s Gutenberg invents printing process		**1462** Ivan III becomes tsar	**1469** Marriage of Ferdinand of Aragon and Isabella of Castile		**1485** Henry VII becomes king of England	**1492** Columbus sets sail; Jews expelled from Spain

This seventeenth-century painting by an unknown Spanish artist depicts am Aztec ruler, perhaps Moctezuma, as he was imagined a century after his death. Images like these, based partly in fact and partly in fantasy, fascinated Europeans in the years after Columbus's voyages to the western hemisphere. (Museo degli Argenti, Palazzo Pitti, Florence/The Bridgeman Art Library)

After reading this chapter, you should be able to answer the following questions:

What were the causes and consequences of Europe's economic expansion after 1450?

What strategies did European rulers use to increase control over their territories?

How did Europe's economic expansion create a global economy?

What factors shaped the formation of Europeans' individual and collective identities and those of the peoples they encountered in global expansion?

EUROPE AFTER 1450 was bustling with renewed energy. The economic stagnation and population decline that had followed the trauma of the Black Death, the turmoil of the Hundred Years' War in France, and the Wars of the Roses in England was easing. By 1450, Europe's population was once again growing, and commerce revived. Both rural and urban dwellers profited from these upswings as increased demand for labor resulted in good wages, laying the foundation for an economically prosperous and expanding Europe.

The years after 1450 also saw a vigorous new generation of rulers in Spain, France, and England who consolidated state power and increased their control over their subjects, often with the help of new, professionally trained legal and financial experts.

At the same time, these rulers continued to fight wars that drained their treasuries and forced them to tax and borrow at unprecedented levels. These European states were stronger and more centralized in 1550 than they had been in 1450 and exercised increasingly effective control over their inhabitants.

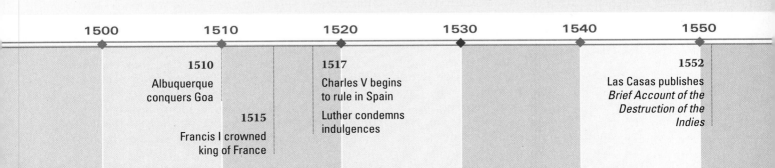

1500	1510	1520	1530	1540	1550

1510
Albuquerque conquers Goa

1515
Francis I crowned king of France

1517
Charles V begins to rule in Spain

Luther condemns indulgences

1552
Las Casas publishes *Brief Account of the Destruction of the Indies*

In other parts of Europe, however, especially in Germany and Italy, the trend was toward smaller regional states instead of large, centralized ones. In the east, the rulers of Moscow broke free from their Mongol overlords, conquered vast territories, and established a Russian empire that stretched from Poland to Siberia.

Europeans also extended their political and economic power over Africa, Asia, and the Americas. When the decline of the Mongol Empire disrupted Europe's land routes to Asia, the Portuguese sought new sea routes to the east and created a trading empire that stretched down the west coast of Africa, where they purchased gold and slaves.

The Portuguese also crossed the Indian Ocean to India and China, where they traded for spices, silks, and porcelain to sell in Europe. At the same time, they ventured to the Western Hemisphere, where they established a colonial empire in Brazil based on African slave labor.

The Spanish established an empire in the Caribbean, Mexico, and Peru that exploited the labor of Indians and then African slaves. Europe's territorial and economic expansion created the first global economy and turned many European states into colonial powers.

Global expansion also raised the troubling issue of the relation of Europeans to the non-European peoples encountered in imperial expansion. The peoples of Africa and the Americas experienced cataclysmic changes, but the century between 1450 and 1550 was, for Europeans, marked by economic, political, and territorial expansion. It was Europe's first modern age.

Economic and Social Change

◆ **What effects did the rise in population after 1450 have on rural and urban communities?**

◆ **How did the revival of the European economy affect the lives of men and women?**

From 1347 to 1351, between a third and a half of Europe's people died from the Black Death. For the next hundred years, population declined; outbreaks of plague, devastation caused by war, and failures of the grain harvest raised death rates to crisis levels and prevented a recovery. Then, about 1450, as plague, war, and famine subsided, the population once again started to grow. Population growth was also accompanied by an economic revival in both the countryside and towns.

Population Increase

Historians using the techniques of modern **demography** have determined that even in the good times after 1450, European death rates were shockingly high. Half the children born died before they reached their twenties. If a person made it to adulthood, however, the chances were good that he or she would live on for another thirty-five years. People over sixty, however, were rare, and the older they were, the stranger they were thought to be. Old people aroused fears: Why had they lived so long? Were they especially blessed by God, or (more likely!) had they made deals with the Devil?

No social or economic group escaped these high **mortality rates**. Death cut down the families of kings and queens along with those of their humblest

demography Statistical study of populations.

mortality rate The number of deaths per thousand in a given population.

Lands of Charles V, by 1556
France
England
Ottoman Empire
Boundary of the
Holy Round Empire

Map 13.1 **Europe in 1556** The political boundaries of Europe in the year of Emperor Charles V's abdication indicate the power of the Habsburgs. © *Cengage Learning*

1. Using the map legend, identify the states of western and central Europe.
2. In what ways do the size and location of the Habsburg lands suggest potential threats to the independence and stability of other European states?
3. Locate the following rivers and trace them from their beginning to their end: the Rhine, the Danube. Now locate Madrid, Antwerp, and Palos.

subjects, with no consideration of social distinctions or levels of wealth.

Prosperity, Marriage, and Population Growth

Once the crisis conditions in the century following the Black Death eased, the low population level created favorable economic conditions for those who had survived. Fewer people meant more available agricultural land, greater food supplies, and a higher demand for labor, which in turn produced higher wages.

These favorable economic conditions affected marriage rates. In the lands of the Roman Catholic

Peter Bruegel the Elder's *The Harvesters* (1556) captures the beauty of a good harvest. Grain stalks shimmer in the sun as men scythe them, while men and women bind them. Other workers take a meal under a tree. This painting presents a powerful image of agricultural abundance and human well-being.

Church, a distinctive marriage pattern had emerged by the mid-fifteenth century. Women married in their mid-twenties and men somewhat later, and about 10 percent of both men and women never married. This pattern contrasted with that of European Jews and Eastern Orthodox Christians, for whom marriage for women coincided with the onset of sexual maturity in the teenage years and was nearly universal.

The reason for late marriage and significant rates of celibacy among the Christians of western Europe lay in the expectation that people should marry only when they could afford to set up their own household. But it took time to establish economic independence, and some people never achieved it. After 1450, when land, food, and wages were abundant, more young people married and established their own households. When these better-fed, healthier people started their families, the **birthrate** rose in much of western Europe. The rise in marriage and birthrates caused an increase in Europe's population. In 1450, Europe's population was about 60 million. By 1550, it was nearly 69 million.

Recovery in the Countryside

In 1450, Europe was still an overwhelmingly agricultural society. Ninety percent of Europeans lived in rural areas, where they engaged in some kind of farming. As in the past, agriculture depended on unpredictable weather conditions that could lead to either abundant harvests or devastating crop failures. Yet despite the precarious nature of agricultural activity, times were good for rural people between 1450 and 1550.

Landlords and Peasants After the Black Death, when population fell and labor was scarce, landlords' power over their peasants often decreased. Serfdom

birthrate The number of live births per thousand in a given population.

virtually disappeared in western Europe, where it was replaced with communities of free peasants who either owned their land, rented it from their lords, or worked as wage laborers.

Below the lord was the peasants' **commune**, which set dates for planting crops and managed the meadows and woodlands belonging to the community as a whole. If the local lord tried to seize these common lands for his own use, the commune would organize villagers' resistance and even encourage riots in defense of them.

In eastern Europe, however, landlords successfully reimposed serfdom on their peasants, seizing peasant lands, setting heavy work requirements, and forbidding peasants to leave their estates. Landlords were able to do this because the kings and other rulers in the region supported their actions.

The Growth of a Market Economy In 1450, many rural communities were largely self-sufficient economically because they produced most of the food, clothing, and other basic necessities they needed. Over the next hundred years, however, many rural people sold their agricultural surplus and bought many goods they had previously produced for themselves. Thus, they became integrated into regional or international markets.

The growth of a market economy affected the value of people's economic activity. Previously, everything men and women did to maintain the material well-being of their families was considered work. With the growth of markets, however, the definition of work began to change. It was now defined simply as activity that produced goods for the market.

This narrower definition of work affected men and women differently. Because women's economic activity focused primarily on their households, they no longer "worked." They simply did "housekeeping." Men were the "workers" because they raised crops for the market.

The devaluation of women's traditional household work was accompanied by the belief that women were incapable of skilled work. They were thought to be too awkward or ignorant to do complicated jobs. Therefore, anything they did was, by definition, unskilled. In fact, however, much of their activity involved considerable skill. For example, many rural women made butter or cheese, but the skill involved was not recognized.

The same attitudes shaped men's and women's wages. At harvest time, when there was a high demand for labor in the fields, men were regularly paid twice what women were although they performed similar tasks.

Growth in the Cities

The developing market economy was also closely linked to the growth of cities. Beginning in 1450, Europe's cities grew until by 1550 about 10 percent of the total population lived in them.

Crowding and Filth Since most cities were surrounded by their old walls, the rise in population made them even more crowded. Houses were crammed next to each other, and streets were full of garbage. Sometimes garbage was dumped into wells, canals, or the local river, polluting the city's water supply, while at others it was piled just outside the city walls. These garbage piles could become so high that they threatened the city's defenses because they could be used for scaling the walls.

Human excrement also presented problems. Feces were placed next to front doors for sale to manure peddlers, who used them to fertilize nearby fields. Urine was sometimes collected in barrels outside leather shops, where it was used in the tanning process. All this waste created a huge stench; often travelers could smell a city long before they could see it.

Overcrowding and filth also led to high urban disease and death rates. Throughout the sixteenth century, cities could never sustain their population levels but relied on a continuous stream of migrants from the countryside. Because of Europe's expanding population, the stream never dried up.

The Urban Community Although cities were crowded and dirty, their inhabitants thought of them as organic wholes whose well-being depended on the harmonious interaction of all the people living in them. It was therefore the responsibility of the well-off to care for the needy by founding hospitals, orphanages, and homes for the elderly.

Men's work in sixteenth-century cities can be classified into four categories. Some men turned agricultural products such as grain into food such as bread, the basic element in the urban diet. Bread was such a basic necessity that urban governments strictly regulated its price and tried to assure its availability in times of grain shortages because they feared riots if the supply gave out.

Other men manufactured cloth and leather goods for clothing. Still others were engaged in construction. With urban populations growing and more buildings under construction, these men were in constant demand. Finally, some men made household furnishings or fashioned the tools that builders used.

Guilds: The Backbone of Society The most prestigious workers in a city, such as weavers of fine woolen or silk cloth or workers in gold, were organized into guilds. Guilds had originated in the Middle Ages but were in their heyday from 1450 to 1550. Like society at large, the guilds

commune An association of peasants supervising and coordinating the collective life of their village.

were organized on hierarchical lines; the men admitted to them were divided into masters, journeymen, and apprentices. Journeymen hoped someday to be admitted to the ranks of the masters, but often they were not because masters worked to keep their membership limited.

Guilds had originated as social clubs for artisans, providing opportunities for drinking and offering protection from a saint adopted as the guild's patron. In the sixteenth century, these older functions were still important, but the guild's main purpose was to regulate the manufacture of specific goods for the marketplace.

Membership in a guild was a prized source of male identity, and members proclaimed their skills and the perfection of their products. They thought of themselves as the backbone of the urban world and were concerned with maintaining an honorable position in society. To this end they carefully policed themselves, punishing the wayward for indecent or immoral behavior. Also, in line with the idea that the community should function as a harmonious whole, the guilds were required by law to maintain the quality of their products in the interests of consumer protection.

Women's Work Guild work was considered skilled and, therefore, usually open only to men. In the Middle Ages, a few women had participated in guilds, but after 1500, most lost their place in them. As in the countryside, most women were confined to housekeeping or low-paid work.

Women did, however, have a significant role in retail trade, operating stalls in marketplaces and serving as city-appointed officers to certify weights, measures, and grain quality. They also worked as seamstresses and lace makers, skilled activities that, like butter and cheese making, were usually undervalued and poorly paid.

Many women spun thread for weaving. Spinning was the slowest process in cloth production, and the need for spinners rose dramatically as weavers tried to meet the growing demand for cloth from a rising population. In the countryside, both men and women worked as spinners. In cities, however, men avoided this occupation as too low paying.

One group did break through the restrictions on women's economic activity—widows. A widowed woman could step in as the head of her dead husband's business and run it on her own. But if she remarried, or had male children who wanted to take it over, she usually returned to a subordinate economic position. Finally, prostitution was the one occupation always open to women. Because it dishonored her, a woman usually chose it only when nothing else was available.

Antwerp City in the Netherlands that functioned in the first half of the sixteenth century as Europe's main trading center.

The Port of Antwerp

Although cities all over Europe were growing, none could rival **Antwerp** in wealth and importance. Located at the western end of the North Sea, Antwerp was an ideal transfer point for the east-west trade that moved through the English Channel and the North Sea to the Baltic Sea. It was also a transfer point between northern Europe, the Iberian Peninsula, and the Mediterranean.

By 1500, Antwerp was the most important commercial center in Europe. With its rise, European trade networks shifted northward, from the Mediterranean. Although Italian cities and merchants continued to play a central role in European trade, Mediterranean cities would never again dominate it.

A Global Trading Center The wharves of Antwerp were piled high with goods from Europe and Asia. One hundred thousand pieces of English woolen cloth were imported each year, and the city was ringed with huge bleaching vats preparing the cloth for finishing in the city's cloth guilds. Spain also sent its prized wool north for spinning and weaving.

Next to the bales of cloth and wool were sacks of wheat, along with wood for urban construction and shipyards, all from eastern Germany and Poland. The sixteenth-century population surge turned eastern Europe into a major supplier of grain and timber for the west.

Bars of copper and silver from mines in south Germany were securely locked away in Antwerp's warehouses, awaiting the arrival of Portuguese ships laden with spices brought around the southern tip of Africa from India and Southeast Asia. The metals would be exchanged for cinnamon, nutmeg, and pepper, and then exported to the Far East where they would pay for another cargo of spices.

Vaults also held chests of diamonds waiting to be cut and sold. Over a thousand representatives of foreign trading companies jostled each other on the city's streets as they inspected cargoes and bargained over prices. In 1500, Antwerp boasted a population of over 100,000, making it one of Europe's largest cities.

The complex trade networks converging on Antwerp, involving thousands of merchant businesses spread over long distances, stimulated the development of the banking and credit networks, developed in the twelfth century, through which traders avoided the inconvenience of hauling about large sums of coins to cover their transactions. Instead, merchants signed notes promising payment from money kept at home. If a merchant's reputation was good, the notes would be accepted as a kind of paper money. The use of these notes laid the foundations for modern banking practices. Because Antwerp was the center for both inter-European and Far Eastern

Musées Royaux des Beaux-Arts de Belgique

How does this painting of Antwerp by an unknown artist from the Netherlands create a picture of the city as Europe's leading commercial center in the sixteenth century?

trade, it functioned as a center of exchange for an emerging world economy.

 Checking In

By yourself or with a partner, explain the significance of each of the following selected key terms:

demography   commune

mortality rate   Antwerp

birthrate

Resurgent Monarchies

◆ **What steps did rulers take to strengthen their realms?**

◆ **What role did religion play in the advancement of royal authority?**

While Europe's population and economy were expanding after 1450, new, energetic rulers extended their control over their subjects and centralized their governments. Civil wars were brought to an end, state control of justice increased, new officials enforced government decrees, and new sources of revenue were created. Above all, a period of warfare erupted in Italy, where the rulers of Spain and the Holy Roman Empire fought the kings of France for control of the peninsula.

Ferdinand and Isabella and the Rise of Spain

In 1469, **Isabella of Castile**, aged eighteen, married the seventeen-year-old **Ferdinand of Aragon**. Their kingdoms shared the Iberian Peninsula with Muslim **Granada** and Christian Portugal and Navarre, and neither was a first-rate state. Moreover, on Ferdinand and Isabella's wedding day, their kingdoms were torn apart by civil war as great nobles challenged the young monarchs' rule. Yet the marriage of these two teenagers laid the foundations for a spectacular rise in the power of Spain.

Consolidating Royal Rule Within ten years, Ferdinand and Isabella had secured their rule, embarking on a tireless campaign of travel and direct appearances and relying on the persuasive power of face-to-face meetings with their unruly subjects. In early modern Europe, kings and queens, God's appointed rulers, were bathed in a sacred aura. As a result, even the most rebellious subjects could be coaxed into obedience when brought personally before the monarch.

The two rulers shrewdly calculated that their success depended as much on

Isabella of Castile (r. 1474–1504) and **Ferdinand of Aragon** (r. 1479–1516) Rulers who launched Spain's rise as a major European power in control of a vast overseas empire.

Granada Last Muslim state on the Iberian Peninsula, conquered by Ferdinand and Isabella in 1492.

negotiation with their people and respect for each kingdom's traditional political institutions as it did on a show of royal grandeur. Thus they did not try to fuse Aragon and Castile into a single monarchy but respected the political independence of each kingdom.

In Aragon, Ferdinand accepted traditions that made him a limited, constitutional monarch. In Castile, the larger and more populous kingdom, he and Isabella took specific measures to strengthen royal power. The nobility was confirmed in its privileges and landed estates, and new titles of nobility were awarded to men who cooperated with the monarchs. At the same time, powerful but rebellious nobles were excluded from a direct role in government.

Lawyers and Taxes Rebellious nobles were replaced by lesser nobles or commoners. These men were more dependent on royal favor for their success than the great nobles. Many had been trained as lawyers. Their legal training gave them orderly habits of mind and a commitment to carefully defined routines for state administration that made the monarchy more efficient.

One of the first benefits of this rule of orderly lawyers was a more effective collection of royal taxes. Isabella and Ferdinand also worked out a policy of cooperation with the towns of Castile. They knew that they were tightly knit communities, jealous of their traditions and suspicious of outsiders who might upset them. Painstaking negotiation in the interests of peace after civil war was the way to bring them into working relations with the royal government. The monarchs also revived urban police forces to clear the country of bandits and established a workable local judicial system.

The War with Granada and the Expulsion of the Jews In 1482, Ferdinand and Isabella went to war with Granada, the last Muslim kingdom on the Iberian Peninsula, using the revitalized urban police forces as their army. In 1492, when Granada fell, the centuries-long Christian Reconquista of the Iberian Peninsula was complete.

The fall of Granada coincided with a new Spanish policy of religious intolerance. In the spring of 1492, Isabella and Ferdinand decreed that Jews were to convert to Christianity or leave their kingdoms. A century earlier, anti-Jewish riots had provoked mass conversions to Christianity.

New Christians/Conversos Jews whom the state forced to convert to Christianity or face persecution and expulsion from Spanish territory.

Spanish Inquisition Church court originally established to try New Christians suspected of observing their old Jewish practices in secret.

Moriscos Muslims in Spain who were forced to convert to Christianity or leave.

But these **New Christians**, or **Conversos**, were often accused of secretly holding to their old Jewish ways. In response, the monarchs created the **Spanish Inquisition**, a church court authorized to examine Conversos about the genuineness of their Christian faith. Over the next dozen years, hundreds of them failed to prove their sincerity and were burned alive as heretics.

Then, in 1491, news of a supposed atrocity swept across Castile. Some New Christians and unconverted Jews were accused of murdering a Christian boy and ripping out his heart for use in magic. A story like this was a standard element in late medieval Christian attacks on Jews, and in 1491 it led to the execution of the accused men, despite the fact that no one reported a missing child. Faced with rising anti-Jewish passions, some Jews responded in kind, repeating old arguments that Christians' souls were created by the Devil.

It was against this background that Ferdinand and Isabella ordered the forced conversion or expulsion of all remaining Jews. About fifty thousand converted, while some forty thousand fled to Portugal, Italy, and North Africa. Many of these refugees eventually returned and submitted to baptism. Thus the edict eliminated Jewish communities but greatly increased the number of New Christians, who continued to be accused of half-hearted conversion.

The Jews who had fled to Portugal were expelled from that kingdom in 1497. Some then moved to Antwerp, where they established a thriving merchant community that prospered from the revival of European commerce. In 1494, Pope Alexander VI proclaimed Ferdinand and Isabella "Catholic Rulers" in recognition of their efforts to suppress non-Christian religions.

The Expulsion of the Muslims Finally, between 1500 and 1502, all remaining Muslims in Granada and Castile were also ordered to convert to Christianity or leave. Some, like the Jews, became Christians. But these **Moriscos** were no more well received than the Conversos, and the sincerity of their conversions was also questioned. Most who left went to North Africa. The forced conversion or expulsion of Jews and Muslims ended the religious pluralism and cultural diversity of Castile and Aragon. The war against Granada had united Castilians and Aragonese in a common Spanish crusade. The expulsion of the Jews and Muslims created a new, exclusively Christian Spanish identity.

Marriage Plans As they consolidated their power and promoted a new identity among their subjects, Ferdinand and Isabella searched for a husband for their eldest surviving child, Joan. They found an ideal match in the son of the Holy Roman emperor, Philip the Handsome. Joan brought Castile, Aragon,

Granada, Naples, Sicily, and Sardinia to the marriage, while Philip brought the **Habsburg** family's land of Austria along with the Netherlands. Theirs was the royal wedding of the century. All that was needed was a child who would inherit this vast collection of territories.

Charles I of Spain, Charles V of the Holy Roman Empire

That child was born in 1500 and named Charles. Charles spent his early years in the Netherlands, where Joan moved after her wedding. A sickly boy, he inherited from his father a large lower jaw that stuck out beyond the upper one and made it difficult to chew food. This "Habsburg jaw" continued to be passed on in the family and can be seen in many paintings of Habsburg rulers, despite artists' attempt to downplay it. In 1517, after the death of his father and grandfather, Charles journeyed for the first time to Spain, where he was to rule as Charles I in place of Joan, who had developed mental problems that prevented her from governing. Charles quickly made Spain his primary place of residence, spending more time there than in his other lands.

The Habsburg Empire The lands Charles inherited rivaled Charlemagne's empire in size, but they were never a united state. Like Ferdinand and Isabella, Charles recognized the political independence of each, respecting its local laws and traditions. Also, like his grandparents, he realized the importance of appearing personally before his subjects. But he ruled over so many lands that he could never be in one of them long enough to satisfy people's desire to see him. This was a constant source of friction. "My life," he complained, "has been one long journey." The journeys became even more frequent in 1519, when he was elected Holy Roman emperor on the death of his paternal grandfather, the emperor Maximilian. In the empire he was called **Charles V**. Although Charles never united his territories into a single state, he did develop a common policy for them by consolidating his rule in each and making sure that none worked at cross-purposes with the others.

This portrait of Emperor Charles V by the Venetian painter Titian (1548) presents him as a warrior, a convention for depicting rulers that stretches back to the pharaohs of ancient Egypt. Charles's forceful gaze, the horse's prancing and fine plumes, and the thrusting lance all point to the Emperor's might. What effect does Titian's choice of a side view of Charles gazing off to the right have on the viewer of this portrait? What would change if the viewer saw the horse and emperor head on?

Museo Nacional del Prado, Madrid/The Bridgeman Art Library

Warfare and Mercenary Armies Coordinating a common policy became particularly important during the long wars with France over Italy, where his role as Holy Roman emperor, along with his inherited lands in southern Italy, made him a central player. For sixty-five years, France and Spain fought for control of the Italian peninsula.

These wars were costly, and they were only one series of Charles's wars. By 1500, Europe's rulers faced a new military world.

Habsburgs Dynastic family originating in Austria that provided many rulers there, and also in the Netherlands, Spain, and the Holy Roman Empire.

Charles V (r. 1516–1556) Heir of Ferdinand and Isabella in Spain and of the emperor Maximilian in the Holy Roman Empire; the most powerful European ruler during the first half of the sixteenth century.

To win a war, it was necessary to fight with the best military forces, and that meant hiring **mercenary armies**. The medieval feudal armies were overmatched by the highly trained soldiers who made warfare their permanent profession. Moreover, weapons technology had changed with the introduction of gunpowder from China, brought west by Arab traders, which made bows and arrows obsolete. But mercenaries and firearms were expensive, and state budgets strained to finance them.

Financing Warfare For his Italian wars, Charles managed to field an army of 150,000 men, the largest Europe had ever seen, but he had to scramble to find ways to pay for it. One way was to push heavily on traditional sources of income such as sales taxes and grants from representative assemblies of subjects like the Castilian **Cortes**. Gold also started to pour in from the Caribbean after Spanish conquests there. But taxes and **New World** wealth never provided enough, so Charles sold **Crown lands**. This was still not enough. So Charles turned to borrowing and contracted ever-larger debts in the form of **annuities**—long-term loans that guaranteed an annual payment to the lender.

Annuities turned out to be the way that cash-hungry sixteenth-century states managed to meet their financial obligations. The success of annuities depended on two things: the availability of lenders and the recruitment of managers to supervise states' growing indebtedness. The demographic and economic expansion of Europe from 1450 to 1550 ensured the former; prosperous times put money in the pockets of many people who then looked for relatively safe ways to invest it. Lending to a state seemed one way. Charles borrowed from bankers in Germany and the Netherlands who were financing the growing trade networks centered on Antwerp, the prize jewel in his inheritance. He also turned to individual subjects who had money to invest.

The rise of a professionally trained class of bureaucrats began with Ferdinand and Isabella's lawyers. Under Charles, men with expert skills were recruited to collect taxes more efficiently. Increasingly, trained managers supervised governments' growing debts and oversaw the new complexity of state borrowing in a time of escalating military costs. Borrowing from banks and subjects turned Charles, and other rulers who did the same, into royal credit risks whose credit ratings were closely watched by would-be lenders.

The Reign Comes to an End By 1550, Charles V was growing weary of rule. He had been personally involved in the Italian and French wars for thirty years. Moreover, the political and religious situation in the Holy Roman Empire was becoming destabilized with the rise of **Protestantism**. He suffered from gout and insomnia. During the sleepless nights, he tinkered with his collection of clocks, taking them apart and reassembling them over and over again. He sank into depression and wept like a child. Finally, in 1556, he decided to abdicate. He granted the position of emperor and his Austrian lands to his younger brother, Ferdinand. His son Philip received the Netherlands, the Italian possessions, the Spanish states, and Spain's vast new overseas empire. Charles then retired to a monastery in southwestern Spain, where he died in 1558.

Francis I and the Kingdom of France

In 1500, the French state, like Spain, was undergoing profound transformations. The Hundred Years' War had strengthened the French monarchy, which now possessed a regular source of revenue from the *taille* tax, a permanent royal army, and the beginnings of a state bureaucracy staffed by experts. But France was fragmented. Although the English had been driven out, except for a toehold around Calais, large swaths of territory, each ruled by a branch of the extended royal family, functioned as virtually independent units within the theoretically unified kingdom. Over the second half of the fifteenth century, however, these branches died out, their lands reverted to the Crown, and the amount of territory directly ruled over by the king almost doubled between 1450 and 1500. Habsburg lands had grown as a result of spectacularly successful marriages; the French state grew as a result of lucky deaths.

Francis I, who ruled from 1515 to 1547, was the most vigorous of the newly powerful French kings. His court was famous for its Renaissance culture. Like Charles V, he traveled throughout his realm, showing himself to his subjects and thereby cementing his rule. Unlike Charles, however, he ruled over a more unified state because political centralization had increased when each previously independent territory reverted to direct royal rule.

mercenary armies Skilled professional armies under the command of generals who sold their services to European rulers.

Cortes In Castile, a representative assembly of Isabella's subjects that advised the queen and negotiated over taxes.

New World Term that Europeans used to refer to the Americas.

Crown lands Lands owned by a ruler as his or her family estate.

annuities Long-term loans to European states guaranteeing an annual interest payment to the lender.

Protestantism Beliefs and practices of Christians who broke with the Roman Church in the sixteenth century.

taille French royal tax first levied during the Hundred Years' War.

Francis I (r. 1515–1547) King of France who centralized royal rule, created at his court a vibrant Renaissance culture, and unsuccessfully fought Charles V for control of Italy.

Reform in the Royal Courts To further this new centralization, Francis ordered all courts, except church ones, to use the French dialect of Paris in their proceedings. Because this French was only one of several dialects spoken at the time, the edict promoted a single common language for use in public affairs throughout the kingdom. At the same time, French nobles stopped using their local dialects and started to speak the refined French of Francis's royal court. The growing use of standardized French, along with political centralization, created a new national identity for the people of the kingdom that slowly replaced older identities rooted in local customs and dialects.

King and Pope Francis also increased royal power when he signed a **concordat** with Pope Leo X in 1516 that gave the king the right to nominate candidates for hundreds of high offices in the French church, thereby increasing the Crown's control of church personnel. In return, Francis repudiated the earlier French position that the pope was subject to the authority of general church councils and recognized him as the supreme head of the Roman Church. Having reestablished good relations with the papacy, the king was now free to pursue his military ambitions in Italy.

The Italian Wars By 1519, when Charles V had inherited the lands ruled over by his two grandfathers, Francis had one great fear: the Habsburgs. From the northeast to the southwest, wherever he looked beyond French borders, he saw Habsburg lands. Francis had tried to break Habsburg power by bribing the imperial electors in the Holy Roman Empire to choose him as emperor, but Charles was the grandson of the emperor Maximilian, and he had bribed the electors as well.

Francis then turned to Italy and tried to make good the French claims to Milan and Naples. But he fared poorly, being captured on a battlefield and taken as a prisoner to Madrid. As the price for his freedom, he was forced to sign a humiliating peace in which he repudiated all his Italian claims and promised Charles the duchy of Burgundy, one of the territories that had reverted to the French Crown.

Back in Paris, Francis repudiated the peace and laid plans to continue the fight. Charles's victories in Italy had created a backlash that allowed Francis to form an anti-Spanish alliance with a number of Italian rulers, including the pope. Then in 1527, Charles won another victory when Spanish and German mercenary armies descended on Rome and sacked the city. Charles's reputation suffered badly from his troops' brutality, and he took his anger out on Francis, proposing, unrealistically, that the two should meet in a duel to settle their dispute.

After 1527, Francis continued the fight against the Habsburgs, but his strategy changed. Now Charles faced the threat of an expanding Protestant movement in the empire and the Netherlands. Although he was no friend of the Protestants in France, Francis allied with the German Protestants and then with the Ottoman Turks in his attempts to weaken Habsburg power. Francis's foreign policy undermined the medieval notion that Europe was held together by a common Catholic Christian faith. Now, it seemed, it was composed of a number of independent states, each of which advanced its own interests without regard to religious allegiance.

Henry II In 1547, Francis died, aged fifty-three and wracked by syphilis, a new disease from America. He was succeeded by his son, **Henry II**, who ruled until 1559.

Although the king was new, French policy remained the same, and Henry continued the war against the Habsburgs. Finally, in 1559, the French and the Spanish signed the **Peace of Cateau-Cambrésis**, which brought the long conflict to an end. The French renounced claims in Italy and ceded some territory to Spain. This settlement caused a good deal of grumbling among powerful French nobles who had shed their blood over three generations on behalf of the "king's just cause" in Italy. Henry, however, ordered festivities to celebrate the peace and participated in one of them, a joust in which men on horseback holding lances charged each other in hopes of dismounting their opponent. As the king's opponent made contact with him, his lance shot into a slit in the king's helmet and pierced his eye. Ten days later Henry was dead.

Consolidation in England Under the First Tudors

Defeat in the Hundred Years' War forced England's kings, for the first time in four hundred years, to confine their rule to their island possessions, except for the French port city of Calais. In 1485, when the Wars of the Roses ended with the death in battle of Richard III, **Henry VII** ascended the throne as the first king of a new royal dynasty, the Tudors. Like his counterparts in Spain and France, Henry embarked on a policy of consolidating royal power. Henry, a Lancastrian, also united Lancastrian and Yorkist factions by marrying Elizabeth of York in 1486.

A Homegrown King The Tudors' roots lay in Wales, a semi-independent territory

concordat Formal agreement between a pope and a ruler of a Catholic state.

Henry II (r. 1547–1559) French king who pursued Francis I's wars in Italy.

Peace of Cateau-Cambrésis (1559) Treaty that ended the Spanish and French war for the control of Italy and established Spanish dominance there.

Henry VII (r. 1485–1509) First Tudor king of England, who ended the Wars of the Roses and consolidated royal power.

under English rule. Henry emphasized his Welsh heritage and presented himself as a truly homegrown ruler, the first since the Norman Conquest in 1066. In the year he became king, Sir Thomas Malory's *Le Morte d'Arthur* was published, recounting the legends about the Welsh king Arthur and his Knights of the Round Table. Drawing on them, Henry named his first son Arthur to emphasize his ancient British background. When Arthur was of age, Henry arranged his marriage to Catherine of Aragon, the younger daughter of Ferdinand and Isabella, to forge a Spanish alliance against England's old enemy, France.

Henry ruled in conjunction with the Parliament, which had gained power during the Hundred Years' War by granting the king taxes to pay for his military expenses. Like Ferdinand and Isabella with the towns of Castile, Henry coaxed the Parliament to cooperate in consolidating the new dynasty.

Henry became king at a particularly favorable time. England, like the rest of Europe, was experiencing demographic expansion and economic growth. Its heartland, the southeast, centered on London, was bustling with agricultural and commercial activity as population rose and ships loaded with wool crossed the North Sea to Antwerp.

Henry took advantage of prosperous times to increase his royal income. He confiscated the property of his opponents in the Wars of the Roses and then made sure his new estates produced maximum revenue. Yet more money came from import and export fees, which rose with expanding overseas trade. The administration of justice also produced revenue because courts charged fees and levied fines. Henry established a series of judicial councils that operated with streamlined rules and speedy efficiency. Understandably, they were popular with his subjects because they offered justice more quickly than older courts bogged down in top-heavy procedures.

England, Scotland, and Ireland Perhaps Henry VII's most important achievement was his imposition of English power on the other parts of the British Isles—Scotland and Ireland. Although Scotland was an independent kingdom, English kings had tried for centuries to bind it closely to their realm. Henry continued this policy by arranging for the marriage of his daughter, Margaret, to the Scots king, a marriage that laid the foundation for a union of the two kingdoms under a single ruler.

Ireland had been under English rule since the twelfth century, when the pope had confirmed Henry II as its lord. In fact, effective English control was confined only to the area around Dublin. But even this area had slipped from the English during the Hundred Years' War and

Henry VIII (r. 1509–1547) King who consolidated Tudor rule over the British Isles and, breaking with the pope over his divorce, launched the English Reformation.

the Wars of the Roses. During his reign, Henry reestablished royal control there.

Henry VIII In 1509, Henry VII died and was succeeded by his younger son, **Henry VIII**, as Arthur had also died. Henry VIII had married Arthur's widow, Catherine of Aragon, to keep his father's Spanish alliance intact. He had to obtain a special papal dispensation to do so because the church forbade marriage between a widow and her brother-in-law. Henry VIII wanted the marriage with Catherine for dynastic reasons: Catherine's chief job was to produce a male heir to the throne. At this she failed; she gave birth to only one child who survived infancy, and it was a daughter, Mary.

The Break with the Pope By the late 1520s, Henry was convinced that Catherine could no longer conceive and sought an annulment of his marriage. Eventually, in the 1530s, Henry broke with the pope over the issue. He forbade papal control of the church in England, got Parliament to approve his divorce from Catherine of Aragon, and married a new wife, Anne Boleyn, the second of six, as it turned out.

Political Centralization and Cultural Unification Like his father, Henry VIII expanded English control over the rest of the British Isles. He abolished Wales' semi-independent status and gave it seats in the English Parliament and got the Irish parliament in Dublin to decree that Ireland was an independent kingdom ruled by the king of England.

England's political control of ever-larger parts of the British Isles was accompanied by a growing cultural dominance as the English dialect of the court and the southeast spread throughout the Tudor realm. The rise of English was partly the result of a new literature, like Malory's Arthurian legends, which was printed in London and distributed throughout the kingdom. English was also spread by men graduating from the country's two universities, Cambridge and Oxford, which started to use it instead of Latin.

The introduction of an English prayer book in churches after Henry VIII's break with Rome spread the use of the language even more. Political centralization and cultural unification laid the foundations for a new English identity that would develop fully during the long reign of Henry VIII's daughter Elizabeth I.

From 1450 to 1550, the monarchs of Spain, France, and England embarked on a policy of consolidating their political power at home by ending civil wars and strengthening royal government. If they fought foreign wars, they faced financial strains that forced them to search for new sources of revenue. The most important source came from borrowing. As a result, a new group of state creditors emerged in Europe. The management of strengthened royal governments

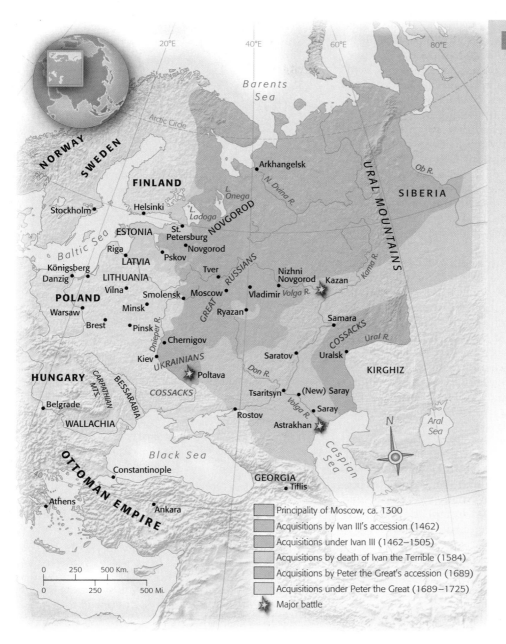

Map 13.2 **The Expansion of Russia, to 1725** From its beginnings as the small Principality of Moscow, Russia expanded to become one of the world's largest states. The acquisitions of Ivan III and Ivan the Terrible made Russia both a European and a central Asian power.
© *Cengage Learning*

1. Consult the legend and identify the stages of Russian expansion.
2. At what point would you say Russia became a significant Asian power?
3. At what point did Russia become a significant European power?

Legend:
- Principality of Moscow, ca. 1300
- Acquisitions by Ivan III's accession (1462)
- Acquisitions under Ivan III (1462–1505)
- Acquisitions by death of Ivan the Terrible (1584)
- Acquisitions by Peter the Great's accession (1689)
- Acquisitions under Peter the Great (1689–1725)
- ✦ Major battle

and complex state finances fell increasingly on a new class of legally trained experts, often of non-noble birth. Finally, these states created new forms of collective identity for their subjects based on a common religion or a common language. As these developments took place, the older ideal of Europe united into one community, Christendom, gave way to a new reality, a Europe made up of independent states whose ambitions often brought them into armed conflict with one another.

Italy, Germany, and Russia

By 1550, large centralized states covered parts of Europe, but other parts continued to be characterized by political fragmentation. Chief among them were Italy and Germany.

Political Fragmentation: Italy In 1450, the Italian peninsula was dominated by five states: Milan, Venice, Tuscany, the Papal States, and the kingdom of Naples. In 1559, when the French and Spanish wars in Italy ended, Spain controlled Milan in the north and the kingdom of Naples in the south and thereby exercised the greatest influence over the peninsula as a whole, but the other states maintained their political independence. Thus regionalism, rather than centralization, characterized the political life of the peninsula for the next three hundred years.

Political Fragmentation: Germany Germany was even more politically fragmented. In theory, the Holy Roman Empire bound all of north-central Europe into a single state. But Emperor Charles IV's Golden Bull of 1356 had given the imperial electors a good deal of political independence, which was gradually claimed by the other rulers of the empire's more than three thousand separate territories, some large and powerful like Saxony or Bavaria, others comprising only a few acres. The Protestant Reformation of the sixteenth century added religious fragmentation to the previously existing political decentralization as the empire's states split into hostile Protestant and Catholic camps. As in Italy, regionalism was to characterize German political life until the nineteenth century.

Ivan III and the Emergence of Russia In far eastern Europe, the decline of the Mongol Empire allowed peoples under Mongol rule to assert their independence. In 1462, the grand prince of Moscow, **Ivan III the Great**, began to consolidate power in a centralized Russian state. Ivan, who married the niece of the last Byzantine emperor, took the title of **tsar**, the Russian form of caesar, to proclaim that he was the successor of the Byzantine emperors, whose court ceremonial he adopted. Moscow was to be the "Third Rome," succeeding Old Rome and Constantinople, now in Muslim hands.

In 1478, Ivan conquered the city of Novgorod and more than doubled his territory as Novgorod ruled lands that stretched east to the **Ural Mountains**. In 1480, he refused to pay tribute to the khanate of the Golden Horde and thereby formally declared Moscow's independence from Mongol rule.

Consolidating the State Ivan III's conquests required a large army to defend his territories. He therefore expanded the army by awarding new soldiers grants of land in return for military service. He also resettled large numbers of landlords: men from Novgorod were moved into older Russian lands, and men from those lands were awarded land in Novgorod. This shift in elite populations lowered the chance of resistance to Ivan's rule by cutting landlords' ties with their old regional power bases while creating clusters of landlord elites in new territories, where they administered justice and collected taxes.

This anonymous portrait of Ivan the Terrible employs traditions of Russian religious art to depict the tsar. The text around his head and the stylized hair and beard echo the icons found in Russian churches. The artist's use of icon techniques is a way of depicting Ivan's majesty and divinely sanctioned rule. Compare this picture of a ruler to that of Charles V on page 377. What is similar and what is different?

Throughout his reign, Ivan increased the tax burden of his subjects, starting a trend that continued into the sixteenth century. In fact, the government was so aggressive in raising taxes that it exhausted the ability of its subjects to pay.

The Rise of Serfdom By the late sixteenth century, landlords and their peasants had started to flee east and south into frontier lands in hopes of a better life. The state responded by ordering peasants to remain where they were to guarantee landlords a workforce for their estates. The result was to turn more and more Russian peasants into serfs bound to the land.

Raising armies, administering justice, and collecting taxes were tasks like those of the centralized monarchies of western Europe. But Ivan's wholesale resettlement of landlords involved governmental interference in the lives of elite subjects that was unlike anything done in the west.

Ivan IV the Terrible In 1533, Ivan III's grandson, **Ivan IV the Terrible**, became tsar. He continued his grandfather's policy of territorial conquest when he marched southeast to the Volga River to seize Mongol **Kazan** and **Astrakhan**. During his reign, Russians also started crossing the Urals to establish settlements in western Siberia.

Ivan III the Great (r. 1462–1505) Grand prince of Moscow who conquered lands, took the title of tsar, and established a centralized state.

tsar (in Russian, "caesar") Title taken by the early consolidators of a unified Russian state.

Ural Mountains Mountain range marking the border between the European and Asian parts of Eurasia.

Ivan IV the Terrible (r. 1533–1584) Ruler of Russia and conqueror of Mongol Kazan and Astrakhan along the Volga River, southeast of Moscow.

Kazan and **Astrakhan** Mongol khanates along the Volga River conquered by Ivan the Terrible.

When Ivan IV died, the tsar ruled over vast, culturally diverse lands. The northern peoples and those in western Siberia were non-Russians who spoke their own distinct languages and worshiped local, non-Christian gods. The people of the center were Slavs who had converted to Orthodox Christianity, and the peoples of the south, in the former Mongol lands, were either Muslims or pagans.

The tsars' policy was to respect these religious differences. Although they were Orthodox Christian in religion, and claimed descent from the Christian rulers of Kiev and Constantinople, Ivan III and his successors officially forbade the Orthodox Church from systematic missionary activity among the non-Christian peoples of the emerging Russian Empire. This policy contrasted sharply with that adopted farther west by Ferdinand and Isabella of Spain.

 Checking In

By yourself or with a partner, explain the significance of each of the following selected key terms:

Ferdinand and Isabella	Francis I
Granada	Henry VII
Charles V	Ivan III the Great
annuities	Ivan IV the Terrible

Europe's Global Expansion

- ◆ **What were the motivations of Europeans who sought long-distance trade and far-off territories?**

- ◆ **What were the unexpected outcomes of expansion?**

Population and economic growth in Europe, along with the rise of strong states headed by energetic rulers, contributed to Europe's global expansion in the sixteenth century. Rising population and a strong economy led to increased demand for the products of Asia and Africa, and vigorous governments helped to organize and finance new commercial ventures. When technological developments turned the wish for new long-distance trade routes on the open seas into a practical possibility, a global economy based on trade began to emerge. At the same time, Portugal and Spain created Europe's first overseas empires in Asia and the Western Hemisphere.

The Motives and the Means

Economic, political, and religious factors, along with technological developments, combined to bring about Europe's overseas expansion. After 1450, when population rose and the economy strengthened, Europeans once again demanded goods from Asia

and Africa. By 1450, however, the realities of trade with those places had changed. Gone were the days when Marco Polo and other Europeans could travel under Mongol protection across Eurasia to trade directly with the Chinese. Now the Ottoman Turks barred the way, and Muslims in Africa kept Europeans out of trade there.

Some Europeans benefited from the new realities; the Venetians established profitable trading posts in Syria and Egypt, where they worked with local Arabs to bring Asian goods to Europe. Others, jealous of the Venetians' success, sought new routes to the east. The Genoese, especially, looked for ways to recover the trade they had lost to the Ottomans on the Black Sea.

Governments and Expansion The rise of strong governments after 1450 also prepared the way for expansion. State sponsorship and financing were crucial in the search for new trade routes. The first states to offer this support were Portugal and Castile. Their location on the Iberian Peninsula positioned them for explorations down the coast of Africa and across the Atlantic. Moreover, Portuguese and Spanish sailors, who had fished in Atlantic waters for centuries and carried cargoes to and from northern trading centers like Antwerp, were accustomed to sailing ocean waters outside the protected Mediterranean. Often, it was the Genoese who organized this rising seaborne commerce. Columbus himself was Genoese.

Religion and Expansion Economic considerations drove states to support the ventures of their merchants, but religious motives were equally important. As Christians, most Europeans believed they were required to spread their faith to all parts of the world, following Jesus' command in the Gospel of Matthew: "Go therefore and make disciples of all nations, baptizing them in the name of the Father and of the Son and of the Holy Spirit." Kings, queens, merchants, and priests all wished to promote Christianity along with trade. Many believed that worldwide conversion to Christianity would prepare for the Second Coming—Jesus' return to earth, when he would judge the world and reign with his saints. Hopes for profits, the spread of Christianity, and Jesus' return, however, would have gotten nowhere had it not been for technological developments that made long-distance sailing on the open seas a practical possibility.

Innovations in Technology In the Middle Ages, Europe's ships were ill suited to long voyages on rough Atlantic waters. Propelled by oars or a simple sail, they were small, with only crude steering devices. By the end of the fifteenth century, however, ships had improved. They were larger, better constructed, fitted with improved rudders for steering, and supplied

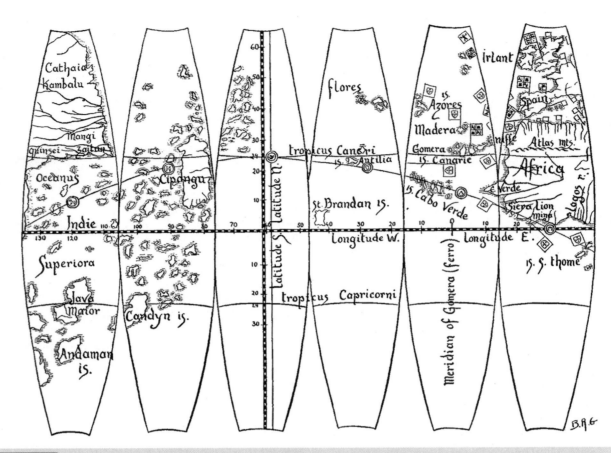

Map 13.3 **Map of Martin Beheim, 1492** Martin Beheim, a fifteenth-century German mapmaker, showed the world as round in 1492. Africa and part of Europe are on the far right. The Madeira and Cape Verde Islands are identified, and then Cipongu (Japan). This is the information Columbus had when he set sail. From *Admiral of the Ocean Sea* by Samuel Eliot Morison. (Copyright © 1942 by Samuel Eliot Morison; Copyright © renewed 1970 by Samuel Eliot Morison. By permission of Little, Brown and Company, Inc.)

1. In addition to Cipongu/Japan and Cabo Verde/Cape Verde Islands, identify Longitude East, Longitude West, and the Azores.
2. At what point does Beheim's information become noticeably less accurate?

with a triangular **lateen sail**, popularized by Arab sailors, that allowed them to pick up the wind regardless of the direction from which it was blowing. They could also carry cannons and thus take advantage of the new gunpowder technology.

Navigational aids had also improved. Mapmaking became more accurate with the spread of navigational manuals and the development of **cartography**, which allowed mapmakers to accurately draw large portions of the known world. Sailors were also able to determine their north/south position (latitude) with greater accuracy, using **astrolabes** or **quadrants** for measuring the distance of heavenly bodies (the sun or known stars) from the horizon. Finding one's east/west position (longitude) was more difficult, but a skilled sailor could calculate it using a magnetic compass, first developed by both Chinese and Arab sailors, along with an hourglass to mark off time and observations about the speed of the ship through the waters. With improved ships, navigational manuals, maps, quadrants, compasses, and hourglasses, sailors ventured farther into the Atlantic and gained knowledge of ocean sailing. By the time of Columbus, they had a good sense of the wind patterns on the Atlantic and were learning how to use them to travel north and south as well as east and west.

Seamen had also discarded some earlier theories about global climate. In the Middle Ages, geographers knew that when one traveled south from Europe, it got hotter and hotter. They therefore reasoned that continuing south would eventually lead

lateen sail Triangular sail, first used by Arab sailors, that could swing to pick up wind coming from different directions.

cartography Science of mapmaking.

astrolabes and **quadrants** Devices allowing sailors to use the stars to find their north/south position (latitude) on the ocean.

to parts of the earth so hot that no human being could survive there. Voyages down the coast of Africa gradually proved this theory wrong.

The Portuguese Empire

Sailors from the kingdom of Portugal, the westernmost state on the Iberian Peninsula, were the first Europeans to systematically explore Africa's west coast. For years, the Portuguese had resented Muslim control of the overland trade routes that carried gold from Africa to the Mediterranean. They were also eager to participate in the spice trade from Asia. In 1415, they captured the Muslim port of Ceuta in Morocco. Portuguese seamen then began inching down the African coast, looking for trading partners who would supply them directly with gold. At the same time, they bought black African slaves from local merchants. Both gold and slaves brought high prices back home, spurring other adventurers to join in the voyages. By the 1480s, the Portuguese had set up trading posts in **Guinea**, the center of the gold and slave trade.

An Empire of Trading Posts From the start, the kings of Portugal took an active part in the explorations, working closely with merchants and finally declaring a royal monopoly over the African trade. A member of the royal family, **Prince Henry the Navigator**, promoted the new technologies that made Atlantic sailing possible.

Portuguese traders did not seize large territories in Africa. Instead, they established fortified trading posts along the coast where they could exchange wine, guns, and wheat for gold and slaves. Life in these posts was difficult; the climate was harsh, and many traders died of tropical diseases, against which they had no immunity. Nevertheless, the trade prospered, and by 1500, Portugal was the chief supplier of gold and slaves to Europeans.

On to India In 1488, **Bartholomew Diaz** made it to the southern tip of Africa, rounding the Cape of Good Hope, as he called it, and sailing into the Indian Ocean. Faced with a mutiny by his crew, he turned back to Portugal before reaching India itself. Then in 1497, **Vasco da Gama** landed on the west coast of India, returning to Portugal in 1499 with a shipload of spices and cotton cloth. Da Gama's success launched the Portuguese drive into the Indian Ocean.

Sailors soon discovered that the best winds for getting around southern Africa were picked up far out in the Atlantic. They therefore sailed due west of the Cape Verde Islands, found these winds, and then turned around and sailed to the southeast past the Cape of Good Hope. In 1500, on one of these trips, the ships sailed farther west than usual and sighted the coast of South America. Soon the Portuguese settled there, calling it Brazil after a local wood used for dying cloth.

Alfonso de Albuquerque The founder of the Portuguese Empire in Asia was **Alfonso de Albuquerque**. Appointed governor-general of Portuguese possessions along the Indian Ocean, Albuquerque sought to take over the spice trade with Europe. He attacked local Muslim merchants' ships at sea, pounding them with his superior shipboard cannons, and led armed expeditions on land against key trading posts. In 1510, he captured **Goa** on India's west coast, killing the Muslim men there and forcing their widows to marry his sailors to establish a Portuguese community. With Goa secured, he attacked the spice-trading center of **Malacca** on the Malay Peninsula. In 1557, the Portuguese established the first European settlement in China at **Macau**.

Albuquerque mixed a passion for trade with a hatred of Muslims. To him, they were liars and cheats; force, not friendship, was the only thing they understood. His dispatches to Portugal reveal the kind of stereotyping that would feed western imaginations for centuries to come. For Albuquerque, smashing infidel control of Far Eastern commerce would allow for the triumphant planting of the cross of Christ in heathen lands. He was the perfect crusader trader.

The Spanish Empire

In the spring of 1492, **Christopher Columbus** began preparations for his westward voyage across the Atlantic. Columbus was no stranger to Atlantic waters. He had lived in Portugal for many years, marrying a Portuguese woman and sailing to the **Canary Islands**, the African coast, and the Madeira Islands, where his wife's family had estates. After failing to get Portuguese backing for a voyage across the Atlantic, he turned to Spain for help (see A New Direction: Isabella of Castile Finances Christopher Columbus's Voyage Across the Atlantic).

Guinea Area near the western bulge of Africa; in the sixteenth century, the center of gold and slave trade.

Prince Henry the Navigator (1394–1460) Member of the Portuguese royal family who encouraged explorations along the coast of Africa.

Bartholomew Diaz (ca.1450–1500) Portuguese sailor who in 1488 rounded the southern tip of Africa and sailed into the Indian Ocean.

Vasco da Gama (1460–1524) First Portuguese trader to land in India and establish direct European trade.

Alfonso de Albuquerque (1453–1515) Governor general of Portuguese possessions along the Indian Ocean; founder of Portuguese Empire in Asia.

Goa Portuguese colony on the west coast of India.

Malacca Muslim port on the Malay Peninsula where goods from spice-growing islands farther east were collected and shipped westward.

Macau Trading post on the south coast of China near Hong Kong.

Christopher Columbus (1451–1506) Genoese sailor and explorer who captained the first European voyages to the Caribbean and South America and claimed lands there for Spain.

Canary Islands Islands in the Atlantic Ocean colonized by Spain.

Isabella of Castile Finances Christopher Columbus's Voyage Across the Atlantic

In January 1492, a forty-year-old Genoese sailor, Cristoforo Colombo, known in the English-speaking world as Christopher Columbus, appeared before Queen Isabella of Castile and her husband, King Ferdinand of Aragon. Columbus was seeking Spanish support for an ocean voyage to the eastern shores of Asia, which he believed were on the far side of the Atlantic Ocean. Twice before, Isabella had turned the Italian down. His third audience with the queen in 1492 was a desperate last attempt. Once again he presented his plans and described the benefits of the voyage. Once again, the queen refused. In despair, Columbus fled the court and galloped north, intending to ask the French king for help. But six miles out of town, royal guards stopped him and brought him back to the city. Isabella had changed her mind.

Later, Ferdinand would claim that he had convinced his wife to finance the voyage. Perhaps. As the only woman in the fifteenth century who ruled as a monarch, Isabella had to assert her royal will while not breaking the conventions of womanliness, which required submission to her husband. Throughout her reign, she acted as a dutiful wife involved in the traditional tasks of running a household, weaving cloth for the family's clothing, and repairing worn garments. Isabella also emphasized her faithfulness to Ferdinand despite his frequent infidelities. Ferdinand's claim that he had the final say in authorizing Columbus's voyage would fit with Isabella's role as the subordinate partner in their marriage.

But Ferdinand's account was challenged by one of Isabella's earliest biographers, the Dominican friar and bishop Bartolomé de Las Casas. Las Casas was an influential person at the court of Isabella's grandson, King Charles I, and had access to official documents and family papers. After Isabella's death, he wrote that the queen took the advice of her financial advisers when she recalled Columbus to court. This, too, is possible. Although Isabella embraced the gender expectations of her age, she was also highly effective in charting her own course of action. She herself had chosen Ferdinand as her husband, defying the wishes of her half brother, the king. The bride and groom were technically ineligible for marriage because, as cousins, they were too closely related in the eyes of the church. But Isabella went ahead with the union after documents were forged in the pope's name permitting an exception to Catholic marriage laws. Although independent when she needed to be, she preferred to work as a partner with Ferdinand, adopting as her motto, "The worth of one is the worth of the other—Isabella as Ferdinand." Isabella's motto cleverly proclaimed both her independence and her wifely relation to Ferdinand. It also emphasized the union of the two Spanish kingdoms that her marriage had achieved.

However she made her decision, Isabella announced that she would pawn her jewels to finance the voyage. (Pawning valuables was one way fifteenth-century monarchs could raise quick cash.) Finances settled, the queen could relish the gains from Columbus's voyage. Spain, like the rest of Europe, was hungry for the gold and spices of the east. But the country was cut off from a land route across Asia by the Venetians and their Muslim trading partners, and from a sea route around Africa by treaties with the Portuguese. A direct westward route was therefore the only one available to the Spanish. Moreover, both the Spanish and Portuguese had discovered and colonized islands in the Atlantic during the past seventy years. Perhaps Columbus would find more on the way to Asia, increasing the likelihood of riches.

Columbus's proposal also appealed to Isabella's fervent Catholic faith; a Spanish presence in eastern Asia would open the way for a Christian encirclement of the Muslim world and even the recapture of the holy city of Jerusalem. This vision exerted a powerful influence on a Spanish queen whose ancestors had extended their rule over a Muslim-dominated Iberian Peninsula. In fact, at the very moment Columbus appeared at court in 1492, Isabella and Ferdinand were celebrating their conquest of Granada, the last independent Muslim state on the peninsula. The Muslim defeat also provoked an attack on the other non-Christian people of the peninsula, the Jews. Shortly after Isabella offered Columbus the money he needed, she ordered the forced conversion or expulsion of all Jews in her lands. In the spring of 1492, just as the unconverted Jews were being shipped out of Spain, Columbus began preparing for his westward voyage.

Isabella of Castile Writes Her Last Will and Testament

On October 12, 1504, twelve years to the day after Columbus landed in the Bahamas, the dying Isabella began to dictate her last will and testament. In it she made arrangements for her burial and the disposition of her worldly goods. She also summed up the major achievements of her reign and asked her successors to honor them.

1 Why would Isabella ask to be buried in a plain grave in Granada?

2 Why does Isabella "beg" her husband and "lord" to carry out her wishes while "ordering" her daughter and son-in-law to do so?

3 How does Isabella's gift of relics to Granada relate to her instructions for her burial?

4 Notice Isabella's description of her motive for conquering new territories. To what degree was it shared by the Spaniards who went to these new territories?

5 Why would Isabella express her concerns for the Indians in her will?

1 I ask and order that my body be buried in the monastery of Saint Francis which is in the Alhambra in the city of Granada … dressed in the habit of the very blessed poor man of Jesus Christ, Saint Francis, in a lowly grave without any bust and only a plain slab on the ground containing an inscription.

2 In addition, because I have wanted to order a simplification of the laws …, identifying the doubtful ones and eliminating the superfluous ones, in order to avoid doubts and any contradictions that have arisen concerning them and the expenses that they might impose on my kingdoms … I beg the king my lord, and I order and enjoin the said princess, my daughter, and the said prince, her husband, to bring together a learned and conscientious prelate with persons who are educated, wise, and expert in law, to examine the said laws and to reduce them into a briefer and less cumbersome code.

3 I command that the jewels which the said princess and prince, my children, have given me be returned to them. And that the relic I have of Our Lord's loincloth be given to the monastery of Saint Anthony in the city of Segovia. And that all my other relics be given to the Cathedral in the city of Granada.

And I entreat and command the said princess, my daughter, and the said prince, her husband, as Catholic princes, to take great care concerning the things that honor God and His holy faith, watching over and securing the faith's safety, defense, and glorification, since for it we are obliged to pledge our persons, lives, and possessions as is necessary. And that they be very obedient to the commandments of holy mother church, as they are obliged to be its protectors and defenders. And that they will not cease the conquest of Africa to fight for the faith against the infidels. And that they will always favor the work of the Holy Inquisition against heretical depravity.

4 From the time when the Holy Apostolic See granted us the Islands and Mainland of the Ocean Sea … our first intention was, from the time we entreated pope Alexander VI, of blessed memory, who gave us the said grant, to attempt to persuade and cause the inhabitants there to convert to our holy Catholic faith, and to send to the said islands and mainland prelates and members of religious orders and clergy, and other learned and God-fearing persons, to instruct the inhabitants and residents there in the Catholic faith, and to teach and instruct them in good behavior, and to put in them the necessary diligence, taking the care stated more fully in the letters of the grant. To this end, I most affectionately beseech the king my lord and I charge and command the said princess, my daughter, and the said prince, her husband, to carry this out as their principal goal with much diligence. **5** They must not in any way allow the Indians, the inhabitants, and the residents in the said islands and mainland to suffer any injury to their persons or property, but must be well and justly treated. And if they have received any injury, they must set it right.

Source: Translated by the author, from Isabella of Castile's Last Will and Testament (1504).

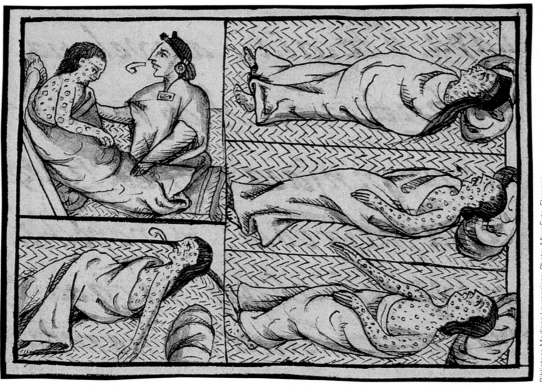

This drawing from about 1550 by an unknown Aztec artist shows the devastation that smallpox brought to the indigenous populations of the Western Hemisphere. At the upper left a local healer speaks to a sick person while others lie dying on mats. What might be the differing reactions of Aztecs and Spaniards to this drawing?

Biblioteca Medicea Laurenziana; Photo: MicroFoto, Florence

When that finally came, he began collecting crews and supplies for the three small ships Queen Isabella had given him.

Local sailors were reluctant to sign on, not because they thought the world was flat and they would soon fall off its western edge (most Europeans knew the world was round) but because they were local tuna fishermen already making a good living in waters close to home. So Columbus had a hard time recruiting the ninety men he needed, some of whom, in the end, were convicts. His task was made especially difficult because he had to work out of the small Spanish port of Palos; the larger ports were clogged with ships carrying away the recently expelled Spanish Jews. Finally, on August 3, 1492, just as a ship carrying the last of the Jews sailed from Palos, Columbus headed out of the port.

Arrival in the Caribbean
After reprovisioning his ships in the Canary Islands, in early September

Columbus sailed west for thirty-three days, landing in the Bahamas on October 12. Because the Spaniards believed they had found islands in the East Indies, they called the local people Indians. Columbus then explored the islands of Hispaniola and Cuba, hoping to set up Portuguese-style trading posts. Finding no cities, he returned to Spain in January 1493, leaving some men behind on Hispaniola. Following a triumphant procession across Spain, Columbus presented Isabella and Ferdinand with gold, parrots, spices, and captives, along with a pineapple, which Ferdinand happily ate.

This was modest booty, but Columbus played up the potential for future profits and managed to get royal backing for three more voyages between 1493 and 1504. In 1494, Spain and Portugal, with the blessing of the pope, signed the **Treaty of Tordesillas**, granting Spain control of Central and South America except for Brazil, which went to Portugal, along with Africa and Asia. Thus the entire world was divided into two zones for these first European empires.

Disease and Decimation The **Taíno** people Columbus encountered on the islands of the Caribbean were friendly and provided him with food

Treaty of Tordesillas Arrangement in 1494 between Spain and Portugal drawing a north-south line west of the Azores; lands west of it went to Spain and lands east (plus Brazil) to Portugal.

Taíno Native people inhabiting the Caribbean islands visited by the Spaniards in the first period of encounter between Europeans and American Indians.

and information, but relations deteriorated when the Spaniards started to claim their land for Spain and rape women. Over the next twenty-five years, as more land was seized for farms, the Taíno, now virtually enslaved, were forced to work it. Even worse were the diseases, such as smallpox and influenza, that swept through the local population.

Since the Western Hemisphere was isolated from Europe, local peoples had no immunity from the diseases the Spaniards brought, and millions died as epidemics swept through Central and South America, often in advance of any European's arrival. The Taíno, who may have numbered 300,000 in 1492, were virtually extinct by 1550, and, overall, the native population of the Americas fell by 90 percent in the century after Columbus's voyages—the greatest demographic catastrophe in recorded history.

The Conquest of the Aztecs For a quarter century after 1492, few Spaniards migrated to the Caribbean. Although some gold was found, it was difficult to grow sufficient food, and Spanish mortality rates were high as men succumbed to local diseases. Columbus himself died in Spain in 1506, disappointed by the meager results of his discoveries. Everything changed, however, in 1519, when a Spanish nobleman, **Hernán Cortés**, landed on the east coast of Mexico with six hundred men, sixteen horses, and six cannons. Like those before him, Cortés was looking for gold.

Unlike his predecessors, he embarked on territorial conquest; in two and a half years his small force conquered the **Aztec Empire** of central Mexico. The Aztecs ruled over many states, which had to supply men and tribute to the emperor in the capital of Tenochtitlán, now Mexico City. Cortés formed alliances with the most discontented states and augmented his own force with their soldiers. If local states refused to join the anti-Aztec coalition, they were intimidated by the invaders, who were mounted on horses, which the local people had never seen before, wore strange body armor, and wielded steel swords. In addition, the noise, smoke, and fire of Cortés's artillery, which was also unknown to the Aztecs, panicked the enemy, as did the attack dogs used in battle. (The Aztecs' only dogs were tiny, resembling modern-day chihuahuas.)

In November 1519, Cortés and his allies entered Tenochtitlán at the invitation of the emperor, Moctezuma II, who may have been influenced by Aztec traditions that prophesied the arrival by sea of a pale-skinned god, Quetzalcoatl. In June 1520, Moctezuma died under mysterious circumstances. Although probably murdered by his own people, the Aztecs blamed the Spaniards for his death and attacked

Cortés. Withdrawing from the city, the Spaniards regrouped and made a successful assault in August 1521. Cortés now controlled the Aztec Empire, and one of his first acts was to demolish the sacred pyramid in the center of Tenochtitlán and replace it with a cathedral.

The Conquest of the Incas Cortés's conquest of the Aztecs launched the first New World gold rush. When news of Tenochtitlán's capture reached Europe, along with gold from Moctezuma's treasury, thousands of Spaniards flocked to Mexico in search of bounty. Among them was **Francisco Pizarro**, an illiterate laborer who had migrated to Hispaniola in 1502 and served in expeditions to Central America, including **Vaso Núñez de Balboa**'s trek across Panama to the Pacific Ocean. In 1531, Pizarro launched an expedition of 280 men and 55 horses against the **Inca Empire**, taking advantage of a political crisis among the Inca to conquer them.

In the late 1520s, the Inca emperor died, a victim of the European-induced epidemics that were raging though Central and South America. Two of his sons, Atahualpa and Huáscar, then fought each other for control of the empire. Arriving during the civil war sparked by the sons' rivalry, Pizarro played the brothers against each other. He used his horses, cannon, and steel swords to slaughter over three thousand Inca soldiers at Cajamarca in present-day Peru after Atahualpa had unwittingly led them into an ambush. Atahualpa was taken prisoner. Huáscar was murdered in 1532, and a year later Atahualpa was also. Pizarro then set up a third brother as a puppet emperor.

Cortés's conquest of the Aztecs and Pizarro's of the Incas finally produced the precious metals that had driven the search for direct trade routes to Asia. It was silver, however, rather than gold, that flowed in ever-increasing quantities toward Spain from mines at Zacatecas in Mexico and Potosí in present-day Bolivia, both started in the 1540s. Following **Ferdinand Magellan's**

Hernán Cortés (1485–1547) Spanish nobleman and conquistador (conqueror) who in 1519 conquered the Aztec Empire.

Aztec Empire Federation of states in central Mexico ruled by an emperor from his capital, Tenochtitlán, the present-day Mexico City.

Francisco Pizarro (ca. 1475–1541) Soldier who in 1531 conquered the Inca Empire with a small Spanish force.

Vaso Núñez de Balboa (1475–1519) Spanish explorer who crossed the isthmus of Panama in 1513 and sighted the Pacific Ocean.

Inca Empire Empire stretching from Ecuador to northern Chile and from the Pacific Ocean to the upper Amazon River.

Ferdinand Magellan (1480–1521) Portuguese commander of a Spanish fleet who circumnavigated the globe in 1519–1521.

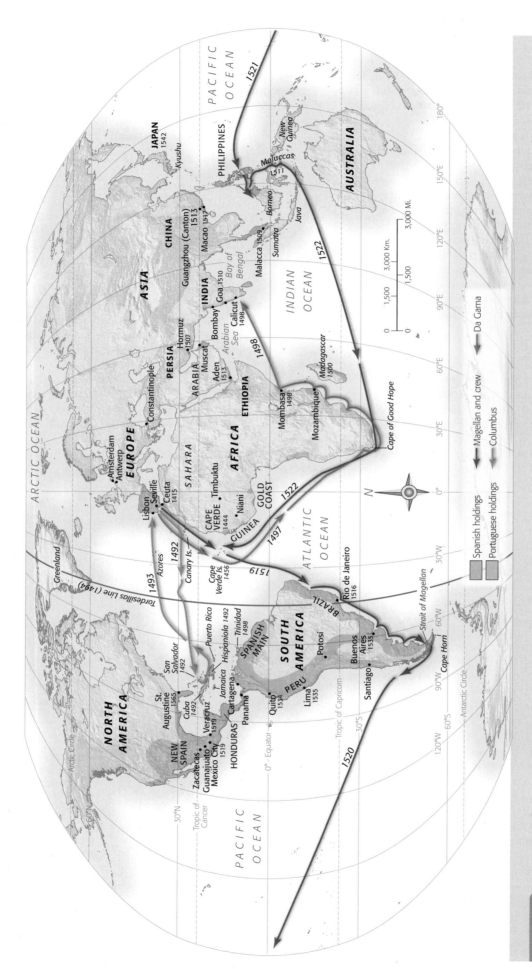

Map 13.4 **World Expansion, 1492–1536** By 1536, Europe's worldwide sea lanes were well established, following the voyages of Vasco da Gama, Christopher Columbus, and Ferdinand Magellan. © *Cengage Learning*

1. Trace the routes of Da Gama, Columbus, and Magellan.
2. Compare the size of Spain and Portugal with the size of their overseas empires.
3. When you look at the Portuguese and Spanish empires of the sixteenth century you can see that they were mainly confined to areas near the coast. What factors can you think of that would explain this phenomenon? Mexico, however, is an exception. Why?

circumnavigation of the globe in 1519–1521, the magnitude of Columbus's voyages and subsequent Spanish conquests began to sink into the European consciousness.

 Checking In

By yourself or with a partner, explain the significance of each of the following selected key terms:

lateen sail	Christopher Columbus
Bartholomew Diaz	Hernán Cortés
Vasco da Gama	Francisco Pizarro
Alfonso de Albuquerque	Ferdinand Magellan

Exploration, Expansion, and European Identity

◆ **How did Europeans come to terms with the peoples of Africa and the Americas, whom they perceived as not like them?**

◆ **How did African slavery develop, and how was it justified?**

Once it became clear that the peoples of the Western Hemisphere were not Asians but previously unknown inhabitants of a "New World," travelers' and missionaries' accounts appeared offering conflicting descriptions of these "Indians." In addition, the creation of Portuguese and Spanish Empires in the New World led to the importation of millions of black African slaves to replace the declining native populations as a labor force. Confronted with strange New World people and the emergence of African slavery in overseas empires, people in Europe were forced to rethink who they were in relation to others and outsiders.

Native Americans in the European Imagination

European attempts to understand Native Americans started with the assumption that there were universal standards for proper human behavior. Early travelers' and missionaries' accounts of New World people based on this assumption were positive. Native Americans were pictured as simple people who lived virtuous lives. They had no private property and no money, and hence no reason to be greedy. They lived in harmony with nature and each other, solving disputes without need of laws and courts. They waged war, but only for just cause. In a word, the Indians were what Europeans ought to be. And so, in the end, these accounts were really about Europe, with the Indians providing a way for moralists to condemn abuses in their own society.

"Good Indian" or "Bad Indian?" Alongside the picture of the "good Indian," an image of the "bad Indian" soon emerged. Indians were accused of eating disgusting things like spiders and worms. Because they wore no European clothes, they were accused of engaging in what Europeans thought were the vilest kinds of sexual behavior, including homosexuality and intercourse with animals. They had no true religion but worshiped satanically inspired idols. Worst of all, they practiced human sacrifice and cannibalism. Both the good and bad pictures of the Indians wove together bits of accurate information with misinformation and a host of European fantasies and fears, and both were believed. Gradually, however, the negative picture gained ground, and by the mid-sixteenth century, arguments were made that the Indians were not really human beings but "**natural slaves**."

The theory of the natural slave went back to the Greek philosopher Aristotle, who stated that there were creatures resembling human beings who nevertheless lacked fully rational minds. Although they could understand and communicate with real humans, they needed human masters to control them. If Indian behavior was as bad as some people said, then it was clear that the Indians were natural slaves because fully rational human beings would reject the things the Indians supposedly did. Moreover, when the theory of natural slavery was applied to the Indians, the Spanish conquest and exploitation of them was fully justified.

Sepúlveda and Las Casas

The attack on the Indians reached a climax in the late 1540s when Charles V's chaplain, **Juan Ginés de Sepúlveda**, defended the theory that they were natural slaves. Sepúlveda's endorsement of the "bad Indian" theory provoked a response from **Bartolomé de Las Casas**. Las Casas was also an influential member of Charles V's court who had known both Ferdinand and Isabella. After 1492, he went to the Caribbean, where he became a landowner, with many Indians working for him. But his

natural slaves As theorized by the Greek philosopher Aristotle, semirational creatures resembling human beings who needed human masters to control them.

Juan Ginés de Sepúlveda (1494–1573) Charles V's chaplain, who denounced the American Indians as less than human.

Bartolomé de Las Casas (1474–1566) Soldier turned priest and bishop who criticized the brutality of the Spanish conquest of America.

Archivo de Indias, Seville/Mithra-Index/The Bridgeman Art Library

This is an idealized portrait of Bartolomé de Las Casas. He is shown as a Dominican friar writing his defense of the Indian populations he encountered as a conquistador and then as a priest and bishop. What techniques does the artist use to convince the viewer of Las Casas's wisdom and virtue?

true calling was to the church, and he became the first man to be ordained a priest in the Americas.

Las Casas's experiences as a landowner had shown him just how brutally the Indians were exploited, and as a priest he campaigned for their better treatment. In 1542, he persuaded Charles V to stop the worst abuses by issuing the **New Laws for the Indies**. In 1545, Las Casas was consecrated a bishop and sent to Guatemala to introduce the New Laws, but local landlords' opposition to the reforms

New Laws for the Indies (1542) Laws issued by Charles V that attempted to stop Spanish exploitation of New World populations.

forced him to return to Spain. When Las Casas read Sepúlveda's attack, he demanded to face him in a debate.

Las Casas argued that men like himself, who had observed Indian culture directly, were the only persons qualified to determine whether Indians were fully human. And he argued eloquently that they were. Las Casas admitted that the Indians often behaved "badly," but he explained that this did not prove a lack of humanity. Their behavior resulted from evil customs that had taken root in their societies. In the past, Christianity had corrected Greek and Roman errors, and it would also correct Indian ones. In 1552, following his debate with Sepúlveda, Las Casas published his *Brief Account of the Destruction of the Indies,* a fiery description of Spanish brutality in the New World that was widely read and influenced many Europeans.

Eurocentrism Las Casas's arguments were thoroughly **Eurocentric.** He believed in the superiority of European civilization and thought that the Indians' conversion to Christianity was the only way to save them from eternal damnation. His recognition of their full humanity and his demands for a just treatment of them, along with his sense of the superiority of European culture and religion, gave voice to many of the principles that guided European colonial expansion in subsequent centuries. Finally, Las Casas, aware of the labor shortage in the Americas created by the decline in local populations, urged his fellow Europeans to import African slaves to fill the gap, a position he later regretted.

The Labor of Africans

New World slavery had its origins in Portuguese exploration of Africa. Beginning in 1420, the Portuguese settled on **Atlantic islands** off Africa's west coast, while the Spanish occupied the Canary Islands. The islands' volcanic soil was ideal for growing sugarcane, and large **plantations** were established to produce it. During the Middle Ages, honey was Europe's chief sweetener. Medieval Europeans had known of sugar, which was imported in small quantities from Muslim lands and used as medicine or a sexual stimulant.

With the colonization of the Atlantic islands, sugar became a European-controlled commodity and the demand for it rose rapidly. At first, the plantations' workforce consisted of Portuguese settlers as well as **indentured servants** fulfilling the terms of their contracts and slaves from the eastern Mediterranean and sub-Saharan Africa. By 1500, however, black African slaves predominated.

Sugar and Slaves For years, tribal warfare in West Africa had involved the capture and enslavement of enemies. Portuguese traders bought these slaves from Africans because they were relatively cheap and could be forced to do the harsh work on the island plantations that free Europeans eventually rejected.

Some African rulers opposed the Portuguese slave trade, but coastal merchants found it economically profitable and even invested in the sugar plantations. Over the sixteenth century, tens of thousands of slaves were brought to the Atlantic islands. Because they came from parts of Africa where agriculture was widespread, they were familiar with field-work and could be trained to handle sugarcane. Soon the islands were the main sugar producers for Europe, sending sugar to Antwerp and other markets.

European Stereotypes and Africans The Portuguese and Spanish not only pioneered the use of African slaves in a plantation system, they also adopted stereotypes about Africans developed first in the Muslim world, where a trade in sub-Saharan African slaves had persisted throughout the Middle Ages. These stereotypes condemned Africans as ugly, lazy, sexually promiscuous, stupid, and evil smelling. Christians had also long identified the color black with sin and the Devil and the color white with purity. The combination of these Muslim and Christian stereotypes laid the foundations for arguments about the racial inferiority of blacks to whites that were to have a long and vicious history.

Columbus, who had lived on the Madeira Islands before coming to Spain, took sugarcane plants with him on his return to the Western Hemisphere in 1493. When settlers realized that cane grew well in Brazil and the Caribbean islands, plantations were established there, and the transatlantic importation of African slaves began. For the next three hundred years, more than eleven million Africans were carried across the Atlantic in one of the largest forced migrations in history.

Europeans justified African slavery in various ways. Some appealed to Aristotle's theory of natural slaves; others cited Christian scripture, which showed that both the Israelites and the first Christians owned slaves. Others turned to Genesis and argued that Africans were the descendants of Noah's son Ham, cursed as a slave because he had seen his father drunk and naked. In a world that believed all human beings were slaves to sin, the idea that some were slaves to other men was easily accepted. In addition, Europe's hierarchical and patriarchal social order, in which wives, children, and servants were subject to the male head of household, made slavery seem like an extension of the general

Eurocentric Idea that Europe and European culture are either superior to or more important than the lands and cultures of other peoples.

Atlantic islands The Azores, the Cape Verde Islands, the Madeira Islands, and São Tomé, where the Portuguese used African slaves to cultivate sugar for the European market.

plantation A large-scale agricultural enterprise producing goods for the European market, often using slave labor.

indentured servants Servants who agreed to compulsory service for a fixed period of time, often in exchange for passage to a colony.

structure of society. As a result, few Europeans questioned it.

New World Slavery Slavery in the Western Hemisphere differed in important respects from the kind practiced in European and Muslim lands. First, slaves were increasingly thought of as black and African. Earlier forms of slavery had been color-blind, and people of many different racial and ethnic communities had been enslaved. In the Americas, most slaves worked on plantations or, after silver was discovered in the Spanish Empire, in mines. This work was in contrast to European and Muslim slavery, in which many different types of work were performed by slaves. Most important, slavery was increasingly considered a lifelong status and one that children inherited from their parents, thus creating a perpetually enslaved class of persons. The idea that one was "born" a slave, not "made" one by capture or some other force, fitted in with European ideas of Africans' racial inferiority.

Checking In

By yourself or with a partner, explain the significance of each of the following selected key terms:

natural slaves

New Laws for the Indies

Juan Ginés de Sepúlveda

indentured servants

Bartolomé de Las Casas

CHAPTER
Review

Summary

◆ The growth of Europe's population, which began after 1450, stimulated an economic expansion based on increasing agricultural activity and the growth of new trading networks.

◆ From 1450 to 1550, most urban and rural workers benefited from a rise in wages, although rates of pay were sharply different for men and women because of prevailing notions about the relative value of men's and women's work.

◆ The gendered distribution of wages echoed the general patriarchal organization of society.

◆ Both urban and rural communities were also arranged hierarchically from the better sort to the lesser sort.

◆ Many communities became less economically self-sufficient as they were linked to large-scale trading networks, but they still retained a strong sense of community identity and mutual responsibility.

◆ The community was conceived of as an organic whole in which anyone's fate was everyone's business. This view explains Europeans' commitment to public hospitals and welfare institutions.

◆ Communities also carefully guarded their local ways of life against outside intrusions.

◆ Rulers in this early modern world benefited from Europe's rising economy, which allowed them to tax and borrow to meet their needs.

◆ But they also had to be careful to respect their subjects' rights and traditions, even as they sought to increase their control over them.

◆ Successful government involved cooperating and negotiating with local elites, whether nobles, landowners, or town fathers, in order to develop working relations with them.

◆ One trend in government was the attempt to forge more centralized states. The means to this end varied.

◆ In Spain, a policy to respect the political independence of Castile and Aragon was balanced against the creation of a new, more homogeneous national identity.

◆ In France and England, it involved the introduction of standardized languages.

- In many states, it involved tying rulers as borrowers to subjects as lenders. It also involved administrative centralization in the hands of experts.

- The creation of empires after 1450 was the most dramatic example of Europe's age of expansion.

- For Portugal and Spain, empire building was directly linked to trade.

- The creation of empires had enormous consequences for both Europeans and non-Europeans.

- For Africans, it had the disastrous effect of expanding and extending the trade in slaves from the small Atlantic islands to the huge plantation economies of the New World.

- In the New World, it involved not only conquest but also the destruction of whole societies, through the unforeseen and largely uncontrollable spread of new diseases. For Europeans like Cortés and Pizarro, empire brought new riches.

- For those like Las Casas, it brought a new urgency to think through the problems of colonial domination and Europeans' relations with other peoples.

Chronology

1420	Portuguese begin the colonization of Atlantic islands
1462	Ivan III becomes tsar
1469	Ferdinand of Aragon and Isabella of Castile marry
1480	Ivan III declares Moscow's independence from Mongol rule
1485	Henry VII (Tudor) becomes king of England
1488	Bartholomew Diaz rounds southern tip of Africa and enters Indian Ocean
1492	Jews are expelled from Spain; Columbus sets sail
1500–1502	Muslims are expelled from Spain
1509	Henry VIII becomes king of England
1510	Alfonso de Albuquerque conquers Goa
1515	Francis I becomes king of France
1517	Charles V (Habsburg) begins rule in Spain
1519	Cortés lands in Mexico
1531	Pizarro invades Inca Empire
1533	Ivan IV becomes tsar
1542	Charles V issues New Laws for the Indies
1552	Las Casas publishes *Brief Account of the Destruction of the Indies*
1556	Charles V abdicates
1557	Portuguese establish trading colony at Macau
1559	French and Spanish sign Peace of Cateau-Cambrésis

© Cengage Learning

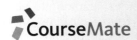
Visit the CourseMate website at **www.cengagebrain.com** for additional study tools and review materials for this chapter.

Test Yourself

To gauge your mastery of the material in this chapter, answer the questions below. More than one answer may be correct.

Economic and Social Change

1. After 1450, European population began to expand because of:

    a. A decline in plague outbreaks.
    b. An increase in religious fervor.
    c. A decline in devastating warfare.
    d. A decline in the outbreak of famine.
    e. All of the above.

2. By 1450:

    a. Serfdom had largely disappeared in western Europe.
    b. Peasant communes set dates for planting crops.
    c. Landlords successfully reimposed serfdom in eastern Europe.
    d. The growth of markets led to a changed definition of work.
    e. All of the above.

3. By 1550 what percent of Europeans were living in cities?

    a. 5 percent
    b. 10 percent
    c. 15 percent
    d. 20 percent
    e. 25 percent

4. Guilds were:

    a. Open to all men and women who worked, regardless of skill.
    b. Regulating the manufacture of the guild's goods for the marketplace by 1500.
    c. Carefully policed by church authorities.
    d. Usually open only to men.
    e. Attacked by government authorities as disturbers of the social order.

5. Antwerp was:

    a. Well positioned as a transfer point for trade between eastern and western Europe and northern and southern Europe.
    b. The second most important commercial center in Europe after Seville.
    c. A trade center for English woolen cloth and Spanish wool.
    d. An important trading center for the wheat and wool from the east.
    e. One of Europe's largest cities.

Now that you have reviewed and tested yourself on this part of the chapter, take time to pull together all the important information by answering the following questions:

◆ What were the causes and consequences of the growth of Europe's population after 1450?

◆ How did the growth of a market economy affect the lives of European men and women?

Resurgent Monarchies

6. Ferdinand of Aragon and Isabella of Castile:

    a. Knew that successful rule depended both on a show of royal grandeur and negotiations with their subjects.
    b. Argued that they did not have to respect the traditional political institutions of their kingdoms.
    c. Staffed their governments with men trained in the law.
    d. Granted limited religious toleration to Muslims while expelling Jews from their kingdoms.
    e. Denounced the work of the Spanish Inquisition.

7. Charles I of Spain (Charles V of the Holy Roman Empire):

   a. Ruled over lands that rivaled Charlemagne's Empire in size.
   b. Fielded an army of 150,000 men.
   c. Paid for his military and other expenses by means of annuities.
   d. Spent more time in the Netherlands than in Spain.
   e. Divided his lands between his son and his grandson.

8. Francis I of France:

   a. Inherited a strengthened monarchy.
   b. Encouraged the use of local French dialects in his law courts.
   c. Weakened royal power when he signed a concordat with Pope Leo X.
   d. Was able to collect revenue from the *taille*.
   e. Allied only with fellow Catholics to fight the Habsburgs.

9. Henry VII of England:

   a. Raised revenue by confiscating the lands of his opponents and imposing fees on England's overseas trade.
   b. Failed to establish effective judicial councils.
   c. Arranged the marriage of his daughter to the king of Ireland.
   d. Tried, but failed, to speak only Welsh.
   e. Married Elizabeth of York to heal the wounds of the Wars of the Roses.

10. Russian tsars:

   a. Allied with the Khanate of the Golden Horde against the Poles.
   b. Thought of themselves as the heirs of the Byzantine emperors.
   c. Spoke only Parisian French at court.
   d. Presided over the expansion of serfdom in their lands.
   e. Encouraged the Orthodox Church to convert all non-Christians in their lands.

Now that you have reviewed and tested yourself on this part of the chapter, take time to pull together all the important information by answering the following questions:

◆ What similar policies did the rulers discussed in this chapter section use to strengthen their rule in their states?

◆ What was unique to each of these rulers' policies?

Europe's Global Expansion

11. Western Europe's ability to think of and profit from new global trading networks depended on:

   a. The Ottoman Turks' closure of traditional trading networks with Asia.
   b. A few Portuguese sailors who struck out into the unknown Atlantic Ocean.
   c. A desire to convert more peoples to Christianity.
   d. All of the above.
   e. None of the above.

12. Which of the following were important innovations for ships planning to sail in the Atlantic Ocean?

   a. Growing use of lateen sails
   b. Higher poop decks
   c. Use of quadrants to determine longitude
   d. Fireproofing in kitchen galleys
   e. Improvements in mapmaking

13. The early modern Portuguese Empire depended on:

   a. The discovery of wind patterns in the Atlantic that allowed ships to sail around the southern tip of Africa.
   b. Strong royal support for exploration along the African coast.
   c. The ability to drive the Dutch from the Indian trade.
   d. The military skills of Alfonso de Albuquerque.
   e. Cooperation from Muslim spice traders in the Indian Ocean.

14. Hernan Cortés's conquest of the Aztec Empire:

   a. Took place in 1542.
   b. Benefited from alliances with discontented states ruled over by the Aztec Emperor.
   c. Was perhaps made easier by the emperor's belief that Cortés was the god Moctezuma.
   d. Launched the first New World gold rush.
   e. Ended with Cortés's murder by rival Spanish commanders.

15. The Spanish conquest of the Inca Empire:

   a. Benefited from a smallpox epidemic in the Inca emperor's lands.
   b. Resulted in Spanish control of silver mines in Bolivia.
   c. Resulted in the deaths of the three thousand Inca soldiers at Cajamarca.
   d. All of the above.
   e. None of the above.

Now that you have reviewed and tested yourself on this part of the chapter, take time to pull together all the important information by answering the following questions:

◆ What technological developments made European expansion possible?

◆ What were Europeans looking for as they began their global expansion, and what were the results of that expansion?

Exploration, Expansion, and European Identity

16. European views of the New World Indians:

   a. Often were comments on European society rather than accurate descriptions of Indian society.
   b. Over time shifted from the view of the "bad Indian" to that of the "good Indian."
   c. Over time shifted from the view of the "good Indian" to that of the "bad Indian."
   d. Contained no accurate information about the Indians.
   e. Contained some accurate information about the Indians.

17. Bartolomé de Las Casas:

   a. Argued against Eurocentric views of the New World Indians.
   b. Argued that Indians were not natural slaves.
   c. Believed in moderate exploitation of the Indians by the Spaniards.
   d. Was the first Catholic priest to be ordained in the Americas.
   e. Had been a landowner in the Caribbean.

18. How many African slaves were imported to New World plantations from 1500 to 1800?

   a. Less than 6 million
   b. 10 million
   c. More than 11 million
   d. 15 million
   e. 20 million

19. Europeans justified African slavery:

   a. By arguing that the Africans were natural slaves.
   b. By arguing that they were the descendants of Ham.
   c. By adopting earlier Muslim views about Africans.
   d. All of the above.
   e. None of the above.

20. Slavery in the New World:

   a. Did not differ from slavery in European and Muslim lands.

   b. Was not color-blind because it identified slaves as black and African.

   c. Usually limited slave labor to plantation work or mining.

   d. Was a lifelong and inheritable status.

   e. All of the above.

Now that you have reviewed and tested yourself on this part of the chapter, take time to pull together all the important information by answering the following questions:

◆ What was the range of European reactions to the Indians of the New World?

◆ What were the causes and consequences of African slavery in the New World?

CHAPTER
14

Reform in the Western Church, 1490–1570

Chapter Outline

1490	1495	1500	1505	1510	1515	1520	1525	1530

1494
Savonarola institutes reforms in Florence

1516
Erasmus translates the Greek New Testament

1517
Luther condemns indulgences

1527
Henry VIII breaks with the pope

This late fifteenth-century marble bust shows Pope Alexander VI (the Spaniard Rodrigo Lanzol de Borja) wearing the triple crown of Saint Peter. This was an officially sanctioned portrait, unlike some others that appeared during his reign. (bpk, Berlin/Skulpturesammlung und Museum fur Byzantinische Kunst, Staatliche Museen, Berlin/ Art Resource, Inc.)

After reading this chapter, you should be able to answer the following questions:

What motivated the leaders of church reform, whether Protestant or Catholic?

What were the similarities and differences in the reform agendas of the several different Protestant reform movements and the Catholics?

How did Protestant and Catholic reform reshape the religious identities of both Christians and non-Christians in western Europe and overseas?

How did religious reformers, rulers, and ordinary people interact in the business of reform?

IN THE SIXTEENTH CENTURY a church renewal movement swept over Europe. Church reform had been a feature of Christian life throughout the Middle Ages, but the movement that gained strength around the year 1500 was unparalleled in intensity and scope. It also split the Catholic Church apart. One branch of reform, known as Protestantism, rejected the authority of the pope, who until then had been the head of western Christianity. The other branch remained loyal to the pope while insisting on the need for basic change within the Catholic Church. Only the Orthodox churches of eastern Europe and the Middle East were largely untouched by these reforms.

In Germany, Martin Luther launched Protestant reform. He was followed by other Protestants who began reforms of their own that sometimes disagreed with Luther's. Thus, Protestants had to choose which reformer to follow. The leaders in Catholic reform were the religious orders of the church and the Roman popes. Together they refashioned Catholicism in ways that lasted until the mid-twentieth century. Because Catholics could

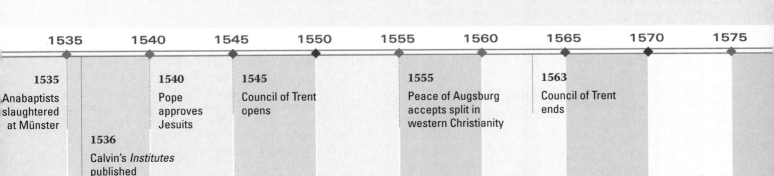

1535	1540	1545	1550	1555	1560	1565	1570	1575

1535 Anabaptists slaughtered at Münster

1536 Calvin's *Institutes* published

1540 Pope approves Jesuits

1545 Council of Trent opens

1555 Peace of Augsburg accepts split in western Christianity

1563 Council of Trent ends

rally around the person of the pope, they remained more united than the Protestants, although they, too, experienced division and controversy.

As reform touched more and more people's lives, both Protestants and Catholics had to rethink what it meant to be a Christian. Both forged new identities while imposing undesirable stereotypes on their opponents. Catholics also launched the first worldwide Christian missionary movement, as priests followed conquerors and merchants into the Americas and East Asia. Both Protestants and Catholics expected Jews to be swept up into church renewal and looked for their conversion to Christianity. When this did not happen, a backlash developed that worsened the living conditions of Jews in western Europe.

In both Protestant and Catholic Europe, reformers expected the mass of Christians to accept the changes they proposed. Often Christians did because there was wide popular support for many of the reforms. Sometimes, however, ordinary people had expectations of their own. When these clashed with those of the reformers, a period of unofficial negotiation took place in which reforms were modified or rejected by the community as a whole.

The Context of Church Reform, 1490–1517

◆ **What developments prepared the way for the church reform of the sixteenth century?**

◆ **What were the similarities and differences between Savonarola's and Erasmus's church reform programs?**

The famine and plague that beset Europe in the fourteenth century intensified religious concerns and raised anxieties about God's wrath and judgment. Above all, people looked to the traditional head of the western church, the pope, for spiritual leadership, but when he did not provide it, they turned elsewhere for religious guidance.

Some found it in the sermons of fiery preachers predicting God's punishment on sinful humankind, while others turned to new forms of piety and to the humanist movement for inspiration. By 1500, spiritual hunger and a growing sense that the western church was ineffective and worldly had set the stage for the waves of religious reform that swept over Europe in the sixteenth century.

Growing Discontent in the Western Church

Around 1500, a number of developments converged to provide the context for the reforming movements that spread throughout the western church during the sixteenth century. After 1450, the Roman papacy, the focal point of the church, tried to recover from the decline in prestige it had suffered during papal residence in Avignon and the Great Schism. Although the papacy successfully countered conciliarism's challenge that church councils held more authority than the pope, the popes of the late fifteenth century did not inspire confidence.

People were looking for a pastor, but none of the men elected to the papacy lived up to their expectations. Some, like Alexander VI, shocked contemporaries with their sexual immorality by keeping mistresses who gave birth to their children. Others, like Leo X, behaved more like Renaissance princes than devout bishops. On hearing of his election to the papacy, Leo reportedly said, "God has given us the papacy and we intend to enjoy it!" Lack of spiritual leadership convinced many that the papacy had become corrupt and worldly.

Hope for a spiritual leader in Rome was fueled by the spread of **Christian humanism**, which emphasized the need to recover pure Christianity by turning to the Bible and the ancient church fathers. At the same time, laypeople in the Netherlands joined clergy to form the **Brothers and Sisters of the Common Life**. The brothers and sisters tried to live the life of Jesus' first disciples—a life of poverty while caring for the sick and feeding the hungry. Their activities and their intense personal devotion to Jesus offered religious comfort to a generation hungry for spiritual renewal. Their devotion also prompted a growing popular interest in the life of Jesus and in the Bible

Christian humanism Humanist movement in northern Europe emphasizing study of the Bible and the early church fathers.

Brothers and Sisters of the Common Life Religious community founded in the Netherlands that cared for the needy, following the example of Jesus.

Catholics, Protestants, and the Eastern Orthodox in 1555 The Religious Peace of Augsburg in 1555 confirmed the division of western Christendom. © Cengage Learning

1. Using the map legend, identify the geographical location of the religious groups found in sixteenth-century Europe, North Africa, and Asia Minor.
2. Which religious community or communities were able to win over the majority of the population in most parts of Europe, north and south, east and west?

and a greater demand for preachers who could talk about scripture and describe Jesus' life and death.

Although the popes did not respond vigorously to rising demands for spiritual leadership, the lower clergy did. By 1500, many clergymen were better educated and more effective in performing their duties than they had been in the Middle Ages. Some installed **pulpits** in their churches to respond to the demand for preaching. Traditionally, preaching had been the task of religious orders like the Franciscans and Dominicans.

When **parish priests** began to preach, these orders resented their intrusion, and tensions led to charges of incompetence and immorality from both sides. Friars complained that parish priests were badly educated, while parish priests accused the friars of preaching to lure women into confession and then use them sexually. Although many of these accusations were exaggerated, they fed a growing belief that the clergy as a whole, not just the pope, was corrupt.

In the absence of strong papal leadership, rulers in many parts of Europe tried to meet their subjects' religious

pulpit Raised and enclosed platform for preaching.

parish priests Clergymen in charge of church life in the basic local unit of the church, the parish.

These two prints attack Pope Alexander VI. The left image, the first a viewer would see, shows the "official" Alexander in his papal robes, carrying a ceremonial cross and wearing the papal triple tiara. The caption reads "Alexander VI Supreme Pontiff." After lifting up the first image the viewer would see the right image of the "real" Alexander, a hideous, hellish monster. The caption reads "I am the pope." Debates over the place of the Roman pope in church life were one of the central features of sixteenth-century church reform. What makes the overlapping images an effective piece of propaganda?

expectations while strengthening their own control over the church in their lands. Ferdinand and Isabella in Spain, along with Francis I of France, showed what determined rulers could do in reforming perceived abuses and regulating relations with the pope. Their efforts inspired others to look to the state as an agent of religious reform.

Finally, the printing revolution that swept over Europe during the fifteenth century allowed for fast reproduction of inexpensive texts and illustrations in large numbers. It was in the Rhineland and the Netherlands that printing first became widespread. In the fifty years between 1450 and 1500, more books were produced using the new technology than during the previous thousand years. After 1500, church reformers quickly exploited the possibilities of rapid, widespread dissemination of their views that the printing press made possible.

Girolamo Savonarola (1452–1498) Italian Dominican friar who tried to carry out church reform in Florence.

God's Wrath and Church Reform

Fear of God's wrath, which lay behind movements like the medieval flagellants, continued to inspire movements of reform. In the 1490s, a Dominican friar in Florence, **Girolamo Savonarola**, denounced corruption in the city and church. He proclaimed that a divine day of reckoning was just around the corner on which the church would be judged and then renewed. Condemning the Florentines' worldliness, he organized "burnings of vanities." In a frenzy of communal purification, people tossed their fancy clothes and jewels onto public bonfires along with playing cards, gambling tables, and pornographic pictures.

For Savonarola, this was the first act in a divinely scripted drama in which Florence would become a truly holy Christian city. He proclaimed that reform would increase Florence's wealth and prestige and would inaugurate a purification of the church throughout the world. Savonarola also prophesied that a French army would invade Italy and win an easy victory over the Italians. When, in fact, the French king Charles VIII invaded in 1494, many Florentines believed that Savonarola's prophesy had come true, and his prestige in the city soared. For the next four years he was Florence's spiritual dictator.

Savonarola Attacks the Pope Savonarola denounced not only the "vanities" of the Florentines but also Pope Alexander VI's sexual immorality. Angered by the attack, Alexander looked for ways to silence him. Faced with mounting papal hostility, Savonarola called for a general council of the church to judge Alexander, thus resurrecting the theology of the conciliar movement that Rome had tried to quash. This was too much for the pope; in 1498, at Alexander's instigation, a church court condemned Savonarola. He was then tortured and burned at the stake.

Savonarola's dictatorship, which had widespread popular support, mixed Christian reform with a strong dose of local patriotism and a belief that a truly Christian Florence could prosper in this world. It expressed a yearning for Christ's return to earth as judge of the living and the dead that was as old as Christianity itself. It also reflected the traditional Christian view that earthly and heavenly things were inseparable; right relations with God led to an orderly, prosperous community life. Savonarola's commitment to a purified Christian community, his belief in a coming day of reckoning with God, and his sense that religion and all other aspects of life were tied together reappeared regularly in the later church reform movements of the sixteenth century.

Humanism and Church Reform

Humanism also contributed to the movement for church reform, thanks to **Desiderius Erasmus** of Rotterdam, the greatest Christian humanist of his generation. The illegitimate son of a priest, Erasmus lost both his parents to the plague when he was a child. His new guardians sent him to various schools, including one run by the Brothers of the Common Life. Later, he complained about the brothers' harsh routine, but their piety deeply influenced him. When his guardians insisted that Erasmus become a monk, he joined a religious order and was ordained a priest. The monastic life, however, was not to his taste, and in 1516 he obtained papal permission to live outside his monastery.

Although Erasmus attended the University of Paris and lectured at Cambridge University in England, he was never drawn to the academic life. Rejecting both the monastery and the university, he set himself up as an independent scholar and traveled widely throughout western Europe. Erasmus shared the humanists' interest in studying the pagan and Christian literature of antiquity. His writings combined an elegant Latin style with biting humor. Like Savonarola, he was fiercely opposed to immorality, but unlike him, he expressed his opposition in wit and satire instead of fiery preaching. Also, like Savonarola, he wanted a reform but not a rejection of the Catholic Church because he accepted the basic teachings of Catholicism, including the pope's preeminence.

The Philosophy of Christ Erasmus's version of reformed Christianity centered on what he called the philosophy of Christ, which was found in the ancient sources of Christianity—the scriptures and the commentaries of the early church fathers. Erasmus believed that the fathers, who were closer in time to Christ than his own generation, were also closer to the original meaning of scripture. Therefore, people should follow the example of Christ in the Gospels as the fathers presented it. Erasmus argued that if certain practices were not found in these early sources, like confession to a priest or clerical celibacy, they were not essential to Christianity.

Erasmus believed that education was the way to get people to accept the philosophy of Christ. He had huge faith in the power of education to change people's lives; study did not simply make people informed or skilled—it made them good. He therefore told teachers that they should teach the young by persuasion, not fear, and should avoid whipping bad students unless absolutely necessary. Since education was to teach the philosophy of Christ based on the scriptures, Erasmus prepared an accurate printed edition of the New Testament in its original Greek and made a correct translation into the more familiar Latin.

During his visit to England, Erasmus met the English lawyer and humanist **Sir Thomas More**. More was famous for his *Utopia*, a witty account of a fictional country where there was no private property, men and women saw each other naked before marriage to show that they were physically sound, and the incurably ill were encouraged to take their own lives. More, a devout Catholic, was not advocating these practices (*utopia* in Greek means "no place"). His intentions were to amuse his readers and to unmask the stupidity and greed of his own society. More also served in the English king's government as chancellor, the highest judicial official in the realm. His service appealed to Erasmus, who believed that Europe's rulers should be agents for church reform.

By the time Erasmus died in 1536, the Protestant Reformation was well under way. Although he remained a Catholic, his emphasis on scripture as the foundation of Christianity, his call for Christians to return to their ancient roots

> **Desiderius Erasmus** (1469–1536) Dutch humanist, theologian, and textual scholar whose writings influenced the movement for church reform.
>
> **Sir Thomas More** (1477–1535) English lawyer and humanist, author of *Utopia* and friend of Erasmus.

for standards of belief and action, and his faith in the power of education to make a better world were all embraced by reformers after him.

 Checking In

By yourself or with a partner, explain the significance of each of the following selected key terms:

Christian humanism

Brothers and Sisters of the Common Life

pulpits

parish priests

Girolamo Savonarola

Desiderius Erasmus

Sir Thomas More

Martin Luther and the Protestant Reformation, 1517–1550

◆ How was Martin Luther's reform agenda similar to and different from that of his predecessors?

◆ What was the impact of Luther's reforms?

By the time Erasmus was a well-established critic of the church, another reformer, Martin Luther, had emerged and was carrying the reforming agenda in new directions. Eventually, Luther argued that reform of the church required a complete rejection of the Roman pope, and rupture with Rome, therefore, became the central feature of his movement. Historians call reformers who broke with the pope Protestants. With the establishment of Lutheran Protestant churches in north Germany and Scandinavia, the religious unity of western Europe was shattered.

Luther's Challenge to the Church

Martin Luther was a broad-faced German monk from peasant stock with a sharp tongue and a brilliant mind whose father had wanted him to become a lawyer. Like Savonarola, Luther was troubled by fears of sin, God's wrath, and judgment. In the summer of 1505, the fears came to a head when he was caught in a violent thunderstorm, during which a bolt of lightning threw him to the ground. He cried out in terror, "Help me Saint Anne!

Martin Luther (1483–1546) German monk who led a church reform movement in Germany that became the Lutheran form of Protestantism.

absolution At the end of confession, words spoken by a Catholic priest, acting as God's agent, that grant forgiveness of a person's sins.

Johannes Tetzel (ca. 1465–1519) Dominican friar whose sale of indulgences angered Martin Luther.

indulgences Documents applying the good works of Christ and his saints to cancel the divine punishment of one's own sins or those of a dead friend or relative.

Scala/Art Resource, NY

Luther was fifty when Lucas Cranach the Elder painted this portrait in 1533. By then Lutheranism was spreading through much of Germany and Scandinavia. Luther gazes out of the picture toward something that would be on the viewer's right. His sturdy face and serene expression convey confidence and calm.

I shall become a monk!" After Luther gave up the law and took monastic vows, the head of his monastery ordered him to study theology, and in 1508 he was appointed professor of New Testament studies at the new University of Wittenberg.

For the next seven years, Luther studied the Bible. He had become a monk to lessen his fears about his sinfulness before God, but the old doubts continued to haunt him. He carefully observed the monastic life and regularly confessed his sins, but the promise of God's forgiveness, which came with the priest's **absolution**, seemed hollow, and he continued to feel unrighteous before God. In 1517, these private doubts burst into public protest when a Dominican friar, **Johannes Tetzel**, began to sell **indulgences** in the territories of the empire.

Indulgences Indulgences were at the heart of the late medieval Catholic religion, and they raised a particularly troubling question for Luther: "How can I become righteous in God's eyes?" The Catholic Church taught that righteousness resulted from two things: human effort and God's help, called **grace**. People could become righteous before God by choosing to do good deeds, called **works**—giving to the poor, going on a religious pilgrimage, and fasting. Above all, righteousness began when one received the **sacraments** of the church, like baptism, Communion, and confession, most of which had to be administered by a priest. When God saw this human effort, he rewarded it with grace, thus helping one to do even better.

In addition to one's own good works, one could become righteous by drawing on the good works of Christ and the saints. They had been so righteous that they had performed a superabundance of good works, which overflowed into a treasury that Christians could draw on to supplement their own less abundant righteousness. An indulgence, issued by the pope, allowed the person obtaining it to use the righteousness of Christ and the saints to cancel out his or her own sins. At its best, the system of indulgences was something like a mutual-aid society based on compassion for sinners, but it often degenerated into an accountant's game of credit (works) and debit (sins) in which specific sums were shifted from the treasury to the sinful man or woman.

Moreover, indulgences could be obtained for someone else, like a spouse or parent, who had died. These dead people were thought to be in **Purgatory**, where they were being punished for their earthly sins. An indulgence for them would cancel some of that punishment and thus hasten their passage into Heaven.

Luther Attacks Indulgences Luther's study of the Bible led him to reject the premise on which the practice of indulgences was based. For him, righteousness before God, called **justification**, did not begin when humans chose to do good works, which then earned God's grace. In fact, Luther believed that while humans had **free will** in the sense that they could choose what they ate for breakfast, when it came to doing things that were good in God's eyes, they had no free will—their sinfulness always made them choose unrighteousness and made them incapable of doing good works. Justification, therefore, had no connection to good works. It was simply God's gift to human beings that made them righteous even though they were still sinners. Christians were simply to trust in this gift and the additional gift of faith that God alone made them righteous. Luther based his position on the apostle Paul, who had written, "He who through faith is righteous shall live" (Romans 1:17).

The Ninety-Five Theses Tetzel came to the vicinity of Wittenberg selling indulgences to fund the building of the new Saint Peter's Church in Rome. He even had a slogan to motivate potential buyers: "When the coin in the change box rings, the soul from Purgatory springs!" When Luther heard of this, he was outraged. Tetzel stirred up the issues of works, grace, faith, and righteousness before God that had preoccupied Luther for years. Luther's response was to pen the **Ninety-five Theses**, propositions attacking indulgences, which were quickly printed up and distributed throughout Germany. They caused a sensation. At first the pope dismissed Luther as just another "drunken monk," but, as the seriousness of his challenge to indulgences sank in, a gulf opened up between Luther and the papacy.

The Impact of Luther's Challenge

The implications of Luther's teaching were profound: if works were irrelevant, and people were justified by faith alone, the whole structure of medieval Catholic piety—based on pilgrimages, fasting, alms to the poor, and indulgences—came tumbling down. Moreover, the sacraments administered by priests were no longer so central. Over the next five years, the rift between Luther and the Catholic Church deepened. In 1518, the pope condemned him as a heretic. In 1519, during the **Imperial Diet**, the Holy Roman Empire's legislative body, which elected **Charles V** emperor, Luther debated publicly with a papal representative, John Eck, and declared that neither the pope nor church councils had final authority to settle theological disputes.

The Break with Rome The pope then excommunicated Luther, who in turn publicly appealed to the princes of the empire to initiate reforms against indulgences. He argued that all believers, not just the clergy, were priests who were responsible for the well-being of the church. This doctrine of the **priesthood of all believers** posed another threat to Catholic

---

grace God's help in making a person righteous.

works Good deeds performed to become righteous in the sight of God.

sacrament Religious practice or ceremony that symbolizes a deeper religious reality; the seven sacraments are baptism, Communion (Eucharist), confirmation, confession (penance), ordination, marriage, and unction in sickness.

Purgatory The place where the souls of the departed were punished for their earthly sins before entering heaven.

justification Luther's teaching that righteousness before God comes from God alone, not from a combination of God's grace and human works.

free will Teaching that people can freely will to do good works and thereby merit God's grace.

Ninety-five Theses Luther's public attack on indulgences.

Imperial Diet Holy Roman Empire's legislative body.

Charles V (r. 1516–1556) Heir of Ferdinand and Isabella in Spain and of the emperor Maximilian in the Holy Roman Empire; the most powerful European ruler during the first half of the sixteenth century.

priesthood of all believers Luther's teaching that all Christians exercised priestly functions in the Christian church.

Christianity, which made a sharp distinction between the ordained priesthood and ordinary Christians. To gain support, Luther printed four thousand copies of his appeal. They sold out in a few days.

In 1521, Charles V, who had remained in Spain during these confrontations, made his first trip to Germany as emperor and summoned Luther to another Imperial Diet in the city of Worms. Asked directly to renounce his teachings, Luther refused, arguing that **scripture alone** was the only authority he would obey. He concluded dramatically, "Here I stand. May God help me! Amen." The emperor then declared him an outlaw, and Luther went into hiding.

Reform in Germany   The local ruler of Wittenberg, who had embraced Luther's theology, shielded him from the imperial authorities. Luther continued to develop his theology, arguing that in the Gospels Christ had instituted only two sacraments, baptism and Communion, not the other rites that Catholics considered sacraments. Soon afterward, Luther began to translate the Bible into German, using Erasmus's edition of the Greek New Testament to make the ancient scriptural sources of Christianity available to ordinary men and women. He also composed hymns like "A Mighty Fortress Is Our God" for people to sing, thus bringing them directly into community worship and strengthening their sense of God's presence among them. And he continued to publish his protests; some three hundred thousand copies of his works were printed and distributed throughout the empire.

The Spread of Reform

Luther's ideas, spread by the printing press, inspired local reformers in both town and countryside. Like Savonarola, they believed that religion was linked to all other aspects of life, and their reform programs had political and social dimensions along with religious ones. In the cities of southern Germany and Switzerland, local religious or political leaders encouraged men and women from the middle ranks of urban society to support reform. These were hardworking people who resented their exclusion from the ruling elite and thought of themselves as the backbone of the town on whom its collective well-being depended. After 1520, they produced a flood of printed pamphlets that, like Luther's, were circulated throughout Germany and constitute a kind of sixteenth-century public opinion poll.

The Urban Reformation   The pamphlets show that Luther's criticism of the pope and his priests was widely accepted. In the decentralized political world of Germany, papal taxes and clerical exemptions from them were often easily imposed and deeply resented. As a result, urban reformers attacked the privileges of the Catholic clergy, demanding that they be taxed like all other citizens.

The Pure Gospel   The urban reformers also believed that community life should be regulated by what they called the **pure gospel**, which stressed the equality of all Christians and rejected the idea that clergy or members of religious orders were somehow more genuinely Christian than laypeople. A number of specific reforms flowed from the idea of the pure gospel. The community, not the local bishop, would appoint clergy. Preachers were to preach on the Bible and nothing else. If disputes arose about the correct interpretation of scripture, the community would decide who was right. Acceptance of the pure gospel, which called for love of neighbor and commitment to the common good, would reinvigorate the collective identity and social solidarity of city dwellers. The reformers were, therefore, particularly receptive to Luther's theology of the authority of scripture alone and the priesthood of all believers.

Faced with the demands of these urban reformers, which were often introduced with a wave of rioting, local municipal authorities had to decide what to do. They were concerned with maintaining public order, so they more or less willingly went along with the reforms.

Zurich and Zwingli   Events in the Swiss city of Zurich show how urban reform progressed. There, a local priest, **Huldrych Zwingli**, after reading Erasmus's attacks on corrupt clergy, urged the town council to inaugurate reform. Zwingli was supported by many townsfolk who believed that both the material and spiritual welfare of the city depended on a purifying reform of the church.

Luther's actions influenced Zwingli, but he went beyond Luther when he banished images of Christ and the saints from the churches and argued that the bread and wine of Communion were not the body and blood of Christ but simple memorials of Jesus' Last Supper with his disciples. Protestant reform thus started to take different and sometimes conflicting paths.

Reform in the Countryside   By 1523, there were signs that urban reform was attracting rural followers. Calls for religious renewal to create a more just Christian community also appealed to German peasants, many of whom were experiencing economic

---

scripture alone Luther's teaching that the Bible was the only authoritative guide for Christian belief and conduct.

pure gospel Reform program of German Protestant reformers in the cities of the empire endorsing some of Luther's reforms but rejecting others.

Huldrych Zwingli (1484–1531) Swiss reformer who accepted some of Luther's theological points but rejected others.

Map 14.2 **Cities and Towns of the Reformation in Germany** This map shows a heavy concentration in the southwest of urban centers caught up in the Protestant reform movement. These centers are mostly in the modern German states of Baden-Württenberg and Bavaria. © *Cengage Learning*

1. Go online and find statistics about the current religious affiliations of people in these states. Do they fit with what you see in this map?
2. Where was Pope Benedict XVI born?

hard times following crop failures and landlords' demands for more rent. Invoking the pure gospel, peasants demanded that their payments to landlords be lowered, that serfdom be abolished, and that they have greater access to common lands. During the summer of 1524, violence broke out in the **Peasants' War**, which engulfed much of southern Germany. In May 1525, an imperial army defeated a peasant force and massacred five to six thousand rebels. After that, the uprising collapsed.

The war shocked Luther, who had a firm respect for social order and obedience to civil authorities. In a pamphlet, *Against the Robbing and Murdering Hordes*

of Peasants, he urged the troops to "smite, slay, and stab" the rebels. Because of the radical nature of its demands, historians have often regarded the Peasants' War as a revolution, though a failed one. It testified to a widespread hunger for fundamental religious and social reform that touched hundreds of thousands of ordinary men and women by the mid-1520s.

State-Sponsored Reform
The years after 1525 saw the continuing spread of Luther's reforms, but the

Peasants' War Uprising, 1524–1525, in southern Germany inspired by Protestant calls for a reform of church and society.

dynamic behind them had changed. No longer were church-based reformers the leaders in the movement, and no longer were German cities in its vanguard. Now the princes of the empire, like the dukes of Saxony and Bavaria, determined whether Protestantism would be adopted in their territories. Rulers also introduced Lutheran reforms in Denmark and Sweden. The state's increasing leadership in reform was partly a backlash following the Peasants' War, as princes and city councils decided that a popular reformation by peasants or the urban middle classes was too dangerous to tolerate. But Luther, under Erasmus's influence, had also prepared the way by calling on rulers to carry out reform.

As the empire split into hostile Catholic and Lutheran states, the emperor Charles V looked on in dismay. Although he wanted to stamp out the Lutheran movement, he was only one of many imperial princes, and he was never able to implement his policy, largely because of distractions from warfare with the Turks in the east and the French in the west. Between 1531 and his abdication in 1556, Charles tried many solutions to the problem of growing religious disunity in the empire: gaining time with a truce between the competing factions; calling for a general church council to resolve the matter; trying to establish a dialogue with the Lutherans; and, finally, in 1546, going to war against the Lutheran princes.

The Peace of Augsburg, 1555 None of these strategies worked, and in 1555, he turned the problem over to his younger brother, the archduke Ferdinand, who accepted the **Peace of Augsburg** in that year. It acknowledged Lutheranism as a religious option in the empire and allowed the rulers of each imperial state to determine whether the state would be Lutheran or Catholic. If the ruler chose Lutheranism, Catholics were free to emigrate to a Catholic state, and vice versa. In fact, emigration was often impossible because of family or economic reasons, and secret Catholic or Lutheran communities developed in a number of states. Thus, dissenting German Christians were forced into a situation rather like that of the Jews and Moors after their expulsions from Spain and Portugal—convert, leave, or practice one's religion in secret.

State rulers now took the lead in reorganizing the church, policing the behavior of clergy, and maintaining Christian morality in the general population. In Catholic states, they still had to share government of the church with the pope. In Lutheran ones, they ruled largely unchecked. Thus, the Peace of Augsburg permanently shattered the religious unity of Germany and established a pattern of Christian religious pluralism that would be one of the hallmarks of European life in subsequent centuries.

Peace of Augsburg First major treaty, 1555, to accept the split in western Christianity between Protestants and Catholics.

 **Checking In**

By yourself or with a partner, explain the significance of each of the following selected key terms:

Martin Luther	Ninety-five Theses
indulgences	Huldrych Zwingli
grace	Peasants' War
works	Peace of Augsburg

The Protestant Reformation Across Europe, 1520–1570

◆ **What were the similarities and differences among the reform programs of Luther, the Anabaptists, and Calvin?**

◆ **What were the distinctive features of Protestant reform in England?**

Along with Lutheranism, other forms of Protestantism developed. One movement, led by radicals, went even further than Luther and Zwingli in rejecting traditional Catholicism. Another, founded by the Frenchman John Calvin, proved to be the most rapidly expanding form of Protestantism. In England, an ambiguous type of reform was eventually introduced from above by the state.

The Anabaptists and Radical Reform

In the early 1520s, when Luther was condemned by the church for pushing church reform too far, he was also attacked by people who thought he had not gone far enough. These were the Protestant radicals. Though never a unified movement, the radicals shared a deep dislike of the ordained clergy and a strong sense that the church should exist for the benefit of ordinary men and women. They were at odds with Luther—a clergyman and university scholar—in rejecting scriptural interpretation by trained professionals. While Luther proclaimed the priesthood of all believers and wanted the Bible in people's hands, he believed the people needed expert guidance in understanding scripture. The radicals replied that every Christian man and woman was capable of correctly interpreting it under the direct guidance of the Holy Spirit.

The radicals were also deeply suspicious of Luther's policy of turning to city or state rulers to help introduce Protestantism.

Separation of Church and State Most radicals argued for a sharp separation of church and state. Some also believed that true Christians should be completely separated from the sinful world surrounding them. Only adults who had received a divine call should become church members; consequently, the ancient practice of infant baptism should be abolished because babies were incapable of receiving or responding to such a call. Soon these radicals were being denounced as **Anabaptists** because they insisted on being rebaptized as adults in a true, voluntary baptism.

Anabaptism first emerged among the craftsmen of the Swiss city of Zurich. They preached adult baptism, called for a separated church, and refused to honor customary civic obligations like paying church taxes, holding public office, or serving in the militia. They even began to hold all their material goods in common, inspired by the first-century church in Jerusalem, which had implemented this form of Christian communalism, as described in the New Testament book of Acts.

Anabaptist separatism was thus deeply subversive because it rejected the generally accepted idea that everyone in a given place should be a church member and that society would fall apart without the unifying force of a common religion. To suppress Anabaptism, Charles V issued an imperial edict in 1529 decreeing the death penalty for anyone who held a separatist view of church-state relations. In some states, executions were carried out by drowning, a punishment thought to fit the crime.

Münster In the northwestern German city of **Münster**, the Anabaptists would not be suppressed. Elected to the city government in 1534, they declared all real estate common property, banned money, and decreed that house doors were to be unlocked and open day and night. Then polygamy was introduced. The reformers justified the practice of men taking multiple spouses by citing the Old Testament, but the practice may have had more to do with remedying a gender imbalance in the Anabaptist community and the need to put women under male rule in individual households.

When Münster's expelled bishop tried to retake the city by force but was defeated, the Anabaptists proclaimed the impending end of the world, with Münster designated as the New Jerusalem. As executions of the wayward began, Catholic and Lutheran rulers were so alarmed that they set aside their differences and joined forces to recapture Münster. Following their victory in 1535, they slaughtered almost all of Münster's inhabitants in one of the greatest bloodbaths of the century.

Jacob Hutter and Menno Simons The catastrophe in Münster permanently discredited all forms of violent Anabaptism. Following it, the radical remnant turned to leaders who denounced violence and embraced **pacifism**. **Jacob Hutter** provided the inspiration for those who fled to Moravia, where they continued to practice Christian communalism and prospered economically in the later years of the

sixteenth century. By 1600, about 20,000 Hutterites lived in peaceful coexistence with their Catholic and Protestant neighbors.

In the northern Netherlands, **Menno Simons**, a Dutch ex-priest, organized churches as a refuge for those Anabaptists who had survived the slaughter of 1535. Simons's churches were based on voluntary membership and adult baptism, but he gave up the New Testament ideal of Christian communalism and called simply for mutual aid among church members. These Mennonites numbered about one hundred thousand at the end of the century. Like the Hutterites, they gained a degree of respectability in the eyes of their non-Anabaptist neighbors.

Beginning in the eighteenth century, many began to emigrate to North America, where their descendants today make up the Amish and Mennonite communities of Pennsylvania and parts of the Midwest. They still live a life separated from the larger world.

John Calvin and Calvinism

John Calvin founded the third major Protestant community of the sixteenth century, **Calvinism**. Luther was already thirty-six when Calvin was born in northeastern France; Calvinism was thus a second-generation Protestant movement. Calvin was sent to the University of Paris to study theology because his father wanted him to become a priest. Then his father changed his mind and sent him to law school. During his school years, Calvin met men who had embraced Protestant reform. His father's death in 1531 freed him to make his own future plans, and he became a reformer.

Calvin was more reserved and private than Luther, who talked openly about his spiritual trials. But he, too, believed that he had undergone a "sudden conversion" in which God subdued his "stubborn heart" and called him to Protestantism. In 1535, the pro-Catholic French government attacked Protestants in Paris, and Calvin was forced to flee under a false name.

Anabaptists (from Greek, "repeated dippers") Radical Protestants who practiced a second, adult baptism.

Münster City in northwestern Germany where a violent Anabaptist movement was defeated by a combined Protestant and Catholic army.

pacifism Opposition to armed force and warfare.

Jacob Hutter (1500–1536) Anabaptist leader in Moravia who embraced pacifism and the practice of Christian communalism.

Menno Simons (1495–1561) Leader of the Mennonite Anabaptist communities in the Netherlands who embraced pacifism but rejected Christian communalism.

John Calvin (1509–1564) Frenchman who founded the Protestant movement known as Calvinism.

Calvinism Teachings and church organization of Protestant churches that considered John Calvin their founder.

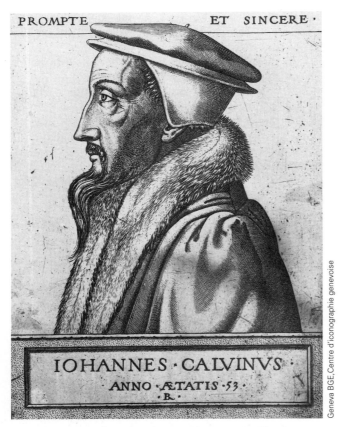

PROMPTE   ET SINCERE·

IOHANNES · CALVINVS ·
ANNO · ÆTATIS · 53 ·
· B ·

Geneva BGE, Centre d'iconographie genevoise

René Boivin's engraving (1562) shows Calvin at age fifty-three, as the Latin inscription at the bottom of the portrait indicates. The caption at the top, in French, asserts that Calvin is "active and honest," affirming his success as a religious leader.

The *Institutes of the Christian Religion* In 1536, Calvin was in Switzerland, beyond the reach of French authorities. There he published the first edition of the *Institutes of the Christian Religion*, a work he revised and expanded for the next twenty-three years. It gained him an immediate European reputation. The *Institutes,* which presented Calvin's version of theology, came to serve as the blueprint for Calvinist reform.

Calvin followed Luther on a number of points, condemning the pope and arguing that scripture was the only source of authority for Christians. He did not, however, accept Luther's teaching on the priesthood of all believers. For Calvin, the clergy were placed above ordinary church members

Institutes of the Christian Religion Calvin's systematic presentation of his Protestant teachings, which served as a blueprint for Calvinist reform.

double predestination Belief that God has predestined some human beings for damnation and others for salvation.

the elect Those whom God has chosen (elected) for salvation.

Consistory Assembly made up of Calvinist ministers and members of city government that enforced Calvinist standards of behavior in Geneva.

to teach and administer discipline in the community. His insistence that the church alone should appoint the clergy was closer to traditional Catholic practice than the procedures adopted in Lutheran lands, where the state controlled clergy recruitment. But Calvin joined Luther in increasing worshipers' personal participation in church services by translating the book of Psalms into French and setting the Psalms to simple tunes that the congregation could sing.

Calvin also agreed with Luther that everyone in a given territory should belong to the same church. But, because of his belief in the doctrine of **double predestination**, he did not think that all church members were necessarily saved. Predestination taught that before the world was created, God foresaw that human beings would sin and thereby merit damnation as the just punishment for their sin. God then decreed that some of these sinners were predestined for Hell while others were predestined for Heaven. Those predestined for Hell suffered just punishment for their sins, testifying to God's justice. Those predestined for Heaven were forgiven their sins and would be reunited with God, testifying to God's mercy.

Calvin often argued that probably only one in a hundred would be saved. Like Luther, he believed that sin had corrupted people's will so that they could do nothing that contributed to their salvation. Therefore, they were saved not through any merit or works of their own but solely as a result of God's loving kindness. Although a person's good works did not earn salvation, Calvin taught that they were a sign that God had chosen the person as one of **the elect** destined for salvation. Since impulses to act as good Christians were an assurance of salvation, Calvinists were quick to nurture their desire for church and state reform.

Calvin also argued that hard work and thrift were signs of election. He believed that the doctrine of double predestination explained why some people refused to join the reformed churches. It also assured believers that, in the end, God would triumph over sinners' opposition to him.

Geneva Calvin's opportunity to put his theology into practice came in 1541, when the town council of the little city-state of Geneva called him to reform the local church. For the next fourteen years, he argued, threatened, and maneuvered to get a reform to his liking. Calvin's cause was helped by an influx of religious refugees from his native country who fled to Geneva to avoid persecution by the French government. These Frenchmen, solidly behind their fellow countryman's agenda, were able to take over Geneva's government in 1555. It was then that Calvin finally gained full control over the church.

Because Calvin thought of the church in territorial terms, everyone in Geneva had to conform to church standards. To enforce reform, he created the **Consistory**, a body made up of Calvinist ministers and members of the city government. The Consistory scrutinized every aspect of Genevans' behavior, imposing fines or imprisonment for infractions. Everything people said or did was to be supervised and controlled. Like the advocates of the pure gospel, Calvinists in Geneva were trying to forge a new Christian identity based strictly on Protestant religious principles.

Throughout the period of Calvin's rule in Geneva, religious refugees from all over Europe continued to stream into the city. It is estimated that between 1550 and 1562 about seven thousand of the city's ten thousand inhabitants were foreigners. These refugees, many of whom were nobility, wanted to introduce Calvin's reforms into their homelands, and their status was particularly important for Calvinism's future success. To meet the refugees' needs, Calvin founded a training institute for future Calvinist pastors, the Genevan Academy, where men were taught the theology of the *Institutes* and the best ways to form church communities, especially under persecution.

The Spread of Calvinism

Calvinism was the most dynamic form of Protestantism after 1550, becoming an international movement with headquarters in Geneva as missionaries left the city to establish Calvinist communities in their native lands. The first to return home were the French.

France and the Netherlands In France, most Calvinists were recruited from the urban middle class, but members of powerful noble families also converted. It was often the women in these families who convinced their relations to embrace Calvinism. For example, **Jeanne d'Albret** introduced Calvinism into the tiny kingdom of Navarre, on the border between France and Spain. By 1560, about 10 percent of the overall French population was **Huguenot**, as the French Calvinists were called, and about 50 percent of the nobility had embraced the new faith. As the Huguenots' numbers grew, confrontations with Catholics also increased, and soon France was on the verge of civil war.

In the Netherlands, Protestantism was fiercely resisted by Charles V. Unlike in Germany, where he was often checked by other powerful imperial princes, Charles governed the Netherlands directly as the local prince, and no powerful noble factions emerged to promote the Protestant cause. When the Lutherans and Anabaptists tried to establish communities in the Netherlands, Charles's government effectively repressed them. By the time he abdicated in 1556, some five hundred dissidents had been executed for heresy. Nevertheless, Calvinist missionaries began to infiltrate the region, establishing secret communities, and, like France, the Netherlands was moving toward armed clashes between Protestants and Catholics.

Scotland In 1558, **John Knox**, returning from Geneva, successfully introduced Calvinist theology into his native Scotland and created a **Presbyterian** form of church administration that eliminated bishops. Knox had the help of powerful nobles who opposed the rule of Mary, Queen of Scots, widow of the French king Francis II and a committed Catholic. In 1559, Knox published *The First Blast Against the Monstrous Regiment of Women*, in which he attacked Mary and argued that female rule was unnatural. Knox's attack appealed to Scottish Calvinists, whose leaders, hardened by organized persecution from Catholic authorities, were prepared to resist rulers if they opposed Calvinist reform. This position directly conflicted with Luther's views about obedience to rulers.

Reform in England

Calvinists in Scotland introduced religious reform from the bottom up. To the south, in England, it was introduced from the top down. In 1521, King **Henry VIII** published a treatise condemning Lutheranism. Shortly thereafter, the pope granted him the title Defender of the Faith in recognition of his service to Catholicism. Twelve years later, however, Rome excommunicated Henry, a surprising turn of events that occurred because succession problems were plaguing the king.

The Break with Rome When the pope refused to grant Henry an annulment from Catherine of Aragon, the daughter of Ferdinand and Isabella, the king turned to the English clergy. With their support, he divorced Catherine and married her lady-in-waiting, Anne Boleyn, who was already pregnant with his child. Anne gave birth to Henry's second daughter, Elizabeth. When the pope learned of Henry's action, he excommunicated him. In retaliation, Henry, in the **Act of Supremacy**, proclaimed himself "the only supreme head on earth of the church of England," a title still held today by British monarchs. In 1536, Henry, still in search of a male heir, had Anne convicted of adultery and beheaded. Following her execution,

Jeanne d'Albret (1528–1572) French noblewoman who introduced Calvinism into the kingdom of Navarre.

Huguenots (from German, "confederation") French Calvinists, so called because they formed a network of Protestant churches.

John Knox (1505–1572) Leader of Calvinist reform of the church in Scotland.

Presbyterian Form of church organization used in the Calvinist Church of Scotland in which ministers known as presbyters or elders were church leaders, eliminating bishops.

Henry VIII (r. 1509–1547) King who broke with the pope over his divorce from Catherine of Aragon and marriage to Anne Boleyn, launching the English Reformation.

Act of Supremacy Henry VIII's declaration that the king of England was the earthly head of the English church.

The Pastors of Geneva Establish Rules for Proper Christian Conduct

Beginning in 1541, the reformed clergy of Geneva, under the guidance of John Calvin, published rules governing the behavior of clergy and laity in Geneva. Calvinism's great strength lay in its ability to forge strong bonds and loyalties between members of a Calvinist community. This could be done by rewarding behavior that conformed to Calvinist community norms while punishing behavior that did not. It could also be done by trying to reconcile quarreling members of the community. The rules of 1541 provided guidelines for carrying out all aspects of Calvinism's community-building agenda.

❶ What picture of the pastor emerges from the prohibition of these vices?

❷ Against whom are these prohibitions directed?

❸ What is the picture of the model Calvinist that emerges from these rules?

❶ Vices which are intolerable in a pastor: Heresy … Rebellion against ecclesiastical order … Drunkenness … Dancing and similar dissoluteness. Vices which can be endured provided they are rebuked: Strange methods of treating Scripture which result in scandal … Buffoonery, Deceitfulness … Rashness, Evil scheming … Uncontrolled anger, Brawling and quarreling.

❷ FAULTS WHICH CONTRAVENE THE REFORMATION …

Those who are found in possession of … images for the purpose of worshipping them shall be sent before the Consistory, and besides the discipline which shall be imposed on them, they shall be sent to [the government].

Those who have been on pilgrimages or similar journeys.

❸ Any person who curses or denies God or his baptism shall on the first occasion be placed on bread and water for nine days; and for the second or third occasions he shall be punished with a more rigorous physical punishment,…

If anyone is found drunk he shall pay three sous on the first occasion and shall be summoned before the Consistory; on the second occasion he shall pay the sum of five sous; and on the third he shall be fined ten sous and be put in prison.

Henry married four more times, finally having a son, Edward, by his fourth wife. All three of Henry's children were to rule England, as Edward VI, Mary, and Elizabeth I.

Although Henry VIII broke with Rome, he had no intention of breaking with traditional Catholicism. Throughout his reign, he resisted any attempt to turn the English church into a Protestant one. Nevertheless, the rift with the pope opened the door to more radical reform, which actually began under Henry. The greatest change came when the king ordered the abolition of English monasteries and the confiscation of their lands on the grounds that the monks and nuns in them were too closely tied to the pope. Most of these lands were then sold to aristocrats to pay for England's foreign wars, and these new owners—who constituted the kingdom's political, social, and economic elite—thus had a vested interest in keeping Roman Catholicism out of England. So Henry's divorce had huge consequences he had not intended.

Edward VI When Henry died in 1547, he was succeeded by his son, Edward VI. Because the boy was a minor, a Regency Council, controlled by Protestant noblemen, was created to govern in his name. In 1552, the council instituted a compromise form of Protestantism in the English church when it imposed the **Book of Common Prayer**, a blend of Lutheran and Calvinist theology. Now congregations could participate directly in worship, using their own language

Book of Common Prayer Official service book of the reformed English church.

Anyone who sings indecent, dissolute, or outrageous songs or dances the fling or some similar dance shall be imprisoned for three days and shall be sent before the Consistory.

No one shall stir up rowdy scenes or altercations, under penalty of being punished according to the seriousness of the case.

If there is ill-will or altercation between any, the minister shall call the guards and shall endeavor, as is his duty, to bring the parties concerned to agreement, and if he is unable to achieve this, the matter shall be brought before the Consistory.

No one shall play dissolute games or any game for gold or silver or excessive stakes, under penalty of five sous and the forfeiture of the money staked.

Any who are found practicing fornication, if they are an unmarried man or an unmarried woman, shall be imprisoned for six days on bread and water and shall pay sixty sous into the public funds.

Although in ancient times the right of the wife was not equal with that of the husband where divorce was concerned, yet since, as the Apostle says, the obligation is mutual and reciprocal regarding the intercourse of the bed, and since in this the wife is no more subject to the husband than the husband to the wife, if a man is convicted of adultery and his wife demands to be separated from him, this shall be granted to her also, provided it proves impossible by good counsel to reconcile them to each other.

❹ On Sunday July 28 [1549] an ordinance … was announced in St. Pierre ordering that girls who had not kept their honor should not henceforward present themselves in church for marriage with the hat which virgins are accustomed to wear, but that they should have their heads veiled; otherwise they could be sent away.

❹ Why would this shaming technique be necessary?

Source: *The Register of the Company of Pastors of Geneva in the Time of Calvin*, ed. and trans. Philip Edgcumbe Hughes (Grand Rapids, MI: William B. Eerdmans Publishing Company, 1966), pp. 38–39, 56–59.

instead of Latin. Had Edward VI lived, the reforms might have succeeded, but in 1553 he died, at the age of sixteen, and was succeeded by his older half sister, Mary, Catherine's daughter.

Mary: England Returns to Rome Mary had never accepted Henry's divorce of her mother and his break with the pope, and as queen she promptly restored the Catholic Church. To seal the restoration, she married Philip II of Spain, the Catholic Church's most energetic defender. Mary then proceeded to execute some three hundred Protestants, many of them Anabaptists, earning her the nickname "Bloody Mary," which has stuck to this day. In the end, England's return to Catholicism was short lived. In 1558, Mary died childless and was succeeded by the last of Henry VIII's children, **Elizabeth I**, the daughter of Anne Boleyn.

Elizabeth I When she became queen, Elizabeth endorsed Protestantism and ended the decade-long alternations between the two forms of Christianity, depending on the ruler. Elizabeth's forty-three-year reign proved decisive in establishing an ambiguous form of Protestantism in England. In 1571, an official theology for the **Church of England** was proclaimed in the **Thirty-nine Articles**, which were silent on a number of hotly contested theological issues, such as Calvin's doctrine of predestination.

Elizabeth I (r. 1558–1603) Daughter of Henry VIII and Anne Boleyn who ruled after the deaths of her half brother Edward VI and half sister Mary.

Church of England Name given to the reformed church in England; also called the Anglican Church.

Thirty-nine Articles Statement of the official theology of the Church of England during Elizabeth I's reign.

Elizabeth and her religious advisers were trying to find a middle ground between Catholicism, Lutheranism, and Calvinism. Political calculations played a central role in this policy. The queen feared a powerful Catholic faction in the English Parliament. She also feared popular agitation if reform went too far. It was Elizabeth's accomplishment to make England Protestant while keeping Catholic opposition fairly well contained. As her reign progressed, more and more Anglicans identified with the queen's theological middle way, seeing it as a distinctively English solution to the huge rift between Protestantism and Catholicism that had engulfed the western church.

By 1570, religious warfare between Catholics and Protestants had broken out in France and the Netherlands. These developments ruled out the possibility of any reconciliation between the rival forms of Christianity on the continent, where, for the next eighty years, there would be armed conflict between Protestants and Catholics.

 Checking In

By yourself or with a partner, explain the significance of each of the following selected key terms:

Anabaptists	Huguenot
John Calvin	John Knox
Institutes of the Christian Religion	Henry VIII
double predestination	Elizabeth I

Institut Amatller d'Art Hispanic

Teresa of Ávila, one of the Catholic Church's great reformers, reinvigorated her religious order, the Carmelites, and wrote spiritual works that were quickly recognized as masterpieces of devotion. As a woman, she faced huge obstacles because women were thought to be unsuited for such serious work. But she won over even her fiercest opponents and at her death was recognized as one of the pillars of the Roman Catholic Church.

Catholic Reform, 1500–1570

◆ **What did Catholic reformers want to change in the church?**

◆ **What were the most important outcomes of Catholic Church reform?**

As Protestantism spread in Europe, the Catholic Church underwent its own reform. In addition to the reform programs of Savonarola and Erasmus, an early sign of Catholic reform was the founding of new religious orders and the reform of old ones. By the 1530s, the papacy had also become involved in reform. Its most important act was to convene a church council in the northern Italian city of Trent. The Council of Trent defined traditional Catholic theology and condemned the Protestants. It also laid down guidelines for the internal reform of the church. Finally, the Catholics inaugurated Christianity's first major missionary campaigns overseas in the Spanish and Portuguese Empires.

Teresa of Ávila (1515–1582) Spanish monastic reformer and spiritual teacher.

Carmelites Order of nuns reformed by Teresa of Ávila to be strictly separated from the larger world.

Reform by Religious Orders

The reform of old religious orders and the foundation of new ones signaled renewal within the Catholic Church. Although their specific goals were often different, all the reforms aimed to increase Catholics' commitment to the moral and spiritual teachings of the church. Most began in Italy or Spain, where Protestantism was less widespread than in northern Europe. None was founded to counteract Protestantism, although some later took up the fight against it.

Teresa of Ávila's reformed **Carmelites** set the tone for women's orders (see A New Direction: Teresa of Ávila Chooses to Reform the Carmelites). Her convents were strictly separated from the larger world because of traditional disapproval of women working actively as teachers or preachers. These nuns maintained their dwellings and prepared their community's food, depending on donations to help with their upkeep. Social distinctions between rich and poor nuns, or noble and common ones, observed in many convents, were abolished.

Teresa of Ávila Chooses to Reform the Carmelites

In 1535, a twenty-year-old woman, defying her father, secretly left her family's house and entered a convent of the Carmelites, a religious order founded in the Middle Ages. There, as "Teresa of Jesus," she did not cease to follow her heart—challenging the male church authorities who oversaw orders of nuns, urging the Carmelites to adhere to poverty, and inaugurating a renewal of church life based in prayer and a personal union with God. Her accomplishments are testimony to the power of one woman's persistence and the strength of personal conviction even in an era dominated by an authoritarian church hierarchy.

Teresa de Cepeda y Ahumada was an unlikely candidate for a nunnery. She was born in 1515 to a wealthy Spanish family, aristocratic in status but also suspect for its recent conversion to Catholicism from Judaism. Many Spaniards thought that Jewish ancestry was a blot that not even Christian baptism could wash away. But Teresa's commitment to Christianity was genuine; even as a child she showed signs of the choice she would make later in life. She liked to "play church" with her brothers and sisters, pretending to be a holy hermit living in a cave. She even dreamed of a trip to North Africa, where she hoped Muslims would chop off her head and make her a Christian martyr.

As a nun, Teresa contended not only with her Jewish background but also with stereotypes that cast women as weak, the playthings of the Devil, and therefore especially prone to error and sin. Clerical enemies dismissed her as a "silly little woman" who had no business writing about monastic reform and the life of prayer. In a clever response, Teresa accepted these charges but turned them upside down, arguing that her ideas and plans must have come directly from God, since she herself was so weak, ignorant, and sinful.

At the same time, Teresa undertook a drastic reform of the Carmelite Order, which had not strictly obeyed its own rules concerning separation from the world. With support from the bishop of Ávila, her hometown, Teresa saw that it did. The nuns were to become the Discalced, or "Barefoot," Carmelites, giving up shoes for sandals and living a life of poverty. These reforms also provoked strong opposition, but she pursued them with firmness and common sense. Although she suffered from ill health, she traveled all over Spain seeking support from the rich and powerful. She regularly rose at five in the morning but often stayed up past midnight to write letters to those who could help or harm her cause. The turning point came when she won the support of the Spanish king, Philip II. Fourteen Carmelite convents accepted her reform program.

Like Catherine of Siena, Teresa was a mystic. Beginning in 1554, she started to experience visions of Christ during her prayers. "His Majesty," as she called Jesus, appeared to her frequently and spoke to her in her heart, as one friend to another. When Teresa told her father confessor and other male clergymen of these visions, they were alarmed and ordered her to write them down in detail so they could examine them for errors. She obeyed. These writings, which described her visions and offered advice on how to pray, soon brought her to the attention of the Spanish Inquisition. But she was able to convince the inquisitors and others that there was nothing heretical or devilish in her experiences or writings.

Soon after Teresa died in 1582, her friends collected her writings and published them. The recently invented printing press, which could rapidly spread an author's works throughout Europe, made Teresa famous. She was immediately recognized as a masterful guide for Catholics who sought a more perfect life of prayer and a closer union with God. In 1612, she was declared a saint of the Catholic Church. But the gender expectations of her age, which classified women lower than men, even shaped the decrees proclaiming her sainthood. She was labeled a "virile woman" with a "manly soul," as male clerics believed that, before Teresa could become an object of public devotion, she had to be made manlike. But her life and writings carried a different message. Here was an intelligent, capable woman who counteracted deep prejudices to renew the life of her religious order, write treatises on prayer that became instant classics of Christian spirituality, and led church reform. In 1969, Teresa was the first woman to be proclaimed a doctor, or authoritative teacher, of the Roman Catholic Church.

Although not all reformed women's orders adopted the strict poverty of Teresa's Carmelites, most followed separation from the world and a rigorous life of prayer, which, they believed, would strengthen the church as a whole. Recruitment to women's orders rose during the sixteenth century. For example, in 1427 two out of a hundred people living in Florence were nuns; in 1622, six out of a hundred were.

The Capuchins The largest reformed male order was the **Capuchins**, a branch of the Franciscans. The Capuchins took strict vows of poverty. They lived in mud huts, went barefoot, and begged in public for their food to show their detachment from worldly possessions and pleasures. They also preached lively sermons on street corners and in churches, urging Catholics to live more in accordance with Jesus' teachings and setting an example by caring for plague victims. In 1542, scandal rocked the order when its head moved to Geneva and became a Calvinist. Nevertheless, the Capuchins continued to attract new members. By 1600, there were almost nine thousand; by 1700, twenty-seven thousand.

The Jesuits The most dynamic new religious order was the **Society of Jesus,** or the **Jesuits.** Its founder was **Ignatius of Loyola,** a nobleman from northern Spain. As a young man he embarked on the classic noble career, service in the army. In 1521, aged thirty, he was badly wounded and forced into a long convalescence. During this period, Ignatius had a profound religious conversion and decided to become a spiritual soldier instead of a military one. In 1522, he offered his old sword to the Virgin Mary and symbolized his new life of dedication to God by exchanging his fine clothes for those of a beggar.

Ignatius wanted to convert Muslims to Christianity in the Holy Land, but an outbreak of plague delayed his departure. As he waited for better travel conditions, he formulated his *Spiritual Exercises*, a training program designed to strengthen one's will to fight for Christ. For thirty days, persons taking the *Exercises* examined their conscience to see where their

Jacopino del Conte painted this portrait of Ignatius of Loyola shortly after Ignatius's death in 1556. The artist bathes Ignatius's face in light to convey his holiness. Compare this picture with the ones of Luther (page 406) and Calvin (page 412). Each artist wants to call attention to his subject's heroic stature. What artistic devices do they employ to achieve this end? How are the devices similar and different?

Courtesy, Curia Generalizia della Compagnia di Gesu, Rome

will to obey God was weak and then concentrated on a word or deed of Christ to strengthen their resolve to follow him. Ignatius's emphasis on training the will to follow Christ was based on the traditional Catholic view that both human effort and God's grace brought about a person's salvation. This view contrasted with Luther's and Calvin's belief in the deep sinfulness of human wills.

For Ignatius, strengthening the will involved a form of prayer called **meditation,** in which one concentrated on a scene from Jesus' life as recounted in the Gospels, breathing the air, feeling the heat, and becoming part of the crowd in order to mentally meet Jesus face to face. Thus Ignatius, like Luther and Calvin, turned to the Bible for inspiration. But he never embraced their doctrine of scripture alone. In fact, part of the *Exercises* laid down "rules for thinking with the church." As a Catholic, Ignatius looked to church tradition and papal authority, as well as scripture, for religious guidance.

As Ignatius formulated the *Exercises*, he also modified his future plans, deciding that more education was necessary to be a successful missionary in the Holy Land. He, therefore, enrolled in a Spanish

---

Capuchins (from Italian, *cappuccio,* "hood") Largest reformed male religious order, named after the hood the friars wore as part of their religious garb.

Society of Jesus (Jesuits) Most important reforming religious order in the sixteenth-century Catholic Church.

Ignatius of Loyola (1491–1556) Spanish nobleman and ex-soldier, founder of the Society of Jesus.

Spiritual Exercises Ignatius of Loyola's training program, designed to strengthen one's resolve to serve Christ and his church.

meditation Form of mental prayer developed by Ignatius that concentrated on a scene from the life of Jesus as recounted in the Gospels.

Erich Lessing/Art Resource, NY

Titian painted *Pope Paul III and His Grandsons* (1546). The old pope, with an arresting face and piercing eyes, looks toward one grandson, an elegant courtier who bows to him, while the other grandson, a cleric, raises his hand in blessing while looking out at the viewer. Paul made both grandsons cardinals. How does this portrait of a Catholic church leader compare to Conte's portrait of Ignatius of Loyola (page 418)? What values are portrayed here?

elementary school (as a nobleman, he had learned how to fight, but not how to read and write). Later he transferred to the University of Paris, where he began his studies in 1528, the year John Calvin entered law school. In Paris, he joined seven fellow students to found the Society of Jesus. In 1537, they were ordained priests and set off for Venice, intending to sail for the Holy Land.

Once again, the trip was canceled, this time because of a war between Venice and the Turks. In 1540, the pope officially recognized the Jesuits, and Ignatius moved to Rome. From there he ran the order in a highly centralized way, rather like a general running his army. He also placed the order at the pope's disposal. From then on, it expanded rapidly and became the single most important reforming order in the church. Like the Capuchins, it concentrated on active service in the world.

Jesuit Schools The Jesuits' most successful service was in education. They founded secondary schools throughout the Catholic world for boys from the middle and upper classes. They believed that, by instilling a deep sense of Catholic identity in these future social and political leaders, they could reinvigorate Catholicism and push back

Protestantism. The Jesuits did not charge students tuition; instead, they expected local authorities to finance their schools and thereby build community involvement in their educational program. They also gave Ignatius's *Exercises* to students and their families, as well as to interested local clergy. The Jesuit schools were spectacularly successful. The quality of instruction was so good that even some Protestants went to them. The Jesuits attacked Protestants in print and from the pulpit, but they welcomed them into their schools in hopes of converting them.

Like the Protestants, the Jesuits and other Catholic reformers also promoted new forms of devotion for the laity. One of the most popular was the recitation of the rosary. Combining traditional veneration for Mary with meditation on Christ's life, death, and Resurrection, the rosary was a widely used means for instructing ordinary Catholics in the church's teachings, heightening their sense of spiritual union with God and forging a strong sense of Catholic identity. In 1556, when Ignatius of Loyola died, the Jesuits had almost a thousand members. Seventy years later, they had fifteen thousand members across the globe and ran 450 schools.

Reform in the Papacy

The pope who recognized the Jesuits was **Paul III**. Paul cautiously embraced church reform, and his reign proved a turning point for the Catholic Church. One of his first reforms was to appoint a special commission to evaluate papal administration. The commission's secret report, issued in 1537, argued that corruption in the church was caused mainly by abuses of papal power. Paul tried to ignore the report, but it was smuggled out to a local printer who made it public, once again demonstrating the power of the printing press. Shortly thereafter, Luther published it with his own scathing comments. Publicly, Paul appeared unruffled by the uproar, but privately he began appointing reformers to the **College of Cardinals**, the body charged with the election of future popes.

The Inquisition and the Index In 1542, Paul established the Roman Inquisition. Modeled on Ferdinand and Isabella's Spanish Inquisition, it investigated and punished heretics in Catholic lands. In 1549, another instrument of repression was set up, **The Index of Prohibited Books**, which listed works Catholics were forbidden to read. Eventually, many of Erasmus's works appeared on it. The creation of the Roman Inquisition and the *Index* signaled a change in outlook for the Catholic Church. Faced with Protestantism, it developed a fortress-like mentality, identifying itself as a militant church guarding against heresy. This new emphasis had a chilling effect on what many Catholics did or said in public.

The Council of Trent Paul III's most significant act was to convene a church council in the city of Trent to address Protestantism and Catholic Church reform. He was not eager to convene the council, fearing it would get out of control or be ineffective, but he conceded to pressure from Charles V, who still hoped to restore religious unity in the empire. The **Council of Trent** met in three separate sessions from 1545 to 1563. The first two sessions (1545–1547 and 1551–1552) reaffirmed traditional Catholic theology. To counter Luther's doctrine of scripture alone, the council declared that *both* scripture *and* the traditions of the church were authoritative for Catholics. Moreover, it decreed that only the Roman Catholic Church, headed by the pope, had the right to interpret scripture.

To counter the doctrine of justification by faith alone, the council decreed that while God's grace saved people, Christians could choose whether they would cooperate with grace or resist it. This position was based on a verse in the Old Testament: "Thus says the Lord of hosts, 'Return to me … and I will return to you'" (Zechariah 1:3). The council, therefore, quoted scripture against Protestants to justify Catholic teaching about the roles of free will, works, and grace in determining a person's salvation and to counteract Protestant teaching about corrupted human wills and double predestination. The council's defense of traditional Catholic belief and practice dismayed Charles V, who saw his hope of reconciliation with the Protestants slipping away.

When the council next met, in 1561–1563, it reaffirmed the practice of indulgences while discouraging their sale, and it endorsed the traditional organization of the church with the pope as its head. Under him were the clergy and then—standing sharply apart—the laity. This last point was reinforced symbolically when the council decreed that at the Mass, the clergy alone would receive the cup of wine, the laity only the bread—a rejection of Luther's priesthood of all believers. The council also reaffirmed the church's seven traditional sacraments. In addition to restating doctrine, the council's last session established guidelines for a thoroughgoing reform of the church.

Paul III (r. 1534–1549) Most important reforming pope of the Catholic Church.

College of Cardinals Body charged with the election of new popes.

The Index of Prohibited Books A list of books that Catholics were forbidden to read.

Council of Trent Catholic Church council, meeting 1545–1563, that reasserted traditional Catholic teaching and created guidelines for Catholic Church reform.

Trent ordered the establishment of **seminaries** in all Catholic **dioceses** for the training of new clergy. It also ordered bishops to visit every church in their diocese to make sure that the buildings were in good repair, that services were properly conducted, and that the clergy were living moral lives. Another decree reaffirmed the traditional position that all women in religious orders were to stay within their convents, separated from society. In 1564, the pope accepted all Trent's decrees while announcing that he alone had the authority to interpret them.

Carlo Borromeo in Milan The reforms of Trent were implemented, slowly and unevenly, throughout the Catholic world. The greatest gains were made in dioceses where the bishop was a committed reformer. One of the first successes came in the northern Italian city of Milan, where the archbishop, **Carlo Borromeo**, founded a diocesan seminary, set up Sunday schools to teach the young the basics of Christian belief and practice, and established religious associations for laypeople. He also gained control over local religious orders, conducted thorough visitations throughout the diocese, and cared personally for the sick and needy. He died in 1584, at age forty-six. In 1610, the pope proclaimed him a Catholic saint.

Borromeo showed the way for reforming bishops elsewhere in the Catholic world. A hundred years after the Council of Trent, that world had been largely transformed. The Catholic Church was more centralized than ever before. Vigorous leadership after 1534 strengthened the position of the Roman popes, while centralized and dynamic orders like the Capuchins and Jesuits spread new ideals and practices to Catholic communities all over the globe. Religious devotion intensified as Teresa of Ávila's treatises on prayer were more and more widely read. Finally, a reformed Catholic identity was further advanced when the church issued new books for worship services that put Catholics literally on the same page throughout the year; all over the Catholic world, on any given day, people in church read and heard the same words during worship. Like the Muslims, whose worship was always in Arabic, the Catholics also shared a common religious language, Latin.

Catholic Missions Overseas

The Catholics were the first Europeans to embark on overseas missionary activity in the Americas and East Asia, believing that converts there could make up for the souls lost in Europe to the Protestant "heresy." Some also thought that spreading Christianity overseas meant the end of the world was near because Christ's command "to make disciples of all nations" (Matthew 28:19) would finally be realized.

Missionaries in the Americas In the Americas, Spanish missionaries debated the best strategy for Christianizing the local people. Some followed Bartholomé de Las Casas in trying to protect them from harsh treatment by fellow Europeans and to preserve those features of their pre-Christian cultures that were compatible with Christianity. Others believed that local peoples were so lacking in human reason that they should be viewed as stubborn unbelievers, like Jews and Muslims. They should be forced to learn Spanish and live in settlements that reproduced European life, thereby replacing their old values and customs with European ones.

If missionaries in the Americas disagreed over strategies for converting local peoples, they all agreed that the process of conversion should be in European hands. Only in the eighteenth century did the church start to train large numbers of Indian men for the clergy. Before then, even the most well-disposed priests doubted that the Indians were ready to lead the church on their own. This attitude resulted from three factors: bewilderment at the complexity and strangeness of the Indians' cultures, a paternalistic sense of the church's obligation to protect or correct local peoples, and a racist sense of the innate superiority of Europeans.

Local peoples reacted to the missionaries' activities in various ways. Some tried to resist any changes in traditional culture. Others, particularly those who came from the old Indian elite, converted fairly easily to both Christianity and European customs. Many, however, found a middle way. They adopted those aspects of Catholicism and European culture that seemed useful and melded them with their older beliefs and practices, creating a new religious identity. Thus in Peru local people went to church— after protecting the building by smearing animal blood on its foundations, an old Inca ritual. This modified Latin American Catholicism still exists, illustrating the complexity of the encounter that took place as the Catholic Church established itself in the Americas.

Missionaries in Japan In Asia, Portuguese missionaries led in spreading Catholicism. One of the first was **Francis Xavier**,

seminaries Schools for the training of the Christian clergy.

diocese Territory presided over by a bishop of the church.

Carlo Borromeo (1538–1584) Catholic archbishop of Milan who implemented the reforms of the Council of Trent in his diocese.

Francis Xavier (1506–1552) Jesuit who led Catholic missions in India and Japan.

who with Ignatius of Loyola had founded the Jesuits. Xavier was active in India and Japan, using as his base the Portuguese trading post at Goa. In 1549 he also traveled to Japan and stayed two years, leaving behind a small Christian community made up of Jesuits and Japanese converts. This mission's success depended on the Japanese political elite. Some local rulers supported the missionaries in hopes of strengthening their commercial ties with the Portuguese. For their part, the Jesuits were careful to respect Japanese customs by dressing appropriately, bathing frequently, and eating only locally acceptable foods. The result was the establishment of a Christian community that numbered some 250,000 by 1600, or about 0.5 percent of the total population.

But after 1593, when Spanish missionaries arrived from the Philippines, quarrels with the Portuguese caused the missionary effort to collapse in the face of imperial rivalries. In 1616, the Japanese government began suppressing Christianity and ultimately executed almost forty thousand men, women, and children, some by crucifixion. Japan then closed its doors to the west. Christianity was driven underground, where it survived for centuries as a secret religion passed on in families and local communities from generation to generation.

Missionaries in China The Jesuits also initiated missionary activity in China. In 1552, Francis Xavier arrived there but died shortly after landing on an island near Hong Kong. The real founder of the Chinese mission was an Italian Jesuit, **Matteo Ricci**, who was born in the year Xavier died. Ricci learned Mandarin, dressed in Chinese clothes, and emphasized the similarities between Catholicism and the traditional Chinese philosophy of Confucianism. Like the Jesuits in Europe, Ricci concentrated on Chinese political and social elites, hoping for conversions in powerful places. He eventually resided at the imperial court in Beijing, where he gained a few converts, though most refused baptism.

Ricci's influence in China was therefore small, but his influence in Europe was considerable. The reports he and other Jesuits sent to Rome were soon published, providing a flood of new information about Chinese culture, philosophy, and history. Here was a people who were unquestionably "civilized" like the Europeans but who had developed without the benefit of Christianity. Debates over the meaning of this puzzle were to swirl about in European intellectual circles for decades to come.

After Ricci's death, the Catholic community in China continued to expand. By the

Adam Schall, a German Jesuit dressed as a Mandarin, was court astronomer for the Chinese emperor in Beijing. Schall calculated the astrologically best dates for the performance of Confucian rites at court. What does Schall's decision to wear Mandarin dress at court rather than his Jesuit robes tell you about the Jesuits' missionary style in China?

Bettmann/Corbis

early eighteenth century, Christians numbered somewhere between two hundred thousand and five hundred thousand, or about 0.2 percent of the total population. Chinese Christians never faced government repression like Japanese Christians, but they achieved only a marginal place in the larger Chinese world.

Matteo Ricci (1552–1610) Italian Jesuit missionary in China who sent new information on Chinese civilization back to Europe.

Checking In

By yourself or with a partner, explain the significance of each of the following selected key terms:

Teresa of Ávila	Council of Trent
Jesuits	Carlo Borromeo
Ignatius of Loyola	Francis Xavier
Paul III	Matteo Ricci

Reformation and Society, 1517–1570

♦ **How was religious reform put into practice?**

♦ **How did the actions of ordinary men and women shape the outcomes of reform?**

From Savonarola on, both Catholic and Protestant reformers hoped that church renewal would bring about a renewal of society as a whole. Reformers, therefore, tried to impose new codes of conduct on their communities, and people had to decide whether to accept or reject them. The result was a negotiation between reformers and the population at large, during which some changes were accepted and others were modified or rejected. This process was at work in three areas: children's education, poor relief, and family life. Finally, both Protestants and Catholics reassessed their relations with the largest religious and social minority in Europe, the Jews.

Educating the Young

In the Middle Ages, primary schooling was mainly reserved for boys destined for careers in the church, the state, law, and medicine. As a result, many men, like Ignatius of Loyola before he decided to become a missionary, saw no reason to study or to learn to read and write. Protestant reformers, however, began to question these traditional ways and to argue for popular educational reform.

Protestant Education Luther's belief in the priesthood of all believers led him to promote elementary education for both boys and girls, along with the establishment of public libraries. His goal was to turn children into good Christians by teaching them how to read the Bible. In 1529, he also published a *Small Catechism* for them, which contained the **Lord's Prayer** along with simple statements of Lutheran theology. Calvin adopted a similar program in his *Geneva Catechism* of 1545.

Leaders in a number of communities adopted Luther's and Calvin's educational agendas, but only after modifying them. While primary schools for boys were established, those for girls lagged behind, reflecting current social values. Few people, including many girls, thought that women's social or work roles were the same as men's; their education could be limited to training as wives and mothers because these were the only respectable roles left for them after the Protestants abolished religious orders.

Catholic Education Catholic reformers sometimes endorsed education for both boys and girls, often for the same reasons as Protestants. A new *Roman Catechism*, published in 1566, taught young people throughout the Catholic world how to recite the Lord's Prayer, the creeds, and the **Hail Mary**. Nevertheless, Catholics established even fewer schools for girls than the Protestants; a late-sixteenth-century educational survey in Venice listed 4,600 boy students but only 30 girls. Catholics, too, thought that cooking, sewing, and other household activities, all requiring little formal education, were women's usual work, although they continued to see life in a religious order as another option.

Catholic boys fared better than girls because efforts were sometimes made to educate more of them than before. For example, the **Piarists**, a religious order founded in 1597 by a blacksmith's son, established primary schools for poor boys so they could meet the entry qualifications for the more advanced Jesuit schools. Since Piarist schools were free, the poor would be given an equal chance with the rich for a quality education. The Piarists met with opposition from people who thought that the lowborn should stay where they were. Overall, both Catholic and Protestant reforms of elementary education, along with the availability of printed reading material, hastened the spread of **literacy** throughout Europe.

Poor Relief

In Europe, the number of poor people grew during the sixteenth century, rising to nearly half the population in the hardest-hit urban and rural areas. It is, therefore, not surprising that Protestant and Catholic reformers called for a rethinking of the problem of poverty. The outcome was a change in attitudes about the poor and the ways communities should deal with them.

In the Middle Ages, the poor were given sacred significance. In the Gospel of Matthew, Jesus identified the hungry, the naked, and the sick with himself. Anyone, therefore, who cared for them was also caring for him. As a result, charity toward the needy made up a major portion of the good works medieval people performed; they looked after the sick and dying and provided food and shelter for the destitute. Above all, they gave to beggars. These practices came under attack

Lord's Prayer The prayer Jesus taught his followers to use, found in the Gospel of Luke and the Gospel of Matthew.

Hail Mary Roman Catholic prayer praising Mary and asking her to pray to Jesus on behalf of the one reciting it.

Piarists Catholic religious order dedicated to the education of poor boys.

literacy Ability to read and write.

from both Protestants and Catholics during the sixteenth century.

Luther on the Problem of Poverty As early as 1522, Martin Luther issued an ordinance governing poor relief in Wittenberg. It outlawed all public begging and mandated that care of the poor was to be transferred from private individuals or groups to the city. Funds for poor relief were to be collected in all the city's churches and then distributed by the municipal government. Only those identified by the authorities as "deserving" would receive help, thus restricting aid to those who were truly unable to work because of age, disability, or sickness. People who simply chose not to work would be left to fend for themselves.

The guiding principle behind Luther's ordinance was his rejection of good works as a means toward salvation. No longer were people to think that giving to the poor helped to save them. Charity was simply a free act of love performed by Christian people for the benefit of other Christians. Luther's reform was rooted in his theology, but his decision to turn poor relief over to the city government had profound consequences: from then on, the state, not the church, was responsible for care of the destitute.

Catholics and the Problem of Poverty Catholic reformers also argued that the state should assume the task of poor relief. In 1526, **Juan Luis Vives**, a Spanish humanist living in the Netherlands, argued that municipal governments should administer all funds for the poor. Vives's work won the support of other Catholics, but his proposals were never fully implemented in Catholic lands. The old practice of individual giving to the poor was too strong to be swept away completely, as the success of the begging Capuchins shows. Moreover, the idea that charity was a praiseworthy good work was reinforced by the Council of Trent. As a result, Catholics tended to create a variety of different systems for poor relief. State authorities administered some funds, religious confraternities collected and distributed others, and private individuals continued to give. Like the Lutherans, Catholics usually tried to distinguish between the deserving and undeserving poor.

Juan Luis Vives (1492–1540) Spanish Catholic humanist living in the Netherlands who supported a state takeover of relief for the poor.

Calvin on the Problem of Poverty Calvin's program for the poor resembled both Luther's and Vives's, with the government of Geneva taking responsibility for the needy. Calvin believed that all wealth came from God and was to be used for the benefit of the community as a whole. Thus the state should tax the rich for the benefit of the poor. He also thought that poverty was a sign of God's anger over sin, but he did not place the sin simply on the shoulders of the poor themselves. If there was poverty, it was because the community as a whole had sinned. Like Luther and Vives, Calvin was shifting poor relief from the church to the state. In the long run, state administration of poverty programs was to be a central feature of the modern European world.

Family Life

A third area in which Protestant and Catholic reformers tried to introduce new social attitudes and practices was family life. As with primary education and poor relief, communities accepted some reforms while modifying or rejecting others. The result was a melding of old and new that resulted from a prolonged contest between reforming elites and ordinary people.

Marriage in the Middle Ages In the western Catholic Church during the Middle Ages, family life was based on the institution of marriage. The church taught that the purpose of marriage was twofold: to provide an outlet for sexual impulses and to bring children into the world. Both purposes were considered acceptable but not ideal. The highest state for Christians was that of permanent sexual abstinence expressed in a life of celibacy, following the example of Jesus and the apostle Paul. Thus clergymen, monks, and nuns were thought to live a better kind of Christian life than married people. For the married, sexual intercourse was permissible only between husband and wife, only on certain days, and only in certain positions. Of course, there were many who failed to live up to these ideals, and some clergymen even expected that people would find it impossible to observe them. Thus many city governments established brothels, arguing that men, especially, were incapable of controlling their sexual passions and that the use of brothels was better than rape and adultery.

Marriage itself was considered a sacrament that the bride and groom administered to each other through the exchange of vows. The free consent of the partners to marriage was thus required. The Council of Trent also required that the marriage take place in public before witnesses, including the priest in the parish where the agreement to marry had taken place. Marriages contracted secretly were not recognized as binding on the couple.

Once a proper marriage had taken place, it would last until the death of one of the spouses way, however, he expanded it by allowing for divorce under special circumstances. Although divorces were frowned on and expensive to obtain, they could be granted for such reasons as adultery, male impotence, a spouse's refusal of sexual relations, desertion, and conviction of a capital crime. Finally, Luther ordered the closure of brothels, arguing that men could control their sexual impulses and confine their sexual activities to marriage.

Luther's reform of marriage served as a model for most other Protestant churches, although some modified various points. For example, the Church of England forbade divorce, and the Anabaptists often insisted on community, not just parental, approval of marriages.

The woman in this sixteenth-century engraving represents, according to the caption, "A Virtuous Woman of Geneva." What aspects of her dress and posture are designed to show her conforming to Calvinist gender norms? (Geneva BGE, Centre d'iconographie genevoise)

Husbands and Wives Protestant reform brought changes to the lives of husbands and wives. On the one hand, those Protestants who married were no longer viewed as second-class Christians because the old ideal of a celibate life was no longer accepted. In addition, marriage was viewed more positively than before. Its purpose was to increase affection and cooperation between spouses, not just to provide an outlet for sexual impulses or to bring babies into the world. Women were viewed as real partners with their husbands in running a household, increasing their honor in society. On the other hand, women lost some of their older religious options as they could no longer enter a women's religious order. From then on, their adult roles were limited to those of spouse or spinster. Even legal prostitution as a choice was taken away when brothels closed.

because divorce was prohibited. It was also widely agreed that after marriage the husband was head of the family, with his wife and all others subject to him.

Luther on Marriage As in other areas of life, Martin Luther swept away many of these traditional attitudes and practices. He declared that marriage was not a sacrament but simply a God-given social institution. He saw it as the foundation of all social order because it created the basic social unit, the family. All men and women, including the clergy, were now to be married, and religious orders, which promoted celibacy, were to be abolished. In 1525, he set the example by marrying an ex-nun, Katherine von Bora.

Marriages were to be public events, and they had to be sanctioned by the couple's parents, not just the future spouses themselves. In these ways, Luther narrowed the freedom of choice for couples. In another

Catholic Reform of Marriage Catholics also reformed marriage practices, although they kept more of the old ways than Protestants. Marriage was still viewed as a sacrament. In addition, the free consent of bride and groom remained the only essential act leading to marriage; parental consent was encouraged but not required. Marriages could not be secret; they had to take place in public before a priest. Divorce was still not allowed. The best one could hope for in a failed marriage was either a permanent separation or an annulment declaring that the marriage had never really existed.

While Catholics differed from Protestants on the matter of divorce, they both agreed that marriage existed for something more than the release of sexual passion and the production of offspring. It was also the place where individuals could find companionship and mutual support. Moreover, women's religious options were greater for Catholics than for Protestants. Special female saints could be invoked during conception, pregnancy, and childbirth, and women could still enter their own religious orders, where they largely governed themselves. In contrast, Protestant authorities had abolished religious orders and prohibited asking saints for their prayers.

Popular Reaction to Reform Faced with the reforming agendas of both Catholic and Protestant clergy, the mass of people had to decide how to react. Many reforms were well received. There was popular support among Catholics and Protestants for closing brothels and for punishment of sexually promiscuous people. Public anger was highest against sexual acts that threatened to disrupt the family or bring dishonor on it, like adultery. Others, like same-sex acts, while technically capital offenses that were deeply offensive to most people, were less of a challenge to social order because they did not result in the birth of children and usually did not tear families apart.

Other reforms were less well received, especially if they seemed too novel or threatening. For example, Luther wanted early marriages as a safeguard against lust. In Germany, where marriages were usually late and took place only when the couple had saved enough money to establish their own households, this reform was rejected. Popular opinion also often won out over the issue of premarital sex. Reformers wanted sexual relations to begin only after marriage, but many couples began them right after their engagement to prevent ill-wishers from using magic that would prevent desired pregnancies; most people believed that their enemies could draw on the Devil's power to inflict harm.

Jews in the Age of the Reformation

The late-fifteenth-century expulsions from Spain and Portugal left western Europe almost empty of Jews as the Iberian Jewish communities were the largest in the Christian world. As Protestant and Catholic reform developed, anti-Jewish sentiment increased and led to further expulsions. In some states, however, authorities permitted Jews to live under severe restrictions.

Luther and the Jews Like Savonarola, Martin Luther believed that church reform would usher in Christ's return to earth. This belief led to attacks on the Jews. With the end of the world at hand, why did they still refuse to convert to Christianity and acknowledge Jesus as their Messiah? In 1543, Luther gave his answer in a pamphlet, *Concerning the Jews and Their*

Ghetto Originally, a district in Venice where Jews were allowed to settle in the sixteenth century.

Lies, where he repeated all the anti-Jewish arguments Christians had made in the Middle Ages. As a result, the Lutheran reformation turned sharply against the Jews; rulers of Lutheran states in the empire ordered their expulsion along with Catholics. Calvin also endorsed the medieval view of Jews as Christ killers and therefore enemies of God. Protestant Europe became increasingly hostile toward Jews. It was only in Catholic Italy that Jews found new places to resettle in the west.

Jews in Catholic Italy In 1516, the government of the Republic of Venice allowed a permanent Jewish community on its territory. Jews were confined to one area of Venice, the **Ghetto**. As a result, some Spanish and Portuguese Jews migrated there from the Muslim lands where they had gone after the expulsions. Those who had been forced to convert to Christianity now returned to Judaism. "Ghettos," modeled on the one in Venice, were also established in Rome and other Italian cities.

Like Luther, reform-minded popes believed that the Jews' refusal to convert to Christianity made them God's enemies. The low point came in 1593, when the pope placed severe restrictions on Jews living in his territories. They were forbidden to sell meat or unleavened bread to Christians. They could not bathe or shave with Christians and could not employ them as servants. Cases they had previously settled in Jewish law courts were now transferred to the state's law courts, run by Christians. Jews could no longer serve as physicians to non-Jews, a role traditionally played by Jewish men in the Middle Ages. Now, their economic activity was confined to the secondhand clothes trade. Finally, they continued to be publicly identified and shamed by the yellow badges they were forced to wear on their clothing.

The pope intended to humiliate the Jews, isolate them socially, and attack them economically. But Jews were not expelled from the Papal States. They were also allowed to live in other states in Italy, often on terms more favorable than those offered by the popes. While Rome shaped its policy for religious reasons, the other states took economic considerations into account. They wanted Jewish settlements for commercial reasons because Jews had good business connections in the Muslim world.

Checking In

By yourself or with a partner, explain the significance of each of the following selected key terms:

Lord's Prayer	literacy
Hail Mary	Juan Luis Vives
Piarists	Ghetto

Summary

- Savonarola's and Erasmus's hopes for church reform were symptomatic of a growing demand for religious renewal in the western church, brought about by the spread of humanism, a decline in the prestige of the papacy and the clergy, a rise in lay-inspired devotion to Christ, and the ability of reformers to use the new technology of the printing press.

- Savonarola and Erasmus raised issues and proposed changes that shaped the programs of many later reformers. One of the first was Martin Luther, the founder of Protestant reform.

- Although other Protestants, like the radicals and Calvinists, disagreed with Luther on some points, their programs were similar enough to create a general Protestant movement.

- Lutheranism was the dominant form of Protestantism in northern Germany and Scandinavia.

- In the second half of the sixteenth century, Calvinism became the most dynamic Protestant movement, spreading throughout Europe.

- After the fall of Münster, the radicals renounced violence and followed leaders who embraced pacifism.

- The outcome of Protestant reform was a permanent split in the western church, characterized by deep hostility on both sides.

- Initially, Catholics who shared the general expectation of church reform did not shape their programs with an eye to the Protestant challenge.

- In the end, however, orders such as the Capuchins and the Jesuits combated Protestantism while reforming the Catholic Church from within.

- Along with the religious orders, the papacy led Catholic Church reform when Paul III convened the Council of Trent.

- The council reaffirmed Catholic teaching, thereby cementing the division between Catholics and Protestants, and created a blueprint for reform that was implemented over the next hundred years throughout the Catholic world.

- Finally, Catholics inaugurated the first overseas missions by western Christians.

- Missionaries often tried to impose European values on converts as they sought to make up for the souls lost in Europe to Protestantism.

- Some local people accepted Christian teachings wholeheartedly, but others rejected them or blended them into their old religions.

- In Europe, the decisive factors determining the success of reform, whether Protestant or Catholic, were the choices made by rulers, nobles, and ordinary people.

- The choices of the elite were the most important in determining whether communities would become Protestant or remain Catholic, but the long-term success of reform within a community depended on popular reception.

- Many reformers thought their programs would restore a united church to a state of purity they believed had existed formerly. In this sense, they were looking backward.

- Some reformers thought that church reform and overseas missions would usher in Christ's Second Coming and thus the end of the world.

- One outcome of reform was the introduction into European life of some basic features of the emerging modern world—the spread of literacy, new state administration of poverty programs, and changing standards for family life.

Chronology

1494	Savonarola institutes moral reforms in Florence		1536	Calvin publishes *Institutes of the Christian Religion*
1516	Jewish Ghetto is established in Venice		1540	Pope approves Jesuits
1517	Luther condemns church indulgences		1541	Calvin initiates reform in Geneva
1521	Luther is excommunicated and declared an outlaw in the empire		1545	Council of Trent opens
1522	Ignatius of Loyola becomes a church reformer		1549	Francis Xavier introduces Christianity into Japan
1524	Peasants' War breaks out in Germany		1555	Peace of Augsburg allows Lutheranism
1525	Luther marries Katherine von Bora		1558	John Knox introduces Calvinism into Scotland; Elizabeth I becomes queen of England
1527	Henry VIII breaks with the pope			
1535	Catholic and Lutheran rulers slaughter Anabaptists at Münster; Teresa of Ávila becomes a nun		1563	Council of Trent ends

© Cengage Learning

Test Yourself

To gauge your mastery of the material in this chapter, answer the questions below. More than one answer may be correct.

The Context of Church Reform, 1494–1517

1. What motivated the reform movement in the western church that grew in the late fifteenth and early sixteenth centuries?

   a. A belief in the growing corruption of the Roman papacy.

   b. A demand for preachers who could talk about Jesus' life and death as described in the Bible.

   c. The ability of reformers to reach a large audience by using the newly invented printing press.

   d. All of the above.

   e. None of the above.

2. Girolamo Savonarola:

   a. Believed that the implementation of his reform program in Florence would usher in a general reform of the church.

   b. Argued that church reform was necessary even if it led to a decline in Florence's prosperity and prestige.

   c. Was supported by Pope Alexander VI.

   d. Was burned at the stake after a church court supported by the pope condemned him.

   e. Had little support among the people of Florence.

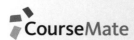

Visit the CourseMate website at **www.cengagebrain.com** for additional study tools and review materials for this chapter.

3. Erasmus of Rotterdam:

   a. Believed that the Bible should be kept out of the common people's hands.
   b. Prepared an accurate edition of the New Testament in its original Greek.
   c. Attacked abuses in the church with fiery preaching of God's judgment.
   d. Believed that Europe's rulers should be agents of reform.
   e. Broke with the Roman pope over the issue of church reform.

Now that you have reviewed and tested yourself on this part of the chapter, take time to pull together all the important information by answering the following questions:

◆ What were the similarities and differences in Erasmus's and Savonarola's views of the Roman papacy?

◆ What role did Christian humanism play in the growing church reform movement?

Martin Luther and the Protestant Reformation, 1517–1550

4. Martin Luther's theology rested on which of the following principles?

   a. Humans possessed free will, which allowed them to do things that God viewed as good and righteous.
   b. Humans were incapable of doing good works because their sinfulness made them choose unrighteousness.
   c. Righteousness was a free gift from God given to humans even while they were still sinful.
   d. Righteousness was a free gift from God given to humans who struggled to do good works and had made some progress toward goodness.
   e. Humans were to accept God's gift of justification by faith alone.

5. Luther eventually argued that:

   a. Church councils were superior to the Roman pope and therefore had more authority than he did.
   b. The sources of authority for Christians were Scripture and church tradition.
   c. The sole source of authority for Christians was Scripture alone.
   d. The Christian priesthood was exercised by all believers.
   e. The printing press was not a particularly effective tool for expressing his theology.

6. Following the Peasants' War of 1524–1525, Lutheran reform in Germany:

   a. Remained mainly in the hands of church-based reformers.
   b. Passed into the hands of the princes of the empire.
   c. Continued to be led by the leaders of Germany's cities.
   d. Endorsed the demands of the insurgents in the Peasants' War.
   e. Turned its back on the demands of the insurgents at Luther's urging.

7. The Peace of Augsburg:

   a. Was signed in 1555.
   b. Was signed in 1565.
   c. Granted full religious freedom to the peoples of the Holy Roman Empire.
   d. Allowed the princes of the empire to choose Catholicism or Lutheranism as the religion of their respective states.
   e. Allowed Catholics in Lutheran states and Lutherans in Catholic states to practice their religion openly.

Now that you have reviewed and tested yourself on this part of the chapter, take time to pull together all the important information by answering the following questions:

◆ Were there elements of Savonarola's and Erasmus's reforming agendas in Luther's reform? What elements were distinctively Luther's?

◆ What elements in the "pure gospel" movement were compatible with Luther's agenda? What elements were not?

The Protestant Reformation Across Europe, 1520–1570

8. The Anabaptists:

   a. Relied on Scriptural interpretation by trained professionals.
   b. Usually held a separatist view of church-state relations.
   c. Usually adopted pacifism after the failure of the Münster rebellion.
   d. Were found in large numbers in southern France.
   e. Were found in large numbers in Denmark.

9. John Calvin:

   a. Accepted Luther's doctrine of the priesthood of all believers.
   b. Continued to use Latin in church services.
   c. Believed that all human beings would be saved.
   d. Believed that a person's good works were a sign that he or she was chosen for salvation.
   e. Implemented his reform agenda in the city-state of Geneva.

10. Calvinists in France:

   a. Were recruited mainly from the middle class.
   b. Attracted few nobles.
   c. Numbered about 10 percent of the French population by 1560.
   d. Were looked on favorably by the French monarchy.
   e. Were known as Huguenots.

11. Henry VIII's reform of the English church:

   a. Maintained most of Catholic theology and practice.
   b. Led to a growth in English monastic life.
   c. Recognized Catherine of Aragon as Henry's wife.
   d. Turned in a Protestant direction when Mary became queen.
   e. Turned in a Protestant direction when Edward VI became king.

Now that you have reviewed and tested yourself on this part of the chapter, take time to pull together all the important information by answering the following questions:

◆ What were the similarities and differences among the reform programs of Luther, the Anabaptists, and Calvin?

◆ What were the distinctive features of Protestant reform in England?

Catholic Reform, 1500–1570

12. Catholic religious orders:

   a. Played little role in the reform and renewal of the Catholic Church.
   b. Played a major role in the reform and renewal of the Catholic Church.
   c. Usually were not founded to attack Protestantism but sometimes turned in that direction.
   d. Were all modeled on the Jesuits.
   e. None of the above.

13. Ignatius of Loyola:

    a. Was French.

    b. Was Spanish.

    c. Had been a major theologian at the University of Paris.

    d. Formulated the Spiritual Exercises.

    e. Learned to read and write as an adult.

14. The Jesuits:

    a. Were an order walled off from the larger world.

    b. Established excellent schools.

    c. Offered the order's services directly to the pope.

    d. Were founded by Paul III.

    e. Were originally founded to convert Muslims to Christianity.

15. Pope Paul III:

    a. Was at first a reluctant reformer.

    b. Reformed the college of cardinals.

    c. Called the Council of Trent into session.

    d. All of the above.

    e. None of the above.

16. Teresa of Ávila's reform of the Carmelite order:

    a. Set the tone for women's Catholic religious orders.

    b. Ordered the Carmelites to work in the world, teaching and nursing the sick.

    c. Originally met with opposition from male churchmen.

    d. Was openly attacked by the kings of Spain.

    e. Showed Teresa to be an important teacher of a Catholic life of prayer.

17. The Council of Trent:

    a. Reaffirmed traditional Catholic teaching that salvation involved, first, God's grace, but also humans' ability to cooperate with or resist divine grace.

    b. Reaffirmed that both scripture and church tradition were authoritative for Catholics.

    c. Ordered the establishment of seminaries in each diocese of the church.

    d. Drew a sharp distinction between clergy and laity.

    e. Ordered women in religious orders to be separated from the larger society and to live within their convents.

Now that you have reviewed and tested yourself on this part of the chapter, take time to pull together all the important information by answering the following questions:

◆ From Alexander VI to Paul III, how did the Roman popes react to calls for reform, and what specific steps did they take to resist or further reforming movements?

◆ What strategies did Catholic missionaries adopt overseas when dealing with non-European peoples?

Reformation and Society, 1517–1570

18. Protestant reforms in children's education:

    a. Put more value on educating girls than boys.

    b. Put more value on educating boys than girls.

    c. Put a premium on religious education.

    d. Produced catechisms for children.

    e. Made attacking the Muslims a top priority.

19. Catholic reformers concerned with the problem of poverty:

    a. Agreed with Protestants that the state had a role in dealing with poverty.

    b. Disagreed with Protestants that the state had a role in dealing with poverty.

    c. Accepted the older idea that individual giving to the poor was an acceptable good work.

    d. Discouraged individual giving to the poor.

    e. Secretly admired the Protestants success in dealing with poverty.

20. Luther:
    a. Declared that marriage was a sacrament.
    b. Believed marriage was not a sacrament.
    c. Accepted the idea of clerical celibacy.
    d. Married an ex-nun.
    e. Declared that a marriage had to be approved by the spouses' parents.

21. Jews in the Reformation era:
    a. Were attacked by Luther who repeated all the medieval charges against them.
    b. Were allowed to settle in the Republic of Venice.
    c. Were ordered by the popes to wear yellow badges on their clothing.
    d. All of the above.
    e. None of the above.

Now that you have reviewed and tested yourself on this part of the chapter, take time to pull together all the important information by answering the following questions:

◆ Compare and contrast Protestant and Catholic views on each of the following: educating the young; reforming family life; and dealing with the problem of poverty.

CHAPTER 15

A Century of Crisis, 1550–1650

1550	1560	1570	1580	1590	1600	1610

1555	1562	1566		1598
Peace of Augsburg accepts split in western Christianity	French Wars of Religion begin	Calvinist revolt in the Netherlands		Edict of Nantes grants tolerance for French Protestants

This is a model of the *San Martino*, a Spanish galleon used as the flagship in Philip II's Armada of 1588 against England. Ships of this type sailed both the Atlantic and Pacific Oceans protecting Spain's global empire and trading network. (© Derek Bayes-Art/Lebrecht Music & Arts/Corbis)

After reading this chapter, you should be able to answer the following questions:

What were the causes and consequences of Europe's economic downturn and population stagnation after 1550?

How did political and religious issues shape the nature of the European states covered in this chapter?

How did the meaning of community change during a century of crisis?

How did religious conflict affect the everyday lives of Europeans?

EUROPE IN 1550 was troubled and turbulent. Rulers fought increasingly expensive and destructive wars and, not content with battling their enemies at home, carried the struggles overseas. The Spanish and Portuguese fought to maintain their empires, while the French, English, and Dutch attempted to seize their rivals' wealth or establish competing empires of their own in the Western Hemisphere and Asia.

After 1550, the prosperity Europeans had experienced since the mid-fourteenth century ended. In both town and country, the numbers of the poor grew, while a small, well-to-do elite struggled to maintain control over the increasingly restless and riot-prone masses. Hard times produced widespread anxiety. People became obsessed with witches, who were feared as agents of the Devil bent on ruining society. Many believed that the troubles they were experiencing were a prelude to Christ's Second Coming to judge the world.

The church reforms of the sixteenth century had created two mutually hostile religious communities in western Europe. Neither the Protestants nor the Catholics

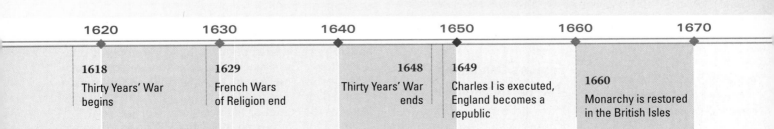

1620	1630	1640	1650	1660	1670
1618 Thirty Years' War begins	**1629** French Wars of Religion end	**1648** Thirty Years' War ends	**1649** Charles I is executed, England becomes a republic	**1660** Monarchy is restored in the British Isles	

accepted that religious unity had been shattered, and both fought ferociously to impose their own ways on their opponents. Capitalizing on his New World wealth and extensive European territories, Philip II of Spain, the son of Charles V, took the lead in the fight for Catholicism. The Netherlands, France, Germany, and the British Isles all saw religious warfare. In some wars, all Protestants joined to fight Catholics; in others, different types of Protestants fought each other. Both Protestants and Catholics committed terrible atrocities. The fierceness of the fighting shows how central the principle of religious unity was for the culture of early modern Europe.

Warfare accelerated economic decline, producing widespread famine and disease. In parts of Europe, population dropped by 50 percent. In the end, neither Protestants nor Catholics succeeded in eliminating their opponents, and religious disunity prevailed. By 1650, most Europeans had accepted it, often unwillingly, as a fact of life. Also by 1650, Spain, having exhausted its resources in the fight against Protestantism, had lost its preeminent position in Europe. France, weathering the crisis of its religious wars, now emerged as the dominant European power.

Although the Jews were not directly involved in disputes between Christians, they, too, experienced hard times when wars broke out in the lands where they lived. Nevertheless, the Jews' condition improved in western Europe, where they settled once again and often prospered. Yet, as a despised minority, Jews were sometimes subjected to terrible attacks.

Europe's Economy and Society

- ◆ **What were the effects of overseas empire building and global trading on Europe's economy?**
- ◆ **What caused the decline in the standard of living for most Europeans, and what effect did this decline have on society?**

Between 1550 and 1650, Europe's economy, which had boomed in the previous hundred years, began to stagnate. Silver from Spanish mines in the Americas caused inflation, which, combined with overpopulation, reduced the standard of living for most Europeans. Hardship was widespread, evident in protests and riots. As communities' traditional sense of solidarity crumbled, the well-to-do became obsessed with maintaining social order. Panic over witches was another symptom of the hard times that struck after 1550.

privateer Private vessel commissioned by a state to attack the commercial and naval ships of another country.

Europe's Continuing Overseas Expansion

During the sixteenth century, Portuguese and Spanish success in creating empires stirred similar ambitions in France and England. At first, the French and English were content to conduct raids against Spanish shipping. In 1523, a French ship seized three ships loaded with Moctezuma's personal treasure and the booty collected by Hernán Cortés's army. Since France and Spain were at war for most of the sixteenth century, this attack was considered part of the larger struggle. In the late sixteenth century, when relations between England and Spain deteriorated, Queen Elizabeth I commissioned the **privateer** Sir Francis Drake to seize Spanish treasure. These raids constituted the first phase of France's and England's entry into empire building in the New World, and by the early seventeenth century permanent English and French colonies were being established.

English, French, and Dutch Colonies in the New World In 1607, businessmen financed the first permanent English settlement in North America at Jamestown in present-day Virginia. In 1625, the English colonized the Caribbean island of Barbados and imported African slaves to work sugar plantations there. The French state also sponsored colonial ventures in America. In 1608, Samuel de Champlain founded the city of Quebec on the Saint Lawrence River as the center of the new colony of Canada.

In 1683, a French nobleman, Robert Cavalier, Sieur de La Salle, led an expedition from the Great

Map 15.1 **Europe in the Age of the Religious Wars** From 1550 to 1650, Europe was engulfed in a series of religious wars. One of the last was the Thirty Years' War, fought from 1618 to 1648 in the Holy Roman Empire. It pitted the Catholic Habsburgs and their German allies against the Protestants of the empire. During the war Sweden, Denmark, the Dutch Republic, Spain, and France were drawn into the fighting. © *Cengage Learning*

1. Consult the map legend and identify the "Spanish Habsburg Lands" and the "Austrian Habsburg Lands."
   a. Why do mapmakers make this distinction for the years after 1550?
   b. Trace the boundary of the Holy Roman Empire. Which lands of the Austrian Habsburgs lie outside the empire? Why are the Spanish Netherlands inside the empire and the United Provinces outside of it?
2. Does the position of the empire in relation to the other states of Europe suggest why so many European states were drawn into the Thirty Years' War?

Lakes down the Mississippi River to the Gulf of Mexico and claimed the lands along the river for France, naming them **Louisiana** in honor of the French king, Louis XIV. At the very end of the century, France claimed the western half of the island of Hispaniola and established sugar plantations there.

The Dutch also established sugar plantations in the Caribbean as, like the English and French, they seized islands originally claimed by Spain. In Asia, the Dutch attacked the Portuguese and gradually replaced them as the major power in the spice trade.

Establishing colonies and attacking empires were costly adventures involving large investments and high risks. To raise the necessary money, Europeans developed a new form of business organization, the **joint-stock company**, in which individuals pooled their capital and received stock shares in proportion to the size of their investment. The joint-stock technique raised huge sums of money but limited the risk factor for each investor. Jamestown was founded by a joint-stock venture, the Virginia Company. The English **East India Company**, founded in 1600, established trading posts on the subcontinent of India, and the Dutch United East India Company, founded in 1602, was profitable for more than a century.

New Foods and New Goods Nowhere were the effects of trade and colonization more far reaching than in the exchange between Europe and the Western Hemisphere. In the century after Columbus's voyages, many new food items were introduced into Europe: chili peppers, beans, pumpkins, squashes, tomatoes, peanuts, chocolate, maize, and potatoes. Maize and potatoes were to become staples in the diets of southern and northern Europeans, respectively.

These strange foods provoked doubt and debate. Some argued that people should eat only foods mentioned in the Bible. Others wondered if potatoes and peanuts, which grew underground, should be fed to animals but not to humans, who were higher up in the ladder of creation. Tobacco, cultivated early in Virginia, provided a satisfying New World smoke, sniff, or chew after a New World turkey dinner, washed down with rum, an alcoholic drink made from American-grown sugar.

The exchange brought even more dramatic changes to the Americas. On his second voyage, Columbus

brought wheat, melons, onions, radishes, grapevines, sugarcane, cauliflower, cabbages, lemons (originally from Asia), and figs to the Western Hemisphere, along with the European rat. Horses, cattle, pigs, goats, dogs, sheep, and chickens came as well, changing forever the animal population of the Americas.

Later European arrivals unknowingly brought weed seed with them in the form of Kentucky bluegrass, daisies, and dandelions, as well as the European honeybee. The European ox pulled plows through soils that had been too heavy to turn over with the Indians' handheld tools.

Trade with Asia also brought more new products to Europe. The first shipment of tea from China arrived at the beginning of the seventeenth century, and rice, a staple in some Asian diets, was soon widely grown in Italy. By the end of the century, coffee, native to the Arabian Peninsula, was grown in the East Indies and then shipped to Europe. Soon it would also be grown in the Americas. The rich prized Asian ebony wood for furniture and delicate Chinese porcelains for their collections of rare items. At a less exotic level, Chinese zinc and Indian tin were imported in ever-increasing quantities.

Thus the entry of new states and private companies into Europe's overseas trade expanded the global trading networks linking America, Europe, and Asia that had begun in the sixteenth century. The result was the beginning of a new era in Europe's economic life based on commerce.

A River of Silver

Spain's silver mines in the Americas, opened in the 1540s, produced huge quantities of precious metal that flowed to Europe and Asia. Contemporary official estimates of silver exports from the Spanish Empire place the figure at some 17,800 tons, but smuggling and unofficial exports may have pushed it as high as 29,000 tons. This amount would have tripled silver supplies in Europe, where the metal was used mainly as money; when news of silver's discovery reached Europe, Charles V's credit rating soared. The most productive mine was in present-day Bolivia at San Luis de Potosí. The other main source was at Zacatecas in northern Mexico. Gold and emeralds were also mined.

From Mines to Markets The silver of Potosí was either minted into coins or melted into bars and then transported to the Peruvian port of Lima. From there it went by ship to Panama, where it was hauled overland to the Caribbean for transfer to Spain. Some silver from northern Mexico was also carried to the Caribbean while the rest went to Acapulco on the Pacific, where it was loaded onto the **Manila galleon**, a large, square-rigged sailing ship sent to the Philippine Islands to purchase Chinese silks and porcelains. The galleon's annual round trip was the single most

Louisiana French colony in the Mississippi valley named after King Louis XIV.

joint-stock company Company in which individuals pool their capital and receive stock shares in proportion to the size of their investment.

East India Company English joint-stock company founded in 1600 to establish trading posts on the Indian subcontinent.

Manila galleon Spanish sailing ship that carried Spanish silver from Mexico to exchange for Chinese silks and porcelains in the Philippine Islands.

profitable voyage in the Spanish Empire, and the millions of silver coins used to pay for trade goods flooded Southeast Asia, where they became the standard international currency.

The silver for Europe, along with goods from China, was collected once a year by armed Spanish ships that arrived in the Caribbean in late summer. After wintering there, they joined up in Havana for the voyage home. This was the most perilous part of the trip because the fleet's valuable cargo made it subject to seizure by independently operating pirates or privateers commissioned by the governments of Spain's enemies.

Silver and the Spanish Monarchy If the Spanish fleet managed to dodge attacks and survive storms at sea, it headed for **Seville**, Spain's largest and richest city. In theory, all precious metals from the Americas had to be registered with the port authorities and then taxed, but smuggling, bribery, false declarations of value, and other techniques were routinely used to evade this requirement. Nevertheless, the government *quinto*, or fifth tax on gold and silver, made up a quarter of the royal income. Other goods were stored on the wharves, but few merchants gathered there to buy them. Instead, goods were shipped north to the trading centers of Antwerp and Amsterdam. Thus Seville never became a major hub in the global commercial network but served simply as a transit point for Spanish overseas riches.

Despite the sizable sum provided by the royal quinto, Charles V and then his son, **Philip II**, found that ruling their lands created costs even the river of silver from the New World could not completely pay. So Philip, like his father, borrowed. During his reign he overextended himself, borrowing more than he could repay and declaring bankruptcy four times. Each bankruptcy created a financial crisis throughout Europe. Lenders disappeared, and expenses piled up until a renegotiation of Spain's debt was worked out. The crisis solved, lenders returned—until the next bankruptcy.

A Revolution in Prices

Around the middle of the sixteenth century, Europe experienced **inflation**, a sharp rise in prices for land, food, and other basic necessities that had major effects on Europeans' day-to-day lives. Several factors explain this **price revolution**.

Silver and the Price Revolution The New World silver flowing into Spain soon spread through Europe as the Spanish government sent it out of the country in the form of coins to pay for the costs of warfare in Italy, the Netherlands, and elsewhere, which never seemed to stop. As silver coins became more and more common, the value of the metal in them declined, and their purchasing power diminished. To counteract the declining value of silver, people with things to sell raised their prices.

Population Growth and the Price Revolution The continuing rise in Europe's population after 1450 also caused the price revolution. At first, population growth stimulated the economy and led to increased agricultural and commercial activity, which benefited many urban and rural workers. By the mid-sixteenth century, however, as population continued to grow, Europe was experiencing a crisis of overpopulation that put pressure on the ability of people to sustain themselves. For example, in agriculture, the growing population required that more and more land had to be cultivated. By about 1550, good land was running out, and cultivation moved to marginal, less productive land. The result was an inadequate food supply and a rise in food prices.

Hard Times The rise in the price of food led, in turn, to two other developments: first, fierce competition for food-producing acreage caused land prices to rise sharply; and second, a glut of workers in need of jobs caused wages to decline. The impact of declining wages might have been offset if rural workers could have raised enough food for themselves on their own plots, but most could not because their landholdings were too small.

To make ends meet, peasants borrowed from local moneylenders. As collateral, they would put up their land or anything else they owned. If they defaulted on the loan, the lender would seize the collateral. So another problem was rising peasant debt. Over the hundred years from 1550 to 1650, rural communities were gradually polarized between a few rich peasants who managed to keep or increase their landholdings and a mass of poor small-scale landowners, landless wage laborers, and sharecroppers who paid rent for the land they farmed by sharing its produce with their landlord.

Urban workers also suffered from rising prices and declining wages brought on by overpopulation. Guild members in the textile industry, which employed thousands in cities across Europe, were particularly hard hit because they faced fierce competition from merchants who hired needy peasants to weave in their homes for low wages and to produce cloth that was not subject to guild regulations. The result was a growing gap between the urban rich and poor that strained relief agencies.

The Little Ice Age To make matters worse, Europe was experiencing a period of climate

Seville Spain's largest city and government-mandated port for all goods going to or coming from the Spanish Empire.

Philip II (r. 1556–1598) King of Spain, the most powerful ruler in late sixteenth-century Europe and leader of the Catholic crusade against Protestantism.

inflation Process by which the cost of goods and services increases and the value of money declines.

price revolution Rise in prices for land, food, and other basic necessities in mid-sixteenth-century Europe.

In this etching by Jacques Callot, a blind beggar stands with his begging cup and canine companion. What features in Callot's rendering of the man would signal to viewers that he was one of the "deserving poor?" (Callot, Jacques, *Beggar with Dog*. Rosenwald Collection, Image © 2007 Board of Trustees, National Gallery of Art, Washington, D.C., 1949.5.302)

The Hunt for Witches

Local political leaders shared the concern for maintaining popular order. In addition to economic hard times and social unrest, they also faced religious turmoil and spiritual anxiety as Europe split permanently into hostile Protestant and Catholic camps. Religious uncertainty lay behind rising beliefs that the world was coming to an end and that the Devil's attempt to destroy good Christians was intensifying. These fears led in turn to a search for **scapegoats** who could be blamed for the troubled times.

For centuries, Europeans thought that some people possessed magical skills that allowed them to cast harmful or helpful spells. These so-called cunning men and women were consulted by people at all levels of society. Both Catholic and Protestant reformers considered them nuisances and tried to draw their followers away from their "superstitious" practices, usually with little effect.

The Stereotype of the Witch By the sixteenth century, however, a belief spread that these cunning folk were not just magicians, but Devil worshippers. As it did, authorities in many parts of Europe inaugurated a crusade against **witches**.

Belief in witches was long standing, but it was only in this period that a sustained campaign against them was launched. After 1550, a stereotype of the witch emerged. Witches were said to be cunning folk who sold their souls to the Devil. In their obscene night rituals, called witches' Sabbaths, they sacrificed infants to Satan, engaged in cannibalism, and performed disgusting sexual acts. In a world where most people's lives were increasingly insecure, fear of bad magic skyrocketed, encouraging people to accuse their neighbors of satanic witchcraft.

Witchcraft Trials As many as 200,000 witchcraft trials were held all over Europe, most leading to convictions. The number of trials varied from place to place. Where lawyers and church officials had strict standards for accepting accusations or were skeptical of them, there were fewer trials. In England, for example, legal procedures prohibiting torture to procure confessions lowered the rates of self-incrimination. Rates were also low in Spain, where the Inquisition doubted that those accused of witchcraft had really made a pact with the Devil. The greatest number of trials—three-quarters of all known cases—occurred in the Holy Roman Empire, in areas where local officials, rather than state or church authorities, were in charge of the process. There, community leaders, clergymen, and other members of the local social elite, fearing social disorder and panicked by their belief in Satan's subversion of society, carried out wholesale prosecutions of people accused of witchcraft.

Women and Witchcraft The vast majority of those accused were older women, most of whom were widowed or single and therefore lacked male protection.

change known as the **Little Ice Age**. Winters were colder and longer than previously; glaciers in the Alps advanced to cover inhabited land; in England, the Thames froze over. Colder, wetter years damaged crops, causing food shortages. Epidemics increased. Declining standards of living, vulnerability to disease, and the growing polarization between rich and poor weakened both rural and urban communities' sense of solidarity and mutual responsibility. The needy protested and rioted more frequently, while the well-off became obsessed with maintaining order among the masses.

Little Ice Age Period of cooler weather in Europe beginning around the start of the fourteenth century.

scapegoats People blamed for other people's bad behavior or embodying their fears.

witches People, usually women, who were believed to have made a pact with the Devil, whom they worshiped.

Some had served as midwives. Most were poor, but some controlled their own property. Those who were quarrelsome or sexually independent were seen as transgressors against prevailing patriarchal values. Women accused of witchcraft were, therefore, associated with dangerous activities, or seen as an economic burden to their communities, or envied for their material wealth, or despised as violators of the community's norms of behavior.

Trials and Torture Witchcraft trials often involved torture to get the accused to confess their activity and then more torture to force them to name accomplices. In cities, torture often produced a chain reaction of accusations. As the numbers of accused grew, the victims bore less and less resemblance to the stereotypical poor-woman witch: men, the rich, and children were named. On average, half of those convicted were executed, and the rest were imprisoned or subjected to other forms of punishment.

The Decline in Trials Beginning in 1650, witch trials declined dramatically, as more and more centralized states took jurisdiction away from local authorities. Lawyers also worked to end persecutions. Although most lawyers still believed in witches, they also believed that legal standards for accusing and trying them had been too lax. Some people also believed in newly proposed scientific views of the world that questioned the Devil's active intervention in human affairs. Thus a sense of fairness, along with doubts about Satan's power, won out over the fear of the Devil's subversion of society by means of witchcraft.

 Checking In

By yourself or with a partner, explain the significance of each of the following selected key terms:

joint-stock company	price revolution
East India Company	Little Ice Age
Manila galleon	witches
Philip II	

This portrait of Philip II by Sanchez Coello (1583) shows the king in the somber dress favored at the Spanish court. His commitment to Roman Catholicism is symbolized by the rosary he holds. How does this style of royal portrait compare with the one of his father, Charles V, in Chapter 13 (p. 377)?

Museo Nacional del Prado, Madrid/Art Resource, NY

his lands. Philip also sought to defend the western Mediterranean from the Ottomans while making war on his own Moriscos and laying the grounds for their expulsion from the Iberian Peninsula. His greatest failure came in the Netherlands, where his attempt to crush Protestantism provoked a rebellion during which the northern provinces declared their independence. These provinces, now organized as the Dutch Republic, soon dominated the European economy.

The Fate of Spain and the Flourishing of the Netherlands

◆ **What were Philip II's successes and failures?**

◆ **What explains the success of the Dutch economy?**

In 1550, Spain, with its silver and empire, was the most powerful state in Europe. Philip II dominated international affairs, making war on Muslims and attempting to eliminate Protestantism throughout

Philip II

In 1556, Philip II succeeded his father, Charles V, as head of the Habsburg dynasty. Despite Charles's grant of the Holy Roman emperorship to his younger brother, Ferdinand I, Philip ruled over a vast assembly of territories: Castile, Aragon, and Granada in Spain; the Netherlands; Franche-Comté on the Rhine; Naples, Sicily, and Milan on the Italian peninsula; Spanish America; and the Philippine Islands (named after him) in East Asia. His global empire was the wonder of the world, and he was the most powerful ruler of his age.

"His Most Catholic Majesty" By the time Philip became king, Protestantism was challenging the Catholic Church throughout central and northern Europe, and Philip undertook its defense, using both military and diplomatic means. He also continued Christian Spain's attack on the Muslim world, now dominated in the west by the **Ottoman Turks**. In Spain, he adopted the title of His Most Catholic Majesty and supported Teresa of Ávila's reform of the Carmelites while collecting manuscripts of her religious writings for his library. He also built a residence, just outside Madrid, the new Spanish capital. Called the **Escorial**, it housed both the royal palace and a monastery where Philip frequently prayed and meditated with the monks. His most important advisers were the priests who heard his confessions and the theologians he kept at his side.

In appearance, Philip hardly looked like the self-appointed leader of the Catholic world. Short and soft-spoken, he presided over a somber court and rarely left the area around Madrid because he thought that "traveling about one's kingdom is neither useful nor decent." In this he unwisely rejected the policy of his predecessors, whose frequent travels throughout their lands kept them in touch with their subjects. Cautious by nature, he kept tight personal control over government, making every important policy decision and spending hours alone in his office pouring over the mountains of memoranda that had to be prepared for his approval.

Before his death, Charles V had urged Philip to fight heresy and to hold onto the lands God had given him. Philip followed this advice. The money he amassed through taxes and borrowing was spent in pursuit of these aims.

The Spanish War Against the Moriscos and the Turks

In the early sixteenth century, the Ottoman Turks continued to push into Christian territory. Hungary fell in 1521, and in 1529 a Turkish army laid siege, unsuccessfully, to Vienna. When the Ottomans conquered Christian peoples in the Balkans, they organized them as a **millet**, or non-Muslim subject people. Millet Christians had to pay special taxes and accept that some of their boys would be recruited into the army as **janissaries**. But they were allowed to practice their religion, and conversion to Islam was discouraged because the taxes Christians paid were an important source of state revenue. Nevertheless, many Christians did convert to improve their position in society. The Christian millet was dominated by Greeks in Constantinople, headed by the Orthodox patriarch there. Jews under the Ottomans were not organized into a millet but were encouraged to immigrate to Turkish lands when western Christian states expelled them.

The Moriscos The Turks also established contact with the **Moriscos**. Following Ferdinand and Isabella's conquest of Granada in 1492, its Muslim population, now called Moriscos, had been forced to convert to Christianity. Then Christians seized their lands and sought to stamp out their culture along with their religion. Speaking Arabic and bathing on Fridays, along with traditional dancing and eating couscous, were forbidden as signs of heresy. Faced with this repression, the Moriscos rose up in 1569. The revolt lasted two years and involved thirty thousand rebels joined by four thousand Turks and North Africans. The revolt was put down in 1571, but hatred remained on both sides.

In 1609, Philip's son, Philip III, ordered all three hundred thousand Moriscos expelled from Spain. Many went to North Africa, while some went to northern Greece and Constantinople. The expulsion of the Moriscos was the last step in the dismantling of the cultural and religious diversity that had characterized medieval Spain. Some Spaniards hailed the expulsion as a purification of the land, but others, like the great novelist **Miguel de Cervantes**, condemned it. In *Don Quixote*, Ricote, an expelled Morisco, laments, "Wherever we are, we weep for Spain, because we were born there and it is our native land."

The Turks In 1571, the last year of the Morisco revolt, Philip destroyed the Turkish navy at **Lepanto** off the coast of Greece; 195 ships in the Turkish fleet of 230 were captured or sunk, thirty thousand Turks were killed or wounded, and three thousand were taken prisoner. Although the Turks assembled another fleet in 1572 and continued to harass the coasts of Italy and Sicily, their dominance of the Mediterranean had been weakened. Then, in 1580, Philip became ruler of Portugal and its empire when the Portuguese king disappeared on a crusade in Morocco against the Muslims. Philip was now at the height of his power.

The Revolt in the Netherlands

Even as Spanish might awed Europe, Protestant forces in England and the Netherlands were rising

Ottoman Turks Muslims who captured Constantinople in 1453, ending the Byzantine Empire and founding the Ottoman Empire.

Escorial Philip II's palace and monastery complex outside of Madrid.

millet Legally defined community for non-Muslims living within the Ottoman Empire.

janissaries Ottoman infantry composed mainly of Christian boys either captured or given in tribute to the sultan to be raised as Muslim soldiers.

Moriscos Muslims in Spain who were forced to convert to Christianity or leave.

Miguel de Cervantes (1547–1616) Spanish writer and critic of Philip II who wrote *Don Quixote*.

Lepanto Naval battle won by Spain over the Ottomans in October 1571.

Map 15.2 **The Netherlands** When the Twelve Years' Truce was signed in 1609, the seven northern provinces of the Netherlands, along with parts of the Duchy of Brabant and the County of Flanders, were put under Dutch control. Spain continued to control the remaining southern provinces. *© Cengage Learning*

1. Refer to the map at the beginning of this chapter, "Europe in the Age of the Religious Wars," and place the northern provinces (the United Provinces) in the larger context of European states.
   a. How large do you imagine the largest and smallest provinces of the Dutch Republic were?
   b. Were there any states in Europe smaller than the United Provinces?
2. What does this tell you about the "Dutch miracle?"

to challenge it. Protestantism had not spread to Spain, but it had to the Netherlands, the Habsburgs' richest territory. Charles V had tried without success to eliminate it there, and Philip tried as well, with even worse results. Philip viewed his Protestant subjects as heretics, but at first he recognized that their growing numbers

required a political solution. Therefore, in 1566, on the advice of his court theologians, he granted religious **toleration** to the Protestants. Shortly thereafter, militant Calvinists went on a rampage across the country, destroying Catholic churches and religious images. Philip now decided on a military solution.

War and Revolt In 1567, a Spanish army marched north to subdue the Protestants. Its commander, the duke of Alba, then tried and executed more than a thousand people. To pay for his army, Alba also imposed a tax on the Netherlanders. Both Protestants and Catholics condemned it and rebelled when it was not withdrawn. Then, in 1572, Calvinist exiles in England returned home and joined the rebellion, seizing the country's northern provinces and electing **William of Orange** as their leader. The general rebellion in the Netherlands forced Philip to recall Alba in 1573.

In 1575, Philip declared a bankruptcy that delayed pay for his troops in the Netherlands. In response, his army mutinied and sacked Antwerp, destroying property and leaving eight thousand dead. This "Spanish Fury" signaled the end of Antwerp as Europe's leading commercial hub. Finally, in 1579, Philip's new military governor was able to consolidate Spain's rule in the southern provinces, thereafter known as the Spanish Netherlands. But the northern provinces were lost when rebels there forced the Spanish army to retreat by opening the dikes that kept the sea out, flooding large parts of the country. Having declared their independence from Spain, the northern provinces reconstituted themselves as the **United Provinces**, or **Dutch Republic**.

The Armada of 1588 Queen Elizabeth I of England had aided the Dutch Protestants, and Philip decided to attack her. In 1588, he sent the **Spanish Armada**—130 ships and 30,000 men—to join with his loyal forces in the Spanish Netherlands and then conquer the island kingdom. The Spanish met a slightly larger and much faster English fleet in the English Channel, where stormy weather and superior English cannon fire broke up the Armada. Only half the Spanish ships returned to their ports.

The defeat was the beginning of Spain's decline. The failure to stamp out Protestantism in the Netherlands, followed by the loss of the northern provinces, was a bitter blow to Philip, who grieved that he had betrayed his father's trust.

toleration Recognition of the right to hold dissenting beliefs.

William of Orange (1533–1584) Calvinist nobleman, also known as William the Silent, who led the Protestant rebellion against the Spanish in the Netherlands.

United Provinces (Dutch Republic) Northern Netherlands provinces that successfully threw off Spanish rule.

Spanish Armada Unsuccessful armed fleet sent by Philip II in 1588 to conquer England.

This engraving from 1647 shows fluteships in a Dutch harbor. The fluteship's deck is narrower than the bulging hull below it, which will be filled with the goods shipped in what the Dutch called the "mother trade" between Dutch ports and Baltic ports in the east.

The Dutch Miracle

It would take decades for Spain to acknowledge Dutch independence, but from the 1590s on, the breakaway provinces were free from serious invasion. Distracted by other wars, Spain was never able to conquer the north. Finally, in 1609, the Spanish signed the Twelve Years' Truce with the rebels.

A Limited Religious Toleration The Dutch Republic was founded by Calvinists who sought to reform church and state. But William of Orange and his successors feared that the rebellion's success would be jeopardized if the Catholics of the north, who made up a third of the population, were alienated. So a policy of partial toleration was instituted. Calvinism was recognized as the state religion, but the church was not allowed to control state policy. Although Catholics were forbidden to worship publicly, they were allowed unofficially to open private chapels. Anabaptists, Lutherans, and Jews also had their places of worship. None of these communities really welcomed the others; each tended to mix socially and marry only with its own kind. But a grudging live-and-let-live attitude prevailed in the country.

The Calling Although Calvinist church members were a minority of the Dutch population, Calvinist values were widely shared. Chief among them was the idea of the **calling**. Calvin had rejected Catholic practices such as renouncing the sinful world by joining religious orders or giving one's wealth to the church or the poor. Like Luther, he believed these acts were useless for salvation. Instead, he urged people to treat their ordinary work as a divine calling through which they could serve God with diligence and to avoid sinful idleness, luxury, and waste.

When giving this advice, Calvin did not have a particular economic agenda in mind, but his ideal of a sober and serious attitude toward one's calling in the world encouraged attentive, thrifty behavior among the merchants, manufacturers, and artisans who heeded it. This attitude was one of the factors behind the Dutch economic miracle of the late sixteenth century.

An Economic Boom The revolt against Spain hurt the economy of the southern Netherlands and hastened the decline of Antwerp. But while the economy faltered in the south, it boomed in the north. Unlike most of Europe, which experienced hard times after 1550, the Dutch Republic flourished. As both population and workers' wages rose, the Dutch economy became the wonder of the age. Its success rested on an adequate grain supply from Poland that prevented the food shortages plaguing other parts of Europe.

calling Calvinist belief that ordinary work was a means for serving God.

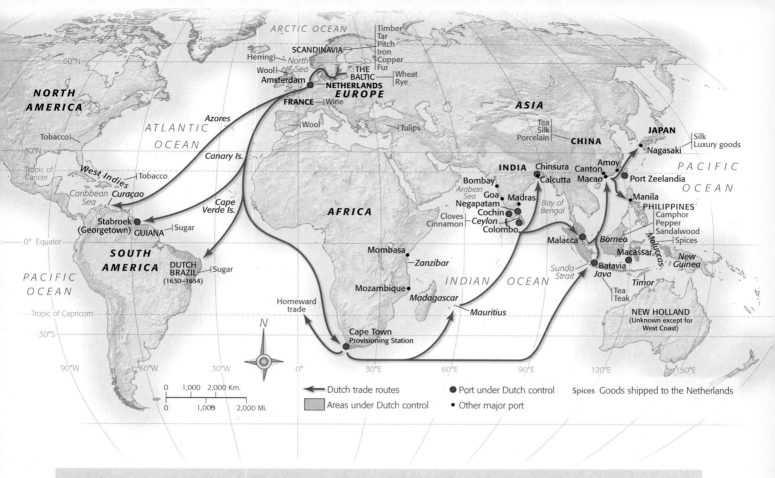

Map 15.3 **Dutch Commerce in the Seventeenth Century** By the seventeenth century the Dutch had developed a complex global trading network. They took over Europe's East Asia trade from the Portuguese, dominated the European seaborne trade routes, traded with their New World colonies, and became the major trading partner with the Portuguese in Brazil. © *Cengage Learning*

1. Locate Amsterdam and the United Provinces on this map.
2. Trace Dutch trading routes and estimate the overall size of the "Areas under Dutch control." Is it larger or smaller than the United Provinces?
3. Look back at Map 13.4 "World Expansion, 1492–1536," in Chapter 13, page 390.
   a. Compare the relative size of Spain and Portugal to their overseas possessions.
   b. Do the same patterns hold of these states and their possessions that hold for the Dutch and theirs?

With the grain supply assured, Dutch farmers were free to specialize in other foodstuffs: butter, cheese, hops for beer, and livestock for meat. In addition, the North Sea provided catches of nutritious herring. Half the labor force was engaged in agriculture, the rest in a variety of industries. There was a need for labor, and workers' wages rose as a consequence. Men worked on large reclamation projects as coastal land was pumped dry with windmills for agricultural use.

Dutch cities grew and with them a demand for servants, carpenters, masons, and other urban workers. High literacy rates and lax censorship created a demand for books, news sheets, and pamphlets offering a wide range of opinions on often-controversial subjects like religion. These, in turn, called for printers and engravers. Shipyards employed others, and the ships they built needed crews. In fact, ships and shipping did the most to stimulate the economy.

Shipbuilding and Trade After 1550, the Dutch became the best shipbuilders in Europe. They also created an international trading network and used their ships to move their goods. The success of Dutch shipbuilding and trade rested on the **fluteship**, a large-hulled boat with a shallow draft. Fluteships carried salt, herring, and cloth east to Poland and other Baltic ports and brought back grain and timber. Some of the imports were used locally, while the rest were sold abroad.

Interestingly, Spain was one of the Dutch Republic's

> **fluteship** Merchant ship with an enlarged cargo hold and shallow draft used in Dutch trade with eastern Europe.

François Dubois's painting of the Saint Bartholomew's Day Massacre, August 24, 1572, graphically depicts the chaos of this event. The barking dog, at center left, seems to give voice to the violence. How does this painting embody Europeans' fears about religious disunity in a community and the related fear of polluting dissent within it? (Musee Cantonal des Beaux-Arts de Lausanne, Switzerland/The Art Archive at Art Resource, NY)

best customers. Although at war with the rebels for much of the time, Spain could not do without Dutch-shipped timber for its navy and grain for its food-hungry territories in Italy. So the Spanish swallowed their principles and traded.

The Dutch also entered the East Asian trade. In 1602, the government licensed the United East India Company to set up trading posts from Persia to Japan. Because Portugal was ruled by Spain after 1580, the Dutch aimed to reduce Spanish power by supplanting Portuguese traders in Asia. After the Portuguese were driven out, the company dominated the spice trade with Europe. It also dominated the inter-Asian trade, picking up cotton cloth in India and trading it elsewhere for goods like porcelain and silk that were then sold in Europe.

After the Japanese government began persecuting Japanese Christian converts and shut off contact with the outside world, the Dutch alone were allowed a trading post there. In 1621, the Dutch government also chartered the Dutch West India Company, which set up posts in Curaçao on the Caribbean and Surinam on the South American coast. Soon the Dutch were trading with Brazil, exporting European goods to the colony and importing African slaves in return for sugar. Dutch settlers also founded the colony of New Amsterdam on Manhattan Island at the mouth of the Hudson River.

The hub of Dutch life was **Amsterdam** in the province of Holland. By the early seventeenth century, Amsterdam had replaced Antwerp as Europe's chief commercial and banking center. Because the republic's commercial activity

Amsterdam Capital of the Dutch province of Holland and commercial center of the Dutch Republic.

spread across Europe and the world, involving people in complex, long-distance economic activity, the Dutch can be seen as the creators of the first truly modern economy.

Checking In

By yourself or with a partner, explain the significance of each of the following selected key terms:

Ottoman Turks   Dutch Republic

Moriscos   Spanish Armada

Lepanto   Amsterdam

William of Orange

Political Contests and More Religious Wars

◆ **What explains the violence of Europe's political contests and religious wars?**

◆ **What were the outcomes of the wars?**

In 1562, France was plunged into religious warfare between Catholics and Protestants that lasted for nearly seventy years. In the end, the Protestants were granted limited religious toleration, but their attempts to create their own semi-independent political communities within France failed. The Holy Roman

Jacques Callot Publishes "The Miseries and Misfortunes of War"

In 1633, Jacques Callot, nearing the end of his life and suffering from a painful stomach disorder, published eighteen large etchings depicting "The Miseries and Misfortunes of War." Military scenes had always been part of his artistic repertory, but the "Miseries" were something different. With them, the respected portrayer of elite life in early-seventeenth-century Europe revealed himself as one of the most powerful protesters against the dark side of war.

Callot was born in 1592 into a noble and devout Roman Catholic family in the duchy of Lorraine. His artistic talent was apparent at an early age, and in his teens he joined a band of gypsies heading south to Rome, where he worked as an assistant in a print shop specializing in religious images at a time when the campaign against Protestantism gripped the city. The papacy urged the Catholic faithful to come to Rome to reinforce their faith through visits to the tombs of saints and the city's magnificent churches. When they left, these pilgrims were eager to take home souvenirs, and prints like Callot's of the famous paintings they had seen in churches were especially prized.

In 1611, Callot moved to Florence to serve the grand duke Cosimo II and his mother, the grand duchess Christine, who, like Callot, was from Lorraine. Cosimo's court was one of the most brilliant and intellectually distinguished in Europe, and Florence was filled with artists and scientists in the grand duke's employ. Here Callot perfected his etching technique using the extra-hard varnish Italian violin makers put on their instruments. This varnish allowed Callot to prepare his copper printing plates by cutting fine, clear lines with his etching needle. The result was a remarkably detailed and precise etching ready to pick up ink for printing. In Florence, Callot continued to produce religious prints, but he also documented the lives of the grand dukes and their lavish court—scenes of operas, precision marching, and tournaments. Soldiers also figured prominently in these works because the rulers of the time were expected to project an image of warrior power. Callot's soldiers were dashing and heroic, mounted on prancing horses and glittering with finely polished armor.

In 1621, Cosimo II died, and the grand duchess Christine, reducing state expenditures, dismissed Callot and other court artists. Callot returned to his father's house in Lorraine, which, in 1630, the French invaded. They invaded again in 1632 and in 1633, when they finally annexed the duchy to France and demanded an oath of loyalty from all locally prominent people, including Callot.

The invasion of Lorraine brought the harsh facts of warfare directly into Callot's family. Plague swept through the duchy, brought in by French soldiers, and Callot's father fell victim to it. It was in this context that Callot decided to create his "Miseries and Misfortunes of War." The series of prints were published in 1633. The first shows an army recruiter luring men to sign up with promises of good pay. A fierce battle scene follows, and then come five prints showing the cruelty of soldiers against civilians as troops pillage a farm, attack a monastery, burn a village, and seize a stagecoach. In these scenes people are stabbed, shot, and burned alive. The next prints show the tables turned on the soldiers, who are tortured and killed by their commanders for military crimes such as desertion. Here men are tied to a rope and hurled earthward from a great height, shot by a firing squad, torn apart on a rack, or burned at the stake, while others hang by their necks like human fruit on the branches of a great tree. We then see wounded and mangled soldiers crowding a hospital, people dying by a roadside, and peasants attacking soldiers in revenge for their atrocities. The series ends with a conqueror rewarding his troops, implying that the horrors, now celebrated as a "victory," will start all over again. Callot presented his prints without any commentary, intending that his artistic skill alone should carry his bitter message; the moralizing lines now seen on many of them were added later.

In 1635, at the age of forty-three, Jacques Callot died in a Lorraine that was ravaged by wartime disease and famine. But his prints endured. They struck home to many of his generation who, like him, were deeply committed Christians, whether Catholic or Protestant, and who were also appalled by the horror and futility of the warfare that had torn Europe apart for nearly a century.

Empire also experienced a religious war. The German war lasted fewer years than the war in France, but it brought non-German states into the fighting, and its destruction was far greater. The peace settlement ending the war granted religious toleration to Calvinists, Lutherans, and Catholics and reduced the emperor's power. Like the French, the Germans had to learn to live with a new religious pluralism. The conflict also accelerated Spain's decline and France's rise as the most powerful state in Europe.

France's Wars of Religion

When Henry II died in 1559, he left his fourteen-year-old son Francis II to succeed him. In the confusion following Henry's death, the powerful **Guise family**, utterly committed to the extermination of Protestantism, seized control of the government. For the next thirty years, as three of Henry's young sons ruled France in succession, plots and fighting broke out between the Catholic Guises and the Protestant Huguenots.

The Saint Bartholomew's Day Massacre In 1572, a Catholic attack on the Huguenots that began in Paris on Saint Bartholomew's Day—thus known as the **Saint Bartholomew's Day Massacre**—spread to the provinces. Some five thousand people died as violence reached extraordinary levels—heads, hands, and genitals were cut off; pregnant women were stabbed in the stomach; and bodies were burned. The massacres put an end to the growth of Protestantism in France.

The brutality of religious conflict demonstrated that both sides believed a fundamental issue was at stake—the belief that all members of a community had to share a common religious commitment for the community to function properly. In early modern Europe, religion was more a matter of community solidarity than of individual belief. Therefore, all religious dissent had to be stamped out to restore communal unity and win God's favor, especially since the Second Coming and Last Judgment were believed to be near at hand. Thus Huguenots and Catholics saw each other not simply as different, but as dangerous polluters of the community. Killing as a rite of purification was not enough; the very bodies of the enemy had to be degraded.

Henry IV and the Edict of Nantes In 1589, the last of Henry II's sons, Henry III, died, assassinated by a fanatical Catholic monk. Since Henry III had no children, the Crown passed to a cousin, **Henry IV of Navarre**, a Huguenot. Henry was eager to end the fighting, but he faced a dilemma. The law of royal succession made him king, but his coronation oath would require him to attack non-Catholic heretics. In 1593, Henry resolved the issue by converting to Catholicism, supposedly saying that "Paris is well worth a Mass." In 1595, when the pope absolved Henry of his Huguenot errors, Henry was able to win over all but the die-hard Catholics.

Henry reassured the Huguenots by issuing the **Edict of Nantes**, granting official toleration, in 1598. This edict brought an uneasy religious peace to France, but at a high price to community unity. The Huguenots were permitted to worship undisturbed, and they were also granted some two hundred fortified towns, along with troops to defend them. These towns were effectively independent from royal control and became a Huguenot state within the state.

To rally support for the edict, Henry showered powerful Catholic and Huguenot nobles with high government positions and large pensions. He also insisted that the king, who was the source of all law and order, should be obeyed regardless of his religion. Henry's emphasis on the importance of law and order vested in the king's authority became one of the basic principles of **absolutism**, which guided French kings' rule for the next two centuries.

The Resurgent French Monarchy

At the grassroots level, Henry IV built on an expansion of government begun by his predecessors, who had sold administrative offices to middle-class lawyers and then forced them to loan the government money. This strategy raised additional revenue and built loyalty, as the new officeholders had a compelling reason to see that the monarchy remained strong. Henry IV used this expanded administrative force to consolidate royal power and initiated tax reform to erase the royal debt and build up a treasury surplus.

Henry's chief minister, the Huguenot duke of Sully, lowered direct taxes while raising indirect ones. The direct tax of the taille took one large bite out of incomes whereas indirect taxes on commodities nibbled slowly away at them, so the pain of taxation was obscured. Most important, Sully imposed the annual *paulette* tax on all officials who had bought their offices. Because their numbers were now so large, paulette payments raised revenues that eventually rivaled the taille as the chief source of royal income.

Although Henry IV won many Huguenots and Catholics over to his policies of religious toleration and administrative consolidation, in 1610 he was stabbed to death by a deranged ex-monk obsessed with the continuing presence of heretics in the kingdom. Henry's heir was his nine-year-old son, **Louis XIII**, who, once king in his own right, resumed war against

---

Guise family Powerful Catholic nobility committed to eliminating Protestantism in France during the French religious wars of 1559–1588.

Saint Bartholomew's Day Massacre Catholic massacre of Protestants in Paris and throughout France in 1572 that ended the growth of Protestantism in the kingdom.

Henry IV of Navarre (r. 1589–1610) Protestant king of Navarre who became king of France, converted to Catholicism, and started to end the religious wars.

Edict of Nantes Decree issued by Henry IV in 1598 that allowed the Huguenots to practice their religion and gave them two hundred fortified towns.

absolutism Doctrine that a king was the sole source of all law in his realm.

Louis XIII (r. 1610–1643) King of France who made war on the Huguenots and took France into the Thirty Years' War to weaken France's political rival, Spain.

A la fin ces Voleurs infames et perdus ,
Comme fruits malheureux a cet arbre pendus

Monstrent bien que le crime (horrible et noire engeance)
Est luy mesme instrument de honte et de vengeance ,

Et que cest le Destin des hommes vicieux
Desprouuer tost ou tard la iustice des Cieux . 2]

Thieving soldiers are executed in this etching from Jacques Callot's *Miseries of War.* A priest blesses the men as they are led up a ladder to be hung. A caption describes the executed as "infamous lost souls . . . hung like unhappy fruit."

the Huguenots. In 1629, he issued the **Peace of Alès**, which dismantled the Huguenots' fortified towns and ended France's Wars of Religion. But the religious toleration granted the Huguenots in 1598 was reaffirmed.

The Habsburg War Against the Turks

Charles V had put his younger brother Ferdinand in charge of the Holy Roman Empire before his abdication in 1556. Thirty years earlier, Ferdinand had also been elected king of Hungary and Bohemia after the previous king died fighting the Ottoman Turks. While Ferdinand had full control of Austria and Bohemia, the Turks conquered most of Hungary, leaving only the northern part in Habsburg hands. Even that was threatened when the Turks, marching up the Danube River, tried in 1529 and again in 1532 to seize all of Hungary and the city of Vienna in Austria. For Ferdinand, a devout Catholic, the Turks posed a greater threat than the Protestants.

Thus, during Ferdinand's reign, and that of his son Maximilian II (r. 1564–1576), various kinds of Protestants increased their followings in all Habsburg lands. Lutherans predominated in Austria, Lutherans and Calvinists flourished in Bohemia, and Calvinists and **Unitarians** gained converts in Habsburg Hungary. "In affairs of religion everyone does as he pleases," one Catholic complained. After Maximilian died in 1576, effective Habsburg rule declined, as a contest between his two sons encouraged the great nobles who controlled the representative assemblies, or **diets**, to seek increased political independence.

The nobles' model for good government was **Poland-Lithuania**, where the nobility elected the king and had the right to rebel against him if he violated his coronation oath. In the Polish Diet, each noble had the right to veto a measure and thus "explode" the diet. They were also free to govern their serfs without royal interference and to choose between Catholicism and some form of Protestantism. When new war with the Turks broke out in 1593, the nobility in the Habsburg lands demanded more religious freedom and greater local control of government in return for funds for the war.

The Thirty Years' War

As Protestantism grew in Habsburg lands, the Catholics launched a counteroffensive. As early as the 1590s, Jesuits from Italy rallied Catholic communities, which soon established a militant anti-Protestant movement. Catholics found their leader in the new emperor, **Ferdinand II**, a fervent Catholic. His determination to put an end to Protestantism launched the **Thirty Years' War**, the most devastating conflict of the

Peace of Alès Treaty in 1629 that ended France's religious wars, allowed Huguenots freedom of worship, but took away their fortified towns.

Unitarians Christians who denied the traditional doctrine of the Trinity.

diets In the Holy Roman Empire under Habsburg rule, representative assemblies dominated by the great nobility that sought increased control of government.

Poland-Lithuania Kingdom formed in 1569 from two previously independent states; included modern Poland, the Baltic states, Belarus, and most of Ukraine.

Ferdinand II (r. 1619–1637) Habsburg emperor who reestablished Catholicism in Bohemia and Austria but failed to do so in the empire as a whole.

Thirty Years' War General war, 1618–1648, between German Protestant princes and their foreign allies against the Habsburgs, who were allied with Catholic princes.

Simplicius Simplicissimus Encounters Some "Merry Cavalrymen"

Jacques Callot was not alone in commenting on seventeenth-century warfare. In 1669, a German innkeeper, Johann von Grimmelshausen, who had fought as a soldier in the Thirty Years' War, published *Simplicius Simplicissimus* (Simplest of Simpletons), a tale that mixes humor and horror in equal measure. It went through three editions in 1669 alone. In the excerpt that follows, young Simplicius/The Simpleton, while working as a shepherd for his father, meets a band of cavalrymen and accompanies them to his home. Here he tells us what happened next.

❶ Why does the author use these remarks to set up what follows?

❷ What effect in the reader does the author try to create when he mixes his account of pillaging with humor?

❶ Though I hadn't intended to take the peace-loving reader into my father's home and farm along with these merry cavalrymen, the orderly progress of my tale requires me to make known to posterity the sort of abysmal and unheard-of cruelties occasionally perpetrated in our German war, and to testify by my own example that all these evils were necessarily required for our own good by the kindness of our Lord. For, my dear reader, who would have told me that there is a God in heaven if the warriors hadn't destroyed my [father's] house....

❷ The first thing these horsemen did in the nice black rooms of the house was to put in their horses. Then everyone took up a special job, a job having to do with death and destruction. Although some began butchering, heating water, and rendering lard, as if to prepare for a banquet, others raced through the house, ransacking upstairs and down.... Still others bundled up big bags of cloth, household goods, and clothes, as if they wanted to hold a rummage sale somewhere. What they did not intend to take along they broke up and spoiled. Some ran their swords into

seventeenth century. At first confined to Bohemia, it soon engulfed the Holy Roman Empire and drew in many European states as it went through Bohemian, Danish, Swedish, and French phases.

The War Begins in Bohemia In 1617, after he was elected king of Bohemia, Ferdinand II ordered Protestant churches closed in two Bohemian towns. Enraged Protestants confronted two of Ferdinand's officials in Prague, the capital of the kingdom, and threw them out of an upper-story window. Surprisingly, they survived. Catholics claimed they had been wafted gently to earth on angels' wings, while Protestants protested that a pile of dung had broken their fall. This "defenestration of Prague" prompted a Bohemian rebellion, which Ferdinand subdued with help from the Spanish Habsburgs. Ferdinand seized rebel lands and gave them to Habsburg supporters. Believing that religious dissent polluted society and offended God, he banned Protestant worship, ordering Protestants to convert or leave. In 1627, a subdued Bohemian Diet declared that the Crown was no longer elective, but rather hereditary in the Habsburg family. The abolition of elective monarchy marked the high point in Ferdinand's reconquest of Bohemia.

The Danes and the Swedes Enter the War The Habsburg victory in Bohemia had repercussions throughout Europe. The Spanish branch of the family used it to seize the Palatinate, a state on the Rhine River, and thereby expand its control of the "Spanish Road" that led north from Habsburg, Italy, to the Spanish Netherlands. Soon the king of Denmark entered the war as leader of the Protestants. But he was defeated and driven out of the empire in 1629. Victorious, Ferdinand II supposedly reaffirmed the 1555 Peace of Augsburg but in reality sought to strengthen Catholicism, not only in Habsburg lands but throughout the empire.

At this point, the Swedish phase of the war began, when the Lutheran king of Sweden, **Gustavus II Adolphus**, assumed leadership of the Protestant cause.

Gustavus II Adolphus (r. 1594–1632) King of Sweden who led Protestant forces against the Habsburgs until his death in battle in 1632.

the hay and straw, as if there hadn't been hogs enough to stick.... Some shook the feathers out of beds and put bacon slabs, hams, and other stuff in the ticking, as if they might sleep better on these. ❸ They flattened out copper and pewter dishes and baled the ruined goods. They burned up bedsteads, tables, chairs, and benches, though there were yards and yards of dry firewood outside the kitchen. Jars and crocks, pots and casseroles, all were broken, either because they preferred their meat broiled or because they thought they'd eat only one meal with us. In the barn, the hired girl was handled so roughly that she was unable to walk away, I am ashamed to report. They stretched the hired man out flat on the ground, stuck a wooden wedge in his mouth to keep it open, and emptied a milk bucket full of stinking manure drippings down his throat; they called it a Swedish cocktail. He didn't relish it and made a very wry face. By this means they forced him to take a raiding party to some other place where they carried off men and cattle and brought them to our farm.... I can't say much about the captured wives, hired girls, and daughters because the soldiers wouldn't let me watch their doings. But I do remember hearing pitiful screams from various dark corners and I guess that my mother and our Ursula had it no better than the rest. ❹ Amid all this horror I was busy turning a roasting split and didn't worry about anything, for I didn't know the meaning of it. ❺ In the afternoon I helped water the horses and that way got to see our hired girl in the barn. She looked wondrously messed up and at first I didn't recognize her. In a sickly voice she said, "Boy, get out of this place, or the soldiers will take you with them."

Source: *The Adventures of Simplicius Simplicissimus* by Hans Jacob Christoffel van Grimmelshausen. A modern translation with an introduction by George Schultz-Behrend, second revised edition. Rochester, New York: Camden House, 1993. Reprinted with permission.

❸ Why does Grimmelshausen order the details of the pillaging in the way he does?

❹ What is the point of this sentence?

❺ Thinking back on this account, why would Grimmelshausen describe the destruction of a clearly prosperous, well-supplied peasant household?

Gustavus Adolphus was a seasoned warrior, having already fought the Danes, the Russians, and the Poles. His chief concern was to expand Swedish power in the Baltic, as he feared that a Catholic Habsburg victory in Germany would threaten his interests. But his death in battle in 1632 spread confusion. When Ferdinand, realizing he would never be able to eradicate Protestantism, offered toleration for Lutherans, the war entered its French phase.

France Enters the War Although Louis XIII and his chief minister, **Cardinal Richelieu**, were devout Catholics, they feared that Ferdinand's reconciliation with the Protestants would increase the power of France's long-standing Habsburg enemy. They, therefore, entered the war, and for the next eleven years, French and Swedish troops continued to fight the Habsburgs. Almost all the fighting was done on German soil, and the devastation was terrible. The Thirty Years' War made the region's economic decline immeasurably worse.

Overall, the population of the empire fell between 15 and 20 percent as the warring armies disrupted agriculture, sacked villages and cities, and spread disease among the civilian population. In areas of the worst fighting, such as Bohemia and the southern Baltic coast, population declined by 50 percent as people died or fled. Cities fell into debt because of the huge bribes they paid the warring armies, whether friend or foe, in hopes of averting pillaging by the troops.

The Peace of Westphalia

The war finally came to an end in 1648 with the **Peace of Westphalia**. It amended the 1555 Peace of Augsburg to allow rulers to choose Catholicism, Calvinism, or Lutheranism as their state religion. Thus Ferdinand II's dream of reestablishing Catholic dominance in the empire died forever. Like the Peace of Alès in France

Cardinal Richelieu (1585–1642) Louis XIII's chief minister, who persuaded Louis to enter the Thirty Years' War against Ferdinand II.

Peace of Westphalia Peace in 1648 ending the Thirty Years' War, allowing states in the Holy Roman Empire to establish their own foreign policies and state religion.

almost twenty years earlier, the Peace of Westphalia ratified a grudging recognition that the state's religious unity had been shattered and that new ways of forming community and community identity would have to be found.

Important political changes also occurred. The empire's boundaries were altered: the Swiss Confederation and the Dutch Republic were now placed outside the empire and recognized as independent states. Within the empire, states were granted the right to develop their own foreign policies without the emperor's approval. Both France and Sweden took imperial territory. Sweden gained control of the southern Baltic shore, and France received three important bishoprics on its eastern frontier.

The French Fight On Although France ended its war in Germany in 1648, war against the Habsburgs continued, with fighting between France and Spain along the borders of the Spanish Netherlands and the Pyrenees Mountains. In 1659, the two countries signed the **Treaty of the Pyrenees**. France extended its rule along the eastern Pyrenees and took important cities in the Spanish Netherlands. To celebrate the peace, the king of Spain agreed to the marriage of his eldest daughter, Anne, to the young king of France, Louis XIV, who had succeeded Louis XIII in 1643. Spain, exhausted by decades of warfare, never regained the position it held under Philip II. France was now the most powerful state in Europe.

Europeans were to fight many more wars after the Treaty of Westphalia, but religious motivations for conflict were never again as strong as they had been in the century before 1648. Now, states formed diplomatic and military alliances to advance their political and economic agendas while curbing those of their rivals, thereby creating an unstable and ever-shifting **balance of power** that prevented any one state from overwhelming the others.

Treaty of the Pyrenees Treaty in 1659 ending the wars between France and Spain and leaving France the most powerful state in Europe.

balance of power Long-time European diplomatic aim for a distribution of power among several states that would prevent the dominance of any one state.

✔ Checking In

By yourself or with a partner, explain the significance of each of the following selected key terms:

Saint Bartholomew's Day Massacre

Henry IV of Navarre

Edict of Nantes

absolutism

Thirty Years' War

Cardinal Richelieu

Peace of Westphalia

balance of power

Reformation and Revolution in the British Isles

◆ **How did the expectations of the English people change, or remain the same, from 1558 to 1660?**

◆ **What were the relations among the English, Scots, and Irish in this period?**

England experienced a golden age during the reign of Elizabeth I, the last Tudor monarch. But during the seventeenth century, the British Isles experienced religious wars when different Protestant groups fought to control state churches. Like their counterparts on the continent, Protestant Scots and English believed that their communities should be united by a single church. Gradually, however, a party formed that called for toleration of different forms of Protestantism, but not of Catholicism. In Ireland, where Catholics predominated, English and Scots prejudice led to a brutal conquest of the island that established Protestant control. Conflict over religion also involved a struggle between the English monarch and Parliament for control of policy, which led to revolution in England, the execution of the king, and the establishment of a republic. In 1660, the republic came to an end and the monarchy was restored.

Elizabeth I

Elizabeth I was one of England's ablest and most popular rulers. At five feet ten inches, she was exceptionally tall for her time, and her flaming red hair, along with her trim, athletic body, caught everyone's attention. Elizabeth was a shrewd ruler who played on her womanhood, challenging contemporary views about women's weakness with her own force of will and political skill while instilling fear in anyone who challenged her. She was exceptionally well educated, speaking French, German, and Italian as well as reading Latin and Greek with ease. When Philip II, anxious to continue his English alliance, proposed marriage, the "virgin queen" turned him down, as she did everyone else, saying, "I am wedded to England." Her subjects hailed her as Good Queen Bess.

The Twin Problems of Spain and Ireland In addition to promoting a moderate form of Protestantism in England, Elizabeth faced two problems—the power of Spain and opposition in Ireland. Philip II's attempt to assert strong Spanish and Catholic control over the Netherlands threatened English economic interests there as the Netherlands had long been the main market for English wool exports. Thus, in 1585, Elizabeth sent an army to aid the Dutch rebels against Philip. The next year, she sanctioned Sir Francis Drake's raids on Spanish colonial shipping. The English now identified themselves as pro-Protestant, anti-Catholic, and anti-Spanish. Thus religious, economic, and political issues deepened the rift between Spain and England, thereby ending the medieval alliance between the two countries that had led to the marriage of Catherine of Aragon to Henry VIII.

Rivalry with Spain also influenced developments in Ireland. Like her father and grandfather, Elizabeth was determined to strengthen English control of the island. But her attempts were met with a local rebellion led by Catholics, who received Spanish help, including the failed Spanish Armada of 1588. In the end, Elizabeth triumphed and transferred vast tracts of Irish land to loyal English Protestants, thus consolidating the conquest of the kingdom.

The English Renaissance Elizabeth's England saw a flowering of literature, known as the **English Renaissance**. **William Shakespeare** wrote many of his plays during her reign, performing them at court and in his own theater, the Globe. Shakespeare's contemporary, **Christopher Marlowe**, wrote equally popular plays, including *The Massacre at Paris*, about the Saint Bartholomew's Day slaughter during France's religious wars. Marlowe's greatest play is *Doctor Faustus*, about a man who sells his soul to the Devil in return for power and knowledge.

Poetry also flourished in Elizabeth's reign. **Edmund Spenser** continued the tradition of epic poetry that stretched back to Dante Alighieri, Virgil, and Homer in his *Faerie Queene*, an elaborate allegory celebrating Protestant England's struggle with Catholicism and Spain. Spenser's friend and fellow poet **Sir Walter Raleigh** also extolled Elizabeth and Protestant England in verse. Both Raleigh and Spenser actively pursued politics.

As a young man at court, Raleigh became a favorite of the queen, who commissioned him to attack Spanish shipping. In 1587 he founded a short-lived colony on Roanoke Island off present-day North Carolina, and in 1595 he led the first English expedition into South America, sailing up the Orinoco River in search of a fabled kingdom ruled by El Dorado, a man covered in gold. No gold was found, but his account of the expedition established him as a master of the literature of discovery and exploration. When Elizabeth began her conquest of Ireland, both Raleigh and Spenser joined her forces and were rewarded with estates confiscated from the rebels.

Mary Stuart, Queen of Scots Elizabeth's refusal to marry was based more on political calculation than on personal preference; she feared the challenges to her power and independence that submission to a husband might bring. As the years passed, however, the problem of succession became acute because her heir was her cousin, **Mary Stuart, Queen of Scots**, the Catholic widow of King Francis II of France and a relative of the Guises. After Francis's death, Mary had returned to Scotland, where she married a Scots nobleman and had a son, James.

Mary's religion caused problems in newly Calvinist Scotland, and in 1568 she fled to England after nobles deposed her and seized James. Elizabeth promptly imprisoned Mary because her Catholicism made her a magnet for those who favored the old church. Rumors of Catholic plots swirled around Mary for years. In 1587, when the rumors seemed to stick, Elizabeth had her beheaded.

The Early Stuart Monarchs

In 1603, Mary Stuart's son, **James VI** of Scotland, succeeded the virgin queen as **James I** of England and Ireland, and, for the first time, the separate kingdoms of Scotland and England were ruled by the same person. James had an excellent mind and published ten works, including a *Counterblast to Tobacco* that denounced smoking as "loathsome to the eye, hateful to the nose, harmful to the brain, [and] dangerous to the lungs." His greatest literary achievement was to sponsor a new translation of the Christian Bible for use in the Anglican Church. Published in 1611 and known as the **King James Version**, it has shaped the English language down to the present.

King and Parliament Two issues dominated James's reign and that of his son, **Charles I**: religion and relations between king and Parliament. Henry VIII and Elizabeth had used Parliament to implement the English Reformation, thereby giving it a permanent place in the country's political life. But the exact nature of Parliament's authority was disputed. Both James and Charles believed that God appointed kings to rule and that they were accountable to Him alone. But they also knew that Parliament had a traditional right to raise taxes. For its part, Parliament believed the king could formulate state policy,

English Renaissance Flowering of English literature during Elizabeth I's reign.

William Shakespeare (1564–1616) England's greatest playwright, author of *The Merchant of Venice*, *The Tempest*, *Othello*, and many other plays and poems.

Christopher Marlowe (ca.1564–1593) Playwright in Elizabeth I's reign, author of the play *Doctor Faustus* and a contemporary of William Shakespeare.

Edmund Spenser (1553–1599) Poet and author of the epic poem *The Faerie Queene*.

Sir Walter Raleigh (ca.1554–1618) Privateer, explorer, poet, and favorite of Elizabeth I.

Mary Stuart, Queen of Scots (r. 1542–1587) Cousin of Elizabeth I and heir to the English throne whose Catholicism led to her execution.

James VI/James I (r. 1567/1603–1625) Son of Mary, Queen of Scots, king who ruled in Scotland as James VI from 1567 and in England and Ireland as James I from 1603.

King James Version Translation of the Bible sponsored by King James I for use in the Church of England and published in 1611.

Charles I (r. 1625–1649) King of England, Ireland, and Scotland who was beheaded by order of Parliament in 1649.

but it claimed the right to criticize policy. James rejected this right. Parliament, he said, was no place "for every rash and hair-brained fellow to propose new laws of his own invention."

At stake in these conflicts was a fundamental political issue: should Parliament simply express opinions, or should it have a voice in policy making? Traditions of strong kingship, stretching back to the Middle Ages, favored the king, but Parliament's power to grant or withhold taxes enabled it to assess the policies its taxes would finance. James and Charles leaned toward royal absolutism, whereas Parliament favored a theory of limited royal rule.

Religion regularly divided king and Parliament. Like Elizabeth, James was a moderate Protestant, but he was married to a Catholic. His moderation and his wife raised suspicions among the **Puritans**, Calvinists who thought that the Anglican Church was not completely reformed. Puritans wanted no bishops, no church ceremony, more sermons, policing of people's behavior, and an effective Protestant foreign policy. Their suspicions of James were overcome in 1605 when the government discovered a Catholic plot to blow up the king, along with Parliament. Thereafter, James followed Elizabeth in treating English Catholics as traitors.

Colonization: Ulster and America Anti-Catholicism also shaped English policy in Ireland. In 1597, another rebellion broke out in **Ulster**, in the northeastern part of the island. It ended just as the plot to blow up the king and Parliament was discovered. In the anti-Catholic backlash, the lands of the rebel Catholic leaders were confiscated and given to English owners, who then colonized them with some one hundred thousand Scottish Protestants. The Catholic Irish, viewed as "savages," were driven onto marginal lands. Later, habits learned in Ireland were transferred to North America, where settlers drove Indian "savages" off the lands they then farmed. Ulster was England's first successful colony.

In North America, the Virginia Colony boomed when tobacco was grown for export. James I may have hated the "pernicious weed," but his subjects loved it and Virginia's economic success was assured. Beginning in the 1620s, other colonies were founded, this time by religious dissidents upset with the monarchy's support of Anglicanism and persecution of Catholics.

The Pilgrims, Protestant Separatists who, like the Anabaptists, believed that the church should be a voluntary association, founded Plymouth Colony in 1620. In 1629, Puritans founded the Massachusetts Bay Colony, and English Catholics emigrated to Maryland in the 1630s. Unlike the colonies of Spain and Portugal, the English settlements were not directly sponsored by the state. Instead, they began as commercial ventures, like the Virginia Colony, or as religious havens.

Charles I James died in 1625, and his son became king as Charles I. Like his father, Charles had an unshakeable belief in his right to rule as he pleased. He also shared his father's views about Parliament. Between 1625 and 1629, the king clashed with parliamentary leaders who criticized his policies and refused to grant him money for his wars against Spain and in support of the Huguenots, questioning the success of his campaigns and criticizing the men in charge of them. Finally, in 1630, Charles decided to govern without Parliament and did not convene it for ten years.

Ruling Without Parliament: Charles and Laud Charles ruled well enough on his own for most of the 1630s. One policy, however, provoked growing opposition—reform of the Anglican Church. In 1633, the king appointed **William Laud** archbishop of Canterbury; Laud introduced new church ceremonies and ordered the clergy to adhere strictly to Elizabeth's 1559 Book of Common Prayer. The Puritans were outraged, seeing Laud's program as an attempt to reintroduce Catholic practices. Some of them left for North America, where they joined their fellow Puritans in Massachusetts.

Others waited for a chance to turn on Laud. Laud's position was further weakened when he stated that the clergy alone, not the local laity, would control church affairs. He also ordered the restoration of church lands that the laity had taken over. These policies angered a large group of landowners with seats in Parliament, who now had economic and political reasons, as well as religious ones, for opposing the king and his archbishop.

Parliament Reconvened Charles and Laud were not content to revamp the Church of England. In 1637, the king imposed the Book of Common Prayer, along with bishops, on the Presbyterian Church of Scotland. In response, in 1639, the Scots rebelled. Charles, now at war with his Scottish subjects, needed funds for an army. In 1640, he resummoned the English Parliament and demanded money from it.

Civil War, Revolution, and the Commonwealth

The new **Long Parliament** was filled with men angry at Laud and the king. It passed a bill stating that the king could not dissolve Parliament without its own permission (which Charles signed, probably inad-

Puritans Calvinists who wanted to eliminate bishops and favored more sermons, policing of people's behavior, and a strong Protestant foreign policy.

Ulster Northeastern part of Ireland colonized by Scots and English Protestants after England's defeat of the local Catholics.

William Laud (1573–1645) Archbishop of Canterbury who enforced Charles I's unpopular religious policies through royal courts.

Long Parliament English Parliament that sat from 1640 until 1660.

In this woodcut print of the execution of Charles I, the blindfolded king, his hat set to the side, puts his neck on the chopping block and waits for the executioner's ax. An Anglican clergyman prays while armed guards and a crowd look on. Thinking back to the portraits of sixteenth and seventeenth century rulers that have appeared in this text, how do you imagine people in Charles's lifetime would react to this woodcut? (Hulton Archive/Getty Images)

vertently). Parliament removed Archbishop Laud and sent him to prison. It also passed an act requiring the king to call Parliament into session on a regular basis. In 1641, Charles was forced to sign a treaty with the Scots that gave the Scottish parliament a role in the appointment of royal ministers and conceded the Scottish parliament's right to oversee policy. The English Parliament promptly demanded the same concessions, and when Charles refused, it proposed a bill abolishing bishops in the Church of England.

At this point, another Catholic rebellion broke out in Ireland, and several thousand Protestants were massacred in Ulster. In 1642, Charles demanded money from Parliament for an army to subdue the Irish. When Parliament refused and started to form its own army, Charles declared war on Parliament.

Civil War England had now fallen into civil war. For the next seven years, the king and his supporters fought Parliament's army. Troops of both sides damaged crops and disrupted trade, and cold temperatures ruined the harvests of the late 1640s. By war's end, popular rebellions against both sides had broken out in various parts of the country.

In 1643, Parliament reorganized the Church of England along Presbyterian lines and then executed Laud. In 1645, Charles, finally defeated in battle,

surrendered to the Scots, who turned him over to the English Parliament in 1647. In 1648, the army purged Parliament of those favoring monarchy.

The King's Trial and Execution The remaining members of Parliament brought the king to trial on charges of treason and murder for his role in the civil war. Charles denied the court's legitimacy, proclaiming that "the king cannot be tried by any superior jurisdiction on earth." But Charles was convicted and publicly beheaded in London on January 30, 1649. When the executioner's ax fell on his neck, a huge groan went up from the crowd surrounding the scaffold, for it was a momentous event. Never before had an English court of law removed a monarch or the English people killed their king. Civil war had become revolution. England was now a republic.

Political Ferment and Debate Even as the civil war raged, the English engaged in an unprecedented debate over the nature of the state and the role of ordinary people in political life. Charles's growing unpopularity led many to go beyond older arguments about the king's relation to Parliament. The Levellers wanted to establish a democratic republic in England and allow all men to vote. Women activists supporting the Levellers petitioned Parliament on their behalf.

Even more radical were the Diggers. Responding to economic hard times, they rejected the institution of private property and supported a form of communal ownership. Levellers and Diggers were always in a minority, but the very fact that they gave public voice to their ideas for reform stimulated popular thought about the nature of England's social order and raised questions about the political and economic identities of English men and women.

Oliver Cromwell

One of Parliament's generals in favor of Charles's execution was **Oliver Cromwell**. In 1649, Cromwell led an army to put down the rebellion in Ireland, where disruptions from fighting and crop failures had produced widespread famine; the Irish population fell by almost 40 percent. Cromwell's invasion delivered the final blows. His army massacred thousands, 80 percent of agricultural land was transferred to the Protestant minority, Catholicism was outlawed, and twelve thousand rebels were deported as penal slaves to Barbados and other English colonies in the West Indies. For the next two hundred years, English Protestant control of Ireland was assured.

With Ireland subdued, Cromwell turned to Scotland. Despite their differences with Charles I, most Scots favored the continuation of monarchy. After the king's execution, **Charles II**, Charles I's elder son, was summoned from exile and crowned Scottish king in 1650. Cromwell then invaded Scotland, forced Charles to flee, and established the rule of the English Parliament there.

When Cromwell returned from Scotland, he quickly dominated the new English **Commonwealth**, as the republic was called. Cromwell believed that God had called him to leadership and guided his actions. In this he was exactly like the king he had helped to execute.

Attacks on Dutch Trading In 1651, Parliament attempted to break the Dutch shipping monopoly with the **Navigation Act**, which required overseas goods destined for England to be carried in English ships or ships of English colonies. The next year, Cromwell supported a war against the Dutch, telling them that

"the Lord has declared against you." The war was short, and the act did little to limit Dutch trade, but it signaled England's rise as a commercial power and marked the beginning of government control of the emerging English Empire.

In 1653, Cromwell took the title of Lord Protector. Parliament continued to meet, but Cromwell and the army actually ruled. In 1655, after suppressing a royalist rebellion, Cromwell established a military dictatorship. Press censorship was instituted, and traditional local officials were replaced by major generals who ran local government and carried out a moral reform of society along strict Calvinist lines.

Although Cromwell ruled as a Calvinist-inspired dictator, he abolished the requirement that everyone attend Calvinist church services, proclaiming, "I meddle not with any man's conscience." He did, however, ban Anglican and Catholic services for political reasons. By the 1650s, growing numbers of Protestants shared Cromwell's embrace of limited toleration.

Cromwell was offered a crown by some followers who wanted him to become King Oliver. He refused it.

The Restoration of the Stuart Kings When Cromwell died in 1658, his son Richard became the new lord protector. Richard, however, did not have his father's political skills and soon retired to his country estates. His departure left England leaderless. Once again, a general stepped in; George Monck marched his army on London and negotiated the return of King Charles II, along with the House of Lords, the Church of England, and all its bishops. Oliver Cromwell's corpse was dug up and publicly hanged.

In 1660, it seemed that England's troubles had come full circle. Anglican monarchists viewed the post-1660 regime as a simple "restoration" of older ways. But in the wake of the Anglican Church being outlawed, a king executed, and a republic created, the merits of absolutist monarchy and limited constitutional government had been debated. There had been calls for democracy, communal ownership of property, and religious toleration. The debates and the conflicts unleashed during the civil war and revolution would shape the future of the English-speaking world.

Oliver Cromwell (1599–1658) General on Parliament's side in English civil war who eventually established a military dictatorship in England.

Charles II (r. 1650/1660–1685) Son of Charles I, crowned king of Scotland in 1650 but ruled there only after 1660, when he was crowned king of England as well.

Commonwealth Name of the English republic from 1649 to 1660.

Navigation Act Parliamentary act of 1651 requiring overseas goods destined for England to be carried in English ships or ships of English colonies.

Checking In

By yourself or with a partner, explain the significance of each of the following selected key terms:

English Renaissance	Puritans
Mary Stuart, Queen of Scots	Long Parliament
James I	Oliver Cromwell
Charles I	Charles II

Christian Reform, Religious Wars, and the Jews

◆ **How did Europe's Jews define themselves as a community in the larger Christian world?**

◆ **How were the Jews in Poland affected by the war that broke out there in 1648?**

The expulsion of Jews from Spain and Portugal destroyed Europe's largest Jewish community. In the early sixteenth century, Italy alone in western Europe had a significant Jewish population. In eastern Europe, Poland also admitted large numbers of Jews. Then, after 1550, Jews returned to western Europe when the Dutch Republic, Bohemia, France, and England once again admitted them. But the rising religious passions of the Christian reformations led to an upsurge of anti-Jewish attacks, including devastating massacres in eastern Poland. Like some Christians, Jews believed that the troubles they experienced were signs of the world's end.

Jews in Poland and Western Europe

Following their expulsion from England and France in the late Middle Ages, western European Jews were permitted to settle in Poland-Lithuania, where the Black Death had reduced the number of people on the agricultural estates of the king and the nobility. Soon Jews were working the land as peasants, supplying local needs as craftsmen, and serving as estate managers. Jews prospered with the growth of grain and timber exports to the west, acting as agents in organizing this trade. They also played an important role as moneylenders. By the end of the seventeenth century, Polish Jews numbered some 450,000, or about 4.5 percent of Poland's population and 75 percent of Jews worldwide.

Whether they lived in towns or the countryside, Jews were governed by local councils made up of prominent community members, who often dressed and acted like non-Jews. Like the Christian population, Jewish communities were hierarchically organized. At the top were a few rich and socially prominent people as well as rabbis and Talmudic scholars. Below them were craftsmen, peddlers, and shopkeepers. Lower still were the poor.

Most Polish Jews were separated from the larger Christian population not only by religion but also by culture. Like the Arabic-speaking Moriscos of Spain, they spoke their own distinctive language, **Yiddish**. Aware of their minority position, the Jews worked hard to maintain a strong sense of community solidarity that fostered a distinctive Jewish identity. At times, however, internal tensions threatened to fracture the community, as when rich Jews adopted non-Jewish ways or well-to-do moneylenders seized land and other collateral from fellow Jews who defaulted on loans.

Beginning in the mid-sixteenth century, Jews started to return to western Europe. The largest Jewish community in the west, Rome excepted, was in Bohemia, where the Habsburgs encouraged Jewish settlement and used Jews as bankers and moneylenders. Bohemian nobles also courted Jews, who served as estate managers like their counterparts in Poland. Even Emperor Ferdinand II welcomed them, despite his determination to eliminate dissident Protestants. In his eyes, heretics were a greater danger to the Christian community than unbelievers. Throughout the Thirty Years' War, both the Habsburgs and the Swedes turned to the Bohemian Jews for the funds they needed to continue fighting.

The Dutch Republic also welcomed Jews. Both **Ashkenazim**, from Poland and Germany, and **Sephardim**, from Spain and Portugal, congregated in Amsterdam. Overall, some eighteen thousand Jews settled in the Dutch Republic. Although this community was smaller than the ones in Poland and Bohemia, it played a crucial role in the booming Dutch economy. Its original members were Sephardim who had economic ties to merchants in the Iberian Peninsula, the Spanish Empire, and Brazil. The Dutch West India Company exploited these contacts to develop trade with Spain and to push into the profitable trade with the New World. Some four thousand Portuguese Jews eventually settled in the Dutch colonies.

France and England also permitted new Jewish settlements. French kings permitted expelled Portuguese Jews to settle in some cities as part of their struggle with Habsburg Spain. In England, Oliver Cromwell fostered a growing Jewish community in London. Like many Protestants, Cromwell believed that the conversion of the Jews to Christianity, along with the destruction of the Antichrist (that is, the pope), would usher in the Second Coming of Christ. He, therefore, welcomed the visit of an Amsterdam rabbi who came to London seeking formal recognition of a Jewish community there.

The rabbi also had a religious agenda; for him, Jews had to settle in all parts of the world as a prelude to the coming of the Jewish Messiah. Although formal recognition of an English Jewish community was not forthcoming, as merchants and clergy resisted, Jews were allowed unofficially to settle in London and engage in trade.

War in Poland

In 1648, the year of the Peace of Westphalia, war broke out in Poland-Lithuania

Yiddish German dialect spoken by the Ashkenazim, derived from German and Hebrew and written in Hebrew characters.

Ashkenazim Jews of Europe who settled mainly in the Holy Roman Empire, Poland, Lithuania, and other eastern regions.

Sephardim Jews from the Iberian Peninsula.

when **Cossacks**, warriors protecting lands bordering on Muslim territory, rebelled in Ukraine. The rebellion was provoked in part by a decision to reduce the number of Cossacks in the Polish army and in part by religious clashes—the Polish Cossacks were Russian Orthodox, and the kings of Poland were Roman Catholics. Catholic-Orthodox tensions were particularly high in the seventeenth century after the **Union of Brest-Litovsk**, which united bishops in Polish Ukraine with the Roman Catholic Church, despite Orthodox Christian opposition.

The Cossack revolt of 1648 inaugurated nineteen years of warfare. Like the Thirty Years' War, it started as a local dispute but was soon internationalized when both Sweden and Russia joined in. In 1655, Sweden, fresh from territorial gains during the Thirty Years' War, hoped to amass more lands on the Baltic's southern shore. The Russian **tsar** also used the war for territorial gain. The Swedes withdrew in 1660 after receiving territory from the king of Denmark, with whom they were also at war. The Russians signed a peace treaty in 1667 that gave them the eastern half of Ukraine.

> **Cossacks** Warriors organized locally to protect frontier lands bordering on Muslim territory; also used by Polish kings and Russian tsars as fighting forces.
>
> **Union of Brest-Litovsk** Agreement in 1596 uniting Orthodox bishops in Polish Ukraine with the Roman Catholic Church.
>
> **tsar** (in Russian, "caesar") Title of the rulers of Russia.

The devastation caused by two decades of warfare was immense. The Polish economy was disrupted, and food shortages occurred, followed by periods of famine. Predictably, armies of all sides spread disease, and epidemics ravaged a population already weakened by disruptions in the food supply. At the beginning of the war, the Cossacks slaughtered Catholics, Jews, and signers of the Union of Brest-Litovsk indiscriminately.

These atrocities matched the worst incidents during the French Wars of Religion. Like the French slaughters, those in Poland were intended to ritually degrade the bodies of a socially polluting enemy. Eventually, all warring sides committed atrocities, and all Poles were victims of them, but Polish Jews suffered disproportionately. The lucky ones fled to Jewish communities in western Europe. Others fled south into Muslim lands, where they were enslaved and then sold in Constantinople. In all, some forty to fifty thousand Jews, a quarter of Poland's Jewish population, perished in the war.

 Checking In

By yourself or with a partner, explain the significance of each of the following selected key terms:

Yiddish   Sephardim

Ashkenazim   Union of Brest-Litovsk

CHAPTER
Review

Summary

- After 1550, the European economy turned downward. A price revolution aggravated an economic crisis brought on by overpopulation.

- Hard times produced widespread anxiety, which in turn led to social unrest, fears that the world was coming to an end, and panic about witches.

- For the next century, religious strife tore Europe apart.

- In Spain, Philip II undertook aggressive campaigns against Muslims and Protestants. He defeated his Morisco subjects in Spain and fought the Turks at sea. He also opposed the Protestant movement in England and fought his own Protestant subjects in the Netherlands.

- When Philip II died in 1598, Protestantism had survived, and Spain's military might was in decline.

- The Netherlands were split in half, and the economically prosperous Protestant provinces of the north were virtually independent from Spanish rule.

- England under Elizabeth I was Protestant and prepared to challenge Spain on the seas and in the New World.

- Henry IV of France had granted religious toleration, along with a good deal of political autonomy, to the Huguenots, but he had also strengthened the French monarchy.

◆ Warfare continued throughout the first half of the seventeenth century.

◆ Europeans believed that religious unity was essential for the well-being of the community, but renewed warfare failed to reestablish the unity lost in the sixteenth century.

◆ Louis XIII defeated the Huguenots and stripped them of their political autonomy, although they still had the right to worship.

◆ In Germany, the Thirty Years' War failed to curb Protestantism in the Holy Roman Empire, and the emperor's power was greatly weakened.

◆ When the war ended, German princes now had a third religious option for their states: Calvinism, Lutheranism, and Catholicism.

◆ In England, Anglicans and Puritans fought each other in a civil war that ended in the execution of Charles I, the dismantling of the Anglican Church, and the establishment of a commonwealth.

◆ In 1660, monarchy and Anglicanism were restored.

◆ All English Protestants agreed that the Catholic Irish must be conquered.

◆ The creation of the Ulster colony and Cromwell's campaign in Ireland established England's dominance of the island. By 1660, it was clear that the religious unity of western and central Europe was shattered.

◆ Europe's Jews were allowed once again to settle in the west, where some benefited from the global trading networks established in the sixteenth century. But Jews were still often despised and sometimes suffered catastrophic losses, like the ones occurring in Poland after the Cossack rebellion of 1648.

◆ Some Jews, like some Christians, hoped for divine deliverance from the troubled times.

Chronology

1540s	Spain's silver mines in the Americas open
1555	Peace of Augsburg allows Lutheranism
1556	Philip II becomes king of Spain; Ferdinand I becomes Holy Roman emperor
1558	Elizabeth I becomes queen of England
1559	Francis II becomes king of France
1562	French Wars of Religion begin
1564	Maximilian II becomes Holy Roman emperor
1566	Calvinists rebel in the Netherlands
1571	Spain defeats Turkish navy at Battle of Lepanto
1572	French Catholics attack Protestants in Saint Bartholomew's Day Massacre
1588	Spanish Armada attacks England
1589	Henry IV becomes king of France
1598	Edict of Nantes grants religious toleration to Huguenots
1603	James VI of Scotland becomes James I of England and Ireland
1610	Louis XIII becomes king of France
1618	Thirty Years' War begins
1625	Charles I becomes king of Scotland, England, and Ireland
1629	Peace of Alès ends French Wars of Religion
1642	English civil war begins
1643	Louis XIV becomes king of France
1648	Peace of Westphalia ends Thirty Years' War
1649	England becomes a republic
1659	France and Spain sign Treaty of the Pyrenees
1660	Monarchy is restored in the British Isles
1667	War ends in Poland

CourseMate Visit the CourseMate website at **www.cengagebrain.com** for additional study tools and review materials for this chapter.

Test Yourself

To gauge your mastery of the material in this chapter, answer the questions below. More than one answer may be correct.

Europe's Economy and Society

1. The joint-stock company:
   a. Limited the risk for an investor to the amount of money invested and stock shares owned.
   b. Raised large sums of money but maximized risk for investors.
   c. Was often used by people investing in overseas trade or colonies.
   d. Was used to found Jamestown in Virginia.
   e. Was used to found Canada, an English colony.

2. Which of the following foods was *not* introduced into Europe from the Western Hemisphere?
   a. Beans
   b. Squash
   c. Tomatoes
   d. Maize
   e. Apples

3. The Manila galleon:
   a. Carried New World silver to East Asia.
   b. Carried Chinese silks and porcelains for export to Europe.
   c. Lost money on most voyages.
   d. All of the above.
   e. None of the above.

4. What were the causes for the inflation that gripped Europe in the mid-sixteenth century?
   a. A decline in the value of silver coins
   b. Overpopulation and a rise in food prices
   c. A decline in population leading to a labor shortage
   d. Food shortages due to poor climatic conditions
   e. A collapse in food supply from the New World

5. The sixteenth-century stereotype of the witch included which of the following characteristics?
   a. Sale of the witches' soul to the devil
   b. The practice of cannibalism
   c. Projectile vomiting
   d. The practice of disgusting sexual acts
   e. Rapid head spinning

Now that you have reviewed and tested yourself on this part of the chapter, take time to pull together all the important information by answering the following questions:

◆ What effects did the rise in the silver supply have in the sixteenth-century European economy?

◆ What caused Europe's witchcraft hunt, and why did it eventually decline?

The Fate of Spain and the Flourishing of the Netherlands

6. Philip II of Spain:
   a. Rejected the previous royal policy of traveling throughout his lands for personal appearances.
   b. Made all important policy decisions himself.
   c. Waged war on his Morisco subjects.
   d. Defeated the Turkish fleet at Lepanto.
   e. All of the above.

7. The revolt in the Netherlands:
   a. Began after Philip decided to impose a military solution on his provinces following a Calvinist attack on Catholic churches.
   b. Led to a Spanish army attack on Antwerp after Philip failed to pay the army's wages.
   c. Led to the independence of the northern provinces of the Netherlands.
   d. Left the southern provinces under Spanish control.
   e. All of the above.

8. The Dutch Republic:

   a. Allowed only Calvinists to worship there.
   b. Allowed Catholics, Anabaptists, and Jews to worship there under certain restrictions.
   c. Unlike other parts of Europe, saw a rise in population and workers' wages.
   d. Had Europe's best shipbuilders.
   e. Traded with all European states except Spain.

9. Dutch traders:

   a. Profited from the founding of the Dutch East India Company.
   b. Traded with Japan.
   c. Traded with Brazil.
   d. Imported African slaves to the New World.
   e. Made Amsterdam Europe's chief commercial and banking center.

Now that you have reviewed and tested yourself on this part of the chapter, take time to pull together all the important information by answering the following questions:

◆ What train of events led to the disappearance of the cultural and religious pluralism that had characterized the Iberian Peninsula in the Middle Ages?

◆ What made the Dutch trading network truly global?

Political Contests and More Religious Wars

10. Henry IV of France:

    a. Issued the edict of Nantes.
    b. Greatly increased the royal debt.
    c. Supported the lowering of direct taxes and the increase of indirect ones.
    d. Taxed men who owned royal office using the paulette.
    e. All of the above.

11. Which characteristics were true in the governance of Poland-Lithuania?

    a. Nobles had a right of rebellion against the king under certain circumstances.
    b. Nobles were strictly subservient to the king.
    c. Nobles could explode the royal diet with their votes.
    d. Nobles were free to rule their serfs as they saw fit.
    e. The form of government was admired by the Habsburg nobility.

12. The Thirty Years' War:

    a. Was launched by the emperor Ferdinand II.
    b. Was launched by the Turks.
    c. Saw fighting in Germany between the Habsburgs, the Swedes, and the French.
    d. Had little effect on the population of the empire.
    e. Led to a significant drop in the population of the empire.

13. The Peace of Westphalia:

    a. Was signed in 1630.
    b. Was signed in 1648.
    c. Allowed rulers in the empire to choose Calvinism, Lutheranism, or Catholicism as the religion of their respective states.
    d. Decreed that the Swiss Confederation and the Dutch Republic were no longer parts of the empire.
    e. Decreed that each state in the empire could develop its own foreign policy, subject to the emperor's approval.

Now that you have reviewed and tested yourself on this part of the chapter, take time to pull together all the important information by answering the following questions:

◆ What made the Thirty Years' War the most devastating conflict of the seventeenth century?

◆ Compare and contrast the motivations for European warfare before and after the signing of the Peace of Westphalia.

Reformation and Revolution in the British Isles

14. Elizabeth I of England:

    a. Was very well educated.
    b. Supported the Dutch rebels against Spain in the Netherlands.
    c. Was secretly a Catholic.
    d. Consolidated the English conquest of Ireland by distributing land there to English Protestants.
    e. Married Philip II of Spain.

15. King James I of England:

    a. Sponsored a revised Latin version of the Christian Bible.
    b. Accepted Parliament's claim that it could criticize royal policy.
    c. Was a moderate Protestant who married a Catholic.
    d. Was a moderate Catholic who married a Protestant.
    e. Was at first resisted and then supported by the Puritans.

16. Charles I:

    a. Rejected his father's views on the king's relation to Parliament.
    b. Accepted his father's views on the king's relation to Parliament.
    c. Ruled without Parliament for ten years.
    d. Criticized Archbishop Laud's reforms of the Anglican Church.
    e. Was forced to reconvene Parliament when he went to war in Scotland over his religious policy.

17. The Long Parliament:

    a. Gave in when Charles I refused to sign a bill agreeing to call Parliament on a regular basis.
    b. Granted Charles money to finance a suppression of an Irish rebellion.
    c. Refused to reorganize the Church of England along Presbyterian lines.
    d. All of the above.
    e. None of the above.

18. Oliver Cromwell:

    a. Massacred thousands in Ireland and outlawed Catholicism there.
    b. Invaded Scotland and established the rule of the English Parliament there.
    c. Refused to establish a military dictatorship but took the title of Lord Protector instead.
    d. Banned Anglican and Catholic worship.
    e. Was assassinated by a Catholic nun.

Now that you have reviewed and tested yourself on this part of the chapter, take time to pull together all the important information by answering the following questions:

◆ What were the constitutional issues dividing the king and Parliament during the reigns of James I and Charles I?

◆ What were the lasting legacies of the English civil war, the execution of the king, and the establishment of the Commonwealth?

Christian Reform, Religious Wars, and the Jews

19. Polish Jews:

    a. Made up 2 percent of Poland's population.
    b. Made up 75 percent of Jews worldwide.
    c. Spoke German.
    d. Lost 25 percent of their population in the war following the Cossack revolt of 1648.
    e. All of the above.

20. In western Europe:

   a. The largest Jewish community was in Bohemia.
   b. Jews were barely tolerated in the Dutch Republic.
   c. Jews in the Dutch Republic played a major role in the Dutch economy.
   d. Cromwell thought that the conversion of the Jews to Christianity was an impossibility in England.
   e. The Sephardim were Jews from eastern Europe.

Now that you have reviewed and tested yourself on this part of the chapter, take time to pull together all the important information by answering the following questions:

◆ How did Jews in Poland-Lithuania foster a sense of a distinctive Jewish community and a distinctive Jewish identity?

◆ Where were Jews found in the Dutch Republic's overseas empire, and what role did they play in it?

CHAPTER 16

State-Building and the European State System, 1648–1789

Chapter Outline

Absolutism in France, 1648–1740

A NEW DIRECTION: *Louis XIV Decides to Rule France on His Own*

- The Sun King at Versailles
- Forty Years of Warfare
- A Unified French State
- Louis XV

LEARNING FROM A PRIMARY SOURCE: *Louis XIV Advises His Son*

The Austrian Habsburgs, 1648–1740

- Leopold I
- The Turkish Siege of Vienna and the Reconquest of Hungary
- The Habsburg Monarchy

The Rise of Prussia, 1648–1740

- Territorial Consolidation
- Taxes to Support an Army
- King Frederick William I

Russia and Europe, 1682–1796

- Peter the Great and Westernization
- Catherine the Great and Russian Expansion
- The Pugachev Rebellion and Russian Society

The English Constitutional Monarchy, 1660–1740

- The Restoration of Charles II
- James II
- The Glorious Revolution
- The Georges from Germany

Two World Wars, 1740–1763

- The Wars
- Eighteenth-Century Warfare
- Winners and Losers

CHAPTER REVIEW

This gilt medallion of Apollo, the Sun God, decorated King Louis XIV's palace at Versailles. Louis, the self-styled Sun King, adopted Apollo as his emblem, and medallions like this were incorporated into many features of the palace. (Reunion des Musees nationaux/Art Resource, NY)

After reading this chapter, you should be able to answer the following questions:

How did governments try to establish good working relations with the people?

What effect did state-building have on the various religious communities of Europe?

What factors worked to develop or retard a collective sense of national identity?

L OUIS XIV WAS ONE of the most successful rulers in the years after the Peace of Westphalia and the very embodiment of absolutism—a style of monarchy that spread across Europe in the seventeenth and eighteenth centuries. Royal absolutism was a way to build the power and effectiveness of the central state. A century of religious warfare had taught Louis and other absolutist rulers that only a strong central government, coupled with a policy of either tolerating or crushing religious dissent, could bring political stability.

Although wars continued to be fought after 1648, religiously motivated warfare declined. Increasingly, the roots of conflict focused on issues of territorial expansion, power, and prestige. By the mid-eighteenth century, European warfare had also taken on global dimensions as states fought each other for control of overseas empires.

To meet the challenges of European and global warfare, rulers increased the size of their armies and brought them under tight state control. Absolute monarchs saw war as a means to enlarge their territories

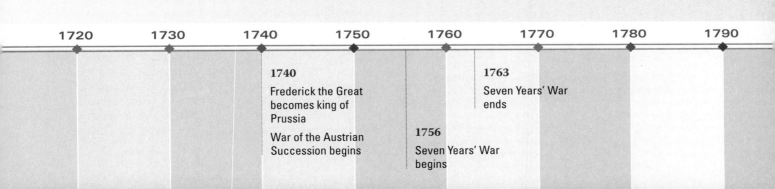

| 1720 | 1730 | 1740 | 1750 | 1760 | 1770 | 1780 | 1790 |

1740
Frederick the Great becomes king of Prussia

War of the Austrian Succession begins

1756
Seven Years' War begins

1763
Seven Years' War ends

and, simultaneously, to deny the territorial ambitions of other states. In their eyes, Europe, and then the world, was like a chessboard on which each state's diplomatic and military moves were met with countermoves from other states.

But war and territorial gains were expensive, and throughout the century after the Peace of Westphalia, states increased taxes, tried to collect them more efficiently, and sought to improve their economies to increase their tax base.

All over Europe, the needs of almost continual warfare drove expansion in state administration and improvements in financial and judicial bureaucracies. State authority aimed to direct economies and to reach more aspects of people's lives. Key to these expansions was the creation of officials accountable to the Crown. In western Europe, loyal middle-class people were recruited into these bureaucracies, while in eastern Europe monarchs drew their officials from the ranks of the lesser nobility.

The goodwill of the public in general was also essential, as was the allegiance of the nobles in particular because they constituted the political and social elite. Some states also tried to increase services to their subjects, such as infrastructure improvement and better policing of town and country.

On the European continent, states tended to develop along the absolutist model pioneered by Louis XIV in France. In Britain, however, the rebellion and revolution of the mid-seventeenth century ended the absolutist ambitions of the early Stuart kings. After 1660, their successors ruled with Parliament in a constitutionally limited monarchy. The joint rule of king and Parliament ensured a high degree of political stability and proved important to Britain's success in empire building, trade, and manufacturing.

In some parts of Europe, warfare and state-building fostered a strong sense of national identity as people embraced the policy perspectives of their rulers and defined themselves as the opposite of their enemies. In other European states, however, the religious and ethnic roots of collective identity were so strong that a common sense of community centered on the state failed to emerge.

Absolutism in France, 1648–1740

◆ **What were the characteristic features of French royal absolutism?**

◆ **What were the outcomes of the French monarchy's attempts to strengthen the state?**

Louis XIV of France dominated Europe in the second half of the seventeenth century. After assuming personal rule (see A New Direction: Louis XIV Decides to Rule France on His Own), he launched wars that added to France's territory. He also continued the policy of stamping out Protestantism in his kingdom, tarnishing his image in Protestant Europe. Eventually continual warfare drained his treasury and forced him to reorganize the French state. His successor built on Louis's successes, expanding state activity in several new directions. But France was also rocked by a new religious crisis, which pitted the state against a dissident Catholic movement.

Map 16.1 **Europe in 1715** In 1715, when Louis XIV died, France was still the dominant power in Europe. But other centers of power—the Austrian Habsburg lands, Great Britain, Russia, and a small newcomer, Prussia—were prepared to challenge France. © *Cengage Learning*

1. After 1715, how did the ambitions of all these states affect the goal of maintaining a European-wide balance of power?

2. Compare the eastern boundary of Sweden and the western boundary of Russia as shown on the first map of Chapter 15 (p. 437) to the boundaries of these two states in 1715. Which was the gainer and which the loser? What advantages came to the winner?

Louis XIV Decides to Rule France on His Own

On March 9, 1661, France's prime minister, Cardinal Jules Mazarin, wracked by gout, kidney stones, and fluid in his chest cavity, died. When news of Mazarin's death was announced, the royal court was abuzz with rumors about who would be next in line for the position. Within hours of Mazarin's death, King Louis XIV made his choice: himself. Standing before the highest officials in the kingdom, he announced: "Up to this moment I have been pleased to entrust the government of my affairs to the late Cardinal. It is now time that I govern them myself. [Monsieur the Chancellor], you will assist me with your counsels when I ask for them. I request and order you to seal no orders except by my command. And you,…my secretaries of state, I order you not to sign anything, not even a passport…without my command."

Courtiers were astonished by Louis's announcement. The twenty-three-year-old seemed more interested in dancing the role of the god Apollo in court ballets and engaging in sexual escapades with young ladies-in-waiting than in sitting at his desk and shuffling through reports on wool weaving in this province or sheep farming in that one. Besides, Louis's announcement that he would rule by himself broke with family tradition. Both his father and grandfather had relied on strong prime ministers to help them with the affairs of state, and since 1643, Cardinal Mazarin had guided France skillfully through the last years of the Thirty Years' War. In the 1640s, France seethed with unrest as taxes rose to pay for the war and great nobles rebelled against Mazarin's policies. There was fearful talk that France—like England—would slip into a civil war. Would monarchy be attacked in France? Would the French king be executed like Charles I? Would the French Calvinists, tolerated but no longer politically independent, rise up like the Puritans and declare a republic? Mazarin had played on these fears of chaos and bloodshed in order to keep the monarchy safe.

By 1653, calm was restored, and the fourteen-year-old Louis XIV's throne was secure. Louis believed that Mazarin had saved the monarchy, and his devotion to his prime minister knew no bounds. For the rest of his life, Mazarin continued to advise the king on policy and even chose his companions, dismissing young men he thought unfit for association with Louis. Mazarin also amassed the largest personal fortune ever known under the monarchy. On his deathbed, he gave it to the king.

Given Mazarin's role in guiding the French monarchy through tumultuous times and the seeming frivolity of the young Louis, it is no wonder that courtiers looked askance at the young king's surprising decision to rule on his own. In the end, however, Louis fooled them all. For the next fifty-four years, until his death in 1715, he refused to appoint a prime minister and directed the affairs of state himself. The discipline, endurance, and stamina this "bureaucrat king" showed in running the government became legendary. Both the successes and the failures of his very long reign rested on his determination to control all the affairs of state.

The Sun King at Versailles

Since 1500, Europe's royal courts had grown in size. In the 1520s, the French court had just over five hundred members. **Louis XIV**'s court had ten thousand, half of them nobles. For the nobles, closeness to the king brought honor, appointments in the royal army, and pensions. Since nobles had a prickly sense of self-worth, a tradition of military service, and extravagant lifestyles that strained their purses, Louis's attentions were highly prized. Thus nobles flocked to the king's court, and, as he established a working relationship with this powerful elite, Louis was also able to keep his eye on them.

Life at Court At court, the entire day focused attention on the king. From his rising to his bedtime, great nobles attended him. At midday, Louis ate alone while courtiers stood and watched. The dinner table etiquette was so complicated that it took three men seven minutes to give the king a glass of wine. Louis believed that he ruled by **divine right** because God had decreed monarchy to be the correct form for France's government and had called Louis to the throne as the eldest legitimately born son of his father.

The elaborate court rituals proclaimed that Louis, as an absolute monarch, was the only real political player in France. He alone made policy and laid

---

Louis XIV (r. 1638–1715) King of France and the most powerful ruler in Europe during the second half of the seventeenth century.

divine right Theory that kings were called by God to rule and that opposition to the king was therefore opposition to God.

Louis XIV of France embodied the ideal of the vigorous, state-building monarch. Throughout his long reign, he dominated European diplomacy and warfare, and his glittering court established standards of grandeur that other monarchs tried to imitate. As a young man, he seemed more interested in the pleasures of the court than in politics. In fact, however, he emerged as one of Europe's ablest and most disciplined rulers following the death of his prime minister, Cardinal Mazarin.

Laurie Platt Winfrey, Inc/The Granger Collection, New York

down the law. He was also the only person who unified the different regions and peoples of France because he alone ruled over them all.

Louis was also the perfect gentleman, famous for his politeness and beautiful manners. Courtiers commented that they rarely saw him lose his temper. If someone misbehaved, a simple look or short comment was enough to convey his displeasure. Like court etiquette, the king's gentlemanly behavior had a political purpose; it reinforced a new trend in noble society that emphasized polite speech and good manners as necessary qualities for the highborn and powerful. Encouraged by noblewomen in Paris, who presided over **salons** in which this conduct was required, the new emphasis on manners disciplined the often violent and crude behavior of nobles.

The setting for Louis's court was **Versailles**, originally a hunting lodge for Louis XIII. Throughout his reign, the king worked to turn his father's modest building into Europe's most magnificent palace. He laid out acres of grounds decorated with lavish fountains. Louis adopted the sun god Apollo as Versailles' symbol and symbolically identified himself with Apollo as the "Sun King," spreading radiance on his lands and subjects. At Versailles, an entire town sprang up to meet the needs of courtiers and their thousands of servants. The palace itself was the centerpiece in a carefully orchestrated propaganda campaign designed to celebrate the king's *gloire*—that is, his glory or renown—in architecture, painting, sculpture, and other artistic media. Above all, Louis's

gloire rose when he led his troops into battle and fought other kings for territory, honor, and prestige.

Forty Years of Warfare

The early years of Louis's reign were marked by peace at home and victory abroad. But after 1668, the king, increasingly worried about the weakness of France's eastern border, launched a series of wars. The greatest of these campaigns was the **Dutch War**. Resenting the "maggots" who dominated European trade and shipping, in 1672, Louis ordered his generals to invade.

Louis Versus the Dutch Faced with French invasion, the Dutch **stadholder**, **William**, broke the dikes that protected his low-lying country and flooded it, as the government had against the Spanish in 1579. The strategy obviously caused much hardship for the Dutch, but it also bogged down the French. In the end, neither side could defeat

salons Meetings in great Parisian homes presided over by well-born women who set the style for discussions of literature, science, and other matters of current interest.

Versailles Louis XIV's palace near Paris begun in the 1660s and housing the king after 1683.

Dutch War France's 1672–1678 invasion of the Netherlands aimed at breaking Dutch control of international trade and shipping.

stadholder Chief executive in the Dutch Republic.

William Stadholder of the Dutch Republic (1672–1702) who later became king of England as William III (r. 1689–1702).

the other, and a peace was signed in 1679. The chief consequence of the war was to alienate William, who was now dedicated to the defeat of France.

To further challenge Dutch economic predominance, Louis's financial minister, **Jean-Baptiste Colbert**, developed a strategy for increasing France's national wealth. Known as **mercantilism**, it regulated economic policy for France's benefit. Consumers were encouraged to "buy French," and the state supported porcelain manufacturers capable of competing with imports from Asia. Monopolies were given to trading companies that would challenge the Dutch in overseas markets.

French Colonies To strengthen the French economy, colonies were encouraged to grow. The population of Canada, known for its exports of furs and fish, rose from three thousand to twenty-five thousand, and the French founded settlements on the Gulf of Mexico at Mobile and New Orleans. These colonies secured the French in the North American heartland watered by the Mississippi and Ohio Rivers. **Saint-Domingue** and other colonies in the Caribbean specialized in cash crops, first tobacco and then sugar. Colbert's mercantilism established a new goal for the monarchy—the development of a national economic policy.

The War of the League of Augsburg The mid-1680s brought a downturn in Louis's fortunes. In 1683, Louis refused to declare war on the Turks when they besieged Vienna. His decision was in line with France's traditional anti-Habsburg policy, but his refusal to help a Christian state attacked by Muslims scandalized many Europeans. Then, in 1689, Louis again went to war on France's eastern frontier, this time against Austria, a war that was quickly joined by the Dutch. The **War of the League of Augsburg** lasted until 1697. Louis, who had the largest army in Europe, strengthened the eastern frontier by conquering the province of Alsace and the city of Strasbourg. But his finances were exhausted. In 1693, crop failures, caused by a drop in average yearly temperatures during the Little Ice Age, led to a terrible famine in which more than a million people perished from hunger and disease.

The War of the Spanish Succession Then an even greater political crisis loomed—the succession to the Spanish throne. Spain was ruled by Charles II, who was childless and feeble-minded. On his death, the vast Spanish possessions would have to pass either to the Austrian Habsburgs or to the French Bourbons, and both had claims to the crown. Although on his death in 1701 Charles had willed his lands to the Bourbons (Louis XIV's grandson, Philip), the Austrian Habsburgs disputed the will and went to war.

This **War of the Spanish Succession** was the most devastating one Louis ever fought. At war's end, Philip remained king of Spain and its empire, but the **Treaty of Utrecht** stipulated that France and Spain could not be united as a single state. The Austrians received northern and southern Italy, along with the Spanish (now the Austrian) Netherlands.

Louis's many wars had increased the size of France by 12 percent and strengthened its eastern borders, now protected with state-of-the-art fortifications. But they had left a bitter legacy. In 1713, France was virtually bankrupt and the economy in a shambles. Moreover, other European states, especially the Dutch Republic and Britain, feared that the Sun King was trying to upset the balance of power, which aimed to prevent any one state from establishing permanent military dominance in Europe.

A Unified French State

Within France, however, the wars had a unifying effect. Continuous warfare after 1688 had led Louis to search desperately for new revenue, and he sold waves of new offices. Then, in 1695, he took the unprecedented step of imposing a tax, the **capitation**, on all his subjects without exception.

The Intendants and the Parlements To supervise the collection of these taxes, Louis relied on his **intendants**, chief local royal administrators appointed on the basis of their ability and loyalty to the Crown. The intendants also gathered information about local conditions for the central government, and their reports allowed the king and his ministers to be better informed about the state of the economy. The result was better policy making.

Thus, in his later years Louis was able to transform the French state. He reduced the power of the royal courts, known as **parlements**, which were now

---

Jean-Baptiste Colbert (1619–1683) Louis XIV's financial minister who implemented French mercantilist policies.

mercantilism State-initiated economic policy encouraging exports, discouraging imports, and stimulating domestic industries.

Saint-Domingue Sugar-producing French island colony in the Caribbean.

War of the League of Augsburg (1689–1697) First of Louis XIV's two great wars fought against Austria, England, and the Dutch Republic.

War of the Spanish Succession (1701–1713) Louis XIV's last great war, with France and Spain allied against the Austrians, Dutch, and English.

Treaty of Utrecht Treaty signed in 1713 between France and the states fighting France that ended the War of the Spanish Succession.

capitation Royal tax imposed on all French subjects in 1695 that introduced the idea of taxation of all people in defense of the state.

intendants In the second half of Louis XIV's reign, the most important local royal administrators, appointed by the king.

parlements France's highest royal courts, which enforced the king's edicts.

forbidden to criticize royal edicts. But their members were guaranteed their right to hold office and encouraged to enforce the law. As royal administration became more efficient, relations between the king and his subjects improved. Well-run parlements appealed to the king's subjects, who increasingly used them instead of church or landlords' courts, believing that they offered fairer rulings.

Taxes and the Army Although taxation was still resented, the better-organized collection of taxes, along with a continuing shift to indirect taxation on items like paper and tobacco, took some of the sting out of payment. Even the royal armies were appreciated. During the religious wars earlier in the century, royal troops had been hated because of their violence and unruliness, but Louis's army, though huge, was well disciplined. His troops were now seen as protectors, welcomed by civilians and local vendors who supplied their needs. Under Louis, the French government functioned more fairly and efficiently.

Curbing the Nobles, Defending Catholicism The unity of France was important to Louis. As a child, he twice had to flee Paris for his safety during a noble revolt against royal rule known as the **Fronde**. When he assumed personal rule of France, he was determined to prevent a similar rebellion. His policy of coaxing the most powerful nobles to his court with promises of honors, careers, and money was designed to tie them closely to the fortunes of the Crown.

Louis also sought to secure religious unity in France, believing the kingdom should have "one king, one law, one faith." In Louis's mind, the French Huguenots were potentially rebellious, so in 1685 he revoked the Edict of Nantes, thereby ending the limited religious toleration Louis's grandfather had granted. Huguenots who failed to convert to Catholicism were forced to flee. Around three hundred thousand, many of them middle-class merchants, left for the Dutch Republic, England, and America, spreading tales of the king's brutality.

The Huguenot exodus cost France dearly because it deprived the kingdom of a commercially skilled group just as the Anglo-French struggle for global commerce was beginning. Those still in France were subject to the quartering of troops in their houses, and in the mountainous south, where many Protestant peasants lived, royal troops burned hundreds of villages. In retaliation, peasants carried on a **guerrilla war** against the royal army.

In Protestant Europe, news of the army's atrocities, coupled with exiles' grim accounts, produced a new image of Louis. The glorious Sun King was now a vicious tyrant. In France, however, most Catholics supported the king's policy. Louis's campaign against the Huguenots resulted not only from a belief that France should be religiously unified but also from fear that the Huguenots were secretly republicans, a charge that bedeviled them after English Calvinists declared a commonwealth in 1649.

Louis and the Pope Louis also quarreled with the pope by supporting the French clergy's adoption of the **Four Gallican Articles**, which proclaimed that church councils were superior to the pope and that the pope could not alter the way the French church was governed. The attack on the Huguenots was designed in part to heal the rupture with the pope. Relations with the papacy were further improved when Louis supported the pope's condemnation of the **Jansenists**, austere Catholics whose notions about human sinfulness struck some Catholics as too close to the views of John Calvin.

During a famine in 1709, Louis took the unprecedented step of issuing a letter directly asking his subjects for help. This appeal went against the principles of absolutism, in which the king was the only political player, but it was well received. As a result, king and subjects bonded in an effort to meet the crisis, and a new sense of collective identity was forged. Now people started to think of themselves as part of a unified nation facing a common task.

Summing Up the Reign Louis XIV's regulation of religious affairs, his control of the French nobility, his efficient royal administration of tax and economic policies, and his establishment of better working relations with his subjects all promoted a growing sense of national unity, exemplifying French royal absolutism in action.

Yet in 1715, seventy-seven years old and dying, Louis reflected on his failings. He told his five-year-old great-grandson and heir, **Louis XV**, "Try to remain at peace with your neighbors. I loved war too much. Do not follow me in that or in overspending."

Louis XV

After 1715, France avoided prolonged warfare. Capitalizing on peaceful times and a smoothly functioning state administration, Louis XV continued his great-grandfather's absolutist policy of expanding the state's activity in new directions; one was policing.

Fronde (1648–1653) Rebellion of the French nobles against Cardinal Mazarin and the regent, Queen Anne, during Louis's early years as king.

guerrilla war An undeclared, irregularly fought war.

Four Gallican Articles Decrees of 1681 proclaiming church councils superior to the pope and denying Rome's power to alter internal rules governing the French church.

Jansenists Austere Catholic reformers who were accused of holding views about human sin similar to the Protestant John Calvin and were condemned by the pope.

Louis XV (r. 1715–1774) Louis XIV's five-year-old great-grandson who became king on Louis XIV's death.

Louis XIV Advises His Son

In 1666, Louis XIV assembled a team of collaborators to help him write his memoirs, which were intended for his young son, another Louis, when he became king. Such memoirs were common in early modern Europe. Charles V had written one for Philip II, and Cardinal Richelieu had composed one for Louis XIII. Although Louis's son died before the king and, therefore, could never follow his father's advice, the Memoirs reveal the preoccupations and principles of Louis XIV some five years after he became his own prime minister.

❶ What do these remarks say about Louis's understanding of his relationship with his subjects?

❷ Why would Louis argue that the happiness and tranquility of France depended on the union of authority in the king?

❸ Why would the king be concerned that a division of political authority would lead to the "greatest misfortunes?"

❹ What do these remarks tell you about the king's personality?

❶ My son, many very important considerations caused me to resolve to leave you, at the cost of much labor in the midst of my most important duties, these memoirs of my reign and principal acts.… I even hoped that in this way I might be the most valuable person in the world to you and consequently to my subjects. For no one with more talent and experience has ever reigned in France, and I do not hesitate to say to you that the higher one's position, the more it has qualities that no one may perceive or understand without occupying it.…

❷ For it is generally agreed that nothing preserves the happiness and tranquility of the provinces with greater certainty than the perfect union of all authority in the person of the sovereign. **❸** The slightest division of authority always produces the greatest misfortunes, and whether the alienated portion falls into the hands of individuals or groups, it cannot remain there except in a state of violence.…

❹ As for the work of [governing], my son,… I imposed upon myself the rule to labor twice daily. I cannot tell you what benefit I received immediately

---

Strengthening the Police Traditionally, cities maintained rudimentary police forces, and the army was the real maintainer of public order. Under Louis XV, the army's policing role declined, and professional police forces were created. Paris saw the first changes. Its police force, which numbered 193 in 1700, grew to 725 by 1760. In the rest of the kingdom, about three thousand men functioned as police. These forces were spread thinly over a population of twenty-four million, but they represented the beginning of a modern, professional police network.

Poor Relief Another area of activity concerned poor relief. Increasingly, the state assumed care of poor children and the elderly, who were housed, clothed, and fed in urban "hospitals." Life in the hospitals was strict; attendance at morning and evening prayers was obligatory, and the able-bodied were forced to work. Some historians argue that the new state program aimed to isolate the socially undesirable from society at large, whereas others see it as the beginning of a modern state-sponsored welfare system.

The Jansenist Problem In religious policy, however, Louis XV struggled, as the problem of the Jansenists remained. While his government continued its predecessor's condemnation of the Jansenists, the Parlement of Paris, following the Four Gallican Articles, declared that the pope was illegally intruding into the French church's affairs. The conflict was intense because in 1715 the Duke of Orléans, the regent for the new child king, had once again permitted the parlements to criticize royal policy. By 1730, the Parlement of Paris was openly defying Louis on the Jansenist issue and challenging the absolutist principle that the king alone made law.

after making this resolution. I felt elevated in spirit and courage, a changed man, discovering in myself unknown resources and joyfully reproaching myself for having ignored them for so long.... I now seemed to be king and born to be so. As for those who were to assist me in my work, I resolved above all else not to appoint a first minister.... For in order to unite in myself all sovereign authority, I resolved after I had chosen my ministers to call upon them when they least expected it, even though their duties might involve details to which my role and dignity would not ordinarily allow me to stoop, so as to convince them that I would follow the same procedure regarding other matters at any time. The knowledge that resulted from this small step, which I took but rarely and more for diversion than because of any principle, instructed me gradually without effort regarding a thousand things that were of value in making general decisions....

❺ Kings are often obliged to do things contrary to their inclinations and good nature. They should enjoy giving pleasure, but they must frequently punish and ruin persons whose good they naturally desire. The interest of the state should take precedence. One should counter one's inclinations and not place oneself in position to regret mishandling something important because some individual's interest interfered and diverted attention from the aims that one should have for the grandeur, the good, and the power of the state.... The mistakes that I have made and have given me infinite pain have been caused by kindness or allowing myself to be too easily guided by others' advice. Nothing is as dangerous as weakness of any kind whatsoever.

Source: From *Louis XIV* by John B. Wolf. Copyright © 1968 by W. W. Norton & Company, Inc. Used by permission of W. W. Norton & Company, Inc.

❺ How did Louis's concern to promote the interest of the state shape his behavior toward others?

Neither side could silence the other, and it now seemed that Louis XV could no longer keep religious peace in the kingdom. Despite this failure, however, absolutism in France had brought the state into new areas of people's lives and made the state more demanding, as well as more responsive, than ever before.

 Checking In

By yourself or with a partner, explain the significance of each of the following selected key terms:

Louis XIV	intendants
Dutch War	parlements
mercantilism	Jansenists
Treaty of Utrecht	Louis XV

The Austrian Habsburgs, 1648–1740

◆ **How was the Austrian Habsburg form of absolutist kingship similar to and different from French royal absolutism?**

◆ **What factors delayed the implementation of state-building in the Habsburg lands before 1740?**

The Habsburg emperor Leopold, a lifelong rival of Louis XIV, successfully contained France's bid for dominance in European affairs, thus maintaining the balance of power. His reign, too, was marked by warfare. Positioned between the French in the west and the Turks in the east, Leopold often had to fight both at the same time.

Austrian National Library, Vienna

In this engraving by Caspar Luyken, Emperor Leopold I is shown in the Spanish style dress worn at his court, far more somber than the fashions favored at Versailles. Leopold looks out at the viewer with piercing eyes. The elongated lower jaw, characteristic of the Habsburgs, is also apparent.

Unlike France, warfare in the Habsburg lands did not accelerate a drive for unity in the state, and Austria was not remodeled along absolutist lines. Its reach was simply too great and its population too diverse—particularly after the reconquest of Hungary—to permit the perfect alignment of the king and the law that had been Louis XIV's aim.

Leopold I

In 1657, on the death of his elder brother from small-pox, the seventeen-year-old **Leopold I** unexpectedly became Holy Roman emperor and head of the Austrian Habsburgs. He had been destined for a career in the church, and at first he did not play the role of monarch very well. Throughout his life he remained deeply religious. He married three times and had sixteen sons and daughters, only five of whom outlived him. He was also withdrawn and bookish as well as an accomplished musician who composed many pieces performed at his court in Vienna.

Like most rulers of his day, Leopold was aware of the political implications of Louis XIV's Versailles and set out to rival him by building his own palace, **Schönbrunn**, on the outskirts of Vienna. Plans to convert the building, which like Versailles had been a hunting lodge, were drawn up during his reign. They included an imposing residence of four hundred rooms as well as gardens and fountains in the manner of Versailles.

The Turkish Siege of Vienna and the Reconquest of Hungary

In 1683, a Turkish army, under the leadership of the Ottoman **grand vizier**, Kara Mustafa, marched up the Danube River and besieged Vienna. Once again, Europe shuddered at the threat of Muslim conquests. Leopold, forced to flee the city, tried to rally support from Christian princes. Many responded, though not Louis XIV, for whom dynastic rivalry was more important than Christian solidarity. In September, after a savage two-month siege of the city, a united force, which had received the pope's blessing, defeated the Turks, and Kara Mustafa fled south.

Reconstructing Royal Rule in Hungary These events opened the way for the Habsburgs' reconquest of Hungary. By 1687, Leopold was master of most of the kingdom and the semi-independent principality of Transylvania. But Leopold did not trust the Hungarians. Earlier in his reign, some of their great nobles had rebelled against him, and others were Protestants. Hungarians were also culturally distinct, dressing in local costumes and speaking their own language—Magyar.

Turkish occupation and the war of reconquest had devastated the Hungarian countryside, and vast stretches of farmland lay unoccupied. To restore agriculture, and also to neutralize possible Hungarian rebellions, Leopold encouraged Serb, Bohemian, and German peasants to resettle the lands, promising them limited freedom from royal taxes and the obligations of serfdom. This resettlement complicated the religious situation in Hungary, where, for a century, Hungarians had been split over religion; along with Catholics, there were Calvinists, Lutherans, Unitarians, Eastern Orthodox, and Muslims. The resettlement also reduced the proportion of Hungarians. In 1526, they had constituted 85 percent of the kingdom's population; by 1700, they made up only 40 percent.

Renewed War and Peace in Hungary Peace in Europe during the 1680s had freed Leopold to concentrate

---

Leopold I (r. 1657–1705) Head of the Austrian Habsburgs, emperor, ruler in Austria, king of Bohemia, and king of Hungary, which he reconquered from the Turks.

Schönbrunn (in German, "beautiful spring") Leopold I's palace on Vienna's outskirts, built on the model of Versailles.

grand vizier Chief minister of the Ottoman sultan.

on Hungary. When the War of the League of Augsburg with France broke out in 1689, he was forced to turn west once again. Then, with Habsburg troop strength reduced in the east, the Turks attempted to retake Hungary, only to be defeated again in 1690. Finally, just as war in the west was ending, in 1697 Leopold scored another smashing victory. At **Zenta**, thirty thousand Turks were slaughtered before the sultan's eyes, for this time the sultan himself had accompanied the Turkish army into Hungary. In 1699, the **Treaty of Carlowitz** confirmed the Habsburg conquests. Although the Ottomans had lost Hungary, they continued to hold the Balkans and challenged the Russians in the northern Black Sea region.

The Rákóczi Rebellion During the War of the Spanish Succession, more trouble flared up in the east, this time a rebellion led by a Transylvanian prince, **Francis II Rákóczi**. Rákóczi typified the touchy Hungarian noble resentful of Leopold's preference for Germans. His father, mother, and stepfather had all led rebellions against the Habsburgs, and he was determined to guarantee Hungary's traditional rights. By 1711, however, he had been defeated, as the Habsburgs were now able to rely on the enlarged non-Hungarian population of the kingdom for support. War and plague devastated the kingdom during the rebellion; almost a half million people perished. Rákóczi eventually sought protection from the sultan and died in exile in Turkey. The **Peace of Szatmár** (1711) united Hungary to the Habsburg lands through a common ruler.

The Habsburg Monarchy

The Habsburgs ruled over lands that were far more socially polarized than Louis XIV's France. At the top were the **magnates**, who were often fabulously rich. Visitors to the magnate Esterházys in Hungary could travel for days before they reached the end of their lands, passing through entire towns that were under the family's exclusive control.

Magnates and Serfs Magnate families were few in number, but their cooperation with the Habsburgs was essential for the smooth functioning of the government, and they dominated Habsburg administration at the central and local levels. Unlike in France, there were few independent cities and towns in the Habsburg lands. The vast majority of people, tied to the land as **serfs**, lived in the countryside.

Serfdom had expanded in the sixteenth and seventeenth centuries as eastern European landlords, all of whom were noble, successfully bound peasants to the soil as a labor force producing grain and timber for the western European market. During the dislocations of the Thirty Years' War, they also bound them to the soil to prevent them from fleeing to more peaceful areas.

Landlords used their serfs to work their estates without compensation. Leopold tried to reduce uncompensated work to three days a week, but his success was limited because direct control of serfs lay with the landlord class, not the Habsburgs. Thus, Leopold's policy had to accommodate noble self-interest before it could become effective.

A Limited Central Government Because Leopold's direct rule over the mass of his subjects was very limited, he never established the kind of centralized, intrusive state that Louis XIV and Louis XV created. The Habsburg state was also characterized by a high degree of ethnic and religious diversity, particularly in Hungary. Habsburg rulers manipulated these groups to their own ends, with the result of enhancing the sense of difference between communities. Unlike in France, no sense of common identity emerged that spanned all the people of the Habsburg hereditary lands.

Leopold died in 1705, leaving two sons, Joseph I (r. 1705–1711) and Charles VI (r. 1711–1740), to rule. But Joseph died during the War of the Spanish Succession.

Charles VI Charles was now the sole surviving Austrian *and* Spanish Habsburg male. He was thus poised to inherit the Austrian territories along with Spain and its lands in the Netherlands, Italy, and America, thus reconstituting Charles V's empire. This was too much for the other European states, which feared that an Austrian Habsburg succession in Spain would upset the European balance of power. They, therefore, supported the division of lands between Habsburgs and Bourbons that was written into the Treaty of Utrecht ending the War of the Spanish Succession.

Warfare did not lead Charles to reform the Habsburg state, as it did in France. Instead, during his twenty-nine-year reign, he devoted his mediocre talents to two basic policies: making sure that his brother's daughters did not succeed him and that his own daughter did. The matter was complicated. The emperor had always been male, so Charles's daughter,

Zenta Battle in 1697 in which the Habsburgs defeated the Turks and reconfirmed Habsburg conquests in Hungary.

Treaty of Carlowitz Treaty of 1699 between the Austrian Habsburgs and the Ottoman Turks confirming the Habsburg reconquest of Hungary.

Francis II Rákóczi (1676–1735) Prince of Transylvania who led the last major rebellion against the Habsburgs in Hungary.

Peace of Szatmár Treaty of 1711 uniting Hungary with the other Habsburg possessions through a common ruler.

magnates Politically powerful nobles in the Habsburg lands who owned vast agricultural estates worked by serfs.

serfs Peasants bound to the land who owed payments and labor service to their landlord.

Maria Theresa, could not follow him in that office. But she could succeed him as ruler of the family's hereditary lands.

The War of the Austrian Succession To this end, Charles coaxed the magnates into recognizing her succession and then sought guarantees from the other European rulers that they, too, would recognize it. When Charles died in 1740, his careful plans exploded. In the **War of the Austrian Succession**, another new ruler, **Frederick II** of Prussia, attacked Maria Theresa during the opening phase of the two world wars that convulsed Europe in the mid-eighteenth century. The new war showed just how weak the Habsburgs had become.

 Checking In

By yourself or with a partner, explain the significance of each of the following selected key terms:

Leopold I

Treaty of Carlowitz

Francis II Rákóczi

Peace of Szatmár

magnates

serfs

Maria Theresa

War of the Austrian Succession

The Rise of Prussia, 1648–1740

◆ **What factors accounted for Prussia's rise in power?**

◆ **What role did the army play in forging a collective Prussian identity?**

Maria Theresa (r. 1740–1780) Daughter of Charles VI and ruler of the Habsburgs' hereditary lands whose husband was elected Holy Roman emperor.

War of the Austrian Succession (1740–1748) Mid-eighteenth century world war, fought on land and sea in Europe, the Americas, and India.

Frederick II (r. 1740–1786) King of Prussia during the War of the Austrian Succession and the Seven Years' War.

Frederick William von Hohenzollern (r. 1640–1688) Known as the Great Elector, ruler who started to create the modern state of Prussia.

North of the Habsburg lands, another state emerged out of the chaos of the Thirty Years' War—Prussia. Prussia was a poor country, lacking the human and material resources of France and the Habsburg lands. But its rulers wanted it to become a major European power. To this end, they consolidated the state's territories, strengthened the state administration, raised revenue, and above all enlarged the army. These ambitious plans meant that the state had to mobilize the country's limited resources to a unique degree.

Territorial Consolidation

In 1640, a twenty-year-old, **Frederick William von Hohenzollern**, known as the Great Elector, became ruler of Brandenburg and a string of other territories that stretched across northern Germany from the Rhineland to the Polish border. In the west, little Cleves and Mark owed him allegiance; in the center were Brandenburg and its capital, Berlin, where he ruled as margrave; to the east was the duchy of Prussia, which he held as a vassal of the king of Poland. These Hohenzollern lands were separated by territories belonging to other rulers, and each had its own jealously guarded political traditions.

Because Frederick William was one of eight German princes entitled to elect the Holy Roman emperor, he had an important place in imperial politics. But his own lands were weak. Those in the center had been devastated during the Thirty Years' War, and some were still under foreign occupation. Overall, the population of his lands had fallen by 50 percent since 1618. But the Peace of Westphalia allowed Frederick William to reestablish princely authority in his territories.

Maneuvering in War In 1655, when Sweden went to war against Poland in hopes of gaining territory on the southern shore of the Baltic Sea, Frederick William faced his first test since the Peace of Westphalia in the treacherous game of warfare and diplomacy that was the norm among European states. At first, he proclaimed his neutrality. When the Swedes suffered temporary losses, he allied with them on condition that they recognize the independence of Prussia from Poland.

When the Poles started to lose, he joined them, again demanding that they abandon any claim to the duchy. At war's end in 1660, he was master of an independent Prussia. Now the Hohenzollern lands were scattered from the Rhineland to the Russian border.

Taxes to Support an Army

For the rest of his reign, the Great Elector set two policy goals: to build up his army and to reorganize his finances to pay for it. Between 1653 and 1688, the army grew from eighteen hundred to thirty thousand. As the one institution established in all territories from east to west, it became the primary unifying force in the elector's state.

Taxes and the Diets A bigger army called for more taxes, and more taxes led to a confrontation between Frederick William and his diets, local political assemblies dominated by the nobility. Like their Habsburg counterparts, the Hohenzollern diets had traditionally granted taxes to the ruler. The elector had obtained a six-year grant from the Diet of Brandenburg in 1653

Map 16.2 **The Growth of Austria and Prussia to 1748** Both Austria and Brandenburg-Prussia were expanding in the first half of the eighteenth century. The Austrians continued adding territories in their southeast, but in the north lost Silesia to Brandenburg-Prussia. Prussian lands were still scattered. © *Cengage Learning*

1. Consult the map legend and trace the stages of Prussia's territorial expansion to 1748.
2. How many territories in the Prussian state were not connected geographically to one or more of the others? What effect could this situation have on state-building in Prussia?
3. Trace the stages of Austria's territorial expansion to 1748.
4. How many territories in the Austrian state were not connected geographically to one or more of the others? What effect could this situation have on state-building in Austria?
5. Drawing on your knowledge of Austrian Habsburg history, what factors explain the marked territorial expansion toward the southeast of western Eurasia?

that he continued to collect on his own authority during the war of 1655–1660.

Also in 1653, he proposed supplementing the grant with a general **excise tax**, taking his cue from the French, who had lowered direct taxes while raising indirect ones. When the local nobility objected that the excise violated their traditional rights of tax exemption, the elector asked only towns to pay it.

Two Tax Systems This solution created two tax systems. The countryside, dominated by nobles, paid a land tax, while towns adopted the excise tax. In creating this twofold system in Brandenburg, the elector split the united opposition of urban and rural taxpayers

excise tax Indirect tax imposed on consumer items and collected at the moment of sale.

Sanssouci Palace at Potsdam. Frederick II built this summer palace near Berlin. It was his answer to Louis XIV's Versailles and Leopold I's Schönbrunn in Vienna. The building is a fine example of eighteenth-century Rococo style architecture and reflects Frederick's refined tastes which were so unlike those of his father. "Sans souci" is French for "Without a care."

to new taxes. When Prussia balked at taxes, Frederick William introduced the two-tiered system there with the same results. Shorn of their taxing power, the diets withered away, and, as in France, political power was increasingly consolidated in the hands of the ruler and his government.

Income from the Royal Domain Frederick William had another source of revenue from his own domain. All European rulers had these private income streams, but the Hohenzollerns were blessed by very large family landholdings, constituting about one-third of their country's agricultural land and worked by 30 percent of the country's serfs. Under the leadership of an efficient administrator, Dodo zu Knyphausen, these domain lands produced ever-larger amounts for the elector's treasury.

Stimulating Economic Growth The elector also encouraged economic growth along mercantilist lines by increasing exports and introducing new

manufacturing centers. As a youth, he had spent time in the Dutch Republic and seen firsthand the thriving economic life there. After 1685, he welcomed some twenty thousand exiled Huguenots. These French artisans, merchants, and manufacturers played a vital role in the economic recovery after the Thirty Years' War.

During his reign, Frederick William had united his far-flung lands into a single state, imposed his right to tax them on a regular basis, and reinvigorated the economy. His growing army made him the most important military figure in Germany after the Habsburgs. In 1688, the elector was succeeded by his son, Frederick, who ruled until 1713.

Frederick spent most of his time in Berlin, presiding over a lavish court in the style of Louis XIV. His one major accomplishment was to adopt the title of King in Prussia in 1701 after obtaining Leopold I's recognition with promises of military aid in the looming War of the Spanish Succession. The title gave Frederick the standing he thought appropriate for his state's new power.

King Frederick William I

In 1713, King Frederick was succeeded by his son, King **Frederick William I**. Although Prussia was Lutheran, Frederick William was a strict Calvinist who believed in the absolutist principle that he was responsible to God alone for his rule. His subjects were to obey him without question. The king hated all elegance and refinement and spent most of his free time with his military men, smoking and getting completely drunk. These "tobacco evenings" sometimes ended with a participant being set on fire, a great joke in the king's eyes. Frederick William also stalked the streets of Berlin, roaring at his subjects, beating them with his cane, and leaving them with broken noses and teeth. Frederick William was a strange, violent, and crude man, but he was also a very successful ruler.

Strengthening the Royal Administration; Enlarging the Army Like his grandfather, the Great Elector, Fredrick William I pursued the twin policies of strengthening the royal administration while enlarging the army. The excise tax was expanded to new commodities, and the land tax was imposed directly on the nobility in East Prussia, as the old duchy was now called. Income from the royal domain was further increased through yet more efficient management. Town councils were abolished and new royal officials put in their place.

A new administrative body called the **General Directory** was created in 1723 that brought together all officials involved in collecting taxes and revenues from the royal domain and supervising the overall economy of the kingdom. The directory improved administrative centralization and efficiency.

A Personal Absolutism The king stood at the apex of this new administrative system. Unlike his predecessors, Frederick William I did not consult regularly with his top officials because he had a low opinion of the men who worked for him, criticizing them for laziness and greed and paying them poorly. Instead, he worked in private, receiving reports and then secretly making decisions that were transmitted in writing to his officials. His was a system of personal absolutism unknown even in Louis XIV's France, where the king always consulted with a handful of trusted advisers.

The king's government produced what Frederick William I wanted above all else—an enlarged army. At his death in 1740, the Prussian army had eighty thousand men, making it the fourth largest in Europe. Command of the troops was given to the Prussian nobility, who also served in the civil administration. The king thus bound the nobility to his government and created a tradition of loyal state service among his nobles that was to last into the twentieth century.

He also guaranteed the nobility's economic preeminence by recognizing their rights as landlords to control the serfs on their estates.

The Prussian Military The military had always been the one institution common to all the Hohenzollern lands, and the state's financial administration was geared to its maintenance. The military budget was met with tax and domain revenues, not with borrowing, as in other states. As he enlarged the army, Frederick William drafted more and more of his own subjects. All parts of the kingdom were required to present men, mainly peasants, for service.

To lower costs, the soldiers were quartered in civilian homes, where they paid for their food and lodging and thereby stimulated the local economy. Because the rank and file of the growing army was made up of Prussians who lived among the civilian population, historians have described eighteenth-century Prussia as a "barracks state."

Frederick II When Frederick William died in 1740, he was succeeded by his son, Frederick II. Frederick was everything his father was not—refined, an accomplished flute player and composer, and a lover of philosophical discussion. He and his father had not gotten along. Relations between ruling monarchs and their successors were often stormy because the next in line attracted those who were out of favor in the current reign. But Frederick William I's treatment of his son was particularly violent. At one point, having beaten Frederick bloody with his cane, he put him in solitary confinement and forced him to witness the beheading of his closest friend on largely falsified charges.

Frederick William I had doubled the size of his army, but he was reluctant to use it in war. Frederick II's first act as king was to attack Charles VI's successor, Maria Theresa, seizing Silesia, her richest territory, and thereby starting the War of the Austrian Succession, the first of two world wars that engulfed the major European states in the mid-eighteenth century.

> **Frederick William I** (r. 1713–1740) King of Prussia who further centralized the state administration and continued to build up the army.
>
> **General Directory** Prussian central administrative agency created in 1723.

 Checking In

By yourself or with a partner, explain the significance of each of the following selected key terms:

Frederick William von Hohenzollern	Frederick William I
excise tax	General Directory
	Frederick II

Russia and Europe, 1682–1796

◆ **How were the state-building efforts of Russia's rulers similar to or different from the reform programs of European rulers farther to the west?**

◆ **How were Russian rulers' relations with their nobility similar to and different from relations between monarchs and nobles farther to the west?**

Beginning in 1700, Russia began to realize Tsar Ivan the Terrible's dream of turning westward to expand its territory. In addition, rulers restructured Russia's state and church, along with its economy and society, along western lines. By the end of the eighteenth century, Russia was a major player in European politics.

Peter the Great and Westernization

Following Ivan the Terrible's death in 1584, Russia sank into a thirty-year period of political instability during which aristocratic factions fought for control of the state. In 1613, stability was restored when the first **Romanov** tsar, Michael, ascended the throne. At the end of the century, another Romanov, **Peter I the Great**, transformed Russia into a major European power. Peter was six feet seven inches tall and powerfully built. His huge size had a personality to match—restless, energetic, and always on the move.

In 1697, he traveled to western Europe under an assumed name, which fooled no one. Settling in the Dutch Republic, he spent hours visiting sawmills, cloth manufacturers, botanical gardens, and museums. But, above all, he visited Dutch shipyards to learn about shipbuilding, and then, having bought his own tools, he worked alongside Dutch shipbuilders. On a visit to England, he went to Anglican church services, attended a Quaker meeting, went to the theater, and visited Parliament, which did not impress him. And, again, he studied ships.

Romanovs Family that ruled Russia from 1613 to 1917.

Peter I the Great (r. 1682–1725) Greatest Romanov tsar who westernized Russia and made the country a major European power.

Great Northern War (1700–1721) War between Russia and Sweden that resulted in Russian dominance of the Baltic.

St. Petersburg City founded by Peter the Great in 1703, which became the Russian capital in 1712.

Poltava Decisive battle of the Great Northern War in 1709 in which Peter the Great defeated Charles XII of Sweden.

Cutting Off Beards and Creating Assemblies Peter worked for the rest of his life to apply what he had learned in the west to Russia. He began with fashion. Immediately on his return to Moscow, he forbade men to grow beards, the traditional sign of manhood in this Orthodox Christian country, and personally cut them off his courtiers. Traditionalists were horrified and protested that their hairless faces made them look like Protestants, Poles, or monkeys. His court was then ordered to dress in western clothes and to meet in "assemblies," where men and women together conversed and engaged in other polite pastimes. This mingling of men and women overturned traditions decreeing the separation of women in special quarters.

The Great Northern War In 1700, the tsar began a two-decade struggle with Sweden, the greatest power in northeastern Europe, for control of the Baltic Sea. Since the sixteenth century, tsars had believed that Russian access to the Baltic, the central sea link between eastern and western Europe, was essential if Russia hoped to be a major European power. Peter acted on this belief in the **Great Northern War**, which marked a turning point in Russian history.

After early Russian victories on the Baltic, Peter took the examples of Louis XIV and Leopold I further by building not a palace but a city, **St. Petersburg**, founded in 1703 on swampy coastal land seized from the Swedes at the mouth of the Neva River. The new city proclaimed his success in securing a Baltic port. In 1712, Peter made St. Petersburg the new capital of Russia, and the next year the court and state administration moved there from Moscow. In 1718, well-to-do landowners were required to build a house there and spend some of the year in the city.

Reforming the Military and Raising Taxes Peter knew that continuing military success in the war with Sweden depended on an unprecedented refashioning of Russia's fighting forces and tax structure. He therefore reorganized his army along western lines, ordering a draft for soldiers and introducing up-to-date western drill and weapons. By 1715, he had an army of 215,000, supplemented by 100,000 Cossacks, locally organized warrior bands used by tsars as fighting forces. Peter also built a Baltic navy from scratch.

To pay for this huge military mobilization, he imposed new taxes on everything from beehives to beards to baths. Overall, taxes skyrocketed during Peter's reign, as they had in France during the Thirty Years' War. To improve his tax base, Peter inaugurated a mercantilist stimulation of the Russian economy by encouraging exports, discouraging imports, and sponsoring new industries in metallurgy, mining, and textiles.

Poltava The decisive battle in the Great Northern War came in 1709 at **Poltava**, where Peter destroyed the Swedish army. Nine thousand Swedes lay dead on the battlefield, and sixteen thousand more surrendered a few days later. The Swedish king, Charles XII,

© Joeri de Rocker/Alamy

The "Tsar Carpenter." This is a copy of a sculpture by Leopold Bernshtam which Emperor Nicholas II presented to the Russian Admiralty in St. Petersburg in 1909 to commemorate the Russian victory at Poltava. It shows Peter the Great at work as a shipbuilder in the Dutch city of Zaandam. The original was destroyed at the beginning of the Russian Revolution in 1918. This copy was presented to Zaandam in 1910. In 1996, the Dutch government gave it to Russia and once again Peter stands in front of the Admiralty. Compare this image with that of Ivan the Terrible in Chapter 13 (p. 382). How has the image of the tsar changed from the sixteenth to the early twentieth century?

who commanded the army, fled into Turkish territory. Although the war lasted another twelve years, the Swedes never recovered from the disaster at Poltava. At the end of the Great Northern War, in 1721, during a solemn ceremony in St. Petersburg, Peter was proclaimed emperor of Russia, a title taken from Rome that was to supplant the traditional one of tsar.

Restructuring Society Peter also continued to restructure Russian society. Traditionally, Russians thought of their society as a three-tiered hierarchy. At the base were the millions of serfs who toiled for their landlords. Serfs, who constituted more than half of the Russian population, were under the complete control of their landlord, needing his permission to marry or leave his estate. They also had to work for

him without pay, often as many as six days a week. In their lack of freedom of choice, they resembled the African slaves laboring in the fields in the Americas more than the European peasants farther to the west.

The landlords in turn worked for the emperor. Peter intensified this traditional pattern, first by demanding more in taxes and military service from the serfs and then by requiring the landlord class to serve for life in either the military or the civilian administration. Candidates for state service had to start at the bottom of their service branch and then work to the top on the basis of personal merit. Peter applied the test of merit to himself when he rose through the ranks of the army and the navy.

This system was codified in the **Table of Ranks**. Administrators received noble status as they moved up. Peter's reform of his civil and military administration was one of the first attempts in modern European history to overturn the idea that nobles had a right to govern in favor of the notion that government should be in the hands of a civil service staffed by experts whose advancement depended on their performance.

To train experts for state service, Peter established engineering, artillery, and medical schools, a school of mathematics and navigation, and a naval academy. In 1725, he established an Academy of Sciences that quickly gained an international reputation for excellence. Peter's insistence on able and expert administrators was central to his program of state-building.

"The Most Drunken Council" Peter loved alcohol, coarse language, and even coarser practical jokes. Throughout most of his reign, he presided over a "Most Drunken Council" that engaged in monumental drinking bouts while mocking Catholic, but not Orthodox, church ceremonies. His practical joking was often violent, as when he forced food down the throat of a courtier, who collapsed in a fit of coughing with blood running from his nose and mouth. Peter's violence matched that of Frederick William I of Prussia and contrasted sharply with the refined manners promoted at the court of Louis XIV and the piety of Leopold I.

Reform of the Church Peter's most radical reform was to abolish the office of **patriarch** in the Russian Orthodox Church. In the Orthodox world, patriarchs were bishops with great prestige and influence. The patriarch of Moscow, who had received the title in 1589, had served as a counterweight to tsars and a check on their power. By Peter's time, however, the patriarchate had been weakened by a schism in

Table of Ranks Decree by Peter the Great in 1722 that restructured civil and military administration into a system of advancement based on merit.

patriarch Title of the most important bishops in the Eastern Orthodox Church.

the church when the **Old Believers** rejected his authority and denounced him as the Antichrist.

The patriarch had tried to reform church practice, and although Russian church councils and the other patriarchs approved the reforms, Old Believers rejected them because they had not been used traditionally in "Holy Russia." Moreover, people unhappy about Peter's policy of cultural westernization looked to the patriarch for support of traditional ways.

Peter never openly attacked Orthodoxy, but his own theological beliefs were heavily influenced by Lutheranism. In 1721, he abolished the patriarchate and replaced it with a **Holy Synod**, which embodied his Lutheran leanings because it reduced the church to a simple department of the state.

Peter's Achievements Peter's plans for the remaking of Russia were far reaching, and many of them looked better on paper than they worked in reality. But his reforms brought a new centralization and rationality to government while demanding more from all Russians and advancing the country as a major European power. Thus, he set Russia on a new course.

Catherine the Great and Russian Expansion

From 1725 to 1762, Russia was allied with Austria against France, the traditional ally of the Poles, the Swedes, and the Turks, all enemies of Russia. The Austrian alliance implemented Peter's policy of bringing Russia directly into the European system of international politics and diplomacy. Domestically, one far-reaching change took place: in 1762, the landlord class was freed from Peter's compulsory state service obligation. From then on, landlords served voluntarily, and many did so because service brought prestige, influence, and wealth.

In 1762, Peter III, Peter I's grandson, became emperor. Peter III was violent, crude, and dimwitted. Raised in Germany, where his Romanov mother had married a duke, Peter feared Russians and loved Germans, thereby alienating many at court. In religion, he also leaned toward Lutheranism and ordered icons removed from Russian churches while demanding that Orthodox clergy dress like Lutheran pastors. No one dared to implement these decrees. Peter was married to Sophie, a princess from a minor German state. Six months after Peter's accession, Sophie

The Granger Collection, New York

For her portrait (c. 1765), Catherine II the Great is dressed in shiny splendor. On her head is the Romanov crown, and in her hands are an orb and scepter, emblems of royal and imperial rule. She gazes straight out at the viewer with a kindly expression, perhaps to convey an image of her womanly concern for her subjects. Compare this portrait of Catherine to that of Peter the Great earlier in this chapter and to Ivan the Terrible in Chapter 13. Is Catherine's depiction more or less in line with the way rulers had been depicted before her? If less in line, why might she have chosen to deviate from the norm? If more in line, why might she have preferred this conventional approach?

plotted with powerful courtiers, one of whom was her lover, to depose Peter in a palace **coup d'état**. He was soon murdered, and the conspirators proclaimed Sophie his successor. For the next thirty-four years, she ruled Russia as **Catherine II the Great**.

Seizing Church Lands; Land for Her Favorites Catherine's first major decision was to continue Peter III's seizure of all ecclesiastical lands, thereby further reducing the church's independence from the state. She then granted large tracts of state land and their peasants to her favorites. This action increased the number of serfs because state peasants were reduced to serfdom when their lands passed into private hands. Catherine also continued her predecessors' policies of exempting the landlord class from compulsory state service and freeing them from taxation

Old Believers Orthodox Christians who rejected the Russian patriarch's attempt to alter church ceremony.

Holy Synod Council of clergy established by Peter the Great in 1721 that made the church a department of the state.

coup d'état (in French, "blow of state") Abrupt overthrow of a government by a small group of conspirators.

Catherine II the Great (r. 1762–1796) German princess who, as Russian empress, was one of Russia's most powerful rulers.

Map 16.3 **The Partition of Poland and the Expansion of Russia** Prussia, Russia, and Austria all benefited from the partitions of Poland. © *Cengage Learning*

1. Consult the map legend and then note the new territories the partitions of Poland added to:
   a. Prussia
   b. Austria
   c. Russia
2. Drawing on your knowledge of these three states, how would the territories added further the state-building agendas of each state?

while forbidding serfs on their lands from directly petitioning the empress for redress of grievances.

Partitioning Poland and Fighting the Turks Like Peter the Great, Catherine dramatically expanded Russia's borders. In 1772, she joined Prussia and Austria, which were also looking to expand their territories, in the first **partition of Poland**. In the 1760s, Prussia and Russia had instigated a civil war in Poland by demanding full toleration for its Protestant and Orthodox inhabitants. Claiming that they were putting an end to that civil war, Austria, Prussia, and Russia proceeded to divide up sections of Poland among themselves.

Two more partitions took place in 1792 and 1795, bringing an end to an independent Poland.

Catherine also fought two wars with the Turks. In 1792, when the second war ended, Russia seized the north shore of the Black Sea and the Crimean peninsula along with the northern Caucasus. These conquests, along with the partitions of Poland, rivaled Peter the Great's advances in the Baltic region and established the modern western boundaries of Russia.

partitions of Poland Divisions of Poland carried out by Austria, Prussia, and Russia in 1772, 1792, and 1795, leading to the end of an independent Polish state.

Catherine encouraged colonization in the lands of the south by urging Russian landlords to move there with their serfs and sponsoring German immigrants in the region. At the end of Catherine's reign, the Russian empire contained dozens of different ethnic and religious communities, 50 percent of whom were Russian. Thus, cultural diversity in the Russian empire rivaled that of the Habsburg lands and similarly retarded the development of a common identity among the peoples ruled by the empress in St. Petersburg.

The Pugachev Rebellion and Russian Society

In 1773, during the Turkish war, a massive rebellion against the empress broke out in the south. It was led by a Cossack, **Emelian Pugachev**, who claimed to be Peter III. Popular revolts led by men pretending to be long-lost tsars were a feature of early modern Russia's political life. So were Cossack frontier rebellions. What made Pugachev's revolt distinctive was its size and its social composition. Thousands rose with him, including many serfs. In 1774, when the Turkish war ended, Catherine was free to turn her professionally trained army against the insurgents, who were no match for the imperial troops, and the revolt fell apart. Pugachev was taken to Moscow in a cage and then executed.

Russian Society in Crisis Although the revolt failed, it was a sign of a deep social crisis in Russia. The elimination of compulsory state service for the landlord class had undercut the traditional structure of the Russian community, in which landlords toiled for the state while their serfs toiled for them. When the landlords were freed of their obligations, many peasants believed they should be free as well. When they were not freed, alienation and anger exploded into revolt. Those who followed Pugachev demanded an end to serfdom, taxation, and the military draft. In 1775, Catherine clamped down. She imposed administrative centralization by reorganizing Russia into fifty provinces and putting the landlords in charge of local government, where they had enough force to control peasant protests.

Russia Becomes a European Power Under Peter I and Catherine II, Russia emerged as a first-rate European military and diplomatic power. Coercion from above was crucial in this transformation. Modernization and westernization also increased privileges for the landowning class and reduced the condition of the peasant population, which (serfs and free peasants together) constituted more than 90 percent of Russia's inhabitants. The gulf between the landowning elite and the mass of inhabitants was as great as, if not greater than, any in Europe.

 Checking In

By yourself or with a partner, explain the significance of each of the following selected key terms:

Romanov	Table of Ranks
Peter I the Great	Catherine II the Great
Great Northern War	partitions of Poland
St. Petersburg	Emelian Pugachev

The English Constitutional Monarchy, 1660–1740

◆ **How did religion continue to play a role in English politics?**

◆ **In what ways did political development in England differ from that in the absolutist regimes on the continent?**

In 1660, after eleven years of civil war, religious controversy, republican government, and Oliver Cromwell's dictatorship, monarchy was restored in the British Isles when Charles I's son, already crowned king of Scotland, was crowned king of England and Ireland. Restoration, however, did not bring either political or religious peace. For the next seventy years, the British Isles were torn apart by conflicts pitting king against Parliament. Religious divisions also persisted, as restored Anglicans refused all compromise with the Puritans.

When the Catholic king James II seemed to have established a permanent Catholic dynasty, he was overthrown, and his Protestant daughter Mary II, along with her husband, the Dutch stadholder William III, were crowned with Parliament's blessing. But Mary and then her successor, Anne, died without heirs, and Parliament again determined who would rule when it chose a German Protestant prince, George I. In this turbulent period, as Parliament made and unmade monarchs, its power grew. Political stability was achieved in the early eighteenth century, when Crown and Parliament started to cooperate in governing the country.

The Restoration of Charles II

The restoration to the throne of **Charles II** in 1660 sparked a repudiation of Oliver Cromwell's Calvinist moral reform of society. The king led the way.

Emelian Pugachev (1742?–1775) Cossack who claimed to be Peter III and led an unsuccessful rebellion of thousands of serfs against Catherine the Great.

Charles II (r. 1660–1685) Elder son of Charles I who became king of England, Scotland, and Ireland.

Charles was a charming, witty man with a taste for good living and an eye for women. A string of mistresses, along with packs of spaniels, shared his bed. "God will not damn a man for taking a little unregular pleasure along the way," he once quipped. In pursuit of pleasure, Charles reopened London theaters and canceled the traditional prohibition against women playing female roles. Now people could revel in worldly comedies like *Love in a Wood* or *The Gentleman Dancing-Master*.

King and Parliament Underneath the glitter of **Restoration** society, the long-standing political conflict between king and Parliament continued to shape events. Like his predecessors, Charles could conduct foreign policy on his own and choose his ministers. He could also call Parliament into session and dismiss it, veto its legislation, and override any parliamentary law by suspending it or dispensing people from its provisions.

For its part, Parliament could impeach royal ministers. It also controlled state finances through its right to raise taxes. In sum, both sides had formidable powers, and neither could gain a permanent advantage over the other. This situation contrasted to the absolutist monarchies on the continent, where power was increasingly concentrated in the hands of the king.

Fights over Religion The issue that provoked the greatest political fights was religion. Although Charles II was officially Anglican, he favored some form of religious toleration in England. But the Parliament elected in 1661 was determined to promote Anglicanism alone and force conformity to the Book of Common Prayer. Therefore, it enacted the **Clarendon Code**, which required all clergymen to swear an oath supporting Anglican theology and prohibited non-Anglican Protestants from worshiping in public. About 10 percent of the clergy refused to accept it and turned their backs on Anglicanism. These clergymen and their supporters, known as **dissenters**, supported the king's more tolerant attitude.

Most Anglicans suspected that the king's policy of religious toleration was shaped by loyalty to his Catholic family—his mother, wife, and younger brother, James, Duke of York, were all Roman Catholics. These suspicions deepened when Charles allied with his cousin, Louis XIV, in the Dutch War of 1672. But Charles was always politically astute, and he postponed his conversion to Catholicism until he was on his deathbed.

The Problem of James: Tories and Whigs The problem of Catholic members of the royal family became especially acute in the 1670s. Although Charles fathered at least seventeen illegitimate children by his many mistresses, he had no legitimate heir to succeed him, so his brother James would be the next king if the rule of strict hereditary succession was applied. The prospect of a Catholic king created a rift among the Anglican elite, which controlled Parliament and ran local government, because Anglicans hated Catholics as well as dissenters.

Soon two parties, the **Tories** and the **Whigs**, fought each other over the issue of succession. Tories supported the Duke of York's right to the crown, even if this meant that Protestant England would have a Catholic king, because they believed that hereditary monarchy was divinely instituted and that opposition to it was a sin.

Whigs wanted a Protestant monarch at all costs. Following the argument of the English philosopher **John Locke**, they believed in the contractual theory of government. The English monarchy was based on a contract between the ruler and his subjects, represented in Parliament, which could be broken for good reason. As battles between the two parties raged, a new politically active press emerged under the relatively moderate censorship regime of the restored monarchy. Press and parties encouraged the English publicly to discuss politics and take sides on issues in ways that were inconceivable under the absolutist monarchies on the continent.

James II

In 1685, when Charles II died, the principle of hereditary succession won out, and the Duke of York became **James II**. James kept up some Anglican appearances, being crowned in public according to the Anglican rite after being crowned in private according to the Catholic one. When one of Charles II's illegitimate sons, the Protestant Duke of Monmouth, rebelled against his uncle, the duke was taken prisoner and executed. At first, many Tories and Whigs could accept James because his heirs were his two Protestant daughters, Mary and Anne, the children of his first marriage. Although James had remarried, none of the ten children by his second marriage had survived past infancy.

James and Religious Toleration Like his brother, James promoted religious

Restoration Name given to the period 1660–1689 in which the restored Stuart kings Charles II and James II ruled.

Clarendon Code Law of 1661 requiring clergy and officeholders to swear allegiance to the Anglican Church and banning non-Anglican Protestants' public worship.

dissenters Non-Anglican Protestants.

Tories Supporters of strict hereditary succession to the crown.

Whigs People who believed in the necessity of a Protestant monarch, even if this meant that the rule of strict heredity would have to be violated.

John Locke (1632–1704) Political philosopher who argued that legitimate government rested on a contract between rulers and subjects.

James II (r. 1685–1689) King of England who was removed from the throne by Parliament.

toleration of both dissenters and Catholics, granting them the right to worship in public and using his power of exempting people from the law to override a provision in the Clarendon Code forbidding non-Anglicans from serving in high civil and military office. This action infuriated the Anglicans, who saw the king's actions as a backdoor way of promoting Catholicism. When Anglican bishops objected, James resurrected King Charles I's hated church courts, and purged Anglican opponents from local government office, replacing them with Catholics and dissenters.

In 1688, England was rocked by news that James's wife had given birth to an eleventh child, a baby boy who would rule as James III. Outraged Protestants tried to argue that the queen had faked a pregnancy and that the baby had been smuggled into the palace in a bed-warming pan. Tories and Whigs alike were horrified at the prospect of a perpetual Catholic monarchy and furious with James's high-handed exempting of the law in favor of non-Anglicans. Joining forces, they asked the stadholder William, the husband of James's daughter Mary, to come to England in defense of Protestantism. When William landed, James panicked. Unable to sleep and suffering from endless nosebleeds, he led an army against William but failed to find him because his generals had no maps. After sending wife and baby out of the country, James fled to France.

The Glorious Revolution

When Parliament reconvened in 1689, it determined who would rule, proclaiming that in leaving the country James had abdicated and then offering the crown to Mary, his daughter, who accepted on condition that William rule jointly with her.

The Bill of Rights Parliament then passed the **Bill of Rights**, which upheld the Whig view that monarchs ruled not by hereditary right but by right of a contract with their subjects. It overturned James II's suspension of parliamentary law, stating that "the pretended power of suspending the laws or the execution of laws by regal authority without consent of Parliament is illegal." It also undercut royal power by denying the king the right to raise an army on his own, saying that "raising

and keeping a standing army within this kingdom in time of peace without the consent of Parliament [is] contrary to law."

This bill also guaranteed subjects' right to petition the government as well as to a jury trial, along with freedom from "cruel and unusual punishments," excessive bail, and excessive court fines. It did not, however, guarantee the right of all subjects to vote for members of Parliament's **House of Commons**. Voting for this lower house, made up of non-nobles, was still limited to a relatively small number of property-owning adult males. Candidates for the Commons also had to meet substantial property qualifications.

In support of Protestantism, Parliament also repealed the most oppressive portions of the Clarendon Code in the **Toleration Act** (1689), which granted religious toleration to all dissenters except Unitarians, people who did not believe in the doctrine of the Trinity. Dissenters, however, were still subject to a law that required all officeholders to take Holy Communion in an Anglican Church.

Overall, the Bill of Rights and the amendments to the Clarendon Code implemented the contract theory of government by strengthening Parliament while providing subjects of the Crown with a wide range of rights that were spelled out in detail and had the force of law.

A Government of Large-Scale Landowners Large-scale landowners controlled Parliament. After 1689, these people also enjoyed control of local government in the countryside with little interference from the king. This situation contrasted with the absolutist monarchies on the continent, where royal control of local affairs was implemented. William knew that his predecessor's dismissal of Anglican landlords from local office in favor of Catholics and dissenters had contributed to his overthrow and did not intend to provoke these powerful people again.

The Rule of Law In 1701, royal judges were given life tenure, subject only to impeachment and removal from office by Parliament. This reform, which created an independent judiciary, was intended to strengthen the **rule of law** called for in the Bill of Rights. William accepted these reforms from below and thereby acknowledged that he ruled by right of contract with his subjects.

William had come to England as part of his grand strategy to defeat Louis XIV. As king he could take England into the War of the League of Augsburg on the Dutch side. Mary reluctantly accepted the crown, believing that she was sinning against her father, who led a French landing in Ireland to reclaim the monarchy. When William defeated James, James fled once again to France, where he died in 1701.

A Constitutional Monarchy The changes brought about in 1689 spelled the end of royal absolutism in

Bill of Rights Parliamentary act passed in 1689 stipulating the basic rights of English subjects; based on the contract theory of government.

House of Commons Lower elected house of Parliament made up of non-noble men (commoners); nobles sit in the upper house, the House of Lords.

Toleration Act Parliamentary act of 1689 granting religious toleration to all Protestants except Unitarians, and also excepting Catholics.

rule of law Principle that law has a higher authority than rulers, governments, and officials; rulers must obey the laws.

In this painting of the House of Commons by Karl Anton Hickel, the Speaker of the House sits with his hat on at the center behind secretaries. The MPs (Members of Parliament) flank him on either side. The man standing is the king's first minister, William Pitt the Younger, who is addressing the House. What impression does this painting give of the way Parliament conducted its business?

the British Isles and laid the foundations for a **constitutional monarchy** in which the monarch and Parliament ruled as partners following the principles of the rule of law.

The reign of William and Mary inaugurated twenty-five years of war against France. Whigs supported William's pursuit of Louis XIV, while Tories grumbled about rising land taxes. The two parties fiercely contested elections to seats in the House of Commons. In principle, Parliament controlled taxation and the Crown controlled foreign policy. But ongoing warfare forced the two sides to work together because William had to explain his policies to Parliament if he hoped to get the money he needed.

Mary died childless in 1694, and when William died in 1702, the crown passed to James II's younger Protestant daughter, Anne. Anne had had nineteen children, all of whom were stillborn or died in infancy. She believed this calamity was God's judgment on her father's removal from the throne. As Anne had no heirs, Parliament determined who would rule when Anne died. In 1701, fifty-seven Catholic Stuarts were passed over in favor of a Protestant granddaughter of James I, Sophia, of the German state of Hanover.

The Act of Union and the "Glorious Revolution" In 1707, Scotland, still an independent kingdom ruled by the English monarch, but suffering from an economic depression and a financial collapse, agreed to accept the **Act of Union** with England to create a united Great Britain ruled over by a Protestant monarch. In 1714, when Anne died, Sophia's son George became king. Later generations in England referred to the events of 1688 and 1689 as the **Glorious Revolution**,

constitutional monarchy Form of government in which the monarch and legislature rule as partners following the principles of the rule of law.

Act of Union Parliamentary act of 1707 uniting Scotland and England in the one kingdom of Great Britain.

Glorious Revolution (1688–1689) Name given to the events leading to the dethronement of James II and the rule of William and Mary.

which kept the state Protestant while advancing the power of Parliament and repudiating absolutist and divine right theories of kingship.

The Georges from Germany

George I was already middle aged when he became king of Great Britain in 1714. He spoke no English and had to communicate with his ministers in French. He also spent half his time in Hanover. The Great Britain he presided over had emerged victorious from the wars against Louis XIV, and his right to the British throne had been recognized by the Treaty of Utrecht ending the War of the Spanish Succession in 1713. The treaty had also awarded Britain Gibraltar, Hudson's Bay, Nova Scotia, Newfoundland, and the *asiento*, which gave the British the exclusive right to import African slaves into Spanish America.

In addition to the *asiento*, Britain was allowed limited rights of trade with the Spanish colonies. These concessions spurred development of the British navy and the establishment of trading posts that were vital to the kingdom's growing colonial empire. The territorial grants in North America intensified the contest between France and Britain for control of Canada.

An Uprising in Scotland and the Decline of the Tories Recognition of George as king provoked James II's baby boy, now grown up, to lead an uprising in Scotland to regain the crown. It failed, but when a number of Tories expressed sympathy for the **pretender**, the Whigs accused them of treason. This charge, coupled with George's clear preference for the Whigs, turned the Tories into a minority party for the next forty-five years.

Sir Robert Walpole The leader of the triumphant Whigs was **Sir Robert Walpole**, a rich landowner and country gentleman. Walpole, unlike his ministerial predecessors, refused the king's offer to ennoble him and give him a seat in the House of Lords, the upper house of Parliament. Walpole preferred to stay in the Commons because he believed he could be more effective there in creating majorities to support royal policies. His skill in winning over both the king and Parliament contributed to the smooth running of the central government, while his decision to remain in the Commons added to the power of that house.

Walpole also tried to calm the partisan passions that had agitated the country since 1660. He emphasized good manners in politics and signaled his willingness to accept moderate Tories into his political coalitions. Thus, in his own way, he agreed with Louis XIV that politeness had its political uses. Under Walpole, Britain enjoyed a period of political stability that contrasted sharply with the turmoil preceding George I's reign.

Britons: A New Collective Identity At the same time, a new sense of collective British identity was forming. Britons enjoyed the rights guaranteed in 1689 and were thereby "free-born," in opposition to what they thought were the "slavish" Catholic peoples of France or Spain. This new sense of identity was given voice in the poem "Rule, Britannia," set to music in 1740: "Rule, Britannia! Britannia, rule the waves/Britons never never never shall be slaves."

After their union with England, Scots could also identify with this sense of national unity, especially since they profited increasingly from British overseas and colonial trade. The Catholic Irish, however, conquered and impoverished, were excluded from the community of the free-born.

George II: "Mixed Monarchy" When George I died in 1727, Walpole survived the change of reign and continued to serve George II. Throughout his career he promoted a policy of peace with the rest of Europe and used this time to consolidate the religious and political gains of the Glorious Revolution. When he left office in 1742, the principle of mixed monarchy, in which a constitutionally sanctioned Protestant king ruled jointly with Parliament, had become the cornerstone of British political life. Finally, the defeat of James II in Ireland in 1689, along with the union of Scotland and England in 1707, consolidated English dominance.

Checking In

By yourself or with a partner, explain the significance of each of the following selected key terms:

Charles II	Toleration Act
dissenters	Glorious Revolution
James II	George I
Bill of Rights	Sir Robert Walpole

Two World Wars, 1740–1763

◆ **How did the competitive European state system affect the conduct of war?**

◆ **What were the outcomes of the two world wars for the states that fought in them?**

In the middle of the eighteenth century, all the major states of Europe were drawn into two great wars.

George I (r. 1714–1727) Elector of Hanover who became king of Great Britain.

asiento Monopoly on the importation of African slaves into Spanish America granted to English merchants by Spain in 1713.

pretender Claimant to a throne.

Sir Robert Walpole (1676–1745) Leader of the Whigs and the most important minister in England from 1721 to 1742.

Table 16.1 **The Eighteenth-Century World Wars and the Diplomatic Revolution**

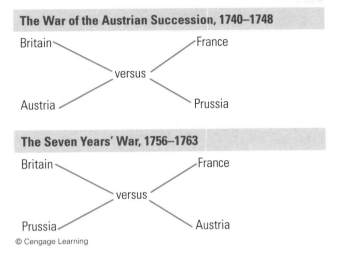

© Cengage Learning

Warfare, a permanent feature of relations between states in early modern Europe, often ended in stalemate, but the midcentury wars fundamentally altered European power relations. Because they were also fought in the overseas empires of Britain, France, and Spain, they had long-lasting consequences for peoples in the Western Hemisphere and Asia.

The Wars

In 1740, Frederick II of Prussia attacked Maria Theresa of Austria, beginning the War of the Austrian Succession. The rulers of Bavaria and Saxony challenged Maria Theresa's right to rule on the grounds that they were more legitimate heirs to Charles VI than she. Frederick, however, accepted the legitimacy of her succession. What he wanted was Silesia, the richest of Austria's territories. Taking advantage of challenges to Maria Theresa's right of succession, he claimed that Silesia rightfully belonged to Prussia and then seized the province.

Britain had been at war with Spain since 1739 over the trading rights conceded to it at the end of the War of the Spanish Succession. In 1740, Britain joined Austria to fight Prussia, renewing the British-Austrian alliance that had been forged in the wars against Louis XIV. The British also attacked the French in North America and India. France, in turn, stood by its traditional ally, Prussia, in order to check Austrian power. In 1748, at war's end, Prussia emerged victorious, keeping Silesia. The war between Britain and France ended indecisively.

The Seven Years' War War broke out again in 1756 between Austria and Prussia over Silesia, this time with Russia allied with Austria against Prussia. Since 1754, France and Britain had again been at war in

North America along the western frontier of the British colonies there. In 1756, they continued the fight in Europe and India during the **Seven Years' War**. Because Austria had recently concluded an alliance with France, Britain also switched sides and joined with Prussia against the two in the **diplomatic revolution**. The war ended in 1763. The complicated alliances in these two wars are summarized in Table 16.1.

Eighteenth-Century Warfare

The complex, ever-shifting alliances and counteralliances that characterized the world wars of the mid-eighteenth century were typical of the culture of war in early modern Europe. War was accepted as an inevitable and ongoing feature of the relations between European states. Rulers did little to counteract this idea; the old ideal of the king as head of the warrior band was too deeply embedded in European tradition.

The growth of large professional armies in the hundred years between 1650 and 1750 reinforced the idea of the inevitability of ongoing warfare.

The Professional Standing Army The professional standing army, pioneered by Louis XIV, became a standard feature in eighteenth-century states. The one exception was Britain, which preferred to keep its army small while offering financial aid to its continental allies' forces. Armies were now better provisioned and disciplined than they had been during the period of religious warfare and were, therefore, less of a danger to the civilian population. Although troops were sometimes quartered in civilians' homes and taxes were imposed for the armies' upkeep, the fear of military pillaging lessened.

The Science of Warfare A science of warfare also emerged, taking several forms. One was an interest in military engineering. In France, Sébastien le Prestre de Vauban improved the architecture of fortresses and supervised their construction along France's northern and eastern frontiers. The idea that impregnable fortresses could protect France from its enemies was to shape French military planning into the twentieth century. Military scientists also produced new drill manuals for soldiers, specifying a series of increasingly complicated battlefield maneuvers, including the Prussian "goose step," which kept soldiers in a straight line.

Not surprisingly, Frederick William I was a pioneer in this field, earning him the nickname "the royal drill sergeant." Soon, other armies were training their troops in similar ways. Army officers, almost always drawn from the nobility, received instruction in

Seven Years' War (1756–1763) World war fought in Europe, North America, and India.

diplomatic revolution Shift in alliances between European states that preceded the Seven Years' War.

Bildarchiv Preussischer Kulturbesitz/Art Resource, NY

In this engraving from a Prussian army manual of 1726 a drill master supervises the marching and field maneuvers for which the Prussian army was famous. Soldiers who fail to follow his commands will have to mount the donkey punishment device shown on the left. What artistic devices does the engraver employ to give the viewer a sense of the precision and orderliness of the troops at drill?

drill and battlefield tactics in new military academies and then applied them to the common soldiers under their command.

The Balance of Power Eighteenth-century statesmen used warfare to enforce the doctrine of the balance of power, based on the assumption that Europe's international system functioned best when power was evenly distributed among states, thereby preventing any one of them from achieving dominance over the others. Thus, the coalitions against Louis XIV were explained as restoring the balance that the Sun King's aggressive military activity had threatened.

Of course, agreement on the balance rested on the agreement of all the interested players. And that was where the problems began. Because one player's "balance" was often another's "domination," European states were thrown into a never-ending defensive and offensive scramble. Religious division played a smaller role in the wars of midcentury than it had a

century earlier. Now issues of territory, power, and prestige were central.

Winners and Losers

When war ended in 1763, there were clear winners and losers. In central Europe, Frederick II was a winner; Silesia was never returned to Austria. But the wars put huge strains on Prussia's finances and military, and at times it looked as if the kingdom would be defeated. In 1762, Frederick was saved when the pro-German emperor Peter III broke Russia's alliance with Austria and signed a peace with Prussia. This was the most consequential act of his short reign.

After 1763, Prussia rested. "Old Fritz," as his subjects called the king, lost his taste for wars of conquest. Now he preferred more peaceful means for gaining territory, such as joining with Austria and Russia in 1772 to partition Poland and finally link Prussia with Brandenburg.

Private Collection, Hamburg/akg-images

In this painting by R. Warthmülle, Frederick II of Prussia inspects a potato field. Potatoes grew well in the sandy soils of Frederick's lands, and he promoted the cultivation of this New World vegetable for its high nutritional value and abundant yield. Well-fed Prussians, he knew, would live to pay taxes and serve in the army. Compare this portrait of Frederick to the one of Louis XIV at the beginning of this chapter. Both were absolute monarchs. What are the similarities and differences in the depictions? What accounts for them?

Reform in Austria: The Army Austria was a loser. Before 1740, the Habsburgs had not followed Prussia and Russia in reforming state finances, strengthening the central administration, and updating the army. The shock of Silesia's loss galvanized Maria Theresa into a frenzy of state-building. She began with the army, founding a military academy, introducing advanced drill and maneuvering techniques, and expanding the government's ability to house and supply its troops. To pay for reform, she overhauled the state's tax structure.

Tax Reform Beginning in 1748, she coaxed the diets of Bohemia and Austria to grant taxes for ten years. In effect, this action made state taxation permanent, and the power of the magnates in the diets to control state finances waned, just as it had in Prussia under the Great Elector.

Administrative Reform To increase government efficiency, she founded a school to train state administrators. In 1761, she decreed that her state council, staffed by experts, could make policy decisions that were binding on her and the state administration. She, therefore, repudiated the king-centered decision making that Louis XIV and Frederick William I of Prussia had developed.

Austria in the Seven Years' War In 1756, when the Seven Years' War began, Maria Theresa's reforms were put to the test and failed. With Silesia still in Frederick's hands at war's end, Austria initiated more reforms, primarily to increase revenue to pay for a better army. This time, however, Maria Theresa tackled the problem by focusing on the economic improvement of the mass of her subjects, the serfs.

Helping the Serfs Like Leopold I, she tried to reduce serfs' uncompensated work for their landlords, decreeing that the traditional minimum of three days a week would now be the maximum. Reform of serfs' lives pitted Maria Theresa against the interests of the landlord class, but she made headway, especially in Austria and Bohemia, when serfs took matters into their own hands by going on rent strikes and fomenting local rebellions against landlord demands.

Reforming the Catholic Church Maria Theresa also imposed new taxes on the Catholic Church. Although she was a pious Roman Catholic who hated heresy, she believed that the church should assume a greater part of the expenses needed to defend the state against competitors. The clergy were taxed without the pope's permission, and the church was forbidden to acquire new land that would be tax-free.

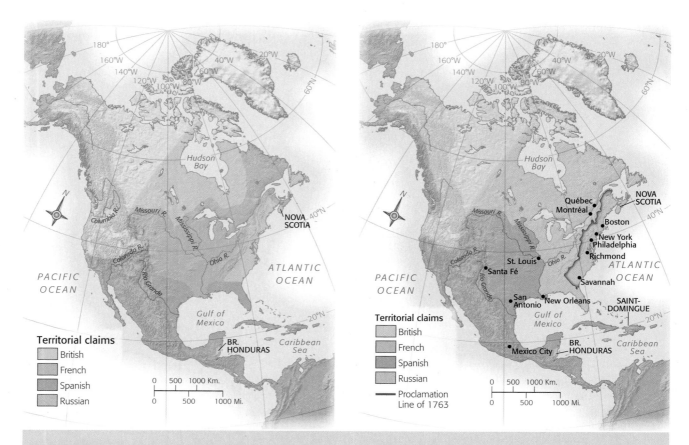

Map 16.4 **European Claims in North America Before and After the Seven Years' War** In losing the Seven Years' War, France lost its continental North American empire. New France went to Britain, and Louisiana went to Spain. France retained only Newfoundland and its island colonies in the Caribbean. © *Cengage Learning*

1. A comparison of these two maps shows very significant territorial gains and losses for Britain, France, and Spain as a result of the world wars of the mid-eighteenth century.
2. Consult a map of North and Central America in 2000. How are North and Central America politically configured today? Did all three European states lose territory after 1756? Which lost the most, which the least?

Partitioning Poland Defense of the Habsburg lands against enemies went hand in hand with attacks on weaker states, as the Polish partition of 1772 shows. Maria Theresa had moral scruples about the partition, but fear of continuing vulnerability in the competitive international system overcame her qualms. Frederick II of Prussia remarked unkindly, "The more she weeps, the more she takes."

Joseph II Maria Theresa died in 1780 and was succeeded by her son, **Joseph II,** who was also determined to strengthen Austria against Prussia. But as his foreign policy never resulted in clear victories, he pushed domestic reforms in a more radical direction. In the 1780s he abolished serfdom. Then, in 1789, using new property tax rolls, he abolished the rents and uncompensated work obligations peasants owed their landlords, replacing them with a single cash payment. He also imposed state taxes on the ex-serfs.

Traditional procedures had denied the state direct jurisdiction over peasants; the state had to work through the noble landlord class. But Joseph's reforms asserted direct state control. Peasants were to keep 70 percent of their income, the rest going in payments to the landlord and the state. Predictably, landlords resisted his radical restructuring of political and social relations, but peasants rose up in support of the reforms. The result was widespread rebellion when

Joseph II (r. 1780–1790) Holy Roman emperor and head of the Austrian Habsburg lands who tried to strengthen his realm through radical reform of its social structure.

Joseph died in 1790. His brother, who succeeded him as Leopold II, restored order by making concessions to the landlords. He reinstituted serfdom and landlords' control of peasants. Serfdom was not permanently abolished until 1848.

Austria's defeat in war led to radical social reforms intended to increase peasant prosperity, which in turn would allow for higher taxes and more money for the army. Thus, the dynamics of Europe's fiercely competitive international system fundamentally shaped the course of Austrian state-building over the second half of the eighteenth century.

Britain a Winner; France a Loser Although Britain and France fought each other in Europe alongside their respective allies, their real contest was overseas in North America and India. In 1763, at the end of the Seven Years' War, Britain was the undisputed winner. British victories drove the French off the North American mainland. Britain also secured its predominant place in India. But the victory in North America created problems of its own that led directly to the American Revolution and indirectly to revolution in France.

 Checking In

By yourself or with a partner, explain the significance of each of the following selected key terms:

Seven Years' War   Joseph II
diplomatic revolution

CHAPTER
Review

Summary

◆ After 1648, Europe's rulers engaged in vigorous state-building. In France, Louis XIV pressed change from above based on the principle of royal absolutism, as did rulers in Prussia, Russia, and, eventually, Austria.

◆ In the British Isles, absolutism gave way to limited constitutional monarchy after the Glorious Revolution, but William III's wars against Louis XIV increased the effectiveness of the central government in Britain while strengthening Parliament's role in policy making and administration.

◆ In all cases, the frequent warfare fostered by the competitive European state system was the prime incentive for strengthening the state.

◆ Successful state-building involved establishing good working relations between rulers and elite groups.

◆ In France and Prussia, nobles' political independence was curbed while their social preeminence was confirmed with honors and opportunities for state service.

◆ In England, after the failure of royal absolutism in 1689, the monarch had to cooperate with the landowning classes who controlled Parliament as well as local government.

◆ In Russia, rulers after Peter the Great wooed the landlord class by canceling compulsory state service but confirming landlords' rights over the serfs on their estates.

◆ Failure to establish working relations with the elite could lead to rebellion, as it did in Austria when Joseph II antagonized the nobility with his attacks on serfdom.

◆ Joseph's abolition of serfdom was motivated in part by a desire to use state power to improve the lives of ordinary people, and the serfs responded by cooperating in the updating of property rolls and rising in support of reform when nobles resisted change.

◆ In France, Louis XIV's reforms also had the same effect; control of the army eased fears of violence and looting, and efficient and fair royal courts encouraged confidence.

◆ Louis XV's reforms of police forces and poor relief offered new services to his subjects.

◆ But when ordinary people's needs were overlooked by rulers, revolt could follow, as Pugachev's rebellion in Russia shows.

◆ After 1648, religious commitments continued to shape identity and sometimes led to conflicts.

◆ Although Protestants throughout Europe denounced Louis XIV's revocation of the Edict of Nantes, the French Catholic population supported it.

◆ In England and Scotland, attacks on Catholics had widespread popular support.

◆ The Old Believers in Russia refused any cooperation with the state-supported Russian Orthodox Church.

◆ In France, Huguenots who refused conversion to Catholicism were also brutally dealt with.

◆ In general, however, the trend after 1648 was toward limited toleration of religious dissenters.

◆ In addition, forms of collective identity shifted from religion toward the national community.

◆ Wars between Britain and France produced a surge of patriotism in each country.

◆ While religious difference contributed to the stereotyping of the enemy, more state-centered issues, such as control of colonies or prosperity in trade, also whipped up patriotic fervor.

Chronology

1640	Frederick William becomes elector of Brandenburg
1657	Leopold I becomes Holy Roman emperor
1660	Charles II is restored as king of England, Ireland, and Scotland
1661	Louis XIV becomes his own prime minister
1672–1679	Dutch War between Louis XIV and the Dutch Republic
1682	Peter I the Great becomes tsar
1685	Louis XIV revokes Edict of Nantes
1688–1689	Glorious Revolution dethrones James II
1700–1721	Great Northern War between Russia and Sweden
1701–1713	War of the Spanish Succession between Louis XIV and most of Europe
1702	Anne becomes queen of England, Ireland, and Scotland
1707	England and Scotland unite to form the kingdom of Great Britain
1711	Charles VI becomes Holy Roman emperor
1713	Pope condemns the Jansenists
1713	Spain grants Britain the *asiento*
1714	George I of Hanover becomes king of Great Britain
1715	Louis XV becomes king of France
1727	George II becomes king of Great Britain
1740–1748	War of the Austrian Succession ends in a draw
1756–1763	Seven Years' War leads to British and Prussian victories
1762	Catherine II the Great becomes empress of Russia
1772	First partition of Poland
1780	Joseph II becomes ruler of the Habsburg lands
1780s	Joseph II abolishes serfdom in the Habsburg lands
1790s	Leopold II reestablishes serfdom in the Habsburg lands

© Cengage Learning

Test Yourself

To gauge your mastery of the material in this chapter, answer the questions below. More than one answer may be correct.

Absolutism in France, 1648–1740

1. Ceremony and good manners at Louis XIV's court were designed to:
   a. Show that Louis XIV was the only legitimate political player in the kingdom.
   b. Curb the violence of great nobles.
   c. Shame middle-class people.
   d. Enhance the king's *gloire*.
   e. All of the above.

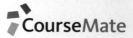 **CourseMate** Visit the CourseMate website at **www.cengagebrain.com** for additional study tools and review materials for this chapter.

2. The most devastating of Louis XIV's wars was:

    a. The Dutch War
    b. The War of the League of Augsburg
    c. The War of the Spanish Succession
    d. The War of the Austrian Succession
    e. The War of the Polish Succession

3. When the War of the Spanish Succession ended:

    a. The French candidate for the Spanish throne was confirmed as king.
    b. The Austrian claimant to the throne was confirmed as king.
    c. A treaty article stated that the kingdoms of France and Spain could never be united.
    d. A treaty article stated that the Austrian lands and Spain could never be reunited into a single Habsburg state.
    e. The French and the Austrians signed an alliance.

4. To unify the French state, Louis XIV:

    a. Used royal intendants to enforce policy and collection information for the government.
    b. Increased the efficiency of royal courts of law.
    c. Imposed a new direct royal tax, the capitation.
    d. Curbed the independence of the parlements.
    e. Reimposed serfdom in eastern France.

Now that you have reviewed and tested yourself on this part of the chapter, take time to pull together all the important information by answering the following questions:

◆ What steps did Louis XIV take to unify the French state and to eliminate the possibility of rebellion and disorder in the kingdom?

◆ What motivated Louis XIV to deny religious toleration to the Huguenots, and what were the reactions to his policy at home and abroad?

The Austrian Habsburgs, 1648–1740

5. The Habsburg reconquest of Hungary:

    a. Followed the lifting of the Turkish siege of Vienna.
    b. Led to the settlement of Bohemians, Serbs, and Germans in Hungarian lands.
    c. Provoked a rebellion by Francis II Rákóczi.
    d. All of the above.
    e. None of the above.

6. Leopold I:

    a. Admired and trusted his Hungarian magnates.
    b. Distrusted his Hungarian magnates.
    c. Presided over a strongly unified state.
    d. Preferred Germans to Hungarians.
    e. Was only a lukewarm Catholic.

7. Charles VI:

    a. Inherited both the Austrian and Spanish Habsburg lands on the death of his brother.
    b. Did all he could to secure his daughter's inheritance of the Austrian Habsburg lands.
    c. Successfully prevented the War of the Austrian Succession.
    d. All of the above.
    e. None of the above.

Now that you have reviewed and tested yourself on this part of the chapter, take time to pull together all the important information by answering the following questions:

◆ How did Leopold I's involvement in the wars against Louis XIV affect his reconquest of Hungary? What were the specific stages in the reconquest?

◆ What was Leopold I's attitude toward the local Hungarian population, and what were his relations with them?

The Rise of Prussia, 1648–1740

8. The Great Elector Frederick William:

    a. Gained the independence of the Duchy of Prussia from Poland.
    b. Greatly increased the size of his army.
    c. Created a unified tax system for both towns and the countryside.
    d. Had little income from his royal domain.
    e. All of the above.

9. King Frederick William I:

   a. Hated all drunkenness and crude behavior.
   b. Created the General Directory to increase government centralization and efficiency.
   c. Increased the size of his army to 80,000 men.
   d. Increased the size of his army to 180,000 men.
   e. Created a tradition of loyal state service by the Prussian nobility.

10. The Prussian army:

   a. Was financed without recourse to borrowing.
   b. Was financed only through heavy state borrowing.
   c. Was recruited by means of a state imposed draft.
   d. Was staffed largely by volunteers.
   e. Housed its troops in specially built cities.

11. Frederick II:

   a. Attacked Maria Theresa of Austria and started the War of the Austrian Succession.
   b. Was attacked by Maria Theresa of Austria who started the War of the Austrian Succession.
   c. Was more refined than his father.
   d. Was less refined than his father.
   e. Played the tuba.

Now that you have reviewed and tested yourself on this part of the chapter, take time to pull together all the important information by answering the following questions:

◆ How did the Great Elector use war and diplomacy to gain full control over the Duchy of Prussia?

◆ What techniques did the Great Elector and King Frederick William I use to strengthen the central state and make its running more efficient?

Russia and Europe, 1682–1796

12. Peter the Great:

   a. Was a shipbuilder in the Dutch Republic.
   b. Built St. Petersburg to secure access to the Baltic Sea.
   c. Reformed the army and the navy.
   d. Required the landlord class to serve for life in either the military or civil administration.
   e. Resurrected the office of Patriarch in the Russian Orthodox Church.

13. Catherine the Great:

   a. Was German by birth.
   b. Continued Peter III's policy of seizing church lands.
   c. Reversed Peter III's policy of seizing church lands.
   d. Reimposed compulsory state service on the landlord class.
   e. Presided over an empire in which ethnic Russians made up only 50 percent of the population.

14. The Pugachev rebellion:

   a. Involved thousands of people.
   b. Was led by a relative of Peter III.
   c. Gave voice to serfs' demands to be freed from their compulsory service to landlords.
   d. Gave voice to demands that the landlord class be freed from compulsory state service.
   e. Led to administrative centralization and landlord control of local government.

Now that you have reviewed and tested yourself on this part of the chapter, take time to pull together all the important information by answering the following questions:

◆ Which reforms of Peter the Great were kept by his successors, and which were modified or eliminated?

◆ How was Russian society organized at the beginning of Peter the Great's reign, and how did it change under his successors?

The English Constitutional Monarchy, 1660–1740

15. Charles II:

   a. Had the right to tax without Parliament's approval.
   b. Had to recognize Parliament's right to raise taxes.
   c. Wanted a policy of religious toleration.
   d. Had to accept Parliament's right to impeach his ministers.
   e. Refused to convert to Catholicism on his death bed.

16. James II:

   a. Accepted a Catholic rite of coronation before accepting the Anglican one.
   b. At first was acceptable to both Tories and Whigs because his heirs were Protestant.
   c. Resurrected Charles I's church courts.
   d. Unexpectedly had a male heir who was baptized a Catholic.
   e. Used his right of suspending laws passed by Parliament to favor non-Anglicans.

17. The Bill of Rights:

   a. Upheld the contractual theory of government.
   b. Upheld the theory that monarchs ruled by hereditary right.
   c. Overturned James II's practice of suspending laws passed by Parliament.
   d. Guaranteed freedom from cruel and unusual punishments.
   e. Allowed the king to raise an army on his own.

18. Sir Robert Walpole:

   a. Chose to lead the British government from the House of Commons rather than the House of Lords.
   b. Chose to lead the British government from the House of Lords rather than the House of Commons.
   c. Tried to outlaw the Tories.
   d. Accepted moderate Tories into his political coalitions.
   e. Wanted to calm the older political passions by insisting on good manners in politics.

Now that you have reviewed and tested yourself on this part of the chapter, take time to pull together all the important information by answering the following questions:

◆ Why was James II driven from the throne?

◆ What were the features of the "mixed monarchy" that emerged out of the Glorious Revolution?

Two World Wars, 1740–1763

19. Maria-Theresa's campaign of state-building included:

   a. Concentrating all policy decisions in her own hands.
   b. Making state taxation permanent.
   c. Expanding the government's ability to house and supply the army.
   d. Freeing the serfs.
   e. Reforms that carried Austria to victory in the Seven Years' War.

20. At the end of the mid-eighteenth century world wars:

   a. Austria regained Silesia.
   b. Austria lost Silesia.
   c. The British took Canada.
   d. The French took India.
   e. The British took India.

Now that you have reviewed and tested yourself on this part of the chapter, take time to pull together all the important information by answering the following questions:

◆ What steps did Maria Theresa and Joseph II take to reform Austrian society and the state, and what were the results of these efforts?

◆ What was the doctrine of the balance of power, and how did it influence the diplomatic revolution of 1756?

CHAPTER 17

The Scientific Revolution and the Enlightenment, 1550–1790

Chapter Outline

1540	1560	1580	1600	1620	1640	1660

1543
Copernicus, *On the Revolution of the Heavenly Bodies*

1637
Descartes, *The Discourse on Method*

This elaborate microscope belonged to Robert Hooke, a seventeenth-century Englishman who published a work on microscopic organisms in 1665. Hooke used the term "cell" to describe the building blocks of the living things he saw. (© Science & Society Picture Library)

After reading this chapter, you should be able to answer the following questions:

What were the basic differences between traditional Christianity and the New Science on views of God, the natural world, and the human world?

How did the Enlightenment draw on and expand the method and findings of the scientific revolution?

How did the principle of autonomous human reason shape the institutions and programs of the Enlightenment?

How did Enlightenment debates reshape Europeans' sense of their identity and the identity of non-European peoples?

IN EUROPE DURING the seventeenth and eighteenth centuries a general shift in scientific theory and method, which had begun in the sixteenth century, gained wider and wider ground. This scientific revolution, which first occurred in astronomy, physics, and anatomy, fundamentally altered people's view of the universe and led to the development of a scientific method that relied more on human reason to arrive at truth and less on the authority of ancient authors and sacred scripture. Now a new intellectual figure, the scientific expert, began to challenge the views of traditional theologians and those who believed that the best human knowledge was found in the works of ancient Greeks and Romans.

The New Science also inspired attempts to apply scientific methods to other fields of inquiry in an intellectual movement known as the Enlightenment. Relying on the scientific method's use of human reason to arrive at truth, the Enlightenment created the modern social sciences. Traditional Christianity also came under scrutiny; many supporters of the Enlightenment

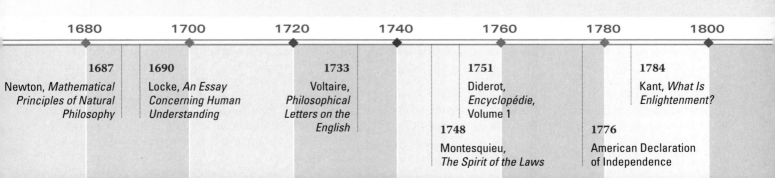

1680	1700	1720	1740	1760	1780	1800

1687
Newton, *Mathematical Principles of Natural Philosophy*

1690
Locke, *An Essay Concerning Human Understanding*

1733
Voltaire, *Philosophical Letters on the English*

1751
Diderot, *Encyclopédie*, Volume 1

1748
Montesquieu, *The Spirit of the Laws*

1784
Kant, *What Is Enlightenment?*

1776
American Declaration of Independence

thought religion should be based on observation of the natural world and the exercise of human reason. Some abandoned traditional Christianity altogether. As a result, the Christian worldview that had dominated European thought for more than a thousand years now competed with non-Christian and even nonreligious alternatives.

The principles of both the New Science and the Enlightenment were spread through new communication networks. Scientific societies, polite salon gatherings, coffeehouses, Masonic lodges, and debating clubs, for all their differences, created environments for discussion of the ideas and methods of both movements. Discussion also filled the pages of a growing number of books, newspapers, and pamphlets, as writers and publishers produced a wide variety of reading material for increasing numbers of literate Europeans.

As more and more people engaged in public discussion of current affairs, a new intellectual and political force arose—public opinion—that could determine an author's success or failure and even sway the policies of kings.

Debate was a central feature of both the scientific revolution and the Enlightenment. Women participated in these debates, and soon their increasing presence in European intellectual life led to a debate over issues of gender equality and the relations between men and women. Growth in commerce and the establishment of overseas colonies around the world also provoked debate about Europe's place in the larger world. By the end of the century, debate also centered on a central feature of commerce and colonization—the institution of slavery. In these debates, as in religion, Christian ideas had to compete with approaches that paid more attention to nature, climate, and biology than to traditional theology.

A Revolution in Astronomy

◆ **What were the central features of the new scientific method?**

◆ **What factors explain the rise of the New Science?**

The religious crises that shook Europe in the sixteenth and seventeenth centuries were accompanied by an intellectual crisis. Beginning as a new theory of the universe that placed the sun, not the earth, at its center, it grew into a questioning of the traditional sources of authority guiding European thought about the natural world—ancient authors, and Christian scripture. Gradually, as the new view of the universe gained acceptance, new sources of authority based on close observation of natural phenomena and the use of independent human reasoning were embraced. These changes are usually described as the scientific revolution.

Ancient and Medieval Astronomy

Following the translation of classical works in the twelfth century, Europeans' views of the universe had been shaped by two ancient Greek authorities: the philosopher Aristotle and the astronomer Ptolemy. For centuries, medieval universities had synthesized their teaching with Christian theology to describe how the universe worked.

The Earth as Center of the Universe In this system, the earth was at the center, created by God to be fixed and unmoving. But in terms of worth, earth was the lowest element in the cosmic scheme. It was the place of decay; as one philosopher put it, our world was "the worst, the lowest, most lifeless part of the universe, the bottom story of the house." It was only in this region, which stretched upward to the moon, that change took place. Here night turned to day; plants sprouted, bloomed,

Map 17.1 **Europe During the Scientific Revolution and the Enlightenment** This map shows that most scientific and Enlightenment centers were in the cities of western and central Europe. © *Cengage Learning*

1. What factors explain this geographical spread?
2. Why do you think intellectual life was focused in cities?

and died; and human beings moved from cradle to grave.

The innate nature of objects determined some of the movement in this region. Thus acorns grew into oaks and kittens into cats because both strove to realize their potential and reach their goal as mature organisms. The same striving toward their goals also characterized nonliving things; fire leapt upward because its proper place was in the heights, while a rock thrown in the air fell because its place was on

the earth. Essentially, objects were urged along by their inner natures to come to rest in their rightful place.

Rest was the natural state of being for objects; it was only motion that had to be explained. In the case of human beings, God's decrees determined the movement of their lives; they hurtled toward death and decay because of their sinful rebellion against God until Christ redeemed them and they found their place of rest in Heaven.

The Heavens Above the moon, a radically different part of the universe reigned. In these regions there was no change or decay. The sun and the planets, made of a uniquely pure and perfect substance, moved endlessly in circles (the noblest form of motion, as Plato had taught). Above them were the fixed stars, which also moved in a circle, propelled by the angels. As all these bodies moved, they created a wondrous music, the harmony of the spheres. Beyond the stars the universe ended, and the mysterious realm of God's Heaven began.

A Plausible Picture of the Universe? This picture of the natural world seemed to work because it was confirmed in multiple ways. First, it corresponded with common sense (sun, moon, and planets *did* move across the sky). Common sense was in turn reinforced by prediction. Ptolemy had shown that it was possible to calculate the trajectories of the planets in advance, and astronomers in the centuries after him had confirmed and refined his calculations. Finally, this view corresponded with what were taken as the revealed truths of Christian scripture.

A New View of the Universe

In the sixteenth century, a new view of the universe challenged the traditional one. As it spread, an intellectual crisis developed, rivaling the crises in faith and certainty created by the Protestant Reformation, the Wars of Religion, and the discovery of the New World—an entire hemisphere with previously unknown plants, animals, and human beings.

Nicholas Copernicus (1473–1543) Polish astronomer who posited a sun-centered universe in which earth and the other planets move around the sun.

Tycho Brahe (1546–1601) Danish astronomer who partly confirmed Copernicus's theory of a sun-centered universe.

Johannes Kepler (1571–1630) German student of Brahe who argued that the planets moved in elliptical orbits around the sun.

Galileo Galilei (1564–1642) Italian astronomer who first used the telescope to view the heavens and argued in favor of the Copernican system.

The Sun-Centered Universe The challenge began with a Polish clergyman in East Prussia, **Nicholas Copernicus**. Seeking to improve Ptolemy's predictions of planetary movement by making them simpler, Copernicus started with the assumption that earth and the planets moved about the sun. His *On the Revolutions of the Heavenly Bodies*, published in 1543, was quickly denounced by both Protestants and Catholics. Nevertheless, Copernicus caught the attention of some astronomers, who began building on his work.

Tycho Brahe and Johannes Kepler One of the first was a Dane, **Tycho Brahe**, who

In an engraving from Johannes Hevelius's *Selenographia* (1647), an astronomer, perhaps Hevelius himself, looks at the heavens through a telescope. After Galileo's pioneering efforts, observatories sprang up all over Europe. Hevelius's observatory, on the roof of his house in Danzig, was one of the best.

World History Archive/Alamy

spent years producing the best logs of planetary movement yet compiled. He also described in detail a new star that appeared in 1572 and, thereby, disturbed the traditional view that the universe above the moon was changeless. But Brahe held the traditional view that the earth was the unmoving center of the universe; for him, the planets moved around the sun, but the sun moved around the earth.

Brahe's work was continued by his pupil, **Johannes Kepler**, who used Brahe's calculations to argue that the planets moved in elliptical, not circular, orbits around the sun and that the speed of their movement varied. Both points also challenged older ideas about the unchanging nature of the upper universe.

Galileo Galilei Galileo Galilei, a professor of mathematics from Florence, continued the work of Copernicus, Brahe, and Kepler. While these men had viewed the heavens with the naked eye, Galileo used the newly invented telescope. He also confirmed Copernicus's theory that the planets and the sun rotated on their own axes and posited that earth did the same. These phenomena further undermined traditional ideas. Galileo also conducted carefully controlled experiments on earthly bodies, rolling metal balls down slopes of varying degrees. He argued that material

The Trial and Condemnation of Galileo

On June 22, 1633, Galileo Galilei, aged seventy, stood before the judges of the Roman Inquisition to hear the sentence passed on him. Galileo was found "vehemently suspect of heresy" for advocating a sun-centered theory of the universe and sentenced to house arrest for life. The judges then banned the publication of all his past works and ordered him to recant his views.

The trial of 1633 brought to a head Galileo's role in the long dispute between the defenders of the Aristotelian understanding of the universe and the supporters of Copernicus, which had been raging for more than twenty years. In 1609, when Galileo began to view the heavens through the newly invented telescope, he saw astonishing things that would turn traditional understandings of the universe upside down—mountains on the moon and moving spots on the sun. How could these phenomena be reconciled with the traditional view that the heavens were free of imperfections and unchanging? Galileo concluded that they could not, and this decision led to the train of events resulting in his condemnation in 1633. But there were many twists and turns along the way.

In 1610, Galileo published his telescopic findings in *The Starry Messenger.* His gifts as a writer made his works widely popular but also stirred up angry opponents among the traditionalists. Friendly readers carried out their own observations and confirmed what Galileo reported while enemies continued to deny the accuracy of his reports and some, it seems, simply refused to use the telescope. As the controversy widened, Galileo's sympathy with the Copernican view became more and more apparent, and in 1614 he was denounced to the Roman Inquisition. Brushing aside the advice of friends in Florence, he decided to go to Rome to defend himself in person.

In Rome, Galileo faced the power and authority of the Catholic Church in the person of Cardinal Robert Bellarmine. Bellarmine, a Jesuit, was one of the most learned theologians of his generation, and he took the challenge of Copernicanism seriously. In the end, he arrived at a carefully crafted position on the matter. Copernicanism, he said, was best taught as a theory about the universe that was not based in fact. If, however, it could be demonstrated *conclusively* through observation that it was factual, it could be embraced with the proviso that contrary statements in Scripture were true but simply not properly understood by human beings.

In 1616, the conflict became even more intense when the Roman Inquisition condemned Copernicanism outright. Bellarmine was told to convey this judgment to Galileo and to order him to stop teaching Copernicanism. Shortly thereafter, books supporting the sun-centered view were placed in the Index.

In 1623, the climate suddenly seemed better for Galileo when a friend and fellow Florentine became pope as Urban VII. When Urban encouraged Galileo to take up the two positions and to make a careful presentation of the pros and cons of each, it seemed possible to reopen the debate. Urban also stipulated that his own traditional views should be presented as well. The result was the *Dialogue Concerning the Two Chief World Systems*, published in 1632. Galileo employed all his wit and skill as a writer in this work, which brought together an Aristotelian, a Copernican, and a neutral commentator. In the end, the Copernican and the neutral commentator demolished the views of the Aristotelian, named Simplicio ("simpleton" in Italian). When readers finished the book, many realized that Simplicio the Simpleton was the one who proposed the pope's views. Urban was furious and Galileo taken aback because he had modeled Simplicio not on the pope but on well-known Aristotelians. The result was the trial, condemnation, and house arrest of 1633.

Beginning in the mid-eighteenth century, the Catholic Church began a slow retreat from its condemnation of Copernicanism and Galileo when it dropped the general prohibition of any book defending Copernicus. Galileo's *Dialogue;* however, along with Copernicus's work, were not formally dropped from the Index until 1835. In 2000, Pope John Paul II issued a formal apology for the trial and condemnation of Galileo.

bodies were naturally in motion, thereby questioning the older idea that they moved only when they were displaced from their homes and rested once they arrived there.

Sir Isaac Newton Galileo's work was built on by others interested in the New Science. The greatest of them was the Englishman **Sir Isaac Newton**. In his *Mathematical Principles of Natural Philosophy* (1687), Newton brought together the work of Copernicus, Brahe, Kepler, and Galileo to present a complete picture of the universe. Planets, rotating on their axes, traveled around the sun in elliptical orbit. Their orbits

Sir Isaac Newton (1642–1727) English mathematician and philosopher who established the modern science of physics.

Sir Isaac Newton was sixty years old when this portrait was painted by Sir Godfrey Kneller in 1702. He had published his *Mathematical Principles* some fifteen years earlier and was at the height of his fame. (National Portrait Gallery, London/The Bridgeman Art Library)

and the variations in their speed were controlled by gravity, a force of mutual attraction that kept the planets from flying off into space. Gravity also explained the behavior of bodies on earth, as described by Galileo. Beyond the solar system, the universe stretched out infinitely. Newton presented his picture mathematically. Although only a handful of his contemporaries understood his advanced equations, his ability to knit the work of his predecessors into an all-encompassing description of the universe proved compelling and established the modern science of physics.

Models of Scientific Knowledge

Just as important as the new view of the universe were the methods developed for proposing it. Taken together, they radically altered traditional European views of how human beings know anything.

Bacon and the Inductive Method Sir Francis Bacon, lord chancellor of England under James I, was an early advocate of an approach to knowledge grounded in careful observation and experimentation. For him, the source of authority for knowledge about the natural world was found in that world itself, not in the writings of Greeks or Romans. He was, therefore, an early defender of a purely **inductive method** of reasoning, which based general statements on observation of phenomena as the only proper way to gain knowledge.

René Descartes Just as influential was a French mathematician and the inventor of analytic geometry, **René Descartes**. Descartes was deeply affected by the intellectual crisis the Protestant-Catholic split had created in western Christendom. The constant attacks of each side against the other had led to massive intellectual confusion. Some maintained that since no human opinion could ever be shown to be definitively true, one had to take a leap of faith and submit to the authority of the church and its teachings. Others embraced a thoroughgoing skepticism about the truth of any human argument. Descartes began by examining himself.

"I Think, Therefore I Am" Self-examination was something Christians had practiced for centuries, but Descartes struck off in a new direction. He decided that he would submit every statement he had heard about humans and their world to radical doubt. If there was any reason, no matter how small, to doubt it, he would treat it as worthless. Statement after statement was tossed aside until, finally, Descartes came upon something that, try as he would, he simply could not doubt: "I think." This undoubted truth became his principle of knowledge. From it he drew another equally firm conclusion: "Therefore I am." I exist as a thinker—that was the starting place for knowledge.

The Deductive Method and Autonomous Human Reason Descartes then went on to reconstruct the world, moving from previously established points to new ones that followed logically from them. This **deductive method**, modeled on geometry, lay behind his *Discourse on Method* (1637). In arriving at reliable knowledge, Descartes departed from Bacon. Instead of looking out at the natural world, he looked inside himself and found an authoritative source for all knowledge—the principle of autonomous, or independent, human reason.

Human reason had always played an important role in traditional Christian views about the sources for human knowledge; the medieval Scholastic movement had placed a premium on logically presented

Sir Francis Bacon (1561–1626) English defender of the New Science who endorsed the inductive method of inquiry.

inductive method Method starting with observation of phenomena and then making general statements about them based on the observations.

René Descartes (1596–1650) French philosopher who argued for the principle of autonomous human reason as the basis for human knowledge.

deductive method The process of drawing logically coherent conclusions from self-evident first principles.

argument. But in the older view, reason was also supplemented by divine revelation, which corrected or completed what human beings could think on their own. For Descartes, human reason stood alone as a reliable source for human knowledge.

The Newtonian Synthesis: The Scientific Method

Newton combined Bacon's and Descartes's methods to argue that any statement about the natural world had to pass two tests. First, it had to correspond to what was found by observation and experimentation. Second, it had to fit logically with all else that was known about the phenomenon being investigated. He thus combined inductive and deductive methods to arrive at knowledge about the world and thereby laid the foundations for the modern **scientific method**. Newton's method impressed people as much as his description of the universe. His mighty mind had swept heaven and earth, revealing for the first time how the universe worked. As the English poet **Alexander Pope** exclaimed:

> *Nature and Nature's laws lay hid in Night:*
> *God said, Let Newton be! and all was light.*

(Excerpted from Alexander Pope's poetry (1688–1744).)

Why Change Occurred

Many factors contributed to the new view of the universe. One stemmed from Renaissance humanists' rediscovery of ancient authors, including Plato. In the medieval west, Aristotle had reigned supreme. With the recovery of other ancient works, it became clear that Aristotle's theories had been contested in their own times and could be challenged again by new approaches to nature.

The Role of Mathematicians and Craftsmen

Another factor concerned the people engaged in the study of nature. Traditionally, philosophers pursued natural studies in a university setting. Much of the new work, however, was done by mathematicians working outside the universities. Copernicus, Kepler, and Descartes worked on their own or sought support from princely patrons.

Mathematicians' prestige rose when they were called on to help with land reclamation and canal building in places like the Dutch Republic or land surveys for taxation purposes in states trying to raise more revenue. Applying mathematics to solve specific problems was also in tune with the humanist emphasis on useful knowledge.

Usefulness also lay at the heart of another tradition contributing to the New Science, that of craftsmen. As sailors ventured out into the Atlantic, the need for precise astrolabes and quadrants to measure their positions had enhanced the work of those who produced these instruments and improved them through experimentation. Thinkers such as

Galileo employed craft traditions of experimentation using metal balls, telescopes, and other devices to examine natural phenomena more precisely. They then wedded observation and experimentation to mathematics.

The Role of Alchemy

Another intellectual pursuit fostering experimentation was **alchemy**. Alchemists believed that nature contained hidden powers that influenced how the world worked and that these powers might be revealed through careful observation of and experimentation with chemical and other natural processes. Isaac Newton, for example, was an accomplished alchemist, and his experiments in a little shed outside his rooms at the University of Cambridge contributed to his endorsement of the inductive method in physics. In addition, his theory of gravity was influenced by the belief that hidden forces determined how the universe functioned.

Vesalius and the Role of Anatomy

Developments in anatomy also fostered increased attention to observation and experimentation. **Andreas Vesalius**, a Flemish professor at the University of Padua in Italy, broke with medieval tradition by conducting his own dissections of corpses during his lectures. Previously, anatomists had lectured from ancient authorities on what dissections would reveal but left the actual cutting to surgeons, who were considered inferior to professors.

Vesalius's dissections, which students loved, revealed that Galen, the greatest ancient medical authority, was incorrect when he stated that the interior wall of the heart separating the ventricles was perforated, allowing for the circulation of the blood. That the heart wall was solid now required a whole new theory of blood circulation. An English student at Padua, **William Harvey**, worked one out in 1628 after examining animals slaughtered for their meat. Harvey combined Vesalius's insistence on direct observation with the craft traditions of butchers to develop his theory and thereby laid the foundation for modern physiology.

The Old Science and the New

Defenders of the New Science argued that it stood in sharp opposition to the

---

scientific method Newton's combination of the inductive and deductive methods to establish a twofold method for scientific inquiry.

Alexander Pope (1688–1744) English poet and literary critic who championed Newtonian physics and the Enlightenment's emphasis on the study of human beings.

alchemy Discipline practiced in the Middle Ages that searched for the hidden relations between natural phenomena.

Andreas Vesalius (1514–1564) Flemish physician who dissected human corpses and corrected some ancient statements about human anatomy.

William Harvey (1578–1657) English physician who described the circulation of blood in the human body.

rigid, unalterable medieval version. In fact, however, the relationship was more complex. For example, both the old and new science insisted on the importance of a logical presentation of an argument. Medieval science had also raised issues like the nature of the terrestrial and celestial realms that preoccupied the New Scientists, and medieval terminology continued in use.

But as the **scientific revolution** progressed, the criteria for making arguments shifted. Scientists who relied more on mathematics, craft traditions, and careful experimentation were developing a new view of the universe as a place full of motion, with much still to be discovered, a view in stark contrast to the unchanging and unchangeable world of Aristotle, Ptolemy, or the Bible.

 Checking In

By yourself or with a partner, explain the significance of each of the following selected key terms:

Nicholas Copernicus	Sir Isaac Newton
Tycho Brahe	Sir Francis Bacon
Johannes Kepler	René Descartes
Galileo Galilei	William Harvey

The Impact of the New Science

◆ **Who participated in the scientific revolution and how did the participants characterize themselves?**

◆ **What was the impact of the New Science on theology and political theory?**

Those practicing the New Science were from many regions of Europe. Their findings were spread by means of a new institution, the scientific society, made up of well-to-do men who thought of themselves as a new type of educated person, the modern man of science. The societies developed procedures for presenting and verifying scientific experiments. They also provided guidelines for reproducing them and published new information for the interested public. As new views of the universe spread, along with the new scientific method and the principle of autonomous human reason, traditional European religious and political thought expanded in new ways.

scientific revolution Name given to the new views of the natural world and the new methods for obtaining them that began in the sixteenth century.

Royal Society One of the earliest scientific academies, founded in London in 1660.

Robert Boyle (1627–1691) Founder of the Royal Society who advanced understanding of air pressure and chemistry.

Scientific Networks

The first scientific societies developed in princely courts. In Prague, the emperor Rudolf II (r. 1576–1612) established one of the first. Rudolph was a moody, reclusive man who fought with his brother for control of the Habsburg empire, but he was also interested in artistic and scientific developments and joined with the king of Denmark to support Tycho Brahe's work. In Florence, Cosimo II not only patronized artists such as the French printmaker Jacques Callot but also supported Galileo and encouraged scientific discussion. In England, Bacon called for a research institute whose members would be royal employees collecting information to enhance state power. In fact, no such institute was created. Scientists' connections with the state were therefore looser than Bacon had hoped. Although Charles II of England and Louis XIV of France granted charters to the **Royal Society** of London and the French Royal Academy of Sciences, respectively, scientists generally worked free of direct royal control.

Membership Membership in scientific organizations was overwhelmingly male. That men interested in science had to have a formal education further limited membership to the economically well-off. Members met to discuss issues of method and to learn what experiments others in the organization had performed. Some societies followed the lead of the English Royal Society and published reports of scientific findings.

Demonstrating Physical Phenomena Demonstrations of observable physical phenomena played an important role in scientific meetings. The correctness and accuracy of observations could be confirmed when many members agreed on them. During meetings, orderly procedures and polite behavior were insisted on. In addition, gentlemanly codes of honor and honesty helped to guarantee that the experimenters could be taken at their word. In printed presentations of experiments, detailed descriptions of equipment, procedures, and results were given so that readers could feel that they, too, had been present when the experiment took place. Detailed description also made possible the reproduction of the experiment.

"Priests of Nature" Members of scientific societies believed they were a new class of people called to interpret the book of nature. **Robert Boyle**, a founder of the Royal Society of London who made important contributions to the study of air pressure and chemistry, called its members "priests of nature" because they revealed God's work through experimentation and observation. Boyle was a deeply religious man. He believed that men performing experiments must be modest and unassuming, in contrast to university debates, which had traditionally been conducted in public with lots of verbal fireworks. Personal ambition, prejudice, and passion had no place in proper scientific work. From these ideas emerged the modern concept of scientific objectivity.

Science and Religion

Newton's theory bound earth to the heavens, describing both as operating under laws that made motion as natural as rest. In his view, the universe seemed to function like a machine or a huge self-regulating clock. After being wound up, clocks ticked away in orderly fashion, following the laws governing their construction. The universe, he proposed, operated in the same way.

In addition, Descartes and others argued that everything in the universe was made up of tiny particles that moved mechanically by universal laws of attraction and repulsion. Rocks, plants, animals, and human beings were like the planets—matter in motion. So it now seemed that there was a man-machine as well as a universe machine. If all this was true, where did God fit in? For a few, the answer was clear: he didn't. For the great majority, however, there was definitely a place for God in the new order.

The Argument from Design Clocks required a clockmaker, and, by analogy, the universe required a universe maker. This widely held belief was reinforced by the **argument from design**. Newton's wonderfully regulated universe could not have come into being without a designer. The microscope, perfected by the Dutch lensmaker Anton van Leeuwenhoek, was also important in this regard because it revealed previously unknown worlds, small in size but intricate in detail, that also pointed to a divine designer.

Innate Ideas Descartes's view that all bodies, including human ones, were simply matter in motion struck many as **atheistic**. But Descartes, a Catholic, believed in the Christian God. He argued that humans were unique. Not only did they have bodies made of matter, which were governed by the laws of attraction and repulsion; they also had minds, which were nonmaterial.

God endowed human minds with the ability to reason, and Descartes reasoned his way to God's existence. For example, he argued that humans were finite beings who yet had a clear and distinct idea of God as an infinite being. Since the idea of an infinite being cannot be conceived by a finite one, it must be an **innate idea** given to humans by God himself. Arguments like these were meant to preserve the basic features of traditional Christian theology while relying solely on the principle of autonomous human reason for arriving at them.

A "Dwarf-God?" If the universe was like a huge clock, did God wind it up at the beginning and then allow it to run on its own? Some of Descartes's arguments seemed to imply this belief, while others made room for ongoing divine intervention. Newton also insisted on God's regular activity in keeping the universe running and denounced the idea of a "dwarf-god" who did nothing more than set the world machine in motion.

The Book of Nature For the New Scientists of the seventeenth century, the universe was not only a great machine, it was also the book of nature. Like the book of scripture, it could be consulted for knowledge of the Christian God. Protestants argued that the book of nature could be enlisted in the battle against Catholic error. A universe operating in a regular way under natural laws had no place for Catholics' superstitious beliefs in miracles performed by saints. The Catholic Galileo argued that knowledge of nature led to a proper interpretation of scripture. Biblical references to the sun's motion around the earth should not be taken literally; they were simply God's concession to "the shallow minds of the common people."

Blaise Pascal One mathematician and scientist, **Blaise Pascal**, took issue with the heavy reliance on observation and reason as the best guides for religious thought. Pascal was a devout Jansenist who worried that Descartes's emphasis on autonomous human reason and innate ideas improperly downplayed the traditional Christian emphasis on revelation as a source of religious knowledge. Pascal gave reason and observation their proper place in the construction of human knowledge: although humans were mere specks in an infinite universe, and frail as reeds tossed about in the wind, they were thinking reeds. But Pascal introduced another source of knowledge: "heart." Heart drew on intuition, allowing a deeper view into the human condition than either reason or observation.

"Heart has its reasons that Reason does not know," Pascal explained. For him, the human condition was characterized by both wretchedness and grandeur. Human wretchedness manifested itself in people's selfish, passion-driven, sin-filled lives as they hurtled toward the abyss of death. Grandeur manifested itself in the deep self-awareness of that wretchedness that "heart" opened up. Life as it is, is not life as God originally

argument from design Widely held belief in the seventeenth century that the complex and beautiful design of nature was proof of a divine designer's existence.

atheism Belief that there is no God.

innate ideas Ideas about God, the human mind, or anything else that seem to be a primary part of human mental equipment.

Blaise Pascal (1623–1662) Scientist and defender of traditional Christianity who stated that "heart" could lead one to the deepest religious truths.

meant it to be. Pascal died before he could present his ideas in a defense of traditional Christianity, but his notes have survived in his *Pensées* (*Thoughts*), one of the great philosophical and religious statements of the seventeenth century and published in various editions since 1670.

Pascal was one of many seventeenth-century scientists whose beliefs were shot through with traditional Christian values and concerns. Bacon believed that the accumulation of natural knowledge would prepare for Christ's return to earth, and Newton believed that human mastery of nature was a step in restoring the human race to Paradise, where Adam was master of the world before he fell into sin.

Science and the State

On April 2, 1662, Jacques-Bénigne Bossuet, a bishop in the Catholic Church, preached a sermon "On the Duties of Kings" before Louis XIV in which he celebrated the theory of absolute monarchy. "You are gods," he said to Louis. "You are all sons of the Most High." These flattering words came from Psalm 82. Bossuet then went on to describe how the king ruled without any human check on his power. Each point was justified by an appropriate quotation from Christian scripture.

Basing politics on the Bible had been practiced since the days of the first Christian emperors of fourth-century Rome. Bossuet was, therefore, the heir to centuries of European political thought. At the same time, however, justifications for absolutism based on the New Science were also being proposed. Descartes's endorsement of the sun-centered universe, for example, was adopted as a model for Louis XIV's monarchy. Just as the planets orbited around the sun, so French subjects should be obedient to the Sun King.

Thomas Hobbes The Englishman **Thomas Hobbes** also drew on scientific thought to argue for absolutism. Hobbes had lived through the turmoil of the English civil war and Commonwealth and had accepted Descartes's idea that human beings were matter in motion. Combining his experience of political instability and violence with his mechanical view of human beings, he argued in *Leviathan* (1651) that people, if left to themselves, would simply attack each other. The prepolitical, or natural, state was "every man against every man" because each human piece of matter in motion would try to fulfill its desires at the expense of the others. "Man is a wolf to his fellow man," he concluded, and all life is "nasty,

Thomas Hobbes (1588–1679) English political theorist who tried to defend absolutism on scientific grounds.

John Locke (1632–1704) English political theorist who argued, like Hobbes, that government rested on a contract between ruler and ruled.

brutish, and short." The solution was to submit to an ironclad authority, a "mortal God," who would rule over everyone and force obedience to laws that restrained the aggressive impulses in people.

Hobbes's defense of absolutism differed from traditional ones by not being based on the ruler's divine right to rule. He believed that the people created the absolute ruler (who might be a king or a parliament) to end the self-defeating violence of prepolitical society. Absolutism was, therefore, based on a contract between ruler and ruled, not on God's will.

John Locke Another Englishman, **John Locke**, also argued that government rested on a contract between ruler and ruled. But he drew quite different conclusions from this premise. Locke was an opponent of absolutism and had fled to Holland when James II became king in 1685. Returning to England with William and Mary, he published *Two Treatises on Government* (1690), in which he justified the Glorious Revolution. Locke had a more optimistic view of human nature than Hobbes. He believed that people could curb their aggressive impulses without coercion from an absolutist government. People entered into a political contract voluntarily and could withdraw from it when it no longer suited their purposes. The chief purpose of government was to protect private property rights. Locke's notions of contractual government and rights of private property supported the overthrow of James II, the repudiation of absolutism, and landowners' control of Parliament under a constitutional monarchy. His thought also had an impact on the American revolutionaries of the eighteenth century.

Although Hobbes and Locke had different views of human nature and endorsed different kinds of states, both tried to construct their politics on the basis of experience and reason rather than tradition and scripture. Their work represents some of the first attempts to construct a "political science."

The Nature of History

Growing enthusiasm for the New Science also provoked a sharp argument over the nature of human history. Traditional seventeenth-century understandings of history were pessimistic. Some stated that history was the sad story of decline and decay from an original high point, sometimes identified as the Garden of Eden and sometimes as Greek and Roman culture. In either case, humanity's passage through time was simply a slide downhill from an earlier golden age.

A less dismal view presented history in cyclical terms. Humanity passed through high stages and then slid into decay until, once again, it started to ascend to a high point that, in turn, would provoke another period of decline. Thus, in a Protestant version of the cyclical theory, the high point of Christianity's first days was followed by a decline as Catholicism spread, until Martin Luther's or John Calvin's day, when Protestantism returned Christianity to its original purity and a high point was once again reached.

Traditionalists sometimes argued that the natural world was subject to decay as well; plants and animals, along with people, had degenerated over time. People who held these traditional views of natural and human history were called Ancients.

The "Moderns" Beginning in the late seventeenth century, a new view of history gained ground, held by people dubbed Moderns. Inspired by the New Science, the Moderns argued against a decay over time of the natural world, citing the timeless, universal laws that Newton had discovered. Moderns also optimistically argued that human history was the story of intellectual progress. Although ancient Greek and Roman poets and playwrights were as good as contemporary ones, ancient scientists had been surpassed. Progress pointed to the overall superiority of Moderns. The battle between Ancients and Moderns continued on into the eighteenth century.

 Checking In

By yourself or with a partner, explain the significance of each of the following selected key terms:

Royal Society	Blaise Pascal
Robert Boyle	Thomas Hobbes
argument from design	John Locke
innate idea	

The Enlightenment

♦ **How did the Enlightenment employ the methods of the New Science?**

♦ **What were the major items on the Enlightenment's agenda for reform?**

Isaac Newton was the inspiration for a new European intellectual movement that emerged in the last years of the seventeenth century. People who joined it described themselves as enlightened because they had embraced Newton's view of the universe along with his scientific method. Historians have adopted the term for the movement itself. The Enlightenment was the most energetic current in European thought during the eighteenth century.

The Early Enlightenment

England, the home of Isaac Newton, was one center for the early **Enlightenment**. The power of Newton's

scientific method inspired his fellow countryman, John Locke, to apply it to a new field of study, the human mind. In 1690, Locke published *An Essay Concerning Human Understanding,* in which he took issue with Descartes's belief that God had planted some innate ideas in the mind. Instead, Locke argued, our minds at birth are like "white paper, void of all characters, without any ideas." Ideas arise only through experience of the world around us. And that experience comes through our senses of sight, hearing, taste, touch, and smell.

A Science of the Mind Locke's *Essay* was one of the foundational documents of the Enlightenment. It showed how Newton's scientific method could be used to establish a new science, that of the human mind, and thereby laid the foundations for the modern discipline of psychology. At the same time, it ratified a central tenet of the scientific method— reasoning on the basis of experience and observation. The *Essay* also had one profound implication. Sense knowledge can come only from the physical, material world because it alone is capable of registering on the senses. That meant that human beings could not directly know the immaterial or supernatural world, even if it exists.

An Unknowable Supernatural World? Thus, the *Essay,* repudiating the notion of innate ideas and limiting human knowledge to sense impressions, cast serious doubt on the reality of divine revelation as an authority for guiding people's lives. Messages from the supernatural beyond seemed less and less likely in Locke's world.

"The Proper Study of Mankind Is Man" Locke's interest in the mind testifies to a central concern of the Enlightenment: the study of human beings. In the sixteenth century, when the western Christian world split into two warring camps—Catholic and Protestant—the problem of God was a central intellectual issue. The scientific revolution brought the study of nature to the fore. In the Enlightenment, attention shifted once again. As Alexander Pope put it:

Know then thyself, presume not God to scan;
The Proper study of Mankind is Man.

(Excerpted from Alexander Pope's poetry (1688–1744).)

The Baron de Montesquieu Another center of the Enlightenment was France, where the **Baron de Montesquieu** took the study of humans in a different direction. A nobleman and a lawyer, Montesquieu sat in the French Parlement of Bordeaux. He made his literary debut

Enlightenment European intellectual movement of the eighteenth century using the scientific method of the New Science.

Baron de Montesquieu (1689–1755) One of the founders of the modern discipline of sociology and author of *The Spirit of the Laws.*

in 1721 with *The Persian Letters,* a witty critique of French society supposedly written by Persian tourists.

In 1748, he published one of the great works of the Enlightenment, *The Spirit of the Laws.* Unlike Locke, who had studied the individual human mind, Montesquieu focused on human beings as a group. Assuming that there was a universal human nature, he then sought the causes for the great variety of human political arrangements—monarchies, republics, despotic states—and found them in environmental factors. A comparative analysis led him to argue that climate and geography played an important role in shaping the features of any given society. He concluded that a society's traditions concerning religion, government, and economic activity also contributed to its distinctive shape, or "spirit."

Government in France Montesquieu argued that good government in France depended on the nobility, seated in institutions like the parlements, which put restraints on both the monarchy and the common people. He also greatly admired the constitutional monarchy of Britain. Montesquieu's interest in the role of natural and historical factors in shaping a society laid the foundations for the modern discipline of sociology.

Voltaire

If any person embodied the Enlightenment, it was the French philosopher and author **Voltaire**. The son of a middle-class Parisian lawyer, Voltaire attended the prestigious Jesuit school of Louis-le-Grand. He then defied his father, who wanted him to enter the law, by deciding to make his living as a writer. In 1718, his first play, *Oedipus,* which recounted the Greek legend of the king who killed his father and slept with his mother, ran on the Paris stage for an unprecedented forty-five nights. This success established the young man as France's foremost author of tragedies. A few years later, he published an epic poem on the reign of Henry IV of France, the *Henriade,* his most popular work.

Voltaire (1694–1778) Social critic, attacker of Christianity, defender of the principle of autonomous human reason, and author of *Candide.*

Bastille Medieval fortress in Paris serving as a royal prison.

philosophes (in French, "philosophers") Name French supporters of Enlightenment ideas gave themselves.

Emilie du Châtelet (1706–1749) Voltaire's mistress and intellectual companion who was an expert in Newtonian physics and mathematics.

The Philosophical Letters on the English In late 1725, a quarrel with a descendant of one of France's greatest noble families landed Voltaire in the **Bastille**, a notorious royal prison. He was released in 1726, on the

In this contemporary portrait, Voltaire is fashionably dressed and wears a wig. His eyes have moved slightly to his right so he can look directly at the viewer. Why might the painter have chosen this way to depict Voltaire? (Mary Evans Picture Library/The Image Works)

condition that he go into exile in England. He did, and his exile set him on the path that made him France's greatest **philosophe**, the name French supporters of Enlightenment gave themselves.

Voltaire stayed in England until 1729, becoming familiar with Newton's and Locke's writings and learning about the English form of monarchical and parliamentary government. In 1733, he published *Philosophical Letters on the English,* a seemingly innocent account of English politics, religion, and society that was, in fact, a scathing denunciation of contemporary France. The issues Voltaire raised in the *Letters* formed the basis for his subsequent career as a reformer.

The subversive tone of the book was not lost on the French authorities, who ordered it burned in public by the royal executioner and issued a warrant for Voltaire's arrest. Fleeing Paris with his new mistress, **Emilie du Châtelet**, he took up residence near the French border in case a quick getaway was needed. Mme. du Châtelet, an accomplished physicist and mathematician, helped Voltaire deepen his understanding of Newton. In 1738, he published *Elements of Newton's Philosophy,* which helped to establish Newton's reputation in France.

The Calas Affair Voltaire was also interested in the improvement of French society. He sought reform of the criminal justice system, especially an end to the use of torture. In 1761, he heard of the perfect case to make his points. In the southern French town of Toulouse, a young Huguenot, Marc-Antoine Calas, was found hanged in his father's shop. It was rumored that Calas was about to convert to Catholicism. Although his family claimed that Calas had committed suicide, the Parlement of Toulouse, dominated by Catholics, charged his father, Jean, with murdering him to prevent his conversion. The elder Calas was found guilty and then subjected to excruciating torture to get him to confess to his crime before his execution. The elder Calas refused, even when his bones were broken, and he was finally strangled to death.

Was the father guilty or not? If he was, for Voltaire he demonstrated Protestant fanaticism; if not, the court demonstrated Catholic fanaticism. Either way, the case demonstrated the barbarity of judicially sanctioned torture. Voltaire turned the **Calas affair** into a European scandal that widely discredited the use of torture in criminal proceedings.

The Attack on Christianity The affair also gave Voltaire the opportunity to attack traditional Christianity, whether Protestant or Catholic. For years he had rejected Christian teaching. Now he openly subjected Christianity to withering ridicule and began closing his letters with the phrase "Stamp out the infamous thing," by which he meant the churches, their ministers and priests, and their teachings. The Jesuits, in particular, came under heavy attack, perhaps because, as Voltaire told Alexander Pope, they had sexually molested him while he was a student at Louis-le-Grand. Although most supporters of the Enlightenment remained Christians, Voltaire's public, passionate attack on Christianity marked a turning point in the religious history of Europe.

Candide Voltaire's campaign to improve human society was waged despite his sense of the limits of reform. When a huge earthquake destroyed the city of Lisbon in Portugal, he published his most famous work, *Candide, or Optimism,* which ridiculed the German philosopher Gottfried Wilhelm Leibnitz and the English poet Alexander Pope, who argued that we live in the best of all possible worlds. Nevertheless, Voltaire endorsed a limited optimism. As Candide says at the end of the novel, "We must cultivate our gardens," by which Voltaire meant that despite calamities like the Lisbon earthquake, which are beyond any human control, some things can and should be changed.

Voltaire also carried on a huge correspondence, exchanging letters with his fellow philosophes, and also with Catherine II of Russia and Frederick II of Prussia, who invited him to his court outside Berlin. No European writer since Erasmus in the sixteenth century was as well connected as Voltaire.

In early 1778, Voltaire, now eighty-three, returned in triumph to Paris. The city's most prestigious theatrical company, the Comédie-Française, performed his tragedy *Irene* and placed his statue in their theater, the only living author to be so honored. At his death, in May of that year, he was arguably the most famous man in Europe. The modern edition of his works fills more than 135 volumes.

Enlightenment Religion

Although Voltaire declared war on Christianity, he was no atheist. He embraced **deism**, a rational religion based solely on the observation of nature. Deism drew on Locke's sense-based psychology, the argument from design, and Newton's clocklike universe. As a religious movement, it denied Christian doctrines of the Trinity, the divinity of Jesus, and the divine authority of the Bible. Most deists also rejected Newton's notion that God intervenes in the universe to keep it going. Deists emphasized the need for humane treatment of human beings, supporting the campaign against judicial torture.

The Fight for Religious Toleration For Voltaire and other deists, like Benjamin Franklin and Thomas Jefferson, deism and religious toleration went hand in hand. Since traditional religion, whether Jewish or Christian, was based on fraud and foolishness, it could never be legitimately defended by attacking those who rejected it. Even acceptable religious belief, like deism, was a matter of individual conscience over which no state or church authority ought to have jurisdiction.

Voltaire's pursuit of these points in the Calas affair met with growing sympathy, and, in 1787, on the eve of revolution in France, Louis XVI signed an edict granting limited religious toleration to the Huguenots. Deist-inspired calls for religious toleration also spread in Britain's North American colonies. After gaining independence, the new United States proclaimed religious toleration in its own Bill of Rights (1791).

Atheism: La Mettrie In addition to battling traditional Christians, Voltaire also denounced atheists. On this score, however, he was fighting a losing battle. By the mid-eighteenth century, more and more philosophes believed that the existence of God could never be proved by an argument from design or demonstrated as necessary for explaining the world and human beings. The **materialism** of Descartes, stripped of its Christian beliefs, could account for everything.

Calas affair Trial, torture, and execution of Jean Calas, who was accused of killing his Huguenot son to prevent his conversion to Catholicism.

deism Religious belief that rejected traditional Christian teachings and tried to base its theology on scientific method.

materialism Argument that material things alone exist, therefore denying the existence of a soul or of an immaterial world.

Voltaire Attacks Christianity

Voltaire wanted to present the ideas of the Enlightenment to a large reading public. He therefore polished a literary style that sparkled with wit and was laced with biting satire and moral outrage. The two pieces presented below illustrate Voltaire's attack on traditional Christianity, "the infamous thing." They were published anonymously, without the approval of the French royal censors, and represent the Enlightenment attack on Christianity in its most radical form. They offended many traditionalists, who dismissed Voltaire as a "filthy little atheist," but they expressed views that many people repeated in the years after Voltaire published his attack.

❶ How does Voltaire turn the technical theological terms he uses here against the doctrine of the Trinity?

On the Trinity

Here is an incomprehensible question which for over sixteen hundred years has exercised curiosity, sophistical subtlety, bitterness, the spirit of cabal, the rage to dominate, the rage to persecute, blind and blood-thirsty fanaticism, barbaric credulity, and which has produced more horrors than the ambition of princes, which indeed has produced enough.

❶ Is Jesus Word? If he is Word, did he emanate from God, is he co-eternal and consubstantial with him, or is he of a similar substance? Is he distinct from him or not? Is he created or engendered? Can he engender in turn? Has he paternity, or productive virtue without paternity? Is the holy ghost created or engendered or produced? Does he proceed from the father, or from the son, or from both? Can he engender, can he produce? Is his hypostasis consubstantial with the hypostasis of the father and the son? And why, having precisely the same nature, the same essence as the father and the son, can he not do the same things as these two persons who are himself?

I certainly do not understand any of this; nobody has ever understood any of this, and this is the reason for which people have slaughtered one another.

Julien Offroy de La Mettrie (1709–1751) French author of the materialist and atheistic works *Man the Machine* and *Man the Plant.*

Moses Mendelssohn (1729–1786) German Jew who said that Judaism's basic beliefs were rationally provable and who worked to end discrimination against Jews.

The universe simply was, and humans were wholly material beings without souls or immaterial minds. At death, they ceased to exist.

In 1746, a French physician, **Julien Offroy de La Mettrie**, argued these points in *Man the Machine*. His work caused a scandal in conservative circles, but, undaunted, he followed it up in 1749 with *Man the Plant*. La Mettrie also preached a gospel of pure physical pleasure, which made him doubly scandalous. In 1751, when he died after gorging himself on pheasant pâté, his enemies said the punishment fitted the crime.

Enlightenment and the Jews Some Jewish thinkers were also caught up in the debates over revealed versus natural religion and atheism. One of the most important was the German Jew **Moses Mendelssohn**. Mendelssohn argued for a Judaism stripped of miracles and other supernatural phenomena. Its basic truths could be proved by reason. He also rejected the idea of Jewish uniqueness, denying that the Jews were a chosen people. But he asserted that, in the larger Christian world, they were an oppressed

The Story of the Banishing of the Jesuits from China

Brother Rigolet: ❷ Our God was born in a stable, seventeen hundred and twenty-three years ago, between an ox and an ass.... [His mother] was not a woman, but a girl. It is true that she was married, and that she had two other children, named James as the old gospels say, but she was a virgin none the less.

The Emperor: What! She was a virgin and she had children!

Brother Rigolet: To be sure. This is the nub of the story: it was God who gave this girl a child.

The Emperor: I don't understand you. You have just told me that she was the mother of God. So God slept with his mother in order to be born of her?

Brother Rigolet: You've got it Your Sacred Majesty; grace was already in operation. You've got it I say; God changed himself into a pigeon to give a child to a carpenter's wife, and that child was God himself.

The Emperor: But then we have two Gods to take into account: a carpenter and a pigeon.

Brother Rigolet: ❸ Without a doubt, Sire; but there is also a third, who is the father of these two, and whom we always paint with a majestic beard: it was this God who ordered the pigeon to give a child to the carpenter's wife, from whom the God-carpenter was born; but at the bottom these three make only one. The father had engendered the son before he was in the world, the son was then engendered by the pigeon, and the pigeon proceeds from the father and the son. Now you see that the pigeon who proceeds, the carpenter who is born of the pigeon, and the father who has engendered the son of the pigeon, can only be a single God; and that a man who doesn't believe this story should be burned in this world and the other.

The Emperor: That is as clear as day.

Source: Extract from Peter Gay, *Voltaire's Politics: The Poet as Realist* (New Haven, CT: Yale University Press, 1959), pp. 246–247. Reprinted by Yale University Press.

❷ Why would Voltaire choose to mock the Jesuits in this little dialogue?

❸ How does Voltaire develop this story for comic effect?

---

people, and he worked tirelessly to end discriminatory legislation against them. He also urged Jews to be more open to the larger European culture. They should stop using Yiddish as a literary language and follow his example of writing in German. Mendelssohn shocked many Jewish traditionalists, but his views appealed to others and were to be influential in the nineteenth century.

Diderot and the *Encyclopédie*

While Voltaire was crusading against Christians and atheists, some of his fellow philosophes were embarking on a highly successful publishing venture. In 1751, the first volume of the *Encyclopédie* appeared.

Under the editorial leadership of **Denis Diderot**, sixteen more volumes followed over the next twenty-one years. The *Encyclopédie* was a huge commercial success, making millions for its publishers.

A Work to Present All Knowledge Diderot wished to present current knowledge on all subjects in a single multivolume reference work. He also wanted to show how all knowledge was interconnected and that the key to it rested on observation, experiment,

Encyclopédie Multivolume work with contributions from philosophes throughout Europe that summed up the philosophy of the Enlightenment.

Denis Diderot (1713–1784) French writer and editor of the *Encyclopédie*.

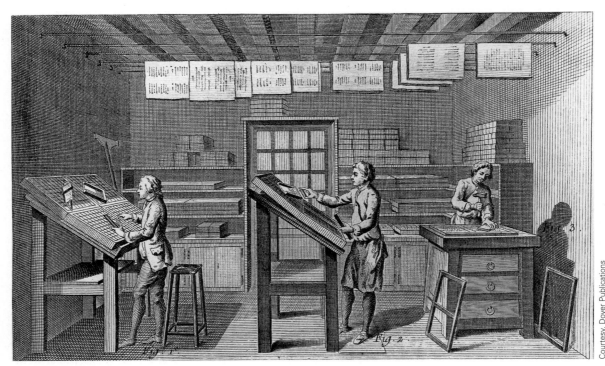

This engraving of a craft process from Diderot's *Encyclopédie* shows a printer's shop. From left to right men set type for a page, arrange lines, and lock the type in place. The type will print four pages at once. Previously printed pages are drying on lines above workmen's heads; when dry, they will be folded to arrange the pages in proper sequence. Diderot's emphasis on craft and manufacturing processes reminded readers of their importance and gave them a new dignity.

and autonomous reason. Throughout the *Encyclopédie,* Diderot drew on the works of Bacon, Descartes, Locke, and Newton. He also got major Enlightenment writers, such as Montesquieu and Voltaire, to contribute articles.

In addition to standard articles on religious, philosophical, scientific, and artistic subjects, the *Encyclopédie* also had groundbreaking contributions on craft and manufacturing processes such as brassmaking, printing, tapestry weaving, and fishing with nets. Inclusion of these articles testified to the importance that craft traditions had played in the emergence of the scientific revolution. They also met Diderot's insistence that the *Encyclopédie* should be useful. Usefulness also lay behind articles like "Asparagus," which not only described the plant and its cultivation but gave five recipes as well.

Evading Censorship Diderot had to work under conditions of government press censorship, which was always on the lookout for unorthodox political or religious ideas and often forced him to make controversial

points in subtle ways. One device he and his associates perfected for sneaking in inflammatory material was a system of clever cross-referencing. For example, in the article on "France," when Louis XIV's revocation of the Edict of Nantes was described, a cross-reference to "Toleration" was given. If Voltaire was the one man who best embodied the ideals of Enlightenment, the *Encyclopédie* was the one work that summed them up.

The Late Enlightenment

As editor of the *Encyclopédie,* Diderot had to be discreet in voicing his own opinions, but his works make clear that he, too, had embraced materialism and atheism. The leading philosophe of the late Enlightenment, however, did not. He was **Jean-Jacques Rousseau,** the son of a Genevan watchmaker. Rousseau was a Calvinist who converted to Catholicism and then embraced deism. His *Profession of Faith of a Savoyard Vicar,* an emotional defense of deism, won Voltaire's praise.

Rousseau's Attack on Civilization Rousseau was touchy, paranoid, and blunt. In the 1750s, he attacked the refined world of the philosophes and their aristocratic patrons. Rejecting the Christian idea of

Jean-Jacques Rousseau (1712–1778) Genevan Swiss social critic, philosopher, and novelist who pioneered modern democratic theory in his *Social Contract.*

The Granger Collection, New York

In this etching Jean-Jacques Rousseau is depicted as a "man of nature" who rejected the refined world of the salons. Leaning against a tree and holding a bunch of wildflowers, he contemplates the beauty of the natural world, which his deist God had created. Compare this etching with the portrait of Voltaire in this chapter. What do you think Voltaire would make of the differences?

original sin, Rousseau believed that human beings were good by nature but that civilization had corrupted them because it encouraged injustice and inequality. His attacks alienated Voltaire, Diderot, and others who believed that civilization was a sign of human progress, not degeneration. Voltaire said he thought Rousseau wanted him to walk around on all fours. In fact, however, Rousseau did not want to abolish civilization; he wanted to reform it.

The Social Contract In 1762 Rousseau published *The Social Contract*, which advocated a democratic society and pioneered modern democratic theory. This work set him apart from other philosophes. For all their radicalism, Voltaire and Diderot were part of the eighteenth-century literary establishment. Like the gentlemen who gathered in the scientific societies of the seventeenth century, they criticized society but did not want to overturn it.

In contrast, Rousseau wanted fundamental change. He argued that the good society is one in which all members voluntarily give up their individual rights and submit to what he called the general will.

Usually, the general will amounted to the will of the community's majority, although Rousseau was careful to say that sometimes it did not. This point has confused some of his readers. What Rousseau really wanted was a community in which people participated in politics and acted openly for the true good of all the community's members. This ideal has served as a benchmark for democratic societies ever since.

The Confessions Rousseau's hunger for openness in human relations prompted him to write his *Confessions*. Published in 1781, three years after his death, the *Confessions* recounted in detail many of the most private facts of his life, among them acts of theft, sex with a sailor, and the abandonment of a child he had fathered. While some were shocked by these revelations, Rousseau's real intent was to demonstrate that he was a man who hid nothing but presented himself fully to other human beings. If all people were as open, society could be fundamentally transformed.

Pamphlet Wars Rousseau's radicalism and rejection of refined aristocratic society was also endorsed by a host of pamphleteers and writers for hire who never made it into Voltaire's or Diderot's elite publishing circles. These people produced political criticism that mixed opposition to government policies with pornographic accounts of the degenerate lives of kings, queens, and nobility. Although these works had roots in earlier traditions of satire and slander, their volume and intensity increased in the late eighteenth century, especially in France after its defeat in the Seven Years' War. Overall, they undermined the legitimacy of traditional government as much as Rousseau's democratic criticisms did.

Immanuel Kant Other parts of Europe were less receptive to the radicalism that swept over France after 1750. In Prussia, **Immanuel Kant** summed up the philosophes' program in *What Is Enlightenment?* (1784): "Dare to know…. Have the courage to use your own understanding is…the motto of enlightenment." Kant, however, never advocated democracy or any real social or political reform. People were free to use their minds to seek the truth but, according to Kant, should submit to the current political, social, and economic orders in which they found themselves.

Immanuel Kant (1724–1804)
Leading German philosophe of the late Enlightenment.

 Checking In

By yourself or with a partner, explain the significance of each of the following selected key terms:

Baron de Montesquieu	Moses Mendelssohn
Voltaire	Denis Diderot
deism	Jean-Jacques Rousseau
Julien Offroy de La Mettrie	Immanuel Kant

Society and the Enlightenment

◆ **What impact did developments in publishing and reading habits have on European intellectual life?**

◆ **What additional trends promoted the Enlightenment?**

Just as scientific societies helped to spread Newtonian physics, so new institutions served to popularize the Enlightenment. Publishers expanded the types of books they produced from religious works to new literary forms like the novel. Newspapers also became increasingly available to readers. This wider array of reading materials, which encouraged readers to digest the news of the day or enter into the world of the novel, offered new ways of thinking about human experience. The Enlightenment's insistence on rational discussion of topics spread through society as new opportunities opened for comment on current affairs in coffeehouses, salons, and Masonic lodges. Critical discussion of issues also spilled over into the political realm as ordinary people commented on rulers' policies and required rulers to justify their actions before a new political force, public opinion.

The New World of Reading

The invention of the printing press in the mid-fifteenth century, along with the Protestant Reformation and Catholic reforms of the sixteenth, ushered in a new era in the history of European book reading. Both Protestants and Catholics used print to attack their opponents and to present their co-religionists with catechisms and prayer books. Most of this popular literature was written in the languages spoken by the people rather than Latin, which was still the official language of learning. In Protestant countries, translations of the Bible also multiplied.

Prayer books, catechisms, and Bibles were read reverently and reread many times; Bible study required returning to passages over and over again, while prayers for the morning and evening were repeated daily. Habits of devout, repetitive reading, a reading style intimately linked to Christian belief, were predominant among literate people in the sixteenth and seventeenth centuries as religious publications multiplied.

novel Literary form of prose fiction that was popular in the eighteenth century and sometimes used to promote social criticism and programs for reform.

Aphra Behn (1640–1689) English novelist who pioneered the form and made a financial success of writing.

lending libraries Institutions allowing readers to borrow books from their shelves and then return them, thus avoiding the need to buy them.

New Types of Literature and New Styles of Reading In the eighteenth century, both the types of literature available to people and styles of reading changed. Throughout the century, religious publications declined dramatically, and **novels**, a new literary type, rose to first place. Novels were particularly popular with women, who were now more likely to read than they had been earlier. Women like the Englishwoman **Aphra Behn** also figured prominently as authors of novels.

Although some people seemed to have read and reread novels many times, and thereby used the same technique for reading them as for Bibles or prayer books, most readers read the latest bestseller only once, then turned to something else.

Newspapers and Lending Libraries In addition to novels, newspapers and political pamphlets became increasingly available in the eighteenth century, especially in Britain and the Dutch Republic where censorship laws were relaxed or abolished. Reading newspapers had often been a collective activity in which one person read aloud to a group, but increasingly newspapers were read privately and silently, like novels, and passed along until the next day's newspaper was available. As the variety of reading material expanded, it is likely that Europeans received more information about the world and, often lost in the contents of the page in front of them, had a wider range of imaginative reading experiences than people had ever had before.

Lending Libraries One of the clearest signs of Europeans' expanding reading habits was the spread of **lending libraries**, which allowed anyone who joined to check books out to read where they wished and thus eliminated the cost of purchasing them.

Changes in Writing and Publishing The nature of writing and publishing changed with new reading habits. Formerly, writers had either worked as economically self-sufficient gentlemen or had sought commissions from wealthy patrons. In the eighteenth century, some thought that the profession of author was beneath the well-born, but others, like Voltaire and Diderot, were eager to make a living from writing. Few became as rich or famous as they, but many managed to survive on wages paid for their work.

Those wages came from publishers. Publishing became big business in the eighteenth century. Publishing houses often specialized in certain types of literature. Some produced cheap editions of fairy tales or almanacs, which peddlers carried in their packs throughout the town and countryside. Others, especially in the Dutch Republic, concentrated on controversial works that might be censored in other countries; Diderot, for example, used a publisher in the Netherlands for the *Encyclopédie*. Many of these

In Pierre-Antoine Baudoin's *Reading,* the woman reads in private. Note how the screen behind her would prevent anyone coming through the door to see directly into the room. Her book is a novel. What has become of it? And what does her posture and facial expression tell the viewer about her reading experience?

works were then smuggled into places like France, where censors were sometimes bribed to look the other way when the books went on sale. Authors also tried to evade censors when they wrote something particularly scandalous; Voltaire was fond of blaming his literary rivals for his anti-Christian works.

Meeting and Shaping Readers' Demands Publishers stayed in business by both meeting and shaping readers' demands and tastes. When a particular type of novel sold, they urged other writers to produce similar works. This worked well for Rousseau, whose *The New Heloise,* a runaway bestseller in 1761, fed a growing late-eighteenth-century taste for novels describing domestic settings that were full of romance, heartbreak, and feeling. His *Emile* (1762), a novel that advocated a "natural" course for children's education based on direct observation and experience at the various stages of a child's development, also sold well. In fact, during his life, Rousseau was better known for these novels than for *The Social Contract.*

Increasing numbers of Europeans could afford books and newspapers, or lending library fees, in part because their disposable incomes rose as Europe entered a new period of prosperity in the early eighteenth century. Moreover, printed material was viewed less as an avenue to God or a source for spiritual improvement than as a means to worldly information and pleasure.

The new world of reading, writing, and publishing constituted a major shift in the intellectual activities of Europeans that the philosophes put to good use for popularizing their ideas and advocating programs of reform. Reading still remained, however, a practice that only a minority of Europeans engaged in, and the ideas of the philosophes were embraced by only a part of this reading public.

Enlightenment Sociability

Along with new types of literature and changing styles of reading, new institutions sprang up in which people could discuss what they read and put into

In this London coffeehouse, as the elegantly dressed owner looks on, a waiter pours coffee for the well-to-do men sitting at tables. What activities are they engaged in? (Note the coffee pots being kept warm in front of the fire.)

practice the central method of the Enlightenment— thought based on autonomous human reason.

Coffee and Tea Houses Chief among them were coffee and tea houses. Europeans' consumption of coffee and tea rose significantly during the eighteenth century as a result of expanded colonial trade and an improving European economy. While both beverages were drunk at home, many people, especially men, liked to take them in cafés where there were newspapers and pamphlets to read, opportunities to buy and sell stocks in joint-stock companies, and people to talk to.

The coffeehouse phenomenon had begun in Restoration London when Whigs took tea or coffee and discussed politics at Old Slaughter's, while the Tories gathered at the Cocoa Tree. Coffeehouses then sprouted up in Paris, Vienna, and other major European cities. The atmosphere in them was informal; one dropped in and left at will.

Originally patronized by the rich and fashionable, coffeehouses became more socially inclusive over the century. Men of different backgrounds who would normally be separated on more formal occasions mixed easily with one another in the coffeehouse atmosphere. And always, politics and other current events were discussed. Because coffee is a stimulant, animated discussion was the rule. Unlike taverns, however, where drinking often led to brawling, coffeehouse conversation was supposed to be orderly and polite, even if heated.

salon Meeting place where current ideas are discussed, in the eighteenth century presided over by a woman.

Freemasonry Social and intellectual movement that originated in England during the eighteenth century and spread across Europe.

Salons Conversation was also the rule in salons. Invented in Paris during the seventeenth century, the **salon** became a central Enlightenment institution for the educated and well-born. Women like Madame du Deffand, the wife of a rich Parisian financier, presided over salons that met in their homes on specified days and discussed topics that the hostess announced. The hostess also set rules for conversation that prohibited shouting, swearing, and name calling. Guests were to converse politely, intelligently, and amusingly about the scientific, artistic, or political matters assigned for discussion. Anyone able to do this would be admitted. Thus, men and women, nobles and commoners, joined in. Although the hostess was usually rich and often noble, salons, like coffeehouses, were relatively informal institutions in which an ability to converse well counted more than wealth or social background. Even religious differences were overlooked in salons, especially in Berlin, where Jewish hostesses brought together Jews and Christians.

Masonic Lodges Masonic lodges also offered a new form of social interaction in which religious or class differences played a minor role. Guilds of masons who laid brick or stone had existed since the Middle Ages, but modern **Freemasonry** began in London in 1717, when a group of middle-class men formed a club in which Newton's science and other issues of current interest were discussed. By the 1720s, 75 percent of the London lodge members also belonged to the Royal Society.

Although Masonic lodges modified old rituals from the medieval guilds when they initiated new members, their main purpose was to create an environment like that of the salons, in which polite conversation on issues could occur. Masonic lodges spread throughout Europe in both Catholic and Protestant countries, despite the pope's condemnation of the movement in 1738 on the grounds that it advocated anti-Catholic ideas.

Like the salons, the lodges downplayed the social and economic differences of their membership. Brotherhood in the lodge made all members equal. These Masonic ideals were articulated in one of the century's great operas, *The Magic Flute,* written by **Wolfgang Amadeus Mozart** and performed in the last year of the composer's life. Mozart made a point of stressing Masonic ideals of human equality. At one point, when a priest exclaims that the hero is a prince, the high priest corrects him: "More than that! He is a man!"

The Enlightenment and Politics

The rational discussion taking place in new social settings also extended to politics, taking different forms in eastern and western Europe. In Scandinavia, Germany, and Russia, Enlightenment rationalism melded with an older political tradition, **cameralism**.

Cameralism Developing in the seventeenth century, cameralism aimed at increasing a state's wealth through direct management of people and resources. Government should intervene in people's lives to make them better fed, better housed, and better behaved so that they could become more productive. Cameralism also emphasized the need for a rational assessment of a state's strengths, weaknesses, and needs as the basis for good government policy. The state itself was compared to a machine. When properly managed, it could regulate society in the interests of increasing its wealth.

Cameralism was taught in eastern European universities to candidates for posts in the state bureaucracy. At the head of the bureaucracy was the ruler, whose job was to see that the machine of government ran smoothly and produced good results. Thus, kings were viewed more as supreme political managers than God-appointed rulers endowed with the sacred authority to govern. Many of the policies of Frederick William I and Frederick II of Prussia, as well as Peter the Great of Russia, were inspired by cameralist principles. Cameralism's emphasis on rational assessment of political needs, along with its conception of government as a well-run machine improving people's lives, fitted into many Enlightenment principles.

Politics in Britain In western Europe, greater discussion of politics by ordinary people gave rise to increased popular participation in politics. In Britain, the political turmoil of the seventeenth century, which led to constitutional monarchy and a permanent role for Parliament in shaping government policy, fostered ordinary people's discussion of political affairs.

Elections to the House of Commons also stimulated political debate, and, occasionally, commoners with widespread popular support could force the king to accept them as government ministers. In 1757, George II thus accepted **William Pitt the Elder**, though he despised Pitt's insistence that Britain's imperial interests were more important than Hanover's, the German principality from which the king and his father had come. It was Pitt who later masterminded the British victories in the Seven Years' War.

Parliament and the Public For its part, Parliament tried to shield its debates from the public by forbidding publication of its proceedings. But intense interest in the kingdom's politics, along with the growth of the press, forced Parliament to back down in the early 1770s. With parliamentary proceedings now publicly distributed, popular discussion of politics intensified.

Politics in France Similar developments also occurred in France. There the monarchy still clung to its absolutist principles, which proclaimed that there was only one political player in the realm, the king. Everyone else was supposed to be a mere spectator watching royal politics from the sidelines. While court etiquette at Versailles and official press accounts of the king's daily activities reinforced this view, it proved increasingly difficult to maintain.

Absolutism Under Siege Prolonged conflicts between the French king and the parlements over Jansenism, during which the parlements published their grievances, made it clear that others beside the king claimed a political role. The growth of the newspaper press and the rise of rational discussion in new social settings also encouraged the king's subjects to become actively engaged in discussion of policies and events.

Public Opinion In both England and France, therefore, public opinion played a growing role in politics. Its advent constituted a major shift in European political life. Monarchs who had previously argued that they ruled by divine grace and operated in a political world, whose rules could not be understood by the mass of their subjects, now had to contend with a growing chorus of voices commenting on and even criticizing what they did.

Although criticism of rulers could lead to charges of treason, it also forced governments to become more open in explaining and

Wolfgang Amadeus Mozart (1756–1791) Composer of symphonies, operas, and many other works who perfected the classical style in music.

cameralism Eastern European tradition of political thought emphasizing rational government policy making that melded with Enlightenment principles.

William Pitt the Elder (1708–1778) British minister during the Seven Years' War.

justifying their policies. As states made increasing demands on their subjects, rulers were increasingly expected to account for their actions.

 **Checking In**

By yourself or with a partner, explain the significance of each of the following selected key terms:

novels	Wolfgang Amadeus Mozart
Aphra Behn	
lending libraries	cameralism
salon	William Pitt the Elder
Freemasonry	

Enlightenment Debates

◆ **How did ideas about Europe's place in the world change during the Enlightenment?**

◆ **How did Enlightenment thinkers confront ideas about difference among human beings?**

Discussion and debate were at the heart of Enlightenment intellectual life. Debating clubs, where men and women could hear opposing views on subjects of current concern, often addressed the degree of likeness and difference in the human community. The philosophes believed in universal natural laws and a universal human nature.

At the same time, they lived in a world where difference separated some people from others and thereby challenged universalism. Debates on human likeness and difference, which raged throughout the eighteenth century, focused especially on three issues: the relation between Europeans and non-Europeans; the institution of slavery; and the relation between men and women.

Europeans and Non-Europeans

As early as the 1540s, the debate over the humanity of non-European people had pitted Bartolomé de Las Casas against Juan Guinés de Sepúlveda. Las Casas argued that New World Indians were fully human, whereas Sepúlveda said they were not. In the sixteenth century, Europeans thought of their culture primarily in religious terms; they lived in Christendom, while others were either infidels (Jews and Muslims) or pagans (everyone else).

During the Enlightenment, as the debate continued, the terms in which it was conducted started to

Abbé Raynal (1713–1796) French priest (*abbé*) and philosophe who argued that the natural world of the Americas was as inferior as its Indian inhabitants.

change. Under the influence of the New Science, natural factors like geology and climate, rather than the traditional religious categories of Christian and non-Christian, were used increasingly to explain diversity in the human community and to shape separate collective identities.

A Degenerate New World? Debate centered on two sets of people: those in the New World and those in the South Pacific. In 1770, a French priest and philosophe, the **Abbé Raynal**, published *The Philosophical History of the Two Indies,* which quickly became a runaway bestseller. Raynal argued, like Sepúlveda, that the Indian natives of the Western Hemisphere were inferior human beings. But Raynal went further, arguing that the natural world in America was as degenerate as the human one.

America, he wrote, had been formed later than Europe, rising from the sea in the recent past. This explained why the climate was damp and cold, making New England, which was on the same latitude as Spain, so snowy in winter. This chilly, watery New World produced plants and animals that were puny compared to their counterparts in Europe.

© Regents of the University of California, UCLA Library

This painting of a New Zealand warrior was made by Sydney Parkinson who accompanied James Cook on his first voyage to the South Pacific. It would seem both familiar and odd to Europeans. Their warriors often wore plumes on their hats, but a cape of fluffy flax and dog skins would never be seen on Europe's battlefields. Why do you think this painting was included in Parkinson's account of his voyage?

Going even further, Raynal stated that Europeans who migrated to North America soon degenerated. Thus, America's geological history produced a climate that was inhospitable to all forms of life.

Jefferson and Franklin Strike Back Raynal's attack provoked a sharp response from the North Americans. In 1781, **Thomas Jefferson** published his *Notes on the State of Virginia,* a spirited refutation of Raynal's work. Was Raynal correct when he wrote that Virginia's Indian men were less manly than Europeans because they had no facial hair? No. The Indians simply chose to pluck out their beards, and such warlike men could not be considered unmanly.

Did the New World produce puny animals? No. Look at the newly discovered bones of a huge American elephant, the **mammoth**. Were Americans of European origin degenerate descendants of their ancestors across the ocean? No. Look at **Benjamin Franklin**.

Franklin was Raynal's cleverest opponent. When the Continental Congress sent him to France in 1776 to seek French aid for the American Revolution, he made a point of refuting Raynal at every turn. Franklin's earlier experiments with electricity made him the ideal man of science, someone who, like Newton, revealed the workings of nature. His invention of the lightning rod made him the philosophe who worked for the betterment of humanity.

At Versailles, Franklin shunned the silks and lace fashionable men favored and dressed in plain brown, presenting himself as a simple American who was, nevertheless, the intellectual equal of any European. The French court was charmed. Franklin was a natural but noble man who showed no trace of deformity.

One evening, he and other Americans found themselves at a dinner party with Raynal. When the theory of American degeneracy came up, Franklin asked all the Americans at the table to stand, and then all the Frenchmen. The Americans towered over the French, and especially over Raynal, whom Franklin dismissed as a "mere shrimp." Soon afterward, Raynal retracted his unflattering picture of America. Franklin triumphed again in 1777, when France signed an alliance with the Americans in their war for independence from Britain.

The People of the South Pacific Debate about non-Europeans also focused on the peoples of the South Pacific. In the 1770s, an Englishman, **James Cook**, and a Frenchman, **Louis-Antoine de Bougainville**, led scientific voyages through the region and published accounts of their expeditions, feeding French and British thirst for travel literature.

The South Pacific was a new frontier for Europeans, and these accounts sparked interest in the local peoples. Diderot wrote a fictional *Supplement to the Voyage of Bougainville* (1772) in which he used Bougainville's account of Tahitians' free and open sexual activity to attack traditional Christian sexual morality as cruel and unnatural.

Raynal's denunciation of a degenerate America and Diderot's titillating account of the Tahitians' erotic freedom were part of a sustained discussion of European civilization and Europe's proper place in the larger world. One central issue was the nature of civilization itself.

Eurocentrism Many Europeans continued to think in **Eurocentric** terms and to assert the superiority of their way of life, and most philosophes encouraged this view. Kant declared that the spread of Enlightenment and of reliance on autonomous human reason was a sign that Europeans, after centuries of immaturity, had finally reached adulthood.

Voltaire celebrated the refined world of salon conversation, seeing it as a sign of a truly civilized world. But Rousseau attacked civilization as a corrupter of humanity's original goodness and purity. Pointing to the tea and coffee drunk in Enlightenment salons, he claimed that overseas trade and colonies promoted an improper love of luxury and harmed other peoples.

Raynal also had his doubts. His depiction of America as an alien and hostile place that Europeans should have avoided arose in part from his belief that colonization had harmed **indigenous people**, as indeed it had. Following their first encounters with Europeans, the native populations of the Americas declined by 90 percent, largely as the result of epidemic diseases that swept through their communities, a demographic catastrophe unparalleled in human history.

Diderot's Tahitians also suffered from European intrusion into their world. In the *Supplement*, a Tahitian complains to Bougainville that "the idea of crime and the fear of disease entered among us only with you." Diderot rejected Rousseau's attack on all civilization but agreed that European colonization had introduced corruption and inequality to other peoples.

Thomas Jefferson (1743–1826) American revolutionary and author of the Declaration of Independence who refuted charges of the New World's inferiority to Europe.

mammoths Extinct American elephants of great size whose bones were found in the eighteenth century.

Benjamin Franklin (1706–1790) American revolutionary, diplomat, and scientist who refuted Raynal's claims of American inferiority.

James Cook (1728–1779) Head of three British Royal Society–financed expeditions into the South Pacific.

Louis-Antoine de Bougainville (1729–1811) French explorer in the South Pacific who gave his name to the bougainvillea, a flowering vine he discovered there.

Eurocentric Idea that Europe and European culture are either superior to or more important than the lands and cultures of other peoples.

indigenous people Original inhabitants of a region, or "natives."

New Ways of Explaining Human Difference As philosophes like Rousseau, Raynal, and Diderot debated the nature of non-European peoples and the worth of commerce and colonies, they increasingly sought nonreligious explanations for differences among human beings and tried to articulate a sense of European identity in non-Eurocentric terms. Europe was simply one human community among many others in the world and could make no valid claims for superiority on religious, cultural, or commercial grounds.

Slavery

"We hold these truths to be self-evident: That all men are created equal; that they are endowed by their Creator with certain inalienable rights; that among these are life, liberty, and the pursuit of happiness." These words in one of the Enlightenment's most famous documents, the **Declaration of Independence** (1776), were written by Thomas Jefferson and proclaimed the philosophes' belief in universal **human rights**. But Jefferson was a Virginia plantation owner who never freed his slaves. This contradiction lay at the heart of Enlightenment debates over slavery.

The Slave Trade By the eighteenth century, trade in slaves from sub-Saharan Africa had gone on for more than a thousand years. During the Middle Ages, Arab traders had brought millions of them into the Islamic world. Beginning in the fourteenth century, the Portuguese brought African slaves to the Atlantic islands. Later Spanish, English, French, and Dutch traders transported Africans to Europe's colonies in the Western Hemisphere, where they worked the plantations that produced the coffee that Europeans drank in their coffeehouses and the sugar that sweetened their tea.

By the end of the eighteenth century, 11 million slaves had been forcibly taken to the Americas to labor for the 2 million Europeans who had migrated there. As demand for slave-produced commodities rose, the slave trade rose also, justified again and again with traditional arguments about biblical passages accepting the practice and the subhuman nature of Africans.

The Philosophes and Slavery The philosophes' attitude toward slavery was mixed. Both Hobbes and Locke endorsed the practice. Although Voltaire had attacked slavery in *Candide*, he came, reluctantly, to accept it as a fact of human life. Montesquieu argued against it, claiming that it undermined a society's moral well-being by oppressing the slaves while giving slave owners too much power. On the other hand, supporters of slavery could point to Montesquieu's argument that the hot, humid climate of the tropics had conditioned the people who lived there to resist work unless forced to do it.

Growing Opposition to Slavery Moral objections had been raised against slavery since the late seventeenth century. In England, several Protestant groups called for its abolition. For example, **Quakers**, who believed that God's "inner light" shone in every human being's heart, argued that the taking of slaves was simply kidnapping and should be stopped, and Quakers in America who owned slaves were urged to free them. Some Anglicans also condemned the trade, arguing that slavery was incompatible with Jesus' gospel of love, despite scriptural passages that sanctioned it. Thus, both Christian and Enlightenment arguments could be made for or against slavery. Over the course of the eighteenth century, however, the balance tipped toward the antislavery position.

Aphra Behn Novelists, poets, and playwrights played a crucial role in this development. Writers of fiction took the lead in arousing sympathy for slaves and an imaginative understanding of the conditions in which they lived. One of the first was Aphra Behn. Her novel *Oroonoko*, published in 1688, described the enslavement of an African prince and his beautiful love, Imoinda. Prince Oroonoko is a physically handsome and morally upright man with an unquenchable love for freedom, and Imoinda displays all the womanly virtues.

Showing her readers that Oroonoko and Imoinda possessed the physical traits and moral qualities that Europeans admired, Behn wanted to evoke admiration for them and outrage over their enslavement. Her novel was eventually turned into a play, and its themes were repeated in a growing body of antislavery literature.

Works like *Oroonoko* and later narratives by slaves who escaped to tell their story drew readers into a world in which slaves were upright and blameless human beings who had suffered terrible cruelty and injustice. The effect was to cut through centuries of dehumanizing stereotypes and indifferent or hostile theological traditions.

By the late 1780s, both the London Committee for the Abolition of the Slave Trade and the French Society of the Friends of the Blacks were campaigning tirelessly for an end to the slave trade and the abolition of slavery. Although both the trade and slavery itself ended only gradually, the antislavery momentum would not, from this point, be reversed.

Declaration of Independence Document justifying separation of American colonies from Britain in 1776 and defending the theory of self-government.

human rights Rights given to all human beings by God or the natural order and that neither the state nor society may take away.

Quakers An English Protestant sect that rejected ceremony and an ordained ministry, relying instead on a mystical "inner light" to guide conscience.

Men and Women

The problem of difference and likeness in human beings, which shaped the debate on slavery, was also addressed in debates over the nature and roles of men and women.

Women participated actively in the Enlightenment. Those who, like Madame du Deffand, presided over Europe's salons were arbiters of intellectual discussion. Those who, like Aphra Behn, joined men as professional writers became respectable public figures. Women also wrote some of the pamphlets that increasingly shaped public opinion, and others, like Mme. du Châtelet, contributed to the spread of Newtonian science. In the arts, France's most sought-after society painter was a woman, **Elisabeth Vigée-Lebrun**. Women's new social, intellectual, and professional activities raised the issue of similarity and difference between men and women and the proper relations between them.

Men and Women as Intellectual Equals To Descartes and Locke, it seemed self-evident that men and women not only possessed a common human nature but were intellectual equals. Descartes had coupled his arguments about the power of autonomous human reason with a discussion of the mind's relation to the body. He argued that the two were radically different; humans' bodies were wholly material and were subject to the laws of matter in motion. The mind, however, was nonmaterial. This **Cartesian dualism** made one thing perfectly clear: mind was not shaped by the body it went with, whether male or female. It floated free in a nonmaterial and, therefore, sexless world.

Locke's picture of the human mind pointed to similar conclusions. If the mind was like a blank sheet of paper, there seemed no good reason to argue for different male and female minds because both were subject to the same stimulus from sense experience.

Many philosophes accepted the implications of Locke's and Descartes's arguments. Diderot did not think that men and women were all that different and agreed with Montesquieu that a woman's sexually based role as a mother was only one part of her life, not its defining characteristic. Voltaire rejected the idea of distinct male and female minds; men and women were intellectual equals, as his collaborator, Mme. du Châtelet, demonstrated.

Acceptance of intellectual equality between men and women, however, did not prevent many philosophes from assigning them separate social roles. Rejecting the traditional idea that men had to rule women because women were prone to irrational and unruly behavior, the philosophes now argued that women should enforce the rules of civilization in society and thereby tame *men's* unruly behavior. The salon hostess performed this task and did so in women's traditional sphere, the household, while other women performed it as mothers who educated their children in proper behavior.

Rousseau on Men and Women Some philosophes rejected outright the idea of gender equality. Chief among them was Rousseau. Resurrecting old ideas about women's inferiority, Rousseau argued that women were irrational. Above all, they should play no public role in society as salon hostesses or commentators in the realm of public opinion. Their actual roles in this regard were simply another symptom of civilization's corrupting effect.

Women belonged at home, breast-feeding their children and obeying their husbands. As creatures of feeling, they played a central role in training children. Men alone, however, should carry on rational discussion and engage in politics.

A growing body of medical literature seemed to support Rousseau's denial of women's equality to men and their banishment from public life. Works by physicians, such as Pierre Roussel's *The Physical and Moral Makeup of Women* (1775), offered a new view of male and female differences that in good Enlightenment fashion claimed to be based on scientific observation.

Rejecting the traditional view that women were simply incomplete men, Roussel and others argued that women were completely different from them. For example, their nervous system, which included smaller brains, made it impossible for them to develop men's rational capacities. Their job was to nurture their babies and their husbands.

Mary Wollstonecraft Rousseau and the medical men found their opponent in **Mary Wollstonecraft**, the author of *A Vindication of the Rights of Woman* (1792) and the ablest defender of women's equality. Wollstonecraft pointed out the basic paradox of their views on women. These men attacked the despotism of kings and rejected the institution of slavery but endorsed the subordination of some human beings to others on the basis of gender.

Wollstonecraft believed with Rousseau that women as mothers should take charge of the moral and emotional education of their children, but she denied that they were inferior to men. If defects existed, she pointed out, they came from the inadequate education women received in a world where the best teaching was available only to men. Wollstonecraft argued that if women were educated with men on an equal basis, their seeming deficiencies would disappear.

Elisabeth Vigée-Lebrun (1755–1842) French society painter.

Cartesian dualism Descartes's idea of the radical difference between material human bodies and nonmaterial human minds.

Mary Wollstonecraft (1759–1797) English writer and feminist who rejected the idea that women were physically and mentally inferior to men.

A New Way of Discussing Men and Women In the Enlightenment, ideas about a universal human nature and gender-neutral minds mixed ambiguously with older ideas about women's inferiority and their proper place in the private, domestic sphere. But the debate among people like Rousseau, Roussel, and Wollstonecraft was conducted in increasingly nonreligious terms. Despite their differences, all sides looked less to Christian scripture and traditional church teaching on gender issues and turned instead to biology, psychology, and an examination of social conventions to demonstrate their respective positions.

 **Checking In**

By yourself or with a partner, explain the significance of each of the following selected key terms:

Abbé Raynal

Thomas Jefferson

Benjamin Franklin

James Cook

Louis-Antoine de Bougainville

Declaration of Independence

Cartesian dualism

Mary Wollstonecraft

CHAPTER
Review

Summary

- The scientific revolution changed European views of earth in fundamental ways. No longer were humans at the center of things; now they spun around the sun in an infinite universe. "These vast spaces terrify me," Pascal lamented in his *Pensées (Thoughts)*.

- Many others, however, were excited by the new understanding of the universe. It rested on a scientific method that relied on autonomous human reason and careful observation to demonstrate that it was true, thereby advancing knowledge far beyond anything achieved in the ancient world.

- So great was the prestige of the New Science that its method was quickly applied to other fields of learning in hopes of turning them into sciences as well.

- The application of the scientific method to an ever-expanding set of problems was at the heart of the intellectual movement known as the Enlightenment.

- The philosophes employed autonomous human reason and careful observation to establish the modern disciplines of political science, psychology, and sociology.

- At the same time, they subjected traditional Christian views on politics, human beings, and human society to systematic criticism. Above all, traditional Christian theology was scrutinized and often rejected, wholly or in part.

- The Enlightenment promoted the principle of rational discussion in a variety of ways. Discussion and debate were put into practice firsthand in

salons, coffeehouses, Masonic lodges, and debating clubs. There people met as equal intellectual partners regardless of their social backgrounds. As more and more people gathered in these new institutions, the habit of collective discussion of and participation in matters of current interest spread.

- The growing numbers of books, newspapers, and pamphlets also aided this sense of participation in current affairs as readers learned of debate and discussion going on in other parts of Europe.

- Although gossip and misinformation jostled uncomfortably with accurate information in this new world of talk and print, participation gradually turned people into a public whose opinions mattered.

- The growing activity of an engaged public would soon manifest itself in demands for more popular participation in political life, a fact that states recognized when they began appealing to public opinion for support of their policies.

- Although rational discussion was central to both the New Science and the Enlightenment, it did not always resolve problems to everyone's satisfaction.

- Ongoing debates over Europe's place in the world, the nature of non-European peoples, the acceptability of slavery, and issues of gender equality demonstrated disagreement as well as agreement. That these debates were conducted in increasingly nonreligious terms indicates a profound shift in western culture and an erosion of Christianity's dominance in Europe's intellectual life.

Chronology

1543	Copernicus publishes *On the Revolution of the Heavenly Bodies*	**1761**	Voltaire takes up the case of Jean Calas; Rousseau publishes *The New Heloise*
1637	Descartes publishes *The Discourse on Method*	**1762**	Rousseau publishes *The Social Contract and Emile*
1651	Hobbes publishes *Leviathans*	**1770**	Raynal publishes *The Philosophical History of the Two Indies*
1687	Newton publishes *Mathematical Principles of Natural Philosophy*	**1772**	Diderot publishes *The Supplement to the Voyage of Bougainville*
1688	Behn publishes *Oroonoko*	**1775**	Pierre Roussel publishes *The Physical and Moral Makeup of Women*
1690	Locke publishes *An Essay Concerning Human Understanding* and *Two Treatises on Government*	**1776**	Declaration of Independence states independence of American colonies from England
1717	First Masonic lodge opens in London	**1778**	Voltaire returns in triumph to Paris
1718	Lady Mary Wortley Montagu introduces smallpox inoculation in England	**1781**	Thomas Jefferson publishes *Notes on the State of Virginia*
1733	Voltaire publishes *Philosophical Letters on the English*	**1784**	Immanuel Kant publishes *What Is Enlightenment?*
1746	La Mettrie publishes *Man the Machine*	**1789**	Olaudah Equiano publishes his *Life*
1748	Montesquieu publishes *The Spirit of the Laws*	**1791**	Mozart's opera *The Magic Flute* is performed in Vienna
1751	First volume of Diderot's *Encyclopédie* is published		

© Cengage Learning

Test Yourself

To gauge your mastery of the material in this chapter, answer the questions below. More than one answer may be correct.

A Revolution in Astronomy

1. Ancient and medieval astronomers:
   a. Based their views on the works of Aristotle and Vesalius.
   b. Based their views on the work of Aristotle and Ptolemy.
   c. Thought there was no sharp distinction between the regions above the moon and those below it.
   d. Thought the earth was the lowest, least worthy part of the universe.
   e. Believed that motion in the universe, not rest, needed to be explained.

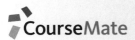

Visit the CourseMate website at **www.cengagebrain.com** for additional study tools and review materials for this chapter.

2. Galileo Galilei:

   a. Rejected the work of Copernicus, Brahe, and Kepler.
   b. Used the newly invented telescope for his observations.
   c. Argued traditionally that earthly bodies were naturally at rest.
   d. Argued that earthly bodies were naturally in motion.
   e. Described craters on the moon and sunspots.

3. Sir Isaac Newton:

   a. Wrote *The Mathematical Principles of Natural Philosophy.*
   b. Argued that the planets, rotating on their axes, traveled around the sun in circular orbits.
   c. Argued that the planets, rotating on their own axes, traveled around the sun in elliptical orbits.
   d. Argued that the universe was infinite.
   e. Was understood by almost all his contemporaries.

4. Sir Francis Bacon:

   a. Emphasized careful observation and experimentation as the best path to knowledge.
   b. Argued that the deductive method, modeled on geometry, was the best way to arrive at reliable knowledge.
   c. Was lord chancellor of England under James I.
   d. Wrote "I think, therefore I am."
   e. Was famous for his hog breeding.

5. The New Science was embraced and advanced by:

   a. Traditionally minded natural philosophers in a university setting.
   b. Mathematicians working outside the universities.
   c. Craftsmen improving instruments through experimentation.
   d. Alchemists interested in hidden powers at work in the world.
   e. People who believed in predestination.

Now that you have reviewed and tested yourself on this part of the chapter, take time to pull together all the important information by answering the following questions:

◆ Compare and contrast the medieval and Copernican theory of the universe.

◆ How did Sir Isaac Newton draw on the work of his predecessors, and what was original to his theory of the universe? What were the component parts of his scientific method?

The Impact of the New Science

6. Scientific organizations:

   a. Were made up mostly of men.
   b. Believed in the careful reporting of scientific experiments in print.
   c. Tried to keep their experiments secret.
   d. Had men in them who thought they were "priests of nature."
   e. Favored argumentative presentation of experiments with lots of verbal fireworks.

7. René Descartes:

   a. Argued that everything in nature could be reduced to matter in motion.
   b. Argued against the theory of innate ideas.
   c. Argued for the theory of innate ideas.
   d. Agreed with Pascal's theory of "heart."
   e. Argued for a "dwarf-god."

8. John Locke:
    a. Believed that people entered voluntarily into government and could withdraw from it if need be.
    b. Favored rule by a "leviathan."
    c. Wrote that man's life was "nasty, brutish, and short."
    d. Defended the Glorious Revolution.
    e. Stated that the chief function of government was to protect property.

Now that you have reviewed and tested yourself on this part of the chapter, take time to pull together all the important information by answering the following questions:

◆ What did religious thought based on the conclusions of the New Science have in common with traditional Christian theology, and where did it differ from that theology?

◆ What characterized the people drawn to scientific societies in the sixteenth and seventeenth centuries?

The Enlightenment

9. Locke's *An Essay Concerning Human Understanding*:
    a. Endorsed the theory of innate ideas.
    b. Rejected the theory of innate ideas.
    c. Argued that human ideas arose through experience of the world.
    d. Used Newton's scientific method to develop a science of the mind.
    e. Asserted that human beings could not directly know the supernatural world.

10. Voltaire:
    a. Wrote *The Spirit of the Laws*.
    b. Wrote *The Philosophical Letters on the English*.
    c. Refused to get involved in the Calas affair.
    d. Openly attacked Christianity.
    e. Was very sympathetic to the Jesuits.

11. Deism:
    a. Accepted the doctrines of the Trinity and the divinity of Jesus.
    b. Drew on Locke's sense-based psychology.
    c. Accepted Newton's theory of a clocklike universe.
    d. Relied on a mystical inner light to guide people to the divine.
    e. Rejected Newton's idea that God periodically intervenes in the universe to keep it going.

12. The *Encyclopédie*:
    a. Aimed to present a summary of all human knowledge.
    b. Was edited by the Baron de Montesquieu.
    c. Had to get around censorship.
    d. Aimed to present useful knowledge.
    e. Was somewhat hostile to the New Science.

13. Jean-Jacques Rousseau:
    a. Believed in the natural goodness of human beings.
    b. Was a pioneer of modern democratic theory and practice.
    c. Was secretive and avoided talking about himself.
    d. Rejected refined aristocratic society.
    e. Wished to be seen as a man who presented himself fully to others.

Now that you have reviewed and tested yourself on this part of the chapter, take time to pull together all the important information by answering the following questions:

◆ How did John Locke's sense-based psychology influence the Enlightenment movement?

◆ What were the various positions on religion put forward by people caught up in the Enlightenment movement?

Society and the Enlightenment

14. The new world of reading in the eighteenth century:

    a. Relied on reading habits that emphasized rereading of works and careful repetition of passages in them.
    b. Fostered the growth of lending libraries.
    c. Broadened people's imaginative reading experiences.
    d. Was largely free of government censorship.
    e. Made publishers more responsive to readers' demands.

15. Coffee and tea houses:

    a. First appeared in Paris.
    b. Were always reserved for the rich.
    c. Eventually brought together men of different backgrounds.
    d. Often saw conversations degenerate into brawls.
    e. Emphasized polite, if heated, conversation.

16. Salons:

    a. Were exclusively meeting places for the rich and well-born.
    b. Were dedicated to frivolity and silliness.
    c. Discussed scientific, artistic, and political topics assigned by the hostess.
    d. Were usually hosted by women.
    e. Brought together men and women from different social and religious backgrounds.

17. Cameralism:

    a. Developed in western Europe.
    b. Viewed kings as supreme political managers.
    c. Viewed kings as God-anointed rulers with sacred authority.
    d. Aimed at increasing a state's wealth through direct management of people and resources.
    e. Compared the state to the human body.

Now that you have reviewed and tested yourself on this part of the chapter, take time to pull together all the important information by answering the following questions:

◆ What kinds of social relations did coffee and tea houses, salons, and Masonic lodges promote?

◆ What accounts for the rise in public opinion since the eighteenth century, and what effect did it have on politics?

Enlightenment Debates

18. The Abbé Raynal:

    a. Wrote that America produced puny plants, animals, and human beings.
    b. Compared Americans to mastodons.
    c. Was challenged by Jefferson in his work *Notes on the State of Virginia.*
    d. Was supported by Benjamin Franklin.
    e. Was called a "fat whale" by George Washington.

19. Aphra Behn:
    a. Supported the institution of slavery.
    b. Attacked the institution of slavery.
    c. Gave her characters the physical and moral qualities Europeans admired.
    d. Made her characters weak and emotionally troubled.
    e. Secretly owned slaves.

20. Jean-Jacques Rousseau:
    a. Agreed with Descartes and Locke that men and women were mental equals.
    b. Argued that women's public role in society was a symptom of civilization's corrupting influence.
    c. Praised the civilizing role of salons presided over by women.
    d. Stated that women should stay at home and breast-feed their babies.
    e. Was a close friend of Mary Wollstonecraft.

Now that you have reviewed and tested yourself on this part of the chapter, take time to pull together all the important information by answering the following questions:

◆ What were the similarities and differences in Europeans' understandings of non-European peoples and their understandings of men and women?

◆ What techniques did novelists use to argue against the institution of slavery?

CHAPTER 18

Trade and Empire, 1700–1800

Chapter Outline

1713

Spain cedes *asiento* to Britain

1720

Last plague epidemic breaks out in France

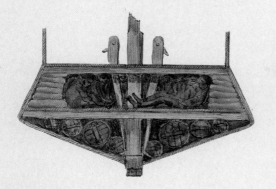

This ink and watercolor drawing by an eighteenth-century French artist shows the cross section of a ship carrying slaves from Africa to European colonies in the Americas. It graphically depicts the cramped quarters slaves were forced to endure on the voyage across the Atlantic. (Bibliotheque de L'Arsenal, Paris/Archives Charmet/The Bridgeman Art Library)

After reading this chapter, you should be able to answer the following questions:

How did changes in overseas empires and trading networks contribute to Europe's economic development in the eighteenth century?

How did Enlightenment thinking influence Europe's economic and social development?

What new forms of individual and collective identity emerged?

How did the Industrial Revolution change the production of goods, and why did it occur in Britain?

BY THE EIGHTEENTH CENTURY a bustling transatlantic economy was fueling Europe's economic growth. In addition, Europe once again experienced population growth, which in turn stimulated economic production and a rise in consumption of goods and services at all levels of society. People bought more clothing, household items, and food. Increased economic activity led European thinkers to explore the reasons for economic growth and to lay the foundations for the modern discipline of economics. These new economists viewed people primarily as rational beings who exercised individual choice as consumers of the goods available in the marketplace.

The Atlantic economy also reshaped the European empires that had been formed in the Western Hemisphere beginning in the sixteenth century. Portugal, founder of the first overseas empire, relied more and more on the riches of Brazil for its continuing prosperity. The Spanish and French empires declined as the British Empire rose, outstripping all others in vitality and prosperity and making London the commercial center

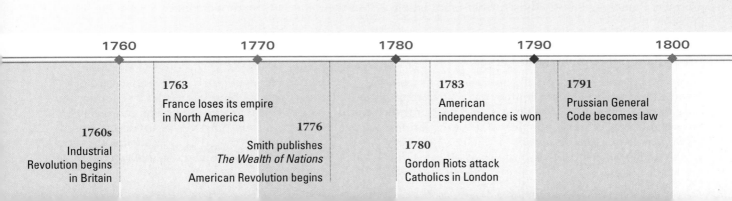

1760	1770	1780	1790	1800

1763
France loses its empire
in North America

1776
Smith publishes
The Wealth of Nations

American Revolution begins

1760s
Industrial
Revolution begins
in Britain

1780
Gordon Riots attack
Catholics in London

1783
American
independence is won

1791
Prussian General
Code becomes law

of Europe. Britain's leading role in the Atlantic economy stimulated manufacturing and early forms of industrialization, thus laying the foundations for the modern economic world. But for the British as for every other New World empire, commerce and wealth depended on the labor of enslaved Africans.

Prosperity in Europe was accompanied by changes in upper- and middle-class behavior, as the well-to-do, influenced by Enlightenment ideas, began to expect greater privacy and comfort in the home and indulged in more spontaneous displays of affection among family members. The poor continued to live more tradition-bound lives, and the social and cultural gap between them and the rich widened. Government officials developed new theories about the causes of poverty and new institutions to eliminate them, while the poor took action by rioting. Food shortages and unacceptable working conditions could provoke popular rioting. So could long-simmering religious hatred. Europeans also began to rethink the basic nature of society, rejecting traditional ideas that emphasized group membership more than individual autonomy. Some people argued that wealth, not birth, was the proper basis for social ranking, whereas others maintained that society was made up of individual citizens bound together in a unified nation.

Economic Recovery

♦ **What new ideas about economic development and the value of work accompanied Europe's economic recovery?**

♦ **What effects did the consumer revolution have on the daily lives of Europeans?**

After 1700, Europe's population began to grow once again. Unlike the sixteenth-century demographic expansion, the eighteenth-century growth did not produce a crisis of overpopulation and economic hard times. Instead, it produced prosperity. But economic growth also caused people to question older ideas about how wealth was generated and to search for the laws that made the economic world function. Europeans also began to consume a greater variety of products than ever before, thus further stimulating the economy.

The Expanding Population of Europe

Europe's sixteenth-century overpopulation crisis was followed in the seventeenth century by a stagnating or declining population in many places. Then, in the early eighteenth century, population again began to grow, increasing from 95 million in 1700 to 146 million in 1800—an increase of more than 50 percent.

Growth was greatest in England and France; in general, western Europe experienced more growth than eastern Europe.

Population Growth: Disease and Hygiene Historians have identified several factors contributing to population increase. The first was the disappearance of bubonic plague. The likely cause for the plague's decline is found in Europe's shifting rodent population as large brown rats, carrying fleas that stayed on them, overtook the earlier black rat population, which hosted fleas that jumped onto human beings. The fleas carried the plague bacillus. This change in the rat population coincided with better government quarantines of infected areas, which reduced the spread of disease.

Other killers, like smallpox, dysentery, and typhoid fever, periodically exploded into epidemics, but their effects were moderated by a growing interest in community and personal hygiene. Recognizing that filth bred disease, urban governments launched campaigns to clear out the garbage and human waste from the cities.

In the eighteenth century, Europeans also began to bathe regularly. Bathing had been common in the Middle Ages, at least in towns with communal baths. After the Black Death, however, many cities closed their baths, thinking that they spread the disease. Later, Protestant and Catholic reformers campaigned

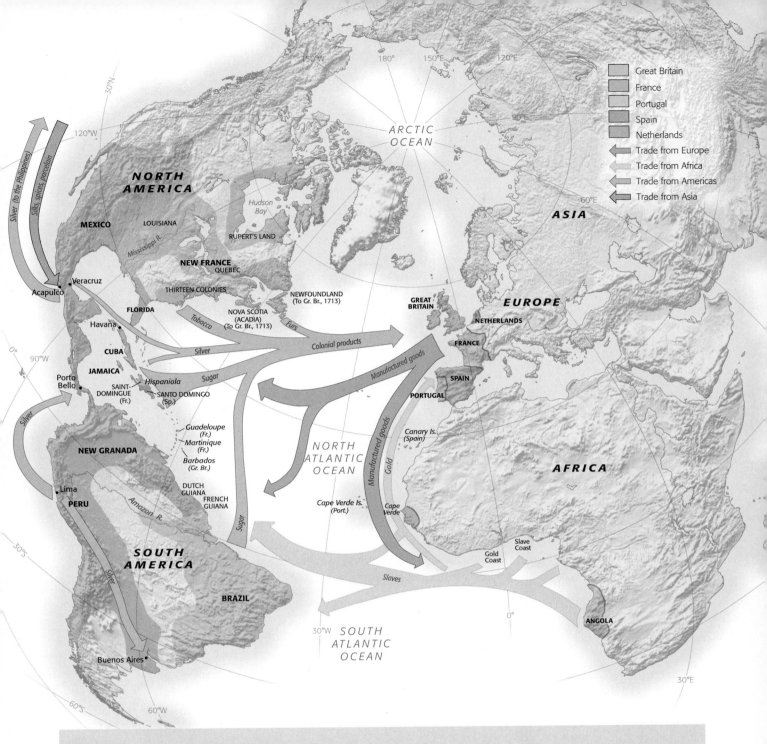

Map 18.1 **The Atlantic World, 1700–1789** By the eighteenth century, Europe's trade had expanded beyond the routes from an earlier time between northern and southern Europe and eastern and western Europe. It now refocused on a cross-Atlantic trade that united Europe, Africa, and the Americas in new trading patterns.
© Cengage Learning

1. Trace the trade routes shown on this map.
2. What role did each of the following play in this Atlantic economy?
   a. Agricultural products
   b. Metals
   c. Manufactured goods

Map labels:
- Great Britain
- France
- Portugal
- Spain
- Netherlands
- Trade from Europe
- Trade from Africa
- Trade from Americas
- Trade from Asia

ARCTIC OCEAN

NORTH AMERICA

ASIA

EUROPE

AFRICA

Hudson Bay

MEXICO · LOUISIANA · RUPERT'S LAND

Mississippi R.

NEW FRANCE · QUEBEC

THIRTEEN COLONIES

NEWFOUNDLAND (To Gr. Br., 1713)

GREAT BRITAIN

NETHERLANDS

FRANCE

SPAIN

PORTUGAL

Veracruz · Acapulco

Silver (to the Philippines) · Silks, spices, porcelain

FLORIDA · Havana · CUBA

NOVA SCOTIA (ACADIA) (To Gr. Br., 1713)

Tobacco · Furs · Silver · Colonial products · Manufactured goods

Porto Bello · JAMAICA · SAINT-DOMINGUE (Fr.) · Hispaniola · SANTO DOMINGO (Sp.)

Sugar

Canary Is. (Spain)

Manufactured goods · Gold

NEW GRANADA

Silver

Guadeloupe (Fr.) · Martinique (Fr.) · Barbados (Gr. Br.)

NORTH ATLANTIC OCEAN

Cape Verde Is. (Port.) · Cape Verde

Lima · PERU

Amazon R.

DUTCH GUIANA · FRENCH GUIANA

Sugar

Slave Coast · Gold Coast

Slaves

SOUTH AMERICA

BRAZIL

Slaves

SOUTH ATLANTIC OCEAN

ANGOLA

Buenos Aires

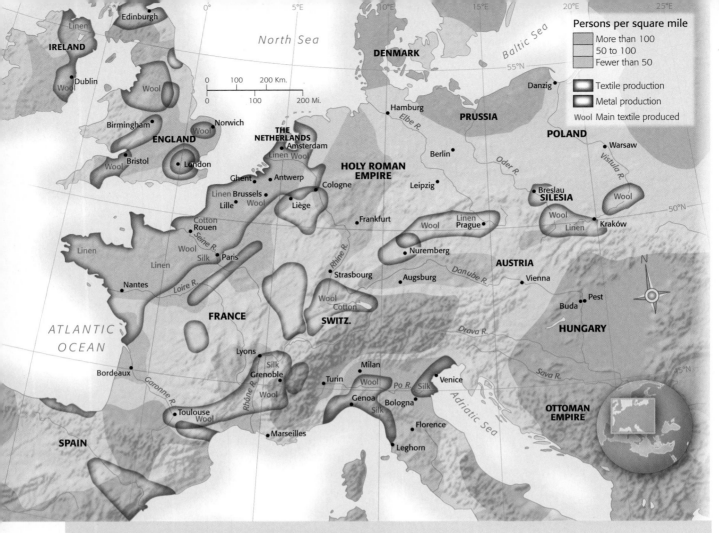

1. Identify the areas of population density from densest to least dense.
2. Now identify the areas of textile and metal production.
3. Overall, is there a significant correlation between population density and textile production? Or is the correlation hard to make?
4. Is there a significant correlation between population density and metal production? Or is the correlation hard to make?

to shut them down, arguing that baths promoted lewdness and sexual license. As a result, Europeans became dirtier and smellier than their medieval ancestors. By the eighteenth century, doctors had started to prescribe cold baths to build up the body, and the resumption of bathing improved hygiene and reduced disease.

Warfare and Population Growth Changing patterns of European warfare also encouraged population growth. The religious wars of the sixteenth and seventeenth centuries devastated the civilian population where they were fought. Armies were huge breeding grounds for disease, which spread beyond their own quarters. Battle also disrupted agriculture and brought on food shortages in a population already straining Europe's agricultural resources. Shortages, in turn, weakened people's resistance to disease. In the eighteenth century, Europe fought some of its wars elsewhere—in the Western Hemisphere and in Asia—and those fought in Europe were shorter and therefore less disruptive than earlier wars.

Moreover, troops were better fed, better supplied, and better disciplined than they had been, making their presence less dangerous to the surrounding civilian population.

Population Growth and Diet Finally, improvements in Europeans' diets encouraged population growth. Better climatological conditions gradually set in after 1700 as the Little Ice Age ended and harvests improved. In addition, some farmers kept up with rising demand by changing the agricultural practices in what has been described as an **agricultural revolution**. The changes developed first in the Rhineland and the Netherlands and then spread to England in the seventeenth and eighteenth centuries.

The Agricultural Revolution Traditionally, farmers had let fields lie fallow, or uncultivated, to restore their fertility. Beginning in the sixteenth century, farmers discovered that instead of taking fields out of production, they could plant clover or turnips, which not only replenished the soil but could also be used as fodder for livestock.

Larger Herds and More Manure Now larger herds could be developed for milk, hides, and meat, so people began breeding livestock to improve quality. In England, local cows were bred with Dutch cattle to increase milk yield, and sheep were bred with specimens that were bigger than normal or that had fine wool coats. Growing herds meant nitrogen-rich manure that could be spread on fields to further increase their productivity. With fallowing eliminated and more manure available as fertilizer, land could be kept in continual production, thus greatly increasing the yield.

The End of the Open-Field System Increased yields created surpluses; so did a reorganization of farmland for agricultural production that ended the open-field system. In the past, cropland was usually divided into individually owned plots that were small but had no barriers between them. Sometimes people owned plots separated from each other by other owners' land. This exposed and fragmented pattern of landholding worked as long as the farming community operated as a single unit, planting and harvesting crops in the same sequence and at the same time. Village councils or the local landlord usually regulated planting and harvesting. After harvest, the community's livestock was allowed to range freely over the fields, grazing on what was left in them. This system discouraged experimentation with new crops and agricultural techniques.

Enclosure Beginning in the middle of the eighteenth century, Britain's Parliament encouraged more efficient and productive use of farmland by passing laws permitting **enclosure** in a given area. Single strips were bought or traded to create large, consolidated blocs of land that were fenced off. Enclosure allowed for economies of scale in agricultural production and made experimentation with different crops and crop rotations possible.

Improving the Soil New land was also brought under cultivation and improved with new techniques. Underground drainage systems were installed in waterlogged fields, and heavy clays were lightened by working in crushed limestone. Improvements in crops, land organization, and soil quality also greatly increased yields. During the eighteenth century, improvements in agriculture spared Europeans from the devastating famines of earlier centuries.

Enclosure increased agricultural productivity, but it came at a social cost. Small-scale owners and poor squatters were forced off their plots, and traditional rights to common grazing after harvest were eclipsed. As the rural poor lost even the chance to maintain livestock, many became landless wageworkers on enclosed farms.

Declining Mortality Rates, Rising Marriage Rates Nevertheless, the decline in epidemic diseases, coupled with improvements in military behavior, people's diet, and agricultural production, reduced mortality rates. During the eighteenth century, more people could count on their children surviving infancy and then living longer, healthier lives. In addition, people had more children because they were marrying earlier than before. In previous centuries, death had been the great social equalizer because rich and poor were equally defenseless in the face of disease. Now, the rich began to live longer than the poor because they were better fed and lived in the cleanest, healthiest environments.

The World of Work

For many Europeans, patterns of work remained as they had been in previous centuries. Despite innovations in agriculture, most peasants toiled in the countryside using age-old techniques for planting and harvesting crops. In cities, guild members continued to think of themselves as the elite of the working world and jealously guarded their privileges. Alongside this traditional world, however, other types of work began to engage growing numbers of people.

The Putting-Out System During the economic slump of the seventeenth century, Europe's peasants and urban working poor, especially in the west, supplemented their incomes by making things at home. Many women spun wool into yarn and sold the surplus—the yarns they did not use themselves. Most likely,

agricultural revolution Improvements in agricultural method and livestock breeding in the sixteenth to the eighteenth centuries that greatly increased crop yields.

enclosure Process of consolidating agricultural land and enclosing it with hedges or fences.

they would put their children to work cleaning and carding (combing) the wool, while husbands would weave on hand looms. Eventually, merchants delivered raw wool to the household and paid cash for finished cloth. This arrangement, known as the **putting-out system**, was Europe's first means of manufacturing.

Merchants got involved because they could pay low and sell high. They might buy raw wool in large volume from sheep farmers, put it out to many different households, and pick up spun yarn or even woven cloth for a pittance—so much for a certain amount, or by the piece. Linen cloth—both coarse and fine—and nails were also produced in the putting-out system.

Workers accepted the arrangement because the entire family could be put to work. But the spread of the system, in which household workers only occasionally saw the merchant who bought their **piecework**, created a personal and physical distance between workers and merchants that did not exist in the older owner-operated workshop of the guild system.

The Pros and Cons of the Putting-Out System When Europe's population once again began to grow in the early eighteenth century, demand for manufactured products rose, offering people further employment. Because prices for food and other basic products tended to rise faster than workers' incomes, there were always people willing to do piecework.

But the putting-out system also carried risks. Merchants would pay for products as long as demand was high, but an unpredictable decline in demand, often in a distant market, would lead to drastically fewer pieces bought and a sharp decline in income for workers. Overall, however, the putting-out system dynamically increased Europe's manufacturing capacity. For example, English linen exports jumped from 180,000 yards in 1730 to 9.6 million yards in 1760.

New Types of Urban Work Other new types of work were urban based. Europe's cities were growing in the eighteenth century, offering work for architects, engineers, bricklayers, stonemasons, street repairers, plumbers, and those who catered to them. In Paris, a kind of "take-out" developed, as people bought prepared food for their meals.

Women found work as dressmakers, seamstresses, linen workers, and clothes washers. Paris had two thousand washerwomen scrubbing along the banks of the Seine River. Women also operated stalls in outdoor markets. As in the past, women's wages lagged noticeably behind men's.

Servants All over Europe, migrants from the countryside to the city often ended up as servants. Servants regularly made up a city's largest single group of workers,

putting-out system System whereby workers manufactured consumer goods for a merchant who supplied them with raw material.

piecework Work paid for by the number of pieces produced.

and Paris may have had more than ninety thousand of them. Usually, servants constituted about 10 percent of the total urban population. Servants benefited from some job security because their employment was continuous and they were given room and board and sometimes clothing. But work in an employer's house also could be dangerous. Angry masters might accuse their servants of theft, and women could be seduced or raped by their employer or fellow servants and then abandoned.

Skilled and Unskilled Servants The servant world was divided into the skilled few and the mass of the unskilled. The skilled worked as butlers, cooks, and personal attendants. They often served the same employer for many years and then retired into the middle class. Most servants, however, worked as footmen, stable boys, or chamber and kitchen maids. These lower servants usually calculated employment opportunities carefully, regularly leaving one employer for another if the new job promised a better wage, a new set of clothes, or better food and lodging.

Male servants viewed their work as a temporary measure until something better came along. Many women worked to save a dowry and then marry a prosperous peasant or artisan in their home village or in the city where they worked.

The Underemployed At the bottom of the urban world were the underemployed. These were men and women who passed in and out of work. Men looked for odd jobs, hauling water or carrying messages across town. Women washed clothes, or took up prostitution when nothing else was available. All of them eked out a life through begging, petty thievery, and occasional work, depending on what seemed the best opportunity from day to day. With Europe's population rising, their numbers probably grew over the century.

Changing Notions of Wealth

As work diversified and patterns of work changed during the eighteenth century, Europeans debated the nature of the economic world. Gradually, new ways of thinking about work and the economy emerged.

Mercantilism During the seventeenth century, states had adopted mercantilism as an economic policy. Mercantilists believed that the world's wealth was limited and that a state needed to increase its overall share at the expense of others. This belief led to programs for stimulating domestic prosperity and establishing favorable trade balances. Mercantilism emphasized the needs of states and their rulers above all else; economic policy was a means of strengthening states locked in the competitive struggle for dominance in Europe. Europe's colonies were absorbed into this mercantilist agenda; their purpose was to provide the things that the mother country needed to secure a greater share of the world's

In this print, Adam Smith, a professor at the University of Glasgow in Scotland, points to a book, perhaps one of his own. Near the book are feather pens and letter paper. Like most writers in the eighteenth century, Smith would have carried on an extensive correspondence with people who shared his intellectual interests.

wealth and to increase its competitive advantage at home and abroad.

The Physiocrats In the eighteenth century, economists started to argue that economic activity did not simply shift wealth from one state to another. Economies were capable of growing, and new wealth could be generated if states stopped interfering in economic life. In France, the **Physiocrats** argued that the government's traditional regulation of the grain trade harmed agricultural productivity and that the economy would work best if the government left it alone. "*Laissez faire, laissez aller!*" ("Leave it alone, let it go!"), they cried. Thus the term **laissez faire** came to stand for a government policy of noninterference in the economy.

The Physiocrats also thought of the economy as a complex mechanism, each part of which depended on the others. In this way it was like the natural world. And, like the natural world, the economy was governed by laws. Just as Isaac Newton had discovered the laws of physics, the Physiocrats proposed to discover the laws of economic activity and to construct a science of economics.

Adam Smith When **Adam Smith**, professor of moral philosophy at the University of Glasgow, visited with the Physiocrats on a trip to France, he became interested in this new science. His *Inquiry into the Nature and Causes of the Wealth of Nations*, published in 1776, quickly became a foundational text for modern economic thought based on the Physiocrats' idea that economies could grow.

Smith adopted the laissez-faire principles of the Physiocrats. Governments, he argued, should regulate economic activity as little as possible, restricting themselves to defending the community against foreign attackers, establishing a judicial system to police people's behavior, and supporting improvements in transportation, such as roads and canals, that would facilitate commerce.

Human Beings as Consumers: The "Invisible Hand" Smith believed that human beings wanted to acquire material goods to make their lives more comfortable. They were consumers by nature. Their economic activity was driven by their own needs and those of their immediate families, not by any concern for the public good. Nevertheless, as individuals pursued their private and often selfish economic interests, the larger economy benefited. An "invisible hand" linked all these private pursuits into an overall economic dynamic that brought prosperity to the whole community.

So, when tea drinkers satisfied their desire for tea by buying tea leaves, a teapot, and teacups, they enriched the merchant who had brought the tea from Asia and the workers in porcelain who had made the pot and cups. These people then used their profits to satisfy their own desires, thereby enriching yet another group of merchants and manufacturers.

The Division of Labor Smith knew that satisfying consumers' desires meant that production of goods had to keep up with them, and he argued that production could grow with the **division of labor**. Each stage in the production of a commodity—Smith used the example of pins—should be done by specialists. Division and specialization would result in a greater volume of production than when one person made one pin, start to finish.

This division of labor was already happening in the putting-out system, as merchants brought raw wool to spinners, picked up yarn

Physiocrats French economists who argued against mercantilist regulation of the economy.

laissez faire (in French, "leave it alone") Economic principle that economies develop best when free of government interference.

Adam Smith (ca. 1723–1790) Scottish philosopher and economist whose *Wealth of Nations* (1776) became a foundational text for modern economic theory and economic liberalism.

division of labor Manufacturing arrangement whereby each stage in production is done by specialists, thus increasing volume of production.

Special Collections/Glasgow University Library

and took it to weavers, and then picked up woven cloth to sell on the market. In their writings, Smith and the Physiocrats analyzed economic behavior on its own terms, and, like the philosophes, they formulated the laws underlying it.

Manual Labor Attitudes toward manual work were also changing during the eighteenth century. Traditionally, manual labor was held in contempt because it involved working with material things like dirt, wood, or animal skins. The material world was thought to be lower than the spiritual world, and, following the story of Adam in Genesis, manual labor was believed to be punishment for sin.

When the philosophes rejected traditional Christian ideas about human beings' inherent wickedness, they also cast aside the idea of work as punishment. No one did this more forcefully than Denis Diderot. His *Encyclopédie* extolled the social usefulness of crafts that depended on working with one's hands and presented readers with detailed articles, accompanied by engravings, of manufacturing processes.

Thus Smith's idea that people could increase their productivity through division of labor was coupled with Diderot's celebration of the workers who produced goods for consumption. Throughout the eighteenth century, a surge in consumer demand across all economic groups created new employment opportunities in a wide range of firms manufacturing consumer products. New attitudes help to explain why the manufacturing sector of the European economy grew so dynamically during the eighteenth century.

The Consumer Revolution

Smith's and Diderot's interest in the production of goods was connected to an important shift in many Europeans' economic behavior that has been described as the **consumer revolution**. As more goods became available, people bought more than ever before, stimulating the production of even more, and more varied, kinds of things to buy.

The Consumer Revolution and the Rich Consumer demand rose over most of Europe, but especially in the states of the northwest—Britain, the Netherlands, western Germany, and France. Imported goods made the array of items to purchase even more enticing. The rich purchased wallpaper, paintings, mirrors, and elaborate clocks, as well as expensive furniture. Fine porcelain began to replace pottery on dining tables and was used for such things as candlesticks that earlier had been made from wood or metal. Cotton clothing, made from fiber imported from India and Europe's American colonies, became increasingly popular, replacing wool and rivaling linen and silk as the fabric of fashion. Snuffboxes for men, elegant scarves for women, and bejeweled walking sticks for both came increasingly into fashion.

The Consumer Revolution and the Middle Classes The rich had always spent heavily on decorative and luxury commodities, and their spending habits in the eighteenth century represented a quantitative but not a qualitative increase in conspicuous consumption. The real change over the century occurred among the middle and lower economic groups in European society; now, for the first time, they bought many of the same items, copying the tastes of the rich. The change is reflected in wills and lists from estate sales.

Now a merchant would have a set of razors for shaving, along with porcelain shaving mugs and washbowls, all of which sat on a wooden stand made of fine wood in the latest fashion. His wife would have several changes of clothes, hung in a new wooden clothes closet set against a wall. Chamber pots placed in toilet chairs became a common feature of their well-appointed bedroom. By the end of the century, some people were installing indoor plumbing and flush toilets that connected to improved sewer systems.

The Consumer Revolution and the Working Poor Even the working poor furnished and decorated their rented rooms. Inexpensive prints hung on their walls, and pieces of pretty porcelain were brought out for special occasions. They bought more bed frames and mattresses than ever before and started to put their children in their own beds instead of adding them to the parental bed, as they had in the past. They also accumulated several changes of clothes, buying from secondhand dealers who sold the used clothes of the rich.

The Pawnshop Several factors lay behind working people's accumulation of possessions. Increasingly, workers were paid in cash rather than kind. The growth of a cash economy offered new forms of investment. Extra clothing and nonessential household items served as a hedge against catastrophic poverty during hard economic times.

If demand for textiles in the putting-out system declined, workers could take their new possessions, purchased when work and incomes were good, and pawn them for cash in the growing number of **pawnshops** that emerged during the eighteenth century. When good economic times returned, the pawned items were redeemed, enjoyed once again, and held in reserve for the inevitable bad times.

A New Sense of Empowerment Moreover, as people became consumers of a variety of products, they developed a sense of empowerment. They saw their choices in the marketplace as reflecting their taste, and they sought to cultivate their taste through knowledge of goods and markets. As they made personal choices about what they wanted to buy, they increased their role as individual actors in the marketplace.

consumer revolution Term used for the eighteenth-century rise in consumer demand that stimulated the economy, especially in northwestern Europe.

pawnshops Institutions that lend money to persons who deposit goods there as security against the loan.

Olof Fridsberg's painting of *Ulla Tessin in Her Study* shows a rich Swedish woman caught up in the consumer revolution. Her study contains many luxury goods—an oriental rug, two desks, a clock, figurines, a Chinese vase, and a Chinese lacquered cabinet on a shelf. Can you identify other consumer items this lady has crammed into her room?

The National Museum of Fine Arts, Stockholm

Adam Smith's picture of an economy based on private individuals' pursuit of their own interests was embodied in the consumer revolution.

Coffee, Tea, Chocolate, Sugar In addition to buying more clothes, accessories, and household items, Europeans also added new foodstuffs to their daily diets. Four items, in particular, stand out: coffee, tea, and chocolate, all of which were drunk, and cane sugar, which started to replace honey as a sweetener. All four depended on the growth in overseas trade and the establishment of colonies. Tea was imported from East Asia, and coffee came from either the Middle East or the Western Hemisphere. Chocolate was raised in tropical colonies. Above all, sugar was produced in ever-larger quantities in the plantations of the Caribbean and Brazil. By century's end, sugar had become a standard item on the tables of both the rich and the poor.

New Foodstuffs and New Manufacturing The introduction of these new foodstuffs often stimulated European manufacturing. For example, as the consumption of tea increased, so did demand for teapots and teacups. A well-to-do hostess, preparing for a tea party, would also have purchased many other new goods—canisters to store the tea, special clippers to cut sugar from the cones in which it came, a tea table, a porcelain pitcher for cream, a sugar basket and tongs for the cut sugar, and teaspoons for stirring.

Checking In

By yourself or with a partner, explain the significance of each of the following selected key terms:

agricultural revolution	Adam Smith
putting-out system	division of labor
Physiocrats	consumer revolution
laissez faire	pawnshops

The Atlantic World

◆ **How did the Atlantic trade link Europe, Africa, and the Americas in an integrated economy?**

◆ **What explains Britain's leading role in this trade?**

During the eighteenth century, trading networks across the Atlantic, which had formed during the sixteenth century, reached their fullest development.

Samuel Gamble Sets Out from London on a Slaving Voyage

On April 7, 1793, Samuel Gamble weighed anchor and eased his ship, the *Sandown*, along the Thames River to the North Sea. Gamble had contracted with a group of British investors in January to gather a cargo of slaves in Africa for sale in the British colony of Jamaica. He had been in the slave trade for years, but this time business conditions were dangerous. France and Britain were once again at war, and the French were attacking British ships on the high seas. The Royal Navy was seizing ships' crews for its men-of-war, and Gamble had replaced twelve seized sailors only days before he set sail. Despite the dangers, Gamble and his backers were willing to put down money for the voyage. High risk meant high yield if the venture was successful.

The *Sandown* was provisioned for long sailing because a roundtrip could last for a year or more. For weeks, supplies had been taken on board: beef, pork, pigs, tripe, potatoes, butter, and beer to feed the captain and crew; lead bars, gunpowder, earthenware dishes, and brandy to trade for slaves; and "big Iron Handcuffs, Neck chains & collars" to bind the slave cargo on the voyage to the West Indies. After leaving the Thames estuary, Gamble sailed along the southern coast of England in a convoy of merchant ships protected by the Royal Navy. Then they headed southwest into the Atlantic. On May 16, some of the ships veered off for the West Indies, while Gamble sailed south for the west coast of Africa. After stopping in Portugal's Cape Verde Islands, where he picked up cotton cloth to trade in Africa, Gamble arrived in what is today Sierra Leone on June 12, prepared to trade his cargo for slaves.

From then on, things went badly. June was the beginning of the rainy season in West Africa, and wet ground brought swarms of disease-carrying mosquitoes. Already, yellow fever was ravaging the coastal areas. This disease often killed within a week, as victims, vomiting blackish blood, fell into a coma while their liver deteriorated, causing them to turn yellow from jaundice. Gamble's stop in Africa had to be short if profits were to be made. He had contracted to carry 250 slaves to Jamaica in time for the beginning of sugar-cane cutting in December, when market demand for new slaves would be

high. But yellow fever had disrupted the African trading networks, and Gamble had to wait nine and a half months before he could collect 234 slaves, 16 short of his contract. They were listed in his journal simply by age, sex, and an assigned number.

As Gamble tried to fill his ship with slaves, and he himself began to shake with fever, some of his sailors fell ill or died. The crew as a whole became, he wrote in his journal, "quite Peevish, fraxious, ill natur'd and Childish." In mid-January 1794, a slave uprising broke out on board, and eight Africans drowned, most likely as they tried to swim to freedom. Troubles continued after the *Sandown* set sail across the Atlantic in March—yellow fever, fights between sailors and slaves, more deaths. The ship's water kegs were leaking, and the *Sandown* had to make an unplanned stop in Barbados to take on more. There sixteen crew members abandoned ship and hired lawyers to get their back wages from Gamble. With the lawyers demanding the removal of *Sandown*'s sails and rudder to prevent it from leaving, Gamble sneaked out of port before daybreak and limped into Kingston, Jamaica, with a crew of five.

Yellow fever awaited him there. It had swirled across the Atlantic on other ships, disrupting the Jamaican slave markets and leaving Kingston's harbor crowded with earlier arrivals from Africa. In any case, Gamble had arrived too late to take advantage of high prices at the beginning of the cane-cutting season. "Slaves complaining of pains in their Bowells," he wrote glumly in his journal on May 25. The next day's entry read, "Slaves as before, they go off very slow (Market glutted)." After taking on provisions and a new cargo, probably of sugar and rum, the *Sandown* joined an armed convoy for the return trip to London, arriving there on October 11, 1794, a year and a half after the outbound voyage.

Gamble and his backers were disappointed in their profits. In a trade economy that pitted high gain against high risk, they had lost.

Source: Excerpts from Samuel Gamble's journal (c. 1793). Included in Bruce L. Mouser (ed.), *A Slaving Voyage to Africa and Jamaica: The Log of the Sandown*, 1793–1794.

Northern Europe's trade with the Mediterranean and East Asia flourished, but the dynamic center shifted decisively to the Atlantic Ocean. The older empires of Spain and Portugal continued to send products to Europe, but they were being overtaken by the French and the British. In the end, it was the British who occupied the central place in an Atlantic trade system. This system was based on the seizure and transport of, ultimately, millions of Africans to the Western Hemisphere, where they

labored as slaves to produce agricultural commodities, especially sugar, to satisfy rising consumer demand in Europe. In return, Europeans manufactured shoes and cheap clothing for slaves and a variety of household items, tools, and luxuries for colonists.

The Atlantic Economy

Samuel Gamble's triangular voyage (see A New Direction: Samuel Gamble Sets Out from London on a

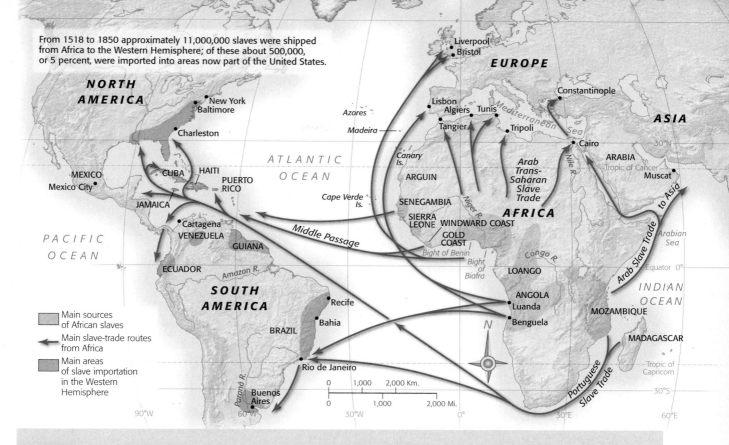

From 1518 to 1850 approximately 11,000,000 slaves were shipped from Africa to the Western Hemisphere; of these about 500,000, or 5 percent, were imported into areas now part of the United States.

Map 18.3 **The Worldwide Slave Trade** In the eighteenth century, slave trading out of Africa went in many directions. Africans from central Africa were taken north to Muslim ports on the Mediterranean, while the Arab-controlled slave trade east from Mozambique to Asia also flourished. Most slaves bound for the New World were taken from Mozambique and from the central and southern west African coast. © *Cengage Learning*

1. How many destinations globally for African slaves can you count on this map? Does the number surprise you?
2. What besides slaves entered the four trading networks shown in this map?

Slaving Voyage) was commonplace in the eighteenth century. British, French, Dutch, and Portuguese slavers sailing from Europe headed to the West African coast. There they turned to resident Europeans with links to local African rulers, who supplied the slaves. Guns and gunpowder, alcohol, cloth, tobacco, and iron bars were traded for the human cargo.

The Middle Passage Once slaves were collected, the voyage across the Atlantic, the dreaded **Middle Passage**, began. For weeks, the ship sailed west, following the trade wind patterns of the North Atlantic. Death stalked the slave ships. On average 10 to 20 percent of the Africans died before reaching the Caribbean, along with 20 to 25 percent of the ship's crew, from diseases contracted in Africa or on board. The Portuguese called these slave ships hearses. Death rates were even higher for Europeans who manned the outposts on the African coast because of malaria and other diseases.

The Impact of the Slave Trade on West Africa The European colonies' import of slaves reshaped the communities of West Africa. Slaves were sometimes captives taken in warfare, and others were simply kidnapped. Some rulers, anxious to take advantage of European demand, extended their power and created centralized kingdoms where the capture and sale of slaves was a central feature of the local economy.

The rich soils of West Africa assured a good food supply, especially after manioc, a nutritious root vegetable, was imported from America. In turn, the food supply encouraged growth of the local population, which slavers could seize for the transatlantic trade. Overall, some 11 million slaves were taken across the Atlantic to toil in American plantations, mainly in the Caribbean and Brazil.

Why Were So Many Slaves Imported to America? The colonies' importation of slaves resulted from an insatiable demand for labor and slaves' high mortality rate; perhaps one-third died within a few years of arriving in the Western Hemisphere. An imbalanced sex ratio also worked against a stabilization of the slave population. Male slaves, considered more desirable for plantation labor because of their strength,

Middle Passage Slave ships' weeks-long voyage across the Atlantic from West Africa to the Caribbean.

Olaudah Equiano Describes Passage on a Slave Ship

In 1789, Olaudah Equiano, a freed slave, published *The Interesting Narrative of the Life of Olaudah Equiano, or Gustavus Vassa, the African*. He claimed that his account was based on his own memories as an African boy of ten taken aboard a slave ship. The claim is currently disputed, but there is no doubt that Equiano's narrative, whether fact or fiction, helped to gain support in England for the abolition of the slave trade.

❶ How does Equiano manage to convey these experiences from the point of view of a ten-year-old child?

❷ Why would Equiano be flogged for not eating?

❸ Why does Equiano make these remarks?

❹ Does this act of kindness lessen or sharpen the horrors of Equiano's account?

❶ The first object which saluted my eyes when I arrived on the coast was the sea, and a slave ship … waiting for its cargo. These filled me with astonishment, which was soon converted into terror…. When I was carried on board I was immediately handled, and tossed up, to see if I were sound by some of the crew, and I was now persuaded that I had gotten into a world of bad spirits and that they were going to kill me. Their complexions too differing so much from ours, their long hair, and the language they spoke, which was very different from any I ever heard, united to confirm me in this belief…. When I looked round the ship too, and saw a large furnace or copper boiling and a multitude of black people of every description chained together, every one of their countenances expressing dejection and sorrow, I no longer doubted of my fate; and, quite overpowered with horror and anguish, I fell motionless on the deck and fainted…. I became so sick and low that I was not able to eat, nor had I the least desire to taste anything. **❷** I now wished for the last friend, Death, to relieve me; but soon, to my grief, two of the white men offered me eatables, and, on my refusing to eat, one of them held me fast by the hands and laid me across, I think, the windlass, and tied my feet, while the other flogged me severely…. **❸** I had never seen among my people such instances of brutal cruelty; and this not only shewn towards us blacks, but also to some of the whites themselves. One white man in particular I saw, when we were permitted [*Sic*] to be on deck, flogged so unmercifully that he died in consequence of it; and they tossed him over the side as they would have done to a brute….

The stench of the hold while we were on the coast was … intolerably loathsome…. The closeness of the place, and the heat of the climate, added to the number in the ship, which was so crowded that each had scarcely room to turn himself, almost suffocated us. This produced copious perspirations, so that the air soon became unfit for respiration, from a variety of loathsome smells, and brought on a sickness among the slaves, of which many died, thus falling victims to the improvident avarice, as I may call it, of their purchasers. This wretched situation was again aggravated by the galling of the chains, now become insupportable; and the filth of the necessary tubs, into which the children often fell, and were almost suffocated. The shrieks of the women and the groans of the dying, rendered the whole a scene of horror almost inconceivable. **❹** Happily perhaps for myself I was soon reduced so low here that it was thought necessary to keep me on deck; and from my extreme youth I was not put in fetters.

Source: From Olaudah Equiano, *The Interesting Narrative of the Life of Olaudah Equiano, or Gustavus Vassa, the African* (London, 1793), pp. 31–33, 45–49, 51–53.

This engraving of Olaudah Equiano appeared in his autobiography, which was published in 1789. He looks out thoughtfully toward the reader. Given eighteenth-century ideas about slaves and Africans, what impression might his European dress have made on the reader of his book? (National Portrait Gallery, Smithsonian Institution/Art Resource, NY)

outnumbered females, and adults were enslaved more frequently than children.

Slavers returned to their home ports loaded with New World products: coffee, chocolate, cocoa, and sugar from the tropics as well as fish, tobacco, and furs from farther north. Above all, it was Europe's demand for sugar that fueled plantation owners' demand for slaves.

Sugar Raising and Refining Sugar raising and refining was a highly complex process that required hundreds of workers laboring in lockstep. When the cane was ripe, it had to be quickly cut and crushed between giant rollers before it dried out and the sap deteriorated. Huge vats heated by roaring fires reduced the sap to a syrup that could be further refined into cones and loaves. Slaves' frenzied cutting and crushing of cane, along with the unbearable heat of the fires beneath the vats, led one Portuguese priest in Brazil to write that "a sugar mill is hell, and all the masters of them are damned."

Clothing and Feeding the Slave Population The need to clothe the huge slave populations of the Americas stimulated the shoe and textile manufacturers of Europe. Food for slave populations was produced in the tropics where they worked, but dried fish was also shipped in from New England. Thus all the lands that bordered the Atlantic—Africa, the Americas, and Europe—were linked in a complex trading system that depended on the forced labor of African slaves.

Mary Evans Picture Library/The Image Works

Sugar was processed on Caribbean plantations where it was grown. In this painting, sugar cane stalks are on the left. In the right rear some slaves crush the stalks for their juice, and in the foreground others tend the vats in which the juice is boiled down until the sugar crystallizes. What might have moved the painter to make the sugar cane stalks on the left almost as large as the palm trees in the background?

The Spanish and Portuguese Empires

After a decline in production during the mid-seventeenth century, Spain's colonial silver mines boomed and produced half of the world's silver in the 1700s. The silver and other trades were organized as they had been in the sixteenth century; the Manila galleon sailed once a year to the west coast of Mexico, from which its goods were transferred to the Caribbean and then shipped with New World silver to Spain in a convoy of merchant ships guarded by men-of-war.

Problems in the Spanish Empire This highly centralized system no longer worked well. By 1700, some 2 million Spaniards had migrated to the Spanish colonies, and their demand for European goods could not be met by the annual trips to and from Spain. Although Spanish law forbade trade with foreigners, smuggling flourished in the empire's ports, where French and British traders brought needed goods from Europe or other parts of the Western Hemisphere and returned to their ports with emeralds, pearls, and cocoa.

The British benefited most from Spain's inadequate trading network. In 1709, during the War of the Spanish Succession, when Britain was fighting both France and Spain, merchants in the western port of Bristol financed a privateer to capture the Manila galleon. The venture was successful, and the galleon's cargo brought a profit of £786,000 to the overjoyed investors. The ship itself was sailed to London, where it became a tourist attraction. In 1713, at the end of the war, the Spanish granted the British the *asiento*, permission to sell slaves in Spanish colonies. In addition, the right to sail into Spanish ports enhanced the possibility for trade in other goods.

Brazil: The Heart of the Portuguese Empire In the fifteenth and sixteenth centuries, Portugal had created an empire that stretched westward from India to outposts in Africa and then across the Atlantic to Brazil. In the seventeenth century, Brazil had produced most of the sugar for Europe. By the 1680s, however, competition from French and British colonies in the Caribbean had led to a decline in prices for Brazilian sugar, and the industry slumped.

Soon afterward, gold was discovered. During the first half of the eighteenth century, gold became the main export, and Brazil was Portugal's most profitable colony. Each new find sparked a fevered gold rush as people from Portugal and the Atlantic islands joined local people in the hunt for treasure.

Treaty of Madrid Treaty between Spain and Portugal in 1750 that revised the boundaries of Brazil by adding more land in the west to the colony.

Gold Reshapes Brazil The influx of these fortune seekers greatly increased the European population in the colony. The slave population also increased because Africans were brought in to work the mines. The largest gold strikes were in Brazil's interior, so, for the first time, Europeans started to move away from the coast, where the sugar plantations were located. The push inland also brought increasing contact between whites and the local Indian population, which declined, like Indians in the Spanish Empire, as the result of disease and exploitation. Historians estimate that the Indian population of Brazil fell by 75 percent during the Brazilian colonial period. Unlike the Spanish, who studied Indian culture even as they exploited the local peoples, the Portuguese showed hardly any interest in the Brazilian Indians except as a labor force.

The Treaty of Madrid Portuguese occupation of the Brazilian interior was capped off by the **Treaty of Madrid**, signed in 1750, which adjusted the boundary between Spanish and Portuguese America, set by the Treaty of Tordesillas, in Portugal's favor. The territory assigned to Portugal west of the old line of demarcation created a colony that covered roughly the same territory as modern Brazil.

By the time the treaty was signed, gold mining was in decline, but the sugar industry was on the upswing as demand and prices rose. Diamonds were also found and sent to Europe in such numbers that their price fell by 75 percent. Sugar, gold, and diamonds ended up making Brazil far richer in resources and income from trade than its mother country.

The French and British Empires

In theory, the French New World Empire was vast, stretching from Quebec in eastern Canada to the Great Lakes and down the Mississippi River to Louisiana and the Gulf of Mexico. It also included the Caribbean islands of Saint-Domingue, Guadeloupe, and Martinique. In fact, however, these lands were sparsely inhabited by European colonists.

Canada In the mid-eighteenth century, Canada contained 60,000 Frenchmen as compared to the 1.8 million European inhabitants of the British mainland colonies. Canada's main export to Europe was furs, especially beaver pelts, which were used for making hats because their tight nap allowed them to shed water easily. French traders paid local trappers and Indians with guns and woolen clothes manufactured in the mother country.

The French Caribbean The Canadians also supplied the sugar islands with grain, timber, and leather goods. The sugar produced there was shipped back to France for refining, along with locally grown coffee. Seventy-five percent of the sugar and 80 percent of the coffee were then re-exported to markets in northern and eastern Europe.

The slave population in the French Caribbean, which far outnumbered the white colonists, stimulated

French manufacturing because textiles were shipped overseas to clothe the African workforce. The sugar island of Saint-Domingue was the single most productive colony of any European empire in the eighteenth century. Despite its profitability, the French, like the Spanish and Portuguese, lost ground to the British. Smaller European populations in the French colonies meant a less dynamic transatlantic economy.

The French in India The French also established trading posts in India, supplanting the Portuguese and Dutch and rivaling the English, who were also expanding their trade on the subcontinent. The main French post was at **Pondicherry**, on the southeast coast, from which silk and pepper were exported to France. In addition to these traditional commodities, printed cotton cloth was exported to supply the growing demand for cotton clothing in Europe.

Britain and the Atlantic Trade Britain benefited most from the Atlantic trade. Its success rested on two things: a slave-worked plantation economy in the Caribbean and the southern half of the mainland colonies combined with a thriving colonial demand for the products of the mother country. In addition, the needs of the mainland colonies' many coastal cities provided other trading opportunities across the Atlantic world.

Beginning in 1651, a series of Navigation Acts passed by Parliament excluded foreigners from the trade between British colonies and the mother country, decreed that all shipping must be in British or colonial vessels, and prohibited American manufacturers from sending their products to Britain if the products would compete there with locally made products.

British Exports to the Colonies London and the ports on Britain's west coast prospered from the trade goods they shipped to all parts of the Atlantic world. In addition to those sent to West Africa for slaves, merchant vessels carried textiles, tools, metal utensils, and a variety of household items to West Indian and North American consumers. Cheap cloth was in demand to provide clothing for the thousands of slaves, and household items like desks, chairs, wallpaper, curtains, china, carriages, and silverware were bought by the white population, who were caught up in Europe's consumer revolution.

Growing Colonial Population Colonial demand also increased because of a rising population. Not only did Britons continue to migrate to the American colonies; birthrates there were exceptionally high and large families the rule. The relatively easy availability of land for agriculture resulted in a high standard of living, perhaps the highest in the world at the time, that allowed colonials to buy nonessential items that pleased them or made their lives more comfortable.

British manufacturers responded to this overseas demand by producing more and more for the overseas market.

Colonial Exports to Britain Colonials also produced products that were shipped either to the mother country for consumption or re-export, or to other parts of the empire. In addition to the sugar, coffee, and chocolate that went from the Caribbean colonies to Britain, rice grown in South Carolina and Georgia on slave-labor plantations was shipped to markets in Portugal, Spain, and Mediterranean ports, where it was a staple in local diets. Indigo from the two colonies was also a highly prized blue dye for textiles. Beaver pelts were also shipped—eighty thousand of them by midcentury. Tobacco grown on slave-labor plantations in Maryland and Virginia was sent to Europe as demand rose. Europeans had imported 9 million pounds of New World tobacco in the 1660s; in 1775, they imported 220 million pounds.

New England No region in British North America prospered more from Britain's Atlantic trade than New England. Despite their cool climate and rocky soil, the New England colonies played a vital role in imperial commerce as the American center for the **carrying trade**. The abundant timber in the region gave rise to a local shipbuilding industry as well as supplying tall fir trees as masts for ships built in Britain. Corn and salt fish were shipped to the sugar plantations of the West Indies in return for tropical fruits, spices, and slaves taken to the mainland colonies.

Molasses, Rum, and Slaves Barrels made from local wood were also sent to the West Indies and filled there with molasses, which New Englanders turned into rum. The rum was then shipped to Africa as payment for slaves who were brought to the Caribbean. Newport, Rhode Island, was the capital of this molasses-rum-slaves trading triangle. Molasses were also sent to the **wine islands** off the northern coast of Africa as payment for **Madeira**, which became the drink of choice for well-heeled Americans. Thus the New England ports of Boston and Newport rivaled British ones in the scope and complexity of their trading networks.

Merchant Networks The merchants who managed the Atlantic trading network had to master the dynamics of moving many different cargoes over long distances to multiple delivery points. None of them could personally know all the people they had to deal with, and all of them knew

Pondicherry Most important French trading post in India.

carrying trade Shipping enterprise that moved commodities from one part of the empire to another.

wine islands Portuguese islands of Madeira and Porto Santo.

Madeira Wine fortified with brandy.

that risk was high. To lessen the dangers of a failed voyage, merchants tried to establish reliable correspondence networks based on kinship, religion, or ethnic identity. Thus merchant families often had members stationed across the world at crucial trading junctures, while Jews and Quakers relied on co-religionists and Scots tended to stick to fellow Scots. Traders also tried to establish a reputation for creditworthiness—a reputation for keeping one's word and being a sound financial risk.

World War and Britain Victorious

The British Navigation Acts had been aimed against the preeminence of Dutch shipping in the emerging global trading networks of the seventeenth century. By 1700, Dutch power was on the wane and England was the major maritime power, thanks to the growth of the Royal Navy. In 1664, the Royal Navy seized the Dutch colony of **New Amsterdam** on Manhattan Island and renamed it New York. The War of the Spanish Succession, known in British America as Queen Anne's War, gave Britain control of Hudson's Bay, Newfoundland, and Nova Scotia (Acadia) in present-day Canada.

War in North America Territorial gains in Canada, along with trade rivalries in India, set the stage for renewed warfare between Britain and France. By the mid-eighteenth century, fur traders in Britain's mainland North American colonies started to cross the Allegheny Mountains into the Ohio River valley and thereby threatened French control of the Mississippi valley. In response, the French built forts and allied with local Indians. War between the two sides broke out in 1754 when a young George Washington led Virginia troops into the Ohio River valley to block French expansion there. He was defeated, but the event was soon embroiled in a larger conflict, the Seven Years' War, known as the French and Indian War in British America.

Britain Wins, France Loses The war's decisive turning point came in 1759, when the British captured Quebec. At war's end, France was forced to cede Canada and all lands east of the Mississippi River to Britain. Louisiana—lands west of the river—was ceded to Spain in compensation for its ceding Florida to Britain. France also lost in India, where it surrendered almost all its trading posts to the British, who consolidated their rule there.

The American Revolution and Britain Subdued

The world wars of the mid-eighteenth century had put huge strains on the finances of all belligerent states. After 1763, the new king, **George III**, and Parliament decided that the American colonies should contribute to the expenses of running an enlarged British Empire. In 1765 the **Stamp Act** levied the first direct tax on the colonies, and the Americans howled in protest. It seemed to them that Parliament was acting in a high-handed, unconstitutional way, just like James II before 1688.

The American Revolution The Americans had embraced the Whig notion that government involved the consent of the governed. But Parliament had no members from the colonies. "No taxation without representation!" summed up the colonists' objections to British policy. Protests over taxes and a lack of parliamentary representation led, within a decade, to the **American Revolution** and, in 1783, to Britain's loss of thirteen very profitable North American colonies.

Crucial to the American victory was help from the French, who had been looking for an opportunity to redress the power balance that tipped in Britain's favor after 1763. The losses at the end of the Seven Years' War had reshaped French notions of what was at stake. In French eyes, the English had violently seized what rightfully belonged to France. In 1777, the French entered the war on the revolutionaries' side, but they paid dearly for their involvement. War costs imposed a crushing debt on the monarchy that led to an unraveling of French state finances and the collapse of the royal government in the late 1780s.

The British in India The British fared better in India than they did in America. After driving the French out of most of their trading posts, Britain's East India Company, which had carried on trade there since the seventeenth century, extended its control indirectly by forming alliances with Indian princes who allowed the company trading rights. Gradually, this indirect rule gave way to direct British control of the country.

 Checking In

By yourself or with a partner, explain the significance of each of the following selected key terms:

Middle Passage	wine islands
Treaty of Madrid	George III
Pondicherry	Stamp Act
carrying trade	American Revolution

New Amsterdam Dutch colony on Manhattan Island seized by the English in 1664 and renamed New York.

George III (r. 1760–1820) British king during whose reign the American Revolution occurred.

Stamp Act British revenue-raising measure imposed in 1765 on the American colonies at the end of the Seven Years' War, provoking American resistance.

American Revolution Rebellion of thirteen British colonies on mainland North America leading to their independence in 1783 as the United States of America.

European Society in the Age of Enlightenment

◆ **How did European ideas of home life change in the eighteenth century?**

◆ **What caused Europeans to rethink the nature of society?**

The consumer revolution coincided with a new emphasis on privacy, comfort, and displays of affection. As population rose, governments began to rethink the problem of poverty, but the poor were not simply an object of study. They also took matters into their own hands through rioting. New ways of thinking about society challenged traditional views emphasizing group membership more than individual autonomy. At the same time, many Europeans also started to think of themselves as members of distinct nations.

Comfort and Privacy

The consumer revolution coincided with new standards of privacy and comfort that changed the lives of Europe's upper and middle classes. Traditionally, nobles and other people of high social standing believed they had to make a public display of their grandeur. They surrounded themselves with many servants dressed in **livery**. They also acted as patrons to networks of clients who joined the servants in waiting publicly on their patron.

In this world of display, privacy meant little, and the houses of the great reflected their public nature. Rooms served multiple purposes; people ate, slept, and received guests in the same space. Servants slept in the rooms of their masters, and both shared their beds with other people of similar standing. The lack of concern for privacy extended to the dining table, where people dipped their fingers into a common bowl, shared drinking cups, and used the edge of the tablecloth as a common napkin.

A New Demand for Privacy Beginning in the eighteenth century, the traditional emphasis on public display began to change. In Europe's cities, the houses of the rich were built for greater privacy. Multipurpose rooms gave way to specialized ones—bedrooms for sleeping; dining rooms for eating; and drawing rooms for conversation, card games, and music. Houses also incorporated a new architectural feature, the hallway. Hallways allowed people to pass from one part of the house to another without entering every room in between, thus increasing each room's privacy. To ensure even greater privacy, servants were no longer housed in the same space as their masters but placed in restricted servants' quarters, and their numbers were reduced to keep domestic space as free from them as possible.

Bedrooms also became more private. Now people slept one to a bed and often one to a room. Dining also became a more private affair. People no longer shared food and utensils. Each person at the table had separate silverware, glasses, and dishes. Food was served onto plates with specialized spoons and forks so that no person's silverware went into prepared food that everyone was eating.

A New Demand for Comfort The growing demand for privacy among Europe's upper and middle classes was accompanied by a demand for comfortable domestic spaces. The older display society had emphasized grandeur, even if that meant that people had to live in uncomfortable surroundings. Although the rich and well-born still put elegance above comfort in dress on formal occasions, they now preferred a more relaxed pattern at home.

Men wore dressing gowns in their private rooms, and women favored looser clothes when they read or visited with friends. Little tea or supper tables covered with simple cloths were placed in front of soft upholstered chairs. Rooms were smaller than before, and thus fires could keep them warmer. Dinner parties also tended to become more informal.

Family Life The emphasis on domestic privacy and comfort also affected family life. Families, now enclosed in the cocoon of the home, often welcomed more openly spontaneous displays of affection and intimacy. Mothers increasingly breast-fed their babies instead of sending them away to **wet nurses** in the country. Parents had always loved their children and shown concern for their futures, but traditional child-rearing practices had stressed discipline: parents punished children's failures and mistakes to prepare them for the rough-and-tumble of the adult world.

During the eighteenth century, however, aristocratic and middle-class parents began to express love more openly, and they praised their children more frequently than before. One reason for Jean-Jacques Rousseau's popularity was his endorsement of these displays of feeling.

Why Did Change Occur? Historians have debated the causes for the rise in domestic privacy, comfort, and displays of familial affection. In part, they resulted from examples given at the highest levels of society, at royal courts. Louis XV of France toned down the public court ritual of his great-grandfather Louis XIV and spent much time in his private apartments with a few close friends. Stiff and silent at formal court events, Louis XV was relaxed and chatty in his private rooms, where he sat with cats on his lap.

No one promoted a comfortable lifestyle more than the French queen Marie Antoinette, wife of Louis XVI. Turning her back on the marble and gilt of Versailles,

livery Clothing with distinctive colors worn by servants of an important person.

wet nurses Women who nursed other women's babies for a fee.

Michel Barthélemy Olliver's *Supper at the Prince of Conti's Residence in the Temple* (1766) shows the prince and his guests enjoying supper in an informal atmosphere. Conti belonged to a junior branch of the French royal family. How does the artist convey a sense of the relaxed nature of this party?

she built a play village, Le Hameau, on the palace grounds. There she and her ladies-in-waiting dressed in country clothes and pretended to be milkmaids. Rousseau's rejection of corrupt civilization and his call for people to live closer to nature inspired Le Hameau. So did the enthusiasm for the "natural" natives of the South Pacific pictured in the travel reports of James Cook and Louis-Antoine de Bougainville. But the new standards for simpler living also shaped it.

Some historians attribute the new privacy to a growing sense of individualism fostered by the Enlightenment's emphasis on each person as an autonomous rational being. Others look to Protestant and Catholic reformers, who called for more modesty in people's daily lives. These reformers also preached that Christians should be bound together by love, thus encouraging an open affection within the family and the idea that affection should take precedence over financial considerations or social advancement when it came to marriage and children. The new emphasis on privacy, comfort, and family affection represented a profound shift in people's sense of how they should relate to others.

The Problem of the Poor

The changes in domestic life in Europe's upper and middle classes had little impact on the mass of working people,

workhouses State-run prison-like institutions housing vagabonds and beggars.

whose lives, as in the past, continued to be lived more in public view and were, therefore, shaped by community opinion and standards. Farthest removed from the world of the well-to-do were the poor. About 10 percent of Europe's population lived in permanent conditions of poverty.

The "Deserving" and the "Undeserving" Poor As in the past, people made a distinction between the "deserving" and "undeserving" poor. Old or sick people, along with the disabled, deserved support, but able-bodied beggars and vagabonds should be forced into work. Throughout the century, these undeserving poor were treated both as a social problem and as a criminal threat. British authorities regularly rounded up beggars along with convicted felons and transported them to its overseas colonies, first to America and then to Australia. In the early eighteenth century, France adopted the same policy and shipped poor men and women to Louisiana.

Workhouses Another way of handling the able-bodied poor was to place them in publicly sponsored **workhouses**, where they were forced to be productive and were re-educated in the value of labor. After the German state of Bavaria cleared its territory of beggars and vagabonds by building a huge workhouse that confined them, other European governments ordered similar institutions.

In England, the law allowed two or more parishes to build a common workhouse for the poor.

In France, Louis XV's government ordered a workhouse for each province. Their inmates either engaged in unskilled work, spinning wool and unwinding silk cocoons, or were drafted to do roadwork.

New Ways of Thinking About Poverty During the eighteenth century, the problem of poverty began to be looked at in new ways. When church reformers of the sixteenth century had called on the state to administer poverty programs, they had argued that it was the government's duty to care for the poor just as a father cared for his needy children.

By the eighteenth century, the view that the state had a fatherly obligation toward the poor was giving way to the argument that poverty relief was a *right* that human beings could demand. The idea of the rights of the poor was stimulated by the Enlightenment notion that human beings were endowed with natural rights that society had to acknowledge. People who accepted this view sometimes argued that poor relief should be supplemented by old-age and medical insurance for the needy. Although insurance programs were never implemented and policy makers concentrated solely on relief or forced work, the idea of a comprehensive state-sponsored welfare system had entered European thought about society.

The Causes of Poverty The Enlightenment also lay behind another new aspect of thought about the poor. Previously, Europeans believed that poverty was the result of human sin, which made the rich greedy and the poor lazy. Programs to eliminate poverty aimed, therefore, to reform the sinner. In the eighteenth century, a more secular approach developed. The Englishman Gregory King and the Frenchman Sébastien de Vauban signaled the change when they called for a careful count of the number of poor people. Once the magnitude of the problem had been established, the state could determine its causes and develop rational policies to deal with it.

The Enlightenment idea that people were naturally good undermined the notion that human sinfulness lay at the root of poverty. Now people looked for social and economic causes and argued that poverty resulted from such things as the rise in the cost of living, shifts in the demand for workers, and problems of overpopulation. On the European continent, the central state took direct control of poverty programs, while in England the state turned the problem over to local government and ordered parishes in the kingdom to undertake the care of the poor. Overall, government-sponsored poor relief was confined to western and central Europe. Farther east, the family or the village commune was called on to deal with its destitute members.

Popular Social Protest

In times of economic crisis—when harvests failed and the food supply dropped or demand for goods produced in the putting-out system declined—the ranks of the poor could swell to almost 50 percent of the population in an affected area. During these bad times, Europeans rioted.

Grain and Food Riots A sudden rise in grain and bread prices often triggered food riots. Because many peasants did not produce enough grain to feed themselves, they had to buy it. When prices shot up, they would lie in wait for wagon convoys carrying grain and attack them—often at stream fords or during the loading of cargo onto riverboats.

In cities, the working poor attacked bakeries. Although the attacks sometimes involved looting, many people, after seizing bread, paid what they thought was a fair price. Records testify to people returning to bakeries following a riot to put their money down on the counter, saying that they had forgotten to pay in the heat of the moment.

Rioters did not think of themselves as thieves and maintained their honor by paying what they could. In times of need, honor was often the only thing poor people possessed, and it was, therefore, carefully protected. Women always played a prominent role in food riots. As the family's food providers, it was their duty to take the lead in putting bread on the table.

The Labor Riot Laborers also rioted to obtain higher wages or better working conditions. Secretly forming organizations with ominous names like "The Conquering and Bold Defiance," weavers destroyed their employers' looms or cut the threads in them. Coal miners also destroyed machinery, throwing it down mineshafts while trying to set fire to the coal.

Antilabor Legislation Employers regularly denounced these riots as the work of wild mobs, and governments looked unfavorably on any form of labor organization. In 1791, the French revolutionary legislature passed the **Le Chapelier Law** outlawing labor unions, and the British **Combination Act** of 1799 made unions unlawful conspiracies. Workers themselves, however, viewed riots and unions as necessary negotiating tactics in a world where they had no legal rights to **collective bargaining**.

Government Authorities and Rioters Government authorities held complicated views about riots. Generally, they took a dim view of popular disturbance in any form and severely punished those they caught. At times, however, they had some sympathy for rioters who seemed to be truly hard pressed by food shortages or deteriorating working conditions and would soften the punishments.

Le Chapelier Law (1791) and **Combination Act** (1799) French and British legislation, respectively, that outlawed labor unions.

collective bargaining Negotiations over working conditions between an employer and an organized group of workers.

In 1780, anti-Catholic sentiment in London exploded in a week of violence known as the Gordon Riots. Rioters destroyed Catholic establishments and homes. In this engraving, they set fire to London's notorious Newgate Prison after freeing the inmates. Attacks on public buildings, including prisons, were common in eighteenth-century riots. How does the artist convey a sense of turbulence and danger in this scene?

Guildhall Library, City of London/The Bridgeman Art Library

Authorities also held women less accountable than men because of widespread beliefs that women by nature were emotional and disorderly. Male protesters took advantage of this view by occasionally disguising their faces with charcoal dust and then putting on women's clothes to protect themselves by symbolically assuming female disorderliness.

The Social Order

Throughout the eighteenth century, theories about how European society should be organized jostled with one another. Traditionalists argued that people were born into their proper social group: children of peasants were peasants, children of nobles were noble. Others argued that levels of wealth, and not the accident of birth, should determine who fell into the upper, middle, and lower groups.

A Society of Orders and Estates In the eighteenth century, most Europeans lived in a society made up of **orders**, also sometimes called **estates**. These were social groupings based largely on hereditary principles. Thus one was born into the estate of nobles or the estate of commoners. Some orders were entered through recruitment; clergy, for example entered their order through the rite of ordination.

orders/estates Form of social organization in which people's identity was largely defined by the groups to which the law assigns them.

privileges Exclusive rights that belonged to members of an order or estate.

Orders could include the family, the official residents of a certain city, and professional or occupational groups like lawyers or members of guilds. People in a society of estates and orders could belong to many of them simultaneously. For example, a French duke living in Paris would be a member of his ducal family, the order of the nobility, and an official resident of Paris. To a large degree, people's sense of self, along with other people's recognition of their place in the community, was defined by their participation in these groups. As a consequence, individuality was less noticed or regarded than group membership.

To enforce this point, European governments defined the orders legally and issued laws stating who were proper members of them. Thus illegitimate children were not legally family members, and vagabonds or the floating population of underemployed poor people were not legally recognized as residents of cities.

Privileges Each order and estate had certain rights that belonged exclusively to it. For example, in France the male head of family had the legal right to request the imprisonment of a disobedient son or daughter, and in eastern Europe the nobility alone had the right to own land. The distinctive legal rights belonging to an order were known as **privileges**. Privilege was something one had a right to that others did not have because it belonged only to one's order. Thus the clergy of France had the right to be exempt from state taxation, but nobles and commoners were taxed in varying degrees.

In a society of orders, one's right to enjoy one's privileges was as strong as other people's right to enjoy theirs, but the privileges varied from order to order. As the conservative English political philosopher **Edmund Burke** put it, "Everyone has equal rights, but not to equal things."

A Hierarchical View of Society A society of orders and estates was also hierarchical. Orders were not only unequal in privileges, they were also unequal in social status. Thus the **Prussian General Code** of 1791 assigned the top position to the nobility, while the middle classes were placed below nobles, and the mass of peasant serfs made up the lowest social order. The law codes of France, the largest society of orders in western Europe, did the same. Societies organized this way recognized that the orders occupied the same general space, such as the kingdom of Prussia or the kingdom of France, but within that space they were walled off from each other by their legally defined privileges and ranked hierarchically. The only thing they had in common was obedience to the king, who presided over all the orders and held them together as a unit—a principle of royal absolutism.

The view of society as comprising orders encouraged people to signal their position in the social hierarchy by surrounding themselves with liveried servants or insisting on their right to wear distinctive kinds of clothing—swords, lace, and bright clothing for nobles; dark-colored, simply cut clothes for commoners. Supporters of the society of orders argued that it was the divinely established form of social organization. People had a duty to live within their order and to respect the hierarchical arrangement of society.

Britain: The Social Importance of Money During the eighteenth century, the idea of society as a hierarchy of orders and estates based on privilege increasingly had to compete with other ways of thinking about the human community. In Britain, the older structure of society had been largely dismantled during the religious and political turmoil of the seventeenth century. Although a privileged nobility, the **peerage**, continued to exist, its numbers were small and its boundaries weak because the younger sons and daughters of peers were classified as commoners.

In its place, a new social structure emerged in which money largely determined people's social position. In this **plutocracy**, an aristocracy made up of peers and commoners, or **gentry**, occupied the highest social position. Membership in it depended on land ownership. Although old landed families often looked down on recent purchasers of land, the newly arrived could count on a general acceptance of their place in the aristocracy.

Britain's dominant position in the Atlantic economy led to the growth of a middle class engaging in trade, manufacturing, and banking. Aristocrats invested in their businesses, sent their younger sons to work in their firms, and welcomed their daughters into their families as well-heeled brides. At the end of the century, the British emphasis on money as a social marker shaped the novels of **Jane Austen**, which are full of discussions about the annual incomes of their heroes and heroines.

Money and Social Standing in France French society was legally organized as a society of orders and estates, but money also played an increasingly important role in determining people's social standing. Wealth bought noble titles for commoners and opened the doors to the best schools for the sons and daughters of the rich, whether noble or not. The consumer revolution, with its emphasis on people as buyers of products, fostered plutocratic conceptions of society, and the increasing importance of money in determining social standing broke down traditional ideas that birth determined one's place in society. In addition, the choices the consumer revolution gave to individuals also undermined the idea that people's identity was largely determined by membership in group-based orders.

The Nation

By the middle years of the eighteenth century, yet another way of thinking about society emerged in which people now argued that a primary component of a person's identity derived from being a citizen of a distinct **nation**. The idea of the nation emerged in both the plutocratic society of Britain and the more traditional society of France. The world wars of the mid-eighteenth century between these two peoples fed a growing sense of national unity on each side.

The British Nation For the British, their common identity was rooted in the belief that they were a unique "island race" united behind a Protestant monarchy and church. The king fostered the sense of national unity by traveling throughout his realm and appearing at carefully staged events that brought rich and poor and men and women together. For many Britons, war with France was a war between antagonistic religious communities. Britons, as defenders of Protestantism, were a

Edmund Burke (1729–1797) Political writer and member of Parliament, Britain's leading opponent of the French Revolution, and the founder of modern conservatism.

Prussian General Code (1791) State law code that defined Prussia as a society of estates.

peerage Legally recognized British titled nobility.

plutocracy Society in which wealth is the main determinant of social standing.

gentry British landowning aristocracy composed of commoners and peers.

Jane Austen (1775–1817) British novelist who depicted provincial life in classics such as *Sense and Sensibility* (1811) and *Pride and Prejudice* (1813).

nation Way of thinking about society that emphasizes common citizenship in a community as a primary component of a person's identity.

free, peaceful, righteous nation, whereas the French were slaves who groveled before a tyrannical monarchy and an oppressive Catholic Church.

The French Nation The French took an equally dim view of the British. They saw themselves as the defenders of enlightened civilization, while the British were addicted to a vulgar materialism that concentrated simply on trade and making money. Hadn't Adam Smith himself referred to them as a "nation of shopkeepers?" French losses in the Seven Years' War fueled the notion that Britain was bent on world domination. The conflict had not been one of king against king, or Protestant against Catholic, but of nation against nation. Thus, by midcentury, the French had forged a new sense of collective identity as they embraced the ideal of a united nation fighting a wicked foreign enemy whose culture and values were incompatible with their own.

The French monarchy, like that of the British, fostered this sense of national identity in the face of a dangerous enemy. But religious concerns were less prominent in the French concept of the nation. While the British thought that Protestantism had united the English, Welsh, and Scots into a single nation, the French thought that the nation was a purely human construction that the French people themselves had willed into existence. Its task was to resist British power and arrogance.

In both France and Britain, people thought that each individual had an active role to play in protecting the nation from enemy outsiders. This sense of individual engagement, along with the rising political importance of public opinion, contributed to a growing popular interest in politics and a desire to participate more directly in the political process.

flying shuttle Weaving device invented in 1733 that doubled a weaver's speed.

spinning jenny Hand-operated spinning device invented by James Hargreaves in 1768 that allowed multiple strands of yarn (or thread) to be spun at the same time.

water frame Water-operated spinning device invented by Richard Arkwright in 1769 that improved the spinning jenny by producing a uniformly strong thread.

factory Building or series of buildings where workers in a particular industry are gathered together to increase the speed and volume of production.

spinning mule Spinning device invented by Samuel Crompton in 1785 that combined features of the jenny and water frame.

✓ Checking In

By yourself or with a partner, explain the significance of each of the following selected key terms:

workhouses	privileges
Le Chapelier Law	Edmund Burke
Combination Act	plutocracy
orders and estates	nation

The Beginning of Industrial Production

◆ **What factors favored industrialization in Great Britain?**

◆ **How did new manufacturing processes revolutionize the production of goods?**

As antagonism between the French and British increased over trade and empire, the beginning of industrialization in Great Britain gave the British the upper hand. At the same time, industrialization had a radical impact on Britons' everyday life. It altered the living habits and psychology of people touched by it—sometimes positively, often negatively, but always unavoidably and without any possibility of returning to an earlier, less complicated era.

Mechanization and Mass Production

Increased international trade and rising consumer demand had fueled growth in British manufacturing under the putting-out system. During the second half of the eighteenth century, continuing increases in population and trade created a need for innovations that would increase productivity, standardize quality, and lower the cost of products. These innovations altered British manufacturing.

Innovations in Cotton Cloth Weaving Cotton cloth weaving was one of the first areas to see radical changes in production. In 1733, the **flying shuttle** doubled the speed at which a weaver could work. The quicker looms demanded more thread, leading James Hargreaves to invent the **spinning jenny** in the 1760s. Previously, spinners produced only one thread at a time; with one person operating Hargreaves's jenny, eight to eleven threads could be spun simultaneously, although the thread produced was unevenly strong. The spinning jenny was further improved by Richard Arkwright who invented the **water frame**, which produced a uniformly strong thread, thereby standardizing quality. Unlike the hand-powered spinning jenny, the water frame relied on a water mill for power.

The Factory The water frame's size and complexity required construction of a special building, the **factory**. Now spinners had to leave their cottages and report to a workplace where their work was supervised, regulated, and timed. Arkwright set up his first factory in 1771, employing nearly six hundred spinners. In 1785, Samuel Crompton patented the **spinning mule**, which combined the best qualities of the jenny and water frame and produced a thread that was both strong and fine. Weavers now could make high-priced, thin cotton cloth as well as cheaper, coarser cloth.

At Josiah Wedgwood's pottery manufactory in Staffordshire, kilns belching coal smoke fired thousands of pieces of china at the same time. The china was then stacked and packed in special containers for distribution around England. In early industrial enterprises, housing for workers was built in the midst of factory buildings. What might be the reasons for this? (Mary Evans Picture Library/The Image Works)

Mechanization Improvements in thread production, however, outstripped the ability of weavers using hand looms to convert thread into cloth, creating a bottleneck in production. In 1785, Edmund Cartwright, an Anglican clergyman, invented the steam-driven **power loom**, eliminating this bottleneck. The power loom also required weavers to leave their homes for power-driven factories. With the power loom, the **mechanization** of the cotton cloth industry was complete; machines now did work that had previously been done by hand. In 1793, the American Eli Whitney invented the **cotton gin**, which quickly separated seed from fiber in the cotton boll.

As American cotton cultivation expanded, British cotton cloth production soared. Between 1750 and 1800, alone, it increased tenfold. The British navy and the merchant marine played an important role by transporting raw cotton from the American South and India to the spinning machines and looms in Britain.

Josiah Wedgwood In addition to cotton cloth, pottery making was at the heart of what would be described as the **Industrial Revolution**. In 1759, **Josiah Wedgwood** transformed British porcelain production. Using the good clay of the English Midlands, Wedgwood opened a porcelain factory, based on Adam Smith's theory of the division of labor. Each stage in production—unloading the clay, mixing it, shaping it into pieces, dipping it in a glaze, placing it in kilns, and firing it—was carried out by specialized worker groups.

In addition, Wedgwood bypassed the individual potter's wheel, which had been used in pottery production for millennia, and shaped his pieces using molds of standardized size. The finished pieces were therefore identical, allowing for easy stacking and storage. Wedgwood hired salesmen to crisscross the country, demonstrating his wares.

Mass Production True to Smith's prediction, division of labor ensured quality control and lowered production costs; for the first time, English porcelain could compete with Asian imports because of lower price. Eventually, Wedgwood replaced workers with steam engines to mix his clay. Division of labor, uniform products, and competitive prices were central to **mass production**, another feature of the early Industrial Revolution.

The Steam Engine The development of steam power was also vital to industrialization. The **steam engine** had been invented by Thomas Newcomen in 1702 and had found practical application in pumping water out of coal mines. But its inefficiency limited use away from coal fields. Broader use of steam power in industry had to wait for the improvements of **James Watt**.

Watt improved on Newcomen's invention, developing a steam engine that was efficient and safe enough to be used in industry. By the 1780s, Watt's engines were pumping water out of mines, driving cotton looms, and powering Wedgwood's clay mixers. The engine's steam was produced by a fire fueled with coke—coal, abundant in England, that had been heated to eliminate impurities preventing it from burning hotly and evenly.

power loom Steam-driven loom invented by Edmund Cartwright in 1785 that doubled the speed of weaving.

mechanization Manufacturing process in which machines replace hand work.

cotton gin Device invented by Eli Whitney in 1793 that allowed easy removal of seeds from raw cotton, thereby making cotton more easily processed for cloth.

Industrial Revolution Changes in manufacturing involving mechanization of production and the use of power sources other than human or animal muscle.

Josiah Wedgwood (1730–1795) English pottery manufacturer whose success came from an efficient division of labor in his manufactory.

mass production Production technique based on the division of labor, uniform products, and competitive prices that increased both quantity and quality of production.

steam engine Engine that uses steam power to supply energy, invented in 1702 by Thomas Newcomen and perfected by James Watt.

James Watt (1736–1819) Scottish inventor who improved Newcomen's steam engine, making it safe enough to be used in industry.

Steam engines were made of iron, and their spreading use stimulated iron production in Britain. Steam, coal, and iron, along with mechanization and mass production, were at the heart of the early Industrial Revolution.

Why Britain?

Britain was the first country in the world to experience the Industrial Revolution. Six important factors made industrialization possible: high levels of agricultural productivity, available skilled workers, ease of transportation, natural resources, political stability, and **capital** for industry.

Agricultural Productivity Before industrialization can take place anywhere, that area's agriculture must be efficient enough to be able to spare workers to leave agriculture for industry. Britain's agricultural revolution had fulfilled that condition, freeing up surplus labor in the countryside that would be absorbed into the industrial working class.

Skilled Workers Another precondition for industrialization was the availability of skilled workers. In Britain this precondition was also present. The growth of the putting-out system, stimulated by Britain's leading role in the Atlantic economy, increased the number of merchant **entrepreneurs** as well as the pool of workers who had mastered many basic processes in the production of goods. Industrialization would build on this basis by using the existing skills of both entrepreneurs and workers. Water and steam power also supplemented human and animal muscles.

Ease of Transportation Geography also helped Britain to industrialize. Because Britain was an island country with many navigable rivers and a well-developed canal system, British industry could transport both raw materials and finished products more economically than its continental competitors. Before the development of the railroad, transporting bulk materials such as coal, wool, or cotton by land was very expensive. Mass industrial production demanded that these materials either be located near the factory (as in the case of coal) or that they be transported cheaply—that is, by water.

Natural Resources Britain was also blessed by nature with a large supply of the raw material that fueled the early Industrial Revolution: coal. The coal belt that extends across Europe from northern England to southern Poland was first exploited in Britain, particularly in such early industrial cities as Manchester, Birmingham, Glasgow, and Sheffield. Because of their endless appetite for coal, the first factories were usually built on top of or next to existing coal fields. Britain was also lucky in that the coal deposits lay relatively close to the surface, allowing easy exploitation of this fuel source.

Political Stability Political factors were no less important. Since the Glorious Revolution of 1688, England had enjoyed peace and political stability. Unlike the continent, Britain was one unified market: no tolls or internal **duties** had to be paid to ship goods from Scotland to England or Wales. The British government also actively encouraged industrial development by such laws as the **Calico Act** of 1721, which restricted the import of cotton cloth, called calico, from India.

Capital Accumulation Britain was also ahead of other European states in the accumulation of capital, thanks to the economic growth produced by the Atlantic trade. Some of this capital came directly from profits in the slave trade, but most of it came from other sources. Although per capita income in Britain in the mid-eighteenth century was probably not significantly greater than that in France, this income was better distributed among larger groups in the population.

More important still, access to capital was easier in Britain than in any other European country, in large part because of the existence of a central national bank. The **Bank of England**, founded in 1694, remained for over a century the only central bank in any major European country. The Bank of England loaned money to smaller banks, thereby helping increase the circulation of capital by making it easier for savings to be funneled into investment. This well-developed system of banks and credit made it relatively easy for British entrepreneurs to obtain financing—venture capital—to build factories, purchase steam engines or power looms, advance credit to purchasers, and the like. The combination of accumulated capital (that is, savings) and a well-developed system of credit helped Britain to industrialize. For all these reasons—agriculture, labor supply, transportation system, natural resources, politics, and capital—Britain managed to take the industrial leap before the rest of the world.

Was the "Industrial Revolution" Revolutionary?

Some scholars have pointed out that *revolution* might be an inappropriate term for this process, which

---

capital Wealth available for investment in the production of goods for the market.

entrepreneur Person who manages economic activity by assuming the risks and enjoying the profits.

duties Taxes, usually charged on products crossing a regional or national boundary.

Calico Act (1721) British act that limited the importation of cotton cloth (calico) from India.

Bank of England National bank established in 1694 that facilitated the circulation of capital during the Industrial Revolution.

began around 1760 but only really took off during the period of French Revolution and the Napoleonic Wars, a period of fifty-five years. The impact of industrialization was revolutionary, however, because it altered work patterns, family life, income distribution, society and culture, the availability of material goods, wealth and poverty, and the thinking of intellectuals and politicians about all these developments.

 Checking In

By yourself or with a partner, explain the significance of each of the following selected key terms:

factory	steam engine
mechanization	James Watt
Josiah Wedgwood	entrepreneurs
mass production	Bank of England

CHAPTER
Review

Summary

- Europe's eighteenth-century population growth stimulated economic growth and led to new forms of work, especially in manufacturing.

- As a result, some theorists began to argue that economies were capable of ongoing expansion, and they searched for the laws that made growth possible, founding the modern discipline of economics.

- As the consumer revolution took root, some economists began to praise all forms of work equally, repudiating the older view that the mental work of philosophers or theologians was superior to manual labor.

- Trading networks across the Atlantic, which had formed during the sixteenth century, reached their fullest development in the eighteenth century.

- The networks also fueled European economic growth, as the French and then the British Empire overtook the older Spanish and Portuguese empires.

- Because of their populous colonies in North America and their sugar islands in the Caribbean, the British developed the most far-reaching and profitable Atlantic trading networks, making London the commercial center of Europe.

- African slaves made possible the commercial exchanges of the Atlantic trading system. They were forcibly imported by the millions to labor in the plantations of the New World, where they cultivated the crops and mined the silver and gold that Europe's people and economies demanded.

- As part of the trading system, Europeans sent manufactured goods to colonies in the New World.

- Well-to-do European consumers developed new standards of domestic life during the eighteenth century.

- Older behaviors emphasizing public display as a sign of high social standing gave way to a concern for privacy and comfort.

- Enlightenment ideals, which stressed life in this world, were partly responsible for these new ways of life.

- Farther down the social scale, the poor continued to live as in the past because their lives were more in public view and were shaped by community-enforced norms.

- The Enlightenment also inspired European governments to reconceive poverty less as a consequence of sin than as the product of social, economic, and demographic conditions.

- The poor also shaped their place in society by means of the riot, the classic form of social protest in the eighteenth-century world.

- Rethinking the problem of poverty was symptomatic of a larger change in social thought, as corporate and hierarchical understandings of society now competed with ideas of status based on land and wealth.

- Some argued that each individual's primary identity was as a citizen of a nation, whose rights and values had to be defended from threatening outsiders.

- Nationalist antagonism between the French and British increased with the beginning of industrialization, which in Britain started as a mechanization of textile production and spread to other forms of manufacture.

Chronology

1713	Spain grants Britain the *asiento*	1771	Arkwright opens the first water-powered factory
1721	Calico Act restricts the import of cotton cloth from India	1776	Adam Smith publishes *The Wealth of Nations*
1733	Flying shuttle doubles weavers' speed	1780	Gordon Riots destroy Catholic property in London
1750	Treaty of Madrid between Spain and Portugal	1780s	James Watt's improved steam engines are introduced in Britain; Prussian General Code becomes law
1760s	Industrial Revolution begins in Britain	1793	Eli Whitney invents the cotton gin
1768	James Hargreaves invents the spinning jenny		
1769	Richard Arkwright invents the water frame		

© Cengage Learning

Test Yourself

To gauge your mastery of the material in this chapter, answer the questions below. More than one answer may be correct.

Economic Recovery

1. Which of the following does *not* explain the growth of Europe's population in the eighteenth century?
   a. The disappearance of bubonic plague.
   b. A growing interest in personal hygiene.
   c. Clearing garbage and human waste from cities.
   d. Better disciplined armies.
   e. The production of more effective medicines for the sick.

2. The agricultural revolution:
   a. First occurred in France.
   b. Eliminated the need to fallow the land.
   c. Allowed for larger herds and more manure.
   d. Led to an increasing fragmentation of individually owned plots of land.
   e. Led to an expansion of grazing rights on the land after harvest.

3. The putting-out system:
   a. Allowed whole families to work in their own homes.
   b. Reduced the role of merchants in the manufacturing process.
   c. Created close personal relations between workers and merchants.
   d. Occasionally led to sharp declines in demand for workers' piecework.
   e. Dramatically increased Europe's manufacturing capacity.

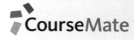

4. The Physiocrats:

   a. Believed in strong government regulation of the economy.
   b. Were opposed to strong government regulation of the economy.
   c. Were active in France.
   d. Were English.
   e. Thought the economy was too complex to be properly understood.

5. Adam Smith:

   a. Believed in strong government regulation of the economy.
   b. Believed people were consumers by nature.
   c. Argued that people looked out for others when making their economic decisions.
   d. All of the above.
   e. None of the above.

6. The consumer revolution:

   a. Stimulated European manufacturing.
   b. Affected all classes of Europeans.
   c. Led to a decline in pawnshops.
   d. All of the above.
   e. None of the above.

Now that you have reviewed and tested yourself on this part of the chapter, take time to pull together all the important information by answering the following questions:

◆ What were the causes and the consequences of Europe's expanding population in the eighteenth century?

◆ How did the Physiocrats' and Adam Smith's notions of wealth and economic activity differ from those of the seventeenth-century mercantilists?

The Atlantic World

7. The eighteenth-century African slave trade:

   a. On average saw a 50 percent death rate among captured slaves during the Middle Passage.
   b. On average saw a 10 to 20 percent death rate among slaves during the Middle Passage.
   c. Made the capture and sale of slaves a central feature in some West African economies.
   d. Took a total of 11 million slaves from Africa to the Americas.
   e. Took a total of 7.5 million slaves from Africa to the Americas.

8. During the eighteenth century, the Spanish Empire:

   a. Produced half the world's silver.
   b. Successfully kept French and British traders out of colonial ports.
   c. Failed to keep French and British traders out of colonial ports.
   d. No longer relied on the Manila galleon.
   e. Each year sent three Manila galleons to Philippine ports.

9. During the eighteenth century, Brazil:

   a. Was the least profitable Portuguese colony.
   b. Was the most profitable Portuguese colony.
   c. Experienced a gold rush.
   d. Saw the colonization of its interior for the first time.
   e. Rejected the Treaty of Madrid.

10. Which of the following statements about the French Empire is *not* true?

   a. French Canada had a population of 60,000 Frenchmen.
   b. French Canada's main export to Europe was furs.
   c. The slave population in the French Caribbean outnumbered the white population there.
   d. The French colony of Saint-Domingue was the single most productive colony of any European empire.
   e. The most important French colony in India was Goa.

11. In the eighteenth century, New England:

    a. Was vital to Britain's carrying trade.
    b. Shipped molasses to the Caribbean where it was made into rum.
    c. Shipped molasses to the wine islands to pay for rum.
    d. Shipped fir trees to Britain for ships' masts.
    e. Developed a thriving shipbuilding industry.

12. At the end of the two midcentury world wars:

    a. Britain gained the area between the Allegheny Mountains and the Mississippi River.
    b. The French were driven out of India.
    c. The British took control of French Canada.
    d. The mainland American colonists began to object to new British taxes.
    e. The French lost Louisiana to Spain.

Now that you have reviewed and tested yourself on this part of the chapter, take time to pull together all the important information by answering the following questions:

◆ What were the goods European states sent to their colonies overseas, and what goods did the colonies send back to Europe?

◆ How was the American Revolution linked to European colonial rivalries and the outcomes of the two world wars of the midcentury?

European Society in an Age of Enlightenment

13. The eighteenth-century demand for greater privacy:

    a. Led to the development of specialized rooms.
    b. Led to the use of the hallway.
    c. Led to the use of bolts on bedroom doors.
    d. Led to the creation of separate quarters for servants.
    e. Led to people eating alone.

14. Eighteenth-century thought about the problem of poverty:

    a. Stated that poverty was the result of human sin.
    b. Started to argue that poverty was caused by such things as rises in the cost of living and overpopulation.
    c. Started with the Enlightenment assumption that people were naturally good.
    d. Blamed overseas colonists for the problem of poverty at home.
    e. Often concluded that no one could ever really know what caused poverty.

15. Rioting in the eighteenth century:

    a. Often occurred when bread prices were high.
    b. Rarely involved workers destroying the machinery of their employers.
    c. Led to anti-union legislation in both Britain and France.
    d. Led to harsh punishments for women rioters, less harsh ones for men rioters.
    e. All of the above.

16. A society of orders and estates:

    a. Was based on the principles of hereditary and occupational recruitment of the various orders composing society.
    b. Encouraged upward social mobility.
    c. Allowed for men and women to participate in several different orders at the same time.
    d. Was rarely backed up by government legal codes.
    e. Held individuality in high regard.

17. Which of the following was true of British society in the eighteenth century?

    a. The younger sons and daughters of noble peers were automatically received into the peerage.
    b. The younger sons and daughters of noble peers were considered commoners.
    c. Birth alone determined one's place in the social hierarchy.
    d. Money largely determined one's place in the social hierarchy.
    e. Landownership more than birth determined whether one did or did not belong to the gentry.

Now that you have reviewed and tested yourself on this part of the chapter, take time to pull together all the important information by answering the following questions:

◆ How did European thought about the poor change during the eighteenth century?

◆ What were the similarities and the differences in British and French concepts of the nation?

The Beginning of Industrial Production

18. Which of the following was *not* central to the early Industrial Revolution?

   a. Coal
   b. Iron
   c. Mechanization
   d. Electricity
   e. Steam

19. A bottleneck in the production of cotton cloth was overcome by:

   a. The creation of factories.
   b. Cartwright's invention of the power loom.
   c. Mechanization.
   d. The invention of the cotton gin.
   e. Josiah Wedgwood.

20. Britain was the first country to experience the Industrial Revolution:

   a. Thanks to an abundance of skilled workers.
   b. Despite few natural resources.
   c. Thanks to high levels of agricultural productivity.
   d. Despite transportation difficulties.
   e. Thanks to a unified British market.

Now that you have reviewed and tested yourself on this part of the chapter, take time to pull together all the important information by answering the following questions:

◆ How was the steam engine employed in mining, cloth manufacturing, and pottery making?

◆ How did Britain's political stability, along with its banking system, promote industrialization?

CHAPTER 19

Revolutionary France and Napoleonic Europe, 1775–1815

Chapter Outline

1775	1780	1785	1790	1795
	1789 French Revolution begins			**1794** Reign of Terror ends
1776 American Revolution begins			**1792** French Republic proclaimed	**1793** Louis XVI is executed

This inkwell, made for a French revolutionary, shows a Catholic priest being crushed by a "Phrygian cap," a hat favored by the revolutionaries. Pro- and anti-revolutionary propaganda like this piece flooded France during the 1790s. (Musee de la Ville de Paris, Musee Carnavalet, Paris/Giraudon/The Bridgeman Art Library)

After reading this chapter, you should be able to answer the following questions:

From 1789 to 1815, what changed and what remained the same in French political, social, and religious life?

How did revolutionaries and opponents of the Revolution in France define their collective identities and those of their enemies?

What was the impact of revolutionary France and Napoleonic rule on Europe?

How did the French define the nation, and what role did nationalism play in French expansion in Europe during the revolutionary and Napoleonic periods?

N JUNE 11, 1775, in the Gothic cathedral of Rheims, a young man of twenty was crowned king of France. The coronation was an ancient ceremony in the kingdom's collective life that bound the French people to the king as his loyal subjects. At the climax of the ceremony, when the archbishop of Rheims lowered the jeweled crown of Charlemagne onto the head of the new king, Louis XVI prayed, "O Christ, may You Yourself crown this king!" Eighteen years later, in Paris, that very same head was severed from its body and lifted from a bloodstained basket to be displayed triumphantly to thousands of the king's former subjects.

In 1775, no one could foresee the king's execution. In retrospect, however, it is clear that the new king faced a growing political crisis. Finally, in 1789, revolution broke out, and thousands of French men and women joined in the movement to reshape the French community from the bottom up. First, France's absolute monarchy was modified into a limited constitutional monarchy. Then, the monarchy was abolished and a republic proclaimed.

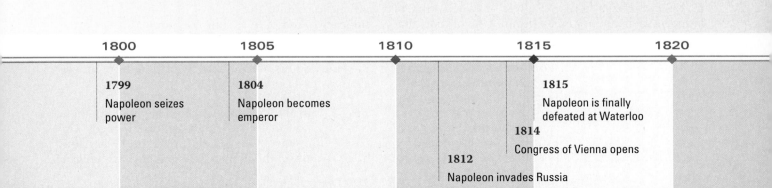

1800	1805	1810	1815	1820

1799
Napoleon seizes power

1804
Napoleon becomes emperor

1815
Napoleon is finally defeated at Waterloo

1814
Congress of Vienna opens

1812
Napoleon invades Russia

When the conservative states of Europe sought to restrain the republic, a revolutionary dictatorship was established to crush France's foreign and domestic enemies. Then, France was a republic again. Then, Napoleon Bonaparte took control and shortly proclaimed himself emperor. During all these years, almost all of Europe was at war against France. France gained control of most of the continent, then lost it all. Napoleon was defeated and exiled. In 1814, the monarchy was back, and Louis XVI's youngest brother was proclaimed king. Then, for a hundred days, Napoleon was back, then gone, and the king returned and remained.

Beneath this dizzying change of regimes in France, fundamental change was taking place that would alter Europe forever. The French revolutionaries created Europe's first modern representative democracy, sweeping away the old world of orders and estates and creating a new world of citizens bound together in a single nation. The revolutionary regime also broke with the Catholic Church, rejecting the centuries-old ties between church and state and creating a secular political and social order. War led to Europe's first mass mobilization of citizens to defend the country from external enemies as well as to a harsh dictatorship that crushed opposition at home.

France's wars spread the revolution outside France, and as victorious French armies occupied foreign territory, Napoleon enforced revolutionary reform across the continent. Written constitutions were introduced, state-sponsored religious discrimination was ended, the principle of equality before the law for all citizens was advanced, and a military draft was imposed. When Louis XVI's brother was restored as king of France, it looked as though the clock had been turned backward. But that was not the case, and Europe was never again as it had been in 1775 when Louis XVI was crowned.

From Crisis to Constitution, 1775–1789

- ◆ **What were the causes of the French Revolution?**
- ◆ **At the end of 1789, how had the political and social order in France changed?**

In 1775, the year Louis XVI was crowned king of France, American colonists began a revolution that challenged British royal authority. Many in France, which aided America's revolutionary war, embraced America's revolutionary rhetoric about fairness in taxation, the rights of citizens, and representative government. At the same time, the French monarchy, nearly bankrupt and facing

Louis XVI (r. 1775–1792) King of France whose monarchy was abolished by the creation of the French Republic.

challenges to its own royal authority, was poised to unravel. Its financial problems peaked in the late 1780s, just as bad harvests forced up the price of bread. An unprecedented crisis quickly escalated into revolution.

The French Monarchy in Crisis

Louis XVI intended to use his absolute political power to rule for the good of his subjects. But absolutism worked only as long as people did not question the king's exercise of that power. By the 1780s, however, many people were questioning it, accusing the king and his ministers of everything from indecisiveness to despotism.

The Crisis in State Finances The chief problem was the king's inability to manage state finances. The cost of the world wars of the midcentury had put huge strains on the French treasury, and for naught,

Map 19.1 **Europe in 1789** In 1789, France was only one of Europe's great powers. © *Cengage Learning*

1. Not counting the Ottoman Empire, how many separate states were there in Europe in 1789?
2. Now turn to Map 16.1 on page 467, "Europe in 1715." What changes occurred over the eighteenth century in Sweden's eastern boundary? What changes occurred in the Italian peninsula?

as France lost its overseas possessions. French involvement in the American Revolution was also expensive. The French government was forced to raise taxes, distributing the burden unequally among its subjects because nobles and clergy were traditionally exempt from some taxes. But state income still regularly fell short of state expenses, so new loans were required. As loans increased, so did interest on them, which only increased shortfalls in revenue. The result was a policy muddle indicating to many that the monarchy had lost its grip on the country's affairs.

Attempts at Reform By the mid-1780s, the king had realized that a complete overhaul of royal finances was needed to solve the problem of declining revenues and rising debt. Hoping to gain the support of the greatest nobles and churchmen, Louis appealed to them to join in a reform of the system. But these powerful people demanded to see the royal accounts before they agreed. Louis took their demand as a direct challenge to his absolute authority and turned it down.

The king then turned for support to the **Parlement of Paris**, but this royal court, too, was reluctant to help and engaged in a fierce struggle over control of policy, claiming that it alone could protect the people of France from government mismanagement. By July 1788, the conflict between Louis and the Parlement had become so severe that public order started to break down as pro-Parlement rioters and royal troops clashed in several provinces of the kingdom.

Queen Marie Antoinette Failure to resolve the financial crisis drove the king into a deep depression. He frequently burst into tears and ate and drank excessively. He also turned increasingly to his wife, Queen **Marie Antoinette**, for political advice. The queen, an Austrian princess, had never been popular; her marriage to Louis in 1770 had been intended to forge an alliance with France's long-standing Austrian Habsburg enemy. Now her extravagant personal spending on clothes and hairdos was also blamed for the financial crisis. Her enemies started calling her Madame Deficit. The queen's new political role, therefore, further enflamed people who had lost confidence in the king's ability to govern.

Crop Failure and State Bankruptcy On July 13, 1788, an unexpected turn in the weather deepened the crisis. A massive hailstorm swept across much of France, with hailstones so big that they killed humans and animals alike. Much of the grain ripening in the fields was destroyed, ruining chances for a good harvest and substantial tax revenues. The losses, the worst incurred in a series of mediocre harvests from the 1760s on, also meant that bread prices would rise sharply, threatening many with starvation. Grain and bread were diet staples; ordinary people spent between a third and a half of their income on them.

Now the government's creditors, individuals and banks at home and abroad, lost confidence in France's ability to pay interest on its debts and refused to lend any more money to the king. In a desperate move to restore confidence, Louis announced that a traditional assembly of his subjects, the **Estates-General**, would convene in May 1789 to deal with the crisis. But lenders were not reassured, and on August 16, 1788, France went bankrupt, suspending payments on its loans.

The Estates-General

The Estates-General had not met in 175 years, and no one in 1788 had a clear idea of how it should be organized. In September, the Parlement of Paris resolved the question by ordering the Estates-General to convene as it had in 1614, in three orders, corresponding to the three estates of the realm. The First Estate was the clergy and religious orders, and the Second Estate was the nobility; together they stood at the top of France's society of orders and accounted for about 3 percent of France's population. The Third Estate was everyone else—the 97 percent of the French population that included merchants, lawyers, shopkeepers, urban workers, landowning peasants, and rural laborers. The estates would meet separately, and each would have one vote, though the Crown allowed the Third Estate to elect as many delegates as the First and Second Estates combined.

The End of Press Censorship At this very moment, the Crown also decided to suspend the old system of royal press censorship. Hundreds of pamphlets debated the implications of the arrangements for the Estates-General: voting by delegates instead of by orders would give the Third Estate a voice.

What Is the Third Estate? The most widely read pamphlet was *What Is the Third Estate?* written by a Catholic clergyman, **Joseph Emmanuel Sieyès**. Though a member of the First Estate, Sieyès argued that the clergy and nobility were parasites in French society. They contributed nothing to the wealth and skills of the kingdom but simply lived off the labor and talents of the Third Estate even as they monopolized political power. "What is the Third Estate? Everything," he exclaimed. "What has it been up to this point in the political order? Nothing." Sieyès wanted the Third Estate's political power to match its economic productivity and social usefulness.

Elections to the Estates-General In this supercharged atmosphere, France went to the polls to elect deputies to the Estates-General. The elections, which took place from January to April 1789, represented the greatest experiment in democratic politics that Europe had ever seen. They were also the largest public opinion poll to be carried out in Europe until the twentieth century, as voters—taxpaying men who were at least age twenty-five—were asked to state their suggestions for reform in books called **cahiers**.

Generally, the cahiers of all three estates called for an end to absolutism and the creation of a

Parlement of Paris France's most important royal court, which resisted the king's absolute rule.

Marie Antoinette (r. 1775–1792) Austrian Habsburg princess married to Louis XVI who as queen of France was his controversial political adviser.

Estates-General Kingdom-wide deliberative body convened in 1789 to deal with the Crown's financial collapse and to reform the government.

Joseph Emmanuel Sieyès (1748–1836) Catholic priest who championed the political rights of the Third Estate.

cahiers Lists of grievances drawn up by voters electing deputies to the Estates-General in 1789.

A FAUT ESPERER Q'EU JEU LA FINIRA BEN TOT.

l'duleur en Campagne Ap. 1789.

A man of the Third Estate staggers under the burden of a priest and an aristocrat, representatives of the parasitic First and Second Estates. Cartoons like this were common in 1789.

Réunion des Musée Nationaux/Art Resource, NY

Table 19.1	The Revolution Unfolds in 1789
January–April	Elections to Estates-General
May	Estates-General meets
June	National Assembly formed Tennis Court Oath
July	Storming of the Bastille
July–August	Great Fear
August	Night of August 4 Declaration of the Rights of Man and the Citizen (Late August) October Days

© Cengage Learning

The Revolution Begins The formation of the National Assembly was the beginning of the constitutional revolution as the deputies' action had no justification in either law or precedent. Over the next several days, a significant number of clergy from commoner families, along with a few members of the nobility, joined the new National Assembly. Some of these privileged defectors were influenced by Enlightenment ideas that government should be based on a contract with the governed. Others joined the patriots out of political calculation, recognizing that there was no other realistic course of action.

The Oath of the Tennis Court These events finally shook Louis XVI into action. He announced that he would address the estates in a special "royal session," but, in the meantime, he prohibited any further meetings of deputies. The problem was that no one informed the deputies of the prohibition! So, on June 21, when the National Assembly tried to reconvene in its usual meeting place, it found the doors locked and barred by royal troops. In a frenzy of excitement and anger, the deputies seized a nearby indoor tennis court and took a solemn oath—the **Tennis Court Oath**—not to disband until they had written a constitution for France.

Two days later, Louis held his royal session, which accomplished nothing, and the Assembly went on meeting. On June 27, the king faced the inevitable and ordered all members of the clergy and nobility to join

representative assembly of citizens that would join with the king in governing. There was also agreement that taxes needed to be restructured and that the exemptions the clergy and nobility traditionally enjoyed should end. (Table 19.1 summarizes the unfolding of the French Revolution in 1789.)

The Estates-General Meets On May 4, 1789, nearly one thousand newly elected deputies to the Estates-General gathered at Versailles. Most looked to the king for leadership in the question of whether the estates would vote by order or by delegate, but it was not forthcoming. Well-intentioned but timid, Louis XVI feared to take the initiative. The deputies, left to figure things out on their own, could do no more than disagree. Weeks passed in stalemate, and tensions mounted dangerously. Finally, in June, the deputies of the Third Estate followed the lead of a minority of self-styled **patriots**, including Sieyès, who had been elected a deputy of the Third Estate, and declared that they were the **National Assembly**, the true representatives of the whole of the French people. Inviting the clergy and nobility to join them in a common meeting, they aimed to proceed with the business of reform.

patriots People who rejected absolutism and supported revolutionary reform of France.

National Assembly First French revolutionary legislature, in session from 1789 to 1791.

Tennis Court Oath Oath of the National Assembly not to disband before a written constitution had been drafted.

This painting of the Tennis Court Oath, based on an unfinished painting of Jacques-Louis David, enshrines the moment in French collective memory. Here representatives of the revolutionary nation stretch out their hands to swear that they will not disband until they have written a constitution. Why has the painter decided to show the curtains billowing in the fresh air and the shaft of light shining directly upon the figure in the center who is reading the oath?

the deputies of the National Assembly. Reluctantly, they did. But the king was humiliated, and at the end of the month he changed his mind again, ordering his soldiers to disband the National Assembly by force. When these troop movements were reported in Paris, fear combined with tension to explode in ways that were to have huge, if unforeseen, consequences for the emerging revolution.

Trouble in Paris, Trouble in the Countryside, Trouble in Versailles

By late June 1789, Paris had become a hotbed of politics as patriot orators, fearful for the fate of the National Assembly, whipped up a feverish state of excitement. Anxiety intensified as food prices skyrocketed following the hailstorm and bad harvest of 1788. Then, on July 11, the king dismissed his latest finance minister, **Jacques Necker**, thought to be the most pro-patriot person in the government.

Paris and the Storming of the Bastille Paris panicked. Rioters, convinced that the king was about to attack the people, broke into arsenals, seizing weapons and ammunition. Soon up to a quarter million people were carrying weapons. On July 14, a huge crowd, armed with cannons, headed toward the Bastille, a medieval fortress that served as a royal prison and had long been a symbol of the king's absolute power.

At first the insurgents tried to negotiate with the prison governor for a surrender of the ammunition they sought. When this failed, they took the Bastille by force, releasing prisoners (there were only seven) and killing the governor, whose head, hacked off with a pocketknife, they paraded triumphantly about the city on the end of a pike. Frightened by the disorder, on July 15, the king recalled Necker to office and ordered the troops around Versailles and Paris to disband. Thus the uprising in Paris saved the National Assembly at Versailles.

Jacques Necker (1732–1804) Louis XVI's financial minister whose dismissal provoked the uprising in Paris on July 14, 1789.

Réunion des Musées Nationaux/Art Resource, NY

Claude Cholat, one of the "conquerors of the Bastille," painted this picture, thereby enshrining another moment in the collective memory of the French people. The awkward perspective indicates that Cholat was not trained in an art academy. How does the work capture the drama of the moment as Cholat remembered it?

Revolution in the Countryside But immediately there was a new crisis, as peasant revolts erupted throughout most of the kingdom. Called the **Great Fear**, these uprisings in the countryside were sparked by the same high food prices and political excitement that had ignited Paris. The peasants believed that they were about to be attacked by people they called brigands and aristocrats.

Rising up in self-defense, they vented their fury against their landlords, looting manor houses and ransacking the offices that housed records of payments to the landlord. These payments, often cited in the peasants' cahiers, included fees for the use of the landlord's mill or bake ovens, which all peasants paid in addition to their regular land rents. Even peasants who owned their own land had to pay them. In the Great Fear, rural communities all over France spontaneously attacked these symbols of remaining feudal dues.

The Night of August 4 Faced with the peasant uprising, the National Assembly feared that all public order was about to collapse. In May, most deputies had wanted a reform of government. Now they realized that fundamental changes were needed. Therefore, on the **Night of August 4**, 1789, in an evening session of the Assembly, some deputies proposed to abolish the feudal dues that peasants were attacking. As it turned out, this limited proposal quickly turned into something extraordinary.

In a flash of enthusiasm, the deputies rushed to renounce all sorts of traditional taxes, payments, and privileges: the clergy gave up the **tithe**, military appointments previously reserved for nobles were opened to commoners, and the tax privileges of many towns and provinces were abolished. By dawn, when the session ended, the deputies had swept away virtually all of France's old society of orders and privilege.

The all-night meeting on August 4 dismantled the old social order of France, just as events in Versailles and Paris, culminating in the storming of the Bastille, had dismantled the old political order. But what was to replace them?

Great Fear Widespread peasant uprisings in July and August 1789 that abolished feudal dues to landlords.

Night of August 4 French legislative session in 1789 that abolished many traditional taxes, payments, and privileges.

tithe (From Middle English: "tenth") Payment required by the Catholic Church from all owners of nonchurch lands.

The Declaration of the Rights of Man and the Citizen Three weeks later, the National Assembly, led by Sieyès and other patriots, gave its answer when it issued the **Declaration of the Rights of Man and the Citizen**, the single most important document produced during the Revolution. In it, France's new regime was laid down in principle. The declaration drew on both Enlightenment thought and the language of the American Revolution, especially as expressed in the Declaration of Independence.

It proclaimed the "natural, inalienable, and sacred rights of man," which included the rights to "freedom, property, safety, and the right to resist oppression." It also guaranteed security from arbitrary arrest and freedom of speech and religion. France was still to have a king, but he was no longer to be absolute; rather, he was to govern according to a new written constitution.

The Revolutionary Principle of Liberty One word summed up the content of the declaration: liberty. Human rights guaranteed by a government representing the people, limited by a constitution, and promoting the rule of law would make liberty possible. The declaration's affirmation that "all people shall have equal rights upon birth and ever after" would have a huge impact across Europe and eventually the world.

The October Days The National Assembly's program for a constitutional monarchy was worked out during August 1789. Now it was up to Louis XVI to state his position on it, and, once again, the king hesitated. Then, in early October, the initiative passed to a new element of the population—the workingwomen of Paris, who were furious about the high cost of bread and believed the king should do something about it. On October 5, six thousand women seized cannons and in pouring rain marched to Versailles to demand food. As the patriots joined them in the streets, the king capitulated. He promised flour for bread and agreed to accompany the marchers back to Paris, where he and his family were resettled in an old palace. A few days later, the National Assembly also moved to the city. These **October Days** shifted the center of power from aristocratic Versailles to turbulent Paris, where the king and the new National Assembly were under the watchful eye of the most militant revolutionaries.

Declaration of the Rights of Man and the Citizen Statement of revolutionary principles, proclaiming universal and inalienable human rights.

October Days Uprising of Parisian workingwomen in 1789 that brought the royal family to Paris.

Old Regime Revolutionary name for prerevolutionary France.

Jacques-Louis David (1748–1825) Important artist who celebrated the Revolution's great turning points in monumental paintings.

Remembering 1789 By October, the events of the previous months were well on their way to becoming legends. The Tennis Court Oath came to symbolize the defiance of the French people in the face of royal despotism, and the storming of the Bastille became the symbol for the overthrow of royal oppression. The Night of August 4 stood for the destruction of the **Old Regime** and the inauguration of the new.

These events were memorialized in monumental paintings, like *The Tennis Court Oath* by **Jacques-Louis David**, and celebrated as national festivals. To this day, July 14, Bastille Day, is France's chief national holiday. The message these events conveyed was clear: In the Old Regime, politics was something done by the king and the court. In the new, politics would be done by the people. This momentous shift in the understanding of politics was at the heart of the French Revolution.

 Checking In

By yourself or with a partner, explain the significance of each of the following selected key terms:

Louis XVI	Great Fear
Marie Antoinette	Declaration of the Rights of Man and the Citizen
Estates-General	
Joseph Emmanuel Sieyès	October Days
Tennis Court Oath	

The Constitutional Monarchy, 1789–1792

◆ **What was new in the revolutionary concepts of the citizen and the nation?**

◆ **What were the causes and effects of the Revolution's break with the Catholic Church?**

From the fall of 1789 to the summer of 1792, France was a constitutional monarchy, with rule by the king and the National Assembly, the new national legislature. Writing a constitution, the Assembly scrapped the old haphazard administrative system, replacing it with uniform institutions and procedures. It also redefined French collective identity, reshaping France as a new nation made up of a community of citizens and defining the nature of citizenship. Many of these changes remain in place today. At the same time, however, new conflicts arose that were equally long lasting. One centered on the rights of women in the new regime. Another raised the problem of slavery in a reformed France. A crucial conflict was the rupture between the Revolution and the Roman Catholic Church.

Réunion des Musées Nationaux/Art Resource, NY

Maximilien Robespierre, the "Incorruptible," is shown here at a writing desk. Although a supporter of the radical democratic left in the revolutionary movement, Robespierre never adopted revolutionary clothing. As shown here, he continued to wear knee breeches and to powder his hair. He also continued to address men as "monsieur" rather than "citizen."

These issues increased the hostility between the revolutionaries and Louis XVI, who never really accepted his new constitutional role. Other European rulers, frightened by revolutionary radicalism, turned against France's new regime. After war broke out between revolutionary France and conservative Europe, France's monarchy fell.

The New Constitution

By November 1789, fear of hunger began to subside following a good harvest that reduced grain prices. Political excitement nevertheless remained high. Dozens of newspapers appeared, with names like *The Daily Thermometer* and *The National Whip*. New political clubs sprang up in Paris, where deputies and their supporters passionately debated legislative proposals.

The Jacobin Club The most famous club was the Society of the Friends of the Constitution, nicknamed the **Jacobin Club** for the building in which it met, once owned by Jacobin Dominican friars. The Jacobins were mainly middle class and often well-to-do.

They supported the democratization of politics, but they also defended the rights of private property and favored an economy free from government regulation. The Jacobin leader **Maximilien Robespierre**, a prim provincial lawyer called "the Incorruptible" because of his dedication to the revolutionary agenda, praised the street violence that had led to the storming of the Bastille and the October march on Versailles.

The Constitution of 1791 By late 1789, the old political and social structures of France had been swept away. Now the National Assembly, following Article 3 of the Declaration of the Rights of Man and the Citizen, which stated that "the principle of all sovereignty resides in the Nation," began to write a constitution for the new regime. The **Constitution of 1791** reinvented French society and politics and redefined what it meant to be French.

The Constitution discarded the old estates and orders, declaring France to be a single nation, uniting all people who resided permanently on French soil. **Sovereignty** now resided in the nation, no longer in the king. The goal of the constitution was to create a community in which each person was equal, with equal natural rights. Ability, not birth, proclaimed the deputies, should determine success and status. Thus, the National Assembly abolished all titles of nobility.

The Departments and the Metric System As French society was pushed to be uniform and unified, the administration of government was made uniform and unified too. The Assembly swept away the overlapping muddle of administrative districts and replaced it with **departments**. Departments were to be alike in size and organized into standardized subdivisions. The departments reflected the revolutionaries' goal of creating efficient administrative districts and implemented the Enlightenment ideal that good government should be based on rational principles. Rationality also lay behind the introduction of the **metric system**, based on the meter, calculated as one ten-millionth of the

Jacobin Club Most important French revolutionary political club, whose members were called Jacobins.

Maximilien Robespierre (1758–1794) Important and powerful leader in the French Revolution and one of the instigators of the Reign of Terror.

Constitution of 1791 Written document establishing a constitutional monarchy in France that went into effect in October 1791.

sovereignty Supreme political power and authority; also a nation's independence or freedom from control of another state.

departments Local French administrative districts, uniform in size.

metric system Standardized system of weights and measurements based on the unit of ten, introduced following the French Revolution.

quarter meridian. From now on, length was to be measured naturally, with a uniform unit based on the size of earth itself.

Citizenship The National Assembly also addressed the issue of citizenship. The idea of citizenship had been discussed during the Enlightenment and was associated with self-government in the tradition of ancient Rome. It had been put into practice during the American Revolution. When it came to implementing citizenship in France, the Assembly, on the advice of Sieyès, backtracked on its principles of unity and uniformity by decreeing that people in the one nation were to be divided into two categories, **active and passive citizens**.

Active Citizens Only men who owned or otherwise controlled a certain amount of property could be active citizens, and only active citizens could vote and hold public office. The deputies believed that property ownership gave men a stake in society that would make them a band of citizen brothers who would act responsibly when making political decisions.

Passive Citizens Women and non-property-holding men were to be passive citizens. Despite these restrictions, these formulations secured France a level of participatory democracy that would not be reached elsewhere in Europe for many decades. About two-thirds of adult French males met the qualifications for active citizens, and Protestants and Jews, who had been discriminated against during the Old Regime, were now admitted to full rights of citizenship.

Women and Citizenship The restructuring of France as a nation composed of equal (male) citizens was summed up in a new revolutionary slogan: "Liberty, Equality, Fraternity." Although women like Olympe de Gouges (see A New Direction: Olympe de Gouges Becomes a Revolutionary), with the support of a few deputies in the Assembly, protested their exclusion from active citizenship, they were not able to change the categories. Most male revolutionaries, influenced by philosophes such as Jean-Jacques Rousseau, considered women too emotional and illogical to participate in political life. Their place was in the home, where they could serve as wives to their patriot husbands and raise children to serve the nation.

For working-class women, Gouges's agenda had little appeal. Food for their families and wages in their traditional occupations were much more important.

active and passive citizens Two categories of citizenship in which only property-owning men (active citizens) were allowed to vote and hold public office.

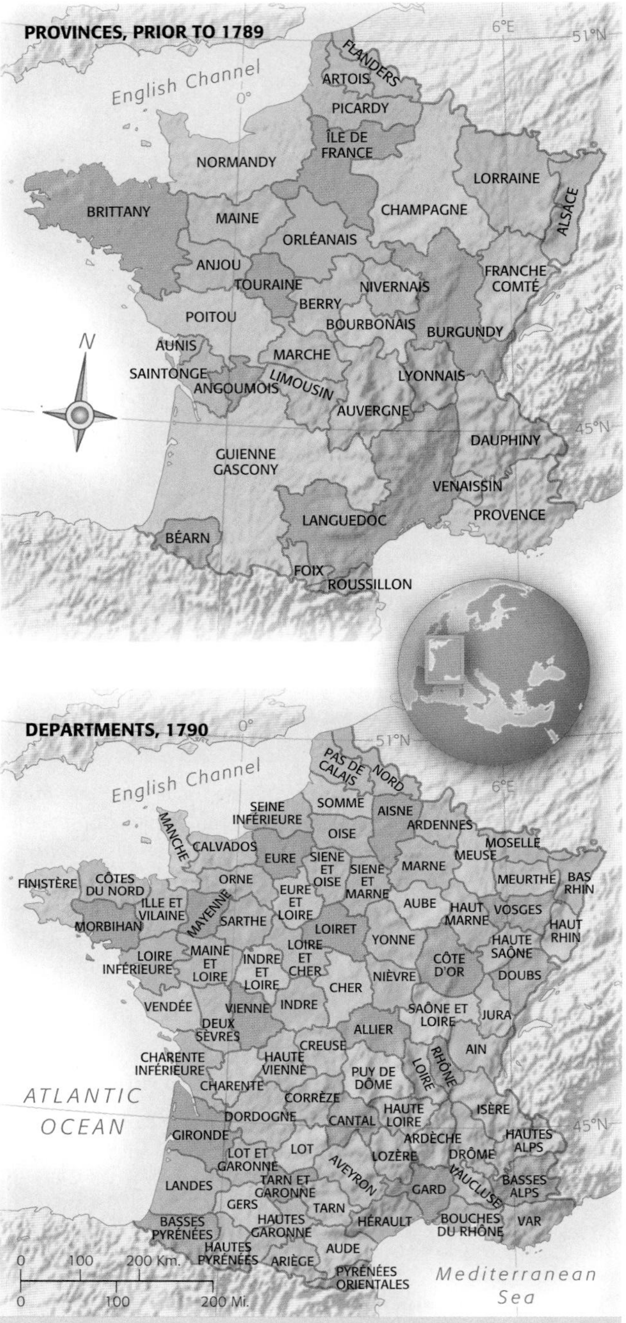

PROVINCES, PRIOR TO 1789

DEPARTMENTS, 1790

Map 19.2 **The Rationalization of French Administration, 1789 and 1790** These maps show the revolutionary reorganization of French territory. The map on top shows the traditional provinces of the monarchy as they were in 1789. The map in the bottom shows the new departments created in 1790. © Cengage Learning

1. Note that the French provinces were very unequal in size. Which was the largest and which was the smallest?

2. How does the map in the bottom illustrate Enlightenment and revolutionary principles of rationality and efficiency?

Olympe de Gouges Becomes a Revolutionary

In 1768, a twenty-year-old widow left her hometown in southern France and headed for Paris to make her fortune. For the next twenty years, Olympe de Gouges struggled to live independently and to establish herself as a playwright in a world dominated by male privilege and aristocratic intrigue. When the French Revolution broke out, she sided with the revolutionaries, calling for a new political and social order based on equality—including equality between men and women.

As a single woman alone in Paris, Madame de Gouges found few respectable options open to her; she could either remarry or work. Vowing not to marry again, she relied on her beauty and wit to get ahead and offered love to men of means, who gave her financial help in return. For ten years, she lived a life of pleasure while quietly amassing enough money to obtain what she truly desired—economic independence. Then, at the age of thirty, she announced she would devote the rest of her life to philosophy by writing plays that praised the ideals of the Enlightenment.

The theatrical world Gouges threw herself into was lively, but not open to new talent. The Crown had granted a monopoly on theatrical performances in Paris to a handful of privileged theaters, which used their power ruthlessly to promote the work of favorites while denying access to others. As a woman without powerful connections, time and again Gouges had the theater doors slammed in her face. She therefore took to publishing her work, often at her own expense, in hopes of building support for the performance of her plays.

In 1789, she wrote *The Slavery of the Blacks*, a controversial play in which the hero, a black, murdered a white man to prevent him from raping the hero's mistress. Finally, this play made it to the stage when the Comédie-Française, the most prestigious theater in Paris, performed it. But after just three performances, it closed. Perhaps the plot was too controversial, or perhaps, as Gouges claimed, the theater management had sabotaged the play to avoid paying her.

By this time, France was in the midst of revolution, and Gouges turned to applying Enlightenment ideals to the crisis at hand. To solve the monarchy's bankruptcy, she called for a voluntary tax to be paid equally by all. She called for a state system of social security and government employment to care for the poor. She denounced the filthy conditions in the maternity wards of hospitals and called for local community ownership of agricultural land to help poor peasants. Above all, she demanded complete political and social equality for men and women. In 1791, she published *The Rights of Woman,* the most important feminist statement of the French Revolution. "Woman," she wrote, "is born free and remains equal to man in rights." This single sentence summed up her years of struggle against the injustices she had experienced and seen around her.

Olympe de Gouges promoted the ideals of France's Revolution, but she never joined revolutionary clubs and refused to take part in the street violence that erupted periodically in Paris. She also never gave up her belief in the French monarchy. She did her best to save the king, even offering to defend him in the trial that led to his execution. For this, she herself was executed. Olympe de Gouges's life was caught up in many of the forces that shaped revolutionary France—resentment at aristocratic privilege, anger at social injustice, excitement over the possibility of fundamental change, and anxiety over the violence that so often accompanied revolutionary action. Most of all, her defense of women's rights raised issues that remained at the center of political debate long after her death.

When these were threatened, workingwomen could be roused to public action that often had profound political consequences, as the October Days had proved.

Although the deputies denied women the vote and the right to hold public office, the legislature eventually endorsed other elements of Gouges's program by expanding women's rights in the important areas of domestic relations and inheritance law. In 1792, divorce, advocated by Gouges but forbidden by the Catholic Church, was legalized. Both women and men were allowed to file for divorce by mutual consent or on account of "incompatibility of temperament." Many women used the new law to separate from their husbands.

Another law benefiting women ordered the equal division of estates among all heirs, male and female. These new divorce and property laws reflected the emphasis on individual rights and the freedom to act even in opposition to Catholic Church teaching or traditional family values.

Citizenship and Slavery Debates over the nation and its citizens sparked a reconsideration of slavery. France had long been considered "free land," but slavery was practiced in French colonies in

Olympe de Gouges Asserts the Rights of Women

In September 1791, just before the Constitution of 1791 went into effect, Olympe de Gouges published her most famous pamphlet, *The Rights of Woman*. In it she demanded equality for both men and women in the new revolutionary regime and asked the outgoing legislature, or the new one created by the constitution, to enact this program. Her decision to model her demands on the Declaration of the Rights of Man and the Citizen of 1789, often following that text word for word while adding the word women, revealed the omissions in that earlier document. She was thus attempting to use the ideals of the Revolution for the benefit of women.

❶ Why would Gouges address her *The Rights of Woman* to the French Queen?

❷ Why does Gouges use the label "citizeness?"

❶ The Rights of Woman: To the Queen

Mothers, daughters, sisters, female representatives of the nation ask to be constituted as a national assembly. Considering that ignorance, neglect, or contempt for the rights of woman are the sole causes of public misfortunes and governmental corruption, they have resolved to set forth in a solemn declaration the natural, inalienable, and sacred rights of woman....

❷ In consequence, the sex that is superior in beauty as in courage, needed in maternal sufferings, recognizes and declares in the presence and under the auspices of the Supreme Being, the following rights of woman and the citizeness.

1. Woman is born free and remains equal to man in rights. Social distinctions may be based only on common utility.

2. The purpose of all political association is the preservation of the natural and imprescriptable rights of woman and man. These rights are liberty, property, security, and especially resistance to oppression.

3. The principle of all sovereignty rests essentially in the nation, which is but the reuniting of woman and man. No body and no individual may exercise authority which does not emanate expressly from the nation.

4. Liberty and justice consist in restoring all that belongs to another; hence the exercise of the natural rights of woman has no other

the Caribbean. There the Declaration of the Rights of Man and the Citizen was a bombshell; white colonials denied that it applied to slaves, while the slaves considered it a signal for revolt. Trouble continued into the spring of 1791, when the Assembly cautiously granted citizenship to a small number of free blacks on Saint-Domingue, France's most important remaining colony, where 57,000 whites and free blacks ruled more than 465,000 African slaves.

François Dominique Toussaint L'Ouverture (1743–1803) Former slave who led the first successful slave revolt in history in the French colony of Saint-Domingue.

In August, there followed a massive uprising led by **François Dominique Toussaint L'Ouverture**, a former slave inspired by Enlightenment thought. Many plantation owners were slain, while others fled to the new United States. The uprising, which ended French control of the island and France's Atlantic trade, was the first successful slave revolt in history. In early 1794, France became the first European country to abolish slavery and to grant full rights of citizenship to ex-slaves. Because citizenship touched on so many aspects of reform, both at home and overseas, it became the central issue in defining the new regime.

limits than those that the perpetual tyranny of man opposes to them; these limits must be reformed according to the laws of nature and reason....

6. ❸ The law should be the expression of the general will. All citizenesses and citizens should take part, in person or by their representatives, in its formation. It must be the same for everyone. All citizenesses and citizens, being equal in its eyes, should be equally admissible to all public dignities, offices, and employments, according to their ability, and with no other distinction than that of their virtues and talents.

7. ❹ No woman is exempted; she is indicted, arrested, and detained in the cases determined by the law. Women like men obey this rigorous law....

10. No one should be disturbed for his fundamental opinions; woman has the right to mount the scaffold, so she should have the right equally to mount the tribune, provided that these manifestations do not trouble public order as established by law.

11. ❺ The free communication of thoughts and opinions is one of the most precious rights of woman, since this liberty assures the recognition of children by their fathers. Every citeness may therefore say freely, I am the mother of your child; a barbarous prejudice [against unmarried women having children] should not force her to hide the truth, so long as responsibility is accepted for any abuse of this liberty in cases determined by the law....

13. For maintenance of public authority and for expenses of administration, taxation of women and men is equal; she takes part in all forced labor service, in all painful tasks; she must therefore have the same proportion in the distribution of places, employments, offices, dignities, and in industry....

Source: *Olympe de Gouges* is the original French pamphlet of 1791 (Olympe de Gouges, "Les droits de la femme. À la reine.") As found in Lynn Hunt, ed. and trans., *The French Revolution and Human Rights: A Brief Documentary History* (Boston: Bedford Books of St. Martin's Press, 1996). pp. 124–126.

❸ How is Gouges turning the ideals of the Revolution as stated in her list of demands to the benefit of women?

❹ Why did Gouges include this article in her declaration?

❺ What is the importance of this article?

The Break with the Catholic Church

The French church had been involved in the new regime from the beginning. Clergy like Sieyès continued to sit in the new National Assembly. Many welcomed the reordering of society into a nation of equal citizens as a fulfillment of the "gentle fraternity" of Jesus, which incorporated everyone equally. The clergymen who were deputies, therefore, accepted the Assembly's increasingly radical restructuring of the church.

The Civil Constitution of the Clergy After abolishing the tithe on the Night of August 4, the Assembly decided to confiscate church property, which constituted about 10 percent of French land, and to use it to back new government bonds and restore confidence in the state's finances. It also withdrew state enforcement of monks' and nuns' religious vows and forbade all future vows. Then, in 1790, the Assembly took even more drastic action, decreeing the **Civil Constitution of the Clergy**. Dioceses were adjusted to conform to new departments, clergy

Civil Constitution of the Clergy Legislative decree of 1790 radically reforming the Catholic Church in France.

were put on state salary, and parish priests were to be elected by active citizens, including Protestants and Jews.

Should the Church Be Consulted? The Assembly issued the Civil Constitution of the Clergy without formal consultation with the church, and while the clergy generally were grudgingly prepared to accept it, they were not prepared to have it imposed on them. In the Old Regime, the king had always consulted with the First Estate over religious affairs. The Assembly argued that since the estates were abolished, consultation was no longer possible.

The issue of consultation was solved, temporarily, by turning to the pope. He was a power outside the nation, but a positive word from him could be taken as final.

The Oath to the Civil Constitution of the Clergy When the Assembly ordered all French clergy to take a solemn oath in favor of the Civil Constitution, only 7 out of 160 bishops complied, though half of the lower clergy stepped forward to take it. Then in May 1791, Pope Pius VI publicly condemned the Civil Constitution.

The Split in the French Church Instantly, the French church was split between those who had taken the oath and those who had rejected it. Because the oath had been phrased to demand loyalty to the Revolution as a whole, clergy who refused it, called **nonjurors**, were quickly branded counter-revolutionaries. Thus the failure to consult the church led to a rupture between the church and the new regime. This was a fateful development. There had been opposition to the Revolution from the beginning, but it was never widespread. Now it increased and solidified.

Traditionally minded Catholics who opposed the Civil Constitution harassed the "constitutional clergy" who supported it, jeering at them in the streets, shooting at their houses, or throwing dead animals onto their doorsteps. The police force representing the new regime attacked these protesters, identifying them as enemies of the nation, and arresting and imprisoning them. As these conflicts widened, opposition to the course of events in the capital mounted, especially in western France, where support for the nonjurors was strongest.

Foreign Intervention

On June 20, 1791, Louis XVI and his family, shocked by the rupture between the new regime and the Catholic Church and fearing for their personal safety, attempted to flee France. The next day they were caught east of Paris, in the town of Varennes. People had recognized the king along the way, but it was the postmaster at Varennes who claimed public credit for the identification after he compared the face of the man before him to the one on a banknote in his pocket.

Louis and his family were immediately returned to Paris under armed guard. With the king back in the capital, the deputies made the best of the situation by claiming that Louis had been "kidnapped." Nobody really believed this accusation because the king had written a letter condemning the new regime in harsh terms. The fiction of kidnapping, however, allowed the deputies to proceed with their constitution making.

The Émigrés Those who shared the king's doubts, however, now thought it best to get out of France. These **émigrés** had first started to leave the country in the summer of 1789. In all, about 150,000 people, out of a total population of 28 million, fled France during the 1790s. Thus, another kind of opponent of the Revolution, unhappy with the revolutionaries' treatment of the king, emerged alongside those unhappy with their treatment of the Catholic Church. These two opposition movements soon joined forces to oppose the Revolution both at home and abroad.

Reactions to the French Revolution Public opinion outside France was sharply divided over the merits of France's revolution. The newly independent Americans fiercely debated the meaning of events in France and formed pro- and anti-French political parties. In Britain, Edmund Burke, a political theorist and member of Parliament, denounced the Revolution's headlong rush to change. "Liberty without wisdom," he argued in his *Reflections on the Revolution in France* (1790), "is folly, vice, and madness." Burke, in turn, was quickly attacked by **Thomas Paine**, an Englishman who had defended the American Revolution in his *Common Sense* and now defended the French in *The Rights of Man*. "From what we now see," Paine wrote, "nothing of reform in the political world ought to be held improbable. It is an age of Revolutions, in which everything may be looked for."

nonjurors Clergy refusing to take an oath supporting the Civil Constitution of the Clergy.

émigrés Counter-revolutionaries who fled France during the Revolution.

Thomas Paine (1737–1809) Englishman who defended both the American and French Revolutions.

The English poet **William Wordsworth**, twenty-one years old and visiting France, also championed the Revolution's assertion of reason and rights: "Bliss was it at that dawn to be alive," he later wrote, "but to be young was very Heaven!" Mary Wollstonecraft not only attacked Burke's views in *A Vindication of the Rights of Man* (1790) but went further in her *Vindication of the Rights of Woman* (1792) to argue, like Olympe de Gouges, for women's full participation in public life.

Heading for War While politicians and intellectuals debated France's Revolution, Europe's governments, based on traditions of royal rule over societies of estates and orders, became increasingly alarmed by the implications of universal human rights and the example of France's democratic government. Monarchs began to suppress local pro-French ferment. For example, the Austrian emperor Joseph II, Marie Antoinette's brother, ordered the state police to arrest revolutionary sympathizers in Vienna. The king of Prussia, Frederick William II, also considered crushing the Revolution and restoring Louis XVI's authority.

Indeed, Louis hoped for just such an invasion, and war between the conservative European states and the Revolution began to seem inevitable. In France, most revolutionaries thought that a war against Austria would end agitation by the émigrés, consolidate the Revolution, and unmask any plotting by the king. In April 1792, in a preemptive strike, France declared war on Austria and its ally Prussia.

The French Monarchy in Peril As it turned out, the war set the stage for the fall of the French monarchy. Austrian troops quickly crossed into France and moved on Paris, with the announced intention of rescuing Louis XVI. Just then, a poor harvest once again sent food prices skyrocketing. Faced with these crises, radical deputies in the legislature, convinced that the king was at the heart of all their problems, started to plan the overthrow of the monarchy. For their muscle, they turned to the old militants of July 1789, now nicknamed the **sans-culottes** (literally, "without knee breeches") because they advertised their democratic principles by wearing long laborers' trousers rather than the shorter breeches with hose favored by the well-to-do.

The Sans-Culottes The sans-culottes were a cross section of Parisian society. Many were artisans and day laborers, but the movement's leaders were often well educated and economically well-off. They championed "equality" over the "liberty" celebrated in the Declaration of the Rights of Man and the Citizen.

Before 1792, many sans-culottes had fallen into the category of passive citizens. Now they demanded full political participation in the Revolution and the right to advance themselves economically and socially. They denounced the "idle" rich, demanding government regulation of private property rights and state-sponsored welfare programs that would provide them with basic necessities like food and jobs. They also called for government controls on the price of bread.

Jacobins and Sans-Culottes The sans-culottes' advocacy of government regulation of the economy put them at odds with the Jacobins and most deputies in the revolutionary legislatures, who favored the laissez-faire principles of the Physiocrats and Adam Smith. To achieve their ends, the sans-culottes advocated the direct use of violence. For the next two years, they played a major role in Paris politics, mobilizing mass street demonstrations and marching on the legislature to demand more and more equality.

The Fall of the French Monarchy On August 10, 1792, the sans-culottes invaded the palace where the king and his family were held. Palace guards put up a bloody fight, but in the end Louis XVI was imprisoned and the Constitution of 1791, in effect for less than a year, was scrapped. New elections took place for yet another legislature, the **National Convention**. In these elections, property and occupational qualifications for voters were abolished. All adult males could go to the polls. This arrangement responded to sans-culotte demands for a more thoroughly democratic regime.

> **William Wordsworth** (1770–1850) English poet famous for his nature poetry and his defense of the French Revolution.
>
> **sans-culottes** (in French, "without knee breeches") Parisian militants who overthrew the French monarchy in 1792.
>
> **National Convention** First republican legislature in France, governing from 1792 to 1795.

 Checking In

By yourself or with a partner, explain the significance of each of the following selected key terms:

Jacobin Club

Maximilien Robespierre

departments

active and passive citizens

François Dominique Toussaint L'Ouverture

Civil Constitution of the Clergy

émigrés

sans-culottes

The Republic and the Reign of Terror, 1792–1795

◆ **What measures did France's new republican government take to secure the Revolution?**

◆ **By 1795, how far had the Revolution traveled since the Estates-General was called to initiate tax reform?**

The National Convention, which met in Paris in September 1792, served as France's government until October 1795. These years saw the proclamation of a republic and the execution of Louis XVI. At the same time, revolutionary France faced both the ongoing foreign war and a new civil war that broke out in 1793. In the end, the republic triumphed, but at a terrible cost, when the Convention created a revolutionary dictatorship that ruthlessly pursued its enemies by means of state-controlled terror. The dictatorship's repression set in motion the forces of its own destruction.

The End of Monarchy and Monarchs

Following the imprisonment of the king and queen, as enemy troops moved closer to Paris, panic swept through the city. A fiery orator from the Jacobin Club, **Georges Danton**, proclaiming that the Revolution needed "boldness, boldness, boldness forever," persuaded the out-going Assembly to create a special tribunal to try people who continued to support the monarchy. Those found guilty of opposition to the new regime were beheaded high on a platform in a public square by a new execution device—the **guillotine**, invented by a French doctor who argued that the fast fall of its heavy blade resulted in a painless and efficient means of execution.

Georges Danton (1759–1794) Radical Jacobin revolutionary who rose to prominence after the overthrow of the monarchy.

guillotine Execution device used by the French revolutionaries for beheading, invented by a doctor as a humane way of executing people.

September Massacres Slaughter of 1,300 prisoners by the sans-culottes in Paris in 1792 that alienated many early supporters of the Revolution.

Mountain and **Girondins** Two revolutionary factions vying for control of the National Convention in late 1792 and early 1793.

Committee of Public Safety Committee of the National Convention created in 1793 and granted dictatorial powers to implement the Terror.

The September Massacres By early September 1792, the Paris prisons were full of people accused of counter-revolutionary activity. Fearful that they were still plotting in their jail cells, the sans-culottes invaded the prisons and slaughtered 1,300 inmates, sometimes mutilating the corpses. These **September Massacres** were publicly defended by Danton and Robespierre as the will of the people, but some who had thus far supported the Revolution were secretly alarmed, seeing in them a chilling example of brutal popular violence. When news of the massacres spread, people throughout Europe and America turned against the Revolution in horror.

The Trial of the King On September 22, the National Convention proclaimed France a republic. Now the problem was what to do with the king. In December, Louis was put on trial before the Convention, where he mounted a dignified defense. But the deputies overwhelmingly found him guilty of "conspiracy against the general security of the state." Now debate turned to the king's punishment.

The Mountain and the Girondins Deputies who argued for execution were known as the **Mountain** because they occupied a steeply rising set of seats in the Convention's meeting hall. The Mountain was also the dominant faction in the Jacobin Club. Robespierre took the lead in pressing the Mountain's case for execution, declaring that the king's conviction required it.

Some deputies, however, wanted a punishment that fell short of execution—perhaps banishment to the United States, as Paine, now a deputy in the Convention, argued. The opponents of execution were known as **Girondins**, because their leaders were from the department of the Gironde. They argued that Louis's execution would energize the Revolution's enemies at home and abroad, thereby increasing the dangers France faced.

Both the Mountain and the Girondins were committed to the new republic, but their power bases were different. The Mountain relied increasingly on the radical Parisian sans-culottes, who had overthrown the king on August 10, whereas the Girondins looked to revolutionary moderates in the provinces. By a narrow vote, including that of Sieyès, the Convention sided with the Mountain and ordered the king's execution. On January 21, 1793, Louis XVI went to the guillotine. His last words to his subjects were deliberately drowned out by a drumroll from the execution squad.

Foreign War and Civil War

The execution of the king caught the attention of Europe's royalty, who now condemned the revolutionaries as "king killers." Shortly after Louis's death, Great Britain and Spain joined the war against France. Austria and Prussia regrouped with a coalition that now included the Dutch Republic and the Italian kingdom of Sardinia.

The Committee of Public Safety Facing enemies on every border, the National Convention formed the **Committee of Public Safety**, made up of twelve

In this engraving of Louis XVI's execution, the executioner displays the king's head to the soldiers and citizens witnessing the event. The king's body still lies on the plank of the guillotine. A basket beside it will receive the head and the body after a priest prays for Louis's soul. Compare this rendering of Louis's execution to that of Charles I (Chapter 15, p. 455). What are the similarities and differences?

Bibliothèques des arts décoratifs/The Art Archive at Art Resource, NY

deputies, led first by Danton and then by Robespierre, who were given dictatorial powers to deal with the wartime emergency. The committee ordered a mass mobilization of French citizens to defend the Revolution: unmarried men were drafted to fight in the army, married men were to make weapons, women were to sew clothes and nurse the wounded, while children and the elderly were to make bandages. Never before had a European government tried to harness the energy of a whole people in the service of the state.

In ordering this mass mobilization, the National Convention appealed to the revolutionary principle of fraternity. Now the revolutionaries identified themselves as a "Nation, one and indivisible" and put this slogan on their flags, their stationery, and even their dinner plates.

The Reorganization of the French Army The most important effect of the mass mobilization of 1793 was the reorganization of the French army. **Conscription** greatly increased the number of men under arms. They were badly needed because the old royal army, which numbered about 165,000 in 1789, had fallen to approximately 130,000 in 1793, owing to deaths, desertions, and the resignations of noble officers who opposed the Revolution.

The new recruits brought the numbers up to 750,000—the largest army Europe had ever seen. It was also Europe's first citizen army, in which volunteers or draftees replaced the professional soldiers of the Old Regime. The new army also offered career advancement on the basis of talent, not birth or wealth, fulfilling one of the principles of 1789. After 1793, many of France's best generals rose up from the rank and file on the basis of ability.

Victory on the Battlefield Many soldiers were fired up with revolutionary patriotism. As one put it, "The war which we are fighting is not a war between king and king or nation and nation. It is the war of liberty against despotism. There can be no doubt that we shall be victorious. A nation that is just and free is invincible." Over the next two years, this new revolutionary army launched mass assaults that crushed opponents and drove enemy troops from French soil, thus ending the foreign threat, and then carried the war outside of France by invading the Dutch Republic and northern Italy.

Insurrection in the Vendée
If the reorganization of the army saved the Revolution in the long run, it also created dangerous short-term problems. In March 1793, when the draft was imposed on peasant communities in western France, the Vendée burst into open insurrection against the National Convention. In 1789, peasants throughout France

conscription Military draft, or forced enrollment of soldiers from among the people.

Vendée Part of western France in open rebellion against the National Convention in early 1793 following the break with the Catholic Church and the execution of the king.

had supported the Revolution, but after the Great Fear ended feudal payments to their landlords, many turned conservative and resisted further change. In the Vendée, the execution of the king and the break with the Catholic Church were especially unpopular.

The Vendée was one example of a gulf opening up between parts of provincial France and Paris, where militant revolutionaries continued to push for ever-more radical change.

Rebellion in Lyon Another hotbed of discontent was the southeastern city of Lyon, second largest in France, where opposition to the Convention's emergency measures sparked a rebellion against the central government. With the Vendée and Lyon in rebellion, the National Convention found itself fighting both a civil war and a foreign war.

The Fall of the Girondins In early 1793, the Mountain blamed the Girondins for both the foreign war and the civil war. Robespierre, Danton, and other members of the Mountain accused the Girondins of being secret counter-revolutionaries. This accusation outraged the Girondins' supporters, who denounced Robespierre as an "insect wallowing in the filth of corruption." Finally, in May 1793, the Mountain purged the Girondins from the Convention with sans-culotte support. In return, the sans-culottes expected the Mountain to enact yet more economic controls and measures against those accused of counter-revolutionary activity.

The Republic of Virtue

Maximilien Robespierre had been active in the Revolution from the beginning, first as a deputy to the Estates-General and then as a fiery orator in the Jacobin Club and a deputy in the National Convention. Now "the Incorruptible" became the Revolution's leader. Elected to the Committee of Public Safety in July 1793, Robespierre and the other committee members moved to crush opposition to the Revolution at home, just as the republic's reorganized armies were crushing France's foreign enemies.

The Reign of Terror In early September, the Convention declared that "terror is the order of the day": enemies of the Revolution would be ruthlessly suppressed by force. Robespierre saw terror as necessary for the establishment of a truly virtuous republican regime: "If the mainspring of popular government in time of peace is virtue, the mainspring of popular government in time of revolution is both *virtue and terror.*

Reign of Terror Government's systematic coercion to defeat the Revolution's enemies, implemented in 1793 and 1794.

Marseillaise Revolutionary battle song favored by the sans-culottes, now the national anthem of France.

Terror is nothing but justice, prompt, severe, and inflexible; it is therefore an emanation of virtue."

In practice, the **Reign of Terror** meant government control of the economy and the execution of those deemed counter-revolutionaries. New laws greatly expanded offenses against the Revolution. Now people the committee identified as high-profile counter-revolutionaries were tried and guillotined, including the imprisoned Girondins, Marie Antoinette, and Olympe de Gouges. Their public beheadings attracted huge crowds.

Crushing Rebellion in the Provinces In the provinces, the committee moved against the rebels in the Vendée, where the army crushed opposition, as self-styled revolutionary "columns from hell" burned, looted, and killed indiscriminately. Tens of thousands of people, mostly peasants, died. The army also besieged Lyon, and when the city surrendered, more executions followed. "Lyon no longer exists," wrote the triumphant agent of the Committee. What remained of the city after the siege was renamed Freed City.

The Politicization of Everyday Life A crisis mentality seized the revolutionaries as they moved to defeat their enemies at home and abroad, and everything took on political meaning. Now revolutionaries scrutinized how people dressed, looking to see if they wore the sans-culottes' long trousers and no longer powdered their hair as men of means had done before 1789.

They listened to how people spoke, making sure they treated each other as equals, using "Citizen," instead of "Monsieur" and "Madame," and addressing each other with *tu*, the familiar French form for "you," instead of the more formal *vous*. They looked to see if people ate and drank from plates and cups with revolutionary slogans on them. They formed processions and marched to the singing of revolutionary songs like the *Marseillaise*—to this day the national anthem of France.

This politicization of all facets of everyday life was one of the most striking features of the Reign of Terror, and one of the most threatening because it narrowed choices down to two—those who were united with the revolutionaries 100 percent and those who were not. The revolutionary ideal of fraternity had now taken on a grimly exclusive meaning.

The New Revolutionary Calendar The most ambitious attempt to ensure that the new republic broke with the monarchical and aristocratic past was the creation of a new calendar. No longer were years to be counted from the birth of Christ. Now they began with the birth of the republic. Thus September 22, 1792, the day the republic was proclaimed, became the First Day of the Year One. Months were renamed after the seasons of the year, and weeks were lengthened from the biblical seven days to ten to accord

Réunion des Musées Nationaux/Art Resource, NY

Jacques-Louis David drew this sketch of Marie Antoinette as she passed by his window on her way to execution in 1793. She sits tall, but her face is drawn. Her hands are tied behind her back so she can easily be positioned on the guillotine's plank, and her hair has been cut to give the blade access to her neck. David knew how royalty had been depicted before he sketched the queen, and you have seen some of those depictions in this book. With those depictions in mind, what do you think David was trying to communicate in this drawing?

with the metric system. Thus time and the seasons were reconfigured in a new republican way.

De-Christianization In the prerevolutionary past, Catholicism had been the official religion of France. It, too, was radically repudiated in a movement known as **de-Christianization**. Unlike earlier attacks on the nonjurors, the de-Christianizers made no distinction between supporters and opponents of the Civil Constitution of the Clergy. All priests and their congregations were roughed up and their churches pillaged. As a result, Catholics were driven underground in much of France. Protestants fared no better; their pastors were assaulted and their meeting places vandalized.

Revolutionary Religion As an alternative to Christianity, the Committee of Public Safety sponsored

new republican religious observances that celebrated the deist divinity of the philosophes. In Paris, a singer from the Paris Opera, dressed as Liberty, presided over a celebration in the former Cathedral of Notre Dame, renamed the Temple of Reason. Robespierre himself presided over a Festival of the Supreme Being. This new religion aimed to cement the unity of all true revolutionaries and provide the republic with its base of virtue.

The Great Terror By early 1794, the crises France had faced during the previous year had subsided. Yet state terror increased as the Committee of Public Safety began to root out fellow revolutionaries accused of deviating from correct republican principles. Thus the Revolution was now devouring its own. Then in June 1794, at Robespierre's urging, the Convention passed a law that denied accused persons any right of self-defense in court, inaugurating the **Great Terror** in Paris. During the next month, more than thirteen hundred people were convicted and executed. The guillotine had to be moved to the edge of the city following complaints about the amount of blood in the streets and the stench from rotting corpses.

The Fall of the Committee of Public Safety Faced with the end of rebellion at home and improved conditions abroad, many deputies believed that the Terror, instituted to meet the crises of civil and foreign war, was no longer needed. They supported yet another uprising in Paris in the revolutionary month of Thermidor (July), during which some members of the Committee of Public Safety, including Robespierre, were arrested and executed. The fall of Robespierre inaugurated a wave of reaction against the Terror, known as the **Thermidorian reaction**. The Convention released political prisoners and closed the Jacobin Club, which was identified with Robespierre. It also dismantled the price and wage controls of the previous year, restoring free-market conditions.

Why Did the Reign of Terror Occur? The Reign of Terror of 1793–1794 was the product of two factors. The first was the pressure of foreign and civil war, to which the Committee of Public Safety responded with realistic, if bloody, repression. But this is not the whole story. The second factor contributing to the Terror had more to do with revolutionary politics than with outside pressures.

Since 1789, the identity of the revolutionary nation had rested on its oneness and indivisibility. The nation could not be divided

> **de-Christianization** Attack on all forms of Christianity initiated by the sans-culottes in 1793.
>
> **Great Terror** Culminating phase of the Reign of Terror in 1794, when more than thirteen hundred people were convicted and executed in Paris.
>
> **Thermidorian reaction** Period in 1794–1795 during which the Terror was dismantled.

against itself. If opposition arose, it therefore had to come from somewhere outside the nation and from people who were opposed to the republic. These people, condemned as counter-revolutionaries, were to be stamped out. It was this kind of thinking that led the Committee of Public Safety to execute fellow revolutionaries who questioned its policies and made Robespierre inaugurate the Great Terror in June.

By the end of the Revolution, some 17,000 people had been officially executed. Another 10,000 to 12,000 were lynched or assassinated for political reasons, and between 6,000 and 11,000 died in prison awaiting trial for political crimes. In all, some 35,000 to 40,000 people perished out of a population of 28 million.

 Checking In

By yourself or with a partner, explain the significance of each of the following selected key terms:

September Massacres	conscription
Mountain	Vendée
Girondins	Reign of Terror
Committee of Public Safety	de-Christianization
	Thermidorian reaction

The Rise of Napoleon, 1794–1804

◆ **How did the Revolution make possible the rise of Napoleon?**

◆ **Which parts of the revolutionary heritage did Napoleon Bonaparte accept, and which ones did he repudiate?**

The revolutionary republic survived for five years following the overthrow of the Committee of Public Safety. France's citizen armies continued to win on the battlefield until, in 1797, all the continental states warring against France made peace with the republic. Only England remained to fight at sea. In 1799, continental war broke out again when Austria and Russia attacked France. That same year, France's leading general, Napoleon Bonaparte, seized power. The early years of Napoleon's rule were marked by significant achievements. He reorganized the French state, brought an end to the war, healed the break with the Catholic Church, and instituted a new law code. In these years there was widespread support for Bonaparte's regime. Some émigrés even returned to France.

Directory Executive committee that ruled France from 1795 to 1799.

Napoleon Bonaparte (1769–1821) French general who seized power in 1799 and ruled France until 1814.

French Expansion

The restoration of free-market conditions following the collapse of the Committee of Public Safety had dire consequences for many sans-culottes. The fall harvest of 1794 proved one of the worst of the decade, creating economic hard times in the capital as the price of bread once again soared. By spring 1795, hardship had provoked two sans-culotte uprisings, which were put down by the army. From then on, a new Ministry of Police kept a sharp eye on sans-culotte leaders and periodically rounded them up for "preventive detention" in the city's prisons. Both the Terror and the Thermidorian reaction used coercion to control political enemies, and both whittled away at the human rights proclaimed in the Declaration of the Rights of Man and the Citizen.

The Directory In October 1795, the National Convention installed a new regime, which consisted of a two-house legislature and a five-man executive committee, the **Directory**. In another retreat from the Revolution, only men owning property could vote and hold public office. The Directory skillfully alternated in supporting republicans and royalists, who re-emerged after the dismantling of the Terror. The Directory tried to keep either from dominating, but the result was permanent political instability and increasing cynicism about a government that stifled dissent.

Yet during this time, the French achieved significant gains in the foreign war. In 1795, Prussia, preoccupied once again with Poland, dropped out of the coalition, as did an exhausted Spain. For France, the next four years saw spectacular military victories and territorial expansion, as the Directory pursued a high-minded desire to create a ring of republics around France and a hardheaded aim to make France the leading power in western Europe.

Napoleon Bonaparte French generals, eager for increased military and political power, also drove the conquests. The most ambitious was **Napoleon Bonaparte**. Bonaparte was born to a minor noble family on the island of Corsica, which France had annexed in 1768. Sent to a French military school at age ten, he was a good student but a loner, hazed by his classmates because of his odd name and modest origins. In 1789, the year the Revolution began, Napoleon was twenty and a lieutenant in the royal army. The Revolution gave him his great chance when it opened careers to talent. Bonaparte sided with the revolutionaries, and by 1793, he had risen to the rank of general.

In 1795, Bonaparte's role in putting down a royalist uprising in Paris led to his appointment as commander of the Army of Italy. In that same year he married Josephine de Beauharnais, the widow of a French nobleman who had been executed during the Terror. Napoleon was deeply in love with Josephine and devastated when he learned of her love affairs with other men after their marriage. From then on, he shut himself off from close relations with people and concentrated on advancing his career.

Victory in Italy In 1797, Bonaparte drove Austria out of northern Italy and negotiated a treaty, thus bringing peace to the European continent for the first time since 1792. Britain alone remained to fight. Bonaparte's Italian victories displayed his qualities as a military commander. He planned carefully, struck fast, and was not afraid to take risks. He also knew how to gain maximum military and political advantage from a win.

The Sister Republics Following the invasion of northern Italy, Bonaparte reorganized his conquered territory into a new state, the Cisalpine Republic, staffed by pro-French locals under his control. In this he followed the pattern established in 1795, when the French had invaded the Dutch Republic and set up the Batavian Republic. In 1797, Napoleon would also establish another republic in Switzerland. The old society of estates and orders was abolished in these **sister republics**, replaced by the French model of a nation composed of citizens.

The sister republics were required to pay France for its war costs, to provide supplies to French troops in their territory, and to maintain their own armies at local expense. In Italy, Bonaparte also organized wholesale looting of churches and palaces, seizing statues and paintings that were shipped to Paris for display in the new **Louvre Museum**, where many can still be seen today.

Bonaparte in Egypt When land fighting ended in late 1797, Bonaparte feared his career would falter, so he began angling for a new command. In early 1798, he and the Directory decided on a campaign in Egypt. If the French had access to the Red Sea, they could threaten the British in India. The French force set off by sea in May, landed near Alexandria, and soon occupied Cairo. Then disaster struck. On August 1, the British navy under Horatio Nelson destroyed the French fleet off Alexandria. With his line of supplies now cut, Bonaparte was bottled up in Egypt. To make matters worse, the Austrians and Russians, alarmed at France's creation of sister republics and a French presence in the Middle East, declared war on France in early 1799.

The Fall of the Directory Now the French were put on the defensive, just as they had been in 1792. The military crisis galvanized a group of politicians disgusted by the failure of the Directory to establish domestic stability. One was a new member of the Directory, Joseph Emmanuel Sieyès, whose pamphlet had touched off the furious debate over

the Estates-General exactly ten years before. Sieyès did not have the power or popularity to lead a plot against the government, so he turned to someone who did: Napoleon Bonaparte.

Bonaparte in Charge Leaving his army in Egypt, Napoleon had slipped through the British naval blockade off the coast and arrived back in France. In November 1799, after the conspirators overthrew the Directory in a coup d'état, Napoleon quickly assumed unchallenged leadership of the government. Now all Napoleon's talents came to the fore—his charm and intelligence, his ability to awe people and inspire their loyalty, and his sense of his own exceptional abilities and destiny.

Order and Administration

The new constitution of December 1799 made Napoleon **First Consul** in a three-man consulate. In fact, however, he was the only one with real power. Members of the new legislature had little say in government; Napoleon, assisted by a council of experts, made all the important decisions. The new constitution did not include the Declaration of the Rights of Man and the Citizen. Opposition to the new government was silenced when a rigid press censorship was instituted. All these changes signaled a repudiation of the Revolution's participatory politics. Yet the repudiation was ambiguous because Napoleon kept up appearances by submitting the new constitution to a carefully controlled popular vote of adult males.

The Prefects In early 1800, Bonaparte reorganized administration throughout France. **Prefects**, put in charge of the departments, were under the strict control of the minister of the interior in Paris, who was second only to Napoleon himself. The prefects were chosen on the basis of administrative experience and political leanings. The First Consul was deliberately upholding the revolutionary ideal of careers open to talent, from which he himself had benefited, while trying to win over all factions except die-hard royalists and radical republicans.

Influenced by Enlightenment thought, Napoleon also believed that governing was a science based on reason and careful observation, which allowed administrators to act logically by objectively analyzing problems and finding rational solutions to them. With this system in place, far less stood between the state and

sister republics French satellite states formed from territories conquered between 1795 and 1799.

Louvre Museum Paris museum of art founded in 1793 and housed in a former royal palace, one of the great museums of the world.

First Consul Title taken by Napoleon Bonaparte when he seized power in 1799.

prefects Napoleon's local government administrators in France.

the citizen in 1801 than had stood between the Crown and its subjects in 1789.

Reform of State Finances One of Napoleon's biggest problems was the continuing crisis in state finances, which had been the immediate cause of the Revolution in the first place. Each revolutionary regime since 1789 had assumed the debts of the old monarchy, but by the late 1790s, these debts had become intolerable. To stabilize the state's finances, Napoleon instituted a standardized system of taxation that fell on all citizens in accordance with the revolutionary principle of equality. Remembering what had happened to the monarchy in 1788, he refused to put his government at the mercy of financiers who could indirectly dictate policy by their lending strategies.

Bonaparte and the Catholic Church In 1801 and 1802, peace returned to Europe as Napoleon signed treaties with the Austrians and the British, confirming France's territorial gains and acknowledging the sister republics. Another peace, which proved more lasting than the others, was signed with the Catholic Church in the form of a new **concordat** between Napoleon and Pius VII, elected pope in 1800. The Concordat of 1801 established French Catholics' right to worship publicly, but it did not renew the ancient connection between church and state. Catholicism was simply recognized as the "religion of the majority of the French," and the state remained separate from the church.

Napoleon himself was a nominal Catholic who thought of religion as a tool for maintaining social and political order. He believed that religious toleration for Catholics was a way to end the political headache caused by the Civil Constitution of the Clergy and de-Christianization. But the Concordat also gave the state tight control over church activities, including the regulation of seminaries. A new national catechism for religious instruction secured church endorsement of the regime. Many French people returned to Catholic worship with fervor, especially in the countryside, where women led the revival, demanding the return of priests and urging neighbors to join once again in communal worship.

Protestants and Jews Protestants also benefited from Napoleon's religious policies; they, too, were allowed to worship openly without harassment. The fate of the Jews, however, was somewhat different. Like the revolutionaries, Napoleon wanted to integrate Jews into society. But he also wanted to place them under state supervision. Although Jews were granted freedom of worship, laws put limits on their economic activities and increased their military obligations. The government assumed control of Jewish moneylending, forbade foreign Jews from settling in France, and ordered Jewish men serving in the army to obey all military rules and regulations, even if these conflicted with Jewish religious observance.

The Reinstitution of Slavery French Jews received limited benefits from Napoleon's regime, but another group saw its condition worsen catastrophically. These were the ex-slaves in the Caribbean. In 1801, Toussaint L'Ouverture, who had led black resistance to French rule a decade earlier, conquered the Spanish half of Santo Domingo and proclaimed himself president of the united island. Initially, L'Ouverture had French support, but in 1802, Napoleon turned against him and sent an army to Santo Domingo. It captured and executed L'Ouverture yet was unable to reassert French control over the former colony, now called Haiti.

In the course of the campaign against L'Ouverture, Napoleon restored slavery in Martinique and Guadeloupe, France's other Caribbean possessions. Thus France, which had been the first European state to abolish slavery in 1794, reinstituted it in 1802. It was not finally abolished until 1848. This act was Napoleon's clearest repudiation of the revolutionary heritage. In 1803, he sold Louisiana, which France had received back from a defeated Spain, to the United States. His failure to retake Haiti convinced him that there was no hope for reestablishing a French empire on the North American continent.

The Napoleonic Code

Napoleon's most lasting achievement was a reform of French law codes. Faced with a confusing and contradictory tangle of laws developed over centuries under the old monarchy, the revolutionary governments of the 1790s had declared in principle that French law needed to be rationalized and standardized as part of the great reorganization of the country into a single, undivided nation. Napoleon carried the principle into practice.

The Reform of Civil Law The most important new code was the Civil Code of 1804, later renamed the **Napoleonic Code**. In it the revolutionary principles of equality before the law and security of persons from arbitrary arrest were reaffirmed. Private property rights were guaranteed, as well as the principle of a free-market economy in which individual economic initiative was encouraged. Workers' rights to form unions or other associations were again prohibited as a form of interference with market forces.

Women in Bonaparte's France The code reversed many of the gains women had made during the 1790s. Laws relating to families upheld patriarchal authority;

concordat Formal agreement between the pope and the ruler of a Catholic state; Concordat of 1801 reestablished Catholics' rights of worship in France but separated church and state.

Napoleonic Code Code of civil law implemented in 1804, applied first to France and then to French-occupied territories in Europe.

Jacques-Louis David painted this official representation of Napoleon's coronation as emperor. Having crowned himself, Napoleon now crowns his wife Josephine. Pope Pius VII, seated, is simply one of the spectators. The painting emphasizes two of Napoleon's governing principles: the separation of church and state and the subordination of women to men. Compare this painting with David's sketch of Marie Antoinette on her way to the guillotine. Does the sketch also show David as a propagandist for revolutionary principles?

the male head of the household stood over all other family members and controlled their property. The revolutionary equality between spouses in filing for divorce was revoked, giving men more grounds for divorce than women. Many of these provisions remained a part of French law until 1965. They reflected Napoleon's view that women belonged in the private sphere, where, he said, men would protect them and make them happy.

The End of Democratic Politics Overall, Napoleon's reworking of the revolutionary legacy, culminating in the Civil Code, promoted what he called "order." In 1789, the rallying cry of revolutionaries had been "liberty." In 1793, the sans-culottes had called for "equality," and the Committee of Public Safety had promoted "fraternity" to unite citizens against internal and external enemies. Now liberty, equality, and fraternity were condemned as excuses for **anarchy**. Under Napoleon, democratic politics ceased. Freedom of speech was silenced by censorship and police surveillance.

Society was dominated by the **notables**, a class of landowners created by Napoleon from the middle classes and the old nobility. Along with civilian administrators and army generals, they were the real powers in France. Once again, French national identity

was based on the Old Regime model of a pyramid with a small and powerful elite at the top.

Emperor Napoleon I In 1802, at the height of his popularity, Napoleon modified the constitution to make himself consul for life. In 1803, after a peace that had lasted a mere fourteen months, France and England went to war again. Britain wanted more access to continental markets for its manufactured goods, and France feared English preeminence at sea.

Soon afterward, Napoleon moved closer toward hereditary rule. In December 1804, he summoned Pius VII from Rome to preside over a coronation ceremony in Paris in which he became Emperor Napoleon I. When it was time to place the new imperial crown on his head, Napoleon crowned himself, asserting the separation of the state from the church. He then whispered to his brother, "If only our father could see us now!"

The new emperor modeled his court on the old one at Versailles and started referring to Louis XVI as "my uncle." In 1808, he created a new imperial nobility. Thus the republican state was

anarchy Absence of government, marked by disorder and lawlessness.

notables Elite group of large-scale landowners created by Napoleon.

eroded, but never completely destroyed: the Napoleonic Code was still in place; legislatures met, even though they had little to do; a written constitution still existed; and changes in the regime were carefully submitted to popular ratification in special elections.

 Checking In

By yourself or with a partner, explain the significance of each of the following selected key terms:

Directory	prefects
Napoleon Bonaparte	concordat
sister republics	Napoleonic Code
First Consul	notables

The Napoleonic Empire, 1804–1815

◆ **What did Napoleon demand from the men who administered his empire and its satellite states?**

◆ **What impact did Napoleon's rule have on Europeans outside of France?**

From 1803 until 1815, France was again at war with the rest of Europe. Beginning in 1805, France won spectacular victories on the continent, crushing Austria, Prussia, and Russia and occupying most of Germany. Conquered territories were added to the ever-expanding French Empire. In 1807, when he controlled Europe from the Atlantic to Russia, Napoleon attempted the economic ruin of his sole remaining enemy, Great Britain. But his policy of closing this vast territory to British manufactured goods stirred up resistance. In 1812, Napoleon invaded Russia, a disaster from which he never recovered. In 1814, a renewed coalition defeated Napoleon and drove him from his throne. Napoleon's empire was short lived, but it had a lasting impact.

Trafalgar Naval battle fought 1805 in which the British destroyed the French navy and gained unchallenged control of the high seas.

Confederation of the Rhine Napoleon's union of all German states except Prussia and Austria.

Grand Duchy of Warsaw Napoleon's restored independent Poland.

Renewed War on the Continent

In 1805, continental war broke out again when Austria and Russia joined Great Britain, at war with France since 1803. Austria was soon defeated for the third time, and the Holy Roman Empire formally came to an end when Napoleon decreed its demise. But the British navy defeated the French navy in the Battle of **Trafalgar** off the Spanish coast. Admiral Nelson, who had destroyed Napoleon's fleet in Egypt, destroyed it once again in this battle, losing his life in the process. From now on, Britain enjoyed unchallenged control of the high seas and imposed a blockade on Napoleon's ports to stop France's international trade. On the continent, Napoleon fared better; Prussia, which joined the Allies in 1806, was quickly defeated, and in 1807 Russia, too, succumbed.

Redrawing the Map of Europe Emperor Napoleon, now at the height of his power, redrew the map of much of Europe. All the states in the old Holy Roman Empire, except Prussia and Austria, were made French allies and consolidated in the **Confederation of the Rhine**, a prelude to German unification in the nineteenth century. An independent Poland reemerged as the **Grand Duchy of Warsaw**.

To organize his vast territory, Napoleon used the techniques of the Directory: the creation of satellite states, now called kingdoms instead of republics, and annexation to France. Napoleon made his numerous brothers and sisters the heads of the satellite kingdoms or relied on close confidants to rule them—Joseph Bonaparte went to Spain, Louis to the kingdom of Holland, and Jerome to the new kingdom of Westphalia. Napoleon expected unquestioning obedience from them.

A French Model for the Satellite Kingdoms Rulers were to remake their kingdoms using France as a model. Written constitutions formed the basis of government. The Napoleonic Code was imposed, sweeping away the society of estates and orders and establishing the principle of equality before the law, careers open to talent, and trial by jury. Local legislatures usually controlled taxation rates, which were lower than those in France. Religious discrimination ended, and Jews were admitted to full citizenship. This last reform was particularly important in Holland and Germany, where there were large Jewish populations. Except in Russia, serfdom was abolished.

Government administration was to be based on the scientific principles employed in France. Military conscription was imposed everywhere, and local people were required to pay the costs of French troops stationed in their territory. Napoleon discouraged concessions to local customs because he thought the French model of government was universally applicable. Many of these reforms outlasted the Napoleonic period, particularly in Holland, Germany, and northern Italy. Even Prussia and Austria adopted some of them, in hopes of combating the French challenge by strengthening their states.

Military Conscription in France Napoleon's stunning victories between 1805 and 1807 were the result of his skill as a general and his ability to raise huge

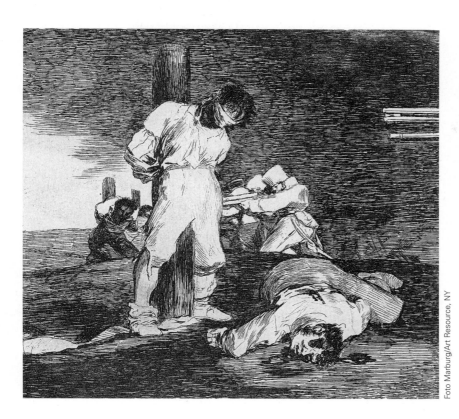

In 1810, the Spanish artist Francisco Goya produced "The Disasters of War," a series of etchings in the tradition of Jacques Callot. This brutal scene of an execution of Spaniards by French solders is titled "And It Cannot Be Changed." How does this painting compare with Callot's understanding of the horrors of war as discussed in Chapter 15?

Foto Marburg/Art Resource, NY

armies by means of conscription. In 1793, France had relied on the mass mobilization of the nation to build up the army to 750,000 men. By 1797, however, the army had fallen to about half this number because of death and desertion. The Directory, therefore, resorted to annual conscription. Napoleon continued the new practice. Some two million French men were conscripted between 1799 and 1814.

At first, the draft was fiercely resisted. Married men were exempt, and potential draftees rushed to marry, sometimes taking wives as old as eighty. If marriage was not an option, men cut off their trigger fingers or hacked away at their shins and testicles to induce debilitating infections. Slowly, however, through persistence and power, the state made its policy stick. By 1806, when the war against Prussia began, the battle against the draft was over; from then on the French submitted to this permanent new intrusion into their lives. Overall, in both the revolutionary and Napoleonic wars, about 916,000 men were lost to the French army, half from death and half from desertion.

The Continental System In late 1806, Napoleon undertook economic warfare against Great Britain. This program, the **Continental System**, closed European ports in French-dominated areas to British merchant shipping. Napoleon reasoned that Britain's economy would slump and its government revenues decline when its traditional continental markets were taken away. As a bonus, French manufacturers would benefit from a market now closed

to British competition. But the system's success depended on the closure of *all* ports, and here the problems began.

France itself could be brought into compliance, but in the satellite states merchants who had profited from trade with Britain protested. Even Napoleon's siblings, under pressure from their subjects, complained. The emperor's response was to annex more territory to France: the kingdom of Holland was absorbed in 1810, as was the north German coast. When Pope Pius VII refused to join the system and excommunicated Napoleon, the pope was put under house arrest and then deported to France, where he lived as Napoleon's prisoner. Italy as far south as Rome was annexed. Pius's imprisonment shocked European Catholics and produced a great wave of sympathy for the suffering pope.

Britain Fights Back, France Responds Britain responded to the Continental System by tightening its blockade on French-controlled ports. The French responded by authorizing privateers to slip through the blockade and harass British merchant shipping. The new United States, a self-declared neutral in the war, was hurt by the blockades and saw its trade with both France and Britain decline. Eventually, in 1812, the United States declared war on Britain in an effort to assert its economic independence.

> **Continental System** Closure of all French-controlled ports to British merchant shipping initiated by Napoleon in 1807 as a form of economic warfare.

Map 19.3 Napoleonic Europe, 1810 By 1810, France was an empire whose boundaries had absorbed many small states to its east. Other states were French allies or dependencies. Napoleon's domination of Europe rivaled Charlemagne's empire and the empire of ancient Rome. © *Cengage Learning*

1. Compare the boundaries of France in 1810 to those of 1789 as shown in the first map in this chapter.
2. Remembering how many separate states there were in 1789 (see the first map in this chapter), count the number of separate states in 1810. What is the difference?
3. Some states were neither at war with France nor part of Napoleon's empire and system of alliances. What are they?
4. Why was Portugal one of the states at war with Napoleon in 1810?

The "Spanish Ulcer" As military intervention and annexation became the means of enforcing the Continental System, Spain entered a period of crisis. Ever since it had withdrawn from the war against France in 1795, the country had been unstable. In 1808, a French army of occupation was sent to close Spain's ports to the British, and Napoleon put his brother Joseph on the Spanish throne. But a riot in Madrid quickly spread into open rebellion across the country, and cries for Spanish national unity in the face of the French occupier grew ever more insistent. More and more French troops were required to keep order. Napoleon denounced the "Spanish ulcer," but the British saw it as an opportunity to reopen the land war against France and sent an expeditionary force to aid the rebels.

Was the Continental System a Success? Despite the problems in Spain, the Continental System was a considerable success. Although British overseas trade never collapsed, it was badly damaged. At the worst of the crisis, Britain survived only by developing new markets in Spain's American colonies, where regulations against foreign traders crumbled in the face of government paralysis at home. On the continent, French traders also opened new markets. French goods now moved east across Europe instead of west to France's Caribbean colonies, as they had before 1789.

Manufacturers in Belgium and central Europe benefited from the exclusion of British goods and the development of a unified continental market. In Poland, however, the loss of British grain markets caused an economic crisis for landlords and their peasants. Overall, French trade advanced under Napoleon, but it never reached the level it had enjoyed in 1789. That would not return until the 1830s.

The Austrian War of Liberation and the French Invasion of Russia

In late 1808, Napoleon marched into Spain with 150,000 men to take direct command of French forces there. Austria seized the opportunity to attack France, urging all Germans to rise up in a "war of liberation." Few German states responded, however, and Napoleon had time to return to France, march east, and defeat Austria for the fourth time. Shortly after signing the peace treaty, Napoleon divorced his wife, Josephine, who had failed to give him an heir. He then married an Austrian archduchess, Marie-Louise, who soon gave birth to a little Napoleon, named the king of Rome.

The Invasion of Russia In Russia, far to the east, Tsar **Alexander I** watched these events and laid his plans. Though required to enforce the Continental System on his coasts, he now believed Russia was strong enough to shake off French domination. He therefore withdrew from the French alliance and resumed trade with the British. Napoleon was furious and began preparing to invade Russia. In June 1812, he moved east with a force of 650,000 troops drawn from twenty countries. It was the largest single army in the field that Europe had ever seen. Throughout the summer, French troops marched farther and farther into Russia, as the Russians withdrew because their army numbered only about 200,000.

Smolensk and Borodino In August, the Russians fought Napoleon at Smolensk, and in early September, they fought again at Borodino, seventy-five miles west of Moscow. These were the bloodiest battles of the revolutionary and Napoleonic wars. After Smolensk, wagons were piled high with amputated arms and legs. Wounded and survivors alike crumpled as food supplies ran out, and hundreds of men died by the roadside from exposure as they slipped into vodka-induced comas. Battle dead and wounded from both sides at Borodino stood at 75,000, including 47 French generals.

The Occupation of Moscow Technically, the French won at Borodino, and the road to Moscow lay open. When Napoleon arrived there in mid-September, however, he found the city practically deserted; once again the Russians had retreated. The French stayed in Moscow for six weeks, waiting for Alexander to sue for peace. But the tsar, in his palace in St. Petersburg, refused. In the meantime, a fire, perhaps started by the Russians, destroyed most of Moscow. With his army exhausted and badly depleted, and with no hope of adequate winter quarters in a burned-out city, Napoleon ordered a retreat to Germany.

The Retreat from Russia What happened next is the stuff of legends: the troops stumbled westward, harassed continuously by Russian units and frozen by the bitter winter that arrived in November. Only 15 percent of Napoleon's army made it back to Germany. For Napoleon, defeat in Russia was the beginning of the end.

Europe's Defeat of Napoleon

In 1813, Austria and Prussia, subsidized by Great Britain, reentered the war after reforming their armies and introducing a French-style draft. Napoleon realized that the next campaign was the one he had to win. The conscription machine in France and the other imperial territories pressed down harder than ever; by the summer of 1813, the emperor had raised an army of 400,000, including 100,000 rounded-up French draft

Alexander I (r. 1801–1825) Russian emperor defeated by Napoleon who then broke with the French, provoking the Russian campaign of 1812.

evaders and deserters. In October, it engaged the Allies in eastern Germany. Napoleon lost and began to retreat westward. As he drew back, the Germans finally rose up in an anti-French revolt, rallying behind their traditional rulers. Years of taxes, conscription, and the hardships of the Continental System were taking their toll. In addition, the French ideal of a united nation of citizens had spread to the occupied peoples. Now they countered the French with their own nationalist fervor.

Abdication After he returned to Paris, Napoleon tried once again to rally his generals and ministers, but they refused to fight on. Finally, in April 1814, he abdicated. The Allies marched into Paris, with Alexander I of Russia at their head. Not far behind was Louis XVI's brother, who had fled France twenty-five years earlier. He was installed as King **Louis XVIII**. Louis XVI's son, who had died in a Paris prison in 1795, was thus honored as Louis XVII.

The Allies exiled Napoleon to the island of Elba, off the coast of Italy not far from his native Corsica. But Napoleon outwitted them one last time. In 1799, he had slipped away from his enemies in Egypt, and now he did it again, secretly setting sail for the south of France. Louis XVIII sent troops to intercept the ex-emperor, but they joined him instead; once again, his fame as a commander carried the day.

The Hundred Days Louis XVIII promptly fled to Belgium, and Napoleon triumphantly reentered Paris, where he was to rule again for a **Hundred Days**. He quickly reorganized the government and prepared yet again for battle. Miraculously, the conscription machine pulled up 100,000 men. On June 18, 1815, Napoleon engaged his old enemies at **Waterloo** in present-day Belgium, where he was defeated for the last time by an English general, the Duke of Wellington, leading a coalition of Prussians, Austrians, and Russians. Once again Napoleon abdicated, Louis XVIII entered Paris, and Napoleon was sent into exile. This time, however, the Allies shipped him into the far South Atlantic, to the island of St. Helena, where he died in 1821 at the age of fifty-two.

The Restored French Monarchy Throughout his years in exile in Allied lands, Louis XVIII had promised a full restoration of the prerevolutionary monarchy if he returned to France as king. But that proved to be impossible; too much had changed since 1789. He therefore issued a Constitutional Charter, which bore a marked resemblance to the Constitution of 1791, as the basis for his rule. The one thing from the past that Louis wanted was a coronation like the one held in 1775 for his brother. But it never took place. The king was old, Rheims was far away, and the revolutionaries had destroyed most of the sacred implements used in the ceremony.

Louis XVIII (r. 1814–1824) Younger brother of Louis XVI of France who became king after Napoleon's defeat.

Hundred Days Period in 1815 of Napoleon's briefly restored rule in France between his return from exile on Elba and his permanent exile on St. Helena.

Waterloo Napoleon's last battle, fought in Belgium in 1815 against an international coalition headed by the British Duke of Wellington.

Checking In

By yourself or with a partner, explain the significance of each of the following selected key terms:

Trafalgar

Confederation of the Rhine

Grand Duchy of Warsaw

Continental System

Alexander I

Louis XVIII

Hundred Days

CHAPTER
Review

Summary

◆ At one level, the era of the French Revolution and Napoleon was characterized by political instability as regimes came and went in a matter of years. From 1775 to 1815, France moved from an absolute monarchy to a constitutional one, and then to a republic, an empire, and back to a restored monarchy.

◆ Beginning in 1792, the wars between France and conservative Europe deeply influenced the policies of these shifting regimes. A similar instability affected the territories France occupied, as lands became sister republics and then kingdoms, or were annexed outright.

◆ On another level, however, it was clear by 1815 that despite political instability, the revolutionary and Napoleonic years had brought about fundamental changes in three areas of European life.

- The democratic experiments of the 1790s, despite their limitations and failures, introduced a new model for political life that was lasting. Frenchmen, endowed with inalienable human rights, became citizens of the state and participants in government.

- Even Napoleon, who detested this democratic world, could not quite stamp it out. Both at home and in the occupied lands, Napoleon relied on written constitutions to give legitimacy to his regime, recognizing the necessity of legislatures and popular voting.

- Although women did not achieve the same level of political participation that men did, demands for their inclusion, first made by revolutionaries like Olympe de Gouges, were to remain central to political debate in the years after 1815.

- The old society of orders and estates based on privilege, abolished first in France and then in Napoleonic Europe, never really returned. The inhabitants of a country were constituted as citizens of a nation. Even Napoleon's reintroduction of nobility did little to alter this new form of society. The notables ignored the old distinctions between commoners and nobles, and the revolutionary ideal of careers open to talent, which had so benefited Napoleon himself in the 1790s, persisted.

- In the end, the occupied peoples adopted the nationalist ideals of France and then turned them against the French.

- Finally, the state's power had grown enormously. The abolition of orders and estates had swept away institutions like the Parlement of Paris that had stood between the state and its subjects. The state had also freed itself from its attachment to the Catholic Church.

- The process of centralized state control, begun by the Committee of Public Safety, was continued after 1799.

- Both at home and abroad, Napoleon used the reorganization of France into standardized units to extend the state's reach into ordinary people's lives. The chief sign of the state's expanded power was conscription.

- The ideals of the Revolution—broad political participation, the end of privilege and the beginning of merit-based advancement, and the increased power of the state—have had repercussions throughout the world.

Chronology

1775	Louis XVI is crowned king of France
1776	American Revolution begins
1788	Parlement summons Estates-General; France declares bankruptcy
1789	Estates-General meets; National Assembly is formed
1790	National Assembly decrees the Civil Constitution of the Clergy
1791	Slaves revolt in Saint-Domingue
1792	France becomes a republic; France declares war on Austria and Prussia
1793	Louis XVI is executed; Reign of Terror begins
1794	France abolishes slavery; Reign of Terror ends
1795	Directory is created
1799	Napoleon seizes power
1800	Napoleon reorganizes French administration
1801	Napoleon and Pius VII sign Concordat
1802	Napoleon makes himself consul for life; Slavery is reestablished in French colonies
1804	Napoleonic Code reforms French law; Napoleon becomes emperor
1806	Continental System closes French ports to British shipping
1812	Napoleon invades Russia
1814	Napoleon is defeated by European allies, abdicates; Louis XVIII becomes king of France

© Cengage Learning

Test Yourself

To gauge your mastery of the material in this chapter, answer the questions below. More than one answer may be correct.

From Crisis to Constitution, 1775–1789

1. The late-eighteenth-century crisis in French state finances was caused by:
   - a. The costs of the two world wars of the midcentury.
   - b. The cost of French intervention in the American Revolution.
   - c. Rising interest rates on state loans.
   - d. State spending on new roads and canals.
   - e. All of the above.

2. In the election for deputies to the Estates-General of 1789:
   - a. The Third Estate had the same number of deputies as the First and Second Estates combined.
   - b. The Third Estate had a third of the delegates and the other two estates had two-thirds of them.
   - c. Voters expressed their grievances in cahiers.
   - d. Voters were prohibited from expressing their grievances.
   - e. Voters were issued government identification cards.

3. The storming of the Bastille:
   - a. Began as a search for ammunition.
   - b. Freed hundreds of prisoners held in the fortress.
   - c. Led the king to recall Jacques Necker to office.
   - d. Led the king to order the royal troops around Versailles and Paris to disband.
   - e. Was soon forgotten in the tumult of revolutionary change.

4. The Declaration of the Rights of Man and the Citizen:
   - a. Drew on Enlightenment thought and the language of the American Revolution.
   - b. Guaranteed freedom of speech and religion.
   - c. Was the single most important document produced in the French Revolution.
   - d. Rejected royal absolutism.
   - e. Proclaimed equal rights for all people.

Now that you have reviewed and tested yourself on this part of the chapter, take time to pull together all the important information by answering the following questions:

- ◆ How did the crisis in French royal finances lead to the collapse of the monarchy?

- ◆ What impact did (a) the events in Paris on July 14, 1789, and (b) the Great Fear have on the National Assembly meeting in Versailles?

The Constitutional Monarchy, 1789–1792

5. In the Constitution of 1791:
   - a. Sovereignty resided in the person of the king.
   - b. Sovereignty resided in the nation.
   - c. Sovereignty was shared by the king and the nation.
   - d. Each person was endowed with equal natural rights.
   - e. The old estates and orders of France were modified.

6. Citizenship in the Constitution of 1791:
   - a. Rested in the revolutionary principles of unity and uniformity in all things.
   - b. Was based on a two-tiered system of active and passive citizenship.
   - c. Favored adult males with a certain amount of property.
   - d. Was open to women.
   - e. Rested on the principle that owning property gave a person a stake in society.

7. François Dominique Toussaint L'Ouverture:

   a. Was a Catholic bishop who embraced the French Revolution.
   b. Was a confidential adviser to Louis XVI.
   c. Was a leading member of the Jacobin Club.

   d. Led the first successful slave revolt in history.
   e. Advised the National Assembly on citizenship issues.

8. Opposition to the Civil Constitution of the Clergy and the oath supporting it:

   a. Was slight among the French Catholic clergy.
   b. Led to a split between the constitutional clergy and the nonjurors.
   c. Was condemned by Pope Pius VI.

   d. Played a major role in increasing and solidifying opposition to the Revolution.
   e. Was particularly strong in western France.

9. The sans-culottes:

   a. Were a cross section of Parisian society.
   b. Were drawn from the poorest sections of Parisian society.
   c. Supported government regulation of private property rights and state-sponsored welfare programs.

   d. Were a leading force in the overthrow of the monarchy in August 1792.
   e. Were opposed to government control of bread prices.

Now that you have reviewed and tested yourself on this part of the chapter, take time to pull together all the important information by answering the following questions:

◆ What were the underlying principles guiding the drafters of the Constitution of 1791? To what degree were these principles realized or violated in the specific provisions of revolutionary reform?

◆ Why wasn't the French clergy consulted during the drafting of the Civil Constitution of the Clergy, and what were the consequences of the failure to consult?

The Republic and the Reign of Terror, 1792–1795

10. The deputies of the Mountain:

    a. Were dominant in the Jacobin Club.
    b. Defeated the Girondins in a struggle to control the National Convention.
    c. Were defeated by the Girondins in a struggle to control the National Convention.

    d. Had their power base among the radical sans-culottes of Paris.
    e. Had their power base in the French provinces.

11. The Committee of Public Safety:

    a. Was created by the National Convention.
    b. Was granted dictatorial powers.
    c. Was led by Robespierre.

    d. Ordered a mass mobilization of citizens to defend the Revolution.
    e. Reorganized the French army.

12. Civil war in France:

    a. Broke out in the Vendée and Lyon.
    b. Broke out in Alsace and Perpignan.
    c. Was put down with little bloodshed during the Reign of Terror.

    d. Could never be successfully ended by the Committee of Public Safety.
    e. Led to the death of tens of thousands of people.

13. The de-Christianization movement:

    a. Attacked any and all types of religious observance.
    b. Attacked any and all types of Christianity.
    c. Promoted religious festivals based on the deist divinity of the philosophes.

    d. Favored the Jewish communities in France.
    e. Was aimed solely against the nonjurors.

Now that you have reviewed and tested yourself on this part of the chapter, take time to pull together all the important information by answering the following questions:

◆ What actions did the Committee of Safety take to defend the Revolution from enemies at home and abroad?

◆ Were the democratic principles of 1789 advanced or compromised by the actions of the Committee of Public Safety?

The Rise of Napoleon, 1794–1804

14. Bonaparte's prefects:
    a. Had to pay the state for the privilege of holding their offices.
    b. Were recruited on the basis of talent and administrative experience.
    c. Were to think of governing as a science based on reason and observation.
    d. Included die-hard royalists and radical republicans.
    e. Were accountable directly to Bonaparte.

15. The Concordat signed with Pope Pius VII:
    a. Established French Catholics' right to worship publicly.
    b. Reinstituted the ancient connection between church and state.
    c. Allowed the state control over Catholic seminaries.
    d. Led to the creation of a national catechism for religious instruction.
    e. Was secretly repudiated by the pope.

16. The Napoleonic Code:
    a. Was Napoleon's most lasting achievement.
    b. Carried out the plans for a revision of the law begun by the revolutionary regimes of the 1790s.
    c. Reaffirmed the principles of equality before the law and freedom from arbitrary arrest.
    d. Reaffirmed the rights women had gained in the 1790s.
    e. Guaranteed workers' rights to form unions.

Now that you have reviewed and tested yourself on this part of the chapter, take time to pull together all the important information by answering the following questions:

◆ How were the French sister republics created, and what were their relations with France?

◆ Which of the revolutionary programs and policies of the 1790s did Napoleon Bonaparte benefit from, repudiate, or maintain?

The Napoleonic Empire, 1804–1815

17. Napoleon's satellite kingdoms:
    a. Were ruled by members of Napoleon's family or close confidants.
    b. Were ruled by powerful generals in the French army.
    c. Were organized along local traditions and ways of doing things.
    d. Were modeled on Napoleonic France.
    e. Were exempt from military conscription.

18. Military conscription in France under Napoleon:
    a. Enrolled five million men into the French army.
    b. Enrolled two million men into the French army.
    c. Led many men to marry in order to avoid the draft.
    d. Represented a permanent new intrusion into French citizens' lives.
    e. Was quickly abandoned after Napoleon's fall from power.

19. The Continental System:
    a. Was implemented to create economic decline in Britain.
    b. Ruined all of Britain's overseas trade.
    c. Had little effect on Britain's overseas trade.
    d. Led to the annexation of more and more territory to France.
    e. Offered French traders new opportunities in the European continental market.

20. Napoleon's invasion of Russia:
    a. Took place despite Alexander I's continuing ban on trade with Britain.
    b. Led to the creation of the largest single army Europe had ever seen.
    c. Culminated in the battles of Borodino and St. Petersburg.
    d. Ended in a successful occupation of Moscow.
    e. Ended in a French retreat.

Now that you have reviewed and tested yourself on this part of the chapter, take time to pull together all the important information by answering the following questions:

◆ What did Austria and Prussia do to defend themselves against France and the Napoleonic empire?

◆ Why did the peoples of the Napoleonic empire rise up against the French at the end, and what did they want as an alternative?

CHAPTER 20

Restoration and Reform: Conservative and Liberal Europe, 1814–1847

Chapter Outline

1810　　**1815**　　**1820**　　**1825**

1814
Congress of Vienna opens

1817
Wartburg Festival celebrates German history, life, and culture

1815
Napoleon is finally defeated at Waterloo

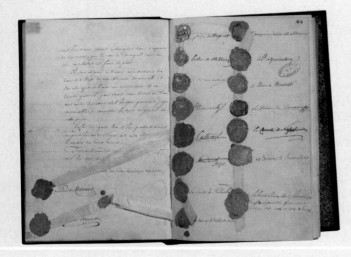

The **"Final Act"** of the Congress of Vienna, signed by all the European powers, included the various treaties that had been agreed upon during the Congress's deliberations. In a very real sense this document redrew the map of Europe and established a political order that in many ways survived into the twentieth century. (Archives Charmet/The Bridgeman Art Library)

After reading this chapter you should be able to answer the following questions:

How did the Congress of Vienna attempt to create a stable Europe after the Napoleonic Wars?

What were the main tenets of Romanticism and the new political movements of conservatism, liberalism, and nationalism?

Why did nationalism have different impacts in Poland, Belgium, the Balkans, and Germany?

Why did political reform take place first in France and Great Britain, then in the rest of Europe?

I N THE DECADES after Napoleon's final defeat, Europeans lived in the shadow of the French Revolution and its ideologies. In 1815, it appeared that the French Revolution had failed. Monarchs held fast to power throughout Europe, from London to St. Petersburg and even in Paris, where a successor to the Bourbons occupied the throne. The peace conference ending the Napoleonic Wars, held in Vienna, established a conservative political system aimed specifically at preventing the spread of liberal and revolutionary ideas. However, appearances were deceiving, as the French Revolution had changed European politics forever. The revolutionary ideals of "Liberty, Equality, Fraternity" continued to inspire active political participation. These ideas dominated the development of political ideologies during these decades.

These ideologies were conservatism, liberalism, and nationalism. Conservatives aimed to retain the power of monarchs, despite the fact that few still believed in the divine right of kings. Liberals called for parliaments, constitutionalism, civil rights, the rule of law, and a withdrawal

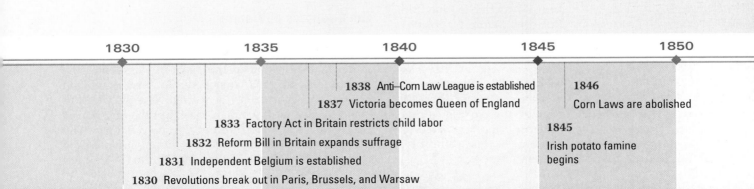

1830   1835   1840   1845   1850

1838 Anti–Corn Law League is established

1837 Victoria becomes Queen of England

1846 Corn Laws are abolished

1833 Factory Act in Britain restricts child labor

1832 Reform Bill in Britain expands suffrage

1845 Irish potato famine begins

1831 Independent Belgium is established

1830 Revolutions break out in Paris, Brussels, and Warsaw of the state from economic matters. Nationalists denounced kings and princes, naming the nation—that is, the entire people—as the ultimate authority in politics. Until 1848, liberals and nationalists often joined forces; most liberals were nationalists. Nationalist movements in the Balkan Peninsula attempted to gain independence from Ottoman rule, and the Greeks succeeded. In central Europe, German and Italian nationalists sought to bring together existing small states into large, unified nation-states. Later in the century they would succeed.

Paralleling and crisscrossing these national movements was a literary and artistic movement known as Romanticism, which championed the individual human spirit. The Romantics rejected the cold rationality of the Enlightenment and looked back in longing to the preindustrial, deeply religious world of the Middle Ages. They celebrated the strong and dynamic individual who— like Napoleon—could change the world. Romantic thinkers and artists also challenged social conventions of the day, openly calling for more freedom in love and sexuality, even as they experimented with new forms of artistic and poetic expression. The Romantics' mystical brand of Christianity clashed with conventional religious institutions and dogmas.

Although most governments in the post-Napoleonic period were conservative, the ideas of the French Revolution continued to influence politics and culture. A series of uprisings in 1830 realized some national and constitutional ambitions, and in Great Britain political reform was achieved through a series of parliamentary acts. Even in conservative-dominated central Europe, liberal and nationalist ideas were spreading and gaining in strength. In 1848, these new ideologies would burst forth in a wave of revolutionary uprisings across the European continent.

The Old Order and New Challenges

♦ **What were the main aims and outcomes of the Congress of Vienna?**

♦ **How did Romantic poets and artists challenge the existing social order?**

Congress of Vienna (1814–1815) International meeting that redrew the European map and restored order after the Napoleonic Wars.

Clemens von Metternich (1773–1859) Austrian statesman, architect of the Congress of Vienna and the Congress System, foreign minister and then prime minister of Austria, 1809–1848.

A quarter century of revolution and war was brought to a close by the defeat of Napoleon at Waterloo in June 1815. But even before Napoleon's defeat, monarchs and diplomats from all over Europe were meeting in the Austrian capital to hammer out a peace settlement. Presided over by the Austrian Prime Minister Prince Clemens von Metternich, this would be a conservative peace.

The Congress of Vienna restored prerevolutionary rulers and drew borders that lasted into the twentieth century. Metternich wanted to restore the preindustrial, absolutist social and political order of the eighteenth century, but he was realistic enough to recognize that he could not set the political clock back to 1788. Instead, he aimed to prevent revolutionary outbreaks and to suppress the new ideologies of liberalism and nationalism by strengthening traditional rulers and the landowning nobility. Even as he did this, however, the new cultural and artistic movement called Romanticism was challenging the conventions of this conservative world.

The Congress of Vienna

After Napoleon's catastrophic Russian campaign of 1812, it was clear that his control of France was weakening. In 1814, as allied troops from Russia and the various German states marched into Paris, Napoleon was exiled—courteously sent to govern the pleasant island of Elba off the Italian coast. But the question of the postrevolutionary order in Europe was open. The **Congress of Vienna**, called by the Austrian Prime Minister **Clemens von Metternich** in mid-1814, aimed

Legend:
- France
- Kingdom of Prussia
- Austrian Empire
- Spain
- United Kingdom
- Russian Empire
- Ottoman Empire
- —— Boundary of the German Confederation

ATLANTIC OCEAN

North Sea

Baltic Sea

KINGDOM OF SWEDEN AND NORWAY
- Oslo
- Stockholm
- Helsinki
- St. Petersburg

Moscow

RUSSIAN EMPIRE

- Riga

SCOTLAND

UNITED KINGDOM OF GREAT BRITAIN AND IRELAND
- Dublin
- IRELAND
- Manchester
- WALES
- ENGLAND
- London

DENMARK
- Copenhagen
SCHLESWIG
HOLSTEIN

KINGDOM OF THE NETHERLANDS
- Amsterdam
- HANOVER
- Antwerp
- Waterloo

- Danzig

KINGDOM OF PRUSSIA
- Berlin
- Göttingen
- Cologne
SAXONY
Elbe R.

Vistula R.
- Warsaw
KINGDOM OF POLAND (Russia)

- Kiev
Dnieper R.

Rhine R.
- Luxembourg
- Paris
LORRAINE
Seine R.

- Frankfurt
- Prague
BOHEMIA

- Cracow
GALICIA
Dniester R.
UKRAINE

FRANCE
Loire R.

ALSACE
BADEN
- Munich
BAVARIA

- Vienna
AUSTRIAN EMPIRE
- Buda • Pest
HUNGARY

BESSARABIA
MOLDAVIA

Garonne R.

SWITZERLAND
LOMBARDY
PIEDMONT
- Milan
Po R.
- Venice
PARMA
MODENA

CROATIA

WALLACHIA

Black Sea

Rhône R.
- Marseilles

LUCCA
TUSCANY
PAPAL STATES

SERBIA
- Belgrade
Danube R.

BOSNIA

PORTUGAL
- Madrid
SPAIN

KINGDOM OF PIEDMONT-SARDINIA
Elba
Corsica (Fr.)
- Rome

Adriatic Sea

BULGARIA

- Istanbul

Ebro R.

Sardinia

NAPLES
KINGDOM OF THE TWO SICILIES

ALBANIA

OTTOMAN EMPIRE

GILBRALTAR (Gr. Br.)

Mediterranean Sea

Sicily

GREECE
- Athens

MOROCCO

ALGIERS

TUNIS

Malta (Gr. Br.)

Map 20.1 Europe After the Congress of Vienna, 1815 The Congress of Vienna redrew the map of Europe in order to strengthen conservative governments. In Eastern Europe multinational empires and not nation-states dominate this map. © *Cengage Learning*

1. Compare this map with Europe before the Napoleonic Wars (p. 586) and in 1918 (p. 783). What has changed? What new countries appear in the later map?

2. Western European countries tend to conform more with the concept of "nation-state" than do countries in central and eastern Europe. Why do you suppose that is so, and what exceptions to that general rule can you see?

3. Why would nationalism be a major threat to the state boundaries set down in this map, in particular in central and eastern Europe?

Supplied by Royal Collection Trust © 2012 Her Majesty Queen Elizabeth II

In this painting from the early 1820s, Metternich gazes haughtily past the viewer, his rich clothing and self-assured posture reflecting the power he exerted in Austria and throughout Europe. How does his poise, his facial expression, even the papers he holds, project a powerful image of a strong, busy, and powerful man?

to set that order. Metternich was a brilliant and complex man who combined wit and charm with cold calculation. When the congress disbanded in 1815, a new conservative, post-Napoleonic Europe had been established.

Besides Metternich, two other statesmen played important roles in the congress's work: the foreign minister of Great Britain, Robert Castlereagh, and Tsar Alexander I of Russia. Prussia's king Frederick William III seemed reluctant to press his concerns, perhaps remembering his military humiliation at the hands of Napoleon and salvation with Russian help. Surprisingly, even defeated France was allowed to send a representative, the cunning but utterly cynical survivor Charles Maurice de Talleyrand, once memorably described as "a piece of dung in a silk stocking." Talleyrand cleverly exploited divisions among the Allies, particularly the widespread fear of growing Russian power, to gain better conditions for France. Castlereagh expressed no interest in territorial gain but aimed to restore a European balance of power in which no European state would ever again be able to dominate the continent. Tsar Alexander I hoped to extend Russian influence in Europe, and Metternich aimed to neutralize it. Talleyrand made the case that only a strong France could ensure each ally's goals.

Frictions over Poland Competing interests came to a head over the issue of Poland. Alexander felt that the partitions of Poland of the late eighteenth century had been immoral and wished to resurrect Poland in some way. More practically, he knew that a reconstituted Poland connected to Russia would considerably enhance Russian influence in central Europe. Understandably, Prussia and Austria opposed this extension of Russian power, though they agreed that Russia should be compensated for its important role in defeating Napoleon. This dispute almost split the congress apart, but in the end a compromise was reached. The kingdom of Poland (or **Congress Poland**) was established as an **autonomous** kingdom, with Alexander as king and Warsaw as its capital. Russia gained the largest amount of Polish territory, but millions of Poles continued to live in Prussia and Austria.

Restoration of Conservative Power in France and German States Talleyrand succeeded in keeping France from being punished. The Bourbons, in the person of Louis XVIII, were restored to France's throne, though not to absolute rule. The king was subject to a constitution and had to share power with a legislature. France had to give up lands occupied after 1795 and to pay a war **indemnity** but remained intact, an important player in European politics.

The German states and principalities that had fought against Napoleon were restored to their rulers, but their total number was reduced from around three hundred to thirty-nine. These ranged in size and importance from Prussia and Austria (the Habsburg empire contained, of course, much non-German territory as well) to tiny Liechtenstein with only five thousand residents.

These German states were loosely connected in a confederation but remained independent entities. Prussia gained the territory west of the Rhine River that Napoleon had incorporated into France. The Netherlands regained independence and acquired the southern provinces that had belonged to Spain and then to Austria. The Spanish Bourbons were restored to power in the person of King Ferdinand VII, who at first promised to work together with liberals, then turned on them and ruled as an absolute monarch. The congress restored the Papal States, including the city of Rome and covering much of central Italy, to the papacy. Thus, the diplomats gathered in Vienna redrew the map of Europe in

Congress Poland Polish kingdom under the Russian tsar created at the Congress of Vienna (1815), enjoying until 1831 its own constitution, legislature, army, and bureaucracy.

autonomous Self-governing but not entirely independent, usually in a certain region or for a certain ethnic/national group.

indemnity Money or goods paid by the losing side after a war to compensate for the cost and damage of military action.

Map 20.2 **Kingdom of Poland, 1815** The Kingdom of Poland was created at the Congress of Vienna and attached to the Russian empire; the Russian tsar was also the king of Poland. The kingdom was ruled by a viceroy and a parliament in the capital, Warsaw. Although most Poles lived in this so-called Congress Kingdom, millions continued to live under Austrian and Prussian rule. © *Cengage Learning*

1. Why would both Poles and Russians be dissatisfied with this compromise solution of the Polish question?
2. Which parts of present-day Poland were included in the Kingdom of Poland? Which are outside it?

a settlement that would set the political course for nearly a century.

Besides the territorial changes set down at the Congress of Vienna, the powers also agreed to work together in concert—the so-called Concert of Europe—to prevent future military and civil disturbances. In this they were astonishingly successful: Europe would see no general war for nearly a century.

The Congress System

The four Great Powers of Prussia, Austria, Russia, and Great Britain (later joined by France) planned regular congresses, like the one at Vienna. Their **Congress System** aimed to root out revolution, even if it meant interference in the internal affairs of sovereign states. Such interference was considered less dangerous than allowing liberal and radical ideas to grow.

The Holy Alliance The guiding principle of the Congress System, urged by Tsar Alexander I, was to be the **Holy Alliance**. Alexander, very much under the influence of Christian mysticism, proposed to his fellow monarchs (not just those present in Vienna) that henceforth they model their policies on principles of the Christian faith. That this suggestion was greeted—at least in private—with a good deal of skepticism and even ridicule reveals that even Christian statesmen and monarchs considered international relations a realm distant from Christian morality. Castlereagh denounced the Holy Alliance as "nonsense," and Metternich called it "a loud-sounding nothing." Nonetheless, the diplomats were reluctant to offend the tsar and at least pretended to be sympathetic to Alexander's proposal.

Threats to the Congress System In fact, the system's real guiding power was Metternich, who sought to limit Russian power in Europe, to expand Austrian influence, and to suppress all the ideas that had come out of the French Revolution. For Metternich, constitutionalism, civil rights, and the rule of law all amounted to the same thing—revolution. For a **multinational state** like Austria, nationalism was every bit as much a threat as liberal ideas. The Congress System was a deeply conservative, even **reactionary**, set of policies that aimed mainly at preventing change.

From the start, however, there were serious practical problems with the Congress System. When the Greeks rebelled against their Ottoman rulers in 1821, setting off the Greek War of Independence, their cause was championed by Tsar Alexander of Russia, but Metternich and Castlereagh opposed any measures that could increase Russian power. The strain between British insular interests and the obligations of the Congress System proved

Congress System Conservative political system put in place at the Congress of Vienna aiming to preserve peace and prevent the spread of nationalism and liberalism.

Holy Alliance Political agreement advocated by Tsar Alexander I at the Congress of Vienna calling for international relations to be based on Christian morals.

multinational state Country in which more than one ethnic group ("nation") resides—for example, the Habsburg, Ottoman, and Russian Empires.

reactionary Exceedingly conservative, wishing not only to prevent change but to retreat into the past.

Berlin/Hamburger Kunsthalle, Hamburg/Art Resource, NY

Caspar David Friedrich's paintings exemplify the romantic sensibility. Often, as in his "Wanderer Above a Sea of Fog" (1818) above, the lone human figures are overwhelmed by the rough and beautiful natural world. Romanticism was also obsessed with death and religion. How are those themes reflected in the images you see in "Abbey Surrounded by Oak Trees" (1809) on the next page?

too much for the already unstable Castlereagh; he took his own life in the midst of the Greek crisis. In the end, Metternich's savvy diplomacy prevented Russia from declaring war on the Ottoman Empire, and the Greeks had to wait another decade for independence.

Castlereagh's suicide pointed to a fundamental contradiction between British interests and European unity in the form of the Congress System. Following more than twenty years of warfare on the continent, the British were extremely reluctant to get involved in European affairs,

Nicholas I (r. 1825–1855) Russian tsar noted for conservatism and his hatred for the political ideals of the French Revolution.

especially in military action. When, in 1823, France intervened against a more liberal order in Spain, Britain openly broke with the alliance. Across the Atlantic, the United States also sought to guard against European intervention. President James Monroe issued what became known as the Monroe Doctrine, declaring that European meddling in the Western Hemisphere would not be tolerated. Alexander I died two years later, and his successor, Tsar **Nicholas I**, was much less interested in European affairs than his elder brother had been. From this point on, the Congress System became little more than a weapon in the hands of Metternich to suppress nationalist and revolutionary movements in central Europe and Italy.

Galerie der Romantik, Berlin/akg-images

The Age of Romanticism

In his attempts to root out nationalism, Metternich set himself against a new cultural movement that was sweeping Europe and would eventually, in a political form, tear apart Austria and the multinational states he sought to preserve. Metternich embraced tradition, privilege, and the existing political order. In contrast, the artistic and literary movement **Romanticism** embraced emotion, individuality, and new forms of expression. Romanticism was everything Metternich was not: mystical, antirational, and passionate. Although often deeply religious, the Romantics opposed most existing institutions—even the church— and demanded freedom for human beings to realize their emotional, cultural, and even sexual potential. Reacting against what it saw as the cold rationality and dull universalism of the Enlightenment, Romanticism celebrated the human soul and mystical nature that connected directly with God.

Romanticism in Literature and Painting The Romantics saw God in nature, as Wordsworth conveyed in his poetry and **Caspar David Friedrich** expressed in his starkly beautiful landscapes. Wordsworth would wander lonely through England's Lake District and return to his cottage to write poems about the glories of nature—and the deeply felt sense of God's majesty in such things as daffodils, clouds, or landscapes. The German poet Friedrich von Hardenberg,

better known as Novalis, portrayed man, woman, nature, and God as merged in an infinite unity. Romantic art also sought out exotic localities, tempestuous nature, and common people as its subjects. In France, Eugène Delacroix's paintings showed exotic scenes (especially in northern Africa and the Muslim world), stormy seas, and his most famous painting of all—a bare-breasted Liberty leading the people to victory over their oppressors. One common aspect of nearly all Romantic art is a burning desire to overcome feelings of personal loneliness and alienation, to submerge individual identity in a cosmic whole combining human, natural, and divine elements.

The Romantics—and it is not by chance that most of these were poets or painters, not stockbrokers or college professors—rejected the Enlightenment's mechanical universe and its method of seeking the truth through studied observation, experimentation, and reason. They were profoundly disturbed by the idea of a clockwork universe in which human beings were just a cog. The most important aspects of life, they contended, cannot be understood by rational scientific

Romanticism Literary and artistic movement of the late eighteenth and early nineteenth centuries that extolled artistic genius and opposed many traditional social conventions.

Caspar David Friedrich (1774–1840) German artist whose landscapes often featured craggy mountains, mighty forests, and Romantic ruins that overwhelmed small human figures.

experimentation. Rather, the irrational—powerful emotions, the sense of beauty, the ecstasy of love—makes us human. In "The Tables Turned," Wordsworth called on a friend to "quit your books," "Our meddling intellect/Mis-shapes the beauteous forms of things—We murder to dissect." In the Romantic view, the scientific method can never fathom the mystery of life or answer fundamental moral questions such as why human beings are here, why we love, and why we suffer. The English poet John Keats, in his famous "Ode on a Grecian Urn," proclaimed: "'Beauty is truth, truth beauty,'—that is all/ Ye know on earth, and all ye need to know."

Romantics also rejected the restraints of middle-class respectability. They mocked hardworking, narrow-minded pillars of society. Instead, they extolled the Romantic hero, a dashing figure who often ended tragically, like **Alexander Pushkin**'s Eugene Onegin and Lord Byron's Don Juan.

The German poet Friedrich Schlegel praised sexual love even outside marriage in his poem *Lucinde*. Novalis's *Hymns to the Night* were inspired by a teenaged girl, though it is clear that his feelings for her were more spiritually exalted than physical. Intellectual women figured prominently in the Romantic movement as organizers of salons where Romantic writers gathered as well as writing themselves. Women like Dorothea (Veit) Schlegel and Mary Wollstonecraft Shelley (daughter of the early feminist Mary Wollstonecraft) worked as equal partners with their writer-husbands and published works of their own.

In their art—and sometimes in their personal lives—the Romantics created a world where man and woman interacted in full equality, the female and the male principles supplementing and inspiring each other. The German writer Johann Wolfgang von Goethe, who had been a great influence on the Romantics, had concluded his epic poem, *Faust*: "The eternally feminine leads us forward." At the same time, the Romantics' conception of "artistic genius" took for granted that most people would not be able to understand or appreciate him—or her! The image of the starving and alienated artist so familiar to us today took on modern form with the Romantics.

Romanticism in Philosophy and Politics Romanticism was an all-embracing philosophy of life that emphasized unity, organic growth, inspiration, and creative genius. While Romantics often combined their mystical longings for the unity of all nature and humanity with religious sentiments, they were rarely Christians in any conventional sense. Furthermore, their emphasis on creative genius bordered on blasphemy: geniuses

The Visual Connection Archive

Active during the reign of Tsar Nicholas I, Russian poet Alexander Pushkin's works reflect the romantic temperament of the age. In this engraving he sits at his desk creating his historical poem "The Bronze Horseman" (1833) in which the famous statue of Peter the Great comes to life and pursues the poem's hero through the gloomy streets of St. Petersburg. How would the figure of a lone man who dares to defy Tsar Peter the Great reflect romantic sentiments?

became in their own way gods, creating new worlds. The established churches could hardly embrace such ideas, even from individuals who opposed the anticlerical Enlightenment. The Romantics were fundamentally **utopian**—visionaries who believed perfectibility was possible in human relationships and societies. But they lacked the detachment and willingness to compromise that are essential to achieving reform in the political arena. Even those Romantic figures like Friedrich Schlegel who wrote on political subjects were not successful in influencing contemporary politics.

Despite its fundamentally utopian nature, Romanticism had an important impact on future politics through its influence of nationalism. Nationalists, embracing the Romantic spirit, rejected universalism and glorified the individual—in this case, the individual language, culture, and nation. Like the Romantics, nationalists in the early nineteenth century rejected existing institutions and looked forward to a golden age in which not just French and German but also languages like Czech, Lithuanian, and Serbian would be cultivated and respected. The Romantics

Alexander Pushkin (1799–1837) Russian nobleman and poet considered Russia's national writer.

utopian (from Greek, "no place") Consisting of unrealistic attempts at reforming human life.

The Grimm Brothers Begin Work on Their *German Dictionary*

In 1838, Jacob and Wilhelm Grimm were middle-aged professors—expelled from their university. They were well known in academic circles for their many pathbreaking studies in the field of linguistics and German philology, the study of words and texts. Individually and together they had published dozens of studies, including a book on German mythology, a grammar of the German language, and collections of German stories, fairy tales, and myths. And linguists speak of "Grimm's Law" to describe a regular shift in consonant sounds (*p* : *v* : *f*) in the development of European languages; for example, *pater* in Latin became *vater* in German and "father" in English. The Grimms' analysis revealed connections among languages derived from Indo-European roots.

The Grimms' collection of German fairy tales was first published in 1812—just as Napoleon was on his way to Moscow. They oversaw the collection of hundreds of stories, often venturing into villages to hear the tales that had been passed down orally from generation to generation. By writing down these narratives for the first time, the Grimm brothers saw themselves as carrying out a patriotic duty to preserve German folk traditions. By the end of the century, these stories would be published in hundreds of editions and dozens of languages.

The Grimms' work aimed to elevate the prestige of German culture and language. They wanted to prove that German culture was every bit as rich as the cultures of unified nations such as England and France. Throughout the century, similar research with the same patriotic purpose would be carried out by Russian, Hungarian, Irish, and Slavic folklorists. In a similar way, the American Noah Webster published his *American Dictionary of the English Language* in 1828 to emphasize the legitimacy of American English. All these early nationalists believed that the development of individual national cultures contributed directly to the enrichment of world culture.

The Grimm brothers' political views combined liberalism and nationalism. When, in 1837, the new king of Hannover (the German kingdom where their university, Georg-August-Universität, was located) cast aside the constitution in effect since 1833, the Grimm brothers, along with five other Göttingen professors, protested. The "Göttingen Seven," as they came to be known, refused to swear an oath to the despotic new king. For daring to stand up for their political principles, they were expelled from the university. Their fame as scholars was now enhanced by admiration for them as political martyrs, and a public collection helped fund their continuing research.

In the same year as their expulsion, the Grimm brothers embarked on their most ambitious project of all: a German dictionary that would "contain the endless richness of our fatherland's language from Luther to Goethe." The Grimms aimed not just to compile definitions of German words but to document the history of the German language and the changing usage of words from late medieval times to the present day. Their *Deutsches Wörterbuch* (*German Dictionary*) was a monumental undertaking. The work went forward slowly, and the first volume (A to Biermolke) was published after sixteen years of work. Wilhelm died in 1859, a year before the second volume appeared. The third volume (E to Forsche) appeared in 1862, one year before Jacob's death. The massive project started by the Grimm brothers was continued by their students and was not completed until the early 1970s. In the twenty-first century, this enormous historical dictionary remains one of the marvels of nineteenth-century philology and is a valuable research tool for specialists in German language and literature.

---

themselves welcomed the French Revolution in its early stages—a nation coming to power—though the bloodshed soon disillusioned them. For many, Napoleon Bonaparte resembled the ideal Romantic hero who swept away old institutions and ideas and brought the ideals of liberty, equality, and brotherhood to the lands he "liberated" (not "conquered").

Romanticism in Eastern Europe In different forms, Romanticism spread across the European continent. The homeland of Romanticism is arguably either Germany or England, but Poles put forth their national poet, **Adam Mickiewicz**, or the patriotic composer and pianist **Frederic Chopin** as archetypical Romantics. Mickiewicz's poetic masterpiece, *Pan Tadeusz*, evokes a lost homeland and a world that no longer exists. Even today it is a rare Pole who cannot recite the poem's first lines: "Lithuania [for Mickiewicz,

Adam Mickiewicz (1798–1855) Polish writer, mainly of lyric and patriotic poetry, born in Polish Lithuania but spent most of his life in exile.

Frederic Chopin (1810–1849) Polish composer and pianist, best known for his expressive Romantic piano works and his dances, especially polonaises, that celebrated Polish nationalism.

a province of Poland], my homeland! You are like health; only he who has lost you can appreciate your true worth." Chopin was born in Warsaw but, like Mickiewicz, spent most of his life in France. His most famous works used traditional Polish folk melodies and musical forms. Both Chopin and Mickiewicz exemplify a fusing of Romanticism and nationalism.

Among Russian writers, Pushkin exhibits Romantic strains, and even more typically Romantic are Mikhail Lermontov's rousing stories and poems of dashing young soldiers, beautiful maidens, unrequited love, and exotic locales along the Black Sea and in the Caucasus Mountains.

 Checking In

By yourself or with a partner, explain the significance of each of the following selected key terms:

Congress of Vienna	Nicholas I
Clemens von Metternich	Romanticism
Congress Poland	Alexander Pushkin
multinational state	Adam Mickiewicz

The Beginnings of Modern Ideology

◆ **On what points did liberals and conservatives of this period differ?**

◆ **Why did conservatives in the early nineteenth century oppose nationalism?**

The nineteenth century has been called the century of "isms." Besides the literary and artistic movement of Romanticism, the most important among these are conservatism, liberalism, nationalism, and socialism. All these modern political ideologies trace their origins back to the French Revolution. Conservatives opposed the Revolution and favored traditional authority and a slow rate of change, carefully directed from above. Liberals generally supported the Revolution's ideals of "Liberty, Equality, Fraternity," though they rejected the violent excesses of the Reign of Terror and Napoleonic period. Nationalists latched onto the Revolution's idea of the "great French nation" in which all citizens were equal in rights and responsibilities. In central and eastern Europe, nationalists—almost always political liberals or radicals—called for democratic nation-states on the French revolutionary model to replace the old multinational states. Conservatives

conservatism Political ideology emphasizing tradition, slow change from above, and respect for existing institutions.

legitimacy Conservative view of the political and social order that assumes the right of kings and the nobility to rule.

like Metternich, on the other hand, rejected nationalist arguments as destructive for existing state structures.

Conservatism

Conservatism is often understood as the political ideology that opposes change. In fact, conservatives recognize that some degree of change in human society is inevitable. In these years, they did, however, oppose the rapid and thoroughgoing change advocated by the French Revolution. Most conservatives were not so much ideological as practical: they saw that change threatened their own position. Metternich is a good example. He believed that "the people" were not capable of choosing their government or governing themselves. Only royalty or the nobility were **legitimate** rulers, and they would direct change from above, based on existing traditions and institutions. For conservatives, religion and the Catholic Church played a fundamental role in maintaining respect for established rules of conduct and obedience to authority. The people themselves are not to be trusted. Conservatives have a pessimistic view of human nature and believe the people must be held in check and told how to behave.

Edmund Burke: Moderate Conservative Perhaps the greatest ideological conservative was the Irish philosopher, political theorist, and member of Parliament Edmund Burke. When the French Revolution broke out, he was almost sixty, and his most famous book, *Reflections on the Revolution in France,* was published in 1790. Burke argued that the French Revolution was doomed to descend into violence and anarchy because it was based on abstract principles instead of firmly rooted institutions. Having swept away the king's legitimacy, Burke warned, the revolutionaries had nothing to put in its place except the abstraction of popular rule that would mean a despotism far worse than Louis XVI's bumbling. Burke did not reject change out of hand but insisted that it must be "organic"—that is, growing naturally out of existing ideas, institutions, and individuals. This metaphor of organic change was to become very common among conservatives.

Burke was certainly no admirer of absolutism. After all, he had defended the American colonists in their revolt against the British monarch. He valued highly the rights enjoyed by British men of his class, talents, and education. He did reject, however, the idea that all men should be treated as equal and should participate on an equal footing in politics. This, he argued, was a recipe for disaster and the worst kind of tyranny. Describing the National Assembly in Paris, Burke wrote, "Their liberty is not liberal. Their science is presumptuous ignorance. Their humanity is savage and brutal." Burke did not reject the ideal of political liberty but insisted that most men—ignorant, lazy, and undisciplined—were not yet ready to appreciate this lofty sentiment. By eliminating the political and moral institutions that helped keep the masses of humanity in line, the French Revolution threatened to unleash a flood of destructive brutality and anarchy.

Pessimistic Conservative: Joseph de Maistre Burke, like Thomas Hobbes before him, thought pessimistically that unfettered liberty would inevitably lead to lawlessness. The terrible events of the Reign of Terror and Napoleonic Wars only served to confirm this pessimism. Perhaps the most extreme political conservative of the post-Napoleonic period was **Joseph de Maistre**. This nobleman from Savoy, on the border between France and Italy, fled his homeland when it was invaded by French armies under General Napoleon in 1792. For the rest of his life, much of which was spent in St. Petersburg, Maistre wrote against the ideals of the French Revolution and liberalism.

Like Burke, Maistre based his political ideology on authority, religion, and tradition. Unlike Burke, Maistre emphasized the pope and the Catholic Church as central to legitimate authority. Maistre argued directly against certain central tenets of the Enlightenment, and in particular despised Jean Jacques Rousseau's famous line "Man was born free, and everywhere he is in chains." Maistre rejected the idea of natural freedom put forth by Rousseau; for him, men were brutish and violent in a state of nature and, without Christianity, were no better than slaves. Only accepting and obeying existing authorities, first among them the pope, prevented the "natural bondage" of humanity from reasserting itself. In other words, mankind's base and sinful nature required the strict control of church and legitimate rulers. Like Burke, Maistre stressed the importance of history and tradition, rejecting written constitutions as harmful abstractions: "Man cannot make a constitution, and no legitimate constitution can be written." In other words, political legitimacy comes only through the slow evolution of traditional authority, never from abstract principles.

Russian Conservatism: The Slavophiles A unique kind of European conservatism in this period arose in Russia, the most conservative of Europe's Great Powers, under Tsar Nicholas I. In the Russian context, **Slavophilism** called for a return to pure Russian Orthodox religious values and a rejection of foreign—specifically western—influences. The Slavophiles demanded the abolition of Tsar Peter the Great's Europeanizing reforms in order to restore Russia's inner harmony and religious purity.

The Slavophiles rejected representative government, institutionalized democracy, and industrial development, arguing in a Romantic vein that such rational western institutions were alien to the Russian soul. At the same time, they argued for the abolition of serfdom, but from a uniquely conservative point of view.

By ending serfdom, the tsar could reestablish the mystical unity that had existed between the Russian people (that is, the peasantry) and himself. Like the Romantics in other parts of Europe, the Slavophiles yearned for mystical unity while championing the uniqueness of their own Russian historical and religious experience. Slavophilism had little effect on Russian governmental policy, but the Slavophiles demonstrated that one could oppose the Russian status quo not only from a left-wing, radical perspective but also out of conservative conviction and religious belief.

The era 1815–1847 was in most respects a conservative, even reactionary one. It is remarkable that this conservatism owed very little to the thinkers discussed here and much more to Metternich's practical politics. These thinkers did, however, share with Metternich many fundamental attitudes. All rejected the legitimacy of written constitutions, representative government, and political change based on abstract rights and reasoning. In this way, conservatism both in theory and in practice lined itself up directly against the most important traditions of the Enlightenment.

Liberalism

Where conservatism rejected the Enlightenment, **liberalism** embraced it wholeheartedly. Liberalism enthusiastically took up the Enlightenment's call to "dare to know," to transform knowledge into practical measures that improve the world. Classical liberalism, like the Enlightenment, put the individual at the center of its political ideology.

Unlike conservatism (and socialism), liberalism emphasized above all constitutionalism and civil rights, including the right to own property, express one's opinions freely, and profess any religion—or no religion at all. The abstractions of law and constitutions so despised by the conservatives lay at the very center of liberal politics. Only through the impersonal rule of law could true liberty be guaranteed for all citizens. Standing above all individuals—rich or poor, noble or peasant—law would regulate the relations of the individual citizen and society as a whole. In this way, the liberals argued, the rule of law assured true equality of rights. Laws also restrict the individual's actions, of course, but liberal theorists recognized that some individual freedoms must be sacrificed for the good of society as a whole. Liberals also stressed the importance of private property for a free society. Owning property gave an individual

Joseph de Maistre (1753–1821) Conservative theorist whose pessimistic outlook on human nature led him to advocate severe limits on human freedom.

Slavophilism ("love of Slavs") Russian social philosophy of the 1830s and 1840s, calling for a return to religious values and a rejection of Tsar Peter the Great's reforms.

liberalism Political ideology emphasizing constitutionalism, civil rights, private property, and the rule of law.

a stake in the existing order and transformed the abstractions of law into concrete rights and duties.

Unlike conservatives, liberals were fundamentally optimistic about human nature and the possibility for transforming the world for the better. The liberals were middle-class men (and, increasingly after the midcentury, women) whose political ideology may be termed the politics of the industrial **bourgeoisie** and educated middle class. Liberals opposed traditional forms of authority like royal absolutism or the pope. On the economy, they differed fundamentally from what present-day Americans understand as liberal, as they firmly opposed government interference. In principle, liberals were in favor of the equality and fraternity of all humanity, though in practice they remained wary of granting full political rights to poorer and less-educated elements in the population. Similarly, very few liberals indeed thought that women were truly equal to men. Rather like the Enlightenment thinkers themselves, they argued that "in time" even these strata would be ready for full political rights—when they were educated. With its insistent call for constitutionalism, civil rights, protection of private property, and the rule of law, liberalism was for this period a markedly progressive political ideology.

Liberalism in Great Britain Great Britain was the homeland of classical liberalism. Classical economic liberalism rests mainly on Adam Smith's renowned work *The Wealth of Nations* (1776). Smith argued that nations enrich themselves not by amassing precious metals and restricting their exports, a central tenet of mercantilism, but by allowing the greatest possible freedom for market forces, in other words, **free trade**. Government should stay out of economic matters, avoid high taxes and tariffs, and let markets set prices. Smith spoke of the "invisible hand" of the market mechanism that through the **law of supply and demand** would maximize economic efficiency. Smith did concede that government could not stay out of the economy entirely because of the need for infrastructure, such as roads and harbors, which the profit motive would not create. On the whole, however, Smith thought that by limiting government expenditures, keeping taxes low, and encouraging free markets, a country would prosper. Economic liberals demanded a laissez-faire economic policy from the state, calling on government to keep out of the economy and let it develop naturally according to market forces.

Political liberalism grew out of Jeremy Bentham's *Introduction to the Principles of Morals and Legislation* (1789), which contained the now famous statement that the aim of legislation should be the greatest happiness for the greatest number of citizens. Bentham, like Adam Smith, believed that enlightened self-interest was the best guide for reforming institutions and politics. Not abstract principles but practical applications should be the reformer's primary goal. Because of his emphasis on practical reforms, Bentham's thought has been called **utilitarianism**. His influence may be seen clearly in the political demands of liberals like James Mill and also more radical thinkers. Like Smith, Bentham held a basically optimistic outlook: if human beings followed their own interests in an enlightened way, a better society would result.

James Mill developed this argument further, emphasizing the role that proper education would play in enabling individuals to recognize their own proper self-interest. Mill argued that the greatest happiness for the greatest numbers may not necessarily require **universal suffrage**, in which everyone had the right to vote, but it certainly did demand a political system in which the participation of educated and propertied individuals was guaranteed. Mill took his own ideas on education seriously enough to apply them to his son, **John Stuart Mill**, perhaps the most famous liberal of all. The younger Mill began to study Greek at the age of three, Latin at eight, and by twelve had read through most of the ancient classics, as well as studying mathematics, history, and philosophy. While morality was a central aspect of this education, religion and poetry were specifically excluded from it.

Not surprisingly, given his father's intense educational regime, as a young man John Stuart Mill underwent a shattering spiritual crisis from which he only gradually recovered. Mill's most famous work, *On Liberty* (1859), forcefully made the case for individual liberty, justice, and toleration. Unlike his father, John Stuart Mill was greatly troubled by the possibility that the spread of democracy could strengthen a tyrannical majority that would limit and crush individual freedoms. Mill defended the right to minority views, which he feared majority rule could threaten.

Liberalism and the Woman Question: John Stuart Mill Mill also believed that women must be recognized as intellectual and political equals—if not superiors—of men, a radical view that he expounded in his *Subjection of Women* (1869). As a philosopher, moralist, and political thinker, Mill was the epitome

bourgeoisie The middle class, especially capitalists, well-to-do investors, factory owners, and educated professionals.

free trade Unrestricted trade between different countries, not hindered by high tariffs or taxes.

law of supply and demand Economic law according to which prices increase when supply is low and demand high.

utilitarianism Practical philosophy, usually associated with Jeremy Bentham (1748–1832), whose goal was the greatest happiness for the greatest number of people.

universal suffrage Right to vote for everyone.

John Stuart Mill (1806–1873) Liberal philosopher who supported universal suffrage, including for women; son of James Mill and author of *On Liberty and Utilitarianism*.

of liberalism. At the same time, his works reflected the progress of industrialization, mass society, and even socialism that challenged the basic tenets of liberalism: individualism, the rule of law, and private property.

Mill's life was intimately related to that of the woman he described in his autobiography as "the most admirable person I had ever known," Harriet Taylor (later Harriet Taylor Mill). Taylor herself published relatively little, but her impact on John Stuart Mill's works was enormous. Mill himself wrote in a highly Romantic vein that when two persons are so close in spirit and mind and spend so much time together conversing on topics of interest to both, then "it is of little consequence in respect to the question of originality, which of them holds the pen." Mill dedicated *On Liberty* to her, calling it "our joint production."

Nationalism

Like liberalism, **nationalism** underwent profound changes as a political philosophy in the course of the nineteenth century. Before 1848, nationalism was generally associated with liberalism and democracy. In the second half of the century, nationalism became more and more closely aligned with conservative forces. The realignment of nationalism after 1848 reflects its triumph, and our present-day acceptance of the **nation-state** (in principle, at least) as the political norm is part of this triumph.

Key Terms: Nation and State To understand the political ideology that nationalists propagated, two often-confusing terms need to be distinguished: *nation* and *state*. In English, as in French, these words are often used as synonyms, but in most of Europe in the nineteenth century, they were completely distinct concepts. Indeed, in most European languages it is impossible to confuse the two: German, for example, distinguishes *Staat* ("state") and *Volk* ("nation").

The state is easiest to define: it is a political entity that levies taxes; finances an army and a state bureaucracy; issues passports; and demands certain obligations of its citizens such as military service, payment of taxes, and obedience to laws. In the classic phrase of the German sociologist Max Weber, the state "holds the monopoly on legitimate violence." Examples of present-day states include Japan, Germany, the Russian Federation, Zambia, Israel, and the United States. It is an example of the linguistic confusion in English mentioned above that the so-called United Nations is in fact an organization of independent *states*.

While states are political units, the term *nations* refers to groups of people bound together by common language, culture, religion, history, ancestry—or some combination of these factors. The Romantics glorified the distinctive qualities of each nation, rejecting the idea that any one nation had the right to consider its language or culture better than any other.

In the nineteenth century, one of the most important markers for claiming nationhood was ethnic and linguistic. Thus, Germans—like the Grimm brothers—championed their own language as the element that made them a single national group, despite the fact that they lived in dozens of separate states. German nationalists in Vienna, Munich, Hamburg, or Berlin all demanded a united Germany. Similarly, Italian nationalists in Rome, Palermo, Venice, and Turin wanted to bring all Italians together in one political unit: Italy.

Nationalism in Eastern Europe In central and eastern Europe there were nations that lacked states altogether. Congress Poland was not truly independent of Russia, and Poles lived elsewhere in Russia, Austria, and Prussia. For Polish nationalists, all Poles should live together in a single Polish state. At least Poles had the historical memory of a strong Polish state; many nations, such as Latvians, Ukrainians, and Romanians, lacked even that.

On a practical level, it was often difficult to decide just where a given nation's boundaries lay, and nations did not usually live in compact, easily defined regions. The people now known as Belarusians and Ukrainians were considered by the Russian government to be branches of the Russian nation, and there was considerable debate on whether they could, or should, be considered separate nations, as they are today. It was also debated whether Croats were a nation or should join an "Illyrian" or **Yugoslav** nation with Serbs, who spoke the same language but followed a different religion. Hence nationalism pulled in opposite directions. Even as it called for members of a nation to live together in one state, it threatened the territorial integrity of such multinational states as the Russian, Habsburg, and Ottoman Empires.

Nationalists also faced difficulties created by class. Some nationalities consisted almost exclusively of peasants, with the upper classes belonging to a different national group. Such was the case for Latvians, whose landlords were German. And there remained the problem of where to put the Jews, who in the context of east-central Europe, at least, certainly fit the criteria of a separate nation with their distinct language (Yiddish), religion, culture, and forms of everyday life. Where—and even whether—Jews would fit in the emerging nation-states of Europe would be known in the late nineteenth century as the

nationalism Political ideology arising in the late eighteenth century that demanded that the nation (a group of people) have control of its own state.

nation-state Independent political unit, usually dominated by one culture or ethnicity, in which the ultimate political legitimacy rests with the people (the nation).

Yugoslav (literally, "south Slav") Group of related languages and ethnicities, including Slovenes, Croats, Serbs, and sometimes Macedonians and Bulgarians.

Jacob Grimm Writes a Foreword to the *German Dictionary*

Before the mid-nineteenth century, the German language suffered from an inferiority complex. Even the celebrated Prussian king Frederick the Great had preferred speaking French over his native German. Most educated Europeans knew little about German literature and culture. And even Germans themselves were not always certain about the correct usage and pronunciation of their language—indeed, often there was no single standard language to guide them, only dozens of dialects.

The Grimm brothers set out to change this situation. They worked to establish a standardized form of German that everyone could accept as "correct." Part of this enterprise was the publishing of a mammoth dictionary. The dictionary would have two main purposes: to document the richness of the German tongue and to standardize usage and spelling of German words. This text is taken from the foreword to the Grimm brothers' *German Dictionary*.

❶ Grimm uses words like *treasure, shrine, sublime monument.* Why do you suppose language is so precious for him as a German? Why might language be more important to a German in this era than, say, someone from England or France?

❷ Grimm describes language as a "mystery" and speaks of the "common folk." How do these two concepts fit into the ideas of Romanticism and nationalism?

❸ Why does Grimm claim that the "endurance of your nation" depends on holding fast to the German language? What does he mean by "nation?" What other European ethnic groups might place similar emphasis on the development of their language?

❹ Look at the map at the beginning of the chapter. How do the geographical limits of the German nation mentioned by Grimm differ from the area where German is spoken today? What happened to bring about this change?

What is the purpose of a dictionary?

❶ It should establish a shrine to the language, preserve its treasure intact, open up the language to everyone. The written word, like the honeycomb, grows and becomes a sublime monument for the folk whose past and present are tied up with it.

❷ Language is known by everyone and is at the same time a mystery. Just as language powerfully attracts the scholar, so too do common folk feel an affinity and interest toward it. "What is that word I can't think of right now?" "There must be better ways of expressing this—let's look it up."

Beloved German compatriots, no matter what your religion or country, come together in the open halls of your ancient ancestral tongue! ❸ Sanctify it and hold fast to language; the strength and endurance of your nation depends on it. ❹ The German language still reaches beyond the Rhine to Alsace and Lorraine, north to Schleswig-Holstein, on the Baltic to Riga and Reval (Tallinn), beyond the Carpathians to Transylvania. And for you, too, German émigrés beyond the salty sea, this book will bring wistful yet pleasant thoughts of your homeland's language.

Source: From the preface to Grimms' Worterbuch (published in 1838).

Jewish question. Before 1848, however, these practical difficulties were rarely considered. Nationalists overwhelmingly felt that national liberation would engender cooperation among different ethnic groups. Like the liberals (and most nationalists were liberals), nationalists were optimistic about human nature, predicting that education and economic development would help put an end to strife and wars.

Before 1848, nationalism often did not yet take a specifically political form. At this point, nationalists emphasized the need to develop the nation's culture and language and worked to expand national consciousness—that is, the feeling of belonging to a nation. In the early nineteenth century, most Europeans, aside from a thin (though growing) stratum of educated people, lacked strong national consciousness: their identity was based rather on belonging to a religion and social group (peasant, noble, artisan, and so on) and having origins in a certain village or town. They often did not think much about the language they spoke, as they had no experience with foreigners. The concept that a peasant speaking some form of German in, say, Bavaria, belonged to the same nation as the king of Prussia would have been completely incomprehensible to these people. Nationalists set out to change this mind-set.

Jacob and Wilhelm Grimm were liberal nationalists. So was **Johann Gottfried von Herder**, a German who spent much of his life in Riga on the Baltic. Herder wrote widely on the philosophy of history, language, and literature and insisted that all cultures and languages have something to add to world culture and world history. All ethnic groups, Herder argued, should develop their own culture, enrich their own language, and create their own literature.

Just as Herder demanded that the German language be treated on an equal footing with French or English, later in the nineteenth century, young Lithuanians would refuse to use Polish, Czechs would reject German, and Jews would insist on using Yiddish or, even more radically, Hebrew in daily life. In his own way, Herder was an individualist Romantic challenging the universalist assumptions of the Enlightenment. He was both a nationalist and a democrat, arguing for equal rights and respect not just for individuals, but for entire cultures.

Nationalism contained in its very essence a strong democratic element. For nationalists, the legitimacy of the state arose out of its unity with the nation. The term *nation-state* describes this unity. Hence politics must be influenced by the sentiments of the nation as a whole. Obviously, very few of those in power in the early nineteenth century could accept such an ideology. Kings might claim to rule for the good of their people, but they rarely welcomed the people's interference in their policies. Nationalists and liberals thus shared an interest in breaking down the royal status quo. Conversely, kings and conservatives like Metternich saw in nationalism one of their greatest enemies.

 Checking In

By yourself or with a partner, explain the significance of each of the following selected key terms:

conservatism
Joseph de Maistre
Slavophilism
liberalism

utilitarianism
John Stuart Mill
nation-state
Jacob and Wilhelm Grimm

Political Pressures on the Continent

◆ **How did nationalist ideology affect politics during this era?**

◆ **Where, and why, did liberal ideas succeed in this era? Where, and why, were they suppressed?**

These new political ideologies of conservatism, liberalism, and nationalism had a direct impact on politics in continental Europe. Conservatism was the driving principle at the Congress of Vienna, but even where monarchs were restored, concessions were made to liberalism in the form of constitutions and elected legislatures. In France, the restored Bourbon king was overthrown by a middle-class revolt in 1830. In Russia, Tsar Nicholas I's conservative regime refused to allow any kind of political reform. But even there and in the Ottoman Empire, nationalist movements challenged the authority of the tsar and sultan by demanding political and cultural rights for specific nations. Across the continent, the growing attraction of liberal and nationalist ideas caused kings and emperors to sit uncomfortably on their thrones.

Restoration and Liberal Revolt in France

The French Revolution and the guillotining of Louis XVI in 1793 changed French politics forever. Even conservatives like Metternich and Talleyrand at the Congress of Vienna recognized this fact. Hence they worked not to restore the absolutist monarchy of 1788. Instead, they put in place a system that kept most power in royal hands but also allowed some political participation for the wealthiest (and most conservative) elements of French society.

Jacob and Wilhelm Grimm (1785–1863, 1786–1859) German linguists famous for their collections of fairy tales and monumental dictionary of the German language.

Johann Gottfried von Herder (1744–1803) German critic and historian who urged small nations to develop their language and culture.

Restoring Monarchy: Louis XVIII The new French king was Louis XVIII, younger brother of the ill-fated Louis XVI. Louis XVIII did not rule as an absolute monarch: he had to share power with a legislature. Louis was a narrow-minded and selfish person whose obesity and atrocious table manners made a horrible impression on Parisian society. He was also a terrible politician. In a few months, he had so alienated the political elite that when Napoleon reappeared on the scene, having escaped from Elba in March 1815, the entire Bourbon court fled. No one was willing to take up arms in defense of Louis XVIII.

Luckily for Louis, Napoleon was soon defeated by the Allies at Waterloo, and Louis returned to Paris. For the next decade and a half, French politics was dominated by Louis and his conservative royalist supporters. Under pressure from Britain and Russia, whose troops were occupying Paris at the time, Louis allowed more moderates into the legislature. In 1818, France paid off its war indemnity, foreign troops left Paris, and, for all practical purposes, France was once again accepted as a fully legitimate Great Power in the Concert of Europe.

The following decade was a period of calm and growing prosperity. The royalists aimed to restore the Catholic Church to dominance in French society, roll back the revolutionary changes of the previous decades, and combat the specter of "democracy" (at this point the word was nearly always used in a negative sense, suggesting mob rule). The French liberals were hindered by a lack of effective leadership and by the vivid memories of chaos and bloodshed during the revolutionary period.

Reaction and Discontent: Charles X In 1820, Louis XVIII died. The new king was his elderly brother, **Charles X**, who was intent on restoring royal absolutism. His coronation at Rheims was a medieval extravaganza; more seriously threatening to the interests of the middle class were his plans to give financial compensation to émigrés who had lost property during the revolutionary years. Other laws considerably tightened censorship and threatened those guilty of sacrilege with severe punishments, even death.

Tensions between Charles X and the Parliament came to a head in 1830, when elections failed to secure a majority for Charles's supporters. Instead of compromise, Charles chose the path of direct confrontation—in effect, a royal coup d'état. He dissolved the legislature and prepared a new electoral law that would deprive even the wealthy bourgeoisie of the vote. This was too much. Led by the brilliant journalist Adolphe Thiers, the liberals demanded a truly constitutional monarchy and the replacement of Charles X by his cousin, the Duke of Orléans. Faced with barricades, street fighting, and a clear lack of broad support, Charles X abdicated in favor of his grandson and left France to spend the rest of his days in Prague. Thus began the reign of the "bourgeois king" **Louis Philippe**—so-called for modest habits and reliance on middle-class political support—which would last for almost twenty years.

Nationalist Movements in Belgium, Italy, and Germany

In France, nationalism played very little role in politics. After all, the French nation and the French state were closely identified with each other, with non-French ethnic groups such as Basques, Bretons, and Catalans far from the capital and not politically organized. In other parts of Europe, however, nationalism was often the single greatest rallying cry for change of the political status quo.

Nationalism Creates Belgium Just to the north of France, nationalism provided the driving force for a revolution in Belgium in 1830. At the Congress of Vienna, the Belgian provinces had been united with the Netherlands. Both economically and religiously, however, these southern provinces differed significantly from Holland. The Belgian provinces were rich in coal, and the textile industry in this region had always been closely linked with England. By 1830, this region was, after England, the most industrialized area in Europe. The Belgian provinces were also predominantly Catholic—unlike the much more Calvinist north—and in great part did not use the Dutch (or Flemish) language, but French.

Discontent with rule from Amsterdam broke into open insurrection in Brussels in late August 1830. When the Dutch king William I was unable to restore order, the Congress System went into action, and the Great Powers called an international conference to decide the fate of the Belgian provinces. The British and French decided to support Belgian independence. The international agreement of 1831 made Belgium a constitutional monarchy, with Leopold of Saxe-Coburg (related not only to German royalty but also to the British ruling house) as its first king. The Great Powers also decreed that Belgium would always remain neutral in international disputes. The creation of Belgium was a triumph for liberal nationalist forces.

Italian Nationalism: Aspirations for Unity Elsewhere liberal nationalists fared more poorly. In Italy, underground nationalist organizations like the radical *carbonari* opposed clericalism and the conservative

Charles X (r. 1824–1830) French king renowned for his refusal to compromise with modern political ideas; swept from power by the July Revolution of 1830.

Louis Philippe (r. 1830–1848) French constitutional monarch, known as the "bourgeois king" for his unpretentious lifestyle and political connections with the bourgeoisie.

carbonari Members of secret societies existing throughout Europe, but especially in Italy, aiming to fight political reaction and work for liberal political reform.

The liberal Italian nationalist Giuseppe Mazzini (left) and radical Giuseppe Garibaldi (right) both dedicated their lives to the cause of Italian nationalism. Mazzini was the thinker and writer, Garibaldi the fighter and revolutionary. How do their outfits in these images reflect their different roles in promoting Italian nationalism? Judging from these images, which one do you find more trustworthy? More exciting?

order. In 1832, **Giuseppe Mazzini** called for all Italians to unite and create a liberal nation-state. In a famous appeal, he urged liberal Italians to form Young Italy—"a brotherhood of Italians who believe in a law of *progress* and *duty,* and are convinced that Italy is destined to become one nation." His writings inspired the **Risorgimento**, a movement calling for a renewal of Italian culture and nationalism. Mazzini organized Young Italy throughout the Italian peninsula, often in dangerous circumstances, and gathered funds for the cause from wealthy supporters. Though Mazzini's supporters often had to operate in secret to avoid arrest, even in the 1830s the membership of Young Italy was estimated at more than fifty thousand people.

One of those inspired by Mazzini's Young Italy was **Giuseppe Garibaldi**. Garibaldi and Mazzini shared more than a first name. They were both born in northern Italy, barely two years apart. Both dedicated their lives to the Italian nation and were key figures in the unification of Italy. But there were also significant differences between the two men. Mazzini was of middle-class origins (his father had been a physician and professor at the University of Genoa); Garibaldi came from a poor fisherman's family. Mazzini was a writer, thinker, and organizer. Garibaldi was an

enthusiast, a revolutionary, and a military man. Indeed, few men so resembled the Romantic hero—passionate, handsome, dedicated to a cause—as Garibaldi did. During the 1830s and 1840s, Garibaldi worked as a sailor, fighting for republican liberties in Italy and South America. Only in 1848 would he return from Uruguay to Europe in hopes of destroying the conservative order set down at the Congress of Vienna. Garibaldi and Mazzini helped pave the way for future upheavals, but during the 1830s and up to 1848, politics in the Italian principalities remained firmly in the hands of conservatives and clericals.

German Nationalism: Challenging Metternich and Conservatism Like supporters of Mazzini and Garibaldi in Italy, young educated Germans opposed

Giuseppe Mazzini (1805–1872) Italian political thinker and revolutionary who advocated bringing together all Italians under a single republican government.

Risorgimento (from Italian, "to rise again") Era of political and cultural nationalism in early nineteenth-century Italy calling for Italian unification and political liberalization.

Giuseppe Garibaldi (1807–1882) Italian political leader who worked to translate Mazzini's nationalist ideas of Italian unification into reality.

the existing political order, calling for a liberal united Germany. German universities were hotbeds of nationalist thought and agitation. There young men (no women would enter German universities until the twentieth century) gathered together in fraternities to discuss politics over beer. After the patriotic fervor of the Napoleonic Wars—in German known as the Wars of Liberation (from Napoleonic rule)—they found it difficult to accept the conservative and antinationalist Congress System.

Liberal nationalists called the first all-German gathering in October 1817 at the Wartburg, the castle where Luther had translated the New Testament into German. At this **Wartburg Festival** they celebrated German history, life, and culture—Luther's challenge to the pope in 1517, the German victory over Napoleon at Leipzig in 1814, and the beauty of the German language. Speeches called on Germans to transcend the political boundaries that divided them. But transforming speeches into political reality proved difficult.

When the somewhat addled young patriot Karl Sand assassinated the reactionary poet August von Kotzebue in 1819, the German authorities moved to restrict the activities of the nationalists. The Carlsbad Decrees of 1819 put severe restrictions on freedom of expression in the press and especially in the universities, which were known for their strong support of nationalist and liberal ideals.

Yet they would not be suppressed. In 1832, at the ruins of a medieval castle in southwest Germany, some twenty to thirty thousand young people gathered and marched, carrying the black-red-gold national banner. At the Hambach Festival, named after the castle where they gathered, German patriotic youth called for national liberation: both from foreign influences—from French culture—but even more importantly from the conservative policies of Metternich. As in Italy, these young radicals organized themselves into a group loosely called Young Germany. And as in the Italian case, Metternich worried over the ideas and appeal of these liberal nationalist groups and set his police to gather information about their subversive actions. It was in this repressive atmosphere that the Grimm brothers, who shared many of the ideals of Young Germany, were harassed and ultimately dismissed from their jobs.

National Liberation Movements in the Balkans

The Ottoman sultan officially still ruled over most of the **Balkan Peninsula**, from the Adriatic Sea to the borders of Austria-Hungary, but local elites held most of the power. These elites were more often Greek than Turkish in culture, though, in some areas, Slavic-speaking Muslims held local control. By the 1790s, many were unhappy with Ottoman rule, with its high taxes, general lawlessness, and the arbitrary behavior of troops and local officials.

Complicating the disorder was competition among the extremely diverse ethnic and religious groups who made their home in the Balkans. Greeks, Romanians, "Turks" (as all Muslims tended to be called), Germans, Hungarians, and many groups of Slavic peoples lived in close proximity. They were Roman Catholic, Orthodox Christian, Muslim, and Jewish, with religion playing a central role in national identity. For example, Croats and Serbs spoke the same language: it was their religion (Catholic or Orthodox, respectively) that divided them. The Muslims of the Balkan Peninsula—who numbered in the hundreds of thousands—were often mistrusted by the nationalists and in many cases fled as nationalists gained power. The small numbers of Jews in the Balkans were significant in the region's commerce and trade. Most Balkan Jews traced their roots to the expulsion of Jews from Spain in 1492 and continued to speak Ladino, a version of Spanish written in Hebrew letters.

Nationalism not only presented a huge challenge for the Ottoman overlords; it also threatened to destabilize traditional life entirely. As throughout eastern Europe, nationalists formed a quite small group of educated, relatively privileged individuals who thought it their duty to agitate for rights on behalf of the entire Serbian, Romanian, or Greek nations. These first nationalists were fervently concerned with developing their own culture, and especially their language.

In the nineteenth century, the languages spoken in the Balkan Peninsula were mainly peasant tongues, lacking many words and expressions necessary to express abstract concepts and to carry out modern scientific research. More crucial still, these languages were seldom written and were not standardized. Each tongue had many local dialects, and speakers of different dialects often had great difficulty understanding one another. Hence the early Balkan nationalists were obliged to push their program on at least two fronts: the cultural (to develop a modern standardized written language and literature) and the political (to gain their own state or autonomy).

Nationalists' programs also had a social component. Elites often differed in ethnicity and religion from the peasant majority. In many regions, such as the future Yugoslavia and Bulgaria, Christian peasants were ruled by Muslim landlords and officials. Thus nationalists combined demands for political independence, cultural rights, and social development of the impoverished masses.

Wartburg Festival Patriotic meeting at Wartburg castle in central Germany in 1817 promoting German national and liberal ideals.

Balkan Peninsula Region between the Black and Adriatic Seas where present-day Bulgaria, Serbia, and Greece are located.

Serbia Nationalist aspirations first came to a head in the Pashalik ("district") of Belgrade, where discontent with Ottoman rule among Serbs ran high. Decades of struggle against Ottoman rule dominated by two Serbian families, the Karadjordević and Obrenović, culminated in the latter family gaining in 1815 the title of supreme prince of Serbia from the sultan. Although Serbia officially remained under Ottoman rule, for most practical purposes, local affairs in the Pashalik of Belgrade were now in the hands of Serbs. Official independence came in 1833, along with an expansion of the borders of Serbia and the establishment of the Obrenović dynasty on the Serbian throne. For the next century, descendants of the two original Serbian rebels, Karadjordje and Miloš Obrenović, would occupy the Serbian (and later Yugoslav) thrones.

Romania To the east of Belgrade, in the Danubian provinces of Walachia and Moldavia (now in Romania), an impoverished peasantry was ruled by a corrupt Greek upper class. The Greek middle class joined Romanian landlords and peasants in an 1821 revolt that was based on a general call for justice and an end to oppression—and not on specific Greek or Romania ethnic demands. The rebels hoped for Russian assistance, but Tsar Nicholas I remained cool to their cause, thus enabling the Ottoman army to crush the rebellion. Although the revolt did not bring independence to the provinces, it did strengthen the position of local (Romanian) nobles, who replaced Greeks in high church and administrative offices. Full autonomy was attained in 1829, and in February 1862 the modern state of Romania was created, officially still under Ottoman control but in practical terms an independent constitutional monarchy. The choice of the name Romania aimed to underscore the new state's connection to classical civilization and the European mainstream.

Greece Nationalist feelings also strengthened in Greek provinces of the Ottoman Empire. Greek nationalists took pride in the heritage of classical Greece, though the language of Plato and Aristotle had splintered into a bewildering array of mutually incomprehensible dialects, their speakers divided by mountainous terrain. The question of what form of Greek to adopt as the official, standard tongue continued to plague Greeks long after political independence had been won. Further complicating matters was the fact that Greek merchants lived all around the Black Sea, including in territory ruled by the Russian tsar.

The Greek War of Independence broke out in April 1821. Greek independence fighters attacked both Ottoman authorities and local Muslims. Christian atrocities were matched by Ottoman reprisals, including the slaughter of thousands of Greeks on the island of Chios and the hanging of the Greek Orthodox patriarch. Reports in the European press of Ottoman atrocities (Christian atrocities against Muslims were generally ignored) pushed the Concert of Europe to intervene in support of the Greeks.

England's Romantic poet Lord Byron and other idealists set off for Greece to fight for Greek independence, often—like Byron—sacrificing their lives. The rebellion ended with a treaty signed in London that created an autonomous (but not independent) Greek state. The new state proved unworkable, and in 1830—in another Concert of Europe action—France and Russia established Greek independence. Greece, like Belgium, was to be a constitutional monarchy, and Prince Otto of Bavaria became its first king. The new Greek state was small, impoverished, and lacked a common language, administration, or educational system. The Greek nationalists had their state; they now had to create the Greek nation.

Autocracy in Russia

While liberal and nationalist ideologies blossomed in much of Europe, Russia's rulers did what they could to insulate their empire from such ideas. After Napoleon's invasion of Russia, Tsar Alexander I became mystical and suspicious of change. Meanwhile, Russian society—at least at the educated upper levels—did not stagnate. Young Russian officers who had participated in the campaign against Napoleon returned home from Paris with new liberal ideas. They desired a greater voice in the affairs of their native land. Some even spoke of constitutions and legislatures, though censorship prevented open discussion of such revolutionary ideas.

The Decembrist Revolt When Alexander I died in 1825, the conspirators decided it was time to act, especially as the question of who should replace Alexander on the throne was confusing. He had left no male heirs, and by law his eldest brother, Constantine, should have succeeded him. But Constantine had given up his right to be tsar when he married a nonroyal woman, though his renunciation of the throne had never been made public. Most Russians were unaware that the younger brother Nicholas was in line to be tsar.

In this confused situation, conspirators aimed to seize power in the name of Constantine and demand a constitution for Russia. But Nicholas was well informed of their plans. These liberal revolutionaries, who have gone down in history as the **Decembrists**, called on the army not to swear allegiance to Nicholas. The Decembrist-led rebels were surrounded by troops loyal to Nicholas on the banks of the Neva River in St. Petersburg. After several hours of fruitless negotiations, Nicholas gave the order to open fire, and the revolt disintegrated on the spot.

Decembrists Supporters of liberal reforms in Russia whose plot was crushed by Nicholas I in 1825.

Réunion des Musées Nationaux/Art Resource, NY

Eugene Delacroix's 1824 painting *The Massacre of Chios* romantically depicts a terrible episode of the Greek War of Independence during which Ottoman soldiers massacred thousands of Greeks. How does this image stir up feelings of solidarity and empathy with the Greeks (and anger at the Turks)? Delacroix's painting style is often described as "romantic"—do you think that is a reasonable description? Why or why not?

The conspirators were soon arrested, tried, and exiled to Siberia or executed. The Decembrists quickly entered into Russian liberal and radical mythology as the "first Russian revolutionaries," but the practical effect of their revolt was negative. Nicholas had always been suspicious of liberal movements, and indeed of any abstract political ideologies, and now his worst fears were confirmed. His rule would be marked by an unwillingness to compromise with these new ideologies. Nicholas insisted that the Russian empire would remain an **autocracy** and that he alone would decide the country's political future.

Russia's Polish Question Nowhere was the contrast between liberal nationalism and the forces of conservatism so stark as in Russian Poland. It was perhaps inevitable that the Russian autocracy would clash with the leaders of the autonomous Congress Poland also ruled by Nicholas I, where many Poles believed that the new tsar was violating their constitutional rights. A rebellion against Russian rule broke out in Warsaw in November 1830, but the rebels, counting on French help for their independence struggle, miscalculated badly. The French were unwilling to provide more than verbal support, and, after initial Polish successes, the Russian army crushed the rebellion. Most Polish peasants refused to support the rebels, seeing in them not national kin but hated landlords. Nicholas abolished the Polish legislature and army and incorporated the Polish provinces more closely into the Russian empire. But the Polish national spirit remained unvanquished, celebrated in the poetry of Mickiewicz and the music of Chopin. Polish patriots continued to sing the now forbidden Polish national anthem, dating from the Napoleonic period, in secret: "Poland is not yet lost / As long as we are alive."

Tsar Nicholas I: The Apogee of Autocracy The Polish uprising confirmed Nicholas's hatred for political abstractions and strengthened his determination to base his rule on tradition and the army. He was never so happy as when inspecting his troops, and

autocracy Form of government headed by a ruler whose power is not limited by constitutional or other political restraints, as in Russia before 1917.

woe to any soldier found with a button unshined or a medal out of place. At one such review, it was said, the tsar was considerably vexed because while the soldiers were lined up in exact rows, their continued breathing upset perfect symmetry. Nicholas wanted the entire country to be just as orderly as his army on the parade grounds.

To prevent the spread of liberal or revolutionary ideas (Nicholas made little distinction between the two), the tsar created a secret police force—the Third Section of the Tsar's Chancellery. Censorship was tightened, reaching truly paranoid levels in the late 1840s, when the phrase "free air" in a cookbook was struck as possibly subversive and censors examined musical scores for signs of secret revolutionary codes.

Yet Russian society under Nicholas could not be shielded from change and foreign influence. It was during Nicholas's reign that there occurred what one historian has called a "parting of ways" between Russian educated society and the Russian government. The Russian **intelligentsia** emerged, a social group whose identity derived not from birth (unlike the nobility or peasantry) but from education and a desire to work for the good of Russia and the Russian people. Such aspirations brought these reformers into direct conflict with the inefficient but all-powerful Russian state—and Nicholas's secret police.

After the midcentury, the Russian intelligentsia would split into liberals who wished to reform Russia and revolutionaries who saw the present system as completely rotten and looked forward to its complete destruction. Nicholas was successful in driving dissent underground during his reign. In the long run, however, his refusal to accommodate new ideas or to share power even on a limited level alienated most educated Russians from their rulers and helped pave the way for a far more destructive revolution.

Checking In

By yourself or with a partner, explain the significance of each of the following selected key terms:

Charles X	Wartburg Festival
Louis Philippe	Decembrists
Risorgimento	autocracy
Giuseppe Garibaldi	intelligentsia

Reform in Great Britain

◆ **Why did the British establishment agree to political reform?**

◆ **What specific liberal reforms allowed Britain to avoid revolutionary outbreaks?**

While Russia staunchly opposed any change in the first half of the nineteenth century, the course of political reform in Great Britain presents a strong contrast. The British middle classes—stronger here in numbers and wealth than anywhere else in Europe—gained significant political rights. These wealthy merchants and industrialists demanded and received a voice in British politics. In triumphs for political and economic liberalism, the parliamentary system was reformed, suffrage considerably broadened, and restrictions on religious minorities reduced.

Even in Britain, many groups remained outside the political system. Reform barely touched the lives of Britain's peasants and factory workers, an impoverished class that expanded rapidly as Britain industrialized. Living and laboring in dangerous conditions, workers sought to organize to improve their lives, but their efforts were opposed by a government committed to a free-market economy. Still, in Great Britain, the existing order was able to bend and modify itself to accommodate new ideologies and social classes, and in the second half of the century most worker demands would be realized. By agreeing to timely reforms, Great Britain avoided the social and political turmoil that occurred in other parts of Europe.

Conservative Domination and Reform

At the beginning of the nineteenth century, political participation in Great Britain was limited to an extremely small group of men (women would continue to be shut out for another century). Both political parties—the conservative **Tories** and the more liberal **Whigs**—were dominated by the aristocracy, but the Whigs were more sympathetic to opening the political system to wealthy middle-class men. King George III was still on the throne, though his off-and-on insanity meant that his son, crowned **George IV** in 1820, often carried out his father's duties. Ruling in his own right, George IV discredited the Crown (and thereby played into the hands of political reformers) by his immoral behavior, including his notorious attempt to divorce his estranged wife, Caroline, and his unwillingness to allow her to be crowned queen.

The first decade after 1815 was dominated by the Tories, who set a very conservative course by passing

intelligentsia Social class of educated, progressive individuals wanting liberal reforms in Russia; later also applied to Russian revolutionaries.

Tories Conservatives, one of the two ruling parties in nineteenth-century Britain.

Whigs Liberals, the Tories' rivals in the British Parliament.

George IV (r. 1820–1830) King of Great Britain and Ireland, hated for his sexual immorality; most notorious for his failed attempt to divorce his wife, Caroline, in 1820.

the **Corn Laws**. These laws, which for all practical purposes prevented the import of cheap grain ("corn") into Great Britain, were designed to reduce British dependence on foreign foodstuffs, but they had a disastrous effect on the poor. By keeping the price of grain—and thus bread—high, they impoverished working people, who had to spend most of their tiny wages on food. In Manchester, which tripled in size between 1801 and 1831 (to a population of 238,000) as peasants from the countryside took jobs in new textile factories, a series of public meetings culminated in 1819 with the notorious **Peterloo massacre**. A cavalry charge dispersing the more than sixty thousand people gathered to petition Parliament for political representation and repeal of the Corn Laws ended with eleven dead and hundreds injured. The government's answer to the public uproar after Peterloo was to restrict civil liberties and free speech. In 1824, however, Parliament repealed the Combination Acts, which had forbidden workers from forming unions. Strikes were still illegal, but the important right of labor to organize had been won.

Broadening Politics: Including Catholics, Dissenters, and Jews The Tory administration also took an important step toward fulfilling the liberal principle that religion should not bar an individual from full participation in political and social life. In 1829, with the **Catholic Emancipation Act**, Catholics and dissenters (non-Anglican Christians) gained the right to participate in Parliament and to occupy all public offices in the realm, with the exception of lord chancellor of England and lord lieutenant of Ireland. The practical effect of this measure was not immediately great—very few Catholics in England and Ireland were wealthy enough to qualify for the vote—but the measure was significant as a further step toward religious toleration in Britain.

English Jews also gained rights in this period. The first bill for Jewish emancipation (that is, completely equal rights with Christians) passed the House of Commons in 1833 but was defeated in the House of Lords. However, individual Jews were knighted (Moses Montefiore, in 1837), admitted to the bar, and elevated into the hereditary nobility (Isaac Goldsmid, in 1841). The process of Jewish emancipation was completed in 1858 when Lionel de Rothschild was—after more than a decade of debate—allowed to take the oath on a Hebrew Bible and take his seat in the House of Commons.

The Reform Bill of 1832 and the Abolition Act of 1833

King George IV died in 1830 and was succeeded by his son William IV. In the parliamentary elections that, by tradition, accompanied the ascension of a new king, the position of the more liberal Whigs and their middle-class supporters was strengthened by the example of France, where the conservative Bourbon dynasty had been toppled, replaced by a new political order under the "bourgeois king" Louis Philippe. Britain's captains of industry likewise wanted to make their importance felt, arguing for a government that would support the interests of manufacturing and trade rather than representing only landowners and landowning interests.

To accommodate the wealthy manufacturers, parliamentary districts, unchanged since the seventeenth century, had to be modernized. Since that time, the huge shifts in population that accompanied industrialization had created entire districts controlled by a few large landowners (**pocket boroughs**) and depopulated districts where only a few dozen people lived (**rotten boroughs**), while large industrial cities like Manchester and Birmingham had no representatives in Parliament at all.

Once in power, the Whigs pushed the **Reform Bill of 1832** through Parliament. Though suffrage was still tied to a property qualification, the new law increased the number of voters by 50 percent and significantly redistributed parliamentary representation to benefit the heavily populated new industrial cities. In short, the Reform Bill of 1832 was a triumph for English liberalism, the first step in a gradual expansion of the political system set in motion by an enlightened class of relatively privileged individuals. Men espousing the liberal ideals of constitutional rule, free trade, and a gradually expanding electorate now increasingly took seats in Parliament. Still, only one in five Englishmen could vote. Reform bills in 1867 and 1884 further extended the franchise, but not until the twentieth century was universal suffrage—for all men and women—achieved.

Corn Laws Series of laws passed in 1815 that prevented the import of grain ("corn") until prices reached a certain (high) level; kept grain and bread prices high; repealed in 1846.

Peterloo massacre Repression of workers' gathering at St. Peter's Fields outside Manchester in 1819, leaving eleven killed and hundreds injured.

Catholic Emancipation Act Act of 1829 allowing Catholics to be elected to Parliament and to serve in most public offices in Great Britain.

pocket boroughs and **rotten boroughs** Electoral districts in Britain that were controlled by a single landowner or where few people lived, respectively, abolished by the 1832 Reform Bill.

Reform Bill of 1832 British reform increasing suffrage and redistributing electoral districts to reflect actual population, thereby giving more representation to industrial cities.

A Liberal Triumph: Abolition of Slavery Liberals had long championed the cause of abolishing slavery. British law did not recognize slavery within England, Scotland, Ireland, and Wales, and in 1807 Parliament had forbidden British vessels and captains from engaging in the slave trade. But in demanding the complete abolition of slavery, liberals found themselves in a perplexing ideological position. The demand for human liberty was, of course, central to liberalism. But so was the protection of private property, and slaves were, after all, a form of property. In 1833, this contradiction was overcome when Parliament passed the Slavery Abolition Act, which abolished slavery throughout the British Empire. At the same time, the enormous amount of 20 million was appropriated by Parliament to pay slave owners for their freed "property." In this way, British liberals succeeded in extending basic human liberty to slaves while compensating their former owners.

The Repeal of the Corn Laws

The expanded Parliament now included middle-class manufacturers who opposed the Corn Laws both out of general commitment to free trade and because the higher cost of bread put pressure on the wages they had to pay workers. Two outspoken opponents to the Corn Laws elected to Parliament in the 1840s were John Bright, son of a cotton manufacturer in Lancashire, and **Richard Cobden**, a calico printer from Manchester. Both proponents of laissez-faire economics, they had founded the Anti–Corn Law League in 1838, an effective and well-financed pressure group that rapidly came to exert influence even on the Tory prime minister, Sir Robert Peel. The league was also extremely successful in appealing to the working class with slogans such as "Give Us This Day Our Daily Bread," taken from scripture. The actual repeal of the Corn Laws came, however, as a direct result of one of the most tragic events of the nineteenth century—the **Irish potato famine**.

The Irish Potato Famine Ireland was, at the time, an impoverished and backward colony of England. The landed gentry was almost entirely Protestant, and often absentee, while the Catholic peasantry eked out a miserable existence on shrinking plots of land, living entirely on potatoes, a New World vegetable adopted by Irish peasants because it produced more calories per planted acre than any other crop. By 1840, it was clear that the land and people were stretched to their utmost limits. Then fungus struck the Irish potato crop, wiping out sustenance for millions. The Protestant landowners and English Parliament

The Irish Potato Famine not only devastated the population of Ireland but also called into question British rule there. Criticism of British policy in Ireland appeared throughout the European and North American press. How does this cartoon make the viewer sympathize with the Irish and encourage hostility toward the English ("John Bull")? How are the Irish depicted?

seemed indifferent to the famine, and from 1845 to the end of the decade, millions in Ireland either starved or left their homes for England or the United States. Around one-third of the Irish population perished or emigrated. To this day, the population of Ireland remains lower than it was two hundred years ago—a fact unparalleled in European demographic history.

In the public mind, the Corn Laws had been a decisive factor in causing the famine by preventing grain imports from abroad. The tragedy thus dealt the Corn Laws a decisive blow, and they were abolished in 1846. This triumph for free trade could not, unfortunately, help the victims of the famine. While grain prices did drop after the abolition of the Corn Laws, not Irish peasants but factory

Richard Cobden (1804–1865) English liberal who in 1838 formed the Anti–Corn Law League to fight for free trade in grain.

Irish potato famine Demographic catastrophe in the mid- to late 1840s caused by a fungus infection, or blight, of the Irish peasantry's staple food, the potato.

workers in Britain were able to take advantage of cheaper bread.

From 1846 until the First World War, free trade and liberalism dominated British economic policy. Presided over by **Queen Victoria**, the Victorian Age represented the pinnacle of British prosperity and prestige. As the first fully industrialized country, Great Britain had a significant economic advantage, while other countries—such as the United States, Germany, and Russia—erected trade barriers to protect their own industries from a flood of cheap British imports. Not until the end of the nineteenth century did the United States and Germany catch up with Britain's industrial head start. The Victorian Age was also the pinnacle of British imperialism. With colonies and dominions in Asia, Africa, and North America, the British were proud to claim that "the sun never sets on the British Empire."

The Chartist Movement and the Factory Acts

Yet not all of Victoria's subjects were content. The middle classes could point to solid gains in political and economic aspects of their lives, but most workers continued in dangerous jobs for little pay. Their discontents were translated into political action by **Chartism**, a workingmen's reform movement that agitated for increased political rights. The movement took its name from the People's Charter, a document published in 1838 that announced six demands: annual Parliaments, universal male suffrage, voting by secret ballot, the elimination of property requirements for members of Parliament, salaries for members of Parliament, and equal electoral districts.

Using modern techniques of political agitation such as mass meetings, pamphlets, and a popular newspaper, the *Northern Star*, the Chartists took their case to Parliament in the form of a petition with several hundred thousand signatures. Parliament rejected the petition overwhelmingly, and when some of the more radical Chartists made statements about armed resistance, the movement's leadership was arrested and jailed. Thus ended the first Chartist movement. Two more petitions were brought to Parliament—and rejected—in the 1840s; afterward, the movement fell apart.

The Factory Acts Though Chartists appeared to have failed in their efforts to improve the political situation of workers, by the early twentieth century five of their six demands had been met. Perhaps even more important for workers' everyday lives, the government continued to intervene—despite laissez-faire liberalism—to improve conditions in mines and factories, which were revealed in a series of government investigations and reports to be appalling.

A series of **Factory Acts** passed in the first decades of the nineteenth century had intended to restrict child labor but lacked enforcement. In 1833, a new Factory Act ruled that children under nine years of age were not to be employed in textile works and set maximum work hours for workers under eighteen. Most important, these laws were to be enforced by a newly created factory inspectorate. An 1842 law prohibited women from underground work in the mines. Most pathbreaking of all, an 1847 act forbade women and children from working more than ten hours a day. Government's responsibility for regulating the conditions of labor was now firmly established, as the interests of public order and safety triumphed over the interests of the manufacturers. Thus, in England parliamentary rule proved capable of reform and of responding to the needs of the people in time to prevent either the middle-class revolt that reformed France or the working-class revolution that in the next century would convulse Russia.

Queen Victoria (r. 1837–1901) English queen whose reign was a period of British prominence in world politics, the world economy, science, trade, and culture.

Chartism Workers' political movement in Britain, 1838–1848, that demanded a People's Charter guaranteeing universal male suffrage and other reforms.

Factory Acts British laws of 1833, 1842, and 1847 that limited the number of hours manufacturers could require children and women to work.

✔ Checking In

By yourself or with a partner, explain the significance of each of the following selected key terms:

Corn Laws	Irish potato famine
Peterloo massacre	Queen Victoria
Reform Bill of 1832	Chartism
Richard Cobden	Factory Acts

CHAPTER
Review

Summary

◆ The period 1814–1847 lacked major upheavals or revolution. We can characterize it as a "breathing space" or rest between the French Revolution/Napoleonic Era and the 1848 Revolution.

◆ The major political ideologies of conservatism, liberalism, and nationalism all derived from the French Revolution and were developed further in this period.

◆ Liberalism opposed rule by monarchs and nobles, advocating instead constitutional rule, parliamentary democracy, and the rule of law.

◆ Nationalism stressed the need for each nation to have its own state, an inherently democratic ideal. Before 1848, liberalism and nationalism went hand in hand.

◆ In this period, conservatives like Austria's Metternich and Russia's Tsar Nicholas I continued to hold most political power. In Great Britain, however, gradual reforms pushed by middle-class liberals spread parliamentary representation to large segments of the population.

Chronology

1814–1815	Congress of Vienna restores prerevolutionary rulers
1815	Napoleon is defeated at Waterloo; British Parliament passes Corn Laws
1817	Wartburg Festival
1818	Mary Wollstonecraft Shelley publishes *Frankenstein*
1819	Peterloo massacre in Manchester kills eleven, wounds hundreds
1821	Greek War of Independence begins
1823	United States issues Monroe Doctrine
1825	Nicholas I becomes tsar
1828	Noah Webster publishes his *American Dictionary of the English Language*
1829	Catholic Emancipation Act furthers religious tolerance in Britain
1830	Greece achieves independence; Revolutions break out in Paris and Brussels
1832	Reform Bill in Britain expands suffrage; Giuseppe Mazzini forms Young Italy
1833	Slavery Abolition Act initiates emancipation of slaves in British Empire; Serbia wins independence
1837	Victoria becomes queen of England
1838	Grimm brothers begin work on their *German Dictionary*
1838	Richard Cobden forms Anti–Corn Law League in Manchester
1845–1849	Potato famine sweeps Ireland
1846	Corn Laws are abolished
1847	Factory Act in Britain reduces working hours for women and children
1848	Revolutions topple governments from Paris to Budapest

© Cengage Learning

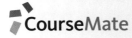

CourseMate Visit the CourseMate website at **www.cengagebrain.com** for additional study tools and review materials for this chapter.

Test Yourself

To gauge your mastery of the material in this chapter, answer the questions below. More than one answer may be correct.

The Old Order and New Challenges

1. The Congress of Vienna was important because it:
   a. Put a definitive end to the period of the French Revolution and Napoleonic Wars.
   b. Redrew the map of Europe.
   c. Attempted to establish a stable, conservative political order in Europe.
   d. Created a political order that allowed Europe to avoid major wars for almost a century.
   e. All of the above.

2. Which of the following countries did *not* send a representative to the Congress of Vienna?
   a. Prussia
   b. France
   c. Russian empire
   d. Germany
   e. Great Britain

3. Which individual opposed and despised the Romantic movement?
   a. Prince Clemens von Metternich
   b. William Wordsworth
   c. Caspar David Friedrich
   d. Friedrich Schlegel
   e. Alexander Pushkin

4. The Congress System:
   a. Aimed to spread democracy throughout Europe.
   b. Was a conservative political system created at the Congress of Vienna.
   c. Developed out of Great Britain's desire for a Holy Alliance of European powers.
   d. Was named after the Congress Kingdom of Poland.
   e. Embraced nationalism and liberal ideas.

5. Romanticism as a literary and artistic movement rejected:
   a. Emotion
   b. Individuality
   c. Exotic locations and landscapes
   d. Nature
   e. Calculating rationality

Now that you have reviewed and tested yourself on this part of the chapter, take time to pull together all the important information by answering the following questions:

◆ In what ways did the Congress of Vienna stabilize European politics after the Napoleonic period?

◆ How did the worldview of Romanticism differ from that of the Enlightenment?

The Beginnings of Modern Ideology

6. Conservatism in the first half of the nineteenth century:
   a. Opposed all forms of political and social change.
   b. Embraced the ideals of the French Revolution.
   c. Was represented by such writers as Edmund Burke and Joseph de Maistre.
   d. Advocated a free market and universal human rights.
   e. Was fundamentally optimistic in its vision of human nature and politics.

7. Which of the following are characteristics of liberalism in the period to 1848?

   a. Accepted monarchism as the best form of government.
   b. Embraced the Enlightenment and, with some reservations, the French Revolution.
   c. Advocated individual rights, constitutions, and free trade.
   d. Believed government should be actively involved in regulating the economy.
   e. Is represented by the writings of James Mill and his son John Stuart Mill.

8. Which of the following statements is true about nationalism in the period to about 1850?

   a. Thought that "nation" and "state" should be congruent (that is, that all Italians should live in Italy, all Germans in Germany, and so forth).
   b. Was generally allied with conservatives such as Metternich.
   c. Considered socioeconomic class more important than ethnic-religious identity.
   d. Threatened, as least potentially, the political stability of states like the Habsburg, Ottoman, and Russian Empires.
   e. Was fundamentally democratic.

9. Which of the following statements does not describe Jeremy Bentham?

   a. Utilitarian philosopher generally associated with liberalism.
   b. English writer, author of *Introduction to the Principles of Morals and Legislation.*
   c. Optimistic in his outlook on human nature.
   d. Considered enlightened self-interest a positive characteristic.
   e. Is mainly remembered as a conservative philosopher.

10. Liberalism and nationalism before 1848 tended to go hand-in-hand because:

   a. Writers like Mill and Smith were strong nationalists.
   b. Both nationalists and liberals tended to be wealthy and educated members of the nobility.
   c. Both ideologies were fundamentally democratic in this period and opposed Metternich's conservative order.
   d. Nationalists were attracted to John Stuart Mill's feminism.
   e. Liberals wanted to use nationalism to oppress ethnic minorities in their empires.

Now that you have reviewed and tested yourself on this part of the chapter, take time to pull together all the important information by answering the following questions:

◆ What did Edmund Burke, Joseph de Maistre, and the Russian Slavophiles have in common? How did they differ?

◆ What similarities in political outlook were shared by liberalism and nationalism in this period?

Political Pressures on the Continent

11. "Restoration" in post-Napoleonic France refers to:

   a. Going back to absolutism, as before 1789.
   b. The European powers' acceptance of Napoleon as a limited monarch in France.
   c. Recreating in France the political system of the 1790s.
   d. Setting up a conservative political order in France, with a king but also a parliament.
   e. Allowing only the rich to have any voice in French politics after 1815.

12. From the 1820s to the 1840s nationalism played an important and disruptive role in which countries?

   a. France
   b. Belgium
   c. Germany
   d. Italy
   e. Russia

13. From the 1820s to the 1840s the Balkan peninsula was:

   a. Ruled by Russia.
   b. Made up of a number of highly diverse religious and ethnic-linguistic groups.
   c. For the most part, under Ottoman rule.
   d. A highly developed, industrial region.
   e. The scene of the Greek War of Independence.

14. The Serbs and Greeks had in common that:

   a. Both were under Ottoman rule in 1800.
   b. Both were mainly Eastern Orthodox Christians.
   c. Both fought the Habsburg empire to gain independence.
   d. Both spoke a language closely related to Russian.
   e. Both gained independence in the 1820s and 1830s.

15. Among the most important events of Tsar Nicholas I's reign was:

   a. A new, more open regime after the death of Tsar Alexander I.
   b. The Polish Insurrection of 1830–1831.
   c. The Decembrist uprising.
   d. The birth of the intelligentsia.
   e. The abolition of censorship.

Now that you have reviewed and tested yourself on this part of the chapter, take time to pull together all the important information by answering the following questions:

◆ Where was nationalism most important in this period? Where least? Why?

◆ Compare this period in France and Russia. What were some of the major differences between these two states?

Reform in Great Britain

16. The Corn Laws were:

   a. A set of regulations to keep American maize out of Britain.
   b. Supported by landowners because they kept grain prices high.
   c. Bitterly opposed by working-class people and manufacturers.
   d. In part responsible for the tragedy of the Irish potato famine.
   e. Were abolished in 1846, an important triumph for the principle of free trade.

17. Which group enjoyed full political rights in Britain before 1848?

   a. Working-class men
   b. Jews
   c. Catholics
   d. The Irish
   e. None of the above

18. Although most inhabitants of the British Isles lacked the right to vote before 1848, Great Britain did make progress in:

   a. Broadening the franchise with the Reform Act of 1832.
   b. Recognizing the evil of slavery by outlawing it in 1833.
   c. Allowing non-Anglican Britons to participate more broadly in politics.
   d. Abolishing "rotten" and "pocket boroughs," thereby making parliament more representative of the actual population.
   e. Giving voting rights to women, but only to those of the wealthiest classes.

19. Among the Chartists' demands were:
    a. Universal suffrage.
    b. Vote by a secret ballot.
    c. Unemployment insurance.
    d. Salaries for members of Parliament.
    e. No property requirement in order to run for election to Parliament.

20. Queen Victoria's reign (1837–1901) can be characterized as:
    a. A period of prosperity and great prestige for the British people.
    b. An epoch of gradual political reform.
    c. The high age of British imperialism.
    d. A period of violent protests against factory owners and the government.
    e. Years in which Britain's relative industrial advantage over the rest of the world steadily grew.

Now that you have reviewed and tested yourself on this part of the chapter, take time to pull together all the important information by answering the following questions:

◆ Why could both conservatives and liberals point to the British system as a political model? What appealed to each?

◆ How did the Repeal of the Corn Laws and the Factory Acts reflect Britain's relatively advanced level of industrialization?

CHAPTER 21

Industrialization and Society, 1800–1850

Chapter Outline

1800	1805	1810	1815	1820	1825

1810s
Luddite revolts protest industrialization in England

1815
Napoleon is finally defeated at Waterloo

1820s
Industrialization begins in Belgium and northern France

1824
British Combination Acts are repealed

The "Rocket," designed by George Stephenson, was one of the first railroad steam engines. When it went into service on the Liverpool and Manchester Railway in 1830, it was considered a technical marvel. The Rocket's design would influence railway locomotives for many decades. With the launch of the Rocket and the railroad between two of England's most important industrial cities, Liverpool and Manchester, the age of rail was born. (© Science & Society Picture Library)

After reading this chapter, you should be able to answer the following questions:

Why did industrialization first occur in Great Britain?

What were the changes that industrialization caused in economics, everyday life, the environment, society, and politics?

What is the definition of the term "class?" Which groups in society belonged to the working and middle classes?

What were the most important socialist critiques of capitalism and industrialization?

INDUSTRIALIZATION TRANSFORMED EUROPEAN society and everyday life in the course of the nineteenth century. Starting first in Great Britain, industrialization soon took the continent by storm, affecting all segments of society, transforming every aspect of life. Skilled artisans and craftsmen found their jobs threatened by mass production in factories, where dozens and even hundreds of workers labored side by side, doing repetitive and monotonous tasks in dangerous conditions. At the same time, the economic power of the middle classes, from factory owners to professional people, grew rapidly, increasing their political power.

The Industrial Revolution transformed Europe on various levels. On a physical level, the coal mines, coal-burning factories, and railroad tracks and trestles altered the European landscape. Soot and pollution literally blanketed industrial cities and their outskirts. Other effects were more subtle. Middle-class people came to think of themselves as "self-made"—that is, they perceived their identity as derived from their work, accomplishments, or training. The thousands of men and

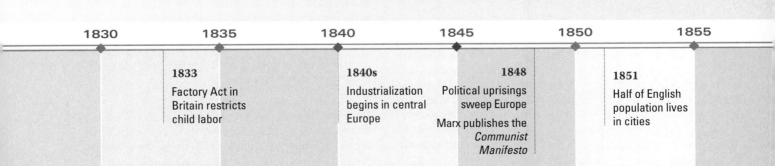

1830	1835	1840	1845	1850	1855

1833
Factory Act in Britain restricts child labor

1840s
Industrialization begins in central Europe

1848
Political uprisings sweep Europe

Marx publishes the *Communist Manifesto*

1851
Half of English population lives in cities

women congregated in factories also began to perceive themselves differently: as members of a new and potentially powerful working class. In both cases, this class consciousness meant that identity was derived not from birth but primarily from one's position within the economy.

Industrialization revolutionized production, efficiently mass-producing huge numbers of items far more cheaply than could be done by hand. But the wealth produced by industrialization was uneven, and the gap between wealthy industrialists and their workers grew. Reformers fought against terrible working conditions, poverty, and exploitation of the workers by the capitalist system. Other reformers thought that justice for workers could be attained by government intervention, cooperation, and reforms. The Factory Acts in Britain in the 1830s seemed to remedy the worst conditions, and eventually workers' pay also rose. But the socialist Karl Marx argued forcefully that only revolution would end exploitation of the working class and create a truly just and humane society.

In many ways the world we know—running by the clock, fast paced, full of mass-produced consumer goods, accepting constant change as normal—is a direct outcome of the Industrial Revolution, which began in the late eighteenth century and continued throughout the nineteenth century. Industrialization rearranged economies, altered the rhythm of daily life, and changed attitudes, first in Europe and North America, then around the world.

The Spread of Industrialization

- ◆ **How did the process of industrialization differ in Britain and in continental Europe?**
- ◆ **How did industrialization create class identities?**

In Britain, the Industrial Revolution took place over several decades in the late eighteenth century and was fueled mainly by technological innovation and private capital. In other parts of Europe, industrialization came later but often developed even more quickly, pushed along by government investment and subsidies. Technology continued to develop rapidly, and new means of transportation—especially the railroad and steamships—seemed to shrink distance and time, encouraging intercontinental trade and migration.

The initial effects of industrialization were usually horrible—pollution, crowded and unsanitary cities, and the disruption of family life. Peasants had lived by the natural rhythms of the seasons, sunrise, and sunset, but the industrial world was regulated by the clock. By the mid-nineteenth century, some benefits of industrialization were evident—an increase in affordable consumer goods, the growth of middle-class prosperity, and, in some cases, even higher wages for industrial workers. Thus, in just half a century, industrialization altered both lifestyles and attitudes, sometimes positively, often negatively, but always permanently.

Industrialization on the European Continent

In the late eighteenth century, as Britain's manufactured goods began to enter continental European markets in increasing numbers, European states became alarmed. Believing that a strong economy was the basis of political power, France restricted British imports until the **Eden Treaty** of 1786, after which British cloth swamped the French market. Some French manufacturers responded to the competition by introducing spinning jennies and water frames in local production. Others blamed the failure of French manufacturers to compete on Britain's passion for world economic domination, which French nationalists had always denounced.

Reasons for the Delay of Industrialization on the European Continent Continental European states soon found that developing their own industries

Eden Treaty Treaty between France and Great Britain in 1786 permitting the import of British manufactured goods into France.

ATLANTIC OCEAN

KINGDOM OF SWEDEN AND NORWAY
- Oslo
- Stockholm

UNITED KINGDOM OF GREAT BRITAIN AND IRELAND
- Newcastle
- Dublin
- IRELAND
- Liverpool
- Leeds
- Manchester
- Birmingham
- London

North Sea

DENMARK • Copenhagen

- Danzig

RUSSIAN EMPIRE
- St. Petersburg
- Riga
- Moscow

Baltic Sea

KINGDOM OF THE NETHERLANDS
- Amsterdam
- Antwerp

KINGDOM OF PRUSSIA
- Essen
- Cologne
- Göttingen
- Berlin
- Warsaw
- Kiev

Elbe R.
Vistula R.
Dnieper R.

- Liège
- Luxembourg
- LORRAINE
- Paris
- Frankfurt
- Prague
- SAXONY
- Cracow

Seine R.
Rhine R.
Dniester R.

FRANCE
- Mulhouse
- ALSACE
- Le Creusot
- Zurich
- Munich
- Vienna
- Buda
- Pest

SWITZERLAND

AUSTRIAN EMPIRE

Loire R.
Garonne R.

- Lyons
- Turin
- Milan
- Venice

Rhône R.
Po R.

- Marseilles

PORTUGAL
- Madrid

SPAIN

Ebro R.

KINGDOM OF PIEDMONT-SARDINIA

TUSCANY **PAPAL STATES**
- Elba
- Corsica (Fr.)
- Rome

Adriatic Sea

- Belgrade

Danube R.

OTTOMAN EMPIRE

- Istanbul

Black Sea

Sardinia

KINGDOM OF THE TWO SICILIES

GIBRALTAR (Gr. Br.)

Mediterranean Sea

Sicily

Malta (Gr. Br.)

- Athens

Legend:
- Railroad
- Coal field
- ○ Industrial area
- Scattered ironworks
- Textile production
- City with population over 500,000

| 0 | 200 | 400 Km. |
| 0 | 200 | 400 Mi. |

Map 21.1 Railroads and Industrial Development in Europe in 1850 By 1850 industrialization had spread from western to central Europe, and railroad construction expanded outward from major cities from Moscow to Manchester. © *Cengage Learning*

1. Where was industry most developed?
2. Which country had the densest railroad system?
3. Where could you go by railroad in 1850? What regions had the fewest railroads?
4. Which regions in central Europe were most industrialized?

would be more complicated than just copying Britain's model. First, Britain jealously guarded its artisans and inventors, making it illegal for them to leave the country. Moreover, on the European continent, water transport was less widely available and more expensive than in Britain. Coal was also in short supply. European guilds were stronger, and their members often actively opposed industrialization as a threat to their livelihood. Finally, much of Europe was simply too poor to provide a market for mass-produced industrial goods. In France, where wealth and educational standards rivaled those in Britain, different taxation systems in various provinces and the innumerable tolls that had to be paid when shipping goods across the kingdom severely handicapped commerce. And just as Britain was making its **industrial take-off** in the 1780s and 1790s, France exploded in revolution.

On the European continent, industrialization had to wait for the end of the Napoleonic wars in 1815. Even then, few regions had the capital, skilled laborers, or resources required for industrializing. From the 1820s, Belgium, northern France, and western Germany began to experience the economic and social transformations of industrialization. By 1850 industry had spread to central Europe, and in 1851 a railroad connected the two largest Russian cities, St. Petersburg and Moscow. Railroads were built, coal mined, and factories and corporations founded. Despite these developments, most of Europe—in particular, the continent's southern and eastern regions—remained mainly agricultural and without significant industry in 1850. British industry remained the most advanced in Europe, as shown by the fact that in 1851 more than half of the English population lived in cities. But by 1850, Britain no longer monopolized European industrial textile production, coal mining, or railroad building.

Industrialization in Belgium

Belgium was the first region on the continent to industrialize. Just across the English Channel, it had long had close commercial ties with Britain, and since the late eighteenth century, British manufactured goods destined for the continent often passed through Belgium. The country also possessed the building blocks of industrialization: good communications by water; raw materials like coal, lumber, and iron ore; a well-trained population with many artisans; and, from 1831, a government favorable to the development of industry. By 1850, Belgium could boast a degree of industrialization unrivaled by any other continental country. At first, Belgian industry concentrated on textiles, but by midcentury a boom in railway building spurred growth in mining and iron production.

Industrialization in France

Industrialization in France followed a different road. As a large and diverse country, quite unlike Belgium, and with its historical suspicion of Britain, France could hardly be expected to follow the British example closely. France did possess the prerequisites for industrialization, such as agricultural efficiency, natural resources including coal and iron, and sophisticated scientists and artisans. For example, French gunsmith Honoré Le Blanc had pioneered the use of **interchangeable parts** in the mid-eighteenth century, and in 1801 inventor **Joseph Marie Jacquard** invented a power loom that could be programmed to produce different patterns of cloth. On the other hand, most French peasants continued to live on their own small farms and were not interested in becoming industrial workers, whereas in England large numbers of landless peasants had little alternative. The French government, again unlike the British, did little to encourage a "pro-industrialization climate"; Le Blanc's innovation of interchangeable parts was not taken up in France and had to wait for another inventor, the American Eli Whitney, to be introduced into manufacturing. The size of France and the lack of economical transport delayed industrialization in many regions until the coming of the railroads.

Traditionally, French manufacturing had concentrated on high-quality luxury items like silk, fine carpets, and exquisite furniture. Entrepreneurs and skilled workers in these traditional manufactures were hostile to the idea of mass production, which, they claimed, was capable of producing only cheap and shoddy articles. Jacquard's looms were attacked and destroyed by angry weavers. Despite the resistance of skilled artisans, industrialization did advance in France. In the Paris region, modern textile factories were established, and the long-standing silk industry in France's second-largest city, Lyon, began to use modern industrial techniques, such as the Jacquard loom. On the whole, however, most French manufacturers continued to produce small amounts of high-quality luxury items rather than the cheap, mass-produced articles of the industrial age.

French industrialization before 1850 was concentrated in **Alsace-Lorraine**, in the northeast, and in the northern part of the country, where coal and iron reserves were located. In the 1830s the first French railroads were built, and in 1842 the government set down a master plan for railroad construction. Private firms built the lines, but with considerable government aid and, later, profit guarantees. This cooperation

industrial take-off The point at which industrialization continues to grow on its own—that is, becomes self-perpetuating.

interchangeable parts Precision manufacture of identical parts so that if the original part breaks or wears out, it can be replaced.

Joseph Marie Jacquard (1752–1834) French inventor and businessman who used punch cards to "program" complicated weaving styles on the power looms called by his name.

Alsace-Lorraine Region of northeastern France in which French industrialization was concentrated before 1850.

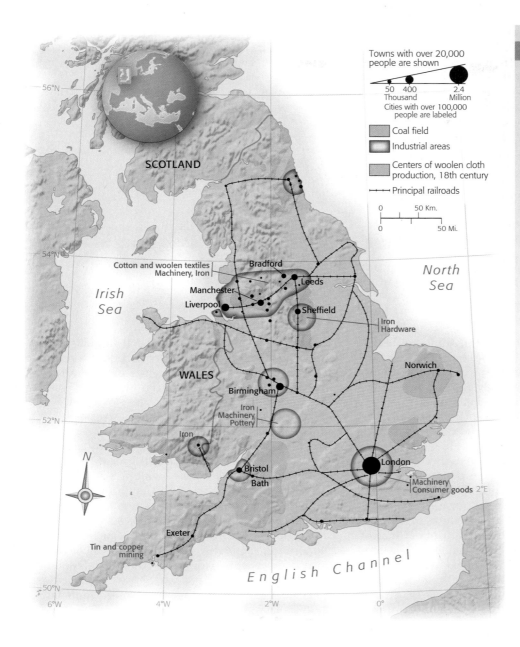

Towns with over 20,000 people are shown

50 Thousand   400   2.4 Million

Cities with over 100,000 people are labeled

Coal field

Industrial areas

Centers of woolen cloth production, 18th century

Principal railroads

0   50 Km.
0   50 Mi.

SCOTLAND

Irish Sea

North Sea

Cotton and woolen textiles
Machinery, Iron

Bradford

Manchester

Leeds

Liverpool

Sheffield

Iron Hardware

WALES

Birmingham

Norwich

Iron Machinery Pottery

Iron

Bristol

Bath

London

Machinery Consumer goods 2°E

Exeter

Tin and copper mining

English Channel

56°N · 54°N · 52°N · 50°N

6°W · 4°W · 2°W · 0°

Map 21.2 **Industrialization in England, ca. 1859** By the middle of the nineteenth century, England was heavily industrialized. Most industrial regions were close to the sea or other waterways and near coal fields. © Cengage Learning

1. Locate Manchester on the map. What about its location made it a prime industrial site?
2. What does the location of railroads tell us about industrialization here?

between government and private business would become typical for the construction of railroads from France to Russia. By 1850, one could go by rail from Paris to Brussels, Frankfurt, Bordeaux, and Marseilles via Lyon. Even greater railroad expansion would come in the second half of the nineteenth century.

Industrialization in the German Lands In the German lands, industry grew on top of coal fields in the **Ruhr** and **Saxony** regions, and entrepreneurs built small factories in the Prussian capital, Berlin. In 1837, August Borsig set up a machine shop there that would become one of the largest locomotive factories in Europe. Ten years later, **Werner Siemens** established a company in Berlin to manufacture telegraph equipment; Siemens remains a major

manufacturer of electronic goods in the twenty-first century. Despite the fact that industrialization had come to many German regions in the 1840s, most Germans continued to live in the countryside and earn their livelihood from the soil. In Prussia, less than 10 percent of the population lived in cities larger than 20,000, even in 1849, and only two Prussian cities boasted populations above 100,000.

Ruhr Region in western Germany that became a center of industrial production and metal industry.

Saxony Region in southeastern Germany, formerly an independent kingdom, important in German industrialization.

Werner Siemens (1816–1892) German inventor and businessman who established his first factory in Berlin in 1847 and was a major figure in the manufacture of electrical goods.

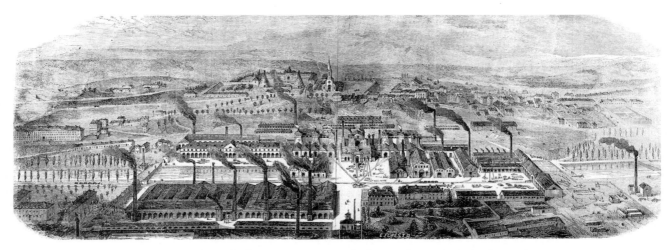

Founded in the late eighteenth century by an English entrepreneur, the Le Creusot ironworks in the Burgundy region to the southeast of Paris became one of the most advanced in France. The company would later develop into France's largest arms manufacturer. What is the first thing you notice about this image? How do you suppose this enormous factory affected people living nearby? (Roger-Viollet/The Image Works)

At the same time, the German Customs Union (**Zollverein**), established in 1834, helped push German industrialization forward by enabling industrialists to sell their products freely across a large area. While the Zollverein did not include all German states, it laid the groundwork for an economically and politically united Germany. Economically, it created a market of 26 million potential customers. Railroads followed rapidly. The first German line ran from Nuremberg to Fürth in Bavaria—a distance of only a few kilometers—in 1835, but by 1850, Germany could boast of nearly six thousand kilometers of railroad lines, nearly double that of France. As in France, in central Europe governments promoted railroad building. Often the Prussian, Saxon, or Austrian governments would guarantee profits for a certain stretch of track to the company willing to undertake its construction. Private investors would then provide the capital for railroad building, confident that their investment would make a reasonable return. In this way, the construction of German railroads involved much more state support than had been the case in Britain.

Comparing with British Industrialization Industrialization on the continent always looked to the example of Britain. For many, like **Friedrich Engels**, this example was negative. Industrialization in Britain had caused misery for thousands of workers, who crowded into the new industrial towns and lived in dark and squalid slums. From the start, continental governments feared the revolutionary potential of impoverished industrial workers, or the **proletariat**, a word that rapidly appeared in many European languages. And they took action in a way that Britain, devoted to laissez-faire economics, did not. Not only did continental governments promote railroads, they restricted the use of child labor and more closely regulated the conditions of industrial work than in Britain, hoping to reduce working-class discontent. In short, governments on the continent always took a much more active role in regulating relations between **capitalists** and industrial workers. They also protected their new industries through high **tariffs** that discouraged the consumption of imported goods by increasing their price. Many argued that Britain's great head start in industrialization made it necessary to shield developing industry from a flood of cheap British manufactures. Britain, in contrast, had long been a promoter of free trade—that is, British trade.

The Revolution in Transportation

New industries required the transport of both raw materials and manufactured goods. At first, rivers and canals were sufficient, but they were rapidly supplanted by railroads. Railroads originated in the coal mines of Britain, where the difficulty of bringing the heavy, bulky coal to the surface called forth a simple but ingenious solution: coal wagons on metal rails.

The Railroad Soon the principle was transferred outside the mines. At first, horses pulled these wagons on metal tracks, but it was only logical that animal

Zollverein German Customs Union, or free-trade area, dominated by Prussia and important in Prussian unification of Germany in 1871.

Friedrich Engels (1820–1895) Karl Marx's closest collaborator, son of a German industrialist who spent most of his life in England.

proletariat Industrial workers or, more generally, people who own absolutely nothing except their own labor.

capitalists Individuals whose income comes from capital—wealth in money rather than land—invested in factories and commerce for profit.

tariffs Taxes charged on imported goods that raise consumer costs and add to government revenues.

The railroad sliced through the countryside, serving as a constant reminder to rural people of the great industrial changes taking place. The rural landscape was transformed by the "iron road" itself, with its bridges and viaducts. The loud, sooty, and dangerous trains that rushed through what had been quiet agricultural regions must have seemed like monsters from another world. In what ways did industrialization change everyday life, even in the countryside?

power would be replaced by steam. The culmination of this process occurred in 1829, when **George Stephenson**'s locomotive, the *Rocket,* won a competition for the new Manchester-Liverpool line by traveling at a top speed of twenty-nine miles per hour over thirty-five miles. The railroad age had begun.

In next two decades, more than six thousand miles of track were laid in Britain. On the European continent, railroad construction was also impressive: by 1850, Berlin, Paris, Vienna, Frankfurt, and other major cities were linked by rail. The first railroad entrepreneurs envisioned these new "iron roads" mainly as a means of bringing bulky raw materials like coal or iron ore to factories and manufactured products to market (such as textiles from Manchester to the port of Liverpool). Very soon, however, railroads were carrying not just freight but also large numbers of people. Railroads made it easier for country people to migrate to the city in search of work, thereby increasing the labor pool for further industrialization.

Steamships Steam engines proved easier to use in locomotives than in ships. Harnessing steam to propel watercraft was plagued by two separate difficulties. First, a high degree of efficiency was required because of a boat's limited ability to carry coal. Second, for an onboard steam engine, safety was extremely important, as an explosion could well mean the destruction of the entire ship, possibly far out at sea. These problems were effectively solved by the late 1830s, however, and by midcentury steamships were

replacing even the swift-sailing clippers on the open seas. Steamships were innovative not only in their use of steam propulsion but also in their construction, being made of iron instead of wood. The use of iron in shipbuilding allowed ships to be larger, more durable, and economically more efficient. In 1838, two iron steamships, the *Great Western* and the *Sirius,* raced across the Atlantic to New York, making the journey in a record-breaking fifteen days. Rapidly, wooden sailing vessels were retired, no longer able to compete.

Road Building Industrialization spurred improvements in roads and overland transport as well. At the beginning of the century, roads in most parts of Europe were worse than they had been during the Roman Empire eighteen centuries earlier. But by 1850, significant improvements had been made, partly in connection with the creation of a European-wide postal system. Post roads with stations where horses could be changed were established along major trade routes from England to Russia. In Britain, by 1830 more than a thousand private "turnpike trusts" had built roads and were then charging tolls to recover their investment. **John McAdam**, a surveyor for

George Stephenson (1781–1848) English railroad pioneer, inventor, and engineer responsible for some of Britain's earliest locomotives and rail lines in the 1820s and 1830s.

John McAdam (1756–1836) Scottish engineer who developed a technique for a harder, less muddy road surface known as "macadam" in various languages.

the Bristol Turnpike Trust, developed a method of road construction that improved foundations and drainage. His method, using gravel and broken rock, formed a hard surface that was more durable and less muddy than dirt roads. Soon similar roads were being built throughout Europe, called in many different languages "macadam."

Canals Water transport was also important for transporting raw materials and manufactured goods. Though the Bridgewater Canal, built in 1761 to carry coal by barge to Manchester, was hard pressed by competition from the Liverpool and Manchester Railroad, the canal's success in generating an entire network of canals around Manchester inspired the Erie Canal in New York State. This canal's completion in 1825, connecting the Hudson River and Lake Erie, opened the American interior to overseas commerce. Even backward Russia improved its canal system, in 1808 rebuilding the Moscow-Petersburg canal first constructed by Peter the Great, and linking the Vistula, Bug, and Dnieper Rivers by canal in 1841 to allow the passage of goods by water from the Baltic to the Black Sea. Many smaller canals throughout Europe connected industry with raw materials and markets, increasingly working together with railroads.

The Social Impacts of Industrialization

The most noticeable—even shocking—impact of industrialization was **urbanization**, the rapid growth of cities. In the first half of the nineteenth century, hundreds of thousands of individuals both in Britain and on the continent left the countryside for work in cities. Factory owners needed large numbers of workers, and these were most readily available in large population centers. New factories built in the countryside to take advantage of water-power, such as the mills established at the falls of the Clyde in Scotland, soon drew so many workers that mills became towns—in this case **New Lanark, Robert Owen's** model factory town. Workers required food, clothing, medical care, and housing,

so more people migrated to the industrialized towns to provide these services. Factory owners and managers in their large houses required servants, who added to the population. For all these reasons, industrial cities grew at breathtaking rates, so fast that available housing was overwhelmed. As thousands of strangers were forced to live and work together in small, cramped spaces, disease and crime were the inevitable result.

Manchester, City of Industry The English city of Manchester offers a spectacular example of population growth. Located some thirty miles from the English port of Liverpool, Manchester had long been a center of wool cloth production, powered mainly by human muscle. But directly under and surrounding the city were huge coal deposits that would fuel the transition to steam power, and the opening of the Bridgewater Canal made coal transport cheap. These three factors—closeness to a port, large reserves of coal, and available skilled laborers—made Manchester the birthplace of industrialization. In 1750, the city's population was 20,000. In the next twenty-five years, the population doubled, but that was before the industrial take-off. By 1831, the population had soared to more than 250,000, and by 1850, it was 400,000.

This rapid growth came at an enormous price: overcrowding, industrial pollution, and filth in the streets that made the stench of Manchester fabled. The air was full of soot and exhaust gases from the coal-powered engines in the factories. A French visitor in midcentury, the journalist Hippolite Taine, described the "dreary streets," full of "masses of livid children, dirty and flabby of flesh. Even to walk in the rich quarter of town is depressing." A medical doctor described this poverty in 1833: "Too often the dwelling of the factory family is no home; it sometimes is a cellar, which includes no cooking, no washing, no making, no mending, no decencies of life." But as the liberal French writer Alexis de Tocqueville observed, "From this filthy sewer pure gold flows."

Negative Effects of Industrialization Unscrupulous landlords threw up cheap, unventilated, and crowded **tenements** in which several families lived in a single room. Water had to be fetched from outdoor wells, often contaminated by outdoor privies. Food was expensive, in part because Britain's 1815 Corn Laws forbade the import of grain. The lack of clean water and the overcrowding made epidemics of diseases like cholera and typhoid common; the polluted air caused respiratory problems that often developed into diseases such as asthma and **tuberculosis**. By the 1830s, British reformers had realized that only government intervention could help solve the problems associated with industrialization.

The pollution and environmental degradation was, literally, breathtaking. Industrial cities were black

---

urbanization Process by which cities grow as population shifts from rural to urban areas; a major effect of industrialization.

New Lanark Cotton mill town on the Clyde River in Scotland where Robert Owen combined profit-making with efforts to improve workers' lives.

Robert Owen (1771–1858) Scottish industrialist and utopian socialist who attempted to incorporate cooperative principles in his factories.

Manchester Textile manufacturing city in northern England.

tenements Cheaply built, crowded, and often squalid multi-story dwellings, often constructed by factory owners to house workers.

tuberculosis Infectious disease that affects the lungs and if untreated often leads to death; a common killer in the nineteenth century, now treatable with antibiotics.

This painting of the industrial city of Manchester in 1851 graphically depicts the enormous impact of industrialization with the dozens of smokestacks pouring pollution into the air, rendering the city's air hazy and difficult to breathe. The stunted trees in the foreground suggest the impact of industrialization on nature. Looking at this image, how do you perceive the impact of industrialization? Comparing the depiction of nature in this painting and those of Caspar David Friedrich (Chapter 20, p. 600), what differences can you point out?

with soot; light-colored clothing would be filthy by the end of the day. One early solution to the problems of air pollution in Manchester and other industrial towns was to build factory chimneys ever higher so that winds would carry the fumes far away from the city. But this method simply spread pollution farther from the factories themselves. Mining ripped up the face of the earth and brought to the surface toxic substances that were simply dumped aside unless they had commercial value. Rainwater ran through these slag heaps, spreading the poison into rivers. In the absence of municipal water treatment plants—no industrial city of the time had any—people were obliged to drink this foul, polluted water. Little wonder that in industrial towns, infant mortality was high and life expectancy low.

Space, Time, and Industrialization Industrialization changed the human sense of space and time. With railroads, cities were hours apart instead of days. But railroads and factories also demanded a more precise keeping of time and spurred on another industry— the manufacture of clocks and watches—as well as standardized time. Railways not only linked major cities but cut through less-developed agricultural regions, ending their isolation. The physical presence of rails traversing the countryside reminded rural

people that the excitement and economic promise of the big city lay mere hours away.

The Duke of Wellington worried that railways "would encourage the lower classes to move about," and they did. Inexpensive fares in third-class carriages made possible travel on a scale hitherto unheard of: 27.7 million railroad journeys were taken in Britain in 1844. Cheap fares encouraged the migration of impoverished rural people into the growing industrial cities, further accelerating their growth. By midcentury, more-distant journeys to America and Australia usually began with a train ride to the port, where emigrants boarded a steamship. Thus the transportation revolution wrought by industrialization had a major impact not just on Europe but on the world.

The Creation of Class One of the most far-reaching effects of the Industrial Revolution was the creation of social categories based on economic, not legal, status. Until industrialization, most people identified themselves by the social category of their birth: peasant, noble, artisan, merchant. These were legal, not merely economic, categories. It was quite possible for nobles to be poor and even (though more rarely) for peasants to be wealthy. Industrial societies, however, are ordered along class lines. One's class derives

Friedrich Engels Denounces Capitalist Exploitation

Friedrich Engels was just twenty-two when his father sent him away from home to keep him out of trouble. Home was Barmen (now Wuppertal), Germany, where the family owned textile mills. The "trouble" was Friedrich's interest in philosophy, which caused him to reject his father's stern brand of Christianity. Hoping to distract his son from such irreligious studies, the elder Engels sent young Friedrich to manage a textile mill outside Manchester, England, in which the family had an interest.

Once in Manchester, young Engels was appalled by what he saw: overcrowded housing; entire districts lacking sewers and clean drinking water; families competing for foul, half-rotten food. The horrifying conditions in which the working people of Manchester lived changed Engels's life, causing him to dedicate his life to exposing the misery caused by industrial capitalism and to helping workers organize to improve their lives. Engels decided to write a book. Though he represented his father's interests at the mill during the day, at night he roamed the slums of Manchester, gathering material for what would be published as *The Condition of the Working Class in England in 1844*.

Engels documented entire families living in a single room, sleeping together in a single bed that was alive with lice and vermin. He recorded the physical effects of grueling work, poor nutrition, and lack of hygiene. These terrible living conditions meant that the majority of industrial workers died before they reached the age of twenty. Even as he gathered his data, Engels was asking himself more fundamental questions: What factors cause such poverty? How could factories that were so efficient at increasing production make the lives of their workers so miserable? In short, Engels wanted to understand the workings of industrial capitalism.

In 1844, Engels returned home to Germany, stopping on the way in Paris to meet Karl Marx. Within two years, the two young men (Marx was only two years older than Engels) would be calling themselves communists and calling for an overthrow of the present economic and political order. But for now Engels went home to write his book. It was published the next year in German, but its dedication was in English: "To the Working Classes of Great-Britain." Engels praised English workers, dedicated his book to them, and urged them to fight for their rights against "the middle classes intend to enrich themselves by your labour."

This was more than a documented report; it was a political manifesto, and Engels called on England's workers to take control of their own destiny. Scholars at the time and later complained that Engels exaggerated the misery wrought by industrialization, provided a one-sided picture of life in Manchester, and based his sweeping accusations against the middle class on his own narrow experience in Barmen and Manchester. These criticisms are reasonable, but on another level they miss the point. Engels was not writing a scholarly analysis; he was trying to change the world. His conclusion was a warning: "The war of the poor against the rich will be the most bloodthirsty the world has ever seen." This war would be a revolution, he claimed, that would usher in a world of justice and dignity for all.

In 1848, only three years after the book's publication, revolutions did sweep the European continent, including Germany. In the same year, Marx and Engels published the famous *Communist Manifesto*, in which they argued that a workers' revolution would soon put an end to capitalism. The workers' revolution did not come in 1848. For political reasons, both Marx and Engels had to flee their native Germany and live in permanent exile in England. There they maintained a fruitful partnership and friendship that lasted until Marx's death in 1883.

Although Engels's *Conditions of the Working Class in England* made him famous among German radicals, it was not published in England until 1891. Still, the book's impact was enormous. For some young Russian socialists, Engels's descriptions of the degradations of industrial capitalism made them hope to avoid industrialism altogether—an aim that Marx and Engels firmly rejected as impossible and undesirable. Instead, Engels argued, radicals needed to harness industrialization's wealth-generating power for the good of all workers and all society. In a sense, Engels did this himself as an individual: he worked all his life as a businessman and manufacturer, devoting much of his income to radical causes and supporting the ever-impoverished Marx family. Ironically, industrial capitalism made Engels a radical and also financed his quest to destroy it.

primarily from one's economic position in society, or as **Karl Marx** would later describe it, one's relation to the **means of production**. The factory owner controlled the means of production (the factory) and derived profit from it; the workers were an element in the means of production, much like the machines they tended.

The idea of class also implies a feeling of belonging together, or **class consciousness**. This consciousness was new in the early Industrial Revolution. Nobles had long distinguished themselves from commoners by dress, manners, and luxurious lifestyle. Now the growing middle classes, or bourgeoisie, differentiated themselves from nobles by their emphasis on the dignity of work and self-improvement, and from the working class by their accent, clean clothes, and soft hands. Workers, crammed together on factory floors and tenement houses, began to recognize their shared interests too. With the coming of industrialization, society was no longer divided into three estates—the nobles, clergy, and peasants of France—or the lords and commoners of England. Now it was divided into capitalists, who had wealth available to invest in the means of production, and workers (the proletariat), who had no source of income other than their labor.

Social Mobility Industrialization also enhanced the possibility for social mobility. An intelligent, hard-working peasant boy could go to work in the city and hope to rise into the lower middle class or, if not he, then at least his children. To be sure, most of those born poor died that way—and died much earlier than their middle- and upper-class contemporaries. But the possibility of becoming a "self-made man" and rising above the class of one's birth was an aspiration—and a reality—for many in this era.

 Checking In

By yourself or with a partner, explain the significance of each of the following selected key terms:

industrial take-off	Manchester
Zollverein	Karl Marx
Friedrich Engels	means of production
Robert Owen	class consciousness

The Middle Classes

◆ **Who belonged to the middle classes?**

◆ **What moral and political values characterized the middle classes?**

In the classic formulation, the middle class was, of course, in the middle—between the aristocracy on one hand and the peasants on the other. In the nineteenth century, the middle classes distinguished themselves from the working classes too. This group grew rapidly as industrialization progressed, and as they prospered, their political importance and influence grew as well. Speaking of "middle classes" in the plural suggests the great variety of occupations and mentalities that this category embraced. But all middle-class people defined themselves not by their birth but also by what they did—their occupation and, increasingly, their education. Their shared interests included pride in their respectability, sobriety, and hard work, often contrasting these "middle-class virtues" with the drunken and wasteful behavior of both workers and those born into great wealth. The middle-class home reflected this proud, sober, and somewhat smug attitude, with a wife who devoted herself entirely to her family, not needing to earn money outside the home. To be sure, this was an ideal not always attained in reality.

A Variety of Middle Classes

Europe had had a strong and growing class of merchants since the Middle Ages, and as commerce grew, so did banking, investing, and shipping. In the eighteenth century, lawyers, doctors, professors, and other educated professionals might have felt that their income and lifestyle gave them something in common with those who had grown rich from trade. And in the nineteenth century, these middle classes expanded rapidly. The spread of industrialism demanded and created capitalists with the liquid wealth, or capital, to invest in new factories. Complex machinery, production methods, and business arrangements created an increased need for engineers, skilled technicians, foremen, and managers as well as distributors and salesmen. All those who filled these positions were members of the middle classes.

Early Industrialists Some of those who established new enterprises were aristocrats, such as the Duke of Bridgewater, who sank his fortune into the Bridgewater Canal. The canal returned an even greater fortune and also brought great earnings to the duke's engineer, James Brindley, a craftsman's son with little education. Brindley was a self-made man who achieved success through this own effort; in fact, biographers attributed his early death to diabetes and overwork. He is representative of a new class of men whose fame and fortune derived directly from industrialization.

Karl Marx (1818–1883) German-born radical scholar and writer, long-time collaborator with Friedrich Engels, and author of *Capital* and *The Communist Manifesto*.

means of production Factories, workshops, and other tools that produce wealth.

class consciousness Identification with other members of one's economic class—for example, industrial workers or middle-class professionals.

Richard Arkwright, a barber whose water frame made him rich, and James Watt, whose improvements on the steam engine made him wealthy, are others. So are Richard Cobden, son of a farmer who gained wealth as a calico printer and prominence as a member of Parliament from Stockport, near Manchester. His close associate in the Anti–Corn Law League, John Bright, was the grandson of a farmer. For these men, social status and identity derived not from birth but from accomplishment. The middle classes were varied and fluid enough to be open to newcomers. Industrialization increased social mobility.

The "Petty Bourgeoisie" Differences within the middle classes were huge. The richest industrialists, for example, married their daughters into aristocratic families; thus their grandchildren would be "upper class" and frequently embarrassed by the grandfather's coarse, unrefined manners. On the other hand, impoverished clerks, owners of small shops, teachers, governesses—the so-called petty bourgeoisie—were in constant peril of sinking down into the "lower depths" of society. The greater possibility for social mobility brought about by industrialization thus cut both ways, enabling the strong, intelligent, and lucky to rise but also making it easy to fall from respected middle-class status into poverty and social disgrace.

Middle-Class Culture

Although some of the self-made men in the new middle classes had limited schooling themselves, they all believed firmly in the value of learning, and they made certain that their sons—and, increasingly, their daughters—had good educations. A secondary or university education almost guaranteed middle-class status, and university enrollments grew steadily throughout the nineteenth century.

New Universities New universities were founded, often specifically to fulfill the requirements of the new, industrializing society, such as University College London, which provided practical educational opportunities to middle-class men and women. In Berlin, a *Bauakademie*—academy of architecture and engineering—was founded by the Prussian state in 1799 and was joined in 1821 by a *Gewerbeakademie*, or business or trade school. These institutions were merged in 1879 to form the Royal Technical Higher School of Berlin, the forerunner of today's Technical University of Berlin. Significantly, these university-level institutions to train engineers and businessmen in Berlin

Accommodations in railroad coaches reflected social class divisions. Aristocrats and the rich traveled in first-class coaches, "respectable" middle-class people in second, and everyone else in third. Although passengers in third (above) and first (below) classes traveled in very different style, the railroad aided social leveling by the simple fact that everyone left and arrived at the same time. Compare the passengers shown in first and third class. How typical (judging from their dress) do you suppose the third-class passengers shown here were?

were founded by the government, whereas University College London arose from private initiative.

In central Europe, the emerging class of the *Bildungsbürgertum*, the educated bourgeoisie, testifies to the importance of education for middle-class status. Despite **Wilhelm von Humboldt**'s revitalization of German universities in the first years of the nineteenth century, training entrepreneurs or technicians was not seen as the university's role. Rather, individuals wishing to pursue such practical studies enrolled in institutions like the business or engineering academies in Berlin. In the decades between 1830 and 1860, the most popular subjects at German universities were theology and law (around 30 percent of students each), medicine and liberal arts (15 percent each), with only 5 percent of German students majoring in science.

Education and the Middle Class

A university education secured one's middle-class status, most likely as a member of a profession such as law, medicine, or the church, but middle-class people valued hard work equally. The enterprising writer, physician, and editor **Samuel Smiles** provided a formula for success in his 1859 book *Self-Help*. Thrift, hard work, and sobriety were important, as were self-denial, good habits, and the ability to learn from mistakes. "Life will always be to a large extent what we ourselves make it," wrote Smiles. As inspiration, he also wrote biographies of self-made men, such as potter Josiah Wedgwood and engineer George Stephenson. Smiles also believed that self-improvement would contribute to the improvement of society as a whole.

Victorian Morality

In their emphasis on practical knowledge, middle-class people may be seen as the heirs of the Enlightenment, but their strict views on sobriety and sexual morality derive rather from Protestant Christian traditions. Young people were admonished to avoid the temptations not only of sexual intercourse before marriage but even of sexual thoughts or masturbation. Many manuals and self-help books for parents and young people warned that "self-abuse" would lead to bad eyesight, insanity, and other misfortunes, including death. Ideally, men and women were to find sexual pleasure only within the bounds of marriage.

Sexual love between members of the same sex was literally unspeakable: the word *homosexuality* was not coined until 1869. It is not by chance that later generations would use the word **Victorian**—referring to the reign of British queen Victoria—to mean preachy, sexually repressed, hypocritical, and narrow-minded. Still, this characterization is at best one-sided. Middle-class ideology in the nineteenth century did have its humorless, self-righteous aspects, but its grinding emphasis on work reflected a desire to validate middle-class identity and to assert that individual dignity should be gauged not by birth but by service to society.

Middle-Class Respectability

As members of a largely new and growing social grouping, middle-class people felt keenly the need to establish and augment their prestige and respectability, often by promoting their values of self-improvement, education, and sobriety among the less fortunate. Smiles argued that only by adopting middle-class values and habits could workers lift themselves out of poverty. Many middle-class women, especially, engaged actively in charity work, sometimes alienating those they intended to help with their strident self-righteousness. The **temperance movement**, for example, was a middle-class reform directed mainly at the working class. Alcoholism was a problem, but workers were often put off by the well-dressed preachy women who scolded them for their drinking habits.

The middle-class belief in hard work as the key to success implied that poverty was something that those who would not work hard enough brought on themselves. Thus the structural causes of poverty, unleashed by industrialization, were obscured. The historian **François Guizot**, who dominated French politics in the 1840s, believed that the opportunity for riches was open to all and that failure to achieve wealth reflected an individual's own limitations and weaknesses. Rather than blaming society for their misery, Guizot argued, the poor had only themselves to blame. If they would stay sober, work hard, and live frugally, they would better their social condition. Many middle-class liberals would have agreed, pointing to their own success as proof that hard work alone brought prosperity and social status.

Religion and the Middle Classes

Middle-class respectability involved both self-control and self-righteousness—overall, an avoidance of extremes. In their churches, the middle classes avoided ostentatious ceremonies, mysticism, and overly emotional displays of devotion. The Church of England and the official Protestant churches in central Europe and Scandinavia reprimanded clergy who showed excessive "enthusiasm" or religious fervor, and pastors who pressed their middle-class parishioners too strongly about their sins might find themselves

Wilhelm von Humboldt (1767–1835) German philosopher, linguist, and statesman, after whom Berlin's main university is named.

Samuel Smiles (1812–1904) Scottish writer who achieved fame through books promising success through hard work, such as self-help, thrift, character, and duty.

Victorian Term referring to the reign of Queen Victoria (r. 1837–1901) and carrying a connotation of sexual restraint, humorlessness, and social conservatism.

temperance movement Movement to ban the use of alcoholic beverages, often affiliated with Christian churches and led by middle-class women.

François Guizot (1787–1874) French historian and politician who believed that the poor must improve their own economic condition through hard work without government aid.

snubbed by the parish. But some Protestants found worship without ceremony and emotion arid and devoid of profound religious meaning. A few left the Church of England for dissenting chapels, and at Oxford, a group of prominent Anglican clergymen who sought to revive certain Roman Catholic rituals drew much attention, particularly when some of them converted to Catholicism.

As Jews began to assimilate into the middle class, dressing and speaking like other members of that class, they also sought to reform their religious practices. The traditional long caftan of the rabbi was exchanged for a sober outfit resembling that of a Protestant pastor. Within the synagogue, a more orderly religious service was inaugurated, sometimes even with choirs and organs, which were quite foreign to Jewish religious traditions. While generally remaining true to their religious laws, avoiding certain foods and keeping the Sabbath (Saturday) holy, these middle-class Jews attempted in all other ways to resemble their Gentile neighbors.

Their **Reform Judaism** was strongest in German areas, but even among the overwhelmingly traditional and Orthodox Polish Jews in Warsaw and Lwów, Reform synagogues were opened in the 1840s. More traditional Jews saw these innovations as the first step to conversion to Christianity, and in their own way, they were right. Later Reform Judaism was to significantly relax the strict requirements to eat only kosher food, to abstain from work on Saturdays, and to orient one's life around prayer, worship, and study. Moreover, many of the middle-class Jews who shed their traditional Jewish garb and habits later abandoned Judaism altogether, as did the children of the preeminent Jewish Enlightenment figure, Moses Mendelssohn. For them, as for the fathers of Karl Marx, English conservative statesman **Benjamin Disraeli**, and many others, social **assimilation** was the first step toward conversion.

The Middle-Class Home

As industrialization spread, concepts of home and work became increasingly separated. In a preindustrial society, artisans lived in or near their workshops, and peasants lived near the fields they tilled, sometimes even sharing their lodgings with their domestic animals. But in industrial societies, just as "work" became associated with a "workplace"—a factory—so, for the middle classes, did the home become distinctly apart from the dirt and noise of manufacturing and the fast-paced and high-pressure world of business. The newly wealthy industrialists built large houses away from their factories, and their wives were expected to create a restful and pleasant haven for their hardworking husbands to return to after a hard day's work. To be sure, these **separate spheres** of home and work were more an ideal than a reality for all middle-class homes, but this ideal had a strong influence on middle-class identity and on ideas of a woman's "proper place." Women's legal status remained unchanged; legally, women were an extension of their fathers or husbands.

Marriage and Family Life Marriage was a vital and central institution of middle-class life; this society rejected as peculiar, and even suspicious, the idea of remaining unmarried, with a few exceptions, such as Roman Catholic priests. The first line of Jane Austen's *Pride and Prejudice* reflects this fact: "It is a truth universally acknowledged, that a single man in possession of a good fortune must be in want of a wife." Founding a family was of vital importance, but first, a middle-class man had to establish himself in business—in effect, earn his fortune. Men were typically older than the women they married and were expected to guide and train their wives as well as to love them. The husband had to earn a sufficient amount to pay for a middle-class home and servants and, of course, to allow his wife to devote herself exclusively to her family without needing to earn money.

Middle-Class Women Middle-class girls were raised to see marriage as their main purpose in life. Not making a suitable marriage was also feared, as it might mean an unpleasant dependency on wealthier relations or a meager livelihood as a "genteel" lady's maid or governess. Once she was married, a middle-class woman's role included running the household, supervising servants, educating her children, and in some cases helping her husband in his professional or scientific endeavors. Outside the home, it was considered proper for a middle-class woman to be active in charitable and religious organizations. Women did not have careers, though they might make their own way as teachers, seamstresses, or milliners—the latter two professions perilously near "working class."

Nineteenth-century novels often examine the dilemmas of bright and sensitive young women of marriageable age. Their authors were themselves women who were trying to make their way as writers—**Charlotte Brontë**, author of *Jane Eyre*, is one example. She and her sister **Emily** published under

Reform Judaism Movement to modernize Jewish life, retaining the religious core of Judaism but eliminating many differences from Gentiles in everyday life.

Benjamin Disraeli (1804–1881) English writer and conservative statesman who was a favorite of Queen Victoria; the son of a converted Jew but very proud of his Jewish origins.

assimilation Process by which one ethnic or cultural group takes on the attributes of another.

separate spheres Middle-class ideal whereby home life was strictly separated from the workplace, with women running the household and men earning money outside it.

Charlotte and Emily Brontë (1816–1855, 1818–1848) English novelists and poets, authors of novels including *Jane Eyre* (Charlotte) and *Wuthering Heights* (Emily).

THE FASHIONS

Expressly designed and prepared for the

Englishwoman's Domestic Magazine

JUNE 1861

The *Englishwoman's Domestic Magazine*'s illustrations reflected middle-class women's desire for respectability and even extravagance in fashion. Increasingly able to afford new outfits frequently, women of the middle class consulted such magazines to learn the latest style. What about the fashions shown here indicate to you that this publication was aimed at middle-class women?

male names, as did **George Sand** (Amandine Aurore Lucile Dupin) in France and **George Eliot** (Mary Ann Evans) in England. By publishing under male names, these pioneering women writers aimed to force readers to take their writing more seriously, and they also sought to avoid criticism by their own middle-class families about earning money with their pen. While some women published—at times with great success—under their own (female) names, they often found that their work was considered by male critics a mere pastime, not real literature.

Middle-class women were not supposed to earn money—just to spend it. Although servants usually did the shopping, it was the "lady of the house" who ordered goods, checked prices, kept accounts, and made sure that neither servants nor merchants were cheating her. Even when she had a housekeeper to perform most of these duties, she was expected by her husband to make sure that all of these activities were carried out properly. The middle-class woman also had to purchase clothes for herself and her family and to furnish her home tastefully. To help homemakers make choices in their selection of furnishings

and clothing, entrepreneurs began to publish books and periodicals devoted to proper, respectable fashions, such as *The Englishwoman's Domestic Magazine*, which began appearing in 1852.

Middle-Class Children Children in middle-class families were trained to be obedient, clean, respectful, and orderly. Physical punishment of children was considered normal, indeed inevitable, though usually the task of the man: respectable French fathers had a small whip for that purpose. At the same time, the ideas of Jean Jacques Rousseau on education and allowing children free time for play and physical development were spreading. Middle-class children were usually educated at home by governesses and tutors, as there was not yet a well-developed educational system. Looking back at their childhood later in the century, many middle-class people recalled the great freedom they had enjoyed compared with later youths, who would be obliged to spend more regimented days in schoolrooms. Because of improved nutrition and sanitation, middle-class families were likely to have many children; it was not unusual for a woman to have ten or more pregnancies in her lifetime. As the century progressed, infant mortality decreased, and the size of middle-class families grew.

Checking In

By yourself or with a partner, explain the significance of each of the following selected key terms:

Wilhelm von Humboldt	Reform Judaism
Victorian	Benjamin Disraeli
temperance movement	George Eliot
François Guizot	

Working Classes

◆ **How did industrialization and urbanization change everyday and family life?**

◆ **How did industrial workers attempt to improve their work situations?**

Industrialization created the working class—or classes. This large group included miners, industrial workers, servants, and artisans, who worked and lived in conditions that were often appalling. Industrialization and urbanization disrupted working-class family life. Increasingly, mothers, fathers, and children went to different workplaces, carrying out

George Sand (1804–1876) French female author of more than eighty novels who took a man's name and dressed in male attire to protest the treatment of women.

George Eliot (1819–1880) Major English novelist, born Mary Ann Evans, whose novels portrayed social and moral problems of the lower middle class.

Realist artist Vasily Perov portrays the misery of the Russian peasants and the indifference of a respectable Russian Orthodox clergyman in this bitter painting, *Tea Drinking at Mytishchi near Moscow* (1862). How does the artist arouse your sympathy for the beggars? What about the portrayal of the priest renders him unsympathetic to the viewer?

Tretjakov Gallery, Moscow/ akg-images

separate tasks. The crowded conditions, combined with the city's many temptations, made the proper upbringing and discipline of children all the more difficult. But workers did not simply accept their lot passively. Working-class people banded together to protect themselves from the worst aspects of early industrialization, organizing unions, demanding better working and living conditions, and insisting on their own dignity in the face of what they saw as middle-class indifference.

Diversity Within the Working Class

Manchester exemplifies the triumphs and contradictions of early industrialization better than any other city. Here huge amounts of money were made by a few, but for the workers, life was harsh, brutal, and short. The workday was long—sometimes stretching to fourteen and sixteen hours, six and even seven days a week. Workers who arrived late were beaten and fined or their pay was docked.

Dangers of the Industrial City Slippery factory floors, complex systems of gears and transmission belts, and the constant presence of fumes endangered life and limb. If injured, workers could expect to be fired instantly. Workers' health also suffered from damp and dank workplaces, sometimes overheated, sometimes chilled by open windows. The air was always filled with smells, fibers, and particles of cloth. Tuberculosis and cholera were common. The reformer and

Edwin Chadwick (1800–1890) English social reformer who worked to improve conditions for the poor through better hygiene and government programs.

Manchester native **Edwin Chadwick** pointed out in 1842 that smoke in Manchester was killing vegetation. In the same report he described workers' housing in another industrial city, Leeds: "walls unwhitewashed for years, black with the smoke of foul chimneys, without water, … and sacking for bed-clothes, with floors unwashed from year to year."

Artisans As industrialization proceeded, artisans often found themselves out of work, replaced by machines. In the early years, artisans' skills had been essential to factory design and operations. But soon mass production deprived tailors, clockmakers, and shoemakers of their livelihood and way or life. Even more directly threatened were weavers and others engaged in textile production. Those who found new employment in mechanized, power-driven textile factories often perceived the change from artisan to worker as painful and humiliating. They resented the constant surveillance of foremen and felt dehumanized by the need to adapt their skills and their personal rhythms to the tempo of the machine. The life of a hand-loom weaver had not been easy, but at least he (weavers were usually men) worked his own hours and was paid a living wage. As artisans were driven out of work and forced to accept factory jobs, they no longer had these satisfactions.

Servants The working classes also included servants. The majority of servants were women, often young girls who came from the countryside to seek employment in the growing number of middle-class households. Hannah Cullwick of Shropshire, for example, lost her parents as a teenager, moved to London, and took a job in the house of a middle-class beer merchant. Remembering her experiences, Hannah described the great gulf between her drudgery as a servant and the life of a "real lady," who "couldn't wash a plate or a saucepan or peal a tato." But the servant class was itself divided into classes. At the very bottom was the harried "girl of all work" who scrubbed, fetched water, washed dishes, and generally carried out any tasks the housekeeper or cook ordered her to do. The cook and chambermaid were her superiors, and they enjoyed a bit more respect. At the very top of the servant class were the housekeeper and butler, who not only dressed and spoke (or attempted to) like the master and mistress but also supervised their fellow servants.

Peasants In the new economy-based social divisions, peasants can be considered working class as well. In Britain, while thousands of peasants left the countryside for work in the cities, some farmers who remained on the land enjoyed increasing prosperity. But peasants in Ireland lived in extreme poverty and suffered from malnutrition and catastrophic famine in the 1840s. French peasants, on the whole, lived more comfortably than peasants elsewhere, a condition that explains in part their reluctance to leave their farms and migrate to cities to work in industry.

Conditions for peasants were worst in eastern Europe, where serfdom remained. Serfs were not only impoverished but could not even leave their village without their landlord's permission. In Russia, the Habsburg empire, and the Balkan Peninsula, serfdom was not abolished until 1848 or later. Legal serfdom, combined with the extreme poverty of these countries, constituted a severe hindrance to industrial development.

Employment for the working classes was fluid. Some young men sought temporary work in the cities before returning to the village to establish a family. Peasant girls often spent several years "in service" before returning home to marry. Servants might take factory jobs, which paid better and gave them more personal freedom. Generally, however, the flow of country people to the city was one way: after living in the city, few young people wished to return to the strict supervision of elders in the boring village. Despite the crowded and unhygienic conditions of early industrial cities, for many workers, life there brought a degree of personal freedom unknown in the countryside.

Working Families

On farms and in farming villages, families worked together; in artisan shops, families were often productive units. Early factories transferred this pattern to a new location. Men, women, and children continued to work side by side. The heavier physical work, such as operating looms, was usually carried out by men. Women predominated among spinners and in other tasks that required less heavy work, as they were assumed to have more manual dexterity than men.

And children worked at a variety of light jobs, handling small spools of thread and reaching into places where adult hands could not fit. Even as industry developed, parents often chose to bring their children along with them to work rather than leave them alone at home.

Women and Children of the Working Classes Long before the factory system, women had worked alongside their menfolk in the putting-out system. Spinning wool (later, cotton) into yarn was an almost exclusively female occupation. Factory owners also liked to hire entire families as a means of reducing individual wages. Sometimes men and women would work in the same factory but in different workshops. Men always predominated in metalworking and mining. Children also worked in coal mines, where boys and girls as young as age eight pushed carts laden with coal up from narrow shafts.

Children's labor brought in much-needed income for their families, but increasingly the working family was separated by work. It no longer functioned as an economic unit. From 1802 onward, the British Parliament passed laws limiting child labor, but it was only after 1833 that these laws were really enforced. Eventually child labor was banned altogether, as reformers argued that childhood should be spent in school or at play—not in mines or textile mills. But few children actually went to school. Instead, they were excluded from factory work largely because of the increasing complexity of machines and industrial processes.

In Prussia, the employment of children under nine in factories was forbidden in 1839. In France, the Child Labor Law of 1841 forbade the employment of children under eight years of age and set down that children under age twelve could not work more than eight hours daily. King Leopold of Belgium proclaimed a similar law limiting child labor in 1842. But such laws were very hard to enforce, in particular because governments seldom wanted to pay for inspectors who would actually check factories for violations.

The employment of women was a different matter. Factory owners often preferred to hire women over men because they could pay women lower wages. Women were also less likely to cause trouble, being much less inclined to alcoholism, insubordination, and union activity. But as industrialization developed, women's work in industry was limited to certain occupational categories, especially in textiles, and was the subject of considerable debate.

Middle-class women were almost entirely shut out of paid labor. But some commentators—usually middle-class men—denounced work outside the home as endangering healthy family life for the working class as well. Others argued that women needed to be protected from the bad effects of factory work on the delicate female body and possible harm to their ability to produce healthy children. Midwives did, in fact, note that the babies of factory women were often delicate and prone to illness, and in 1847 Parliament limited the working day of women and children in textiles to ten hours. Nevertheless, women continued to work, as their wages were often necessary for the family's survival and, if single, they enjoyed the independence wage work gave them.

Everyday Life Working families' domestic life was vastly different from life in middle-class homes. Working women kept their own house and did their own washing and cooking in dwellings that were sparse and at times even squalid. Young babies had to be "farmed out" to wet nurses so that the mother could continue working. Frequently these babies died in their first months of life, and estimates of child mortality up to the age of five reach as high as 50 percent in the early to mid-nineteenth century.

One common practice for keeping infants still was to give them drugs such as **laudanum** or a highly alcoholic "cordial." Malnutrition and the conditions of early factory work had very negative consequences for these children's health. One doctor wrote that children working in the Manchester cotton mills were "almost universally ill-looking, small, sickly, barefoot and ill-clad … a degenerate race." Military leaders also complained that young men who had grown up in working-class families were smaller in stature, thinner, and less hearty than peasant lads. More generally, parents came to recognize that children—despite the pennies they might earn working in a factory—were a drain on the family's resources. As industrialization and urbanization progressed, birthrates almost always declined.

Taverns and Drinking Culture Working men sought refuge from the conditions of factory and tenement in the taverns, which were generally off-limits for respectable women. Drinking was more than an attempt to forget one's misery in an alcoholic haze; visiting the pub was an integral part of male working-class comraderie. A working man who never visited the tavern would be considered abnormal—asocial and probably thinking too highly of himself. But the money spent on drink meant that much less remained for the family's support. Not by chance women spearheaded the temperance movement, calling on men to abandon the bottle and spend more time with and money on their families.

laudanum Opium dissolved in alcohol, a popular though habit-forming sleep aid in the nineteenth century.

Charles Dickens (1812–1870) Famous English novelist, author of *Oliver Twist, A Tale of Two Cities,* and *A Christmas Carol,* among many others.

Fyodor Dostoevsky (1821–1881) Russian writer, author of *Crime and Punishment, The Brothers Karamazov,* and other novels.

Methodism Religious movement in nineteenth-century Britain that preached self-control, frugality, and hard work, appealing primarily to working-class people.

Criminality, Amusements, and Methodism Many working families barely earned a living, and the lures of the criminal world described in nineteenth-century novels were real. Like Fagin's band of boy thieves in **Charles Dickens**'s *Oliver Twist,* orphans in London's slums engaged in pickpocketing and other petty crime. Like Sonya Marmeladov in **Fyodor Dostoevsky**'s *Crime and Punishment,* young women turned to prostitution to support their families. Gin, opium, games of chance, cockfights, bearbaiting: a variety of unsavory and illegal pastimes were available in industrial cities, enriching some but impoverishing many. Yet the industrial cities held opportunities that peasant life could not offer: taverns, theaters, coffeehouses, and the dream of advancement—the chance, however slim, of making one's fortune.

Moreover, family life was not entirely dismal. Parents and children celebrated holidays and played games together. Religion provided comfort and companionship. Working-class people in Britain were often attracted to **Methodism**, a religious movement founded by John Wesley in the eighteenth century that preached self-control, frugality, hard work, and self-respect. Methodism gave working-class people a sense of mission, dignity, and community.

Methodist preachers (often themselves of working-class origin) emphasized that working people were separate from, but in no way inferior to, members of the middle and upper classes. Methodism stressed the fundamental Christian beliefs that honored the meek and humble over the rich and powerful, specifically identifying working people with Christ's teaching that the "poor in spirit" would inherit the "kingdom of heaven" and the "meek" would "inherit the earth." On a practical level, Methodist preachers often set up Sunday schools to teach workers and their children how to read and write. Methodist worship services were emotional occasions during which preachers and congregation would shout, groan, leap up, faint, and sing praises. Methodist revival meetings, often held in the open air, attracted thousands of enthusiastic worshipers in the early decades of the nineteenth century.

Working-Class Consciousness and Trade Unionism

Industrialization brought workers together in densely packed spaces. Most did not enjoy their work. Their lives were constricted by factory rules and hours, and whatever independence they might have formerly enjoyed as farmers or artisans was gone. So was pride in their craft and in the products they made: many early mass-produced goods were less durable and attractive than items produced by skilled artisans. Moreover, in the factory no one worker made something from start to finish. In a textile factory, for example, spinners spun the thread and weavers wove it into cloth. In a garment factory, one person cut the

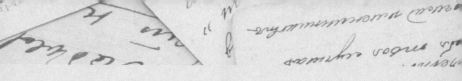

Friedrich Engels Describes the Condition of the Working Class in England

Friedrich Engels, the son of a German textile manufacturer, saw the impact of industrialization in England firsthand when his father sent him to work in a family owned textile mill there. The conditions in which working-class people labored in England appalled Engels, compelling him to write his first book, *The Condition of the Working Class in England in 1844*. Engels was only twenty-five when the book was published. It gained widespread attention and favorably impressed young Karl Marx, who soon became Engels's friend and collaborator.

❶ Name some of the ways that industrialization transformed England's society. According to Engels, how typical was England in this respect in 1844?

❷ What does Engels mean when he claims that England is "composed of classes wholly different" and "a different nation" in 1844 than it had been sixty years earlier?

❸ Why would artisans be attracted to a growing town around a factory?

❹ Describe the steps by which a factory town becomes an industrial city, according to Engels.

❺ What did Engels have in mind when he wrote of London's "marvels of civilisation?"

❻ Why do you think workers' housing, clothing, and food were of such bad quality?

❶ Sixty, eighty years ago, England was a country like every other, with small towns, few and simple industries, and a thin but *proportionally* large agricultural population. ❷ Today it is a country like *no* other; with a capital of two and a half million inhabitants; with vast manufacturing cities; with an industry that supplies the world and produces almost everything by means of the most complex machinery; with an industrious, intelligent, dense population, of which two-thirds are employed in trade and commerce, ❸ and composed of classes wholly different; forming, in fact, with other customs and other needs, a different nation from the England of those days. The Industrial Revolution is of the same importance for England as the political revolution for France.

A manufacturing establishment requires many workers employed together in a single building, living near each other and forming a village of themselves in the case of a good-sized factory. ❹ They have needs for satisfying which other people are necessary; handicraftsmen, shoemakers, tailors, bakers, carpenters, stonemasons, settle at hand. ❺ The inhabitants of the village, especially the younger generation, accustom themselves to factory work, grow skilful in it, and when the first mill can no longer employ them all, wages fall, and the immigration of fresh manufacturers is the consequence. So the village grows into a small town, and the small town into a large one.

❻ Londoners have been forced to sacrifice the best qualities of their human nature, to bring to pass all the marvels of civilisation which crowd their city.... What is true of London, is true of Manchester, Birmingham, Leeds, is true of all great towns. The dwellings of the workers are everywhere badly planned, badly built, and kept in the worst condition, badly ventilated, damp, and unwholesome. The inhabitants are confined to the smallest possible space, and at least one family usually sleeps in each room.... The clothing of the workers, too, is generally scanty, and that of great multitudes is in rags. The food is in general, bad.

Source: From The Condition of the Working Class in England in 1844, by Friedrich Engels.

cloth, another stitched only sleeves, another finished buttonholes. This division of labor was efficient, but it made work repetitive and monotonous. Workers often felt like they were cogs in a machine. Without any control over their work, they sensed they had lost a part of their humanity. Karl Marx would later attribute this sense to what he described as factory workers' **alienation** from the product of their labor.

Working-Class Resistance Increasingly, working people recognized their common interests and joined together to press for political changes that would aid them. The workers of Manchester who gathered at St. Peter's Field in 1819 were protesting the Corn Laws that kept the price of grain artificially high. Chartist protests of the 1830s and 1840s were democratic, aiming to gain political rights for working men, though women also participated. **William Cobbett**, the most famous working-class radical, argued tirelessly against child labor and the unfairness of a society in which some enjoyed great wealth while many could not provide for their most basic needs. "No society," he proclaimed, "ought to exist where the labourers live in a hog-like sort of way." Cobbett's protests help bring about Britain's 1832 Reform Act, but for many political change was too slow and not enough.

Some workers resorted to violence. In the second decade of the nineteenth century, textile workers in Britain's industrial cities occasionally destroyed their machines. As they claimed to be followers of "General Ludd," a mythical figure, they came to be known as **Luddites**. In France, artisans attacked the hated symbol of industrialization, the Jacquard loom. In the city of Lyon, the weavers' guild staged a public execution for the Jacquard loom in 1806, smashing it to bits, then setting the fragments ablaze. A generation later, worker dissatisfaction boiled over in a series of bloody riots and insurrections. The largest uprising occurred in 1831, again in Lyon, where thousands of workers, most from the silk industry, took to the streets. Government repression of these outbreaks took hundreds of lives. On a more personal level, workers avenged themselves on hated foremen by waylaying them after work, sometimes stuffing them headfirst into a sack, then soundly beating it.

Other forms of worker resistance took milder forms. Common was the practice of "blue Monday," in which workers—often hung over from overindulgence on their one day of rest—failed to show up for work. Workers also engaged in petty theft or purposely worked at a slow pace. But all these methods had one great disadvantage: the employer could at any moment, without justification, fire workers. Thus any kind of protest, absence, or work slowdown could bring unemployment—a word that is itself a product of industrialization.

Working-Class Organizing: Trade Unions Machine breaking and other forms of resistance were random and unorganized, and so were many strikes, when workers just illegally walked off the job. But coordinated efforts increasingly testified to a strengthening working-class consciousness. In Britain, the Combination Acts of 1799 and 1800 severely limited workers' ability to "combine"—that is, to organize for better wages and working conditions. This law made it necessary to disguise workers' organizations as self-help societies that collected money from members to provide support in case of injury, illness, or family emergencies. In Russia, even these organizations were illegal, and in most of Europe, **trade unions**, worker organizations that demanded higher wages and better working conditions, were suppressed until after 1850.

Britain, however, repealed the Combination Acts in 1824, allowing workers to organize openly. The repeal also permitted strikes in certain cases, but while the number of strikes did increase after 1824, most often factory owners found it easy to intimidate or simply fire union organizers and other troublemakers. Nevertheless, Parliament also took action, passing Conspiracy Laws in 1825 that again restricted the right to strike.

British unions concentrated on trying to limit work hours. The 1847 act that limited the workday for women and children to ten hours was an early success, though somewhat ironic, as women were excluded from union membership. Trade unionists claimed that working women depressed working men's wages, preferring instead to press for a "family wage," sufficient for a husband to allow his wife to stay home and raise a family. Most trade unions combined practical activities like schools and clubs with larger appeals for international working-class solidarity. So did the working-class newspapers that began to appear in France in the 1830s and 1840s, though their readership was limited.

Before 1850, working-class organizations were weak and largely ineffective. In most European countries, such as Russia and Germany, workers had no right to organize whatsoever. In Britain and France, laws restricted the ability of workers to organize and strike. Governments tended to side with factory owners against the workers, seeing investors and capitalists as necessary for economic development of the state. Improvements for workers would not come

alienation Marx's concept of the breakdown, under capitalism, of workers' pride in and identification with the product of their labor.

William Cobbett (1763–1835) English political reformer who advocated radical working-class politics, elected to Parliament after the Reform Act of 1832.

Luddites Workers and artisans who destroyed the machines depriving them of a livelihood during early stages of industrialization; now anyone who opposes technological change.

trade unions Organizations having the aim of protecting workers' rights, improving working conditions, and enhancing workers' prosperity.

until their organizations were stronger and their perspective put forward in a coherent ideology.

 **Checking In**

By yourself or with a partner, explain the significance of each of the following selected key terms:

laudanum

Charles Dickens

Fyodor Dostoevsky

Methodism

alienation

William Cobbett

Luddites

trade unions

Critics of Industrialization

◆ **How did society's view of poverty change with industrialization?**

◆ **What were the main differences between utopian socialism and Marx's scientific socialism?**

Industrialization created enormous wealth and great poverty at the same time, and the inequality between capitalist entrepreneurs and wageworkers struck many thinking people as outrageous. These critics of industrialization called for a more equal sharing of profits and even created complex schemes for perfect societies. These first socialists later were themselves criticized by Karl Marx, who insisted that their cooperative, nonviolent methods were doomed to failure. Only by organization and violent revolution, he argued, could the injustices of industrialization be righted.

Poverty in Industrial Societies

Poverty has existed as long as human society, but the poverty created by industrialization was not only more noticeable but also more frightening than rural poverty because it was concentrated in cities, close to the institutions of government and to the ruler's residence. Early concepts of the deserving (hardworking, but unlucky) and undeserving (lazy, drunken, unruly) poor were hard to apply to the situation in industrial cities.

Workers had much more money than peasants; but they also had to pay for everything, at prices that were very high, whereas peasants usually paid little or nothing for their hut or humble housing and often grew at least some of their own food. Peasant poverty fluctuated with crop yield, but there was always a social safety net, as relatives, neighbors, and even the landlord would usually help out in cases of extreme need. In the anonymous industrial city, no such safety net existed. Unlike the noble landlord, the factory owner rarely knew his workers and did not consider himself responsible for them.

Worker poverty also fluctuated with the success or failure of industrial enterprises and economies increasingly subject to boom-and-bust cycles. Because of the difficulty of obtaining reliable credit, businesses often went bankrupt, throwing all their employees out of work. Sometimes, as in the U.S. Panic of 1819, overproduction caused a general depression throughout the economy as one factory after another was forced to close down. But one very great difference between poverty before and after the Industrial Revolution must be noted. Previously, poverty meant being on the edge of starvation, and the periodic famines that swept Europe killed thousands. After industrialization, such famines no longer occurred. England and Ireland offer an example; both experienced bad harvests in the early 1840s, but industrialized England did not experience famine, whereas agricultural Ireland, also beset by the potato blight, did. The criticisms of industrialization focused less on absolute poverty than on the sharp difference in conditions of life between factory owners and their workers. These critics pointed out the inequitable distribution of wealth in a capitalist system, though they did not generally use that word. **Capitalism** is an economic system in which the means of production are privately owned and operated by individuals for a profit and in which the market plays a dominant role. Modern capitalism developed alongside industrialization, increasing the efficiency of production, extending markets around the world, but also bringing with it new social problems.

Early Socialists

The liberal response to the poverty caused by industrialization was to promote a free market that would, liberals believed, eventually increase prosperity for all. Middle-class liberals extolled individual rights, property, and rule by the most competent. They were inherently **elitist** in their insistence that wealthier and better-educated segments of society dominate in politics but at the same time potentially **egalitarian** in their emphasis on self-help, education, and hard work as the means for improving one's own economic and social condition. Other political thinkers held that the economic and political system itself made it impossible for workers to improve their lives. The discrepancy between the egalitarian ideals of middle-class liberalism and its elitism in practice fueled political **radicalism**, in particular in

capitalism Economic system characterized by private property and a market economy developed by industrialization in the nineteenth and twentieth centuries.

elitist Belief that a small and superior group of individuals (the elite) has the moral right and responsibility to make important social and political decisions.

egalitarianism (from French, "equal") Belief that all people should have the same social, political, and—in its most radical version—economic rights.

radicalism Political ideologies that strive for thoroughgoing political and social changes.

the form of **socialism**. Many early socialist writers and leaders were themselves from middle-class backgrounds, most famous among them Karl Marx and Friedrich Engels.

Socialism vs. Liberalism Liberalism championed the individual's right to property, whereas socialism put the primary emphasis on the welfare of society as a whole. Socialists disagreed on the status and morality of private property, but all agreed that the rich should share their wealth, for both moral and practical reasons. Such a social sharing was moral because every human being had a right to minimal standards of decent food and housing. It was practical because by lessening the misery of the working masses, the more fortunate classes would defuse anger and hostility that could otherwise explode into violence.

Like liberalism and nationalism, modern concepts of socialism derive from the French Revolution, which proclaimed "fraternity," or solidarity among all citizens, whether rich or poor. During the French Revolution, socialist ideas were championed by the radical **François Babeuf**. Shocked by the continued existence of poor and rich, Babeuf demanded not just legal equality for all citizens but "real equality"—that is, an elimination of differences in wealth and social status. Real equality could be achieved, Babeuf argued, only by a total elimination of private property and by state control of goods and even state-sponsored employment programs. While Babeuf made little impact at the time—he was executed in 1797—his ideas of a state in which all material goods would be shared formed a cornerstone of socialist thought.

Utopian Socialists Babeuf's ideas influenced the so-called **utopian socialists** of the early nineteenth century. The term itself comes from Karl Marx, who described these thinkers as "utopian"—that is, naive, unrealistic, and impractical—to distinguish them from his own thought, which Marx termed "scientific." Like Babeuf, the utopians looked forward to a harmonious society in which material differences would be minimized. They did not, however, advocate the total abolition of private property, nor did they foresee a violent revolution that would overturn capitalism. In the details of the social transformation they proposed, the three main utopian socialists—**Claude Henri de Saint-Simon, Charles Fourier**, and Robert Owen—differed significantly. What united them was a desire to harness industrialization to improve life for all classes, to avoid social conflicts, and in the end to create a just, attractive, and humane society.

Saint-Simon Claude Henri de Saint-Simon, born in 1760 to a noble family, was a grown man during the French Revolution and as an aristocrat came close to meeting his end at the guillotine. He fought on the American side during the Revolutionary War, made a fortune as a speculator during the 1790s, went bankrupt, and spent time in an insane asylum. Despite his aristocratic background, Saint-Simon detested kings, the nobility, and bishops. He admired British society, seeing it as a system that rewarded merit and hard work. Like the British liberals, Saint-Simon admired intelligence and the entrepreneurial spirit. But in contrast to the liberal belief that competition in a free market would benefit all, Saint-Simon emphasized social cooperation and planning, led by a dedicated, well-educated elite.

Saint-Simon's last major work, *The New Christianity* (incomplete at the time of his death in 1825), attempted to place his ideas on economic justice and a new society in a Christian framework. Surveying the history of Catholicism and Protestantism, he criticized both for failing to respond to the problem of poverty. His New Christianity, he claimed, would rejuvenate Christianity's fundamental rejection of violence and call for compassion. He charged rulers to: "Hearken to the voice of God that speaks through me. Return to the path of Christianity.... Remember that Christianity commands you to use all your powers to increase as rapidly as possible the welfare of the poor." These ideas gained considerable prominence among businessmen, intellectuals, and politicians in France, but Saint-Simon's most significant contribution was his linking of industrial growth to general social improvement rather than simply to individual enrichment.

Fourier Charles Fourier, the most visionary of the utopians, demanded a far more thorough transformation of society than Saint-Simon. Fourier was an eccentric and difficult man. He came from a family of cloth merchants and earned his living in trade. At the same time, he spent his free moments concocting a utopian scheme of grandiose proportions aimed to solve the economic, social, and even spiritual problems of society. Human beings are motivated, Fourier proposed, by twelve main passions, ranging from friendship and ambition to love of intrigue and the five senses (taste, smell, touch, sight, and hearing). While all of these passions are present in every human

socialism Political movement of the nineteenth and twentieth centuries that aimed to end industrial poverty by spreading profits throughout society.

François Babeuf (1760–1797) French revolutionary who demanded not only legal but also economic equality among all citizens.

utopian socialists Early socialists such as Saint-Simon, Fourier, and Owen who believed that the profits of industrialization should be used to improve living conditions throughout society.

Claude Henri de Saint-Simon (1760–1825) Early socialist of noble birth whose ideal society was led by an elite of technocrats.

Charles Fourier (1768–1830) French thinker who envisioned socialist communities (phalanges) having a division of labor based on passions and abilities.

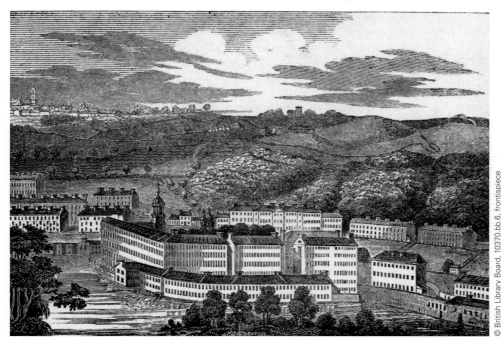

Robert Owen's community of New Lanark, in the Scottish lowlands, was an example of utopian socialism that worked. A practical businessman with a social conscience, Owen built huge brick textile factories at the falls of the River Clyde. He also provided brick dwellings for workers, paid them fair wages, and ran schools for their children. How typical do you think New Lanark was among industrial establishments of its time? What would be the positive and negative sides of living in such a "company town?"

being, the proportion of each differs greatly. Using complex and quite incomprehensible mathematical principles (Fourier left behind several notebooks containing nothing but equations and mathematical notations), he arrived at the idea of the *phalange.*

Each phalange would include 1,620 individuals, carefully selected to include a variety of "passionate types." These small communities would live and work together, each carrying out the tasks best suited to his or her (Fourier firmly believed in women's equality) passions and abilities. For example, children, who love muck and filth, would carry out trash and clean sewers. While the division of labor would be retained, it would be based on the most fundamental drives and desires of human beings and would thus enhance, not suppress, their humanity.

While inequalities in income and wealth would continue to exist in the phalange, these differences would not cause social discontent because all individuals would freely choose their own jobs and income. Children would be brought up and educated communally within the phalange, total equality would exist between women and men, and restrictions on sexual relations would disappear. Best of all, because the phalange would put human passions to their best use in a just and cooperative community, the need for coercive government, police, armies, and prisons would disappear. Fourier believed fervently that if only one phalange could be set up, its success would rapidly transform the world into a community of phalanges.

Fourier's scheme seems eccentric, but it addressed real social problems and proposed serious methods of combating them. Industrialization had condemned millions to boring, repetitive, and meaningless work in which they themselves became like machines. It had destroyed social networks that protected the poor. It had also had a devastating effect on the natural environment. Fourier's scheme attempted to give people back their humanity, to end exploitation, and to create a social order consistent with fundamental human psychology (Fourier's "passions"). Although no phalange was ever set up, Fourier's ideas in various forms certainly influenced actual egalitarian communal settlements, such as Brook Farm and the Oneida community in the United States as well as the Israeli **kibbutzim**.

Owen Robert Owen, like Fourier, believed in the inherent goodness of human nature, but Owen attempted to build practical cooperative communities. He was himself a successful industrialist who used his cotton

kibbutzim Collective agricultural settlements set up by Jewish settlers in what is now Israel in the late nineteenth century and continuing to the present.

mill at New Lanark to try out his principles. Owen believed that cooperation rather than competition would enable him to make a profit while spreading industry-generated wealth among the workers. Under his management, New Lanark became a model community in which workers enjoyed high living standards in the apartments he built for them, pleasant and hygienic surroundings, and free education for their children.

Owen tried to interest his fellow industrialists in his cooperative principles, but with little success. The community he set up in New Harmony, Indiana, failed after only a few years. In his later years, Owen was active in the trade union movement and encouraged the establishment of **consumer cooperatives** for workers, but he died a disillusioned man. Despite his failure to persuade contemporary businessmen to adopt the system of factory-paid housing and schools, his ideas influenced later industrial-residential complexes from the Soviet Union to Fiat's factory city of Turin, Italy.

The importance of the utopian socialists lies not so much in the communities that applied their ideas but in their ideas themselves, which later socialists would build on and develop. For example, Fourier's idea that a unified economic system would create a more efficient and humane society was taken up by Karl Marx and later in the Soviet Union. Fourier was also one of the first to advocate total equality between the sexes and to denounce bourgeois marriage as a form of prostitution, ideas that would be further developed by Friedrich Engels and later socialist and feminist thinkers. Saint-Simon's ideas were extremely influential in mid-nineteenth-century France (many cabinet ministers and businessmen considered themselves "Saint-Simonists"), and he can be seen as an early advocate of "technocracy," or rule by technologically trained elites. Owen's ideas have found practical application in various cooperative communities.

Karl Marx

Like most socialist thinkers, Karl Marx was middle class, not working class. His father was a lawyer of Jewish origin who converted to Christianity when Karl was a young boy, growing up in western Germany. Marx attended university in Bonn and Berlin, where he studied philosophy under **G.W.F. Hegel**, whose systematic thought would prove an important source for Marx's own ideas. Marx's passionate personality, which gained him many friends and many bitter enemies, developed early. As a university student, he believed that philosophy was the best method for understanding the world. Soon, however, Marx was ready to go beyond philosophy: "Philosophers have only interpreted the world in various ways," he stated. "The point, however, is to change it." Marx's quest to change the world would make him one of the most loved and hated figures in the late nineteenth and twentieth centuries.

Threatened with arrest by the Prussian authorities in the 1840s because of his radical views, Marx left his homeland. After the publication of *The Communist Manifesto* in 1848, he always lived abroad. During this decade he also married, started a family, and began his famous collaboration with Friedrich Engels. Meeting first in Paris in 1844, the two men quickly formed one of the closest and most productive friendships in history. Engels's *Condition of the Working Class in England* (1845) showed that he was far more familiar with the actual conditions of industrial workers than Marx was, but Marx possessed the greater theoretical mind. Engels was less of an original thinker than Marx but far more practical and easygoing—and much more successful in business. Few days in the next four decades went by without letters between the "Moor" (Marx) and the "General" (Engels), as they jokingly referred to each other.

The Communist Manifesto Marx's most famous early work, coauthored with Engels, *The Communist Manifesto,* appeared during the revolutions of 1848. In a few dozen pages, the *Manifesto* denounced bourgeois society as hypocritical, exploitative, and doomed to destruction: "A specter is haunting Europe—the specter of Communism." Marx used the term **communism** to distinguish his more radical thinking—based on class struggle and an inevitable violent revolution—from the less confrontational schemes of earlier socialists. *The Communist Manifesto* set down in stirring language both an ideological justification and a practical program for a thoroughgoing revolution: "Workers of the world unite!"

Marx, Hegel, and the Dialectic of History Marx's program was based on the philosophy of Hegel, who had argued that history progresses in a **dialectical** way. That is, in history, an idea that becomes prominent is inevitably challenged by its opposite, and the resolution of these two opposing principles produces a higher idea. Marx's philosophical innovation was to apply this principle to the material world and to argue that this struggle over ideas would produce revolutionary change in the economic, political, and social structure of society.

consumer cooperatives Organizations of consumers who band together to obtain better prices from producers and share any profits derived from sales.

G.W.F. Hegel (1770–1831) Important philosopher of the nineteenth century whose philosophy of historical progress was crucial for Marx.

communism Radical political philosophy proposed by Karl Marx, advocating the abolition of private property and an inevitable violent workers' revolution.

dialectical Process of thought that achieves a higher synthesis by reconciling two contradictory ideas ("thesis" and "anti-thesis").

For Marx, history could be understood as class struggle: slaves versus slave owners, serfs versus lords, and now the proletariat versus the capitalists. Marx allowed that the capitalists had previously played a progressive and even revolutionary role in history by challenging the old economic order based on landed wealth and replacing it with industrial capitalism. Now, however, the leading position had to shift away from the capitalists—the bourgeois middle class to the industrial workers, the proletariat. In the end, Marx insisted, the working masses would rise in revolt, strip the bourgeoisie of their wealth and power, and create a just, egalitarian society.

Marx and Revolution Marx's practical program was violent revolution, which he saw as the natural outcome of inevitable class struggle. It would be naive, he wrote scornfully, to imagine that the bourgeoisie would relinquish their wealth and power without a fight. Here Marx differed significantly from the utopian socialists, who stressed cooperation over violence, and he termed his program "scientific" to distinguish it from theirs. The utopian socialists, Marx claimed, had a faulty understanding of history, economics, and society. Thinking that persuasion and cooperative efforts could do away with the proletariat's misery, Marx thundered, was both absurd and reactionary. Rather, workers had to organize and seize power themselves to achieve a just society. The contours of this future society may be seen by the specific goals mentioned in *The Communist Manifesto:* free education for all children, the abolition of inheritance and landed property, state control of credit and transportation, a **progressive income tax**, and an end to the distinction between urban and rural areas by spreading cultural and educational institutions outside of cities.

The impact of Marx's writing on the revolutions of 1848 was minimal. But Marx put forth his ideas about class struggle and the need for revolution at this time and then spent the rest of his life gathering and analyzing data to support his thesis. In the second half of the nineteenth century, the influence of his and Engels's ideas would grow. By the end of the century, self-proclaimed Marxist parties existed in most European countries. Even more important, liberals and even conservatives came to recognize that to avoid "communist revolution," they needed to respond to worker demands for improved working conditions and increased pay.

> **progressive income tax** Tax on money earned, with high earners paying a greater percentage of income than individuals earning less.

 Checking In

By yourself or with a partner, explain the significance of each of the following selected key terms:

capitalism	Claude Henri de
socialism	Saint-Simon
François Babeuf	Charles Fourier
utopian socialists	G.W.F. Hegel

Summary

- Industrialization began first in Great Britain in the late eighteenth century.

- By 1850, industrialization had spread to Belgium and parts of France, the German lands, and elsewhere in continental Europe.

- Industrialization made cities grow, often causing terrible living conditions.

- Industrialization helped create the socioeconomic category of class, a consciousness based on one's place in the economy.

- Middle-class people saw themselves as "self-made" and respected education, sobriety, and hard work.

- Working-class people, despite the appalling conditions of work, also strove for respectability with such movements as Methodism.

- Working-class organizations strove for better working conditions, shorter hours, and to exclude children from the industrial workforce.

- Utopian socialists like Saint-Simon, Fourier, and Owen tried to solve the problems of industrialization through cooperation.

- Karl Marx, who termed his own thinking "scientific socialism," argued that only violent revolution would bring justice to the working class.

Chronology

1799–1800	English Combination Acts prohibit strikes and unions	**1834**	Zollverein (German Customs Union) established to promote trade
1801	Joseph Marie Jacquard invents the automated loom	**1835**	First German railroad opens
1810s	Luddites revolt in England	**1838**	Iron steamships compete in race across the Atlantic to New York
1815	British Parliament passes Corn Laws	**1839**	Prussia forbids the employment of children under nine in factories
1815	End of Napoleonic Wars	**1840s**	Beginnings of industrialization in central Europe
1820s	Industrialization begins in Belgium, northern France	**1847**	British Factory Act limits the number of hours women and children can work in textile factories
1824	Repeal of Combination Acts permits labor unions	**1848**	Revolutions sweep Europe; Marx and Engels publish *The Communist Manifesto*
1829	First steam locomotive, the *Rocket,* travels from Liverpool to Manchester in test race	**1851**	First major Russian railway opens, linking Moscow and St. Petersburg; Half of English population lives in cities
1830s–early 1840s	Chartists protest British Corn Laws	**1859**	Samuel Smiles publishes *Self-Help*
1831	Belgium's independence encourages industry		
1831	Workers in Lyon destroy Jacquard loom to protest industrialization		

© Cengage Learning

Test Yourself

To gauge your mastery of the material in this chapter, answer the questions below. More than one answer may be correct.

The Spread of Industrialization

1. Industrialization on the European continent lagged behind Great Britain because:

a. Great Britain had better supplies of iron ore and coals in easy-to-get-to places.

b. As an island country, Britain avoided most of the disruption and destruction of the Napoleonic wars.

c. Few European countries had access to waterways that could rival Britain's.

d. Britain worked hard to prevent its technological advances from spreading to Europe.

e. Britain's "head start" in industrialization made it hard for European industry to compete.

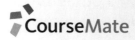

Visit the CourseMate website at **www.cengagebrain.com** for additional study tools and review materials for this chapter.

2. Industrialization in France:

a. Was hindered by artisan and luxury-manufacture traditions.
b. Was held up by the Napoleonic Wars.
c. Was actively encouraged by government policy before and after 1815.
d. Soon spread throughout the country, not being concentrated in certain regions.
e. Quickly surpassed Britain in part due to the invention of interchangeable parts by Joseph Marie Jacquard.

3. Railroads were important for industrialization on the continent because:

a. They transported both raw materials and finished goods.
b. The manufacture of rails, locomotives, and railroad wagons was itself a major industrial branch.
c. They brought new people into cities who often ended up working in industry.
d. They eliminated class distinctions entirely.
e. They completely eliminated the need for transport on roads, waterways, and by steamships.

4. The English city of Manchester is important for early industrialization because:

a. It was a spectacular example of urbanization, with its population growing twenty-fold over the century from 1750.
b. It made a number of factory owners very rich indeed.
c. It demonstrated the ability of industry and the natural environment to coexist, as industrialists worked to prevent pollution from their factories.
d. It was an excellent and healthy place to work.
e. Its poverty encouraged social activists like Friedrich Engels to demand radical reform or even revolution.

5. Industrialization's social and political effects included:

a. Strengthening of class consciousness, the feeling of belonging to a specific economic group.
b. A general lowering of living standards over the long run.
c. Dismay on the part of conservatives who feared the now more mobile lower classes.
d. Far higher level of industrial pollution in and around new manufacturing centers.
e. A heightened level of physical and social mobility.

Now that you have reviewed and tested yourself on this part of the chapter, take time to pull together all the important information by answering the following questions:

◆ Where did industrialization begin on the European continent? What countries lagged behind?

◆ How did new forms of transportation created by industrialization change everyday life?

The Middle Classes

6. Professions that in nineteenth-century Europe would be considered "middle class" included:

a. Noble landowner
b. Teacher
c. Lawyer
d. Rich factory owner
e. Industrial worker

7. Middle-class culture stressed:

a. The unfettered genius, just as did the Romantics.
b. Hard work and sobriety.
c. Individual achievements and property.
d. Education.
e. Religious ecstasy, as in revival meetings.

8. Middle-class households in the nineteenth century were characterized by:

a. Mothers who usually worked outside the home.
b. A distinction between home and workplace.
c. Women as consumers and managers of the household economy.
d. A respect for education and hard work.
e. An assumption that nearly any normal person would marry.

9. Which of these important historical figures would be considered middle class?

    a. Friedrich Engels
    b. Samuel Smiles
    c. The Duke of Wellington
    d. George Eliot
    e. Jane Austen

10. Reform Judaism appealed to many middle-class Jews because it:

    a. Reduced the visible external differences between Jewish and Christian worship.
    b. Aimed to integrate Jews into the mainstream of social and political life.
    c. Allowed Jews to resemble their Christian neighbors in nearly every way.
    d. Encouraged the growth of antisemitism.
    e. Declared that Jews formed their own nation and should move to Palestine.

Now that you have reviewed and tested yourself on this part of the chapter, take time to pull together all the important information by answering the following questions:

◆ How were the middle classes set off from "upper" and "lower" classes?

◆ What were some of the characteristics of "middle-class respectability?"

Working Classes

11. Which of the following professions would not be considered "working class" in nineteenth-century Europe?

    a. Teachers
    b. Doctors
    c. Skilled factory workers
    d. Peasants
    e. Servants

12. What impact did industrialization have on the working classes?

    a. It greatly increased the number of peasants working the land.
    b. It brought thousands of young girls to the growing cities to work as servants.
    c. It increased artisan work for tailors, shoemakers, and the like.
    d. It increased job stability and decreased mobility.
    e. It brought the family together as all family members now worked together in the factory as never before.

13. What were the negative impacts of industrialization on working people?

    a. Long and dangerous working hours.
    b. Wages that were less than peasants generally earned.
    c. Crowded and unhygienic living conditions.
    d. Increased use of drugs and alcohol.
    e. Larger numbers of women turning to prostitution to pay the bills.

14. In the first half of the nineteenth century, trade unions:

    a. Grew in strength as industrialization developed in England and elsewhere.
    b. Were illegal in most European countries.
    c. Were heavily influenced by Karl Marx and his theory of alienation.
    d. Had to contend with hostility from government and factory owners alike.
    e. Began to organize in Britain after the repeal of the Combination Acts in 1824.

15. Children were employed without restriction in factories until approximately:

    a. The 1830s in Britain, though an initial law had been passed in 1802.
    b. 1841 in France.
    c. The 1880s in Belgium.
    d. 1839 in Prussia.
    e. 1920 in Russia.

Now that you have reviewed and tested yourself on this part of the chapter, take time to pull together all the important information by answering the following questions:

◆ Who made up the "working classes?"

◆ How did industrialization affect family life and gender relations?

Critics of Industrialization

16. Which were changes in poverty caused by industrialization?
    a. Industrialization increased absolute levels of poverty.
    b. Industrialization created a greater gap between the rich and the poor.
    c. Industrialization concentrated poverty so it was more noticeable.
    d. Early capitalism tended to run in booms and busts, creating large levels of unemployment (and hence poverty) at certain intervals.
    e. Criticisms of industrialization by socialists demanded a return to preindustrial relations.

17. Who among the following thinkers is not an early socialist?
    a. Charles Fourier
    b. Friedrich Engels
    c. Claude Henri de Saint-Simon
    d. Robert Owens
    e. François Babeuf

18. Karl Marx's political philosophy differed from that of the "utopian socialists" primarily in:
    a. His antagonism toward capitalism and liberals.
    b. His elitist concept of cultivating a small group of professional revolutionaries.
    c. His insistence that not reform but only violent revolution based on the class struggle would bring about meaningful change.
    d. A program to create cooperatives to reform capitalism without violence.
    e. An extremely radical approach toward gender relations that would, among other things, end all restrictions on sexual relations.

19. The utopian socialists:
    a. Invented this term to describe their own political philosophy.
    b. Included Fourier and Saint-Simon.
    c. Were led by Karl Marx and Friedrich Engels.
    d. Emphasized cooperation with capitalism and reform rather than violent revolution.
    e. Influenced later experiments in communal living, such as the Israeli kibbutzim.

20. Marx and Engel's *The Communist Manifesto* is important because:
    a. It caused the Revolution of 1848.
    b. It set down a clear political program based on class struggle and violent revolution.
    c. It was immediately popular among workers and was quickly translated into dozens of languages.
    d. It applied Hegelian historical principles to socioeconomic relations, concluding that class struggle was the prime mover in history.
    e. It was a bestseller and made both men rich.

Now that you have reviewed and tested yourself on this part of the chapter, take time to pull together all the important information by answering the following questions:

◆ On what grounds did socialists criticize liberalism?

◆ How did individual "utopian socialists" plan to reform capitalism to create a better, more just society?

CHAPTER 22

The Triumph of the Nation-State, 1848–1900

Chapter Outline

1800	1805	1810	1815	1820	1825
		1810s Luddite revolts protest industrialization in England	**1815** Napoleon is finally defeated at Waterloo	**1820s** Industrialization begins in Belgium and northern France	**1824** British Combination Acts are repealed

The Bologna Civil Guard is depicted here as upholding the city's finest traditions. The words "sovereign people," "honor," and "fatherland" make clear that the guards saw themselves not just as citizens of a city, but as Italians. This image reflects the liberal civic nationalism that succeeded in unifying Italy during these years. (Alfredo Dagli Orti/Art Resource, NY)

After reading this chapter, you should be able to answer the following questions:

What was importance of the revolutions of 1848?

How did the ideologies of liberalism and nationalism affect the revolutions of 1848?

What were the main events and individuals that led to the unification of Germany and Italy?

How and why did nationalism shift from a liberal to a conservative ideology after 1848?

Where and under what circumstances did democratic institutions like constitutions and parliaments spread throughout Europe in the decades after 1848?

What were some of the different ways state (government) power grew in this period?

THE WORLD AS WE KNOW it—politically, economically, socially—took shape in the second half of the nineteenth century. While political "isms" like nationalism, liberalism, and socialism can be traced back to the French Revolution and earlier, from the 1850s onward these ideologies fundamentally altered political and social life. It was precisely during this period that many Europeans identified with and demanded rights for their nations. Similarly, although the Industrial Revolution had started in Britain in the late eighteenth century, only during the second half of the nineteenth century did large-scale industrialization begin to affect the lives of people all over Europe and elsewhere in the world. The growth of technology and industrialization came together with new forms of politics to create a new and more democratic Europe after 1848. In that year, liberal democratic institutions existed in few European countries, and constitutionalism as a practical political program was almost unknown. By 1906, even conservative states like the German and Russian empires had adopted some aspects of constitutional government.

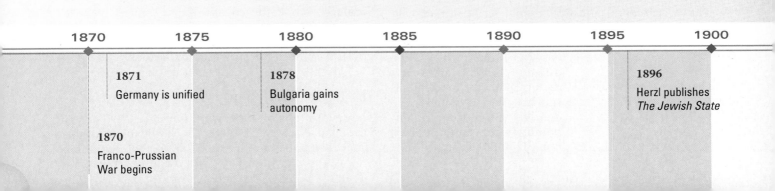

1870	1875	1880	1885	1890	1895	1900

1871
Germany is unified

1878
Bulgaria gains autonomy

1896
Herzl publishes
The Jewish State

1870
Franco-Prussian War begins

Perhaps the single most potent political force of this period was nationalism. Increasingly, people identified themselves with a national group instead of with their village, social class, or religion. Europeans came to accept the nationalist principle that all members of one nation should live together politically as citizens of a single state. At the same time, the definition of who belonged in a certain nation was contested, and many conservative multinational states opposed nationalism as a dangerous, even revolutionary, idea.

Political leaders, recognizing the force of nationalism, began to define their actions in terms of the "national will." The spread of nationalist rhetoric meant that even kings and emperors found it necessary to wrap themselves in the national banner. Before 1848, nationalism and liberalism tended to be aligned, both opposing the prevailing conservative and monarchist order symbolized by Clemens von Metternich in Vienna. After 1848, it was the conservatives who used nationalist ideology for their own political aims.

By the end of the nineteenth century, nationalism had gained broad acceptance, especially in western and central Europe. Even so, nationalism was not without its opponents. The growing socialist movement argued against the aggressive demands and divisions of nationalism, calling for working men of all nations to unite against the capitalists. Socialists emphasized class identity over nationality. The Catholic Church also opposed nationalism, particularly after the formation of the secular and implicitly anticlerical Italian state in the 1860s. The rulers of conservative multinational empires in central and eastern Europe understood that nationalism threatened their empires' very existence. In different and often contradictory ways, Habsburg, Ottoman, and Romanov rulers attempted to neutralize the growing power of nationalist ideology. In the end, however, not nationalism but these empires were swept away.

The Revolutions of 1848

◆ **What changes did the revolutionaries of 1848 demand?**

◆ **What were the short- and long-term outcomes of the uprisings in 1848?**

In 1848, revolutions across Europe ended the conservative, antiliberal, and antinational period initiated at the Congress of Vienna and symbolized by the Austrian Prime Minister Clemens von Metternich. While different circumstances in each capital city and region sparked the uprisings, all demanded a broadening of political rights and recognition of nationalist concerns.

revolutions of 1848 Series of upheavals that shook Europe from Sicily to Paris to Berlin to Vienna, bringing first liberal change, then generally conservative reaction.

In the short run, all were unsuccessful. The Prussian king and Austrian emperor were threatened but remained on their thrones. In France, the newly elected president, Louis Napoleon, declared himself Emperor Napoleon III and crushed political opposition. Still, the failure of 1848 helped pave the way for the triumph of national ideas—though not of liberalism—some twenty years later, when the nation-states of Italy and Germany were created. Similarly, while the constitutions granted in 1848 were not always respected, the precedent of constitutional rule had been established and would gain political authority in subsequent decades.

The Tide of Revolution

The **revolutions of 1848** swept through nearly every European country. Only those on the periphery—Great Britain, Scandinavia, Russia, the Ottoman

Map 22.1 **Political Europe in 1900** The force of nationalism can be seen in the changing boundaries of European states between 1815 and 1900. Observe the political boundaries on this map from 1900, then compare it with the map of Europe after the Congress of Vienna (p. 597). © Cengage Learning

1. What are the most significant changes between these maps?
2. What new countries appeared over that time?
3. Where did nationalism play the most important role in determining political boundaries?
4. Which countries can be termed "nation-states" and which are not?

Empire—were spared. But even in these undisturbed regions, rulers and privileged classes were shocked and terrified. In Russia, for example, the government increased censorship and repressed radical thinkers. In Britain, increased police surveillance following the Chartist agitation prevented revolution, but Queen Victoria regarded the events on the continent with worry.

The first uprising began in January 1848 in Sicily. Street demonstrations in Palermo and Naples forced the reactionary ruler of the Kingdom of the Two Sicilies, as the southern Italian state was known, to form a liberal government and issue a constitution. These liberal concessions in one of the most conservative regions of Europe electrified rulers and liberals alike.

1848 in France Then, in February 1848, Louis Philippe, France's "bourgeois king," was forced to **abdicate**. Since his coronation in 1830 as "King of the French," Louis Philippe had attempted to steer a compromise course between the demands of royalist aristocrats and the new, wealthy bourgeoisie. Most Frenchmen, even of the middle class, continued to be shut out of the political process.

In the mid-1840s, middle-class protesters began to join with broader peasant and working-class movements demanding relief in the face of bad harvests and unemployment. Because political meetings were illegal, in 1847 a banquet campaign was launched. The king could hardly forbid Frenchmen from eating! As everyone understood, the main purpose of these banquets was not cuisine but politics; banquet speakers called for an extension of the vote, even universal male suffrage. When the government tried to prevent a "monster banquet" in February 1848, clashes with police and would-be banqueters and students escalated into major street battles. Seeing no way out of the situation, Louis Philippe abdicated and fled to London. France was declared a republic, and the revolutionaries began the task of creating a new government.

With the monarchy swept away, the liberals and radicals began to quarrel. When the **national workshops**, set up in March 1848 to provide relief and work for the jobless, could not keep pace with growing unemployment, moderate liberals began to grumble about supporting the lazy at the taxpayers' expense. Business leaders, too, denounced the national workshops as unfair competition and an unbearable tax burden. Yet thousands of impoverished men continued to stream into Paris, and many feared the collapse of public order.

Elections in April revealed another growing divide—between Paris and the provinces. Voters in the provinces overwhelmingly supported moderate or even conservative candidates, whereas in Paris radicals managed—barely—to send radical and socialist delegates such as **Louis Blanc** to the National Assembly. Meanwhile the turmoil on the streets of Paris intensified. On May 15, large crowds declared the parliament dissolved and attempted to set up their own radical government. This attempt ended in failure and arrests, but tensions continued.

1848 in Central Europe As Metternich once quipped, "When Paris sneezes, Europe catches cold." News of the Paris upheavals quickly reached Berlin, Vienna, and other central European cities, where liberals soon demanded similar political concessions from their rulers. In the Habsburg lands, street fighting in May forced the imperial family to abandon Vienna for a more easily guarded country estate. Metternich resigned and fled the city alone. In Berlin clashes between the army and local citizens left many dead. The outrage over the killings was so great that Prussian king **Frederick William IV** felt himself compelled to issue a constitution and salute as heroes the bodies of those shot by his own troops.

Liberal Germans, casting themselves as representatives of the German nation, demanded a unified Germany and organized elections for a **constituent assembly**, which met in late spring at Saint Paul's Church in Frankfurt. Among the more than four hundred elected representatives who gathered to write a constitution, with political rights for all, were lawyers, government officials, and professors, including the Grimm brothers, now at work on their German dictionary. Although there were also four artisans, thirty-four landowners, and one peasant, this **Frankfurt Assembly**, in which 90 percent of the representatives were educated, was indeed a "parliament of scholars."

The nationalism apparent in the Frankfurt Assembly's anticipation of a unified Germany was also at work in Hungary. The Hungarian elite, especially, resented the power of the central government in Vienna. In March, led by the fiery speaker **Louis (Lájos) Kossuth**, they demanded an end to imperial rule and the establishment of a Hungarian parliament. The Austrian Habsburgs were at first conciliatory, but

abdicate To give up one's position as ruler, usually said of kings.

national workshops Paris institutions set up in 1848 to give work to the unemployed at government expense.

Louis Blanc (1811–1882) French socialist who advocated the right to work and the abolition of competition.

Frederick William IV King of Prussia (r. 1840–1861) who issued a constitution during the Berlin revolution of 1848.

constituent assembly Meeting to draw up a constitution or to agree on basic fundamentals of a governing system.

Frankfurt Assembly Representatives elected throughout German states who met in Frankfurt (1848–1849) to draft a liberal constitution for a united German Empire.

Louis (Lájos) Kossuth (1802–1894) Hungarian statesman who led his people in revolt against the Habsburg (Austrian) empire during 1848 and 1849.

During 1848, revolutionaries built barricades in the streets of many cities, as in this image of a barricade built during the March 1848 uprising in Berlin. The rebels fly the black-red-gold tricolor of German liberalism and fight for a united, liberal Germany against the Prussian king's troops. How does this image reflect the patriotic feelings of the German nationalists in 1848?

when the newly elected Hungarian parliament voted to create its own army and currency, the emperor sent in troops, and a regular war ensued between Austrian (imperial) and Hungarian forces.

1848 in Italy In the Italian states, revolution also seemed to triumph in the spring of 1848. The insurrections spread from Naples to Milan (then belonging to the Habsburg empire), Venice (where a republic was declared), and Rome. In Rome, the rebels took over the city as traditional authorities fled—and the pope sought refuge outside of town in the fortress of Gaeta. Giuseppe Mazzini and Giuseppe Garibaldi worked together to build a "Rome of the People," establishing freedom of the press, setting up secular schools, and handing over some church property to the poor.

The Restoration of Authority

If in spring the revolutionaries seemed to be winning, by early summer the forces of traditional authority had gained strength, and by fall the revolutions had been stamped out nearly everywhere. In Paris, tensions between moderates and radicals led to a bloody clash set off by the moderates' abolition of the national workshops in late June. These might have been dismantled without bloodshed had the government moved slowly. Instead, the overnight action sparked an armed workers' uprising, in which more than 1,500 people, including the archbishop of Paris, were killed. After suppressing the uprising, government forces massacred more than three thousand workers. The violence, known as the June Days, demonstrated that liberal governments, like monarchies and conservative regimes, were willing to use violence against political opponents. After June 1848, the forces of moderation and order were firmly in control in Paris.

In December 1848, French voters overwhelmingly chose Louis Napoleon, a nephew of the great Napoleon, as president of the French Republic. Their longing for order after a year of revolution would help pave the way to his dictatorship as Emperor **Napoleon III**, beginning in 1852. Thus the immediate outcome in France of the 1848 revolution was not a liberal republic but the Second Empire, which lasted until 1870.

Nationalism and Authority in the Habsburg Lands The situation in the Habsburg empire was complicated by its numerous nationalities and the strife between them. When the Hungarians declared their independence from Vienna, the Hungarian dependency of Croatia aligned itself with the Habsburg emperor. Similarly, German liberals in Prague were offended when the eminent Czech historian František Palacký refused to participate in elections to the Frankfurt Assembly. Palacký pointed out that he was not a German but a Czech who was loyal to the Habsburg empire. Believing that cultural and political rights of small nations like his were better assured in a large multinational empire than in a nation-state like the one the representatives at Frankfurt envisioned, Palacký declared, "If Austria did not exist," he wrote, "it would be necessary to invent her."

Unlike the Germans and Hungarians, smaller national groups in the Habsburg empire did not aspire to political independence but hoped only to be allowed to use their own language in schools, publishing, and perhaps in government offices. The **Slavic Congress**, held in Prague in June 1848, asserted its loyalty to the Habsburg empire while advocating recognition for Slavic languages (Czech, Slovak, Croatian) as equals of German. It also called for closer relations between the Slavic peoples of the Habsburg empire and Slavs in the Russian and Ottoman empires. The congress was dissolved at gunpoint by forces loyal to the new Habsburg emperor, **Francis Joseph**.

By late 1848, the emperor was back in a now subdued Vienna. The imperial army had established order in northern Italy and in the Czech lands and was gearing up for battle with the Hungarians. But the Hungarians proved hard to defeat, surrendering only after Russian units had come to the aid of the Austrians. Francis Joseph repudiated the constitution he had agreed to in 1848 and vowed to rule as an absolute ruler. As in France, in the Habsburg lands it appeared that the upheavals had all been for nothing.

Liberals Defeated in the German Lands In the German Confederation, the revolution ended less violently. Except in Berlin, German states had generally avoided clashes with their citizens. Most German princes retained power after 1848, though mainly after promising liberal political reforms. Since May, the Frankfurt Assembly had been debating plans to unify Germany: Should Germans unite under Habsburg rule, the so-called *grossdeutsch*, or "big German," solution, or should a new German Empire be formed with the Prussian king at its head, the *kleindeutsch*, or "small German," solution? At first, most delegates favored the *grossdeutsch* solution. But Francis Joseph could not agree to being the head of a German national state when over half of his subjects in the Austrian and Hungarian lands were non-Germans. After this refusal, the Frankfurt Assembly offered the crown of the future German Empire to King Frederick William IV of Prussia. Frederick William indignantly refused, calling the offer "from the gutter" and the crown a "diadem moulded out of the dirt and dregs of revolution, disloyalty and treason."

Rebutted by Austrian emperor and Prussian king, the Frankfurt Assembly found itself in an impossible position. Lacking the will or ability to revolt against existing German princes, it was attacked as too conservative by radicals and workers. Ironically, the assembly was rescued by Prussian troops, and the "scholars" were unceremoniously sent home. Sporadic attempts at revolution were countered everywhere in the German lands by military action.

By the end of 1849, the revolutions were over. In Paris, a moderate liberal government had demonstrated brutality toward its opponents. In the Italian lands, most of the same rulers were in place, despite a flurry of granted constitutions and promised political rights. In Berlin, the Prussian king was in control, and thousands of liberals and radicals were under arrest, in hiding, or already in exile. Friedrich Engels and Karl Marx would live the rest of their lives in England, but many "Forty-Eighters" fled to the United States. In Vienna, the Habsburg emperor was once again firmly in power. Despite the apparent calm, however, few of the political, national, or social demands of the revolutionaries had been dealt with, and the issues would be raised again. In retrospect, 1848 was a watershed.

1848 as a Watershed Year

The role of ideology in the revolutions of 1848 is complex. There is no doubt about the importance of liberal ideals such as constitutionalism, civil rights, and the rule of law to those who tried to overthrow regimes in Sicily, Paris, Vienna, and Berlin. But when moderate liberals were confronted with radical and socialist demands and the destruction of private property, they joined with conservatives in calling for order. In central Europe, nationalist revolutionaries promoted liberal ideas, only to find themselves opposed by other liberal nationalists who remained loyal to traditional authority. In central Europe, nationalist slogans

---

Napoleon III (r. 1852–1870) Louis Napoleon, nephew of Napoleon Bonaparte, who was elected president of France in 1848 and declared himself emperor in 1852.

Slavic Congress Assembly of Slavic nations—Poles, Balkan peoples, Czechs, Ukrainians, and one Russian—in Prague in 1848 that called for cultural recognition for Slavs.

Francis Joseph (r. 1848–1916) Habsburg emperor of Austria from 1848 and king of Hungary from 1867.

Map 22.2 **Revolutions of 1848** In 1848 revolutions swept many European countries. © *Cengage Learning*

1. Which countries were most affected by these revolutions?
2. Where did revolutions not happen, and why?

combined with liberal ideas and proposals. Socialist ideas were also discussed, though the actual influence of socialism in 1848 was small.

Liberalism, Socialism, and Nationalism Liberalism was certainly the most important political ideology in 1848. The revolutionaries called for constitutions, popular representation, and an end to censorship. In Paris, liberalism momentarily triumphed, then was challenged from the left. In central Europe, middle-class liberals learned that the masses of workers and peasants were not always willing to follow their lead, especially if liberal policies did not also promote low bread prices, decent wages, and employment opportunities.

Marx and Engels's *The Communist Manifesto*, published in 1848, had been written before the revolutionary outbreaks, and its immediate influence was small, in part because it was available only in German. Socialist ideas such as the abolition of inheritance and landed property, state control of credit and

transportation, and free education had not yet gained broad support. Only in Paris did avowed socialists like Louis Blanc, father of the national workshops, play a significant part in the revolutions. On the whole, rebelling workers and peasants in 1848 knew nothing about socialism. Their demands were more tangible: lower taxes, cheaper food, jobs. Only later in the nineteenth century would Marx's pamphlet become basic reading for a mass audience.

Nationalism played a very visible role in 1848, though it scored few victories. Neither Germany nor Italy was united, the Hungarian attempt to secure autonomy and national rights was put down by Vienna, and the Slavic Congress in Prague was dissolved. In most parts of Europe, most people did not yet think in national terms. People spoke local dialects that were often far from standard written forms of, say, the German language that the Grimm brothers were working so hard to define. People identified themselves more often as inhabitants of a village, as Catholics, or as Jews than as Hungarians or Czechs or Germans. But nationalist movements in 1848 helped popularize the idea that languages like Czech, Ukrainian, Romanian, Slovak, and Croatian deserved respect—and rights. Crucially, the central idea of nationalism—that a state must defend the values of a nation—was expressed by revolutionaries from Paris to Berlin, from Palermo to Budapest. Although the revolutions of 1848 did not establish nation-states in central Europe, they helped spread the ideals of nationalism.

Changes in Political Ideology After 1848 After 1848, the political center shifted significantly to the left. Few thinking Europeans continued to defend divine-right monarchy, and increasing numbers of educated middle-class people embraced political liberalism or even socialism as solutions to society's problems. The liberals are particularly interesting in this context. Before 1848, they constituted a small minority in the politics of every European country save Britain. After midcentury, liberal ideas and liberal figures took on new importance not only in Britain, France, and other western European countries, but even in Russia, the Habsburg lands (after 1867, Austria-Hungary), and southern Europe. Thus the liberals who were defeated in 1848 had by 1900 become an important—in some cases, a predominant—part of the political landscape. And by this time they recognized that the greatest challenge to liberalism came not from conservatives but from the growing socialist movement.

Yet conservatism was not dead. The peasant unrest of 1848 convinced rulers to abolish the last vestiges of serfdom in Europe, except in Russia. After 1848, the peasantry in western and central Europe became a bulwark of conservative and religious forces. The Catholic Church, badly shaken by the year's events, which had temporarily forced Pope **Pius IX** to flee from Rome, turned away from any kind of liberal reform. Until nearly the end of the century, the Catholic Church would be a solid bulwark of traditional authority, condemning constitutions, nationalism, and popular representation in government.

Many of the rejected national demands of 1848 were resurrected a generation or so later. Italian unification took place in the 1860s, partly through Garibaldi's continued efforts. The Hungarian demands to Vienna in 1848 were granted two decades later in the **Compromise of 1867**, which gave the Hungarians domestic autonomy in the empire. The Slavic Congress of 1848 can be seen as a precursor of the Pan-Slav movement of the 1870s that aimed to unite all Slavic peoples from the Adriatic to the Pacific under the Romanovs. Thus immediate failures of 1848 masked future triumphs.

 Checking In

By yourself or with a partner, explain the significance of each of the following selected key terms:

revolutions of 1848	Napoleon III
national workshops	Slavic Congress
Frankfurt Assembly	Francis Joseph
Louis (Lájos) Kossuth	Compromise of 1867

New Nation-States and Nationalist Tensions

◆ **How, in politics and personalities, were the processes of German and Italian unification similar?**

◆ **How did nationality identity differ in Poland, Bulgaria, and Norway? How do you explain these differences?**

In the second half of the nineteenth century, nationalists translated their ideas into political realities. The greatest triumph of the national principle was the creation of two large, unified states in the middle of Europe: Italy and Germany. Both had conservative constitutions under powerful monarchs (the Prussian king took on the title of Kaiser [emperor], to the disappointment of liberal nationalists. Norway and Bulgaria also became independent states in this era. Nations lacking states stressed ethnic unity and linguistic solidarity. Throughout Europe, nationalism became exclusionary. Across the Atlantic, the United States experienced a mass immigration of European peoples.

The Unification of Italy

Since the 1830s, the idea of the Italian nation had been promoted by Giuseppe Mazzini, who exemplified the enthusiasm and almost mystical quality of early, liberal nationalism. His impassioned writings reminded Italians of their glorious Roman past and called for national unity, democracy, and equal rights for all. Mazzini inspired thousands of his countrymen to think beyond the boundaries of their local town or community and aspire to be "Italians." He demanded "a sacred devotion to the fatherland" and urged Italian men to "cancel from your minds every idea of superiority over Women." Mazzini's importance lies in his writings and the enthusiasm for the Italian idea he spread.

Pius IX (r. 1846–1878) Pope who became a staunch conservative, refusing to acknowledge Italian unification and condemning all forms of modernity.

Compromise of 1867 Agreement between Austria and Hungary dividing the country into two autonomous parts, linked by a common budget, military, and foreign policy.

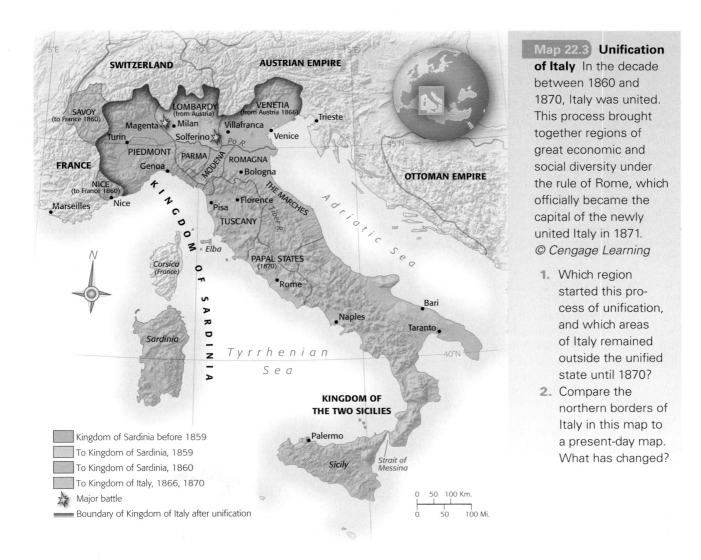

Map 22.3 **Unification of Italy** In the decade between 1860 and 1870, Italy was united. This process brought together regions of great economic and social diversity under the rule of Rome, which officially became the capital of the newly united Italy in 1871. © Cengage Learning

1. Which region started this process of unification, and which areas of Italy remained outside the unified state until 1870?

2. Compare the northern borders of Italy in this map to a present-day map. What has changed?

First Steps Toward Unification The idea of a united Italy had a lot to overcome, as following the revolutions of 1848 Italy was still divided into numerous sovereign political units. In the northwest, centered on the city of Turin, was the small but stable kingdom of Piedmont-Sardinia, ruled by the House of Savoy. Southern Italy was dominated by the Kingdom of the Two Sicilies, which stretched from the island of Sicily to Naples. In between were the Papal States, including Rome and Bologna, an area in which the pope not only was the spiritual head but also ruled as a secular lord, much like the dukes of Milan or Modena. In the northeast, the provinces of Veneto and Lombardy remained under Austrian rule. As Metternich had famously put it, Italy was no more than a "geographical expression."

In 1859, Napoleon III, who supported the idea of an Italian state in the hopes of strengthening French influence in the region, agreed to help Piedmont drive Austria out of northern Italy. The prime minister of

Piedmont, **Camille Cavour**, saw the alliance with France as a means to position his state as the nucleus of a future united Italy. In his own personal beliefs, Cavour reflected the changes in nationalism before and after 1848. In that year, he had urged the king to issue a constitution, had sponsored some liberal policies, and had worked to end Austrian rule in northern Italy. Ten years later, Cavour continued to pursue the goal of expelling the Austrians from Milan and Veneto, but now specifically with the aim of enhancing the power of his king, Victor Emmanuel II.

Crowning the King of Italy, 1861 First Lombardy (with its capital of Milan), in 1859, and then Veneto, in 1866, were ceded by Austria to the kingdom of Piedmont-Sardinia. In the south the unification movement was

Camille Cavour (1810–1861) Prime minister and adviser to the King of Sardinia, Victor Emmanuel II, who in 1861 became the first king of united Italy.

spearheaded by Garibaldi, backed up by his famous Red Shirts. This informal—though effective—army fought its way across Sicily, defeating the kingdom of the Two Sicilies. In 1860, this vast region joined Piedmont, as did the central Italian states of Tuscany and Parma. Thus by 1860, the entire Italian peninsula except for Veneto in the north and the Papal States around Rome were under the rule of Victor Emmanuel II, who would be crowned king of Italy in 1861. These last two areas would become part of the new kingdom of Italy by 1870, though the pope would not reconcile himself to the new political situation. Surrounded by Italian territory that he refused to recognize, Pope Pius IX remained in self-imposed imprisonment in the **Vatican** for the rest of his life.

Liberal Nationalists' Disappointment with United Italy Italian unity had been achieved, but the resulting constitutional monarchy was very far from the democratic ideal envisioned by Mazzini and Garibaldi. Mazzini died in 1872, bitterly disappointed by the form in which his dream had been realized by the less idealistic—but more realistic—Cavour. The new Italy was a constitutional monarchy with universal male suffrage, but the king and his ministers held much more power than the parliament. The problems of illiteracy and poverty, especially in the southern half of the country, were an enormous challenge to the new rulers and would continue to be so well into the twentieth century. In 1870, most subjects of King Victor Emmanuel spoke not standard Italian but dialects, and retained strong regional identities. As one statesman put it, "We have made Italy; now we must make Italians."

The Unification of Germany

"Germany" immediately after 1848 was like Italy: no more than a geographical or cultural expression. Dozens of German states existed, from powerful Prussia to the tiny city-state of Hamburg. When the 1848 revolutionaries offered the crown of a new German Empire to the king of Prussia, he rejected it. His brother would accept it in 1871 as William I, but under vastly changed circumstances. As in Italy, conservatives gained most from German unification. In particular, one man was responsible for Prussia's rapid rise to dominate a unified Germany. This was the Prussian Chancellor Otto von Bismarck.

Otto von Bismarck and German Unification Bismarck combined great energy, determination, and loyalty to the Prussian ruling house with cold calculation. He resembled Metternich in intelligence and ruthlessness, though Bismarck lacked Metternich's elegance and refined manners. Born into a moderately wealthy landowning family, Bismarck had been shocked by the revolutions of 1848 and disappointed by the king's concessions to the liberals. A staunch conservative who had served in the Prussian Landtag (parliament) and as ambassador to Russia and France, Bismarck rose to power by chance. In 1862, King William I became entangled in a dispute with the Landtag over the state budget, in particular the funding for the Prussian army. In despair, the king appointed Bismarck chancellor, hoping that he would be able to find a compromise. Instead, Bismarck directly defied the Landtag, acting as if it did not exist. Bismarck's brash behavior revealed the weakness of Prussia's parliament in the face of a strong and ruthless statesman.

Bismarck declared that the biggest mistake of the 1848 liberals was their attempt to unite Germany through "speeches and majority resolutions" rather than "blood and iron." By this he meant military might and warfare. In the next decade, Bismarck waged three wars that would realize the primary goal of the liberals in the Frankfurt Assembly—a united Germany. The first war came as Denmark attempted to take over the province of Schleswig, previously an independent duchy. Prussian and Austrian troops invaded Schleswig early in 1864, forcing the king of Denmark to withdraw his claims. Austria and Prussia were to administer the territory jointly, an arrangement Bismarck knew would soon lead to conflict. After various frictions and provocations, Austria and Prussia went to war in mid-1866.

The Prussians humiliated the Austrians at a single decisive battle. The peace terms Bismarck offered were mild: Austria lost no territory and paid no war indemnity, but henceforth, Austria would be excluded from the North German Confederation carved by Prussia from the old Austrian-dominated German Confederation set up at the Congress of Vienna. Now the North German Confederation, dominated by Prussia, stretched from the Dutch border in the west to the Russian empire in the east; to the south Austria remained isolated.

The Franco-Prussian War Bismarck had eliminated his chief rival in the German lands. Now he looked to eliminate his chief rival on the continent—France—which felt threatened by the rise of a unified, aggressive German state. Again Bismarck skillfully manipulated events—the candidacy of a Hohenzollern prince for the throne of Spain—to push strained Franco-Prussian relations over the brink. In a brilliant, though dishonest, media maneuver, Bismarck took a telegram—the Ems Dispatch—he had received from King William I on this matter, doctored it in a

Vatican Seat of the Catholic Church and the pope's residence, in central Rome on the Tiber River.

Otto von Bismarck (1815–1898) Prominent conservative Prussian statesman, chancellor (prime minister), and architect of German unification in 1871.

Map 22.4 **Unification of Germany, 1871** Germany was unified in great part through the efforts of Prussian Chancellor Otto von Bismarck. © *Cengage Learning*

1. Where were German speakers left outside unified Germany?
2. Why did France and Russia feel uneasy about German unification?

---

way that was insulting to the French, and leaked the provocative document to the press. Napoleon III foolishly took Bismarck's bait and declared war on Prussia.

The **Franco-Prussian War** (1870–1871) was a disaster for France and for Napoleon III personally. The French badly underestimated the training and equipment of the Prussian forces and were further hampered by poor military leadership. At the Battle of Sedan in early September 1870, the Germans encircled a large French force, capturing more than a hundred thousand men, including Emperor Napoleon III

himself. The French declared their emperor deposed and formed a provisional government, which sued for peace.

The Paris Commune Radical Paris, though surrounded by German troops, was outraged and disgusted by the actions of the provisional government. Rather than surrender, the adult male citizens of Paris voted in

Franco-Prussian War (1870–1871) Conflict provoked by Bismarck, resulting in the defeat of France and end of Napoleon III's reign; also led to German unification.

With his bald head and bushy mustache, German Chancellor Otto von Bismarck was a favorite of caricaturists, as in this cartoon from the early 1890s. Bismarck is shown getting ready to leave (he was forced to resign by the new Kaiser) and looking in disgust at the new Kaiser William II, who gazes lovingly at a newborn labeled "socialism" while reclining on a throne bristling with weaponry. The goddess of Germania looks on in consternation. How accurate is this image's depiction of Bismarck and Kaiser William II? What biases do you detect here?

Bettmann/Corbis

March 1871 to declare the **Paris Commune**. The Commune passed legislation granting free education, moderating rents, reducing church power, and generally supporting the working class.

Two months later the provisional government, which had temporarily withdrawn to Versailles, sent troops to storm Paris and crush the Commune. More than twenty thousand people were killed, more than during the entire Reign of Terror of the French Revolution. This slaughter of mainly working-class people by the middle-class government would long be remembered by socialists, as would the myth of the Commune as the first workers' state. Writing immediately after the crushing of the Commune, Marx exclaimed, "Within sight of the Prussian army that had annexed to Germany two French provinces, the Commune annexed to France the working people all over the world."

In January 1871, before the Commune and even before a peace treaty could be negotiated, King William I had himself crowned "Emperor of the Germans"—symbolically—in Louis XIV's magnificent Hall of Mirrors in the Palace of Versailles. Bismarck had achieved his goal—a united German Empire. In the peace settlement, Germany took from France two German-speaking provinces along the Rhine River—Alsace and Lorraine—and received from France an indemnity of $2 billion. Germany was united, but the French swore revenge.

The American president, Ulysses S. Grant, congratulated the new German government on forming a federal union like the United States and expressed the hope that Germans would soon enjoy the benefits of democracy. In fact, the German constitution did grant universal male suffrage (to those aged twenty-five and older) in elections to the **Reichstag**, or federal parliament, but German states retained considerable autonomy. The Reichstag's power was balanced by that of the Bundesrat, or federal council, in which Prussia exercised great influence. Most of all, the emperor—or Kaiser—held enormous power, dictating foreign policy, acting as commander in chief of all armies, and having the right to declare **martial law**, close down parliament, and interpret the constitution. In short, while German states such as Bavaria, Baden,

Paris Commune Radical regime in Paris after Franco-Prussian War, brutally suppressed by the French government in May 1871.

Reichstag German federal parliament for united Germany that met in Berlin starting in 1871 and was elected by universal male suffrage.

martial law Temporary strengthening of government powers, including the suspension of certain civil rights, during public disturbances or other emergencies.

The Basilica of Sacré-Coeur was built in a working-class area of northern Paris to commemorate the lives lost in the Franco-Prussian War and ensuing Paris Commune. Despite its official aim to reconcile all victims of 1870–1871, it quickly became a symbol of conservative Catholicism in France. Why would working-class Parisians view this huge church in their midst as a foreign entity? What role did the Catholic church play in French society at this time?

Bettmann/© Age fotostock/SuperStock

and Saxony could maintain their own armies and issue their own postage stamps, Prussia and its Kaiser dominated German politics. The authoritarianism and militarism traditional to Prussia would often—if unfairly—be perceived by outsiders as "typically German."

Bismarck as German Chancellor Having engineered unification, Bismarck was secure in his position as—now—*federal* chancellor, though Kaiser William sometimes grumbled that Bismarck wielded more power than he. But Bismarck had to contend with a Reichstag considerably more diverse and demanding than the Prussian Landtag. Representatives from the Catholic south of Germany and the organization of the Catholic **Center Party** inspired fears of undue influence from the Vatican, so Bismarck embarked on an anti-Catholic campaign, the **Kulturkampf**. New laws removed priests from the state bureaucracy (most were teachers), closed down Catholic schools, outlawed Jesuit institutions, and instituted **civil marriage**. German Catholics in the south and the millions of Polish subjects of the Kaiser in the east saw these measures as a direct attack on their religion. The Vatican supported their resistance with an 1875 declaration threatening to excommunicate anyone who complied with these laws. At this point, Bismarck sought a compromise with Catholic leaders, but Catholic Germans continued to view rule from Berlin with suspicion.

After the failure of the Kulturkampf, Bismarck sought to suppress what he perceived an even greater threat to the German Empire—the socialists. He had long mistrusted working-class organizations, and after two unsuccessful attempts on the life of Kaiser William I in 1878, Bismarck pushed the Reichstag to forbid German socialists to organize, meet, and publish their programs. Despite this law, which remained in force until 1890, German socialists steadily gained votes in Reichstag elections, from just over 300,000 in 1881 to almost 1.5 million in 1890. Cleverly, Bismarck then implemented some of their demands, including state-sponsored unemployment insurance, health care, and retirement benefits, to undercut their appeal and ensure workers' loyalty to the state. Germany's social welfare programs were the first, but in the twentieth century nearly every European state would adopt similar policies, advancing government responsibility for aiding sick and poor citizens.

Nations Seeking States

By 1871, Italy and Germany were unified nation-states in which conservative nationalism had triumphed. Hungary, too, had achieved a degree of independence. After its defeat by Prussia, Austria conceded to the Hungarians essentially what they had demanded in 1848. In the Compromise of 1867, Hungarians gained almost complete autonomy, a fact reflected in the country's new name: Austria-Hungary. Hungarians handled domestic affairs independently. They had their own parliament, used their own language without restriction throughout their part of the empire, and obliged non-Hungarians to use that language in schools and government offices.

Center Party Catholic political party in Germany, organized in 1870.

Kulturkampf (in German, "struggle for culture") Bismarck's attack on Catholic schools, institutions, and political influence in the 1870s.

civil marriage Legal bond between two persons, usually man and wife, recognized by the state but not necessarily by religious authorities.

Only in matters of foreign policy, state defense, and the overall budget did Hungary have to compromise with Austria. Austria and Hungary also shared the same ruler.

Nations Without States: National Minorities

But many, perhaps most, nationalities in eastern and southeastern Europe lacked political autonomy. They lived as **national minorities** in the multinational empires of Russia, Austria-Hungary, and the Ottomans. As groups such as Ukrainians, Estonians, Romanians (in Hungary), Croatians, and Slovaks pressed their demands for autonomy, the multinational states were forced to give increasing attention to their **minorities question**—how does a state deal with a minority that refuses assimilation, insisting on using its own language and maintaining its own separate national culture instead of blending in with the majority? Newly independent states like Romania also wrestled with this problem—in Romania, particularly with regard to its Jewish and **Roma** ("gypsy") citizens. Despite pressure from the western powers, Romania refused to grant full citizenship to members of these ethnic groups, treating them like foreigners.

Poles: An Exceptional Stateless Nation

Poles were a unique national minority in nineteenth-century Europe. They looked back to a large and powerful Polish state in the medieval and early modern period, before it was partitioned by Russia, Austria, and Prussia in the late eighteenth century. Polish written culture was well developed, and a Polish nobility continued to exist, despite the disappearance of the Polish state. While the Polish peasantry did not always identify with the "Polish nation" in midcentury, the existence of a Polish nation—without a state—could not be questioned, even by hostile Russians and Prussians like Bismarck. The Polish case stood in marked contrast to that of neighboring Slovaks, Belarusians, and Ukrainians, who lacked a long tradition of statehood or written culture.

The majority of Poles lived under Russian rule in the so-called kingdom of Poland, but after the Polish insurrection of 1830, little remained of its autonomy. A second insurrection in 1863 failed disastrously. In its aftermath, thousands of Poles were arrested, had their property confiscated, and were exiled to Siberia or fled abroad. Government schools used Russian as the language of instruction, Poles were excluded from many government jobs, and strict censorship was applied to the Polish press. The next generation of Polish intellectuals, known as the Warsaw positivists after the French intellectual movement of that name, emphasized economic and cultural development over national unity. They recognized that developing a strong, literate, and prosperous Polish nation was under present circumstances more important than fighting for independence.

From the 1890s onward, however, the cautious approach of the positivists did not satisfy the more impatient socialist and nationalist Polish youth. They argued for direct action against the repressive Russian empire, even for revolution. The **Polish Socialist Party** was both nationalist in its political ideas (demanding an independent Polish state) and socialist in its economic ideas (demanding state ownership of factories and means of communication).

At the end of the 1890s, it was challenged by the **National Democratic Party**, which stressed nationalism and rejected socialism. Led by **Roman Dmowski**, the National Democrats were aggressive and exclusivist in their approach, refusing to accept non-Poles, and especially Jews, as a part of the Polish nation. Dmowski argued that the large Jewish minority living among the Poles had taken over middle-class occupations, pushing out Poles. Thus, for a healthy Polish nation to develop, Dmowski's argument continued, the Jews must either assimilate totally—shedding Jewish culture and identity—or leave Poland. Dmowski's appeals exemplified the beginnings of mass politics in Poland. On the one hand, he and his National Democrats helped organize Poles against Russian and Prussian cultural and political oppression; on the other, he rallied Poles to reject their Jewish neighbors and to embrace an aggressive, almost biological, form of nationalism.

Bulgaria Breaks Away from the Ottoman Empire

While the Poles would have to wait until the twentieth century for independence, Bulgarian religious and national leaders wrested their own state from the Ottoman Empire by manipulating international tensions. The Ottomans tolerated

---

national minority Ethnic/national group not making up the majority of a state's population—for example, in the Russian empire, Jews, Poles, Ukrainians, and Latvians.

minorities question Problem of what cultural and political rights to give to national minorities.

Roma Nomadic people living especially in eastern Europe who trace their origins back to India, sometimes incorrectly referred to as "Gypsies."

Polish Socialist Party Political party founded in 1892 that combined socialist ideology with the demand for an independent Polish state.

National Democratic Party Nationalist and antisemitic Polish party formed in 1897 that advocated limiting the number of non-Poles—especially Jews—in a future Polish state.

Roman Dmowski (1864–1939) Polish politician and leader of the nationalist and antisemitic National Democratic Party.

Patriotic images like this one inspired Bulgarians to fight for their independence from the Ottoman Empire in the late 1870s. In this poster, as in many others, the nation was depicted as a woman surrounded by symbols of state. Here we see the Bulgarian flag and the two-headed eagle that represented Bulgaria's link to the Russian empire. How does this image present a heroic vision of Bulgarian patriotism? How might Turks or Serbs respond to this image and its ideals?

St. Cyril and Methodius Library/Visual Connection Archive

Bulgarian Orthodox Christianity, but the ruling class in the region was made up primarily of Muslims. By the late nineteenth century, growing numbers of middle-class Bulgarians, most educated in missionary or church schools, came to resent their subordination to Muslim Ottoman authorities. They turned to Russia, which shared its religious traditions, spoke a similar language, and also used the Cyrillic alphabet. Russia had long seen itself as the protector of Orthodox Christians in the Ottoman Empire.

Launching an uprising in the spring of 1875, Bulgarian nationalist leaders drew all Europe's attention to their oppression, especially after violent reprisals by Ottoman forces took the lives of many thousands of Christian Bulgarians. Britain's former Prime Minister **William Gladstone** produced an overwrought account of the massacre, *The Bulgarian Horrors and the Question of the East*. When, in 1876, another

Balkan Slavic people in the mountainous province of Bosnia-Herzegovina rose up against Ottoman rule, Russia intervened, in defense of Orthodox Christian Serbs and Montenegrans. In the **Russo-Turkish War**, Russian troops crossed neutral Romania, invaded Bulgaria in the spring of 1877, and the following year defeated the Turks.

The terms Russia imposed on the Ottomans included a huge independent Bulgaria stretching from the Black Sea to the Aegean. This prospect alarmed Europe's Great Powers, which feared Russia would now gain undue influence in the Balkans and upset the balance of power. At the Congress of Berlin in 1878, Germany, Austria-Hungary, Great Britain, and France forced Russia to accept a much smaller Bulgaria with a German prince, Alexander of Battenberg, as its king. The Bulgarians had received their state, not because of popular agitation or nationalist revolution but through the intervention of Russia. The Ottoman province of Bosnia-Herzegovina was placed under Austrian administration.

Norway Splits from Sweden Norway gained its independence in an entirely different way. Assigned to the Swedish Crown in 1815 at the Congress of Vienna, Norwegians cherished a separate identity derived from their rugged terrain, folk culture, and historical traditions linked to Denmark. The language used by educated Norwegians differed little from Danish, while the folk dialect was closer to Swedish. As subjects of the Swedish king, Norwegians enjoyed political and civil rights found in few other European countries. Still, Norwegian nationalists insisted on an independent Norway. After some negotiation, the Swedes agreed to a "divorce," and Norway became independent in 1905. This achievement of statehood by peaceful means stands out as a historical rarity.

William Gladstone (1809–1898) British politician and prime minister; important figure in the Liberal Party.

Russo-Turkish War (1877–1878) Major war in the Balkans with Serbia and Russia fighting against the Ottoman Empire.

 Checking In

By yourself or with a partner, explain the significance of each of the following selected key terms:

Camille Cavour Reichstag

Otto von Bismarck Kulturkampf

Franco-Prussian War William Gladstone

Paris Commune

Theodor Herzl Creates Modern Zionism

In 1895 journalist Theodor Herzl was in Paris covering the trial of Captain Alfred Dreyfus, who had been accused of spying for the Germans. Like Herzl himself, Dreyfus was an assimilated, Europeanized Jew. The trial was held more than a century after the French Revolution had promised equal rights to Jewish citizens. But the trial was unfair: Dreyfus's Jewish background was held against him. In the streets crowds shouted "Death to the Jews!" Herzl was shocked, and he wrote in his diary, "I recognized the emptiness and futility of trying to 'combat' antisemitism." He concluded that Jews would always be outsiders in the European countries in which they dwelled. They would be exiles—as Hebrew teachings phrased it—until they had their own Jewish state. Jews were not just a religious group; they were a nation.

Herzl had experienced antisemitism. As a student at the University of Vienna in the early 1880s, he had been denied admission into a prestigious fraternity because of his Jewish origins. He had been furious, for he felt himself Austrian by culture, upbringing, and language, and more patriotic than most. Being Jewish was just a personal religious matter. But the young Herzl learned a hard lesson: for a Jew, no matter how assimilated, wealthy, and intelligent, some avenues were closed. Herzl graduated and became a well-known playwright and journalist in Vienna, indistinguishable from other middle-class Viennese, with an unhappy marriage, a lifestyle that outstripped his income, and a love for wit and culture.

Vienna was a thriving center for German Jewish culture, with such distinguished writers as Stefan Zweig and Arthur Schnitzler, composers like Alban Berg and Arnold Schoenberg, and of course the renowned psychiatrist Sigmund Freud. In this environment, surrounded by other Jews like him—German speaking, cultured, successful—Herzl tried to believe that Jews could retain their religion and still live in harmony with their Christian neighbors. But that was before he covered what became known as the Dreyfus affair.

Despite the absurdity of the accusation and the flimsy evidence against him, Dreyfus was court-martialed and exiled to Devil's Island off the coast of South America. It was later discovered that the army had manipulated and forged evidence against him. By that time, Herzl was already a Jewish nationalist, a Zionist. In 1896 he published a small book entitled *The Jewish State,* which proposed a political solution to what Europeans called the Jewish question—the proper relation between Jews and the states where they lived. Once Jews had their own state, Herzl argued, the other nations of the world would respect them. Other central and eastern European Jewish thinkers had reached similar conclusions before Herzl—in part, in reaction to the shock of the 1881 wave of anti-Jewish violence in the Russian empire—but he apparently did not know any of them. Even the term *Zionism* had been used before Herzl, but he gave the movement new political force and vigor.

In 1897, Herzl summoned a "symbolic parliament" of European Jews to the Swiss city of Basel. At this First Zionist Congress he issued a call for all Jews to unite to create a Jewish state. Though he did not specify where that state would be founded, the obvious place was Palestine—for Jews, Eretz Israel ("land of Israel"), an Ottoman province between Egypt and Syria. After all, Jews prayed every year at Passover to meet again "next year in Jerusalem." Most Jews in western Europe did not respond to Herzl's call. Feeling secure and patriotic in France, Britain, and Germany, they firmly rejected the idea of a Jewish nation and feared that Zionism could worsen anti-Jewish feelings. But in eastern Europe, particularly in the Russian empire, Herzl's call was received with joy. Visiting Russia in 1903, Herzl was lauded as "king of the Jews" in towns throughout the Pale of Settlement, where Russian Jews were forced to reside.

Herzl did not live to see his ideal realized. When he died in 1904, very few people believed that Zionism could succeed—the political, economic, and religious obstacles seemed too great. But, as Herzl once remarked, "If you will it, it is not a dream." Forty-four years after Herzl's death, two thousand years after the Jewish people were sent into exile, the state of Israel declared its independence. The Jewish people had their own state.

The Expanding Role of the State

After 1848, political participation increased throughout Europe. By the end of the century, almost all males in Britain and France could vote, as they also could in newly united Italy and Germany. In the stateless nations in the Ottoman and Habsburg empires, agitation for political rights strengthened. Everywhere leaders used education as a means of influencing citizens to identify with the state, its culture, and its interests. States also intruded into the economy to encourage local industry and keep out foreign competition. Across Europe, the role of the state in citizen's lives expanded.

Mass Politics and Nation Building

The term **nation building** cannot be separated from the concept of nation-state. It describes the process by which the political unit (state) attempts to transform its population into a "nation." Nation building was also connected with new legislative assemblies and the expansion of political participation after 1848. As individuals voted in elections, held office, debated political issues, read newspapers, and traveled (often seeking employment) throughout their countries, they gained a sense of national identity that transcended local and religious ties.

The Nation-State in Great Britain In Britain the nation-state was firmly established by the nineteenth century, and parliamentary traditions were strong. In 1832, in a triumph of British liberalism, the Reform Acts had granted the vote to middle-class men. The Reform Acts of 1867 and 1884 extended suffrage to male heads of households; further extensions brought almost universal male suffrage by the early twentieth century. Regional identities remained strong, but they did not challenge the dominance of a British identity fostered by London.

Throughout this period, Great Britain was plagued by the Irish question—what to do with the Irish, poverty-stricken, Catholic peasants in a mainly Protestant and industrialized British nation. The horrific famine of the mid-1840s had reduced the population of Ireland by over one-third and poisoned relations between Irish Catholic peasants and their Protestant landlords. One proposed solution to the Irish question was home rule—autonomy for the Irish provinces with their own parliament in Dublin.

Irish demands for home rule increased at the end of the nineteenth century.

Changes in French Politics France also enjoyed a strong national tradition, prestigious culture, and prosperity. The centrality of Paris and the strength of the central state apparatus and of French culture overshadowed the linguistic and cultural diversity (Basque, Breton, Provençal) existing within France's borders. The extensive rebuilding of Paris in the decades before 1870 added to its glamour and attraction as the center of the French nation. To be French meant to be part of the "great nation" that included all citizens of the French Republic. Local identities hardly had a chance to take shape as separatist or national movements. After the French Revolution, being French had nothing to do with religion. French identity was political: one could "become" French by accepting the responsibilities of being a loyal citizen.

The expansion of the electorate in France followed a more abrupt path than in Britain. Following the 1848 revolution, universal male suffrage was established, but under Emperor Napoleon III, starting in 1851, democracy ended in France for two decades. The disastrous Franco-Prussian war ushered in the **Third Republic**, and from 1871 onward, Frenchmen would always enjoy voting rights.

Elsewhere in Europe political rights also increased. In newly unified Italy and Germany, all men could vote. Even in backward Russia, most men could vote in **Duma** elections after 1906, though the votes of the wealthy counted far more than those of peasants and workers. Universal male suffrage came to Austria (though not to Hungary) in 1907. In Finland, still an autonomous principality within the Russian empire, women were granted the vote in 1906. Women could also vote in local elections in some western states in the United States. Democracy was far from universal even in the early twentieth century, but great strides had been made in that direction since 1848.

Technology and Nation Building Technology played a role in nation building. Steam presses and advances in papermaking technology made newspapers cheap and abundant after the 1860s, and increased literacy meant that more people read them. Newspaper reading helped establish and spread a standard form of the language and thus weakened local dialects. Industrial development also strengthened national feelings. Railroads

nation building Creation of a strong nation-state, with institutions to educate the population in obedience and patriotism.

Third Republic (1870–1940) Longest continuous republic in French history, beginning with the defeat in the Franco-Prussian war and ending with military defeat by Hitler.

Duma Russian legislature, granted by Tsar Nicholas II in 1906 and lasting until the Revolution of 1917.

The "Grand Boulevards" of Paris, planned and built during the reign of Emperor Napoleon III and generally associated with his prime administrator, Georges-Eugène Haussmann, today give the impression of a well-ordered city. But at the time they entailed an enormous amount of destruction, demolishing much of medieval Paris and pushing many working-class people out of the central city to the suburbs. This photograph, from 1852, shows the clearing of the area near the Louvre. How did the recasting of Paris under Haussmann change the city for the better? What negative aspects did these changes have?

Scala/White Images/Art Resource, NY

encouraged mobility between town and countryside and reduced differences between peasants and town dwellers, reinforcing the idea that "we are all Frenchmen" (or Germans, or Russians, or Italians). The telegraph, which dates from 1844, twenty years later spanned the European and American continents, helping bring citizens in closer contact and aiding governments in administering their territories.

The impact of this expanding political participation was enormous. With mass political participation came the need for governments to respond to public opinion. Some governments used secret subsidies to influence the opinions newspapers expressed. For example, it was an open secret that the Russian government paid large sums to the Belgian daily *Le Nord*, which then gave favorable coverage of Russian affairs. Governments also paid editors to print favorable news and suppress embarrassing information. Most governments attempted to limit the information reaching their citizens through censorship, but as the amount of information freely available to citizens grew, politics

could no longer remain confined to a few wealthy families.

New Political Parties The new political power of peasant and working-class men changed the agendas of political parties. Conservative parties attempted to gain peasant support by appealing to Christian (often Catholic) values and denouncing "godless" urban socialists and, in some cases, the Jews. Liberal parties increasingly modified their laissez-faire attitudes to support limits on employment of children and the length of the working day and provision of assistance to ill or injured workers. Nationalist politicians often took up antisemitic slogans, blaming Jews as being responsible for higher prices.

Working-class political organizations grew steadily. In England, the **Labour Party**, founded in 1900, rapidly challenged both the Tories and the Liberals, whose party had developed from the Whigs. In other countries, socialist parties sought to represent labor, though they were often harassed or disbanded by governments. The **Social Democratic Party of Germany** was powerful enough to attract more votes than any other party in the 1913 elections, but it was still kept out of the government. In France, when a socialist, Alexandre Millerand, accepted a cabinet post in 1899, he was soundly criticized by other socialists for participating in a bourgeois government. Russian socialists, on the other hand, were forced to operate underground. These illegal groupings were split between the peasant-based **Socialist Revolutionaries**, who embraced terrorist methods, and the Marxist Social Democrats, who themselves split into **Bolshevik** and **Menshevik** factions in 1903 over questions of party strategy. Everywhere,

Labour Party British political party founded in 1900 with the help of trade unions to represent the interests of the urban working class.

Social Democratic Party of Germany Europe's most powerful and popular socialist party in the late nineteenth and early twentieth centuries.

Socialist Revolutionaries Russian underground political party, founded in 1901, that carried out terrorist acts against the tsarist government.

Bolsheviks and **Mensheviks** Two branches of the underground Russian Social Democratic Party, the more radical of which was the Bolsheviks.

socialists believed that as the numbers of working-class people grew, their triumph over capitalism was increasingly certain.

Mass politics took varied and even contradictory forms. When the British Prime Minister William Gladstone, a Liberal, toured the country by rail in the 1870s to influence voters, he was participating in mass politics. When, in the 1890s, the Polish political leader Roman Dmowski and the National Democrats published the newspaper *Kurier Wszechpolski* in Austrian Galicia, in part so it could be smuggled into the Russian empire, they were also participating in mass politics. Mass-circulation newspapers attempted to influence public opinion with their coverage of events and exposés of political corruption. French writer **Émile Zola**'s article denouncing the French army's attempt to frame Captain Alfred Dreyfus, "J'Accuse!" ("I Accuse"), is a famous example of such an exposé.

Education and the Nation-State

Before 1848, few European states compelled their citizens to attend school. By 1914, universal schooling was accepted as a goal—though it was not yet a reality—throughout Europe and increasingly around the world. Literacy and access to education were coming to be seen as a primary responsibility of governments. In most countries of western, northern, and central Europe, parents were obliged to send their children to school. States recognized the importance of schools for forming the population into well-trained workers and patriotic citizens.

Spreading Education Everywhere, literacy improved, though at unequal rates. At midcentury, more than 70 percent of the population in Scandinavia, Germany, Scotland, and the United States was literate; by 1913, the figure was over 90 percent, not only in those countries but also in Great Britain (including Ireland), Australia, New Zealand, Austria, and France. Even in backward Russia, nearly half of the population was literate by this time. Generally, literacy rates were higher in urban than rural areas, among men than women, and in Protestant countries than in Catholic countries, probably because of Protestantism's emphasis on Bible reading.

The spread of mandatory elementary education, though not rapid, was steady. From the late eighteenth century onward, Prussia obliged parents to send their children to school. In France, a law promising free, compulsory, and universal elementary education was passed in the wake of the 1848 revolution, though it took several decades to be implemented. Great Britain instituted universal primary education in 1871, and this system grew rapidly in the next few decades. Even in Russia, where the spread of literacy was hampered by poverty and the government's distrust of teachers,

who were suspected of revolutionary sympathies, the numbers of primary schools increased significantly in the decades up to 1914, and plans were under way to introduce free and universal primary education.

Technical Education The nature and philosophy of education changed radically, with its practical—rather than moral or religious—aspects getting more attention. In Prussia, traditional classical high schools, or *Gymnasien*, that emphasized Latin and Greek were supplemented by more practical secondary schools teaching mathematics and science to prepare workers for a new industrial economy. New institutions of higher learning—in particular the technological universities—concentrated on producing well-trained chemists, engineers, and other specialists vital to Germany's growing industries. In other countries, too, science and technology found a place in the curriculum, and technological institutes were set up in St. Petersburg, Warsaw, and Boston, where the Massachusetts Institute of Technology was founded in 1861.

In many parts of Europe, the state sought to reduce the influence of the church on education. The secular French state instituted state-run primary schools with state-employed teachers, the *instituteurs*, who saw themselves as countering the forces of backwardness and reaction they perceived as embodied in the Catholic Church and the local priest. In Germany, one purpose of Bismarck's Kulturkampf was to eject the Catholic priest from the classroom. In other European countries, the tension between state education and religious authority was less open, but everywhere conservatives and traditional religious leaders felt uneasy about mass education, worrying that it could promote radical thinking and atheism.

Education and Patriotism Mass education also aimed to strengthen patriotism. Italian schools insisted that the pupils use standard Italian, a language that children in many regions could barely understand. Ukrainian and Belarusian children were taught—if at all—in Russian because the government claimed that their languages were only dialects of Russian. But the patriotic lessons taught in schools went beyond language. In Italian schools, children learned that they had inherited the glories of ancient Rome. Russian pupils were taught that the tsar was a kindly father looking out for all his subjects in their broad motherland, which covered one-fifth of the earth's surface. British children learned pride in their democratic traditions and love for the queen and the British Empire, on which "the sun never sets." In Prussia, the values of order and discipline were stressed.

Émile Zola (1840–1902) French writer, author of "J'Accuse," an article accusing the French army of trying to frame Dreyfus.

Education and Class Even while opening up opportunity for a few gifted individuals, mass education also reinforced existing class lines. While more peasants and workers now sent their children to school, few could afford secondary or higher education. The British public school system prepared the sons of the gentry and upper middle class to enter Oxford and Cambridge and from there to occupy positions of power in government and industry. University students came overwhelmingly from the middle class and upper levels of society, and higher education was far from common. In 1900 there were fewer than thirty thousand university students in France and fewer than fifty thousand in Germany—less than 1 percent of the population in both cases. At the same time, less privileged people were getting more and more education that allowed hundreds of thousands to take up jobs as bank clerks, government bureaucrats, teachers, and telegraph operators. Mass education thus helped expand the middle class, which in turn increased demands for broader political rights.

The Growing Power of the State

Nation building aims to convince citizens that they have a stake and a voice in the nation-state. The nation-state's political legitimacy derives in the end from the nation—that is, all citizens taken as a whole. But the state also demands that citizens fulfill various obligations: paying taxes, serving in the military, obeying the law. Now citizens were asked to fulfill these obligations as part of a social contract between themselves and the nation-state. At the same time, citizens increasingly expected the state to protect them not only from domestic or foreign enemies but from the devastation of sickness, poverty, and old age. In the second half of the nineteenth century, state power expanded in the form of increased government intervention in everyday life, but in return the state promised order, more protection for weaker segments of society, and international prestige.

Increasing State Intervention in the Economy Classical liberalism argued that the state should interfere as little as possible in economic matters, holding that legal equality would give all citizens equal access to fame and fortune. By the last decades of the nineteenth century, even liberals allowed that the state had a role to play in the economy. The failed example of France's national workshops of 1848 began to seem like a reasonable idea during periods of high unemployment. Most state intervention in the economy, however, aimed to assure investors' profits.

In the building of railroads in Russia and Austria, for example, where investors put forth capital, the state guaranteed a certain percentage return, at least for a specific period. The state also sought to assure decent working conditions. From Britain to Russia, government factory inspectors examined working conditions with the power to fine or even shut down workplaces that were dangerous. For some factory owners, such measures seemed an outrageous example of government interference in their businesses.

The technology of war also contributed to nation building and the growth of state power. By the 1870s, nearly every European country, with the exception of Britain, demanded military service from its male citizens. Serving in the Russian or French or Italian army helped young peasant lads to see themselves as part of a larger group—the nation. Before 1917, more Russian boys were taught to read in the army than in schools. Similarly, bringing together young men from different parts of France and Italy helped encourage use of the standard language rather than local dialects and impressed on the soldiers that they served not only their family, village, or region but the entire nation. And the existence of a strong national army was a matter of pride and international prestige: few Europeans could imagine a self-respecting nation-state without a well-trained army in flashy and distinctive uniforms. Throughout Europe the cost of these armies was nearly universally the largest item on the state budget.

Rising Taxes To intervene in industrial development, educate citizens, and build strong armies, states needed taxes. With the exception of Great Britain, which introduced an income tax—levied only on those with higher incomes—in 1842, European states collected revenue from tariffs and **indirect taxes**, such as taxes on salt, kerosene, and matches. In Austria-Hungary the state had a monopoly on the sale of tobacco products, and in Russia the state budget was covered in large part by taxation on vodka. Tariffs and indirect taxes pushed up prices and fell disproportionately on the poor. Throughout Europe taxes rose in the course of the nineteenth century.

indirect taxes Taxes levied on products of common use, like salt, alcoholic beverages, or kerosene, as opposed to direct taxes, such as income tax.

 **Checking In**

By yourself or with a partner, explain the significance of each of the following selected key terms:

Third Republic	Socialist Revolutionaries
Duma	Bolshevik
Labour Party	Menshevik
Social Democratic Party of Germany	Émile Zola

Nationalism and Its Opponents

◆ **What links developed in the later nineteenth century between nationalism and racism?**

◆ **Why did anarchists, socialists, and the Catholic Church oppose nationalism? In each case, what aspects of nationalism did they dislike?**

Despite its growing influence, nationalism was not without opponents in this period. Some objected to its increasingly aggressive, even racist, aspects, which pitted nation against nation in contests that defined some as inferior, others as superior. Both conservatives and radicals, for different reasons, saw nationalism as a destructive, even evil, movement. The conservative multinational empires in central and eastern Europe opposed nationalism as a threat to their continued survival. The Catholic Church condemned both the democratic politics of some nationalists and the racism of others. Socialists denounced nationalism as a tool of the ruling classes to distract ordinary people from real social and economic issues, to disguise exploitation with nationalist slogans, and to increase profits through the sale of armaments.

Integral Nationalism, Racism, Antisemitism, and Zionism

After 1848, conservatives took up the nationalist ideas and slogans that had been the hallmarks of liberalism before the uprisings. After 1860, nationalists began to preach a more exclusionary and aggressive creed, stressing struggle and dominance rather than cooperation and mutual assistance. At the same time, conservatives recognized the utility of nationalism as a tool for rallying the masses. By painting radicals and socialists as internationalists, the conservatives suggested that leftists would support foreign interests over patriotism. Most important, now everyone was expected to identify with one nation, not with a local village or religious faith. This growth in national self-consciousness was encouraged by government schools, mass publications such as newspapers and calendars, and various political parties.

Nationalism Learns to Hate: Integral Nationalism Toward the end of the nineteenth century, nationalism took on increasingly narrow and aggressive forms. This phenomenon has been termed **integral nationalism**, to stress its all-encompassing character and distinguish it from earlier liberal nationalism. These nonliberal nationalists stressed struggle between nations and domination of other nations.

Dmowski in Poland, for example, argued that only a struggle between Poles and Ukrainians would determine whether the Ukrainians would survive as a nation.

Another key ingredient of integral nationalism was a narrow definition of the nation, focusing in particular on who *did not* belong and usually seeing a nation as a community of birth, not an identity that one could choose. German nationalists came to insist that birth determined German identity. Although France and the United States theoretically defined their nations as open to anyone accepting their political ideals, discrimination belied this open, liberal attitude.

Racism Narrow and exclusionary definitions of the nation came together with the rise of racialist thought. As Europeans engaged in a new wave of colonizing in Africa and Asia, the idea of race emerged as a biological reality and object of study. Though race is now understood as lacking a scientific basis and the diversity of humankind as being unclassifiable in such terms, scientists and philosophers in late-nineteenth-century Europe developed a racial system of human classification based on a strict hierarchy, with white Europeans on top. This **scientific racism** claimed that humanity was divided into three races with different physical, mental, and sexual capacities.

Antisemitism Racism and integral nationalism fused most notoriously in **antisemitism**. The word itself was first used by the obscure German writer **Wilhelm Marr** in 1879 in his pamphlet *Victory of the Jews over the Germans* to describe a new phenomenon. While religious hatred and discrimination against Jews had long existed in Christian Europe, antisemitism attacked not the Jewish religion but all those of Jewish birth ("race"), no matter what their religious beliefs, as enemies of all Europeans and their society (the term **Aryan** was often used in this context to mean non-Jews). Antisemites insisted that Jews by their very nature could not be part of European nations, much to the anger of middle-class Jews, who, believing in assimilation, considered their religion no obstacle to their strongly felt identity as patriotic Frenchmen, Germans, or Poles.

---

integral nationalism Form of nationalism common in the later nineteenth century, characterized by an aggressive stance toward other ethnic groups.

scientific racism Nineteenth-century biological theory that claimed humanity is divided into three races with different physical, mental, and sexual capacities.

antisemitism Anti-Jewish political movement arising in Germany in the 1870s and spreading to many countries, in particular in eastern Europe.

Wilhelm Marr (1819–1904) German writer who coined the word *antisemitism*, arguing that Jews posed a major threat to European peoples and culture.

Aryan Designation for non-Jews, implying that Jews belonged in a specific "semitic" race, whereas other white Europeans belonged to the "Aryan" race.

Theodor Herzl Speculates on the Impact of Jewish Immigration to Palestine

When Theodor Herzl proposed the creation of a Jewish state in 1896, he focused not on a location or an exact form of government but on the simple fact that Jews should have their own state to shelter them from persecution and to foster their national pride. In his writings, however, he envisioned an economically modern state that would be liberal and democratic in its politics. He also envisioned good relations between Jews and Arabs. In this passage from *Old-New Land*, a fictional English visitor speaks with an Arab landowner about the impact of Jewish immigration to Palestine.

❶ Why does Herzl have an English visitor address this question to an Arab?

❷ Why, according to Reschid, do the Palestinian Arabs appreciate their new Jewish neighbors?

❸ Why does Herzl have Kingscourt comment on Reschid's European education? Which culture does Kingscourt see as superior?

❹ Who is the target of Herzl's indirect criticism here?

❶ "One question, Reschid Bey," interrupted Kingscourt…. "Were not the older inhabitants of Palestine ruined by the Jewish immigration? And didn't they have to leave the country?"…

❷ "What a question! It was a great blessing for all of us," returned Reschid. "Naturally, the land-owners gained most because they were able to sell to the Jewish society at high prices…."

"But I wanted to ask you, my dear Bey, how the former inhabitants fared—those who had nothing, the numerous Moslem Arabs."

"'Your question answers itself, Mr. Kingscourt," replied Reschid. "Those who had nothing stood to lose nothing, and could only gain. And they did gain: Opportunities to work, means of livelihood, prosperity. Nothing could have been more wretched than an Arab village at the end of the nineteenth century…. Now everything is different. They benefited from the progressive measures of the New Society whether they wanted to or not…."

"You're queer fellows, you Moslems. Don't you regard these Jews as intruders?"

"You speak strangely, Christian," responded the friendly Reschid. "Would you call a man a robber who takes nothing from you, but brings you something instead? The Jews have enriched us. Why should we be angry with them? They dwell among us like brothers. Why should we not love them?…"

Reschid's gentle words had moved everyone, Kingscourt included. That gentleman cleared his throat. "Hm-hm! Quite right. Very fine. Sounds reasonable. ❸ But you're an educated man, you've studied in Europe. I hardly think the simple country or town folk will be likely to think as you do."

❹ "They more than anyone else, Mr. Kingscourt. You must excuse my saying so, but I did not learn tolerance in the Occident [the West]. We Moslems have always had better relations with the Jews than you Christians."

Source: Translated by the author, taken from Herzl's *Alt-Neuland*.

UN DINER EN FAMILLE

— Surtout ! ne parlons pas de l'affaire Dreyfus !

Ils en ont parlé.

A pair of French cartoons illustrates the bitter controversy caused by the Dreyfus affair within French society—and even within individual families. The first cartoon reads "Above all let's not talk about the Dreyfus Affair"; the second—"They talked about it." Why did the Dreyfus Affair cause such strong feelings? Who was Dreyfus, and what was he accused of?

Antisemites held that Jews unfairly monopolized commerce and banking; were dishonest in their dealings with non-Jews; and exercised a corrupting moral influence through their activities as journalists, lawyers, and doctors. Jews were identified with modern capitalist society—disrespectful of social traditions while energetically and unscrupulously accumulating wealth and power. Antisemitic political parties, such as Dmowski's National Democrats, appealed to workers and lower-middle-class voters, whose economic and social position were threatened by industrialization and large-scale capitalist commerce.

Antisemitism, the Dreyfus Affair, and Zionism
Antisemitism gained significant popular support in the 1870s and 1880s in places where Jewish populations were substantial, as in Austria-Hungary and Russian Poland, and where Jews were noticeable in society, despite their small numbers, because of their achievements in business or the free professions, as in Germany. But antisemitism within European society was so general that when the Austrian journalist **Theodor Herzl**, covering the **Dreyfus affair** in Paris, witnessed public demonstrations of hatred toward all Jews, he concluded that no Jew was safe, not even in enlightened, republican France (see Learning from a Primary Source: Theodor Herzl Speculates on the Impact of Jewish Immigration to Palestine). Declaring that Jews constituted a nation, not just a religious community, Herzl initiated a movement, known as **Zionism**, calling for the establishment of a Jewish state in the historical home of the Hebrews in Palestine.

The final decades of the nineteenth century were traumatic for Europe's Jews. In 1881, in the wake of the assassination of Tsar Alexander II in St. Petersburg, a wave of **pogroms**, or organized attacks on Jewish life and property, swept the southwestern provinces of the Russian empire (today's Ukraine). Despite the small number of deaths in the pogroms, their moral impact was devastating. Most Jews—and Russian liberals—concluded that the Russian government itself was behind the attacks (a view now rejected by historians), and by the end of the 1880s, tens of thousands of Jews were leaving Russia every year, mainly for the United States.

Theodor Herzl (1860–1904) Viennese journalist who founded modern Zionism.

Dreyfus affair Series of trials between 1894 and 1906 involving the false accusation of Captain Alfred Dreyfus, a Jewish officer on the French general staff, of spying for the Germans.

Zionism View that Jews were not merely a religious community, but a nation; also a movement advocating the formation of a modern Jewish state in Palestine.

pogrom In Russia in 1881 and later, organized attacks on Jews and Jewish property.

Armenians Christian ethnic group living in the Russian and Ottoman empires, subject to violent attacks under Sultan Abdul Hamid II.

Strains in the Multinational Empires

Nationalism also threatened the conservative multinational empires of eastern and central Europe. The Ottoman Empire, Austria-Hungary, and Russia were all defined by dynastic loyalties and contained within their borders a wide diversity of groups increasingly conscious of their national and ethnic identities. Their demands for cultural and political rights undermined the stability of these empires.

The Ottoman Empire The Ottoman Empire was a kaleidoscope of ethnic diversity, including, at mid-century, Slavs, Albanians, Arabs, and others—it was not a "Turkish" state. Sultan Abdül Hamid II himself was born to an **Armenian** mother, and among his wives were women of various ethnic groups. In the Ottoman Empire, religion was much more important than nationality. Religious toleration was practiced, though Islam was considered the most perfect religion. In practice, business and commerce were dominated by Christians and Jews, and the population of Istanbul—the former Constantinople—was more Christian than Muslim in 1900. National and ethnic strife were not entirely absent, however, in the Ottoman state. When Armenians, for example, were suspected of disloyalty to the sultan, they were subjected to violent attacks.

In the course of the nineteenth century, Greeks, Romanians, Serbs, and Bulgarians gained their independence from the Ottoman Empire, while Bosnia-Herzegovina was transferred to Austria. These territorial losses were just one sign of Ottoman weakness. Though the sultan exercised absolute power in principle, in reality the empire's unwieldy size and inefficient bureaucracy meant that he could never be sure his orders would be carried out in distant provinces. Local elites from the Balkans to northern Africa often took control into their own hands. Eventually, the economic problems of the Ottoman state became so acute that in effect the empire went bankrupt, and state budgets had to be approved by the empire's European creditors.

The Russian Empire The Russian empire was even larger and more diverse than the Ottoman Empire. Stretching from Finland to the Pacific Ocean, it covered one-fifth of the earth's dry land. Like the Ottoman Empire, Russia was not a nation-state. The census of 1897 indicates that not quite half of Nicholas's subjects were ethnically Russian. The empire encompassed Ukrainians, Poles, Jews, Lithuanians, Germans, pagan Udmurts, and Muslim Tartars. Germans predominated among Russia's diplomats, and German names—Benckendorff, Totleben, Kaufmann—were common among the highest officials and generals of the empire. The Finns enjoyed broad autonomy, having their own coinage, postal system, and legislature. The legal status of most non-Russians in the empire was, however, far less favorable.

The ethnic diversity of the Russian empire is reflected in this 1900 poster showing representatives of a half-dozen peoples (including a Georgian, Chechen, Armenian, and Lezgin) all in native dress. These peoples lived in the Caucasus Mountains that separated Russia from the Ottoman Empire, a region conquered by the Russian empire in the nineteenth century. How is cultural difference depicted in this image? What other ways of showing ethnic diversity could have been used?

Visual Connection Archive

Russia had been considered a major European power only since the Napoleonic Wars, and this status was severely shaken by its defeat in the **Crimean War** (1854–1856). Tsar Nicholas I died a broken man in the midst of the war, admonishing his son Alexander II to learn from his mistakes. While no liberal, Tsar Alexander II recognized that only sweeping reforms could save Russia's status as a great power. In 1861, he emancipated the serfs in the first of a series of **Great Reforms** that ended in 1876 with universal military service. Censorship was also lightened, but Alexander refused to create an elected legislature, even of an advisory sort.

Even before the Great Reforms, religious toleration had been practiced in the Russian empire, but the Russian Orthodox Church was officially the "reigning religion," its primacy taken for granted. Catholics were regarded as untrustworthy, and Russian officials closely monitored the movements and actions of Catholic priests and bishops. The Jews were worst off: their residence, with few exceptions, was restricted to the western part of the empire, the so-called **Pale of Settlement**; they were discriminated against in government jobs and secondary and higher education.

Russia differed from the Ottoman or Habsburg Empires, however, in the predominance of one religion and one language. While the tsar's subjects were generally free to speak their native tongues at home, Russian was the usual language in government offices and schools, courts, and universities. The Russian tsar had to be Russian Orthodox in religion, but in the nineteenth century, every tsar married a foreign princess, though they all converted to Orthodoxy as a condition of marriage. The last tsar, Nicholas II, married a German princess, Alix—or Aleksandra Fyodorovna, as she was known after her conversion—who had been brought up in England at the court of Queen Victoria. At home, the imperial family usually spoke English, though sometimes German and French, as well as Russian.

In the second half of the nineteenth century, the tsar attempted to introduce a more centralized administration using Russian. This process, usually described as **russification**, did not aim to make Finns, Poles, Jews, and others into Russians, but rather to create a more unified empire where Russian could serve as the means of communication among all of the empire's inhabitants. Nevertheless, russification caused great resentment among non-Russian elites who, like Dmowski, would form the nucleus of nationalist movements throughout the empire. By 1900, nationalism

Crimean War (1854–1856) War fought on the Crimean peninsula in which Russia's defeat by France and Britain led to Tsar Alexander II's Great Reforms.

Great Reforms (1861–1876) Series of Russian reforms that included emancipation of the serfs, lessening of censorship, and reform of the military and judicial systems.

Pale of Settlement Area in the southwestern Russian empire—roughly equivalent to present-day Belarus, Lithuania, and western Ukraine—where Jews were allowed to reside.

russification Effort to culturally assimilate minority national groups in the Russian empire, in particular in the second half of the nineteenth century.

was a powerful antigovernment force, in particular in the empire's western borderlands. At the same time, Russian nationalism was also growing, often exhibiting an aggressive anti-Polish and anti-Jewish attitude. Among the many problems facing the Russian empire in the early twentieth century, nationalism was one of the most threatening.

Austria-Hungary Whereas the Russian empire adopted a policy of russification and repression, Austria-Hungary attempted reconciliation. After the Compromise of 1867 divided the empire into two separate halves, Austria and Hungary ran their own domestic affairs separately, sharing military and diplomatic affairs. They also shared, of course, a ruler: Francis Joseph was emperor (Kaiser) in Vienna, but king (*király*) in Budapest. The rights of minority nationalities were assured by law throughout Austria-Hungary, but in practice the Hungarians tried to impose their language on the Slovaks and Romanians who lived in Hungary. Anyone wishing to gain an education and rise socially would have to master the difficult Hungarian language. Rather like in Russia, this harsh policy had the opposite effect of what Budapest hoped for. Slovak and Romanian peasants were easily propagandized by nationalists, who pointed out that they would have better economic, cultural, and educational opportunities in their own national states.

In Austria, the national issue was a source of constant political complications. Among the larger non-German groups were Czechs, Poles, and Ukrainians (Ruthenians). Poles were given broad autonomy in the eastern region of Galicia, where they lived in large numbers. Somewhat later, the Ukrainians of eastern Galicia were granted special language rights. Little by little, Czechs also made significant gains, such as being able to use their language in schools and state offices. The 1882 split of Prague University into German and Czech institutions was also a major achievement for the Czechs. These concessions served to embolden rather than satisfy the nationalists. At the same time, German nationalism was on the rise, and in Vienna it was difficult to piece together a lasting government coalition from the various battling parties. Some were already predicting that the Habsburg Empire would not survive the death of its elderly ruler, Francis Joseph, who had been on the throne since 1848.

Syllabus of Errors Document issued by Pope Pius IX in 1864 condemning many modern beliefs, including rationalism, socialism, communism, and liberalism.

Leo XIII (r. 1878–1903) Successor of Pius IX, pope who attempted to find ways of reconciling Catholic faith and the modern world.

De rerum novarum (*About Modern Things*) Document issued by Pope Leo XIII in 1891 condemning socialism and the exploitation of workers and calling for cooperation between classes.

Second Socialist International (1889–1914) Loose organization of working-class political parties dominated by Marxists.

Universalism in the Roman Catholic Church

The Roman Catholic Church had no reason to favor nationalism. When Rome was incorporated into Italy in 1870, Pope Pius IX refused to acknowledge the Italian state. At the time, he was pushing the Vatican Council to adopt the doctrine of papal infallibility, which holds that papal pronouncements on matters of faith and dogma must be accepted by all Catholics. With this new doctrine, Pius hoped to strengthen the church's position against all forms of modernism, from nationalism and socialism to progress, liberalism, and lay education. Pius's negative opinion of nearly all aspects of modernity may be seen in his *Syllabus of Errors* of late 1864. Here he condemned, among other things, rationalism, socialism, liberalism, and attempts to reconcile church doctrine with scientific discoveries. Pius's total rejection of constitutionalism and modern politics cut the ground out from under moderate Catholics who had been attempting to reconcile their faith with modern life.

Pope Leo XIII's *De Rerum Novarum* In 1878, Pius IX died and was succeeded by a far more conciliatory pope, **Leo XIII**. He was no less an enemy of nationalism, socialism, and rationalism than his predecessor, but he recognized that the church needed to find a compromise that would allow Catholics both to participate in modern life, including politics, and to remain faithful to their religion. Pope Leo's social views were set down in his encyclical *De rerum novarum* of 1891. Here he took a moderate position, though he condemned socialism and the liberal principle of absolute property ownership rights. True Catholics, he set down, must neither support socialist movements nor exploit others economically. Capitalist exploitation was, Leo stressed, every bit as sinful as socialism. The pope called on the Catholic faithful to support those parties that best exemplified Christian values—for example the Center Party in Germany. Nonetheless, the church continued to emphasize its international, indeed universal, role in human affairs.

Internationalism in Politics

Socialists were even more opposed to nationalism than the Catholic Church. In 1864 socialists set up the "International," bringing together socialists from different countries. In particular the **Second Socialist International**, organized in 1889 after Marx's death, worked to strengthen ties between socialists of various nationalities in different countries. Socialists pledged themselves to international solidarity and solemnly declared that they would never go to war. Practically speaking, however, they admitted that socialist organizations would need to be created on a national level. Sometimes national and socialist agendas were pursued simultaneously. The Polish Socialist Party, for example, aimed to overthrow the existing political order and establish an independent—and socialist—Polish republic.

Hulton Deutsch Collection/Corbis

Pope Pius IX started his papacy as a liberal, but the revolutions of 1848 transformed him into a staunch conservative. He opposed liberalism, socialism, and nationalism—including the unification of Italy. His rejection of Italian unification led to tensions between the Catholic Church and the Italian nation-state that were not resolved until the twentieth century. Which aspects of modernity did Pius IX reject?

Anarchism Some who sought to overthrow the political order described themselves as **anarchists**. Like the socialists, anarchists looked forward to a world of shared prosperity, diffusion of political power, and the destruction of the powerful centralized state. But while socialists increasingly accepted the Marxist program of industrial development and a worldwide revolution, anarchists used more flexible tactics, from education and propaganda to **terrorism** and assassination. Some anarchists thought that killing a powerful political leader would strike a blow against state repression. The most famous anarchist, **Mikhail Bakunin**, once famously declared, "The urge to destroy is also a creative urge!" Among the victims of anarchist attacks were Tsar Alexander II (1881), President Sadi Carnot of France (1894), Spanish premier Antonio Canovas de Castillo (1897), Empress Elisabeth of Austria (1898), and U.S. President William McKinley (1901).

Pacifism Where the anarchists often used violent means to achieve peaceful ends, **pacifists** aimed to prevent war at all costs. As technology and militarism advanced, the prospect of war became evermore horrific. Why not, the pacifists argued, take the millions spent on armies and weapons and use it for better housing, sanitation, cultural facilities, and education? Perhaps the most famous pacifist of this period was the **Baroness Bertha von Suttner**. Daughter of an Austrian field marshal, Suttner became a worldwide celebrity in 1889 with the publication of her bestselling novel *Lay Down Your Arms!* Suttner dedicated the remainder of her life to encouraging pacifism and working to prevent war.

One of her greatest achievements was to persuade the Swedish industrialist and inventor of dynamite, **Alfred Nobel**, to fund an annual prize for those promoting the cause of peace. The Nobel Peace Prize, along with prizes for chemistry, medicine, and literature, was first awarded in 1901. Appropriately, Suttner herself was awarded the Nobel Peace Prize in 1905. The pacifist movement could point to several successes during this period, including the establishment of international treaties on the conduct of war known collectively as the Geneva Conventions that resulted from meetings called by Tsar Nicholas II in 1899, and the Hague conferences and tribunals (1899–1907), which used arbitration as one method of settling diplomatic disputes.

anarchists Political radicals of the late nineteenth century who distrusted central government authority and advocated violent means to overthrow the existing political order.

terrorism Use of violence to intimidate individuals, ruling groups, or entire nations to achieve an individual's or group's political-ideological goals.

Mikhail Bakunin (1814–1876) Russian anarchist and revolutionary who espoused a political ideology opposed to all forms of state authority.

pacifists Individuals who oppose war and violence on principle and seek peaceful solutions to state conflicts.

Baroness Bertha von Suttner (1843–1914) Austrian writer and pacifist organizer whose novel *Lay Down Your Arms!* (1889) gained her an international reputation.

Alfred Nobel (1833–1896) Swedish industrialist who funded the Nobel prizes, which he hoped would encourage world peace and the development of culture.

Checking In

By yourself or with a partner, explain the significance of each of the following selected key terms:

antisemitism	Great Reforms
Theodor Herzl	*Syllabus of Errors*
Dreyfus affair	anarchists
pogroms	Alfred Nobel

CHAPTER Review

Summary

- The revolutions of 1848 were a major watershed in European history.

- After 1848, nationalism tended to be adopted as a political tool by conservatives, as in the unification of Italy and Germany.

- After 1848, nationalism and the ideal of the nation-state became broadly accepted as a political norm, despite the continued existence of multinational states like the Russian empire and Austria-Hungary.

- In the late nineteenth century, nationalism became increasingly aggressive, even racist, and often allied with antisemitism.

- The increased acceptance of nationalism was challenged and criticized by socialists, pacifists, and the Catholic Church—each for different reasons.

Chronology

1848	Marx and Engels publish *The Communist Manifesto*
1848–1849	Political uprisings sweep Europe
1852	Louis Napoleon declares himself Emperor Napoleon III
1854–1856	France and Britain defeat Russia in Crimean War
1859	Napoleon III and Piedmont defeat Austria in northern Italy; Italian unification begins
1861	Victor Emmanuel II is crowned king of Italy; Tsar Alexander II emancipates Russian serfs
1861–1865	America fights Civil War
1863	Polish rebellion against Russian rule fails
1866	Prussia defeats Austria, opening the way for German unification
1867	Austria grants Hungary semi-autonomy
1870–1871	Franco-Prussian War ends with French defeat
1871	Prussian king William I becomes emperor of Germany; Paris Commune is crushed by French government
1875	Ottomans crush Bulgarian uprising
1877–1878	Russians defeat Turks in Russo-Turkish War
1878	Bulgaria wins autonomy from Ottoman Empire
1894	Dreyfus is convicted of espionage
1896	Herzl publishes *The Jewish State*
1897	First Zionist Congress is held in Basel, Switzerland
1901	First Nobel prizes (for peace, chemistry, medicine, and literature) are awarded
1901	Queen Victoria dies; end of Victorian age

© Cengage Learning

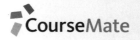 **CourseMate** Visit the CourseMate website at **www.cengagebrain.com** for additional study tools and review materials for this chapter.

Test Yourself

To gauge your mastery of the material in this chapter, answer the questions below. More than one answer may be correct.

The Revolutions of 1848

1. The revolutions of 1848 touched most European countries, but not:

   a. France
   b. Prussia
   c. Russia

   d. Italy
   e. Hungary

2. In Paris, the revolution of 1848:

   a. Was set off by a banquet campaign.
   b. Forced the abdication of King Louis Philippe.
   c. Put Louis Blanc on the throne.

   d. Was initially characterized by an alliance between middle-class liberals and radicals.
   e. Saw the setting up of national workshops to help the unemployed.

3. In central Europe, such as the German states, Austria, and Hungary, 1848 was characterized by:

   a. Strong feelings of nationalism.
   b. Demands for constitutions from kings and other rulers.
   c. The breaking away of Hungary from Austrian rule.

   d. The triumph of nationalism in the form of a unified Germany.
   e. The crowning of Kossuth as King of Hungary.

4. Among the most significant outcomes of the revolutions of 1848 was:

   a. Establishment of a more liberal political order under Francis Joseph in Vienna.
   b. The coming to power in France of Louis Napoleon, who would later proclaim himself Napoleon III.
   c. The Slavic Congress in Prague, which urged all Slavic peoples to unite under Russian rule.

   d. The failure of the Frankfurt Assembly to unite Germany.
   e. The introduction of a constitution in Russia for the first time.

5. Historians think of 1848 as a watershed year because:

   a. It was successful in gaining national rights for Germans, Italians, and Hungarians.
   b. Marx and Engels published *The Communist Manifesto* in that year and in subsequent decades the influence of socialism would grow steadily.
   c. Pope Pius IX embraced the revolutionary movement and liberalized Catholicism.

   d. Despite the failure of nationalist demands in 1848, these movements paved the way for future successes like the Austro-Hungarian Compromise of 1867.
   e. Democratic constitutional regimes were established in Germany, Austria, and Italy.

Now that you have reviewed and tested yourself on this part of the chapter, take time to pull together all the important information by answering the following questions:

◆ What were the short- and long-term causes of the revolutions of 1848? What role did ideologies play?

◆ How did the demands and outcomes of the revolutions of 1848 differ in western and east-central Europe?

New Nation-States and Nationalist Tensions

6. Who was Giuseppe Mazzini?

   a. The prime minister of Piedmont-Sardinia.
   b. An Austrian minister who opposed nationalism.
   c. A colorful freedom fighter and Italian nationalist, known best as leader of the "Red Shirts" who fought for Italian unity.
   d. The first king of united Italy.
   e. An intellectual and fervent Italian patriot whose ideas helped unify Italy.

7. Who was Otto von Bismarck?

   a. King of Prussia after 1871.
   b. Conservative Prussian leader and chancellor (prime minister) who helped unify Germany.
   c. Liberal nationalist who opposed war.
   d. Hohenzollern Prince who fought to keep Prussia independent.
   e. Leader of the Paris Commune.

8. The Franco-Prussian War:

   a. Brought an end to the rule of Napoleon III in France.
   b. Was a disaster for Prussia.
   c. Was the final step toward the unification of Germany.
   d. Gave rise to the Paris Commune, which opposed the French government's desire to make peace with the Germans.
   e. Ended with the transfer of Alsace-Lorraine to German rule.

9. The position of Poles among national minorities in the nineteenth century was unique because:

   a. Unlike Ukrainians or Estonians, Poles had had their own state until the late eighteenth century.
   b. The Polish peasantry always identified with the Polish nation.
   c. Educated Poles actively supported both socialist and nationalist parties.
   d. Poles used the Cyrillic alphabet to write their language.
   e. Polish nationalists like Roman Dmowski argued for the integration of Jews into the Polish nation.

10. How were Bulgaria and Norway affected by nationalist movements?

    a. Bulgaria fought for and won independence from Russia.
    b. Norway split away from Sweden peacefully in the early twentieth century.
    c. Thanks in part to Russian help, Bulgaria broke away from the Ottoman Empire in the late 1870s.
    d. Due to the similarity of their language and culture, Norwegians and Swedes voluntarily united in one state in 1815.
    e. Bulgaria accepted a Russian prince as their king because of their religious and cultural similarities with Russians.

Now that you have reviewed and tested yourself on this part of the chapter, take time to pull together all the important information by answering the following questions:

◆ Nationalism can serve as both a unifying and a divisive ideology. Give examples of both.

◆ Why were liberal nationalists disappointed in the way that Germany and Italy were united?

The Expanding Role of the State

11. The process of nation building is concerned with:
    a. Building a strong nation-state.
    b. Creating institutions such as legal codes and parliaments to enhance state stability.
    c. Educating the populace in a sense of patriotism and loyalty.
    d. Strengthening the majority culture, though local differences may continue to exist.
    e. All of the above.

12. Among the factors pushing nation building in different countries were:
    a. Cheap newspapers that encouraged mass literacy in standard languages.
    b. Advances in communication like railroads and telegraph that increased identification with the country as a whole, not just to a village or region.
    c. Military training bringing together young men from all over the country.
    d. Broader suffrage, giving more citizens a "stake in the system."
    e. Appeals to universal Christian values and denunciations of Jews.

13. Education expanded broadly in the mid- and later nineteenth century because:
    a. Stable nation-states needed citizens literate in standard languages.
    b. New kinds of institutions, like technological institutes, were founded to train a new technological elite.
    c. The Catholic Church cooperated with nation-states to set up national educational systems.
    d. Increasingly, parents were not allowed to keep their children from attending school.
    e. Working-class people were increasingly able to send their children to universities.

14. Signs of the growing power of the state in the nineteenth century include:
    a. State investments and guarantees in building railroads in Austria and Russia.
    b. Compulsory military service in nearly all European countries (except Britain).
    c. The introduction of income taxes in most European countries.
    d. Factory inspections to enforce safety and labor laws.
    e. Increasing numbers of indirect taxes, such as those on matches, vodka, and tobacco.

15. Which of the following could *not* be considered a form of mass politics?
    a. Prime Minister Gladstone touring Britain by rail to explain his government's policies to the people.
    b. Émile Zola accusing the French army of a cover-up by publishing a newspaper article.
    c. Blaming Jews for economic problems, as conservative parties often did.
    d. Emperor Napoleon III's decision to declare war on Germany in 1870.
    e. The development of working-class organizations like the British Labour Party and the German Social Democratic Party.

Now that you have reviewed and tested yourself on this part of the chapter, take time to pull together all the important information by answering the following questions:

◆ What are some ways in which technology helped in the process of nation building?

◆ What are some of the pros and cons of the development toward increasingly powerful states in the later nineteenth century?

Nationalism and Its Opponents

16. What is the main difference between "liberal" and "integral" nationalism?

   a. Liberal nationalism developed mainly in the first half of the nineteenth century, integral nationalism after 1848.
   b. Integral nationalism stressed domination over other nations, often combined with an aggressive pride in one's own nation.
   c. Liberal nationalism is associated with figures such as Herder and Mazzini, integral nationalism with antisemitism and racism.
   d. Liberal nationalism was generally located on the political left, integral nationalism on the right.
   e. Integral nationalism believed that all cultures and nations had equal rights to develop.

17. Which of the following were core beliefs of antisemites?

   a. If Jews converted to Christianity, they could be accepted as equal citizens.
   b. Jews were dishonest in their business dealings.
   c. Jews had a negative effect on Christian society as journalists and lawyers.
   d. Since Jesus Christ was born into a Jewish family, it was necessary to be respectful of the Jewish religion.
   e. Even if a Jew spoke perfect French, dressed like a Frenchman, and was a patriot for France, he could never be a proper Frenchman.

18. In which ways did multinational empires differ from nation-states?

   a. Many diverse ethno-cultural and religious groups speaking different languages lived in multinational empires.
   b. Nation-states were generally dominated by a single language.
   c. Multinational empires were located in eastern, not western, Europe.
   d. Multinational empires tried to force their entire population to speak a single language.
   e. Nation-states never contained any ethnic-linguistic minorities.

19. In the later nineteenth century, the Catholic Church:

   a. Tended to be associated with conservative movements.
   b. Did not, despite its conservatism, favor integral nationalism.
   c. Remained consistently reactionary and even racist in its worldview.
   d. Was ruled over by Pope Pius IX, who was very conservative, but from 1878 by the more moderate Pope Leo XIII, who tried to find compromises between Catholic doctrine and modernity.
   e. Openly supported many new elements of modern politics, including antisemitism.

20. Which of the following did pacifists, anarchists, and socialists have in common?

   a. All opposed terrorist methods.
   b. All supported the Second Socialist International after Marx's death.
   c. All agreed that in some cases political violence was justified, indeed necessary, for progress.
   d. All collaborated with Alfred Nobel in the creation of the Nobel Peace Prize.
   e. All opposed nationalism.

Now that you have reviewed and tested yourself on this part of the chapter, take time to pull together all the important information by answering the following questions:

◆ What aspects of modernity did antisemites detest and blame on the Jews?

◆ How did multinational empires attempt to maintain stability in this period? Which of the three empires considered here was most (and least) successful in this?

CHAPTER 23

The Culture of Industrial Europe, 1850–1914

Chapter Outline

The Second Industrial Revolution
- New Materials, New Industries, New Technologies
- Communications and Transportation Networks
- New Places and Patterns of Work
- The New Concept of Leisure

Mass Society
- Mass Consumption
- Public Health
- Families and Feminism

Art and Industrial Society
LEARNING FROM A PRIMARY SOURCE: *Marie Curie-Skłodowska Recalls Her Youth in Russian Poland*
- From Realism to Abstraction in Art
- Realism and Naturalism in Literature
- Art for the Masses

Science and Social Science
- The Science of Society
- The Influence of Charles Darwin
- Chemistry and the New Physics

A NEW DIRECTION: *Marie Curie-Skłodowska Chooses to Study Physics*
- The Battle Between Science and Religion
- Critiques of Reason

CHAPTER REVIEW

1850	1855	1860	1865	1870	1875	1880

1851
Crystal Palace Exhibition opens in London

Half of English population lives in cities

1867
Nobel patents dynamite

1869
Suez Canal opens in Egypt

1872
Nietzsche publishes *The Birth of Tragedy*

1879
Edison invents the electric lightbulb

A poster advertising Cook's Travel Services. Thomas Cook was one of the pioneers of tourism, beginning with rail trips to London to see the Great Exhibition of 1851 and by century's end—as one sees in this advertisement—offering everything from seaside jaunts to round-the-world adventures. Tourism was just one example of the new forms of leisure that were becoming prevalent during this period. (NRM/SSPL/The Image Works)

After reading this chapter, you should be able to answer the following questions:

What was the second Industrial Revolution? How did it differ from earlier industrialization?

How did the second Industrial Revolution affect everyday life, society, and culture in different parts of Europe?

What is meant by the concept of "mass society?" Why was this concept increasingly important from the late nineteenth century on?

What were some of the most important advances in natural science (physics, chemistry) and social sciences in this period?

What caused the conflict between religion and the new science? How did scientists and religious believers attempt to reconcile these differences?

INDUSTRIALIZATION GENERATED profound shifts in social, political, and cultural ideas. Technological advances from the telegraph to the bicycle radically created new rhythms of everyday life. No less radical were new intellectual movements that rejected religion and attempted to apply the scientific method to all realms of human experience, from social relations to the body and sex. Artists and musicians challenged accepted modes of expression, creating works of art that shocked and enraged conservative critics. Women sought a more visible place in society, even demanding political rights. The clash between traditional social and cultural expectations and new ways of experiencing the world led some to fear that the old and the new could never be reconciled.

New technology and the spread of industrial production had a broad impact on the population, helping to create what we know as mass society. Great population growth brought together people in ever-larger cities, most arriving by railroad. The divide between "city" and "countryside" became far more easily traversed.

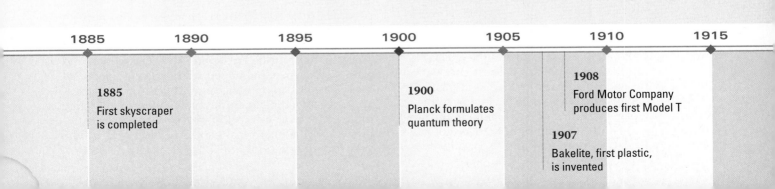

1885	1890	1895	1900	1905	1910	1915

1885
First skyscraper is completed

1900
Planck formulates quantum theory

1908
Ford Motor Company produces first Model T

1907
Bakelite, first plastic, is invented

Significant numbers of workers and peasants came to enjoy certain levels of political freedom, comfort, and leisure time.

Despite economic differences and class prejudices, more and more people came to expect that their children would be better educated, healthier, and better off materially than they had been. The idea of progress gained broad support. Yet not everyone enjoyed social advancement, political participation, and cultural development, especially those in southern and eastern Europe. And not everyone welcomed the leveling effect on culture that the growth of mass society brought with it. Some denounced it as soulless, shallow, and mediocre.

Art and science also changed radically. Realism in art, which aimed to reproduce images found in nature, gave way to abstraction, which aimed to express the artist's individual perceptions of the world. Scientific research in new fields, such as work on radioactivity, compelled scientists to completely re-examine previous understandings of the physical world. The theories of Charles Darwin and Sigmund Freud sparked great controversies.

This was a period of contrasts and contradictions. Economic and industrial developments utterly transformed some regions while others—in particular, the Balkan and Iberian Peninsulas, southern Italy, and much of the Russian empire—changed relatively little. The growth of mass culture clashed with individualistic ideologies. Atheistic materialism gained many adherents, but the majority of Europeans retained their religious faith. Changes in economies, in technology, and in science, society, and everyday life were rapid and overwhelming, and yet, looking back after 1918, many who lived through these decades wistfully recalled the stability of the era. For most Europeans, this was a time of prosperity, peace, and cultural richness.

The Second Industrial Revolution

◆ **What technological advances were made during the second Industrial Revolution?**

◆ **How did technological advances alter work and leisure?**

In the second half of the nineteenth century, in particular after 1870, industrial and technological changes so profoundly altered European life that the era is called the second Industrial Revolution. These innovations included the widespread use of steel and electricity in industry, major breakthroughs in chemistry, the increasing use of petroleum to supplement coal and other power sources, and a variety of new inventions that revolutionized transportation and communications.

All these new industries created new categories of jobs and required corporate organization on a scale previously unknown. Industrial advances increased pay and decreased working hours, allowing Europeans to consume more material goods and enjoy more leisure than ever before.

The prosperity of the period gave new possibilities to artists and writers, whose works were viewed and purchased by large numbers of people. Science played a dual role in these changes, both enabling new, more efficient industrial techniques and calling into question long-held views about humanity's place in the world. For some, the discoveries and claims of science threatened traditional religious beliefs. This was an optimistic era, believing in progress and eagerly anticipating new advances. At the same time, some worried darkly that cold scientific rationality and mediocre mass society could destroy the very foundations of moral life and society.

New Materials, New Industries, New Technologies

The stages of early industrialization in Britain and on the continent had been driven by the mass production of textiles in factories using first water power and then coal-driven steam engines. The railroad was a second driving factor in the economic upsurge that spread to the continent following the Napoleonic Wars. In the second half of the nineteenth century, however, while textiles and iron continued to be vital to the industrial economy, new materials and processes—steel, chemicals, petroleum—revolutionized industrial production.

When the Flatiron Building in New York City was completed in 1902, it was the tallest building in the world. "Skyscrapers" became a symbol of American dynamism for Europeans, but steel also revolutionized construction in Europe. What was the connection between mass production of steel and new possibilities for very tall buildings? Looking at this image, what elements of the Flatiron Building seem modern? What seems old-fashioned, compared with later skyscrapers?

engines and cars, steamships, and increasingly sophisticated weaponry.

Steel also allowed new forms in architecture: its strength and flexibility meant that buildings could expand upward to an unprecedented degree. The skyscraper—an American invention—was the result. The ten-story Home Insurance Building in Chicago was erected in 1885, but expansion skyward was limited by the need to climb stairs. In 1887, this problem was solved with the invention of the high-speed elevator, and by the early twentieth century New York City had a number of skyscrapers, including the beautiful Flatiron Building with twenty-one stories, completed in 1902.

Modern Chemistry Creates New Products Rapid advances in textile production during the first half of the nineteenth century created a need for dyes, which scientists in Britain, France, and Germany figured out how to synthesize from coal tar. The first artificial dye of purple hue was given the French name *mauve.* Soon red ("magenta"), brown, and other colors were synthesized. These cheap new dyes meant that inexpensive brightly colored clothing now could be mass produced.

By the late nineteenth century the German chemical industry had far outstripped all competitors, producing some 90 percent of the world output of synthetic dyes as well as new medicines (most famous of all was aspirin), artificial materials such as Bakelite (an early plastic, 1907), and cellophane (1912). Artificial fertilizers began to be produced in the 1840s, and chemists found new uses for poisons—such as the insecticide DDT, discovered in 1874, though not used until much later. The poisonous gas ammonia that formed an important part of many fertilizers was also used in the development of explosives. In 1867, Swedish businessman Alfred Nobel took out a patent for dynamite, which allowed highly explosive liquid nitroglycerine to be used more safely by combining it with a fine powder and packaging the mixture in tubes. The German firms founded in this era—such as BASF, Bayer, and Hoechst—continue today to be among the largest multinational chemical firms in the world.

Another innovation in chemistry was the process that produced cheap paper from wood pulp, which fostered the growth of mass-circulation newspapers and journals. The use of this cheap paper and mechanized printing, using steam-powered presses, made possible cheap newspapers such as *La Presse* in Paris (founded 1836) and the *Daily Telegraph* in London (founded 1855). The telegraph allowed fast-breaking stories from around the world to be reported almost instantly, and newspapers often printed special editions to cover major events. The invention of the linotype machine in 1886, which mechanized typesetting, allowed newspapers to get stories into print faster. Advances in printing allowed for more illustrations in newspapers and magazines. And the use

Mass-Produced Steel The most important of these was mass-produced steel. Steel combines the advantages of pig iron (being hard and durable) and wrought iron (being flexible and resistant to cracking). The advantages of steel had long been known, but before the mid-nineteenth century, there had been no economical method of mass-producing steel. Then, in the 1850s and 1860s, the **Siemens-Martin (open-hearth) process** revolutionized steel production. In 1861, before these innovations had begun to spread throughout Europe, the total steel output in Britain, France, Germany, and Belgium was around 125,000 tons. By 1871, production had more than tripled and in 1913 topped 30 million tons—over eighty times the amount made in 1871. This massive output went into rails, railroad

Siemens-Martin (open-hearth) process Technological advance that allowed mass production of steel.

National Motor Museum/HIP/The Image Works

Early automobiles, like this 1899 Renault, were expensive and unreliable. Very few people aside from the very rich could afford cars, and many conservative aristocrats scorned the risky and smelly machines. Early automobiles were often called "horseless carriages." Looking at this image, what elements of this early auto justify that description?

of **lithography** from the 1830s onward allowed artists to create drawings, etchings, and other artworks in multiple copies, making artwork more affordable for a mass audience.

New Forms of Energy The original Industrial Revolution was fueled mainly by coal, but coal was difficult to mine and expensive to transport, especially to countries that lacked natural deposits, so industrialists sought new forms of energy. Coal gas came to be used for streetlights in all major cities early in the nineteenth century. Later it was replaced by natural gas, often discovered when drilling for oil, and petroleum products, from kerosene to gasoline, were increasingly sought after.

Kerosene was widely used in lamps, where it produced greater light with less danger of fire than candles. Petroleum was also adopted for use aboard steamships, where the liquid fuel eliminated the need for stokers, and the reduction in labor costs helped offset the higher cost of the fuel itself. Two other distillations of petroleum, gasoline and diesel fuel, were used to propel the first automobiles; the diesel engine was patented in 1892, and the Ford Motor Company's Model T—the first mass-produced automobile—rolled off the assembly line in 1908. By 1900, the petroleum industry was growing enormously, especially in Russia and the United States, making **John D. Rockefeller** one of the world's richest men.

Electricity is not so much a source of energy as a novel means of transmitting power over distance. Knowledge of electricity was not new, but the innovation of the late nineteenth century was to harness electricity for practical use and to perfect methods

of generating and supplying it over long distances. The harnessing of electricity meant that industrial plants could be located away from coal fields or other sources of energy, such as water power. Unlike bulky steam engines, small electric motors could be transported from one location to another.

Within the factory, the use of electricity eliminated many of the dangerous belts and pulleys that had connected the steam engine to machinery. As cables and insulation to carry electricity became more efficient, hydroelectric power could be generated and used over a broad area. The spread of electric light, using **Thomas Edison**'s invention of the lightbulb (1879), proceeded in tandem with the establishment of public power stations. The first of these was set up in England by the **Siemens brothers** in 1881, and by 1914, electricity for offices, industry, and households was available in all major cities of Europe, though only the richest and most up-to-date families had electricity in the home.

Communications and Transportation Networks

Perhaps no invention symbolized the compression of time and space during this period better than the telegraph, invented in the United States in the late 1830s. By the late 1860s, telegraph lines ran from one end of Europe to the other and were even connected by transatlantic cable to the United States. By the end of the century, all continents were connected by underwater cable, meaning that a message could go from London to Johannesburg to Calcutta to Sydney to Vancouver in a matter of minutes.

Telegrams and Telephones Telegrams were sent using **Morse code**, a system of dots and dashes representing letters invented for this purpose, and flew through wires as electrical impulses. The telegraph required skilled operators who could translate the dots and dashes into words, offices where individuals could send messages, and messenger boys (in this period, nearly always male) to bring telegrams— often with bad news—to offices and residences. The impact on government, industry, and private life was enormous. At the beginning of the nineteenth century, news could travel no

lithography Printing method used widely from the 1830s that produced text and color images used in posters and illustrated magazines.

John D. Rockefeller (1839–1937) Founder of the Standard Oil Company, which dominated the American petroleum market.

Thomas Edison (1847–1931) American inventor of the microphone, record player, and the first commercially practical lightbulb.

Siemens brothers German brothers (Werner, Wilhelm, and Carl Heinrich) who, starting in 1847, established branches of their electrical firm in England, Germany, and Russia.

Morse code System combining dots and dashes representing letters, invented by the American Samuel Morse for sending messages over the electrical telegraph.

faster than horses or pigeons. By 1900, news traveled at the speed of light from one corner of the globe to the other. On a practical level, the telegraph enabled, for example, the tsar in St. Petersburg to check up on governors in distant Kamchatka or Tashkent, businessmen to keep in touch with offices abroad, and ordinary people to contact loved ones, though usually only in emergencies because of the high cost.

In 1876, the American Alexander Graham Bell perfected a device that carried not just electrical impulses but actual sounds over a wire: the telephone. Unlike the telegraph, the telephone provided a direct link from person to person, though few working-class people could afford the new invention at first and some aristocrats, such as Emperor Francis Joseph of Austria-Hungary, refused to speak on the telephone at all. Still, many in business and government quickly recognized the advantages of the telephone, and by 1900 telephone exchanges had been set up throughout Europe and North America, from London to Moscow, Berlin to Los Angeles. In Germany, the Siemens and Halske Company enjoyed a near monopoly in building telephone networks. In 1912, among the ten cities with the most telephones per capita, five were in the United States, three in Scandinavia, and two in Germany. The invention was also used to transmit other forms of sound, such as musical performances and news. By the 1890s, the *théâtrophone* in Paris allowed subscribers to hear the latest operas and concerts, and in Budapest thousands subscribed to a service providing news, musical performances, plays, stock market reports, and lectures by telephone.

The "Wireless" Radio Soon another invention of the 1890s, the wireless or radio, made telephonic concert and news services obsolete. Perfected for practical purposes by the Italian **Guglielmo Marconi**, wireless telegraphy, as it was then called, seemed useful primarily for communication between ships at sea. In 1899, the first distress signal from a ship at sea was sent. When the state-of-the-art ocean liner the *Titanic* went down on its first voyage on the night of April 14, 1912, it sent out distress signals; unfortunately the telegraph operator on the nearest ship was not on duty. A ship three times as far away did receive the signals, but

when it arrived some two hours later, most of the *Titanic* passengers were already dead in the frigid waters of the North Atlantic. Wireless and telegraph communications meant that by the following morning, people all over the world could read in their local newspapers that the ship had struck an iceberg and had sunk rapidly with the loss of more than 1,500 lives. But few heard of the tragedy by radio, which did not become a common household appliance until the 1920s or later.

Canals and Steamships The world was connected not only by telegraph wires and cables but also increasingly by steamship service and railroads during these decades. For the British, the steamship was vital in linking the homeland with India, though in the 1850s the one-way trip took around a month. The opening of the **Suez Canal** in 1869 cut travel between the Mediterranean Sea and the Indian Ocean in half and speeded up mail service between Britain and its colony India.

Steamship travel between Europe and the Americas became increasingly rapid, cheap, and—in the first- and second-class cabins—comfortable. By the 1890s, a steamship ticket from Italy to Argentina had become so inexpensive that many Italians traveled to Argentina to work as agricultural workers there during spring and summer, then returned to do the same in Italy, taking advantage of the reversed seasons in the Northern and Southern Hemispheres. Travel from northern Europe to New York took less than two weeks, and millions of immigrants made that journey in search of economic and political freedom. The **Panama Canal**, which opened in 1914, connected the Atlantic and Pacific Oceans. Cutting through mountainous terrain, it was a marvel of engineering.

Railroads Connect East and West By the 1870s, railroads linked all the European capitals (Istanbul, or Constantinople, the name used by nineteenth-century Europeans for the city, followed in 1883). European capital and engineers also extended railroads through South America, India, Africa, and Russia. The **Trans-Siberian Railroad**, begun in 1891, helped Russia transport hundreds of thousands of soldiers to Manchuria to fight the Japanese in the Russo-Japanese War a little more than a decade later. Military planners recognized the key role that efficient railroad transportation could play in warfare. The fact that Germany had the most developed railroad network in Europe was perceived as a direct threat by the French and Russian general staffs.

The increased traffic on rail and road required new bridges. In 1849, Buda and Pest were finally linked by a permanent bridge over the Danube, a first step to the unification of the two cities. The Royal Albert Bridge, designed by engineer and railroad innovator Isambard Kingdom Brunel, opened in 1859, stretching 455 feet over the river Tamar in southern England.

Guglielmo Marconi (1874–1937) Italian physicist best known for perfection of radio ("wireless telegraphy"); awarded the Nobel Prize in Physics in 1909.

Suez Canal An artificial waterway connecting the Red Sea and the Mediterranean, built by the British and French and opened in 1869.

Panama Canal An artificial waterway connecting the Atlantic and Pacific Oceans, built from 1904 to 1914 by American military engineers.

Trans-Siberian Railroad Russia's ambitious railway project connecting Moscow with the Pacific Ocean, begun in 1891 and completed in 1916, which caused friction with Japan.

Most famous of all was the Brooklyn Bridge, completed in 1883 after a decade of construction. Spanning almost 1,600 feet, it connected Manhattan with what was then a still mainly rural Brooklyn. Building bridges involved new materials like dynamite and steel; similar techniques and materials were used by Gustave Eiffel in the tower named for him in Paris, completed in 1889.

New forms of transportation also took to the air. Germany became a leader in the production of dirigibles or blimps, flying an airship called a zeppelin (named for the German Count Zeppelin) for the first time in 1900. An even more startling development was the Wright brothers' successful flight in 1903, opening the skies to heavier-than-air flying machines. Although few people actually traveled by air, thousands watched in awe as dirigibles and primitive airplanes, whose impact on warfare, the economy, and culture in the new century would be profound, took to the skies.

New Places and Patterns of Work

As Europe industrialized, it also urbanized as hundreds of thousands of people left farms and villages for better wages and a more exciting life in the cities. In 1800 there was only one city—London—with a population of over 1 million; only twenty-three cities had more than 100,000 inhabitants. By 1900, London's population had grown to over 4 million and five more European cities had over 1 million inhabitants (Paris, Berlin, Moscow, St. Petersburg, and Vienna); 135 cities had populations over 100,000. Manchester had by then topped 600,000.

The population of Berlin increased from around 500,000 at midcentury to over 2 million sixty years later. The Polish textile town of Łódź (not by chance known as the Polish Manchester) exploded in size, from a mere 519 inhabitants in 1809 to more than 300,000 at the end of the century. Throughout Europe, cities such as Budapest, Rome, Madrid, and Hamburg grew impressively.

Living Conditions in Cities Most of the newcomers to cities lived in wretched and expensive lodgings and tenements. In some cases, overcrowding was so severe that beds were rented out in two or more "sleeping shifts" on a twenty-four-hour basis. Hygiene and health suffered greatly in such places, and tuberculosis was rampant, claiming thousands of lives yearly. But running water and central heat were increasingly available, even for the less well-off, and electric tramways and—in Paris and London—subways made it possible for workers to live in less crowded, leafy suburbs and commute to work.

London's "underground" was the first to open, in the 1860s, and the Paris "metro" dates from the first decade of the twentieth century. By that time, even smaller cities such as Warsaw and Stockholm

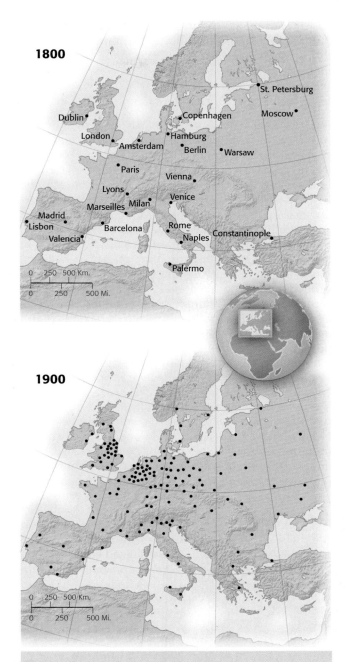

Map 23.2 **European Cities with Populations over 100,000, 1800 and 1900** The rapid growth of population combined with migration from rural to urban areas in Europe is reflected in the significant increase in large cities during the course of the nineteenth century, as shown in these maps. © *Cengage Learning*

1. Which of these cities are located in regions that industrialized before 1850 ("first" industrialization)?

2. Which regions and countries show the greatest density of urban centers? How does this correlate with their rate of industrialization?

had streetcars and trams connecting the suburbs and downtown. Public transportation allowed workers to live farther from the factories, and cities became increasingly differentiated by social class. In Berlin's West End, the bourgeoisie built villas, while workers lived across town in tenements.

New Professions, Shorter Working Hours Many of the people riding the streetcars to work were employed in new **white-collar** positions. As prosperity increased, so did the places to spend or save that money. Department stores, such as the **Bon Marché** in Paris and KdW (Kaufhaus des Westens) in Berlin, also opened in Budapest, Milan, and elsewhere. But saving money was also a middle-class concern; the number of banks increased and, with them, the number of clerks. Similarly, the number of lawyers, physicians, and dentists went up markedly, and these professionals employed even larger numbers as receptionists and assistants. Government bureaucracies also burgeoned as the state's role in the economy and everyday life grew. Most of these new positions were filled by young men, but women were able to find employment in banks, department stores, and professional offices. They were, however, expected to quit work upon marrying.

By the late nineteenth century the average workday had shrunk in western and central Europe, partly because of technological innovations and partly under pressure from organized labor. As fewer workers, both in offices and in factories, lived adjacent to their places of work and workdays shrank to ten and even eight hours, the routine of transport/work/transport became common. Through all layers of society in the industrialized countries, one fact was constant: the entire day was no longer taken up by work, freeing up precious hours for **leisure**.

The New Concept of Leisure

As the predominant form of work became employment with a fixed number of hours per day, contracted to an employer, employees also found they had "free time," time after work that was open to other pursuits. The concept of leisure was new, and it was much enjoyed in the second half of the nineteenth century, especially as the workday shrank to about ten hours and the idea of a work-free weekend took hold. Most Europeans had both more time and more money for leisure activities than had their grandparents' generation. Electric lighting meant that dance halls and nightclubs could stay open well into and even through the night. Alcohol consumption increased considerably, worrying religious authorities and middle-class moralists who had chosen for themselves more "high-brow" entertainment such as concerts, operas, and plays.

Popular Amusements Nearly everyone in large cities frequented cafés and dance halls. There one could eat and drink, listen to music, experience light comic and dramatic performances, and, of course, dance. Some cafés catered to a select middle-class audience, but for commercial reasons, most desired the largest possible number of patrons and served anyone who enjoyed drinking, dancing, listening to music, and watching clown shows and comedy acts. By the 1890s, the Spanish flamenco and Argentine tango competed with more traditional popular music and dance for public attention.

Magic lantern slide shows were increasingly popular, allowing mass audiences to experience—at least visually—travels to exotic destinations around the world. Around 1900, the moving picture became technically and commercially viable, and cinema houses sprang up in all major European cities. In the United States, by far the leader in this new technology, millions went to the "picture show" every week. The early picture shows were often long on sensation and short on memorable artistic value, but the new medium of film opened up vast possibilities for artists in the new century.

Photography The new technology of photography, perfected in the late nineteenth century, allowed amateurs to make pictures with their own cameras. The word *Kodak*, specially created by American businessman George Eastman in 1888 to market his small cameras, passed into several languages. Photographic technology, which produced an image as exact as the best sketch or painting, had an important impact on artists, who no longer needed to copy the world but could instead portray their own impressions of light, color, and shadow. Photography also facilitated the spread of another popular diversion: pornography.

Railroads and Tourism Railroads made travel for pleasure possible for the masses. When the Great Exhibition of the Works of Industry of All Nations, better known as the **Crystal Palace Exhibition**, was opened in London in 1851, about one-fifth of the people of England visited, in part on package tours from the travel entrepreneur Thomas Cook. Many of the visitors had never been far from their hometown or village. After the St. Petersburg–Warsaw railroad opened in 1862, travelers could embark from Moscow in a sleeping car and emerge in Paris a few days later. From 1883

white collar Employment that does not involve physical labor, such as that of professionals (lawyers, doctors, teachers) and office workers.

Bon Marché First department store, opened in Paris in 1852 and catered primarily to middle-class people.

leisure Time for relaxation or recreation, new in the later nineteenth century owing to industrial and social advances.

magic lantern Early form of the modern slide projector that projected images painted on glass plates onto a screen.

Crystal Palace Exhibition Great Exhibition of the Works of Industry of All Nations, opened in London's Crystal Palace in 1851.

Solomon R. Guggenheim Museum, New York/The Bridgeman Art Library

Henri Rousseau's 1908 painting, *The Football Players,* reflects a growing interest in sports and other leisure-time activities among middle- and even working-class Europeans. Not only the football itself was mass-produced but also the outfits worn by the players. One or two generations earlier, before the second Industrial Revolution, games were much less standardized. Rousseau's artistic treatment of these men is obviously stylized, but what elements of modern football-soccer do you see depicted here? Looking at the image, name at least two objects that would not have been present (or only in very different form) before the industrial revolution Weeks. Like industrialization itself, most modern forms of leisure, tourism, and sport began in England and spread to the rest of Europe in the second half of the nineteenth century. English words themselves invaded other languages, so that Russians and Germans speak of "sport," Swedes enjoy "fotboll," Italians engage in "turismo," and Poles refer to a bicycle as a "rower" after one British company (Rover) that manufactured them.

onward, they could take the Orient Express from Paris through six countries, ending up in the exotic Ottoman capital, Istanbul. Russian aristocrats could now spend their summers on the French Riviera.

Wealthy Europeans traveled by railroad to spas such as Baden-Baden and Karlsbad (Karlovy Vary in the Czech Republic), where they "took the waters," relaxed, played cards, flirted, and engaged in other diversions. Christian pilgrims numbering in the hundreds of thousands annually took the train to Lourdes, where the peasant girl Bernadette Soubirous claimed to have seen a vision of Virgin Mary in 1858. And even workers of modest means could take suburban railroads for day trips to the countryside.

The rich could travel in comfort, riding in first class or even hitching their own private railcars onto trains. They stayed in new and magnificent luxury hotels such as the Hotel Adlon in Berlin, where the Kaiser put up his own guests.

Sports Workers also enjoyed sports, both as active participants and as spectators. First in Britain, then throughout Europe, football in the forms of soccer and rugby brought together enthusiasts in increasing numbers. By the early twentieth century, it is estimated, some half million British men regularly played. Golf, spreading outside Scotland, became the sport of choice for the well-to-do. After the chain-driven bicycle was perfected in the early 1890s, cycling swept western Europe. Social conservatives were outraged by the mobility and personal freedom that bicycles gave women, as well as by the new fashions that allowed them to ride astride these new iron horses. Tennis in its modern form was invented in the 1870s and rapidly gained popularity, not least of all because it was the rare sport—golf was another—that middle-class men and women could play together.

Leisure created new industries. Originally, blown-up pig bladders were used as soccer balls, but their irregular shape made the game unpredictable. In 1855, the American inventor Charles Goodyear applied the process of vulcanizing rubber that he had invented a decade earlier to the manufacture of soccer balls. This first "modern" soccer ball did not yet have today's familiar white-and-black pattern but was regular in shape. Soon others adopted Goodyear's technique, and a new industry was born. The same desire for a more regular, predictable game led to the mass production of baseballs, bicycles, tennis rackets, and sports outfits.

Checking In

By yourself or with a partner, explain the significance of each of the following selected key terms:

Siemens-Martin (open-hearth) process

Thomas Edison

Guglielmo Marconi

Suez Canal

Panama Canal

Trans-Siberian Railroad

Bon Marché

Crystal Palace Exhibition

Mass Society

◆ **How did economic changes alter society and family life?**

◆ **What impact did science have on society?**

In the second half of the nineteenth century mass production in industry and mass consumption in department stores influenced the social order. High levels of literacy, political participation, and (relatively speaking) material affluence in western Europe reduced differences between social classes and expanded opportunities for social advancement. Measured by these criteria, mass society appeared first in Britain (excluding Ireland), Scandinavia, France, Belgium, and the Netherlands. Central and southern Europe, Russia, and the Balkans lagged behind.

By the early twentieth century, access to education and to some level of political participation had come to be expected, increasingly by women as well as men. Greater numbers of people were now able to enjoy better food, brighter clothes, and a longer life. Advances in the biological sciences led to new medicines and vaccines. The new opportunities for employment and consumption also influenced women's place in the home and in society, opening the way for a new movement, feminism.

Mass Consumption

The benefits of technological innovation came first to the wealthy, but in the second half of the nineteenth century, they expanded rapidly to the urban poor and peasants out in the countryside. Mass production created a **mass society** in which prosperity spread among different classes. This heightened affluence and widespread education meant that obvious external differences between "high" and "low," such as clothes and speech, were reduced. Factory-produced textiles and manufacture of garments made clothing so cheap and colorful—reflecting the availability of cheap synthetic dyes—that few peasants even in less developed countries like Russia continued to make their own clothes. In fact, peasants could now afford several changes of clothes, including undergarments—a novelty at the beginning of the century, but a basic by 1900.

Consumption as Leisure: The Department Store

Cheap newspapers and magazines, distributed widely by the thickening rail networks, meant that even people in remote regions could see and seek to imitate the latest fashions from Paris or St. Petersburg. And mass production brought prices down so that more and more middle- and sometimes working-class people could afford to dress fashionably. The famous department store Bon Marché was hailed as "a cathedral of commerce for a congregation of consumers" by the ironic French writer Émile Zola.

The name Bon Marché means both "good market" and "inexpensive" in French—and the idea of a store for the masses was the creation of a self-made man, Aristide Boucicaut, and his wife, Marguerite. Their first store, opened just after the 1848 revolutions, introduced the novelty of clearly marked prices and welcomed people—mainly women—to come and look over the merchandise without obligation to purchase. The revolutionary concept of allowing potential customers to look without necessarily buying amounted to the invention of shopping as a pastime—and was wildly successful.

In 1869, Boucicaut resolved to build a large new store using the most modern architecture. When the palatial structure opened in 1887, it delighted customers with its sumptuous decorations, sweeping marble staircases, and electric elevators. Shoppers are still delighted by Bon Marché, a palace in which to shop and be seen shopping. Boucicaut was a masterful businessman, offering such novel services as a catalogue of merchandise, free delivery, a money-back guarantee, and various sales like the "white month" in January. Zola wrote a novel about the department store—*The Ladies' Paradise* (1883)—and a metro station was given Boucicaut's name.

Thousands of attractive young women were hired as department store clerks, though previously selling had been regarded as unseemly for women. Women also joined the growing lower middle class as teachers, nurses, postal clerks, typists, and telephone operators. Although large numbers of young women continued to work as servants into the twentieth century, the higher pay, greater personal autonomy, and social prestige of these new occupations attracted many. Although the salaries were low, the job allowed—indeed required—women to dress and behave like members of a more privileged class. Conservatives found this blurring of social distinctions outrageous and complained that it was becoming impossible to distinguish "people of good family" from servants by dress, and increasingly even by speech and manners.

Public Health

The population of Europe more than doubled between 1800 and 1900 (from around 200 million to 430 million), despite the departure of millions of emigrants for the Americas. This population explosion can be explained partly by better nutrition and the lack of massive epidemics or major wars after 1815, but improvements in medical knowledge and treatment were also a factor.

Microorganisms, Germs, and Disease Medical research paralleled work in physics: both were searching for invisible causes for certain phenomena. In physics, these were gamma rays, x-rays, and radiation; in medical science, the invisible cause was the germ, which was discovered in the 1880s. But long before that, scientists knew that *something* spread diseases, and they devised practical programs to prevent disease transmission. In the eighteenth century it had

mass society Modern society characterized by universal legal rights, education, a large middle class, and a high level of equality among classes.

been discovered that using matter from cowpox pustules created an effective vaccine against smallpox. Similarly, the connection between dirty water, rotting waste, and disease had long been made—but most continued to think that disease was spread by foul smells.

Around 1820 cholera, a disease spread by unclean water, spread from India and Central Asia to Russia and western Europe. Crowded towns with minimal hygiene and limited access to clean water were an ideal breeding ground for the disease, which caused epidemics in a number of cities. In London a major outbreak in 1854 allowed the physician **John Snow** to promote his theory that the disease spread not through the air but by bad water. Snow's data showing that all the cholera victims had drunk water from a single source, the Broad Street pump, convinced even his critics. Snow was also one of the first physicians to use chloroform and ether to deaden pain. His most famous patient was Queen Victoria, who was grateful for his treatments during childbirth.

Around the same time in France, **Louis Pasteur** was demonstrating that heating wine to 55 degrees Celsius killed the disease-causing microorganisms in it. His technique, called pasteurization, was later applied to beer and milk. Pasteur also pioneered methods for vaccinating against a number of diseases, including rabies and anthrax. Perhaps most important for medical practice, Pasteur demonstrated methods of sterilization that reduced the risk of infection in surgery and hospitals. Pasteur's suggestion that tiny particles of organic matter floating through the air could contaminate matter and cause fermentation was seized on by the English surgeon Joseph Lister, who showed that treating wounds with carbolic acid significantly reduced infections. Lister's antiseptic technique cut in half the number of deaths from infection following surgery and was later immortalized in the mouthwash Listerine.

Germs and Hygiene: From the Laboratory to the Hospital Pasteur's pathbreaking work in microbiology was continued by **Robert Koch** in Germany. Previously scientists had suspected the existence of microorganisms too small to be seen under the microscope; Koch proved their existence by isolating the cholera bacillus in 1883. He showed that every disease had its own microbiological cause and devised treatments and vaccines for these diseases. During the last part of his life, Koch devoted himself to the cause and treatment of the infectious lung disease tuberculosis, that plagued of factory workers and city dwellers. In 1905, Koch was awarded the Nobel Prize in Medicine in recognition of his achievements. Until the mid-nineteenth century, a sick person was *more* likely to die if admitted to a hospital, where unhygienic conditions often led to infections and death, than if treated at home. **Florence Nightingale**, who helped organize military hospitals in Istanbul during the Crimean War, returned to Britain to improve hospital care there. She virtually invented the profession of nursing, which from the start was an almost exclusively female occupation—and in Catholic countries often carried out by nuns. Building on the discoveries of Snow, Pasteur, and Lister, Nightingale worked throughout her long life to create modern, antiseptic, but welcoming hospitals. By the early twentieth century, the chances of dying after surgery, during childbirth, or in a hospital had been much reduced.

Families and Feminism

The technological and economic changes wrought by industrialization penetrated all aspects of public and private life. In the industrial cities, families no longer functioned as production units, and children came to be recognized as more of an economic burden than a benefit. Medical advances reduced infant mortality rates, so a woman who gave birth to, say, a dozen children could reasonably assume (at least in western and central Europe) that ten would survive to adulthood. But these children would be expensive to raise and educate, especially as the number of years required for a good education increased. In these decades, family planning in the form of contraception and medical abortions became widespread. Nearly everywhere, both were illegal, but laws did not prevent women from attempting to limit the number of their offspring.

Women, Falling Birthrates, and Education Throughout Europe, birthrates went down, but unevenly. French politicians, not coincidentally all male, expressed grave concern at France's falling birthrate, the lowest among the Great Powers. The German birthrate, though relatively high, went down steadily in this period. Birthrates remained high in the least developed areas, such as Russia, Italy, Spain, and the Balkan Peninsula.

Among the middle classes, having fewer children meant that women had more time for other activities. Before 1848, women could not study at most universities, but during the second half of the nineteenth century these barriers gradually broke down. Women seeking higher education often went to Switzerland

John Snow (1813–1858) English physician who proved that cholera is spread by drinking water and who pioneered the use of chloroform to deaden pain.

Louis Pasteur (1822–1895) French scientist who developed a process for heating liquids to kill disease-causing organisms, now known as pasteurization.

Robert Koch (1843–1910) German bacteriologist who established that many diseases such as anthrax, tuberculosis, and cholera were caused by bacterial infections.

Florence Nightingale (1820–1910) English reformer and creator of nursing as a profession who was instrumental in creating hygienic, well-organized hospitals.

to receive training as doctors, lawyers, or economists, such as the famous Polish-Jewish socialist **Rosa Luxemburg**. Other exceptional women, like **Marie Curie**, studied in Paris, though not all professors—or male students—were comfortable with women students. Although few women succeeded in surmounting the great economic and social obstacles and completing the university course, these first successful pioneers demonstrated that women were in no way intellectually inferior to men.

Women's Rights Yet women's educational opportunities, especially in secondary and higher education, remained limited, and it was often difficult for an educated woman to earn her own living. The laws of most European countries did not recognize women as adults. Very often a woman could not even open a bank account, sign a contract, or purchase property without her husband's (or, if single, her father's) permission.

Women also had little protection against abusive husbands. Despite the passage of the Matrimonial Causes Act in Britain in 1857, which allowed divorces without separate acts of Parliament (previously any divorce needed to be approved by Parliament as a specific, separate act), few women could afford the expense—and social scandal—of a divorce trial. Similarly, in France, divorce was made legal from 1884 onward, but the procedure was so complicated and expensive that few actually used it. In many countries, like Russia, divorce was not a possibility, and men who grew tired of their wives often simply abandoned them, along with their children. Socialists like Friedrich Engels mocked the morality of middle-class sexuality and family life, calling it little more than a legalized form of enslavement and prostitution.

Demanding Legal Equality: Feminism Despite their legal disabilities, women were increasingly literate and active in society. Whether raising children or working in factories, hospitals, or offices, women were increasingly well informed on contemporary cultural and scientific subjects. Some, like Florence Nightingale, chose to forgo marriage to devote themselves to other causes. Others, like the middle-class feminist **Emmeline Pankhurst**, dedicated themselves to achieving equal rights and opportunities for women, including the vote. Pankhurst, whose daughters Christabel and Sylvia

also became notable feminists, embraced radical tactics such as arson, vandalism (like dumping jam into mailboxes), and public protests. For these activities Pankhurst was arrested several times, going on hunger strikes in jail and being force-fed. Such activities were controversial, but they attracted attention to women's unequal status before the law and in the economy. Feminists in other European countries and in the United States did not always agree with these tactics, but they recognized that such radical actions forced the male establishment to take women seriously.

Feminism—use of the word to refer to the struggle for women's rights dates from this period—was mainly a middle-class phenomenon, for women workers and peasants were usually more concerned with better wages and work conditions than specific gender-based demands. Socialists denounced feminism as a bourgeois diversion, arguing that true equal rights for women would come only with socialist revolution. But the idea that women should have the same professional and political rights as men was gaining ground.

 Checking In

By yourself or with a partner, explain the significance of each of the following selected key terms:

Louis Pasteur	Marie Curie
Robert Koch	Emmeline Pankhurst
Florence Nightingale	feminism
Rosa Luxemburg	

Art and Industrial Society

- ◆ **What impact did the economic and social changes of the late nineteenth century have on the visions and techniques of artists and writers?**

- ◆ **How did mass production and mass society influence art and literature?**

Industrialization so deeply permeated all aspects of life in the late nineteenth century that art was profoundly altered as well. Art reflected the new industrial mass society both in its subjects and, even more strongly, in its techniques and artistic vision. Photography and the mass production of images through lithography and other techniques called into question the need for realistic art. Artists also worried that the mass production of cheap objects would degrade people's ability to appreciate the beautiful. Yet though artists experimented with new techniques, most people continued to prefer traditional realism and bought mass-produced images in the thousands and millions. Increasingly, artists found themselves out of tune with mass society.

Rosa Luxemburg (1871–1919) Polish-Jewish socialist who worked with V. I. Lenin and was murdered in 1919 by right-wing nationalists after a communist uprising in Berlin.

Marie Curie (1867–1934) Polish-born chemist and physicist who studied radioactivity and radium, the winner of two Nobel prizes.

Emmeline Pankhurst (1858–1928) English crusader for women's suffrage who was often arrested for her radical activities.

feminism Movement for equal rights for women, including legal equality and the right to vote.

Marie Curie-Skłodowska Recalls Her Youth in Russian Poland

In an autobiographical memoir that appeared in 1930, Marie Curie described the major events and milestones of her life. This memoir was published together with autobiographical sketches by American activist Jane Addams, Japanese feminist Sugimoto Etsu Inagaki, and other women. The editor of this volume, Helen Ferris, wanted to provide young women with positive role models and evidence that women could make their mark on society. In this passage, Marie Curie recalls teaching Polish children under repressive Russian rule in the 1880s.

❶ Why did the Russian government oppose education for these Polish children? Why might the Russian government see education as dangerous?

❷ How important do you think the example of other successful women was for inspiring Marie to try to find a way to study abroad? What do you think motivated Madame Curie to write this short memoir?

❸ What were the advantages and drawbacks of solitary study for Curie?

❹ What does this passage reveal about family responsibilities in this period? How do they differ from family obligations today?

❺ How does this belief in study as a moral force compare with the teachings of Comte and the positivists?

❻ Why could Polish young people in the 1880s think of study as a patriotic activity? Can you imagine any students in the twenty-first century having the same attitude, and, if so, where and why?

❶ Since my duties with my pupils did not take up all my time, I organized a small class for the children of the village who could not be educated under the Russian government.... We taught the little children and the girls who wished to come how to read and write, and we put in circulation Polish books which were appreciated, too, by the parents. Even this innocent work presented danger, as all initiative of this kind was forbidden by the government and might bring imprisonment or deportation to Siberia.

My evenings I generally devoted to study. **❷** I had heard that a few women had succeeded in following certain courses in Petrograd or in foreign countries, and I was determined to prepare myself by preliminary work to follow their example....

❸ My solitary study was beset with difficulties. The scientific education I had received at the lyceum [high school] was very incomplete; it was well under the bachelorship program [high school curriculum] of a French lyceum; I tried to add to it in my own way, with the help of books picked up at random. This method could not be greatly productive, yet it was not without results. I acquired the habit of independent work, and learned a few things which were to be used later on.

❹ I had to modify my plans for the future when my eldest sister decided to go to Paris to study medicine. We had promised each other mutual aid, but our means did not permit our leaving together. So I kept my position for three and a half years, and, having finished my work with my pupils, I returned to Warsaw, where a position, similar to the one I had left, was awaiting me....

❺ Another means of instruction came to me through my being one of an enthusiastic group of young men and women of Warsaw, who united in a common desire to study, and whose activities were at the same time social and patriotic. It was one of those groups of Polish youths who believed that the hope of their country lay in a great effort to develop the intellectual and moral strength of the nation, and that such an effort would lead to a better national situation.... **❻** We agreed among ourselves to give evening courses, each one teaching what he knew best. There is no need to say that this was a secret organization, which made everything extremely difficult.

Source: Helen Ferris, ed., *When I Was a Girl: The Stories of Five Famous Women as Told by Themselves* (New York: MacMillan, 1930).

Jean-François Millet's 1857 painting *The Gleaners* depicts women's backbreaking work of gleaning fields after harvest. Like many other realist works by Millet, this painting shows a scene from the everyday life of poor peasants. In what ways can this image be seen as an example of Realist art? At first glance, industrialization appears not to have reached this area—but what objects can you see that could be products of industrial mass production?

Musée d'Orsay, Paris/Giraudon/The Bridgeman Art Library

Realism Movement in literature and painting that aimed at the objective reproduction of reality without idealization.

Jean-François Millet (1814–1875) French painter concerned with depicting social problems in a realistic style.

Honoré Daumier (1808–1879) French artist best known for his bitingly sarcastic caricatures of contemporary political figures and bourgeois society.

Ilya Repin (1844–1930) Russian Realist artist who specialized in painting enormous scenes from Russian past and contemporary life.

Edouard Manet (1832–1883) French painter who chose scandalous subjects and influenced the later Impressionists.

Salon de Paris Exhibition of paintings sponsored every other year by the Academy of Painting and Sculpture.

From Realism to Abstraction in Art

The scientific and technological advances of the mid-nineteenth century made artists look at the world in a new way, leading to a new artistic movement calling itself **Realism**. Realists rejected conventions dictating that the proper subjects for painting should be lofty—scenes from classical Greece, for example, or the Bible. Instead, they took their subjects from among working people, the peasantry, and events of everyday life. Among the most famous Realists was **Jean-François Millet**, whose paintings often depicted peasants at work, their faces grim and resigned. Realist painters were often political radicals who wanted to convey social and political opinions in their works. The caricatures of **Honoré Daumier**, for example, acidly criticized the existing social order. In Russia, the paintings of **Ilya Repin** revealed the stark misery of the Russian lower classes.

From Realism to Impressionism The paintings of **Edouard Manet** also laid open society's more sordid side. He shocked his contemporaries by making a well-known prostitute the subject of his painting *Olympia*. In the same year, 1863, Manet again outraged critics by painting together a pair of fully dressed gentlemen and an unabashedly naked woman in *The Luncheon on the Grass*, alluding to the hypocrisy existing in relations between men and women. Manet's technique remained Realist in his careful and objective attention to detail, but his subjects were deemed scandalous.

Midcentury French art had two main centers, both in Paris: the Academy of Painting and Sculpture, where young artists learned realistic techniques and painted exalted scenes; and the **Salon de Paris**, which exhibited new paintings sponsored by the academy every other year. Having one's work accepted for display at the Salon was the ambition of all young artists, as it meant success and often wealth. But the works of Manet and others who did not accept the Academy's narrow view of art had no chance of being accepted to the Salon. Angry at this conservatism, the rejected artists organized their own Salon des Refusés—an exhibition of refused paintings beginning in 1863.

In the 1870s, artists began to experiment with new ways of depicting reality. Instead of striving

Ilya Repin's works exemplify the Realist style in Russian art and often portray the poorest Russians, as in this painting, *Volga Barge-Haulers,* 1870–1873. Like other Realists, Repin did not intend merely to show a scene from Russian life: he wanted to shock viewers and remind them of the grinding poverty and social injustice present in their country. Compare this image with Millet's *The Gleaners* (see p. 702). What similarities and differences do you see in subject matter and style?

for photographic realism, artists like **Claude Monet** sought to capture the artist's perception of light and shadows—a technique labeled **Impressionism** by a hostile critic. The label stuck but soon lost its negative connotation. The Impressionists sought to convey not an image of an object but rather the artist's perception and technique for depicting color, light, and shadow. Monet's paintings of haystacks at different times of day showed how the play of light created entirely different colors and images. Impressionists such as Edgar Degas, Auguste Renoir, and Georges Seurat painted the new amusements of the day—dance halls, boating trips, and cafés. The great graphic artist **Henri de Toulouse-Lautrec**, who was close to the Impressionists, raised the poster to an artistic form, thereby blurring the distinction between art and advertising. Toulouse-Lautrec's posters advertising the Chat Noir (Black Cat) nightclub, the singer Jean Avril, and Le Moulin Rouge (Red Mill) dance hall became classics.

Going Beyond Impressionism During the last decades of the nineteenth century, Paris became the center of the entire art world. American painters like James McNeill Whistler and Mary Cassat came to live and paint there; Cassat remained in France all her life. The Spaniard **Pablo Picasso** arrived in Paris in 1899 and also spent most of his life there. With its academic traditions, the masses of young artists rebelling against those traditions, government support for the arts, and a large wealthy and sophisticated society of art lovers, Paris attracted thousands of artists from everywhere in Europe and throughout the world.

The Impressionists emphasized the artist's perception over any single objective vision of reality, but at the beginning of the twentieth century new movements progressed even further from visual realism. The Viennese painter **Gustav Klimt** combined realistic and abstract elements in such works as *The Kiss* (1907–1908), in which the kissing faces of a couple are surrounded by colorful geometric patterns. Increasingly, artists aimed to go beyond surface reality. Picasso's influential and shocking *Demoiselles d'Avignon* of 1907

portrays the "Young Ladies of Avignon" as flat expanses of pink paint with exaggerated eyes and noses. Picasso and other so-called **Cubists** depicted the same object as seen simultaneously from various angles, resulting in a multifaceted, fractured image that represented the mind more than the eye.

The movement away from Realism in art culminated in **abstract art**. In abstract works, such as those of the Russian Vasily Kandinsky and the Swiss Paul Klee, swirling shapes and colors do not represent any specific "real" objects but aim instead to depict the artist's emotions and perceptions of the world. The **Futurists**, who published their "Manifesto" in 1909, took these new artistic techniques and added a political twist, provocatively calling for the destruction of past artistic and literary works to open the way for the new. In *Nude Descending a Staircase* (1912), the Futurist Marcel Duchamp used Cubist techniques to portray his subject—movement. These new trends in nonrepresentational art would have a great influence on the art of the twentieth century but failed to find broad acceptance or understanding in their own time.

Claude Monet (1840–1926) French Impressionist painter best known for his studies of light on landscapes, such as haystacks and the Rouen Cathedral.

Impressionism Artistic movement in France beginning in the 1870s that aimed to reproduce the painter's impression of light on a scene.

Henri de Toulouse-Lautrec (1864–1901) French artist who created bright and compelling posters advertising nightclub singers and dance halls.

Pablo Picasso (1881–1973) Spanish painter, founder of the Cubist school, and lifelong experimenter with abstract techniques.

Gustav Klimt (1862–1918) Viennese painter whose portraits integrated rich abstract patterns with realistic and expressive human faces.

Cubists Painters who challenged traditional realism by breaking up three-dimensional figures into different "cubes."

abstract art Art depicting the artist's view of the world through free use of color and shapes.

Futurists Artistic movement beginning in 1909 with a "Manifesto" that stressed energy, movement, even violence in visual and literary art.

Gustav Klimt, *The Kiss*, 1907–1908. Klimt was at the same time an extremely popular portraitist and a controversial and innovative artist in turn-of-the-century Vienna. This painting, one of his most famous, incorporates abstract, ornamental surfaces and sinuous human figures locked in a passionate embrace. Does this image appeal to you? Why or why not? How do the abstract shapes in the painting (especially on the figures' "cloaks") symbolize masculine and feminine? Why do you think Klimt chose to stray from strictly realistic portraiture to this more abstract style? (Osterreichische Galerie Belvedere, Vienna/The Bridgeman Art Library)

Realism and Naturalism in Literature

Realism was not limited to the visual arts. Writers such as Charles Dickens in England, Ivan Turgenev in Russia, and Gustave Flaubert in France all wrote Realist fiction, aiming to describe life objectively and with an eye toward social criticism. Dickens's heroes such as the orphans Oliver in *Oliver Twist* (1838) and Pip in *Great Expectations* (1861) struggle to improve their social position, eventually succeeding in being accepted in middle-class society. Turgenev's most famous novel, *Fathers and Sons* (1862), highlights the generational conflict between the liberal gentry "fathers" and the radical younger generation during the Great Reform period in Russia. In Flaubert's *Madame Bovary* (1856), a woman locked in a loveless marriage to a dreary though not evil man seeks joy by taking a lover and is ultimately destroyed by her choice. Flaubert's sympathetic description of an adulteress led in 1857 to a court case against the novel for obscenity, but the writer was acquitted.

Turgenev's contemporary **Fyodor Dostoevsky** also wrote novels in the Realist style. But Dostoevsky, who despised Turgenev as a weak liberal overly fond of western European culture, combined psychological depth with political and religious passion. As a young man in the 1840s, Dostoevsky had been condemned to death for his involvement in a liberal reading circle. The death sentence was called off at the very last moment, after the first of the condemned had already been bound to a post to be shot. Dostoevsky was exiled to Siberia, where he rejected liberalism and rediscovered his Christian faith. In his best-known novel, *Crime and Punishment* (1866), an impoverished university dropout, a would-be great man like Napoleon, plans the perfect crime—the killing of a vile moneylender. After carrying out the murder, his guilt proves that no man is above God's law. In another work, *The Possessed* (or, translated more accurately, *The Devils*, 1871–1872), Dostoevsky delves into the psychology of Russian radical terrorists of the late 1860s.

Going beyond Realism, Émile Zola described his own approach as "naturalist," and he exposed—in extensive scientific detail—the unhealthy aspects of modern society. In a series of very popular novels, he depicted several generations of two families beset by poverty, alcohol, prostitution, and other social ills, implying that their ills are inherited and inevitable. His characters are miners, café owners, prostitutes,

Fyodor Dostoevsky (1821–1881) Russian Realist novelist whose expansive narratives examine conscience, character, and redemption.

Tretyakov Gallery, Moscow/The Bridgeman Art Library

Vasily Perov's famous 1872 painting of the novelist Fyodor Dostoevsky shows the writer's intense gaze and haggard expression. Subject to epileptic seizures and plagued by an addiction to gambling that never allowed him to achieve material prosperity, in certain ways Dostoevsky resembled one of his own tortured characters. What elements of composition and style in this painting convey a brooding, intense personality?

printed by the thousands. On the other, artists were disturbed when their images were poorly copied and distributed in distorted, cheapened form. Some purists also attacked Toulouse-Lautrec and the Czech poster artist Alphonse Mucha for "prostituting" their art in posters that advertised cigarettes, bicycles, singers, and dance halls. For others, the brightly colored posters were a form of art available for the enjoyment of those who could never afford a painting. Posters bridged the gap between "high" and "low"—a single, dynamic, brightly colored figure presented in a style unconventional enough to catch the attention. The success of these poster artists is apparent in the continued popularity of their images a century later.

Technology and Art for the Masses Lithography and photography also made possible a great proliferation of illustrations in books, periodicals, and as prints. In Russia, hardly a peasant home was without the *lubok*: a cheap lithographed print sold by peddlers. These prints were mass-produced on zinc plates and then often brightly colored by hand. Favorite subjects for the *lubok* were popular heroes, images from Russian history or mythology, and religious scenes. Similar mass-produced prints brightened the homes of the poor in other parts of Europe, though middle-class critics complained of their low artistic value, crude workmanship, and garish colors.

But it would be wrong to distinguish too sharply between "popular art" for the masses and works by "great artists" such as the Impressionists and Cubists. In Paris, tens of thousands flocked to the Salon, especially on days when admission was free. Poster art was broadly exhibited and accepted, and even the paintings of great artists were quickly available in prints and popular magazine illustrations.

Some artists seized on mass production to argue that it should aim to produce beautiful things. William Morris, founder of the **Arts and Crafts movement** in Britain, designed books, tapestries, and even wallpaper, applying medieval designs to modern uses. His burning desire to see artistic beauty incorporated into everyday life came together with his commitment to equality as a socialist who worked with Karl Marx's daughter, Eleanor. Morris aimed to merge the useful and the beautiful. "Have nothing in your house that you do not know to be useful or believe to be beautiful,"

and their clients, whose lives are described without moralizing. Zola dismissed criticism that his novels were rough, inelegantly written, and full of the sordid. "I am little concerned with beauty of perfection," he wrote. "All I care about is life, struggle, intensity. I am at ease in my generation."

Literature was also mass-produced. All the works mentioned here were bestsellers both in their original language and in translation. Inexpensively produced books were readily available, and bookshops in railroad stations provided reading material for travelers. Nearly all novels were first published in newspapers in serial form, helping boost circulation. Unfortunately for authors, it was very difficult to make a living from writing, as effective international **copyright** protection dates back only from 1887.

Art for the Masses

Advances in technology—especially lithography and photography—were both welcomed and denounced by artists. On the one hand, lithography allowed a work of art such as Toulouse-Lautrec's posters to be

copyright Legal protection for authors and artists, giving them specific rights to profit from the works they create.

lubok Brightly colored print, often of a religious or historical scene, mass-produced and sold by peddlers to Russian peasants.

Arts and Crafts movement
Effort led by English artist and designer William Morris to merge beautiful design and workmanship with industrial techniques.

he advised. But Morris and his followers failed to find a broad following. His decorations and graceful designs were simply too expensive for most peasants and working-class people.

 Checking In

By yourself or with a partner, explain the significance of each of the following selected key terms:

Realism	Pablo Picasso
Honoré Daumier	abstract art
Ilya Repin	Fyodor Dostoevsky
Impressionism	Arts and Crafts movement

Science and Social Science

◆ **How did science expand and change in the late nineteenth century?**

◆ **How did new scientific theories challenge religious ideas, and how did religion accommodate science?**

During the nineteenth century it appeared that the Enlightenment promise of understanding the world entirely through scientific observation was being fulfilled. The application of the scientific method to the study of human behavior and society created new academic disciplines—the fields of anthropology, psychology, and especially sociology. Some argued that the natural world and human society could be understood without recourse to any metaphysical basis—that is, without any belief in God. Geological discoveries that the earth was far older than had been thought called into question the literal interpretation of the Bible.

Even more shocking to traditional religious sensibilities was the theory of evolution advanced by Charles Darwin. By suggesting that human beings evolved from less complex animals, evolution struck at the very heart of traditional religion: the idea that humanity was created in God's image. Even time and space were no longer constants, as Albert Einstein's theories in the field of physics showed. Some religious leaders of nearly every faith furiously attacked the new science, whereas others pointed out that scientific observation cannot provide a basis for morality and argued for a reconciliation between science and religious faith. The arguments that started in these decades continue to fuel controversy more than a century later.

The Science of Society

Sociology was the newest and perhaps the most ambitious of the new fields of inquiry into human existence. As its name suggests, sociology saw itself as the "science of society," claiming that human society can be studied, quantified, and understood like any other part of the natural world. Indeed, nineteenth-century sociologists called their discipline the queen of sciences, from which all other human sciences derived. Others were less sure that scientific methods could explain the inner workings of human society, and some feared that trying to do so would strip away the mysteries of human relations and impoverish life.

Auguste Comte and Positivism The beginnings of sociology may be found in the philosophy of **Auguste Comte**, a student of Claude Henri de Saint-Simon. To understand world history, Comte proposed the law of three stages, which explained history as the steady progress of humanity's understanding of the world through rational observation. The first stage of history he called the "theological," the era when people's primary means of explaining the world was through reference to God. The second stage was the "metaphysical," during which religious explanations were supplanted by a belief in ideas as reality—for example, G.W.F. Hegel's theory of history. The third and final stage, and one that Comte wanted to usher in with his own work, he named the "positive"— thus, his philosophy came to be known as **positivism**. In the positive era, the world would be explained exclusively by verifiable scientific data and method, and all branches of human knowledge would come together in a unified scientific system. The natural and social sciences would supplement each other, but both would share a common methodology based on mathematics and the scientific method.

Comte's call for a scientific study of society and the idea and method of positivism were widely influential. In the second half of the nineteenth century, the discipline we now know as sociology was created in great part along Comtian lines. Among its most famous practitioners was **Émile Durkheim**, who used **empirical** methods and statistics to examine the common values that held societies together. In his *Division of Labor in Society* (1893), Durkheim argued that the division of labor—so hated by Marx—actually had positive effects on society by allowing "organic solidarity" to arise, in which the various parts of society worked together like organs in a healthy body. His classic work on suicide, first published in 1897,

Auguste Comte (1798–1857) French thinker, inventor of the word *sociology* and proponent of positivism.

positivism Comte's philosophy of knowledge emphasizing empirical observation and the idea that all natural and human phenomena can be explained in scientific terms.

Émile Durkheim (1858–1917) French sociologist influenced by positivism who used empirical methods and statistics to study society.

empiricism Belief that all knowledge can be derived from scientific observation.

attributed rising suicide rates (a widespread fascination of the period) to a breakdown in commonly held values.

Comte's insights also found resonance in Germany. There, two sociologists, Friedrich Tönnies and Georg Simmel, made the now classic distinction between *Gemeinschaft,* a traditional community of shared values, and *Gesellschaft,* a modern industrial society in which individuals seldom knew their neighbors and felt no strong emotional attachment to the people around them. **Max Weber** looked into the inner workings of authority and obedience. He used the term *charisma* to explain why some political leaders are successful in commanding respect and power. His short work *The Protestant Ethic and the Spirit of Capitalism* (1904–1905) aimed to explain the role that religious and moral values played in the development of modern capitalism. In their own ways, all of these early sociologists were attempting to come to terms with the social change and dislocation of this era. Their work reflected concerns also present in the works of Karl Marx, whose *Das Kapital (Capital)* appeared in three volumes between 1867 and the 1880s.

The Influence of Charles Darwin

Perhaps the greatest challenge to traditional values and outlooks on the world was presented by the thought of **Charles Darwin**. Darwin was the son of a self-made man, a physician who grew wealthy from his tireless work and financed his son's studies and, crucially, a trip around the world on the *HMS Beagle* (1831–1836), during which Darwin sketched and gathered samples of thousands of exotic species. He wrote many books on topics ranging from fossils to barnacles, orchids to carnivorous plants, worms to coral reefs, and, most famously, *On the Origin of Species* (1859) and *The Descent of Man* (1871).

Evolution and Natural Selection Darwin's primary contribution to science was not the idea of **evolution**—many previous thinkers, including his own grandfather, Erasmus Darwin, had noted the possibility of evolutionary change in nature. What Darwin offered, however, was an explanation of how evolution took place: **natural selection**. In his revolutionary *On the Origin of Species,* Darwin suggested, drawing on examples taken from his extensive career as a naturalist, that in any population of animals, certain features give individuals a greater chance for survival. For example, a bird that feeds mainly on nuts and seeds needs a strong bill to crack these open. Over time, natural selection favors these strong-billed birds, and the species evolves in that direction. For birds feeding on fruit or insects, however, other characteristics are more important.

Random mutations that enhanced survival played a key role in evolution. At the time, Darwin could not explain just how mutations arose and how these changes were transmitted to future generations. The discovery of the gene and the rediscovery in 1900 of the experiments in genetics carried out earlier by **Gregor Mendel** helped buttress Darwin's theories. *The Descent of Man* put forth the even more controversial thesis that humanity had descended from less advanced primates. Darwin's theory described a state of constant struggle for survival. Thus, even the smallest genetic advantages, he posited, could favor the survival of one species over another. Darwin's notion of the gradual improvement of species over time—the less favored individuals dying out—went along with the era's belief in the progress of human society.

Social Darwinism and Eugenics Darwin's theories had a huge impact, and not only on the scientific community. His ideas were broadly debated by fellow scientists, who compared him with Galileo and Isaac Newton, and in the popular press, where he was ridiculed as "the monkey-man." The greatest long-term effect of Darwinism outside of biology, however, came from those who applied the concept of natural selection to human society. So-called **social Darwinists** such as **Herbert Spencer** argued that human societies also evolved through struggle, what Spencer called "the survival of the fittest," and that a society's health depended on the strongest elements being allowed to develop themselves freely.

Spencer was careful not to equate the "fittest" with the most aggressive or physically able, but others used these ideas to oppose social programs that aided the poor and weaker elements in society. Social Darwinists now used the language of science to validate the long-held opinion that the poor were to blame for their own poverty. Many social Darwinists also advanced arguments about European "racial superiority" over the peoples of Asia and Africa. Allied with such ideas was the new discipline of

Max Weber (1864–1920) German sociologist who considered religious belief, charisma, and bureaucracy central influences on political and social life.

Charles Darwin (1809–1882) English scientist who formulated the theory of natural selection and authored *On the Origin of Species* (1859).

evolution Biological theory that diverse animal and plant species developed over time through a combination of genetic mutation and environmental influence.

natural selection Darwin's theory that better-adapted species survive (and reproduce) while others are eliminated.

Gregor Mendel (1822–1884) Austrian monk credited with the discovery of the theory of genetic heredity.

social Darwinists Theorists who applied Darwin's theory of natural selection to human society, arguing that poorer and weaker segments of society deserved their fate.

Herbert Spencer (1820–1903) English philosopher and political theorist who coined the phrase "survival of the fittest."

No 10   5 Cmes

LA Petite LUNE

Bureaux : rue Coq-Héron, 5 || Dessins de GILL || Abonnem^{te} : Paris, 3 fr. — Dépar^t 3 fr. 50

DARWIN

ARBRE DE LA SCIENCE

(Voir à la page 2.)

Darwin's controversial theory of evolution made him a world-wide celebrity—though he had to endure many caricatures of himself as a "monkey man," as in this August 1878 issue of the French satirical journal. Why did Darwin's suggestion that humanity may have evolved from other primates shock conservatives?

Archivo Iconografico, S.A./Bibliotheque nationale de France

Russian anthropologists and ethnographers, for example, described the everyday life and beliefs of Siberian and Central Asian native peoples. In St. Petersburg, exhibitions of the dress, art, and lifestyle of these exotic peoples were organized—showing not only artifacts like clothing, carpets, and dwellings but sometimes individuals of these ethnic groups as well. Peasants also interested anthropologists, such as **Olga Semyonova Tian-Shanskaia**, who studied Russian peasant life. Anthropologists generally saw themselves as representatives of a superior civilization, which they contrasted with the object of their research, so-called primitive or savage peoples, doomed to extinction by human progress, whose culture was put on display in museums and exhibitions.

Chemistry and the New Physics

In chemistry and physics, too, new research was fundamentally changing the understanding of the physical world. Dmitri Mendeleev's periodic table, first published in 1869, advanced chemistry by classifying elements according to atomic weight and periodical—that is, recurring—properties. Mendeleev's arrangement of the elements allowed chemists to predict characteristics of unknown elements according to their atomic weight and place in the table, thus paving the way for later discoveries, such as Marie Curie's radium.

Up to this time, following Isaac Newton, physics had understood all phenomena and motion as the result of the action of one particle on another. But this mechanical view made it difficult to understand the action of light and other invisible rays that traveled rapidly across space and appeared to have no mass. For Newtonian physics to work, scientists had theorized that a substance called ether permeated the universe, though it had never been discovered or measured. The search for ether would lead to the discovery of many other invisible rays and forces that in the end would establish the existence of fields of force that operated over great distances. Through experimentation and rational analysis, scientists postulated a physical world more complex than previous generations had imagined.

One practical challenge was to understand the nature of electricity. The work of James Clerk Maxwell, though mainly on a theoretical level, paved the way for practical applications of electricity for use in lighting and motors. Maxwell also predicted the existence of radio waves and theorized that light itself was a form of electromagnetism. The German scientist Heinrich Hertz proved Maxwell correct by broadcasting and receiving radio waves in the late 1880s. In late 1895, Wilhelm Röntgen discovered x-rays, a form of electromagnetic radiation. This discovery spurred others—the Curies among them—to search for other forms of radiation. All of these discoveries were rapidly developed into practical inventions by

eugenics, which sought to improve society by discouraging the reproduction of "undesirable elements." Increasingly in the early twentieth century, advocates of eugenics and scientific racism argued that certain races were inferior not only because of environment but in their very genes. Some even called for the sterilization of those judged to be physically or mentally inferior.

Anthropology The new field of anthropology also sought to describe and explain human diversity, especially as Europeans encountered different societies, religions, political structures, and kinship patterns in their colonies.

eugenics Pseudoscience aiming to improve humanity by encouraging those with "desirable traits" to reproduce; now discredited as racist.

Olga Semyonova Tian-Shanskaia (1863–1906) Russian ethnographer who collected folk songs and important data on the Russian peasantry.

Marie Curie-Skłodowska Chooses to Study Physics

Maria Skłodowska, better known to the world as Madame Curie, chose to dedicate her life to science. Born at a time when women scientists were rare and almost unthinkable, she left her native land, obtained a university education, and made her mark in scientific research. Her life reflects a period when dynamic women could defy social norms and succeed. Her career parallels the enormous growth in the importance of scientific discovery for the economy and everyday life.

Maria was born into an educated middle-class family in Warsaw in late 1867. Her father taught physics and mathematics at a Warsaw gymnasium. Her mother was also educated and served as the director of a local school for girls. But, as Poles, her parents could not teach in government schools, and the salaries they received in private schools were meager. Education in Poland was, at the time, under severe restraints. Following the Polish insurrection of 1863, Russian authorities curtailed the use of the Polish language in schools. Almost all teachers had to be native Russians, and they treated Poles with contempt and hostility. It was in this atmosphere that Maria Skłodowska received her primary and secondary education. Then, when Maria was only nine, her mother died, leaving behind four children.

Finishing high school at age fifteen, at the top of her class, Maria was forced by family circumstances to seek employment as a governess. Many years later, she remembered these years with pleasure, recalling that she had set up secret circles to teach children literacy in Polish, an activity strictly forbidden by the Russian authorities. She also studied at the underground "flying university" that Polish intellectuals had set up for young Poles. But even so, educational opportunities in Russian Poland were limited, so Maria vowed to continue her education abroad as soon as possible. Gathering her meager savings, she left for Paris in 1891 and two years later met Pierre Curie. The two married in July 1895.

Pierre Curie had just completed his doctorate in physics and was teaching at a Paris secondary school. The Curies' economic situation was far from enviable, but their work carried them through. Soon they had two daughters, but Marie (as she was now known) refused to give up her scientific work. With the help of a servant, she balanced her roles as mother and scientist. Pierre's teaching position and Marie's occasional tutoring brought in modest sums, and they were forced to carry out their research in their spare time and in a small laboratory that was little more than a shack outfitted with homemade equipment. Marie was interested in the study of x-rays—peculiar rays emitted by uranium salts—and, as she put it, "decided to undertake an investigation."

For several years the Curies studied the nature of what we now call radioactivity. In 1903 they were awarded the Nobel Prize in Physics along with the French physicist Antoine Becquerel. When Pierre was killed in an automobile accident in 1906, Marie continued their work on her own. She discovered two new elements, polonium and radium, for which she was awarded the Nobel Prize in Chemistry in 1911. At this time she was named to the faculty of the prestigious Sorbonne in Paris, the first woman to be so honored. Under her leadership, research in chemistry and physics blossomed there. Her daughter Irène Joliot-Curie also became a distinguished scientist. Marie Curie died in 1934, one year before Irène and her husband Frédéric were awarded the Nobel Prize in Chemistry.

Marie Curie's discoveries advanced scientific knowledge of radioactivity, which would be expanded on later to produce both nuclear power and atomic arms. But her choice to dedicate her life to science had other important consequences. Her dedication to science challenged conventional views of national minorities and the capabilities of women. After Marie Curie, young women could more easily envision their own place as scientists, professors, and even Nobel prizewinners.

---

other scientists and by industry: electricity was put to work in the electric lightbulb, phonograph, and innumerable other inventions by Edison; Hertz's findings were translated into the radio by Marconi; Röntgen's x-rays found practical application in health care and his name became the German word for "to x-ray."

Albert Einstein The revolutionary work of **Albert Einstein** built on these scientists' research, but, in another sense, completely reformulated physicists' understanding of the universe. In 1905, the young scientist published a paper proposing the **special theory of relativity**, suggesting that as particles approach the speed of light, their speed cannot be predicted by Newton's laws of motion. Two years later Einstein developed these ideas further, leading to the now famous equation $E = mc^2$—energy

Albert Einstein (1879–1955) German physicist most famous for his theory of relativity.

special theory of relativity Einstein's theory stating, among other things, that the speed of light is always constant while distance and time are relative to the observer.

is equivalent to mass multiplied by the square of the speed of light. Einstein postulated that light travels through empty space at a constant speed, thereby eliminating the need for any medium like ether. Einstein's theory of relativity also challenged concepts of absolute space and time because these were shown to depend on the relative velocity of the particle and the observer.

Within a few years, Einstein's theory was being hotly debated by scientists, many of whom attempted to verify or discredit relativity experimentally. As Einstein's special theory of relativity gained acceptance on both sides of the Atlantic, he followed it with the general theory of relativity in 1915, which dealt with gravity. In this theory, Einstein predicted that starlight passing near the sun would be curved by the pull of gravity. This prediction was verified in 1919 during a solar eclipse, and Einstein suddenly became an international celebrity. He was awarded the Nobel Prize in Physics in 1921.

Few scientists at the time could appreciate Einstein's relativity theories or the radical new understanding of the atom, the quantum theory, advanced by the German physicist **Max Planck** in 1900 to explain the behavior of energy within the atom. While physicists struggled with the implications of relativity and quantum theory, for many in the general public these disturbing new ideas symbolized a destruction of certainty. Just as Darwin had called into question accepted notions about the natural world and its origins, Einstein and Planck stripped away certainty from even the most fundamental elements of perception: time and space.

The Battle Between Science and Religion

Darwin's theories, especially regarding human evolution, stirred great controversy, and some of his main opponents were religious leaders who understood evolution as directly challenging not only the biblical story of creation but the majesty of God. Anglican bishop Samuel Wilberforce of Oxford decried Darwin's work as "a tendency to limit God's glory in creation," and the Catholic cardinal Henry Edward Manning denounced Darwin's ideas as "a brutal philosophy—to wit, there is no God, and the ape is our Adam."

The controversy between science and religion went far deeper, representing a profound crisis of consciousness in the nineteenth century. Geological discoveries, in particular those associated with the British geologist **Sir Charles Lyell**, had already proved that the earth was vastly older than the number of generations in the Bible between Adam and Jesus Christ. In addition, the fossil remains of dinosaurs and other animals not mentioned in the Bible further eroded conventional Christian faith in literal biblical truth. Although most Europeans still professed Christianity, the content of their beliefs changed under the weight of scientific evidence. The biblical account of creation came, for example, to be understood more and more in a symbolic rather than a literal way.

Religion, Science, and Atheism In the second half of the nineteenth century, many Europeans came to reject religious belief as unscientific, irrelevant, or even immoral. As early as the 1840s, Marx had exclaimed that religion was the "opiate of the people." In other words, religion diverted people's attention from the real causes of their poverty and, most important, hindered their action to bring about social justice. Marx and other socialists were atheists, rejecting religion, but they believed fervently in progress, science, and humanity's ability to better itself. This radical rejection of a religious worldview was also shared by the fictional hero in Turgenev's *Fathers and Sons*, Evgeny Bazarov, whose views were summed up by a friend: "He doesn't believe in principles, but he believes in frogs [to dissect]." Like Bazarov, many young radicals rejected religious authority and demanded that any principles, whether moral, political, or scientific, be proved by empirical methods. In a sense, they were simply reformulating Comte's positivism. Not religion but empirical scientific methods—in both the social and physical sciences—would bring about true progress.

Science Versus Tradition For most people, however, a world without God was unthinkable. Even scientists were not generally atheists, though they often did not accept all aspects of church dogma. Most continued at least to cherish a belief in a Supreme Being, however defined. Even though Pope Pius IX condemned materialism in the *Syllabus of Errors* of 1864, and "modernism" was denounced by the later Pope Pius X in 1907, many educated Catholics sought to reconcile their religious beliefs and elements of modern thought. In the **shtetls** of eastern Europe, Jewish boys were punished for daring to read "modern" authors—even in Hebrew translation. Traditional Jews claimed that the Torah, Talmud, and other religious works contained enough of human wisdom to satisfy anyone, but their attempt to shut out the modern world was in the long run doomed to failure. Some Jews discarded religious beliefs entirely in their desire to become modern, rational Europeans; others pointed out that great Jewish scholars from earlier ages had studied natural science, claiming that the study of science was but another way of understanding the greatness of God's creation.

Max Planck (1858–1947) German physicist and author of quantum theory who won the Nobel Prize in Physics in 1918.

Sir Charles Lyell (1797–1875) English geologist whose *Principles of Geology* (1830–1833) suggested that the world must be far older than hitherto imagined.

shtetls (in Yiddish, "small cities") Towns inhabited mainly or exclusively by Jews, in particular in eastern Europe.

While religion could not ignore new scientific discoveries, neither could scientific materialism be entirely satisfying for most people. The scientific method could explain much, but it was mute when faced with life's most basic question: Why are we here? Even Comte conceded the existence of a Supreme Being in his positivism, and Darwin fudged: "There is a grandeur in this view of life, with its several powers, having been originally breathed by the Creator into a few forms or into one." Rationality and empirical experimentation could only explain so much of human existence.

Critiques of Reason

Toward the end of the nineteenth century, the optimism that came with prosperity, scientific advances, and the philosophy of positivism began to falter. Some thinkers saw mass production less as a triumph than a threat, burying differences and local peculiarities in sterile uniformity. Max Weber warned darkly about the "iron cage" of bureaucracy. The German philosopher **Friedrich Nietzsche** called on gifted individuals to resist mass society, which he termed "the common herd." Austrian psychiatrist **Sigmund Freud** used scientific methodology to probe into the irrational motivations of human behavior. Just as artists were rejecting representations of the external world for explorations of individual perceptions, writers such as Gustave Le Bon and Henri Bergson described the limits of rationality in human experience, arguing that passion and intuition played a key role in social and individual behavior. Despite advances in science, politics, and technology, both seemed to say that human behavior remains profoundly determined by basic, even primitive, drives and passions.

Friedrich Nietzsche Nietzsche himself bore both physical and psychological scars from his service as a medical orderly in the Franco-Prussian War. Returning home, he (Friedrich Nietzsche) rapidly published his first book, *The Birth of Tragedy* (1872), which gained him a European-wide reputation though among specialists his theses were rejected. *The Birth of Tragedy* emphasized the role of passion and ecstasy (which Nietzsche associated with the Greek god Dionysus) in the genesis of Greek tragedy, an argument that was so novel and suggestive that Nietzsche became a celebrity outside of academic circles as well.

In the next decade and a half, Nietzsche produced thousands of pages of books, essays, polemics, and poetry, returning time and again to the themes of personal freedom and intellectual and moral self-reliance. He despised many aspects of modern life, including mass society, and lashed out against liberal democracy, German nationalism, antisemitism, and traditional moral standards—in particular, the "slave morality" of Christianity. He denounced mass society, which he perceived as his era's "herd mentality" and preference for the safe and comfortable. Instead, he demanded that human beings recognize their own freedom, admit that "God is dead," and then celebrate the enormous liberation that this fact implies. Nietzsche's philosophy emphasized the role of the will and passion over cool, calculated reason, and his insistence that humans discard all traditional values and create their own moral world is perhaps the most radical modern restatement of Immanuel Kant's famous dictum, "Dare to know!"

Nietzsche was never a systematic philosopher, and the sheer sparkle and wit of his writing may get in the way of his ideas. These qualities, combined with his meandering writing style, open his works to many different interpretations. In the twentieth century, the German National Socialists (Nazis) tried to appropriate his ideas for their cause, claiming that Nietzsche's superman—a man whose passion and will would create a new moral world—was identical to the Nazi Aryan ideal. But this interpretation is directly contradicted by Nietzsche's denunciation of Germany's antisemites as typical of the herd mentality. Nietzsche scorned biological explanations of human differences. On the other hand, his no less vehement attacks on such Christian values as forgiveness, charity, kindness, and mercy seem at times to parallel Nazi ruthlessness. In the light of rationality, elements of Nietzsche's thought seem contradictory, but he claimed that his philosophy operated at a higher—or deeper—level, concerning the innermost reaches of the human soul.

Sigmund Freud Nietzsche died in 1900, one year after Sigmund Freud's most famous work, *The Interpretation of Dreams,* appeared. Although the two men were utterly different in background, professional training, and temperament, both had an enormous impact on modern consciousness. Freud was born into a lower-middle-class Jewish family and lived nearly his entire life in Vienna. Like many young Jews of his generation, he studied medicine, aiming to dedicate his life to medical practice and research and discarding traditional religious belief along the way.

As early as the 1880s, Freud noticed in some of his patients—who were primarily middle-class women—symptoms that could not be explained by physical illness alone. Gradually he developed his theory of **repression**, claiming that patients repressed—that is, denied and refused to acknowledge

Friedrich Nietzsche (1844–1900) German philosopher renowned for his demand for a complete revision of human ethics and who notoriously despised mass society.

Sigmund Freud (1856–1939) Austrian psychiatrist who emphasized the role of fundamental and prerational drives, including sexual desire, in human behavior.

repression Freud's theory that memories and desires not acknowledged by a person's conscious thought can lead to physical and mental disorders.

on a conscious level—traumatic memories, usually of a sexual nature. Having diagnosed the problem, Freud began to develop a treatment. Like others before him, Freud differentiated between conscious and subconscious levels in the human psyche. On the conscious level, we may be rational, considering pros and cons and thinking through the consequences of our actions. But Freud insisted that our rational decisions were always liable to be influenced and sometimes overpowered by the subconscious. His "talking cure" (today we know it as psychoanalysis) aimed to reveal the subconscious by a steady probing of a patient's memories, reactions, behavior, and dreams. Dreams were a key component because for Freud they often revealed repressed desires that existed at a subconscious level.

To describe the human personality, Freud divided the psyche into three components: the id, ego, and superego. The id consists entirely of drives, hungers, and desires; a baby, for example, may be seen as an example of pure id. The ego develops as the child encounters reality and realizes that not all wants can be filled. The superego, the last part of the personality to develop, incorporates the moral values, taboos, and behavioral models that children internalize as they mature. According to Freud, all three components

exist in every human being; none are inherently bad or good. Hysteria and other neuroses appear, however, when the three are out of balance. For example, in any society, individuals must control and regulate their instinctual drives. But for some neurotics the demands of the superego become so intense that they make normal life impossible.

Freud's thought combines the rationalist method of the later nineteenth century with a recognition of the limitations of rationality. In his own life, Freud was very much the model of the positivist scientist, rejecting the idea of a Supreme Being and insisting on an empirical approach in psychology. But he also recognized that in human behavior, irrational—or at least subconscious and prerational—elements often prevailed.

Checking In

By yourself or with a partner, explain the significance of each of the following selected key terms:

positivism	eugenics
Max Weber	Albert Einstein
Charles Darwin	Sigmund Freud
social Darwinists	

CHAPTER
Review

Summary

- The second Industrial Revolution, based on electricity, steel, and modern chemistry, changed the world profoundly.

- Technological advances allowed for mass production of clothing, newspapers, and many other consumer goods.

- Communications were also revolutionized with increased railroad building, steamships, and the telegraph and telephone.

- Science made considerable advances, and the fields of social sciences, such as sociology, aimed to explain human society and behavior.

- The new science, in particular Darwin's theory of evolution, presented a challenge to the traditional religious worldview.

- By the end of this period, thinkers like Friedrich Nietzsche and Sigmund Freud called into question positivism's trust in rationality, pointing out that human behavior could not be explained by reason alone.

Chronology

1851	Crystal Palace Exhibition takes place in London	**1888**	Kodak box camera is perfected by George Eastman
1859	Charles Darwin publishes *On the Origin of Species*	**1891**	Work begins on the Trans-Siberian Railroad
1862	Ivan Turgenev publishes *Fathers and Sons*	**1892**	Rudolf Diesel patents the internal-combustion engine
1863	Edouard Manet paints *The Luncheon on the Grass* and *Olympia*	**1899**	Sigmund Freud publishes *The Interpretation of Dreams*
1867	Alfred Nobel patents dynamite	**1900**	Max Planck formulates quantum theory
1867	Karl Marx publishes volume 1 of *Capital*	**1903**	Wright brothers successfully fly the first airplane
1869	Suez Canal opens in Egypt	**1904**	Max Weber begins publication of *The Protestant Ethic and the Birth of Capitalism*
1872	Friedrich Nietzsche publishes *The Birth of Tragedy*	**1905**	Albert Einstein publishes paper on special theory of relativity
1876	Alexander Graham Bell invents the telephone		
1879	Thomas Edison invents the electric lightbulb	**1907**	Bakelite, the first plastic, is invented
1885	First skyscraper, the Home Insurance Building in Chicago, is completed	**1908**	Ford Motor Company produces first Model T

Test Yourself

To gauge your mastery of the material in this chapter, answer the questions below. More than one answer may be correct.

The Second Industrial Revolution

1. The second Industrial Revolution began:

   a. After 1848.
   b. After 1865.
   c. After 1870.
   d. After 1880.
   e. After 1890.

2. Which of the following was *not* a new source of energy in the second Industrial Revolution?

   a. Natural gas
   b. Coal
   c. Kerosene and gasoline
   d. Electricity
   e. Diesel fuel

3. Which of the following industrial branches and processes was *not* new to the second Industrial Revolution?

   a. Lithography
   b. The Siemens-Martin process for producing steel
   c. The cotton gin
   d. Advances in artificial dyes
   e. Mass production, including of automobiles

4. Which of the following manufactured goods depended on steel?

   a. Railroad engines, cars, and tracks
   b. Skyscrapers
   c. Automobiles and steamships
   d. Modern weaponry such as artillery and rifled guns
   e. The telegraph

5. Which of the following countries became the leader in producing artificial dyes for use in the textile industry?

   a. Russia
   b. Germany
   c. France
   d. Great Britain
   e. United States

Now that you have reviewed and tested yourself on this part of the chapter, take time to pull together all the important information by answering the following questions:

◆ How did the second Industrial Revolution revolutionize transport and communications?
◆ Why did many Europeans have more leisure time, and how did they use it?

Mass Society

6. The Bon Marché in Paris, one of a number of department stores that appeared in late nineteenth-century Europe, featured:

   a. Personalized service by salespeople.
   b. A policy of allowing customers to look at goods without buying them.
   c. An attractive place for respectable middle-class women to spend time and money.
   d. A no-returns policy.
   e. Inexpensive, though low quality, goods.

7. Women found new work opportunities as:

   a. Sales clerks in department stores.
   b. Railroad engineers.
   c. Postal clerks.
   d. Police women.
   e. Telegraph operators.

8. Between 1800 and 1900 the population of Europe:

   a. Was stagnant.
   b. Grew by 25 percent.
   c. Grew by 50 percent.
   d. Grew by more than 100 percent.
   e. Fluctuated wildly.

9. Nineteenth-century European women:

   a. Had limited access to secondary and higher education.
   b. Were usually not considered as adults.
   c. Had little protection against abusive husbands.
   d. Often could not sign a contract on their own.
   e. Were increasingly literate and active in society.

10. The changes brought about by industrialization resulted in:

   a. The urban family remaining the basic production unit.
   b. Children in a family being recognized primarily as an economic benefit.
   c. A decline in family planning and abortions.
   d. A decline in the number of years needed for a good education.
   e. A decline in birthrates throughout Europe.

Now that you have reviewed and tested yourself on this part of the chapter, take time to pull together all the important information by answering the following questions:

◆ How did increased prosperity and better public health help create mass society?
◆ How was feminism reacting to the novelties of mass society? Where were feminists most active?

Art and Industrial Society

11. Realist painters such as Daumier, Repin, and Manet often:

   a. Chose to paint lofty subjects like biblical heroes.
   b. Painted everyday people and events.
   c. Were politically conservative.
   d. Were on the political left.
   e. Wanted to use their art to effect social change.

12. In the late nineteenth century the center of the art world was:

   a. New York
   b. London
   c. Paris
   d. Berlin
   e. St. Petersburg

13. Russian writer Fyodor Dostoevsky's novels:

   a. Depicted the life of the Russian aristocracy, as in *War and Peace*.
   b. Supported socialism and praised revolutionary ideals.
   c. Delved into the psychology of Russian terrorists of the late 1860s.
   d. Described a young man who thought he was above God's law.
   e. Exhibited the author's strong Christian feelings and rejection of socialism and liberalism.

14. The French novelist Émile Zola:

    a. Described his writing as "naturalist" and claimed that it presented reality in a scientific way.
    b. Depicted alcoholism, prostitution, and poverty in his novels.
    c. Was originally a liberal, but became conservative after a prison sentence in Siberia.
    d. Frequently moralized about the sordid lives of his characters.
    e. Once stated that he was "little concerned with beauty of perfection."

15. The Arts and Crafts movement:

    a. Put medieval designs to modern uses.
    b. Stated that the useful should be merged with the beautiful.
    c. Stated that the useful and the beautiful were two separate things.
    d. Was inspired by socialist principles.
    e. Produced things that were generally too expensive for working-class people.

Now that you have reviewed and tested yourself on this part of the chapter, take time to pull together all the important information by answering the following questions:

◆ In what ways can art of this period be termed part of "mass society?" How did new art forms and techniques reach out to a broader audience?
◆ How did Realist writers like Dickens, Dostoevsky, and Zola depict the realities of their age?

Science and Social Science

16. Auguste Comte:

    a. Believed that the world could be explained only through the use of verifiable scientific method and data.
    b. Was one of the founders of sociology.
    c. Believed that the natural and human sciences could be united by a common method.
    d. Divided history into three stages, the highest of which he termed the "positive" age.
    e. Influenced such renowned social scientists as Durkheim and Weber.

17. Charles Darwin's *Origins of Species:*

    a. Argued that human beings were descended from apes.
    b. Was a violently atheistic book.
    c. Was based on data collected by Darwin while on a trip around the world.
    d. Proposed the theory of natural selection to explain the proliferation of species and the extinction of some.
    e. Was less controversial than his later book *The Descent of Man.*

18. The social Darwinists:

    a. Applied Darwin's concept of natural selection to human society.
    b. Often embraced the "science" of eugenics.
    c. Sometimes argued that racial superiority placed Europeans above Asians and Africans.
    d. Strongly supported government programs to help the poor.
    e. Were associated with the English writer and philosopher Herbert Spencer.

19. Among the scientific discoveries that revolutionized physics and chemistry in this period was:

    a. Mendeleev's explanation of gravity.
    b. Maxwell and Hertz's work on electricity.
    c. Albert Einstein's special theory of relativity.
    d. Marconi's discovery that under certain conditions the speed of light can speed up or slow down.
    e. Max Planck's quantum theory.

20. Friedrich Nietzsche:

    a. Celebrated mass society.
    b. Advocated liberal democracy.
    c. Championed German nationalism.
    d. Condemned antisemitism.
    e. Accused Christians of having a "slave mentality."

Now that you have reviewed and tested yourself on this part of the chapter, take time to pull together all the important information by answering the following questions:

◆ What did Comte's "positivism" have in common with physics and chemistry?
◆ What common ground existed between religious critiques of science and critiques of reason presented by Freud and Nietzsche? Where did they differ?

CHAPTER 24

The Age of Imperialism, 1870–1914

Chapter Outline

1850	1855	1860	1865	1870	1875	1880

1857
Sepoy Rebellion begins

1865
Tashkent falls to the Russians

1867
French annex Cochinchina

1869
Suez Canal opens in Egypt

1877
Queen Victoria becomes empress of India

Nigerian carving of Queen Victoria. Queen Victoria, from 1876 also "Empress of India," symbolized the age of imperialism. Among the colonies of the British Empire was Nigeria, where this intricate carving of the empress was produced. The carving uses local traditions of highly developed wooden sculpture to depict the Empress as mighty, benevolent, dignified, and serene in her power. (Pitt Rivers Museum, University of Oxford (1965.10.1))

After reading this chapter, you should be able to answer the following questions:

What is meant by the term "imperialism?" Why did European power throughout the world expand so quickly in this period?

Where did the new imperialism have its greatest impact? Why?

What impact did imperialism have on the Muslim world, Asia, and Africa?

Why did most Europeans support imperialism? What were the arguments of Europeans who opposed it?

EUROPEAN EXPANSION AND colonialism did not start in 1870. Spain and Portugal had established American colonies in the late fifteenth century, and Russian domination of Siberia in northern Asia dates from the seventeenth century. But the imperialism of the late nineteenth century was new. Europe's industrialization and new technologies made it possible, and more of Europe's nations than ever before got involved in the race for expansion. In little more than a generation, Europeans extended colonial rule over much of the globe.

Colonies provided Europeans with raw materials and markets. They were good for European economies. Imperial rule also fascinated Europeans, whose very identity became linked with their countries' role as overlords in Africa, Asia, and the Muslim world. Europeans were proud of their culture and believed it superior to any other civilization in the world. The scientific and technological advances of the nineteenth century, rising literacy rates, and the general advance in standards of living convinced them that their rule of other lands was a benefit.

In 1870, there were a few European colonies and settlements on the edges of Africa. By 1900, the entire

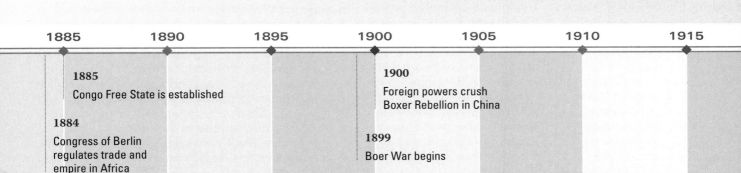

1885	1890	1895	1900	1905	1910	1915

1885
Congo Free State is established

1884
Congress of Berlin regulates trade and empire in Africa

1900
Foreign powers crush Boxer Rebellion in China

1899
Boer War begins

continent had been divided up among the European powers. The largest colonial territories were held by Britain and France, but Portugal, Belgium, and Germany also ruled over thousands of square miles and hundreds of thousands of Africans. Only two independent states remained in Africa by 1914—Ethiopia in East Africa and Liberia on the west coast.

Asia was also colonized by Europeans. The largest and richest colony of all was there: British India. France extended colonial rule in Indochina (now Vietnam, Laos, and Cambodia), and the Dutch exerted control over the islands now known as Indonesia. Although China was never colonized directly, western powers interfered in Chinese domestic affairs. And Japan, industrializing from the 1870s onward, became a colonial power in its own right, conquering Taiwan at the end of the century. In all, around half a billion Asians and Africans fell under colonial rule.

The new imperialism extended to the Muslim world, as the Ottoman Empire, the most important Muslim state of the time, was challenged by incursions from Russia and other European powers. An even larger number of Muslims lived under imperial rule in British India and, by the end of the nineteenth century, in Russian Central Asia. Muslim intellectuals, who wondered why their culture had been unable to withstand these threats, formulated programs of reform to meet the challenge of imperialism.

Some Europeans, too, opposed and criticized imperialism, denouncing it as a highly exploitative and racist form of capitalism. These opinions would be influential into the twenty-first century.

Motives and Methods of the New Imperialism

◆ **What political and technological advances paved the way for the new imperialism?**

◆ **How did Europeans attempt to justify imperialist expansion?**

new imperialism Extension and strengthening of European colonial rule, mainly in Africa and Asia, from approximately 1870 to 1914.

Leopold II (r. 1865–1909) Belgian king who established personal rule over a large part of central Africa (later the Belgian Congo).

Cecil Rhodes (1853–1902) British businessman and colonial official who made a fortune in diamonds and was prime minister of Cape Colony in Africa.

Many explanations have been offered for European expansion between 1870 and 1914. These include economic motivations, political and demographic factors, national rivalries, a desire to spread Christianity, and the idea that Europeans (and North Americans) had a moral responsibility to spread their culture and technology around the world. European governments did not follow any well-thought-out plan in expanding their colonial empires. Rather, they reacted to specific circumstances, always seeking to prevent other European powers from gaining on them. The conviction of European superiority also pushed imperialism forward. So did the new technologies of the second Industrial Revolution. All these factors help explain how, and why, millions of non-Europeans were brought under European rule.

Economic Motivations

The desire for new markets and the need for the raw materials of industry certainly fueled the **new imperialism**. Britain looked to India as a market for its textiles and other industrial products. King **Leopold II** of Belgium derived huge profits from rubber plantations in the Congo, and **Cecil Rhodes** became vastly wealthy from exploiting African labor in the gold and diamond mines of southern Africa. Industrial society demanded rubber for industrial uses, but also for tires on bicycles and a new invention, the automobile. Similarly, palm oil was in great demand as a machine lubricant. Fruits such as bananas and pineapples were also imported from colonized areas. These products could be obtained only in tropical regions, many of which came under European rule at this time.

Still, the direct connection between economic motivations and the establishment of political control

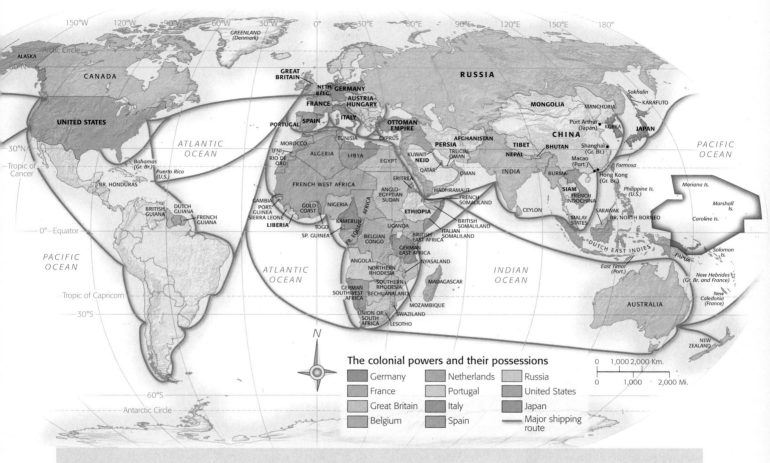

Map 24.1 **European Colonies Around the World, 1900** By 1900, European countries had established colonies on every inhabited continent. Already-existing colonies in the New World, Asia, and Oceania were joined by huge territories dominated by European powers, most notably in Africa. © *Cengage Learning*

1. On which continents were the majority of European colonies?
2. Which European countries had the greatest number of colonies?
3. Which parts of the world were most and least affected by the new imperialism?
4. Which of these colonies had been established since 1850?

is not often clear. Britain enjoyed economic and political dominance of India and southern Africa *before* imperialist domination was established. For Germany, the establishment of colonies in Africa and the Pacific made no economic sense; these colonies cost German taxpayers millions. Furthermore, throughout this period, more western European capital flowed to Russia, the United States, and South America than to territories under formal colonial rule. Thus, economic motivations alone cannot explain the late-nineteenth-century drive for colonial rule.

Domestic Politics and National Rivalries

A more convincing explanation of imperialism is found in the domestic politics of the major European powers. Large numbers of Britons, Frenchmen, Germans, and others came to identify their own national pride with colonial possessions.

The Popularity of Imperialism After their humiliating defeat in the Franco-Prussian War, the French, for example, were able to take pride in an expanding colonial empire. And Germans, who had won the war, felt the need for a colonial empire too. Having failed to suppress the Social Democrats even through the strategy of adopting some of their programs, Chancellor Otto von Bismarck turned to empire to enhance his political popularity. In the late nineteenth century, Europe was swept by "imperialist fever." Even sober politicians not usually concerned with popular opinion—such as Bismarck in Berlin—found it necessary, or at least useful, to adopt imperialism as a political program.

National rivalries contributed to imperial expansion. The establishment of one colony almost inevitably led to the perceived need to grab more territory to "protect" it. In this way, European rivalries contributed to European expansion. For example, in the early 1880s, the French government declared formal control over Tunisia in northern Africa mainly because it feared Italian expansion westward from Libya. Similarly, the British occupied Egypt in 1882 partly to deny the French any influence. At first, they did not intend to maintain permanent political control, but facing a power vacuum and fearing that hostile Egyptian groups would take over, the British stayed. Control of Egypt also allowed the British to secure the sea route to India once the Suez Canal was constructed. Protection of the canal then became an end in itself. Thus, securing access to existing colonies also served as a justification for taking new ones. All along the route to India, the British secured stopping and fueling points for ships. Aden, at the tip of the Arabian Peninsula, was deliberately taken for this purpose.

Competition Among Colonial Powers in Africa

As Britain and France carved up Africa, other European powers demanded their place in the sun. Italy grabbed Libya from the Ottoman Empire in 1912 and established control over Eritrea and Somaliland in East Africa. Germany occupied Cameroon, German Southwest Africa (now Namibia), and German East Africa (roughly today's Tanzania). Germany also took control of a large group of Pacific islands, thereby coming into conflict with another young imperial power, the United States. None of these colonies brought wealth or significant new markets to the home country. Rather, their main purpose was to satisfy the patriotic fever of Germans and Italians who felt that without colonies their countries would be second-rate powers. In this way, domestic politics pushed imperialism, often against the wishes and advice of the imperialist powers' foreign ministers and foreign policy experts.

Christian Missions

Churches and missionaries also played a vital role in imperialist expansion. Most often, Christian missionaries had established footholds before official colonial control was declared. To be sure, missionaries sincerely desired to bring education, health care, and other benefits of European culture to Africans and Asians. They often built schools and hospitals. Missionaries seldom forced Christianity on the native peoples, hoping instead to win converts by good example. At the same time, they taught European concepts of sexual morality and gender relations and often insisted that natives dress in a "modest" European manner, all of which undermined native cultural values. When local rulers attempted to restrict or expel missionaries, even without using violence, the European powers often intervened. Thousands and eventually millions of Asians and Africans embraced Christianity, but these numbers represented a grave loss to native cultures and religions.

David Livingstone One well-known missionary was **David Livingstone**. As a small boy in Scotland, born to a working-class family in 1813, young David was influenced by accounts he heard and read of Christian missionaries in China and the Muslim world. In 1840, he left England for Africa, where he was to spend the rest of his life spreading the gospel, healing the sick, and fighting European exploitation—including enslavement—of Africans.

Livingstone became famous for his expedition seeking the source of the Nile River and his discovery of Victoria Falls, now shared by Zimbabwe and Zambia. His life in the African bush and his dedication to helping Africans, even against other Europeans, made him a controversial figure, however. In 1871, the American reporter Henry Stanley went to Africa in search of Livingstone, famously greeting him with the words, "Dr. Livingstone, I presume?" Stanley described the elderly missionary as "a living skeleton."

Livingstone died in his tent in 1873 and was buried in London, in Westminster Abbey. At his funeral, he was praised for his efforts to spread Christian morality through good example. Livingstone's motivations for the extension of European culture contrast sharply with those of Rhodes, indicating the complexities of imperialist motivations.

Missionaries Helping Colonized Peoples Missionaries translated the Gospels into African languages, wrote grammars and dictionaries, and thereby helped transform tongues previously only spoken into written languages. Many stood up for native rights against European administrators. They did not always get along with European traders, but their example—the clothes they wore and houses they kept—provided Africans with incentive to purchase European manufactured goods. Thus, in spite of their own intentions, missionaries encouraged economic links between industrial Europe and underdeveloped colonies.

The "White Man's Burden"

Many Europeans, not only missionaries, saw the spread of European civilization as a precious gift to "dark peoples" of African and Asia: the figure of speech referred to alleged intellectual and cultural backwardness as much as to skin color. The English poet **Rudyard Kipling** called this impulse the **white man's burden**. Kipling was born in India, which is the setting for his well-known children's books, such as *The Jungle Book* (1894) and *Kim* (1901). In 1899, in the context of the Spanish-American War that had begun a year earlier, he addressed these lines to the

David Livingstone (1813–1873) Scottish missionary, explorer of Africa, and discoverer of Victoria Falls.

Rudyard Kipling (1865–1936) English writer and poet, born in India, best known for his adventure stories, which often took place in exotic colonial locations.

white man's burden Phrase taken from a poem by Rudyard Kipling urging Americans—but implicitly all "white men"—to spread western civilization.

Cecil Rhodes Writes His Own "Confession of Faith"

From an early age, Cecil Rhodes had a mission—to spread British culture, values, and education. Rhodes never wavered in his belief that the world would be better off under British rule. In 1877, at age twenty-four, Rhodes set down his ideas in a "Confession of Faith" for himself. The document was never published in his lifetime.

❶ What do you think Rhodes meant by "the most despicable specimens of human beings?"

❷ What would happen to these people if Rhodes's plan was realized?

❸ What kind of "extra employment" do you think Rhodes had in mind here? How did imperialism increase jobs at home?

❹ What does Rhodes mean when he speaks of "race?" How does his usage differ from our present-day understanding of that word?

❺ Do you think that Rhodes's emphasis on duty was typical of the nineteenth century? Typical of someone twenty-four years old? Why or why not?

❻ Why do you suppose that Rhodes proposed a secret society to pursue his aims?

❶ I contend that we [English] are the finest race in the world and that the more of the world we inhabit the better it is for the human race. Just fancy those parts that are at present inhabited by the most despicable specimens of human beings what an alteration there would be if they were brought under Anglo-Saxon influence, look again at the extra employment a new country added to our dominions gives. I contend that every acre added to our territory means in the future birth to some more of the English race who otherwise would not be brought into existence. Added to this the absorption of the greater portion of the world under our rule simply means the end of all wars….

❷ Why should we not form a secret society with but one object the furtherance of the British Empire and the bringing of the whole uncivilised world under British rule for the recovery of the United States for the making the Anglo-Saxon race but one Empire….

❸ Africa is still lying ready for us it is our duty to take it. It is our duty to seize every opportunity of acquiring more territory and we should keep this one idea steadily before our eyes that more territory simply means more of the Anglo-Saxon race more of the best, the most human, most honourable race the world possesses. **❹** To forward such a scheme what a splendid help a secret society would be a society not openly acknowledged but who would work in secret for such an object….

What has been the main cause of the success of the Romish [Roman Catholic] Church? The fact that every enthusiast, call it if you like every madman finds employment in it. Let us form the same kind of society a Church for the extension of the British Empire. A society which should have its members in every part of the British Empire working with one object and one idea….

Source: From Rhodes's Confession of Faith, an essay included in *The Last Will and Testament of Cecil John Rhodes* (1902).

United States, urging Americans to join in the imperialist enterprise:

> *Take up the White Man's burden—*
> *Send forth the best ye breed—*
> *Go bind your sons to exile*
> *To serve your captives' need;*
> *To wait in heavy harness*
> *On fluttered folk and wild—*
> *Your new-caught, sullen peoples,*
> *Half-devil and half-child.*

Excerpt from Rudyard Kipling's poem,
"The White Man's Burden."

The condescending attitude of the imperialists is evident here. At the same time, Kipling emphasizes that imperialism is not a program for exploitation and self-aggrandizement but a duty: *"to serve your captives' need." He sees imperialism as a "civilizing mission" that is self-sacrificing. The next stanza describes it as: "To seek another's profit, / And work another's gain." Kipling may be termed a romantic imperialist who perceived imperialism as an uplifting moral crusade that, while not always so understood by the natives ("new-caught, sullen peoples"), would in the end bring about better conditions for their lives.

*Excerpt from Rudyard Kipling's poem, "The White Man's Burden."

Imperialism and "Civilizing Missions" Imperialists firmly believed in western superiority in civilization, culture, and even genetic makeup. Earlier in the nineteenth century, Americans had justified their expansion from the Atlantic to the Pacific Ocean as **manifest destiny**, claiming that God and the natural order had ordained American control over the entire continent. In a similar way, Europeans extolled the virtues of their social order, technology, and religious beliefs and assumed that non-Europeans would be grateful to be "uplifted" and assimilated into the European political and economic systems and moral values.

Scholars such as the French sociologist and journalist Paul Leroy-Beaulieu argued that France had a "civilizing mission" to the world. In other words, French culture was a valuable commodity that could improve the lives of Asians and Africans. The British politician Joseph Chamberlain argued much the same for British culture. In a speech to Parliament in 1897 he exclaimed, "I maintain that our rule does, and has, brought security and peace and comparative prosperity to countries that never knew these blessings before." Chamberlain praised the "work of civilization" that British imperialists carried out in India, Africa, and other lands. But these attitudes contained within them a contradiction. Even as imperialists claimed that they brought civilization to colonized peoples, they frequently exploited the labor of those peoples, denying them the rights and privileges taken for granted by Europeans. The large gap between the rhetoric of imperialism and its more brutal reality meant that sooner or later imperialism would collapse.

Racism and Paternalism Racism certainly played a part in the ideology and practice of imperialism. By the second half of the nineteenth century, scientific theories of race had divided humanity into Caucasian, Negroid, and Mongoloid races, which some argued were different species and others arranged in a strict hierarchy, with Europeans (Caucasians) on top. European racial theorists believed it was self-evident that the white, or Caucasian, race had progressed further than the others. Both the categories and the argumentation revealed not scientific facts but prejudices and convenient self-justifications for European dominance. Nonetheless, these ideas about the races were widely held.

Beaulieu and Chamberlain were not overtly racist, but their assumption that European culture was superior to that of Asia or Africa was paternalistic. **Paternalism**'s greatest blind spot was its inability to recognize and respect the humanity of non-Europeans. Kipling's description of native people as "half-devil

and half-child" reflects this view. Imperialists did not understand that their values were not necessarily universal and that from the colonized people's point of view, imperialist efforts to "enlighten" might well be experienced as oppression and even as the destruction of time-hallowed traditions. Hypocrisy was inherent in this system that claimed to protect and nurture native peoples while in reality privileging European economic and political interests.

The Importance of Technology

European domination over most of the world's surface would have been impossible without the technological advances of the second Industrial Revolution. Among these, advances in communications, transportation, and medicine are most important.

Telegraph and Railways in the Service of Imperialism The telegraph vastly simplified the administration of world empires by making nearly instantaneous communication possible. By the 1860s, England was connected to India by telegraph over land lines, but messages had to be sent and retransmitted many times, often by operators not entirely fluent in English. When underwater cables were laid in the late 1860s and 1870, communications between Britain and India became far faster and more reliable. By 1895, nearly two hundred thousand miles of underwater cables connected Europe with America, Asia, Africa, and Australia, and more than six hundred thousand miles of land telegraph cables sped messages to their destinations.

When, at the end of the nineteenth century, the increasingly dense telegraph network was supplemented by a growing telephone network, colonial administrators were able to be in continuous and almost instant communication. At any sign of unrest, an administrator out in the countryside could telegraph the nearest military outpost with a request for troops. In this way the telegraph helped imperial administrators stifle resistance and revolt.

Developments in transportation similarly facilitated imperial administration. The imperial powers constructed railroads in the colonies, most impressively in India, which by 1900 had more than twenty-five thousand miles of railway lines—more than France or Britain itself. Just as Rhodes dreamed of connecting British colonies throughout East Africa by a Cairo-to-Capetown rail line, German imperialists dreamed of a Berlin-to-Baghdad railroad that would strengthen German influence in the Ottoman Empire. Neither line was completed, but railroads were built in many African colonies, making the extraction of raw materials and the penetration of European military control possible. Steamship lines, too, shortened distances. The trip from England to Australia, which had taken more than four months in the early nineteenth century, was down to a month by the century's end.

manifest destiny North American ideology that saw the extension of the United States to the Pacific Ocean as fulfillment of a divine plan.

paternalism Attitude toward or control of one group (here, colonialized people) by another (here, Europeans) that resembles a father's rule over his children.

Tropical Illness and Modern Medicine As Europeans ventured into new climates in Africa and Asia, they encountered new microbes. In Africa, particularly, death rates among European explorers up to the mid-nineteenth century were extremely high. Among the diseases, **malaria** was probably the most devastating. Before the late nineteenth century, little was understood about germs. The disease was attributed to "bad air"—in Italian, *mal'aria*—because it was not yet understood that the disease was spread by germ-carrying mosquitoes.

By trial and error, Europeans came to recognize that constant doses of the bark of the cinchona tree were effective in staving off the worst symptoms of malaria. The bark contained quinine, which began to be commercially produced in the 1830s. Quinine became the constant companion of the imperialist in tropical areas, and the typical imperialist cocktail, a gin and tonic (containing quinine), became a pleasant means of administering a daily dose. By the end of the century, the role of germs in sickness was established, and British scientists made significant advances in studying tropical diseases. For all that, mortality continued to be high among Europeans serving in tropical regions, in particular in equatorial Africa.

Political, ideological, economic, and technological factors all contributed to the new imperialism's massive extension of European power around the globe. Imperialists saw themselves as the bearers of a superior cultural and political order. At the same time, many of them gained huge profits and prestige derived from the labor and natural resources of the colonized lands. Imperialists took for granted the superiority of European thought and culture, seeing the native populations as ignorant and backward savages to be "brought up" to European standards. Despite the imperialists' often sincere belief in their own "civilizing mission," their failure to appreciate the validity of other cultures led quickly to conflicts, resentment, and resistance.

Checking In

By yourself or with a partner, explain the significance of each of the following selected key terms:

new imperialism	Rudyard Kipling
Leopold II	white man's burden
Cecil Rhodes	manifest destiny

The Scramble for Africa

◆ **How did settler colonies in Africa differ from other kinds of colonies?**

◆ **What economic factors propelled Europeans to colonize Africa?**

Africa provides the most startling example of the new imperialism. In 1870, while there were European outposts along the coasts, the African interior was almost totally unknown to Europeans. By 1914, the continent was almost completely colonized. Africans resisted imperialism, but the superiority of European weaponry doomed resistance to failure. But competition for control led two groups of European settlers to fight against each other in the Boer War.

Settler Colonies in South and North Africa

Historians differentiate between **settler colonies**, in which colonists came in large numbers, often including entire families, and settled permanently, and colonies where only a few, usually male, administrators lived temporarily and then returned to Europe. Settler colonies were usually located in temperate regions such as Argentina, the United States, and Australia, where the majority of the current population is descended from settlers, not native to that place.

South Africa and Algeria In Africa in the nineteenth century, there were only two large-scale European settler colonies. One was located at the temperate southern tip of Africa, where Dutch farmers (or Boers) had originally settled in the seventeenth century, later joined by English colonists. During the Great Trek of 1836–1846, the Boers moved north into land previously inhabited by Africans. Around 1900, perhaps 10 percent of the total population in South Africa was of European descent, but they dominated the economy and political system there. It was these white settlers who gained most from the establishment of the Union of South Africa in 1900.

Thousands of Indian laborers and professionals also made these colonies their home. Most numerous, of course, were the native African peoples of the region, who often saw their land and livelihoods taken over by Europeans in this period. To fight against these injustices of colonial rule, the South African Native National Congress was established in 1912. This organization, later called simply the **African National Congress**, helped abolish white privilege and establish a more democratic order in South Africa in 1994.

In northern Africa, French Algeria can be considered a settler colony. By 1848, around one hundred thousand Europeans had settled there, and by the early twentieth century, around one million French men and women made their home along Africa's Mediterranean coast. Some 40 percent of the population was of European

malaria Infectious parasitic disease transmitted by mosquitoes, particularly widespread in tropical areas but preventable by constant doses of quinine.

settler colonies Colonies inhabited by settlers of European origin, always located in temperate regions such as North America, Australia, and South Africa.

African National Congress Organization established by Africans in 1912 to defend their rights that eventually brought a more democratic order to South Africa.

These two youths were among the many in King Leopold's Congo colony whose hands were cut off by soldiers and policemen who forced local people to produce rubber for export—or else. The printing of photographs like this one in European newspapers and magazines helped publicize the brutality of imperial rule in central Africa. How effective do you think such images were in changing Europeans' views of imperialism? Looking at this photograph, what emotions do you think contemporary Europeans would feel?

Courtesy, Anti-Slavery International

called humanitarian purposes. In fact, he financed private expeditions—sending Henry Stanley, among others—throughout the Congo River basin for his own economic gain. By the late 1880s, the Congo was in essence Leopold's own private estate, an estate of some nine hundred thousand square miles with millions of inhabitants. Though he set up the Congo Free State in 1885, Leopold ruled the area directly, with the help of his Force Publique, a brutal and corrupt mercenary army. Treating the Congo as a financial investment, Leopold extracted as much rubber, ivory, and palm oil as possible with a minimum of expense, gaining vast riches in the process. African workers were forced to produce quotas of rubber. Failure to do so brought brutal punishments, including the hacking off of hands and feet. Though the king and investors grew rich, the brutality appalled Europeans, and in 1908 European pressure obliged Leopold to turn over the colony to the Belgian state, which would rule over the area as the Belgian Congo until 1960. The cruelty and inhumanity of exploitation in the Congo inspired **Joseph Conrad**'s novella *Heart of Darkness*.

The Berlin Conference and German Colonies

In Germany, Chancellor Bismarck seized on tensions among Africa's colonial powers to enter Germany in what has been described as the scramble for Africa. In 1884, he called the **Berlin Conference**, specifically to press Leopold to agree to free trade in the Congo. At this congress, the United States joined Great Britain, France, Russian, Austria-Hungary, and the Ottoman Empire in recognizing Leopold's authority over the Congo in exchange for the right to trade there.

Germany's African Colonies Bismarck used the occasion to declare German control over Southwest Africa, Togo, and Cameroon, to be followed by East Africa (today's Tanzania) a year later. Also during these years, 1884–1886, Germany established colonies in the South Pacific, straining relations with the United States. By establishing colonies, Bismarck was pursuing both international and domestic goals. In foreign policy, he aimed to enhance German power and prestige in the world. At home, Bismarck was responding to pressure from the **German Colonial Union**. By 1884 it appeared that if the German state did not act quickly, all chances for African colonies would be gone, the continent taken over by the British and French. So Bismarck acted swiftly and, in the short run, very successfully, as his popularity soared.

The new German colonies lacked any obvious economic or political rationale. Furthermore, Bismarck's action infuriated the British who regarded German colonies as a threat to British interests.

After attempting to administer the colonies through private chartered companies, in the 1890s, the German government took them over directly. In their effort to crush native resistance and establish

descent. Unlike South Africa, Algeria was from the 1840s onward considered by the French government to be an integral part of that country. However, the native Arabic-speaking Muslim population had no political rights under the French, and Europeans also dominated the economy.

The Belgian Congo

One of the largest and most profitable colonies in Africa was established by the private initiative (and funds) of the king of Belgium, Leopold II. Neither the Belgian government nor the Belgian public showed much interest in an African possession when Leopold, acting on his own, established the Association Internationale du Congo in 1876 for what he

Joseph Conrad (1857–1924) English writer of Polish origin whose novels such as *Heart of Darkness* and *Lord Jim* often examined the morality of colonialism.

Berlin Conference Meeting in Berlin of the United States and European powers in 1884 that regulated European trade and imperial control in Africa.

German Colonial Union Political pressure group formed in 1882 to press the German government to seek overseas colonies.

Map 24.2 **Partition of Africa, 1870–1914** Between 1870 and 1914 nearly all of Africa came under European colonial rule. As these maps show, British and French colonies predominated, but several other European powers also participated in "the scramble for Africa." © *Cengage Learning*

1. Which European countries had a presence in Africa before 1870?
2. Where were French colonies most prevalent? British colonies?
3. What Africa countries remained independent in 1914? Why?

control of German Southwest Africa, German colonial officials, small in number and inexperienced, carried out horrifying massacres, especially after the **Herero Revolt** of 1905–1907. This policy of **genocide** was widely criticized in Europe. On the whole, German colonies in Africa failed to bring Germany either economic or political gains.

The Boer War

In South Africa, the discovery of gold and diamonds in the 1880s attracted thousands of Englishmen and other Europeans to the region.

Herero Revolt Rebellion against colonial rule in German Southwest Africa followed by a German massacre of the Herero people in 1905–1907.

genocide Attempt to kill an entire people or nation.

In this missionary school in German East Africa (Dar Es Salaam, now Tanzania), African children learn to read under the gaze of the German Kaiser and his wife. As the writing on the chalkboard indicates, these children were learning to read not only in German but also in their own native African language.

Among these new arrivals was Cecil Rhodes, whose investments in the gold and diamond mines of Kimberley made him a millionaire. The huge influx of prospectors caused the Dutch farmers, or Boers, great worries. They had earlier left their original colony near the Cape of Good Hope and trekked north to avoid English rule. Now it appeared that the English were pursuing them once again, threatening their farms and way of life. To preserve their independence, in 1899 the Boers, led by their gruff leader Paul Kruger, took a stand against the British.

The resulting **Boer War** of 1899–1902 caused great suffering and death among Africans, but the central dispute was between Europeans, in particular, the Boer's desire to retain their own autonomy and the British insistence on extending their

Boer War Conflict between the British Empire and Dutch settlers (Boers) in South Africa from 1899 to 1902, ending in a costly British victory.

rule to include areas of Boer settlement. The British expected to win quickly and easily, but they were wrong. Nearly five hundred thousand British men fought in the Boer War; around one-tenth of these lost their lives. In the end the British prevailed, however, and they granted the Boers broad autonomy and home rule. But after this expensive and bloody war between Europeans in a colonized country, many Europeans began to question whether imperialism was economically or morally defensible.

Checking In

By yourself or with a partner, explain the significance of each of the following selected key terms:

settler colonies

African National Congress

Joseph Conrad

Berlin Conference

German Colonial Union

Herero Revolt

genocide

Cecil Rhodes Creates the Rhodes Scholarship

For Cecil Rhodes, as for many other young, energetic Europeans of the late nineteenth century, establishing colonies around the world was not just an adventure or means of gaining wealth but a moral duty. They wanted to spread European values and culture around the world.

Born in 1853 into a middle-class family in a country town in England, Rhodes had been singled out early as an intelligent boy. His adoring and powerful mother sheltered him in his early years, and he grew up self-confident, sure of his own destiny. At the age of sixteen, he set off for Africa with his parents' blessing. In the 1870s, he divided his time between Africa and Oxford, earning his degree in 1881. Already by this time—before his thirtieth birthday—he had made a fortune in South African diamonds. His ambitions helped extend British power far to the north, into a region named Rhodesia (today Zambia and Zimbabwe) in his honor.

As a businessman and government official, Rhodes was known for ruthlessness and an authoritarian style that created enemies among his white contacts and fear among Africans. As prime minister of Cape Colony, he authorized a military excursion that he hoped would unite South Africa as a British colony. Its failure led the House of Commons to pronounce him guilty of grave breaches of duty, and he was forced to resign. Rhodes died a rich but embittered man in 1902, not even fifty years old.

But Rhodes had already made provision for funding the Rhodes Scholarships, for which he is best known today. Though a businessman and colonial official, Rhodes was also a visionary who believed that English culture should conquer the world. Convinced of English superiority, Rhodes maintained that the more the world came to resemble England, the better. So to preserve and spread English culture, Rhodes funded scholarships that would allow the most talented men (women could not enter most British universities at the time) to study in England—at the oldest of English universities, Oxford.

At first, Rhodes proposed thirty-six scholarships for "young colonials" from New Zealand, Australia, Canada, and South Africa. Later, scholarships were added for young men from the United States and Germany. In all cases, Rhodes's aim was the same: to produce cultured, educated English gentlemen. Rhodes had little interest in producing scholars or independent thinkers: among the qualifications he listed for selecting scholarship winners were "manly sports," "qualities of manhood," and "moral force of character," as well as "literary and scholastic" excellence. Rhodes Scholars, he hoped, would not be mere bookworms but would carry on his own values and those of upper-class, wealthy Britons dedicated to the good of the empire.

Rhodes set down that the scholarships would be open to all male candidates, regardless of "race or religious opinions." Rhodes did not mean race as it is understood today; he meant nationality, and by this he intended that the Dutch in South Africa—Britain's rivals for control—should be eligible. He certainly never expected Africans or Asians to apply. In practice, however, the scholarships have been awarded to individuals of diverse races and backgrounds and from many countries.

Rhodes's legacy has enabled hundreds of young men and women (the latter only since 1977) to complete their education at Oxford. Among Rhodes Scholars are some of the most distinguished scholars, political leaders, and social activists of the twentieth century: Count Bernstorff, a German diplomat executed for conspiring against Hitler; Edwin Hubble, the astronomer after whom the Hubble Space Telescope is named; Daniel Boorstin, former librarian of Congress; David Souter, Supreme Court justice; and former U.S. President William J. Clinton. Add to this list hundreds of distinguished scholars, diplomats, and politicians from Pakistan, India, Canada, Australia, and other countries.

The British Raj in India

- **What was the nature of British rule in India?**
- **Why was British rule in India so important for the empire?**

British dominion over India was always a special case, with its specific mystique and tradition. Even the language used to refer to this colony was unique— "the jewel in the crown" of empire. The British presence in India dated from the seventeenth century, and domination continued in various forms until 1947. Besides the unprecedented length of British control, the huge size and complex culture of the territory made India a colony unlike any other. The enormous diversity of religions, languages, and customs in India complicated British rule, especially as the extension of British colonial power in India did not follow a well-considered plan. Rather, economic interests were gradually transformed into political dominion in reaction to threats of foreign encroachment,

Cecil Rhodes was one of the best-known advocates of the new imperialism of the late nineteenth century, and he reflected the mind-set of the age. A cartoon in the English humor magazine *Punch* showed Rhodes as a colossus whose mighty stride took in the entire African continent. It related specifically to Rhodes's pet project of a railroad running the length of Africa, from Cairo to the Cape of Good Hope, a project that was never realized. How does this cartoon portray Rhodes as an exuberant imperialist? (Reproduction with permission of Punch Ltd, www.punch.co.uk)

the perceived and real weaknesses of native Indian administrations, and resistance to British rule. More than any other colony, India influenced British home politics, national identity, and culture. The impact of British rule on Indian culture was no less significant.

Commerce and Trade

European traders had visited the Indian **subcontinent** from the sixteenth century onward. By the eighteenth century, both French and English traders were competing over Indian goods like calico cloth, spices, and luxury items.

Beginnings of the Raj: The British East India Company At first, British interests in India were strictly commercial. The British East India Company had one aim: profit. It operated through warehouses and posts along the Indian coast, where agents traded with Indian merchants, but by the early eighteenth century the trading posts in

Bombay, Madras, and Calcutta were fortified. Following Britain's victory in the Seven Years' War (1756–1763), French competition ended. Still, as the **Mughal Empire** weakened, company officials continued to worry about their own safety and the future of trade there. In this insecure political situation, British state institutions gradually moved in.

A governor-general of India was first named in the late eighteenth century. Though supposedly just the agent of the British Parliament and the Crown, he ruled in the absolutist style. Some regions he ruled directly; in others he ruled through subordinate Indian princes. But from the first, the ideological basis of British rule in India was contradictory. British liberals saw it as aiming to produce Indians capable of self-rule, "a class of persons Indian in colour and blood, but English in tastes, in opinions, in morals, and in intellect," explained Thomas Babington Macauley, a Whig member of Parliament and East India Company leader. Until this class could be trained, however, India was controlled by a British administration that, while generally honest and efficient, was conservative and on the whole quite alien, even hostile, to Indian traditions.

The Sepoy Rebellion

The **Sepoy Rebellion** of 1857 demonstrated that Indian soldiers in British service, called sepoys, had long been dissatisfied over issues of pay and rumors that the British would force them to convert to Christianity. When they were issued new cartridges greased with fat made from cows (sacred to Hindus) and pigs (forbidden to Muslims), they refused to load their weapons. The mutiny spread rapidly through northern India. British response was brutal: thousands of Indian soldiers were massacred and entire villages were destroyed. This response was justified by pointing to lurid stories of sepoys committing murder and rape, specifically of "dark men" sexually abusing English women. The British believed they had to protect both "the white race" and "English womanhood."

Following the rebellion, British rule of India was fundamentally transformed. The British East India Company was disbanded and control of the colony transferred to the Crown. Large numbers British soldiers were sent to the colony. Whereas in 1857 European soldiers were outnumbered ten to one by native troops, by 1885 there were 73,000 British and 154,000 Indian soldiers. The costs of administration and the army were a heavy burden for Indian taxpayers.

Religious Policy of the Raj Official British policy aimed to avoid interference in religious matters, but, as the mutiny demonstrated, few British administrators understood the complexities of religious relations in India. Traditional religions involved the worship of many gods, but the large Muslim population, making up a significant proportion of native rulers, was strictly **monotheistic**. The Church of England,

subcontinent British India, including present-day Pakistan and Bangladesh ("sub" refers to its location on Asia's bottom edge).

Mughal Empire Muslim empire in India lasting from 1526 to 1857.

Sepoy Rebellion Revolt of Indian soldiers (sepoys) in northern India in 1857–1858, put down with brutality by the British.

monotheism Belief in the existence of only one God.

Map 24.3 **Growth of British India** India was by far the largest and most important British colony from the late eighteenth to the mid-twentieth century. As this map shows, British India—which included the present-day countries of India, Pakistan, Bangladesh, and Burma—was partly under direct British rule and partly ruled by Indian princes subordinate to the British. © *Cengage Learning*

1. Where was British rule in India first established?
2. What present-day countries once formed part of British India?

although not a militant missionary force, was influential through its influence on British administrators. As Christians, they found it difficult to understand and appreciate a religion not based on belief in a single God. Wishing to rationalize administration, the British encouraged the creation of a more coherent Hindu religion out of thousands of separate, often local, rites, beliefs, and rituals. At the same time, Hindus perceived British rule as favoring monotheistic Muslim Indians,

thereby exacerbating relations between the diverse religious groups of the subcontinent.

The Jewel in the Crown

In the late nineteenth century, the British **Raj** in India continued to expand. Steamships brought officials and

Raj (from Hindi, "rule") British Empire in India.

The Delhi Dunbar of 1903 was an enormous celebration of British rule in India that brought together dozens of Indian princes, hundreds of British soldiers and officials, and huge crowds who watched the splendid processions and ceremonies. Why do you think the British orchestrated such a huge celebration at this time? What impression might this celebration have made on Indians?

©British Library Board, OIOC Photo 430/78(30)

their families back and forth between England and Calcutta, the capital of British India. It became common for ambitious young men to make a career in India, amassing a fortune or pension, then returning to England in retirement. Some Englishmen, however, remained in India their whole lives. Their children were known as "Anglo-Indians," the most famous of whom was probably the writer Rudyard Kipling.

Relations Between Colonizers and Colonized
Even for Anglo-Indians, however, relations with Indians were seldom on an equal basis. With only a few exceptions at the highest levels of society, the English in India knew native people as servants. An Englishwoman could not be alone with an Indian man without endangering her reputation. Racial categories and hierarchies—with the Englishman on top—dominated English colonial identity in India as well as at home. The injustice of this racially defined colonial rule helped bring about the formation of the **Indian National Congress** in 1885, an organization that would work to free India from British rule.

The allure of India also affected Englishmen who would never leave home. Visual art, songs, and literature—like Kipling's *Jungle Book*

Indian National Congress
Organization formed in 1885 demanding the end of colonial rule in India.

and *Kim*—created an image of India as a place both familiar and alien, full of exotic scenes, wild animals, and exquisite dangers. British identity derived great pride in the domination and influence over this vast region, so many times larger than England itself. In 1877, Queen Victoria took the title of Empress of India in well-orchestrated ceremonies both at home and in India itself. The stately processions of Indian princes, elephants, and native soldiers in uniforms thrilled Englishmen in Manchester and Leeds. Their own lives might be dull and routine, but as Englishmen they, too, were part of these imperial pageants.

British Order and Indian Culture

British liberals claimed that in India their goal was an honest administration, a market economy, and individual self-development. They aimed to reduce corruption, to increase efficiency, and in the long run to bring prosperity and enlightenment to the peoples of India. The British regime sought to uplift and educate, rooting out customs such as the isolation of upper-class women from men (purdah) and the suicidal burning of widows on their deceased husbands' funeral pyres (suttee). In time, the British hoped, all aspects of life, from administrative practices to religion to social roles, would be transformed by their benevolent rule.

Paternalistic Rule in India Rapidly, however, the British liberals recognized that to introduce their own ideas of culture and standards of hygiene in India they would have to oppose the popular will. They justified these measures as "for the Indians," though not "through them." In the words of the English liberal John Stuart Mill, "Despotism is a legitimate mode of government in dealing with barbarians, provided the end be their improvement." But when Indians wished to retain traditional ways and their own cultural values, the British denigrated them as backward and ignorant. Some British administrators were disillusioned by the perceived lack of interest in the Indian community for "self-betterment."

Even those Indians who embraced British education, values, and the English language discovered that they were not accepted as equals by most Europeans. The group most receptive to British culture, the middle-class Bengali babus, was mocked as being effeminate and incapable of independent action. The word *babu,* which in Bengali denoted a respected educated figure, when used by the British meant a half-educated, slavish, and rather contemptible figure who was neither British nor Indian and neither man nor woman.

The **gendering** of British colonialism differentiated sharply between the manly "martial races" such as the Sikhs and the "effeminate" Bengalis. Predictably, imperialists equated manliness with strength, goodness, and progress, while so-called effeminate tendencies bore a negative connotation of corruption, weakness, and backwardness. The British ascribed to themselves manly virtues such as bravery, decisiveness, and energy. The Indian masses, in contrast, were denigrated as passive, backward, and unambitious.

British Cultural Influences in India British rule did have some positive aspects for Indians. It united the subcontinent as never before. The educational system, while still leaving most Indians illiterate, made significant strides in creating an educated Indian elite—the very class that would be instrumental in challenging and ending British rule in the twentieth century. By 1857 there were five universities in India, and increasing numbers of young Indians entered the civil service. In 1900, Calcutta University, with eight thousand students, was the largest university in the world. Even earlier, privileged Indians had begun to attend elite British universities. In 1888, **Mohandas Karamchand Gandhi**, who would lead India's independence movement and preach nonviolent resistance to colonialism, left India to study law in London.

The English language provided a common means of communication for educated Indians, who spoke hundreds of different native languages. As this new middle class of Indians developed, they could not help contrasting the liberal British ideals of democracy and equal rights with their own situation. The most talented Indians, even if trained at Oxford, could not reach the highest levels in the colonial bureaucracy or in private British firms. Nor could native Indians join exclusive British associations like the Bengal Club. The resentment and frustration of the educated Indian middle class fueled demands for an end to British colonial rule that would come in the twentieth century. Economically, British rule in India brought mixed results. One was **deindustrialization** of the subcontinent, even as railroads and telegraph lines were built. British manufacturers, particularly of cheap British cloth, put native industries out of business. On the other hand, British rule connected India to the world economy.

Checking In

By yourself or with a partner, explain the significance of each of the following selected key terms:

Mughal Empire

Sepoy Rebellion

Raj

Indian National Congress

Mohandas Gandhi

Imperialism and the Muslim World

◆ **Where did Muslims come under colonial rule in the late nineteenth century?**

◆ **In what ways did the Russian and Ottoman Empires confront imperialism differently?**

The Muslim world also felt the impact of the new imperialism, and not only in India. As Russia expanded its influence in southeastern Europe (the Balkans) and beyond the Caucasus Mountains on its southern border, hundreds of thousands of Muslims were affected. Nor could the Ottoman Empire, the only major Muslim state in the world at this time, defend itself from European imperialists.

In northern Africa, southeast Europe, and elsewhere, Ottoman influence was replaced by European influence. At the very end of the nineteenth century,

gendering Considering certain peoples or activities intrinsically linked with the male or female gender, in the latter case often with a negative connotation.

Mohandas Karamchand Gandhi (1869–1948) Indian political and spiritual leader who fought for Indian independence and emphasized nonviolent struggle.

deindustrialization Process of reducing the level of industry in a country, generally in colonized regions, especially India.

a new challenge to the Muslim world arose—the Zionist movement, which called on Jews to return to their ancestral homeland, Palestine, at the time an Ottoman province. European successes called forth new movements among Muslims that aimed for new forms of modern, nationalist, and democratic politics.

Russian Expansion

After the British in India, Russians had more contact with Muslims than any other Europeans. From the sixteenth century onward, the tsar had counted among his subjects Tartars and other Muslim peoples. As Russia expanded, a variety of religious and national groups came under Russian rule, including many Muslims. By 1700, Russia had extended its dominion over thinly populated Siberia all the way to the Pacific. A century and a half later, Russian control stretched across the Bering Strait, over Alaska, and down the American west coast as far south as present-day California. Amid the Great Reforms of the mid-1860s, however, Russia abandoned its American territories, selling Alaska to the United States in 1867. Russian expansion would now take place not in the New World but in the heart of the old: **Central Asia**.

Central Asia The boundary between "southern Siberia" and "Central Asia" is fluid, and Russian settlers had been moving gradually into what is now Kazakhstan at least from around 1800. In the second half of the nineteenth century, however, the Russian empire—already the largest on earth—took over vast territories in Central Asia. Like the European colonial powers in Africa, the Russians did not set out to control this region. They did not intend to settle Russians in Central Asia, only to prevent any other power from gaining a foothold there. In this respect, Russian expansion into Central Asia followed a common colonial pattern.

In 1865, Tashkent fell to the Russians, followed later in the decade by the khanates of Bukhara and Khiva. The ruling **khans** remained in place but now formally recognized the tsar's authority. In the 1870s, Russian troops engaged in military action against the warlike Turkmen who dominated the territory to the east of the Caspian Sea, establishing Russian control there by the end of the decade. Thus, by 1887, the conquest of **Turkestan** (the contemporary Russian term for Central Asia) was completed and Russian rule extended to the borders of Persia and Afghanistan.

British Discomfort at Russian Expansion The Russian advance did not go unnoticed by other western powers. In particular, the British were deeply concerned about the possibility of Russian influence in Central Asia and how it might affect British rule over India. These fears were rather exaggerated: the Russians had neither the intention nor the means of threatening the British colony. In the end, Afghanistan remained as a buffer between Russian and British **spheres of influences**, and in the early twentieth century Persia was partitioned between a northern Russian zone and a southern British zone.

Russia's new possessions in Central Asia did little to enhance the Russian economy, despite some cotton exports. The Russians did build railroads and extend telegraph lines to the new territory in the interests of more efficient administration. On the whole, however, few Russian merchants appeared in these new lands, and local economies experienced little change. The costs of administering these regions far exceeded any new tax revenues.

These territories were dominated by Muslim culture and populated by peoples speaking **Turkic** languages (as well as Tadjik, which is related to Persian). Persian and Arabic remained the most powerful languages in written culture; local languages were spoken but rarely written. The Russian rulers and settlers did not make serious attempts to russify or convert local populations. Like the British in India, they tended to live apart from native peoples and to return to Russia once their service was completed.

Russian Culture and Central Asia Central Asia exerted a powerful influence on Russian artists and ethnographers, many of whom visited the newly conquered lands to study the peoples and the architectural monuments there. The popular artist **Vasily Vereshchagin**, for example, resided for a time in Tashkent and produced many drawings and paintings on Central Asian themes. The region was also hailed by Russian nationalists. "Asia will prove the outlet for our future destiny," proclaimed the popular novelist Fyodor Dostoevsky. But well into the twentieth century, Central Asia remained impoverished, remote, and, aside from a few large cities, largely untouched by Russian or other western influences.

Despite some efforts to spread the Russian Orthodox religion in Central Asia, neither the Russian

Central Asia Geographical area including present-day states of Kazakhstan, Tajikistan, Uzbekistan, Kyrgyzstan, and Turkmenistan.

khan (in Turkic, "lord" or "ruler") Term used to describe Islamic rulers in Central Asia.

Turkestan (in Turkic, "Turk-land") Central Asian region inhabited by Turkic peoples.

sphere of influence Region over which a state exerts indirect political power, usually to prevent another state from extending its influence there.

Turkic Designation for a number of related languages such as Tartar, Uzbek, Kyrgyz, Turkmen, and Kazakh.

Vasily Vereshchagin (1842–1904) Russian realist painter, best known for his paintings of exotic Central Asia scenes.

Vasily Vereshchagin's artistic works often showed scenes from regions in Central Asia that had recently been incorporated into the Russian empire. This 1869 painting of the exquisite tomb in Samarkand of Timur or Tamerlaine, the Mongol conqueror who died in 1405, combined exoticism with a deep interest and respect for Central Asian culture. What elements of European exoticism can you point out in this image?

government nor the Orthodox church was particularly interested in converting Muslims. Few missionaries ventured out into Central Asia or Siberia. Those who did, moreover, did not attempt to convert the native populations directly. Instead, they established schools, where they taught in non-Russian languages as a first step toward "civilizing" native peoples. Only a few such schools were set up, however, and in the late 1860s the governor-general of Turkestan, Konstantin Kaufman, banned missionary activity in this huge, newly conquered Russian colony. Instead of gaining converts, Russian rule in Central Asia indirectly encouraged a movement for modern Islamic education known as **Jadidism**. As in colonized areas elsewhere in the world, the Russian presence in Central Asia ended up provoking the development of local nationalisms aimed against the imperial power.

The Ottoman Empire

In the nineteenth century, Muslims around the world looked to the Ottoman Empire as the religious and political center for their religion. The sultan held the title of Caliph, the spiritual head of all Muslims. Even more important, the holy cities of Mecca, Medina, and Jerusalem were all located in Ottoman territory. Thus the decline of Ottoman political power and loss of Ottoman territory were of concern to all Muslims.

Shrinking Ottoman Power in Europe In 1800, the richest and most populous lands of the Ottoman Empire were in Europe, on the Balkan Peninsula. By midcentury,

Jadidism (from Arabic, "new method") Movement attempting to reconcile Islam with modernity, especially in the Russian empire from the 1870s.

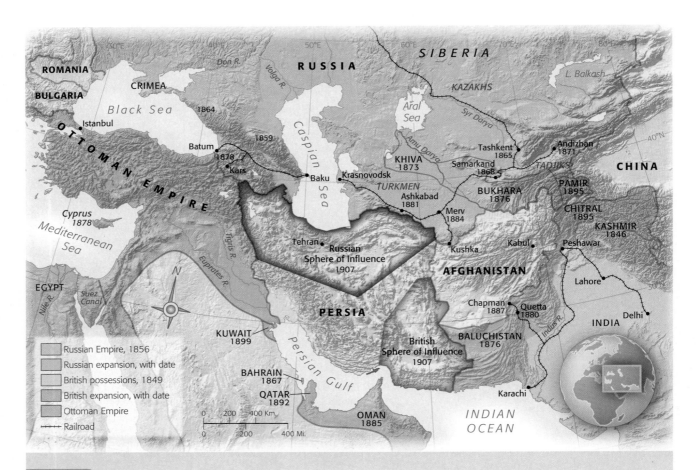

Map 24.4 **Central Asia** The Russian empire extended its borders southward from the 1860s to include most of Central Asia. By the late nineteenth century, the Russian empire extended to border Afghanistan on the south, causing great concern among British officials in India. © *Cengage Learning*

1. In expanding into Central Asia, what countries did the Russian empire threaten?
2. Looking at this map, how do you explain that the British were so upset about Russian expansion into Central Asia?

Ottoman influence over these lands had been considerably reduced, though the officially Romanian, Greek, Serbian, and Bulgarian regions remained within the empire. A key event showing the weakness of the Ottoman Empire was the Crimean War, fought ostensibly over which European power—Russia or France—had the right to protect Christians in the Ottoman Empire. Russia lost the war, but the very fact that European powers could demand—and get—the right to protect Christian Ottoman subjects showed the empire's weakness. The sultan could not, of course, offer similar protection to Muslims living under colonial rule in Egypt, French Algeria, or Russian Central Asia.

During the era of new imperialism, Ottoman influence was further reduced. The creation or expansion of Greek, Romanian, Serbian, and Bulgarian states in the Balkans was accompanied by the migration—often forced—of hundreds of thousands of Muslims to the Ottoman interior. Similarly, as Russia expanded its borders to the south, establishing control over present-day Armenia and Azerbaijan, many Muslims preferred to flee rather than live under the new Christian rulers. The Ottoman Empire was helpless to oppose the widening Russian influence.

Muslims, Christians, and Zionists

Another challenge to the Ottoman Empire and Muslim world was the new Jewish nationalist movement, Zionism. This movement, led by Theodor Herzl, aimed at the establishment of a Jewish state in ancient

Palestine, or what Jews called Eretz Israel, centered on Jerusalem. In the 1890s, this region was under Ottoman rule, and although numerous Jews and Christians lived there, the majority of the population was Muslim. The first Zionist settlers arrived in Palestine in the 1880s, and after that, large groups of Zionist pioneers came from Europe to establish Jewish settlements in this Ottoman province.

Initially, neither local Muslims nor the Ottoman authorities were concerned about the Zionists. After all, their numbers were small—around twenty thousand by 1903—and Jews had long lived in the region, even constituting the majority in Jerusalem. Still, the Ottoman sultan refused to grant the Zionist leader Herzl a charter officially sanctioning Zionist settlement, preferring to allow or forbid such activity on a case-by-case basis.

In the early twentieth century, **Arab nationalism** was beginning to take form. At first, however, this movement was primarily anti-Ottoman, wishing to foster an Arab identity based primarily on language and culture and only secondarily on the Muslim religion shared with the Turks. Not until the second decade of the twentieth century would Arab nationalists begin to see Zionism as a serious threat to the region and to their own identity.

Checking In

By yourself or with a partner, explain the significance of each of the following selected key terms:

Central Asia	Vasily Vereshchagin
Turkestan	Jadidism
spheres of influence	Arab nationalism

The Far East

- **How did economic and administrative practices differ in Asia and Africa, and between different colonial powers?**
- **How did Japan and China react to the threat of European imperialism?**

In East Asia or, to use an imperialist term, the Far East (far, of course, from Europe), imperialism also had a major impact. Some regions, such as Indochina and Indonesia, were controlled directly by European powers. But even in the two large East Asian countries that were not directly colonized—Japan and China—European influence had a profound effect. Western ideas as diverse as constitutionalism and Christianity entered these societies, influencing some Asians in a positive way while calling forth resentment and resistance from others. Both the violent and failed Boxer Rebellion in China and the peaceful reform of Japan's military and

political institutions reflect the power of European imperialism of this period.

The French in Indochina

While the French had long held colonial outposts in Asia, including India, French expansion into Southeast Asia dated from the 1850s. French missionaries in the region caused friction with local rulers, whose anti-Christian measures induced the French emperor Napoleon III to intervene. A treaty of 1862 forced local rulers in **Indochina** (today Vietnam, Cambodia, and Laos) to concede religious toleration for Christians. The treaty gave France a foothold in the southern part of what is now Vietnam, including the city of Saigon, and in 1867 France annexed this territory, known as Cochinchina. From there the French extended direct rule into most of present-day Cambodia and Laos to protect Catholic missions, establish naval bases, and defend French commercial interests in China. Emperor Napoleon III's foreign policy was explicitly imperialist, as he sought to enhance French prestige in the world.

Economically, the most important product of Indochina was raw silk, but reports of rich mineral wealth in the hills of Vietnam also lured French investors and adventurers. A small group of French settlers derived profit from plantations that produced rubber and teak wood. On the whole, however, French taxpayers paid a heavy price for France's colonial ventures. Few Frenchmen were interested in settling in the new colony, though many hundreds served there in administrative and military roles. The French also set up schools where, by the end of the century, young Vietnamese, Laotians, and Cambodians were learning to read and write French from the same textbooks used in Paris. Among the students were future leaders of Indochinese liberation movements, including **Ho Chi Minh**.

In India, higher British administrators brought their wives and raised their families, but French administrators in Indochina generally did not, often taking wives and mistresses from the local population. So-called native wives and their offspring did not receive equal political protection. Very often, at the end of their tour of duty, the men simply returned to Europe, abandoning their local wives and children.

In contrast to the British colonies, which were often ruled using already-existing political structures and local

Arab nationalism Movement beginning in late nineteenth century declaring that all Arabs constitute one nation and should be liberated from foreign rule.

Indochina Region in Southeast Asia under French colonial rule in the later nineteenth century, today Vietnam, Laos, and Cambodia.

Ho Chi Minh (1890–1969) Vietnamese national leader who in Paris helped found the French Communist Party and later led the Vietnamese independence movement.

This French board game, based on Jules Verne's novel *Around the World in Eighty Days*, emphasized the exotic territories now colonized by European powers like France. What technological innovations of this period allowed Verne's traveler to travel around in the world in less than three months?

Archives Charmet/The Bridgeman Art Library

rulers, the French had a more ambitious agenda. At least initially, they hoped to assimilate their colonial subjects and to make them into genuine Frenchmen. Soon, however, the realities of colonial administration, the difficulties in financing an adequate school system, and resistance from native peoples considerably interfered with this aim. Moreover, racial and nationalist prejudices made the French unwilling to allow native peoples in Indochina the same legal rights and financial advantages enjoyed by French colonists and officials.

The Dutch in Indonesia

The Dutch had been active in Southeast Asia since the sixteenth century, when Dutch explorers had opened the way for the spice trade that had been a great source of Dutch wealth. Like the British in India, the Dutch managed trading posts and spice warehouses through a trading company—the Dutch West India Company—but did not exercise direct rule over the region that is today Indonesia. In contrast to the French, the Dutch were not interested in "civilizing" the native population, whose Islamic faith had been brought to the region centuries earlier by Arab traders. The Dutch carried out little missionary activity and, on the whole, left existing native political and

Qing dynasty Ruling house of China from 1644 to 1912, also known as Manchus.

Opium Wars Conflict between Britain and China from 1839 to 1842 that ended in Chinese defeat.

unequal treaties Treaties favorable to western powers (and Japan) extorted by force or threat from China during the nineteenth and early twentieth centuries.

judicial structures and Muslim institutions in place. At no time did the Dutch attempt to influence the mainly Muslim Indonesian population to abandon their faith. Dutch schools for natives aimed primarily to train minor officials to serve in the local colonial bureaucracy.

Between 1830 and 1870, the Dutch West Indies produced huge profits for the Netherlands, but only by exploiting native labor and generating serious local discontent. After about 1870, Dutch trade with the Dutch West Indies declined. In contrast to Vietnam, where French influence may still be discerned a half century after the end of French colonial rule there, Dutch colonial control left few traces in Indonesia.

Concessions in China

China, the largest and most populous country in Asia, had long been a major cultural influence. By the mid-nineteenth century, however, under the corrupt and weak **Qing dynasty**, China could not compete against the military and economic might of the European imperialists. China's defeat in the 1840s by the British during the **Opium Wars** revealed its weakness. Subsequently, the Chinese accepted massive imports of opium from British India, enriching British merchants but weakening Chinese society.

Chinese Weakness: The Unequal Treaties Thus began the era of **unequal treaties**. Western imperialist powers negotiated concessions at treaty ports that assured them favorable trade arrangements and a minimum of Chinese interference. As part of the concessions, the Chinese agreed that the imperialist power could administer its own tax system and legal system.

The British took over Hong Kong and had a concession in the major city of Shanghai. The Germans received a concession in the port city of Qingdao (Tsingtao), establishing a beer factory that continues in operation today. The French also gained favored treatment in China. In many areas in China, foreign businessmen could trade without interference or taxation from the Chinese government. Concessions deprived the Chinese state of much-needed taxes, while westerners—and some well-placed Chinese businessmen—reaped huge profits.

China's political weakness was also apparent in foreign policy. Defeat in the Sino-Japanese War of 1894–1895 forced China to relinquish the island of Formosa (Taiwan) to Japan. In the early twentieth century, with Russian and Japanese power growing in northeast Asia, China lost its influence over Korea. A few years later, China bowed to Russian pressure, allowing the Russians to build a railroad across its Manchurian province to the north and to establish nearby naval bases. By the early twentieth century, foreign influence in the form of concessions, naval bases, and trade privileges had compromised Chinese sovereignty.

Christian Missionaries in China Christian missionaries set up schools and health clinics throughout China, winning a significant number of converts. For ambitious Chinese parents, missionary schools provided some education for daughters and, for sons, a means to a higher education, usually abroad. Following this path, the future nationalist leader **Sun Yatsen** received a Christian education and then left China to attend medical school in Hawaii.

Despite the missionaries' sincere desire to educate and help the Chinese people, their teachings inevitably came into conflict with Chinese customs. For example, the ancestor worship so important for Chinese culture was seen by Christians as a form of idolatry. Christian missionaries also encouraged not only education for females but an end to female infanticide and the traditional practice of binding young girls' feet so they would be the desirable tiny size in adulthood. Foreign missionaries worked with their Chinese pupils and converts to translate western ideas into Chinese, but often without any understanding of the implications of western practices within Chinese society. Many Chinese thus feared and resented the spread of Christianity. In 1870, in Tianjin, these feelings exploded into attacks on foreigners. The so-called Tianjin Massacre did not, however, reduce missionary activity in China.

The Boxer Rebellion By the late nineteenth century, this enormous cultural and economic influence of foreigners had called forth a strong and violent reaction from Chinese patriots, the **Boxer Rebellion.** The Boxers were a group of young Chinese men who combined training in martial arts with a burning desire to free China from foreign domination, which they found humiliating. In 1900 the Boxers attacked foreign missionaries, businessmen, diplomats, Chinese converts to Christianity, and generally all forms of foreign influence. Their violence alarmed westerners, and the imperialist powers reacted swiftly to put down the rebellion. Thousands of German, French, American, British, Japanese, and Russian troops rushed to Beijing, where they ended a siege of foreign embassies. Order was restored, but the prestige of the Qing dynasty was fatally weakened. Young Chinese intellectuals increasingly called for limitations on foreign influences and the restoration of Chinese sovereignty throughout the entire territory of China.

The Westernization of Japan

Japan forms an exception to many generalizations about late-nineteenth-century imperialism. The Japanese were successful in using western models to their own advantage and, in the end, against the western powers themselves. For the previous two centuries, foreign entry into Japan had been limited to two small trading posts. Then, in 1853, the American commodore **Matthew Perry** arrived in Tokyo harbor and, after months of negotiation, forced the Japanese to open up to foreign trade in 1854.

The Meiji Restoration The Japanese were shocked at the foreigners' command of new and unfamiliar technology, in particular modern firearms. Rather than falling under foreign rule, however, the Japanese under a new emperor known as Meiji ("the enlightened one") carried out their own administrative, military, and economic reforms. By the end of the century, Japan was rapidly industrializing. Railroads connected the most important Japanese cities, and the Japanese army had been reconstituted along Prussian lines. The success of the **Meiji Restoration** may be seen in the Japanese defeat of China in the Sino-Japanese War.

Japanese Expansion Japanese influence in Korea led inevitably to frictions with Russia, which was also seeking to expand its power in East Asia. Beginning in the 1890s, construction of the Trans-Siberian Railroad, linking Moscow and the Pacific Ocean, was one means by which Russia hoped to promote its influence in Siberia and even settlement of the region. The railroad's terminus at Vladivostok was just a few hundred miles from Japan and even closer to Korea. Russia obtained the right to build the railroad directly across the northeastern

---

Sun Yatsen (1866–1925) Chinese physician and political leader who aimed to transform China with patriotic, democratic, and economically progressive reforms.

Boxer Rebellion Antiforeign revolt in China in 1898–1900.

Matthew Perry (1794–1858) American naval officer who in 1854 persuaded the Japanese government to allow American trade with previously closed-off Japan.

Meiji Restoration Reform of Japanese politics and economy under Emperor Meiji (r. 1867–1912).

In this Japanese print of the Meiji period (ca. 1860), traditionally dressed samurai set out in boats to confront Commodore Matthew Perry's looming "black ships." By signing a treaty in 1854 opening Japan to foreign trade, the Japanese reversed centuries of isolation and began a rapid process of industrialization and westernization in their country. How does this image contrast the western ship and Japanese boats? (British Museum/The Art Archive at Art Resource, NY)

Chinese province of Manchuria, to Japan's considerable annoyance. The Chinese also allowed the Russians to build a naval base on Chinese territory at Port Arthur (now Lüshun), to the south of Korea, which Japan could only see as a direct threat. Fearing further Russian inroads into China and Korea, in 1904 Japan carried out a surprise attack on the Russian base at Port Arthur.

The **Russo-Japanese War** that ensued turned out to be an international and domestic disaster for Russia. To the shock of not only Russians, but all Europeans, the Japanese prevailed on the seas—destroying the Russian fleet—and on land. For the first time in centuries, a European power was defeated by an Asian country. The success of Japan's modernization was evident in its army trained on the Prussian model and its navy of western-style warships. The American President Theodore Roosevelt helped negotiate a peace between

Japan and Russia, which ended the war in 1905. The Japanese used their victory to extend their power in the region, and in 1910 they formally annexed Korea.

In Russia, the war caused a crisis, the **Russian Revolution of 1905**. When marchers who had peacefully gathered outside the Winter Palace in St. Petersburg were brutally dispersed, causing dozens of deaths, the country exploded into violent protest and strikes. **Tsar Nicholas II** seemed completely out of touch—unable to influence events and unwilling to compromise with widespread demands for political reform. General strikes that paralyzed the country in October forced him to reduce censorship, increase religious freedom, and grant a parliament, the Duma. While limited in its powers, the Duma provided a place for political debate until 1917.

Russo-Japanese War Conflict in 1904–1905 that began with a Japanese surprise attack on a Russian naval base and ended in Russian defeat.

Russian Revolution of 1905 Insurrection in Russia set off by military defeats in the Russo-Japanese War that forced political concessions from Tsar Nicholas II.

Tsar Nicholas II (r. 1894–1918) Russian emperor and cousin by marriage of Kaiser William II, killed by the Bolsheviks in 1918, after the Russian Revolution.

 **Checking In**

By yourself or with a partner, explain the significance of each of the following selected key terms:

Opium Wars

unequal treaties

Sun Yatsen

Boxer Rebellion

Meiji Restoration

Russo-Japanese War

Russian Revolution of 1905

Tsar Nicholas II

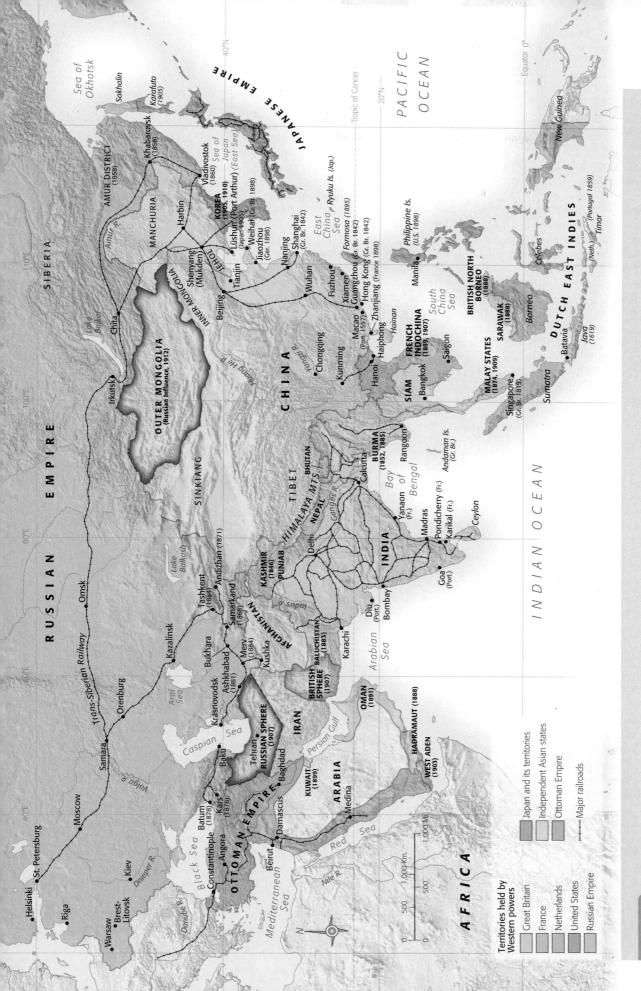

Map 24.5 **Asia in 1914** In 1914 one found both independent countries (Japan, China, Siam [Thailand]) and a number of European colonies (British, French, Dutch) in East Asia. Japan had also extended its rule over Korea to the north and Taiwan to the south. By the early twentieth century, the Trans-Siberian Railroad connected Moscow with the Pacific. © Cengage Learning

1. Why did Japan feel threatened by this railroad?
2. Looking at the railroads on the map, which countries appear most developed? Most backward?

Territories held by Western powers

- Great Britain
- France
- Netherlands
- United States
- Russian Empire

- Japan and its territories
- Independent Asian states
- Ottoman Empire
- Major railroads

Consequences and Critics

◆ **What impact did imperialism have on the global economy and European culture?**

◆ **Who opposed imperialism in Europe and elsewhere, and why?**

Even as the new imperialism extended European influence throughout the world, it also called forth resistance and condemnation. Its benefits were greatly unequal, as western powers profited while colonized regions did not. Ironically, the western ideals of liberty and democracy that the imperial powers boasted they were bringing to the unenlightened peoples of the world inspired anticolonial movements among African and Asian intellectuals. But critics in Europe, too, argued that imperialism was a capitalist sham, an attempt to divert attention from injustice and inequality at home. In both negative and positive ways, imperialism had a profound effect on European politics and culture.

A Global Economy

In the late nineteenth century, European colonial empires did much to link up the world and to create a single global economy. But the linkage was uneven. Raw materials like cotton flowed from the colonies to Europe, and European goods like cloth were purchased by the colonies. British textiles were exported to Africa and India. The Indian railways used rails and locomotives that for the most part were imported from England. Textiles from Russia found a market in Central and East Asia. Because the European colonizers had little interest in developing colonial industry, the colonies became economically dependent on European industry. In some cases, colonies deindustrialized. So as profits flowed to Europe, wages and living standards remained very low in nearly all colonial areas.

Trade Around the Globe In addition, colonial economies were reshaped to meet the needs and desires of western imperialist powers. Tea, sugar, and chocolate had become staples in the European diet; in this era even Russian peasants began to drink tea daily. The plantations that produced these commodities expanded, and the economies of entire colonies and tropical nations were built around a single export. Bananas, which began to appear on tables in North America and Europe, are only the most prominent example. The companies that managed these commodities were

Omdurman Battle in 1898 in present-day Sudan, in which thousands of African warriors were massacred by a British army using machine guns.

western; the laborers were native peoples. Again, the profits flowed to Europe.

Now guano from Peru and nitrites from Chile enriched the fields of European farmers. Rubber for tires, belts, and gaskets, indispensable for modern machinery, had to be extracted from trees that grew only in tropical regions such as Malaya (a British colony, now Malaysia), Indochina, and the Belgian Congo. Palm oil, another tropical commodity, was used in the manufacture of soap—a product then exported back to the colonies. Cinchona trees were also cultivated to provide the quinine on which the health of Europeans in tropical regions depended. Copper was imported from mines in the Belgian Congo; tin came from Malaya. Huge amounts of Indian cotton were imported to be transformed into cloth in British mills. Diamonds and gold from South African mines adorned wealthy Europeans.

New inventions and technological innovations facilitated global exchange. Starting in the late 1870s, for example, refrigerated steamships carried frozen meat from the United States, Argentina, and even New Zealand to the ports of Europe, pushing out less efficient meat producers. But on the whole, European economies were not challenged by colonial economies. Colonial markets were relatively small compared to European markets, and Europeans sold far more manufactured goods to each other and in the Americas than they did to their colonies. Europeans did invest in colonies, however. Global links were economic; they were only partly the result of direct colonial rule.

Indigenous Resistance

As the Sepoy Rebellion and the Boxer Rebellion indicate, colonized peoples in Asia did not simply accept European colonial domination. In the Battle of **Omdurman**, too, Africans fought against European colonizers. But native troops, armed with traditional weapons, were massacred there by British troops using machine guns. European technological superiority meant that native peoples needed to seek other means of resistance.

Different Forms of Resistance After European colonies had been established, the colonized had to struggle for their rights within the existing colonial system. Some resistance assumed a heroic public form, such as Gandhi's organizing of Indian residents in South Africa to demand their rights in the 1890s. Other resistance was more subtle. Indigenous peoples might refuse to carry out the orders of colonial administrators, avoid paying colonial taxes, or shun European cultural and educational institutions. Some resisters insisted on wearing native clothing, despite imports from Europe,

THE FORMULA OF BRITISH CONQUEST

PEARS' SOAP IS THE BEST

PEARS' SOAP IN THE SOUDAN.

"Even if our invasion of the Soudan has done nothing else it has at any rate left the Arab something to puzzle his fuzzy head over, for the legend PEARS' SOAP IS THE BEST, inscribed in hugh white characters on the rock which marks the farthest point of our advance towards Berber, will tax all the wits of the Dervishes of the Desert to translate."—Phil Robinson, *War Correspondent (in the Soudan) of the Daily Telegraph in London, 1884.*

Mary Evans Picture Library/The Image Works

Pears' soap advertisements like this one emphasized the "civilizing mission" of British imperialism. Bringing order, science, and hygiene to supposedly backward world regions was one of the prime justifications of imperialist rule. Why would a British company use an image like this one to sell its product? What surprises you about this image? What elements of this ad would you see as common for this period?

or on speaking native languages, despite schools that taught English or French.

The education that colonized peoples received at colonial schools proved to provide them with the most effective weapon of resistance. Learning of European constitutional government and political rights, native peoples came to challenge the racial hierarchies evident in the colonies. Pointing out the contradictions of a system that promised civilization and justice but refused equal rights to native peoples, resistance leaders exposed the hypocrisy of imperialism and demanded rights for themselves and their peoples. To the European imperialists they quoted European thinkers and ideals such as liberty, democracy, and individual rights. They pointed to the vast contrast between the luxury in which colonial officials lived and the impoverishment of natives.

Before 1914, however, resistance to imperialism was only beginning to be organized. In most African and Asian colonies, European administrators continued to dominate, at least officially. Away from cities and European settlements, however, life generally continued along traditional lines. At the same time, increasing numbers of educated Asians and Africans were formulating ways of resisting European dominance. Full-fledged independence movements would emerge in the mid-twentieth century.

Imperialism and European Culture

Though the dominators, not the dominated, Europeans were affected by the lands they ruled. Literature, music, visual arts, architecture, and even advertising took up themes and images of imperialism. Popular novels praised the bravery of the colonists while hinting at forbidden romantic attachments.

Exoticism in Art, Music, and Literature Painters produced scenes of entrancing foreign places, often featuring ruins, exotic vegetation, and—of course—beautiful native women. In music, the most "imperial opera," *Aïda,* by Giuseppe Verdi, was commissioned specifically for the opening of the Suez Canal in 1869. The story hinges on a beautiful Ethiopian slave, Aïda, and her love for an Egyptian general in the era of the pharaohs. The opera was a hit: apparently few minded the absurdity of a made-up story about ancient Africans sung in Italian for the benefit of European audiences.

Literature of the late nineteenth and early twentieth centuries reflects imperialist themes. Kipling's many stories and novels about life in British India were bestsellers of the day. The poet Alfred, Lord Tennyson celebrated the empire in verses such as "The Fleet" (1885) and "On the Jubilee of Queen Victoria" (1887). In France, **Pierre Loti** published dozens of novels that reflect the European fascination with the peoples and customs of the colonies. Set in exotic regions, they nearly always involve a romance between a strong European man and a beautiful non-European woman. The plots are unrealistic, but Loti's novels were very popular, and in 1891 he was elected to the **French Academy**, the prestigious scholarly and literary society, at the unprecedented young age of forty-one.

International Exhibitions International exhibitions in Paris in 1867 and 1900 also reflect European fascination

Pierre Loti (1850–1923) French writer who authored novels set in exotic climes and featuring romances between a European man and a non-European woman.

French Academy French cultural institution established in 1635 whose members make judgments on the proper use of the French language.

Musée d'Orsay, Paris/Giraudon/The Bridgeman Art Library

Many of Paul Gauguin's paintings from Tahiti, like Arearea (1892), depict beautiful Tahitian women in an exotic tropical landscape. Gauguin's own biography—abandoning a respectable middle-class profession and leaving his family to pursue pleasure and painting in the South Seas—reflects the lure colonial regions had for nineteenth-century Europeans. How does Gauguin convey exoticism in this image through his style and subject matter?

with the colonies. Here Parisians and visitors could "experience" an African village, listen to Tunisian musicians, or wander through a reproduction of a Cairo street. These exhibitions aimed both to educate the populace about the colonies and to promote European superiority. Ethnographic museums served similar purposes. In Paris at the Museum of the Colonies, and in museums in Moscow and St. Petersburg, colonial peoples themselves were put on display. The purpose was always to demonstrate the "savage" ways of "the uncivilized" and to reassure Europeans of their superiority.

The interests of imperialism were evident in the visual arts as well. In Russia the painter Vereshchagin depicted the land and peoples of Russia's newly conquered territory in Central Asia. After French stockbroker **Paul Gauguin** abandoned his family and went to live in Tahiti, he painted Tahitians in their own environment. Popular postcards and prints familiarized Europeans with far-off colonies and spurred interest in the colonial endeavor. Images in advertising, too, drew on imperialist themes. In Britain, advertisements extolled Pears' Soap as one of the benefits that Britons could bring to Africa and Asia.

Capitalism and Imperialism

The heyday of imperialism lasted barely two decades, ending with the Boer War. While no crisis of

Paul Gauguin (1848–1903)
French painter who painted Tahitian life and culture.

European imperialism was obvious in the first decade of the twentieth century, the arguments of the anti-imperialists were already being developed. The first critiques concentrated on its cruelty toward subject populations. Later these were overshadowed by Marxist critics who portrayed imperialism as part of a decaying capitalist world order.

Hobson's Imperialism In 1902, **John A. Hobson** argued in *Imperialism: A Study* that Britain's imperial expansion was a short-term attempt to avoid social conflict. British workers at first benefited from the cheap produce and labor of the colonies, but Hobson predicted that soon their position would be undermined by this vast pool of cheap labor. Hobson saw a major cause for imperialism in the search for markets and investment opportunities abroad. For him, imperialism was both hypocritical and dangerous. Imperialists falsely claimed to be bringing higher culture to subject peoples, and Britain's nondemocratic rule over the colonies posed a threat to democracy at home. By placing colonial peoples at the very bottom of the social hierarchy, Hobson claimed, imperialism falsely elevated the status of England's working class.

Lenin Criticizes Imperialism Some of Hobson's arguments were taken up a bit more than a decade later by the Russian Marxist **Vladimir Ilyich Lenin.** Lenin's *Imperialism: The Highest Stage of Capitalism* (1916) portrayed imperialism as a symptom of a larger ill: capitalism. Thus, when capitalism would be overthrown by socialism, imperialism would also be destroyed. Following Karl Marx, Lenin pointed out that since the early years of industrialization, profit levels had declined steadily. Capitalists were thus forced to seek new and more lucrative investment opportunities outside Europe. Although in retrospect it is evident that colonial markets and investment were of secondary importance even in the heyday of imperialism. Lenin's exposure of imperialism as an economic, political, and moral dead end seemed convincing to many contemporary Europeans.

> **John A. Hobson** (1858–1940) English economist and influential critic of imperialism.
>
> **Vladimir Ilyich Lenin** (1870–1924) Russian Marxist revolutionary and leader of the Bolsheviks.

 Checking In

By yourself or with a partner, explain the significance of each of the following selected key terms:

Omdurman	Paul Gauguin
Pierre Loti	John A. Hobson
French Academy	Vladimir Ilyich Lenin

CHAPTER
Review

Summary

- In the period 1870 to 1914, European countries established colonial rule over huge parts of the globe.

- Africa was the most affected continent in this "new imperialism."

- Russia, France, and Germany established new colonial rule in Asia; Dutch and British rule continued in previously established colonies.

- Among the reasons for the new imperialism were technological advances, national prestige, and economic motives.

- The new imperialism went hand-in-hand with racism, the idea that European peoples and their descendants were biologically superior to Asian, African, and Amerindian peoples.

- The new imperialism's effects were contradictory and controversial, from exploitation of native peoples to the spread of education and the use of European languages.

Chronology

1836–1846	Boers take Great Trek north away from English colonists in southern Africa
1839–1842	British defeat the Chinese in the Opium Wars
1853–1854	United States forces Japan to open to foreign trade
1857–1858	British put down Sepoy Rebellion in India
1865	Tashkent falls to the Russians
1867	French annex Cochinchina (southern Indochina)
1869	Suez Canal opens
1877	Queen Victoria becomes empress of India
1882	British occupy Egypt
1884–1886	Germany establishes African colonies
1885	Indian National Congress is founded; Congo Free State is established
1887	Russia completes conquest of Turkestan (Central Asia)
1894–1895	Japanese annex Formosa (Taiwan)
1898	Spanish-American War begins
1899–1902	British defeat Boers in the Boer War
1900	Foreign powers crush Boxer Rebellion in China
1902	Hobson publishes *Imperialism*
1904	Japanese attack on Russian naval base at Port Arthur
1905–1907	Herero Revolt takes place in German Southwest Africa
1908	Leopold II turns over the Congo Free State to Belgium
1910	Union of South Africa is established
1912	South African Native National Congress is established; Italy invades Libya
1916	Lenin publishes *Imperialism, the Highest Stage of Capitalism*

© Cengage Learning

Test Yourself

To gauge your mastery of the material in this chapter, answer the questions below. More than one answer may be correct.

Motives and Methods of the New Imperialism

1. Which of the following were motives for the new imperialism?
   a. National prestige.
   b. The desire to protect already-held colonies.
   c. Profit, especially in seeking valuable raw materials.
   d. Spreading Christianity.
   e. The desire to spread "civilization" and western values.

2. Which of the following methods were used during the new imperialism?
   a. New weapons technology such as the machine gun
   b. The compass
   c. Steamboats
   d. Tropical medicine, such as the use of quinine against malaria
   e. The telegraph

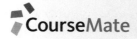 Visit the CourseMate website at **www.cengagebrain.com** for additional study tools and review materials for this chapter.

3. Which of the following world regions did the new imperialism not affect directly?

   a. South America
   b. The Near East (present-day Israel, Palestine, Jordan, Lebanon)
   c. Indochina (Vietnam, Laos, Cambodia)
   d. Africa
   e. Central Asia

4. The "white man's burden" was:

   a. A poem by Rudyard Kipling directed to Americans in the midst of the Spanish-American War.
   b. A paternalistic and implicitly racist call for "white men" to "enlighten" the rest of the world.
   c. A racist ideology based on social Darwinism.
   d. To support imperialism, but not by exploitation or mistreatment of non-Europeans.
   e. Romantic in its belief that imperialism could serve the best interests of colonialized people.

5. Which statements about important figures in the period of new imperialism are correct?

   a. Chancellor Bismarck was from the start a fervent advocate of imperialism, and Germany quickly established a large empire in Africa and Asia.
   b. Cecil Rhodes was an English businessmen who made a fortune in southern Africa.
   c. David Livingstone was an important military leader for the French in Algeria.
   d. King Leopold II of Belgium established an enlightened colony in Mozambique that aimed to better the lives of the African inhabitants.
   e. Rudyard Kipling was born in British Syria and fought against the Russians during the taking of Samarkand.

Now that you have reviewed and tested yourself on this part of the chapter, take time to pull together all the important information by answering the following questions:

◆ How important were economic considerations among the causes of the new imperialism?

◆ What part did racism play in the new imperialism? Were all imperialists racists?

The Scramble for Africa

6. Settler colonies in Africa:

   a. Only existed after 1870.
   b. Were established along the Atlantic coast already in the fifteenth century.
   c. Made up 40 percent of the total population of the continent.
   d. Existed only in two places, South Africa and French Algeria.
   e. Were already established before the mid-nineteenth century.

7. The Belgian Congo is important historically because:

   a. It established large chocolate and waffle factories in Central Africa.
   b. It was originally owned as the personal property of King Leopold II.
   c. It exhibited a level of brutal exploitation unusual even for this period.
   d. It spearheaded efforts to make imperialism more humane.
   e. It gained independence from Belgium before the first World War.

8. German participation in the new imperialism was characterized by:

   a. Its tardiness, as Germany only united in 1871.
   b. A concerted aggressiveness that led to Germany ruling more than one-third of Africa by 1910.
   c. Initial hesitancy on the part of Chancellor Bismarck who later embraced imperialism because of its popularity among Germans.
   d. Spreading lederhosen as a practical outfit in sub-Saharan Africa.
   e. Considerable ruthlessness, as in the repression of the Herero Revolt of 1905–1907.

9. The Scramble for Africa:

   a. Took place primarily from 1870 to around 1914.
   b. Involved various European countries taking control of the great majority of the African continent.
   c. Left only two independent countries in Africa, Liberia and Ethiopia.
   d. Made Italy one of the largest colonial powers in Africa.
   e. Allowed Cecil Rhodes to build a railway from Cairo to the Cape entirely within British colonial territories.

10. The Boer War:

    a. Occurred in the 1860s when Britain invaded Egypt.
    b. Was primarily a conflict between two colonial groups in southern Africa, Boers and the armed forces of the British Empire.
    c. Was precipitated in great part by the discovery of gold and diamonds in South Africa.
    d. Did not affect local Africans in southern Africa.
    e. Caused many Europeans to question whether imperialism was worthwhile.

Now that you have reviewed and tested yourself on this part of the chapter, take time to pull together all the important information by answering the following questions:

◆ What factors explain the quick penetration by European powers of the African continent in this period? Why didn't this happen earlier?

◆ Where were the colonial holdings of different countries (Britain, France, Belgium, Germany, Portugal) located? Which of these holdings were acquired in this period?

The British Raj in India

11. The term "British Raj" refers to:

    a. A new colony acquired by Great Britain in this period.
    b. Britain's rule over its most important colony, India.
    c. A British colony that had a major influence on British culture and national identity.
    d. A colony that was itself significantly influenced by British culture.
    e. The British-installed King of India.

12. Which of the following statements about British rule in India is correct?

    a. British administrators took great pains to convert Indians to Christianity.
    b. The Sepoy Rebellion led to a significant increase of British troops in India.
    c. The British government had exercised direct rule over India since the sixteenth century.
    d. The British East India Company mainly wanted to spread British culture in India.
    e. In the eighteenth century both Britain and France had trading posts in India.

13. On religious policy in the British Raj, which of the following statements is most correct?

    a. Britain favored the Hindus because of their monotheistic religion.
    b. Missionaries were encouraged by the British authorities to press hard for conversions.
    c. Few British administrators understood very much about Indian religions.
    d. Queen Victoria demanded religious uniformity in her Indian colony.
    e. Muslims, who made up the poorest segments of the Indian populace, welcomed British protection against almost universal Hindu rule.

14. Which of the following statements about British rule in India are correct?

    a. British rule was based on a feeling of affinity and equality with Indians.
    b. There were always more Indian than British troops in the Raj, even after the Sepoy Rebellion.
    c. The bulk of administrative costs of the Raj were borne by British taxpayers.
    d. Serving in India was considered an unusual hardship by ambitious young Britons.
    e. The unfairness of British colonial rule led to the formation of the Indian National Congress in 1885.

15. Which of the following were actual effects of the Raj on Britain and on India?

    a. A deindustrialization of India because most industrial products were imported from Britain.
    b. Construction of one of the most extensive railroad nets in Asia.
    c. Spread of the English language in India.
    d. Acceptance before 1900 by Britons that their imperial rule in India had to be brought to an end soon.
    e. Widespread popularity of Mohandas Gandhi in Britain by 1900.

Now that you have reviewed and tested yourself on this part of the chapter, take time to pull together all the important information by answering the following questions:

◆ How did India differ from other British colonies? Why was it called "the jewel in the crown?"

◆ What were the stages of British rule in India? What attitudes changed from the late eighteenth to early twentieth century?

Imperialism and the Muslim World

16. Which of the following statements about Islam and the new imperialism are correct?

   a. Imperialism had little or no effect on Muslims.
   b. In this period Russia extended its rule over Muslims for the first time.
   c. The strength of the Ottoman Empire meant that Muslims could ignore the new imperialism.

   d. The Russian empire's expansion into Central Asia brought many thousands of Muslims under Russian rule.
   e. Muslims in Africa, Central Asia, and India all experienced imperial rule in this period.

17. Russian rule in the second half of the nineteenth century:

   a. Expanded in Central Asia to include Muslim peoples in Turkestan.
   b. Expanded into North America, including Alaska.
   c. Was mainly following economic interests when it expanded into Central Asia.

   d. Expanded into Central Asia, but did not make serious efforts to convert or russify the local population.
   e. Sparked a modernist movement among Muslims in the Russian empire known as Jadidism.

18. During the nineteenth century, the Ottoman Empire:

   a. Ceased to exist.
   b. Expanded to include new territories in Africa and western Asia.
   c. Almost disappeared entirely from Europe with the independence or autonomy of countries like Greece, Bulgaria, Serbia, and Romania.

   d. Declined in territory and power, but still included the holy cities of Mecca, Medina, and Jerusalem.
   e. Enthusiastically endorsed and supported the Jadidist movement.

19. Zionism in this period can be defined as:

   a. Arab nationalism.
   b. A political movement in favor of the strengthening of the Ottoman Empire.
   c. Following the ideas of Theodor Herzl who wanted an independent nation-state for Jews.

   d. Jewish nationalism.
   e. Wishing to eject Arabs from Palestine and replace them entirely with Jewish settlers.

20. Russian expansion into Central Asia:

   a. Took place primarily from the 1860s onward (aside from northern Kazakhstan).
   b. Followed a well-thought-out plan from St. Petersburg.
   c. Worried British authorities in India.

   d. Brought large populations, mainly Turkic-speaking Muslims, under Russian rule.
   e. Was not much noticed among educated Russians of the time.

Now that you have reviewed and tested yourself on this part of the chapter, take time to pull together all the important information by answering the following questions:

◆ Why might Muslims of the Ottoman Empire have been concerned about European expansion in this period?

◆ What were some of the most important effects of Russian expansion in Central Asia?

The Far East

21. French and Dutch colonial rule differed in what ways?

   a. The Dutch colonies in Asia had been established centuries earlier.
   b. French direct rule in Indochina developed out of intervention to protect French missionaries.
   c. French administrators brought their wives and families from France; the Dutch tended to marry local women.

   d. The Dutch West Indies produced larger profits before the era of new imperialism.
   e. Dutch imperialists set up an impressive school network, which is why their language continues to be spoken widely in modern Indonesia.

22. French colonial expansion in the Far East:

   a. Centered on the territory of Indochina.
   b. Was promoted by Napoleon III for reasons of national prestige.
   c. Did not involve economic interests.
   d. Left no trace in the postcolonial world.

   e. Involved relatively few French colonists, far less than in British India.

23. During the era of new imperialism, China:

    a. Was split up by three foreigner rulers.
    b. Retained its independence but had to relinquish some ports and territories including Korea and Taiwan.
    c. Witnessed a rise in nationalist, antiforeigner sentiment that culminated in the Boxer Rebellion.
    d. Demonstrated more flexibility in coming to terms with European imperialism than did the Japanese.
    e. Was influenced by Christian missionaries who often set up their own schools in China.

24. Compared with China, Japan:

    a. Was more successful in adapting western techniques to enhance its own national power.
    b. Was less affected by imperialism, being isolated from the rest of the world until the twentieth century.
    c. Used western techniques to push forward its own industrialization in the late nineteenth century.
    d. Enhanced the power of the emperor in the so-called Meiji Restoration.
    e. Was forced to make humiliating concessions in so-called unequal treaties with western powers.

25. Which of the following statements about the Boxer Rebellion is correct?

    a. It aimed for a thoroughgoing westernization of China.
    b. It took place in China around 1900.
    c. It was led mainly by patriotic young Chinese men who trained in martial arts.
    d. It ended with the expulsion of all foreigners from China.
    e. It helped shore up the prestige of the Qing dynasty.

Now that you have reviewed and tested yourself on this part of the chapter, take time to pull together all the important information by answering the following questions:

◆ How did French and Dutch colonial rule differ from that of the British in India?

◆ In what ways was Japan "an exception to many generalizations about imperialism?"

Consequences and Critics

26. Which of the following are examples of a new global economy in the late nineteenth century?

    a. Export of spices from Asia to Europe.
    b. Mass importation of beverages like tea from Asia to Europe.
    c. Technology-dependent trade, such as the sale of frozen meat by Argentina to Europe.
    d. Importing sugar from the New World to Europe.
    e. Trade in rubber for tires and gaskets, palm oil for soap, and minerals like copper and tin from colonies.

27. Which of the following statements accurately characterize relations between imperialists and indigenous peoples?

    a. During this period indigenous peoples were almost completely incapable of resistance.
    b. Incidents like the massacre of native troops at the Battle of Omdurman showed that direct resistance to colonial power could be suicidal.
    c. Forms of resistance included refusing to pay taxes, wearing traditional garb, and speaking local languages.
    d. Indigenous resistance severely undermined British and French colonial rule before 1914.
    e. Indigenous people used the education received under colonialism to point out the hypocrisy of imperial rule.

28. European culture's depiction of indigenous culture in the colonies was:

    a. Entirely negative, based on the idea that natives were primitive and backward.
    b. Minimal as Europeans were not much interested in imperialism.
    c. Often combined eroticism, a fascination with the exotic, and unrealistic plots.
    d. Sometimes quite positive, as in the paintings of Vereshchagin and Gauguin.
    e. Frequently paternalistic, as in the advertisements for Pears' Soap extolling the hygienic benefits brought by British imperialism to Africa and Asia.

29. Among the pre-1914 critiques of imperialism was:

    a. The argument that imperialism bred unrest and Marxism and thus must be ended.
    b. Hobson's criticism of imperialism for causing British labor costs to rise.
    c. Lenin's argument that imperialism was the final stage of capitalism.
    d. The economic argument that imperialism sought markets abroad to make up for diminishing profit rates in the developed world.
    e. Hobson's claim that British imperialism aimed to avoid social conflict at home by exploiting cheap labor abroad.

30. Summing up, which of the following were outcomes of the new imperialism?

    a. Increased global trade, including tropical products like rubber and bananas being imported to North America and Europe.
    b. A more peaceful world because there were fewer nation-states.
    c. Enrichment of native peoples in Africa and Asia from the sale of rubber, guano, bananas, and other products.
    d. Significant impact of exotic themes and locales like Egypt, India, and Central Asia in European art, music, and literature.
    e. General feeling among many Europeans that their country's colonial holdings were proof of their own superiority over nonwhite peoples.

Now that you have reviewed and tested yourself on this part of the chapter, take time to pull together all the important information by answering the following questions:

◆ How did Hobson's and Lenin's critiques of imperialism differ? How influential were their ideas at the time?

◆ What did Ho Chi Minh, Sun Yatsen, and Mohandas Gandhi have in common?

CHAPTER 25

War and Revolution, 1900–1918

Chapter Outline

1902	1904	1906	1908	1910

1905
Tsar Nicholas II crushes revolt in Russia

1908
Austria-Hungary annexes Bosnia-Herzegovina

This poster is just one example of the many forms of propaganda that all warring powers used during World War I. Here it is suggested that any young man not going off to war would be betraying not just his fatherland but also the women in his life—mother, sisters, wife. The women here appear sad but stoic, accepting the sacrifice of their sons and brothers for the war effort. (Private Collection/Photo © Bonhams, London/The Bridgeman Art Library)

After reading this chapter, you should be able to answer the following questions:

What were the main causes, both long- and short-term, of World War I?

Why was the actual war very different from what most Europeans expected? How did World War I change politics, economy, and everyday life?

What were the main causes of the Russian revolutions of 1917?

Why did the Germans finally lose the war?

Why do some historians argue that World War I ended the European era in world history? Do you agree?

USING THE TECHNOLOGIES developed during the second Industrial Revolution, World War I devoured the financial and human resources of Europe. To manage the Great War, as it was called at the time, governments harnessed civilian populations as never before. State intervention in the economy and society grew considerably during the war and changed everyday life. State propaganda ceaselessly reminded citizens why they needed to continue the fight. Throughout Europe—and the world—women took up jobs vacated by men sent to the trenches.

In August 1914, many Europeans welcomed war. For some, the chance for heroism and glory appeared attractive. Nationalists saw the war as a chance to enhance the prestige and strength of their nation-state or even to achieve a long-desired independence. Some radicals—such as V. I. Lenin—saw the war as an opportunity to overthrow the old order with socialist revolution.

Europe at war's end looked very different from anyone's expectation in 1914. The horrific and senseless massacres of trench warfare convinced many Europeans that nothing could ever justify war again. Millions

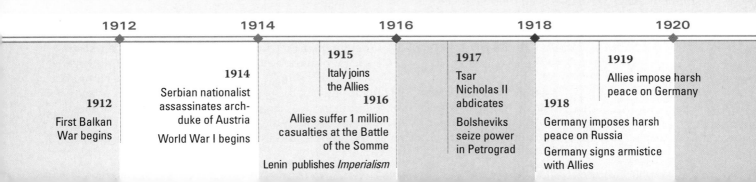

1912	1914	1916	1918	1920
		1915 Italy joins the Allies	**1917** Tsar Nicholas II abdicates	**1919** Allies impose harsh peace on Germany
	1914 Serbian nationalist assassinates archduke of Austria World War I begins	**1916** Allies suffer 1 million casualties at the Battle of the Somme	Bolsheviks seize power in Petrograd	**1918** Germany imposes harsh peace on Russia Germany signs armistice with Allies
1912 First Balkan War begins		Lenin publishes *Imperialism*		

and millions of soldiers and civilians had died, and an influenza epidemic killed millions more. Poverty and political unrest, as well as the Bolshevik Revolution in Russia, threatened to further destabilize the entire continent. Nothing was as it had been. The safe, secure world of aristocratic and middle-class Europeans was gone forever. But if the world was more dangerous, it also had the potential, at least, to be more democratic.

A New Century, 1900–1914

◆ **In the early years of the twentieth century, what made a general European war seem likely?**

◆ **How did nationalism help cause the outbreak of World War I?**

By 1900, three generations had passed since a major war had swept Europe. The balance of power set down at the Congress of Vienna, though rattled by the unification of Germany and Italy, seemed to be effective in keeping the peace. But relations between the Great Powers were strained, in particular by the huge growth of German industry and the aggressive style of the German Kaiser William II. Wars in the Balkan Peninsula threatened to draw Russia into local conflicts.

Advances in technology meant that any new war would be far more deadly—and more expensive—than any previous war. Optimists hoped that the threat of the enormous killing power of modern weaponry would make states find peaceful solutions. Others pointed to the system of alliances as a factor that would prevent war: every major power knew it would be very difficult to localize a conflict, and even a small outbreak threatened a continent-wide conflagration. Ironically, the very alliances that were intended to protect Europe from war ended up playing a major role in the continent's descent into war in 1914.

An Unbalanced Balance of Power

As the twentieth century began, the balance of power established at the Congress of Vienna almost a century earlier remained shakily in place. France, Austria (since 1867 Austria-Hungary), Britain, and Russia continued to play important roles on the European continent. After 1871, however, following Germany's victory in the Franco-Prussian War, the balance was increasingly threatened by the growing might of the Prussian-dominated German Empire.

Kaiser William II (r. 1890–1918) Prussian king and German Kaiser, noted for his impetuous and unsteady character.

The German Threat Germany, with a population of nearly 70 million and an industrial output rivaling Great Britain's and exceeding that of France, sought to expand its economic, political, and cultural power. A latecomer to imperial ambitions, it seized colonies in Africa after the Berlin Conference in 1884. Ruled since 1890 by the insecure and belligerent **Kaiser William II**, Germany directly threatened the European status quo. The newly independent states of Italy, Romania, Serbia, and Bulgaria also complicated the international scene. Major powers scrambled to form new alliances that would retain the balance of power under greatly changed circumstances.

The French felt most threatened by a powerful Germany. Since the end of the Thirty Years' War in 1648, France's foreign policy had aimed to keep the Habsburgs to the east divided and weak. But Otto von Bismarck had successfully isolated Austria and then united German-speaking lands under Prussian leadership. Germany's victory over France in 1871 had gained it Alsace-Lorraine and its king the title of Emperor. Avenging this national humiliation remained a burning issue in French politics. With their low birthrate, moderate industrial growth, and underdeveloped railroad network, the French could not hope to take on the German army alone: they needed an ally.

The Franco-Russian Military Alliance The obvious candidate was Russia, whose large population, enormous territory, and long border with Germany offset its technological and economic backwardness. Although relations between Russia and Germany had traditionally been friendly, Russia was disturbed by Germany's growing industrial and military power. France courted Russia, and in 1894 the two signed a military alliance in which each promised to come to the other's aid if attacked by Germany. Thus the most conservative major power in Europe, Russia, joined forces with its ideological opposite, republican France. Ideology mattered less than the menace of a common foe.

The Triple Alliance This agreement, however, heightened the prospect of Germany's worst strategic nightmare: a two-front war. To counter this threat, Germany sought alliances with Austria-Hungary and Italy, both second-rate military powers. Austria-Hungary was continuously embroiled in domestic crises between the Austrian and Hungarian halves of the empire, and in Austria proper there were clashes

Map 25.1 **Europe in World War I, 1914–1918** The First World War divided Europe into two warring camps. Only the edges of the continent—Ireland, Scandinavia, and the Iberian Peninsula—were not affected.
© Cengage Learning

1. What differences can you see on this map between the war's progress on the eastern and western fronts?
2. Where was Germany most successful?
3. What alliances and strategic interests caused Europe to divide up in this way?
4. Which countries did not choose sides immediately in this conflict? Why not?

over the use of local languages in schools and administration. Austria-Hungary was also concerned about the pro-Russian regimes in Serbia and Bulgaria, new states in the Balkans, and thus welcomed German military support against these Slavic nations.

The junior member in this alliance, Italy, had its own troubles trying to hold together the mainly rural and impoverished south with the wealthier and industrialized north. In 1896, eager to seize an African colony for itself, Italy had been defeated by Ethiopia. The military pact Germany signed with Austria-Hungary

and then, in 1882, with Italy was known as the **Triple Alliance**.

Great Britain's Diplomacy The wild card in international politics was Britain. Traditionally wary of continental entanglements, the British refused to join any military alliance. But the rapid growth of German industrial and military strength deeply disturbed

> **Triple Alliance** Military alliance concluded in 1882 by Germany, Austria-Hungary, and Italy.

British leaders. From the time of the Napoleonic Wars, British policy had aimed to prevent the domination of the European continent by any one power. Now Germany seemed ready to do just that, especially after it began an aggressive program of naval construction in 1907.

Germany's belligerent behavior in international affairs had already alienated British public opinion as well as its Foreign Office, especially Germany's seizure of colonies in Africa. Although Britain held back from a formal alliance, it reached a friendly understanding, known as the **Entente Cordiale**, with France in 1904. It reached a similar agreement with Russia in 1907. Now the **Triple Entente** balanced the Triple Alliance, but instead of ensuring general peace, the new alliance system seemed headed for war.

The Schlieffen Plan To prepare for the two-front war it feared, in the early twentieth century the German General Staff adopted the **Schlieffen Plan**, named for the general who developed it. In case of war, German armies were to strike quickly and decisively against the French before wheeling to the east and taking on the Russians. Thus, Germany could fight each enemy separately rather than dividing its forces between the two fronts. To knock out the French army, the Germans would march through Belgium toward the North Sea, bypassing the French border fortresses, then swing around toward Paris. For the plan to work—for hundreds of thousands of troops to move into position to threaten Paris—speed was of crucial importance. The Germans would also have to count on Belgium's cooperation or at least hope that Britain would not object to this violation of Belgian neutrality, guaranteed by Britain and the other major powers at the time Belgium won independence in 1831. In 1914, this proved to be a fatal miscalculation.

Rivalries

The alliance system seemed to stabilize the strains in international relations caused by national pride and imperial rivalries. For the French, regaining Alsace-Lorraine was a matter of pride. For Russia, there was a worry that the Ottomans were so weak that another power might seize the Bosporus and Dardanelles Straits, thereby cutting off Russian access to the Mediterranean Sea. In Africa, German and British interests came into direct conflict. In the 1890s, Kaiser William II made matters worse by publicly expressing his support for the anti-British Boers of South Africa.

Empires and Nationalism National identity in Britain was connected closely with imperial prestige. In central and eastern Europe, however, nationalism was directed *against* existing empires—both Russia and Austria-Hungary. In Russian lands, Poles and Finns sought concessions or even independence; Poles, especially, aspired to the resurrection of Poland, which had been partitioned into oblivion in the eighteenth century. In Austria-Hungary, Romanians, Serbs, Czechs, and Italians hoped to gain broader political and cultural rights. Young nation-states in the region, such as Romania, Serbia, and Bulgaria, further encouraged such nationalist agendas. Russia considered itself the protector of the ethnically Slavic and religiously Orthodox peoples in the Balkans, including Bulgarians, Montenegrans, and Serbs. Russian public opinion strongly supported such **Pan-Slav** sentiments.

Germany Versus Russia European rivalries were not only political, however. They were also economic. Since 1870, both Germany and Russia had experienced very significant industrial growth, including the building of railroads that often served strategic aims. The rapid growth of German manufacturing presented French and British firms with a frighteningly efficient competitor, while modern industry in Moscow, St. Petersburg, Warsaw, and other cities of the Russian empire had the potential to threaten Germany directly. Thus, Germans felt great relief at the poor showing of the Russian army and navy in the Russo-Japanese War of 1904–1905. When the Revolution of 1905 shook the political order in Russia to its foundations, Germans mistakenly concluded that it would take Russia at least a decade to recover. Then, when the Russian economy shortly boomed again, German leaders became alarmed.

Arms Manufacture Of Europe's many industries, arms manufacturing was among the biggest, employing thousands of workers and producing large profits. National and imperial rivalries generated an arms race that was good business for these manufacturers, which successfully lobbied their governments against any reductions in military budgets. New technologies meant that a country's weaponry had to be replaced quickly. Among the military innovations of the years before 1914 were airplanes, the machine gun, poison gas (though an agreement had been signed promising not to use it), and enormous artillery pieces that could destroy the most massive fortifications.

Nationalism in the Balkans

By the end of the nineteenth century, formerly Ottoman territories on the Balkan Peninsula were now

---

Entente Cordiale Set of agreements signed between France and Great Britain in 1904 pledging cooperation, but not a formal military alliance.

Triple Entente Agreement signed in 1907 by Russia, France, and Great Britain pledging closer relations.

Schlieffen Plan German war plan of the early twentieth century that aimed to avoid a two-front war by a quick and massive attack first on France, then on Russia.

Pan-Slavism Movement from later nineteenth century emphasizing Russia's kinship with other Slavic nations, especially those under Ottoman and Habsburg rule.

Ottoman Empire
Predominantly Serbs and Croats
Predominantly Romanians

Map 25.2 **The Balkans Before World War I** The two Balkan Wars of 1912–1913 both weakened the Ottoman Empire and revealed hostilities among the young Balkan states. Bulgaria's territorial loss to Serbia was one reason Bulgaria sided with Germany and Austria during World War I. © *Cengage Learning*

1. How much of the Ottoman Empire was left in Europe in 1914? Why might this motivate the Ottoman Empire to enter the war against the Allies?

2. The map shows regions outside Serbia and Romania where many Serbs and Romanians lived. Why would this become an important factor during and after World War I?

independent states: Romania, Serbia, Bulgaria, Greece, Montenegro, and Albania. Bosnia-Herzegovina, occupied by Austria-Hungary since 1878, was formally annexed to that country in 1908. The Russians were furious, but their army, much weakened following defeat by Japan, was unable to help their Slavic allies. Both Russians and Balkan Slavs—especially Serbs—were now convinced that Austria-Hungary harbored aggressive intentions. Each of the states in the Balkans had contested borders with its neighbors

and significant numbers of national minorities inside its borders. All were united, however, in hatred for the Ottoman Empire. Religious loyalties added to the tensions, as, except for Albania, which had large numbers of Roman Catholics and Muslims, the people of the Balkans were Eastern Orthodox, whereas the Ottomans were Muslims. During the First Balkan War of 1912, the Balkan League of Serbia, Montenegro, Greece, and Bulgaria attacked the Ottoman territories of Kosovo and Macedonia and nearly swept the Ottoman forces out of Europe. Austria-Hungary, which had significant interests in the Balkans, prepared for war until the threat of Russian intervention caused it to back down.

But the Balkan League could not hold together for long. The large territorial gains by Bulgaria excited the anger and resentment of its neighbors. In 1913, the Second Balkan War broke out when Serbia, Greece, Romania, and Montenegro banded together and attacked Bulgaria. When the Bulgarian armies had already been severely weakened, Ottoman forces crossed the border to take back some of the territory lost in 1912. The end result of the two **Balkan Wars** was a weaker Bulgaria, a stronger Serbia, and anger in Austria-Hungary over growing Serbian power, which was promoted by Russia. The 1913 peace established in the Balkans seemed temporary.

Checking In

By yourself or with a partner, explain the significance of each of the following selected key terms:

Kaiser William II	Schlieffen Plan
Triple Alliance	Pan-Slav
Entente Cordiale	Balkan Wars
Triple Entente	

The Unexpected War, 1914

◆ **How did the reality of war differ from expectations?**

◆ **Why, and how, did Europe's conflict engage the entire world?**

On June 28, 1914, a young Serbian nationalist named Gavrilo Princip shot and killed the heir to the Austro-Hungarian throne, Archduke Francis Ferdinand. The archduke had not been popular, and at first little notice was taken of the assassination. Foreign ministers and other dignitaries continued their vacations, not suspecting a major crisis. Only some weeks later, when Austria-Hungary presented harsh demands to the Serbian government, did

> **Balkan Wars** Two wars, in 1912 and 1913, among countries of the Balkan Peninsula, the first ending with defeat for the Ottoman Empire, the second with defeat for Bulgaria.

Gavrilo Princip Decides to Assassinate Archduke Francis Ferdinand

Gavrilo Princip was born into a Bosnian Serb family in the summer of 1894. His family was of a modest peasant background, supplementing the meager harvest from their small plot of land by working at various odd jobs. For a time, Gavrilo's father, Petar, served as postman for the Grahovo Valley where the family lived. Petar was an unusual man who never swore or touched liquor. As a young man in the 1870s he had participated in the revolt against the Ottoman Empire that culminated in the occupation of Bosnia-Herzegovina by Austria. Gavrilo's mother, Nana, was a strong, uneducated woman who gave birth to nine children, six of whom died as infants. Indeed, when the baby Gavrilo was born on a hot day in July of 1894, Nana held little hope that the small child would survive. At the Serbian Orthodox priest's insistence, the baby was christened Gavrilo, after the Archangel Gabriel.

Gavrilo was a small, quiet boy who loved reading and resembled his mother, with her light blue eyes and curly hair. His love for study sometimes led to conflicts within the family; literacy itself was rather new and by no means universal in this region. Despite his father's opposition, nine-year-old Gavrilo was sent to a nearby village school. After a difficult first year, he did well in his studies. For his hard work, he received a prize of a volume of Serbian heroic poetry which, it was later recalled, he would read to assembled friends and relatives back home. When Gavrilo completed the four-year village school course, his brother Jovo learned that the Military School in Sarajevo was accepting healthy boys for a free course of study. So it was that in August 1907 the village lad Gavrilo found himself in the capital of Bosnia, ready to begin his studies toward a career as a Habsburg officer. His brother Jovo accompanied him, and persuaded Gavrilo that it would be wrong to be trained to serve the enemies of his own people—the Habsburg Empire. So Gavrilo entered not the military school but a merchants' school in Sarajevo, where he spent three years.

It was at this time that Gavrilo began to come under the influence of Serbian (and Yugoslav) nationalism. All Serbs and other south Slavs (Yugo-Slavs), he came to believe, should live together in one state. The young and sensitive teenager, who also dreamed of becoming a famous Serbian poet, became inflamed with the idea of serving his nation. Like other young Bosnian Serbs of his generation, he looked to Belgrade, the Serbian capital, as the Mecca of his national aspirations. Early in 1912 Gavrilo was expelled from school in Sarajevo because of his participation in demonstrations against the Austrian authorities; he decided to continue his studies in Belgrade. Gavrilo spent nearly two years in Belgrade, the exciting years of the Balkan Wars in which Serbia triumphed, gaining territory that more than doubled the state in size. It was also at this point that he met other young Bosnian Serbs and decided to participate in the assassination of a high Austrian official in Sarajevo.

At first the conspirators planned to assassinate the Austrian governor in Bosnia-Herzegovina, General Oskar Potiorek. But when the conspirators discovered that the heir to the throne, Archduke Francis Ferdinand, would be visiting the Bosnian capital on Vidov Dan (St. Vitus's Day), the anniversary of the Serbian defeat at Kosovo in 1389, they chose him instead as their target. All of the conspirators were young, mostly in their teens. All were committed to the ideal of a Yugoslav state.

The assassination attempt on June 28, 1914, did not, however, go as planned. The first assassin, Nedeljko Čabrinović, himself the son of a police agent in the pay of the Austrians, threw a bomb that bounced off the hood of the Archduke's car and exploded, hurting several people but leaving the Archduke unscathed. Gavrilo heard the explosion and thought that the attempt had been successful, but then saw that the Archduke was unhurt. In a fury, Francis Ferdinand rushed to the Sarajevo town hall where he upbraided the horrified local officials. He then gave orders to proceed to a local military hospital to visit one of the officers injured in the blast. As they passed through town, his driver took a false turn, then stopped to turn around—in front of the astonished Gavrilo Princip. Taking aim, Gavrilo fired several times, killing both Francis Ferdinand and his wife.

Gavrilo and his co-conspirators were found guilty of assassinating Francis Ferdinand and his wife, and several were sentenced to death. As for Gavrilo himself, under Austrian law he could not be executed because on the date of his crime he was not yet twenty years old—his twentieth birthday mere weeks away. He was sentenced to solitary confinement in the dank fortress of Theresienstadt in Bohemia, a punishment that amounted to a death sentence spread out over several years. Questioned by a prison doctor in 1916 Gavrilo explained that he did not regret his action, but felt sorry that he had killed Sophie, Francis Ferdinand's wife. Several times he repeated that he could have had no idea that a world war would result from his action. He insisted that he and his co-conspirators had acted as idealists, not as criminals. The harsh conditions in prison were too much for Gavrilo's frail health; he died on April 28, 1918, not quite twenty-four years of age. Celebrated by Serbian historians as a hero, this young man has also been denounced as a terrorist and a fanatic. As so often in history, both sides are correct.

European leaders begin to realize the danger of the situation. By then it was already too late: within days, Europe was at war.

Imperial rivalries and military competition among European states had heightened international tensions to the point that any compromise seemed like fatal weakness. The complex alliance system, designed to prevent war, instead increased the likelihood that a small, regional conflict would become general. Economic interests such as those of major armament manufacturers backed up the alliance system. Individual states hoped that war would bring territorial gains, and stateless nationalities like the Poles saw war as a chance to gain their own nation-state.

The causes of the war were multiple, but no one expected it to turn out as it did. Rather than the quick, patriotic war Europeans expected, the war became a drawn-out, murderous international conflict, the first genuine world war in which battles took place around the globe. Both on the front and at home every element of society was called upon to serve the war effort.

The Slide into War

The assassination of the heir to the Habsburg throne did not immediately appear to threaten European peace. However, in the next weeks the harsh demands of Austria-Hungary—backed up by Germany—on the Serbian government made war inevitable.

Assassination, Ultimatum, and War The assassination of the Austrian archduke Francis Ferdinand set off a fatal chain of events, tied to alliances and war plans. The shooting took place in Sarajevo, capital of Bosnia-Herzegovina, the province annexed by Austria-Hungary just six years earlier. The assassin, Gavrilo Princip, was connected with the Black Hand, a nationalist group with ties to Serbia that dreamed of a unified Slavic state.

On July 23, encouraged by its German ally, Austria presented Serbia with an **ultimatum**, a set of nonnegotiable demands so harsh that they could not be accepted by a sovereign state. For example, the Austrians demanded not only that all forms of anti-Austrian **propaganda** be stamped out but that this campaign be carried out by Austro-Hungarian officials. As expected, the Serbians could not accept all the ultimatum's demands, and on July 28, exactly a month after the assassination, Austria-Hungary declared war on Serbia.

Europe Falls into War Russia felt obliged to support its Serbian ally, though Tsar Nicholas II recognized that military action against Austria-Hungary would compel its ally, Germany, to declare war. Yet to abandon Serbia at this moment would have meant a humiliation for Serbia's Great Power protector, Russia, and so, on July 30, reluctantly, the tsar ordered a general **mobilization**. Now he hoped to avert a war through a personal appeal to Kaiser William, his cousin by marriage. Unfortunately, two days of frantic telegrams between "Nicky" in St. Petersburg and "Willy" in Berlin (the two communicated in English) came to nothing, and on August 1, Germany declared war on Russia. On August 3, convinced that France was about to attack from the west, Germany declared war on France and, following the Schlieffen Plan, marched into neutral Belgium. Technically in defense of Belgium, on August 4, Great Britain (whose king was also a cousin of "Nicky" and "Willy") declared war on Germany. "The lamps are going out all over Europe," observed British foreign minister Sir Edward Grey, "We shall not see them lit again in our lifetime."

Allies Versus Central Powers Europe quickly divided into two warring camps: the **Allied Powers**, led by France, Great Britain, and Russia; and the **Central Powers**, Germany and Austria-Hungary, joined by Bulgaria and the Ottoman Empire. Serbia, Romania, and Belgium sided with the Allies, and Spain, Greece, Switzerland, Holland, and the Scandinavian countries remained neutral. Italy infuriated the Central Powers by refusing to honor its alliance and then, on May 23, 1915, declaring war on Austria-Hungary and thereby joining the Allies, lured by promises of territorial gain in a postwar settlement. Both the Allies and the Central Powers promised territorial gains and other enticements to bring neutral powers onto their side, a fact that would complicate postwar settlements.

War Enthusiasm

Europeans from London to Moscow greeted the outbreak of war in August 1914 with patriotic demonstrations. Huge crowds gathered in the public squares of cities. In St. Petersburg, Russians attacked and gutted the German Embassy, and it became dangerous to be heard speaking German. In Munich, a twenty-five-year-old Austrian named Adolf Hitler cheered with the crowds on Odeonsplatz, then returned home and thanked God that he had lived to see the outbreak of war. In Paris, men rode to war in train cars marked "To Berlin!" In Berlin, Kaiser William II told the Reichstag that he "no longer recognized parties, only Germans."

ultimatum Harsh demand requiring an immediate positive answer to avoid dire consequences.

propaganda Efforts to influence public opinion, often using dishonest or misleading means.

mobilization Calling up of military reserves and putting armies in place for battle that generally precedes a war.

Allied Powers Wartime coalition of France, Great Britain, Russia, Serbia, and others, in the end a total of twenty-four countries including the United States.

Central Powers Opponents of the Allies in World War I, most importantly Germany and Austria-Hungary, later joined by the Ottoman Empire and Bulgaria.

Among the crowd on Ode-onsplatz in Munich cheering the outbreak of war on August 2, 1914, was a delighted Adolf Hitler. Like many men throughout Europe, the young Austrian welcomed war as an exciting adventure and an oppor-tunity to put his nationalist sentiments into action. Why did so many Europeans greet war's outbreak with positive feelings?

Heinrich Hoffmann/Hulton Archive/Getty Images

Forms of War Enthusiasm European men rushed to polling stations to enlist, and women showered them with flowers. Mothers, wives, and sweethearts duti-fully sent their men off to war. Patriotism, a longing for adventure, and a desire for revenge came together in a feverish enthusiasm for war. The young soldiers expected to be home, triumphant, by Christmas. Military planners, too, expected a quick, mobile war with one or two decisive battles, like all the smaller wars that had been fought since Napoleon was finally defeated in 1815.

The war was initially so popular that even paci-fists hesitated to oppose it, and those who did often brought trouble on them-selves. In Russia, the Social-Democrats who refused to vote to fund the war were promptly arrested. The Russian socialist **Alexandra Kollontai** openly called for resistance to the war—from the safety of neutral Scan-dinavia. Others, following the idea of the long-time pacifist Bertha von Suttner, who had recently died, agi-tated for a "peace without victory." In the summer of 1915, an International Con-gress of Women in the neu-tral Netherlands called on all warring countries to lay down their arms. By that point, however, none of the

Alexandra Kollontai (1872–1952) Russian revolutionary and diplomat, commissar for social welfare in 1918 and head of the women's section of the Communist Party.

First Battle of the Marne Crucial battle near the Marne River, just north of Paris, in early September 1914, in which the French stopped the German advance.

Tannenberg Battle in East Prus-sia in August 1914 in which the Germans decisively defeated the Russian army.

warring countries were ready to compromise and make peace.

As the Schlieffen Plan dictated, the German army advanced rapidly and by September 1, 1914, threatened Paris. At this point, the French army and the British Expeditionary Force launched a counter-offensive. This **First Battle of the Marne** forced the exhausted and overextended German troops to re-treat. By mid-September the opposing sides began to dig themselves in along a line stretching from the English Channel to the border of Switzerland. The stalemate of trench warfare on the western front had begun.

War in the East: Battle of Tannenberg On the eastern front, Russia mobilized more rapidly than expected. Pressed by their French allies to attack, on August 15 two Russian armies invaded East Prus-sia, forcing the German high command to transfer troops from France to the eastern front, a transfer that may have been decisive in the Schlieffen Plan's failure. Russian troops still outnumbered the Ger-mans in East Prussia, but they were poorly led and supplied. At **Tannenberg**, the Germans won a decisive victory, with some 100,000 Russian sol-diers taken prisoner. Never again in this conflict would Russian troops threaten German soil. Aus-tria was a different matter. Russian armies invaded the Austrian province of Galicia, remaining there until 1916. Even more embarrassing for Austria, the small Serbian army successfully defended the Serbian capital, Belgrade, until finally defeated by a much larger combined Austrian and German force in October 1914.

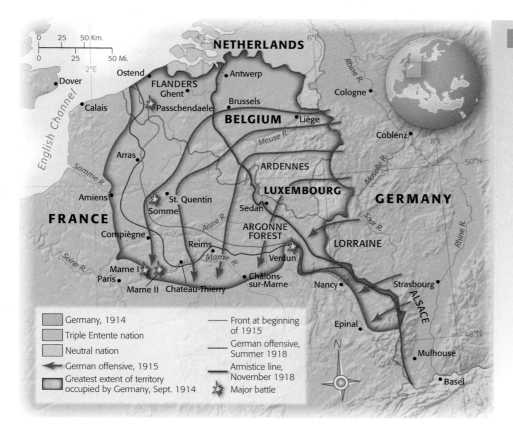

Map 25.3 **Western Front, 1914–1918** The western front remained mainly stable from autumn 1914 to spring 1918 with trenches stretching from the English Channel to Switzerland.
© *Cengage Learning*

1. Why did the German military plan demand a violation of Belgian neutrality?
2. Looking at the map, can you give reasons why the Germans did not succeed in taking Paris in August 1914?
3. What was the logic behind the broad German sweep across Belgium?

Map legend:
- Germany, 1914
- Triple Entente nation
- Neutral nation
- ← German offensive, 1915
- Greatest extent of territory occupied by Germany, Sept. 1914
- Front at beginning of 1915
- German offensive, Summer 1918
- Armistice line, November 1918
- ★ Major battle

It was already clear that expectations for a short, glorious war were an illusion. **Casualties** had mounted to the hundreds of thousands, and ammunition had begun to run short. Governments were forced to take drastic measures to boost arms production. On all sides, military planners and civilian authorities had known huge amounts of resources would be needed at the start, but no one had anticipated the need for long-term military and economic organization. The war they had expected developed in a way they did not expect.

Trench Warfare

No one had anticipated that movement on the western front would stop altogether, but by fall 1914 soldiers on both sides had dug in. Across northern France were hundreds of miles of trenches in which thousands of men lived, fought, and died in a sea of mud, blood, rats, and vermin. The great technological advances in weaponry produced by the armaments industry were countered by primitive defenses built of earth and barbed wire. Generals continued to use old tactics of massive frontal assaults, however. Periodically, an attempt to break through to the enemies' front trench would end in slaughter and failure or, at best, the gain of a few yards of territory.

Life in the Trenches On the Allied side, a typical front trench was about six to eight feet deep, about four feet wide, and separated from the German front trench by a narrow strip of land—**no man's land**—fifty yards to a mile wide, with masses of coiled barbed wire in front of each set of trenches. A few hundred yards behind the front, or firing, trenches were parallel support and reserve trenches. All these trenches were connected by perpendicular communication trenches that enabled men to move between the rear and the front. German trenches were similar but, in general, deeper and more elaborate. British and French soldiers who saw them were impressed by their neatness. Behind the trenches were rail lines that brought in fresh troops and supplies and evacuated the wounded and men on leave. Between the two lines of enemy trenches were the killing fields. During the day, stepping into no man's land would mean instant death, but at night this area was busy with scouting expeditions and soldiers repairing defenses.

Those who experienced trench warfare and survived recalled filth, stench, and constant noise. Imagine thousands of men living in close quarters in a muddy hole in the ground with few opportunities for personal hygiene. Add a climate in which rainfall and

casualties Deaths and injuries in battle.

no man's land Territory between the two opposing enemy lines of trenches that had to be crossed in an attack.

In this photograph taken by French photographer Jacques Moreau in 1916, soldiers in a forward trench in the Champaign region of northern France have a quick bite to eat. Note the different levels in the trench, enabling men to walk safely in the middle but allowing the use of periscopes to peer out over the top of the trench facing no man's land. What about the soldiers and their surroundings strikes or surprises you? How typical do you suppose this scene was? Would it have been much different a year earlier or later?

Archives Larousse, Paris/Giraudon/The Bridgeman Art Library

dark gloomy weather are the norm. Then there was the odor of decomposing corpses fed upon by large rats. The racket of constant artillery and small-arms fire, together with flares illuminating the night sky, made sleep difficult.

The nervous strain of trench warfare produced a psychological disorder newly described as **shell shock**, which left thousands of men incapable of fighting any longer or carrying out everyday activities at home. Constant shelling pulverized farmhouses, barns and yards, roads and forests. Chemicals from thousands of explosive shells poisoned the earth itself, leaving it useless for agriculture. Once-familiar landscapes became eerie, lifeless moonscapes later depicted by painters like **Paul Nash**. Tense monotony alternated with solitary deaths (if, for example, one forgot to crouch down in the more shallow parts of the trench) and, periodically, the mass slaughter of an offensive.

"Going over the Top" Attempts to break through the line followed a common pattern. First, artillery shelling, often lasting days, aimed to destroy forward machine-gun placements and barbed-wire defenses and force the enemy back from the front trenches. Relentless shelling also aimed to wear down and "soften" the enemy psychologically.

Then, always at dawn, came the order to advance. The nervous men were awakened and given a stiff drink to buck up their nerves. The artillery would cease its shelling, a clear signal of impending attack. At the sound of a whistle, hundreds of men would "go over the top" of the front trench and run headlong into no man's land—and into machine-gun fire.

Only a few made it as far as the barbed-wire barriers in front of the enemy trenches. Fewer still actually made it into the empty enemy trench, where they could do little more than sit tight, hoping for the arrival of reinforcements before enemy soldiers were able to rush back to their front trenches. Usually death arrived before reinforcements, and the stalemate was reestablished. Desperate to break this stalemate, in the spring of 1915 the Germans lobbed canisters of poison gas into enemy trenches, inflicting blindness and miserable deaths on unprepared French and British soldiers. Gas attacks and gas masks soon became standard on both sides.

The Battles of Verdun and the Somme Two battles in 1916, each lasting months, epitomize the desperation and gruesome absurdity of warfare on the western front. In February, the Germans launched a massive assault, aiming to capture the French fortress at **Verdun**. Calculating that the French would go to extreme lengths to defend this town, which had been fortified after defeat in the Franco-Prussian War, the German command aimed simply to kill as many

shell shock Psychological disorder, sometimes lasting decades, caused by the extreme stress faced by men under the constant barrage of explosions during war.

Paul Nash (1889–1946) English painter whose disorienting, surreal paintings depicted the bizarre world of the trenches.

Verdun French fortress attacked by Germans in 1916, resulting in almost 700,000 casualties.

Paul Nash's ironically entitled painting *We Are Making a New World* (1918) shows a landscape devastated by shelling with the sun rising ominously over the horizon. Nash was a volunteer in the British Army who was later promoted to officer and experienced trench warfare firsthand. How does Nash's use of color and shading enhance this image's strange, alien quality?

Imperial War Museum, London/The Bridgeman Art Library

French soldiers as possible. The propaganda value of the fortress far overshadowed its military importance. "They shall not pass!" declared the French general **Henri Pétain**. But the French lost more than 350,000 men, and before the battle was over, ten months later, the Germans had lost 330,000. Today Verdun is a mausoleum and a cemetery, its defenses still harboring live mines and closed to visitors.

On July 1, to take the pressure off the French at Verdun, the British launched a massive attack at the **Somme** River, along a twenty-mile front, and were later joined in the battle by the French. Despite the use of a new weapon, the tank, the Allies were unable to dislodge the Germans. When the fighting finally ended in mid-November, the Allies had suffered one million casualties—and had advanced six miles.

War on the Seas and in the Air

The war was also fought by sailors and, for the first time in history, men in airplanes. The main importance of naval action was the bottling up of German ports by the British navy. Airplanes were used in reconnaissance and to bomb enemy targets.

Gallipoli With the British army bogged down in the trenches, the British Admiralty, headed by young **Winston Churchill**, urged an assault on the Central Powers' southern ally, the Ottoman Empire. Churchill calculated that an attack on the **Gallipoli** peninsula would break through Turkish defenses and open the way to Istanbul, knocking Turkey out of the war.

In this largest **amphibious** operation of the war, troops from Australia and New Zealand under British command seized the beaches of Gallipoli in late April 1915. Contrary to expectations, however, Turkish troops on bluffs overlooking the beach rained down bullets and shells on the Allied positions. In the end, Churchill could not muster sufficient troops and **materiel** to break the Turkish defenses, and the British gave up the attempt. Churchill and Britain were humiliated by the defeat, and Turkey remained in the war. Together the belligerents suffered more than 500,000 casualties.

The Battle of Jutland Despite this setback, the British navy continued to dominate the seas, blockading Germany's North Sea harbors. Given British naval superiority, the German navy preferred caution

Henri Pétain (1856–1951) French general in World War I who later, during World War II, served as president of Vichy France, the Nazi puppet state.

Somme Battle in 1916 near the Somme River in which the British and French failed to break through German lines, resulting in one million Allied casualties.

Winston Churchill (1874–1965) English politician of aristocratic background who backed the disastrous Gallipoli campaign, nearly destroying his political career; as prime minister during World War II, he inspired British victory.

Gallipoli Peninsula in western Turkey where an Allied attack using Australian and New Zealander troops from April to December 1915 ended in failure.

amphibious Military action using both land and sea troops.

materiel Military hardware such as guns, tanks, and ammunition.

to bold moves until mid-1916, when the two fleets clashed at the Battle of **Jutland**, off the west coast of Denmark. Although the German fleet was smaller, it inflicted heavy losses on the British. In the end, the battle was indecisive. The British blockade continued, but the German navy still dominated the Baltic, standing between the British navy and its Russian allies.

The U-Boat Vastly more important than this conventional naval battle was what the Germans called the war on commerce, carried out almost entirely by a new type of warship, the submarine, or **U-boat**. The British could be starved into submission, thought the Germans, if their submarines could prevent the delivery of food and raw materials, and Britain's naval blockade of Germany justified this measure.

In early 1915, the Germans announced **unrestricted submarine warfare**, warning that any ship entering British waters, including those of neutral countries, could be attacked and sunk. Because of the vulnerability of submarines when on the surface, there would be no warning before an attack. This policy, which violated traditional rules of war for engagements on the high seas, antagonized the United States, which had declared neutrality but traded actively with Britain.

Although millions of tons of Britain-bound shipping fell prey to submarines, it was the sinking of the British passenger liner *Lusitania* on May 7, 1915, with the loss of over a hundred American lives, that intensified anti-German feeling in the United States, despite the Germans' contention that the ship had been carrying an illegal cargo of arms. Rapidly the British developed antisubmarine measures, including mines, aerial surveillance, depth charges, and, most effective of all, the use of armed escorts of naval shipping—the **convoy system**—which was introduced in May 1917.

Airplanes in War While not as effective as U-boats, "flying machines" also played a part in World War I. Airplanes scouted out enemy positions, attacked enemy troops, and dropped bombs and propaganda leaflets. Their pilots were known as aces; perhaps the most famous was Manfred von Richthofen, the "Red Baron." Aces engaged in aerial "dogfights," but in the final year of the war airplanes were also used in mass formation to support ground troops—an actual military advance. Both sides also developed anti-aircraft guns. The planes themselves changed rapidly in these four years, as tens of thousands were built and destroyed. By 1918 the first all-metal fighters were appearing. German airships, called zeppelins after their inventor, were used to bomb London and military targets in England. Bulky, slow, and inflated with flammable gas, they were extremely vulnerable to attack by aircraft. This bombing of civilian areas blurred the traditional line between the fighting front and the "home front." World War I was the first **total war**.

A World at War

Many eighteenth- and nineteenth-century European conflicts had taken place far from Europe, but this war in Europe's heartland affected the entire world. At the same time, technological advances, such as the submarine, brought warfare to the high seas. More than anything else, Europe's unprecedented economic and colonial domination of the world brought nearly every continent into the conflict and made it difficult for independent states to remain neutral. Eventually twenty-four states were drawn in on the Allied side—from the African Republic of Liberia to China, Japan, and Siam (Thailand) in Asia; Brazil, Cuba, Guatemala, and Honduras in South and Central America; and, eventually, the United States. Of the total world population of 1.6 billion, some 1.4 billion lived in states officially engaged in the conflict.

Africans and Asians in War Thousands of Asians and Africans from Europe's colonies fought on the western front, where their bravery was noted, challenging Europeans' sense of racial superiority. Young men from Australia and New Zealand fought at Gallipoli; Canadians and South Africans also helped the British war effort. Battles also took place in the colonies. In Africa, the Allies attacked the German colonies of East Africa, Togoland, and Southwest Africa. Fighting was particularly bitter in East Africa, involving British Kenya in the north down to present-day Zambia. Both European and African troops fought in these regions, and many African homes, crops, and herds were destroyed.

Nationalism During the War National and ethnic groups took advantage of warfare to press their own ambitions. In Russian Central Asia, Kazakhs revolted in 1916 against forced labor and war taxation, venting their anger on recently arrived Russian colonists.

Jutland Naval battle in 1916 between Britain and Germany off the coast of Denmark that ended in a draw.

U-boat (from German *Unterseeboot*, "undersea boat") Submarine.

unrestricted submarine warfare German policy of attacking without warning any ship entering British waters during World War I.

Lusitania British passenger ship torpedoed by a German submarine off the coast of Ireland in May 1915, drowning more than 1,000 passengers, including 120 Americans.

convoy system Grouping merchant ships together with an escort of armed naval vessels, successfully used to protect shipping from U-boats.

total war War in which all elements of the population, economy, and politics are obliged to serve the military effort.

The revolt was put down with massive bloodshed. Half a world away in Dublin, on Easter Day 1916, Irish nationalists led a revolt against British rule, demanding an independent Ireland. The **Easter Uprising** was quickly repressed, but the anxiety of the British government over the Irish question increased. Both Allied and Central Powers attempted to incite the minority national groups under enemy rule. The Russian tsar and German Kaiser, for example, each sought to gain Polish loyalty by promising the Poles increased national rights after the war. In the Ottoman Empire, the British encouraged nationalist Arabs to revolt against their Turkish overlords as the young English officer **T. E. Lawrence**—"Lawrence of Arabia"—dressed in Arab garb to lead Arab troops against Turkish positions. Today the military cemetery at Mount Scopus, Jerusalem, bears witness to the thousands of British and Arab troops that died in that conflict.

Even before the fighting had ended, the future of the region had been decided. In 1916 the British and French negotiated the **Sykes-Picot Agreement**, dividing up former Ottoman territories in the Middle East between themselves. When it became clear that the British government did not intend to grant the Arabs real independence, Lawrence resigned in disgust. An even more complicated appeal to a national minority in the region was the **Balfour Declaration** of November 1917, in which the British government indicated its willingness to set up a Jewish "national home" in Palestine. Support for Zionism, the British thought, would strengthen Jewish sympathy throughout the world for the Allied cause.

The Armenian Massacre In another part of the Ottoman Empire, the border region between Russia and Turkey, an unprecedented attack on a civilian population occurred: the **Armenian Massacre**. Relations between Christian Armenians and Muslim Turks (and Kurds), never cordial, had become severely strained by accusations that the Armenians had been spying for the Russians. During the winter of 1915–1916, Ottoman authorities gave orders to deport Armenians from their native villages near the front with Russia. In the course of these deportations, Turkish military units killed many unarmed Armenians or allowed them to perish in the harsh winter. Up to 1.5 million Armenians died in these operations, which nearly wiped out the Armenian community in Turkey. As an instance of genocide, the Armenian Massacre stands as a precursor to even more horrific ethnically based attacks on civilian populations later in the twentieth century.

The participation by colonized people in the European war effort radicalized movements opposing European rule and weakened the legitimacy of imperialism. If Indians, for example, could shed blood for the Allied cause, Indian nationalists argued, why could they not also rule themselves? In Africa, too, the economic effects of the war fueled nationalist and anticolonial sentiments after 1918.

 Checking In

By yourself or with a partner, explain the significance of each of the following selected key terms:

Allied Powers
Central Powers
First Battle of the Marne
Battle of Tannenberg
Winston Churchill

unrestricted submarine warfare
Balfour Declaration
Armenian Massacre

Total War, 1914–1918

◆ **How did war influence everyday life and family relationships?**

◆ **In what ways did governments aim to control their citizens?**

The Great War broke down the distinction between the military and noncombatants. Entire societies were harnessed for the war effort. Governments intruded into the economy and everyday life of their citizens as never before, making this the first total war. The right to free speech was limited. Shortages affected households and diets. Women took up new jobs as millions of men left for the front, unions and employers agreed to avoid conflicts to increase war production, and political parties vowed to work together. Like the mass mobilization during the French Revolution, but far more encompassing, the state demanded that citizens devote full energies to crushing the enemy.

State Control and Intervention

Within months of the outbreak of war, all governments realized that supplies of foodstuffs and raw materials were threatened. State intervention in the form of rationing, restrictions, and planning aimed to safeguard these precious supplies.

State Intervention in the Economy The German government rapidly set up a

Easter Uprising Nationalist rebellion in Dublin in 1916 that demanded Irish independence and was bloodily suppressed by British authorities.

T. E. Lawrence (1888–1935) English soldier and scholar known as "Lawrence of Arabia" who led the Arabs against Turkish domination during World War I.

Sykes-Picot Agreement Treaty of 1916 dividing up Ottoman territory in the Middle East between Great Britain and France.

Balfour Declaration Official statement by the British government in November 1917 in favor of a Jewish "national home" in Palestine, a major victory for Zionism.

Armenian Massacre Killing of as many as 1.5 million Christian Armenians by the Muslim Turkish military and Muslim Kurds in 1915–1916.

Raw Materials Department in the War Ministry to secure raw materials vital to war industries. In Russia, Tsar Nicholas II proclaimed that, for the duration of the war, no vodka would be distilled. This measure, designed to reserve millions of tons of grain to feed Russian soldiers, had the unintended side effect of eliminating the government's largest source of income, the tax on vodka.

In Britain, the government negotiated a settlement between unions and big business to assure that war production would not be interrupted by strikes. As the war dragged on, government intervention in the economy became more radical. In 1915, Britain **nationalized** the railroads. In May 1916, the British government moved the clock forward one hour to take advantage of summer daylight—the first daylight savings time.

Food Rationing To prevent hunger, governments stepped in to manage the production and sale of foodstuffs. With overseas food supplies cut off by the British naval blockade, Germany began to ration bread in early 1915. By mid-1916, labor shortages in agriculture and the effect of German submarine attacks forced the French and British governments, also, to introduce food rationing. In France, the beloved baguette was outlawed as wasteful, as were ice cream and most forms of candy. By late 1916, Germans had ration cards not only for bread but for meat, potatoes, milk, sugar, butter, soap, and eggs. Even so, supply could not keep up with demand. Governments introduced various food substitutes, such as vegetable beefsteaks, artificial eggs, and "war bread," which contained a limited amount of white flour.

Military Conscription and Raised Taxes Government intervention was most direct in military conscription. Compulsory military service, long in force in most countries, was expanded. Britain's 1916 Military Service Act drafted men between eighteen and forty. All across Europe, almost all young men were either serving in the army or working in war industries. Those not serving in the armed forces found themselves scorned or even physically attacked as cowards.

To pay for the costs of the war, governments raised taxes and took out loans. For the Allies, most loans came from the United States. Even these measures could not cover war costs, however, and everywhere governments printed money, thereby starting an inflationary cycle that would continue into the 1920s.

nationalization The taking over of private enterprise by a government, sometimes with compensation, sometimes not, often in emergencies.

War Propaganda

Throughout Europe, governments attempted to control what citizens could know

Hoover Institution Archives

Propaganda merged with commercial purposes during World War I. This advertisement for a Hungarian brewery suggests that its beer was so delicious that the enemy soldiers would come running—and surrender—just to get a glass. Do you think this is an advertisement from early or late in the war? Why? Looking at the uniforms, which soldiers belonged to which army?

about the war's progress. The German people did not know that German troops had destroyed the priceless library at Louvain, in Belgium, and the people of England and France did not know that the Allies had bombed civilians in Karlsruhe, Germany. Propaganda campaigns sought to keep up morale and convince citizens that right was on their side. The enemy was always characterized as vicious, cunning, and hardly human. The Allies portrayed German troops as "the Hun," murderous creatures bent on looting and destruction. German atrocities in Belgium were said to include bayoneted children and raped nuns. German propaganda countered with stories of German prisoners being tortured by Allied captors, all the while depicting German soldiers as defenders of culture pitted against effeminate French decadence and Russian barbarism.

Culture in the Service of War Politicians' speeches, press editorials, posters, and even songs warned citizens to be ever vigilant, to avoid defeatism, and to work for the war effort. In Germany, the poetic "hit" of the war was Ernst Lissauer's "Song of Hatred Against England," for which the author was awarded the **Iron Cross**, a military decoration. Postcards bore such gruesome rhymed inscriptions as "Jeder Schuss ein Russ" ("Every shot, a Russian") and "Jeder Stoss ein Franzos" ("Every bayonet thrust, a Frenchman"). Similarly, patriotically minded Russians could send New Year's greetings on cards depicting a Cossack lopping off a German soldier's head and bearing the message, "Happy New Year! A successful blow!" French posters called on citizens to save wine for the troops and to support the war by buying war bonds.

Films also bolstered spirits, and because one-third or more of the people of Europe—at least those in cities—attended the movies at least once a week, their effect was significant. In Germany, melodramatic war films, such as *How Max Won the Iron Cross,* inspired patriotism. Among the Allies, **Charlie Chaplin**'s comedies enjoyed immense popularity, including his rare, unheroic portrayal of a frontline soldier in *Shoulder Arms,* produced in 1918. Moviegoers were also treated to newsreels, which showed a very sanitized and upbeat version of the week's military developments.

Sanitizing the Reality of War Propaganda everywhere dealt in half-truths and some outright lies. In London one could visit a model trench that, as returning soldiers complained, hardly resembled the real thing. In fact, soldiers found the patriotic falsehoods spread at home to be sickening. Even civilians on the home front grew weary of the emphasis on the positive and upbeat as news of casualties mounted and food in the cities grew scarce. In the end, it is doubtful that the large expenditures on propaganda had any significant effect on the final outcome of the war.

Besides controlling the flow of information, governments restricted civil rights. Fearing civil unrest immediately after the declaration of war, in August 1914 the British Parliament passed the Defence of the Realm Act, known as **DORA**. This act essentially placed Britain under martial law for the duration of the war, allowing police to question and arrest individuals without a warrant and severely restricting freedom of speech. Individuals like the philosopher **Bertrand Russell** who dared to question the war or to advocate pacifism were harassed and even imprisoned. In Germany, when the radical socialists **Karl Liebknecht** and Rosa Luxemburg denounced the war at a **May Day** rally in 1916, calling for it to be transformed into a class war, they were arrested, tried for treason, and imprisoned. Even in the United States, the declaration of war in 1917 was quickly followed by the **Espionage and Sedition Acts**, which outlawed agitation against the war effort or criticism of the government.

Domestic and Family Life

In this war, every segment of society fought in one way or another. All were admonished to "do your part."

Wealthy and middle-class women volunteered as nurses. Retired people put their savings into war bonds to help finance the purchase of weaponry. Schoolteachers instilled patriotic and military virtues in their pupils and encouraged their students to prepare "care packages" to be sent to the men on the front. From the top to the bottom of society, people tried to economize and waste less, with more modest meals for the British royal family setting an example.

Women in War The deterioration in quality and quantity of basic consumer goods and foodstuffs meant that most German women were fully occupied simply finding food for their families and mending clothing that could not be replaced. German women also supplemented their income by taking in work, such as the home production of gas masks, uniform items, and sandbags. Numerous posters called on women to subscribe to war bonds as one way of doing their part to help their men in the trenches.

Women also began to take jobs previously reserved for men. In Britain, female "postmen" and bus conductors startled onlookers at first. In Russia, a famous propaganda poster showed a women working at a lathe. German women also worked in armament factories, and everywhere women worked as nurses. With doctors overwhelmingly occupied at the front, nurses took their place at home in treating civilian ailments.

Although no army put women into combat, the British organized auxiliary units, such as the WAACs (Women's Army Auxiliary Corps) and Wrens (British Women's Royal Naval Service), in which women carried out office duties and also served as nurses. In Germany, the military command established the "Women's Home Army" to keep up morale and detect spies. Strikingly, Russia formed and trained a "Women's Battalion of Death," a volunteer unit that also functioned to shame male soldiers whose morale was low.

Mobilizing the Family Even the most intimate spheres of life were militarized. A French poster showed a newborn baby lamenting

Iron Cross High military honor awarded for bravery to Prussian and German soldiers from 1813 to 1945.

Charlie Chaplin (1889–1977) British film actor and producer who created the Little Tramp character and whose silent comedies were extremely popular.

DORA Defence of the Realm Act, a law that curtailed civil liberties in Britain during World War I.

Bertrand Russell (1872–1970) British mathematician, philosopher, and pacifist.

Karl Liebknecht (1871–1919) German left-wing socialist who spent most of the war in jail for his socialist and antiwar agitation.

May Day International labor holiday, celebrated since the late nineteenth century throughout the world except in the United States.

Espionage and Sedition Acts Laws in United States passed in 1917 restricting free speech to prevent antiwar statements ("sedition") and spying ("espionage").

"Alas! I arrived too late." Another showed a soldier surrounded by beaming women proclaiming, "Let's do our part for repopulation." In this way, even the newborn and the unborn were mobilized for the war effort.

Old family patterns were disrupted by the absence of fathers who were at the front. Women assumed new responsibilities that helped break down old stereotypes and encouraged demands for economic and political equality. In Britain, greater numbers of women in wage work outside the home strengthened the arguments of women's suffrage activists. By war's end, they had achieved the vote for women. Children, too, became more independent and self-reliant. Men returning from the front were sometimes shocked by the new attitudes of their wives, sisters, and children. Entire societies felt the impact of the new social and economic roles for women that developed during wartime.

✓ Checking In

By yourself or with a partner, explain the significance of each of the following selected key terms:

Iron Cross

Charlie Chaplin

DORA

Bertrand Russell

Karl Liebknecht

Espionage and Sedition Acts

Russia in Revolution, 1917

◆ **What caused the Russian monarchy to collapse?**

◆ **What caused the Provisional Government to collapse in November 1917?**

Stalemate, scarcities, mounting casualties, and millions of deaths: war stalked all of Europe, but the Russians were most miserable of all. Russia was the largest, poorest, least industrialized, and most politically repressive of the large European states. Russia also had the largest army in Europe, a heavy burden on its limited resources. By late 1916, overwhelmed by rising prices and widespread shortages of food and fuel, and facing another cold, dark winter, Russians were desperate. Strikes broke out as workers protested the excessive profits earned by arms manufacturers while their own low wages failed to keep up with inflation.

Anger with the tsarist regime mounted with military disasters and the seeming indifference of the tsar and his German-born wife. In March 1917, popular discontent exploded to sweep the tsar from power. Suddenly Russia found itself without a real government. As rival groups competed, a small band of radical socialists took advantage of the political instability to seize control and impose a new economic, social, and political order. Denouncing the "imperialist war," the new leaders of Russia urged soldiers on all sides to join in a class struggle that would topple corrupt empires and destroy capitalism itself. Exhilarating for some and horrifying for others, the Russian Revolution posed a direct challenge to existing economic, social, and political powers around the world.

The March Revolution

Repeated military setbacks made the tsar's many subjects heartily sick of war and bitter about the failures of his leadership. They believed that his German wife, Alexandra, sympathized with the enemy. Suspicions of treason at the highest level of government were reinforced by the presence in the imperial palace of a notorious peasant healer, **Grigory Rasputin**. The tsar and his wife appreciated Rasputin's ability to ease the bleeding of young Alexis, the heir to the Romanov throne, who suffered from hemophilia. Most Russians, however, falsely believed Rasputin to be a German spy and Alexandra's secret lover. Foolishly, Nicholas refused to send Rasputin away.

Failure of Leadership in St. Petersburg Nicholas's refusal to acknowledge ugly facts made him unable to deal effectively with Russia's deteriorating military situation and rising social unrest. A man who hated conflict, the tsar politely banished strong personalities from his presence and simply ignored criticism or advice from public figures or the press. In September 1915, he made a fatal decision when, in direct opposition to his advisers and despite his complete lack of military expertise, he left Petrograd—the new, more Russian-sounding name given to St. Petersburg in 1914—to join the general-staff headquarters near the front lines. As his advisers had feared, the tsar's presence at headquarters both distracted the officers there and meant that the Russian public connected every military defeat with the tsar's person. Back in Petrograd, Alexandra and Rasputin, together in the imperial palace, fueled more rumors that the "German woman" and her degenerate peasant lover were the real rulers of Russia. The truth was simpler: Russia lacked any effective leadership.

The March Revolution Every morning in the Russian capital, women lined up before dawn in front of shops that might have some bread and milk to sell. On March 8, 1917, however, many shops had received no food at all, and women were turned away empty handed. As they trudged home, worrying how they would feed their families, they came upon radical women demonstrating in support of **International Women's Day**. The two groups came together, and soon the entire capital city was in an uproar, with ten thousand women demanding equal rights for women,

Grigory Rasputin (1869–1916) Siberian peasant healer whose ability to ease the suffering of Tsar Nicholas's son Alexis gained him entry to the Russian imperial family.

International Women's Day International holiday celebrating the achievements of women, whose demonstrations for "bread and peace" in Petrograd on March 8, 1917, grew into workers' riots that deposed Tsar Alexander II.

Stock Montage

This wartime cartoon mocked Tsar Nicholas II and his wife Alexandra as mere pawns in the hands of the sinister bearded Rasputin. In fact the Siberian peasant healer's influence on policy was negligible, despite what many Russians thought. How does the artist's technique underscore Rasputin's evil power? How are Nicholas and Alexandra portrayed?

a Russian republic, and an end to the war—demands summed up in the slogan "Bread and Peace." As workers went out on strike and even middle-class professionals took to the streets, the local chief of police telegraphed news of the riots to Nicholas. The president of the Duma sent a similar telegram, begging Nicholas to take notice of the people's demands. Instead, the tsar chose repression, commanding the local authorities to crack down on demonstrators.

Nicholas failed to appreciate how much the power of local authorities had eroded. Very quickly, control of the city passed over to the rebels. It soon became dangerous for those associated with the tsarist regime to show themselves in public. Policemen were beaten to death. When Nicholas finally decided to return, railway workers sabotaged the route, stranding the emperor outside the capital. Conservative Duma members persuaded the tsar to abdicate to preserve Russia. His patriotism touched, Nicholas signed away his power and thus ended more than three centuries of Romanov rule in Russia.

The Provisional Government

News of the tsar's abdication was greeted in the streets with shouts of "Long live the Russian republic!" Support for the monarchy seemed to evaporate overnight. Former Duma members of the center and moderate left formed a new government that was rapidly recognized by the Allied Powers. This **Provisional Government** was to rule Russia for most of 1917. Its leaders proclaimed a free, liberal, and democratic Russia. They issued a blanket **amnesty** for political prisoners, ended all restrictions on non-Russians (thereby giving Russia's Jews and Muslims equal rights), and promised to convene a constituent assembly to draw up a constitution for the new republic. The Provisional Government also pledged to continue the war effort against Germany, hoping that the Allies would offer significant material support to the new, democratic Russia. Outside of Petrograd, however, the end of tsarist rule brought little change; even local administrators were seldom replaced.

Dual Power The Provisional Government, representing mainly middle-class Duma members, espoused such liberal ideals as the rule of law, civil liberties, and private property. Almost immediately, it was challenged by the more radical, socialist **Petrograd Soviet**, a council that represented factory workers and soldiers. Issuing Order No. 1 in early March, the Soviet called on each military unit to form committees of elected representatives, demanded that officers show proper respect to the common soldiers, and proclaimed that no military orders were to be honored unless approved by the Petrograd Soviet. The Provisional Government felt unable to oppose this order directly. As unpopular officers were killed or, more frequently, simply warned to disappear, the conservative officer corps found it exceedingly difficult to maintain discipline.

As Order No. 1 vividly demonstrates, after March 1917 there were two centers of power in Russia. The Provisional Government was the internationally recognized government, but it lacked power and legitimacy at home. It saw itself as a caretaker, in place only until a permanent constitution could be drafted and put into effect. The Petrograd Soviet, on the other hand, had little time for such liberal and parliamentary niceties. Inspired by the Petrograd Soviet, workers' councils sprang up in other cities and in the countryside to push for a radical solution to Russia's wartime problems.

Bolsheviks Return Home Soon after the blanket amnesty, political prisoners in Siberia and political exiles around the world began to make their way home.

Provisional Government Temporary Russian government in March–November 1917 that was led by former Duma members and deposed by the Bolshevik Revolution.

amnesty General pardon by government.

Petrograd Soviet (in Russian, "council") Radical council that represented socialist workers and soldiers and shared power with the more moderate Provisional Government.

Lenin Proposes His "April Theses"

When V. I. Lenin returned to Petrograd in April 1917, the enthusiasm for the democratic revolution of March had not yet worn off. Even socialist parties—including Lenin's own Bolsheviks—had agreed to support the Provisional Government until the war was won. Within days of his return, Lenin shocked his Bolshevik colleagues with his "April Theses," which demanded a far more radical and confrontational course of action. In any other country at war—including the United States—Lenin would have been arrested for his demands to end the war and for revolution. The fact that he was able to publish these radical comments openly shows that, indeed, as he himself commented, Russia after the March revolution was "the freest country in the world."

❶ Why did Lenin term the war "predatory?" What did capitalism have to do with that?

❷ Why would overthrowing capitalism bring about a "truly democratic peace?"

❸ Was the Provisional Government conservative or antisocialist? What does Lenin mean by "annexations" here?

❹ What social groups might support Lenin in his call for nationalizing large estates?

❺ Would peasants welcome the placing of land under the control of local Soviets?

❻ Why did Lenin specifically mention that banks should be nationalized (he does not mention any other kind of business or industry)?

"[Thesis 1: Against the war]
   ❶ The war … unquestionably remains on Russia's part a predatory imperialist war owing to the capitalist nature of that government….
   The class-conscious proletariat can give its consent to a revolutionary war….
   ❷ It is necessary … to explain the inseparable connection existing between capital and the imperialist war, and to prove that without overthrowing capital *it is impossible* to end the war by a truly democratic peace….

[Thesis 3: Against the Provisional Government]
   ❸ No support for the Provisional Government; the utter falsity of all its promises should be made clear, particularly of those relating to the renunciation of annexations….

[Thesis 5: For revolution]
   Not a parliamentary republic—to return to a parliamentary republic from the Soviets of Workers' Deputies would be a retrograde step—but a republic of Soviets of Workers', Agricultural Labourers' and Peasants' Deputies throughout the country, from top to bottom….
   Abolition of the police, the army, and the bureaucracy….

[Thesis 6: Agrarian program]
   ❹ Confiscation of all landed estates.
   ❺ Nationalisation of all lands in the country, the land to be disposed of by the local Soviets of Agricultural Labourers' and Peasants' Deputies….

[Thesis 7: For the nationalization of banks]
   ❻ The immediate amalgamation of all banks in the country into a single national bank, and the institution of control over it by the Soviet of Workers' Deputies.

Source: From Lenin's April Theses (1917).

The support of war-weary soldiers like these marching in Petrograd under the banner of communism was crucial for the success of the Bolshevik takeover in November 1917. By continuing to push the war effort, the Provisional Government lost support among many workers, soldiers, and peasants. Why would soldiers march through the streets carrying a banner calling for "Communism?"

RIA/Novosti

In April, Vladimir Ilyich Lenin, the leader of the radical **Bolsheviks**, arrived in Petrograd after a complicated journey, supported by the German authorities, from his exile in Switzerland. Quickly he published a fiery article demanding an end to the war in the Bolshevik newspaper *Pravda*. His clear and radical program appealed to many, and support for the Bolsheviks grew.

The Bolsheviks had two things other political parties in Russia lacked: the dynamic leadership of Lenin and an easily understood program summed up in the slogan "Peace, Land, and Bread." But the Bolsheviks were a small and extreme group, and no one thought they would eventually triumph.

Alexander Kerensky Meanwhile, the Provisional Government was also moving to the left politically. In July, **Alexander Kerensky**, a socialist lawyer and the only man to hold posts in both the Provisional Government and Petrograd Soviet, became prime minister. Kerensky enjoyed great popularity at first. His talents as an orator were considerable, though when he preached to the troops at the front that they had a sacred duty to give their lives for Mother Russia some scorned him as the "persuader-in-chief." Unfortunately for Kerensky, his speeches proved unable to prevent the collapse of the Russian army. A major Russian offensive launched in the summer of 1917 turned into a rout.

As a moderate socialist, Kerensky faced serious enemies on both the right and the left. The military

despised him as an illegitimate upstart, and the Bolsheviks saw him as ineffectual. In a sense, both were correct. But Kerensky was in an impossible situation. Having neutralized the Bolshevik threat after a coup attempt in July, in early September Kerensky had to fend off a military coup led by the popular Cossack general Lavr Kornilov. To defeat Kornilov, Kerensky released many Bolsheviks from jail, including **Leon Trotsky**, another dynamic leader. The Bolsheviks regrouped, and within weeks Kerensky faced them again, now more dangerous, well organized, and armed.

The November Revolution

Hiding outside of Petrograd, Lenin pelted his comrades in the capital with enraged letters and instructions. In mid-October he entered Petrograd in disguise to persuade his party comrades that the time had come to seize power. Opposition to Lenin's timetable was considerable, but his powers of persuasion were even stronger. Trotsky's support proved critical.

Bolsheviks Radical wing of the Russian Social-Democratic Party in 1917 led by Vladimir Lenin, whose program called for "Peace, Land, and Bread."

Alexander Kerensky (1881–1970) Moderate socialist and prime minister of the Provisional Government who was deposed by the Bolsheviks.

Leon Trotsky (1879–1940) Russian revolutionary who along with Lenin helped bring the Bolsheviks to power in 1917.

Despite press coverage of the Bolshevik plan to grab power, the Petrograd Soviet refused to believe it could succeed and would not align itself with Kerensky and the Provisional Government.

Executing the Revolution On the night of November 6, the Bolsheviks executed a carefully planned takeover of Petrograd. Bridges across the river Neva were occupied, and the Bolshevik party's **Red Guards** surrounded the main railway stations, central post office, and other strategic buildings. The Provisional Government found itself trapped inside the Winter Palace, unable to communicate with the outside. Except for a few cadets and the ill-trained Women's Battalion of Death, no one defended Kerensky and the recognized government of Russia.

Very much like the tsar's regime some eight months earlier, the Provisional Government collapsed. As Lenin put it later, "Power lay on the street; we merely picked it up." The following day, the Bolsheviks broke into the Winter Palace and arrested the members of the Provisional Government except for Kerensky, who, disguised as a woman, escaped in an American Embassy automobile. Though the Bolsheviks faced stiff opposition and street fighting in Moscow, in the countryside peasants were far more concerned with seizing the land they had been promised by the Bolsheviks. By the end of November, Lenin and his party comrades found themselves unexpectedly in control of the world's largest country.

Bolshevik Rule The Bolsheviks themselves did not expect their power to last. They hurried to proclaim Russia the first socialist state in history and rapidly issued decrees calling for peace, nationalizing land for peasants, establishing worker control of factories, and affirming equal rights for all religious and national minorities. Alexandra Kollontai became commissar for people's welfare. To the embarrassment of the Allied Powers, the Bolsheviks published secret treaties concerning promises about postwar settlements revealing, among other things, that Russia was to receive territory from Turkey after the war—agreements that the Allies had earlier denied. The long-delayed elections to the constituent assembly were allowed to take place, but when it convened in January 1918, the Bolsheviks shut it down after only one day. Already the Bolsheviks were curtailing the liberal freedoms gained by the March revolution.

The Bolsheviks had never pretended to be liberals. They had never advocated equal rights or toleration for all political views. When they came to power, they were well aware of how weak their position was and how many enemies surrounded them. In December 1917, they established the secret police known as the **Cheka**—the Extraordinary Commission to Combat Counterrevolution, Sabotage, and Speculation. The Cheka and its agents, Chekists, ruthlessly sought out and arrested anyone suspected of opposing Bolshevik power. By mid-1918, all conservative and liberal parties had been shut down, their newspapers confiscated, and their leaders driven underground or into exile. By the summer of 1918, the enemies of the Bolsheviks had organized themselves to fight the new order in Russia. The **Russian Civil War**, between the Reds (Bolsheviks) and the Whites (diverse groups opposed to the Bolsheviks), was to last until 1920. Some of the first victims were Nicholas II and his family, killed in July 1918 on the orders of Lenin, who feared that the ex-tsar might fall into the hands of the Whites.

✔ Checking In

By yourself or with a partner, explain the significance of each of the following selected key terms:

Provisional Government	Leon Trotsky
Petrograd Soviet	Red Guards
Bolsheviks	Cheka
Alexander Kerensky	Russian Civil War

The Turning of the Tide, 1917–1918

◆ What events led to the defeat of Germany and the Central Powers?

◆ Why did so many Germans refuse to believe that they had been defeated?

After two and a half years of war, by early 1917 despair and frustration prevailed on all sides. The ideals and enthusiasm of the summer of 1914 had been long forgotten as governments and military leaders desperately cast about for some way of ending the conflict. Two events of 1917 broke this deadlock: the revolutions in Russia and the decision of the United States to enter the war on the Allied side. With the arrival of American finances, troops, and equipment, chances for a victory of the Central Powers faded. The year 1918 began with German victory on the eastern front but ended with defeat in the west. Few Germans realized at the time how crushing this defeat would be. But even the exhausted Allies had little cause for celebration in 1918.

War Exhaustion

Based on the military situation in early 1917, it would have been difficult to predict World War I's final outcome.

Red Guards Troops organized by the Bolsheviks that were instrumental in their victory in the Russian Revolution of November 1917.

Cheka Secret police established in Soviet Russia in December 1917 to eradicate enemies of the Bolshevik regime.

Russian Civil War War between the Bolshevik government ("Reds") and its opponents ("Whites") from 1918 to 1920, ending in victory for the Reds.

Despite the stalemate in the west, the German army had advanced into Russia. Warsaw was taken in mid-1915, and by late 1916 Germans had taken Wilno (now Vilnius, Lithuania) and occupied much of eastern Ukraine, Belarus, and Lithuania. Austrian armies took back Galicia, which had been occupied by the Russians in the first months of the year and, after unexpectedly fierce fighting, succeeded in neutralizing Serbia.

War Exhaustion in Austria-Hungary The military and domestic situation in multinational Austria-Hungary, however, was unstable. Czech and other Slavic troops often deserted across the Russian lines, and even German-speakers in the empire questioned openly the utility of continuing "Prussia's" war. Early in 1916, Emperor Francis Joseph died after a reign of nearly seventy years, depriving Austria-Hungary of a unifying symbol.

Later that year, a young man entered a Viennese café, approached the Austrian prime minister, cried out, "We want peace," then shot him and waited quietly to be arrested. A Russian offensive in the summer of 1916 had brought the Austro-Hungarian army close to collapse, until German troops intervened. Behind the scenes, the young Austro-Hungarian emperor sent out secret peace feelers to the Allies, only to be found out and severely rebuked by the Kaiser. By 1917, the war enthusiasm of a few years earlier was dead, all sides longed for an end to the bloodletting, but no one could see a way out.

Calls for Peace In such a situation, the peace movement gained momentum. In previous years radical socialists, including Lenin, Kollontai, and Luxemburg, had met in Switzerland to issue a manifesto, drafted by Trotsky, calling for "a peace without annexations or war indemnities." These socialists argued that the war should end without any country gaining new territory or demanding payment from their enemies. They believed that the present war was absurd and immoral, serving the interests of the armaments industries, the imperialist powers, and the rich. They demanded, instead, a war against the existing order, in which the working people of all nations would band together and turn weapons on the hated capitalists and generals. No mainstream socialist party could accept such a radical program, but as the stalemate continued on the battlefronts, and misery on the home fronts deepened, calls for peace were also issued by mainstream leaders, including U.S. President **Woodrow Wilson** and the pope.

Strikes and Mutinies In 1917, in Britain, France, and Germany, hundreds of thousands of workers went out on strike, breaking their no-strike pledges. Even wage increases could not keep up with the steep rise in prices, but strikers were also protesting this senseless war. Influenced by left-wing arguments, they increasingly rejected the idea of shared interests with factory owners. Similarly, soldiers distrusted their generals and loathed the politicians back home. For many, it appeared that incompetent leaders were merely spouting hollow lines about patriotism to mask their inability to end a war that by now nobody wanted. In April 1917, at several places on the western front, French soldiers simply refused to "go over the top." Their disobedience was simply a reasonable unwillingness to carry out unreasonably murderous orders, but these mutinies shook the military leadership, who feared that the soldiers would turn their weapons against their own officers and mutinies would spread.

Russian soldiers, whose morale and material conditions had been shaken by the March revolution in Petrograd, retreated in disorder in the midst of a summer offensive. Shortly after seizing power in November, the Bolsheviks initiated cease-fire talks with the Germans. Germany had already defeated Romania earlier in 1917 and had exacted very harsh peace terms from that country. At the same time, the Central Powers' Bulgarian and Turkish allies were barely hanging on, plagued by low morale and shortages of food and ammunition. The loss of vast Ottoman Middle Eastern territories to the British by late 1917 created a crisis of confidence in the Turkish leadership.

Battle of Caporetto Amid general war weariness, only the Germans appeared to have some reason for hope. In late September 1917, the combined German and Austrian army inflicted a crushing defeat on the Italians at Caporetto. The Italian army nearly disintegrated, thousands deserted, and three hundred thousand men were taken prisoner by the German and Austrian armies. This decisive victory, combined with the Russian collapse, encouraged many Germans to believe that the war would end favorably in 1918. Such wishful thinking failed to appreciate the decisive turn in the war's fortunes caused by the United States joining the Allies.

The Entry of the United States

Until 1917, the United States had avoided taking sides in the European conflict. Most Americans could not see how their interests were involved in the European war and preferred to remain neutral. Even after the public outrage over the sinking of the *Lusitania* in May 1915, President Wilson remained unwilling to press for American intervention. His election campaign of the following year was conducted under the slogan "He kept us out of war."

Woodrow Wilson (1856–1924) U.S. president, 1913–1921, who brought the United States into war "to make the world safe for democracy" and authored the Fourteen Points.

But just a month after his second inauguration, Wilson signed a declaration of war against Germany.

The Zimmermann Telegram Two foolish actions by the German government had altered American public opinion. In January 1917, the German foreign minister, Arthur Zimmermann, telegraphed the German ambassador in Mexico, instructing him to offer Mexico the return of lands lost in the 1840s to the United States if Mexico would support Germany against the Americans. The British intercepted the telegram and revealed its contents to the American government. The reaction was predictably furious, and when the telegram was published in the American press in March, anti-German war sentiment ran high.

Resuming Unrestricted Submarine Warfare At the beginning of February, the Germans announced the resumption of unrestricted submarine warfare, disregarding the effect that such a move would have on American public opinion. The sinking of several American merchant ships strengthened calls for intervention. The March revolution in Russia heightened the contrast between the militarist regime in Berlin and democratic governments in Paris, London, and now Petrograd. All these factors came together in Wilson's request on April 2, 1917, for a declaration of war. Wilson stated that world peace was the goal: "The world must be made safe for democracy."

The Impact of America's Entry into the War The impact of the American entry into the war was felt first financially. American loans and credits, previously somewhat restrained by considerations of neutrality, opened up fully for the Allied Powers. American factories retooled for war production, and more than 20 million men registered for military service. American soldiers began to arrive in France in June 1917, though it was not until 1918 that American troops actually went into battle. Just as in European countries, the American government intervened in the economy. The War Industries Board in Washington coordinated production and distribution of essential goods. As American troops and manufactured goods streamed across the Atlantic, the Central Powers were reaching their last reserves.

German Victory over Russia

With the American entry into the war, the Germans knew that their only chance for victory was to crush the Allies before American troops could arrive in significant numbers. That seemed possible when the Bolsheviks pulled Russia out of the war. Lenin recognized that the very survival of his new socialist regime depended on making peace, and the Russian army had essentially ceased to exist. As Lenin himself put it, peasant soldiers had "voted with their feet" by deserting to head home and obtain their share of agricultural land being seized from the landlords.

Treaty of Brest-Litovsk In the autumn of 1917, the Germans had taken Riga and were threatening the Baltic approaches to Petrograd, with little to stop them. On December 15, 1917, representatives of the Bolsheviks and the Central Powers met in the Belarusian town of Brest-Litovsk and agreed on an **armistice**. Both delegations remained in the city to hammer out details of the peace. The deliberations between Bolsheviks, led by the fiery orator Trotsky, and the German delegation, made up mainly of stiff Prussian generals and sober diplomats, revealed the enormous political differences between the two sides. The Soviet representatives demanded "peace without annexations or war indemnities" and **national self-determination** for Ukrainians, Poles, and other non-Russians under German occupation. The Germans were astounded that the Bolshevik representatives dared make demands, considering their military weakness. When negotiations broke down, the German army simply advanced farther into Russian territory, encountering almost no resistance.

Back in Petrograd, Lenin was furious. He scolded Trotsky for his arrogance and warned that Germany's conditions for peace would now be even harsher. He was right. In March 1918, the Bolsheviks accepted the **Treaty of Brest-Litovsk**. Russia signed away over a quarter of its prewar population and arable land as well as over half its coal fields and iron manufacturing. This vast region, stretching from the Baltic Sea to Ukraine, was carved into new states dependent on Germany. Even though relatively few ethnic Russians lived in these lands, the loss of this huge territory was a severe blow to the young government, one that no democratic government could have survived. The new border with Finland and Estonia ran threateningly close to Petrograd, and for security reasons the Russian capital was moved to Moscow, where it remains to this day.

armistice Temporary cease-fire reached before the official treaty ending hostilities.

national self-determination Right of ethnic groups or nations to autonomy, often falsely interpreted to mean the setting up of independent nation-states.

Treaty of Brest-Litovsk Harsh peace imposed on Soviet Russia by Germany in March 1918 that stripped Russia of large territories on its western borders.

German Defeat

In January 1918, Woodrow Wilson issued his famous **Fourteen Points**—a plan of the future peace based not on revenge but on the liberal principles of freedom, justice, and free trade. Among the most important of the Fourteen Points were the demands for "open covenants of peace, openly arrived at," national self-determination, an independent Polish state, arms reduction, free navigation of the seas, and the creation of a postwar international body—the **League of Nations**—that would regulate relations between states and prevent future wars. Through private conversations, many Germans and Austrians learned of the speech despite their governments' efforts to suppress the information. For them, the Fourteen Points appeared to open the possibility of peace negotiations. Others, however, denounced Wilson's speech as mere propaganda. As long as there was a chance for military victory, in any case, the German government expressed no interest in Wilson's proposal.

Germany Seeks Peace Hoping to win the war quickly, the Germans launched major offensives on the western front in the spring of 1918, but they failed, with several hundred thousand casualties only weakening the Germany military further. By autumn, even the German High Command recognized they had lost the war. Thinking that a civilian government could win milder terms from the Allies, and seeking to evade their own responsibility for the defeat, the military leadership persuaded the Kaiser to abdicate. As strikes and political demonstrations rocked German cities, a new government was formed, dominated by moderate socialists. In this way, the burden of defeat fell not on generals and the Kaiser but on the fledgling democratic government of Germany.

Under the armistice agreement, the Germans promised to withdraw from Belgium, return Alsace-Lorraine to France, surrender submarines and rail stock, and destroy artillery. All Allied prisoners of war were to be released immediately, and the Treaty of Brest-Litovsk was annulled. The Germans agreed to pay for war damages. The Allied naval blockade of Germany would continue until a final peace settlement was reached. Though the provisions were harsh, the German delegation signed, one member taking comfort by observing, "A nation of seventy million suffers, but does not die." At the eleventh minute of the eleventh hour of the eleventh day of the eleventh month of 1918, the guns went silent on the western front.

Chaos and Consternation at War's End The fighting was ended, but the final conditions of peace were still to be negotiated and the German people were already stunned at the harsh armistice terms. Though

Jaroslav Hašek's literary creation, *The Good Soldier Švejk* was an ordinary soldier—a kind of Czech "Sad Sack"—in the Austro-Hungarian army during World War I. Good-natured and portly, Švejk has been seen as a reflection of Czech national character, but the effort of this "little man" to survive in an absurd war is a universal theme. Švejk showed no particular patriotism or eagerness to fight, only a desire to survive. How typical do you think that attitude was during the war? (Jaroslav Hasek (1883–1923), Osudy Dobreho vojaka Svejka; Za Svetove Valky (Prague: Ceskoslovensky Spisovatel) Photo: Visual Connection Archive)

the German generals knew well that the war had been lost, propaganda at home had predicted victory. Ordinary Germans had no way of knowing that their army was on the brink of collapse. German troops remained in position in northern France, and no Allied troops had crossed onto German soil. Corporal Adolf Hitler, temporarily blinded in action, heard the news in his hospital bed and wept.

Central and eastern Europe were in chaos. The Russian and Austro-Hungarian Empires had ceased to exist. Independence was declared in Poland, Ukraine, Czechoslovakia, Finland, and Lithuania. In Vienna, an Austrian Republic was proclaimed; its parliament asked to be accepted into the German Reich. German sailors mutinied and took over the northern port city of Kiel. In other German cities, from Berlin to Munich, radicalized soldiers and workers set up soviets on the Russian model. Budapest, capital of

Fourteen Points President Woodrow Wilson's blueprint for peace and postwar negotiations based on the principles of freedom, justice, and free trade.

League of Nations Postwar international body proposed by Woodrow Wilson to regulate relations between states with the goal of preventing future wars.

the new Hungary, also experienced a short-lived soviet government. As workers, soldiers, and sailors took to the streets, the middle classes feared for their property and lives. In Moscow, Lenin hoped this was the dawn of the world revolution. Not just a war had ended, but a world.

End of the European Era

More than eight million Europeans died in World War I, and about twenty million young men had been wounded, many permanently disabled. The worldwide influenza epidemic of late 1918–1919 killed as many as forty million more. In many areas, public order had broken down, and governments were in disarray. Four empires—German, Russian, Ottoman, and Habsburg—had collapsed, millions of people had been uprooted, and class warfare had broken out in many parts of central and eastern Europe.

War's Destruction   The war caused widespread destruction. Roads and railroads were destroyed. Entire villages and towns ceased to exist. Factories were breaking down without proper upkeep and investment. The total cost of the war is difficult to calculate, but the famous English economist John Maynard Keynes estimated that it represented Europe's entire industrial output of several years.

From London to Constantinople, from Moscow to Marseilles, Europeans were poorer in 1918 than in 1914. Except for Britain, industrial production contracted. Commercial trade ceased, and the center of international finance shifted from London to New York. Agriculture also suffered, and food shortages

were so widespread, especially as the naval blockade continued, pending the peace settlement, that millions faced starvation in the winter of 1918. On the other side of the world, Japan prospered during the war and increased its influence in the region at the expense of China. The American economy also boomed as its capital and goods streamed into Europe, further reducing the European proportion of world economic output.

Psychological Impact   The war had a permanent effect on the European psyche. Trench warfare and total war made optimism about the future—and belief in the past—hollow. The notion of human progress was undone. Disorientation, depression, and rage were the surviving emotions, reflected in the paintings of Paul Nash and George Grosz and in the highly unmilitary figure of Jaroslav Hašek's *Good Soldier Švejk.* Literary critic Paul Fussell has suggested that World War I even altered European perceptions of the natural world. Sunrise had long been the symbol of a new day, full of hope and possibilities. But for soldiers in the trenches, dawn was the most terrifying time of all—the time of the call to "go over the top." After World War I, nothing, not even the sunrise, would be the same.

 Checking In

By yourself or with a partner, explain the significance of each of the following selected key terms:

Woodrow Wilson	Treaty of Brest-Litovsk
armistice	Fourteen Points
national self-determination	League of Nations

CHAPTER
Review

Summary

- A major war had long been expected, but the length and ferocity of World War I surprised many Europeans.

- Nobody had predicted the frustrating and murderous trench warfare that even poison gas, massive artillery barrages, and aircraft could not break for three years on the western front.

- The Russian empire collapsed under the stress of the war in March 1917, and the liberal Provisional

Government was swept away by the communists in November 1917.

- World War I strengthened the role of state intervention in the economy and in everyday life.

- When the Germans sued for peace in late 1918, every European country was exhausted; the real victor of the conflict was the United States whose influence in the world grew hugely.

Chronology

1904–1905	Japan defeats Russia in Russo-Japanese War	**1915**	Turks defeat Allies at the Battle of Gallipoli; Italy declares war on Austria-Hungary (May 23)
1905	Dissatisfaction with tsarist rule sparks empire-wide revolution in Russia	**1916**	Battle of the Somme ends without significant advances (July–November)
1908	Austria-Hungary annexes Bosnia-Herzegovina	**1917**	Russian Revolution begins; Tsar Nicholas II abdicates (March); United States enters World War I on Allied side (April); Bolsheviks attempt coup in Petrograd (July); Bolsheviks seize power in Petrograd (November)
1912	First Balkan War weakens Ottoman Empire		
1913	Second Balkan War strengthens Serbia		
1914	Archduke Ferdinand is assassinated (June 28); Austria presents Serbia with an ultimatum (July 23); Austria-Hungary declares war on Serbia (July 28); Germany declares war on Russia (August 1); Germany declares war on France and invades Belgium (August 3); Great Britain declares war on Germany (August 4); World War I begins (August); Germany defeats Russia at the Battle of Tannenberg (mid-August); French defeat Germans in the First Battle of the Marne (September)	**1918**	Treaty of Brest-Litovsk ends war for Russia (March); Germans launch offensives on the western front (spring); Armistice ends World War I (November 11)
		1918–1919	Worldwide influenza epidemic kills millions

Test Yourself

To gauge your mastery of the material in this chapter, answer the questions below. More than one answer may be correct.

A New Century, 1900–1914

1. Change in the European "balance of power" since midcentury included:

   a. Creation of a unified and increasingly powerful Germany.
   b. Unification of Italy.
   c. The growing military and economic power of Austria-Hungary.
   d. A military alliance between France and Germany.
   e. The cooling of relations between Russia and Germany.

2. The Schlieffen Plan:

   a. Was drawn up by the French military chief of staff.
   b. Was created to counter the threat of a two-front war.
   c. Aimed to knock out France before turning on Russia.
   d. Counted on Britain joining Germany in a war against France.
   e. Foresaw a long, drawn-out war.

3. Which of the following statements about alliances in the early twentieth century is correct?

   a. Most countries avoided committing to alliances.
   b. Britain stayed out of military alliances, so Germany hoped in a conflict it would remain neutral.
   c. Germany's main alliance partner was Austria-Hungary.
   d. Italy and France were close allies.
   e. The military alliance between Russia and France in 1894 threatened Germany with a potential two-front war.

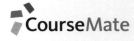

4. Nationalism in this prewar period:

    a. Was more of a threat to France than to Russia or Austria-Hungary.
    b. Was strong and growing in many parts of Europe.
    c. Strongly supported the empire among Britons (not Irishmen).
    d. Threatened the stability of Austria-Hungary because nationalities like Czechs, Serbs, and Italians demanded greater rights.
    e. Included Pan-Slavism, which stressed cultural-religious ties between Russia and Balkan peoples like Serbs and Bulgarians.

5. The Balkan Peninsula in the decade before 1914:

    a. Was a peaceful region where countries generally cooperated with each other.
    b. Saw two wars that considerably aggravated relations between Serbia and Bulgaria.
    c. Was generally pro-Austrian in sentiments and diplomatic relations.
    d. Feared invasion by the Ottoman Empire and turned to Russia for protection.
    e. Included a number of small, unstable countries whose rivalries with each other threatened to pull larger European powers into a more general conflict.

Now that you have reviewed and tested yourself on this part of the chapter, take time to pull together all the important information by answering the following questions:

◆ Why did nationalism present different difficulties for states in western and eastern Europe?

◆ How did the shifting alliances between countries help set the stage for general war in 1914?

The Unexpected War, 1914

6. The outbreak of World War I in 1914 can be called "unexpected" because:

    a. Nobody anticipated a European conflict in this period.
    b. Europeans expected the war to be over in a few months.
    c. No one anticipated trench warfare.
    d. After the assassination of Francis Ferdinand, immediate war was expected, not a war over a month later.
    e. The unexpected quickness of Russian mobilization, among other factors, caused the failure of the Schlieffen Plan.

7. Which of the following statements about events leading up to the outbreak of World War I is true?

    a. Within days of the assassination of Francis Ferdinand, Europe was at war.
    b. True to Germany's expectation, Britain preferred to remain neutral.
    c. Immediately upon war's outbreak in early August, Italy invaded Austria-Hungary.
    d. Personal telegrams between the cousins, Kaiser William and Tsar Nicholas, were unable to prevent war.
    e. Europe's major powers quickly coalesced into two groups: the Allied Powers and the Central Powers.

8. Trench warfare was characterized by:

    a. Little movement of frontlines between the hostile armies.
    b. Shallow trenches, quickly built to ensure temporary shelter.
    c. Combat consisting mainly of hand-to-hand fighting with little use of artillery.
    d. A system of elaborate deep trenches and underground bunkers reaching from the Swiss border to the British channel.
    e. Almost no attempt to break the stalemate, as generals did not want to sacrifice men needlessly.

9. Among the new military technologies employed in World War I were:

    a. The submarine, used very effectively by the Germans in an attempt to starve Britain into submission.
    b. Nuclear-powered warships used in particular by Italy against Austria-Hungary.
    c. Airplanes and zeppelins, employed both as bombers and for reconnaissance.
    d. Dreadnoughts, which allowed Germany to dominate the seas throughout the conflict.
    e. Poison gas, first used by Germans but then employed by the Allies as well.

10. Geographically speaking, World War I:

    a. Forced every European country to join; neutrality was not an option.
    b. Had major effects throughout Europe and even into Central Asia, as the Kazakh Uprising of 1916 showed.
    c. Brought dozens of countries on all continents except Antarctica into the conflict.
    d. Involved fighting in Africa, particularly between colonial forces of different powers, supported by African troops.
    e. Provided the background for the Armenian Genocide in 1915–1916.

Now that you have reviewed and tested yourself on this part of the chapter, take time to pull together all the important information by answering the following questions:

◆ Why did so many Europeans greet the war with enthusiasm? What did they hope to get out of the war?

◆ How did new technologies affect the nature of war in this conflict?

Total War, 1914–1918

11. Which of the following impacts did World War I have on the "home front?"

    a. A ban on producing vodka in Russia.
    b. More women took jobs outside the home, including in armaments factories.
    c. Great Britain took the railroads under government ownership.
    d. Germany, unlike Allied countries, refused to introduce rationing.
    e. Higher government taxes entirely covered the costs of war.

12. Which of the following statements accurately shows the increase in state interference in everyday life during World War I?

    a. Governments took over most private property to finance the war effort.
    b. Taxes increased nearly universally.
    c. Huge government spending on the war fueled inflation.
    d. The British government introduced daylight savings time for the first time.
    e. The French outlawed a number of tasty treats from baguettes to candy.

13. Propaganda during World War I:

    a. Strove to present an accurate, unbiased picture of the war.
    b. Generally portrayed the enemy as subhuman or monstrous.
    c. Often enjoyed considerable popularity, as with Lessauer's hit "Song of Hatred Against England."
    d. Was often believed by citizens because they did not yet have radios or any other means to get a more balanced view.
    e. Was used mainly by the Central Powers and avoided by the Allies.

14. Civil liberties (like freedom of speech and assembly) during World War I:

    a. Were restricted primarily in Russia and Germany.
    b. Were ended entirely with a strict censorship in all countries that prevented any discussion of the war.
    c. Were narrowed in Britain by DORA.
    d. In Germany did not allow criticism of the war, as the arrests of Luxemburg and Liebknecht in 1916 showed.
    e. Even took a beating in the United States with the restrictive Espionage and Sedition Acts.

15. Which of the following effects did World War I have on domestic life?

    a. All segments of the population were urged to help the war effort.
    b. For the first time women began to work in textile factories.
    c. Effects were minimal, especially for richer people like the British royal family.
    d. Women were recruited into auxiliary units and in Russia even to a combat unit, "The Women's Battalion of Death."
    e. Family life in general was not much affected by the war.

Now that you have reviewed and tested yourself on this part of the chapter, take time to pull together all the important information by answering the following questions:

◆ How did propaganda present a one-sided picture of the war? How successful was it?

◆ How did this war, often called the first "total war," differ from earlier conflicts in its impact on society and everyday life?

Russia in Revolution, 1917

16. What was the situation in the Russian empire in early 1917?

   a. Though there had been some military reversals, on the whole morale was high.
   b. Russians expected their army to take Berlin in the spring.
   c. Russians were hungry and cold, and it appeared that their government was inefficient, corrupt, and possibly infiltrated by German spies.
   d. The tsar agreed to share power with parliament in a confidence-building measure.
   e. Military failures and breakdowns in the supply of bread and coal destroyed confidence in the government.

17. The March 1917 Revolution is important because it:

   a. Forced the tsar to abdicate and put the liberal Provisional Government in power.
   b. Brought the Bolsheviks to power.
   c. Took Russia out of the war.
   d. Was a spontaneous people's uprising on International Women's Day.
   e. Passed sentence on and executed Nicholas II for treason.

18. The period between March and November 1917 in Russia was characterized by:

   a. Unchallenged and effective rule of the Provisional Government, a mainly liberal temporary government.
   b. Continued government support of the war effort, despite many Russians' dissatisfaction with the conflict.
   c. Considerable repression, as the Provisional Government strengthened censorship and arrested its opponents.
   d. "Dual Power" in which the official government was influenced by the more radical Petrograd Soviet.
   e. An extremely liberal political atmosphere in which radicals were amnestied and one could print nearly anything in the newspapers.

19. The November Revolution is important because:

   a. It brought the Bolsheviks to power.
   b. It led to the creation of the first socialist country in history.
   c. It represented the final triumph of liberalism in Russia.
   d. Stalin was the leader of this revolution and he would rule until the 1930s.
   e. It took Russia out of the war.

20. The liberal Provisional Government failed to maintain itself in power because:

   a. It was too repressive, causing many citizens to rebel.
   b. It depended too much on support from the army, like General Kornilov.
   c. The Bolsheviks were a well-organized and well-led opponent.
   d. The Provisional Government's amnesty allowed radicals like Trotsky and Lenin to return to Russia.
   e. It failed to appreciate how deeply unpopular the war had become and insisted on continuing the war effort.

Now that you have reviewed and tested yourself on this part of the chapter, take time to pull together all the important information by answering the following questions:

◆ What mistakes did Nicholas II make that helped bring about his downfall? Could he have retained power, and if so, how?

◆ What mistakes did the Provisional Government make that weakened their power?

The Turning of the Tide, 1917–1918

21. Which of the following events reflect or were caused by the widespread war exhaustion starting around 1916?

    a. Austria-Hungary's separate peace with Italy.
    b. The assassination of the Austrian prime minister in 1916.
    c. The Russian Revolutions of 1917.
    d. Call by radical socialists meeting in Switzerland to transform the conflict into a war against the existing order.
    e. Refusal of some French soldiers in 1917 to "go over the top" and attack the enemy.

22. The United States entered the war in April 1917 because:

    a. Woodrow Wilson had long promised to use American power to defeat the Germans.
    b. Most Americans felt a patriotic need to support the French and British against the Central Powers.
    c. Russia's March 1917 revolution allowed Wilson to portray the conflict as a struggle against anti-democratic militarists in Berlin.
    d. Unrestricted submarine warfare by the Germans had angered many Americans.
    e. Publication of the "Zimmermann telegram" shocked Americans who saw in it a clear threat to U.S. national security.

23. The Treaty of Brest-Litovsk:

    a. Ended the war between Finland and Germany in 1916.
    b. Took Austria-Hungary out of the war in early 1918.
    c. Ended the war between Germany and Soviet Russia.
    d. Made Lenin and the Kaiser allies for a time.
    e. Took a huge amount of prewar Russian territory and created states dependent on Germany out of this territory.

24. Germany signed an armistice in late 1918 because:

    a. Liberal and socialist politicians tricked the Kaiser into it.
    b. The German government wished to consolidate gains in the east in alliance with Lenin.
    c. Spring offensives, though initially successful, had collapsed and the German military leadership recognized that they could not win the war.
    d. Germans expressed their dissatisfaction with the war in strikes and political demonstrations.
    e. Ordinary Germans recognized that their armies had been defeated.

25. Which of the following were direct outcomes of World War I?

    a. The collapse of the Ottoman and Russian Empires.
    b. Huge destruction, including some eight million dead and twenty million wounded.
    c. A near bankrupting of European governments, nearly all of whom were now in debt to the United States.
    d. The end of all European colonial empires, with independence for the former colonies.
    e. A great diminishing of the optimism and belief in scientific progress that had characterized the nineteenth century.

Now that you have reviewed and tested yourself on this part of the chapter, take time to pull together all the important information by answering the following questions:

◆ What different forms did war exhaustion take in the years 1916–1918?

◆ Why could the Central Powers not win against the western Allies, though they did win against Russia?

CHAPTER 26

A Decade of Revolutionary Experiments, 1918–1929

Chapter Outline

1916	1917	1918	1919	1920	1921	1922
		1918 Russian civil war begins	**1919** League of Nations is established Versailles Treaty imposes a harsh peace on Germany			**1922** Mussolini seizes power in Italy

Isadora Duncan (1877–1927), the British dancer who charmed America and Russia, became a symbol of the experimental spirit of the modernist movement. She performed barefoot, adopting a natural style that rejected the formal and more constrictive aesthetics of classical ballet. Generations of choreographers and dancers since then, such as Josephine Baker and Martha Graham, have been inspired by her philosophy and teachings. (Ullstein Bilderdienst/The Image Works)

After reading this chapter you should be able to answer the following questions:

What are the weaknesses and strengths of the postwar treaties?

What were the challenges posed to European political stability by new political movements and economic developments?

Why was the Soviet Union such a radically new type of state?

What are the defining elements of fascism?

What were the challenges to cultural and social norms posed by cultural developments?

WITH A RADICALLY ALTERED MAP of Europe as a result of the war, in the decade after 1918 many Europeans began, or were forced, to reconsider their social, cultural, and political identities. Many abandoned their allegiance to the nationalist or liberal ideals that had yielded few positive results in the Great War. Others found new hope in nationalism, especially ethnic groups from the newly formed states in Eastern Europe. Women demanded political and economic power, workers fought for social justice, peasants for property rights, newly created states struggled for recognition, and artists offered entirely new ways of defining beauty and the individual.

This period saw both a rush toward creating a brand new world from the ashes of war and a withdrawal aimed at imposing stability on a world that had unraveled. As empires collapsed, new states sprang up, forcing a veritable new order. Europe redrew national borders, reformulated the principles of state sovereignty, and redefined the nature of international relations. Democracy became the new foundation for political legitimacy. The postwar peace conference that mapped

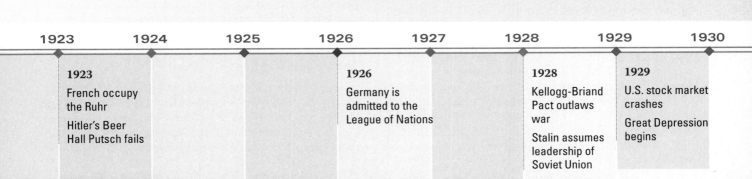

1923	1924	1925	1926	1927	1928	1929	1930

1923
French occupy the Ruhr

Hitler's Beer Hall Putsch fails

1926
Germany is admitted to the League of Nations

1928
Kellogg-Briand Pact outlaws war

Stalin assumes leadership of Soviet Union

1929
U.S. stock market crashes

Great Depression begins

these changes pleased no one and left many issues unresolved. Mounting economic problems such as postwar payments and debts plagued much of the continent.

To address these new conditions, Europeans tried a broad range of political experiments, from social democracy in Germany and Scandinavia to fascism in Italy. In Russia, the Bolsheviks won a civil war and embarked on a new and untested communist system. New state institutions forcefully eliminated any real and potential enemies and tried to transform peasants into workers, and women and men into equal participants in the building of communism. Avant-garde artists created a new revolutionary style.

New social and intellectual movements flourished all over Europe. Women tried on new public identities in popular culture and new political roles in countries where they won the vote. Some challenged economic, social, sexual, and cultural limits. Philosophers, theologians, and artists reacted against the destruction of the war with a renewed commitment to moral values and hope in Christianity. The 1920s also saw the growth of a pacifist movement.

The notion of progress had been strenuously tested by the war and the frailty of the human condition exposed. Europeans met these challenges in different ways—some by living in the moment and enjoying the freedoms of popular entertainment and consumption, others by searching for absolutes in politics, philosophy, or art. At the heart of many of these responses was the hope that a brand new world could be forged out of the ashes of the war. Some politicians, reformers, and intellectuals tried to find a middle ground, but their voices were barely heard in the chaotic atmosphere of the 1920s. By 1929, Europe was becoming polarized between two extremist political regimes—fascism and communism—and democracy was losing ground.

The Search for Stability, 1918–1924

◆ **What various strategies did political leaders use to restore Europe after the war?**

◆ **What problems stood in the way of political stability?**

When European leaders met in 1919 to write the peace treaties, the mood was grim. The war was over, but violence continued. Four empires—the Habsburg, German, Ottoman, and Russian—lay in shambles. Revolution had engulfed Russia and spread in Germany and Hungary. The economies of all the combatants were devastated. Cities, factories, and fields lay in ruin; people starved. Yet few leaders were ready to rebuild Europe and secure a lasting peace through democracy. Instead, they focused on

immediate objectives, such as increasing their territory and population, reducing war payments, and solidifying their own political position at home. The peace negotiations were driven as much by internal as by international considerations. They also were driven by secret treaties made during the war. As a consequence, the ideal of national self-determination promoted by U.S. President Woodrow Wilson stood little chance of success. In the end, the victors were dissatisfied, and the defeated were humiliated. Even before the ink dried on the paper of the last peace document (1923), radical movements were undoing the stability of Europe.

The Peace Treaties

As peace negotiations opened in January 1919 at the old royal palace in Versailles, the representatives of the victorious Allied Powers, who dominated the agenda—all gray-haired men in tails and top hats—embodied the old European order established a

Boundaries of German, Russian, Austro-Hungarian, and Ottoman Empires in 1914
Areas lost by Austro-Hungarian Empire
Areas lost by Russian Empire
Areas lost by German Empire
Areas lost by Bulgaria
Areas lost by Ottoman Empire
Demilitarized Zones
Areas controlled under mandates from the League of Nations, 1920
Boundaries of 1926

Map 26.1 **Europe Following World War I** Europe's political map was greatly altered by the peace settlements following World War I. With four empires wiped off the map, and new, smaller states cobbled out of the territories lost by these former great powers, Europe entered a new era of the nation-state. © *Cengage Learning*

1. If you compare the borders of European states after the peace treaties with those of 1914, as shown on Map 25.1 (page 753), who were the winners and who were the losers after the war in terms of territorial changes?

2. Which winning countries seem most vulnerable in terms of borders with countries on the losing side of the war?

3. Which countries seem most stable territorially?

In 1919, Prime Minister *David Lloyd George* of the United Kingdom, *Vittorio Orlando* of Italy, Premier *Georges Clemenceau* of France, and President *Woodrow Wilson* of the United States met at Versailles to decide the fate of Europe. Does their pose reflect great power interests prior to the war or the new vision of self-determination at the heart of the peace treaties?

Bettmann/Corbis

century before at the Congress of Vienna. But revolutionary changes were at hand: the map of Europe would be redrawn, a new international system would redefine state relations, and democracy would replace aristocratic privilege as the fundamental basis for political power.

Self-Determination Wilson arrived in Paris with an idea for a European order based on national self-determination: Poles should govern themselves in an independent Poland, and Italians should live in Italy. This principle seemed a rational and just solution to some of the problems that had caused turmoil in Europe since the nineteenth century and contributed to the beginning of World War I. Ethnic minorities had come to see themselves as fundamentally oppressed because they generally did not receive the same benefits of economic development and state support for their education and culture as members of the majority ethnic group. Yet the ethnic map of Europe was so complicated as to make self-determination impossible. Polish nationals lived in areas where there were significant Russian and German populations. Italians and South Slavs were mixed in Istria and other areas along the Adriatic Sea. So no matter where the national boundaries were set, some ethnic groups would still be minorities. Generally though, the winners in Europe's Great War liked Wilson's ideas and supported them as a basis for peace and stability in Europe as well as a justification for

Versailles Treaty First peace treaty of World War I; established Germany's guilt in starting the war and punished it through reparations and demilitarization.

territorial gains. Those who had sided with the Allies—such as the Poles and Romanians—gained, while those aligned with the Central Powers lost.

One outcome of self-determination was an array of new and significantly reshaped countries. Among the winners, France, Greece, Italy, and Romania gained territories and populations. From the losers, new countries were created: Czechoslovakia was carved out of Austria-Hungary; Finland, Estonia, Latvia, and Lithuania emerged from Russia's western borderlands; Poland was re-created from the unification of territories lost by Germany, Russia, and Austria-Hungary; Turkey was a diminished version of the Ottoman Empire; and Yugoslavia was created by uniting Serbia with South Slavic territories lost by Austria-Hungary. The western European states' interest in creating these new countries had a great deal to do with self-determination and also with their fear of Bolshevism. The new countries that bordered the Soviet Union would be a buffer zone against communist contamination from the east.

Problematic Outcomes By contrast, Austria, Bulgaria, Hungary, Germany, and Russia lost territories. Most severely reduced were Germany, held responsible for starting the war, and Russia, whose Bolshevik regime had signed a separate peace with Germany. Neither was represented at the negotiations. For all these countries, save the Soviet Union, revision of the **Versailles Treaty** and the supplemental treaties (see Table 26.1) was an important aim in the internal politics of the next two decades, undermining any quest for stability and democratic government.

Table 26.1   World War I Peace Treaties

1918 Brest-Litovsk: Germany with Russia
1919 Versailles: Allies with Germany
1919 St. Germain: Allies with Austria
1919 Neuilly-sur-Seine: Allies with Bulgaria
1920 Trianon: Allies with Hungary
1920 Sèvres: Allies with Turkey
1921 Riga: Poland with Soviet Union
1924 Lausanne: Allies with Turkey and Greece

© Cengage Learning

Other wartime arrangements undermined the spirit of reconciliation and justice promoted by Wilson. To convince Italy to enter the war, the Allies had secretly offered it Istria, where the majority of the population were South Slavs. Serbia, also an ally of France and Britain, had been promised the same area. In the end, Italy received a good part of this territory, in flagrant disregard for the principle of self-determination. Another victim of the secret treaties was the Ottoman Empire. The Sykes-Picot Agreement (1916) had promised France and Britain various Ottoman territories in the Middle East. After the war, contradictory promises made by some British leaders, such as T. E. Lawrence, to Arab nationalist groups, and by other British politicians to Jewish Zionist groups (the Balfour Declaration) produced a conflict over Arab and Jewish homelands in Palestine that remains unresolved to this day.

Thus, a great deal of debate at Versailles focused on what counted more—the promises made by the Allies during the war or the new and popular principle of self-determination. The solutions varied, and though the states involved in these disputes were pacified, they were not necessarily satisfied. The greatest casualty, however, was the very principle of self-determination. If secret treaties counted more than the rights of ethnic groups who inhabited the disputed territories, the new states learned quickly that they were still at the mercy of Great Powers.

Minorities Protection The Great Powers tried to address potential interstate conflicts in two ways. First, they made sure the peace treaties protected minorities. The borders of Czechoslovakia, Poland, Romania, Yugoslavia, Greece, and Turkey were recognized only if these states agreed to treat ethnic and religious minorities, especially Jews, as equal citizens. Yet these provisions fostered some instability: they gave rise to protests inside states, especially by ethnic majorities, and from outside—from states that had lost populations. On a personal level, consider the dilemma of an educated ethnic Hungarian, a city employee in Kolozsvár, in the heart of Transylvania. After 1919, when Hungarian Kolozsvár became Romanian Cluj, he lost his job because he did not speak the language of the new administration—Romanian. His identity changed overnight: he lost his economic position, his social standing as a respectable government employee, and his cultural position as a member of an important European nation, Hungary. Though the same person living in the same place, he was recast as a member of a powerless ethnic minority. It is not difficult to imagine how those who had been part of Europe's privileged old order felt after 1919 and how quickly they looked to revise the peace treaties. **Revisionism** set the stage for future interethnic conflict.

The League of Nations The Great Powers also tried to maintain peace through the new League of Nations, created in the peace settlement. This international organization gave sovereign states the means for communicating and solving problems through open, peaceful negotiations rather than through secret treaties. The League also monitored the protection of minorities and various international humanitarian organizations, such as the Red Cross. But it was weak from the beginning because the United States—fearing European entanglements—refused to join, and Germany, Russia, and Turkey were excluded. Other Great Powers wavered between playing a strong role and disengagement. The League was important for upholding international principles such as human rights and for regulating arms trafficking, labor practices, and the treatment of displaced persons. But it did not have the strength to enforce its decisions. Its most severe punishment was to expel countries that did not comply.

The League did have an important role regarding the status of colonies, however. Former German colonies in Africa and Asia were transferred to Britain, France, Japan, and the United States as **trust territories** or **mandates,** and large parts of the former Ottoman Empire were also placed under British authority. Through its new mandate system, the league monitored the treatment of the native populations by colonial governments and facilitated cooperation among colonial powers, which were now also obligated to report to the League on their colonies. The goal of this system was to prepare native populations for self-government. One prominent example was the role of Britain in facilitating the development of modern political institutions and elites in Iraq, which moved from its **protectorate** position in 1919 to gaining full independence in 1932.

---

revisionism Political aim of revising the World War I peace settlements.

trust territories and **mandates** Former colonies and territories of losing countries given by the League of Nations to the winning countries to oversee.

protectorate Political entity that formally agrees by treaty to enter into an unequal relationship with another, stronger state.

In most cases, the League found it difficult to enforce its supervisory role without military force. Yet the participation of colonial troops in the war and the promises of the League had awakened the hope of self-rule and greater freedom among native peoples, and the League was ineffective in easing the resulting tensions. Especially in Palestine, another British mandate, clashes between the local Arab population and resolute Jewish settlers continued into the 1930s and beyond.

Still, the League represented a major departure from the system of international relations of the nineteenth century, in which small states had been virtual clients of the Great Powers. Some of these uneven power relations continued after the war, but recognition of all member states as equals allowed small and new states to carve out a more independent position in international relations. This more democratic and inclusive setting helped generate a new culture of diplomacy, in which alliances and negotiations were discussed openly. Even though the League was ultimately unsuccessful in preventing another world war, it did bring about greater stability in the 1920s. It also served as a learning ground for the creation of the United Nations after World War II.

Revolutionary Upheavals

The Bolshevik threat also shaped the ultimate outcome of the peace negotiations. With revolution in Russia and millions of armed soldiers on their way home to ruined economies and impoverished families throughout Europe, all states were afraid of revolution. In a few cases, this fear was real. In Germany, the Communist and Socialist Parties seemed on the rise, and several bloody uprisings took place between November 1918 and January 1919. They were crushed relatively quickly and violently, with leaders Rosa Luxemburg and Karl Liebknecht brutally murdered on the spot. A young corporal, **Adolf Hitler**, made himself known in the crushing of the communist uprising in Bavaria.

The Bolshevik Uprising in Hungary In Hungary, a Bolshevik revolution in March 1919 helped bring about a short-lived (133 days) Soviet Republic under the leadership of **Béla Kun**. The Bolshevik success here owed much to the Hungarians' dissatisfaction with the results of the war. As junior partners of the Austrians, they had endured great material and psychological losses. Kun's regime did not alleviate this suffering, focusing instead on brutally suppressing its enemies. In a swift reaction, the Great Powers allowed Slovak and Romanian forces to invade the country. The results were disastrous for Hungary. The Kun regime was crushed, but Romania and Czechoslovakia extracted large territorial concessions for their role in "saving" the Hungarian people. The result was the Treaty of Trianon (1920), which reduced Hungary to one-third its prewar size, with large groups of Hungarians living outside its borders. The brief and violent Soviet Republic proved a costly experiment. It rendered Hungary small, landlocked, and vengeful, eager to revise the peace treaties.

Proto-Fascists in Italy Another short-lived revolutionary experiment was the **Republic of Fiume**, the brainchild of Italian poet **Gabriele D'Annunzio**. This small Adriatic port was part of Istria, the area claimed by Italy and Yugoslavia on the basis of secret treaties at the beginning of the war. South Slavs constituted a majority in Istria, but the city of Fiume had an Italian majority. Wilson sided with Yugoslavia. Given the controversy over this city, D'Annunzio decided to take matters into his own hands and seized municipal institutions in September 1919. The poet became a military dictator, revered by his followers and feared by the general public.

Fiume was finally granted to Italy, but its ultimate fate was less important than the style of rule and **charismatic leadership** D'Annunzio modeled for **Benito Mussolini**, the future fascist leader. D'Annunzio's dramatic public speeches swayed huge crowds, more through performance and style than content. His followers marched through the streets in black shirts and leather boots, creating the impression of a highly unified and threatening military force. Adopting a look of youthful vengeance and an aura of absolute obedience, these young men seemed ready to renounce their individuality and devote themselves to their leader. The masterful way in which D'Annunzio reshaped identities impressed Mussolini, who adopted the rhetoric, uniforms, and ideas first experimented in Fiume.

Irish Nationalism Other victors also confronted revolutionary uprisings. The turmoil in Ireland intensified after 1919. Newly elected members of the Irish parliament declared independence and a bitter civil war ensued (1919–1921), claiming many victims and ending in a peace treaty that laid the foundation of the **Irish Free State** (1922–1937). This state comprised all of Ireland except the six counties of Northern

---

Adolf Hitler (1889–1945) Leader of the Nazi Party and dictatorial ruler of the Third Reich who initiated World War II by attacking Poland.

Béla Kun (1886–1938) Leader of a short-lived Bolshevik regime in Hungary crushed by Romanian and Slovak forces.

Republic of Fiume Revolutionary experiment led by Gabriele D'Annunzio, whose dictatorship and militarized police state were precursors of fascism.

Gabriele D'Annunzio (1863–1938) Italian writer who led the Republic of Fiume.

charismatic leadership Leadership style that uses emotional appeals to arouse followers and compel loyalty.

Benito Mussolini (1883–1943) Fascist dictator of Italy, the first to successfully challenge democracy in Europe; after 1936, a close ally of Adolf Hitler.

Irish Free State Irish state established in 1922 with dominion status, consisting of all of Ireland except Northern Ireland, which remained under direct British rule.

Ireland and received **dominion** status identical to that of Canada. There was much debate over the requirement to swear allegiance to the British king and especially over the status of Northern Ireland, which remained under direct British rule. The close final vote to ratify the treaty, 64 to 57, virtually ensured that separatist movements, such as the **Irish Republican Army** (IRA), would continue against the British. Unlike most other movements for national liberation in Europe at that time, in Ireland religion rather than language identity was at issue. In the Irish Free State, Catholicism was the dominant religion, whereas Catholics were a religious minority in Northern Ireland, where Protestants dominated. Yet despite tensions, Catholics and Protestants in Northern Ireland lived in relative peace for the next forty years.

Political challenges from the left and right thus threatened peace in Europe. Most governments and parties equated stability and democracy with suppressing Bolshevism. Liberals, social democrats, and nationalists united against this common enemy; yet some nationalist parties were also aggressive and potentially destabilizing, especially when they fought against the peace treaties. German nationalists in both Germany and Czechoslovakia, for example, used the principle of self-determination to argue that Czechoslovakia, with its large German minority, did not respect the peace treaties and would therefore be Bolshevik-friendly. Opponents of the peace treaties often used anti-Bolshevism to argue their cause.

War Reparations and Economic Crisis

While the peace treaties sought political solutions to Europe's turmoil, economic stability proved elusive. The cost of the war had been enormous in financing the military effort and rebuilding destroyed lands and industries. Between the deficits that built up to finance the wars and the overall drop in economic production, all European states emerged from the war with major deficits, looking toward the United States for help.

Paying Off the War Debt The victorious Allies, wanting the Central Powers to pay these costs, imposed **reparations** as part of the peace treaties. By far the largest reparations were demanded of Germany, both as revenge and as a means for the political leaders at Versailles to gain popular support at home. Coupled with the treaty's war guilt clause, in which Germany had to admit responsibility for starting the war, and its demand for disarmament, including demilitarization of the Rhineland, reparations reinforced Germany's humiliation and aimed to prevent it from becoming a major power again. The notion of making losers pay for the costs of armed conflict was not new, but the size of the payments was unprecedented. An international commission set reparations at 132 billion gold marks (today about $331.79 billion),

or two years' worth of Germany's gross national product.

The German Crisis The British and French pressed Germany to start payments immediately, as both needed to repay the United States billions of dollars in war loans. The Americans were in a hurry to see the loans repaid, and with weak economic performance and potential political instability at home, Britain and France were relying on war reparations as an important revenue source. The French were particularly inflexible. But after making its first payment of 2.5 billion gold marks in 1921, the German government defaulted the following year. Great Britain was willing to work out a **moratorium** and potential reduction of the payments, but France and Belgium, which had suffered much greater material and human losses in the war, stood by the Versailles agreement and proceeded to occupy Germany's heavily industrial Ruhr district in order to extract the debt payment in kind.

The **Ruhr occupation** (1923–1925) had a twofold effect on the young German democracy. First, it unified Germans in their opinion of the 1919 Versailles Treaty as unjust and of the victorious powers as abusive. This view fostered the growth of nationalist parties, including the **National Socialist German Workers' Party**— the **Nazis**. In addition, by extracting from Germany some of its most important economic resources (the Ruhr produced 80 percent of Germany's steel and coal), the occupation helped generate a severe economic crisis. The German government only made things worse by printing more money, which led to **hyperinflation**. For white-collar workers, small business owners, and the lower middle class generally, buying power vanished overnight. The hard-won savings of a middle-class professional that once might have paid for a car now barely bought a loaf of bread. Suitcases filled with paper money were not enough for a week's groceries. The professionals and

dominion Status in which former colonies recognize the British monarch as the head of the state but control their internal and foreign affairs.

Irish Republican Army Military organization recognized in 1919 by the parliament of the *Republic of Ireland* as its army, revived in 1970 as a paramilitary terrorist organization.

reparations War payments demanded by the victors from the losers.

moratorium Delay in the payment of the war debt.

Ruhr occupation Occupation (1923–1925) by French and Belgian troops of Germany's industrial Ruhr district to enforce the war reparations clause of the Versailles Treaty.

National Socialist German Workers' (Nazi) Party Rightwing party that recruited followers by promoting nationalism-socialism, with a nationalist-racist perspective.

hyperinflation Rapid devaluation of a currency that reduces its buying power overnight.

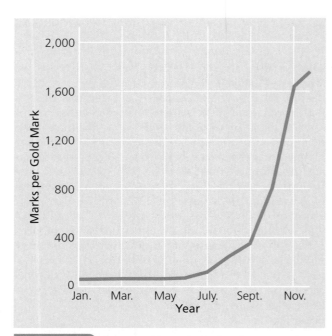

Figure 26.1 **German Hyperinflation in 1922** After 1918 Germany suffered an economic breakdown, due to the punitive war debt payments the state was obligated to assume. It was only after the Dawes Plan came into effect in 1924 that Germany began to recover its economic power. How was the buying power of an average German citizen affected by the change in the value of the German mark between September and November 1922?

Source: Wilkinson, James D.; Huges, H. Stuart, Contemporary Europe: A History, 9th Edition, © 1998, pp. 136. Reprinted by permission of Pearson Education, Inc., Upper Saddle River, NJ.

Dawes Plan Financial agreement concluded by France, Britain, and the United States in 1924 that solved the crisis of war reparations and loans.

Aristide Briand (1862–1932) French foreign minister who orchestrated reconciliation with Germany and the Kellogg-Briand Pact.

Gustav Stresemann (1878–1929) German prime minister and later foreign minister who brought stability to Weimar Germany in the 1920s.

Kellogg-Briand Pact Agreement renouncing war, signed in 1928 by fifteen European countries and the United States and ultimately by sixty-three states.

small businessmen who had been the backbone of Germany's social and economic stability were instantly converted into impassioned and desperate critics of the new German republic.

The Ruhr crisis brought in other mediators, including a commission headed by American statesman and banker Charles G. Dawes. Its recommendations, known as the **Dawes Plan** (1924), set reparation payments at more realistic levels and helped rebuild the economies of other European countries, including Germany's. The United States loaned money to Germany to finance its war debt.

Germany then paid installments to France and Britain as part of its reparations. These payments enabled France and Britain to repay their war loans to the United States. By the second half of the 1920s, Europe's economies seemed restabilized.

With inflation under control in Germany and reparations payments steady, a new mood of reconciliation dominated Franco-German relations. In 1925, the two countries finally accepted their post-1918 common border. The League of Nations, despite the absence of the United States, was active and had a growing membership that after 1926 included Germany. That same year **Aristide Briand**, the French foreign minister, and **Gustav Stresemann**, his German counterpart, received the Nobel Peace Prize for their "unprecedented attempt to base politics on the principle of mutual friendship and trust." In 1928, under the leadership of Briand and U.S. Secretary of State Frank B. Kellogg, fifteen countries signed the **Kellogg-Briand Pact**, which "condemned and renounced war as an instrument of national policy." Though the pact suggested greater U.S. involvement in European affairs, it had no means of enforcement, so it represented more a hope for peace than a guarantee. Still, international relations were now conducted in a relatively democratic and open fashion, a major shift from the prewar order.

 Checking In

By yourself or with a partner, explain the significance of each of the following selected key terms:

Versailles Treaty

Adolf Hitler

Béla Kun

Benito Mussolini

Ruhr occupation

National Socialist German Workers' Party (Nazis)

Dawes Plan

Kellogg-Briand Pact

Postwar Political Experiments, 1924–1929

◆ **What new forms and responsibilities of government emerged during this period?**

◆ **Where and in what ways was democracy successful, and what were its failures?**

In the second half of the 1920s, Europe stabilized. Governments rebounded from the disappointments of the peace treaties and hyperinflation. In western Europe, the most successful political parties were conservative and moderate; liberals and social democrats lacked popular trust. New parties tried to take advantage of this vacuum, most prominently the Italian fascists. In eastern Europe, a combination of older liberal and new agrarian parties had the greatest impact on the young states. Only in Scandinavia was there continuity between the prewar and postwar politics. But everywhere, except for Italy, democratic forms of government seemed solidly in place.

Politics in Western Europe

In the five years after 1918, the politicians of the most powerful European countries—Great Britain, France, and Germany—lost the confidence of their constituents. They had failed to fulfill the promises made before and during the war. Disappointment with the peace treaties and subsequent economic crises further eroded their standing.

Political Contests in Britain and France In Britain, the most important political casualty of the war was the Liberal Party, which never recovered from the growing division over wartime policies. Though **David Lloyd George** had won at Versailles, his position at the helm of the Liberal Party wavered, as many politicians and followers were displeased with the economic and political costs of his aggressive wartime policies. He tried to rebuild his popularity and the unity of the party, but allying himself with Conservative politicians cost him dearly, sending many followers toward the growing Labour Party. While the Liberals floundered, between 1920 and 1929 the Conservative and Labour Parties fought for political power. The Conservatives provided an economic platform and an ideology of security that spoke to the older basis of this party, the upper classes, and also to many among the middle classes who had lost faith in the Liberals. For most of the decade, the Conservatives controlled Parliament and pushed stringent measures to protect business interests, often at the expense of the working and lower middle classes. Yet the British economy did not fully recover from its wartime losses.

Leading the anti-Conservative opposition was the Labour Party, which developed rapidly from a marginal, class-based party to a more popular and broad-based party with socialist ideological leanings that attracted workers in the public service sector and lower ranks of the middle class. Though the Labour Party held power for only a brief nine-month period under **Ramsay MacDonald** (1924), it forced the Conservatives to confront workers' concerns such as the length of the workweek and unemployment benefits as mainstream issues. Just as important was the growing union movement, loosely coordinated with the Labour Party but institutionally independent, which in 1926 forced the Conservatives to deal with workers' concerns through a general strike. The strike failed, but the work rights demanded by the strikers entered the vocabulary of both dominant parties.

In France, the disappointment that followed the peace treaties produced a quick succession of governments. No party—centrist, conservative, or left wing—was able to keep power for long. Only after 1926, under the Republican centrist **Raymond Poincaré**, did a more secure government emerge. He stabilized the currency and secured prosperity, which gave people hope for the future.

Stability in Weimar Germany Germany faced the greatest political challenges after 1919. All prewar political leaders were compromised by defeat, and following the collapse of the monarchy, a new political system had to be created. The political leaders who drafted the progressive democratic constitution and other political institutions in the city of Weimar—which gave its name to the new government, **Weimar Republic**—had the difficult task of gaining the trust of an embittered population. Some nationalist leaders were blamed for the outcome of the war, some liberal leaders had been assassinated by radical nationalists, and some on the left had been tainted by the communist uprisings in 1918–1919, so it was unclear who could fill this vacuum.

The key figure turned out to be Gustav Stresemann, a successful businessman and politician who came from a monarchist conservative background. Before the war he had strongly supported German nationalist aspirations and traditions embodied by the emperor but had looked with some favor upon measures benefiting workers. Above all, he was a realist who knew by 1918 that the old system was bankrupt. For him, democracy was a pragmatic, rather than ideological, choice.

Between 1920 and 1923, when he assumed leadership of the government for one brief year, Stresemann went from opposing the Weimar constitution to supporting it for the sake of stability. After the war, he created the German People's Party to revise the Versailles Treaty, secure economic growth, and offer some support for workers. Stresemann's election as prime minister in 1923 marked a turning point for the Weimar Republic. He stabilized internal politics and, resolving the Ruhr occupation crisis, rebuilt Germany's international stature. Under him, radical right- and left-wing movements were effectively put down, notably the Nazi Party's attempt under Hitler to seize power in Bavaria known as the **Beer Hall Putsch**.

David Lloyd George (1863–1945) British politician who led Britain through World War I and the postwar settlement as the Liberal Party prime minister, 1916–1922.

Ramsay MacDonald (1866–1937) First leader of Britain's Labour Party to become prime minister.

Raymond Poincaré (1860–1934) French politician, president between 1913 and 1920, then twice premier.

Weimar Republic Name of the German state between 1919 and 1933, taken from the city where its democratic constitution was written.

Beer Hall Putsch (in German, "beer hall riot") Violent failed attempt by Hitler and the Nazi Party to take over the Bavarian local government in 1923.

Stresemann's successors were able to maintain stability partly because of his achievements. Although the Weimar Republic proved short lived, it was one of the most democratic and progressive states in Europe, with universal suffrage and protections for workers much more comprehensive than in Great Britain or France, from regulation of the workweek to state unemployment insurance.

Politics in Eastern Europe

After 1918, eastern Europe was responding to dramatic changes in borders and new ethnic compositions and struggling to organize stable governments. Democratic institutions and mass parties were new, so the main concern was order rather than the return to prosperity sought in the west. And while some countries—Czechoslovakia, Poland, the Baltic states, Greece, and Turkey—adopted republican governments to foster democracy, the rest—Hungary, Yugoslavia, Romania, Albania, and Bulgaria—opted for more traditional constitutional monarchies. Neither choice brought stability and democratization, however, as both were compromised by corruption.

The Czechoslovak Democratic Model The only new state to demonstrate relative political stability and economic growth was Czechoslovakia. Like all the other new states in eastern Europe, Czechoslovakia experienced interethnic tensions (among Czechs, Slovaks, and Germans) and political weakness. There were so many parties that no single one could capture the majority in parliament. In almost every election, it was necessary to form coalitions among two or three parties, rendering any government unlikely to follow a clear political agenda. But, unlike other eastern European states, Czechoslovakia was fortunate to have a visionary president, **Tomáš G. Masaryk**, who followed a policy of tolerance toward ethnic minorities. Masaryk was skillful at negotiating and maintaining the trust of the population. He also kept his country out of regional conflicts. Just as significant was his faith in the democratic institutions created after 1918.

Stability Through Autocracy Elsewhere in eastern Europe, leaders manipulated the new democratic institutions to maintain power or sometimes disregarded them altogether in the name of stability. These young democracies had little chance to function properly. In Poland, for instance, **Józef Piłsudski** used his position as leader of the military and war hero to undermine the powers of the parliament. Between 1926, when he executed a military coup to replace the

Tomáš Garrigue Masaryk, Czechoslovakia's first president, came to be known as the father of modern Czechoslovak democracy. Many of his ideas about governing through compromise in order to maintain stability came from the years he spent in the United States. He was also a visionary in this part of Europe in his strong feminist convictions.

Hulton Archive/Corbis

government in power with his own, and until his death in 1935 he sought economic stability, international security, and tolerance for minorities—all worthy goals. But he sacrificed any balanced division of power among the branches of government, showing through his actions that democracy could not work in his country. Piłsudski himself never assumed leadership of the country and preferred instead to manipulate policy making through indirect threats and intrigues. Poland's failure to build democracy was typical of most other eastern European states.

In the former Ottoman lands, Greece and Turkey also aimed for stability and prosperity within their new borders, often disregarding democratic aspirations. Greece had been the first constitutional government in the Balkans and by 1920 had almost a century of political experience with modern parliamentary rule. But experience did not improve its chances at establishing a stable democracy. Instead, Greece became embroiled in expansionist dreams at the expense of Turkey. After 1918, it pursued a series

Tomáš G. Masaryk (1850–1937) First president of Czechoslovakia and a strong supporter of democracy.

Józef Piłsudski (1867–1935) Military leader of Polish liberation forces in World War I and most important political figure between 1926 and 1935.

Stock Montage

Mustafa Kemal took on the surname "Atatürk" to fashion himself as the father of modern Turkey. His main goal was to position Turkey as a modern player in the international arena, rather than a mere survivor of the remnants of the Ottoman Empire. Can you identify elements of his agenda for modernization and secularization from this photograph?

Fascism

While eastern Europe struggled to create democratic institutions, Italy abandoned them altogether. Benito Mussolini established a **fascist** dictatorship that was the decade's first successful challenge to democracy. His model was D'Annunzio's police state in Fiume. Born to a blacksmith and a schoolteacher, Mussolini was a talented writer and speaker. In his youth he joined the Socialist Party and edited left-wing publications. His radical pacifism landed him in jail in 1911. Already he was dreaming of organizing a revolutionary mass movement of workers. But in the fall of 1914, he switched to an aggressive prowar position. In 1917, after he was accidentally wounded by a grenade (not on the battlefield), he turned to writing for a nationalist paper and to promoting his heroic participation in the war.

The Power of Paramilitary Troops Having once spoken for the workers, Mussolini was skillful at exploiting postwar fears of unemployment with proworker rhetoric. In 1919, when strikes led by communist and socialist unions broke out, Mussolini used the popular anti-Bolshevik rhetoric of the time to depict these actions as a threat to Italy's stability. His call attracted young war veterans and other men looking for a good fight. These recruits were organized in closely knit **paramilitary** groups that operated in a strictly hierarchical fashion, copying the army, and took their orders strictly from their leader. They became the *fasci italiani di combattimento*, or "Italian gangs of combat," the predecessors of the Fascist Party.

Mussolini's fascists terrorized members of opposing parties and by 1921 had become a feared group in Italian politics. In October 1922, Mussolini threatened to march on Rome with his fascist troops and seize power from the weakened parliament unless he was named prime minister. King Victor Emmanuel III gave in. Mussolini moved swiftly to eliminate all political parties and establish a one-party authoritarian state in which he personally controlled all branches of the government and a powerful military. On the surface, he continued to maintain a parliamentary system, but

of disastrous military campaigns, only to be defeated and humiliated by **Mustafa Kemal Atatürk's** armies. The territorial losses and repatriation of more than 1.2 million Greeks sent Greek politics into turmoil. In the first half of the 1920s, the king was forced to abdicate, and a new republican system was proclaimed, but it proved ineffective and in 1935 the king returned to the throne. The cradle of democracy proved inauspicious ground for building democratic institutions and practices after 1918.

Turkey also failed in its attempt to foster democracy. Atatürk focused his entire career as president of the new republic (1920–1938) on consolidating parliamentary rule, a secular government, and a new type of military, striving to embody this new spirit through his own rejection of traditional garb and even of wearing the fez. He also pursued modernizing social programs, such as compulsory education for all children and many reforms to empower women. Yet his style of government was not unlike that of Piłsudski, preaching democratization while practicing heavy-handed **authoritarian** tactics. Yet, although substantially diminished in terms of size, during the 1920s Turkey, reshaped by Atatürk, was militarily stronger, more homogeneous, and effectively **secularized**.

Mustafa Kemal Atatürk (1881–1938) President of Turkey from 1920 to 1938 who pursued modernization and secularization in the name of democracy.

authoritarian Concentrating power in the hands of a ruler.

secularization Change in a society from close identification with religious institutions to a more separated relationship, including transfer of institutions from ecclesiastical to civil control.

fascism Radical-right political movement initiated by Benito Mussolini in Italy that replaced parliamentary democracy with authoritarian regimes emphasizing order.

paramilitary Group of civilians trained and organized in a military fashion.

Mussolini's "Italian gangs of combat," the *fascisti*, aimed to embody a new type of man. What are the values represented by their uniforms and expressions on their faces?

United States Holocaust Memorial Museum

only members of his Fascist Party could be elected, and "debate" meant obedience to the party line set by Mussolini himself.

Mussolini as Dictator Despite the existence of government institutions that suggested a division of power among the executive, legislative, and judicial branches, all power rested in the hands of Il Duce— "the leader." At times, Mussolini held as many as seven positions in government ministries, trying to run everything from public works to propaganda and the army. He was obsessed with managing every aspect of government, even making hiring decisions about minor personnel. The light in his office was kept on for the entire period of his rule, and little boys and girls would be told that Il Duce was always there, laboring to bring happiness to the Italian people.

Mobilizing the Nation Italian fascism became an important model for other European politicians critical of democratic parliaments who wished to establish strong authoritarian regimes. Mussolini's regime was particularly attractive because its **corporatist** structure combined political and social stability with the promise of economic growth, thus attempting to solve all the dilemmas of postwar Europe. Eliminating political parties and labor unions, which he claimed were destabilizing, Mussolini instead channeled citizens into corporations run by the state, which would supposedly enable

corporatism System of government that organizes society into industrial, occupational, and professional groups that channel political expression and repress dissent.

them to express their political views and protect their interests. Corporations would, for example, mediate conflicts between employees and employers without disturbing economic production through strikes. In reality, however, corporations were set up mainly to control workers and to disable protests against business leaders and the state.

Special corporations were created for women. These institutions aimed to control women's public activities and at the same time give the illusion that they were actively contributing to the nation's betterment. Mothers' organizations that promoted child care and household management told women it was their patriotic duty to be good mothers and wives and gave them a sense of pride in their domestic chores. But this propaganda also underscored what was *not* proper for women—to engage in employment outside the home and activities outside the family. Feminist ideas about women's economic and political independence were depicted as antipatriotic and dangerous. Women's corporations were meant as much to shape the identity of women as solely mothers and wives as to allow women a place to come together in public.

Corporations successfully changed social and political institutions, but the fascists had more trouble with religious institutions. Mussolini was an unabashed atheist, and his paramilitary troops often showed little respect for the Catholic Church. Yet for most people being Italian was the same as being Catholic. The church had such a central role that it was really impossible to either ignore or fight it. It took Mussolini many years to come to an agreement over the status of the church, the clergy, and Catholic organizations in Italy, but in 1929 he signed a concordat with the pope that recognized the autonomy of Vatican and reinforced the dominance of the church in education and marriage law. Relations with the church continued to be rocky in some areas, but most Italians were pleased with this agreement, which greatly increased Mussolini's popularity.

Fascist Economics Finally, the fascist government attempted to solve the problem of economic underdevelopment by increasing agricultural productivity, enlarging the male workforce, and creating public works such as roads and irrigation. There was a program to reclaim land, a program to improve wheat production, a program to promote agricultural self-sufficiency (encouraging purchases exclusively from the internal market), a program to increase the birthrate, and a program to improve transportation and build highways and railways. The economy was still primarily in the hands of private entrepreneurs and farmers, but the state played an important role in regulating business practices (for example, by eliminating trade unions and dictating priorities in production), communications, and commerce, especially international trade. To some unstable European states, the fascist government's strong grip over both business and labor seemed to have solved the era's political and economic difficulties.

Policing the Nation Yet fascist solutions were neither simply pragmatic nor wholly positive. Workers' rights were reduced for the benefit of industry; farmers' production was closely scrutinized; and women's rights were severely restricted for the benefit of families, their bodies closely monitored for the purpose of reproduction, especially through **pro-natalist** and anti-birth control policies.

Those who were not willing to abide by these restrictions, or who were defined as dangerous on account of their convictions, ethnicity, or religion, were severely persecuted. To be communist, non-Italian, feminist, or, especially after 1936, Jewish was a dangerous identity. These populations were threatened by economic and social discrimination, subsequently by isolation, and, starting in the late 1930s, by extermination. Thus, in addition to positive definitions of what it meant to be a true Italian, Mussolini imposed categories of unacceptable identities on some.

The Power of Propaganda But in the 1920s, Mussolini was able to hide these negative aspects of his regime through masterful propaganda. Newspapers, films, radio broadcasts, parades, museums, and other state institutions and activities portrayed him as a man of the people and a resolute leader ready to listen and respond to the needs of all Italians. Most people could not imagine their country without Mussolini at the helm: "Italians of my generation carried the portrait of Mussolini within themselves, even before they were of an age to recognize it on the walls," remembered a writer who grew up in the 1920s. Mussolini's image was in every government office and classroom, and his personal style directed fashion trends. Both men and women were attracted to Il Duce—the first political leader to turn his baldness into a symbol of virility and strength. In making himself such a vivid model of the new Italian, Mussolini helped transform the ideals of a whole generation. Marching in the streets by the thousands, in their stylish black uniforms, young men experienced power as intoxicating; on the sidewalks, young women swooned. Their emotions rendered them loyal followers in the hands of the charismatic and cunning Duce.

Social Democracy in Scandinavia

A very different approach to the economic and social problems of the postwar period can be seen in the Scandinavian countries, which used the tools of democracy. Here a tradition of charitable work and support for state intervention in matters of employment had existed since the late nineteenth century. Questions regarding the role of government in education, public health, child care, unemployment, and pensions were often the subject of debate in parliament. Social democratic and labor parties had a large presence in Scandinavian parliaments both before and after the war, and they guaranteed that social welfare measures would continue to be on the agenda. In 1923, Norway introduced old-age pensions. Denmark endorsed the principle of full rights for government social services, such as education, health care, and pensions for all citizens, irrespective of class or gender. Sweden launched a system of unemployment benefits, state support for health, and life insurance.

Scandinavian countries were thus at the forefront in establishing the **welfare state**, and their innovative reforms averted both social unrest and state bankruptcy. Yet the Scandinavian context was unique in Europe. With the exception of Finland, Scandinavia had been sheltered from war. The small size and ethnic homogeneity of these countries also helped preserve their stability. Quite simply, the sense of crisis and despair that dominated most of Europe in early 1919 was not present in Scandinavia. Instead, reforms that built on the prewar social welfare agendas proceeded, as the dominant political parties were never discredited by the war. Continuity, rather than upheaval, best describes the political and social development of Scandinavia in the 1920s.

pro-natalism Policy encouraging women to have more children, pursued by most European governments after 1918 to replenish the postwar population.

welfare state State in which the government assumes responsibility for social needs such as public health, education, and unemployment insurance; pioneered in Scandinavia.

Checking In

By yourself or with a partner, explain the significance of each of the following selected key terms:

Weimar Republic	fascist
Beer Hall Putsch	paramilitary
Mustafa Kemal Atatürk	corporatist
authoritarian	welfare state

The New Soviet State

♦ **What were the essential components of the Soviet state?**

♦ **How did the Bolsheviks reshape society and individual identities?**

The most radical experiment of the 1920s was the Soviet state. Out of a bloody civil war, the Bolsheviks were able to create a smaller but stronger country in which they reinvented the state and reshaped society according to Marxist-Leninist ideology. The Bolsheviks succeeded because of the unprecedented level of control imposed on every aspect of public life, rendering the Communist Party all-powerful and individuals fearful of the party's every move. The Bolsheviks also tried to attract people to the party by promising a better life for workers and peasants. By 1929, the Soviet Union had consolidated into a stable police state.

The Civil War

Russia left the Great War in 1918 after the Treaty of Brest-Litovsk, but the country was soon embroiled in a civil war between the Bolsheviks and their supporters, known as the Reds, and an alliance of supporters of the old order, known as the Whites, that included military officers, nobles, and anti-Bolsheviks (supporters of liberalism and democracy) inside Russia and out. In their attempt to stamp out the Bolshevik threat, France, Britain, the United States, and Japan sent troops and financial help to the Whites. In addition, the newly independent Baltic republics and Poland, which wished to secure their territorial gains, also pursued a war against the Bolsheviks.

Trotsky and the Victory of the Reds Though fighting a desperate war on its borderlands—from the Baltic and Siberia to the Crimea—the Bolsheviks won. What they lacked in experience and military power they made up for in organization and unity of purpose. They had charismatic,

Comintern International organization set up by the Russian Bolsheviks in 1919 to promote communist revolutions all over the world.

driven leaders who inspired great loyalty in their followers. Among them was War Commissar Leon Trotsky, described by an American observer as "the most dramatic character" and the "only great organizer" of the Russian Revolution. Trotsky was a skilled military leader who turned some of the most difficult battles of the civil war into victories. With his wild hair and piercing glare behind wire-rimmed glasses, Trotsky inspired many people, especially among the poor, to join the Reds. Like Mussolini, Trotsky represented a new style of leader whose ability to project virility, demand action, and use violence made them attractive to the generation that came of age during the war.

By contrast, the Whites were divided in their aims and strategies, and the foreign aid they received was half-hearted. By 1922, these supporters were pulling out their war-weary armies and the Reds were winning in the Crimea and Siberia. Poland remained a serious threat, but the new states of eastern Europe did not challenge the Bolshevik regime itself. By 1922, the Reds had won the war by simply giving up some territories in the west, then consolidating their control over the rest of the country.

Beginnings of a New Order The civil war set in motion some important trends later formalized as components of the Soviet regime. In 1918, the Bolsheviks nationalized almost all industry, legislated the obligation for all adults to work, and placed the government in charge of commercial activities. Another element of the civil war that became permanent was a secret police apparatus, the Cheka, which employed brutal methods to silence enemies. In its first six years, the Cheka killed more than two hundred thousand people. Overall, the human losses in these years, due to military conflict, starvation, and various epidemics, is estimated by some at above 4 million.

In 1919, the Bolsheviks also created the Communist International, or **Comintern**, as a means for promoting world revolution, an extension of Trotsky's belief in the mission of the Soviet Union to transform the world into a "workers' paradise." This organization provided financial support and ideological guidance to communist movements abroad. In exchange, the Soviets demanded that all Communist Parties of the Comintern abandon cooperation with socialist and other left-wing noncommunist organizations; they were to take orders only from Moscow. These developments prefigured the more aggressive policies of political purging and terror, state-controlled economy, and communist imperialism that came to define the Soviet Union in the 1930s.

But in 1922, the Bolsheviks had the more basic tasks of creating a stable political system and reinvigorating the economy. The communist regime of those years was more open to experiments in economic production, propaganda, and social programs than at any other time.

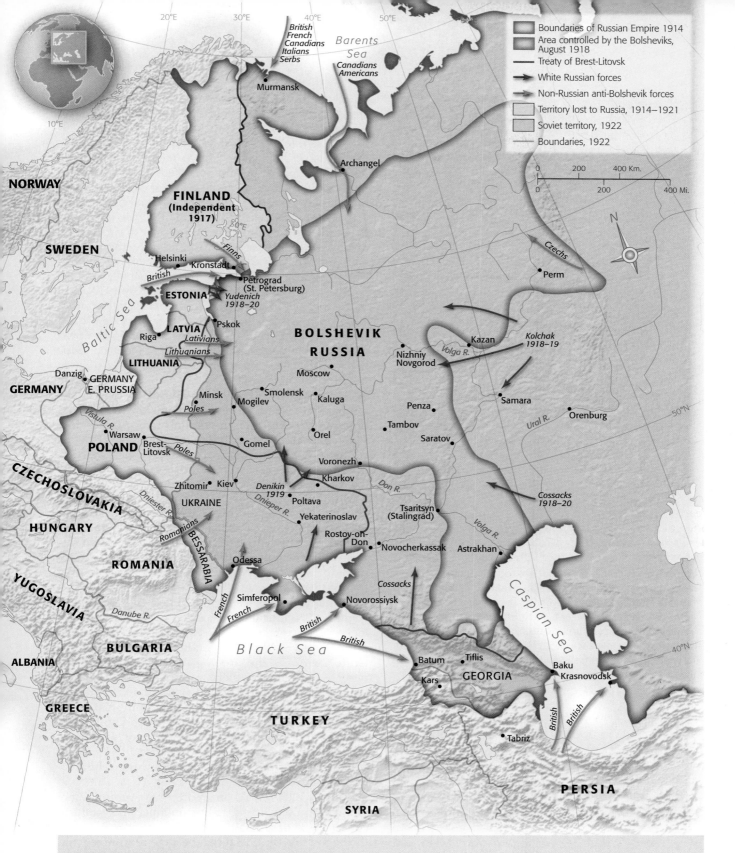

Map 26.2 **The Russian Civil War, 1918–1922** The Russian Civil War proved to be a second conflict of attrition after World War I, engulfing large parts of Russia and lasting almost three years. The victory of the Reds (Bolsheviks) came at a high human and territorial price, as Russia lost many of its western imperial lands. © *Cengage Learning*

1. Looking at the shifts in the territory controlled by Bolshevik forces, as well as the 1914 versus 1922 borders, how would you describe the territorial challenges to Russia during this period?
2. Where were lasting changes most radical? What countries had the most to gain from these losses?

"Workers of the World Unite!" declares this Soviet poster in large red letters. The Soviet propaganda of the 1920s focused on the success of the workers' revolution in crushing the forces of oppression, depicted here through the crown and royal mantle, as well as the shield and broken chains, on which the worker steps with calm confidence. What relationship between workers and peasants does the poster suggest? What role does it depict for women?

Union of Soviet Socialist Republics (USSR) Official name of the Soviet Union, a federation of four, and eventually fifteen, autonomous republics, the largest and most powerful of which was Russia.

Zhenotdel Women's Section of the Soviet Communist Party, which focused on policies and issues such as employment, day care, and domestic work.

The Communist Regime

In December 1922, the **Union of Soviet Socialist Republics (USSR)** came into being. The ideological and legal foundations of this state combined the writings of Karl Marx and Friedrich Engels with V. I. Lenin's own ideas.

Ideological Foundations

One fundamental principle of the new order was equality, understood very differently from the definition offered in the U.S. Declaration of Independence. Instead of focusing on equal rights for pursuing individual goals, the Soviets focused on economic equality: all people who worked were *equally* entitled to the fruits of their labor. This principle also implied that differences in wealth and class were fundamentally unjust, as they were based on the oppression of one class (the workers) by another (the bourgeoisie). The Soviet state set out to eliminate these injustices, first by taking all property and means of production away from the bourgeoisie and nobility and then by enabling workers to gain control over the economy. The proletariat, or workers, the producers of goods, were to control the fruits of their labor. By 1922, most of the means of production were under state control. The system the Bolsheviks imagined was entirely untested. No other country in the world had attempted such a fundamental transformation of the economic and social system overnight.

Strategies for Political Consolidation

The Soviet Union also had to address problems of political stability and control. The revolution took place before workers had achieved full "consciousness" of class conflicts, one of the Marxist prerequisites for a communist revolution. Lenin made it an important goal for the Bolshevik regime to consolidate political power both by inclusive means, educating the workers and peasants, and by exclusionary tactics, eliminating enemies of the Bolsheviks. Propaganda and a secret police with an extensive network of informants were essential for this effort, and both had been solidified during the civil war. By 1922, they were essential in building state institutions and programs.

Finally, the Soviet regime aimed to open opportunities for political participation to people who had lacked a voice before 1917. This goal was also incorporated into Soviet propaganda: the party would listen to the needs and problems of the oppressed and defend their rights; these promises would induce people to join the party and its affiliated organizations. The Women's Section of the Communist Party, or **Zhenotdel**, was one such institution. The Bolsheviks had critiqued the inferior status of women in Russian society and attempted to attract them to the Communist Party through this department. Initially led by Alexandra Kollontai (see A New Direction feature), it also served as an advocacy group where women could voice social, economic, and political concerns. Though democratic and experimental at the beginning, by 1928 it had become centralized and authoritarian and was eventually dissolved.

For all its positive propaganda, the exclusionary policies of the Soviet regime raised questions even among the faithful. Did the ends justify the means? Supposedly, communism was about democratic equality and justice. Yet the road to it was paved with violence, and the new institutions of the Soviet Union concentrated power in the hands of a small party elite.

Snark/Art Resource, NY

By the mid-1920s, there were furious debates within the party over centralization, with Trotsky in fierce opposition. In addition, although the party claimed that individuals had choices and that the state was interested in their ideas, most institutions suppressed ideas and actions that were contrary to the official party line. Soviet citizens received protection from the state only insofar as they were willing to serve the state with unquestioning loyalty.

The New Economic Policy and Struggle for Leadership

As the Soviet regime was attempting to deal with enemies at home and in the borderlands, its economy worsened.

Economic Challenges Nationalizing all industry did not lead to economic growth. In 1921, industrial production was just 13 percent of the prewar volume. Many of the best-trained professionals left the country, peasants refused to work for the state, and workers went on strike. Lenin realized that the regime needed to adopt a pragmatic economic policy to win the civil war and consolidate political control. In the spring of 1921, he inaugurated the **New Economic Policy (NEP)**, which allowed for the rebirth of private property and free commerce. The state retained control over large- and medium-size industries, such as steel and heavy machinery, but small businesses could be privately owned. Under the NEP, three-quarters of retail trade shifted back into private hands. In the countryside, the state allowed peasants to sell their own harvests rather than have the state requisition them at fixed prices. The recovery of the economy was remarkable. By the end of the 1920s, the Soviet Union had reached 1914 levels in agricultural production.

Factionalization and Stalin's Victory But the social and political costs of this recovery seemed too high to many Bolsheviks. The NEP had fostered the rebirth of an entrepreneurial class that was a nuisance to local communist administrators. On the one hand, the regime spoke about the need to eliminate class oppression and give workers control over the means of production. On the other hand, the state allowed for the kind of exploitation it condemned, based on pragmatic considerations. This double standard weakened the control of the Soviet regime and troubled faithful party members.

A struggle over the political costs of the NEP ensued in the **Politburo** the highest decision-making body of the Communist Party. Lenin's death in January 1924 rendered this debate more complex because Politburo members became divided. Trotsky and his leftist supporters wanted to continue the revolutionary struggle in the world at all cost. This group also opposed the NEP as a deviation from communism and was concerned about the growing centralization of the

state, which clashed with the democratic foundations of communism. Their strongest opponents were the centrists, led by **Joseph Stalin**, who called for building socialism in the Soviet Union, de-emphasizing the struggle for worldwide revolution. Stalin stressed the principal role to be played by Russia in the USSR and suggested the need to further centralize the state. This position was favored by Russian communists with nationalist leanings.

In the end, Stalin won the struggle by working behind the scenes in the Politburo and among his loyal lower party appointees. Few anticipated his victory, as he was less respected than Trotsky. Stalin was, however, a cunning man who advanced his career through power politics. Born in the Georgian Caucasus as Joseph Dzhugashvili, he joined a Marxist group while studying to become a priest and later worked with local Bolsheviks. He undertook dangerous actions on behalf of the movement, ending up in jail and exile, but he was neither a theoretician like Lenin nor an organizer like Trotsky. He simply happened to have a good instinct for showing up in the right place at the right time and knowing whom to flatter and whose weaknesses to exploit.

By the early 1920s, Stalin had risen to the top of the Bolshevik hierarchy, but neither Lenin nor the other leaders thought he would be Lenin's successor; they assumed that would be Trotsky. Stalin was clever, however, in exploiting Trotsky's criticisms of the NEP and other policies as evidence of disloyalty; eventually Trotsky was eliminated from leadership and sent into exile. Then Stalin removed all remaining opponents. By 1928, he dominated all institutions of the state in dictatorial fashion, much like Mussolini in Italy, but without the fascist leader's personal allure.

The New Soviet Man and Woman

The Bolsheviks wanted nothing short of a complete transformation of society. They depicted capitalism as a system that bred greed, narrow-minded materialism, and pettiness among people and described their own aims in terms of transforming individual and collective identity to foster fairness, selflessness, and dedication to the common good.

Class Enemies To eliminate class differences, supposedly the root of all capitalist problems, the party used brutal policies. In addition to abolishing private property in the early days of the civil war, the Bolsheviks

New Economic Policy (NEP) Economic plan allowing limited capitalism adopted by Lenin in 1921 to alleviate Russia's deep economic crisis.

Politburo Highest decision-making body of the Soviet Communist Party.

Joseph Stalin (1879–1953) Dictatorial leader of the Soviet Union from 1929 to 1953, who transformed the Soviet Union into a police state run by fear and deceit, and into a military and economic superpower.

Alexandra Kollontai Becomes a Revolutionary

At age twenty-two, Alexandra Kollontai seemed to have achieved everything expected of a young aristocratic woman. The daughter of a general in Russia's imperial army, she was well educated, privileged, and active in St. Petersburg's high society. She married an army officer and gave him a son. She was obedient and devoted. Then she read August Bebel's *Woman and Socialism*. His ideas that under capitalism women were fundamentally subjugated through the institution of marriage and could achieve full independence only under socialism convinced her that she was enslaved.

She started attending lectures by radical socialists and visiting factories to see the conditions in which the workers, especially women, of St. Petersburg labored. Her secure and privileged life now seemed nothing more than a gilded cage, and she knew she could never go back to it. At age twenty-five, she abandoned her husband and child, disowned her aristocratic heritage, moved out on her own, and embarked on a remarkable career of revolutionary activism.

Beginning in 1898, she worked with underground Marxist organizations in Russia and abroad. She was an outspoken organizer of women workers, an important opponent of World War I, and leader of the International Women's Day demonstration for bread and peace that triggered the overthrow of the tsar in March 1917. In November 1917, she was at the forefront of the armed Bolshevik uprising.

Though a devoted Bolshevik, Kollontai was never satisfied with just following the party line; she insisted on speaking her mind and following her convictions, regardless of the consequences. Thus, in 1918 she found herself to be the sole opponent of the Treaty of Brest-Litovsk, which she viewed as abandoning the Finnish communist movement, and resigned from her government position as commissar for social welfare. She remained an inconvenience to the Bolshevik leadership throughout the early 1920s, never afraid to stand up to anyone, even V. I. Lenin.

Cleverly, Lenin dealt with Kollontai's radicalism by sending her abroad. In November 1922, she was appointed to the Soviet legation in Norway, then sent to Mexico and to Sweden. Far from Moscow, Kollontai was free to criticize the Bolshevik regime without posing a real threat inside the center of power. Yet she continued to play an important role in the Soviet Union. She was among the first female diplomats in the world to serve at such a high level and was regarded in the diplomatic international community as a very able colleague. Even when sidelined, Kollontai was a trendsetter.

Kollontai's radicalism was most remarkable in her work as the first leader of the Women's Section of the Communist Party (the Zhenotdel). Following Bebel's principles, she advocated an end to marriage and the nuclear family in favor of living in free unions and raising children in communal settings, where domestic chores—cleaning, cooking, and child care—would be shared. She lived by her convictions but was unable to inspire others to do the same. Most women were not ready to abandon the satisfaction and security of marriage and motherhood, and men resisted her radical ideas. Yet Kollontai's choice for freedom and courage to reshape her identity according to her radical beliefs made her a symbol of revolutionary experiments in politics and social relations that marked the decade after the Great War.

---

also wished to eliminate all "oppressors," especially the social and economic elites of the tsarist regime—the aristocracy, businessmen, and the professional middle class. In the first phase of this social revolution, the Bolsheviks imprisoned or killed most members of the nobility. The bourgeoisie was also a class enemy, but it was a larger and less clearly defined category. Initially, the Soviet regime eliminated businessmen, easily targeted as exploiters of workers, by nationalizing their wealth and killing many. But if the bourgeoisie included all those who owned private property, it would include peasants as well.

Class enemies also included white-collar workers, professionals, and some educators. Those employed in state institutions, such as bureaucrats and teachers, became targets because of their allegiance to the tsarist regime. Doctors and engineers were viewed as a threat because they belonged to professions with standards independent of the political regime, and the Soviets could not tolerate independence. Doctors, chemists, and engineers often had to join the party to maintain their professional standing.

Education and Secularization As large numbers of qualified individuals were removed from professions badly needed in the economy, education, and social services, the party embarked on its own program of education and training to fill gaps. The government considered eliminating illiteracy (above 50 percent in 1918) an important social goal and created many public schools, but quality was poor. Progress and access to higher education were linked to class background, with priority given to sons and daughters of workers, often at the expense of academic qualifications. The first generation of teachers, doctors, and engineers produced by this system were more likely to be faithful party activists than skilled professionals.

Alexandra Kollontai Advocates a New Type of Woman

While away from the Soviet Union, Kollontai published other radical writings, including the book from which the following selection is taken, *The Autobiography of a Sexually Emancipated Communist Woman*, first published in Norway in 1926.

❶ Kollontai uses the terms "unfit" and "natural selection" to connect capitalism to a certain scientific theory of the nineteenth century. What is she referring to?

❷ What is Kollontai implying about marriage?

❸ How do working women revolt against past "truths?" Does Kollontai criticize or celebrate this challenge?

❹ What does Kollontai's criticism here imply about bourgeois women's movements?

❺ Is the women's movement for liberation separate, or does it have to be part of a larger working-class movement? Why?

But who are they, these single new women? The single woman—she is a child of the large-scale capitalist economic system. ❶ There is no place in the ranks of those earning their own livelihood for the "unfit," that is to say, the women of the old type. Here, too, therefore, a "natural selection" among the women of the different social strata is discernible: only the stronger, more resistant disciplined natures arrive in the ranks of those "earning their own livelihood." ❷ The weak, inwardly passive, cling to the family hearth, and when the insecurity of existence tears them away from the protection of the family, to catapult them into the stream of life, supinely, they let themselves be driven by the waves of legal or illegal prostitution: they enter into a marriage of convenience or they walk the streets.

❸ The influence of women earning their own livelihood spreads far beyond their own circle. With their criticism, they "poison" the minds of their contemporaries, they smash old idols, they raise the banner of revolt against those "truths" with which women have lived for generations. By liberating themselves, the new, single women, earning their own livelihood, also liberate the passive-backward spirit, as this has been molded down the centuries, of their contemporary sisters.

❹ But whereas with the women of the working class, the struggle for the assertion of their rights, the strengthening of their personality, coincides with the interests of the class, the women of other social strata run into unexpected obstacles: the ideology of their class is hostile to the transformation of the feminine type. In the bourgeois milieu, woman's "rebellion" bears a far sharper character, its forms are set in bolder relief, and here the psychological dramas are far sharper, more variegated, and more complicated. ❺ The new type of woman, inwardly self-reliant, independent, and free, corresponds with the morality which the working class is elaborating precisely in the interests of its class. For the working class the accomplishment of its mission does not require that she be a handmaid of the husband, an impersonal domestic creature, endowed with passive, feminine traits. Rather, it requires a personality rising and rebelling against every kind of slavery, an active conscious equal member of the community, of the class.

Source: *The Autobiography of a Sexually Emancipated Communist Woman*, by Alexandra Kollontai (1971, Herder & Herder).

The Soviets used education to promote secularization and a rational understanding of Marxist economy. Though presented as scientific, the Marxist worldview was akin to a religious vision of history. Communists described eliminating class struggle as scientifically predictable. Yet there was no way of proving such developments. Instead, it was through a leap of faith that the Bolsheviks spoke of the certain "withering away of the state" and the inevitable victory of communism throughout the world. Like other religious zealots, revolutionaries such as Trotsky and Kollontai were willing to sacrifice both themselves and all who stood in their way for the fulfillment of this destiny.

Organized religion, however, was seen as irrational and a threat to Soviet ideology. The Orthodox Church, the state religion in tsarist Russia, emphasized faith in the afterlife and accepted the hardships of this life as normal, something to be embraced, not overcome. Social inequality was a fact of life. These beliefs clashed with the staunch atheism of the Bolsheviks. In addition, the Orthodox Church was rich and influential. It owned large estates and economic interests and commanded a great deal of respect, even fear, among the Russian population. From the beginning of their struggle in 1918, the Bolsheviks persecuted members of this and all other religious institutions, clergy and laypeople alike. These persecutions continued throughout the 1920s, forcing believers to retreat to private places of worship, including homes and forests. Yet the complete elimination of all religious organizations did not become a goal of the Soviet Union until after 1928.

Reshaping Gender Roles In their ambition to transform Russian society, the Soviets also sought to reshape private lives, including family and gender relations. The Bolsheviks were quick to replace religious marriage with civil marriage. Young couples now came to city hall to be married before a judge in a ritual that incorporated statements of loyalty to the Soviet regime and the Communist Party. Some party leaders, like Kollontai, believed that marriage itself should be eliminated, as it institutionalized the oppression of one-half of humanity, women, by the other half, men. Only free love, without the constrictions of marriage, would end this oppression. There were some early attempts to create communal housing for those who lived together but were not married and also to give children born out of wedlock full legal rights. The more radical leadership of the party envisioned a future in which children would be brought up in communal housing where domestic chores would be shared.

But the Communist Party shied away from such radical change. Bolshevik leaders themselves lived in traditional marriages and considered Kollontai's ideas threatening to social stability. By the end of the 1920s, the party had come around to condemning those who were not married and extolling the virtues of the proletarian family. Nuclear families remained the foundation of social stability, yet with more freedom to enter and exit such unions for both partners. In particular, divorce was liberalized, allowing women protection against domestic violence, which had not been recognized as a basis for dissolving marriages under previous divorce laws.

Women also gained more reproductive control. Early on, the Soviet regime legalized abortion and made it inexpensive. The liberalization of abortion would be short lived, however. By the end of the decade, the Communist Party had revised its policies, partly out of fear of depopulation. Under Stalin, abortion was made illegal again.

A lasting change, however, involved the support for and protection of women's employment and education as well as the creation of state child-care institutions for working mothers. These measures helped women become more economically self-sufficient and can thus be viewed as progressive reforms, similar to social welfare measures in Scandinavia during the 1920s. Yet the Soviet regime was interested only in increasing the workforce and fashioning loyal citizens through education. The Soviets looked upon women as an important means for fulfilling these aims rather than as oppressed individuals. Women would not have a choice of motherhood or employment. Rather, they would have to join the workforce and leave child rearing in part to state institutions such as kindergartens and schools.

Checking In

By yourself or with a partner, explain the significance of each of the following selected key terms:

Comintern	New Economic Policy (NEP)
Union of Soviet Socialist Republics (USSR)	Politburo
Zhenotdel	Joseph Stalin

Social and Cultural Experiments

◆ **How did social reformers and intellectuals respond to the aftermath of war?**

◆ **How did the war and technology transform culture and entertainment in this era?**

Social reformers, intellectuals, and artists throughout Europe tried to cope with the disruptions of war in radical ways as well. The experience of total war forced both men and women to re-examine many assumptions about their roles in the family and society. This process prompted important changes in gender relations, but fewer than reformers, especially feminists, hoped to achieve. Artists grappled with loss and destruction by fashioning entirely new artistic styles, some democratic and socially engaged and others an escape into dream worlds. Widespread violence had become an everyday experience, and many embraced it as a potentially positive force in art. Others recoiled from the memory of this violence and turned to pacifism and religious faith. Some of these trends had started before 1914 but were greatly reshaped by war's destruction and transformation of European society. These experiments produced some of the most remarkable works of literature and art of the twentieth century as well as important developments in popular entertainment.

Change and Frustration in Gender Roles

The war had brought upheaval in gender roles, and with the resumption of peace, many wondered if the changes would continue. More than in any previous conflict, the experiences of soldiers had been so vastly different from those of civilians that a great gap opened between husbands and wives, mothers and sons, fathers and daughters.

Pushing Women Out of the Workforce The experience of total war had placed both soldiers and civilians in direct contact with violence, but the physical and psychological burdens of trench warfare often crippled soldiers in unprecedented ways. Returning soldiers suffered from deep psychological trauma and were unable to communicate their suffering to noncombatants. So many soldiers had gruesome injuries that the sight of a maimed body became commonplace. Deep psychological and physical scars forced veterans to question their masculinity and often strained relationships at home; domestic violence increased. These men yearned to have their old jobs and the prestige they had enjoyed before the war, but nothing could go back to the way it had been.

Many women had entered "male" professions and jobs during the war. After 1918, both government and private businesses preferred to rehire men, however, even for positions in which women had been effective and had accepted lower wages. The idea that men were breadwinners and women were nurturers remained strong, but not all women returned to the home. Many continued to work, but in jobs that were less secure and poorly paid, including domestic and secretarial work and factory work in the food industry. Women also were increasingly important as consumers, as evidenced by the greater diversity in goods available at both the low and high ends of the markets. An aggressive fashion industry focused on "working girls" and independent women. The image of the flapper, or "new woman," was plastered all over fashion magazines and movie posters. These changes suggested new identities opening up for women.

Yet little changed for women in the domestic sphere. They were still considered primarily responsible for child care, cooking, and tending to the home. Unlike the Scandinavian welfare experiments and the Bolshevik revolution in women's family responsibilities, governments in the rest of Europe paid little attention to child-care questions. Consequently, women found it difficult to both work and take care of their families, or they did so with enormous effort and little support.

Fighting for Political Rights Still, in the realm of politics women made important gains, achieving voting rights except in France, Italy, Spain, and the Balkans, where they could vote only in local elections. The extent of women's suffrage varied and often included educational, marriage, and age criteria at a time when universal male suffrage was the norm. But even as feminists celebrated this victory, they also wondered how much power women had really gained. Though women could vote, their concerns were not necessarily reflected in party platforms, nor were female politicians successful in the first decade after the war. Traditional parties, even liberal and socialist ones with pro-women platforms, were unwilling to put forth female candidates. Questions about women's rights seemed subordinate to the pressing issues of the Bolshevik threat, war debt, inflation, unemployment, and revisionism.

Pro-Natalism Politicians appealed to women as mothers and wives, asking them to place family and nation above their individual selves and help rebuild their nation. In France, for instance, a pro-natalist campaign for replenishing the human losses in the war involved a stern government demand that all women of childbearing age, regardless of economic status, produce as many children as possible to regenerate the fighting force. Women were described as patriotic and selfless if they responded to this call and as heartless materialists if they indicated interest in attaining economic independence or limiting their families. There was no comparable campaign to shame men into fatherhood.

Most European governments were concerned with population growth and hoped to revive the birthrate with positive incentives, such as monetary rewards and patriotic propaganda, and negative measures, such as the criminalization of abortion. Some reformers with similar concerns took a different position on reproduction. They saw sexual satisfaction as key to a couple's desire to reproduce and have a happy family. In the decade after the war, a diverse movement advocating sexual reform emerged. It was a response, in part, to the marital problems many couples were having after years of separation during the war. Husbands who came back with psychological traumas and physical disabilities were often unable to perform sexually; and women, who had gained tremendous self-confidence during the war years, found themselves more interested in an active role in sexual relations. Reformers wrote manuals for couples, encouraging the exploration of mutual sexual satisfaction, and doctors provided sex advice to husbands. Sex advice columns began to appear in women's magazines. Even though the ideas about what constituted normal sex and pleasure were conventional, removing the taboo on discussing such matters in public and emphasizing women's sexual needs were important and lasting changes.

Bildarchiv Preussischer Kulturbesitz, © 2007 Artists Rights Society (ARS), NY

Hannah Höch's collage *Cut with a Cake Knife* (1919) is an example of the Dada movement, which flourished during and right after World War I. Höch's work explored the contradictions of contemporary society in an aggressively ironic feminist vein. What are some of the visual elements and symbols she uses in her critique?

Intellectual Responses to the War

The destruction wrought by war prompted the rise of important intellectual movements in the decade after 1918. Among the cries for revenge and revolution, some intellectuals took a stand for peace. The postwar pacifist movement was in part a continuation of prewar pacifism and in part a reflection of Europe's political strategy to keep the peace, but it was no longer linked to particular political ideologies and organizations. It was more of an individual reaction to the horrors of war, a conclusion that no ideology—nationalism, liberalism, communism—could justify the enormous human losses.

Pacifism Many pacifists came from socialist or religious backgrounds, but some were completely non-ideological. Among the most prominent figures were the German physicist **Albert Einstein** and British writer **Vera Brittain**, who spent the war as a volunteer nurse and wrote as early as 1914: "The destruction of men seems a crime to the whole march of civilisation." Einstein's strong pacifism was unusual for a prominent scientist. In the following decade, he continued to be an outspoken critic of fascism and antisemitism at a time when other scientists were retreating into their labs or committing their research to the service of states with destructive agendas. The impact of the peace movement was small by comparison to the more forceful and well-organized fascist and communist ones. Yet the personal courage of individuals who stood up against the aggressive nationalism of the coming decade represents an important legacy.

Religious Rejuvenation Some intellectuals and artists reacted to the destruction of the war by taking on an overtly atheistic and often Marxist position on religion, whereas others sought spiritual rejuvenation, prompting a revival of Christianity. Among these were several prominent thinkers of the time. In Britain, T. S. Eliot and Aldous Huxley turned away from secularization to find spiritual and intellectual solace in religion. The French philosopher and atheist **Gabriel Marcel** converted to Catholicism. Marcel attempted to find a concrete philosophy of being engaged in the world, but through spirituality, and moved away from abstractions such as truth or progress toward a focus on the everyday experience of pain, joy, and other basic human emotions.

Artistic Experiments

In contrast, in the arts, the decade of the 1920s was spectacular. Writers, painters, dancers, musicians—all types of artists and performers—revolutionized both high culture and popular entertainment. These experiments were connected both to a longer tradition of the avant-garde in the arts, dating from the end of the nineteenth century, and to the war, whose trauma had a direct impact on basic questions about beauty and goodness in the face of overwhelming destruction.

Futurism Several movements in the art world flourished during this period. The Futurists believed in a future marked by technology, power, and even violence. They saw war as a positive tool for cleansing all that was putrid in society and preparing for an era of strength. Futurists became close allies of radical political movements. In Italy, **Filippo Marinetti**, whose paintings depicted movement and speed on canvas, served as Mussolini's minister of the arts. In Russia, poet **Vladimir Mayakovsky** led a generation of Futurist writers who promoted Bolshevism.

Surrealism Even though the Futurists were original, they did not produce the lasting masterpieces created by the **Surrealists**. These visionaries sought alternatives to the "reality" of the visible world in the inner world of dreams and nightmares, the subconscious and suppressed, which they considered more truthful to the human condition and suffering than the decade's obsession with wealth and social stability. Adapting the new interest in psychoanalysis to art, they rebelled against rationality, ignored politics, and explored the mind. The first Surrealist manifesto, authored by the French writer **André Breton**, appeared in Paris in 1924 and declared this movement a revolution, outlining in form and content how Surrealism was to alter human consciousness. Artists, poets, and filmmakers rallied to his call to explore the subconscious and reject immediate reality.

The movement continued to flourish until World War II, with Spanish artist **Salvador Dali** and Belgian painter **René Magritte** as some of its most spectacular practitioners. Dali's haunting work portrayed a dream world, in which distortions of everyday objects were rendered in photographic detail and placed in hallucinatory settings. Dali lived his art, appearing in public in bizarre costumes, sporting a fantastic mustache, immaculate yet always strange. In keeping with Surrealistic principles, he showed no interest in politics. Unlike the colorful Dali, Magritte was far more cerebral and understated, and his paintings reached into dream worlds by a scrupulous, photographic rendition of objects in surprising settings. This paradoxical juxtaposition of the real and unreal, rather than distortion, became Magritte's signature.

Expressionism Other artists more directly engaged with political and social upheavals became affiliated with **Expressionism**. This movement had been developing since the beginning of the twentieth century but took on more social and political tones after the war. German artist **Käthe Kollwitz**, for example, had been a committed socialist and pacifist before the war, depicting the social problems of the working class, especially women and children. The loss of her son in the early days of the war brought on a deep personal crisis. In contrast to the dream world of the Surrealists, her stark woodcuts projected the pain and suffering of people whose emotions were a direct response to the outside world and real events.

Artistic Avant-Garde in the Soviet Union Much more committed to linking artistic experimentation and political engagement were the artists who were active during the first decade of the Soviet Union. Among early devoted supporters of Bolshevism were writers such as Mayakovsky and artists such as **Marc Chagall**. In the early 1920s, Chagall developed his unique dreamlike combination of color and religious imagery. Cinema directors such as **Sergei Eisenstein** produced remarkable films like *Battleship Potemkin* that revolutionized cinema.

His techniques in framing, lighting, and composition were stark and expressive, unlike anything that had been seen on the silver screen before.

Soviet artists were not, however, free of state control. Chagall fell out of favor with the Soviet leadership and had to leave the country in 1923 because of tensions with the party and increased antisemitism. Mayakovsky committed suicide in 1930 after his work was severely criticized by party officials. Eisenstein was able to pursue his creative work only by making movies that did not challenge the ideology of the Communist Party. His prominent films from the 1920s were, in fact, powerful propaganda for the Soviet regime. Under Stalin's dictatorship, many writers and artists were silenced, imprisoned, or killed for their art.

Experiments in Architecture and Design

After the war, some architects and designers sought to redefine the relationship between the practical and the artistic by simplifying architectural and interior design.

A New Focus on Functionality Grouped around Walter Gropius in Germany, these designers, artists, and architects became known as the **Bauhaus school**, the most influential design movement in the first half of the twentieth century. The motivation of these architects and artists was connected to the horrors of the war. They sought to blend style and functionality, eliminating excesses they identified with the high bourgeois culture before the war and stripping away nationalism in style. Adherents of the Bauhaus school were optimistic: by eliminating the excesses of

Surrealism Artistic movement of the 1920s and 1930s that explored the realm of dreams and altered reality to find the deeper truth of human experience.

André Breton (1896–1966) French writer and founder of Surrealism.

Salvador Dali (1904–1989) Spanish-born artist who became the most famous Surrealist.

René Magritte (1898–1967) Belgian Surrealist painter famous for his superimposition of photographically depicted objects in unrelated three-dimensional spaces.

Expressionism Artistic movement that aimed to represent the connection between the inner emotional world and outer social reality.

Käthe Kollwitz (1867–1945) German Expressionist artist who portrayed the plight of working-class women and children.

Marc Chagall (1887–1985) Russian Jewish painter whose art combined romantic images of lovers, nature, and traditional Jewish symbols with harsh political commentary.

Sergei Eisenstein (1898–1948) One of the greatest film directors of the twentieth century, who used pioneering film techniques as powerful propaganda for the Bolsheviks.

Bauhaus school Innovative German movement of architectural and interior design that sought to make living spaces and furniture designs functional and affordable.

the past, artists and architects hoped to build a more stable environment accessible to people of different classes.

Another important force in design was **Le Corbusier**, a Swiss-born French engineer and artist—and one of the greatest architects of the twentieth century. Le Corbusier had a vision similar to that of the Bauhaus school—streamlining design, making it affordable and accessible to people of different social classes, and creating a new type of urban environment. Reacting against the cramped and alienating living conditions of the working classes before the war, he envisioned living quarters that were open, transparent, and connected to the community. His aim was to create a new society, and his *Toward a New Architecture* (1923) revolutionized urban planning. The Bauhaus school and Le Corbusier's work helped transform the appearance of old and new cities all over Europe, from Prague to Paris, as well as cities in Brazil, Algeria, and India.

Art Deco The idea that the best in design should be available to people of all incomes generated the movement known as **Art Deco**, which aimed to make everyday objects simple, sleek, and affordable through mass production. Technological advances and assembly-line methods first introduced by Henry Ford in his Detroit automobile plants helped cut production costs. By the end of the 1920s, Art Deco furniture, china, household appliances, and window treatments graced the grand houses of the rich, the homes of the middle classes, and even the bungalows of the working classes. The gap between highbrow and lowbrow culture in the realm of consumer goods was closing up.

Private Collection © DACS/Peter Newark American Pictures/The Bridgeman Art Library

The artistic persona of Josephine Baker, the enormously popular African American jazz dancer in Paris, challenged the aesthetic norms of old Europe and reinforced concepts of race in European culture. How is race depicted in this poster?

Le Corbusier (1887–1965) Swiss-born French architect whose innovations aiming to eliminate class distinctions influenced city planning throughout the world.

Art Deco Architectural and design style that emphasized simplicity in style and aimed to make quality designs affordable to all through mass production.

jazz Innovative American musical form that combined elements of African rhythm and slave songs with popular music and later avant-garde European influences.

Josephine Baker (1906–1975) African American dancer who charmed European audiences in 1925 and popularized the music and dance associated with jazz.

Isadora Duncan (1877–1927) British dancer who transformed traditional ballet technique into a more natural and emotion-filled movement style.

Popular Entertainment

High art joined popular culture in this amazing decade to give new status to entertainment, particularly dance and music.

Popular Music and Modern Dance Cabarets had been popular since the 1910s, but after the war they were transformed by new trends, particularly American **jazz**, which swept working-class music halls and high-class art gatherings from Paris to Bucharest. Jazz was electrifying, showcasing improvisation and defying old classifications in its combinations of African rhythms and slave songs with popular ragtime and the blues. Introduced to Europe by African American soldiers serving in France, jazz made audiences yearn to know more about American popular culture and entertainment.

Soon Europeans were doing the Charleston, with swings and heel kicks said to have originated with black dance styles on the islands off South Carolina. And in 1925, dance was further revolutionized when a U.S. traveling show captivated Paris with wild new jazz rhythms and the sensuous dances of its young African American star, **Josephine Baker**. Baker became an idol overnight, appealing to people of all walks of life who sought to discard the stuffiness of the prewar forms of entertainment for a more democratic and participatory type of dance and music. Baker's freedom and sensuality made her a lasting symbol of American culture in Europe.

At the same time, British dancer **Isadora Duncan** was transforming classical ballet into a new form of performance that emphasized expressive movement and grace rather than virtuosity. Duncan appeared

Fritz Lang's *Metropolis* (1927) presented an image of modernity and technological progress that was both alluring and foreboding. The icon at the center of the movie was emphatically female. What does the poster communicate about women and modernity?

on stage barefoot, in willowy silks instead of the stiff classic tutu; her movements aimed to convey emotions rather than showcase technique. Her new style of modern dance connected the Royal Opera House

and rowdy cabarets into one seamless continuum of celebrating human creativity and sensuality.

A new invention, the phonograph, also made musical choices more accessible to mass audiences. For a few pennies, anyone could hear the sounds of a favorite band at home, practice trendy new dance steps, and throw a party instead of sitting in the audience at a music hall for an evening's entertainment. Just as revolutionary was the introduction of inexpensive, mass-produced radios, which, starting in the late 1920s, transformed the music industry and news media. Soon the sounds of jazz and other popular music blasted out of windows and courtyards in almost every neighborhood.

Film Film was by far the most important and inexpensive form of entertainment for the masses during the 1920s. German film makers produced some of the most memorable films. The most important directors, such as **Fritz Lang**, were the Expressionists, who used simple plots to exaggerate human emotions, especially suffering, through distorted camera angles, lighting, and creative editing. Lang's best-known movie is *Metropolis* (1927), which examined the relationship between technology and progress by personifying technology as a female with both enticing and ultimately destructive characteristics. The movie also presented the suffering of the lower classes but expressed hope that technology could overcome social problems.

Listening to jazz, dancing the Charleston, and watching movies enabled working people, even the poor, to forget the war and escape the boredom of their hard lives. These forms of popular entertainment also allowed them the freedom to imagine other roles for themselves—as famous dancers, actors, or musicians. The new entertainment styles blurred the distance between the highly educated and privileged elites and the lower masses: fame seemed to be something almost anyone—in the excitement of the 1920s—could achieve.

Fritz Lang (1890–1976) German Expressionist film maker, later active in Hollywood.

Checking In

By yourself or with a partner, explain the significance of each of the following selected key terms:

Vera Brittain	Expressionism
Filippo Marinetti	Käthe Kollwitz
Surrealists	Bauhaus school
Salvador Dali	Josephine Baker

Schulz-Neudamm, Metropolis, 1926. Lithograph, 83" x 36½". Gift of Universum-Film-Aktiengesellschaft Digital Image © The Museum of Modern Art/Licensed by Scala/Art Resource, NY

CHAPTER
Review

Summary

- The end of World War I challenged the old political and social order, relations among states, and the roles of individuals in society.

- Self-determination sowed the seeds of discontent among European states.

- War debt repayments generated economic hardship all over Europe.

- Political leaders, social reformers, intellectuals, artists, workers, and average citizens sought new identities in the new Europe.

- Experiments of the decade offered radically new solutions and ideas, with varied success.

- Established democracies resisted successfully against revolutionary upheaval.

- In newly created countries, democratic institutions had greater difficulty in gaining legitimacy.

- The most radical challenge of the period was the successful establishment of a communist regime in Russia.

- The Soviet Union established itself as the international leader of all communist movements, through radical social programs inside the country and international outreach.

- Mass campaigns for education and secularization showed the will of the Bolshevik regime to reshape the minds and souls of every citizen.

- Fascism represented another important challenge against political and territorial stability.

- Fascism and communism provided important models for radical politicians in Europe in the following decade.

- Women experienced empowering changes but also frustration, especially with regard to family relations, especially in the Soviet Union.

- Lasting experiments in the realm of culture produced many of the century's masterpieces and avant-garde movements.

- Spectacular growth was seen in the realm of popular entertainment, from music to film.

Chronology

1918–1922	Reds and Whites engage in Russian Civil War
1919	Comintern is established; Bolshevik revolution in Hungary creates short-lived Soviet Republic; League of Nations is established; Treaty of Versailles officially ends World War I; Fiume Republic is established
1921	Lenin inaugurates the New Economic Policy in Russia
1922	Mussolini seizes power in Italy; Irish Free State is established
1923	Hitler attempts to seize power in Bavarian Beer Hall Putsch
1923–1925	Britain and France occupy Ruhr, precipitate German economic crisis
1924	Ramsay MacDonald becomes first Labour Party prime minister of Great Britain; Dawes Plan resets German reparation payments; First Surrealist manifesto is issued in Paris
1925	Josephine Baker performs American jazz dances in Paris
1926	Germany is admitted into the League of Nations
1928	Kellogg-Briand Pact renounces future war in Europe; Stalin assumes leadership of Soviet Union

© Cengage Learning

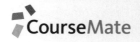
Visit the CourseMate website at **www.cengagebrain.com** for additional study tools and review materials for this chapter.

Test Yourself

To gauge your mastery of the material in this chapter, answer the questions below. More than one answer may be correct.

The Search for Stability, 1918–1924

1. Self-determination is:

   a. The right of a person to determine where he or she should live.
   b. The right of a state to determine the ethnicity of each person living inside its borders.
   c. The authority of the League of Nations to protect the borders established in the post-war peace treaties.
   d. The right of any individual nationality to govern itself through its own sovereign state.
   e. None of the above.

2. Which of these states had revisionist aims after World War I?

   a. Hungary
   b. Czechoslovakia
   c. Germany
   d. United States
   e. Habsburg Empire

3. The League of Nations was:

   a. The first international organization to offer membership to all sovereign states.
   b. A protector of human rights.
   c. Instrumental in transforming the authority of colonial states.
   d. Fully supported by the United States.
   e. A financial organization.

4. Which of these revolutionary challenges were successful?

   a. Bela Kun Regime
   b. Republic of Fiume
   c. Irish Free State
   d. Communist uprising in Germany
   e. None of the above.

5. The Dawes Plan:

   a. Crippled the German economy.
   b. Challenged the League of Nations.
   c. Enabled European war debtors to repay their war loans.
   d. Established the foundations of the World Bank.
   e. Was rejected by the U.S. legislature.

Now that you have reviewed and tested yourself on this part of the chapter, take time to pull together all the important information by answering the following questions:

◆ What actions did political leaders undertake to restore European order after the war?

◆ What problems frustrated these efforts?

Postwar Political Experiments, 1924–1929

6. Between 1918 and 1919, which were the most successful political parties in Great Britain and France?

   a. Communists
   b. Liberals
   c. Fascists
   d. Anarchists
   e. None of the above.

7. The Weimar Republic succeeded in becoming a functioning democracy by:

   a. Suppressing the nascent fascist movement.
   b. Suppressing the freedom of the press.
   c. Stabilizing hyperinflation.
   d. Challenging the Versailles borders.
   e. Offering strategic reforms for workers' rights.

8. What new state in Europe embraced democratic political institutions and did not challenge them through authoritarian behavior?

   a. Soviet Union
   b. Poland
   c. Czechoslovakia

   d. Turkey
   e. None of the above.

9. Italian Fascism:

   a. Empowered women to vote and seek employment in any area.
   b. Did away with private property.
   c. Established Benitto Mussolini as the dictatorial ruler of Italy.

   d. Had a strong paramilitary wing.
   e. Did not recognize the authority of the Vatican.

10. The welfare state refers to state-run and regulated programs regarding which areas?

    a. International relations
    b. Taxation
    c. Education

    d. Health care
    e. Child care

Now that you have reviewed and tested yourself on this part of the chapter, take time to pull together all the important information by answering the following questions:

◆ What new ideas about the powers of the government emerged during this period?

◆ Where was democracy successful and where did it fail? Why?

The New Soviet State

11. The Civil War:

    a. Was won by the Reds.
    b. Enabled Russia to retain its prewar territories.
    c. Inaugurated new forms of secret police brutality.

    d. Turned Leon Trostky into a Bolshevik hero.
    e. Ended in 1924.

12. The Bolshevik State aimed to:

    a. Do away with private property.
    b. Bring about full equality between men and women.

    c. Educate workers and peasants.
    d. Eliminate all class enemies.
    e. All of the above.

13. The New Economic Policy:

    a. Allowed for the return of private property.
    b. Enabled Russia to restore its prewar economic power.
    c. Became a permanent feature of the Bolshevik regime.

    d. Was supported by Leon Trotsky.
    e. Enabled Stalin's rise to power.

14. The new Soviet man would ideally have the following profile:

    a. Be religious.
    b. Be a profit-making entrepreneur.
    c. Be educated.

    d. Be a worker.
    e. Be a tsarist supporter.

15. The Bolshevik regime radically altered the lives of women in Russia by:

    a. Offering them educational opportunities.
    b. Allowing women to pursue any professions open to men.
    c. Giving them voting rights.

    d. Organizing a special women's section of the Bolshevik Party.
    e. Doing away with marriage as a bourgeois institution.

Now that you have reviewed and tested yourself on this part of the chapter, take time to pull together all the important information by answering the following questions:

◆ What were the essential elements of the Soviet state?

◆ What actions did the Bolsheviks undertake to reshape society and individual identities?

Social and Cultural Experiments

16. After the war women:
    - a. Became prominent entrepreneurs.
    - b. Gained voting rights everywhere.
    - c. Were often forced out of their jobs by returning veterans.
    - d. Were pressured to marry and reproduce.
    - e. Were able to project a more independent image through new fashions.

17. Pacifists:
    - a. Established many political parties.
    - b. Established a successful international movement.
    - c. Had among their supporters war veterans.
    - d. Succeeded in changing the rules of the League of Nations.
    - e. Had among their ranks many socialists.

18. The art avant-garde movements of the 1920s included:
    - a. Expressionism
    - b. Surrealism
    - c. Romanticism
    - d. Realism
    - e. Dada

19. Bauhaus architecture sought to:
    - a. Blend style and function.
    - b. Generate a new brand of German furniture.
    - c. Give rise to various national styles.
    - d. Build functional and affordable housing for the working classes.
    - e. Build stylish homes for the European elites.

20. In the 1920s, popular entertainment innovations included:
    - a. The photograph
    - b. The radio
    - c. The phonograph
    - d. The television set
    - e. Jazz

Now that you have reviewed and tested yourself on this part of the chapter, take time to pull together all the important information by answering the following questions:

◆ How did social reformers and intellectuals respond to the aftermath of war?

◆ What were the new directions in culture and entertainment during this era?

CHAPTER 27

Democracy Under Siege, 1929–1945

Chapter Outline

1929	1930	1931	1932	1933	1934	1935	1936	1937

1929
Great Depression begins

1932
Great famine begins in Ukraine

1933
Hitler comes to power in Germany

1936
Civil war begins in Spain

Great Purges begin in Soviet Union

A product of modern technological research in the area of pest control, cyanide B (zyklon-B) was repurposed during World War II to "enhance" the "efficiency" of the process by which the Final Solution was to be achieved. Initially it was used in small doses to delouse the clothing and other belongings of inmates arriving in the Nazi concentration camps. Eventually, the odorless gas released by the pellets shown here was used in large indoor spaces to asphyxiate large numbers of inmates, who would die within twenty minutes of inhaling the lethal doses of this gas. (© David Sutherland/Corbis)

After reading this chapter, you should be able to answer the following questions:

How did the challenges to democracy from 1929 to 1945 help transform European civilization?

Were the experiments of Hitler and Stalin an aberration of western civilization or the product of its ideas, science, and technology?

At what price did the Allies win the war?

M ANY EUROPEANS WITNESSED with alarm the profound political crisis of the 1930s as Europe's democracies plunged into a severe depression. Some became more committed than ever to socialist ideas. Others rejected democracy itself as the problem and turned toward antidemocratic solutions. Of the options taken in the 1930s, the dictatorships in Italy, Germany, and the Soviet Union seemed the most successful in managing the economic crisis, eventually restoring full employment and production growth while democracies struggled. But the success of the Soviets and the Nazis was due largely to their oppressive internal policies, which controlled workers and resources in ways democracies could not. The Nazis' racist ideology and the Stalinist paranoid concept of internal enemies institutionalized terror in both countries. Adolf Hitler and Joseph Stalin also aimed to undo the international system that had been developing through the League of Nations. In particular, Hitler's rearmament and expansionist policies challenged the Versailles Treaty, and democratic states stood idle until it was too late.

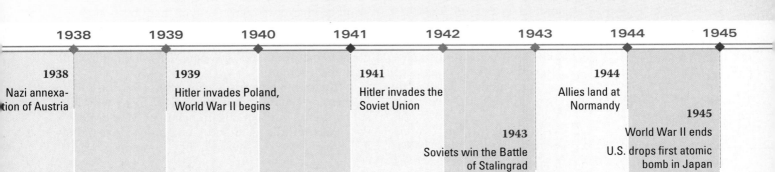

1938	1939	1940	1941	1942	1943	1944	1945

1938
Nazi annexation of Austria

1939
Hitler invades Poland, World War II begins

1941
Hitler invades the Soviet Union

1943
Soviets win the Battle of Stalingrad

1944
Allies land at Normandy

1945
World War II ends

U.S. drops first atomic bomb in Japan

Still, faced with Hitler's challenge to European international order in 1939, after 1941 the western democracies joined forces with the Soviet Union and by 1945 had defeated Germany and its allies. World War II, with its unmatched carnage, involvement of civilians, use of new military technology, and extermination of innocent people, especially the Jews, radically transformed Europe for a second time in less than a half a century.

Responses to the Great Depression, 1929–1939

- ◆ **What were the causes of the Great Depression?**
- ◆ **What were the political consequences of the Great Depression?**

In the fall of 1929, the bubble of prosperity burst, bringing on severe economic problems and major political upheaval. After the 1929 stock market crash in the United States, European banks and enterprises lost much of their capital and millions of people lost their jobs. The political impact of the world depression that followed was huge, as most governments lost the trust of the voters, yet starving workers had nowhere else to turn. Everyone looked toward the state for solutions, but no one knew how to deal with this economic and social crisis of unprecedented scale. Only in Britain, France, Belgium, Czechoslovakia, and the Scandinavian countries was democracy able to pass this difficult test. Most other countries slid toward regimes that offered security and strength at the price of democracy. With Italy providing an example of successful management of the economic depression, authoritarian regimes rose all over eastern and southern Europe. Germany also abandoned its fragile republic under the spell of Adolf Hitler.

John Maynard Keynes (1883–1946) British economist whose theories revolutionized the supply-demand equation and inspired government policies to encourage economic growth.

Great Depression Global economic crisis that began in October 1929 and lasted throughout the 1930s.

deflationary Referring to a fiscal policy aimed at preventing inflation.

The Great Depression

By the end of World War I, New York had replaced London as the financial capital of the world, and by 1929, European economies had become highly dependent on the American economy. The Dawes Plan for payment of the war debt tied the finances of Britain, France, and Germany to the economic well-being of the United States. During the 1920s, the growing availability of American goods and the lure of American popular culture in Europe also strengthened economic ties across the Atlantic. Thus, when the New York stock market crashed in October 1929, its effects were felt immediately in Europe. American banks and financiers started to call in short-term loans, depleting European banks, especially in Germany and Austria, of sizable resources. By the end of 1930, 1,350 American banks had closed; 2,293 more did so in 1931. Between 1929 and 1934, almost 33 percent of American banks had failed.

Run on the Banks In Europe, panic ensued. As people withdrew cash from banks and closed their accounts, the capital available to businesses shrank, leading to the collapse of major European banks, including the Kreditanstalt, Austria's largest bank. Unable to pay their workers, these businesses started to fire workers by the thousands. Even the 1931 American moratorium on war debts could not reverse the downward spiral, though it did ease international tensions. Unemployment in Germany reached 3 million in 1930 and skyrocketed to almost 6 million by 1932—almost 40 percent of the workforce. In the United States, 25 percent of the workforce was unemployed. By 1933, economic production had fallen by 50 percent in the United States and by 40 percent in Germany. (See Table 27.1.)

Economic Theories About the Depression Some economists, such as **John Maynard Keynes**, believed that the **Great Depression** was also connected to the **deflationary** policies of the 1920s, which had followed the hyperinflation scare of the early 1920s. Businesses and individuals had been afraid to borrow, thus slowing economic growth, and banks had also become more conservative, charging higher interest rates. Other scholars have seen the Great Depression as a more acute case of the cyclical process of economic growth and slowdown characteristic of all capitalist economies.

Whatever the causes, the effects of the Great Depression were profound. Many of those who had spent their youth in the trenches of World War I were now middle aged and had families. When they lost their jobs or businesses, they grew despondent.

Map 27.1 **Axis Victories in World War II, 1942** World War II tested the limits of European civilization and democratic legacies. The threat was greatest in the spring of 1942, when Adolf Hitler's Axis alliance controlled most of Europe and North Africa. © *Cengage Learning*

1. What European states disappeared during World War II?
2. What might have been the weaknesses of the Nazis at the moment of their greatest victories in World War II?
3. What seem to be the Allies greatest challenges in fighting against the Nazis?

Some, unable to feed their families or make payments on their homes, slipped into deep depression and abandoned their families. Women's economic status was also badly hurt, though some were able to find part-time work in the service industry—as cooks, servants, and sometimes as sex workers.

Democracies' Responses

If dependency on American investments and banks along with deflationary policies were the initial causes of economic collapse in Europe, the depth and duration of the Great Depression were also a consequence

Table 27.1 The Great Depression

Indices of Industrial Production, 1929–1938, in Major European Countries (1937 = 100)

	1929	1930	1931	1932	1933	1934	1935	1936	1937
France	123	123	105	91	94	92	88	95	100
Germany	79	69	56	48	54	67	79	90	100
Italy	90	85	77	77	82	80	86	86	100
Great Britain	77	74	69	69	73	80	82	94	100

Unemployment (in Thousands)

	1929	1930	1931	1932	1933	1934	1935	1936	1937
France	neglig.	13	64	301	305	368	464	470	380
Germany	1,899	3,070	4,520	5,575	4,804	2,718	2,151	1,593	912
Italy	301	425	734	1,006	1,019	964	—	—	874
Great Britain	1,216	1,917	2,630	2,745	2,521	2,159	2,036	1,755	1,484

Source: Stromberg, Roland N., *Europe in the Twentieth Century*, 4th Edition, © 1997. Reprinted by permission of Pearson Education, Inc., Upper Saddle River, NJ.

of the choices various states made after 1929. Politicians tried to balance state budgets and avoid expenditures. Following the lead of the United States, European governments quickly imposed higher tariffs to protect their own industries. The result was a decline in international trade that further reduced production and employment. Keynes argued that economic recovery could be achieved only by abandoning the obsession with balanced budgets and the **gold standard** and by instituting government programs to put people back to work. A larger employed workforce, he pointed out, would increase the tax base, and more taxes would reduce budget deficits. Under President Franklin D. Roosevelt, the United States weathered the Great Depression in part through a broad range of government-supported public works programs that implemented Keynes's ideas.

Toward National Unity in Britain But in Britain, politicians were not open to these solutions. Labour Prime Minister Ramsay MacDonald, elected in May 1929 on the promise of securing workers' interests, could not cope with the massive unemployment that hit Britain by 1930 (a 60 percent rise just during that year). His government opted for conservative economic solutions for the economic depression. Hopelessly, it attempted to keep the budget balanced, and it refrained from setting up the kinds of public works programs developed in America. Instead, MacDonald chose to cut compensation for the unemployed. Such a move by a Labour prime minister seemed so much at odds

gold standard Fiscal policy that pegs national currency to gold reserves.

Library of Congress

One of millions of people worldwide left homeless and on the verge of starvation by the Great Depression, this "Migrant Mother" became an iconic image. Florence Thompson was photographed in 1936 in California by the American documentary photographer Dorothea Lange. What emotions can you see on her face? What do the turned away faces of her children suggest?

with that party's ideology that half his ministers resigned.

In an unprecedented move, MacDonald compromised with the Conservatives to create a **National Unity Government**, with himself as prime minister, which he led until 1935, though he was expelled from the Labour Party for betraying workers' interests. Despite political and economic turmoil, the National Unity Government managed two important accomplishments. First, the Conservatives agreed to support issues important to Labour, such as government-regulated health insurance and Housing Acts that mandated the building of affordable, safe housing. By the late 1930s, politicians of all leanings recognized housing, education, and public health as services for which the state had responsibility, and Britain was on its way to becoming a welfare state. Though private enterprise ran many social services, the government monitored their quality and helped the poor gain access to decent housing and health care.

The chief accomplishment of the National Unity Government in Britain, however, was to simply hold on to the principles of democracy. Both communist and fascist movements grew in Britain during the 1930s, gathering strength from the sheer desperation of the economic crisis. But most politicians resisted the temptation to play upon fears in order to increase their following. British politicians followed well-established democratic rules, and average citizens respected this position, although they were often dissatisfied with the results.

Democracy Tested in France France, too, adopted deflationary measures to cope with the downturn in economic production and rise in unemployment. The French were even more conservative than the British, keeping the franc on the gold standard at a time when every other European country and the United States had abandoned it. By 1935, when most European countries had begun to recover, France was registering its highest unemployment rates (464,000, in contrast to 13,000 in 1930) and its lowest index of industrial production since 1929 (30 percent lower).

Yet France, too, resisted the fascist temptation and defended democratic institutions, weathering a major political scandal in 1934 and a demonstration by two hundred thousand protesters that was brutally crushed by the police. Though fascist organizations in France had more than 750,000 members, mainstream politicians and average citizens rejected fascist appeals and in 1936 put a strong antifascist coalition in power.

Authoritarian Solutions

Most of Europe's political elites, however, responded to the Great Depression by undermining or abandoning democratic institutions. Where such institutions were recent, both politicians and ordinary citizens were quick to equate economic problems with a fundamental weakness of democracy and to look for other political solutions.

Catholic Authoritarian Regimes In Austria, Spain, and Portugal, the response was an alliance between conservative politicians and the Catholic Church. In these countries, the Roman Catholic Church was one of the most stable institutions, shaping not only religious outlook but also political life. In Austria, the Christian Socialists, one of the two largest parties in the country, had a conservative Catholic outlook on moral values and social responsibilities. The party favored government control over education that would be strictly Christian, a traditional social hierarchy with the Catholic aristocracy at the top, and the exclusion of Jews from important positions of public authority. In the early 1930s, both Austria and Portugal replaced democratically elected governments with strong conservative leaders who were devout Catholics. These leaders gave the Catholic Church important educational, propaganda, and social responsibilities. The school curriculum came under the control of the Catholic Church, as did many other social services. Church-controlled censorship of literature and other cultural endeavors were also introduced.

The Spanish Civil War In Spain, the struggle between conservative militarist and Catholic political forces and their secularist left-wing opponents proved more violent and led to a civil war. The **Spanish Civil War** lasted three years (1936–1939) and destroyed trust in democracy in Spain and among many Europeans generally. The country went from a republican government in 1931 to a titular monarchy in 1939, which was headed by the authoritarian general **Francisco Franco**, the leader of the pro-Catholic right-wing forces. The son of a naval postmaster, Franco had, at age thirty-four in 1926, become the youngest general in Europe. Before 1936, he had served under a right-wing nationalist coalition to purge the military of supporters of the left. Through military skill and successful maneuvering among his rivals, he built a reputation as a strong leader and a unifier. Although many regarded Franco as a supporter of fascism, he was in fact a pragmatist who used the support of fascist forces, especially from Italy and Germany, to win the civil war. By 1939, when Franco's Nationalists won against the

National Unity Government
Coalition government in Britain during the first half of the 1930s, headed by Labour leader Ramsey MacDonald but dominated by the Conservatives.

Spanish Civil War (1936–1939)
War won by the right-wing Nationalists, supported by the Nazis, over republican left-wing forces, supported by the Soviets.

Francisco Franco (1892–1975)
General and leader of the Nationalists in the Spanish Civil War and dictator of Spain from 1939 until his death in 1975.

George Orwell Commits Himself to Socialism

In 1930, Eric Arthur Blair became George Orwell. It wasn't just about choosing a pen name but rather about giving up his privileged identity as the son of a respectable servant of the British Empire in India. Instead of following the path to easy security and middle-class respectability opened by his family, at age nineteen Blair turned his back on elite schools to join the imperial police in India for some adventure. At age twenty-four, disgusted with its racist policies, he quit to live among the poor.

Having decided to follow his dream of writing, Blair, now Orwell, aimed high. He wanted nothing less than to become the moral conscience of his country, writing from conviction and experience, unlike many of the pseudo-bohemian writers of the time who enjoyed material privileges while writing about the poor. He didn't want just to move his audiences but instead aimed to challenge and force them to rethink their identities and act on their beliefs. True to this conviction, Orwell took a job as a dishwasher in Paris and lived in a poorly heated room for many months. It was during these days of self-imposed poverty that he began to understand class inequalities and gain sympathy for socialism as the best direction for democracy.

In his quest to become a good and socially active writer, in 1934 Orwell took on the assignment of writing about the life of coal miners in northern Britain. The result, *The Road to Wigan Pier* (1936), movingly described the appalling conditions of these workers but received mixed reviews from his left-wing editor. Always holding on to his aim of being the moral conscience of his peers, Orwell did not hesitate to criticize British socialists, whom he viewed as armchair critics rather than active reformers.

To demonstrate his own dedication to the cause of democracy through socialism, in 1936 Orwell went to Spain, where a civil war was pitting left-wing forces against a right-wing militarist regime. He arrived as a journalist but couldn't stay away from the action and joined the left-wing armies. His experiences in Spain reinforced his commitment to socialism as profoundly democratic but made him wary of the contribution of the Soviet Union to this cause. Soviet manipulations of the left-wing forces opened his eyes to the controlling and antidemocratic nature of the Soviet regime. These experiences were penned in *Homage to Catalonia* (1938).

Still hungry for action and eager to make a difference, Orwell tried to serve in the British army during World War II but was discharged because of injuries he had received in Spain. Instead, he worked for the British Broadcasting Corporation (BBC) as a reporter, a job that revealed to him the nature of wartime propaganda and the antidemocratic ways in which the British government manipulated information.

Orwell's passionate commitment to "turn political writing into an art" led him to write his last two and most important books, *Animal Farm* (1945) and *1984* (1949). Both reflected his desire to remain the moral conscience of Britain. Exposing the absurdity of sloganeering with expressions such as "war is peace" and "ignorance is strength," he pointed to the deep political corruption, both on the left and on the right, as the root of the tragedies he had witnessed all over Europe in the 1930s and 1940s. These books also represented an impassioned plea on behalf of peace and democracy and against totalitarianism, but they were not exclusively anticommunist, as they came to be depicted later on. Until the end of his life in 1950, Orwell remained committed to his belief in socialism as the most radically democratic ideology of the times, more progressive than liberalism or communism.

Republicans, more than one million people had been placed in prison by Franco's victorious dictatorship. The Catholic Church became Franco's right arm in enforcing strict censorship over culture, education, and other public services.

Carol II (r. 1930–1940) Romanian king who ruled in an authoritarian fashion.

dictatorship Autocratic form of government headed by a single all-powerful ruler, the dictator.

Dictatorship in Eastern Europe In other young democracies, especially in eastern Europe, political leaders and average citizens blamed democratic institutions and ethnic minorities for the economic crisis. Their solution was to dissolve parliaments, suppress the voice of ethnic minorities, and establish authoritarian ethno-nationalist rule. In Romania, for instance, the young king **Carol II** claimed he was the only leader interested in the unity of the country, thus undermining all political parties. He dealt with the economic crisis by allowing antisemitic propaganda and policies to flourish as he militarized the economy, reviving floundering branches of industry by emphasizing the production of armaments. In 1938, he made himself a virtual dictator. By then, **dictatorships** had replaced parliamentary systems in many

Museo Nacional Centro de Arte Reina Sofia, Madrid/Art Resource, NY, © ARS, NY

Pablo Picasso painted *Guernica* (1937) as a political-aesthetic reaction against the mass killings by right-wing forces led by Francisco Franco during the Spanish Civil War. Specifically, Guernica, a small town in northern Spain, was bombed in 1937 by German planes supporting Franco. Though muted in color, the painting became a dramatic symbol of pacifism. What does the image of the mother with the infant in her arms suggest in relation to the war? What other symbols of pacifism can you identify in the painting? What images does Picasso use to represent violence?

eastern European states, including Latvia, Poland, Hungary, Greece, and Yugoslavia. Eastern European leaders used the revisionism of ethnic minorities as an excuse to build up the military. The increasing obsession with militarization led to a veritable arms race in the area. Acquiring military equipment from Nazi Germany in return for agricultural goods that could not find a market in western Europe relieved some of the economic crisis for these countries but also rendered them greatly dependent on Germany for their military needs.

The rhetoric and paramilitary organizations of the authoritarian regimes in eastern Europe resembled those in fascist Italy. In fact, fascist movements were particularly strong in Romania, Hungary, and Yugoslavia. But they did not foment fascist coups like Mussolini's. Instead, the dictators of these countries merely took on a fascist style, with uniformed supporters marching in the streets. Authoritarian regimes in the rest of Europe remained much more conservative in scope and ideology. They were interested in maintaining stability and preventing broad social and political upheaval rather than in generating the kind of changes Mussolini had brought about in 1922.

The Rise of Nazism

By contrast, between 1930 and 1933, Germany experienced a political and social revolution that brought to power the most radical movement since the Bolsheviks—the Nazis. After the 1929 crash, Germany faced obstacles similar to other young democracies. Political parties had a fluid following, and many people had come to question the democratic institutions of the Weimar Republic, which had been set up in the shadow of the much-hated Versailles Treaty and were only a decade old. Just months before the crash, Gustav Stresemann—a central figure for the Weimar's stability—died. Moreover, Germany was hit harder by the depression than any other state in Europe. The Social Democrats, who led the government at the time of the crash, lost power, their representation in parliament shrinking from 30 percent in 1928 to 20 percent in 1932. No other party was strong enough to succeed, so a series of political compromises followed. Various governments tried different approaches, first obtaining a moratorium on war reparations (1931) and then implementing a major land reform. Many politicians were angered by these moves, and average citizens lost faith in the democratic processes that seemed to bring very little stability and even less economic relief to the country. Meanwhile, a political party once marginal and ridiculed by mainstream politicians was growing rapidly. Electoral support for the Nazis increased from 2.5 percent in 1928 to 18 percent in 1930 and to 37 percent in July 1932. The reasons for this meteoric growth were many. First and foremost, the Nazis had a charismatic leader unmatched by any other German politician—Adolf Hitler.

The Rise of Adolf Hitler Hitler came from a lower-class Austrian family and had left home at age sixteen to become a bohemian artist in Vienna. Unable to get into the Fine Arts Academy, he became a drifter, living in homeless shelters and eking out a living as a street peddler until 1914, when he volunteered in the German army. Having fought bravely in the war (he was decorated twice), Hitler was dismayed by Germany's loss and looked for a way to continue his service in a paramilitary organization. His ambitions brought him, in 1919, to the organization that became the Nazi Party a year later. Here Hitler discovered his great talent as a speaker and fundraiser, turning the Nazis into a notable party by 1923. His supporters were a motley crew of disillusioned veterans, drifters like himself, and "little men" who were suffering from the effects of the war and postwar inflation. After the failed 1923 Beer Hall Putsch, Hitler was thrown into jail. The Nazis were made illegal but continued their activities, including the publication of Hitler's *Mein Kampf*, written in prison.

Hitler's Ideology: Mein Kampf Hitler was not a great thinker, as *Mein Kampf* shows. The book is a muddled collection of nationalist and racist, primarily antisemitic, ideas. Using the work of racist theorists of the nineteenth century, Hitler developed a genetically determined hierarchy of ethnicities, with the Aryans (Germans, Scandinavians, Britons) at the top and Slavs and Jews at the bottom, the latter categorized as "subhuman." The book argued for the idea of **Lebensraum**—that because the German nation needed more territory in order to thrive, it ought to expand eastward into Poland, Czechoslovakia, and beyond. Hitler was singularly able to distill the frustrations of many Germans into a few simple messages: Germans had been served poorly by the Weimar Republic, which had been a result of the unfair Versailles Treaty; the enemies of the German people were both outside (especially the Soviets) and inside (communists, Jews, and the capitalists who had profiteered from the postwar economic problems). Eliminating these enemies was the key to bringing Germany back to its former imperial glory.

The Paramilitary Dimensions of the Nazis By the time the Nazis re-emerged as an important political party during the Great Depression, Hitler was a seasoned leader and spellbinding speaker, with a loyal paramilitary organization—the Storm Detachment or SA—and a band of personal bodyguards, the **Schutzstaffel**, or **SS**. His ability to construct a spectacle around the Nazis was another reason for their growing popularity. In a time of growing disaffection and demoralization, Hitler's Brown Shirts marched around as a solid unit—a symbol of Germany's once-great virility and military prowess, now stymied by the Treaty of Versailles and the Social Democrats. Much like Mussolini, whose mastery of ceremony had been a model for the Nazis, Hitler understood well that a powerful show of force sometimes meant more than speeches and ideology. He attracted many students and younger followers simply with the sense of community and strength he seemed to radiate: "Long ago you heard the voice of a man … and it struck to your hearts, and it awakened you, and you followed his voice…. It is faith in our nation that has made us small people great, that has made us poor people rich, that has made us vacillating, dispirited, anxious people brave and courageous."

The Appeal of Antisemitism The appeal of the Nazis rested on posing simple solutions for complicated problems and playing on the fears of a population caught in a deep economic crisis that other parties could not end. It was not just the die-hard antisemites who voted for the Nazis. The party attracted educated and uneducated, poor and well-to-do, men and women, workers and entrepreneurs, and religious and secularized Germans. But the largest group of Nazi supporters were those either hurt badly by the depression—small artisans and shopkeepers, some workers, farmers—or those who had come to see in the Weimar government only a betrayal of Germany and defeat by outside forces—soldiers who had fought in the war, men laid off while women still worked, students, and antisemites.

By November 1932, the Nazis were the strongest party in the Reichstag. Hitler did not have a mandate to form a single government (the Nazis had received only 33 percent of the vote), but he was not interested in sharing control and no other leaders were willing to give him full powers. Then in January 1933, he became chancellor and embarked on a swift process of undermining all democratic institutions of the Weimar Republic through steps that were technically legal. In February, a mysterious fire in the Reichstag building allowed Hitler to ask for emergency powers to go after the culprits, whom he identified as communists. With the president's approval, Hitler suspended all free speech and asked for new elections, which gave the Nazis 44 percent of the vote. The new parliament moved quickly to outlaw the Communist Party and pass the **Enabling Act**, which gave Hitler extraordinary powers in making executive decisions in all matters of "national security," placing him above accountability to the legal and judicial branches of government. The act enabled Hitler to become a dictator and to begin reshaping Germany

Mein Kampf (*My Struggle*) Book written by Hitler in 1925 in which he formulated his ideas of racial purity and his goal of exterminating the Jews.

Lebensraum (in German, "living space") Idea that Germany needed to expand eastward to secure the healthy growth of the Aryan race.

Schutzstaffel (SS) (in German, "protective squadron") Hitler's personal bodyguards in the early days of the Nazi Party.

Enabling Act Decree passed by the Reichstag in 1933 that enabled Hitler to legally eliminate all political enemies and assume full dictatorial powers.

according to his vision of a racially pure thousand-year empire—the **Third Reich**.

Checking In

By yourself or with a partner, explain the significance of each of the following selected key terms:

John Maynard Keynes	*Mein Kampf*
Great Depression	Schutzstaffel (SS)
Spanish Civil War	Enabling Act
Francisco Franco	Third Reich

The Soviet Union Under Stalin, 1929–1939

◆ **What were the Soviet Union's successes and failures in the decade of the Great Depression?**

◆ **What were the new elements added by Stalin to turn the Soviet Union into a totalitarian state?**

As Europe struggled with the Great Depression and political instability, the Soviet Union seemed on an unstoppable track toward modernization, industrialization, and full employment. With membership in the League of Nations, it gained international respectability. In the 1930s it was a model for many disillusioned people in the west. As a force in the antifascist struggle, the Soviet Union emerged as a first-rank international power. The reality of Stalin's rule, however, was grim: modernization and stability were accomplished only with much brutality. Stalin's newly powerful country was a ruthless police state.

Domestic and Foreign Policy

While the rest of Europe was entering a period of economic crisis, the Soviet Union was relatively free of the vagaries of the free market, as it had not been involved in the Dawes Plan or affected by the rise of American banking in the world of international finance. Fully in control of the country's political apparatus, in the late 1920s Stalin turned his attention toward improving the Soviet Union's international standing and developing the economy.

A More Moderate Course in Foreign Policy During the early 1930s, the Soviet Union reversed its policy of fostering world revolution, focusing instead on international security issues. The most important foreign policy concern was to counter the rise of threats in the west (Nazi Germany) and in the east (Japan). The Soviets pursued this goal with a two-pronged strategy: diplomatic and military. In the realm of diplomacy, the foreign commissar

Maxim Litvinov played the most important role. A skillful diplomat, he projected an image of cosmopolitan sophistication, unlike most other representatives of the Soviet Union. During the 1920s, when the country was still an international **pariah** and had no diplomatic ties with the Great Powers, Litvinov had become involved in disarmament discussions in the League of Nations. Through his relentless efforts, France (1932) and then the United States (1933) finally reestablished diplomatic relations with the Soviet Union, opening the way for the its admission into the League in 1934 and for increased international economic ties.

Establishing the Command Economy Another component of the Soviet effort to build up international strength was militarization. While Litvinov was praising disarmament in the League of Nations, Stalin was focusing on the armament industry as an important component of economic planning. The military was building new weapons, such as tanks and new types of bombs. The military leadership was fully committed to this program and conducted intensive campaigns for training and diversifying the fighting forces.

The Five-Year Plans Internally, Stalin's goal was nothing less than turning an agricultural nation into an industrial powerhouse. In 1929 he proclaimed: "We are becoming a land of metals …, automobiles…, tractors, and when we have put the USSR on an automobile and the peasant on a tractor, let the noble capitalists … attempt to catch up." This ambitious goal, however, needed unprecedented planning and government control. Stalin ended the New Economic Policy (NEP) and called on his economic advisers to create a series of **five-year plans** that would set up a **command economy**: all aspects of the economy—from securing natural resources to research and development, employment, and commerce—would be controlled by the state rather than the market. The supply of goods would be determined by ideological goals—industrialization and modernization—rather than by consumer needs and wants. The first five-year plan focused obsessively on high production

Third Reich Title used for the period of Nazi rule in Germany.

Maxim Litvinov (1876–1951) Soviet foreign commissar in the 1930s who orchestrated the admission of the Soviet Union to the League of Nations.

pariah Outcast; a nation that is diplomatically shunned, its leadership and actions not recognized as legitimate.

five-year plans Centralized formula for economic planning initiated by Stalin in 1928 to direct and coordinate production in all sectors of the economy.

command economy State-controlled economy in which all aspects of the economy are controlled by the state in a centralized manner.

targets in heavy industries, subordinating production in all other areas to this primary goal: it called for an increase of 300 percent in the production of electricity, coal, pig iron, and steel. "There is no fortress that the Bolsheviks cannot storm," boasted the party leadership.

In the first few years, these industries achieved huge levels of growth because they were so rudimentary at the start. In addition, Stalin empowered factory managers and directors of heavy industry enterprises to use any necessary means, often simply reallocating natural resources and transportation from other economic sectors and using forced labor instead of paid workers for some of the most ambitious projects, such as the Volga–White Sea Canal. But by the third year, the rate of growth had slowed down. Without comprehensive planning for the entire economy, the state risked halting production in some sectors, such as agriculture and light industries, to achieve the official quotas in the heavy industry. For instance, if trains were made available only for mining and steel industries, production and delivery in other sectors of the economy became blocked. In the end, the first five-year plan was a failure by its own goals, but it still produced some outstanding results—a growth of over 100 percent in steel, electricity, and machinery production, although some of these statistics were manipulated. But by the end of the third five-year plan, in 1939, the Soviet Union was outproducing Britain and France, both still mired in depression, and was, after the United States and Germany, the third-largest industrial power in the world.

Worker Dissatisfaction The greatest failure of the five-year plans pertained to the welfare of the workers. To the Soviet state, the only thing that mattered was the growth of production; the basic material needs of average people were unimportant. Only work and its products—the finished good—had quantifiable value. In practice, this meant that Soviet industries were built without any regard for worker safety. The Soviet workplace looked a lot more like the filthy capitalist enterprises criticized by Friedrich Engels and Karl Marx a century earlier than the workers' paradise envisioned by V. I. Lenin.

The Soviets used both rewards and coercion to mobilize the labor force and increase productivity, especially in heavy industries. Workers who more than met production goals received higher pay and other benefits, such as better housing. In addition, convict labor continued to be used in mining, lumbering, and building roads and waterways. Most workers

collectivization Soviet policy for turning all agricultural land into state-owned farms and peasants into wage laborers.

kulaks Entrepreneurial peasants who enriched themselves during the NEP years.

put up with these measures, some out of conviction and others out of fear or need.

Collectivization Peasants, however, resisted more stubbornly as the Soviets converted agriculture into a state-owned sector. The five-year plans called for **collectivization**—the confiscation of private land to create state-owned farms where production targets set by the state dictated the crops to be grown and the quantities to be produced. Peasants became wage-laborers who could keep only small plots of land and a few animals around the house for basic household needs. From the perspective of the state, collectivization was a rational way to consolidate small holdings and increase productivity. Large state farms, with machinery unaffordable to most farmers, could produce better crops and larger yields, to everyone's benefit. But for peasants, collectivization robbed them of their identity. To be a peasant in Russia meant to have land, not just live on it. A man's dignity, in particular, was tied to his ability to feed his family from his land. Communist officials who pushed for collectivization were aware of this problem. But they believed the peasants, especially the newly enriched **kulaks** from the NEP period, needed to be broken. Collectivization was as much an ideological and social goal—eliminating a class enemy and creating a larger proletariat—as it was an economic aim.

The Great Famine Collectivization was accomplished at appalling human costs and failed miserably to reach its economic goals. In the winter of 1932–1933, outrageous production quotas induced a general famine, especially in the Ukraine. Forced by the state to give up even the animals and crops they would have needed to survive through the winter, between 5 and 7 million peasants starved to death. The lucky ones were able to find shelter and food with relatives in the city. Others were reduced to eating tree bark and bugs—and even cannibalism. Young mothers, unable to feed their infants, killed them. By the end of 1933, ruthless methods had forced most peasants to give up their land. By 1940, all agricultural land was in the hands of the state.

Yet this apparent victory masked important failures. First, peasants had been forced to give up their land through imprisonment, torture, exile in Siberia, and, in many cases, execution. The number of victims of this brutal process is still disputed, but it was certainly in the millions—6 to 10 million, according to various scholars. Some of the best working hands were eliminated in the first years of collectivization, and survivors were broken psychologically and physically. Second, the peasants did not go down without a fight. Many burned their crops and killed their livestock rather than see them in the hands of the government. As a result, the cattle population decreased by over 40 percent and the pig population by almost 50 percent between 1928 and 1931. Such violence continued into the late 1930s because peasants simply could not see collective farms as anything other than theft by the state.

The one goal in which collectivization succeeded was ideological. Peasants were forced to become workers, with no other resources for survival. In the next generation, the very notion of taking pride in one's land was wiped out. The communists had eliminated another social enemy from the old regime and reshaped the identity of the rural population into a subservient, if resentful, category of workers. Using violence, Stalin was on his way to refashioning the New Soviet Man and Woman.

Stalin's Totalitarian State

Having subdued the peasantry, Stalin turned toward intimidating other internal enemies—distrusted members of the party. This campaign began in 1936 and lasted until 1939, starting with the party's upper hierarchy and then widening to include family, friends, and other connections. By 1934, there had been significant disagreement among party leaders over industrialization and collectivization. Most in the Politburo leaned toward slowing down the pace and ending the most brutal policies. Unable to persuade or intimidate his opponents, Stalin turned the **NKVD**, the secret police, on them. The terror employed by the NKVD was not new for the Soviet regime, but the scale of the **Great Purges** that followed was unprecedented.

The Great Purges The first victims were high-ranking old Bolsheviks, some in the Politburo, followed by the most prominent army leaders and eventually the very leaders of the NKVD who had engineered the first purges. Stalin's diabolical system ensured that responsibility for the purges would always fall on the shoulders of his henchmen. Most old Bolshevik elites perished or were exiled, 70 percent of the Central Committee was removed, a significant number of officers were exiled or executed, and most of the leadership of the NKVD was also killed. In 1939, less than 2 percent of the delegates who had attended the 1934 party congress remained. By the end of the decade, the purges had produced a new generation of party, army, and secret police leaders personally subservient to Stalin.

The purges were a conscious policy engineered by Stalin to eliminate all opposition through execution and fear. Most people learned not to speak in public. A comment about how crowded the bus was might land one in jail. Criticism of food in a cafeteria might bring an NKVD agent to the table. Individuals disappeared so often in public places, never to be heard of again, that most people came to believe that the secret police were everywhere and that everyone was a potential informer, including children, spouses, and other close family members.

Labor Camps By 1939, several million people had been harassed and arrested by the NKVD in connection with alleged opposition. Many were executed; many more were sent to forced-labor camps, the **gulags**, where a majority perished from the brutality of the guards and the dreadful living conditions. An infamous camp was Solovetsky, an island in the Arctic Circle. Those who survived were used as slave labor, building railroads and hydroelectric stations as well as working in coal, gold, and copper mines.

Purges and the NKVD succeeded in transforming high-ranking communist officials and average citizens alike into fearful, powerless pawns in the hands of the state. They completed Stalin's social revolution. Through relentless and arbitrary brutality, the Soviet Union was now a **totalitarian** police state. The fate of all citizens rested in the hands of the party and on the whims of the Great Leader. The party and the state were one. The state controlled the economy and, through the secret police, intruded itself into everyone's daily life. A member of the Politburo could become a victim of Stalin's rage as easily as a poor peasant. In fact, the closer one was to the center of power in Moscow, the tighter the control exercised by Stalin's apparatus of fear. His ability to control Soviet society through terror was unmatched by any leader in the twentieth century, save Hitler.

The Cult of Personality Yet Stalin was not content to project the image of a feared tyrant. He wanted to impress Soviet citizens and the world with his great accomplishments. Through a costly and sophisticated propaganda machine, he built a mythical cult of personality that depicted him as a beloved father of the country. One propaganda ode from this period declared: "O great Stalin, O leader of the peoples, / Thou who broughtest man to birth. / Thou who fructifies the earth, / Thou who restorest to centuries …, O thou, / Sun reflected by millions of hearts." Writers were pressed into composing such poems; to write in opposition to Stalin meant certain death.

But many were in awe of Stalin and honest in their praises. A movie producer who later became a critic of the regime confessed: "The strangest thing to me is that I was absolutely sincere. I thought all this was a necessary part of building communism. And then

NKVD (Russian acronym for "People's Commissariat of Internal Affairs") Soviet secret police under Stalin that organized the massive purges of the 1930s.

Great Purges Campaigns of political repression and persecution in the Soviet Union orchestrated by Joseph Stalin during the late 1930s.

gulag (Russian acronym for "Chief Administration of Corrective Labor Camps") Soviet forced-labor camp system in which political enemies of the state were confined and literally worked to death.

totalitarianism State system in which the state has total control over politics, economic life, and society at large.

I believed Stalin." Western intellectuals disillusioned with the weak democracies and their inability to fight the fascist threat were also impressed by Soviet accomplishments. The Spanish painter Pablo Picasso, for instance, came to glorify the Soviet Union under Stalin. Engineers and scientists from Europe and the United States were likewise enthusiastic. But many of those who went to the Soviet Union during the 1930s also disappeared into the gulag. It was safer to admire the Soviet Union from afar than to experience it up close.

 Checking In

By yourself or with a partner, explain the significance of each of the following selected key terms:

Maxim Litvinov	kulaks
five-year plans	Great Purges
command economy	gulags
collectivization	totalitarian

The Third Reich, 1933–1945

- ◆ **What distinguished the Third Reich from other political regimes of the 1930s?**
- ◆ **What methods did the Nazis employ to achieve total control over German society?**

In Germany, Hitler was also creating a totalitarian state. A pragmatist, he used the economic elites and existing political institutions to gain support and eliminate his enemies. But he was as quick to destroy inconvenient allies, making himself—like Mussolini and Stalin—the supreme leader, the Führer. The Nazis did not come to power with a clear political agenda other than Hitler's concepts of racial purity and the need to revise the Versailles Treaty. But in a few years, violence against internal enemies, in particular Jews, and expansionism became the hallmarks of the Third Reich.

Hitler's Consolidation of Power

Hitler won his mandate in 1933 by vowing to do away with internal enemies. First on the list were the communists, the purported villains behind the Reichstag fire. After the Enabling Act, he eliminated all political parties and trade unions. Labeling his moves as security measures, in 1934 he ordered his SS troops to kill all conservative leaders who had opposed him before 1933 as well as leaders of his own storm troopers. This **Night of Long Knives**, Hitler's first internal purge, paved the way for his dictatorial rule by terror, much like Stalin's purges that began during the same period.

Nazi Racism as State Ideology Within six months Hitler had consolidated all political power in his hands. With other political parties gone, the Nazis moved to control civic and public institutions in the name of national and economic reconstruction. The foundation of this policy was the racist ideology set out in *Mein Kampf*. There Hitler argued that the very racial identity of Jews and Slavs made them a threat to the German nation and its dominant **Aryan race**, which supposedly had superior intellectual, physical, and moral qualities. To ensure the purity and well-being of this race, Jews—whom Hitler considered morally and physically subhuman, materialistic, and physiologically unable to work for the nation's greater good—had to be eliminated. To this end, Hitler used some of the popular ideas at that time, especially eugenics, to suggest swift, "scientific" ways to sort out those who were "desirable" from the rest and to eliminate the biological threat posed by "undesirables." The eugenicist theories adopted by the Nazis considered the health of an individual as a function primarily of genetic makeup, implying that it was impossible to cure or rehabilitate those genetically deficient. Eugenicist solutions ranged from preventing intermarriage with the "healthy" population and denying any social services to the genetically inferior to outright sterilization and **euthanasia**. Under the guise of national reinvigoration—"creating a Germany for Germans"—Hitler's goal was to create a racially pure state.

This irrational ideology worked because it was convenient: it offered an easy scapegoat for Germany's ills and did not force non-Jews to take responsibility or look for difficult solutions. But, in time, Jewishness came to be defined in increasingly complicated ways to include individuals who did not identify themselves as Jews but rather as Germans. Men and women who were Catholics, for example, and had Aryan blond hair and blue eyes, were considered Jewish if the state could uncover one Jewish grandparent. Thus the Nazis forced all people into trying to conform to racial stereotypes and hide any elements of their identity that might raise the suspicions of the dreaded **Gestapo**, Hitler's secret police.

Hitler's division of people into desirables and undesirables went beyond Aryans and Jews, however. Based on his racist theories, the category of undesirables broadened throughout the 1930s to include all

Night of Long Knives First purge of the SA, in which Hitler's personal political enemies and disloyal followers were killed in one night in 1934.

Aryan race Pseudoscientific idea of the racially superior group that made up the German nation.

euthanasia Forceful termination of one's life in a presumably painless way.

Gestapo (German contraction for Geheime Staatspolizei, "secret state police") Nazi secret police that implemented Hitler's policies of total control.

Jews, Roma (Gypsies), and Slavs (for example, Poles) as well as socialists and communists (said to have joined with Jews in a "Judeo-Bolshevik plot" again Germany), homosexuals, members of some religious denominations (for example, Jehovah's Witnesses), feminists, disabled persons, and anyone who supposedly suffered from a genetic disease or from tuberculosis, syphilis, or alcoholism.

Nazi Policies of Extermination The policies for dealing with undesirables aimed to eliminate them. Starting in 1933, the Nazis sterilized Roma and then others deemed "unfit" to reproduce. Doctors and judges, not the Gestapo, were the primary administrators of this policy. In 1933 the first **concentration camp**, meant to advance the elimination of undesirables, was established at Dachau, a town north of Munich. Here initially communist and other left-wing dissidents were taken to perform hard labor in subhuman living conditions intended to starve them to death. Later, these "labor" camps were turned into more effective killing factories, where most of Europe's Jews were exterminated.

The Nuremberg Laws The policy of segregating and later eliminating Jews began to take shape in 1935 through the **Nuremberg Laws**. These stripped Jews of citizenship, forbade them to marry non-Jews, and restricted their economic and social activities to the Jewish community. Jewish doctors could treat only Jewish patients; Jews could shop only at Jewish stores. Now Jews who saw themselves as Germans and did not identify with Jewishness in terms of religion, customs, or language were forced to assume a Jewish identity.

Controlling the Aryans But the Nazis were equally intent on controlling the desirables. Aryan women had to abide by the regime's pronatalist policies, which limited their social role to the home and children. Those who bore no children were considered disloyal to the Führer and punished, while unwed mothers of Aryan children were praised as patriotic Germans. People had to continually show their loyalty to the Nazi state to avoid the terror of the Gestapo, which could at any moment arrest people on the suspicion of treason or for being undesirables. By the late 1930s, the Third Reich had become a totalitarian state under the complete control of the Nazis and their supreme Führer, much like the Soviet Union was under Stalin.

Still, for ethnic Germans there was room for economic and social improvement in Hitler's racist state. During their first five years in power, the Nazis virtually eliminated unemployment, reducing it to less than 1 percent (though that figure did not include more than 1 million noncitizens—Jews and others imprisoned or simply stripped of citizenship). For those who were citizens, incomes were going up,

business opportunities were growing due to Hitler's remilitarization of the economy, and housing was becoming more affordable. Industrial production rose by nearly 30 percent between 1932 and 1938, a success similar to Stalin's accomplishments. And, like Stalin, Hitler also built these successes on the bodies of those forced to give up their wealth, freedom, and life. But unlike Stalin, Hitler successfully rallied the wealthy business class to engage in his plan of economic recovery. From an economic standpoint, the Nazi regime turned out to be more capitalistic and less socialistic than it had claimed at the beginning.

Antisemitic Propaganda Intense antisemitic propaganda also worked to justify the actions of the Nazis and gain the cooperation of many average and well-educated Germans. School textbooks were revised to include discussions of racial purity and the threat of marriages with Jews and other "inferior" races. Hitler also skillfully used movies and radio as propaganda tools. The Nazis harnessed the talents of outstanding artists such as film director **Leni Riefenstahl** to produce arousing and flawless documentaries and feature films designed to seduce average citizens into identifying with the ideals of the Third Reich. The most notable was *Triumph of the Will*, a cinematic masterpiece in communicating a racist message with eloquence and in revealing how the Nazis hoped to transform the German people into a homogeneous, energized, militarized, and obedient unit. Hitler also encouraged the production of affordable radios so he could reach most Germans on a regular basis. In addition to music, listeners got a daily dose of antisemitic propaganda through newscasts, speeches, and even humor.

Finally, the Nazis turned to sports, already an important pastime in Europe, and determined to demonstrate the superiority of the Aryan race in the Berlin Olympics of 1936. Athletes were carefully selected and trained in a grueling regimen that did produce many medal winners. But the Nazis also suffered some embarrassments, especially in the resounding victories of the African American track-and-field athlete Jesse Owens, whose supposed racial inferiority did not prevent him from breaking eleven Olympic records.

Intense propaganda was successful in transforming German society. By the late 1930s, educated people supported the Nazis. Doctors, for example, were willing to go along with sterilization programs and to pressure those with a good racial

concentration camp Camp for the internment of political prisoners and "undesirables," especially as organized by the Nazi regime.

Nuremberg Laws Edicts issued by the Nazis in 1935 that deprived Jews of German citizenship and initiated their segregation from German life.

Leni Riefenstahl (1902–2003) Famous German film director who made propaganda films for the Nazis.

This Jewish synagogue was vandalized by Nazi party members on the night of November 9–10, 1938, which came to be known as Kristallnacht (Night of Broken Glass). What message was the Nazi regime communicating to the Jewish population and to non-Jews about Jewish civilization and sacred spaces?

Mary Evans Picture Library/The Image Works

"pedigree" to have children. By the late 1930s, German industrial power was second only to that of the United States.

The Nazi Challenge to Europe

Hitler's dream of an Aryan state included an essential expansionist component. He was dedicated to revenging the German losses in World War I and wanted to recover all territories in which German populations lived, to save them from oppression by inferior races such as Slavs and Jews. His concept of Lebensraum aimed to justify the conquest of Poland and Russia so that Germans could resettle these lands and make them productive by using the native populations as slave labor. Not everyone grasped the extent of Hitler's idea of world domination until the beginning of World War II, but most Germans supported revising the Versailles Treaty and strengthening the military.

Gaining Allies in the East Initially Hitler focused on projecting a nonconfrontational international position. Germany was isolated in Europe, so he worked to increase trade with countries weakened by the Great Depression, especially in eastern Europe. Although these were also territories slated for occupation, where Slavic people he deemed inferior lived, Hitler was pragmatic. His offers to trade guns for grain and natural resources were received with interest by impoverished authoritarian regimes in Bulgaria, Romania, and Hungary. Such international agreements served to rearm these countries and also to provide Germany with important resources, especially Romania's oil, for its economy and for a future war.

With new markets for their guns, in clear violation of the Versailles Treaty, the Nazis began to rebuild the armament industry, using the very capitalists whom they had criticized before 1933. Starting in 1935 Hitler built a new air force, the Luftwaffe, and encouraged the creation of new offensive weapons through a vast program of research and development. The draft was introduced (1935), increasing the fighting forces to half a million, in flagrant defiance of the Versailles Treaty. But the first significant violation of the treaty came in March 1936, when German troops marched into the Rhineland, the region on the French border that was supposed to remain demilitarized as

Adolf Hitler and Benito Mussolini appeared together on many occasions to underscore their strong alliance and personal friendship. In reality, Hitler thought of Mussolini as an inferior, if useful partner in his plans for world domination.

Table 27.2	Nazi Challenges to the Versailles Treaty
March 1935	Establishment of German air force and military conscription
March 7, 1936	Occupation of demilitarized Rhineland
March 13, 1938	Annexation of Austria
March 1939	Occupation and dismemberment of Czechoslovakia
August 23, 1939	Molotov-Ribbentrop Pact
September 1, 1939	Invasion of Poland

© Cengage Learning

a buffer zone. The western democracies failed to respond strongly to this challenge, protesting through the League of Nations but taking no action. These violations of the Versailles Treaty are summarized in Table 27.2.

The Axis Alliance This inaction was a vital mistake because it bolstered Hitler's self-confidence, his popularity at home, and his appeal to similar regimes beyond Germany. Italy also had expansionist ambitions and in 1935 had invaded Ethiopia. By the end of 1936, the **Berlin-Rome Axis** had been formed, an alliance of like-minded states that would later include Japan, a militarist and expansionist power already embarked on conquest in East Asia and the Pacific. The alliance was based on their mutual imperialist interests, their profound disregard for democracy, and their fear of the Soviets.

Resistance and Appeasement

Hitler's rise to power challenged the Soviet Union. In 1935, the Soviet Union began to focus resolutely on the threat Hitler posed to the stability of Europe. The cornerstone of the new Soviet position in

international affairs was collective security. The threat of war in both the west and the east forced the Soviets to consider cooperation with capitalist countries, something unthinkable a decade earlier. But Stalin argued that this position did not contradict the goal of world communist revolution. It simply focused on eliminating the most imminent threat, fascism. This position led to his signing of mutual-aid pacts with France and Czechoslovakia in 1935, directed primarily against Germany.

Establishment of the Popular Fronts The same pragmatic vision led to a reversal of Comintern policies in 1935 from noncooperation to coalition building with other antifascist parties. This radical change paved the way for the formation of the **Popular Fronts** in Spain and France as well as the coalition in China against the Japanese threat. In France, the Socialist **Léon Blum** was able to talk the Communist, Socialist, and Radical Parties into forming the Popular Front in 1936. Blum was the first Jewish prime minister in France; his victory was an important symbolic challenge to the Nazis and on behalf of democracy, inclusiveness, and social responsibility of the state toward all citizens.

Blum quickly introduced major changes: the forty-hour workweek, the paid two-week vacation, the right of workers to collective bargaining, and other social programs. Under Blum, the Bank of France and the armaments industry were also nationalized. These changes signaled a major shift in defining government responsibilities but were not endorsed by everyone. Blum was attacked by members of his coalition and by opponents on the right. He resigned in June 1937 but

Berlin-Rome Axis Agreement between Mussolini and Hitler in 1936 to support each other in their expansionist goals.

Popular Fronts Moderate left-wing coalition governments during the 1930s that brought political stability, social reforms, and some economic recovery from the Great Depression.

Léon Blum (1872–1950) First Jewish prime minister of France, a Socialist who led the Popular Front government in 1936.

Hugo Jaeger/Time Life Pictures/Getty Images

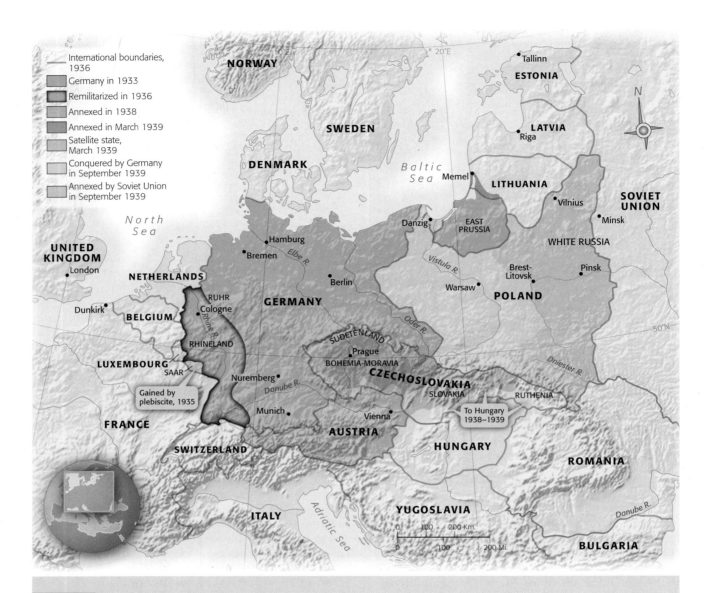

Map 27.2 **The Expansion of Germany** Between 1939 and 1942, Nazi Germany aggressively pursued its goals of acquiring Lebensraum for its Aryan German population. Its success would prove to be short-lived, however, especially as the Axis powers started to overstretch their resources. © *Cengage Learning*

1. What happened to Poland, Austria, and Czechoslovakia between 1938 and 1939?
2. How did these changes threaten European international order?
3. What direction did German territorial expansion have? Can you explain that in reference to Nazi ideology?

Thomas Mann (1875–1955)
Great German writer of the twentieth century who was persecuted by the Nazis for his staunch criticism of their antisemitism.

Virginia Woolf (1882–1941)
Pacifist English writer who drew attention to gender inequalities.

remained an important force in the coalition and resumed leadership briefly in 1938, in strong support of the Spanish Republic's struggle against Franco.

Artists Defend Democracy While politicians tried ineffectively to defend democracy against radical challenges, writers, popular culture stars, and religious leaders tried to address, if not solve, the crises of the day. The art and literature of the 1930s became more engaged with current events than had been the case in the more escapist 1920s. Writers like the German novelist **Thomas Mann** made it a personal quest to salvage the humanist spirit in Germany and the spirit of tolerance toward Jews. In Britain, **Virginia Woolf** confronted women's continued inequalities and militarization in her book *Three Guineas* (1938).

The fate of the world was sealed during this secret meeting in Moscow on August 23, 1939. Soviet Foreign Minister V. M. Molotov and German foreign minister Joachim von Ribbentrop sign a nonaggression pact, while Joseph Stalin (in the back second from the right) smiles as he presides over the proceedings, which were held in an inconspicuous office.

Bettmann/Corbis

But a far more powerful and effective critique of the social problems of the times and the rise of fascism came from an unlikely source, the silver screen. Charlie Chaplin effectively depicted social and economic inequalities while offering an amusing and deeply humane picture of the poor. In *Modern Times* (1936), his famous Little Tramp character became a symbol of humanity's vulnerability in a world run by machines and obsessed with mechanized progress. Similarly, *The Great Dictator* (1940) confronted the racist irrationality of Nazi Germany through comedy and farce involving a Jewish barber (the Little Tramp) standing in for Hitler at a Nazi mass rally.

Reactions of Religious Leaders Some religious leaders, such as the German Lutheran pastor **Dietrich Bonhoeffer**, attempted both to criticize the inhuman policies of the Nazis and to minister to their religious communities. Bonhoeffer went so far as to establish the underground pacifist Confessing Church, which remained active throughout World War II, at great peril to its leader and his following. Throughout the 1930s and the war, Bonhoeffer voiced his strong opposition to the Nazis; he was executed in April 1945 for his role in a plot to assassinate Hitler.

Other prelates, such as Eugenio Cardinal Pacelli, later Pope **Pius XII**, chose a policy of compromise with the Nazis to protect the Catholic Church. Though Pacelli spoke on several occasions against the Nazis and was critical of their antisemitic policies

in some of his writings, he also orchestrated a concordat in 1933 that established official relations between the Nazi regime and the Vatican. Critics saw the concordat as condoning the Nazis' assumption of dictatorial powers and the beginning of the Vatican's abandonment of the German Catholics into Hitler's hands. Supporters of Pius XII saw the concordat as a practical means for the Vatican to exercise some pressure on behalf of Catholics in Germany.

Yet many in Europe and America stood idle during this period of increasing tensions and violence. Burdened by their own antisemitism, many democratic countries refused entry to the Jews who were desperately trying to flee the Third Reich. The governments of both Britain and the United States, where many German (and later Austrian and eastern European) Jews sought refuge, were reluctant to lift immigration quotas. One of the most egregious incidents was the refusal by the American government to grant entry to ten thousand Jewish children, a request made insistently by First Lady Eleanor Roosevelt.

Nazi Expansion into Austria and Czechoslovakia As there were no protests from abroad, Hitler

Dietrich Bonhoeffer (1906–1945) German Lutheran pastor who openly criticized the Nazis and organized an underground church during the Third Reich.

Pius XII (r. 1939–1958) Pope who failed to take a strong stance against the Nazis under the pretext of neutrality.

continued his quest for aggrandizement. Claiming to respond to the wishes of Austrians—as true Aryans—to be part of the great German nation, in March 1938 he annexed Austria through coercion and manipulation. This action emboldened him to move toward the next target, Czechoslovakia, where a large German minority was concentrated mainly in the western region of the Sudetenland. But Czechoslovakia could not be easily intimidated. Its democratic government had strong military and mutual assistance pacts with France and the Soviet Union. Hitler gambled and requested that the Sudetenland be ceded to Germany, prompting an international crisis.

At the **Munich Conference** in September 1938, the British and French caved in to the German demands, justifying their desertion of Czechoslovakia as a small price to pay for securing peace. This policy of **appeasement** was meant to reduce the German threat under the misguided notion that Hitler's quest for Lebensraum could be satisfied by the Sudetenland. In fact, appeasement signaled to all countries in the east that the European order and frontiers could be violated and that they could be abandoned by the western democracies at any moment. Within six months, Czechoslovakia was divided into annexed (Sudetenland), occupied (Bohemia and Moravia), and independent (Slovakia) territories controlled by the Nazis. Slovakia became a puppet state ruled by the Catholic priest Josef Tiso, whose full cooperation with the Nazi policies of exterminating Jews was never denounced by the Vatican.

The Nazi-Soviet Pact As Hitler was preparing his next step—the invasion of Poland—Britain and France finally determined to stand up to Hitler's challenge by guaranteeing Poland's integrity. But it was not clear whether either of these countries was willing or prepared to honor that promise or whether they were merely making a gesture. Either way, Hitler had so much confidence by now that he was completely unimpressed. In addition, he now turned cunningly toward another potential ally, the Soviet Union.

On August 23, 1939, the two mortal enemies, Hitler and Stalin, signed a nonaggression agreement known as the **Molotov-Ribbentrop Pact**, for the foreign ministers who negotiated it. Many were surprised about this about-face in Soviet-Nazi relations. The pact went against the Nazi racist idea that the Slavs and Bolsheviks were enemies of the Third Reich; it also contradicted all the antifascist statements and alliances of the Soviet Union since 1935. Instead, the pact was a pragmatic move. Stalin had been excluded from the Munich Conference, and as the Soviet Union was isolated by France and Britain, he sought another partner in Europe. The Soviets also wanted to recover some of the territories lost in World War I. Thus the pact included several secret clauses that pertained to the division of Poland and the Baltic countries, as well as to the recovery of Bassarabia from Romania. Hitler wished to pursue his drive toward the east but wanted to ensure that the Soviets would not precipitate a two-front war. The solution was to divide Poland. On September 1, 1939, Germany launched a surprise attack on Poland from the west. On September 3, Britain and France honored their commitment to Poland by declaring war on Germany. World War II had begun.

Checking In

By yourself or with a partner, explain the significance of each of the following selected key terms:

Night of Long Knives	Léon Blum
Nuremberg Laws	Munich Conference
Berlin-Rome Axis	appeasement
Popular Fronts	Molotov-Ribbentrop Pact

World War II, 1939–1945

- ◆ **How did World War II differ from previous wars?**
- ◆ **What military strategies, technological developments, and other factors enabled the Allies to win the war?**

World War II was unprecedented in the extent of the destruction it wrought on the entire world, the degree to which it involved civilians, and the depth of the moral questions it raised. New military technologies, fighting strategies, psychological manipulation, and scientific discoveries ensured that this would be a war unlike any other. By the end of the conflict, the entire world had been touched by war; almost 70 million people had perished, most of them in Europe; and democracy had been challenged to the core. (See Table 27.3 for major events of the war.) Although the Allies defeated the Axis, Europe lay in ruin and democracy was not secure. Communism became Europe's next important challenge, as Stalin emerged victorious in eastern Europe.

Germany's Early Triumphs

Hitler managed to occupy the western half of Poland in four weeks. Tanks and motorized armored troop carriers raced across the border, supported by air power and paratroopers, introducing the world to a new type of warfare, **blitzkrieg**. The Poles fought desperately, but their military strength was inferior to

---

Munich Conference Emergency meeting in 1938 in which Britain and France gave in to Hitler's demand for the Czech Sudetenland.

appeasement Policy of giving in to an opponent's requests to prevent further demands.

Molotov-Ribbentrop Pact Non-aggression agreement of 1939 that secretly divided the Baltic countries and Poland between the Soviets and the Germans and allotted part of Romania to the Soviet Union.

blitzkrieg (in German, "lightning war") German attack strategy involving massed air force cover and rapid, motorized tank and troop movements that overwhelmed opponents.

Table 27.3 Major Events of World War II

September 1939	Poland occupied by Nazis and Soviets
May 1940	Churchill becomes prime minister of Britain
June 1940	Nazis occupy France
Fall 1940	Battle of Britain
March 1941	Lend-Lease Act
April 1941	Nazis occupy Greece and Yugoslavia
June 1941	Operation Barbarossa: Nazis invade Soviet Union
December 1941	Pearl Harbor; United States enters the war
November 1942	Allied invasion of North Africa
February 1943	Germans surrender at Stalingrad
July 1943	Soviet victory at Kursk
September 1943	Allied invasion of Italy
June 1944	Operation Overlord: Allied invasion of Normandy and liberation of France
August 1944	Warsaw Uprising
February 1945	Yalta Conference
May 8, 1945	Soviets liberate Berlin; Germans surrender
August 6 and 9, 1945	United States drops atomic bombs in Japan
August 14, 1945	Japanese surrender

© Cengage Learning

that of the Nazis, and their allies Britain and France offered little help. When the Soviets invaded Poland from the east on September 17, the Poles surrendered within ten days. The Soviets also proceeded to occupy Latvia, Estonia, and Lithuania and to incorporate them as Soviet Republics. Only Finland resisted Soviet demands, fighting back and scoring some victories, but it, too, was ultimately defeated in the winter of 1939–1940.

Nazi Victories in Western Europe In the spring of 1940, Hitler turned west, invading Denmark and Norway and then attacking the Netherlands and Belgium, which fell in two weeks. France was next. In mid-June 1940, German troops marched into Paris, and Henri Pétain, the hero of Verdun, signed over to German occupation the northern three-fifths of the country. The south, **Vichy France**, became a German puppet state under Pétain. This defeat was the greatest humiliation France had ever experienced, and it showed the whole world the aims and methods of the Third Reich.

Britain Fights Back Britain offered some aid to Belgium in May but had had to evacuate its troops to prevent their capture by the Nazis. In response to the fall of Norway, Winston Churchill assumed leadership of the country and radically shifted the British position from uncertain support for its allies to standing fast against Hitler, who now began an intensive bombardment of Britain's industries and cities in preparation for invasion. During those difficult months, Churchill provided what the British people needed—an unbounded energy and faith in the army, air force, civilians, and democracy that proved inspiring. In June 1941, he declared resolutely: "We shall go on to the end.... We shall never surrender."

Churchill had been in British politics for a long time, but he had never made more than a temporary mark. As an officer he had first served in India and Africa, then entered politics in 1901. As head of the British navy, he was responsible for the disastrous loss at Gallipoli early in World War I, which discredited him for the next twenty-five years. By the mid-1930s, he was considered a political maverick, always sure to take unpopular positions and often, critics said, too eager to jump into half-baked plans. But Churchill was also a passionate speaker, and his powerful warnings about the threat to democracy posed by the two great evils of fascism and communism grabbed the attention of the public and politicians alike. By 1940, he seemed the only leader with the vision and courage to change the course of the British policy of appeasement and the magnetism to carry the country with him: "Let us therefore brace ourselves to our duties, and to bear ourselves that, if the British Empire and Its Commonwealth last for a thousand years, they will say, 'That was their finest hour.'"

Between July and October 1940, Britain and Germany engaged in intensive air combat, known as the **Battle of Britain**. Initially the Nazis pursued a policy of strategic bombing of air bases. Their success depended almost exclusively on the strength and versatility of the Luftwaffe, while the British Royal Air Force (RAF) had a sophisticated system of command and coordination among its pilots enhanced by a radar network and good intelligence work in Germany. These advantages gave the RAF great precision in intercepting enemy planes (over 80 percent at times) and coordinating aerial attacks. By contrast, though the Nazis had excellent planes and pilots, they were often less precise and had to resort to riskier blanket bombing. In September, the Nazis shifted to a strategy of bombing civilian targets, bent on

Vichy France Puppet state established by the Nazis in southern France during World War II, named so for its capital in Vichy.

Battle of Britain Nazi air campaign against the British Isles in the fall of 1940 that became Germany's first major defeat.

terrorizing the population and killing more than 23,000 civilians. But by October 1940, the RAF had outmaneuvered the Germans. The Battle of Britain was significant because it was the first time since 1939 that the Nazis had suffered defeat, and it severely weakened the strength of the Luftwaffe. It also convinced Hitler to shift his attention to other areas, though the Nazis continued their attacks on Britain until June 1941.

U.S. Support for the Allies Churchill also gambled on assistance from the United States and initially received limited help. But the heroic resistance of the British galvanized support from President Roosevelt's government, which in March 1941 passed the **Lend-Lease Act**, granting "all aid short of war" to Britain. Later that year, the two leaders met to formulate a statement of war aims, the **Atlantic Charter**, which announced a commitment to restoring democracy in Europe. Finally, Churchill gambled in sending British troops to the Mediterranean to fight Italian forces bent on conquering Egypt and Greece. This strategy left the British Isles vulnerable but created an important diversion in the south, as Hitler had to send German reinforcements to a new battlefront in North Africa and the Balkans. For the first six months of 1941, German forces concentrated on taking Algeria, Morocco, Tunisia, Greece, and Yugoslavia.

The Nazis Invade the Soviet Union By June 1941, the Axis controlled almost all of Europe, from Norway to the Mediterranean and from France to Poland. Britain stood alone, with support from the United States. The blitzkrieg strategies had worked well for Hitler, and he now prepared to turn east again, toward the Soviet Union, to pursue his Lebensraum policy. The about-face against his former ally was anticipated in Britain, where intelligence concerning **Operation Barbarossa** had leaked in May. Churchill tried to warn Stalin, but to no avail. Other signs made it increasingly clear that Hitler was mounting a large-scale operation against the Soviet Union, especially a series of alliances that drew Hungary, Romania, and Bulgaria into the Axis.

Thus, when the Nazis finally embarked on Operation Barbarossa on June 22, 1941, no one except Stalin was surprised. The campaign was unprecedented in size and scope, including more than three million Axis troops, an air force of thousands, and more than three thousand tanks. The Soviets had a formidable army as well, in terms of size and equipment, but they lacked leadership. In addition to the purge of the officer corps, which demoralized the remaining personnel, the military was also paralyzed by Stalin's inability to come to terms with Hitler's betrayal. Quickly, the Germans drove to Kiev, where they took more than six hundred thousand prisoners in just one battle. By the end of October, they were besieging Leningrad and threatening Moscow in the north, while advancing toward oil fields in the south. **Joseph Goebbels**, Hitler's propaganda minister, announced that the war was over: the Soviets had lost more than two million soldiers, three hundred thousand square miles of land, and thousands of planes and tanks. Germany seemed invincible, but important developments in 1942 turned the tide of the war.

Allied Victory

The Axis had driven across a large portion of the Russian steppe, but the vast distances, harsh climate, and rudimentary roads proved their greatest obstacles. As winter arrived, the Germans and their allies were unable to get fresh troops and supplies to the front. In addition, the Soviets conducted a scorched-earth policy of burning fields, removing livestock, and disassembling industrial enterprises before retreating east. Blitzkrieg collapsed into a war of attrition. German troops grew demoralized as temperatures plunged to minus 60 degrees Fahrenheit. Many Germans froze to death, while the Russians went into hiding.

The U.S. Enters the War Meanwhile, the British and the Soviets soon had a new and important ally, the United States, which was compelled to declare war on the Axis following Japan's surprise attack on **Pearl Harbor** on December 7, 1941. Roosevelt sent an important infusion of food, supplies, and armament to the Soviets, helping them rebound from the massive losses incurred in 1941. Thus, when the Germans reopened their offensive in August 1942 by attacking **Stalingrad**, an important industrial center at the edge of European Russia, the Soviets were ready to fight back. In addition to Stalingrad's being a gateway to Asian Russia and oil resources in the south, taking the city renamed for the Soviet leader had become an obsession for Hitler.

For Stalin, the city was also symbolic, and he used all available propaganda to promote the idea that

Lend-Lease Act U.S. commitment in 1941 to grant massive financial and military support to the Allies.

Atlantic Charter Agreement between Churchill and Roosevelt in 1941 stating Allied goals for the war, including the commitment to restoring democracy in Europe.

Operation Barbarossa Code name for the Nazi invasion of the Soviet Union in June 1941.

Joseph Goebbels (1897–1945) Hitler's propaganda minister who played a central role in the Final Solution.

Pearl Harbor U.S. naval base in Hawaii bombed by Japan on December 7, 1941, drawing the United States into World War II.

Stalingrad (today Volgograd) Soviet city held under siege by the Nazis for six months where the Soviets scored one of the most important victories in 1942.

saving it was the same as saving the Russian soul. The war was no longer between communism and fascism; it was now the Great Patriotic War, in which soldiers and civilians, men and women, parents and children were called on to help Father Stalin and save Mother Russia from the Germanic invasion. Film director Sergei Eisenstein made his masterpiece, *Ivan the Terrible*, in the midst of war, depicting the medieval ruler as both despot and great patriot—the man who saved Russia from foreign threats. Stalin wanted to be seen this way—ruthless against foreigners but an ally of the simple people, who followed him faithfully. The morale of the people proved crucial to the defense of Stalingrad, which withstood months of house-to-house fighting before the Germans surrendered on February 2, 1943, their troop strength diminished from five hundred thousand to eighty thousand. Stalingrad had been reduced to rubble, and Soviet victory came at the great price of over 1.5 million casualties.

Turning the Tide of the War   The crushing defeat at Stalingrad slowed down the Nazis, but it was fighting at **Kursk**, between February and July 1943, that permanently turned the tide of the war in the east. At Stalingrad, Nazi troops had been at a tactical disadvantage because they were engaged in urban warfare, for which they were inadequately prepared; but at Kursk, they could use blitzkrieg techniques. At the same time, however, the Soviets had learned much about Nazi military strategy and had been able to upgrade their armaments, especially tank power and antitank guns. Defeated by the Soviets at their best game, the Nazis were profoundly demoralized and began to retreat.

In North Africa, German forces had also been pushed back by the British, now joined by American troops. By May 1943, the Germans had withdrawn entirely from the region. With North Africa secured, the Allies were able to launch an invasion of Sicily, a steppingstone to the invasion of Italy in September 1943. Mussolini was forced from power but remained in the hands of the Germans, at the helm of a puppet republic in northern Italy.

In addition, the Allies pursued a strategy of all-out air attacks on Germany. The policy of strategic bombing—attacking important military, industrial, and transportation centers—failed in its immediate goals of destroying the military capacity of the Nazis, but it did cut production. Night bombing afforded greater protection from anti-aircraft guns but also reduced precision in hitting targets and increased civilian losses. Some 300,000 Germans died and 750,000 were maimed in Allied air raids. But it was clear that Hitler would be defeated only by an invasion.

Allied Victory   On June 6, 1944, **Operation Overlord** began. In one of the most intense military operations

of the war, the Allies crossed the English Channel to land more than two million soldiers (Americans, British, Poles, Belgians, Canadians, Norwegians, Dutch, and French) and millions of tons of military equipment in Nazi-occupied France. Securing the first strip of beach involved heavy casualties, but months of careful planning paid off. Now the Germans had to fight a three-front war—east, west, and south—and could do little more than resist while retreating. Paris was liberated by August, Brussels in September, and that month the first Allied troops crossed into Germany.

In the east, the Soviets were also advancing steadily. In January 1945, they liberated the concentration camp at Auschwitz and took Warsaw; in April, advance units of the American and Soviet armies met south of Berlin on the Elbe River. Mussolini met his end on April 28, killed by Italian partisans while trying to escape. He was then publicly hung so that crowds could freely abuse his body. Two days later, trying to avoid the humiliation of capture, Hitler committed suicide together with his wife, Eva Braun, in his Berlin bunker. On May 8, the Soviets finally liberated Berlin and brought the war to an end on the European front. Three months later, the United States used a newly developed weapon against Japan, the **atomic bomb**. The Japanese surrendered on August 14, and World War II was over.

The Human Costs   The total human toll of the war was as high as 70 million people, by some estimates, with Europe suffering roughly half of the casualties. Approximately 20 million of these were soldiers, and the remaining 50 million were civilians. The astronomic number and ratio of civilian to soldier casualties were unprecedented. Those who suffered the most were in eastern Europe: Yugoslavia lost 4.5 million people, a higher ratio of its population than Germany's 7.7 million casualties, while in Poland, Warsaw alone had more casualties in absolute numbers than Britain and the United States combined. The vast majority of the Jewish population exterminated in the war came from eastern Europe. The extent of material destruction was equally unprecedented, with eastern Europe again experiencing the highest losses as two waves of occupation and destruction—the Nazis and then the Soviets—swept through the area between 1939 and 1945.

Technology and the Allied Victory   The Allies won the

Kursk Battle in which the Nazis received a crushing defeat through Soviet blitzkrieg tactics.

Operation Overlord Code name for the Allied invasion of France in June 1944.

atomic bomb Bomb powered by nuclear energy, with unprecedented destructive capability, developed first by scientists in the United States.

Map 27.3
Allied Victory in Europe Soviet, British, and U.S. troops, supported by numerous resistance movements in Axis-occupied territories, turned the tide of war after 1942. © Cengage Learning

1. What would you describe as the position of Nazi Germany in Europe in 1942?
2. What were the obstacles faced by the Allies at that point?
3. By looking at the movement of military forces over this map and the reoccupation of Axis-controlled territories by different Allied forces, which country bore the brunt of the effort?

war by outperforming their enemies in military technology, intelligence gathering, science, diplomacy, and mobilization on the home front. On the eastern front, the Soviets spared no expense and converted more than 50 percent of their industrial production to building tanks that were larger and more powerful than Germany's. The British developed radar technology essential to the RAF success in the Battle of Britain. The Allies also used new technology to break the German and Japanese military codes. And the Americans invested nearly $2 billion and employed more than 130,000 people in the **Manhattan Project**, the vast nuclear engineering complex that worked steadily between 1942 and 1945 to develop the atomic bomb before the Germans did and to use it to force the Japanese surrender.

Victory and Allied Diplomacy Another key to Allied victory was diplomacy. The ability of Churchill, Stalin, and Roosevelt to work together, despite their fundamental ideological differences

Manhattan Project Extensive science and development program in the United States in 1942–1945 that produced a nuclear bomb.

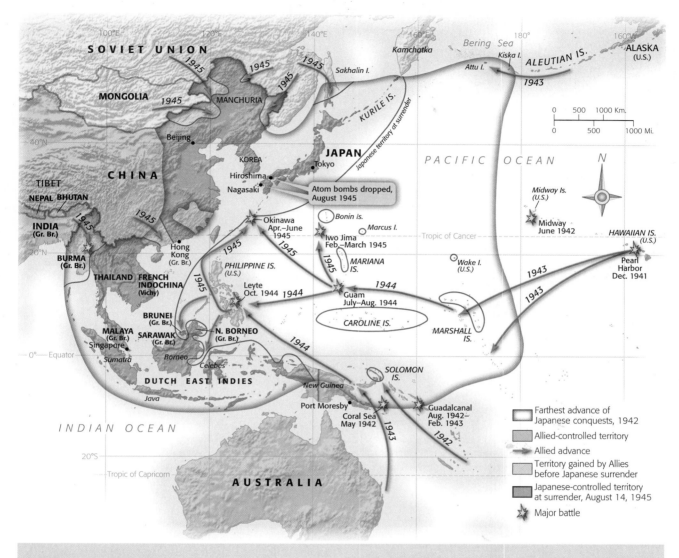

Map 27.4 **War in Asia** In the war against Japan in the Pacific, a different configuration of the Axis versus Allies conflict took place. © *Cengage Learning*

1. Who bore the brunt of the war effort?
2. What other supporting countries helped in the effort against the Axis?
3. What other features of the conflict that are different from the European theater of war can you discern from this map?

and deep distrust between Stalin and his western allies, was one of the remarkable successes of the war. The three met on two important occasions during the war, in Teheran in 1943 and Yalta in 1945. The **Yalta Conference** was particularly important as it laid the foundation for the creation of the United Nations, determined policies for liberating and dividing Germany, allowed postwar Poland and eastern Europe to fall primarily within the Soviet sphere of influence, and arranged for the Soviet Union's entry into the war against Japan. The last two provisions were the result of an informal exchange between the Americans, who desperately wanted support against Japan, and the Soviets, who sought to control the political future of eastern Europe. The Yalta Conference would play a major role in the political reconfiguration of Europe after the war.

Yalta Conference Meeting of Churchill, Roosevelt, and Stalin in 1945 to discuss postwar peace.

In February 1945, Winston Churchill, Franklin Roosevelt, and Joseph Stalin met in the Russian resort town of Yalta, in the Crimea, to map out plans for ending the war in Asia and for establishing order in postwar Europe. Roosevelt was already ailing; he died in April. In July, Churchill was voted out of office. The Yalta Conference was the last time the leaders of the three great powers were able to work together peacefully for more than forty years. How would you describe the mood of the three leaders? What differences do you notice among them?

Mobilization, Collaboration, and Resistance

The Allies could not have won the war without the unprecedented mobilization of civilians, who worked in war industries and other essential capacities and, in occupied regimes, participated in resistance movements. Women, especially, served in new capacities. They were allowed to join, and in some cases were even drafted into, the military. But only in the Soviet Union did they serve as combatants, from ambulance drivers to pilots. More important, however, women were mobilized for economic production and auxiliary services, such as medical aid, supplies, and various public service jobs, from secretaries to bus drivers. Their service was significant in Britain and especially in the Soviet Union, where women already constituted almost half of the labor force. During the war, female employment in Soviet industries climbed to an unprecedented 60 percent.

Mobilizing the Home Front In Germany, the mobilization of civilians was carefully weighed against fears of demoralization. Hitler allowed the production of consumer goods as a means of diverting the

anxiety of families whose sons and husbands were away at war. The standard of living of Aryan Germans remained close to the prewar levels long after Soviets, Italians, and Romanians were asked to give up their personal comforts. By contrast, in Britain, people were asked to conserve, give up, and buckle down throughout the war. The constant bombings during the Battle of Britain both frightened civilians and helped build their resolve. The tremendous losses incurred by the Soviets during the first year of combat also worked as powerful propaganda in the hands of the communist government, which used patriotism to recruit the help of civilians and then celebrated their heroism, especially after Stalingrad.

Civilian help was also essential in occupied territories, such as Slovakia, Vichy France, and Croatia, where the Nazis set up puppet governments. To supply the war machine with much-needed armaments and other industrial products, food supplies, and fuel, the Nazis depended heavily on collaboration with native populations. Even in places like Poland, where the official policy was to exterminate all Jews and where more than 2.5 million non-Jewish Poles perished in the war, the Germans needed to work with the Polish population at the local level. This policy was also implemented in the Czech lands, France, the Netherlands, Serbia, and Greece. The peoples of occupied countries faced difficult choices—either collaborate with the Nazis or become their victims.

Many learned to work within this harsh system and to play by its methods. In Prague, for example, a Czech man working for the German authorities stopped saluting his Jewish neighbors on the street, fearful that he might be suspected of being a Jew himself. Soon he asked his son not to play with their Jewish neighbor, until one day the Jewish family was gone. Though he was sad and afraid, he was also relieved. Occupation forced most people to spy, lie, and vilify fellow humans in order to survive, corrupting their human dignity.

Resistance Movements Despite fear and violent reprisals, resistance movements developed in all occupied territories and even in Germany, some spectacular in scope and results, others merely symbolic. In Germany, the most remarkable were the efforts of military leaders to assassinate Hitler in 1943 and 1944. These officers were attempting to rescue the German war effort from Hitler's increasingly irrational leadership, but they were not necessarily opposed to either the racist ideology or the expansionist goals of the Third Reich. They all failed, and the officers were executed.

More widespread resistance movements developed in the France, Yugoslavia, the Soviet Union, and Poland. In France, the Free French, under the leadership of **Charles de Gaulle**, provided a focus for courage and hope. The Free French military contributions were modest, but they helped de Gaulle establish himself as the liberator of his people.

The most successful partisan movement in occupied Europe was that of the Yugoslav Communists, led by **Josip Broz Tito**. His well-organized guerilla army liberated Yugoslavia with only indirect assistance from the Allies, and largely independent of the Soviets. This movement was more successful because of broad popular support, Tito's tight leadership, and Germany's weak control in Yugoslavia. But Tito accomplished this remarkable feat by also committing atrocities against other partisan movements and civilians.

In Poland, an underground Polish Home Army acted to thwart German operations with great bravery. They were also able to supply important intelligence to the Allies. In the final months of the war, a large part of this resistance force perished in the **Warsaw Uprising**, which attempted the liberation of the city from Nazi occupation in August 1944. Despite promises to come to the aid of the Poles, Stalin kept the advancing Soviet armies from providing any support to the uprising, which was violently crushed. Though valiant in its efforts to liberate Poland, the Home Army did little to help

Table 27.4   The Final Solution

March 1933	Dachau concentration camp opens
September 1935	Nuremberg Laws
October 1939	First Polish ghetto
October 1941	Auschwitz concentration camp is opened for the extermination of Jews
January 1942	Wannsee Conference
January 27, 1945	Soviets liberate Auschwitz and its remaining 7,000 inmates
April 1945	Allies liberate last concentration camps

© Cengage Learning

Polish Jews and was generally reluctant to accept Jews as members.

The Final Solution

The unprecedented level of brutality against civilians is one of the deepest moral challenges posed by World War II. Millions of innocents on both sides of the conflict were imprisoned, placed under siege and starved to death, forced into slave labor, raped, and bombed, initially with conventional artillery and at the very end with nuclear bombs. But by far the most horrifying aspect of World War II was the Nazi policy of destroying the Jews of Europe. Eliminating the Jews from German society had been a fundamental concept of the Nazis since before 1933. And yet the technologies to bring about the **Final Solution**—the physical extermination of all Jews—did not come together until the war. This diabolical policy came into being in a combination of Hitler's irrational theories of racial purity and with the expertise of architects, engineers, doctors, biologists, and other people well grounded in the foundations of science and reason, many of whom subscribed to the long-held assumption that there was a "Jewish problem" in Europe. The progression of the Final Solution is summarized in Table 27.4.

Planning for the Extermination of All Jews The decision to pursue a policy of genocide against all Jews was made official at the **Wannsee Conference** in

Charles de Gaulle (1890–1970) Leader of the Free French, the partisan movement that worked to liberate France, and first president of postwar France.

Josip Broz Tito (1892–1980) Leader of the Yugoslav Communist Party and of the most successful partisan movement in World War II.

Warsaw Uprising Revolt by the partisan Polish Home Army in the fall of 1944 against the Nazis.

Final Solution Nazi concept of exterminating all European Jews as a response to the so-called Jewish problem in Europe.

Wannsee Conference Meeting of high-ranking Nazis in early 1942 that officially decided to exterminate all Jews.

Map 27.5 **The Holocaust**

Nazi genocidal policies toward European Jewry resulted in the murder of more than six million Jews. Most were from eastern Europe, where all of the death camps were located. © *Cengage Learning*

1. What state had the highest losses?
2. Where were most of the camps located?
3. What state had the fewest losses?

Map legend:
- ■ Extermination camp
- ● Concentration camp
- ✱ Major ghetto
- **7,680** Estimated Jewish death toll, by country
- Under Axis control
- Allied nations
- Neutral nations

Map labels:
NORWAY 762, SWEDEN, FINLAND 7, ESTONIA 2,000, LATVIA 71,500, Jungernhof, LITHUANIA 143,000, Kaunas, SOVIET UNION 1,000,000, Minsk, Maly Trostinets, DENMARK 60, North Sea, Baltic Sea, GREAT BRITAIN, NETHERLANDS 100,000, Bergen-Belsen, Bialystok, Warsaw, Treblinka, Pripyat' R., BELGIUM 28,900, GERMANY 141,500, Chelmno, Lódz, Lublin, Sobibor, POLAND 3,000,000, Drancy, LUX. 0, Auschwitz, Cracow, Belzec, Lwów, Bogdonovka, Mostovoi, BOHEMIA & MORAVIA 78,150, Majdanek, Pechora, Vapniarka, FRANCE 77,320, Dachau, Bratislava, SLOVAKIA 71,000, TRANSNISTRIA, SWITZ., AUSTRIA 50,000, Budapest, HUNGARY 569,000, Kishinev, Fossoli, Bozen, Zagreb, Iasenovac, Belgrade, ROMANIA 287,000, Odessa, SPAIN, CROATIA, 60,000 SERBIA, Danube R., Black Sea, ITALY 7,680, BULGARIA 0, ALBANIA, GREECE 67,000, TURKEY, Mediterranean Sea, Elbe R., Rhine R., Seine R., Loire R., Oder R., Vistula R., Danube R., Po R.

January 1942, though the specific means by which the estimated 11 million Jews of Europe were to be killed was not yet discussed. Experiments with mass killings through conventional and chemical weapons had already been tried both before the war in Germany and during the eastern campaigns in Poland, Byelorussia, Ukraine, and Russia. The rounding up of the Jews was assigned to special troops, the **Einsatzgruppen**, small mobile killing units made up of the cruelest SS and Gestapo recruits. The Einsatzgruppen were to eliminate other undesirables also, including communists, Roma, Jehovah's Witnesses, and Slavs.

The Ghettos Another important policy was to place all Jews in occupied territories in **ghettos**, where they were sealed off from the non-Jewish population. In Warsaw, for instance, the European city with the largest Jewish population, several thousand Poles were moved out to make room for around half a million Jews, crowded into a few city blocks. Before being sent to concentration camps, these people were first stripped of all possessions and forced into crowded, unheated, and lice-infested rooms. Jews unable to

Einsatzgruppen (in German, "mission groups") Nazi death squads created at the beginning of the war to round up and execute Jews and other "undesirables."

ghetto Small, sealed-off areas in Nazi-controlled cities where the Jewish population was forced to live.

George Orwell Reflects on Nationalism

In May 1945, Europe lay in ruins, beyond recognition. George Orwell had reported on the war for the BBC and had seen both Nazi racism and British nationalist propaganda take their turn at vilifying the enemy. To Orwell, it seemed hardly suitable to stand proud because the Allies had just won the war in Europe. Instead, he wrote a sobering reevaluation of the nationalism that had fueled the war effort on both sides.

❶ Do you agree with Orwell's distinction between patriotism and nationalism? Are there instances when defending one-self can actually mean military aggression and securing more power for one's nation?

❷ Do you agree with this statement? How, then, is one to explain the popularity of the Nazis?

❸ How can the proletariat be the object of passionate nation-alist feeling? Is it equivalent to hold a religious, versus racist, versus class identity at the heart of one's nationalism? Are there important differences among these categories of identity?

❹ Looking back at the case studies before Orwell's eyes in 1945, do you see this combina-tion of self-delusion and intense passion as a strength or a weak-ness of nationalist movements?

❶ By "nationalism" I mean first of all the habit of assuming that human beings can be classified like insects and that whole blocks of millions or tens of millions of people can be confidently labeled "good" or "bad". But secondly—and this is much more important—I mean the habit of identifying oneself with a single national or other unit, its interests. Nationalism is not to be confused with patriotism. By "patriotism" I mean devotion to a par-ticular place and a particular way of life, which one believes to be the best in the world but has no wish to force on other people. Patriotism is of its na-ture defensive, both militarily and culturally. Nationalism, on the other hand, is inseparable from the desire for power. The abiding purpose of every na-tionalist is to secure more power and more prestige, not for himself but for the nation or other unit in which he has chosen to sink his own individuality.

    ❷ Confronted with a phenomenon like Nazism, which we can observe from the outside, nearly all of us would say much the same things about it. But here I must repeat what I said above, that I am only using the word "nationalism" for lack of a better. Nationalism includes such movements and tendencies as communism, political Catholicism, Zionism, antisemi-tism, Trotskyism and Pacifism. It does not necessarily mean loyalty to a government or a country, still less to one's own country, and it is not even strictly necessary that the units in which it deals should actually exist.
❸ To name a few obvious examples, Jewry, Islam, Christendom, the Pro-letariat and the White Race are all of them objects of passionate national-istic feeling: but their existence can be seriously questioned, and there is not definition of any one of them that would be universally accepted.

    It is also worth emphasizing once again that nationalist feeling can be purely negative. There are, for example, Trotskyists who have become simply enemies of the USSR without developing a corresponding loyalty to any other unit…. A nationalist is one who thinks solely, or mainly, in terms of competitive prestige…. He sees history, especially contempo-rary history, as the endless rise and decline of great power units, and every event that happens seems to him a demonstration that his own side is on the upgrade and some hated rival is on the downgrade….
❹ Nationalism is power-hunger tempered by self-deception. Every nationalist is capable of the most flagrant dishonesty, but he is also— since he is conscious of serving something bigger than himself— unshakably certain of being in the right.

Source: Excerpt from "Notes on Nationalism" from The Collected Essays, Journalism, and Letters of George Orwell, Volume III: As I Please 1943–1945 edited by Peter Davison, copyright © by the estate of the late Sonia Brownell Orwell and renewed 1996 by Mark Hamilton. Reprinted by permission of Houghton Mifflin Harcourt Publishing Company, A M Heath, and The Random House Group Ltd. All rights reserved.

Bettmann/Corbis

British troops liberated the Nazi concentration camp at Bergen-Belsen in April 1945, too late to save young Anne Frank, who had died there of typhus in March, but British food and medical care did help some, such as these starving prisoners, to survive. Bergen-Belsen, in Germany proper, was initially a detention and transit camp, but an estimated 50,000 people died there, largely of disease. Those who survived the camps were physically, emotionally, and psychologically traumatized, and had great difficulty adjusting to life in postwar Europe. What do the looks and general appearance of these prisoners communicate about the experience of the concentration camps?

Scientific Genocide In the camps, Nazi engineers and architects designed gas chambers made to look like shower rooms, and scientists identified **Zyklon B**, an insecticide, as a cheap and effective lethal gas. Labor camps in Poland were transformed into extermination camps; at Auschwitz alone, 1.5 million Jews perished. By April 1945, when the last camps were liberated, over 6 million Jews had been killed as well as more than 4.6 million other people classified by the Nazis as undesirables.

The Moral Failure of Europe The tragedy of European Jewry is incomprehensible in rational terms and raises questions about what could have been done to save Jews and others and why such efforts failed. Those who committed these crimes against humanity abound. In Germany, they were not only Nazi fanatics but also ordinary citizens who either willingly helped or looked the other way. In occupied territories, non-Jews were under intense pressure to collaborate with the Germans, and some did so more easily than others. The Allies had detailed knowledge of concentration camps and atrocities as early as 1942, but they failed to impede the program by bombing the camps or the railroads that led to them. Pope Pius XII, who was aware of anti-semitic laws and violence committed by Catholics in Italy, Poland, Germany, and Slovakia did not condemn these actions, failing in his role as moral and spiritual leader of the Roman Catholic Church. The general public in Europe and the United States was more concerned with defeating Hitler than saving the Jews. Antisemitism was a mainstream attitude in the western world. Though it did not necessarily translate into support for Hitler's ideas, it meant that sympathy for the Jews was limited, and Jews themselves, like the American secretary of the treasury Henry Morgenthau, hesitated to use the example of the Jewish plight to mobilize support for the war.

Yet individuals and communities also acted courageously to assist Jews and others persecuted by the Nazis. Towns in France helped Jews escape to Switzerland, and several were wiped out by the Nazis as a consequence. The Danes and Bulgarians were notable for their efforts to hide Jews and their refusal to hand them over to the Germans. But brave acts were rare, and no effort, it seems, could stop the Nazi intention to exterminate the Jews of Europe.

Finally, the Jews of Europe were themselves in disbelief about the Final Solution. Many German, Hungarian, Polish, and French citizens of Jewish ancestry had become culturally integrated into their national cultures and thought of themselves as part of the nation rather than as a racially defined group. Only under the Nazis were they forced to identify themselves as Jews. Jewish resistance against the Holocaust developed rather slowly and with limited effect, partly because of the dangers involved and partly because Jews were themselves a diverse group.

leave the ghettos were gradually starved to death through inadequate food supplies. Some also perished because of unsanitary and overcrowded conditions, which fostered tuberculosis and other epidemics.

The Nazis used deceit and fear to manage the ghettos. They set up Jewish councils and police, dividing communities by forcing Jews to monitor one another and compete for inadequate food supplies and menial jobs, while Nazi death squads periodically entered the ghettos to kill people at random. Jewish leaders were required to select and round up those who would be sent to concentration camps. Some of these leaders committed suicide; others were killed by their own communities. Upon his arrival at Auschwitz, the leader of the Lódz ghetto was beaten to death by Jewish inmates, who viewed him as the filthy tool of the Germans. The Nazis were clever in setting Jews against Jews, forcing them to victimize each other and question the very core of their identity.

Zyklon B Type of insecticide used by the Nazis for efficient extermination of the Jews in the death camps.

In Belorussia, as the Nazis and their local collaborators began implementing Nazi genocidal policies, Jewish men and women organized military units that struck back, with the support of the Soviet Union. Why did these Jewish partisans turn toward the Soviet Union for support? (Courtesy, Leonid Smilovitsky, The Goldstein-Goren Diaspora Research Center)

The failure to stop the Holocaust had significant consequences in Europe after the end of the war. Although democracy was saved, Europeans and Americans were forced to look within themselves for the source of this profound failure of western civilization. Genocide had succeeded in advanced European countries because the technology was available to implement it, and the people generally were willing to use or allow it.

 Checking In

By yourself or with a partner, explain the significance of each of the following selected key terms:

Atlantic Charter	Manhattan Project
Operation Barbarossa	Yalta Conference
Joseph Goebbels	Warsaw Uprising
Kursk	Wannsee Conference

CHAPTER
Review

Summary

- From 1929 to 1945, democracy was severely challenged in Europe by radical movements from the right and the left.

- The Great Depression destabilized all European economies, bringing about high unemployment, loss of capital, and political unrest.

- Two totalitarian dictatorships, Germany and the Soviet Union, were able to address economic problems more successfully than democratic countries.

- Remilitarization and antidemocratic policies were key to their economic recovery.

- Nazi state ideology of racist extermination was made clear in the 1930s, but encountered weak responses from the European states and the United States.

- The failure of the western democracies to stand up to Hitler's early defiance of the Versailles Treaty played a role in emboldening him.

- World War II brought unprecedented destruction and transformed the relationship between civilian and military involvement in war, encompassing the entire populations of the combatant countries.

- New military technology widened the scope and intensity of destruction and made military operations more complex than ever before.

- The Nazi extermination of entire populations and the atrocities committed by both occupiers and liberators (especially the Soviets) laid bare horrors that belied all concepts of civilization and progress in Europe.

Chronology

1928–1933	Stalin initiates first five-year plan in Soviet Union
1929	Great Depression begins
1931	United States initiates moratorium on war debts
1933	Hitler comes to power in Germany; Dachau labor camp established in Germany
1934	Soviet Union is admitted to League of Nations
1935	Mussolini invades Ethiopia
1936	Popular Front is formed in France; Spanish Civil War begins; Great Purges begin in Soviet Union
1939	Nazis take over Czechoslovakia; Franco wins Spanish Civil War; Hitler and Stalin sign Molotov-Ribbentrop Pact; World War II begins
1940	Nazis occupy Norway, Denmark, the Netherlands, Belgium, and France; Nazis bomb England in Battle of Britain
1941	U.S. Lend-Lease Act grants war aid to Britain; Nazis invade Soviet Union in Operation Barbarossa; United States enters the war after Japanese bomb Pearl Harbor
1942	Wannsee Conference plans Jewish genocide
1943	Soviets win decisive battles at Stalingrad and Kursk
1945	Soviets liberate Auschwitz; Churchill, Roosevelt, and Stalin meet at Yalta Conference; United States drops first atomic bombs in Japan; World War II ends

© Cengage Learning

Test Yourself

To gauge your mastery of the material in this chapter, answer the questions below. More than one answer may be correct.

Responses to the Great Depression, 1929–1939

1. The Great Depression is a:
   a. Geographic feature of the Alps.
   b. Historic event that lasted a week.
   c. Massive trauma experienced by all Europeans at the loss of democratic regimes.
   d. Global economic slump that lasted almost a decade.
   e. All of the above.

2. In Europe, which country had the largest number of unemployed persons during the Great Depression?
   a. France
   b. Italy
   c. Germany
   d. Great Britain
   e. Romania

3. The Government of National Unity in Britain succeeded in:
   a. Ending unemployment.
   b. Providing support for affordable housing.
   c. Providing support for health insurance.
   d. Bringing down the Conservative Party.
   e. Co-opting the communists into the government.

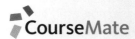 Visit the CourseMate website at **www.cengagebrain.com** for additional study tools and review materials for this chapter.

4. The Spanish Civil War:

   a. Brought down the Republicans.
   b. Led to the establishment of a military fascistic regime.
   c. Ended the monarchical rule in Spain.
   d. Restored trust in democracy in Spain.
   e. Brought an end to the domination of the Catholic Church.

5. Lebensraum refers to:

   a. Germany's quest for peace in Europe.
   b. Hitler's ideology of territorial expansion.
   c. The Nazi view of Germans as racially superior and entitled to world domination.
   d. The legitimacy of obliterating Poland and incorporating it into Germany.
   e. The Nazi quest for revisionism in response to the Versailles Treaty.

Now that you have reviewed and tested yourself on this part of the chapter, take time to pull together all the important information by answering the following questions:

◆ What were the causes of the Great Depression?

◆ What were the political consequences of the Great Depression?

The Soviet Union Under Stalin, 1929–1939

6. In the 1930s the Soviet Union attempted to improve its international standing by:

   a. Lending money to countries hit by the Great Depression.
   b. Taking a more moderate position in foreign relations.
   c. Appointing Maxim Litvinov as foreign commissar.
   d. Building its military power.
   e. Joining the League of Nations.

7. The Five Year Plans aimed to:

   a. Industrialize important sectors of the Soviet economy.
   b. Collectivize agriculture.
   c. Improve the welfare of the workers and peasants.
   d. Build the infrastructure (roads, waterways, electricity) of the country.
   e. Make an automobile available to each citizen.

8. Collectivization:

   a. Led to confiscation of most land from individual peasants.
   b. Enabled kulaks to thrive.
   c. Enabled Soviet agriculture to improve productivity.
   d. Led to a horrific famine that killed millions of people.
   e. Was embraced by peasants as progressive.

9. The Great Purges:

   a. Were undertaken through the NKVD.
   b. Protected high-ranking Bolsheviks from lower-ranking ones.
   c. Led to the development of the gulags.
   d. Enabled Stalin to gain greater legitimacy.
   e. Began in 1930.

10. Stalin attempted to control Soviet society through:

   a. State controlled economic planning.
   b. The confiscation of private property.
   c. Establishment of a police state.
   d. A sophisticated propaganda machine.
   e. A meritocratic reward system.

Now that you have reviewed and tested yourself on this part of the chapter, take time to pull together all the important information by answering the following questions:

◆ What were the Soviet Union's successes and failures in the 1930s?

◆ How did Stalin turn the Soviet Union into a totalitarian state?

The Third Reich, 1933–1945

11. The Nazi ideology contended that:

   a. Jews were an inferior race of humans.
   b. The superior Aryan race was a scientific reality.
   c. Jews were the cause of Germany's economic problems after World War I.
   d. Aryans should marry non-Aryans so as to improve the racial quality of all populations.
   e. Feminists represented a threat to the German nation.

12. The Nuremberg Laws:

   a. Established citizenship on the basis of racial purity.
   b. Stripped Jews of all political and social rights.
   c. Sterilized all Jews.
   d. Forbade the marriage of Jews and non-Jews.
   e. Only applied to non-secular Jews.

13. Which of these famous personalities spoke out against Hitler during the 1930s?

   a. Virginia Woolf
   b. Pope Pius XII
   c. Benito Mussolini
   d. Charlie Chaplin
   e. Leon Blum

14. Appeasement:

   a. Led to the creation of a strong European alliance.
   b. Forced Czechoslovakia to surrender to Hitler.
   c. Brought fear to European countries in the east.
   d. Demoralized the democratic regimes in France and Britain.
   e. Was promoted by Stalin.

15. Which of these territories were occupied by Germany through forceful military struggle before September 1939?

   a. Rhineland
   b. Austria
   c. Sudetenland
   d. Slovakia
   e. None of the above

Now that you have reviewed and tested yourself on this part of the chapter, take time to pull together all the important information by answering the following questions:

◆ What were the distinguishing features of the Nazi regime?

◆ How did Germany manage to challenge the European international order?

World War II, 1939–1945

16. Germany was able to advance quickly between 1939 and 1941 because of the:

   a. Nonaggression pact with the Soviet Union.
   b. Blitzkrieg military strategy.
   c. Atomic bomb.
   d. Use of slave labor on the front.
   e. Military weakness of the Allies.

17. The Allies were able to turn around the tide of the war starting in 1942 because of:

   a. Use of new technologies.
   b. Entry of the United States in the war.
   c. Partisan movements in Nazi occupied territories.
   d. Soviet military successes at Kursk and Stalingrad.
   e. Successful diplomatic maneuvers among the Allies.

18. The Final Solution was made possible by:

   a. The state ideology of antisemitic racism.
   b. Collaboration between political leadership and the scientific community in Germany.
   c. Hitler's hatred of Jews.
   d. Insufficient opposition against antisemitism in Germany and the Nazi-allied states.
   e. The failure of the Allies to destroy concentration camps.

19. Which international accord established the Allied goal of restoring democracy in Europe after World War II?

    a. Lend-Lease Act
    b. Yalta Agreement
    c. Atlantic Charter
    d. Wannsee Conference
    e. Molotov-Ribbentrop Pact

20. The most successful partisan movements in World War II developed in:

    a. Finland
    b. Italy
    c. Yugoslavia
    d. Poland
    e. France

Now that you have reviewed and tested yourself on this part of the chapter, take time to pull together all the important information by answering the following questions:

◆ How did World War II differ from previous wars?

◆ What military strategies, technological developments, and other factors enabled the Allies to win the war?

CHAPTER 28

Europe Divided, 1945–1968

Chapter Outline

1944	1946	1948	1950	1952	1954	1956

1945 World War II ends

1946 Cold war begins

1947 Marshall Plan aids western European recovery
Britain grants India independence

1948 Communist take-overs of eastern Europe are complete

1949 NATO is founded

1953 Stalin dies

1956 Hungarian Uprising is crushed

On October 4, 1957, the Soviet Union became the first country to reach the "final frontier" and successfully launch a man-made satellite into space, the beginning of the space race. *Sputnik I* became a symbol of the technological achievements of the communist superpower in its contest with the United States for global leadership, who managed to upset this relationship only in 1969, when Buzz Aldrin placed a U.S. flag on the moon. In 1967, the Soviets still celebrated their undefeated primacy in space with this special issue stamp. (Visual Connection Archive)

After reading this chapter, you should be able to answer the following questions:

How did the cold war change the international system?

What differences can you identify in the process of postwar reconstruction in western versus eastern Europe?

What important differences in politics, social developments, and culture emerged between western and eastern Europe during this period?

How did the new world order affect the process of decolonization?

Why did 1968 become a pivotal year in the history of Europe, and what changes did it bring about?

ILITARY HOSTILITIES ENDED in August 1945, but peace did not immediately follow. Instead, many Europeans experienced occupation by "liberating" armies and retribution for war crimes. Yet war memories were quickly silenced by new challenges. By 1949, the United States and the Soviet Union were struggling for global power and parceling up the world into zones of influence. Europe became the first and initially most important site for superpower confrontation, as it was divided between East and West, communism and capitalism, totalitarianism and democracy. Europeans had to realign their identities. For some, like Ana Pauker, the new era meant transforming their societies in the likeness of the Soviet Union. For others, the end of one war was the beginning of a new one to protect democratic values against communism. This war—a cold war—was fought at the highest level of military and diplomatic planning, usually in great secrecy; yet it touched the lives of every person living in Europe and throughout the world.

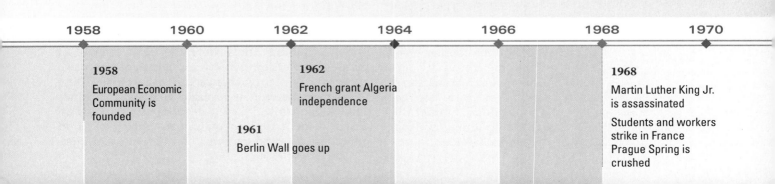

1958	1960	1962	1964	1966	1968	1970

1958
European Economic Community is founded

1961
Berlin Wall goes up

1962
French grant Algeria independence

1968
Martin Luther King Jr. is assassinated

Students and workers strike in France

Prague Spring is crushed

By the late 1950s, western Europeans had settled into a comfortable view of themselves as the "real" Europe and their enemies as distant contenders. In France and Germany, in particular, economic reconstruction brought about great hopes that Europe could regain its leading role in the world. In the meantime, eastern Europeans were thrown into the challenges of building communism according to Stalin's vision of it. The communist regimes employed harsh policies but achieved some measure of success in modernizing their economies. By the late 1950s, the separation between East and West was entrenched. It took another generation to challenge this division. In the wake of anticolonial movements and a new antiestablishment youth, Europeans were forced to look across the East-West divide more carefully and to re-examine their values as events during 1968 shook the political establishment.

The Iron Curtain, 1945–1958

◆ **What conflicts over Europe's future paved the way for its division?**

◆ **How did international relations change in the first two postwar decades?**

The end of World War II brought to Europe a tense and precarious stalemate among the winning Allies. There was no comprehensive peace treaty. The United States and Great Britain were at odds with the Soviet Union over the future of the liberated territories and their own role in the process. Initially, each victor had its own methods for dealing with Nazi war crimes. The issue of what to do with the people displaced by the war also posed significant problems. But everything came under the shadow of a growing rift between the United States and the Soviet Union. By 1948 the Soviet Union had given up the pretense of cooperating with the West and forcefully put an end to democratic politics in eastern Europe. The rift became a division, with the United States assuming the role of protector of western European democracy and capitalism. The Soviet Union became the protector of oppressed peoples everywhere and the counterforce, through the spread of communism, against western imperialism. The United Nations added another dimension to the polarized international system.

percentages agreement Secret agreement reached by Churchill and Stalin in 1944 regarding the division of eastern Europe.

Nuremberg Trials Postwar trials of Nazi leaders and collaborators, held in Nuremberg, Germany, in 1945–1946.

de-Nazification Destruction of Nazism and its influence.

Occupation and De-Nazification

At the end of World War II, millions of Europeans were homeless and impoverished. Entire cities and economies lay in ruin. The political leadership of many countries had either perished or been thoroughly compromised by collaboration with the Nazis. To ensure a stable transition to postwar peace, the United States, Britain, France, and the Soviet Union occupied and divided the territories formerly controlled by the Third Reich and its allies. Germany, Austria, and the city of Berlin were divided into four occupation zones, while other areas of Europe fell under the control of the liberating ally.

The Percentages Agreement In 1945, Soviet troops had liberated all the countries east of Berlin and were fully in control of them. A 1944 **percentages agreement** between Winston Churchill and Joseph Stalin assigned Romania and Bulgaria to the Soviet sphere of influence, Czechoslovakia and Greece to the West (Britain, France, and the United States), with Yugoslavia and Hungary in a fifty-fifty arrangement. Subsequently, at Yalta (1945), Poland was placed in the hands of the Soviets, while Czechoslovakia's fate remained open.

De-Nazification To be viewed as liberators, the Americans, aided by the British and French, swiftly rounded up Nazi Party members and collaborators. The **Nuremberg Trials** were the most famous of the **de-Nazification** war crime trials that took place everywhere in Europe between 1945 and 1948. These international tribunals brought charges of "crimes against humanity," a new legal concept rooted in Enlightenment notions of human rights, to sit in judgment on Nazi racism and the Final Solution.

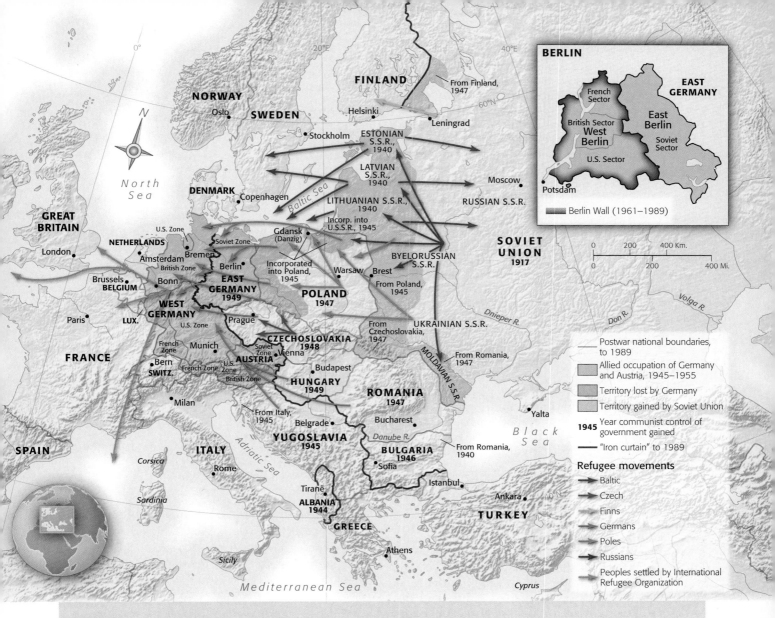

Map 28.1 **Europe Following World War II** Between 1945 and 1989 Europe became divided into two camps struggling for legitimacy in an ideologically polarized world. © *Cengage Learning*

1. How do the territorial changes after World War II compare to those after World War I?
2. What countries witnessed the most population displacement?
3. What changes on this map reflect the bitter division between East and West?

But many high-ranking Nazi officials involved in the death camps and most rank-and-file party members escaped trial. Many of them now cast themselves as victims or innocent bystanders. During his trial at Nuremberg, **Hermann Göring**, head of the Luftwaffe, rejected the notion of collective guilt. "It is the leaders of the country who determine the policy," he said cynically, "and it is always a simple matter to drag the people along, whether it is a democracy or a fascist dictatorship."

Using the Nuremberg model, in eastern Europe, as the Soviet sphere was increasingly called, the

Soviets orchestrated trials against many military and political leaders who had worked with the Nazis or, more recently, opposed the Soviets. Invariably, those tried were found guilty and executed or sent to prison. In eastern Europe, the de-Nazification trials became both a form of intimidation and an attempt to legitimize the communists—the Communist Party being the only political party that appeared untainted by wartime

Hermann Göring (1893–1946)
Nazi leader, founder of the Gestapo and head of the Luftwaffe, who was convicted at the Nuremberg Trials.

collaboration with the Nazis. With so many politicians removed, the trials paved the way for the future communist takeovers and created a myth that responsibility for war crimes rested exclusively on the shoulders of the Germans and other foreign fascists.

The de-Nazification trials failed to find all Nazi collaborators and punish them. The prosecutors had neither the ability nor the political will for such a vast task, and many collaborators went into hiding or committed suicide. But the trials did enable survivors to achieve a degree of closure on the Nazi past and get on with their lives. In addition, in light of the growing competition with the Soviet Union, the western allies found it politically expedient to complete de-Nazification quickly in order to shift focus toward economic reconstruction.

Displaced Persons

To get on with their lives, however, many Europeans first had to try to find a home. Entire cities were in rubble, and many Germans and others had fled west as the Soviet armies advanced. At the end of the war, between 11 and 20 million individuals were displaced persons.

Resettling Germans Moreover, entire populations were resettled. At the **Potsdam Conference** in July 1945, the western allies agreed that eastern European governments in Poland and Czechoslovakia could forcibly remove all Germans from their countries. In Poland, hundreds of thousands of ethnic Germans were expelled. A similar policy sent hundreds of thousands of Poles from western Ukraine and Belorussia to Poland. Czechoslovakia also expelled its Germans. There was much debate over who exactly was a German, as there were many ethnically mixed marriages and individuals whose families had long lived in the contested areas. A Czech woman married to a Sudeten German would likely become a candidate for expulsion, even though she and her husband had been born subjects of Czechoslovakia and his family had lived there for generations and had become subjects of the Nazi state only after 1938. Often resettlement was abused by envious neighbors who wanted a piece of property or simply revenge for some past wrong. The process reinforced the power of the state to decide the identity and fate of its inhabitants. Ultimately, more than 13 million ethnic Germans, mostly in eastern Europe, were forcibly removed. In expelling Germans, Czechoslovakia and Poland enforced the racist definitions of nationality developed by the Nazis. Ironically, the western defenders of democracy were

Potsdam Conference Meeting in July 1945 at which the United States, Britain, and the Soviet Union decided how to administer postwar Germany.

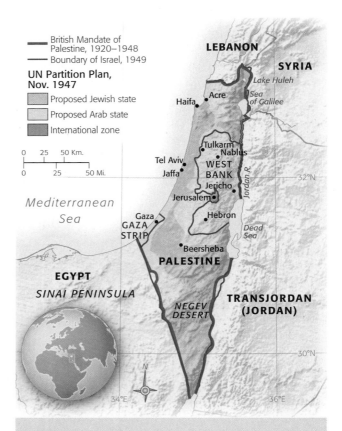

Map 28.2 **UN Mandate for Israel and Palestine, 1947** The UN Mandate, which created the legal framework for international recognition of Israel, left the status of the Arab inhabitants of Palestine unresolved. The conflict that rages today between Israel, Palestinians, and the Arab states in the Middle East originated with the formation of the state of Israel in 1948. © *Cengage Learning*

1. What problems might derive from the shape of the proposed Jewish state?
2. How might problems arise from the borders of the proposed Palestinian state?
3. What does this map suggest about territorial stability in the region, especially looking at the actual borders of 1949 versus the proposed 1947 partition?

enabling the elimination of populations promoted by the Nazis.

Achieving Ethnic Homogeneity Those forced out left almost everything behind. They walked or rode bicycles or donkeys; the lucky had horse-driven carts. In the process, children were sometimes separated from parents and wives from husbands. More than 100,000 families ended up living across the East-West divide, unable to keep in touch with each other for a generation. The process of moving millions of people away from their homes and into potentially hostile communities generated psychic wounds that began to heal only later, primarily through forgetting. An important political result was the reshaping of most of eastern Europe into more ethnically homogeneous countries. Poland, for instance, became almost entirely Polish and Catholic, with Jews, Germans, and Ukrainians gone.

Among the displaced persons were more than 250,000 Jews, located primarily in the American zone, where they were placed in camps. Jewish leaders from Palestine, such as **David Ben-Gurion**, worked with the western allies to decide the fate of these people. More than 130,000 of them settled in British-controlled Palestine, which became Israel in 1948. Those who stayed in Europe were subjected to antisemitic discrimination and even postwar pogroms, which generated additional emigrations to Israel.

Beginnings of the Cold War

The wartime alliance between the United States and the Soviet Union against a common enemy dissolved into an adversarial relation, as the victors could not agree on postwar goals for Germany and the rest of Europe. Both nations emerged from the war as superpowers, with great international prestige, and each embarked on a struggle for political, economic, and moral-cultural world supremacy. No other state could match their strength, and most European states owed their survival to one or both of them. In this contest, the engagement of the United States in European affairs was a greater departure from past behavior than for the Soviet Union. After World War I the Soviets had aided communist movements in Europe, but the United States had pursued isolationism. After World War II, however, the development of Europe cannot be understood without the essential involvement of the United States.

Constructing the East-West Ideological Divide

Europe became the playing field in a struggle between the opposing options of the Americans and the Soviets: liberal democracy versus communism, private property versus state ownership, capitalism and free-market economies versus state-controlled ones, freedom and material comforts versus equality and social justice. Both sides wanted to erase whatever gray areas existed in each European country between these poles. New identities and allegiances were created in connection with the two superpowers, and new enmities developed among old neighbors. The Hungarians, who had been the Austrians' partners in ruling the Habsburg Empire a century earlier, were now to be their enemies by virtue of the barbed wire that separated the two countries. East Germans, under Soviet occupation, were to begin thinking of their West German relatives and friends as imperialist traitors. This division of Europe into East and West came about as a result of the superpower confrontation.

Soviet Wartime Losses and Strategic Claims In the contest over world domination, the two superpowers gave different explanations and used different methods. The Soviet Union had lost more people (over 30 million by some accounts) and resources than any other war combatant and wanted to recoup the economic resources spent fighting the war. In fact, since Germany had experienced 80 percent of its casualties at the hands of the Soviets, Stalin was not exaggerating when he claimed that Europe owed the Nazi defeat to his country. To rebuild the Soviet economy, he wanted Soviet troops in the occupied zone to oversee the production and subsequent transfer of goods to the Soviet Union. The Soviets also acted out of fear. Having been attacked by Germany twice in the twentieth century, they wanted a buffer zone in eastern Europe, where friendly political regimes and military resources would protect Soviet security.

The United States as Defender of Democracy The United States, on the other hand, had an overwhelming interest in bringing back democracy and capitalist markets to the regions it had liberated. One lesson from World War I was that a punishing peace could lead to resentment and revenge. This time, the victors focused on rebuilding a Germany committed to their ideals. In addition, the Great Depression's costly economic and political consequences also pointed toward rebuilding markets as a better strategy than exacting high war payments. Strong capitalist economies would bolster political stability, American strategists concluded. These goals were not entirely altruistic. The American economy had grown during the war, and businesses were looking for new markets. European countries had already become deeply dependent on American goods and dollars, and they were a good investment.

The means by which the Soviets pursued their goals in eastern Europe were in keeping with Stalin's personality. He fundamentally distrusted those not under his control. He sent some of the toughest military leaders and most unquestioning loyalists from the communist parties in eastern Europe, such as Ana Pauker, to oversee postwar regimes. The Soviets manipulated the western observers and used any legal means available, as well as illegal and violent ones, to eliminate all political enemies and place Soviet pawns in power. Political legitimacy and the well-being of the populations involved were low on Stalin's agenda.

David Ben-Gurion (1886–1973) Zionist leader central to the establishment of the state of Israel and its first prime minister.

Stalin had a formidable opponent in U.S. President Harry Truman, who, as vice president, had never trusted the Soviet Union. Following President Franklin D. Roosevelt's death in April 1945, the simple man from Missouri brought his common sense to the presidency and his own strong views about the postwar peace. He followed a careful line of encouraging a stable international environment through the **United Nations (UN)** and an increasingly hard line against the Soviets.

The Truman Doctrine In Europe, Truman was committed to prosperity and democracy through positive, though anti-Soviet, incentives. Instead of sending troops to defend American interests, in March 1947 he issued the **Truman Doctrine**, which offered to help countries fighting communist expansion, specifically Turkey and Greece, where communist partisans in a civil war were receiving help from Yugoslavia and the Soviets. Greece was considered key to the political stability in the Mediterranean and American overseas markets. With substantial American support, the military establishment defeated the communists and imposed its own authoritarian rule.

In addition, the 1947 **Marshall Plan** allocated more than $13 billion in grants and loans to rebuild Europe's economies. This money helped rebuild roads, industries, and housing. The plan found unprecedented support among Americans and generated a host of programs that paved the way for the European Union. American aid came with a price, however. The United States encouraged France, Britain, and Germany to hunt down communist sympathizers who might have infiltrated leftist parties and be plotting communist takeovers. The Marshall Plan also served to further separate western from eastern Europe, where countries occupied by Soviet troops were never in a position to accept U.S. aid.

Stalemate over Berlin In Germany, the Soviets dismantled industrial plants in their occupation zone and took no interest in preventing the starvation of German civilians, which drew the criticism of the West. In response, in February 1948 the Soviets set up a blockade to isolate the western zones of Berlin from access by Western powers. To avert military conflict, the United States sent in supplies by means of the **Berlin airlift**, flying in up to 13,000 tons per day. By May 1949, the Soviets had backed down, and Germany became divided into the Federal Republic of Germany, known as West Germany, and the German Democratic Republic, known as East Germany. Berlin itself was divided into East and West Berlin. Though stabilized, Germany remained at the epicenter of the contest between the United States and the Soviet Union for the next forty years—the **cold war**.

The Cold War Goes Global Other developments helped shape the cold war. After the contentious creation of Israel in 1948, the Middle East became an important ground for competition between the Soviets, generally backing Arab states and insurgents, and the Americans, generally supporting Israel, especially from the late 1960s onward. In addition, in 1949, **Mao Zedong** led a successful communist revolution in China, a development that made the Americans more fearful of the spread of communism. Communist China complicated American strategies, as it operated independently of the Soviet Union, unlike other communist states. Finally, after the Soviets exploded an atomic bomb in 1949, the prospect of nuclear war intensified. Fear of total annihilation kept the Soviets and the Americans at some distance, while their ambitions kept them in uncomfortable proximity and often in indirect military confrontation in the regional struggles they wanted to manipulate.

Nuclear Arms Race The Soviets' development of nuclear weapons after 1949 ushered in an arms race. Starting in the 1950s, both the United States and the Soviet Union expended huge sums on military technology and espionage, as each tried to keep up with the other. In 1953, the United States spent $50 billion, or almost 40 percent of the federal budget, on the military. Spending by the Soviet Union for the same purposes reached 25 percent of its revenues during the same period. This obsession with being militarily prepared for global conflict created a predicament, as neither country had enough intelligence about the other's capacity to make reasoned judgments, and the political leadership was easily persuaded about the need for military spending. Unprecedented levels of military spending only increased the fear of conflict and fed the perceived need to spend more.

International Security

The piecemeal peace agreements of the first postwar years secured a somewhat stable relationship between the superpowers in Europe. But the most important step for creating a different international order was

United Nations (UN) International organization founded in 1945 to facilitate collaboration among nations; replaced the League of Nations.

Truman Doctrine Policy statement issued by U.S. President Harry S Truman in 1947 announcing the U.S. commitment to fight the spread of communism everywhere in the world.

Marshall Plan Economic recovery plan established by the United States in 1947 that offered grants and low-interest loans to noncommunist European states.

Berlin airlift (1948–1949) U.S. shipment of supplies to Western-controlled sectors of Berlin following a Soviet blockade.

cold war Name by which the 1945–1991 standoff between the superpowers, the United States and the Soviet Union, came to be known.

Mao Zedong (1893–1976) Leader of the communist revolution and, from 1949, the communist regime in China.

Other NATO members:
U.S.A.
CANADA

U.S. loan of $3.5 billion, 1946
Exploded first atomic bomb, 1952

Exploded first atomic bomb, 1949

Berlin blockade, 1948–1949

Communist coup, 1948
U.S.S.R. invasion, 1968

Joined NATO, 1955

Exploded first atomic bomb, 1960

Zones of occupation ended, 1955

Uprising, 1956

Tito-Stalin schism, 1948

Left COMECON, 1961
Withdrew from WP, 1968

Truman Doctrine, 1947
Joined NATO, 1952

Truman Doctrine, 1947
Joined NATO, 1952

Legend:

$ Participant in the Marshall Plan

Members of NATO, formed in 1949

Members of CMEA, formed in 1949, and the Warsaw Pact, organized in 1955

Non-aligned communist country

Member of the European Community, formed in 1958

East European Stalinism

■ Prison camp
• Major prison
• Labor camp
○ Town renamed after Stalin
▲ Mountain peak renamed "Stalin"

0   200   400 Km.
0   200   400 Mi.

Map 28.3 **East European Stalinism** Between 1945 and 1953, the Soviet Union consolidated its grip over the political institutions and economies of its eastern European satellites. Yugoslavia alone remained a thorn in Stalin's side. Magocsi, Paul R., *Historical Atlas of East Central Europe*, cartographic design by Geoffrey J. Matthews, Seattle: University of Washington Press, 1993. Reprinted by permission.

1. What elements of political control and violence are highlighted on this map?
2. Where does the grip seem tightest?
3. Why do you think that is the case?

the establishment of the United Nations (UN) in 1945. Unlike the League of Nations, which it never joined, the United States was a founding member of the UN. This organization was similar to the league in its aim to facilitate collaboration among all states by giving all members the same rights regardless of size,

military power, or wealth. But the UN was different from its predecessor in how it achieved these goals. It included a governing body, the **Security Council**,

Security Council Leading body of the United Nations in matters of international security.

on which China, France, Great Britain, the Soviet Union, and the United States sat as permanent members, along with ten rotating members. The UN also acquired financial resources and a military force to take action when necessary. Its large budget enabled it to manage international programs for public health, child protection, and cultural exchange, giving states large and small, poor and rich, access to new opportunities for peaceful cooperation, such as the successful antimalaria campaigns in Africa and assistance in underdeveloped areas to increase productivity and eradicate poverty.

Human Rights The UN's **Universal Declaration of Human Rights** (1948) specified unprecedented rights and freedoms, such as the freedom to move from one location to another, the right to education, and the right to be protected from unemployment. Though not legally binding, the declaration became a powerful means whereby citizens could hold their governments accountable for human rights abuses in an international arena. The autonomous International Criminal Court at The Hague became an important forum for punishing human rights abuses and war crimes. Thus, the UN revolutionized international relations and brought pressure and resources to bear on broad issues from human rights to poverty and health.

NATO However, other international organizations reduced hopes for peaceful solutions to international problems. In 1949, the **North Atlantic Treaty Organization (NATO)**, a military defense alliance aimed primarily against the Soviets' alleged plans for armed global conflict, was created, with collective security as its cardinal principle— an attack on one member was an attack on all, and the security of each individual member depended on the security of all. NATO forced uniform policies on its members and required that each be in a permanent state of military preparedness. The establishment of NATO signaled a formal division of the postwar world between the western democracies, with the twelve NATO members— the United States, Britain, France, Canada, Italy, the Netherlands, Belgium, Luxembourg, Portugal, Denmark, Norway, and Iceland, later joined by West Germany, Greece, and Turkey—at the forefront, and the Soviet-dominated communist camp on the opposite side.

Universal Declaration of Human Rights Declaration adopted by the United Nations General Assembly in 1948 outlining universal basic human rights.

North Atlantic Treaty Organization (NATO) Defensive alliance established by Britain, France, and the United States in 1949 with Canada and other western European allies.

Committee for Mutual Economic Assistance (CMEA) Soviet organization created in 1949 to coordinate economic production and trade in communist bloc countries.

Warsaw Pact Organization of communist states created in 1955 as a counterpart to NATO.

Soviet Economic and Security Counterparts The Soviet Union retaliated by calling for the creation of a communist alliance. First, the **Committee for Mutual Economic Assistance (CMEA)** was formed in 1949 as a counterpart to the Marshall Plan, serving to increase Soviet control over eastern European economies. Subsequently, the **Warsaw Pact** was created in 1955 as a direct response against the rearming of West Germany and as a counterpart to NATO. But the Warsaw Pact increasingly policed its own communist member states.

In this new international order, European states were pawns rather than major players. Military buildups provide an example. Although NATO presumed that all members would participate actively in military defense, the United States and Britain led in armament production, and when Charles de Gaulle attempted to upgrade France's nuclear program, he was hastily rebutted by the Americans and the British. The power imbalance was even more evident in the Warsaw Pact, with the Soviets supervising the production and sale of armaments, even when the factories were in Czechoslovakia.

 Checking In

By yourself or with a partner, explain the significance of each of the following selected key terms:

Nuremberg Trials	Universal Declaration of Human Rights
de-Nazification	
David Ben-Gurion	North Atlantic Treaty Organization (NATO)
Marshall Plan	
Mao Zedong	Warsaw Pact

The Revival of Western Europe

- **Why was western Europe so successful in rebuilding its economic power?**
- **What were the political consequences of the commitment to economic recovery?**

Given the magnitude of the material destruction and political disarray at the end of the war, western Europe's record recovery has been rightly called a miracle. By 1950, the region was producing at a level 30 percent higher than before the war (see Figure 28.1). This great achievement owes much to the immense financial resources poured into the economies of western Europe, to international stability (if not without tension), and to the expansion of the welfare state, which secured internal social and political stability.

The Economic Miracle

Thanks to the Marshall Plan, France and Italy had surpassed their prewar levels of production by 1950,

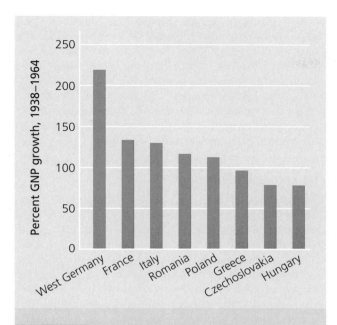

Figure 28.1 **Economic Growth in Europe,
1938–1964** Between 1945 and 1964, western
Europe experienced a virtual economic miracle.
In part due to the Marshall Plan, and in part due to
successful internal political and economic policies, Germany, France, and Britain regained their
economic prominence. What country had the
highest GNP growth? Where did the lowest growth
happen? What do these figures suggest about the
differences between eastern and western Europe
during this period?

Source: Wilkinson, James D.; Huges, H. Stuart, *Contemporary Europe: A History,*
10th Edition, © 2004, p. 422. Reprinted and electronically reproduced by permission of Pearson Education, Inc., Upper Saddle River, NJ.

but West Germany had the most impressive success. Between 1945 and 1950 production shot up
25 percent, 15 percent higher than in 1938. Many
West German cities destroyed during the war
were completely rebuilt to accommodate former
inhabitants and to make room for the more than
12 million refugees from the communist East. By
the 1960s, West Germany was the undisputed economic leader in western Europe in industrial production, research and development, and its ability
to put its swelling population to work. Even with
a tremendous growth in population, the country
had virtually no unemployment until the 1960s,
when a majority of West Germans were living
in unprecedented comfort, able to fill their apartments and homes with refrigerators, television
sets, and automatic washing machines.

Rebuilding the West German Economy It is no
wonder, then, that **Konrad Adenauer**, the leader who

oversaw this economic miracle, continued to dominate
the political scene until the 1960s. The founder of the
Christian Democratic Union, he was the first postwar
chancellor. Like other successful western political
leaders after the war, he had a record of resistance to
the Nazis, a commitment to rebuilding capitalist democracy, and a center-right political orientation. An
active opponent of Hitler, he had spent part of the
war in a concentration camp, but he was *not* a sympathizer of the left. He used his reputation to push
economic recovery and political distance from East
Germany. Under his leadership, the great German industries and private business were rebuilt and workers were guaranteed decent wages and health care.
The Old Man, as he came to be known, masterfully
developed a new image of Germany that highlighted
the nation's industrious and democratic spirit. His
politics gave hope to West Germans and attracted
their loyalty, discrediting claims by communist East
Germany that it also represented the German people.
Adenauer's Christian Democrats, committed to economic recovery and social stability, dominated German politics until 1963. Table 28.1 summarizes key
events in western Europe during the postwar period.

Recovery in France

In France, economic recovery was also remarkable,
but it was not accompanied immediately by political stability. France had largely escaped physical destruction during the war, and its population had suffered smaller losses than had most other countries.
However, France had experienced great shame and
humiliation. Reconstruction thus had much to do
with resurrecting faith in a vigorous France.

Charles de Gaulle Charles de Gaulle overshadowed
all other politicians during this period, even though
he did not hold office between 1946 and 1958. Raised
in a well-educated Catholic family, de Gaulle embodied some of the oldest and proudest French traditions.
He grew up among history and philosophy books and
in adolescence opted for a military career in which he
could live out his patriotic sentiments. He served in
the infantry, almost died at Verdun in 1916, and subsequently volunteered to fight against the Bolshevik Russians in 1919–1920. His family's political leanings were
monarchist, but de Gaulle became a republican. Still,
party divisions were never to his taste, as he preferred
either the strict hierarchy of the army or the direct voice
of the people at the ballot box. Above all, de Gaulle saw
two fundamental traits in his countrymen: "The desire
of privilege and the taste of
equality are the dominant
and contradictory passions of
the French of all times."

France had had a vibrant
socialist movement since the
nineteenth century, and it
was prominent in anti-Nazi

Konrad Adenauer (1876–1967)
Christian Democratic conservative opponent of Hitler who was
elected the first chancellor of
West Germany in 1949.

Table 28.1 **Western Europe in the Postwar Period**

1945–1946	Nuremberg Trials
1946	National Health Service Act in Britain
1947	Marshall Plan
1949	Division of Germany; Konrad Adenauer elected chancellor of West Germany
1951	European Coal and Steel Community formed
1955	West Germany joins NATO
1958	European Community established; Fall of French Republic; de Gaulle coup and birth of Fifth Republic
1961	1 million Volkswagen Transporters sold
1962–1965	Second Vatican Council
1968	Student movements and national strike in France

© Cengage Learning

resistance. The resistance had also been fertile ground for the communists, yet de Gaulle, who represented the conservative nationalist wing of European politics, led the liberating French forces in 1945. Until 1958, France was bitterly divided between left and right. The left claimed legitimacy based on its wartime efforts, but the communists became compromised by connections with the Soviet Union. The right, dominated by de Gaulle's party and other nationalist movements, had U.S. support. More than nineteen governments rotated in and out of power during this period.

The Price of Stability In 1958 a political crisis brought de Gaulle into office and launched the **Fifth Republic** under a new constitution that gave broad powers to the presidency and limited those of the parliament. He was a more difficult ally for the Americans than Adenauer but no friend of the Soviet Union

Fifth Republic Current French political regime established by Charles de Gaulle in 1958 through a presidential coup.

Robert Schuman (1886–1963) First premier of postwar France, instrumental in forming the European Union and the European Coal and Steel Community.

European Coal and Steel Community (ECSC) Organization established in 1951 that created a common customs, production, and labor market for coal and steel.

or the communists. As premier, de Gaulle helped restore people's faith in France as a great nation. His victory in French politics had come primarily at the expense of the left, which became increasingly marginalized in the decade after the war, accused of being a tool of Soviet expansionism. The decline of the left in France was like that in other western European countries with strong socialist and communist movements, such as Germany and Italy.

The European Community

The hardening of the East-West division between 1947 and 1958 served to broaden ties among western European states. These countries began to create stronger internal markets and to cooperate in trade, economic production, and employment policies. Given the nationalist jealousy that had dominated relations between France and Germany since the nineteenth century, this cooperation was remarkable. But European politicians and economists had learned the hard lessons of the Great Depression and were ready to take new directions. In addition, the Marshall Plan stipulated that the recipients were to cooperate in areas of investment, production, and trade.

Ending French-Germany Enmity The main architect of these bold policies was **Robert Schuman**, an economist and the first premier of postwar France. Together with other French and German economists and politicians, he put forth a plan to end enmity between Germany and France, promising greater stability and prosperity for both countries. "The solidarity in production thus established," he explained, "will make it plain that any war between France and Germany becomes not merely unthinkable, but materially impossible."

Economic Growth Through Collaboration Discussions led in 1951 to the creation of the **European Coal and Steel Community (ECSC)**, with six members—Belgium, France, Germany, Italy, Luxembourg, and the Netherlands. Trade tariffs were lifted for some products, workers from member countries could cross borders to find employment, and investment in coal and steel production across borders was encouraged. The union offered opportunities to entrepreneurs, paving the way for multinational corporations, as well as workers, and extending protections to them in all member states.

The ECSC was a great success, increasing steel and iron production by 75 percent in its first three years, with industrial production rising by 58 percent. It made possible the creation of the European Atomic Energy Community (1957), which oversaw the development of atomic energy for civilian purposes, and finally the European Economic Community (EEC). The 1958 EEC Rome Treaty provided the institutional foundations for four areas of cooperation

A visionary French economist and politician, Robert Schuman successfully convinced the French public and his West German counterparts to put their nationalist disputes behind them and to cooperate for the benefits of prosperity and democracy in their respective countries and in Europe more broadly. What specifically in his vision helped change French-German relations?

among members: administrative (Council of the European Union), legislative (European Parliament, largely on paper), economic (European Commission), and judicial (European Court of Justice). The EEC also became known as the **European Community** or the Common Market. This transformation did not mean the end of political independence for the members but ensured cooperation and joint planning to enhance economic growth.

The success of the European Community was also linked to the optimism and self-sacrifice present everywhere in Europe after the war. Most people focused their energies on stability and economic well-being rather than politics. Thus, political leaders could take swift steps toward recovery in the major industries at the expense of consumer goods. The spirit of cooperation also developed among political parties, which began to make connections across borders with others of similar leanings—from left-wing socialists to center-right Christian Democrats. NATO also induced military cooperation among members.

Continued Tensions Yet nationalism continued to pose problems for the European Community. De Gaulle, for example, used France's veto to block Great Britain's membership in this organization in 1963 and 1967.

His opposition was based on his negative view of Britain's postwar subservience to the United States and also on his skepticism about Britain's willingness to accept all EEC responsibilities. De Gaulle's concerns were not groundless: given its success in postwar recovery, Britain was slow to show interest in the European Community.

Great Britain and the Welfare State

After the war, Britain's political and economic problems forced its leadership to focus inward. Though a wartime hero, Churchill was defeated by Labour Party contender **Clement Attlee** in July 1945. The election outcome reflected a widespread desire among the public to shift away from deep involvement in European and world security. For more than five years the British public had been told to sacrifice for others, and they did so at great human and material cost. Now they wanted the government to look out for them.

Rise of the Welfare State in Britain The Labour Party interpreted its victory as a mandate for welfare programs. The state established firm control over important areas of the economy and public services, from transportation to utilities. The Bank of England was nationalized, as were the coal and steel industries. The National Health Service Act of 1946 placed health insurance under state control while still allowing for private practice. This pioneering law made health care accessible to virtually all British citizens. A similarly radical reform established government-funded pensions for all working citizens—a social security fund. Britain thus became a leader in welfare policies and a model for other European countries, which were encouraged to adopt similar policies. The sweeping welfare measures worked both because of the conciliatory mood of the Conservatives, who continued the policies of the Labour Party after they came to power in the 1950s, and because of the generous financial help—more than $3 billion—of the Marshall Plan.

Educational Opportunities
The state also expanded educational opportunities. The 1944 Education Act made education mandatory until age fifteen and increased government funding to create the necessary schools, as well as scholarships for university students. More poor pupils than ever before were able to finish secondary schools and attend college, a development that took place just as rapid modernization escalated the need for educated professionals and skilled

European Community Precursor of the European Union, founded in 1958 with the creation of the European Economic Community, the European Coal and Steel Community, and the European Atomic Energy Commission.

Clement Attlee (1883–1967) British prime minister from 1945 to 1951 and Labour Party leader who oversaw the establishment of the welfare state and the end of British colonialism.

Ana Pauker Submits to the Communist Party

In August 1944, Ana Pauker rode into Bucharest atop a Soviet tank, returning to the city of her troubled youth as a liberator (or conqueror). She had traveled a long and difficult path from her birth to an impoverished Jewish family in northern Romania, at a time and place where antisemitism was popular and where women were regarded as second-class citizens. Intelligent and fearless, she worked hard against this double discrimination and the roles traditionally assigned to women like her. She first chose to study Judaism and then went on to join the Communist Party during World War I, having opposed Romania's entry into the war. Though she spent some years abroad after the war, she returned to Romania to lead underground activities against Romania's unstable governments. During the 1920s and 1930s, she served several prison sentences, the last one at the same time that her husband, Marcel Pauker, was imprisoned by the Soviets during the Great Purges.

Pauker denounced her husband at his 1938 trial in Moscow. At that moment, she understood clearly that she had to pick one of her conflicting loyalties—family or the communist revolution. If she questioned the Moscow party line, she would be betraying her ideological convictions. She chose ideology. By betraying her husband, she aligned herself with Moscow and made herself ready to win control in Romania after the war.

After she returned to Romania in 1944, she retained this all-consuming loyalty. She willingly gave up leadership of the Communist Party in recognition that, as a woman and Jew, she was a liability to the party. Only by downplaying these identities could she be a decision maker in the government. As shadow leader of the party in the Politburo, she oversaw the purging of the precommunist political leadership and the transformation of the state into one modeled after Stalin's vision. In 1948, *Time* magazine named her "the most powerful woman alive."

Yet by 1951, Pauker had come into conflict with other Romanian communist leaders, as well as Stalin, especially over collectivization. Having given so much of her personal life to the party, Pauker assumed she could independently make the most important decisions in this aspect of economic reform. She wanted to collectivize slowly, to ensure that peasants would not come to resent the party. Though she did not come from a peasant family, she cared about the fate of peasants, and though she felt deep personal loyalty to Stalin, she also cared about Romania. Still, many in Romania perceived her as a "foreigner" because of her Jewish origins. In an atmosphere of growing antisemitism, Pauker's competitors in the party used this conflict to accuse her of betraying communism. Only her personal friendship with Stalin saved her life. But in 1953 Pauker was forced to denounce herself as a traitor and renounce her membership in the Communist Party. Once more she sacrificed herself for the sake of the party.

Few people mourned Pauker's departure from the party leadership, as her ruthless style was much feared. But, unlike other communists, Pauker seems to have wanted power not so much for herself but rather in order to carry out her convictions. She passed away two decades later, in anonymity and still much hated by many Romanians.

---

workers in the industrial and service sectors. Simultaneously, important shifts in agricultural production pushed new waves of people into urban areas. The population of the countryside fell by 50 percent as urban growth exploded.

Women on the Margins Women, however, lagged behind as beneficiaries of these new social welfare programs. Quotas imposed for access into secondary education, even when state mandated and funded, ensured that the number of girls who attended the best schools was always smaller than the number of boys, despite girls' overall superior academic performance. And though more women than ever before were employed, their wages lagged 30 to 50 percent behind men's. They also received insufficient support for child care and often had to leave the labor force for this reason.

Overall, however, the growth of work opportunities, education, and inexpensive or free public services from the state made it possible for record numbers of workers to partake in the consumer culture and enjoy leisure activities. British workers attended concerts, participated in sports, took paid vacations, and traveled abroad. Tourism took off, with more than 100 million people taking trips every year. The working class was looking like and identifying more with the middle class, and old stereotypes about national characteristics weakened as people traveled in other countries and worked together in Common Market projects.

 ## Checking In

By yourself or with a partner, explain the significance of each of the following selected key terms:

Konrad Adenauer	European Community
Fifth Republic	Clement Attlee
Robert Schuman	
European Coal and Steel Community (ECSC)	

The Restructuring of Eastern Europe

◆ **What were the important steps in the communist takeovers in eastern Europe?**

◆ **What was the effect in the region of Stalin's death?**

By 1948, the communists were in power everywhere in eastern Europe, revolutionizing politics, and in the next two decades internal and external forces solidified these regimes. In some cases, communist leaders preferred to follow Moscow to ensure their own political survival. In other cases, local communists attempted to gain legitimacy by portraying themselves as leaders of their nation. But the Soviets reacted swiftly against all who deviated from the interests of communism as defined in Moscow and put down any important attempts at reform. By 1968, all the communist leaders who had dreamed of reform and autonomy from Moscow were gone, generating broad disillusionment with all communist ideals.

The Communist Takeovers

In 1945, the communists were a tiny political group in eastern Europe, except for Czechoslovakia and Yugoslavia. Most members of these parties had perished at the hands of the Nazis or their own governments during the war. Some had escaped to Moscow, as Stalin worked hard to recruit European communists who, like Ana Pauker, were fully devoted to Soviet goals for eastern Europe. By 1945, these communists had been returned to their countries to begin organizing mass movements and building political power.

Eliminating Political Contenders The only other potential contenders for political power were the representatives of the governments in exile, especially the Poles and Czechoslovaks, as well as the leaders of parties that had not cooperated with the Nazis. The Soviets were able to eliminate many of these during the de-Nazification trials. And with the Soviet troops on the ground at the end of the war, noncommunist politicians stood virtually no chance of resuming office in the new regimes unless they cooperated with the Soviets.

The noncommunist Czechoslovak leader **Edvard Beneš**, for example, had kept channels of communication with Moscow open throughout the war, and after the war his country was not occupied. Instead, the Soviets used Beneš's political and moral authority to smooth the transition to the postwar regime. Beneš won the 1946 presidential election as head of a coalition government led by communists and socialists, who had been fairly strong in Czechoslovakia in the 1920s and 1930s. In contrast to other eastern

European countries under Soviet domination, these elections were not outright rigged. By 1947, however, the Soviets had made it clear that Czechoslovakia was not to accept Marshall Plan aid. The electoral popularity of the Czech Communist Party quickly dropped to 20 percent. In February 1948, the Soviets helped the communists force a political coup. Beneš refused to sign the new constitution, which banned all parties save for the Communist Party, and died soon afterward.

In Romania, where the Communist Party had only about a thousand members, the Soviets played a more direct role in the communist takeover. Under the strict oversight of Soviet generals and their troops, Pauker and a handful of other Moscow protégés imprisoned, exiled, or executed all noncommunist politicians. This loyal leadership also followed Moscow's orders in taking over all newspapers and radio stations, the police, the military, and labor unions. By 1947 the communists controlled the elections and orchestrated the victory of their party. The communist takeovers in Hungary, Poland, East Germany, and Bulgaria were similar.

Communist Victory By 1948, the Communist Parties had outmaneuvered their political opponents everywhere in eastern Europe, often due to the presence of Soviet troops. But the victory of communist regimes was also due to the lack of viable political options and to the collapse of democracy long before the Soviet occupation. In Poland, many saw the Soviet Union as the only power interested in securing the Polish borders against future aggression from the West, and Polish communists cast themselves as patriots protecting their nation from another German invasion.

To oversee relations with Communist Parties abroad and the new governments of the communist bloc, as communist eastern Europe came to be called, the Soviets established the **Cominform**. Under direct Soviet control, it was a ruthless instrument for purging various Communist Parties. As relations with the West worsened, Stalin became convinced that he was surrounded by enemies, that he could not trust even allies, and that his efforts to win the war had gone unappreciated. The Cominform's close control over the affairs of European Communist Parties reflected his increasingly paranoid view.

Yugoslavia's Independent Course

Yugoslavia was the only country in eastern Europe where the communist victory was due overwhelmingly to internal forces. Communist partisans had effectively struggled against

Edvard Beneš (1884–1948) President of Czechoslovakia after World War II who resented the communist takeover in 1948 and resigned.

Cominform Postwar international organization, directed from Moscow, that coordinated Communist Parties abroad, including those in western Europe.

Jakub Berman Defends the Communist Takeover in Poland

In an interview conducted by Teresa Toranska, a young Polish journalist, in the early 1980s, Jakub Berman, one of the main leaders of the Polish communist regime in the early Stalinist years, staunchly defended the legitimacy of that regime. Like Ana Pauker, Berman had spent the war in Moscow. He returned to his native Poland as part of the Soviet "liberation" of the country but was very much perceived, again like Pauker, as a foreign occupier, in part because he was Jewish. This interview reveals the huge gap between Berman and Toranska's generations in their understanding of communism.

❶ How does Berman describe the communist takeover? Do you agree with this assessment?

❷ How does Berman depict the role of the Soviet Union? Why would the Poles be "lucky" to have ended up in the Soviet camp?

❸ According to Berman, how did the reconfiguration of international relations after World War II impact Poland's political fate?

Berman: ❶ After all the disasters that had befallen this country, we brought in its ultimate liberation, because we finally got rid of those Germans. We wanted to get this country moving, to breathe life into it; all our hopes were tied up with the new model of Poland, which was the only chance it had had throughout its thousand years of history. We were bound to succeed, because we were right; not in some irrational, dreamed-up way we'd plucked out of the air, but historically—history was on our side….

Toranska: You're considered the cause of all the evil that has befallen this nation….

Berman: That's the result of mental backwardness…. Two great powers arose. ❷ We found ourselves in the Soviet sphere of influence, which was lucky for us. They had to meet with resistance on the part of a population raised on and accustomed to an entirely different set of ideas…. Was it plausible at any moment to imagine that Poland would be again the country it had been between the wars? … You have to be deaf and blind not to see that we, the Polish communists, rescued Poland from the worst…. ❸ Our efforts were stifled by the extraordinary pressure of the cold war atmosphere and by a genuine threat from America…. She wanted to invest in Europe (hence the Marshall Plan) in order to make it dependent on her…. For us to break away from the Soviet Union would have meant losing the recovered territories. Poland would have become the duchy of Warsaw…. The world *has* changed, can't you see that? There aren't any sovereign states any more, only semisovereign ones…. Poland can't be uprooted from the Soviet bloc. Poland lies on the road between the Soviet Union and western Europe, and its position is clear: either/or. There are no half shades, because Poland can't float in the air.

Source: Excerpt from Jakub Berman's interview with Teresa Toranska, published in her book *Them: Stalin's Polish Puppets* (1988).

the Nazi occupation and liberated Yugoslavia's territory. To be sure, the Yugoslav communists also abused their power, especially at the expense of populations who had collaborated with the Germans, such as the Croatians. But by 1947, the Yugoslav Communist League was popular and widely viewed as the legitimate political leader.

An Ambitious Leader Josip Broz Tito, the leader of the communist partisans, became the undisputed leader of Yugoslavia, and he stood up against Stalin's designs for eastern Europe. Born to a Slovenian mother and Croat father, Tito embodied a Yugoslav identity devoid of ethnic nationalism. Moreover, he was a veteran communist, initially favored by Moscow. He had fought for the Reds in the Russian Civil War, was trained in Moscow afterward, and ruthlessly followed Stalin's line during World War II. Thus, he considered himself untouchable and after 1945 embarked on an independent plan to industrialize and modernize the economy. He also sought to speed up communist revolution in the Balkans by giving military aid to communists in Greece and Albania. At a time when all regional relations were subject to Soviet oversight, he sought closer relations with Bulgaria independently of Moscow.

Stalin Reacts Stalin perceived these moves as a direct challenge to his authority, and Tito's insistence on remaining autonomous soon incurred the wrath of the Soviet leader. Increasingly paranoid about the growing strength of his ideological and personal enemies, Stalin was fixated on punishing anyone who disobeyed. After repeated warnings, Stalin summoned Tito to Moscow in 1948. When the Yugoslav leader failed to appear, Stalin denounced him as a capitalist spy and expelled him from the Cominform. Tito stood his ground and survived, due to internal support and significant help from the West. The United States, perceiving him as an important tool in the cold war, lavished financial aid on Yugoslavia, over $600 million in 1950–1953 alone. In some ways Yugoslavia became another pawn in the superpower game for world domination.

Tito's Winning Bid Yet Tito also remained independent of both superpowers, challenging the notion that the world had to be divided into two camps. He became a role model for many **Third World** countries emerging from colonial rule and, after 1948, founded the **Non-Aligned Movement**. Tito saw a great opportunity among newly liberated colonial territories such as India and Indonesia to create a bloc of states independent of the Soviet and American alliances. This movement focused on increasing trade relations among members to reduce their economic dependency on the two superpowers and lobbying the UN to represent their interests, especially in situations of international crisis. For instance, as a supporter of Arab nationalism in the Middle East, Tito used non-alignment to represent the interests of the **Palestine Liberation Organization (PLO)** against Israel.

Anti-Tito Purges

While Tito purged his internal political enemies and skillfully used his position to advance his interests in the international arena, other Soviet bloc countries bore the brunt of the Tito-Stalin split. Stalin took his anger out on the eastern European regimes, as the Soviet Union helped orchestrate vast purges of the communist leadership between 1948 and 1953. Many leaders who had been in Moscow during the war and ruthlessly followed Stalin's orders in the early postwar years were now put on trial for fabricated charges of collaboration with western "imperialist" forces against their own people. In reality, these were sham trials, staged to satisfy Stalin's growing fear of imagined enemies and to reinforce the threat that the communist police state could eliminate anyone at any time, even its highest leaders. Ostensibly aimed at all communist leaders who had been friendly to Tito before 1948, the anti-Tito campaign actually proved an opportunity for revenge among Communist Party factions, as exemplified in Romania by the purge of Ana Pauker at the hands of her rival, **Gheorghe Gheorghiu-Dej**.

Fear and Violence The years 1948 to 1953 were dominated by fear and violence, similar to the Great Purges in the Soviet Union but with the important difference that these purges came about through both internal rivalries and Soviet interference. For many loyalists, this interference tainted the ideals of communism. Any legitimacy the Communist Parties claimed on the basis of having fought the fascist threat and struggled for social justice now eroded. As leaders fell and were replaced by others, who in turn could fall at any time, people learned to keep their heads down in fear and to distrust party ideology. Those who rose to the top of the party hierarchy were not idealists but opportunists.

Antisemitism and the Purges The most bitter disillusionment came in Czechoslovakia in 1951 with the

Third World Term coined in 1952 to identify the nations that aligned with neither the West (the First World) nor the Soviet bloc (the Second World) during the cold war.

Non-Aligned Movement Grouping of states initiated by Josip Broz Tito in 1948 that did not wish to be caught in the East-West cold war and tried not to choose sides.

Palestine Liberation Organization (PLO) Organization founded in 1964 by Palestinians fighting for an independent Palestinian state in territories claimed by Israel after 1948.

Gheorghe Gheorghiu-Dej (1901–1965) Leader of communist Romania from 1948 to 1965 who carried out a ruthless campaign of collectivization in the 1950s.

Slánský trial. Like Pauker, Rudolf Slánský had been a ruthless communist, but now he was accused of having spied for the West and plotting against the Soviet Union. Slánský's Jewish background was used against him, and others who were purged with him were Jewish survivors of concentration camps and idealistic communists. Antisemitism had become a feature of Soviet policies in Russia and beyond. In Czechoslovakia, the communist-controlled press identified the Jewish communist leaders alternatively as Zionists and as fascist radicals, once picturing Slánský in an SS uniform. Most troubling, people generally accepted the absurd antisemitic accusations not only out of fear but also because they often shared antisemitic attitudes. By 1953, most of the top echelon of the communist leadership and government officials in the communist bloc had been removed from power, stripped of their party membership, like Pauker, or executed, like Slánský.

State-Controlled Economies

While implementing these purges, the communist regimes in eastern Europe also began economic reconstruction with direct Soviet support. Initially, the Soviets focused on rebuilding Russia, and they did so by directly extracting resources from the communist bloc, from wheat and cattle to entire factories. The Soviets justified these seizures as war reparations. Thus, there was little economic growth in eastern Europe during the first few years of communist domination.

Soviet Economic Control Moscow sent observers, usually with military personnel, to oversee economic planning in each country. Instead of imposing a Soviet-style command economy, planners required each country to specialize in certain areas so that the region would collectively achieve economic growth. This clever plan ensured that no one state could gain economic autonomy. Thus East Germany, Poland, and Czechoslovakia, which were already more industrialized, were to focus on industrial goods, while Romania, Bulgaria, and, to some extent, Hungary were to provide raw materials and agricultural goods to support the industries and consumer needs of the other countries. The Soviets provided energy sources for industrial production in exchange for finished industrial products, at prices set by the Soviets. The Committee for Mutual Economic Assistance coordinated economic exchanges among these countries, with support from the Soviets, but in reality the Soviets controlled all the economic exchanges. For instance, the sale of Czech-produced cars in Poland was subject to Soviet approval.

Economic Growth and Its Price This formula for economic growth had some payoffs: by 1950, some industrial products, like steel, had surpassed prewar production. But these successes came at great cost for both agricultural and consumer goods. In addition, just as in the Soviet Union, the performance of the economy was judged by production rather than its value on the open market. For this reason, the quality of goods remained inferior to goods produced in western Europe.

Although the goals of economic restructuring were everywhere the same, the processes varied, depending on the relationship of the local communist leadership with Moscow. For instance, the collectivization of agriculture was pursued aggressively in Romania but not in Poland. Polish communists viewed collectivization as potentially destabilizing, while the Romanians were more willing to apply violent means to accomplish it. As a result, by 1958 the Romanian state fully controlled agriculture, and the regime was able to persuade the Soviets to withdraw all troops. The Poles relied on Soviet troops, however, to secure their western borders, which were not recognized by West Germany until the 1960s. Without the incentive of Soviet troop withdrawal, Polish communists allowed most peasants to keep their land but controlled the sale of agricultural products instead.

Changing the Social Landscape of Eastern Europe Economic restructuring produced a social restructuring like that in the Soviet Union in the 1920s and 1930s. Using the Soviet model, each Communist Party attempted to create a larger urban proletariat and eliminate all class enemies, including the old middle classes and rich peasants. In addition, many religious leaders were imprisoned, and writers and artists with a "bourgeois" background were censored or imprisoned to make way for a new atheist communist spirit. Ultimately, the communist regimes in eastern Europe wanted to replicate the total social control achieved by the Soviets in their own country.

Stalin-Mania The stamp of Soviet domination was made visible also through the renaming of places after Stalin. The old Romanian city Braşov became Stalin; the highest peak in the Tatra Mountains in Poland was renamed Stalin; and one of the largest squares in Budapest took on Stalin's name as well. But no Poles, Bulgarians, or Romanians rushed to name newborns after the Soviet leader, as many in the Soviet Union had done in the first decade of communist control. Many feared Stalin's close embrace; few admired him in the way Russians had looked up to V. I. Lenin in the 1920s.

De-Stalinization

In 1953 Stalin suddenly died. Soviet leaders and the population at large were petrified: Stalin's presence had been so overwhelming that virtually nobody knew how to behave in his absence. The funeral

Slánský trial Anti-Titoist purge trial in 1951 against Rudolf Slánský, leader of the Czechoslovak Communist Party.

Erich Lessing/Magnum Photos

The Hungarian Uprising of 1956 gained mass support when it shifted from a communist conflict between elites to a national uprising of the Hungarian people against Soviet imperialism. What does this photograph, taken in the midst of the uprising, suggest about the attitude of the Hungarian rebels in relation to the Soviet Union and the communist regime?

became a performance for anticipating Stalin's successor, as he had not given the issue much thought. Thousands crowded to see the corpse, laid beside Lenin's in the mausoleum in downtown Moscow. Party members paid their respects out of loyalty and fear of the unknown future; average people were mostly curious to see the great man dead. The pallbearers and funeral speakers were viewed as the potential successors, especially **Georgy Malenkov**. He was prime minister and assumed the position of party general secretary.

Krushchev's Rise to Power   In the following months, a fierce battle took place in the Politburo. Initially, the decision was to revive the principle of collective leadership. At the same time, however, two opponents began to vie for first place: Malenkov and **Nikita Khrushchev**. Khrushchev had been faithful to the party and loyal to Stalin and also cultivated an image as a simple man of the people. Born to an impoverished peasant family, he was the first among

them to learn to read and write. He had fought in the Civil War and had worked hard and ruthlessly to become the leader of the Moscow party organization in 1935. At the height of the Great Purges, Khrushchev was one of Stalin's henchmen in Moscow and the Ukraine, where he eliminated opponents of collectivization. By 1953, he had a forceful presence in the Politburo and controlled the main party newspaper, *Pravda*.

The Secret Speech   Within a year, Khrushchev's newspaper succeeded in tarnishing Malenkov's attempts to paint himself a reformer interested in improving living standards. Like Stalin, Khrushchev worked behind the scenes, and he orchestrated Malenkov's resignation. Between 1955 and 1956, he outmaneuvered other contenders for first place in the collective leadership of the party and in February 1956 made a dramatic move that catapulted him to the top. At the Twentieth Party Congress, Khrushchev delivered a **Secret Speech** that denounced the abuses of Stalin's era and called for a reassessment of that legacy, together with punishment for Stalin's henchmen. Declaring himself the true heir of Lenin, he placed himself in opposition to those who had supported Stalin.

The speech became a watershed in Soviet and communist history. It called for reassessment and encouraged internal criticism of the party, overturning the doctrine of infallibility established by Stalin. Khrushchev made good on this promise by freeing some political prisoners of the Stalin regime, in both the Soviet Union and eastern Europe. Some labor camps were closed down, and the **KGB**'s powers were reduced. At the same time, purges against Stalin's supporters began all over the eastern bloc.

From De-Stalinization to Rebellion   When Khrushchev opened the pages of *Pravda* to criticisms of the party and suggestions for reform, even Poles and Hungarians began reading it, interested in the changes it outlined. But many were aware of Khrushchev's past and realized that his call for reform had limits. That he avoided explanations, but claimed the mantle of Leninist leadership, was a signal to proceed cautiously. The most important test case for **de-Stalinization** came

Georgy Malenkov (1902–1988) Soviet communist leader who lost to Nikita Khrushchev in becoming Stalin's successor.

Nikita Khrushchev (1894–1971) Stalin's successor as leader of the Soviet Union and Soviet Communist Party who criticized Stalin's excesses and opened up a period of mild liberalization.

Secret Speech Speech by Khrushchev in 1956 to a closed party meeting that criticized Stalin and marked the beginning of his campaign to purge Stalin's supporters.

KGB Soviet Union's premier security, secret police, and intelligence agency, from 1954 to 1991.

de-Stalinization Elimination of Stalin's followers from the leadership of Soviet bloc Communist Parties after Stalin's death.

Table 28.2 Eastern Europe in the Postwar Period

1947	Communist takeover in Czechoslovakia
1948	Tito expelled from Cominform; Beginning of purges
1948–1949	Berlin blockade
1949	Formation of CMEA
1951	Slánský trial
1953	Stalin dies; Khrushchev comes to power
1955	Warsaw Pact formed
1956	Khrushchev's Secret Speech; Hungarian Uprising
1958	Soviet troops withdrawn from Romania
1961	Berlin Wall constructed
1964	Brezhnev comes to power
1968	Prague Spring and Soviet suppression

© Cengage Learning

the border and into Budapest, guns and homemade bombs were not enough to stop them. More than half a million Hungarians were imprisoned as a result, several thousand were killed in the initial clashes and the subsequent purges, and thousands managed to flee the country. Eastern European leaders learned the hard way that de-Stalinization would have to proceed at the speed and in the direction approved by Moscow.

Yet de-Stalinization did bring improvements. As people learned to live by the new rules, the violent purges ended. The state began spending more money on housing, public health, and basic consumer goods. Workers now had paid vacation time and opportunities to travel in other countries of the communist bloc. By the beginning of the 1960s, Stalin's legacy seemed a distant memory. His name was removed from Soviet encyclopedias and his photograph taken down in public buildings; places named Stalin were renamed once again. Table 28.2 summarizes key events in Eastern Europe during the postwar period.

✓ Checking In

By yourself or with a partner, explain the significance of each of the following selected key terms:

Edvard Beneš	Slánský trial
Cominform	Nikita Khrushchev
Non-Aligned Movement	de-Stalinization
Palestine Liberation Organization (PLO)	Hungarian Uprising

in Hungary in 1956, where two communist factions vied for leadership. One faction, led by **Imre Nagy**, adopted Khrushchev's liberalizing attitude and gained the support of the younger generation and lower-ranking party members, while the other wanted to preserve the Stalinist controls over political and economic life.

Initially Khrushchev supported the reformers, who became emboldened. Yet in October 1956, the party conflict gave way to a popular uprising that called for the expulsion of all Soviet forces. Nagy announced Hungary's withdrawal from the Warsaw Pact. The insurgents looked with hope to the West, but the United States was unwilling to risk its stable relations with the Soviets to support the **Hungarian Uprising**. And in western Europe, while the conservative parties took the same approach as the United States, their left-wing counterparts followed the Soviet line. A brief and bloody struggle ensued, with the Soviets prevailing through violence. As Soviet tanks rolled over

Imre Nagy (1896–1958) Hungarian communist leader who broke with Moscow in 1956 and attempted to establish an independent socialist path for Hungary.

Hungarian Uprising Nationwide uprising against the Soviet occupation and communist regime in 1956 that was violently crushed by the Soviets.

Superpower Conflicts and Colonial Independence Movements, 1945–1968

◆ **What role did the American-Soviet conflict play in the colonial struggles for independence?**

◆ **What were the consequences of the liberation movements?**

Europe's transformation into the two opposing camps of the cold war coincided with a revolution in the European colonies, most of which gained independence in the two decades after World War II. Yet the degree of actual political and economic autonomy of these postcolonial states varied greatly. Many continued to depend heavily on Europe, now with support from the Americans as well, while others opted to embrace the Soviet side of the cold war. Yet some states chose a third way, non-alignment. Overall, the East-West divide became replicated all over the postcolonial world, with the United States and the Soviet Union coming into conflict in Southeast Asia, the Middle East, and Africa.

Corbis

The Korean War, the first cold war military confrontation, resulted in a stalemate that continues today. It was also the first combat action in which black and white U.S. troops were officially integrated. How successful was the U.S. military intervention in the war?

Superpower Confrontations

In the 1950s, the United States and the Soviet Union became embroiled in Korea in their first direct military confrontation of the cold war. A postwar settlement had divided the former Japanese territory into a communist Democratic People's Republic in the north and the Republic of Korea in the south.

The Korean War What started as a war between the two in 1950 quickly became internationalized in the bipolar world of the cold war. After the Soviets sent military support to the North, the Americans went before the UN Security Council to request a military intervention on behalf of the South. The Security Council agreed, primarily because the Soviets, boycotting the UN at the time, were not present to veto the decision. The United States thus sent in troops under the guise of South Korean requests for help and UN endorsement. In reality, the **Korean War** was a heated conflict unfolding between the Soviets' pursuit of a zone of influence in Korea and the Americans' implementation of the Truman Doctrine to aid those fighting the spread of communism. The new Chinese communist regime also became involved, sending military aid to the North Koreans. A truce in 1953 left Korea divided, with families split across the border and unable to communicate. The Soviets and Chinese celebrated a communist victory, while the United States boasted success in stopping the spread of communism.

Yet the Korean War was an abysmal failure. It brought the two superpowers into a military conflict that left nothing resolved; troops remain poised at the border today. The outcome of this conflict for the world scene was twofold: it established that the two superpowers were willing to use military power in their contest for world domination, and it showed the great military and human costs of such actions. If Korea could be a setting for war among the superpowers, then all political leaders of liberation movements in colonial territories had to think carefully about the choices they made.

The Race for Outer Space In the following decade, the contest between the Soviets and the Americans circled the globe and escalated to outer space. Under President Dwight Eisenhower, the United States expanded its military alliances and placed nuclear missiles around the world, from France to Pakistan and the Philippines. The Soviets also built a missile arsenal. In 1957 they launched *Sputnik 1*, the first space satellite and a scientific achievement that placed them ahead of the Americans in the space race.

Dividing Berlin The Soviets attempted to parlay this success by threatening to hand over control of access to West Berlin to the East Germans, hoping to force the Americans out of the city and ending the flow of

Korean War (1950–1953) Military conflict between communist-backed North Korea and United States–supported South Korea.

Sputnik 1 Soviet satellite that in 1957 was the first to be launched into earth orbit and began the Soviet-American space race.

In June 1963, U.S. President John F. Kennedy stood on a platform above the Berlin Wall, addressing 12,000 West Berliners and a few East Berliners silently watching on the other side of the wall. Speaking on the themes of freedom and citizenship, he asserted, "Ich bin ein Berliner" (I am a Berliner). What does this image of Kennedy standing above a crowd in West Berlin and looking over to East Berlin suggest about U.S. policies during the cold war?

Berlin Wall Wall built through Berlin by East Germany in 1961 to prevent its citizens from escaping into West Germany.

Cuban Missile Crisis Standoff between the United States and the Soviet Union in 1962 over Soviet equipping of Cuba with nuclear missiles.

Fidel Castro (1926–) Leader of Cuban communist revolution in 1956 and president of Cuba between 1959 and 2008.

decolonization Process by which European imperialist powers moved to withdraw from colonial holdings and ready colonies for independence.

Commonwealth of Nations Association of independent states, originally former British colonies, that was created in 1947 to enhance economic and cultural cooperation.

Germans from East to West. After a three-year standoff, in 1961 East Germany put up the **Berlin Wall**, dividing the city. There was little the Americans could do about it. The wall became a powerful symbol of what the cold war meant for average people.

Near Nuclear Disaster The most dangerous confrontation of the Soviets and Americans came in 1962, during the **Cuban Missile Crisis**. After **Fidel Castro** came to power in Cuba in 1959, he was courted by both the Americans and the Soviets. For the United States, Cuba had great economic and strategic interest because of its proximity. For the Soviets, Cuba could be an outpost for nuclear missiles, to counter the American bases in Turkey and Pakistan. After a failed American attempt to depose Castro in 1961, the Soviets offered to bolster the Cuban defenses by bringing in nuclear weapons. For a few days in October 1962, President John F. Kennedy and Khrushchev came close to nuclear war. Each leader called on the other to back down, while both were in fact mobilizing out of fear that the other would strike. Then, when the Americans promised not to invade Cuba and to withdraw their missiles from Turkey, the Soviets removed the missiles from Cuba. The crisis made both powers aware of the need for constant communication.

Colonial Independence Movements

As American and Soviet economic and military power expanded, most European countries with colonies realized that their reduced political, military, and economic resources made it impossible for them to maintain control over vast territories outside of Europe.

British Decolonization In Britain, the Labour Party favored liberating the colonies as a matter of ideology and pragmatic consideration. The British led **decolonization** by offering colonies independence and a new, autonomous relationship with Great Britain through the **Commonwealth of Nations**, which focused on economic relations. India was a relatively successful model. Given the large population and great variety of traditions and cultures that existed on the subcontinent, the Indian nationalist movements were remarkably united in their negotiations with the British. The leadership of Mohandas

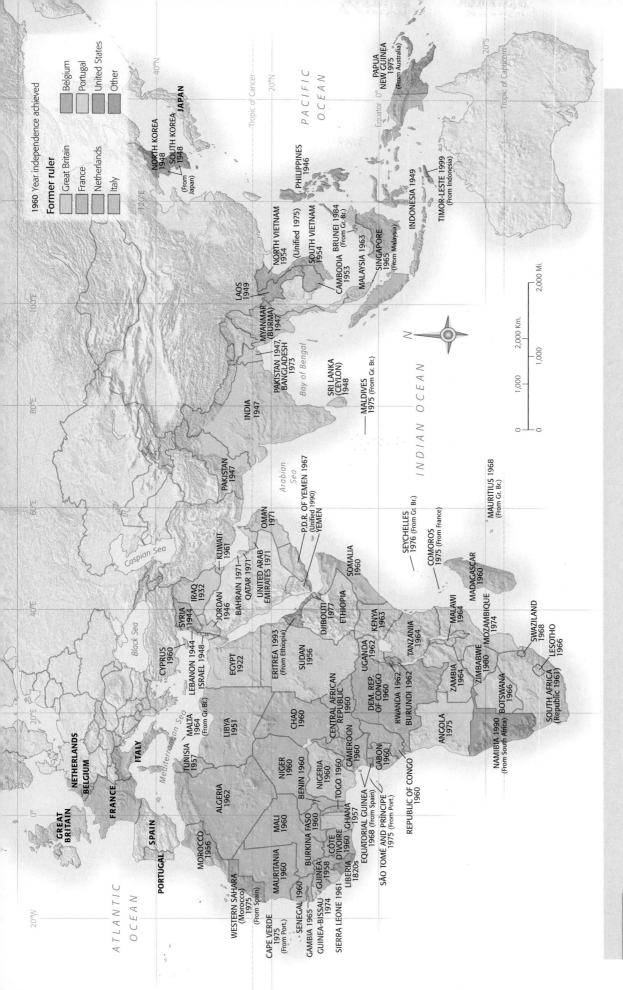

Map 28.4 **Decolonization Movements, 1945–1968** Between 1945 and 1968 most European colonies gained independence. For some, like Ghana, the process was peaceful. Others, like Vietnam, fought bloody wars. The United States and the Soviet Union became involved in these struggles as the new world power brokers. © Cengage Learning

1. If you look at the dates on the map, how would describe the decolonization process of the British colonies?
2. What about the French colonies?
3. What territory was last to be decolonized?

1960 Year independence achieved

Former ruler

Great Britain
France
Netherlands
Italy

Belgium
Portugal
United States
Other

Gandhi gave these movements cohesion and a strategy of peaceful resistance to colonial rule. His protégé **Jawaharlal Nehru** became the first prime minister of independent India. Both resisted the strategy of outright military conflict over India's borders, a serious threat as India was culturally and ethnically divided, most importantly between Hindus and Muslims. In 1947, British India devolved into Muslim-dominated Pakistan and Hindu-dominated India. Border conflicts between the two countries continue today.

The British pursued a similar disengagement policy in their African colonies but proceeded more gradually, as these colonies had not yet developed an indigenous intellectual and economic elite like that in South Asia. In addition, as the white settlers in these African territories were far more numerous than those in Asia and unwilling to give up their homes, the process of decolonization was more contentious and violent. West Africa, Ghana, and Nigeria were the first to gain independence peacefully. By contrast, a great deal more conflict occurred in Kenya, where white settlers wished to retain their economic privileges after independence, by force if necessary, while indigenous radical groups such as the **Mau Mau** fought for a radical break from the British. After five years of violence, the British won the war but lost the colony. Having become financially overextended, the British pulled out their troops. Kenya became independent in 1963.

French Decolonization The French wanted to preserve greater control over colonies in Africa and Asia and chose to repress independence movements. In Asia, de Gaulle attempted to persuade Vietnam to remain part of the French Union. This arrangement allowed colonial territories to gain more autonomy and become more democratic through enfranchisement of the local population. But administration, education, and commerce would remain heavily dominated by French-educated and-speaking elites.

But the postwar Vietnamese political factions proved impossible to control. The communists were a growing pro-independence group that secured help from the new regime in China. In 1954, the communist leader Ho Chi Minh defeated the French, despite massive financial help from the United States. Vietnam was divided between the communist-controlled north and the western-supported south. The loss of Vietnam produced a political crisis in France that eventually brought colonial rule to an end.

Yet Vietnam remained an important battleground in the cold war. In the early 1960s, the United States sent military advisers and then troops into South Vietnam to forestall what President Lyndon Johnson saw as the threat of communist revolution everywhere in Asia. The **Vietnam War** became increasingly brutal but did not bring any resolution. In 1973, under pressure from the American public, who watched the atrocities committed by both sides every day on television, President Richard Nixon reached a truce with North Vietnam and pulled out.

Algeria and the Challenge to French Democracy
The French had troubles with their overseas territories in Africa as well, with the costliest conflict in Algeria. More than 1 million European settlers had lived there for generations, and the territory had been formally integrated into France as an administrative region. Therefore, when a revolt broke out in 1954, shortly after the humiliating defeat in Vietnam, the French felt a threat to the homeland, and repression of the rebels became a core political issue. Yet the Muslim rebels were committed to fighting for independence from French rule. The **Algerian War** divided France both at home and in North Africa, bringing down the Fourth Republic in 1958. In this civil war, some white settlers and European French citizens sided with the pro-independence insurgents, while some of the North African indigenous populations sided with the French colonial administration. By and large, however, the division was racial—whites against nonwhites—and the abuses committed during the war only reinforced racism in French society. De Gaulle was able to save the state from the brink of collapse in 1958 through a new constitution that strengthened the power of the president and military establishment against the parliament. Yet he eventually gave up Algeria in 1962.

The rest of French Africa, where the French were less invested politically and culturally and the number of European settlers smaller, gained independence with less strife. After Algeria, the French administration was eager to grant independence to the rest of its colonies. Yet, as the level of indigenous economic development remained low, these countries continued in their economic dependence on France.

Emerging Conflicts over the Middle East Although disengagement and decolonization dominated the political fate of former colonies in Asia and Africa, the Middle East became a new battleground for the two superpowers, primarily because of its tremendous oil resources. The United States gradually replaced the British in the area, trying to broker

Jawaharlal Nehru (1889–1964) Leading figure of the Indian independence movement who became the first prime minister of India in 1947.

Mau Mau (in Kikuyu, "burning spear") Pro-independence Kenyan rebels who advocated violent methods against white settlers in order to reclaim land and political power for indigenous Africans.

Vietnam War (1959–1975) Successful effort by the communist North Vietnamese to take over South Vietnam, which was supported by the Americans and the French.

Algerian War (1954–1962) Civil war in which Algerian nationalists eventually defeated the French colonial administration and established an independent state.

These three leaders of the Non-Aligned Movement—Egypt's Gamal Abdel Nasser, Yugoslavia's Josip Broz Tito, and India's Jawaharlal Nehru—saw themselves as the advocates of independence for their nations and critics of imperialist oppression. What does this image convey about the lifestyle of these leaders of oppressed people?

between the newly established state of Israel and its hostile Arab neighbors while competing with the Soviet Union for alliances with oil-rich Arab leaders.

The development of Arab nationalism was accelerated by the creation of Israel and the failure of the United Nations to create a Palestinian Arab state. On the one hand, Israel came to define itself and be viewed increasingly as a promoter of progressive ideas and of western civilization. After 1967, it was sturdily on the side of American interests in the area. On the other hand, some Arab populations in Palestine and the rest of the Middle East began to look toward the Soviet Union as a better broker for their interests. After 1964, when the PLO established itself as the foremost leader in the Palestinian struggle for statehood, the organization was quickly recognized by and sought the material support of the Soviet Union and other communist states, such as Yugoslavia.

Yet neither communism nor capitalism was the choice of the political leaders of the Middle East. Instead, the region produced a blend of Arab nationalism with strong Muslim influences. Many territories remained kingdoms, and postcolonial states established authoritarian governments with only a thin veneer of parliamentary life. Political institutions in these countries often resembled premodern theocracies, and their oil resources brought great wealth to ruling elites. States like Saudi Arabia could display the trappings of material civilization in step with Europe while its justice system and suppression of

women remained violent. Until the 1970s, neither superpower intervened directly in the internal ideological preferences of these states so long as they could benefit from access to the region's oil resources.

The Non-Aligned Movement

By the late 1960s, European colonial rule had come to an end almost everywhere. This process was uneven and very costly in some instances, and it brought about radical change in international relations. The UN General Assembly became dominated numerically by relatively poor postcolonial states. By 1980, the Non-Aligned Movement had grown from 25 to 117, becoming the largest bloc in the UN and acting forcefully as a faction when important matters came to a vote. Thus, the non-aligned bloc was able to direct financial assistance to underdeveloped areas, such as South Asia and Africa. This bloc regarded Europe sometimes positively, as an important patron in cultural and economic relations, and at other times with bitterness, as the seat of imperialist oppression. Almost half of the presidents of the assembly have come from postcolonial states of the non-aligned bloc.

Postcolonial Realignments in the Cold War Postcolonial regions became a new arena for superpower struggle. The Soviets invested heavily in economic and educational exchanges with the newly independent African states, accompanied by a heavy dose of communist ideology. African rulers often found the Soviet propaganda about western imperialism appealing. By contrast, the United States backed regimes that supported its economic interests. American oil investments in the Persian Gulf, for example, prompted U.S. support for an authoritarian monarchy in Iran that replaced the nationalist republican independence movement.

States such as Indonesia, Egypt, and India maintained more distance from the two superpowers. One important moment in this process was the **Suez Canal Crisis**. In 1956, during the Hungarian Uprising, Egyptian leader **Gamal Abdel Nasser** nationalized the canal. With encouragement from the Soviets, the Egyptians hoped to secure control over this strategic body of water that had been under French, British, and more recently American control. But Khrushchev did not send direct military aid. Thus, in winning the conflict, Nasser established an independence position, able to broker between the superpowers without a direct commitment to either side. Like Tito before him, Nasser also secured hefty financial support for Egypt from both superpowers.

 Checking In

By yourself or with a partner, explain the significance of each of the following selected key terms:

Korean War	Jawaharlal Nehru
Berlin Wall	Vietnam War
Cuban Missile Crisis	Algerian War
Commonwealth of Nations	Suez Canal Crisis

Cultural Developments and Social Protest

◆ **Why was there a moral and spiritual crisis in the 1950s?**

◆ **What were the generational divides behind the revolt of the 1960s?**

In the 1950s and 1960s, European culture took many new turns, especially as the very meaning of being European was questioned and redefined. Although a consensus seemed to develop in the 1950s about European identity and culture, a new generation of intellectuals and rebels in the 1960s helped shake it up. Now Europe became divided between old and young, between conformist and anti-establishment factions.

Suez Canal Crisis Military attack on Egypt by Britain, France, and Israel in 1956 after Egypt seized the Suez Canal from British administration.

Gamal Abdel Nasser (1918–1970) President of Egypt from 1956 to 1970 who nationalized the Suez Canal.

Consumption and Conformity

After the war, western Europeans sought to forget the past, work hard, and acquire material goods. Instead of participating in mass political movements, they sought recognition for individual achievements. Initially success measured by material goods meant simply having a job, a place to live, and food on the table. But as the economic miracle began to make consumer goods more affordable, the culture of consumption took off. At first, people wanted refrigerators, radios, and comfortable furniture. By the 1960s, they wanted a television, a car, and the leisure activities that a car made possible.

Consumer Culture in Western Europe The availability of inexpensive consumer goods was closely connected to technological advances made during and after the war. Plastics made everything cheaper—and also created an unprecedented level of dependency on oil. As consumer goods proliferated, their very availability induced people to want to have more of what other people had. The desire to conform increased as the possibility for purchasing the same goods grew. This kind of social pressure was not new, but it had never before been expressed on a massive scale that defied social class divisions. Ironically, while struggling to be individually successful, people now proclaimed their status by fitting in; conformity and anonymity gave a sense of security. This reaction seemed natural after the wartime years, when many had lived the experience of being singled out in painful ways.

Conformity Without Consumption in Eastern Europe Nothing parallel to the consumer culture developed in eastern Europe, but the new communist regimes did place great emphasis on conformity. This conformity was, however, imposed without mercy from above and enforced by manipulating fear. Behavior regarded as deviant was harshly punished, with imprisonment or exile to labor camps. Priests and religious believers were often singled out. Some theological institutes were closed. All denominations were persecuted, but not to the same extent. For instance, members of the Greek Catholic Church, made illegal in Romania in 1948, were harshly punished for any public religious displays, whereas members of the Roman Catholic Church in the same country were allowed to continue their religious practices in limited ways.

Under the pressure for conformity to the strict party line, people quickly learned to live double lives. A member of an illegal faith might openly abandon his or her religious allegiance but continue religious practice in hiding. Because the communist regimes could not police a person's every action, most eastern Europeans became skilled at shifting between public and hidden identities.

By the beginning of the 1960s, the communist regimes were also using the mass media to enhance conformity and social stability. Radio and television programs, films, and magazines—some glossy and appealingly designed—became effective communist propaganda machines. Starved for information and entertainment, people in eastern Europe often embraced these propaganda products as a form of relaxation and escape.

Moral and Spiritual Crisis

As western European culture became more conformist and consumer oriented, it also became increasingly secular and even unconcerned with questions of morality and spirituality. For many, the war and the Holocaust had unraveled the very concept of civilization. In the first decade after the war, a few intellectuals and spiritual leaders attempted to offer answers to the deep moral questions opened up by the wartime violence, corruption, and utter degradation of the human condition. Yet these answers proved unsatisfactory to the following generation, who challenged the solutions offered by their predecessors.

Ideological Commitment or Moral Alienation Intellectuals such as **Albert Camus** and **Jean-Paul Sartre** tried to claim social relevance for literature through personal engagement against injustice. In the Algerian War, these writers took opposite sides— Sartre for postcolonial independence, Camus for retention of links with France. Sartre's position derived from his ideological commitment to communism, whereas Camus arrived at his stance through direct experience in his native Algeria. Their quarrel became famous in intellectual circles, but, powerful as they were, their writings offered no moral guidance or satisfactory answers to their readers. In fact, it was Camus's gradual distancing from the ideological commitment of Sartre that resonated most strongly. The condition of the postwar generation was one of moral alienation.

New Departures Among Religious Institutions This context provided some important opportunities for the Catholic and Protestant churches in western Europe to regain spiritual relevance. But it was not the churches that grew. Instead, it was the Christian Democratic political parties that grew, especially in France, Germany, and Italy and especially when they demonstrated a concern for social justice and progressive measures relating to workers' rights and social welfare. But these parties also represented a social and cultural conservatism that had little appeal to the generation born after the war, which seemed detached from the challenges of the postwar years and unable to find moral and spiritual guidance either in religious parties or in religion itself.

Jean Paul Sartre and Simone de Beauvoir were the most celebrated couple in postwar France—intellectuals committed to political and social causes. Yet de Beauvoir remained for a long time in the shadow of Sartre, her feminism viewed secondary to his existential philosophy. How do they appear in this photograph?

In response to this moral crisis, Pope **John XXIII** attempted to provide a new direction for Catholicism. At the **Second Vatican Council**, he presented a broad agenda for changes in all areas of the church's organization and social engagement while attempting to preserve its fundamental mission. Decisions at this series of meetings, from 1962 to 1965, allowed churches to use local languages, gave reformist bishops more autonomy, and permitted greater involvement in social activism—for instance, on behalf of the poor in Latin America.

If the primary struggle of churches in western Europe was against the moral and spiritual alienation of

Albert Camus (1913–1960) Algerian-born French writer and philosopher who opposed Algerian independence and was awarded the Nobel Prize in Literature in 1957.

Jean Paul Sartre (1905–1980) Most famous French philosopher of the twentieth century, an open communist sympathizer.

John XXIII (r. 1958–1962) Reformist pope who spearheaded changes in language use and liturgical rituals and initiated the Second Vatican Council.

Second Vatican Council Meeting of cardinals and bishops of the Roman Catholic Church between 1962 and 1965 to promote church reform.

The English rock band The Who turned youthful rebellion into performance art. In addition to playing well-crafted compositions with great style, Pete Townshend (guitar) and Keith Moon (drums) also took to smashing their instruments on stage at the end of performances. What qualities about their performance does this image suggest?

the population at large, in the communist bloc, churches and religious believers fought for their very survival in the face of political persecution. The communist regimes tolerated and gradually used some churches both to appease religious believers and to inform on them with the help of corrupt priests. In other instances, however, religious institutions became the seat of spiritual survival against communism. In Poland, the Catholic Church preserved a degree of integrity and moral authority unparalleled anywhere else in eastern Europe. In fact, religiosity among Poles grew, and many gravitated to the church as the one institution uncorrupted by communism. Protestant denominations also offered a secure and morally uplifting refuge. But most eastern Europeans became estranged from religious experience through the aggressive anti-religious campaigns of the communist regimes.

Youth and the Counterculture

By the mid-1960s, a new postwar generation was questioning the direction of prosperity and security in western Europe and rejecting the values and lifestyles of their elders. The clash of generations arose from several factors. First, while the direct experience of deprivation and death made the prewar generation overly preoccupied with material comforts, abundance made the postwar generation indifferent to the value of material goods. Those born after 1945 were marked by the culture of conformity and consumption in two ways: on the one hand, they fully enjoyed the fruits of the economic miracle, the availability of cheap material goods, books,

records, and other forms of entertainment and information; on the other hand, they wanted more meaning in their lives than the satisfactions their parents found in material goods. They deplored the conformity and cultural boredom of their elders and wanted to engage in meaningful choices and spread their comforts among others less fortunate. Finally, the postwar generation had much greater access to college education.

Rock 'n' Roll A new pop culture best expressed the mood of this new generation. Rock and roll developed first in America, but by the mid-1960s, European bands like the Beatles and The Who had taken the new musical form and made it theirs. Rock music anthems like "My Generation" were rebellious and appealing precisely because rock 'n' roll was loud and rough. Young people loved it as much as their parents hated it. Some performers brought broader political and social content to their lyrics. Bob Dylan, the most powerful voice of the postwar generation, wrote verses that resonated with young people all over western Europe: "I learned to hate the Russians / all through my whole life / If another war comes / it's them we must fight / … with God on my side."[1]

In film, New Wave Cinema merged a social and political critique with a harsh style that echoed the loudness of rock music. The films of French director

---

[1] Lyrics from Bob Dylan, "With God on Our Side," from *Times They Are A-Changin'*, Columbia Records, New York, 1964. Reprinted by permission of Bob Dylan Music Company, Special Rider Music Company.

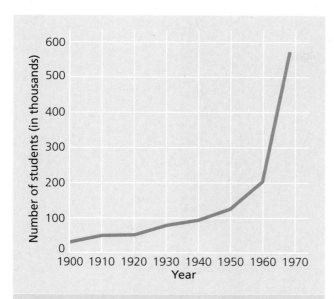

Figure 28.2 Enrollment Figures for French Universities from 1900–1968 After World War II, western Europe was fundamentally changed by the great growth in college attendance. The beneficiaries of this growth were especially the poor and women. What decade saw the highest rate of growth?

Source: Wilkinson, James D.; Huges, H. Stuart, *Contemporary Europe: A History,* 9th Edition, © 1998, p. 425. Reprinted by permission of Pearson Education, Inc., Upper Saddle River, NJ.

From Peaceful Protests to Violent Clashes King's murder signaled the end of the peaceful civil rights movement and the beginning of more belligerent African American protests. At the same time, protests against the Vietnam War were taking a more radical form. On campuses across America, originally peaceful marches often ended as violent clashes with the police. Television news reports showing long-haired hippies being clobbered by steel-helmeted police made this generational clash real for everyone. To some, the young appeared unruly, self-indulgent, and irresponsible. To others, they were heroic for shaking up the political establishment and addressing large issues such as racism, sexism, postcolonial imperialism, and naked military aggression.

The Student Rebellions in France A similar style of protest emerged in Europe, as student antiwar and anticolonial protests erupted from London to Berlin. But the most powerful student movement was centered in Paris, where, in May 1968, under the inspired leadership of **Daniel Cohn-Bendit**, it made common cause with the French workers. Born in the year the war ended, Cohn-Bendit embodied many of the characteristics of his generation. He came from a German Jewish family that, having fled the Nazis during the war, had returned to West Germany afterward. His background made him painfully aware of the cost of postwar western European reconstruction—the abandonment of moral imperatives for the sake of material well-being. In the impassioned works of Marxist revolutionaries, Cohn-Bendit found inspiration for challenging all that was accepted around him and struggling for social justice in ways that the traditional left seemed to have abandoned. The national strike Cohn-Bendit led put France on hold for almost a month and helped bring down de Gaulle. Similar student protests across Europe evidenced the reengagement of youth in politics, in support of the anticolonial struggle, social justice, the guerrilla fighters in Algeria and Vietnam, and communist leaders such as Mao in China.

Jean-Luc Goddard confronted materialism, sexuality, and political violence. He and other film makers broke free of the conventions and conservative aesthetics of their predecessors. Film, they contended, should not be an escape. It should depict life, and life was neither heroic nor even coherent, but full of violence, breakdown, and loss.

Education and the Youth One central unifying element of this new generation was its unprecedented access to education. In France, for instance, university enrollment went up by almost 200 percent in the 1960s, especially among women and working-class people (see Figure 28.2). This dramatic change forced important questions about the quality of education and the political agenda of its content. In the ensuing battles over democratizing university education, both students and teachers became increasingly radicalized and involved in political protest, giving rise to a new wave of left-wing activists and politicians.

1968

These generational tensions came to a head in the extraordinary year 1968. In an explosive set of coincidences, the world seemed headed toward a revolution. In the United States, the charismatic civil rights leader **Martin Luther King Jr.** was assassinated.

Prague Spring The most important political challenge of 1968 came from inside the communist bloc, in Prague. Until the late 1960s, the Czechoslovaks had avoided de-Stalinization because of their success in industrial production. As long as their industrial production worked to the benefit of the Soviet Union, Khrushchev left the Czechoslovaks alone. By the early 1960s, however, the productivity of the Czechoslovak economy

Jean-Luc Goddard (1930–) Prominent French New Wave film maker.

Martin Luther King Jr. (1929–1968) African American Baptist minister and nonviolent leader of the American civil rights movement in the 1960s.

Daniel Cohn-Bendit (1945–) German-born charismatic left-wing leader of the student protests in France in May 1968.

While Czech students protested Soviet oppression in Prague and American students protested the
Vietnam War on college campuses, in May 1968 French students took to the streets to support a
general strike that brought the country to a standstill and forced politicians of the older generation
to pay attention to the students' calls for change. How would you describe their protest activities
as seen here?

was decreasing, and growing numbers of party members called for economic, social, and cultural reforms.
Alexander Dubček, a reformer who had spent the
wartime years fighting in the anti-Nazi resistance,
convinced the Soviets, responding to pressure from
dissidents, to allow him to experiment with liberalizing reforms. For a few brief months during the **Prague
Spring**, Dubček attempted to create "socialism with
a human face"—abolishing
censorship of the press, allowing criticism of the communist leadership, and reviving workers' councils.
He tried to combine social
policies that would benefit
all citizens with policies that
would accelerate economic
growth. He even pardoned
political prisoners, including religious believers, who
had been harshly perse-
cuted in the 1950s.

The reforms in Czecho-
slovakia proved too radi-
cal for the Soviets, who recalled the 1956 Hungarian
Uprising, even though the
Czechoslovak movement

proposed not to end communist rule but to reform
it. In August 1968, **Leonid Brezhnev** sent tanks into
Czechoslovakia to wipe out all opposition. All Warsaw Pact members save Romania also sent in troops.
The military intervention was out of proportion,
given the fact that Czechoslovak reformers did not
put up armed resistance, and the West came to associate the communist leadership of eastern Europe
with this crude military response. The crushing of the
Prague Spring brought to a tragic end the era of de-
Stalinization and reform. Over the next two decades,
while the western European youthful protesters became influential in politics, culture, technology, and
commerce, their counterparts in eastern Europe spent
years in jail or learned not to challenge the system.
A lucky few escaped into the West.

 Checking In

*By yourself or with a partner, explain the significance
of each of the following selected key terms:*

Albert Camus   Daniel Cohn-Bendit

Jean-Paul Sartre   Alexander Dubček

Second Vatican Council   Prague Spring

Martin Luther King Jr.   Leonid Brezhnev

Alexander Dubček (1921–1992)
Leader of the Czechoslovak Communist Party during the Prague
Spring who initiated liberalizing
reforms but was forcibly removed
from power.

Prague Spring Short-lived period
of liberalization in Czechoslovakia
in 1968 that was violently crushed
by the Soviets.

Leonid Brezhnev (1906–1982)
Soviet leader between 1964 and
1983 who oversaw the reversal
of the liberalization efforts of the
Khrushchev regime.

Summary

- World War II transformed Europe into a pawn in the struggle between the two superpowers of the cold war—the United States and the Soviet Union.

- Europe became divided into two camps, East and West.

- The capitalist West became a place for rebuilding democracy and the cradle of the new welfare state.

- In the communist East dictatorial regimes came to power under Soviet control.

- New multinational organizations like the UN, NATO, and the Warsaw Pact marked an entirely new international order in which European states were often relegated to the sidelines in the contest between the Soviet Union and the United States.

- European colonial powers engaged in a process of relinquishing power over their non-European territories.

- Decolonization was sometimes peaceful and other times violent, playing a direct role in political stability in Europe.

- The generation born after World War II came to challenge the wisdom of the materialist values of the reconstruction generation, bringing in a new mood of social and political engagement, moral responsibility, and self-sacrifice.

Chronology

1945	Potsdam Conference discusses how to administer postwar Germany	**1951**	European Coal and Steel Community (ECSC) is established
1946	National Health Service Act ensures health care	**1953**	Stalin dies
		1954	Vietnam gains independence
1947	India gains independence; Truman Doctrine commits the United States to fight communism worldwide; U.S. Marshall Plan offers reconstruction aid to western Europe	**1954–1962**	Algerians win independence from the colonial French government
		1955	Warsaw Pact is formed
1947–1948	Communists take over Romania, Czechoslovakia, Hungary, Poland, East Germany, and Bulgaria	**1956**	Khrushchev delivers Secret Speech criticizing Stalin; Hungarian Uprising is crushed by Soviets; Egypt nationalizes the Suez Canal
1948	Stalin expels Tito from Cominform; Stalin begins purges of eastern European communist leadership	**1958**	European Economic Community is formed
		1958	French Fourth Republic falls; De Gaulle succeeds in French presidential coup
1949	Indonesia gains independence; North Atlantic Treaty Organization (NATO) is founded; Committee for Mutual Economic Assistance (CMEA) is founded; Mao Zedong leads communist takeover in China	**1961**	Soviets construct Berlin Wall
		1962	Cuban Missile Crisis
1950–1953	Korean War ends in stalemate	**1968**	Prague Spring is crushed by Soviets; Students and workers create national strike in France

Test Yourself

To gauge your mastery of the material in this chapter, answer the questions below. More than one answer may be correct.

The Iron Curtain, 1945–1958

1. Which of these countries ended up overwhelmingly under the Soviet sphere of influence according to the informal percentages agreement between Stalin and Churchill?

   a. Yugoslavia
   b. Czechoslovakia
   c. Hungary

   d. Romania
   e. Bulgaria

2. The Nuremberg Trials:

   a. Divided Germany into two countries.
   b. Brought to justice Nazi wartime criminals.
   c. Became a model for de-Nazification all over eastern Europe.

   d. Created a new system of international law.
   e. Introduced the legal concept of "crimes against humanity."

3. The post–World War II peace settlements differed from World War I because the:

   a. United States decided not to pursue an isolationist position in international relations.
   b. Soviet Union had become a world power.
   c. Ethnic map of Europe was significantly different.

   d. Victors wanted to avoid the rise of a strong Germany again.
   e. Ideological goal of rebuilding democracy, rather than self-determination, was the guiding principle of the Western allies.

4. The Truman Doctrine:

   a. Identified communism as the primary threat to democracy.
   b. Forced all European countries to take sides with or against the United States.
   c. Offered financial incentives to Poland to rebel against the Soviets.

   d. Aimed to stamp out communism in Greece.
   e. Helped rebuild the western European economic infrastructure.

5. NATO:

   a. Invited all European states to join.
   b. Focused on defending member countries against the alleged Soviet plans for global military domination.

   c. Included Turkey among its first members.
   d. Allowed all members to plan individually for their military preparedness.
   e. Gave equal voice to all members.

Now that you have reviewed and tested yourself on this part of the chapter, take time to pull together all the important information by answering the following questions:

◆ What international conflicts in the early postwar period paved the way for Europe's division?

◆ How did international relations change in the first two postwar decades?

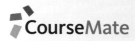

Visit the CourseMate website at **www.cengagebrain.com** for additional study tools and review materials for this chapter.

The Revival of Western Europe

6. The highest economic growth in Europe in the first two decades after World War II took place in:

   a. Poland
   b. France
   c. Italy

   d. Germany
   e. Hungary

7. Left-wing parties were successful in establishing themselves as important players in the early postwar period in:

   a. Germany
   b. France
   c. Great Britain

   d. Greece
   e. None of the above.

8. The European Coal and Steel Community:

   a. Established an international company for mining and heavy industry.
   b. Helped eliminate German-French enmities.
   c. Enhanced the production of steel and iron of the members by over 75 percent.

   d. Excluded Britain.
   e. Benefited from support from the Marshall Plan.

9. The early postwar political changes in Britain included:

   a. Establishing firm state control over the economy and public services.
   b. Nationalizing the Bank of England.
   c. Creating a National Health Service.

   d. Expanding educational opportunities for women in secondary education.
   e. Creating state pension funds for all workers.

10. Charles de Gaulle:

    a. Brought political stability to postwar France.
    b. Advocated for greater power for the parliament and more limited powers for the executive.

    c. Saw himself as a Catholic first and a Frenchman second.
    d. Was an enthusiastic ally of the United States.
    e. Was a socialist.

Now that you have reviewed and tested yourself on this part of the chapter, take time to pull together all the important information by answering the following questions:

◆ By what means was western Europe successful in rebuilding its economic power?

◆ What were the political consequences of the commitment to economic recovery?

The Restructuring of Eastern Europe

11. The communist regimes came to power in eastern Europe due to:

    a. Popular support.
    b. Soviet support.
    c. A lack of political alternatives.

    d. The use of military force.
    e. The elimination of all other political contenders.

12. Josip Broz Tito:

    a. Fought for the Reds in the Russian Civil War.
    b. Tried to help the Greek communist partisans against Soviet wishes.
    c. Was an ardent Stalinist.

    d. Was purged in 1948.
    e. Considered himself a Croat.

13. The anti-Tito purges eliminated from power:

    a. Presumed enemies of Stalin.
    b. All of the communist leaders from the wartime years.
    c. Many Jewish leaders of the communist regimes.
    d. Many loyalists of the communist party.
    e. All of the above.

14. The Committee for Mutual Economic Assistance (CMEA) aimed to:

    a. Rebuild the economies of its members by enhancing industrial production in vital areas in all of the countries.
    b. Assign different economic roles to each member.
    c. Help to rebuild the Soviet economy through exchanges with the CMEA members.
    d. Collectivize the agriculture of all the members in the same fashion.
    e. Create a large landless proletariat class in all communist bloc countries.

15. Stalin's death brought about which of the following changes?

    a. Loosening of internal control by the communist parties all over eastern Europe.
    b. The rise to power of Nikita Khrushchev.
    c. The closing down of some labor camps.
    d. A new independent regime in Hungary.
    e. More social benefits for workers across the communist bloc.

Now that you have reviewed and tested yourself on this part of the chapter, take time to pull together all the important information by answering the following questions:

◆ What were the important steps in the communist takeovers in eastern Europe?

◆ What was the effect in the region of Stalin's death?

Superpower Conflicts and Colonial Independence Movements, 1945–1968

16. The Korean War:

    a. Was won by the Soviet Union.
    b. Saw the presence of the first racially integrated U.S. troops in combat.
    c. Represented an implementation of the Truman Doctrine.
    d. Was endorsed by the Security Council of the United Nations.
    e. Was the first time the cold war superpowers came into close military conflict.

17. The global struggle between the Soviet Union and the United States manifested itself through:

    a. The competition to send the first satellite into space.
    b. Building walls around borders to prevent citizens from escaping.
    c. Offering financial rewards to allies.
    d. Threatening each other with nuclear war.
    e. Welcoming all refugees from the other side.

18. The last European colonial possession to gain independence was:

    a. Namibia
    b. Brunei
    c. Zimbabwe
    d. Angola
    e. Mozambique

19. The Algerian War:

    a. Ended French colonial rule.
    b. Found no supporters in France for Algerian independence.
    c. Exposed racism in France.
    d. Led to the establishment of a new constitution in France.
    e. Inspired other similar movements among Algeria's neighbors.

20. The Non-Aligned Movement:

    a. Played off the superpowers against each other.
    b. Was more sympathetic to the Soviets than to the United States.
    c. Was more sympathetic to the United States than to the Soviets.
    d. Stayed away from both superpowers.
    e. None of the above.

Now that you have reviewed and tested yourself on this part of the chapter, take time to pull together all the important information by answering the following questions:

◆ What role did the American-Soviet conflict play in the colonial struggles for independence?

◆ What were the consequences of the liberation movements?

Cultural Developments and Social Protest

21. Under the communist regime religious institutions were:
    a. Something everyone could embrace freely.
    b. Persecuted.
    c. Closed down everywhere.
    d. A site for opposition against the communist state.
    e. None of the above.

22. The Second Vatican Council:
    a. Attempted to bring about changes in the structure and mission of the Catholic Church.
    b. Changed the language of the mass to local languages.
    c. Supported social activism.
    d. Advocated for women to become clergy.
    e. Allowed bishops to have greater autonomy.

23. The generation born after World War II:
    a. Lived better lives than their parents.
    b. Embraced the values of the generation of sacrifice that came before them.
    c. Wanted more meaning in their lives.
    d. Embraced rock and roll.
    e. Had greater access to higher education than any generation before them.

24. The year 1968 was remarkable because of the:
    a. Anti–Vietnam War protests.
    b. Assassination of Martin Luther King Jr.
    c. Fall of the French government.
    d. End of communist rule in Czechoslovakia.
    e. Violent clashes between student protesters and the police across western Europe and the United States.

25. The Prague Spring:
    a. Was the result of support for reform on the part of the communist leadership in Czechoslovakia.
    b. Was a violent clash between armed Czechoslovak forces and Soviet ones.
    c. Was brought to an end violently by Leonid Brezhnev.
    d. Tried to bring about socialism with a human face.
    e. Ushered in an era of greater freedom in eastern Europe.

Now that you have reviewed and tested yourself on this part of the chapter, take time to pull together all the important information by answering the following questions:

◆ Why was there a moral and spiritual crisis in the 1950s?

◆ What were the generational divides behind the revolt of the 1960s?

CHAPTER 29

Lifting the Iron Curtain, 1969–1991

1966	1968	1970	1972	1974	1976	1978

1968
Prague Spring is crushed

1973
Arab oil embargo begins

1972
West Germany recognizes East German border

Antiballistic Missile Treaty is signed

1977
Charter 77 movement in Czecho-slovakia

1978
Polish Cardinal becomes Pope John Paul II

The wall erected in 1961 to separate West and East Berlin became a symbol of the cold war. When fearless citizens from communist East Germany climbed on the wall and began to dismantle it in October 1989, everyone around the world and especially in other communist bloc countries understood they were witnessing the end of Soviet hegemony in eastern Europe. Images like this emboldened people in Hungary, Czechoslovakia, Romania, and Bulgaria to speak and act against their own rulers. By January 1990, all communist regimes in eastern Europe, save for Yugoslavia, fell from power. (Thomas Kienzie/AP Images)

After reading this chapter, you should be able to answer the following questions:

What were the important challenges to democracy in Europe during this period?

What important changes took place in European politics in Europe over this period?

How did European identities change during this period?

What important new trends in European culture and societies can you identify during this period?

What brought down the communist regimes?

HE 1968 REVOLTS SHOOK the establishment and put traditional political parties on the defensive, forcing them to redefine themselves if they were to speak to the postwar generation. These challenges also pushed governments in the East and West to learn to live with the idea of permanent threat brought about by the cold war while achieving internal political stability.

Inside western Europe, the political challenges of the 1970s and 1980s came not from traditional political organizations but rather from radical new political formations, like the Greens, feminists, and antinuclear activists. These groups did not propose choosing between capitalism and communism but rather moving beyond the cold war divide and recognizing the greater problems that threatened the well-being of all people, from nuclear obliteration to gender inequality.

An economic crisis that started with the oil embargo of 1973 and continued into the 1980s complicated the political choices of western Europeans, who had to contend with economic depression, unemployment, inflation, and a severe slowdown of the postwar "economic miracle." The European Community also became involved in unprecedented global economic connections.

1980	1982	1984	1986	1988	1990	1992

1980
Polish Solidarity movement begins

1985
Gorbachev becomes leader of Soviet Union

1989
Berlin Wall falls

1991
Soviet Union collapses

1983
First Green Party member is elected to West German parliament

1979
Thatcher becomes British prime minister

The economic crisis of the 1970s also brought about radical change in eastern Europe and the Soviet Union. Governments looked for new markets and took advantage of a relaxation of tensions to increase trade. People in the communist bloc started to get a taste of consumer goods through popular culture, travel, and even access to coveted western status symbols, like blue jeans. The same economic crisis finally forced Soviet leader Mikhail Gorbachev to acknowledge that the Soviet Union was financially unable to maintain its hold in eastern Europe and to concede that each state in the bloc should follow its own path. Within three years, all eastern European communist regimes had fallen like a house of cards, and the Soviet Union itself had disappeared, ending the communist experiment initiated by revolution in 1917.

Politics in Western Europe

◆ **What role did the relaxation of international tensions play in western Europe?**

◆ **How did political parties change in the 1970s and 1980s?**

In the 1970s, tensions between western and eastern Europe relaxed, and governments began to consider issues on which they could cooperate, such as human rights initiatives. At the same time, the West faced important internal challenges, such as an energy crisis after 1973 and the emergence of radical terrorist groups from Northern Ireland to Italy. Leftist parties were less able to deal with these problems than their center-right counterparts, who gained political control in many places by 1980. Yet, especially in southern Europe and in France, left-wing parties held the power throughout the 1980s. The Common Market expanded but was also burdened by the weaker new members that joined in this decade.

détente (in French, "release from tension") Easing of political relations between the Soviet Union and the United States in the 1970s.

Antiballistic Missile Treaty Treaty signed in 1972 by the Soviet Union and the United States reducing their nuclear arsenals.

Willy Brandt (1913–1992) West German chancellor from 1969 to 1974, Social Democrat and architect of détente.

Relaxed Tensions and Renewed Cooperation

The 1968 protests challenged western European parties to define a new kind of politics in which people could participate more directly and be counted. At the same time, the dominant presence of the two superpowers raised questions of European autonomy in international relations, especially in Europe. These two concerns combined to produce two new directions in European politics: a focus on internal stability and a stabilization of international relations.

Détente In the United States, the violent protests of 1968 helped secure the victory of a Republican law-and-order presidential candidate, Richard Nixon. Once defeated by the charismatic John F. Kennedy, Nixon returned to politics by casting himself as a representative of stability and reason. With his secretary of state, Henry Kissinger, Nixon engineered a major shift in international politics, the policy of **détente**. From reconsidering the Vietnam War to opening relations with communist China, Nixon led the way toward relaxing the tough stance that had defined relations between the democratic and communist blocs in the previous decades. He also sought to reengage the United States in Europe by building bridges of communication across the East-West divide.

By the end of the 1960s, not only Nixon but also his Soviet counterpart Leonid Brezhnev and many politicians in western Europe realized that the cold war had achieved a balance of power and military escalation was unlikely. An important departure in the 1970s was the decision by Nixon and Brezhnev to limit their military buildups, evident in the **Antiballistic Missile Treaty** (1972). In agreeing to limit their antiballistic missile systems and put a cap on military spending, the Americans and Soviets conceded that military parity was sufficient for both to feel secure and that to continue spending would in fact increase the possibility of conflict, especially nuclear war. This kind of self-limiting thinking was a complete reversal from the military planning of the late 1940s and represented a major step toward a more peaceful international environment.

West Germany's Eastern Politics No longer content to be pawns in the superpower game, European political leaders played an active, even pioneering, role in this process. In West Germany, Chancellor **Willy Brandt** initiated a policy of normalizing relations with East Germany and, years before Nixon and Brezhnev, worked on a policy of reconciliation between the

Expansion of European Community

- Original members, 1967
- New members, 1973
- New member, 1981
- New members, 1986
- Members of CMEA

Map 29.1 **From European Community to European Union** In the 1970s and 1980s, the European Community became a source for European integration in economic matters and a springboard for cultural change toward a shared European identity that stood for democratic values, greater tolerance, and decreased nationalist tensions. © Cengage Learning

1. Who were the original members of the Common Market?
2. How much did it grow before 1989?
3. How large a part of the European continent did the Common Market represent in comparison to countries in the CMEA?
4. How does the change in the map of the Common Market suggest changes in the actions and sense of identity of the European Community?

West and the East. His accession to power in 1969 signaled a momentous change in West Germany: it was the first time since the 1920s that the Social Democrats were in power. Brandt had an unimpeachable past. He had been a Social Democrat since the age of seventeen, and in 1933, when the Gestapo tried to arrest him, he fled to Scandinavia, where he became an outspoken journalist and antifascist activist until the end of the Third Reich. He saw these years not as a cowardly flight but rather as "a chance to serve the 'Other Germany,' which did not resign itself submissively to enslavement."

In the Bundestag, which had replaced the Reichstag as West Germany's parliament, Brandt made his mark as a defender of democracy and socialism against communist dictatorship. He was the mayor of West Berlin when the first bricks in the Berlin Wall went up in August 1961. Finding that the contest between the superpowers made him powerless to attend to the well-being of ordinary Germans, he took on a pragmatic view of cold war politics. By 1969, when he was elected chancellor, he had become the foremost spokesman of **Ostpolitik**, the policy of taking small, steady steps toward normalizing relations with East Germany and, by extension, serving as a model for better relations between the East and West in Europe. He was a pioneer in the détente shift in international relations.

Brandt successfully cultivated an international image acceptable to both the United States and the Soviet Union and, at the same time, independent of their whims. Though his politics were far to the left of those of the Christian Democrat Konrad Adenauer, Brandt appeared to Nixon as a peaceful and loyal ally and to Brezhnev as a reasonable representative of socialism.

Brandt proceeded to make good on his promise to open up relations with the East by traveling to Moscow and signing an important nonaggression pact with the Soviets, which paved the way to recognizing the border between East and West Germany in 1972. This action of legitimating the post-1945 rearrangement of European states was, in fact, the final peace treaty of World War II. And this time Europeans themselves acted on their own behalf rather than at the beckoning of the superpowers, as had been the case in 1945. Brandt also normalized relations with other eastern European countries, most prominently Poland. Possibly the most famous of his gestures of reconciliation was his visit to Warsaw in 1970, where he knelt before the memorial to the Warsaw Ghetto heroes and begged the forgiveness of the Polish nation for the horrors committed by the Third Reich. Brandt's public career was crowned by the Nobel Peace Prize, which he received in 1971 for his leadership role in East-West relations.

If Ostpolitik and détente meant relaxation, tolerance,

Ostpolitik (in German, "eastern politics") West German policy of reconciliation with the communist East.

Conference on Security and Cooperation in Europe Meeting of all European states, the United States, and Canada in 1972–1975 to rethink East-West relations.

Bettmann/Corbis

In a symbolic gesture, in December 1970 West German Chancellor Willy Brandt knelt before the Warsaw Ghetto Uprising memorial, asking forgiveness from the Polish people for the violence of the Nazi regime. The gesture greatly improved West German–Polish relations and helped decrease East-West tensions generally in the 1970s. What does his demeanor and facial expressions in this photograph communicate?

and the willingness to sit down at the negotiating table, they also encouraged greater scrutiny and manipulation of the flow of information between East and West. It was a gamble on both sides, and it proved very costly for Brandt. A few dramatic cases of Soviet agents in West Germany caught with important German secrets encouraged the perception that western leaders who promoted détente were not watchful and tough enough on communist threats from over the wall. Brandt became the victim of one such scandal. Although he had not been personally responsible for the actions of a Soviet spy who had infiltrated his administration, Brandt lost legitimacy at home and finally resigned in 1974. But the policy of détente continued in the hands of other European leaders and with the support of U.S. Presidents Gerald Ford and Jimmy Carter.

Stability and Human Rights Brandt's policy of opening up trade with the East in order to improve the quality of life under communism provided an important starting point for a broader international process of European cooperation, and this gave birth to the **Conference on Security and Cooperation in Europe.**

The conference represented the first attempt to broadly rethink European international relations not only in terms of the cold war superpower contest, but also in terms of the interests and needs of the European states. All European states participated, as well as the United States and Canada. The process itself, together with the **Helsinki Final Act** (1975) it generated, created a new forum for collaboration between East and West, especially in the area of human rights. All signatories recognized existing European borders and committed themselves to protecting their citizens' human rights, including freedom of religion, free speech, freedom to move or travel, and the right to due process. The Final Act became a guiding principle for the Carter administration's foreign policy. For Europeans, it represented a new basis for international relations that went beyond the political interests and ideologies of the United States and the Soviet Union.

The conference also gave rise to institutions for implementing these agreements. **Helsinki Watch** became one of the important **nongovernmental organizations (NGOs)** reporting on human rights violations, both in the West and in the East. As Helsinki Watch and other NGOs worked with western governments to guide the implementation of the Final Act, they became new players in international relations. Often lobbying on behalf of the powerless, they also worked with western governments to expose abuses by regimes that did not acknowledge their violations of basic human rights and to bring international pressure to bear on them. The United States, for instance, offered reduced tariffs to eastern European countries that abided by the provisions of Helsinki and threatened to cut off economic benefits to regimes with human rights abuses.

Security and Economic Challenges from the Middle East

As tensions across the East-West divide relaxed, European countries faced new security and economic challenges from the Middle East. In October 1973, in alliance with Syria, Egyptian President **Anwar el-Sadat** attacked Israel, to regain territories lost by both states in the **Six-Day War** (1967). The **Yom Kippur War** grew in complexity as Arab states lent support and troops to Egypt, while Israel enlisted the support of the United States and western Europe.

The Oil Crisis Arab states, viewing western support of Israel as a conspiracy against Egypt's legitimate reconquest of territories Israel had seized, retaliated through an **oil embargo** that lasted until March 1974. The embargo sent the world economy into a decade-long crisis. The immediate effect was soaring oil prices, which generated a rise in the price of virtually all products. In addition, most European states were unable to provide sufficient energy resources for their economies. Some went so far as to ration the use of oil and other energy resources. In the United States, the government introduced unprecedented supply and price regulations.

The energy crisis signaled two important long-term trends in Europe and elsewhere. Economic processes were becoming increasingly **globalized**, so it was no longer possible for the West to be economically self-sufficient. And western Europeans, with only meager internal oil resources, resolved to deal with the crisis by looking into alternative energy resources, from hydroelectric to wind and nuclear. Overall, the energy crisis induced greater cooperation among members of the Common Market in finding alternative fuels and markets that would buffer them from fluctuations in the global economy. During the oil crisis, the Common Market provided important benefits to its members, such as access to nuclear power and coal, but its success was also measured by its general prosperity and growth, as Brandt had been able to reconcile the French to the idea of allowing Great Britain to join in the very year of the oil embargo.

Member countries continued to negotiate and move forward toward a **European Monetary Union**. But in 1979, a second oil crisis brought about by the 1977 **Iranian Revolution**, together with a spike in the value of the dollar, made European currencies more vulnerable on the international markets. As European economies slowed down, further discussions of the monetary union ended. The strongest western European economies—the

Helsinki Final Act Accord signed in 1975 by all European states that introduced human rights as a principle in international relations.

Helsinki Watch Nongovernmental organization created to oversee the implementation of the Helsinki Final Act's human rights provisions.

nongovernmental organization (NGO) Voluntary nonprofit organization often focused on humanitarian issues.

Anwar el-Sadat (1918–1981) President of Egypt who contributed to the rise of Arab nationalism in the 1970s.

Six-Day War War fought in 1967 between Israel and its Arab neighbors Egypt, Jordan, and Syria; won by Israel.

Yom Kippur War War in 1973 between Egypt and Israel over the Sinai Peninsula and Golan Heights, which had been conquered by Israel in 1967; won by Israel.

oil embargo (1973–1974) Refusal by Arab petroleum-exporting countries to ship petroleum to countries that had supported Israel in the Yom Kippur War.

globalization Increasing global connections among national and international economic and cultural forces, starting in the 1970s.

European Monetary Union Unification in 1990–1999 of the fiscal policies of European community members, with the goal of creating a single currency.

Iranian Revolution Nationalist uprising in 1977 that ousted the Iranian monarchy and destabilized the global oil supply.

German and the British—turned inward to solve their problems with rising unemployment and low economic performance instead of pursuing further collaboration with the Common Market.

The End of Détente Overall, by 1979, the era of détente was ending. There were some important changes—the stabilization of European borders and recognition of human rights as an important component of international politics. Yet trust did not catch hold, and ideologues on both sides of the cold war skillfully exploited the fears of average voters about loss of stability. In addition, the Soviets changed their international stance significantly. On Christmas Eve 1979, they invaded Afghanistan. The reason for this intervention seems to have been the fear of the spread of Islamic fundamentalism from Afghanistan into Soviet-controlled Central Asian territories. But the United States read the **Afghanistan invasion** as a challenge to the balance of power in the Persian Gulf, a region to which it had become vulnerable since the 1973 oil embargo. The Americans reacted swiftly and sent military help to the Islamic Afghan rebels who opposed the Soviets.

Thus, a significant change in U.S. relations with the Soviet Union and western Europe took place in the 1980s. American voters viewed Carter's stance on human rights and his response to the Iranian Revolution as weak, and they put Ronald Reagan, an unabashed hawk in international relations, in the White House. The United States shifted toward a renewed military buildup against the Soviet Union, which responded with similar moves. Until 1985, relations between the two superpowers remained extremely tense. NATO became an important institution for rallying western Europe support behind Reagan's vision of military buildup as the guarantee for peace, with Britain as the most outspoken ally. Other Europeans saw themselves cast again as second-tier participants in the superpower contest.

Yet, despite such challenges, western European states moved along toward European integration. The major successes of the 1980s were Greece, Portugal, and Spain, which quietly abandoned authoritarian rule between 1970 and 1975 and in the 1980s were welcomed into the Common Market. By this time, vestiges of the old dictatorships were largely gone in the politics of these countries, while their economies began to flourish and a culture of **pluralism** also developed. Their Common Market membership enhanced their political stability in the face of continued challenges from extremist movements.

Afghanistan invasion Military invasion by Soviet Union in 1979 to prevent the spread of Muslim fundamentalism to the Soviet Republics in Central Asia.

pluralism State of society in which diverse groups can participate while maintaining their interests and traditions.

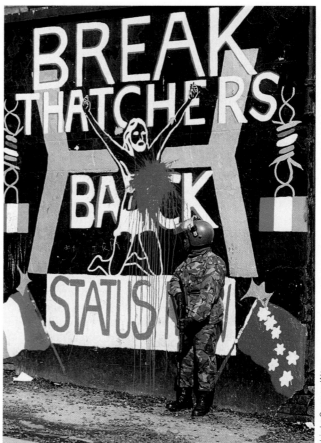

From the late 1960s to the present, the walls of many urban neighborhoods in Northern Ireland became a venue for the Irish Republican Army's quest for legitimacy. This mural, painted during the 1980s, is critical of Margaret Thatcher's government. What symbols does it use, and what values and attitudes to they communicate?

The Transformation of the Left

In the 1970s and 1980s, domestic politics in western Europe saw an ebb and flow among traditional parties, but two trends were about to transform them. First, traditional politics seemed to draw less voter support. As 1968 had shown, average citizens were less interested in what politicians had to offer through the regular channels of political platforms and elections. Second, new types of movements—grassroots politics and radical, secret terrorist organizations—attracted more followers.

Crisis in Northern Ireland In Britain, where the Labour Party had come to power in 1973, the oil crisis of that same year undermined economic prosperity. Unemployment stayed high, the economy did not bounce back, and the pound remained weak. When the party proved incapable of effective solutions, it lost power in 1979.

The Labour Party also lost support because of its inability to deal with the rise of protests in Northern

Ireland. In the late 1960s, the **Northern Ireland Civil Rights Association** sponsored peaceful street protests and began documenting the abuses of the **Unionist** government against Catholics. The government's violent crackdown led to actions by the Irish Republican Army (IRA) that brought the level of violence to unprecedented heights. Car bombings in Protestant communities and assassinations of government loyalists became staple activities of this group. The situation in Ireland soon became a permanent crisis in British politics, with both British and Irish nationalists unwilling to compromise. Instead, violence and terrorism became a way of life for the next generation—both Protestants and Catholics.

In an era of rapid secularization elsewhere in Europe, the people of Ireland went in a different direction, taking religious identity as a rallying point. Religious spaces, religious rituals, and overall religious practice became nationalist and overtly political. The voice of religious authorities on these divisions mattered less than the use of religious language by politicians and terrorists. Friendships across this harsh divide became dangerous, shunned by both communities, even though children grew up speaking the same language and playing the same games.

Communism and Terrorism in Italy In Italy the communists made important gains in the early 1970s. The recovery of the Communist Party after the 1956 and 1968 uprisings in Hungary and Czechoslovakia was due to the ability of the Italian communists to project their party as humane. Under **Palmiro Togliatti**, Italian communism succeeded in becoming both a nationalist movement, highlighting the "Italian way," and also a party consistently committed to social justice. Thus, for most of the 1970s, the Communists and the Christian Democrats shared power and succeeded in preserving stability and prosperity.

Yet a parallel development, prompted by a grassroots dissatisfaction with these political compromises, gave rise to terrorist movements on both the left and right. By 1978 the **Red Brigades**, a radical left-wing communist terrorist organization, were regularly staging kidnappings and other terrorist attacks, such as bombings. Their most prominent action was the 1978 murder of **Aldo Moro**, who had been instrumental in the left-center-right compromise. Eager to blame each other for the violence, the left and right broke off their alliance.

The nationalist terrorist movement in Northern Ireland and the communist terrorist movement in Italy were but two examples of a more general trend in Europe. The year 1968 had opened a new era of grassroots politics, of taking ideas to the streets and using new technologies, especially television, to force action and change outside parliamentary debate, legislation, and election. These terrorist movements were not widespread; most were small, secret organizations that could not operate on a large scale.

But, in the beginning at least, they did resonate with a broader population. The IRA specifically used dissatisfaction among the Irish in general to strike against established political institutions.

Stability in France In France, however, traditional left-wing governments dominated the 1980s. In 1983, **François Mitterrand** gained power and remained president of France for two terms, the first socialist head of government since Léon Blum in 1936. But Mitterrand was moderate and continued many policies of his center-right predecessor, **Valéry Giscard d'Estaing**. After attempting to nationalize important financial institutions and initiate an increase in wages and social benefits, Mitterrand found such policies ineffective in addressing larger problems such as trade deficits and the devaluation of the franc. Within a year, his government returned to many of the previous center-right policies. Yet Mitterrand improved some social services and welfare measures, such as shorter working hours and increased pension benefits.

Spain and Greece also saw the emergence of socialist governments. The Spanish Socialist Workers' Party secured both stability and steady economic growth, despite repeated challenges from the right. King **Juan Carlos I** played an important role in restraining the military establishment against the democratic left. The financial commitment of the European Community was also important in this process.

The Antinuclear and Environmental Movements

The 1968 protests expressed opposition to the colonial wars, and as the Vietnam War continued into the 1970s, the peace movement also grew. Many involved in these movements saw

Table 29.1 Antinuclear Protests

1971	Demonstrations against nuclear power plants in France and Germany
1972	Antiballistic Missile Treaty
1978	UN first special session on disarmament
1981	Millions of western Europeans participate in antinuclear street protests
1981–1991	Women's protest at Greenham Common military base in England
1983	Antinuclear Green Party wins twenty-seven seats in West German parliament
March 1983	U.S. Strategic Defense Initiative announced; Relations with Soviet Union reach all-time low
October 1983	Protests of millions in western Europe against U.S. intermediate-range nuclear force (INF) deployments
1983–1984	Over forty thousand women resume protests at Greenham
1987	Reagan and Gorbachev sign intermediate-range nuclear force treaty
May 1991	Last U.S. cruise missile leaves Greenham Common military base, site of a decade of antinuclear protests organized by women

© Cengage Learning

Campaign for Nuclear Disarmament Antinuclear British organization founded in the 1950s that became a leader in the peace movement of the 1970s and 1980s.

Green Party West German party founded by antinuclear and environmental activists in 1979.

Greenham Common Military air base in England that became the site of a long-standing antinuclear protest from 1981 to 1991.

Chernobyl City in Soviet Ukraine where the greatest nuclear disaster to date occurred in April 1986, resulting in widespread nuclear contamination.

Mikhail Gorbachev (1931–) Soviet leader between 1985 and 1991 whose reforms paved the way to the fall of communism in 1991.

themselves as outside the division between capitalism and communism; they viewed themselves as advocates of a world free of the threat of war and of the arms race that dominated U.S.-Soviet relations. They hailed the Antiballistic Missile Treaty of 1972 as a victory and committed themselves to continuing reductions of the nuclear arsenal. Yet even as the energy crisis of the early 1970s made nuclear power attractive to some, fears of a nuclear disaster gained new dimensions. Table 29.1 summarizes antinuclear protests during this period.

The antiwar and antinuclear/environmental movements were closely connected and drew support from a wide range of scientists, student activists, housewives, and people of any or no political persuasion. In Britain, the **Campaign for Nuclear Disarmament**, founded in the 1950s, became the leading organization of the antinuclear movement. It served as a political lobbying force and also a link for people beyond national boundaries, ideologies, and religious beliefs. Other environmental NGOs built communities on an ethic of caring that crossed national borders and promoted a new global identity. Free from the adversities of the ballot box, these NGOs often acted swiftly and also across borders, especially in moments of crisis.

Rise of Environmental Parties The same concern for environmental issues gave birth to a new left-wing party in Germany, the **Green Party**. The party grew from small local groups that lobbied on behalf of ecological concerns starting in the early 1970s and attracted voters dissatisfied with the social and environmental policies of the traditional left. This trend was not exclusive to West Germany, but it developed faster and had broader appeal there, in part because of the committed sense of citizenship that was particular to post-1945 German political culture. In the 1980s, the Greens remained a marginal presence in the Bundestag but made steady gains in local politics. Throughout this period they continued to work closely with local environmental NGOs in a new blend of community activism and parliamentary politics.

Popular Protests Against Nuclear Weapons After 1981, as the Reagan administration resumed its military buildup in Europe, the antinuclear movement offered increased resistance. Though the British government welcomed the American missiles, the popular support of the generation who had welcomed the Americans as liberators during World War II was almost gone, as the numbers of this generation dwindled through death. Their sons and daughters, taking security and prosperity as a given, opposed nuclear threat of any sort—from West or East. Thus, when the Reagan administration announced the deployment of new Pershing II intermediate-range missiles on U.S. bases in western Europe, almost one million people marched in Bonn, London, and Rome in opposition; a month later, half a million protesters gathered in Amsterdam. These protests continued throughout the 1980s, most famously at the **Greenham Common** military base, where an all-woman camp established in 1981 continued until 1991, when the last nuclear missiles were removed from the site.

Nuclear Disaster and Its Consequences In April 1986, an explosion at a nuclear power station in **Chernobyl**, in Soviet Ukraine, forced all Europeans to face the reality of environmental nuclear disaster. Though the details were at first suppressed by the Soviet leader, **Mikhail Gorbachev**, the effects were so severe and widespread that Chernobyl became an

For ten years, thousands of women kept a continuous presence at the Greenham Common military base west of London. They camped, held vigils, and engaged in various other forms of protest to signal their commitment to creating a nuclear-free Britain. What does this image suggest about the attitudes and relationships of these protesters?

instant symbol of the dangers of nuclear power. More than thirty thousand square miles of land were contaminated and, according to a 1994 study, almost five million people in the region were affected. In western Europe, environmental pressure groups forced the closing of nuclear power plants: France, which had been a leading producer of nuclear energy, had to retool its energy sources. By the end of the 1980s, concerns over the possibility of nuclear disaster had breached political divisions between East and West to become a common cause across Europe.

The New Conservatism

In the 1980s, with the traditional left losing support and new grassroots movements still politically underdeveloped, West German and British parliaments were dominated by conservative regimes. In West Germany the Christian Democrats, led by **Helmut Kohl**, assumed control in 1982. As chancellor, Kohl continued the policies of Ostpolitik and the effort to change political culture in Germany. German laws, culture, and educational policies openly acknowledged and discussed the atrocities of the Third Reich and worked to prevent any recurrence.

More than any other European state, Germany was quick to condemn extremism and avoid aggression. Kohl also oversaw a tremendous economic recovery of the country that made Germany the backbone of the Common Market, producing one-third of its exports in the 1980s.

The Iron Lady In Britain, the electorate brought back the Conservatives in 1979 under the leadership of **Margaret Thatcher**, the first woman prime minister of Britain. She dominated politics throughout the 1980s, orchestrating a decisive shift in foreign and domestic politics. Thatcher came to be known as the Iron Lady for her resolute support for the Reagan administration's rearmament policies and for her stiff refusal to consider the social welfare costs of her government's support for business and industry. Whether people admired or despised her, Thatcher articulated a new path for conservative politics. Her years in power

Helmut Kohl (1930–) Christian Democratic chancellor of West Germany from 1982 to 1998 who continued Ostpolitik.

Margaret Thatcher (1925–) First female British prime minister who led the Conservative government between 1980 and 1992.

Reagan Presidential Library

British Prime Minister Margaret Thatcher and U.S. President Ronald Reagan, here at the presidential retreat Camp David in 1986, are generally considered the two staunchest defenders of a tough policy of nonnegotiation with the Soviet Union during the 1980s. How would you describe the relationship between the two leaders, as depicted here?

care, education, and birth control. But Thatcher was not one to fit any particular cliché of a female politician, and she followed her own path. Born in 1925, she became interested in politics as a chemistry student at Oxford. In 1953, as a brand-new mother of twins, she also passed the bar and soon returned to work as a tax specialist. After she won a seat in Parliament at age thirty-four, she fully dedicated her public life to working for the Conservatives. She served in several cabinets in the 1960s and in the 1970s drew attention as a leader of the Conservative opposition by condemning détente and supporting rearmament: "The men in the Soviet Politburo put guns before butter," she quipped, "while we put just about everything before guns."

Thatcher and Militarism These policy stands won her the "Iron Lady" nickname, and she proceeded to make good on it in the 1980s. In foreign policy, she reinvented the "special friendship" with the United States that still defines the relationship between the two countries. She vocally supported Reagan's nuclear rearmament policies and gladly offered British military bases for stationing U.S. nuclear missiles. No other European state took such a friendly view of Reagan's policies regarding the Soviet Union, but her aim was to restore Britain's international position as a partner with the United States in the cold war.

Thatcher was unapologetically imperialistic, opposing nationalist movements in Wales and Scotland, and offered symbolic victories that drew even the working classes to support her government. Britain's easy victory in the 1982 **Falklands War** helped solidify her reputation. The British Navy came out in full force to confront Argentina's takeover of the tiny Falkland/Malvinas Islands. The conflict lasted only a few weeks, but it inflicted serious casualties on the Argentineans while yielding a victory for Britain that stirred those nostalgic for empire. For many in Britain, disaffected by dull leaders and ineffective government, Thatcher seemed to have commanded respect, regardless of party.

Lessening Government Role in the Economy In domestic politics, Thatcher deregulated many industries in communications and energy and refused to bow to the pressures from trade unions. The new climate helped generate economic growth, but it also brought higher unemployment rates and diminished spending on social programs. Thatcher favored limiting state interference in social services provided by private businesses. Thus, while she retained national health care, she allowed private providers greater freedom. The aim was no longer to serve all populations, especially the poorest, but to harmonize the well-being of private businesses with access to these services.

Although Thatcher did continue funding for public education, her careful pulling back from the universal commitments to social welfare of postwar

and her policies have reshaped the relationship between the traditional left and right, making Thatcherism an important force in contemporary politics even today. The focus on individual freedoms rather than social programs and on encouraging business rather than favoring labor unions became the trademarks of this movement.

As a woman, Thatcher was an improbable leader of the Conservatives, a party in which women were underrepresented and that generally lined up with areas of political and economic life that were dominated by men—from the armaments industry to the landed aristocracy. Most western European women who entered politics after World War II gravitated to left-wing parties, which tended to have woman-friendly positions on issues such as child care, health

Falklands War (1982) Conflict won by Great Britain against Argentina over a small archipelago off Argentina, the Falkland/ Malvinas Islands.

governments represented an important and permanent departure. She had her share of opponents among the British politicians and public, but her policies of favoring the free market and diminishing state services were never fully reversed after she lost power. Thatcherism became a political hallmark of the late twentieth century.

 Checking In

By yourself or with a partner, explain the significance of each of the following selected key terms:

détente	Greenham Common
Helsinki Watch	Mikhail Gorbachev
Six-Day War	Helmut Kohl
Iranian Revolution	Margaret Thatcher

Social Change in the West

◆ **How did western European societies change during this period?**

◆ **How did western European identities alter?**

Despite growing prosperity and opportunities for social advancement in western Europe, the years after 1968 saw challenges from various groups. Women demanded greater social, political, and economic power. Demographic change spurred social change as birthrates decreased and working populations aged. Newly arrived immigrants and guest workers tested the ability of western governments to deliver the same social services to all those who lived and worked in their countries.

The Feminist Revolution

By 1970, women had made dramatic gains in many areas. More women were employed outside the home and received college degrees than ever before. Yet their economic opportunities were more limited than those of men, their wages were significantly lower (by about one-third), and they were still expected to be primarily wives and mothers. A woman with a college degree in business would more likely become a secretary than a manager. Left-wing parties, which advocated economic and social equality, remained unsympathetic to glaring gender inequalities in politics and the workplace. They were willing to offer social assistance to workers but not to consider housework as labor that was entitled to respect and protection.

The Personal Is Political Even in left-wing movements, women were relegated to secondary roles—making signs, typing, and making coffee—behind the masculine façade of the protests. Disillusioned, many

women left these movements and formed their own, vowing to promote gender equality in structures that rejected the male patriarchal model. "The personal is political" was the motto of this feminist movement, which focused primarily on the social and economic empowerment of women rather than their relationship to men. Celebrating women's identities as women and defining them as worthy of public concern was at the heart of this new movement. Thus, giving birth was viewed not as a personal and private event but as a unique female experience with deep social, emotional, and political implications for the whole community. Feminists also addressed the problem of "compulsory heterosexuality." Lesbian activism developed during this period as a form of celebrating women's identities unencumbered by relations with men. This was the age of universal sisterhood.

Difference and Equality The most prominent intellectual figure of the women's movement in Europe, **Simone de Beauvoir**, defined the struggle for women's liberation as an individual quest to gain respect for differences. Her study of women's cultural and psychological conditioning, *The Second Sex* (1949), became an important manifesto for European feminists, who focused especially on family issues. They sought the right to divorce, access to birth control (including abortion), and child care for working mothers. This emphasis was in contrast to American feminists, who also embraced these issues but who generally focused less on difference and complementarity than on equality in economic power and in politics. American feminists, for example, demanded "equal pay for equal work" and full representation in government, business, sports, and education.

New Social Rights: Divorce and Birth Control De Beauvoir herself had not been interested in taking a public stance on women's issues until 1971, when she signed the **Manifesto of the 343**, acknowledging that she had had an abortion. Since abortion was a criminal act in France, signing this document was an act of civil disobedience, and it became a springboard for securing women's access to birth control. Abortion was legalized three years later, one year after it was also decriminalized in the United States. Other Catholic countries followed suit—Italy in 1978 and Spain in 1985—with women's groups applying the pressure. In 1990, Belgium became the last western European country to decriminalize abortion.

Catholic countries also eventually legalized divorce. Left-wing governments in Italy (1974) and

Simone de Beauvoir (1908–1986) French philosopher and author of *The Second Sex* (1949), a central text of the second-wave feminist movement.

Manifesto of the 343 Manifesto in support of legalizing abortion in France, signed in 1971 by 343 Frenchwomen who acknowledged they had had illegal abortions.

AP/Wide World Photos

The growing availability of the birth control pill revolutionized women's relationship to reproduction and opened up new debates about the relationship between sexuality and reproduction. What are some of the positions that various individuals and institutions took on this debate?

Spain (1981) gave in to grassroots pressure in which women played a major role. Women were only loosely organized in informal networks that focused mostly on coping with women's burdens. But as more women became educated and understood their burdens as discriminatory treatment that could be changed, they started to act differently in their daily lives. They applied pressure to the Italian government by marching in the streets, a traditional form of protest; but they also withheld household "services" such as cooking and cleaning. These methods made the point, as 60 percent of Italians came to support legalization of divorce in this most Catholic of western European states.

Women's actions on behalf of abortion and divorce had broad effects throughout society. The birthrate dropped significantly, and marriage patterns changed. Couples married later and became more committed to long-term monogamous relationships than in the past. Overall, women were now able to lead freer lives, with more economic and social choices than ever before.

Finding Their Own Political Parties But in traditional politics, women remained marginal. The percentage of women in elected national offices remained disproportionately low, at 5 to 10 percent, with a slightly higher level in local government. Women tended to be appointed to "feminized" government positions—in social services, education, public health, or the arts. At the same time, however, Thatcher's position in Britain, though she represented a conservative party and did not encourage female participation in politics, proved an important milestone toward redefining women's politics.

In leftist parties, women did assume leadership positions. **Petra Kelly**, for example, of West Germany's Green Party, was elected to a seat in the Bundestag in 1983, and she set new directions. At age thirty-six, she was younger than most other members. She focused on environmental safety and antinuclear activism as unifying concerns, "beyond left and right." She was a feminist without making feminism the center of her political struggle. Her strong belief in the need for women's equality was shaped by her experience of growing up in the United States in the 1960s, and she was always quick to point out gender biases in the Green movement itself. Kelly was part of a generation that took gender equality as a given and simply acted accordingly.

New Populations

Between 1960 and 1990, the natural population growth in European Community states declined by three-quarters. The birthrate decreased dramatically everywhere in western Europe but most remarkably in Catholic countries that legalized abortion during this period. In Spain, for example, the birthrate dropped from 21.5 per thousand in 1960 to 10.3 per thousand in 1990. The downturn in the birthrate raised concerns about a shrinking workforce. At the same time, the number of elderly people who were entitled to retirement benefits was growing. The average age expectancy for western European men in 1980 was 71, and for women 77, while retirement ages averaged 60 for men and 55 for women. Thus, western European states needed to provide retirement and health care benefits for an average of twelve years for each retired person. Overall, it seemed that the number of people contributing to the workforce was going down while the number of those entitled to social services was rising.

Guest Workers To fill needs in the labor force, western European governments opened up their borders to **guest workers** and immigrants. People with skills for critical economic needs were permitted to live temporarily in European Community states as guest workers. The needs most often cited were for low-paying, menial jobs, such as domestic service and janitorial work, and for hard labor in dangerous settings. The migrants had the right to work. They had to pay taxes, but they did not have the right to apply for permanent residency, nor did they have the same social rights as citizens. Health care, education, pensions, and vacations were not guaranteed to guest workers. Nor was there any attempt to acculturate them to the language and customs of the host country. Guest workers remained on the margins of their host societies.

New Muslim Populations Yet foreign nationals reshaped the demographic profile of western Europe.

Petra Kelly (1947–1992) West German feminist who helped found the Green Party and became the first Green Party member to serve in the West German Bundestag.

guest workers Citizens of foreign countries temporarily allowed to live and work in western European countries.

Petra Kelly, the first Green Party candidate elected to the West German Bundestag, combined street activism and legislative work on behalf of her deeply held ecologist, pacifist, and feminist beliefs. How does she appear in comparison to Margaret Thatcher?

Policies encouraged immigration from the old colonies in Asia, Africa, and the West Indies, and large numbers of Muslims came to work in Germany, the Netherlands, Denmark, Spain, France, and Britain. At first guest workers seemed largely invisible, but as their populations grew, cultural differences were exposed. Western European governments were largely unprepared for the presence of large groups of unassimilated migrants. Moreover, just as Italians, Danes, and Germans were starting to identify themselves as Europeans, there were new populations to define themselves against—new people of color and adherents of different religions. Thus new tensions arose over what it meant to be European.

Tensions also arose as guest workers lived in poverty while they worked in prosperous settings. A Turkish worker cleaning toilets in the Frankfurt International Airport, for example, saw the lifestyle available to Germans and knew it would never be possible for him. The loneliness and resentment of guest workers was compounded as they observed ethnic Germans repatriated from eastern Europe gaining citizenship and access to full social services. The significance of race in eligibility for citizenship was clear. The race line was a particular problem for children born to guest workers in the host country: Were they to be "tolerated," or could they become citizens with full rights? As temporary workers lived in host countries for decades, a new generation of children was exposed to the possibility of losing their rights if their parents

were deported. And, because they attended European schools and spoke European languages, they began to identify themselves as Europeans. Thousands of families struggled with divided identities.

Checking In

By yourself or with a partner, explain the significance of each of the following selected key terms:

Simone de Beauvoir	Petra Kelly
Manifesto of the 343	guest workers

Growing Crisis in the Communist East

◆ **What impact did détente have for the people of the communist bloc?**

◆ **How did the Soviet Union change from the 1970s to the late 1980s?**

For most eastern Europeans, 1968 represented the end of hope. Yet, by the late 1970s, Ostpolitik and détente had increased the availability of consumer goods, allowed people to travel more freely inside the bloc and beyond, and made room for dissidents to express their criticisms. The 1973 economic crisis did not hit eastern Europe as hard as it did the West. But by the beginning of the 1980s, severe inflation and underproduction were forcing the Soviet Union to rethink its economic and foreign policy. At the same time, popular protests in Czechoslovakia and Poland forced communist regimes there to use increasingly brutal repressive measures. Communism was weakening.

Détente and False Prosperity

When Brezhnev pulled Soviet bloc troops from Czechoslovakia in 1969, the hope of reform—so strong during the Prague Spring on 1968—seemed dead. The leaders of the dissident movement had been imprisoned or purged. By directly participating in the invasion, eastern European communist regimes had also signed on to the **Brezhnev Doctrine**, a commitment to crush dissent.

Consumer Goods and Political Stability But the communist leaders understood that military force and fear alone were not sufficient to suppress opposition. The era of détente made possible a shift in economic planning from heavy industries toward consumer goods. For the first time, radios and television sets became available. New countries in addition to Czechoslovakia, such as Romania, began to produce their own cars. Only a generation earlier, most transportation had been either by horse and cart or on foot; in contrast, this new emphasis in economic policy was breathtaking. Items formerly considered luxuries were now mass-produced, and western consumer goods began to be imported.

For many eastern Europeans, the early 1970s was an age of prosperity. For the first time, a factory worker could get in his car and take his family on a trip to another country. A Bulgarian teenager could wear jeans and makeup. Polish students spent their summer vacations camping in Romania, sipping Cuban rum and Pepsi at dance clubs that played the latest tunes from the Swedish pop band ABBA. Workers from non-aligned Yugoslavia went to West Germany to work and returned home with western cars, whiskey, or plain cash. Though salaries were relatively low, many people now dreamed less of life in the free West than of vacations and new furniture.

The communist regimes shifted economic priorities partly because oil from the Soviet Union was available at a time when the rest of the world was suffering from the oil crisis and partly because cheap loans were a stimulus. West Germany had been the first to extend cheap loans to East Germany, but soon Poland, Yugoslavia, Romania, and others benefited. After the Helsinki Act, the United States and western European countries extended special loans and lower tariff rates to eastern European countries that agreed to protect human rights and allow the freedom of religion.

This deal afforded the communist regimes new means of "buying off" the loyalty of their citizens. But it also compelled these regimes to conceal their human rights abuses, if not to curb them. And the availability of western goods, especially movies, VCRs, and books, also made many increasingly aware of the prosperous lifestyle of the noncommunist West. People did not regard the new goods as proof of the success of the communist regimes but rather as proof of West's ability to offer superior products.

The Return of Dissent By the end of the 1970s, the veneer of economic well-being was wearing off. Because they were not producing goods that could be sold abroad, most eastern European states could repay foreign loans only by raising prices for basic goods, such as bread and milk, which had long been subsidized. But wages were not raised, and in 1976–1977 strikes erupted from the Jiu Valley in Romania to Gdańsk, Poland. At the Lenin shipyards in Gdańsk, violent clashes between workers and police were followed by a crackdown. The government canceled the price hikes but avoided dealing with the underlying economic issues. People went back home, bruised and fearful, but it was clear that the consumerist policies of the early 1970s had backfired.

By the mid-1970s, even the Soviet Union was experiencing economic troubles. There was a sense of stagnation—that things were not getting any better during a period when people expected more. Voices from inside the Soviet Union rose to criticize Brezhnev. **Andrei Sakharov**, a brilliant physicist who had helped develop the Soviet hydrogen bomb, gave up his privileges when he openly discussed Soviet treatment of dissenters and put his life in danger by speaking out on behalf of human rights. For these efforts, he received the Nobel Peace Prize in 1975, but he was unable to collect it. Placed under house arrest, he continued his activities from his tiny apartment in Gorky and remained one of the important leaders of the movement for peace and human rights until his death in 1989.

Charter 77 and Solidarity

By 1977, it was becoming clear that the governments of eastern Europe had failed in their attempt to win loyalty through consumerism. Centralized economic planning could not sustain the growing demand for consumer goods at the low prices people had come to expect. And with increased expectations about consumer goods, those inside communist countries were more likely to become dissatisfied when such goods disappeared or became too expensive.

Brezhnev Doctrine Policy of Soviet military intervention to secure the interest of communism in Soviet bloc countries, established by Leonid Brezhnev in 1968.

Andrei Sakharov (1921–1989) Soviet physicist who was the most prominent human rights and antinuclear activist during the Brezhnev era.

Václav Havel Chooses Dissent

To live in truth: this is the deceptively simple choice Václav Havel, the first president of post-communist Czechoslovakia, made most of his life. In a brave letter to the communist leadership, he wrote: "Even a purely moral act that has no hope of any immediate and visible political effect can gradually and indirectly, over time, gain in political significance." This strong faith in the power of each individual to make a difference in the world by living a moral life guided the famous playwright in his own life and imposed on him costly personal choices—from social isolation to imprisonment—but it also made him an inspiration to people throughout the communist bloc.

During the short-lived Prague Spring, from January to August 1968, Havel was at the forefront of the reform movement that sought full freedom of the press, religion, and assembly in addition to important social and economic changes advocated by the reformist party leadership. Thirty-two at that time, and thus older than most of the students who stood beside him, Havel publicly criticized the injustices of the communist regime even though, as a prominent playwright, he had much to lose. But he believed in truth telling, and in an open letter to the communist leadership, he laid out the major abuses of the regime.

These actions made him a target of the repression that came in 1969, after the Soviets rolled their tanks through Prague. Havel was blacklisted, his plays removed from all theaters: he was forced to choose between being a playwright without a stage or abandoning his political principles. Havel chose neither. He remained an unconcealed opponent of the regime, but as he was not allowed to publish or stage his plays, he created an underground publishing house and arranged to have his plays staged in unlikely places, from barns to restaurants. As he could not make a living as a playwright, he took on a day job stocking barrels in a brewery. In this way, he continued to provide an inspiring example of how one could not only survive but also live in truth under a regime of lies, exposing it for what it

really was. His underground press published many texts that opposed the regime, contributing to the development and recognition of an important body of works. Many of these publications were also smuggled abroad, making Havel, his cohort of writers, and, more broadly, Czechoslovakia a place to which western Europeans and Americans looked for signs of a crack in the Soviet bloc.

Havel's best-known act of opposition was his central role in co-writing and publicizing a petition against the Czechoslovak government in 1977. Charter 77, as it became known, pointed out real but undisclosed facts about the abuses of the communist regime, which in 1975 had signed the famous Helsinki Final Act that guaranteed citizens' basic human rights. Charter 77 became the foundation for a new movement for rehumanizing social relations, restoring human dignity, and reenergizing moral conviction. In its most public challenge, the petition asked the government to release the members of a rock band who had been imprisoned for their lyrics and for loud aesthetics—supposedly "unbecoming" of a musical group in a communist state. Charter 77, and Havel in particular, challenged the regime to show how it could claim to support freedom of speech and personal movement while treating people as subjects of a tyranny. For his role in Charter 77, Havel was imprisoned in 1979 and suffered great abuses. In 1983 he almost died from an untreated case of pneumonia, and only under great international pressure was he finally released to recover in a regular hospital. By now he had become a larger-than-life hero of the underground intellectual and civil rights reform movement in the communist world. In 1989, he emerged as leader of the anticommunist opposition and was soon elected as president of a democratic Czechoslovakia. After Slovakia declared its independence in 1991, he remained the president of the Czech Republic until his retirement in February 2003.

Source: From a letter written by Václav Havel (1936–2011).

The strikes were the most visible sign that the workers' states were facing the revolt of the workers. In Gdańsk, the strikes gave birth to an underground organization, the **Workers' Defense Committee**, which offered assistance to those who lost their jobs in the strikes. This network provided the foundation for an alliance of workers, lawyers, and intellectuals that was a first in eastern Europe.

Dissent and Human Rights The Czechoslovaks followed the Polish example with **Charter 77**, which called on the government to abide by the Helsinki Final Act. It listed actions taken by the government, such as imprisoning citizens without due process, which contravened the agreement signed by the Czechoslovak government in 1975. This petition was signed by more than a thousand people, including

Workers' Defense Committee Polish underground organization founded after the 1976 Gdańsk labor strikes to provide assistance to the participants.

Charter 77 Document signed by Czechoslovak citizens in 1977 protesting the communist government's noncompliance with the Helsinki Final Act.

prominent writers such as **Václav Havel** but also by engineers, workers, and other average people. The petition refused to define itself as a political movement; it simply stood as a grassroots act. Thus it became the foundation for a new type of **civil society** that tried to change political culture and government policies from outside traditional political channels. Like citizens in the West, but for different reasons, eastern Europeans were tired of traditional politics and turned toward grassroots activism to express their criticism. For those living under a dictatorship, the price of such actions was high. Predictably, the leaders of Charter 77 were imprisoned and stripped of their rights. But the crackdown did not match the purges of the early 1950s.

The Workers' Rebellion The most devastating challenge to a communist regime came in 1980, when another wave of strikes swept through Poland following a government announcement that it would raise the price of basic foods. The deep economic problems that lay behind the previous round of strikes had not been solved. Poland was defaulting on its international loans, and its economy collapsed. People were forced to wait in line for everything from bread to shoes, as the state became unable to deliver even basic goods.

The strikes in the Gdańsk shipyards were led by **Lech Wałęsa**, a young worker with boundless energy, great charisma, and an unshaken belief in the Catholic Church. Wałęsa was not well educated, nor was he a party member. He was truly of the people, and many came to see him not only as a workers' representative but also as a Polish patriot. Throughout Poland, most factory workers, teachers, rural workers, and even some party members struck in sympathy with the Gdańsk workers. Poland's economy came to a standstill.

The Violent Crush of Solidarity With other dedicated workers, Wałęsa established **Solidarity** to negotiate better working conditions and wages. The organization was independent of communist control and at its height had more than 10 million members. This organization gave hope to most Poles that they could organize themselves and function independently of the communist regime. Entire communities gave everything they had to make this effort work, from Catholic priests, who described the actions of Solidarity in their sermons, to housewives, who turned their apartments into miniature publishing houses, hostels, and cafeterias. By December 1981, the communist regime regarded Solidarity as enough of a threat to send tanks into the streets of Warsaw. For a year, Poland was under martial law. Solidarity leaders were imprisoned, and the state imposed harsh control over all media. But the organization was too strong to be eliminated.

Opposition Underground In the following years, Solidarity supporters formed an underground network known as the **flying university**. The government tried to shut it down but had neither the will nor the resources to succeed, as many Poles were no longer afraid. Writers expelled from official publications immediately found employment as teachers and editors in the underground classes set up in churches and farmhouses. Those who still had official jobs used their economic resources to help people in the underground. Virtually everyone in Poland, including party members, either knew someone who was an underground activist or helped in such activities.

The Polish Pope The Polish dissident movement was unique in eastern Europe for its long-term worker activism and the organizational structure of the Workers' Defense Committee and also because of the role of the Catholic Church, which opened its doors to the flying university and Solidarity activists after 1981. In addition, in 1978, the Catholic Poles gained one of their most important spokesmen in the international community through the election of Karol Cardinal Wojtyła as Pope **John Paul II**. The first Polish pope, John Paul was an inspiration for all Catholics in Poland and gave them renewed faith. The pope himself became an outspoken, if diplomatic, critic of the communist bloc. Even though there were large groups of Catholics in Slovakia, Hungary, Romania, and Croatia, nowhere else did the Catholic Church provide such a catalyst for mass dissent in the last decade of communism.

Reform in the Soviet Union

In 1985, Mikhail Gorbachev became the new Soviet leader, turning out to be the right man at the right time, as Soviet leaders and the general population had come to see the necessity for change. As the old generation of party activists from World War II passed away, younger people, who had not lived under unconstrained Stalinist terror, came to expect reform to be possible. Gorbachev exemplified this new generation of leaders. He had been just eight years old when Germany invaded the Soviet Union, and when Stalin died he was pursuing a law degree in Moscow.

Václav Havel (1936–) Czech playwright and dissident who became the first president of post-communist Czechoslovakia.

civil society Nongovernmental institutions and social networks that help negotiate civil rights, social justice, and a public space outside of direct state control.

Lech Wałęsa (1943–) Shipyard worker who led 1980 labor strikes in Gdańsk, Poland, and leader of the Solidarity union and movement.

Solidarity First noncommunist workers' union of any communist regime in eastern Europe, founded in August 1980 in Poland.

flying university Underground Polish educational network that was a training ground for dissidents in the 1980s.

John Paul II (r. 1978–2005) Pope who inspired Polish Catholics and encouraged their opposition to the communist regime.

Václav Havel Calls on the Power of the Powerless

This essay, written a year after the founding of Charter 77, is Václav Havel's most famous piece. It was first published abroad in an English translation and came out in its original Czech only after 1989; before that, mimeographed copies circulated in the underground. The parable of the greengrocer has become a legendary statement of the corrupting power of totalitarian regimes and the apparently simple, potentially costly, yet fundamentally liberating means of escape from the vicious circle of living within a lie. Note that in calling people to live in truth by rejecting the communist regime as fundamentally untruthful, Havel does not embrace capitalism. He sees the consumerism of western capitalist societies as a coercive conformity, pressuring individuals into other forms of living within a lie.

❶ This is one of the most famous mottos of *The Communist Manifesto*, which adorned the front page of many communist newspapers in the Soviet bloc. Why does he do it?

❷ Why does Havel pick a greengrocer for this parable?

❸ How does the ritual of displaying the slogan help dictatorship become anonymous? What does it mean for power to become anonymous?

❹ If the greengrocer helps create the conditions to which he had to adapt, then is he a victim of the regime? Is he powerless?

❺ Are these two forms of noncompliance acts of opposition against the regime? What is their meaning and for whom?

❻ What would be the consequences of living within the truth? Is that an easy choice to make and maintain?

The manager of a fruit and vegetable shop places in his window, among the onions and carrots, the slogan: **❶** "Workers of the world, unite!" … I think it can safely be assumed that the overwhelming majority of shopkeepers never think about the slogans they put in their windows, nor do they use them to express their real opinions. **❷** That poster was delivered to our greengrocer from the enterprise headquarters along with the onions and carrots. He put them all into the window simply because that is the way it has to be. If he were to refuse, there could be trouble. He could be reproached for not having the proper "decoration" in his window; someone might even accuse him of disloyalty. He does it because these things must be done if one is to get along in life. It is one of the thousands of details that guarantee him a relatively tranquil life "in harmony with society," as they say….

We have seen that the real meaning of the greengrocer's slogan has nothing to do with what the text of the slogan actually says. Even so, this real meaning is quite clear and generally comprehensible because the code is so familiar: the greengrocer declares his loyalty (and he can do no other if his declaration is to be accepted) in the only way the regime is capable of hearing; that is, by accepting the prescribed *ritual,* by accepting appearances as reality, by accepting the given rules of the game. In doing so, however, he has himself become a player in the game, thus making it possible for the game to go on, for it to exist in the first place…. **❸** Because of this, dictatorship of the ritual, however, power becomes clearly *anonymous*….

[A] woman who ignored the greengrocer's slogan may well have hung a similar slogan just an hour before in the corridor of the office where she works. She did it more or less without thinking, just as our greengrocer did, and she could do so precisely because she was doing it against the background of the general panorama and with some awareness of it, that is, against the background of the panorama of which the greengrocer's shop window forms a part…. **❹** The greengrocer and the office worker have both adapted to the conditions in which they live, but in doing so, they help to create those conditions….

❺ Let us now imagine that one day something in our greengrocer snaps and he stops putting up the slogans merely to ingratiate himself. He stops voting in elections he knows are a farce. He begins to say what he really thinks at political meetings. And he even finds the strength in himself to express solidarity with those whom his conscience commands him to support. In this revolt the greengrocer steps out of living within the lie. He rejects the ritual and breaks the rules of the game. He discovers once more his suppressed identity and dignity. He gives his freedom a concrete significance. **❻** His revolt is an attempt to *live within the truth*….

Source: The Power of the Powerless, Václav Havel, © 1985 M.E. Sharpe. Reproduced by permission of Taylor & Francis Books UK.

In some ways Gorbachev was typical: an ambitious, hardworking, and talented party activist, rising through the ranks very quickly to become, at age forty-nine, the youngest member of the Politburo. His relative youth made him attractive to those desiring reform.

A New Openness Once in power, Gorbachev moved swiftly to eliminate most of the upper and midlevel old party leadership, replacing them with younger men he personally trusted. Such a change might have appeared autocratic, but he followed this power consolidation with a much more radical change. Starting in 1986 he introduced the policy of **glasnost**, or openness, which was an invitation to both party members and the media at large to discuss domestic problems honestly. Initially, the policy was not intended as full freedom of speech. Gorbachev hoped to control reform by positioning trusted party members as critics of the status quo and the advocates of change. He anticipated criticisms of Joseph Stalin and Leonid Brezhnev but also a positive re-evaluation of some Leninist legacies, especially the NEP years, as well of Nikita Khrushchev, all intended to reinforce commitment to the central ideals of communism.

The Price of Glasnost The gamble was fundamentally wrongheaded: Gorbachev believed openness would strengthen communist rule and restore the faith of satellite regimes. But reform was too little, too late. Both inside the Soviet Union and elsewhere, many took glasnost to mean openness *not* to choose communism and tested Gorbachev's willingness to deliver on his promise. Within three years the Soviet Union was falling apart.

Still, glasnost had important accomplishments, especially in encouraging the growth of independent organizations that became the kernel of a new civil society, much like Solidarity in Poland. Gorbachev himself oversaw the restoration of civil rights to many political prisoners, including Sakharov, and a new respect for human rights. The new openness also had an intolerant underside. For instance, the organization **Pamiat'**, dedicated to the victims of communism, had openly antisemitic overtones and encouraged new forms of **xenophobia**.

Restructuring Economic and Political Processes Gorbachev saw glasnost as part of a broader agenda, which also included **perestroika**, or restructuring. In 1988, he introduced open elections and set new time limitations to political office. In effect, he was institutionalizing a more democratic process that prized change, rather than stability, as the key to healthy politics.

glasnost (in Russian, "openness") Policy of encouraging constructive criticism of the Communist Party that was introduced by Mikhail Gorbachev in 1985.

Pamiat' Nongovernmental Soviet organization that fostered antisemitic, radical-right nationalism.

xenophobia Intense fear of foreigners.

perestroika (in Russian, "restructuring") Failed economic reforms aimed at decentralizing state control of the economy, initiated under Mikhail Gorbachev.

In the economy, perestroika proved more challenging, as some reformers called for decentralizing planning and production, which would have meant a system-wide overhaul. Previous economic reform had focused on fighting corruption, reviving worker control on the factory floor, and replacing political leaders with able technocrats. Gorbachev himself gained popularity by firing corrupt factory managers and giving speeches about making peasants the new masters of the land. But the Soviet economy was too large and sluggish to be changed just by introducing new laws and possibilities for freer market relations. All signs pointed toward the need to let the market, rather than the party, set prices and production priorities. But neither the party leadership nor the population at large was ready for such a radical change.

Resistance to Change The very culture of work needed to be transformed so as to encourage personal incentive and creativity. But neither the manager of a textile factory nor the workingwoman on the floor could make such a switch in thinking. The communist regime had so successfully reshaped the identity of the New Soviet Man and Woman that workers identified more closely with the fixed paycheck they took home every month than with productivity or creativity at work. The security of access to free public health, education, and a meager pension rendered workers as supporters of this status quo. Similarly, the communist regime had successfully directed factory managers to respond to party directives: they were not used to having to make decisions about what the factory would produce, for whom, and at what cost. These decisions were made in Moscow, and the manager's job was to simply implement them.

So when Gorbachev's reforms allowed the opening of small individual enterprises and gave more power to factory managers, the response was mixed. Most managers were unwilling to really change: their choice was most often to maintain things as they had been. Workers were no less conservative. And allowing prices to reflect the true market value of products brought inflation, which devalued the savings most people had gathered for years under their mattresses. By the end of the 1980s, the Soviet gross domestic production figures had declined by 17 percent and retail prices had increased by 140 percent. The communist system was collapsing, though the speed with which it unraveled caught the whole world by surprise.

Checking In

By yourself or with a partner, explain the significance of each of the following selected key terms:

Brezhnev Doctrine	Lech Wałęsa
Charter 77	Solidarity
Václav Havel	John Paul II
civil society	glasnost

Cultural Leaps over the Wall

◆ How did cultural concerns shared by people on both sides of the Iron Curtain transform European identities?

◆ What role did these cultural trends play in challenging the division between West and East?

In the 1970s and 1980s, cultural divisions between East and West became muted. People on both sides of the Iron Curtain had similar cultural concerns. They embraced sexuality as a part of their identity. Intellectuals challenged faith in progress, and many people turned to new religious practices. In eastern Europe these shifts did not directly challenge communism, but they did show the extent to which people no longer believed in government propaganda and tried to create alternative identities.

Whose Sexual Revolution?

The four decades after World War II saw a virtual revolution in sexual identities. Men and women became more open about sex as integral to their identity. New technologies for birth control made it easier to separate reproduction from sexual intercourse. And with methods that allowed both partners to control the process, men and women both became generally more sexually active—earlier and with more partners.

Sexual Inequalities But this new openness did not necessarily bring greater sexual equality between men and women. In the West, feminists lobbied for greater access to birth control, especially the contraceptive pill, as a means for women to eliminate unplanned pregnancies. Yet the pill, first available in Europe in the late 1960s, and other contraceptives increased pressure for women to become sexually active. By the early 1980s, the average age when a girl became sexually active in Sweden was fifteen years and two months and for a boy, two months later. For almost half of these young women, their first sexual encounter was not consensual.

Women Workers and Birth Control in Eastern Europe In communist Europe, with abortion having become legal after World War II and with methods of birth control available, especially interuterine devices, there was also a revolution in sexuality. But the revolution here was directed from the top down, as the communist regimes wanted to separate production from reproduction to facilitate the entry of a maximum number of women into the workforce. Indeed, in some eastern European countries, almost 40 percent of women worked, but usually in low-level, poorly paid jobs. More women entered technical professions than in the West (engineering was especially popular), but, as elsewhere, women were less likely to rise to the top of their professional ranks than men.

Pronatalism Under Communism By the late 1960s, concerns for women as active workers were replaced by fears of depopulation. Everywhere in Europe, the birthrate was decreasing dramatically, and the total population of many countries was going down. In western Europe, the solution was to bring in guest workers. But communist bloc governments looked to other methods. The most dramatic solution was found in Romania, where, in 1967, on the advice of sociologists and doctors, the government of **Nicolae Ceauşescu** recriminalized abortion and eliminated all forms of birth control. Women went overnight from being free to choose any form of birth control to being forced to undergo monthly gynecological examinations to monitor any pregnancy. Women's identity shifted from being partners in the labor force and public life to becoming birthing vessels. Yet mothers were given little assistance by the state, and the quality of health care and child care indicated that the regime was interested primarily in the number of children born.

The Slow Acceptance of Homosexuality Another important aspect of the sexual revolution was the emerging acceptability of homosexuality as an identity. Underground gay communities and culture had existed for a long time, but in the late 1960s and early 1970s politicians began to consider decriminalizing homosexual acts. Sweden had led the way in 1944. In the 1970s and 1980s, gay rights activists in the West largely achieved decriminalization and a degree of cultural tolerance. Sexual equality was added to the list of human rights that most western European governments protected by law. By contrast, in the communist East homosexuality remained criminalized, and many gay persons were placed in abusive psychiatric wards.

Then, in 1983, the AIDS (acquired immune deficiency syndrome) crisis reignited worldwide fears of sexual promiscuity, especially regarding male homosexuals. Despite medical research indicating that heterosexuals were often as likely as homosexuals to become infected with the AIDS virus and that the source of infection could be blood transfusions rather than sexual contact, the myth that AIDS was a homosexual illness or punishment for sexual deviants persists in many places.

These important changes in how sexuality was defined had much to do with social practices, medical advances, and public policy. But equally important was the role of popular culture. The emergence of rock and roll and of youth culture as a product that could be easily marketed, together with the growth of television, helped popularize sexual freedom. Rock stars openly flaunted their sexuality, and their fans imitated these trends. Movies, television programs, billboards, and newspaper advertisements promoted

Nicolae Ceauşescu (1918–1989) Dictatorial leader of communist Romania from 1965 to 1989.

sexually explicit images, reinforcing the notion that people's sexual desires and actions were not shameful taboos but integral components of their identity.

Sexuality in Pop Culture Popular culture generally did little to challenge traditional gender and sexual identities. James Bond movies celebrated masculine sexual promiscuity and the ideal of the sexually submissive woman. Later in the 1970s, the lifestyles of rock stars like David Bowie and Elton John challenged the staunchly heterosexual aggressive masculine ideal, but most people in western Europe were not ready to accept their sexual choices as anything more than eccentric. In eastern Europe attitudes changed even more slowly, though by the 1980s an infatuation with western popular culture had introduced important aspects of the sexual revolution in the communist bloc. As men traveled abroad, they brought back copies of pornographic magazines and sexually explicit movies. Yet, untouched by feminism, many women in eastern Europe came to equate freedom from communist oppression with the freedom to be erotically provocative in ways that western feminists might decry as turning themselves into sexual objects for the enjoyment of men.

Religious Revival

In both West and East, the generation coming of age in the 1970s and 1980s turned away from established religious traditions. In the West, those who rejected the increasingly consumerist and materialist society sought a new spirituality. In the East, many who were alienated from the ideas of communism and from the religious institutions that had not opposed communism also became interested in nontraditional religions. Buddhist and Hindu practices, particularly yoga, offered spiritual fulfillment for some. Following the trend set by famous stars like the Beatles, some westerners traveled to Asia to immerse themselves in local traditions. People retreated into either private or highly informal ways of expressing their religious beliefs rather than supporting established religious institutions. Church attendance declined even as interest in spirituality grew.

Catholicism and Resistance to Oppression Ireland and Poland were exceptions, however, as in both the Catholic Church became a focus of national resistance to oppression—imperial in Ireland and communist in Poland. In Northern Ireland, the Catholic population, whether they supported the IRA or not, found in the Catholic Church a space in which to cultivate Irish national identity as separate from Protestant English nationalism. In Poland, there was an upsurge of religious attendance as young people found the

Michel Foucault (1926–1984) French philosopher and prominent postmodernist author.

church a refuge from their bleak political and economic life.

The Persistence of Antisemitism Other developments revived affiliation with traditional religions. In the case of Judaism, antisemitic policies in eastern Europe and the Soviet Union prompted Jews to reassert their religious identity and request permission to emigrate to Israel. In Poland, the turning point was 1968 when Jewish students and intellectuals were targeted in the crackdown against the protest movements. In the Soviet Union, the Jewish population began to demand the implementation of the Helsinki Final Act, but only after Gorbachev came to power were a considerable number of emigration requests granted. With a significant influx of eastern European Jewry in the 1980s, the population of Israel changed dramatically. Many immigrants arrived in Israel barely familiar with the religious and cultural traditions of their new home and had to make a radical transition to assume their role as citizens.

Growth of Islam As Jews were leaving Europe, another religious group was growing—Muslims, who arrived as guest workers. Because of their poverty and cultural marginalization by the larger community, most guest workers remained conservative in their religious practices. Their children were often raised in the spirit of strict Muslim traditions in the midst of larger secular communities often intolerant of Islam. These economic and cultural factors combined to reinforce the marginalization of Muslims in their host countries, even in France, where this group had become the second-largest religious denomination by the beginning of the twenty-first century.

Postmodernism

Some Europeans experienced new or renewed religious affiliations, but others questioned the essence of faith in progress and western civilization itself. In the formulations of French philosopher **Michel Foucault**, the most important thinker of the postmodern movement, these two critiques were closely intertwined. Born in 1926, Foucault was active in the 1968 political protests. Yet, as a homosexual, he was a closet minority even within that progressive vanguard. In the 1970s he published a series of studies that questioned the concepts of "knowledge" and "truth," arguing that both were products of specific ways of thinking and thus fundamentally subjective.

Power and Positionality In the postmodernist universe, action was part of a complex web of relations, and individual ideas and deeds did not have meaning outside that web. Postmodernists suggested it was foolish to believe that any political or social system could be reformed from within. The fundamental injustices were in the imbalances of power between those who had economic and other resources and those who started from marginal positions. Thus it was impossible to pinpoint the causes and consequences of any action. The theory generated a fundamental dilemma: if there was no way of establishing a clear relationship between any two actions of even one individual, then knowledge was nothing more than an illusion. To "know" was to insert one's own beliefs into the interpretation of facts. This critique did not point to any way out. The only response was irony and skepticism.

An Age of Contradictions For many intellectuals in both the West and East, postmodernism expressed the contradictions of their age—the promises of plenty and the persistence of poverty, access to education and growing ignorance, the ideals of freedom and the shackles of consumerism. In particular, the ironic stance proposed by postmodernists was a survival tool for many writers behind the Iron Curtain. They were themselves caught in a web of powerlessness vis-à-vis the political leadership, for political repression made it impossible to be true to one's calling as a writer and at the same time the calling compelled them to try to express their ideas. It is no wonder, then, that some of the most original and sophisticated thinkers of the postmodern movement came from eastern Europe. For example, the Slovenian philosopher **Slavoj Žižek**'s preoccupation with the ways in which language is shaped by power, and power by language, was an extension of his experience growing up with a regime in which lies were the norm.

The Americanization of European Popular Culture

While some intellectuals worried about the meaning of postmodernism, most Europeans became addicted to American television. Comedy shows like *Married with Children* and *Roseanne* became very popular in Britain and Germany. At seven o'clock in the evening, families across the entire continent could watch the evening news in their native language or broadcasts of American sitcoms. Late-night shows that tried to replicate David Letterman's format sprang up everywhere. There were local alternatives, but the popularity of the American programs was undeniable.

American musicians from Willie Nelson to Madonna regularly sold out all their European performances. American fast-food franchises such as McDonalds opened everywhere in Europe, including Budapest and Moscow. Some worried that eating Big Macs and watching reruns of *Roseanne* would make European culture bland. In fact, Europeans still read more and watch less television than Americans, and they are less likely to eat fast-food. It is not clear whether economic reasons or cultural preferences are

behind these differences. But it seems that Europeans have self-consciously attempted to preserve some distance between their consumption of American popular culture and material goods, on the one hand, and their identification with their local and regional European culture, on the other.

 Checking In

By yourself or with a partner, explain the significance of each of the following selected key terms:

Nicolae Ceauşescu   Slavoj Žižek

Michel Foucault

The Collapse of the Soviet System, 1989–1991

◆ **What were the immediate causes of the collapse of communism in eastern Europe?**

◆ **How was the fall of communism different among the communist bloc countries?**

By 1989, Gorbachev's attempts at reform in the Soviet Union were failing. Talk of perestroika was not followed by spectacular results at a time when most people were expecting a dramatic rise in their quality of life. Yet the final blow to Gorbachev's reforms resulted from his unwillingness to hold back the new nationalist wave sweeping through both the Soviet Union and its eastern European clients. Even as he was struggling to revive the Soviet Union's viability, his actions prompted dissident movements in eastern Europe to overthrow the communist regimes. With no hope of support from Moscow, most of these regimes gave up without a struggle. Romania, however, experienced a bloody revolution that brought the end of communism at a much higher price. By the end of 1991, the communist bloc had ceased to exist.

The Velvet Revolution

Under glasnost, many informal groups with an openly non-Russian national character developed in various Soviet Republics. They were more outspoken and well-organized in the Baltic Republics, where massive rallies in 1988 showed popular support for economic independence from Moscow. Perestroika was interpreted there in a nationalist-separatist direction. In addition, by 1988 Gorbachev was speaking clearly about the need to let European nations follow their own paths. This policy reversed the interventionist Brezhnev Doctrine and signaled the beginning of Soviet disengagement from its imperialism in eastern Europe. Though Thatcher and Reagan took credit for pressuring the Soviet leader into making such

Slavoj Žižek (1949–) Postmodernist Slovenian philosopher and literary critic.

Table 29.2 The Fall of Communism

1976–1977	Massive strikes in Poland and Romania
1977	Charter 77 movement in Czechoslovakia
1978	Polish cardinal becomes Pope John Paul II
1980–1981	Solidarity movement in Poland
1985	Mikhail Gorbachev becomes leader of the Soviet Union
1988	Anti-Soviet demonstrations in Lithuania
April 1989	Roundtable talks between Solidarity and Polish communist regime
June 1989	Anticommunist protests in Tiananmen Square, Beijing
September 1989	Hungary opens border with Austria
September 11, 1989	125,000 East Germans cross into Austria via Hungary
November 9, 1989	Berlin Wall comes down
November 10, 1989	Bulgarian communist leader Todor Zhivkov deposed
November 17–December 29, 1989	Peaceful street demonstrations and deposition of communist regime in Czechoslovakia
December 16–21, 1989	Massive street protests in Romania; thousands killed
December 22, 1989	Romanian communist dictator Nicolae Ceauşescu flees
March 1991	Baltic Republics gain independence from Soviet rule
August 19–21, 1991	Failed coup by authoritarian communist group in Moscow
December 1, 1991	Ukraine declares independence from Soviet Union
December 8, 1991	Commonwealth of Independent States is established
December 25, 1991	Soviet flag lowered for last time from Kremlin

© Cengage Learning

statements, Gorbachev's position was, in fact, an extension of the glasnost and perestroika policies he had promoted since his arrival in the Kremlin in 1985. The fall of communism is summarized in Table 29.2.

Ending the Brezhnev Doctrine In eastern Europe, the reversal of the Brezhnev Doctrine was perceived by most of the older party leaders as a personal threat to their authority. Reformers moved quickly to secure a peaceful transition to a younger and more dynamic party leadership. In Poland, Solidarity was the first noncommunist organization to become the engine of change. In early 1989, it held roundtable talks with communist officials who hoped to secure a peaceful transition to a regime that would allow the party to retain some political power. But free elections resulted in a complete victory for Solidarity and in the peaceful ousting of the communists.

Peaceful Protests and Departures A wave of activism followed. In the summer of 1989, Estonians,

Latvians, and Lithuanians formed a peaceful human chain more than four hundred miles long in opposition to Soviet rule. The rest of eastern Europe awaited Moscow's reaction to these political challenges. Yet nothing happened—no troops crossed into Poland, no tanks entered the streets of Riga. This lack of response prompted the Hungarian government to open up its border with Austria. In a few days, the East Germans started to leave in droves for West Germany through Czechoslovakia, Hungary, and Austria. The road was tortuous, the lines at the border were long, but nobody could stop the exodus. Driving beat-up Trabants, riding old motorcycles, or walking, people camped out on the side of the road, sharing food, music, and their strong hope that they were finally getting out.

Bringing Down the Wall By October 1989, the East German leadership had acknowledged defeat and opened up the border with West Germany. In a frenzy of youthful hope and pent-up hate for the regime, people took axes, hammers, and household knives to

Map 29.2 **The Fall of Communism, 1989–1991** Between 1989 and 1991 most of the communist states in Europe collapsed, bringing the cold war to an end. © *Cengage Learning*

1. How would you describe these changes in comparison with those after World War I, in terms of borders?

2. How would you describe the changes in comparison with those after World War II in terms of level of violence?

3. Similarly, how would you compare post–World War II and post-1989 changes in borders?

---

the Berlin Wall and tore it down. News of what was happening in Berlin was flashed instantly by Radio Free Europe and Voice of America throughout the communist bloc. From Warsaw to Tirana, people celebrated in the streets or rejoiced quietly at home.

In November–December, the **Velvet Revolution** brought down the Czechoslovak government. Although massive student demonstrations in Prague on November 17 were brutally suppressed by the police, peaceful street marches continued. Almost half a million Czechoslovaks joined the protests after the first signs of repression. Unlike in 1968, the government had neither the force nor the political will to continue. Instead, the communists retreated. On December 29, Václav Havel was elected as president by the "power of the powerless."

Violent Struggle in Romania

In two countries, however, the fall of communism proved much more violent. In Yugoslavia, a bloody civil war set the country on a path of self-destruction that would last a decade. In Romania, a much shorter violent popular uprising became the means by which communist dictatorship was forced out. Nicolae Ceaușescu was alone in disregarding Moscow's encouragements for reform, but that was not a new stance.

The Costs of Romania's Independent Road Since the 1960s Ceaușescu had acted independently, securing good relations with China when the Soviets were in conflict with that country and, in the 1970s, emulating North Korea by breaking all links with the outside world to show that Romania needed no economic assistance from the West or the East. In reality, the Romanian economy suffered from the same problems of soaring prices and lack of energy resources as the rest of the continent.

By 1989, basic goods such as bread, milk, and

Velvet Revolution The peaceful fall of communism in most of eastern Europe in 1989.

toilet paper were unavailable, and Romanians were simply struggling to survive. On December 16, people took to the streets of Timișoara to protest the imprisonment of a prominent local Hungarian clergyman. Despite the climate of terror that had increased in the 1980s, thousands joined the crowd. Then the police attacked, killing some civilians. The street uprising seemed to calm down by evening.

A Violent End A few days later, on December 21, Ceaușescu decided to demonstrate his power by holding a public gathering in Bucharest. The plan backfired. Within minutes there was loud booing, and the dictator fled the scene. A few hours later he and his wife were seized by a group of secret police, military, and political leaders. By the end of the year, the **National Salvation Front** was in charge. Ceaușescu and his wife had been executed after a sham trial, and some top communist leaders were in prison. But many midlevel communists were part of this new government, led by an old party activist who had known Gorbachev since his youth, **Ion Iliescu**. The Romanians had rid themselves of the most horrible aspects of communism, but they had not achieved a democratic regime. Still, the year 1990 began with great optimism in eastern Europe. The Iron Curtain had been lifted.

The End of the Soviet Union

In the Soviet Union, 1990 began with the recognition that the communist experiment had failed to achieve a viable workers' state. The Soviet political and military establishment realized that Gorbachev's reformist talk had permitted the lawful and peaceful exit of the eastern European communist bloc states and that even Soviet Republics no longer wished to be part of the Union. The Baltic states had already made that clear, and after Gorbachev pulled troops out of Afghanistan in 1989, a growing wave of independence movements swept the republics of Central Asia. Nationalism, whether secular or strongly Muslim in orientation, was challenging the authority of communism and the Russian party elites everywhere.

The Communist Leadership Divided By August 1991, the party had become sharply divided into two factions: one led by **Boris Yeltsin**, the president of the Russian Republic and a young former supporter of Gorbachev, now disappointed with perestroika's lack of success; the other, a conservative faction, now led by Gorbachev, which tried to undo many of the reforms of the 1980s. The unforeseen consequences of his reforms had pushed Gorbachev to retreat. He was fundamentally still a supporter of the communist project and could not embrace the disintegration of the Soviet Union even though he had provided the means for it. Thus, for a brief period of time, Gorbachev attempted to rein in the nationalist independence movements, with strong support from the military establishment and older party leaders.

Crisis in the Kremlin Yet Gorbachev was also troubled by his abandonment of the principles of glasnost and perestroika. So, by early 1991, he returned to his reformist stance and, under strong international pressure, allowed the independence of Latvia, Lithuania, and Estonia. By August, together with Yeltsin, he had prepared a new treaty for a looser union with the remaining Soviet Republics. This treaty set the stage for the creation of a **Commonwealth of Independent States (CIS)**, which offered its members autonomy in the management of internal affairs while the CIS would coordinate foreign affairs, security, and some economic policies, such as trade.

In a last-ditch effort to save the status quo, a group of eight conservative party leaders tried to seize power and establish a hard-line authoritarian regime. Working with the KGB, they detained Gorbachev at his summer home on August 19. But Yeltsin remained in Moscow, where he appeared in public, made statements broadcast in the state-controlled media, and rallied around him the support of the people and even many military troops. The most defiant moment of Yeltsin's opposition to the **August coup** came when he stood atop a tank that was supposed to separate the Duma from the population and spoke on live television surrounded by large crowds of supporters. Russians everywhere instantly realized that the army was divided, the coup was a sham, and Yeltsin was the man of the hour. Within three days the conservative coup collapsed and Gorbachev returned to Moscow.

From Reform to Breakup But the real winner was Yeltsin, who had stood up to the hard-liners and confronted the army through an act of passive resistance. Instead of operating behind closed doors to outmaneuver his opponents, as the conservatives had done, Yeltsin had instead stood with the people to protest the abuses of the government. Earlier, when Soviet troops had threatened to intervene in the Baltic Republics, he had flown to Riga to stand by protesters.

National Salvation Front Emergency government that came to power in Romania in 1989 after dictator Nicolae Ceaușescu fled.

Ion Iliescu (1930–) Communist leader of the National Salvation Front in postcommunist Romania who became the first president of the country after elections in 1990.

Boris Yeltsin (1931–2007) First president of postcommunist Russia, 1991–1999, who oversaw the dismemberment of the Soviet Union and privatization of the economy.

Commonwealth of Independent States (CIS) Alliance of former Soviet republics that oversees some trade, economic reform, and defense issues.

August coup Attempt in August 1991 by communist hard-liners to bring an end to the reforms of Yeltsin and Gorbachev that was crushed by a popular uprising.

In August 1991 Boris Yeltsin became an instant symbol of revolt against the old Soviet system as he stood with civilians and soldiers on the top of this tank, demanding the resignation of the Soviet leadership. Shortly after these events he outlawed the Communist Party in the Russian Soviet Socialist Republic. How is this image of transition in political power different from that of the Berlin Wall in October 1989?

Now, when the party threatened to take over the government, he called on the people and the lower army ranks to stand by him as a Russian patriot.

Yeltsin thus became the face of democratic Russia. As president of the Russian Republic, he shortly outlawed the Communist Party there, closed down communist newspapers, and transferred most state authority from the Soviet Union's federal level of government to his own Russian Republic. On December 1, Ukraine, the second most populous republic of the Soviet Union, proclaimed its independence. By Christmas Day 1991, the Soviet Union had ceased to exist. The hammer and sickle flag in Red Square was lowered, and the Russian flag raised. The seventy-year communist experiment had ended, and Russian nationalism was restored.

The collapse of the Soviet Union was surprisingly more peaceful than its beginnings, and it signaled the end of the cold war. Arguments remain over the most important causes for this collapse: the strong military stance of Reagan and Thatcher, Gorbachev's reforms, or dissent movements in eastern Europe. Although the West had won the cold war, the meaning of this victory for Europeans at large was still to be determined because the communist bloc states remained weak economically and politically.

Checking In

By yourself or with a partner, explain the significance of each of the following selected key terms:

Velvet Revolution

National Salvation Front

Ion Iliescu

Boris Yeltsin

Commonwealth of Independent States (CIS)

August coup

CHAPTER
Review

Summary

- ◆ Between 1968 and 1991, Europe went from being divided to becoming open to the flow of people, ideas, and goods from all regions.

- ◆ During détente, the actions of western and eastern political leaders helped increase the exchange of ideas and goods across the cold war divide.

- ◆ In eastern Europe dissidents bravely challenged their governments to honor human rights.

- ◆ Tensions between the superpowers increased after the Soviet invasion of Afghanistan, yet in the mid-1980s Gorbachev reversed the Soviet position in eastern Europe.

◆ By the end of 1991, the communists had lost power everywhere in eastern Europe except Yugoslavia.

  ◆ In western Europe traditional parties were confronted with new types of activism, from the Greens to radical nationalist and terrorist movements.

  ◆ The decade-long economic crisis that began in 1973 created new challenges for political stability, as Europe became more vulnerable to shifts in the global economy.

  ◆ Western European governments achieved renewed prosperity and stability in the 1980s by scaling back welfare programs and privatizing some economic sectors.

◆ While people in the East looked to the West, some western Europeans questioned the faith in progress in their societies.

  ◆ Religion remained an important site for political opposition in some areas.

  ◆ The feminist, environmental, and antinuclear movements created new alliances and forms of grassroots activism.

  ◆ Demographic shifts brought important changes, from an aging population and lower birthrate to a more ethnically, religiously, and sexually diverse mix of people.

  ◆ The fall of communism was overall a bloodless transition.

Chronology

1972	West Germany recognizes the East German border; United States and Soviet Union sign the Antiballistic Missile Treaty
1973	Great Britain, Ireland, and Denmark join the Common Market; Egypt and Israel engage in the Yom Kippur War; Arab oil embargo begins
1974	Abortion is decriminalized in France
1975	European states sign the Helsinki Final Act
1976–1977	Massive strikes erupt in Poland and Romania
1977	Charter 77 movement in Czechoslovakia begins
1978	Polish cardinal Karol Wojtyła becomes Pope John Paul II
1979	Soviets invade Afghanistan; Margaret Thatcher becomes British prime minister
1980	Solidarity movement begins in Poland
1981	Greece joins the Common Market; Spain legalizes divorce; Millions march in antinuclear protests in western Europe
1982	Britain defeats Argentina in Falklands War
1983	François Mitterrand becomes president of France; Petra Kelly, first Green Party representative, is elected to the West German parliament; AIDS crisis begins
1985	Mikhail Gorbachev becomes leader of the Soviet Union
1986	Explosion at the Chernobyl nuclear power plant spreads contamination
1989	Berlin Wall is taken down; Communism falls in eastern Europe
1991	Soviet Union collapses

© Cengage Learning

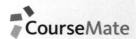

Test Yourself

To gauge your mastery of the material in this chapter, answer the questions below. More than one answer may be correct.

Politics in Western Europe

1. The 1970s détente meant:

   a. Recognizing all borders of postwar Europe.
   b. The attempt to limit militarization of the superpowers.
   c. A policy of reconciliation between West Germany and eastern Europe.
   d. Freedom for all citizens in Europe to travel across borders.
   e. Emphasizing the need protect human rights through international cooperation.

2. The Yom Kippur War:

   a. Led to an oil embargo.
   b. Created new tensions between the Arab world and Israel supporters.
   c. Led to soaring prices in every area of economic activity all over the world.
   d. Returned the Sinai Peninsula to Egypt.
   e. Led European countries to turn to other forms of energy, such as electrical and nuclear.

3. Left-wing parties regained popularity in the 1970s in:

   a. Italy
   b. France
   c. Spain
   d. Britain
   e. Greece

4. The antinuclear movement in the 1970s:

   a. Succeeded in closing down all nuclear military bases in Britain.
   b. Mobilized millions of peaceful protesters.
   c. Brought about the establishment of environmental parties in Europe.
   d. Led to the closing down of the Chernobyl nuclear station.
   e. Led to new international cooperation among political activists in Europe.

5. Margaret Thatcher:

   a. Deregulated state control over economic production.
   b. Was trained as a physicist.
   c. Reduced the state's commitment to social welfare programs.
   d. Won the Falklands War.
   e. Closed down the Greenham Common military base.

Now that you have reviewed and tested yourself on this part of the chapter, take time to pull together all the important information by answering the following questions:

◆ What role did the relaxation of international tensions in the 1970s play in Europe, East and West?
◆ How did political parties in western Europe change in the 1970s and 1980s?

Social Change in the West

6. In the 1970s, feminists began to develop their own political movements because they:

   a. Were unable to gain access to higher education.
   b. Found little support among traditional parties for their fight for equal wages with men.
   c. Remained secondary players in the established political parties.
   d. Rejected heterosexuality.
   e. Wanted housework to be considered as an economically significant occupation.

7. Simone de Beauvoir was:

   a. The leader of the feminist party in France.
   b. A philosopher.
   c. A supporter for decriminalizing abortion.
   d. A proponent of the notion that men and women were equal in every way.
   e. The partner of writer Jean Paul Sartre.

8. What was the last European country to decriminalize abortion in 1990?

   a. Italy
   b. Spain
   c. Belgium
   d. France
   e. Poland

9. The feminist movement's wide-ranging impact on European societies in the 1970s and 1980s included:
   a. An increase in the birthrate.
   b. A change in marriage patterns.
   c. Significant growth of women being elected to national office.
   d. The development of the environmental parties.
   e. The development of different types of grass-roots political protest.

10. The most significant population changes in western Europe between 1960 and 1990 were a:
   a. Growth in age expectancy.
   b. Decrease in the birthrate.
   c. Growth in migration from western Europe.
   d. Growth in marriage rates.
   e. Growth in Muslim populations.

Now that you have reviewed and tested yourself on this part of the chapter, take time to pull together all the important information by answering the following questions:

◆ How did western European societies change during this period?

◆ How did the feminist movement change western European society?

Growing Crisis in the Communist East

11. The communist regimes tried to prevent dissent movements in the 1970s by:
   a. Making western consumer goods, such as jeans, available.
   b. Enforcing the Helsinki Final Act.
   c. Making western music available.
   d. Allowing some people to travel to western Europe as guest workers.
   e. Allowing free elections.

12. Andrei Sakharov:
   a. Developed the Soviet hydrogen bomb.
   b. Traveled widely in the world to discuss the human rights abuses in the Soviet Union.
   c. Lived for many years under house arrest.
   d. Traveled to Oslo in 1975 to collect the Nobel Peace Prize.
   e. Was a prominent member of the Communist Party in the Soviet Union.

13. Václav Havel:
   a. Was a prominent Czech playwright.
   b. Worked in a brewery for several years.
   c. Opposed Charter 77.
   d. Embraced capitalism as the solution to the communist lie.
   e. Was imprisoned for his political ideas.

14. Solidarity:
   a. Successfully established the largest independent workers' union in the communist bloc.
   b. Was led by John Paul II.
   c. Was crushed by the military.
   d. Was supported by the Soviet Union.
   e. Brought the Polish economy to a standstill through a national strike.

15. Perestroika:
   a. Was promoted most actively by Mikhail Gorbachev.
   b. Successfully led to the restructuring of the Communist Party.
   c. Was embraced by the population at large.
   d. Led to the development of free markets in the Soviet Union.
   e. Led to the collapse of the Soviet Union.

Now that you have reviewed and tested yourself on this part of the chapter, take time to pull together all the important information by answering the following questions:

◆ What impact did détente have for the people of the communist bloc?

◆ How did the Soviet Union change from the 1970s to the late 1980s?

Cultural Leaps over the Wall

16. The availability of new forms of birth control in Europe led to:
   a. Fewer unplanned pregnancies.
   b. Greater pressure for women to become sexually active.
   c. More work opportunities for women.
   d. More sexual intercourse before marriage.
   e. Women's independence.

17. In the 1970s and 1980s homosexuality was:
   a. Decriminalized in many western European countries.
   b. Embraced as a biologically based sexual preference.
   c. Linked to the AIDS global crisis.
   d. Becoming more visible in popular culture.
   e. Rejected universally as a form of social deviance.

18. The Catholic Church became a focus of resistance to political oppression in:

    a. Spain
    b. Ireland
    c. France

    d. Poland
    e. Italy

19. Postmodernism represents:

    a. The quest for absolute truth.
    b. An expression of the deep political and cultural contradictions of the 1970s and 1980s.
    c. A philosophy of doubt in progress.

    d. The renewed hope that political reform was possible from within a system.
    e. The notion that all power relations were mutually constituted by the powerful and the powerless.

20. In the 1980s most Europeans:

    a. Embraced fast-food.
    b. Embraced migrant Muslim populations and Islam as core aspects of European societies.
    c. Continued to watch less television than the Americans.

    d. Rejected American popular music.
    e. Became interested in nontraditional religious movements.

Now that you have reviewed and tested yourself on this part of the chapter, take time to pull together all the important information by answering the following questions:

◆ How did cultural concerns shared by people on both sides of the Iron Curtain transform European identities?

◆ What role did these cultural trends play in challenging the division between West and East?

The Collapse of the Soviet System, 1989–1991

21. In what countries did peaceful protests lead to the collapse of communism?

    a. Poland
    b. Czechoslovakia
    c. Romania

    d. Albania
    e. East Germany

22. What types of activities led to the collapse of communism in Europe?

    a. Strikes
    b. Street demonstrations
    c. The departure of over a hundred thousand citizens through newly opened borders

    d. Free elections
    e. Military action

23. The collapse of communism in Romania was different because of the:

    a. Romanian leadership's rejection of perestroika.
    b. Violent crackdown on street protests by the regime.
    c. Hurried execution of Nicolae Ceauşescu.

    d. Descent of the country into war.
    e. Independent course the regime had pursued in relation to Moscow since the 1960s.

24. The Commonwealth of Independent States:

    a. Was a last ditch attempt to quell the independence movements in the Baltics.
    b. Succeeded in retaining the authority of the Russian Communist Party.
    c. Led to the rise to power of Boris Yeltsin.

    d. Brought about a failed attempt to imprison Gorbachev.
    e. Represents a loose alliance of former Soviet republics.

25. The collapse of the Soviet Union did not see much violence because:

    a. The army was divided on the issue of military repression.
    b. Boris Yeltsin gained the trust of the army's lower ranks through passive resistance.

    c. The hard-liners were afraid to use the secret police forces to take out their enemies.
    d. The street protests were peaceful.
    e. The media supported the opposition.

Now that you have reviewed and tested yourself on this part of the chapter, take time to pull together all the important information by answering the following questions:

◆ What were the immediate causes of the collapse of communism in eastern Europe?

◆ How was the fall of communism different among the communist bloc countries?

CHAPTER 30

Europe in a Globalizing World, 1991 to the Present

Chapter Outline

1990	1992	1994	1996	1998	2000

1991

Yugoslav civil wars begin

Soviet Union collapses

1993

European Union is inaugurated

1995

World Trade Organization is established

Dayton Agreement

1996

Poland, Czech Republic, and Hungary join NATO

1999

Kosovo War brings NATO intervention

2000

Milosevic resigns

Starting in January 2011, the youthful faces of Egyptian men and women brandishing the national flag in Tahrir Square, Cairo, have become a symbol of hope for a democratic future in the Middle East. (Khalil Hamra/AP Images)

After reading this chapter, you should be able to answer the following questions:

What has the end of the cold war meant for Europe?

How has the European Union reshaped the European political and economic scene?

What are the most important changes in international security and cooperation since the end of the cold war?

How successful has Europe been in retaining a powerful role in the process of economic globalization?

What role have European states played in the War on Terrorism in relation to the United States?

What important changes since 1991 have reshaped European identity today?

IN 1991 EUROPE found itself confronting new challenges, the first of which was to undo the economic and political legacies of the cold war. Liberal democracies won the war, and the postcommunist European states now took on new significance for western Europe as trading partners, a source of labor, and simply as neighbors. The creation of the European Union (EU) and then its enlargement eastward have been important steps toward European integration.

Overall, democracy has been secured in Europe, and Europeans now live in greater stability and prosperity, with greater tolerance toward each other's differences. Where such tolerance remains challenging is in accepting the increasing Muslim influences in European societies. Although Muslim workers and their families are allowed to live in Europe, they generally have been treated as outsiders, even when local Islamic traditions go back hundreds of years.

Europeans have once again become strong players on the international scene as a leading force in the global economy. Though far from united, Europeans

2002		2004		2006		2008		2010

2002
Euro goes into circulation

2001
Terrorists attack the United States

2003
Iraq War begins

2004
European Union gains ten new members

Angela Merkel becomes the first woman chancellor of Germany

2005
European Union Constitution is defeated

2007
Romania and Bulgaria join the EU

2008
Iceland's currency collapses, EU orchestrates bailout

Kosovo declares independence

Barack Obama becomes the first African American president of the United States

2009
Ratification of Lisbon Treaty

Great Britain withdraws all troops from Iraq

2010
Beginning of Arab Spring

have also been active in international conflicts, from the Yugoslav Wars of the 1990s to the War on Terrorism since 2001 and most recently the Arab Spring (2010), which has shaken several political regimes around the Mediterranean. Internally, the greatest challenges have been preserving democratic principles in the European Union while stretching its boundaries to include countries of the postcommunist bloc. Externally, the most important challenge has been how to negotiate with the United States their collective position as winners in the cold war in economic and international security matters. Who has paid the cost of this victory and who is reaping the benefits have remained subjects of contention in American-European relations. Many have tried to preserve the particular character of European culture in this era of increasing homogenization and the dominance of global economic and political concerns.

Eastern Europe After Communism

◆ **What impact did the postcommunist transition have on eastern European states and societies?**

◆ **To what extent have these countries become more democratic?**

The West won the cold war. By the end of 1991, the Soviet Union was defunct and all but one eastern European country had renounced communism. Within a few years, Russia became a friendly competitor and sometimes ally of liberal western Europe, the most remarkable achievement in politics of the last three decades. In eastern Europe, however, Yugoslavia remained a vestige of the old communist order, now transformed into an ethno-nationalist dictatorship. As the postcommunist countries claimed a place in the larger European "home," new challenges arose for countries embarking on democratization. The only politicians with experience were the communists, and the most popular ideas uniting the citizenry were nationalist and often nondemocratic. Eastern European politicians had to deal with internal political and social problems while also responding to outside pressures from the West for transparency, increased economic freedoms, and reduced corruption. For Russia, Romania, and Bulgaria, these challenges were difficult to meet, but Poland, Hungary, the Czech Republic, and Slovakia managed the 1990s effectively. The postcommunist transitions have led countries of the Soviet bloc in different directions, and political democratization has not always brought economic betterment, nor has international investment been a guarantee for democratization. The relationship between the free market and democratic politics remains problematic in this part of Europe.

Russia from Foe to Partner

Russians woke up on Christmas Day 1991 to a brand-new state: a noncommunist Russia and its Commonwealth of Independent States (CIS). At the helm was Boris Yeltsin, the jovial and forceful politician who had stood up to the fearful Gorbachev and staunch communist old-timers to demand reform and democratization. Yeltsin was hugely popular in the days of the August 1991 coup, when he stood atop a tank and asked the Russian people to protect him and the reformist politicians from the abuses of the communist leadership. He sounded and looked like a man of the people, and his wild stunt worked in rousing the population.

Yeltsin: From Rebel to Reformer Yet Yeltsin was not an outsider to Communist Party politics. He had been handpicked by Mikhail Gorbachev to pursue perestroika in the mid-1980s as party chief in the Moscow region. But dutifully following the rules was not Yeltsin's way. He was certainly ambitious and wanted to rise high in the party. But he had been a thrill seeker since childhood, when he pursued many sports competitively, from volleyball to boxing. As a teenager, he learned the skills of the construction trade and then in college became an engineer and joined the party. He soon rose to top leadership in Sverdlovsk. In 1985 he catapulted into the Politburo, becoming the youngest member and Moscow party chief, where he was broadly popular for his tough stand against corruption.

Unceremoniously fired in 1987 for his daring reforms that pushed perestroika and glasnost too far, Yeltsin returned to a humble job in the construction industry. But in 1989, Gorbachev's reforms in electoral law enabled the people of Moscow to bring Yeltsin back to the Duma. With broad popular support, Yeltsin quickly rose to become the most outspoken

Expansion of European Union

- Members, 1989
- German reunification, 1990
- New members, 1995
- New members, 2004
- New members, 2007
- Candidates, 2012

Map 30.1 **The European Union in 2007** Since 1993, the European Union has been a powerful force in refashioning European identities. Originally an international economic organization, it has gained political and cultural dimensions. © *Cengage Learning*

1. How has the membership of the EU changed since 1989?
2. What proportion of the EU do the original members represent at the present time?
3. What does this change suggest about the relationship between western and eastern Europe?
4. How do you view the nonmember status of various countries in Europe in relation to the development and specific features of the EU?

and trusted reformist of the Communist Party elite, in 1990 creating a Democratic Platform group that demanded radical change in the party's leading role, as well as decentralization of the state structure.

By August 1991, when conservatives attempted a coup, Yeltsin was the popularly elected president of Russia. This victory emboldened him to contest the power of the Soviet federal authorities. In fact, he swiftly dissolved the Communist Party in Russia and proceeded to fire officials appointed on the basis of party loyalty. In all these radical changes, Yeltsin risked a great deal of personal and professional safety, but it was in his nature to gamble and think big.

By early 1992, Yeltsin commanded the admiration of the entire world: the amazingly sudden and peaceful transformation of the Soviet Union from the "evil empire" of U.S. President Ronald Reagan's rhetoric into multiparty Russia was one of the most important developments of the post–cold war period. Politicians in the West celebrated the victory of the United States over the Soviet Union. The Soviet people themselves celebrated the end of communist rule as though waking from a bad dream. But these celebrations were short-lived. Within months, the reality of the aftermath of political, social, and economic collapse set in.

Russia's Difficult Democratization Yeltsin continued to rule Russia throughout the decade, but his popularity and success were never as high as in 1992. Politically the country became democratic in that the communist monopoly was replaced by a multitude of political parties, but many of them were undemocratic. Measures to transform the state-controlled economy into a market-driven one benefited a narrow stratum of people while most became impoverished. And in matters of national unity and international security, Yeltsin satisfied neither die-hard nationalists nor progressive reformers.

In 1992 the only Russian politicians with experience were communists, and most people who were not already involved in the party had no desire to participate in politics. Therefore, even though Yeltsin's regime introduced full political freedoms, most political parties represented small groups interested in political gains rather than voters' interests. Most prominent among these groups were newly enriched businessmen, who were able to gain control over important economic resources illegally and wanted to protect their businesses. The oil industry became a particularly powerful force in several parties.

Other groups were motivated by the nationalist desire to make sure the new Russia served Russians above other nationalities. These groups grew in the early 1990s because they spoke to the electorate in terms the people understood. They blamed poverty and personal insecurity on outsiders—the West or enemies within the CIS, such as Ukraine, Georgia, and Moldova, former Soviet republics now seeking independence from the Russians. Though these parties acknowledged social and economic problems, their solutions, such as increasing military spending to alleviate poverty, were ineffective. Yeltsin tried to balance these new factions and the communists but could not manage to create a popular, reform-minded party of his own.

Economic Corruption and Collapse Given the lack of parties that offered solid solutions to the economic and social problems of the broad electorate, most people did not fare better in these early years of Russian democratization. The economy was swiftly **privatized**, with the state selling or simply giving up its previous control over most economic enterprises, from factories to beauty salons. By 1995, over half of all economic activity was in private hands. It was in these private enterprises that almost 90 percent of the industrial workforce was employed. New service sectors developed, while large public enterprises and services, such as health care, social services, and education, remained largely in the hands of the state. State employees such as coal miners and teachers sometimes did not get paid for months, and inflation reduced the buying power of the ruble. Thus, even when the checks arrived, many public employees could not support their families. In 1993 more than 30 percent of the population was living in poverty.

During the same period, there was a marked increase in the activities of criminal gangs, who took advantage of irregularities and simply took over many services and state enterprises. The state did not have enough reliable law enforcement agents to deal with corruption. Thus, while some of the signs of privatization looked encouraging, the overall welfare of the people declined. For a majority of Russians, the benefits of democracy were not apparent, and many began celebrating the old national holiday of the Soviet Union (November 7) with parades and even mourning Joseph Stalin's death.

In August 1998 the Russian stock market completely collapsed. Under pressure from international financial organizations such as the **World Bank** and the **International Monetary Fund**, which had loaned Russia billions of dollars for its economic reform, the government was forced to devalue the ruble. This move was completely unexpected, as Yeltsin had promised time and again never to devalue the ruble. Many lost their life savings and their trust in

---

privatization Replacement of state ownership of property with private ownership in the postcommunist states.

World Bank International financial organization controlled by developed countries in the West that offers discounted loans for economic reform to developing countries.

International Monetary Fund International financial organization started in 1946 that is responsible for managing the global financial system.

the banking system overnight. The ruble slowly recovered some of its value, but faith in the stock market and in Yeltsin's brand of reform was never fully restored.

Irredentist Challenges Yeltsin's decade in power was also plagued by crises in former Soviet territories. **Chechnya**, where the native Islamic majority had never accepted the Russian takeover of 1859, made a bid for independence in the early days of postcommunism. In 1994 Yeltsin sought to regain control through military invasion. Three years of military conflict ensued, and Yeltsin's popularity plummeted when he signed a shaky truce with the Chechen rebels in 1997. By 1999, Chechnya had become a haven for traffic in illegal weapons and drugs, as well as a training ground for Islamic radicals.

After a decade of political, economic, and international challenges, Yeltsin finally decided to step down. Suffering from severe health problems and battling alcoholism, he had taken steps to secure his successor in the summer of 1999, when he appointed **Vladimir Putin** as premier. On December 31, Yeltsin called Putin into his office and handed over the presidency to him. This choice of a successor may be Yeltsin's most troubled legacy.

The Dismemberment of Yugoslavia

In the 1990s Yugoslavia plunged into a bloody civil war that destroyed the country, brought appalling human losses, and prompted the first major military intervention by NATO. The political and economic troubles that destroyed Yugoslavia had begun as early as 1968, when a new wave of nationalism became apparent in various regions of the country. Yugoslavia had been created after World War I, primarily as an extension of Serbia's ambitions for unifying all the South Slavs; Croats, Bosnians, and Slovenes were brought into this union as unequal partners. World War II had further antagonized the various ethnic groups, as Serbs massacred Croats and Croats massacred Serbs under the watchful eye of the Nazi occupiers. After 1945, Josip Broz Tito had attempted to create "brotherhood and unity" among these embattled ethnic groups.

From Yugoslavism to Rabid Nationalism When Tito died in 1980, hope for brotherhood and unity vanished. Politicians began to depict inflation and other economic problems in ethnocentric terms. In 1986, a brash Serbian lawyer, **Slobodan Milošević**, attracted attention by laying blame for the Serbians' economic problems on the Croats, Bosnians, and Kosovar Albanians. As president of Serbia, Milošević was still a high official in the Communist Party, but he had already begun his transformation into a Serbian ultranationalist. By 1991, he had emerged as the most outspoken proponent of Yugoslavia as the country of Serbs first

Table 30.1 The Dissolution of Yugoslavia

1989	Slobodan Milošević becomes president of Serbia; Kosovo loses autonomous status
1991	Slovenia declares independence; Yugoslavia fails in military attempt to prevent it; Croatia declares independence; Civil war begins
1992	Bosnia civil war begins
1993	UN peacekeeping troops on the ground
1995	NATO air strikes; Dayton Agreement
1996	Active military resistance in Kosovo against Serbian government begins
1999	NATO-U.S. air strikes against Serbia
2000	Milošević resigns
2001	Milošević is in the custody of the International Criminal Tribunal for the former Yugoslavia
2003	Yugoslavia ceases to exist, becoming "Serbia and Montenegro"
2004	Slovenia joins the EU
2006	Montenegro declares independence from Serbia
2008	Kosovo declares independence from Serbia; Radovan Karadzić arrested for war crimes and brought into the custody of the International Criminal Tribunal for the former Yugoslavia

© Cengage Learning

and other nationalities second. With the state fully in control of politics, the media, and the army, Milošević embarked on a campaign to discredit non-Serbians and liberal economic and political reformers. Table 30.1 summarizes the dissolution of Yugoslavia.

War and Ethnic Cleansing Slovenes and Croats reacted by declaring independence in June 1991. The Slovenes were able to walk away from the Yugoslav union without any contest, but Croatia and then Bosnia, which declared independence in 1992, became engulfed in civil war. Between 1991 and 1995, Serbs, Croats, and Muslim Bosnians engaged in **ethnic cleansing**, killing each other relentlessly on the basis of

Chechnya Region in Central Asia controlled by Russia since 1859, which has a strong independence movement led by radical Islamists.

Vladimir Putin (1952–) President of Russia, 2000–2008 and since 2012, and prime minister between 2008 and 2012, popular because of his nationalist credentials and anticorruption platform.

Slobodan Milošević (1941–2006) Socialist dictatorial president of Serbia and Yugoslavia who was deposed by popular protests and died while on trial for genocidal war crimes.

ethnic cleansing Eliminating an "enemy" ethnic group by exiling, killing, and raping its members and destroying or taking away their property.

Map 30.2 **The Breakup of Yugoslavia** Between 1991 and 2006 the federal, multiethnic Yugoslavia fragmented into small and relatively poor independent states. Slovenia became a success, but Montenegro is still struggling to become an economically viable state. © *Cengage Learning*

1. What does the ethnic map of Bosnia–Herzegovina suggest about the internal challenges of this state?
2. What advantages does Slovenia have in relation to other former Yugoslav countries in terms of location and ethnic makeup?

Geneva Conventions Four international treaties that forbid the mistreatment of civilians and prisoners of war during wartime.

sanctions Punitive measures adopted by a country or group of countries against another state for political reasons.

Dayton Agreement Peace agreement signed in 1995 that ended the Bosnian civil war and established the grounds for an independent Bosnia and a Serbian Republic.

ethnic identity. Most of the fighting took place outside Serbia proper, but Milošević's actions as supreme commander of the Yugoslav army and in helping Serbian paramilitary groups in Croatia and Bosnia played a central role in the atrocities committed by the Serbian forces. The exiling, killing, raping, and seizure and destruction of property had the sole purpose of eliminating the presence of these other ethnicities. More than twenty thousand women, most of them Muslim, were

systematically raped in Bosnia as part of the Serbian and Croatian ethnic-cleansing campaigns.

Peace Through Compromise By 1994, enraged world opinion prompted belated action against these outrageous crimes. The internationally sanctioned **Geneva Conventions** forbade the mistreatment of civilians and prisoners of war, and the UN attempted to impose **sanctions** and sent in observers, but these measures had little effect. After the publication of evidence about several massacres, the UN finally approved air strikes by NATO, its first military intervention ever. By December 1995, the war was over, and all parties signed the **Dayton Agreement**, which recognized both an independent Muslim-Croat federation and a Serbian Republic in Bosnia, with a UN peacekeeping force to oversee the postwar transition.

Rikard Larma/AP Images

Between 1991 and 1995 Yugoslavia endured the bloodiest civil war in Europe since 1918. Serbs, Croats, and Bosnians fought with each other, and many civilians were murdered, giving rise to the term "ethnic cleansing." These Muslims are at a funeral of forty-seven civilians killed by Serbs at the beginning of the war and later unearthed in the village of Ahatovici, near Sarajevo, on Sunday, July 7, 1996. How would you describe the posture of the woman at the front of the procession?

This agreement offered a peaceful resolution, but it also created some important problems. In particular, it implicitly endorsed the right of the Milošević government to fight any future pro-independence movements.

"Rejoining" Europe: Economic Recovery Most post-Yugoslav countries pursued economic and political reconstruction with the aim of "rejoining" Europe. Slovenia quickly developed a free market while maintaining important components of the communist welfare system. By 2010, this country had a per capita Gross Domestic Product of over $28,000. It was a complete success story. By contrast, Croatia had more problems, especially given the staunchly nationalist and sometimes illiberal bent of its government in the early 1990s. With much of the economy trying to reinvent itself outside the Yugoslav markets, and with many of its resources having been diverted to civil war, Croatia was slower to move toward a democratic system and a free-market economy. Yet, by the end of the 1990s, nationalist excesses were diminishing, trade with western Europe was picking up, and the economy was growing so fast that Croatia had become a candidate for EU membership.

The Kosovo War Milošević tried to pull together Yugoslavia's remaining resources. His corrupt regime controlled the media, the military, and political parties with support from abroad, especially Russia. To revive his popularity among nationalist followers, he turned to Kosovo, where tensions between the overwhelmingly Albanian majority (80 percent) and the powerful Serbian minority had festered for a long time. Tensions increased as Kosovars suffered increasingly from economic problems and political oppression. In the summer of 1998, as many as three hundred thousand Kosovo Albanians were forced to flee their homes,

going elsewhere inside Yugoslavia or across the border to Albania, Macedonia, and Greece. This mass exodus raised international concern.

In February 1999, with one civilian massacre by the Serb forces confirmed, American, British, and Russian negotiators attempted a settlement between the Kosovo Albanians and Serbs. Serbians and their Russian supporters walked out of the talks, and on March 24, NATO began air strikes against Serbia. The **Kosovo War** lasted just a few months. Its most spectacular features—the American bombing of the Chinese Embassy and Serbian hospitals—received much media attention, while the number of casualties was disputed because few independent observers were allowed on the ground. The number of Kosovo Albanian refugees skyrocketed to more than one million. When the NATO bombing ended on June 10, it was not clear who had won. Inside Serbia, Milošević declared victory. Though his version defied facts by depicting Serbs as victims of a worldwide conspiracy and U.S. President Bill Clinton as another Hitler, Milošević gained popularity in Serbia after the war. Instead of weakening him, the NATO campaign had the adverse result of mobilizing more Serbs, who cast themselves as patriots defending their country against a foreign invasion.

Toward a Precarious Peace The massive abuses in Kosovo ended, though instances of ethnic hatred have erupted periodically since 1999. The area's stability still depends on the continued presence of UN troops. Kosovo declared independence in 2008 and has been recognized as an autonomous state by 76 states (22 of the 27 EU members among

> **Kosovo War** (March–June 1999) Military conflict between NATO forces and Serbia over abuses against Kosovo Albanians.

In October 2002, Slobodan Milošević was brought down by a popular street uprising in which young people and Internet communication played an important role. Serbia has struggled since then to fashion an international image of a viable democracy. How does this image compare to the collapse of the Berlin Wall (p. 879) and fall of the communist regime in Moscow (p. 903)?

Darko Dozet/AP Images

them). Serbia still considers it officially part of its territory, yet Belgrade has virtually no say in internal affairs. Most refugees (eight hundred thousand) returned, and autonomous government institutions were set up to represent the Albanian population.

The Kosovo War did not bring down Milošević, but in October 2002 a popular revolt, with street protests all over Belgrade, removed him from power. His replacement was Vojislav Koštunica, a constitutional lawyer with strong Serbian nationalist credentials and a more internationally acceptable reputation. The Milošević regime was brought down by its own massive corruption, the impoverishment of the population, general fatigue after a decade of fighting, and the growing sense that their country had become an outcast in Europe.

Postcommunist Transitions in Eastern Europe

The transformation of the other eastern European countries from members of the communist bloc to members of the European international community has been more successful. They have developed constitutional, pluralist governments, with free elections, multiple parties, freedom of the press, and a free-market economy. But each has had specific problems to deal with, and their solutions have differed widely.

The Peaceful Dismemberment of Czechoslovakia Like Yugoslavia, Czechoslovakia was created after World War I. And like Yugoslavia, Czechoslovakia was dismembered in the early postcommunist years under the weight of nationalist pressures. But rather than starting a civil war, the Czechs and Slovaks went their separate ways on the basis of national referenda. At the end of 1992, the population simply voted to split up the country into two republics. Václav Havel, the playwright president, oversaw this peaceful democratic process and accepted its outcome. The important difference between Yugoslavia and Czechoslovakia was that the political leadership of the latter refused to pursue a violent path even though nationalist enmities existed. Instead, leaders trusted the newly developed democratic institutions, even when these institutions turned them out of power.

Nationalism Returns to Eastern Europe Hungary also embraced democratic politics, but with a stronger nationalist element. Some popular politicians of the 1990s openly espoused antisemitism and pushed for special protection for ethnic Hungarians living in other countries. Yet such ethnocentric issues did not play any role in the economic policies pursued by either center-right or left-wing governments. Overall, Hungary was successful in maintaining a talented labor force, attracting foreign investments, and improving the quality of life of its citizens.

Poland saw the return and then departure of Solidarity leader Lech Wałęsa. In 1980, Wałęsa had been a charismatic unifier of opponents to communism, but after 1989 he was ill prepared to assume the responsibilities of governing a democratic regime. He had neither the vision nor the skills to offer good solutions to the challenges of privatization and to the increasing activism of the Catholic Church. Still, though Solidarity lost its initial appeal, it did give rise to numerous other parties and provided the groundwork for a generation of democratic politicians. Poland was also fortunate in that it proceeded quickly with privatization and implemented tough reforms that brought healthy economic growth by the end of the decade.

In social and cultural policies, however, Poland seemed to cling strongly to the past. Having been a main force of opposition under communism, the Catholic Church, with the direct support of Pope John Paul II, proceeded to create its own political following. The church cultivated socially conservative politicians who wanted to make abortion illegal and advocated Catholic "family values," pursuing anti-gay propaganda campaigns. The public presence of the church grew, from television programs to educational institutions. Still, though many in Poland see the Catholic Church as a privileged institution, it coexists alongside secular social and cultural organizations that pursue their own agendas and values.

The Visegrád Four and European Integration The Czech Republic, Slovakia, Hungary, and Poland thus implemented democratic reforms and successfully managed antidemocratic forces. They were also the first to engage successfully in regional cooperation. Coming together as the **Visegrád Four** in 1991, they agreed to coordinate internal reforms from education to the environment, with the goal of joining the EU. By building regional trade, the four countries turned their communist economies into competitive capitalist ones. Key to their success were three factors: agreement among the political leadership, public support, and economic and administrative infrastructures that were compatible with reform. In addition, long-standing personal links forged in the communist era among the underground oppositions in Poland, Czechosolvakia, and to some extent Hungary fostered institutional cooperation. Moreover, both the EU and the United States regarded the economies of these four countries as the most advanced of the former communist states and invested in them both political hopes and financial resources.

The Baltics Look West Latvia, Lithuania, and Estonia traveled a different road from direct Soviet control to successful democratization. In these Baltic countries, the legacies of communist politics and state economies were more difficult to undo. In Estonia, where a large ethnic Russian population had been brought in, the ethnic antagonism between the two groups ran deep, especially since positions of power had been occupied overwhelmingly by Russians. While Latvians found it relatively easy to tolerate the presence of the Russians without any fears of further russification, the Estonians (and to some extent the Lithuanians) saw ethnic Russians as agents of imperialism even after the dissolution of the Soviet Union. Indeed, Russia remained vocally concerned about the large Russian minority in Estonia but had little power to act on its behalf. Under the influence of growing nationalism, the Estonians have implemented some policies to diminish the public presence of the Russian minority, such as mandating a majority of classroom hours in Estonian, even in towns where only ethnic Russians live. Overall, however, with unemployment relatively low and new economic opportunities opening up, the people of the Baltic states remained relatively content in the 1990s. All three countries have stable democracies.

Slow Reform in Romania and Bulgaria Romania and Bulgaria, however, failed to become fully functioning democracies. They did hold free elections in which a multitude of parties competed. But these parties were closer to the kinds of factions that developed

in Russia under Yeltsin, led by old Communist Party activists and interested in protecting narrow interests. Political corruption continued to dominate the electoral process, with few checks and balances. Corrupt judges protected corrupt legislators, and local law enforcement agencies worked with administrators to protect each other's interests.

In Romania, Ion Iliescu, a disgruntled protégé of Nicolae Ceauşescu, won the first presidential election and then proceeded to win again after a four-year interregnum by a more reform-minded coalition. Most successful Romanian politicians of this decade espoused some form of nationalism, from mild to radical. There was a short revival of a neofascist party, and one openly antisemitic and anti-Hungarian party won 20 percent of the vote in the 2000 presidential elections.

Romania's most debilitating problem was that no government in the 1990s pursued a thorough policy of privatizing large state enterprises and encouraging investments in competitive new businesses. Instead, political clients won investment bids through bribery and squandered many of the state and private resources for personal gain. Foreign investment was also discouraged by Romania's inability to protect private property. By 2000, the Romanian economy lagged behind that of every country in Europe save Albania.

Bulgaria fared marginally better. Though plagued by political corruption, its service and tourism industries outperformed those in Romania. Nor did nationalism play a strong rallying role, although small Muslim enclaves remained relatively impoverished and received inadequate support from the government. The country was also relatively less affected by organized crime than Romania and Russia, whose economies were sapped of important revenue resources by these criminal organizations.

Overall, economic growth in Romania and Bulgaria has been impeded by the harsh political and economic legacies of the communist period as well as a lack of investment incentives or interest from western countries. By the time these regimes achieved internal political stability, curbed corruption, and created legislation friendly to foreign investment, the initial enthusiasm of the West to invest in the postcommunist countries had vanished.

> **Visegrád Four** Group formed in the early 1990s by Hungary, Poland, the Czech Republic, and Slovakia to coordinate internal reforms toward joining the EU.

 Checking In

By yourself or with a partner, explain the significance of each of the following selected key terms:

World Bank	Slobodan Milošević
International Monetary Fund	Dayton Agreement
Chechnya	Kosovo War
Vladimir Putin	Visegrád Four

European Integration

◆ How has the EU transformed European politics and economies?

◆ What impact has the EU had on European security matters?

Due to these remarkable changes among the post-communist states, eastern Europe both transformed and was transformed by the European Union. With the Soviet threat removed, western Europe perceived the future differently. The former communist countries became participants in a larger framework of European integration. This process of challenging established divisions and offering new ways of connecting European states and people created unprecedented opportunities to redefine Europe as a political, economic, and cultural community. In the 1990s the Common Market underwent important institutional changes, from a loose economic union to a fiscal unit, a political institution, and a cluster of cultural and social institutions that are today truly multinational and reach into every corner of the continent. Europeans tackled international security challenges on the basis of cooperation. Yet, internal political contests and nationalism continued to test the boundaries of international collaboration. Table 30.2 summarizes the development of the European Union.

From Community to Union

After 1985, when **Jacques Delors** became the president of the **European Commission**, the highest executive authority of the Common Market, the European Community embarked more forcefully on a plan to create a single-market entity. Delors and other euro enthusiasts pointed to the outstanding track record of the participating countries since the inception of the Common Market in terms of economic growth, employment, and per capita income, suggesting that greater institutional cooperation among member countries would increasingly benefit them.

The growing complexity of economic activities since the 1970s also suggested that greater political cooperation would be needed to sustain the well-being of member countries. To enable the workforce to move across borders in order to effectively match skills and needs, states would have to work out better policies regarding migration, labor rights, and social welfare policies. Closer coordination of taxation, interest rates, and other fiscal measures would also help businesses operate across borders. For

Jacques Delors (1925–) French Socialist politician and president of the European Commission from 1985 to 1994 who promoted the creation of the EU.

European Commission Executive branch of the EU, responsible for drafting legislation and enforcing regulations.

Table 30.2 Development of the European Union

1951	European Coal and Steel Community (ECSC) is established
1957	Treaty of Rome establishes the European Economic Community (EEC), made up of Belgium, France, Italy, Luxembourg, the Netherlands, and West Germany
1973	Britain, Denmark, and Ireland join the EEC
1981	Greece joins the EEC
1985	Portugal and Spain join the EEC
1992	Maastricht treaty creates the European Union (EU); European Economic Community is renamed the European Community (EC) as part of the EU
1995	Austria, Finland, and Sweden join the EU; Schengen Agreement goes into effect
2002	The euro becomes EU currency
2003	First EU constitution is drafted
2004	Cyprus, the Czech Republic, Estonia, Hungary, Latvia, Lithuania, Malta, Poland, Slovenia, and Slovakia join the EU
2007	Bulgaria and Romania join the EU
2009	Slovakia becomes the sixteenth member of the Eurozone; Lisbon Treaty is ratified by all members
2010– 2012	Financial bailout of Greece by the EU, IMF, and World Bank

© Cengage Learning

example, for an enterprise such as Airbus, with capital and profits in France, to expand its operations outside of France meant depending on the willingness of Spain and Britain to protect its business interests and accept its practices. Since the inception of the Common Market, such arrangements had developed through bilateral agreements. By the 1980s, many believed that an international political institution would improve cooperation and serve the interests of both employers and employees.

Obstacles and Opposition The unification of institutions and standardization of economic regulations, from taxation to the labeling of agricultural products, was to take place between 1985 and 1992. The process of ratification was cumbersome, for the national governments of Common Market members had to individually ratify all changes. This arrangement respected the sovereignty of each member state but rendered the process vulnerable to political change in any member country.

At the beginning there was a great deal of enthusiasm for the idea of a single market, increased opportunities for investment, and the unrestricted movement of workers and goods across borders. But by 1990 the enthusiasm was largely gone, as politicians, corporations, and consumers began to see that regulations meant to free up access to markets and goods also had a restrictive impact. For instance, agricultural producers were to test, package, and label their goods in accordance with new Common Market regulations. Smaller organic farmers suffered in the process because their costs of production and shipping increased significantly. If they passed these costs on to consumers through higher prices, they would make themselves less competitive than multinational corporations, such as McDonald's, which could produce certified genetically modified products more cheaply.

Monetary Unification At a series of intergovernmental meetings in 1991, member countries addressed such issues. Achieving a European Monetary Union demanded a complex plan of coordinating fiscal policies among members. And since such a massive fiscal restructuring had never before been attempted, policy makers and ordinary people alike worried about potential negative consequences. A policy of moving to one single currency, the **euro (€)**, was outlined, with the ultimate goal of having one European Bank and the euro in circulation by 1999. That change actually occurred in 2002.

Political Cooperation Sovereignty In addition, the question of political integration raised nationalist fears about the expanded powers of the European Commission and European Parliament at the expense of national governments. The formula of a loose federation was worked out by the end of 1991. No one country could dominate either of these bodies. Additionally, any legislative measures by the European Parliament would have to be approved by a broad international margin, and the most important measures, such as a European constitution, would have to be ratified by each member. Furthermore, the European Parliament would have the power to check the executive powers of the European Commission.

Another thorny issue was the growth of the German share of the Common Market, especially with the unification of the two Germanies in 1990. Suddenly, this country counted for a quarter of the total population and 27 percent of the European Community's production. Concerns that a strong and ambitious Germany might again threaten the stability of Europe were allayed only when well-respected politicians, in particular French President François Mitterrand and German Chancellor Helmut Kohl, pursued a campaign for European integration: "We consider it necessary to accelerate the political construction of the Europe of the Twelve. We believe that it is time to transform relations as a whole among the member states into a European Union … and invest this union with the necessary means of action."

Free Movement Across Borders The idea of free movement of people across borders became vastly more complicated with the opening of borders in eastern Europe after the fall of communism and the incoming flood of eastern Europeans. A unified EU policy on immigration actually reconstructed the East-West divide. In 1995, most EU members (save Ireland, Britain, and Denmark) began implementing the **Schengen Agreement**, which eliminated the need for citizens of signatory states to obtain visas to travel and work inside the Schengen space. Citizens of most other countries still had to apply for entry, but once they obtained a visa from one of the signatory states, they could travel without additional visas elsewhere in the Schengen space. In practice, it became more difficult for most people outside the Schengen territory to obtain work or permanent residence visas in any of the signatory countries, but it was easier to obtain travel visas. For people from postcommunist eastern Europe, still having to apply for a visa was a humiliating reminder of their outsider status in Europe.

Birth of the EU In February 1992, the Common Market foreign ministers signed the **Maastricht treaty**, which created the European Union, the most important milestone toward European integration since the creation of the European Coal and Steel Community in 1951. Although it was expected that member countries would ratify the treaty without much resistance, there was opposition in Denmark and Britain, where politicians and the populace at large preferred national policies in certain crucial areas. In Britain, the Conservatives retained the policy of deregulating industries and upholding the strength of the pound. In Denmark, the vote went narrowly against the treaty in order to retain environmental and other public policy standards higher than those of the EU; the Danes also feared German domination. In both cases, however, opposition stemmed less from nationalist pride and anxieties than from concern about specific economic and social policies. After a year of negotiations with both countries, the Maastricht treaty went into effect in November 1993 and the European Union came into being.

The European Union in Operation

The EU consists of a set of existing institutions, now with expanded powers, as well as some new bodies.

Executive Powers The highest executive body is the

euro (€) Currency introduced in most EU member countries starting in 2002.

Schengen Agreement Treaty signed by seven members of the Common Market in 1985 allowing the free passage of people and goods across their borders, which went into effect in 1995.

Maastricht treaty Treaty signed in 1992 and ratified by all members of the Common Market in 1993 that brought the EU into being.

European Council, composed of heads of state or government and the president of the European Commission. Since 1993, the European Council has met several times a year to discuss issues of interest at the national and international level and on occasion to iron out tensions among member states. This body does not deal with the specific implementation of day-to-day measures passed by the European Parliament but only with broad issues, such as the balance between national political autonomy and international cooperation.

The **Council of Ministers** is charged with implementing EU goals on a practical level. A cross between an executive and legislative body, the Council of Ministers attempts to find a balance in unifying everything from energy to taxation policies so as not to run counter to national prerogatives and to maintain cooperation. For instance, the use of nuclear power for the energy needs of a particular state has to be reconciled with the environmental regulations of the EU as a whole.

The European Commission, whose president also sits on the European Council, also mediates between national and EU interests but works solely as an elected body of the EU. Before 1993, the European Commission was the primary initiator of legislation and also served as the executive power in dealing with the Council of Ministers and the European Council. After 1993, the European Commission lost some of its legislative authority to the European Parliament, especially in matters of the EU budget. The EU Parliament has also helped restrain the executive powers of the European Commission, especially those of its president.

Legislative Powers The development of the **European Parliament** from a symbolic body to a legislative assembly with EU-wide powers from taxation to education is one of the most important political developments in Europe since Maastricht, and it has started to reshape European political parties at large. The number of seats assigned to each country varies but is not strictly proportional, so smaller countries have disproportionate influence. Thus, these smaller countries can form coalitions to block passage of laws they view as harmful to their interests. Yet representatives in the European Parliament tend to act not only according to their national flags but also according to their ideological platforms, and the body divides more consistently along ideological than national lines. Thus French delegates are as likely to be at odds with each other over environmental concerns, such as the use of genetically modified organisms in agriculture, as they are to be at odds with their German colleagues. Delegates who are members of Green parties, for example, tend to vote as an international bloc on environmental matters, regardless of what other representatives from their home countries think.

Expanding the Union In the 1990s, the EU began to consider the question of enlargement to include countries from the former communist bloc. This issue was first broached in 1990, after German reunification, when the political and economic legacies of communism were assumed directly by West Germany, which was already the strongest economy in the Common Market. When the Visegrád Four began to lobby for admission, the EU had to consider the impact of such a change on its economic strength and also the very criteria for admission. Greece, Portugal, and Spain had all been accepted as members in the 1980s on the premise that they had potential for democratic politics rather than a proven record. Yet to many EU leaders, the admission of Greece, because of its weak economy in the 1980s, set an unfortunate precedent. Still, some members, such as France, Germany, and Italy, supported the notion of rewarding the stable postcommunist democracies with EU membership. Supporters of enlargement eastward also pointed to the potential larger markets and increased stability in Europe as advantages for the EU. Ultimately, market expansion and European stability became the criteria for enlargement in the next phase. Yet how these criteria were applied in some cases raised questions. For instance, many argued that having Estonia, Latvia, and Lithuania, with their sizable Russian minorities, in the EU would, in fact, create new tensions between the EU and Russia, reducing European stability.

By February 2003, eight of the postcommunist countries (the Czech Republic, Estonia, Hungary, Latvia, Lithuania, Poland, Slovakia, and Slovenia) had finally been accepted into the union, along with two other applicants (Cyprus and Malta), bringing the number of member states to twenty-five. In January 2007, these ten countries were joined by two additional postcommunist states, Romania and Bulgaria. The success or failure of this larger union remains to be seen, especially with the euro becoming the new currency in three of these states (Estonia, Slovakia, and Slovenia). But several issues will continue to be of concern. The larger union means a larger bureaucracy. If all the existing rules regarding governance, balance of power between the Commission and the Parliament, and representation of all languages in the running of the EU are to be maintained, the daily activities of EU institutions are likely to become more expensive and more cumbersome.

The EU Constitution and the Lisbon Treaty With so many new members in the EU, discussions about changing its legal framework resulted in a new constitution, which was initially signed in October 2004 but had to be ratified by each member state before

European Council EU advisory body composed of the heads of state or government of member countries and the president of the European Commission.

Council of Ministers Main legislative body of the EU, composed of ministers from each country, that carries out EU goals in legal measures and policymaking.

European Parliament The directly elected parliamentary body of the European Union.

The European Parliament has the power to vote (as we see it exercised in this image) on important policies that affect the people, economies, and political institutions of all member countries. What does this photo suggest about the size of the EU Parliament? What does the image suggest about the level of participation of its elected members?

going into effect. In 2005 France and the Netherlands failed to ratify it, bringing the process to an impasse. Discussion resumed through a series of negotiations among member states and resulted in the **Lisbon Treaty**, which was ratified by all members and went into effect in December 2009. The treaty fundamentally altered the executive and legislative powers of the EU, generally making individual members and their citizens accountable to new fiscal, judicial, and human rights standards. Individual citizens are now able to hold their national governments to higher standards in terms of human rights, from gender and sexuality issues to racial discrimination. (These same human rights provisions have brought about a backlash against the EU from nationalist parties.) The Lisbon Treaty has made it possible to demand greater fiscal accountability from individual members, a change that has played a major role in Europe's recovery during the current economic crisis.

Nation-States in a New Context

The EU has not meant European unity, even among the older member countries. Between the early 1990s and the late 2000s, in Britain, Germany, and Spain, right-wing governments were replaced by left-wing ones, though not necessarily for the same reasons.

Leftist Coalitions In Britain in 1997, the Labour Party returned to power with **Tony Blair** as prime minister when the public reacted against the Conservative government's aggressive policies of privatizing national industries and reducing social programs.

Blair pursued business-friendly internal policies and a commitment to the EU. To Conservative skepticism about the impact of the EU on the British pound and industries, Blair responded with enthusiasm for the EU's social and political components. Still, he was careful to continue his support for the pound, even as the rest of the EU was adopting the euro.

The shift toward the left in Germany was both a product of EU integration and the condition for it. Helmut Kohl was a central player in promoting Maastricht and EU enlargement, but he faced problems at home connected to reunification, including fluctuating unemployment, the democratization and privatization of the former East Germany, and important disparities in the standard of living. The socially conservative chancellor lost some of his popularity during this period, as voters in both parts of reunified Germany began to identify the Christian Democrats with the economic and social problems of reunification.

As a result, the Social Democrats came to power in 1998, with the younger **Gerhard Schroeder** as the first German chancellor to have grown up after the war and also the first to rule

Lisbon Treaty Treaty signed by all EU members in 2007 that became the new constitution of the union in 2009; it gives the EU additional legislative, executive, and judicial powers, including protection of individual citizens against human rights abuses by national governments.

Tony Blair (1953–) Labour Party prime minister of Britain from 1997 to 2007, credited with creating a more centrist position for the British left.

Gerhard Schroeder (1944–) Social Democratic chancellor of Germany from 1998 to 2005 who led a coalition government with the Greens.

in a coalition with the Greens. Schroeder was a disappointment to the more left-leaning Social Democrats and the Greens, as he increased German military involvement in NATO and was unable to reduce unemployment. Still, he secured a second term in 2002. Among his important achievements were the lowering of taxes, preservation of government funding for education, and recognition of homosexual civil unions.

In Spain, a centrist government dominated politics after 1996, overseeing the country's full integration into the EU and a healthy economic growth since 2000. But it lost popularity by 2004 because of Spain's active role in the **Iraq War**. After **al-Qaeda** engineered a series of bombings in Madrid in March of that year, killing and injuring hundreds of people, the Socialist Workers' Party under the leadership of **José Luis Rodríguez Zapatero** won a close victory. From a staunchly Catholic conservative country under Francisco Franco, Spain has become a leader in political reforms that surpass the most ambitious EU civil rights policies. In 2005, the Socialist Workers' Party government passed a law that recognizes same-sex marriages and engineered a reconciliation with terrorist Basque separatist groups. Re-elected in 2008, Zapatero struggled to reform taxation, social welfare, and various fiscal policies to enable Spain to return to fiscal solvency.

Iraq War War begun in March 2003 when a U.S.-led coalition overthrew Iraqi President Saddam Hussein in an attempt to establish a new, democratic regime.

al-Qaeda Islamic terrorist organization established by Saudi Arabs in 1988 to fight against the Soviet Union in Afghanistan.

José Luis Rodríguez Zapatero (1960–) Socialist democrat politician who served as prime minister of Spain for two terms (2004–2012), overseeing government reforms in response to the economic crisis, the eruption of terrorist al-Qaeda attacks, and reconciliation with the Basque separatists.

Jacques Chirac (1932–) French president from 1995 to 2007, leader of the center-right party Rally for the Republic and outspoken critic of American policy in Iraq.

Nicholas Sarkozy (1955–) President of the French Republic (2007–2012), leads a center-right government that attempted to deregulate government control in the economy and limit the powers of the presidency while enhancing those of the Parliament.

Center-Right Governments

By contrast, in France and Italy left-wing governments gave way to center-right ones. In France, **Jacques Chirac**, the leader of the center-right party, Rally for the Republic, won the presidential election in 1995 in a close contest with the socialists. Chirac had built a strong career as a successor of the Gaullist tradition since the 1970s, and after several unsuccessful bids, he emerged as president in the middle of a decade of slow economic growth and high unemployment. Despite his promise of opposing further EU integration, he became an advocate of the euro. Though he was implicated in several high-level corruption scandals, he managed to distance himself from former close

Paul White/AP Images

In March 2004, a series of related bombings on commuter trains in Madrid killed 191 and wounded more than 2,050 people. The heavily used commuter system of the Spanish capital came to a standstill. Though horrified by these events, Spanish politicians and the Spanish public only grew increasingly critical of U.S. President George W. Bush's so-called War on Terror. How would you describe the scene in this attack?

allies who were prosecuted. Chirac also maintained his popularity in France because of his staunchly anti-American position on the Iraq War.

In 2007, the center-right **Nicholas Sarkozy**, who proved tough on Muslim rioters two years earlier as Minister of the Interior, won a resounding victory as Chirac's successor. Sarkozy has made a mark for himself through critical views of EU expansion, especially regarding Turkey, and through his pro-American stance, which sets him apart from his predecessor. More recently, he has been criticized by both the left and the right in France, the former for racist remarks and actions against Muslim and Roma immigrants, and the latter for his inconsistency in terms of government deregulation of economic life. In the 2012 elections, Sarkozy lost to Francois Hollande, the Socialist candidate.

Between 2001 and 2006, Italian politics were likewise dominated by a center-right government led by

Silvio Berlusconi, a media mogul turned politician. Having made millions of dollars in the entertainment industry, especially television, in the 1990s Berlusconi developed a party devoted to defeating the communists with a nationalist, business-friendly platform. Like Chirac, Berlusconi was involved in several high-profile corruption scandals that eventually led to his resignation in 2011.

Stability and Power: Putin's Russia A nationalist authoritarian mood has been growing in Russia since 2000, when Vladimir Putin assumed the presidency. Chosen by Yeltsin as acting president in 1999, Putin easily won election in 2000 and then re-election in 2004. Putin was able to retain his position of power in the center of Russian politics by winning the office of prime minister in 2008, when Dmitri Medvedev, at that time prime minister, was elected president. In 2012, Putin outmaneuvered a strong street opposition movement to wing the presidency for another term.

Many outside were puzzled by the broad popularity of an ex-agent of the KGB. But Putin seemed to embody qualities much in demand as Russia's economic and political stability floundered. His healthy lifestyle and personal self-restraint were a powerful contrast to Yeltsin's hedonistic outbursts. Even more important, his devotion to Orthodox Christianity bolstered his popularity in Russia, where church attendance has been growing.

Even those who are not particularly religious have embraced Putin's style as embodying Russian national aspirations. Whether dealing with foreign crises, the military, terrorism, or corruption in politics and the economy, Putin has placed his actions in the context of Russia's need to maintain its international standing as a powerful state. He has reasserted the legitimacy of Russian interference in the affairs of independent ex-Soviet states, such as Georgia and Ukraine, where Russia openly supported the pro-Russian presidential candidate in 2004. Such measures have led ethnic Russians to consider Putin their defender and a strong leader, even when his policies do not serve the immediate economic and social needs of the majority of Russian citizens. While nationalist sentiments continue to be a strong force in Russia, recently many voters have come to see his party as corrupt and removed from the needs of average Russians.

Authoritarian tendencies of the Putin regime have become most apparent in the media. Freedom of the press has been rolled back through intimidation, government control of important outlets, and the elimination of political opponents. A number of journalists have been assassinated in the past decade, and the state has been slow to investigate these murders and begin trials of those accused in the respective cases. Likewise, foreign nationals have had increasing difficulties traveling, conducting business, or doing research in Russia.

Alexander Zemlianichenko/Pool/Reuters/Corbis

Though a faithful employee of the Soviet secret police, the KGB, and of a state that believed religion was an opiate of the masses, Vladimir Putin has become an open supporter of the Orthodox Church, an institution fundamentally linked to Russian culture and identity. What power does the Patriarch seem to have, as seen in this photograph from Putin's inauguration as president in Moscow in 2001?

Euroskeptics and Right-Wing Electoral Victories
By 2004, the rightward shifts in some national elections combined with some negative reactions to the effects of EU integration produced a general shift to the right in the European Parliament elections, in which various right-wing parties and coalitions garnered more than 60 percent of the vote. Almost one-quarter of these representatives were outright opponents of the EU. Yet the financial troubles that have plagued individual EU economies since then resulted in very different electoral results by 2009, when right-wing parties and euroskeptics counted for less than 12 percent of

Silvio Berlusconi (1936–) Television mogul, leader of a center-right coalition, and prime minister of Italy (2001–2006 and 2008–2011).

Angela Merkel Completes Unification

In 1989, when Germany was searching for a new identity and path in Europe, nobody in the East or West would have predicted that by 2009 the daughter of a Lutheran Pastor from East Germany would become the most powerful woman in the world, according to *Forbes* magazine. How Angela Merkel rose from her station in life to this remarkable position of power illustrates the important opportunities that opened up for many in Europe after the end of the cold war, and suggests the boundless possibilities for change on the continent in the future, both internally and globally.

Merkel was born Angela Dorothea Kasner in Hamburg (then West Germany) in 1954. Her father was a Lutheran pastor and her mother a member of the Social Democratic Party. When she was a few months old, her father was called to head a parish in East Germany, so Merkel grew up under the communist regime. She was extremely gifted in the sciences and went on to obtain a doctorate in physics in 1978 and later worked as a researcher at the Central Institute for Physical Chemistry of the Academy of Sciences in East Berlin. She only became interested in political issues in 1989 as part of the "Democratic Awakening," when pro-democracy street protests took place in many East German cities in the months before the fall of the Berlin Wall. As a spokeswoman for this movement and for the speedy reunification of Germany, she was elected to Parliament in the first East German free elections in 1990, and subsequently joined the Christian Democratic Union (CDU).

She slowly rose through the ranks of that party, which dominated the process of reunification under then Chancellor Helmut Kohl. When he was ousted from party leadership because of murky financial dealings, Merkel was elected the first chairwoman of the CDU. Merkel was unusual in many regards: she was the first woman to lead the party, as well as the first non-Catholic to do so, and the first politician from the former communist regime. For a party that stood for family values, as a divorcee without children she also hardly fit the ideal German woman. She was also the first person with such an outstanding academic background. In fact, it is likely that her impeccable academic credentials, together with her reputation for hard work and personal integrity, enabled her to overcome any questions of inadequacy that other elements of her biography might have invited.

From 2000 on she ably rebuilt the reputation of the CDU and won the 2005 elections, becoming the first woman top political officer in the history of Germany. Due to her rising popularity, she was re-elected by a wide majority in 2009. Merkel was one of the main architects and an active lobbyist for the Treaty of Lisbon, pressuring some of the less enthusiastic EU members to sign on. In this regard, she also played an important role as a unifier. As chancellor of the strongest economic power in the EU during a period of global recession, Merkel has successfully brought Germany to a position of strong economic growth and fiscal solvency. Under her leadership, Germany has come to embody a balance of pro-business and pro-welfare policies that, combined with fiscal self-restraint in terms of government spending and debt accumulation, have established new standards for all EU members.

---

the vote. Debates over the EU's future are guaranteed to remain wide-ranging, from questions about enlargement to specific economic, social, and cultural policies.

In addition, in internal elections center-right parties and euroskeptics have been on the rise again, east and west, scoring important victories in the national parliaments of the member states. Elections since 2005 have brought to power the Conservatives in Britain under David Cameron, and the Christian Democrats in Germany under the leadership of the first East German and first woman chancellor, **Angela Merkel**. In Hungary and Slovakia, in 2010, center-right governments were elected after the social-democratic governments in those countries failed to address the onset of the economic crisis of the late 2000s.

European Security and International Organizations

The EU has successfully met the political challenges of the post–cold war period, but it has been less effective in international security matters, where the changing roles of the UN and NATO have also intruded on European states' potential for representing their interests as a bloc. Though the UN had been influential in the postcolonial world in security matters and had tried to mediate between the two superpowers and other states, it had not played an important security role in Europe. The ethnic-cleansing atrocities and utter internal chaos of the

Angela Merkel (1954–) Leader of the Christian Democratic party in Germany, the first woman and also first East German to be elected chancellor (2005–).

Yugoslav civil wars, however, convinced the UN to send a peacekeeping force. EU members generally supported this idea, and British, French, and Italian troops figured prominently among peacekeepers. The UN intervention was framed not in terms of countering threats to European security but rather as a globally significant means of halting human rights abuses. Thus the EU remained marginal in decision making.

NATO's Military Role in Europe The ineffectiveness of UN troops forced the international community to consider more drastic measures, and NATO stepped in to oversee a military intervention against the rebel Serbs in Bosnia. Traditionally, NATO had focused on securing western Europe against threats from the communist East. In the 1990s, however, it transformed itself, partly through this intervention, into a broader alliance to secure democratic Europe, east and west, against external or internal threats. Russia, no longer the main enemy, played a sometimes friendly, if passive, role. Though aligned with Milošević, it never challenged NATO militarily.

As part of its expanded mandate of preserving security and democracy in Europe, NATO also embarked upon a process of eastward enlargement, building **Partnerships for Peace** with postcommunist countries as a bridge toward their full membership in the alliance. Partnerships with thirty countries allowed for increased cooperation in matters of military training, ground operations, and logistical links for future strategy planning. NATO requirements forced reforms, including civilian leadership at the top of the armed services administration and increased expenditures on armaments, equipment, and personnel. In 1996, the Czech Republic, Poland, and Hungary were admitted to NATO, paving the way for admission of most other postcommunist eastern European states in the next decade. Thus, NATO became the broadest military alliance representing the security interests of Europe.

The U.S. and European Security The U.S. role in NATO remained central, however, as its largest and most important funding and armament source. Some European states, such as France, urged a more European-centered framework for solving international conflicts on the continent, but most others, especially the postcommunist countries of eastern Europe, were happy to have American troops and military support in their countries, as they were still concerned about Russia's interests in the area. The Kosovo War became the first test of the new members' and partners' commitment to upholding their military obligations, and Poles, Czechs, and Romanians all gave significant help. Since 2000, however, the operations of NATO in Europe have remained minimal, limited to peacekeeping in Serbia, while

the bulk of operations have shifted to the Middle East and Central Asia.

 Checking In

By yourself or with a partner, explain the significance of each of the following selected key terms:

Schengen Agreement	Iraq War
Maastricht treaty	al-Qaeda
Lisbon Treaty	Angela Merkel
Tony Blair	Partnerships for Peace

Europe and Globalization

◆ **How has globalization transformed the economic power of Europe in the world?**

◆ **What have been the great international challenges since 1991?**

Since the early 1990s, a combination of technological, political, and market forces have transformed the world economy into a dynamic, close-knit web of processes. The growth of the EU played a central part in this change, securing Europe a privileged role in globalization. As the speed of global communication has increased, Europeans have become increasingly involved in world affairs and culture while non-Europeans have remained interested in Europe. But the international security problems that emerged after the cold war have been challenging, and Europeans have often been divided over crises in the Middle East and international terrorism.

Economic Globalization

In the 1990s, economic production and trade became more closely interwoven on an unprecedented global scale, owing to several developments. New technologies, such as accurate and instant communication of information, computerized assembly lines, and new types of large trucks and refrigerated crates, made it easier to produce and transport more goods anywhere from the United States to Taiwan. Support for free trade among the most powerful countries in the world facilitated the exchange of goods across borders. An already high standard of living in the developed countries meant that people expected access to cheap consumer goods. To feed this process, many American and European businesses, such as Unilever, started to look for production sites with low costs, loose labor and environmental protections, and high product quality. Postcommunist eastern Europe fit this profile, as did China,

Partnerships for Peace NATO project to increase cooperation in military matters between its members and postcommunist states.

Vietnam, and other places in the developing world. Evian and Nissan production facilities sprouted from Hungary to Taiwan.

New International Structures and Economic Power The most important institutional supporter of globalization has been the **World Trade Organization (WTO)**, created in 1995 to oversee the **General Agreement on Tariffs and Trade (GATT)**. First signed in 1947, this agreement encouraged free trade in order to generate economic prosperity in the early postwar years. There was no institution to oversee the agreement, which remained loosely enforced by individual countries. For instance, the countries of the Common Market abided by GATT, but countries in eastern Europe and Latin America were less inclined to allow cheaper western goods to be introduced in their markets. Instead, most developing countries pursued policies that protected internal production so as to reduce their dependency on imports. Equally important were the ideological considerations of countries like China, which feared that the impact of western goods might destabilize communism.

But with the end of the cold war, many of these considerations became obsolete. Beginning in 1995, the WTO has allowed countries to become members on the basis of stable trade policies and stable governments. The 149 member countries benefit from reduced tariffs, preferential trade agreements, and access to international loans through connections with the International Monetary Fund (IMF) and the World Bank. Entry into this group and policymaking are both accomplished through consensus, not majority vote, an arrangement that has tended to give the wealthiest economies greater power than members with weaker economies. It has also facilitated the operation of large multinational corporations in foreign markets, to the detriment of small producers everywhere, especially in less developed countries. And since most multinational corporations are still overwhelmingly controlled by investors in the United States, western Europe, and Japan, the WTO has enhanced the economic power of these areas at the expense of the rest of the world.

EU's Economic Competitiveness Individually, European countries and corporations might have been at a disadvantage against the greater economic power of the United States or, more recently, China and Russia. But the EU framework has enhanced their competitiveness in the scramble for new markets and cheap labor in the developing world. In the early 1990s, the markets in eastern Europe were flooded with chickens from the Netherlands, milk from Italy, and shoes from Spain. These products were often partially manufactured in eastern Europe, but still under western brand names. The flow of goods was overwhelmingly west to east for the first decade after 1989. But western producers have now set up shop in many eastern European locations and are beginning to ship their goods, for example, from Budapest to Paris. For the postcommunist countries now in the EU, this process has reached near-parity, with the new members having achieved greater buying and production power. The EU has also used members' links with former colonies, forging strong relations with developing economies from Indonesia to Nigeria. British Petroleum, for example, is working in South Korea to develop technologies that will be used in Cameroon and Nigeria to extract oil and natural gas.

The Global Economic Recession The spectacular growth of interdependency in economic processes, from foreign trade to stock trade, prices, and availability of capital, bore bitter fruit in the second half of the 2000s. The collapse of several important banks and international companies, due initially to the deregulation of the mortgage industry, has led to a worldwide recession that has affected entire countries, private individuals, and multinational corporations alike. Iceland became the first such victim in 2008, when three of its main banks folded and the currency collapsed. The severe problems faced by its economy became a warning for the EU, which has recently assumed a more aggressive role in terms of limiting access to loans and other financial assistance to other members, such as Greece, Portugal, and Spain. Countries facing major debt and currency devaluation have been pressured to drastically reduce welfare programs and establish new banking and business regulations to prevent future disasters for the EU.

Multinationals based in the EU have generally done better, given the continuing strength of the euro, though individual citizens have fared worse, with rising taxes, decreasing salaries, and vanishing benefits. Some countries, such as Germany, have managed to retain more of their social welfare programs and even see some economic growth. By and large, however, the possibility to predict future economic problems in the EU remains limited, given the linkages of all aspects of European economies with markets and resources that are well beyond the control of the EU.

Antiglobalization Activism Producers have successfully used the WTO and other international organizations like the IMF to secure business interests, but human rights, environmental, and consumer activists have not been effective in curbing the deleterious effects of globalization. Questions about product safety, abusive labor practices such as child labor and sweatshops, and environmental damage have not received much attention in private corporations' business

World Trade Organization (WTO) International organization created by GATT in 1995 to implement GATT's free-trade principles.

General Agreement on Tariffs and Trade (GATT) International agreement promoting free trade, first signed in 1947, and most recently signed by 123 countries in 1993.

practices, nor have they been the subject of serious international state-sponsored agreements. Even when states have tried to increase legal regulations against such abuses, multinational corporations such as Shell or Nike, with higher annual revenues than some European countries, have used the WTO effectively to lobby on behalf of deregulation in the name of free trade. More recently, however, Amnesty International and other human rights groups have forced the question of human rights abuses by member countries or members-to-be. A precondition for China's admission to the WTO, for example, was the reduction of abuses in labor practices.

International organizations have also been ineffective in dealing with other global problems, such as **global warming**, world poverty, and the AIDS epidemic. Scientists have linked the **greenhouse effect** to rapid industrialization and have urged governments to come to a global agreement over basic environmental regulations that would prevent further erosion of the earth's atmosphere. In 1997, representatives from 160 countries met in Kyoto and signed an agreement to cut greenhouse gas emissions by 10 percent, but the United States, the world's larger industrial producer of greenhouse gases, declined to ratify it. Without U.S. support, the **Kyoto Agreement** remains ineffectual.

World Health Issues Nor has globalization alleviated world poverty. The UN has worked to bring economic help to the world's poorest areas, such as Africa and South Asia, but even as farmers produce more than enough to feed the world's population, neither the UN's direct aid policies nor the WTO's advocacy for free trade has eliminated starvation as a cause of premature death.

Since the 1990s, another significant global concern has been the persistence of malaria and the spread of the AIDS virus, especially in Africa. More than 25 percent of the population in parts of Africa have the AIDS virus. Although western pharmaceutical companies have developed preventive anti-HIV vaccines and treatments for those already infected, most of the people who need these medicines are too poor to afford them. Likewise, malaria, for which preventive vaccines have existed for more than a generation, still kills millions of people each year in the poorest areas of the world. The most effective programs for containing these two epidemics have been international philanthropic nongovernmental organizations rather than the World Bank, the UN, or the WTO.

International Security and Terrorism

Since the 1990s, a sweeping transformation has occurred in international relations. Though the Americans and western Europeans were partners in winning the cold war, the United States has largely determined the international agenda since 1991. Security concerns in the West changed from the contained fears about relatively stable communist states to a vague terrorist threat, largely located in the Middle East and in Muslim communities, but often without a state sponsor that could be held accountable through the conventional means of international relations. Overall, this change has reduced the effectiveness of the UN as a means for peacefully alleviating security threats. Its function has shifted instead to poverty, AIDS, and other human rights issues. Though peacekeeping remains one of its functions, the UN has not used its troops to great effect anywhere in the world since the 1990s, from Bosnia to Rwanda. Instead, the United States has come to rely primarily on NATO and other bilateral and broader agreements to further its security interests. Europeans have participated in this process either as members of NATO or more recently as individual allies of the United States in the **War on Terrorism**.

Conflicts in the Middle East The most intense site of conflict has remained the Middle East. In 1991 Iraq, under the leadership of **Saddam Hussein**, invaded Kuwait, a country rich in oil resources and with close economic ties to the United States. The noncompliance of the Iraqi leader with the UN resolution demanding his withdrawal prompted an international military response. In the **Gulf War**, the United States led a coalition of more than thirty states that included significant forces from Great Britain, France, and Egypt. Even the postcommunist countries sent in specialists to lend logistical support.

This conflict signaled an intensification of tensions that had been building up in the Middle East since World War II. Since the inception of Israel in 1948, the United States, Britain, and other western countries have been committed to its security as an outpost of democratic rule and western civilization. These are precisely the reasons that Arab countries in the Middle East came to view the West with mistrust and Israel as a symbol of western imperialism in the area. While Jordan remained relatively friendly to the West, since the mid-1950s, Egypt,

global warming Increase in the average temperature of the air and oceans in recent decades and its projected continuation.

greenhouse effect Effect of gases emitted by human activities, especially pollution.

Kyoto Agreement Agreement signed in 1997 by 160 nations to reduce greenhouse gas emissions; not ratified by the United States.

War on Terrorism Term used by the George W. Bush administration to refer to military, political, and legal actions taken to curb the spread of terrorism since 2001.

Saddam Hussein (1937–2006) Iraqi president from 1979 to 2003 who fought against the United States in the 1991 Gulf War and was deposed during the Iraq War.

Gulf War (1991) War between an international coalition led by the United States against Iraq in response to Iraq's invasion of Kuwait.

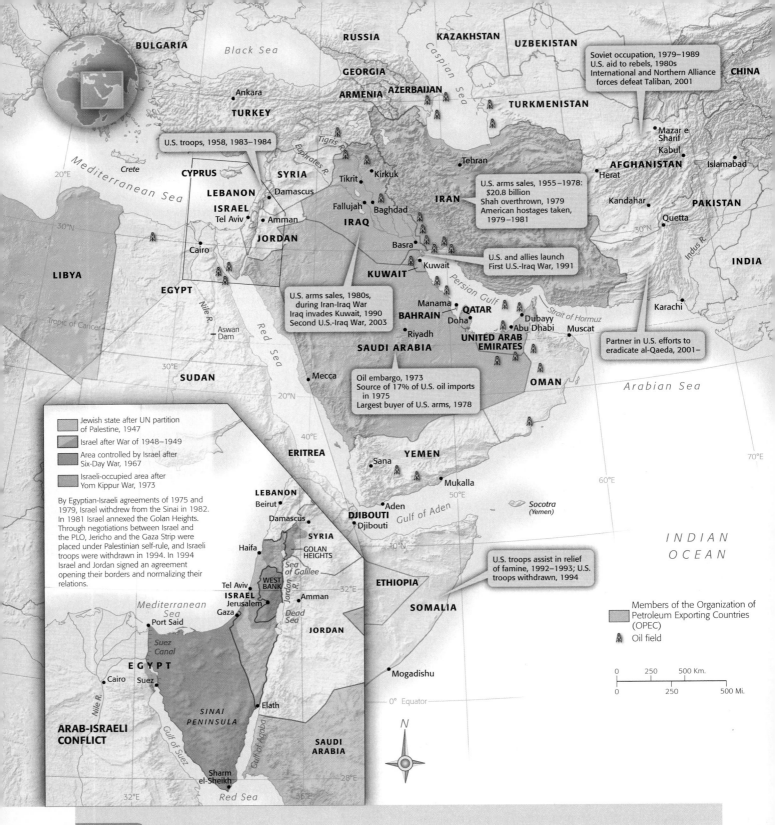

Map 30.3 **Israel-Palestine Since 1948** The state of Israel and the stateless Palestinians have been at the heart of struggles in the Middle East for economic resources, political legitimacy, and international support.
© Cengage Learning

1. Can you estimate how much Israel has expanded the territories it controls since its founding in 1947?
2. What are the states with which Israel has ongoing border tensions?
3. What percentage, roughly speaking, of the border of the state of Israel is or has been recently contested?

Syria, and later Iran and Iraq became open supporters of Arab nationalist claims at the expense of Israel, on occasion testing the strength of this state through military campaigns at its borders.

The Rise of International Terrorism The fate of the Muslim and Christian Palestinians in Israeli territories has remained a point of contention between Arab nationalists and Israel. By the 1970s, as peaceful negotiations had not yielded much success for the Palestinian cause, a new method of struggle emerged—**terrorism**. At the 1976 Olympics in Munich, Israeli athletes were taken hostage and killed by Arab nationalist terrorists. After that globally publicized incident, the Palestine Liberation Organization and other such groups continued to pursue terrorist actions against Jewish citizens of Israel and other states. Antisemitism was an important component of these terrorist groups' agenda.

In Iraq, Saddam Hussein managed to fashion himself as a regional protector of Arab nationalism against the West. Hussein had come to power in 1979 as a secularizing popular nationalist, and the United States had assisted his regime because he seemed to offer a counterbalance to the radical Islamic regime in power in Iran since 1977. From the beginning, Hussein cleverly played American concerns and Soviet regional interests to his advantage, securing financial help from both superpowers during the cold war. Content to have him in power and as a supplier of oil for western needs, the United States overlooked the human rights abuses of the regime against religious and ethnic minorities. But when Hussein refashioned himself as a paragon of Arab nationalism against Israel and the West, and attacked Kuwait in 1991, the West reacted with military intervention. During the Gulf War, Hussein launched missile attacks against Israel. This anti-Israeli and more broadly antisemitic agenda continued during the 1990s, when Iraq offered cash to the families of **suicide bombers** who attacked Israelis.

Growing Tensions Although the American-led coalition scored a sweeping victory, the Gulf War left complicated legacies that came to haunt the UN, the EU, and the international community in general. Inside Iraq, Hussein became solidly entrenched. The country's Shi'ite and Kurdish peoples suffered harsh reprisals, including the use of chemical and biological weapons, and the traumatic environmental and psychological effects of the war on both civilians and soldiers are still unfolding. During the 1990s, the European allies in the war remained convinced that UN sanctions and inspection teams could curb Hussein's abuses, but the American leadership began to lose faith in such methods.

One of the most important consequences of the Gulf War was the destabilization of the Middle East, with Israel enlisting the support of the United States and some European governments while many Arab Muslim states began to see themselves as more in conflict with the West than as allies of the Americans in putting down Hussein's bullying actions in the region. European countries that had supported the United States in the 1991 war resisted drawing the same clear lines as the Americans between supporting Israel and vilifying its Arab foes, including the Palestine Liberation Organization. In 1993, when President Bill Clinton hosted Israeli and Palestinian leaders and orchestrated the **Oslo Agreements** as a step toward a peaceful resolution of their conflict, Europe remained in the background. Many in Europe viewed the United States as unfairly favoring Israel, though Britain steadily supported the American role.

The War on Terrorism Terrorist attacks continued in the 1990s in Africa, Southeast Asia, and Europe, but the most important challenge to the post–cold war international order came on **September 11, 2001**, when an al-Qaeda attack brought down the World Trade Center in New York and destroyed part of the Pentagon in Washington, D.C. The 9/11 attacks killed more than three thousand people from more than sixty countries and were the most severe attack on American soil since Pearl Harbor. Although al-Qaeda and similar organizations had undertaken terrorist actions over the previous decade, the attacks on September 11 were perceived as unprecedented in the United States and prompted a major foreign policy shift by the George W. Bush administration.

Within days, President Bush declared a War on Terrorism and embarked on an aggressive policy of employing all American intelligence, diplomatic, and military resources to respond to this grave terrorist threat. Although a significant number of European nationals were killed during the 9/11 attacks, European countries responded to the American call to action in different ways. The initial military campaign in Afghanistan, one of whose goals was to find and capture **Osama bin Laden**, the al-Qaeda leader and mastermind behind the 9/11 attacks, was broadly supported by governments in Europe.

terrorism Violence or other harmful acts against civilians, often by disempowered groups trying to force political change.

suicide bombers Individuals who carry out terrorist attacks by setting off explosive devices that also kill themselves.

Oslo Agreements Agreements signed by Israel and the PLO in 1993 to establish an independent Palestinian state and subsequently repudiated by both sides.

September 11, 2001 Day on which al-Qaeda terrorists crashed hijacked passenger planes into the World Trade Center in New York and the Pentagon in Washington, D.C.

Osama bin Laden (1957–2011) Militant Saudi Arabian Islamist who founded al-Qaeda in 1988 and organized the 9/11 attacks on the United States; spent the next decade in hiding in Afghanistan and Pakistan, where he was finally ambushed and killed by American forces.

In February 2003, U.S. Secretary of State Colin Powell went before the UN General Assembly to convince the international community that Saddam Hussein was concealing chemical and biological weapons, and to request the approval of the Security Council to commence military action against Iraq. Here he holds up a vial of anthrax, a life-threatening infectious disease reputed to be in the terrorist arsenal. How is Colin Powell making use of his position to drive home the argument for war?

Elise Amandola/AP Images

NATO members sent military, logistical, and humanitarian support. The European public was less eager to support these actions, however, and massive antiwar protests took place all over western Europe, reminiscent of the peaceful street protests of the 1980s. Unlike in the 1980s, however, when activists had a broad antinuclear agenda but did not single out the Americans, these protests generally identified the United States as the sole country engaged in military and economic imperialism. In 2011 military operations in Afghanistan continued, to the tune of over $8 billion per month. The total cost of this war as born by U.S. taxpayers was more than $1.29 trillion by the end of 2011.

The Iraq War When President Bush shifted his focus in the War on Terrorism from Afghanistan to Iraq, European political leaders responded in an increasingly negative manner. The UN was at that time involved in overseeing economic sanctions and inspections to make sure Iraq was destroying its military capabilities, as Saddam Hussein had agreed to do following his defeat in the Gulf War. Starting in 2002, reports about Iraq's nuclear and chemical capabilities in defiance of the 1991 agreements and UN resolutions led the Bush administration to contemplate military action against Iraq. In late 2002 the European countries on the UN Security Council (Great Britain, France, Russia, and Spain) made it clear that they would not support military action by the United States until all peaceful options, especially the international inspections, had been exhausted. In 2003, the inspectors openly stated that there were no weapons of mass destruction left in Iraq.

Colin Powell (1937–) U.S. secretary of state under George W. Bush, 2000 to 2004.

In a last attempt to convince the UN that collective military action was necessary, in February 2003 U.S. Secretary of State **Colin Powell** presented an impassioned report on Iraq's severe violations of the UN resolutions. Some, like Britain and Spain, were convinced, but most other countries were not. The United States went to war against Iraq a month later, its preemptive strike justified as intended to destroy nuclear and biochemical weapons capabilities, but these capabilities proved to be an illusion, as Powell later acknowledged.

The Iraq War split the European political leadership and population, but not along the old cold war lines. The French, Russians, and Germans vehemently opposed the war, and the British, Dutch, Italians, and Spaniards supported it. These different responses were based on different fears regarding terrorist actions; different views on the U.S. disregard for the UN as well as U.S. policies on the Middle East, especially the Israeli-Palestinian conflict; and pragmatic assessments of economic benefits and costs in the aftermath of the war. For instance, the Spanish were concerned about terrorism at home and supported the Americans as a deterrent to their own internal enemies, whereas the Russians opposed the intervention because they did not want to invite terrorist activities in volatile places like Chechnya. The French and Germans resented the American disregard of the UN. The postcommunist countries generally identified Hussein with the kind of tyrannical government that had dominated their region for fifty years and so were eager for a direct military alliance with the United States that would stand against Russia. Romania and Bulgaria welcomed American bases that would deploy troops to Iraq. Yet the level

Since 2003 hundreds of thousands of people have marched through the streets of European and North American cities to protest against the American-led War in Iraq. Here British citizens are seen at a massive antiwar protest. Great Britain, which had the second largest number of troops in Iraq, withdrew all of its troops in 2009. How would you describe this protest?

of anti-Americanism in Europe has never been so high, among both politicians and the general public.

A decade later, Iraq is ruled through free parliamentary elections and has a new constitution. Almost 4,500 U.S. soldiers have died to date in this conflict. Estimates regarding the Iraqi casualties vary widely, but most observers agree that more than 100,000 Iraqis have died since 2003 in connection with the war.

Instant Communication and the Internet

Even as they remain divided over international politics, Europeans and Americans have become more closely connected than ever through new means of communication, information exchange, and entertainment. The end of the twentieth century brought communications revolutions that have made distances insignificant and provided instant access almost anywhere on earth. The new technologies have brought people greater freedom to relate to each other and to become "virtually" anyone; they have also brought greater power to those who create and implement these technologies.

Connected Through TV Cable television, first introduced in the United States in the 1970s, became wildly popular across Europe in the 1990s. Many people in the postcommunist countries went from having access to one or two government-controlled channels to having twenty or more public and private channels through inexpensive cable packages. Overnight, a person sitting in his living room in Sofia, Bulgaria, went from watching the daily dose of communist speeches to being able to choose everything from Scooby-Doo cartoons to live coverage of the O. J. Simpson trial. The impact of the diversity of mostly American programs and channels was tremendous all over the globe.

The Internet Revolution Another component of the communications revolution was the **Internet**, which, since its inception in 1992, has become the most important means for information gathering and exchange in today's world. Ubiquitous in Europe, it has proved to be an equalizer, as differences in access arise largely from differences in education and technical know-how rather than from economic status. Internet cafés that charge low access fees can be found in even the most provincial settings, and most people under age thirty have an Internet account. Young people have a sense that they can always be connected to others anywhere in the world, and they share ideas and music with people they have never met. But the spread of the Internet has not necessarily encouraged communication across cultures or languages. It has become more of a

Internet Global computer network created in 1992 that makes it possible to instantly connect to people and information around the world.

resource for creating parallel communities of people with similar tastes and interests. Fans of Lady Gaga, for example, create websites to communicate about her; they rarely explore other types of music. White supremacist groups, too, have found niches where their biases are reinforced by all participants rather than challenged by those who oppose their racist ideologies.

Above all, the Internet has facilitated the possibility of imagining multiple identities, of turning the concept of the self in a community into a more fluid and less concretely bound thing. Fact and fiction blend together in the virtual space, making it easy to converse across national borders and to imagine being anyone or anywhere. The free flow of ideas challenges national allegiances, and authoritarian regimes, such as China, have censored the Internet. But users have ways of getting around such controls.

The Twitter Generation and the Arab Spring The most spectacular events to date in terms of the political uses of the Internet and instant telecommunications have involved the use of cell phones, YouTube, and Twitter to document egregious political abuses by authoritarian regimes in countries such as Iran, Moldova, and Kyrgyzstan. In all these places, popular street uprisings and government violence against the protesters were instantly documented and then broadcast all over the world at lightning speed, at a time when no independent media had access to the events. Though such methods have drawn the attention of the international community, the impact inside these repressive regimes has been unclear.

By contrast, in Tunisia, Egypt, and Libya, protesters have made successful use of the new technologies to get organized, publicize their views, and expose the abuses of the regimes against which they are fighting. In Tunisia and Egypt, the results have been dramatic, bringing about a new sense of hope for the possibility of peaceful reform and democratization in these countries. In other countries, similar tactics have brought about critical remarks, some diplomatic action, and, in the case of Libya, military intervention that helped opposition forces to bring down the abusive regime of Muammar Gaddafi. The **Arab Spring** has brought hope and trepidation in the world about internal and international trajectories of the countries in the Middle East.

Arab Spring Series of uprisings that began in December 2010 in Islamic countries in North Africa and the Middle East that have resulted in important reforms by the existing regimes, the overturn of some regimes, as well as brutal reprisals by others.

Organization of Petroleum Exporting Countries (OPEC) International organization that oversees price and supply fluctuations in the production and sales of oil.

Checking In

The Future of the West

◆ **What important challenges are likely to reshape the West in the near future?**

◆ **What is the meaning of western civilization in the global future?**

The face of the West is likely to become less specifically "western" in the twenty-first century. Even as Europeans are holding on to old institutions, from politics to social relations and culture, they are debating the meaning of these institutions both inside Europe and beyond. Demographically, with migration on the rise and large birthrate differentials among various social categories of Europeans, the face of the West is also likely to change significantly in the next generation. In the short run, the most important challenges and frictions remain between Christian and Muslim populations. In the long run, it is not clear whether the primacy of western civilization, as asserted in the past few thousand years, is likely to endure.

Old Institutions, New Directions

In the twenty-first century, the West seems to have retained important institutions, but their future is somewhat uncertain. Nation-states are still the basic political units of government. Nationalism remains an important rallying force for politicians and average citizens, from Washington to Moscow to Beirut. But the multinational EU has created a new model for international political organization and peaceful cooperation among states. Whether the EU can retain this healthy balance remains to be seen after its next round of enlargement, especially if Turkey becomes a member.

New Economic Competitors In the global economy, most traditional economic institutions have taken on new elements. Small businesses continue to exist, but they are rarely able to operate without some direct or indirect assistance from multinational companies. With oil controlled by the **Organization of Petroleum Exporting Countries (OPEC)** and in the hands of a tiny group of multinational corporations, no one government can dictate the use of these resources, and small businesses are very much at the mercy of rising oil prices. A weaver in Bloomington, Indiana, may succeed or fail in selling her product not only on the basis of its quality or the demand for weavings but ultimately also on the basis of competitive pricing. Yet the costs for producing those weavings—from paying for yarn transported from elsewhere to paying for the electricity and other utilities in the workshop—are controlled by global market forces, especially the rising cost of energy. Despite such growing concerns, the United States is likely to remain the most powerful economic unit in the global economy, with the EU as a smaller partner or competitor. China is the only economy that might challenge the undisputed first place of the United States.

Changing Social Institutions Even basic social and cultural institutions and traditions are likely to be greatly transformed. The traditional definition of marriage as a social institution, initially sanctioned by religious authorities in the Middle Ages and in the twentieth century identified as a secular institution, has recently been challenged. Gay couples all over the world have demanded changes in the law to recognize same-sex unions as legal marriages. This challenge is testing the boundaries of secularization in the West. For instance, evangelical Christian organizations in the United States have successfully prevented the legalization of same-sex marriage. Yet in South Africa and Europe, even in staunchly Catholic Spain, gay marriages have been legalized without considerable opposition. In the realm of civil rights, the EU remains more committed to the traditions of social inclusiveness and tolerance than the United States, where liberty from government interference is still valued more than government protection for the disadvantaged and socially marginal.

The Future of Organized Religion Religious institutions are also being challenged from within the ranks of the clergy. With the decrease in young men's willingness to join the Catholic priesthood, some religious reformers have suggested the need to reconsider clerical celibacy. Others have suggested that women should also be allowed into the priesthood. Some other Christian denominations, such as the Episcopalians and Methodists, have undertaken reforms toward greater gender and even sexual inclusion, but the Catholic Church has refused to consider any such reforms. Following the death of Pope John Paul II, the election of another conservative cardinal, Pope **Benedict XVI**, has made the church's direction clear and reinforced the primacy of the West and Europe in defining the future of the Catholic Church. Even as the largest areas of growth of the Catholic

Church are in Asia, Africa, and Latin America, it was a German pope who was selected to lead the church in 2005. But the Catholic Church no longer holds a central religious, social, or cultural role in defining what it is, or means, to be European.

Who Is a European?

The reassertion of European leadership in the Catholic Church is part of continued efforts to define who may be a European and who may not. Thus, just as Catholic institutions remain essentially tied to Europe, Muslim institutions remain defined as largely nonwestern. The growth of Muslim populations in many European states, such as Holland, Denmark, Spain, Britain, France, and Germany, is forcing non-Muslims to ask themselves about their relationship with these often deeply religious communities that uphold seemingly non-European traditions and cultural values. For instance, a video that depicts the culture of Holland for its immigrant populations includes images of topless women and gay couples kissing as examples of the tolerance and liberal tradition that the Dutch government is proud of. But the video does not also include images of Muslim women in traditional veils, suggesting the limits of what liberal democratic Europe is willing to embrace.

Overall, the decreasing birthrate among secular and Christian Europeans, and the parallel rising birthrate among Muslim Europeans, is posing a serious question about what being a European might mean a generation from now. Israel faces a particularly perplexing dilemma, as the sharp differences in birthrates between Jews and Arabs in that state indicate that in the next generation Muslims will constitute more than a quarter of the Israeli population.

Democracy and Europeanness Politically, democratic forms of government have become an important marker of Europeanness. The enlargement of the EU has been tied to how well applicants can demonstrate potential (Greece, Portugal, and Spain) or success (the postcommunist applicants) in creating a democracy. Yet radical antidemocratic movements are still present everywhere in Europe, both as political parties and as militant terrorist cells. One thing is certain: the clear-cut East-West divide between those who belong to the European core and those who are at the margins is vanishing. Not everyone wants to welcome every country, from Iceland to Russia, into the new European home, but it is becoming increasingly difficult to justify any divisions along these lines.

Education and Urbanization Europeanness has also become identified more

Benedict XVI (r. 2005–) German-born pope who has continued the conservative policies of Pope John Paul II.

Pope Benedict XVI Speaks of the Future of Christianity

In August 2006, in preparation for his first trip to his native Bavaria since assuming the pontificate, Benedict XVI spoke to a Vatican spokesman about his goals for the trip and more generally about his vision for the role of the Roman Catholic Church. The pope's background as a German growing up in the Third Reich has made him the object of criticism by both liberal secular intellectuals and non-German (and especially non-European) Catholics. Pope Benedict XVI has been an outspoken advocate for living in strict accordance with Catholic dogma and has condemned some reformist interpretations of the Second Vatican Council. Regarding relations with other religions, he has spoken about love and reconciliation but also condemned certain Islamic practices in ways that have brought a strong reaction from Muslim leaders.

❶ What does Pope Benedict see as the most important spiritual challenge in the West today? How is it tied to globalization?

ZDF: How do you see the present situation of the Catholic Church in Germany?

Benedict XVI: **❶** I would say, first of all, that Germany is part of the West, with its own characteristic colouring obviously, and that in the Western world today we are experiencing a wave of new and drastic enlightenment or secularization whatever you like to call it. It has become more difficult to believe because the world in which we find ourselves is completely made up of ourselves, and God, so to speak, does not appear directly anymore. We do not drink from the source anymore, but from the vessel which is offered to us already full, and so on. Humanity has rebuilt the world by itself, and finding God inside this world has become more difficult. This is not specific to Germany: it is something that is valid throughout the world, especially in the West. Then again, today the West is being strongly influenced by other cultures in which the original religious element is very powerful. These cultures are horrified when they experience the West's coldness towards God. This "presence of the sacred" in other cultures, even if often veiled, touches the Western world again, it touches us at the crossroads of so many cultures. The quest for "something bigger" wells up again from the depths of Western people and in Germany. We see how in young people there is the search for something "more," we see how the religious phenomenon is returning, as they say, even if it is a search that is rather indefinite. But with all this the Church is present once more and faith is offered as the answer....

closely with highly urbanized and well-educated societies that are secular yet tolerant of religious difference. The vast majority of Europeans live in cities, yet some are choosing to reject the overcrowded, traffic-jammed, polluted urban setting for the simpler country life. This choice has been a response to the excesses of globalization and an embrace of the local resources it endangers. Yet this "simple life" is facilitated by new communication technologies, such as cell phones, luxuries many cannot afford.

Most Europeans have graduated from high school and have attended institutions of higher education. Education has been an important tool in providing greater equality to all people, regardless of gender, class, ethnicity, or religion—one of the great successes of the post-1945 welfare state. Yet the cost of these state services has become so burdensome

BR: Holy Father, Christianity has spread around the world starting from Europe. Now many people think that the future of the Church is to be found in other continents. Is that true? Or, in other words, what is the future of Christianity in Europe, where it looks like it is being reduced to the private affair of a minority?

Benedict XVI: I would like to introduce a few subtleties. ❷ It is true, as we know, that Christianity began in the Near East. And for a long time its main development continued there. Then it spread in Asia, much more than what we think today after the changes brought about by Islam. Precisely for this reason its axis moved noticeably toward the West and Europe. Europe—we are proud and pleased to say so—further developed Christianity in its broader intellectual and cultural dimensions. But I think it is important to remind ourselves about the Eastern Christians because there is the present danger of them emigrating, these Christians who have always been an important minority living in a fruitful relationship with the surrounding reality. There is a great danger that these places where Christianity had its origins will be left without Christians. I think we need to help them a lot so that they can stay. But getting back to your question: Europe definitely became the centre of Christianity and its missionary movement. Today, other continents and other cultures play with equal importance in the concert of world history. In this way the number of voices in the Church grows, and this is a good thing. It is good that different temperaments can express themselves, the special gifts of Africa, Asia and America, Latin America in particular. Of course, they are all touched not only by the word of Christianity, but by the secular message of this world that carries to other continents the disruptive forces we have already experienced. ❸ All the Bishops from different parts of the world say: we still need Europe, even if Europe is only a part of a greater whole. We still carry the responsibility that comes from our experience, from the science and technology that was developed here, from our liturgical experience to our traditions, the ecumenical experiences we have accumulated: all this is very important for the other continents too. So it is important that today we do not give up, feeling sorry for ourselves and saying: "Look at us, we are just a minority, let us at least try and preserve our small number!" We have to keep our dynamism alive, open relationships of exchange, so that new strength for us comes from there.

Source: Benedict XVI's Speech on the Future of Christianity (5 August 2006). © Libreria Editrice Vaticana, 2007. Reprinted by permission of Libreria Editrice Vaticana.

❷ How does Pope Benedict describe the origins of Christianity?

❸ How does Pope Benedict describe the role of Europe in the Catholic Church today?

as to endanger the quality of public education. As a result, private institutions are proliferating, creating new levels of competition and possibly inequality in terms of access to high-quality education.

Religiousness and Secularism Even though secularism and religious tolerance have remained important components of Europeanness, since the 1990s, debates over the acceptance of religious differences, especially with regard to Judaism and Islam, have grown. Antisemitism and anti-Muslim attitudes are on the rise, especially since 9/11. The recent ban in French schools against the headscarves that all observant Muslim girls must wear calls into question the level of religious tolerance in the cradle of modern European democracy. Turkey's bid for membership

Over the past few years the Muslim population in Europe has become more assertive about their civil rights and have demanded that their cultural differences be respected in public institutions and policies. On January 18, 2004, Muslim French women were protesting in Paris against the banning of headscarves in public schools. Their banners read: "Sarko (A reference to Nicolas Sarkozy, then Minister of the Interior, and elected French president in June 2007), French Islam Doesn't Need Foreign Interference!"; "Why, in the country of the rights of man, women don't have the right to wear what they want?"; and "Beloved France, where is my freedom?" What values are these women embracing with their actions and words?

in the EU remains an important test for the question of European definitions of western civilization. If Turkey continues to be rejected, it means that Europeans are fundamentally unable to consider Islamic traditions and culture, even in their most secularized forms, as an integral part of the West. Yet if Turkey does become an EU member, its presence will initiate a fundamental redefinition of who is a European and what core values western civilization can embrace.

Even though European people like to represent their identity and culture as very different from the American identity and culture, the lifestyle of the average person in Europe is increasingly similar to that of the average person in the United States. The European past, long a mark of European distinctiveness, is becoming more difficult to discern in the face of a shared popular culture. A Polish college student in Warsaw is much closer in her fashion preferences, job options, and hobbies to an American college student in Chicago than she is to her Polish parents who grew up under communism. It is increasingly the past, rather than the future, that is likely to define the West as somehow unique in the world.

 Checking In

By yourself or with a partner, explain the significance of each of the following selected key terms:

Organization of Petro-leum Exporting Coun-tries (OPEC)

Benedict XVI

CHAPTER
Review

Summary

- ◆ Since 1991 Europe has become increasingly democratized.

- ◆ States have had to cut back welfare programs, but overall public services from health care to education remain important benefits.

- ◆ Since the mid-1990s, European companies have become serious competitors of U.S. companies in the world market.

- ◆ In terms of economic growth, the EU has been a success, even in countries hit most seriously by the global recession.

- ◆ Europe has not been able to act as a unit in international affairs, especially after the terrorist attacks of 9/11.

- ◆ There has been a growth in popular anti-American attitudes, but governments have sometimes reacted differently than their populace.

- ◆ There is increasing homogeneity across Europe in terms of markers for social advancement, consumer tastes, and the tendency of people to identify themselves as European along with their other national and regional identities.

- ◆ Europeanness has become tied to a past culture, something significantly unique to their continent, rather than to the current and future aspirations of people living in Europe.

Chronology

1991	Gulf War begins; Soviet Union is dissolved
1991–1995	Serbs, Croats, and Bosnians fight ethnic-based civil wars in Yugoslavia
1992	Internet society is chartered
1993	Israel and the Palestine Liberation Organization sign Oslo Agreements; EU comes into being after ratification of the Maastricht treaty
1995	World Trade Organization is created; Dayton Agreement ends Bosnian War, establishes an independent Bosnia and Serbian Republic of Bosnia
1996	Poland, Czech Republic, and Hungary join NATO
1997	Tony Blair is elected prime minister of Great Britain
1998	Russian stock market collapses
1999	NATO begins Kosovo War against Serbia
2000	Vladimir Putin is elected president of Russia; Fall of Milošević government
2001	Al-Qaeda hijacks passenger planes to attack the World Trade Center in New York and the Pentagon in Washington, D.C.
2002	Euro becomes European currency; MTV opens local broadcast channel in Romania
2003	Iraq War begins
2004	Al-Qaeda terrorists bomb commuter trains in Madrid; Ten new members, mostly postcommunist countries, join the EU; Russians reinvade Chechnya; George W. Bush is re-elected president of the United States
2005	Same-sex marriage is legalized in Spain; Angela Merkel becomes the first woman chancellor of Germany
2007	Romania and Bulgaria join the EU
2008	Iceland's currency collapses, EU orchestrates a bailout; Kosovo declares independence; Barack Obama becomes first African American president of the United States
2009	Ratification of Lisbon Treaty; Great Britain withdraws troops from Iraq
2010	Beginning of the Arab Spring

© Cengage Learning

Test Yourself

To gauge your mastery of the material in this chapter, answer the questions below. More than one answer may be correct.

Eastern Europe After Communism

1. Yeltsin was successful in:
   a. Bringing an end to the communist one-party state in Russia.
   b. Enabling the privatizing of the Russian economy.
   c. Creating a democratic political party of his own.
   d. Ending the activities of criminal gangs.
   e. Eliminating irredentist threats in Chechnya.

2. The Yugoslav Wars of 1991 to 1995:

   a. Restored the international prestige of Serbia.
   b. Brought about the dissolution of Yugoslavia.
   c. Were ended through international intervention by the UN and NATO.
   d. Allowed for families to resettle in order to be in their preferred ethnic group.
   e. Brought about the independence of Kosovo.

3. The Kosovo War:

   a. Brought about NATO intervention.
   b. Brought down Slobodan Milošević.
   c. Was fought between Serbia and Albania.
   d. Brought about the independence of Albania.
   e. Internationally embarrassed the United States because of their wrongful bombing of the Chinese Embassy in Belgrade.

4. The Visegrád Four was:

   a. A military alliance.
   b. An informal group of four countries that coordinated economic reforms.
   c. A group bound to each other in terms of political reform.
   d. Successful because of personal links of the leaders going back to the communist era.
   e. A group of four presidents.

5. The less successful postcommunist countries in terms of political democratic and economic reforms were:

   a. Poland
   b. Lithuania
   c. Romania
   d. Slovakia
   e. Bulgaria

Now that you have reviewed and tested yourself on this part of the chapter, take time to pull together all the important information by answering the following questions:

◆ What impact did the postcommunist transition have on eastern European states and societies?

◆ To what extent have these countries become more democratic?

European Integration

6. The EU has created internationally binding agreements among member states in the area of:

   a. Monetary union
   b. International relations
   c. Travel
   d. Taxation
   e. National elections

7. Which of the following postcommunist countries are now in the Eurozone?

   a. Poland
   b. Hungary
   c. Slovenia
   d. Bulgaria
   e. Slovakia

8. The Lisbon Treaty:

   a. Took the place of the failed EU constitution.
   b. Has imposed higher standards of protection of human rights on all member countries.
   c. Has not been ratified by France.
   d. Has generated higher standards of fiscal accountability for all member states.
   e. Has established a timeline for the adoption of the euro in all EU countries.

9. Vladimir Putin has been popular in Russia because he:

   a. Projects the image of a moral, healthy leader.
   b. Has supported democratic movements in post-Soviet countries.
   c. Has upheld Russia's Great Power image.
   d. Has enhanced the freedom of the press.
   e. Has had a friendly relationship with the United States.

Now that you have reviewed and tested yourself on this part of the chapter, take time to pull together all the important information by answering the following questions:

◆ How has the EU transformed European politics and economies?

◆ What impact has the EU had on European security matters?

Europe and Globalization

10. Economic globalization has:
    a. Enabled states to compete more successfully against multinational corporations.
    b. Favored international institutions such as the EU.
    c. Enabled environmental organizations to better lobby on behalf of concerns about pollution.
    d. Led to the enforcement of higher standards of human rights protection.
    e. Enabled smaller producers to make more profits by gaining access to larger markets.

11. What global critical problems remain unresolved?
    a. The spread of AIDS
    b. Global warming
    c. Malaria
    d. Child labor
    e. Starvation

12. The War on Terrorism:
    a. Was initiated by the United States.
    b. Has been targeting primarily Islamic extremists.
    c. Was prompted by the abuses of Saddam Hussein against his own people.
    d. Was justified because of the presence of weapons of mass destruction in Iraq.
    e. Has cost the United States over a trillion dollars.

13. Which European states initially strongly supported the Iraq War?
    a. Great Britain
    b. France
    c. Spain
    d. Romania
    e. Italy

14. New access to technology has been successfully used to help overturn political regimes in:
    a. Iran
    b. Egypt
    c. Jordan
    d. Saudi Arabia
    e. Tunisia

Now that you have reviewed and tested yourself on this part of the chapter, take time to pull together all the important information by answering the following questions:

◆ How has globalization transformed the economic power of Europe in the world?

◆ What have been the great international challenges since 1991?

The Future of the West

Now that you have reviewed and tested yourself on this part of the chapter, take time to pull together all the important information by answering the following questions:

◆ What important challenges are likely to reshape the West in the near future?

◆ What is the meaning of western civilization in the global future?

ANSWERS TO THE TEST-YOURSELF MULTIPLE-CHOICE QUESTIONS

Chapter 1

1. b	2. b, c	3. a, c, d
4. a, c, d, e	5. a, c, d	6. c
7. b, c, d	8. a, d, e	9. b, c
10. b	11. c	12. e
13. a	14. b, c, e	15. d

Chapter 2

1. a, c, d	2. c, d	3. c
4. d	5. b	6. c
7. c, d	8. a, b	9. a, b, d
10. a, b, c	11. a, b, d, e	12. a
13. a, b, c, d	14. a, b	15. b, c, d

Chapter 3

1. a, c, d	2. a, c	3. d
4. a, b	5. b, c, d	6. d
7. b, c	8. c	9. a, b, e
10. a	11. b, d	12. c
13. c, d	14. c	15. a, c

Chapter 4

1. b, c, d	2. a, c, d	3. b, c, d
4. a, b, d	5. b, c, d	6. d
7. a, b, d	8. b	9. b, c, d
10. c	11. a, c	12. b, d
13. a, b	14. c, d, e	15. a, c, e

Chapter 5

1. c	2. c, d, e	3. d
4. a, d	5. a, b	6. a, b, c
7. a, c, d	8. c	9. b
10. a, b, d	11. a, c, d	12. d
13. c	14. a, c, d	15. c

Chapter 6

1. a, c, d	2. a, d	3. a, b, d
4. a, c, d	5. d	6. b, c
7. b, c, d	8. d	9. a, c, d
10. a	11. a, b, d	12. a, b, d
13. b	14. a, b, c, d	15. a, d

Chapter 7

1. a, b, d	2. a, d	3. a
4. a, c, d, e	5. a, c, d	6. d
7. a, b, c	8. b	9. a, b, c
10. a, d	11. a, b	12. a, b, d
13. d	14. b, d, e	15. c
16. a, b, d	17. c	18. a, c, d
19. b		

Chapter 8

1. b	2. b	3. a
4. d	5. a	6. b
7. a	8. d	9. b
10. e	11. c	12. d
13. b	14. c	15. b
16. d	17. e	18. e
19. a	20. e	

Chapter 9

1. c	2. d	3. a
4. e	5. b	6. e
7. b	8. a	9. c
10. e	11. d	12. c
13. d	14. a	15. b
16. c	17. e	18. a
19. b		

Chapter 10

1. a	2. c	3. a
4. c	5. d	6. e
7. b	8. e	9. a
10. c	11. c	12. b
13. a	14. e	15. d
16. b	17. a	18. e
19. c	20. c	21. e
22. a	23. e	24. b

Chapter 11

1. a	2. c	3. e
4. d	5. b	6. c
7. a	8. c	9. b
10. a	11. a	12. e
13. c	14. d	15. b
16. b	17. c	18. a
19. c	20. e	21. c
22. d	23. a	24. d
25. b		

Chapter 12

1. c	2. e	3. a
4. e	5. a	6. b
7. e	8. d	9. e
10. c	11. b	12. d
13. a	14. d	15. b
16. a	17. e	18. d
19. b		

Chapter 13

1. a, c, d	2. e	3. b
4. b ,d	5. a, c, d, e	6. a, c
7. a, b, c	8. a, d	9. a, e
10. b, d	11. a, c	12. a, c, e
13. a, b, d	14. b, d	15. d
16. a, c, e	17. b, d, e	18. c
19. d	20. b, c, d	

Chapter 14

1. d	2. a, d	3. b, d
4. b, c, e	5. c, d	6. b, e
7. a, d	8. b, c	9. d, e
10. a, c, e	11. a, e	12. b, c
13. b, d, e	14. b, c, e	15. d
16. a, c, e	17. a, b, c, d, e	18. b, c, d
19. a, c	20. b, d, e	21. d

Chapter 15

1. a, c, d	2. e	3. a, b
4. a, b, d	5. a, b, d	6. e
7. e	8. b, c, d	9. a, b, c, d, e
10. a, c, d	11. a, c, d, e	12. a, c, e
13. b, c, d	14. a, b, d	15. c, e
16. b, c, e	17. e	18. a, b, d
19. b, d	20. a, c	

Chapter 16

1. a, b, d	2. c	3. a, c
4. a, b, c, d	5. d	6. b, d
7. b	8. a, b	9. b, c, e
10. a, c	11. a, c	12. a, b, c, d
13. a, b, e	14. a, c, e	15. b, c, d
16. a, b, c, d, e	17. a, c, d	18. a, d, e
19. b, c	20. b, c, e	

Chapter 17

1. b, d, e	2. b, d, e	3. a, c, d
4. a, c	5. b, c, d	6. a, b, d
7. a, c	8. a, d, e	9. b, c, d, e
10. b, d	11. b, c, e	12. a, c, d
13. a, b, d, e	14. b, c, e	15. c, e
16. c, d, e	17. b, d	18. a, c
19. b, c	20. b, d	

Chapter 18

1. e	2. b, c	3. a, d, e
4. b, c	5. b	6. a, b
7. b, c, d	8. a, c	9. b, c, d
10. e	11. a, d, e	12. a, b, c, d, e
13. a, b, d	14. b, c	15. a, c
16. a, c	17. b, d, e	18. d
19. b	20. a, c, e	

Chapter 19

1. a, b, c	2. a, c	3. a, c, d
4. a, b, c, d, e	5. b, d	6. b, c, e
7. d	8. b, d, e	9. a, c, d
10. a, b, d	11. a, b, c, d, e	12. a, e
13. b, c	14. b, c	15. a, c, d
16. a, b, c	17. a, d	18. b, c, d
19. a, d, e	20. b, e	

Chapter 20

1. e	2. d	3. a
4. b	5. e	6. c
7. b, c, e	8. a, d, e	9. e
10. c	11. d	12. b, c, d
13. b, c, e	14. a, b, e	15. b, c, d
16. b, c, d, e	17. e	18. a, b, c, d
19. b, d, e	20. a, b, c	

Chapter 21

1. a, b, c, d, e	2. a, b	3. a, b, c
4. a, b, e	5. a, c, d, e	6. b, c, d
7. b, c, d	8. b, c, d, e	9. a, b, d, e
10. a, b, c	11. a, b	12. b
13. a, c, d, e	14. a, b, d, e	15. a, b, d
16. b, c, d	17. b	18. c
19. b, d, e	20. b, d	

Chapter 22

1. c	2. a, b, d, e	3. a, b, c
4. b, c, d	5. b, d	6. e
7. b	8. a, c, d, e	9. a, c
10. b, c	11. e	12. a, b, c, d
13. a, b, d	14. a, b, d, e	15. d
16. a, b, c, d	17. b, c, e	18. a, b, c
19. a, b, d	20. e	

Chapter 23

1. c	2. b	3. c
4. a, b, c, d	5. b	6. a, b, c
7. a, e	8. d	9. a, b, c, d, e
10. e	11. b, d, e	12. c
13. c, d, e	14. a, b, e	15. a, b, d, e
16. a, c, d, e	17. c, d, e	18. a, b, c, e
19. b, c, e	20. d, e	

Chapter 24

1. a, b, c, d, e	2. a, c, d, e	3. a, b
4. a, b, d, e	5. b	6. d, e
7. b, c	8. a, c, e	9. a, b, c
10. b, c, e	11. b, c, d	12. b, e
13. c	14. b, e	15. a, b, c
16. d, e	17. a, d, e	18. c, d
19. c, d	20. a, c, d	21. a, b, d
22. a, b, e	23. b, c, e	24. a, c, d
25. b, c	26. b, c, e	27. b, c, e
28. c, d, e	29. b, c, d, e	30. a, d, e

Chapter 25

1. a, b, e	2. b	3. c, e
4. b, c, d	5. b, e	6. b, c, e
7. d, e	8. a, d	9. a, c, e
10. b, c, d, e	11. a, b, c	12. b, c, d, e
13. b, c, d	14. c, d, e	15. a, d
16. c, e	17. a, d	18. b, d, e
19. a, b, e	20. c, d, e	21. b, c, d, e
22. c, d, e	23. c, e	24. c, d
25. a, b, c, e		

Chapter 26

1. d	2. a, c	3. a, b, c
4. c	5. c	6. e
7. a, c, e	8. c	9. c, d
10. c, d, e	11. a, c, d	12. e
13. a, b, e	14. c, d	15. a, b, c, d
16. c, d, e	17. b, c, e	18. a, b, e
19. a, d	20. c, e	

Chapter 27

1. d	2. c	3. b, c
4. a, b	5. b, c, d, e	6. b, c, d, e
7. a, b, d	8. a, c, d	9. a, c
10. a, b, c, d	11. a, b, c, e	12. a, b, d
13. a, d, e	14. b, c, d	15. e
16. a, b, e	17. a, b, c, d, e	18. a, b, c, d, e
19. c	20. c	

Chapter 28

1. a, c, d, e	2. b, c, e	3. a, b, c, d, e
4. a, d, e	5. b	6. d
7. c	8. b, c, d, e	9. a, b, c, e
10. a	11. b, c, d, e	12. a, b, c
13. a, c, d	14. b, c, e	15. b, c, e
16. b, c, d, e	17. a, b, c, d	18. a
19. a, c, d	20. a	21. b, d
22. a, b, c, e	23. a, c, d, e	24. a, b, e
25. a, c, d		

Chapter 29

1. a, b, c, e	2. a, b, c, e	3. a, b, c, e
4. b, c, e	5. a, c, d	6. b, c, e
7. b, c, e	8. c	9. b, d, e
10. a, b, e	11. a, c, d	12. a, c
13. a, b, e	14. a, c, e	15. a, e
16. a, b, d	17. a, c, d	18. b, d
19. b, c, e	20. a, c, e	21. a, b, d, e
22. a, b, c, d, e	23. a, b, c, e	24. a, c, d, e
25. a, b, d		

Chapter 30

1. a, b	2. b, c	3. a, e
4. b, d	5. c, e	6. a, c, d
7. c, e	8. a, b, d	9. a, c
10. b	11. a, b, c, d, e	12. a, b, e
13. a, c, d, e	14. b, e	

Index